Teacher Education Programs
In the United States
A Guide

Compiled by Modoc Press, Inc.

With the support and cooperation of the
American Association of Colleges for Teacher Education (AACTE)

 AMERICAN COUNCIL ON EDUCATION
PRAEGER
Series on Higher Education

Library of Congress Cataloging-in-Publication Data

Teacher education programs in the United States : a guide / compiled by Modoc Press Inc.
      p. cm. — (ACE/Praeger series on higher education)
    "Published in cooperation with the American Association of Colleges for Teacher Education, Washington, DC."
      Includes bibliographical references and index.
      ISBN 0–275–98156–8 (alk. paper)
      1. Teachers—Training of—United States—Directories.   2. Education—Study and teaching—United States—Directories.   I. Modoc Press.   II. American Association of Colleges for Teacher Education.   III. American Council on Education/Praeger series on higher education.
LB1715.T424 2004
370'.71'1—dc22   2004014776

British Library Cataloguing in Publication Data is available.

Library of Congress Catalog Card Number: 2004014776
ISBN: 0–275–98156–8

First published in 2004

Praeger Publishers, 88 Post Road West, Westport, CT 06881
An imprint of Greenwood Publishing Group, Inc.
www.praeger.com

Printed in the United States of America

The paper used in this book complies with the
Permanent Paper Standard issued by the National
Information Standards Organization (Z39.48–1984).

10 9 8 7 6 5 4 3 2 1

Table of Contents

Foreword

Teacher education is a rapidly expanding enterprise that involves hundreds of colleges and universities across the United States. These institutions are not only responding to the ever growing need to prepare more teachers for our nation's K-12 schools, they also are creating new linkages to local school districts, developing innovative educational technologies, offering dynamic new programs, and increasing program rigor.

Each year, more colleges are adding teacher education to their program offerings with many baccalaureate level institutions seeking graduate status by offering master's degrees in education for K-12 teachers and other school personnel. Increased federal investment in teachers' professional development has accelerated this trend. All types of institutions – public, private, research, comprehensive – and all kinds of postsecondary institutions – historically black colleges and universities, religious, polytechnical – offer programs to prepare pre-kindergarten, elementary, middle and secondary school teachers in traditional subject areas such as mathematics, science, language arts, social studies, foreign languages, arts and music, as well as specialties such as special education and counseling.

What characterizes all of these programs is their dependence on faculties beyond education (arts and letters, science and technology) and their heavy reliance on local K-12 schools for practicums and other clinical experiences for their students as well as research sites for their faculties. Because most of these programs are funded as lower division didactic social science programs (and not as clinical or even upper division social science programs), they usually generate large sums of revenue for their host institutions, which are allocated to non-teacher education programs.

The directory that follows documents the many facets of teacher education on the nation's college campuses. It highlights:

- **The size of the enterprise.** Some 1,400 colleges and universities offer one or more preparation programs for preservice teacher candidates, and this directory describes two-thirds of these programs.

- **The productivity of teacher education programs.** Approximately 250,000 degrees in education are offered annually. Nearly 15 percent of all post-secondary degrees are in teacher education.

- **The reliance on more rigorous requirements for entry into the preparation program, such as completion of two years of general education, a GPA of at least 2.5 on a 4.0 scale, passage of one or more admission tests, and interviews with faculty.** Graduates typically must satisfactorily complete a student teaching experience and pass at least one exit examination administered by the state to be licensed to teach in the state or to gain licensure reciprocity with other states.

- **The diversity of program offerings and degree programs** – from early childhood education to school leadership.

- **The colleges' heavy reliance on state controls.** The course of study is often set by the state education agency, with the focus on licensure requirements for candidates in teaching.

- **The dependence on professional or specialized accreditation.** The majority of programs included in this directory are accredited by National Council for Accreditation of Teacher Education (NCATE), the premiere accrediting organization for institutions that offer teacher education programs.

Rapid Enrollment Growth

Enrollment growth in teacher education has been rising in response to the demand for more PK-12 teachers and the expectation that high-quality teachers can transform PK-12 schools. Enrollments have grown steadily by about 6 percent per year since the mid-1990s, when the U.S. Department of Education picked-up the "teacher shortage" theme of the National Commission on Teaching and America's Future, and projected a shortage of more than 2.4 million teachers. Candidates saw opportunities in teaching and came to teacher education programs to become licensed. That growth has been sustained due to the economic downturn (and loss of job opportunities in other sectors) and because of policy maker insistence that "highly qualified teachers matter." Enactment of the federal *No Child Left Behind Act* (P.L.107-110) reinforced the message that teachers with "deep subject matter knowledge" and the skill to communicate with "all children" could make a profound difference in the learning of students. Both undergraduates and graduates responded by enrolling in college and university programs for teacher education.

Alternative Providers

Another response to the demand for more and better teachers is the expansion of the enterprise and the experimentation with alternative routes to certification. Virtually every college and university has responded by expanding their offerings beyond the "traditional" program and catering to the needs of a broader range of candidates. These "initial" but often post-baccalaureate certification programs have been met with receptivity by local schools in need of particular kinds of teachers (mathematics, science, special education, and bilingual education).

While a number of states pioneered in the development of alternative routes to certification during the 1980s, it was not until the administration of George W. Bush that the movement gained momentum. Encouraged and funded by the U.S. Department of Education following passage of NCLB, local school districts (e.g., Los Angeles and Dallas), state agencies and intermediate units (Texas), for-profit companies (e.g., Sylvan, DeVry, Walden, Apollo and Capella), and on-line providers (e.g., Western Governors University) gained the authority to prepare teachers and built expansive programs to cater to both preservice candidates and practicing teachers (who pursued additional or alternative certification -- e.g., to become a reading specialist or an elementary school principal). While many of their efforts predated enactment of NCLB, they responded to the opportunities in this federal program and encroached in significant ways on the traditional markets of "so-called" traditional colleges and universities. They often met institutional accreditation guidelines and flourished as the U.S. Department of Education sought to "break the monopoly" of traditional teacher education programs.

At a time when most traditional or standard programs in teacher education are "over-subscribed," the effect or potential impact of these alternative providers has not been felt. Faculty seem insulated from the competitive effect of these alternative providers as enrollments in traditional preparation programs have not declined, and "placements" of graduates have not been affected. The same continues to be true for faculty relative to the competition presented by more traditional colleges and universities who have sought to become "national" providers of teachers and operate across the country (and internationally). Among the largest of these programs are those offered by: Lesley College (MA) and Ottawa University (KS), National University (CA), and National Louis University (IL). All of this suggests that teacher education is a highly dynamic enterprise with more and more providers offering courses and experiences similar to those highlighted in this directory.

The Expanding Role of Community Colleges

Yet another set of alternative providers in teacher education are the community colleges, which are expanding their traditional missions to include: (1) more professional courses in teacher education - sometimes including field experiences in K-12 schools - leading to associate of arts degrees in teacher education, (2) baccalaureate level programs in teacher education, and (3) post-baccalaureate programs that cater to degree holders who want to switch careers or pursue teacher certification. This is a significant movement in teacher education that likely will recast the composition of "providers" and challenge the preeminent position of baccalaureate and graduate level institutions.

Teacher education will continue to be a highly competitive market for alternative providers and community colleges, and the education schools and colleges and universities listed in this directory will need to confront these challenges in the future. Cooperation and collaboration with these emerging providers will be necessary (and strategic) as the landscape of teacher need and teacher demand is transformed.

David G. Imig
President and CEO
American Association of Colleges for Teacher Education
June 2004

About This Directory

This directory is a compilation of informative data for 872 institutions that offer teacher education programs. Data were collected via questionnaire, Internet search, and the various databases maintained by the National Center for Educational Statistics. Information is applicable to the 2002-2003 academic year.

Member institutions of the American Association of Colleges for Teacher Education are included as well as other regionally accredited institutions that responded to inquiry via questionnaire. Institutions accredited by the National Council for Accreditation of Teacher Education (NCATE) are identified in their respective institutional entries. All institutions included have been accredited by the responsible regional accrediting agency and all institutional programs listed have been approved by the applicable state agency responsible for teacher certification.

Regional accreditation is awarded by the following organizations:

MSA — Middle States Association of Colleges and Schools

NASC — Northwest Association of Schools and Colleges

NCA — North Central Association of Colleges and Schools

NEASC— New England Association of Schools and Colleges

SACS — Southern Association of Colleges and Schools

WASC — Western Association of Schools and Colleges

Fees and expenses usually increase on a yearly basis. Those listed with each main entry apply to the 2002-2003 academic year. For current information, users are advised to contact the institution or search the institution's web site. Telephone, FAX, e-mail, and web site information are cited prominently in the institution's entry.

Undergraduate and graduate admission requirements vary from school to school and program to program. Specific information is given under Admission Requirements: Undergraduate and Graduate.

Various testing programs are required by the governing state organizations These vary from those examinations developed by the state to the most commonly used test series, PRAXIS I and II, preprofessional skills tests developed by the Educational Testing Service

Licensure is granted by a state approving body. Reciprocity is available almost universally. The National Association of State Directors of Teacher Education and Certification (NASDTEC) organization should be contacted to determine reciprocity. Many state directors of teacher credentialing have signed interstate agreements through NASDTEC that expedite the certification process.

Sample Entry

TOWSON UNIVERSITY
College of Education
Teacher Education Unit
Hawkins Hall, room 301
8000 York Road
Towson, Maryland 21252-0001
Phone: (410) 704-2570
Fax: (410) 704-2733
E-mail: coe@towson.edu
Internet: http://www.towson.edu

Institution Description: Towson University is an institutional member of the University of Maryland System. It was established and chartered as Maryland State Normal School in 1866. The name was changed to State Teachers College at Towson in 1935 and to Towson State College in 1963. The present name was adopted in 1976.

As the first teacher-training institution in Maryland, Towson University has been preparing men and women for teaching careers for over 135 years. Programs of study lead to the baccalaureate degree in education with certification in early childhood, elementary, and special education.

Institution Control: Public.

Calendar: Semester. Academic year August to May.

Official(s): Dr. Thomas Proffitt, Dean.

Faculty: Full-time 74.

Degrees Awarded: 310 baccalaureate; 320 master's.

Admission Requirements: *Undergraduate:* Graduation from an approved secondary school or GED; College Board SAT or ACT composite. *Teacher education specific:* Completion of education foundations course; completion of a minimum of 60 semester credits; PRAXIS I test scores; must meet state qualifying score on PRAXIS II prior to graduation. *Graduate:* Baccalaureate degree from a regionally accredited institution. *Teacher education specific:* Teaching credential where required by the program pursued; recommendations; faculty interview.

Fees and Expenses: Undergraduate: in-state $3,956 per academic year; out-of-state $11,602. On-campus room and board: $6,322. Other expenses: $2,150. Books and supplies: $675.

Financial Aid: Resources specifically for eligible students enrolled in teacher education programs are awarded on the basis of financial need and academic merit. The institution has a Program Participation Agreement with the U.S. Department of Education for eligible students to receive Pell Grants and other federal aid. Funding for prospective and current teachers in various awards is available for qualifying students. *Contact:* Vince Pecora at (410) 704-4286 or e-mail at vpecora@towson.edu.

Accreditation: *Regional:* MSA. *Professional:* NCATE. *Member of:* AACTE. *Approved by:* Maryland State Board of Education.

Undergraduate Programs: The Department of Early Childhood Education offers programs of study that include: early childhood education, the major in elementary education with eligibility for early childhood education certification. The programs require completion of a general education core, professional studies, field experiences, and student teaching. A minimum of 120 semester hours must be completed for the degree award.

The Department of Elementary Education offers the major in elementary education, the major with eligibility for early childhood certification, the integrated elementary education-special education major, and the elementary education major with a minor in selected disciplines.

The Department of Reading, Special Education, and Instructional Technology is responsible for courses that are not limited to a single teacher education program. The programs include a major in special education, the major in integrated elementary education-special education.

The Department of Secondary Education offers 13 certification programs in the secondary subject areas of biology, chemistry, earth-space science, English, French, geography, German, school health, history, mathematics, physics, social science, and Spanish. The programs of education for junior, middle, and high school teachers are designed to bring about close integration between teaching methods and the practical experience of student teaching.

Graduate Programs: Master's degree programs are offered in the areas of early childhood education, elementary education, instructional technology, reading, secondary education, and special education.

The Doctor of Education degree program in instructional technology focuses on the development of instructional expertise to meet the present and future needs of technology integration in instruction across the education spectrum.

Licensure/Reciprocity: Maryland. Students seeking teaching certification in a state other than Maryland should consult with that state's teacher certification office early in their program of study to insure compliance with requirements. Many state directors of teacher credentialing have signed Interstate Agreements through NASDTEC that expedite the certification process.

ALABAMA

ALABAMA AGRICULTURAL AND MECHANICAL UNIVERSITY

School of Education
307 L.R. Patton Building
4107 Meridian Street
Normal, Alabama 35762
Phone: (256) 372-5500
Fax: (256) 372-5636
E-mail: jvickers@aamu.edu
Internet: http//www.aamu.edu

Institution Description: Alabama Agricultural and Mechanical University is a state institution and land-grant college. The university was established as Huntsville Normal School and offered first instruction at postsecondary level in 1875. It became Alabama Agricultural and Mechanical College in 1948 and the present name was adopted in 1969.

Through its program areas, the School of Education provides a variety of programs leading to the Bachelor of Science degree. Teacher certification at the Class B level is offered, along with special courses, conferences, workshops, and consultant services for the continuing development of educational programs in the state, region, and community.

Institution Control: Public.

Calendar: Semester. Academic year August to May.

Official(s): Dr. John Vickers, Jr., Dean.

Faculty: Full-time 78.

Degrees Awarded: 544 baccalaureate.

Admission Requirements: *Undergraduate:* Graduation from an accredited secondary school or GED; minimum 2.0 GPA; College Board SAT or ACT composite. *Teacher education specific:* Apply to the School of Education; PRAXIS I exams; faculty interview.

Fees and Expenses: Undergraduate: in-state $3,040 per academic year; out-of-state $5,560. On-campus room and board: $4,500. Books and supplies: $800.

Financial Aid: Resources specifically for eligible students enrolled in teacher education programs are awarded on the basis of financial need and academic merit. The institution has a program participation agreement with the U.S. Department of Education for eligible students to receive Pell Grants and other federal aid. *Contact:* Financial Aid Office at (256) 372-5400.

Accreditation: *Regional:* SACS. *Professional:* NCATE. *Member of:* AACTE. *Approved by:* Alabama State Department of Education.

Undergraduate Programs: All baccalaureate degrees require the successful completion of the general education requirements plus specific courses in the student's area of concentration. Students may select from the fields of early childhood education, elementary education, middle school education endorsements, special education, N-12 programs in art, music, physical education and secondary education. The majority of secondary education programs require two areas of concentration. Under the rules of the Alabama State Department of Education, secondary school teachers are licensed to teach only in academic areas endorsed on the professional certificate.

Licensure/Reciprocity: Alabama. Students seeking teaching certification in a state other than Alabama should consult with that state's teacher certification office early in their program of study to insure compliance with requirements. Many state directors of teacher credentialing have signed Interstate Agreements through NASDTEC that expedite the certification process.

ALABAMA STATE UNIVERSITY

College of Education
915 South Jackson Street
Montgomery, Alabama 36101-0271
Phone: (334) 229-4250
Fax: (334) 229-4908
E-mail: VDeshields@asunet.alasu.edu
Internet: http://www.alasu.edu

Institution Description: The university was established in 1874. It became a junior college in 1920 and a four-year institution in 1929. It became Alabama State College in 1954 and the present name was adopted in 1969.

The College of Education awards the Bachelor of Science and the Master of Education degrees plus the Educational Specialist degree in programs that lead to certification in teaching and leadership positions.

Institution Control: Public.

Calendar: Semester. Academic year August to May.

Official(s): Dr. Vivian DeShields, Dean; Dr. Linda Bradford, Chairperson, Curriculum and Instruction.

Faculty: Full-time 42.

Degrees Awarded: 223 baccalaureate; 211 master's.

Admission Requirements: *Undergraduate:* Graduation from an accredited secondary school or GED; College Board SAT accepted; ACT composite preferred. *Teacher education specific:* Application to the College of Education; PRAXIS I exams; faculty interview. *Graduate:* Baccalaureate degree from a regionally accredited institution. *Teacher education specific:* Alternative fifth-year programs lead to the Master of Education degree and certification for those who did not complete a teacher education program at the undergraduate level.

Fees and Expenses: Undergraduate: in-state $2,904 per academic year; out-of-state $5,808. Graduate: Tuition charged per credit hour. On-campus room and board: $3,500. Books and supplies: $800. Other expenses: $2,310.

Financial Aid: Resources specifically for eligible students enrolled in teacher education programs are awarded on the basis of academic merit and financial need. The institution has a Program Participation Agreement with the U.S. Department of Education for eligible students to receive Pell Grants and other federal aid. *Contact:* Financial Aid Office at (334) 229-4323.

Accreditation: *Regional:* SACS. *Professional:* NCATE. *Member of:* AACTE. *Approved by:* Alabama State Department of Education.

Undergraduate Programs: Bachelor of Science degree programs are offered in early childhood education (grades N-3); elementary education (grades K-6); nursery through grade 12 (N-12); art education; health education; music education; physical education, and reading. secondary education programs (grades 6-12) are offered with area emphases in biology, business and office education, chemistry, English, French, history, and language arts, mathematics, political science, general science, social science, and Spanish. All programs require the successful completion of 129 credit hours.

ALABAMA STATE UNIVERSITY—*cont'd*

Graduate Programs: The graduate programs in the areas of instructional support offer concentration for the principal, superintendent, supervisor in educational administration, school counselor, and library media specialist. The fifth-year alternative program leads to the Master of Education degree and teacher certification.

Licensure/Reciprocity: Alabama. Students seeking teaching certification in a state other than Alabama should consult with that state's teacher certification office early in their program of study to insure compliance with requirements. Many state directors of teacher credentialing have signed Interstate Agreements through NASDTEC that expedite the certification process.

ATHENS STATE UNIVERSITY

School of Education
Teacher Education Program
300 North Beaty Street
Athens, Alabama 35611
Phone: (256) 233-8100
Fax: (256) 233-8220
E-mail: admissions@athens.edu
Internet: http://www.athens.edu

Institution Description: Athens State University is a state institution providing upper division degree study only. It was established as Athens Female Academy in 1822. It became coeducational as Athens College in 1931 and became Athens State College in 1975, The present name was adopted in 1998.

Students who are admitted to the Teacher Education Program are expected to accept the challenge of a rigorous course of study, demonstrate attainment of skills and knowledge, and exhibit appropriate professional behavior.

Institution Control: Public.

Calendar: Quarter. Academic year September to August.

Official(s): Dr. Mary Lou Maples, Dean.

Faculty: Full-time 50.

Degrees Awarded: 378 baccalaureate.

Admission Requirements: *Undergraduate:* Graduation from an accredited secondary school with a 2.0 GPA. *Teacher education specific:* Apply to the Teacher Education Program by July 20 for admission prior to fall semester; minimum 2.75 GPA; complete specific courses in English composition and fundamentals/foundation of education with a grade of C or better; score a minimum of 320 on Basic Skills Test.

Fees and Expenses: Undergraduate: in-state $2,904 per academic year; out-of-state $5,808. On-campus room and board: $3,500. Books and supplies: $800. Other expenses: $2,310.

Financial Aid: Resources specifically for eligible students enrolled in teacher education programs are awarded on the basis of academic merit and financial need. The institution has a Program Participation Agreement with the U.S. Department of Education for eligible students to receive Pell Grants and other federal aid. *Contact:* Financial Aid Office at (256) 233-8122.

Accreditation: *Regional:* SACS. *Professional:* NCATE. *Member of:* AACTE. *Approved by:* Alabama State Department of Education.

Undergraduate Programs: The Bachelor of Science in Education degree programs offer approved majors in biology, chemistry, collaborative teacher K-6, collaborative teacher 6-12, comprehensive science, elementary education K-6), history, early childhood education P-3, language arts, mathematics, physical education, social science, career technical education, and post-secondary education. Students must maintain a GPA of 2.75 in general education courses, professional education courses, and teaching field requirements. The degree requires the completion of 192 quarter hours.

Licensure/Reciprocity: Alabama. Students seeking teaching certification in a state other than Alabama should consult with that state's teacher certification office early in their program of study to insure compliance with requirements. Many state directors of teacher credentialing have signed Interstate Agreements through NASDTEC that expedite the certification process.

AUBURN UNIVERSITY

College of Education
Haley Center 3084
Auburn University, Alabama 36849-5245
Phone: (334) 844-4446
Fax: (334) 844-5785
E-mail: kochafr@auburnu.edu
Internet: http://www.auburn.edu

Institution Description: Auburn University is a state institution. It was established by the Methodist Episcopal Church, South and chartered as East Alabama Male College in 1856. Control was transferred to the state and its name was changed to Alabama Agricultural and Mechanical College in 1872. The present name was adopted in 1960.

The College of Education was established in 1915. It offers both teacher certification programs and academic programs which do not lead to teacher certification. Students who have already earned undergraduate degrees and want to pursue teacher certification may work with Teacher Education Services for either a second undergraduate degree or the nontraditional master's certification program.

Institution Control: Public.

Calendar: Quarter. Academic year September to June.

Official(s): Dr. Frances Kochan, Dean; Dr. Robert Wowsey, Associate Dean; Dr. Emily Melvin, Assistant Dean.

Faculty: Full-time 90; part-time 5; adjunct 10.

Degrees Awarded: 1,489 baccalaureate; 594 master's.

Admission Requirements: *Undergraduate:* Favorable consideration will be given to accredited secondary school graduates whose college ability test scores and high school grades give promise of success. *Teacher education specific:* Student must pass all Alabama Prospective Teacher Test; complete pre-teaching; 2.5 GPA in all coursework; satisfactory department interview. *Graduate:* Baccalaureate degree from an accredited institution. *Teacher education specific:* appropriate formula score (GPA and GRE); letters of recommendation; faculty interview.

Fees and Expenses: Undergraduate/ graduate: in-state $3,650 per academic year; out-of-state $10,950. Other fees: $1,689. On-campus room and board: $6,050. Books and supplies: $900.

Financial Aid: Resources specifically for eligible students enrolled in teacher education programs are awarded on the basis of academic merit and financial need. *Contact:* Michael Reynolds, Director, Financial Aid Office at (334) 844-4367 or reynom2@auburn.edu.

Accreditation: *Regional:* SACS. *Professional:* NCATE. *Member of:* AACTE. *Approved by:* Alabama State Department of Education.

Undergraduate Programs: The baccalaureate degree program requires the completion of a teacher education core (diversity of learners and settings in education; child development, learning, motivation, and assessment; adolescent development, learning, motivation, and assessment I and II). Departmental specific core courses include counseling and counseling psychology; curriculum and teaching, educational foundations, leadership, and technology; health and human performance; rehabilitation and special education. All other general education requirements must be completed for a total of 192 quarter hours.

Graduate Programs: Master of Education degree programs are offered with concentrations in counseling and counseling psychology; curriculum and teaching; educational foundation; leadership technology; health and human performance; and rehabilitation and special education. Specific courses are required.

Licensure/Reciprocity: Alabama. Students seeking teaching certification in a state other than Alabama should consult with that state's teacher certification office early in their program of study to insure compliance with requirements. Many state

directors of teacher credentialing have signed Interstate Agreements through NASDTEC that expedite the certification process.

AUBURN UNIVERSITY AT MONTGOMERY
School of Education
P.O. Box 244023
7300 University Drive
Montgomery, Alabama 36117-3596
Phone: (334) 244-3413
Fax: (334) 244-3835
E-mail: auminfo@mickey.aum.edu
Internet: http://www.aum.edu

Institution Description: Auburn University at Montgomery is a state institution that was established in 1967.

The School of Education offers degree programs at the baccalaureate, master's, and specialist levels. The school's comprehensive program is designed to integrate content, operative, reflective, and collaborative knowledge as a framework for the teacher education programs. Over 1,300 students are enrolled in these programs.

Institution Control: Public.

Calendar: Semesters. Academic year September to August.

Official(s): Dr. Janet Warren, Dean; Dr. Jennifer Brown, Associate Dean.

Faculty: Full-time 40.

Degrees Awarded: 151 baccalaureate; 168 master's.

Admission Requirements: *Undergraduate:* Graduation from an accredited secondary school or GED; ACT composite. *Teacher education specific:* Apply to School of Education and meet all education course requirements for admission; PRAXIS I exams; faculty interview. *Graduate:* Baccalaureate degree from an accredited institution; acceptable GPA in all coursework undertaken; *Teacher education specific:* PRAXIS II and III exams; faculty interview.

Fees and Expenses: Undergraduate: in-state $3,620 per academic year; out-of-state $10,400. Graduate: Tuition charged per credit hour. On-campus room and board: $4,610. Books and supplies: $600. Other expenses: $2,360.

Financial Aid: Resources specifically for eligible students enrolled in teacher education programs are awarded on the basis of academic merit and financial need. The institution has a Program Participation Agreement with the U.S. Department of Education for eligible students to receive Pell Grants and other federal aid. *Contact:* Financial Aid Office at (334) 244-3571.

Accreditation: *Regional:* SACS. *Professional:* NCATE. *Member of:* AACTE. *Approved by:* Alabama State Department of Education.

Undergraduate Programs: The School of Education offers Bachelor of Science programs in art education, early childhood education, elementary education, physical education, secondary education, special education, and speech communication education. Specific courses are required in each of these program areas plus the university core curriculum for a total of 120 semester hours.

Graduate Programs: Graduate degrees at the master's level are offered in counselor education, early childhood education, educational leadership, elementary education, physical education, reading education, secondary education, and special education. For further information regarding program requirements, contact Dr. Ray Braswell at the School of Education.

Licensure/Reciprocity: Alabama. Students seeking teaching certification in a state other than Alabama should consult with that state's teacher certification office early in their program of study to insure compliance with requirements. Many state directors of teacher credentialing have signed Interstate Agreements through NASDTEC that expedite the certification process.

BIRMINGHAM SOUTHERN COLLEGE
Division of Education
900 Arkadelphia Road
Birmingham, Alabama 35254
Phone: (205) 226-4810
Fax: (205) 226-3065
E-mail: educate@bsc.edu
Internet: http://www.bsc.edu

Institution Description: Birmingham Southern College is a private liberal arts college affiliated with the United Methodist Church. It was established in 1859.

The Division of Education offers majors in K-6 education, eleven areas of secondary education and their P-12 programs (art, dance, and music). In addition, a major is offered in education for students who wish to pursue careers that do not require a teaching certificate.

Institution Control: Private.

Calendar: Semester. Academic year September to May.

Official(s): Dr. Clint E. Bruess, Chair.

Faculty: Full-time 5; part-time 1; adjunct 1.

Degrees Awarded: 30 baccalaureate.

Admission Requirements: *Undergraduate:* Graduation from an accredited secondary school or GED; College Board SAT or ACT composite score. *Teacher education specific:* Students who wish to pursue a teaching career must make formal application after completing at least 15 units of work; GPA of 2.5; faculty recommendation; passing score on Alabama Basic Skills Test.

Fees and Expenses: $17,650 per academic year. On-campus room and board: $5,360 to $7,330. Books and supplies: $600.

Financial Aid: Resources specifically for eligible students enrolled in teacher education programs are awarded on the basis of academic merit and financial need. *Contact:* Ronald Day, Financial Aid Office at (205) 226-4670 or rday@bsc.edu.

Accreditation: *Regional:* SACS. *Professional:* NCATE. *Member of:* AACTE. *Approved by:* Alabama State Department of Education.

Undergraduate Programs: All elementary education majors are prepared to teach in any academic setting for kindergarten through 6th grade. The graduates will receive both elementary and special education certifications from the Alabama State Department of Education. This dual certification allows students to make their own choice of school settings ranging from classrooms to special education facilities. Requirements are necessary in three areas; general studies, professional studies, and major studies.

The secondary education program leads to Alabama Class B certification for grades six through twelve. Candidates for this certificate must complete coursework in general studies, professional studies and a major. Single majors are available in biology, French, German, history, mathematics, and Spanish.

All baccalaureate degree programs require the completion of 128 credit hours.

Licensure/Reciprocity: Alabama. Students seeking teaching certification in a state other than Alabama should consult with that state's teacher certification office early in their program of study to insure compliance with requirements. Many state directors of teacher credentialing have signed Interstate Agreements through NASDTEC that expedite the certification process.

FAULKNER UNIVERSITY
Department of Education
5345 Atlanta Highway
Montgomery, Alabama 36109-3378
Phone: (334) 272-5820
Fax: (334) 386-7200
E-mail: kmack@faulkner.edu
Internet: http://www.faulkner.edu

Institution Description: Faulkner University (formerly Alabama Christian College) is a private, independent, nonprofit institution affiliated with the Churches of Christ in Montgom-

FAULKNER UNIVERSITY—*cont'd*

ery. The university was established as Montgomery Bible College in 1942 and its name was changed to Alabama Christian College 1953. The present name was adopted in 1985.

The Department of Education is committed to the preparation of elementary and secondary school teachers who will demonstrate both Christian character and a high degree of of professional competence. Program are offered by the Divisions of Elementary Education, Secondary Education, and Physical Education.

Institution Control: Private.

Calendar: Semester. Academic year August to July.

Official(s): Dr. Robert Lester, Chair, Department of Education.

Faculty: Full-time 7.

Degrees Awarded: 9 baccalaureate.

Admission Requirements: *Undergraduate:* Graduation from an accredited secondary school or GED. *Teacher education specific:* Application to the Department of Education after completion of specified prerequisite courses; faculty interview.

Fees and Expenses: $9,300 per academic year. On-campus room and board: $4,600. Other expenses $2,200. Books and supplies: $900.

Financial Aid: Resources specifically for eligible students enrolled in teacher education programs are awarded on the basis of academic merit and financial need. The institution has a Program Participation Agreement with the U.S. Department of Education for eligible students to receive Pell Grants and other federal aid. *Contact:* Financial Aid Office @ (334) 386-7195.

Accreditation: *Regional:* SACS. *Approved by:* Alabama State Department of Education.

Undergraduate Programs: The primary purpose of the elementary education major is to provide a student with sufficiency in the areas of study that are considered important in teaching children. Completion of the requirements for an Alabama Class B teaching certificate (grades kindergarten through grade 6). Students must complete 30 semester hours of professional education, 71 semester hours of core curriculum courses, and 33 semester hours in the field.

A student majoring in secondary education may choose from the areas of biology, chemistry, history, general social science, English language arts, or mathematics education. Each subject area requires completion of 3 components: general studies, professional education, and a subject area concentration.

The program offered by the Department of Physical Education broadens a student's choice of activities and increases body control. In addition to general curriculum requirements, completion of 33 semester hours of physical education courses is required in the N-12 major.

Licensure/Reciprocity: Alabama. Students seeking teaching certification in a state other than Alabama should consult with that state's teacher certification office early in their program of study to insure compliance with requirements. Many state directors of teacher credentialing have signed Interstate Agreements through NASDTEC that expedite the certification process.

HUNTINGDON COLLEGE
Department of Education and Psychology
Teacher Certification Program
1500 East Fairview Avenue
Montgomery, Alabama 36106-2148
Phone: (334) 833-4222
Fax: (334) 833-4428
E-mail: admis@huntingdon.edu
Internet: http://www.huntingdon.edu

Institution Description: Huntingdon College is a coeducational liberal arts college related to the United Methodist Church. The college was established and chartered as Tuskegee Female College 1854. Its name was changed to Alabama Conference Female College in 1872 and to Woman's College of Alabama in 1909. The present name was adopted in 1935.

The Department of Education offers baccalaureate programs leading to teacher certification at the elementary, middle school, and secondary levels.

Institution Control: Private.

Calendar: Semester. Academic year August to May.

Official(s): Dr. Anna T. Koslowski, Chair, Department of Education and Psychology.

Faculty: Full-time 4.

Degrees Awarded: 12 baccalaureate.

Admission Requirements: *Undergraduate:* Graduation from an accredited secondary school or GED; minimum 2.25 GPA; College Board SAT or ACT composite score. *Teacher education specific:* Students interested in preparation for teaching certification are encouraged to declare their intentions as early as possible; formal application to the Teacher Education Program; completion of 57 semester hours of which 39 semester hours are in the general studies program; satisfactory score on the Alabama Prospective Teacher Test; faculty interview; successful completion of 70 hours of preprofessional laboratory experiences in a school setting prior to the student's junior year.

Fees and Expenses: $13,800 per academic year. On-campus room and board: $5,820. Other expenses $240. Books and supplies: $700.

Financial Aid: Resources specifically for eligible students enrolled in teacher education programs are awarded on the basis of academic merit and financial need. The institution has a Program Participation Agreement with the U.S. Department of Education for eligible students to receive Pell Grants and other federal aid. *Contact:* Financial Aid Office at (334) 833-4428.

Accreditation: *Regional:* SACS. *Approved by:* Alabama State Department of Education.

Undergraduate Programs: The college offers the following programs leading to certification by the Alabama State Department of Education: secondary teaching field programs (grades 7-12) and P-12 teaching programs (preschool through grade 12). Secondary teaching field programs require completion of a major in a teaching field (chemistry, English/language arts (comprehensive), history, and mathematics. The programs require 48-57 credit hours in the college core, 36-33 credit hours in professional studies. P-12 teaching field programs include: art, dance, music education, and physical education.

Licensure/Reciprocity: Alabama. Students seeking teaching certification in a state other than Alabama should consult with that state's teacher certification office early in their program of study to insure compliance with requirements. Many state directors of teacher credentialing have signed Interstate Agreements through NASDTEC that expedite the certification process.

JACKSONVILLE STATE UNIVERSITY
College of Education and Professional Studies
Department of Educational Resources
700 Pelham Road North
Jacksonville, Alabama 36265-1602
Phone: (256) 782-5445
Fax: (256) 782-5169
E-mail: swebb@jsu.edu
Internet: http://www.jsu.edu

Institution Description: Jacksonville State University was established, chartered, and offered first instruction at postsecondary level in 1883. It became a 4-year institution and its name changed name State Teachers College in 1929. The college then became Jacksonville State College in 1957 and the present name adopted in 1967.

The College of Education and Professional Studies prepares students for careers in a variety of professions. Programs in the college enable graduates to become creative decision makers who can effectively solve problems using concepts and practices appropriate for each discipline.

Institution Control: Public.

Calendar: Semester. Academic year August to July.

Official(s): Dr. Sheila Anne Webb, Dean; Dr. Cynthia Harper, Associate Dean; Dr. Kathleen Friery, Department Head.

Faculty: Full-time 63; part-time 12; adjunct 32.

Degrees Awarded: 1,507 baccalaureate; 745 master's.

Admission Requirements: *Undergraduate:* Graduation from an accredited secondary school or GED; College Board SAT or ACT composite score. *Teacher education specific:* Admission to the College of Education and Professional Studies; student must have earned a minimum of 60 semester hours of college credit with at least 48 semester hours in the general studies area; 3 written recommendations from professors in the general studies area; classroom observation at the level and in the teaching area in which a degree or certification is sought; faculty interview; other requirements may apply.

Fees and Expenses: Undergraduate: in-state $3,240 per academic year; $6,480 out-of-state. On-campus room and board: $3,000. Books and supplies: $1,000.

Financial Aid: Resources specifically for eligible students enrolled in teacher education programs are awarded on the basis of academic merit and financial need. *Contact:* Diane Price at (256) 782-5165 or dprice@jsucc.jsu.edu.

Accreditation: *Regional:* SACS. *Professional:* NCATE. *Member of:* AACTE. *Approved by:* Alabama State Department of Education.

Undergraduate Programs: The Department of Educational Resources offers undergraduate programs in secondary teacher education and service courses in educational psychology and instructional media. Secondary degree programs (grades 6-12) are offered with emphases in biology, collaborative (special education), English/language arts, French, general science, geography, German, health, history, home economics education, mathematics, social science, Spanish, and technology. Add-on middle school endorsements (grades 4-8) are available in biology, English/language arts, geography, general science, history, mathematics, social science. The baccalaureate programs require the completion of 128 credit hours.

Graduate Programs: The department offers courses leading to teacher certification in the alternative fifth-year program for persons holding an undergraduate degree. Students may earn a Master of Science in Education degree in the following secondary fields: biology, English/language arts, history, mathematics, general science, social science.

Licensure/Reciprocity: Alabama. Students seeking teaching certification in a state other than Alabama should consult with that state's teacher certification office early in their program of study to insure compliance with requirements. Many state directors of teacher credentialing have signed Interstate Agreements through NASDTEC that expedite the certification process.

JUDSON COLLEGE
Department of Teacher Education
302 Bibb Street
Marion, Alabama 36756
Phone: (334) 683-5100
Fax: (334) 683-6675
E-mail: admissions@judson.edu
Internet: http://www.judson.edu

Institution Description: Judson College is a private church-related (Southern Baptist) liberal arts college for women. The college was established as Jackson Female Institute in 1838. The present name was adopted in 1904.

The Department of Education begins student teaching experience in the freshman year. The campus-based teacher workshop gives students extensive classroom experience with access to a computer center and laboratory with the latest educational curriculum and software.

Institution Control: Private.

Calendar: Semester. Academic year September to June.

Official(s): Dr. Frankie K. Oglesty, Head, Department of Teacher Education.

Faculty: Full-time 5.

Degrees Awarded: 6 baccalaureate.

Admission Requirements: *Undergraduate:* Graduation from an accredited secondary school or GED; ACT composite score preferred; College Board SAT accepted. *Teacher education specific:* Approval by Teacher Education Department advisor; student should declare intent to enter the program as early as the student's freshman year.

Fees and Expenses: $8,150 per academic year. On-campus room and board: $5,300. Books and supplies: $700. Other expenses: $2,580.

Financial Aid: Resources specifically for eligible students enrolled in teacher education programs are awarded on the basis of academic merit and financial need. The institution has a Program Participation Agreement with the U.S. Department of Education for eligible students to receive Pell Grants and other federal aid. *Contact:* Financial Aid Office at (334) 683-5157.

Accreditation: *Regional:* SACS. *Approved by:* Alabama State Department of Education.

Undergraduate Programs: Available majors offered by the department include early childhood education, elementary education, secondary English (grades 6-12), secondary mathematics, physical education (grades 6-12, K-12 specialist), and music education specialist (grades K-12). All programs leading to the Bachelor of Science in Education require general education courses and specific major program area courses for a total of 128 semester hours.

Licensure/Reciprocity: Alabama. Students seeking teaching certification in a state other than Alabama should consult with that state's teacher certification office early in their program of study to insure compliance with requirements. Many state directors of teacher credentialing have signed Interstate Agreements through NASDTEC that expedite the certification process.

MILES COLLEGE
Division of Education
Teacher Education Program
5500 Myron Massey Boulevard
Fairfield, Alabama 35064
Phone: (205) 929-1000
Fax: (205) 929-1453
E-mail: info@mail.miles.edu
Internet: http://www.miles.edu

Institution Description: Miles College is a private college affiliated with the Christian Methodist Episcopal Church. It was established as Miles Memorial College in 1905. The present name was adopted in 1911.

The Division of Education offers programs leading to the Bachelor of Science degree and to professional teaching certification. Prospective early childhood/elementary teachers and secondary education teachers are provided considerable depth and involvement within the professional and major field curriculum.

Institution Control: Private.

Calendar: Semester. Academic year August to May.

Official(s): Dr. Hattie G. Lamar, Dean, Academic Affairs.

Faculty: Full-time 5.

Degrees Awarded: 38 baccalaureate.

Admission Requirements: *Undergraduate:* Graduation from an accredited secondary school or GED; ACT composite score. *Teacher education specific:* Apply for admission to the Teacher Education Program (TEP) during the semester in which the student will have earned 60 semester hours; interview with the TEP Committee; cumulative GPA of 2.60 or above; passing score 300 or above on the Content Mastery Examination for Teachers.

Fees and Expenses: $5,008 per academic year. On-campus room and board: $3,770. Books and supplies: $790. Other fees: $2,275.

Financial Aid: Resources specifically for eligible students enrolled in teacher education programs are awarded on the basis of academic merit and financial need. The institution has a

MILES COLLEGE—cont'd

Program Participation Agreement with the U.S. Department of Education for eligible students to receive Pell Grants and other federal aid. *Contact:* Financial Aid Office at (205) 929-1665.

Accreditation: *Regional:* SACS. *Approved by:* Alabama State Department of Education.

Undergraduate Programs: The elementary education major program leads to a Bachelor of Science degree and to Class B teacher certification in the areas of early childhood and elementary education. The program is designed to prepare teachers for grades P-6. Student must complete general education requirements and the professional studies component for a total of 120 credit hours.

The division also offers programs in secondary education leading to the Bachelor of Science degree and to professional teaching certification. These programs include biology education, chemistry education, language arts education, mathematics education, and social science education. The student must complete general education requirements and the professional studies component for a total of 120 credit hours.

All education majors must enroll in student internship which is the intensive and extensive practicum required for all majors. The student-internship program provides the student opportunities to interpret and synthesize theory through a variety of planned experiences in the school and community.

Licensure/Reciprocity: Alabama. Students seeking teaching certification in a state other than Alabama should consult with that state's teacher certification office early in their program of study to insure compliance with requirements. Many state directors of teacher credentialing have signed Interstate Agreements through NASDTEC that expedite the certification process.

OAKWOOD COLLEGE

Department of Education

7000 Adventist Boulevard, N.W.
Huntsville, Alabama 35896
Phone: (256) 726-7000
Fax: (800) 824-5312
E-mail: Fbliss@oakwood.edu
Internet: http://www.oakwood.edu

Institution Description: Oakwood College is a private college affiliated with the General Conference of Seventh-day Adventists (SDA). The college was established as Oakwood Industrial School in 1896 and its name changed to Oakwood Manual Training School in 1904. The college became Oakwood Junior College in 1917 and became a senior college with its present name in 1944.

The Seventh-day Adventist Christ-centered philosophy of education is foundational to all that is studied in the Department of Education. While supporting a distinct separation between public education and religious instruction, students in the teacher training program are taught skills needed for success in parochial and public classrooms.

Institution Control: Private.

Calendar: Quarter. Academic year September to June.

Official(s): Dr. Francis Bliss, Department Chair.

Faculty: Full-time 5.

Degrees Awarded: 24 baccalaureate.

Admission Requirements: *Undergraduate:* Graduation from an accredited secondary school or GED; minimum 2.0 GPA; ACT composite score. *Teacher education specific:* Apply to Department of Education and declare intention to pursue a teaching career; PRAXIS I exam scores; faculty interview.

Fees and Expenses: $10,194 per academic year. On-campus room and board: $5,852. Other expenses $5,440. Books and supplies: $1,000.

Financial Aid: Resources specifically for eligible students enrolled in teacher education programs are awarded on the basis of academic merit and financial need. The institution has a

Program Participation Agreement with the U.S. Department of Education for eligible students to receive Pell Grants and other federal aid. *Contact:* Financial Aid Office at (800) 624-5321.

Accreditation: *Regional:* SACS. *Professional:* NCATE. *Member of:* AACTE. *Approved by:* Alabama State Department of Education.

Undergraduate Programs: The Department of Education offers a curriculum that prepares students for elementary and secondary school teaching, graduate study, and employment in administration, teaching supervision, and support services. The curriculum allows students to apply for the Alabama Class B certification (except in religion), certification in other states, and the Seventh-day Adventist Basic Teaching Certification.

Degree programs offered include biology 6-12, business 6-12, chemistry 6-12, elementary K-6, English language arts 6-12, family and consumer sciences 6-12; mathematics 6-12 music vocal/choral P-12, music (instrumental) P-12, physical education P-12, religious education 7-12, social studies 6-12.

SDA certification for elementary education is for grades 1-8 and for secondary education grades 7-12.

Licensure/Reciprocity: Alabama. Students seeking teaching certification in a state other than Alabama should consult with that state's teacher certification office early in their program of study to insure compliance with requirements. Many state directors of teacher credentialing have signed Interstate Agreements through NASDTEC that expedite the certification process.

SAMFORD UNIVERSITY

Orlean Bullard Beeson School of Education
Teacher Education Program

800 Lakeshore Drive
Birmingham, Alabama 35229-2240
Phone: (205) 726-2011
Fax: (205) 726-3673
E-mail: admiss@samford.edu
Internet: http://www.samford.edu

Institution Description: Samford University is a private institution affiliated with the Baptist State Convention. It was established as Howard College and chartered in 1841. The present name was adopted in 1965.

In addition to extensive undergraduate program offering, the Orlean Bullard Beeson School of Education offers a variety of options for graduate study to qualified applicants. To accommodate the growing number of graduate students who pursue degrees part-time while continuing full-time employment, the graduate programs are tailored to fit a busy schedule. The courses are offered primarily in the evenings.

Institution Control: Private.

Calendar: Semester. Academic year June to May.

Official(s): Dr. Richard Franklin, Dean.

Faculty: Full-time 10, part-time 7.

Degrees Awarded: 78 undergraduate; 49 master's.

Admission Requirements: *Undergraduate:* Graduation from an accredited secondary school or GED; College Board SAT or ACT composite. *Teacher education specific:* Application to the Teacher Education Program; successful completion of 3 required education courses; passing score on the Alabama Basic Skills Test; completion of 60 credits of coursework with a GPA of at least 3.0 on a 4.0 scale in the areas of general education, the major, and professional studies; faculty interview. *Graduate:* Baccalaureate degree from an accredited institution; acceptance into a graduate program.

Fees and Expenses: $12,294 per academic year. On-campus room and board: $5,234. Other expenses $3,532. Books and supplies: $840.

Financial Aid: Resources specifically for eligible students enrolled in teacher education programs are awarded on the basis of academic merit and financial aid. The institution has a Program Participation Agreement with the U.S. Department of Education for eligible students to receive Pell Grants and other federal aid. *Contact:* Financial Aid Office at (205) 726-2905.

Accreditation: *Regional:* SACS. *Professional:* NCATE. *Member of:* AACTE. *Approved by:* Alabama State Department of Education.

Undergraduate Programs: Students who successfully complete a prescribed program at the baccalaureate level in teacher education will be eligible for the Alabama Class B teacher's certificate in their area(s) of specialization. Completion of the program is contingent upon achieving a 3.0 GPA on all work attempted; satisfactory performance as a teacher during the professional semester; completing and orally presenting a professional portfolio; receiving a passing score on the major field assessment examination prior to the end of the professional semester. All baccalaureate degrees require the completion of 128 credit hours.

Graduate Programs: The master's, education specialist, and doctoral degree programs in educational leadership are based on the premise that principals and other educational leaders should be "chief learning officers" in their organizations. The programs are designed to provide school administrators with the knowledge and skills to lead high-performing schools and school systems. Students work in teams to solve authentic problems of practice and complete school improvement projects designed to improve teaching practices and student achievement.

Licensure/Reciprocity: Alabama. Students seeking teaching certification in a state other than Alabama should consult with that state's teacher certification office early in their program of study to insure compliance with requirements. Many state directors of teacher credentialing have signed Interstate Agreements through NASDTEC that expedite the certification process.

SPRING HILL COLLEGE
Division of Teacher Education
4000 Dauphin Street
Mobile, Alabama 36608-1791
Phone: (251) 380-43477
Fax: (251) 460-2184
E-mail: aadams@shc.edu
Internet: http://www.shc.edu

Institution Description: Spring Hill College is a private college sponsored by the Society of Jesus, Roman Catholic Church. The college was established and and offered first instruction at postsecondary level in 1830. Spring Hill College is the third oldest Jesuit college and the first institution of higher education in Alabama.

The goad of the Division of Teacher Education is to prepare students to teach in our diverse society. The program combines liberal arts education and strong teacher preparation courses.

Institution Control: Private.

Calendar: Semester. Academic year August to May.

Official(s): Dr. Ann A. Adams, Chair.

Faculty: Full-time 4; adjunct 5.

Degrees Awarded: 101 baccalaureate; 92 master's.

Admission Requirements: *Undergraduate:* Graduation from an accredited secondary school or GED; 2.0 GPA; counselor recommendation; College Board SAT or ACT composite. *Teacher education specific:* Application to the Division of Teacher Education; completion of general education requirements in the lower division courses; pass specified tests. *Graduate:* Baccalaureate degree from an accredited institution. *Teacher education specific:* Faculty interview; recommendations; pass specific professional exams.

Fees and Expenses: $17,230 per academic year. On-campus room and board: $6,170. Other expenses: $2,060. Books and supplies: $900.

Financial Aid: Resources specifically for eligible students enrolled in teacher education programs are awarded on the basis of financial need and academic merit. *Contact:* Betty Harlan, Director of Financial Aid at (251) 380-3460 or bharlan@shc.edu.

Accreditation: *Regional:* SACS. *Professional:* NCATE. *Member of:* AACTE. *Approved by:* Alabama State Department of Education.

Undergraduate Programs: Undergraduate majors (early childhood, elementary education, secondary education) lead to teacher certification. Coursework combines lectures, discussion in the classroom and extensive laboratory experiences in the local schools. The professional sequence culminates in a full-time internship in an approved school.

Students who major in early childhood education follow a degree program designed to meet the requirements for teacher certification in nursery through grade three.

The elementary education major follows a program that meets the requirements for teacher certification in grades 1 through 6.

Students who major in secondary education follow a program that leads to teacher certification at the high school level (grades 7-12). Single, dual, or comprehensive teaching fields are selected from the following fields: biology, chemistry, English, history, language arts, mathematics, political science, social sciences, and Spanish.

Teacher education students who participate in one retreat and who complete selected courses to fulfill their theology requirements are eligible to receive their basic catechetical certification from the Archdiocese of Mobile.

Graduate Programs: The Master of Science program is offered in early childhood education, elementary education, and the teaching of reading. The Master of Arts in Teaching program is available for people who have a bachelor's degree in a field other than education. Two areas of study are offered: early childhood education and elementary education.

Licensure/Reciprocity: Alabama. Students seeking teaching certification in a state other than Alabama should consult with that state's teacher certification office early in their program of study to insure compliance with requirements. Many state directors of teacher credentialing have signed Interstate Agreements through NASDTEC that expedite the certification process.

STILLMAN COLLEGE
Teacher Education Program
3600 Stillman Boulevard
P.O. Drawer 1430
Tuscaloosa, Alabama 35403
Phone: (205) 349-4240
Fax: (205) 366-8816
E-mail: admissions@stillman.edu
Internet: http://www.stillman.edu

Institution Description: Stillman College is a private, historically black, four-year institution affiliated with the Presbyterian Church (USA) and the College Fund/UNCF. It was established as Tuscaloosa Institute in 1876. It became a junior college in 1937, a 4-year institution in 1948. The present name was also adopted in 1948.

The Teacher Education Program includes preparation for students who wish to be elementary teachers as well as those who desire to teach a student area a the secondary level. The program maintains the Teacher Education Center, a resource laboratory for students majoring in a teacher education area.

Institution Control: Private.

Calendar: Semester. Academic year August to May.

Official(s): Dr. Debra Baird, Chairperson.

Faculty: Full-time 11.

Degrees Awarded: 13 baccalaureate.

Admission Requirements: *Undergraduate:* Graduation from an accredited secondary school or GED; College Board SAT or ACT composite. *Teacher education specific:* Admission into the Teacher Education Program requires successful completion of the admissions test designated by the State Superintendent of Education; successful completion of Stillman College general education requirement completed prior to application for admission; overall GPA of 2.5 on a 4.0 scale; faculty interview.

Fees and Expenses: $7,848 per academic year. On-campus room and board: $4,236. Other expenses $1,400. Books and supplies: $750.

STILLMAN COLLEGE—cont'd

Financial Aid: Resources specifically for eligible students enrolled in teacher education programs are awarded on the basis of academic merit and financial need. The institution has a Program Participation Agreement with the U.S. Department of Education for eligible students to receive Pell Grants and other federal aid. *Contact:* Financial Aid Office at (205) 366-8844.

Accreditation: *Regional:* SACS. *Professional:* NCATE. *Member of:* AACTE. *Approved by:* Alabama State Department of Education.

Undergraduate Programs: The Teacher Education Program is comprised of a set of prescribed field experiences, entry and retention requirements, courses, and regulations to prepare students for state certification and successful careers at the elementary and secondary levels. Students who complete a program will be eligible for the Alabama Class B teacher's certificate in the area(s) of their specialization. A total of 124 credit hours must be completed for the degree award.

Licensure/Reciprocity: Alabama. Students seeking teaching certification in a state other than Alabama should consult with that state's teacher certification office early in their program of study to insure compliance with requirements. Many state directors of teacher credentialing have signed Interstate Agreements through NASDTEC that expedite the certification process.

TALLADEGA COLLEGE

Division of Social Sciences and Education
Education Department
627 West Battle Street
Talladega, Alabama 35160
Phone: (256) 362-0206
Fax: (256) 362-2268
E-mail: ehall@talladega.edu
Internet: http://www.talladega.edu

Institution Description: Talladega College is a private, nonprofit college affiliated with the United Church of Christ. The college was established as as a primary school 1867 and normal school training began in 1868.

The primary mission of the Education Department is to educate, challenge, and motivate its students to become productive, professional teachers and leaders in society. The purpose of the secondary education program is to prepare qualified persons for entry level position sin the public education delivery system and to provide a pool of qualified teachers for admission to graduate training programs in selected fields of teaching.

Institution Control: Private.

Calendar: Semester. Academic year August to May.

Official(s): Dr. Edward Hall, Dean.

Faculty: Full-time 3.

Degrees Awarded: 9 baccalaureate.

Admission Requirements: *Undergraduate:* Graduation from an accredited secondary school or GED; minimum GPA 2.35; College Board SAT or ACT composite. *Teacher education specific:* Admission to the college does not qualify a student for admission to the teacher education program. Applicants must submit application to the Department Chair after completing a minimum of 60 semester hours; GPA of 2.5 on all college work attempted; personal interview; satisfactory score on the Alabama Basic Skills Test.

Fees and Expenses: $6,727 per academic year. On-campus room and board: $3,622. Other expenses $1,140. Books and supplies: $1,178.

Financial Aid: Resources specifically for eligible students enrolled in teacher education programs are awarded on the basis of academic merit and financial need. The institution has a Program Participation Agreement with the U.S. Department of Education for eligible students to receive Pell Grants and other federal aid. *Contact:* Financial Aid Office at (256) 761-6236.

Accreditation: *Regional:* SACS. *Professional:* NCATE. *Approved by:* Alabama State Department of Education.

Undergraduate Programs: The Education Department offers programs leading to the Bachelor of Arts and teacher certification (grades 6-12) in biology, chemistry, English, French, history, mathematics, and music. The baccalaureate degree programs require the completion of 123 credit hours. Teacher certificates are issued by the Alabama State Department of Education upon recommendation from the Certification Officer at Talladega Colleges. Students have five years from program completion to apply.

Licensure/Reciprocity: Alabama. Students seeking teaching certification in a state other than Alabama should consult with that state's certification officer early in their program of study to insure compliance with requirements.

TROY STATE UNIVERSITY

College of Education
Department of Curriculum and Teaching
University Avenue
Troy, Alabama 36082
Phone: (334) 670-3365
Fax: (334) 670-3548
E-mail: dkelley@troyst.edu
Internet: http://www.troyst.edu

Institution Description: Troy State University is a public institution with branch campuses at Dothan and Montgomery. It was established and chartered as Troy State Normal School in 1887 and became Troy State Teachers College in 1929. The name was changed to Troy State College in 1957 and the present name was adopted in 1967.

Troy State University offers teacher education programs with majors in secondary education, preschool-12th grade, and elementary education. Successful completion of all program requirements leads to recommendation for the Alabama Class B teaching certificate.

Institution Control: Public. Academic year August to May.

Official(s): Dr. Donna D. Kelley, Director of Teacher Education.

Faculty: Full-time 20.

Degrees Awarded: 155 baccalaureate.

Admission Requirements: *Undergraduate:* Graduation from an accredited secondary school or GED; minimum grade average C; College Board SAT or ACT composite. *Teacher education specific:* Admission to the college does not qualify a student for admission to the Professional Education Program. Students must apply to the department after completion of all required general education studies courses; GPA of 2.50; faculty interview.

Fees and Expenses: Undergraduate: in-state $3,532 per academic year; $6,752 out-of-state. On-campus room and board: $4,496. Books and supplies: $420.

Financial Aid: Resources specifically for eligible students enrolled in teacher education programs are awarded on the basis of academic merit and financial need. The institution has a Program Participation Agreement with the U.S. Department of Education for eligible students to receive Pell Grants and other federal aid. *Contact:* Financial Aid Office at (334) 670-3186.

Accreditation: *Regional:* SACS. *Professional:* NCATE. *Member of:* AACTE. *Approved by:* Alabama State Department of Education.

Undergraduate Programs: Secondary education majors are offered in the areas of biology, chemistry, English/language arts, French, general science, health education, history, Latin, mathematics, social sciences, and Spanish. Pre-school-12th grade majors are offered in art education, music education (instrumental or vocal/choral); and physical education. elementary education majors K-6 are offered in collaborative teaching K-6. General studies courses cannot be used to meet requirements for both a teaching field major and general studies. Some education majors have special general education requirements.

Licensure/Reciprocity: Alabama. Other states may grant professional certification to students completing the teacher education program, although some states may have additional requirements.

TROY STATE UNIVERSITY DOTHAN

College of Education
500 University Drive
Dothan, Alabama 36304
Phone: (334) 983-6556
Fax: (334) 983-6322
E-mail: sjones@tsud.edu
Internet: http://www.tsud.edu

Institution Description: Troy State University Dothan (TSUD), a member of the Troy State University System, is a nonprofit, state-assisted institution. TSUD is a comprehensive, coeducational, commuter university. The campus was established as a resident center at Fort Rucker in 1961 and was named Troy State University at Fort Rucker in 1967. Classes were first offered in Dothan in 1974 and the campus became Troy State University at Dothan/Fort Rucker in 1975. The present name was adopted in 1996.

The mission of the College of Education is to prepare educators, counselors, and administrators to be life-long, reflective, informed decision makers effectively trained to achieve the goals, competencies, and skills identified by the Alabama Department of Education as requisite for educating children and youth.

Institution Control: Public.

Calendar: Semester. Academic year September to August.

Official(s): Dr. Sandra Lee Jones, Dean.

Faculty: Full-time 13.

Degrees Awarded: 67 baccalaureate; 70 master's.

Admission Requirements: *Undergraduate:* Graduation from an accredited secondary school with a minimum of 23 Carnegie units; College Board SAT or ACT composite. *Teacher education specific:* Admission to the Teacher Education Program requires the completion of the minimum of 33 credit hours in general studies and permission of an assigned advisor. *Graduate:* Baccalaureate degree; minimum 3.0 GPA; faculty recommendations. *Teacher education specific:* Students with a baccalaureate degree who are changing majors and/or specialization and who have 2 years appropriate successful teaching experience will complete a 3-9 hour internship.

Fees and Expenses: Undergraduate: in-state $3,220 per academic year; $6,440 out-of-state. Graduate tuition charged per credit hour. On-campus room and board: $4,632. Other expenses $3,080. Books and supplies: $300.

Financial Aid: Resources specifically for eligible students enrolled in teacher education programs are awarded on the basis of financial need and academic merit. The institution has a Program Participation Agreement with the U.S. Department of Education for eligible students to receive Pell Grants and other federal aid. *Contact:* Financial Aid Office at (334) 963-6556.

Accreditation: *Regional:* SACS. *Professional:* NCATE. *Member of:* AACTE. *Approved by:* Alabama State Department of Education.

Undergraduate Programs: The College of Education offers programs of study in the areas of collaborative education (k-6), collaborative education (6-12), early childhood education, elementary education, early childhood/elementary education (dual program), secondary education (concentrations in biology, English language arts, comprehensive general science, history, mathematics, social science). All baccalaureate degrees require the completion of 128 semester hours.

Graduate Programs: The Master of Science in Education degree is offered in the areas of early childhood education, elementary education, secondary education, special education, Alternative Class A programs, and instructional support programs. Completion of 36 to 48 semester hours is required for the degree award.

Licensure/Reciprocity: Alabama. Students seeking teaching certification in a state other than Alabama should consult with that state's teacher certification office early in their program of study to insure compliance with requirements. Many state directors of teacher credentialing have signed Interstate Agreements through NASDTEC that expedite the certification process.

TROY STATE UNIVERSITY MONTGOMERY

College of Education
231 Montgomery Street
Montgomery, Alabama 36103-4419
Phone: (334) 241-9577
Fax: (334) 241-9508
E-mail: lkitchens@tsum.edu
Internet: http://www.tsum.edu

Institution Description: Troy State University Montgomery offers programs in education for working adults. The institution is an adult, evening, and commuter school.

The College of Education offers graduate degree programs in counseling and human development and graduate degree programs in education.

Institution Control: Public.

Calendar: Semester. Academic year September to August.

Official(s): Dr. Len Kitchens, Dean.

Faculty: Full-time 8.

Degrees Awarded: 13 master's.

Admission Requirements: *Graduate:* Baccalaureate degree from a regionally accredited institution; *Teacher education specific:* Apply to the College of Education; specific achievement tests; GRE; faculty interview.

Fees and Expenses: $3,142 in-state per academic year; $6,214 out-of-state. Books and supplies: $840.

Financial Aid: Resources specifically for eligible students enrolled in teacher education programs are awarded on the basis of financial need and academic merit. The institution has a Program Participation Agreement with the U.S. Department of Education for eligible students to receive Pell Grants and other federal aid. *Contact:* Financial Aid Office at (334) 241-9520.

Accreditation: *Regional:* SACS. *Professional:* NCATE. *Approved by:* Alabama State Department of Education.

Graduate Programs: There are four programs of study in education: Master of Science in elementary education or adult education and Master of Arts in Teaching. Also offered is a program leading to Education Specialist in general education administration. The Master of Science in elementary education is a certified degree program. It is focused on grades 1-6 and is comprised of 30 semester hours of coursework (15 semester hours of core courses and 15 semester hours of electives appropriate to the program of study.

Licensure/Reciprocity: Alabama. Students seeking teaching certification in a state other than Alabama should consult with that state's teacher certification office early in their program of study to insure compliance with requirements. Many state directors of teacher credentialing have signed Interstate Agreements through NASDTEC that expedite the certification process.

TUSKEGEE UNIVERSITY

College of Liberal Arts and Education
Department of Curriculum and Instruction
Old Montgomery Road
Tuskegee University, Alabama 36088
Phone: (334) 727-8144
Fax: (334) 724-4384
E-mail: gathrigh@tusk.edu
Internet: http://www.tusk.edu

Institution Description: Tuskegee University is a private, independent, nonprofit institution of higher learning. It was the first black college to be designated as a Registered National Historic Landmark (1966) and the first black college to be designated a National Historic Site (1974). The university was established as Tuskegee Normal School in 1881 and became Tuskegee Institute in 1937. The present name was adopted in 1985.

The Department of Curriculum and Instruction is responsible for the preparation of professional educators. The department prepares students for professional teaching careers in schools and for careers as educationists in other agencies.

Institution Control: Private.

TUSKEGEE UNIVERSITY—cont'd

Calendar: Semester. Academic year August to May.
Official(s): Dr. Benjamin Benford, Dean.
Faculty: Full-time 12.
Degrees Awarded: 17 baccalaureate; 2 master's.
Admission Requirements: *Undergraduate:* Graduation from an accredited secondary school or GED; minimum 2.5 GPA preferred; SAT score of 900 or ACT of 18. *Teacher education specific:* Apply to the department as early in course of study as possible; basic skills tests; faculty interview. *Graduate:* Baccalaureate degree from a regionally accredited institution; GRE and other specified exams. *Teacher education specific:* faculty interview; completion of specified requirements and exams.
Fees and Expenses: $10,784 per academic year. On-campus room and board: $5,600. Other expenses: $2,514. Books and supplies: $875.
Financial Aid: Resources specifically for eligible students enrolled in teacher education programs are awarded on the basis of academic merit and financial need. The institution has a Program Participation Agreement with the U.S. Department of Education for eligible students to receive Pell Grants and other federal aid. *Contact:* Financial Aid Office at (334) 727-8212.
Accreditation: *Regional:* SACS. *Professional:* NCATE. *Member of:* AACTE. *Approved by:* Alabama State Department of Education.
Undergraduate Programs: The department offers undergraduate teacher education programs in elementary education, English/language arts, general science, and mathematics. All baccalaureate degrees require the completion of general education courses, core education courses, and professional participation studies (student teaching). A variable number of credit hours are required for the degree (average 130 credit hours).
Graduate Programs: Graduate programs offered by the department are the Master of Education in general science which is primarily for candidates with undergraduate science education degrees. The Fifth Year Nontraditional Master of Education in general science is primarily for candidates whose undergraduate degree is in a science field but not teacher education. Credit hour requirements vary by program.
Licensure/Reciprocity: Alabama. Students seeking teaching certification in a state other than Alabama should consult with that state's teacher certification office early in their program of study to insure compliance with requirements. Many state directors of teacher credentialing have signed Interstate Agreements through NASDTEC that expedite the certification process.

UNIVERSITY OF ALABAMA

College of Education
739 University Boulevard
Tuscaloosa, Alabama 35487-0132
Phone: (205) 348-6010
Fax: (205) 348-5666
E-mail: admissions@ua.edu
Internet: http://www.ua.edu

Institution Description: The university was established and chartered in 1820.

The mission of the College of Education is to offer professional programs to prepare educators to be effective decision makers. The college provides comprehensive instructional programs in educational research and seeks to enhance policy-making and professional development at state, regional, and national levels.
Institution Control: Public.
Calendar: Semester. Academic year August to May.
Official(s): Dr. W. Ross Palmer, Dean.
Faculty: Full-time 127.
Degrees Awarded: 213 baccalaureate; 231 master's.
Admission Requirements: *Undergraduate:* Graduation from an accredited secondary school or with completion of 20-course pre-college curriculum or GED; either SAT or ACT required.

Teacher education specific: Apply to College of Education after completion of all general education courses; faculty interview. *Graduate:* GPA of 3.0 on a 4.0 scale in the last 60 semester hours in a degree program or 3.0 for a completed graduate degree program. *Teacher education specific:* The applicant must have score on the appropriate entrance examination that is acceptable for regular admission.
Fees and Expenses: Undergraduate: in-state $3,556 per academic year; out-of-state $9,624. Graduate: Tuitions charged per credit hour. On-campus room and board: $5,824. Other expenses: $2,392. Books and supplies: $700.
Financial Aid: Resources specifically for eligible students enrolled in teacher education programs are awarded on the basis of financial need and academic merit. The institution has a Program Participation Agreement with the U.S. Department of Education for eligible students to receive Pell Grants and other federal aid. *Contact:* Financial Aid Office at (205) 348-6756.
Accreditation: *Regional:* SACS. *Professional:* NCATE. *Member of:* AACTE. *Approved by:* Alabama State Department of Education.
Undergraduate Programs: The College of Education offers teacher education programs in the following areas: elementary education; interdisciplinary teacher education; music education; and secondary curriculum, teaching, and learning (science, language arts/social science, ESL/bilingual, reading, mathematics, and foreign language).
Graduate Programs: Graduate programs offered by the College of Education include collaborative teacher program, multiple abilities program, early childhood special education; gifted and exceptional children education. Contact the college for specific program requirements.
Licensure/Reciprocity: Alabama. Students seeking teaching certification in a state other than Alabama should consult with that state's teacher certification office early in their program of study to insure compliance with requirements. Many state directors of teacher credentialing have signed Interstate Agreements through NASDTEC that expedite the certification process.

UNIVERSITY OF ALABAMA AT BIRMINGHAM

School of Education
Department of Curriculum and Instruction
1530 3rd Avenue South
Birmingham, Alabama 35294
Phone: (205) 934-4011
Fax: (205) 934-5371
E-mail: UndergradAdmit@uab.edu
Internet: http://www.uab.edu

Institution Description: The university was established and offered first instruction at the postsecondary level in 1966.

The Department of Curriculum and Instruction offers numerous undergraduate programs which lead to a Bachelor of Science degree and professional certification. Students who are preparing to teach are expected to participate in a series of planned assignments in community and/or school settings both before and during admission to the Teacher Education Program.
Institution Control: Public.
Calendar: Semester. Academic year September to June.
Official(s): Dr. Joe Burns, Chair.
Faculty: Full-time 25.
Degrees Awarded: 190 baccalaureate; 308 master's.
Admission Requirements: *Undergraduate:* Graduation from an accredited secondary school or with completion of 20-course pre-college curriculum or GED; either SAT or ACT required. *Teacher education specific:* Apply to College of Education after completion of all general education courses; faculty interview. *Graduate:* GPA of 3.0 on a 4.0 scale in the last 60 semester hours in a degree program or 3.0 for a completed graduate degree program. *Teacher education specific:* The applicant must have score on the appropriate entrance examination that is acceptable for regular admission.

Fees and Expenses: Undergraduate: in-state $3,880 per academic year; out-of-state $7,810. Graduate: Tuition charged per credit hour. On-campus room and board: $7,218. Other expenses $2,438. Books and supplies: $900.

Financial Aid: Resources specifically for eligible students enrolled in teacher education programs are awarded on the basis of academic merit and financial need. The institution has a Program Participation Agreement with the U.S. Department of Education for eligible students to receive Pell Grants and other federal aid. *Contact:* Financial Aid Office at (205) 934-8223.

Accreditation: *Regional:* SACS. *Professional:* NCATE. *Member of:* AACTE. *Approved by:* Alabama State Department of Education.

Undergraduate Programs: The Department of Curriculum and Instruction offers numerous undergraduate programs which lead to a B.S. degree in education and/or Alabama Class B professional certificate in the student's program area. Students may prepare for any of the following teaching areas: early childhood education, grades N-3; elementary education, grades 1-6; high school education, grades 7-12, art education, grades N-12; foreign language, N-12; general music, N-8; instrumental music, N-12; vocal/choral music, N-12; and speech communication/theater, grades N-12.

Graduate Programs: Programs of study are offered which lead to a Master of Arts in Education degree and to an Education Specialist degree. These programs are designed so that the students may receive the Alabama Class A and Class AA certificates in certain fields. Students may also earn a Doctor of Philosophy in early childhood education.

Licensure/Reciprocity: Alabama. Students seeking teaching certification in a state other than Alabama should consult with that state's teacher certification office early in their program of study to insure compliance with requirements. Many state directors of teacher credentialing have signed Interstate Agreements through NASDTEC that expedite the certification process.

UNIVERSITY OF ALABAMA IN HUNTSVILLE

Department of Education

Morton Hall 243
301 Sparkman Drive
Huntsville, Alabama 35899
Phone: (296) 824-6180
Fax: (256) 824-2387
E-mail: piersman@uah.edu
Internet: http://www.uah.edu

Institution Description: The campus was established as a resident center for the University of Alabama in 1950. The present name was adopted in 1966. It began and undergraduate program and awarded first baccalaureate degree in 1968. The campus became an autonomous institution 1969.

The mission of the Department of Education is to prepare teachers who are academically strong, competent in theory and practice, and prepared to help resolve the educational needs for our society. The department, in conjunction with the College of Liberal Arts and Science, offers undergraduate certification programs in art education, elementary education, secondary education, and music education.

Institution Control: Public.

Calendar: Semester. Academic year August to May.

Official(s): Dr. Mary L. Piersma, Department Chairperson.

Faculty: Full-time 8; adjunct 2.

Degrees Awarded: 231 baccalaureate; 53 master's.

Admission Requirements: *Undergraduate:* Graduation from an accredited secondary school; College Board SAT score of 1050; ACT composite score of 23 or higher. *Teacher education specific:* 2.5 overall; pass APT test. *Graduate:* 3.0 GPA; passing score on GRE or Miller Analogy Test. *Teacher education specific:* 2.5 GPA in major at undergraduate level; maintain 3.0 GPA.

Fees and Expenses: Undergraduate: in-state $3,556 per academic year; $9,624 out-of-state. Graduate tuition charged per credit hour. On-campus room and board: $5,824. Other expenses: $2,392. Books and supplies: $700.

Financial Aid: Resources specifically for eligible students enrolled in teacher education programs are awarded on the basis of academic merit and financial need. *Contact:* Andrew Weaver at (256) 824-6942 or weavera@uah.edu.

Accreditation: *Regional:* SACS. *Professional:* NCATE. *Member of:* AACTE. *Approved by:* Alabama State Department of Education.

Undergraduate Programs: Programs offered by the Department of Education are designed to prepare for professional certification at the Class B level. Students may pursue the baccalaureate degree in art education (Pre-K-12); elementary education (K-6); secondary/high school education (6-12) with majors in biology, chemistry, English/language arts, French, general science, German, history, mathematics, physics, social science, and Spanish; and music education (Pre-K-12).

Graduate Programs: The College of Liberal Arts offers programs of study leading to the Master of Arts degree in English, history, psychology, and public affairs, Class A teacher certification is available with formal degree programs in English and history, as well as the disciplines of biology, chemistry, mathematics, and physics. Teacher certification may be achieved through either traditional or nontraditional fifth-year approaches. Those students who have earned graduate degrees in appropriate disciplines may be eligible for certification only programs.

Licensure/Reciprocity: Alabama. Students seeking teaching certification in a state other than Alabama should consult with that state's teacher certification office early in their program of study to insure compliance with requirements. Many state directors of teacher credentialing have signed Interstate Agreements through NASDTEC that expedite the certification process.

UNIVERSITY OF MOBILE

School of Education

5735 College Parkway
P.O. Box 13220
Mobile, Alabama 36663-0220
Phone: (800) 946-7267
Fax: (251) 442-2523
E-mail: education@free.umobile.edu
Internet: http://www.umobile.edu

Institution Description: The University of Mobile, formerly known as Mobile College, is a private college affiliated with the Southern Baptist Church. It was chartered in 1961 and offered first instruction at the postsecondary level in 1963. The present name was adopted in 1993.

The primary concern of the School of Education is to provide academic programs that encourage self-development and to enable graduates to develop professionally in an environment that emphasizes Christian ethical values.

Institution Control: Private.

Calendar: Semester. Academic year begins August to April.

Official(s): Dr. Larry V. Turner, Dean, School of Education.

Faculty: Full-time 11.

Degrees Awarded: 49 baccalaureate; 12 master's.

Admission Requirements: *Undergraduate:* Graduation from an accredited secondary school or GED; College Board SAT or ACT composite. *Teacher education specific:* Application to the School of Education as early in college enrollment as possible; completion of general education requirements and specified courses in the field of education. *Graduate:* Student must hold a baccalaureate degree from an accredited institution; overall undergraduate GPA of 2.75 on a 4.0 scale. *Teacher education specific:* Test scores obtained on the GRE; provide copy of teacher certificate.

Fees and Expenses: $8,940 per academic year. On-campus room and board: $5,000. Books and supplies: $500.

UNIVERSITY OF MOBILE—cont'd

Financial Aid: Resources specifically for eligible students enrolled in teacher education programs are awarded on the basis of academic merit and financial need. The institution has a Program Participation Agreement with the U.S. Department of Education for eligible students to receive Pell Grants and other federal aid. *Contact:* Financial Aid Office at (251) 442-2252.

Accreditation: *Regional:* SACS. *Professional:* NCATE. *Member of:* AACTE. *Approved by:* Alabama State Department of Education.

Undergraduate Programs: The elementary education program is designed to prepare students to acquire the knowledge, understanding, and necessary skills. Teaching skills are refined through in-class modeling and field experiences that help the student to practice methodology and decision-making that are grounded in well-researched theories. The program consists of formal training in educational methods, theory, and pedagogy.

A major in early childhood Education learns the development characteristics of young children, their learning styles, and classroom experiences that are appropriate for early childhood programs. A major requires, in addition to the general preparation sequence from liberal arts, sixteen courses (48 semester hours) in teacher education, 9 semester hours in student teacher, and 9 semester hours in approved electives.

Graduate Programs: The Master of Arts in Education degree is offered in programs leading to Class A certification in the areas of early childhood and elementary education. The programs require completion of core courses and teaching field courses for a total of 33 credit hours.

The alternative certification program is available for non-education baccalaureate degree majors. The major for the undergraduate degree must be in a content area approved for certification by the Alabama State Board of Education.The program requires the completion of core courses and teaching field courses for a total of 45 semester hours.

Licensure/Reciprocity: Alabama. Students seeking teaching certification in a state other than Alabama should consult with that state's teacher certification office early in their program of study to insure compliance with requirements. Many state directors of teacher credentialing have signed Interstate Agreements through NASDTEC that expedite the certification process.

UNIVERSITY OF MONTEVALLO

College of Education
Department of Curriculum and Instruction
Station 6392
Montevallo, Alabama 35115
Phone: (205) 665-6030
Fax: (205) 665-6337
E-mail: counce@montevallo.edu
Internet: http://www.montevallo.edu

Institution Description: The University of Montevallo is a state institution. It was established as the Alabama Girls' Industrial School 1896 and its name was changed to Alabama College in the 1920s. Men were admitted as full-time students in 1956 and the present name was adopted in 1969.

Institution Control: Public.

Calendar: Semester. Academic year August to May.

Official(s): Dr. Jack Riley, Dean, College of Education; Dr. Beth Counce, Chair, Department of Curriculum and Instruction.

Faculty: Full-time 11.

Degrees Awarded: 49 baccalaureate; 103 master's.

Admission Requirements: *Undergraduate:* Graduation from an secondary school with 15 units or GED; 2.0 GPA on a 4.0 scale; College Board SAT or ACT composite. *Teacher education specific:* Before entering the teacher education program, students observe teaching in public schools while taking an introduction to education course. *Graduate:* Baccalaureate degree from a regionally accredited institution; faculty interview. *Teacher education specific:* Faculty interview; various certification exams/tests.

Fees and Expenses: Undergraduate: in-state $3,506 per academic year; out-of-state $6,766. Graduate: Tuition charged per credit hour. On-campus room and board: $3,754. Other expenses: $2,646. Books and supplies: $600.

Financial Aid: Resources specifically for eligible students enrolled in teacher education programs are awarded on the basis of academic merit and financial need. The institution has a Program Participation Agreement with the U.S. Department of Education for eligible students to receive Pell Grants and other federal aid. *Contact:* Financial Aid Office at (205) 652-3576.

Accreditation: *Regional:* SACS. *Professional:* NCATE. *Member of:* AACTE. *Approved by:* Alabama State Department of Education.

Undergraduate Programs: The department offers undergraduate degree programs in early childhood education and in elementary education. The programs satisfy requirements for Alabama Class B certification in those areas. Certification in both areas may be obtained. Students must complete a semester-long internship in a public school during the senior year. A total of 130 semester hours must be completed for the degree including general education courses, subject area major, and professional studies.

Study for a certificate in elementary education allows for a middle-school endorsement with the completion of additional courses. The endorsement may be granted in biology, English/language arts, general science, physical science, history, mathematics, and social science.

Secondary school certification qualifies the recipient to teach at the secondary-school level (grades 6-12) and requires completion of professional education courses, and internship, and courses in the teaching field(s).

Graduate Programs: Graduate programs include the Master of Arts (English); Master of Science (speech/language pathology); Master of Music; Master of Education (counseling, early childhood, elementary, preschool to 12th grade, secondary education, educational administration). Contact the department for particular requirements for each field.

Licensure/Reciprocity: Alabama. Students seeking teaching certification in a state other than Alabama should consult with that state's teacher certification office early in their program of study to insure compliance with requirements. Many state directors of teacher credentialing have signed Interstate Agreements through NASDTEC that expedite the certification process.

UNIVERSITY OF NORTH ALABAMA

College of Education
UnA Box 5031
Wesleyan Avenue
Florence, Alabama 35632-0001
Phone: (256) 765-4252
Fax: (256) 765-4464
E-mail: fihattabaugh@una.edu
Internet: http://www.una.edu

Institution Description: The University of North Alabama is a state institution. The campus was established when faculty and students of LaGrange College (established 1830) moved to Florence to open a new institution by the Methodist Church as Wesleyan University in 1855. Operations were suspended in 1862 and the facilities were donated to the state and reopened as Florence Normal School in 1872. After several name changes, the current name was adopted in 1974.

The College of Education offers baccalaureate and graduate programs in teacher education with various options in subject areas.

Institution Control: Public.

Calendar: Semester. Academic year August to May.

Official(s): Dr. Fed Hattabaugh, Dean.

Faculty: Full-time 26; part-time 1; adjunct 7.

Degrees Awarded: 321 baccalaureate; 286 master's.

Admission Requirements: *Undergraduate:* Diploma from an approved high school; composite of 18 or higher on ACT; 830 or higher on SAT; GPA at least 2.0. *Teacher education specific:* GPA

3.0; completion of general studies requirements; C or better in Fundamentals of Speech and English Composition; completion of introductory education class. *Graduate:* Baccalaureate degree from a regional accredited institution; satisfactory test scores and GPA requirement specified for the particular program. *Teacher education specific:* Certification in required field; 3.0 overall GPA; minimum score on MAT or GRE.

Fees and Expenses: Undergraduate: in-state $127 per credit hour; out-of-state $254. Graduate: in-state $148 per credit hour; out-of-state $296. On-campus room and board: $5,202 per academic year. Books and supplies: $800.

Financial Aid: Resources specifically for eligible students enrolled in teacher education programs are awarded on the basis of financial need. *Contact:* Ben Baker at (256) 765-4279 or bbaker@una.edu.

Accreditation: *Regional:* SACS. *Professional:* NCATE. *Member of:* AACTE. *Approved by:* Alabama State Department of Education.

Undergraduate Programs: Students can major in elementary education or secondary education in various academic fields. In addition to general education courses and professional study courses, a semester of internship (12 semester hours) is required. Completion of all requirements leads to Alabama teacher certification.

Graduate Programs: The College of Education offers degree programs of study for teachers already certified at the baccalaureate level. An alternative master's degree program is offered in some secondary subject fields for individuals not certified at the baccalaureate level.

Licensure/Reciprocity: Alabama. Students seeking teaching certification in a state other than Alabama should consult with that state's teacher certification office early in their program of study to insure compliance with requirements. Many state directors of teacher credentialing have signed Interstate Agreements through NASDTEC that expedite the certification process.

UNIVERSITY OF SOUTH ALABAMA

College of Education
Department of Curriculum and Instruction
UCOM 3600
75 North University Boulevard
Mobile, Alabama 36688-0002
Phone: (231) 380-2738
Fax: (231) 380-2748460-7023
E-mail: coe@southalabama.edu
Internet: http://www.southalabama.edu

Institution Description: The University of South Alabama is a state institution. The university was established and chartered in 1963. The first baccalaureate degree was awarded in 1967.

The College of Education offers many advantages to the student pursuing a degree in education. The Department of Curriculum and Instruction prepares undergraduate and graduate students for elementary, middle level, and high school classrooms through several programs. Through a series of courses and experiences emphasizing reflection and decision-making in teaching, students develop knowledge, skills, and attitudes necessary for effective teaching.

Institution Control: Public.

Calendar: Semester. Academic year August to May.

Official(s): Dr. Thomas L. Chilton, Dean, College of Education; Dr. Phillip Feldman, Chair, Department of Curriculum and Instruction.

Faculty: Department of Curriculum and Instruction: 17 full-time.

Degrees Awarded: 199 baccalaureate; 213 master's.

Admission Requirements: *Undergraduate:* Either graduation from accredited secondary school or GED; College Board SAT or ACT composite; GPA of at least 2.0. *Teacher education specific:* Completion of general studies requirements; completion of introductory education class; other special tests may be required. *Graduate:* Baccalaureate degree from a regional accredited institution; 3.0 overall GPA. *Teacher education specific:*

Satisfactory test scores as specified for the particular program; teacher's certificate in required field; 3.0 overall GPA; minimum score on MAT or GRE.

Fees and Expenses: Undergraduate: in-state $127 per credit hour, out-of-state $254. Graduate: in-state $148 per credit hour, out-of-state $296. On-campus room and board: $5,202 per academic year. Other expenses: $1,854. Books and supplies: $800.

Financial Aid: Resources specifically for eligible students enrolled in teacher education programs are awarded on the basis of academic merit and financial need. *Contact:* Emily Johnson, Director, Financial Aid at (251) 460-2631 or ejohnson@southalabama.edu.

Accreditation: *Regional:* SACS. *Professional:* NCATE. *Member of:* AACTE. *Approved by:* Alabama State Department of Education.

Undergraduate Programs: The program in elementary education is designed to prepare teachers for kindergarten through 6th grade. Satisfactory completion of the program and accompanying tests lead to Alabama certification. The degree requires the completion of 64 hours in general education courses plus specified courses including professional studies, internship, educational foundations, and the teaching field and curriculum area.

The secondary education program offers concentration in English/language arts, mathematics, and social sciences. A minimum of 64 hours in general studies plus specified courses in professional studies and teaching field.

The Preschool Through Grade 12 option is designed to prepare students to teach art or music at any grade level from preschool to grade 12. In addition to the general education requirements, students must complete specified courses in professional studies and the teaching field (art or music).

Graduate Programs: Graduate programs offered by the Department of Curriculum and Instruction include Masters of Education programs in early childhood education, elementary education; Alternative Masters in elementary education; and high school (grades 7-12) in the content areas of language arts, mathematics, science, and social studies. Master's programs with content areas in music or art for grades N-12 are also offered.

Licensure/Reciprocity: Alabama. Students seeking teaching certification in a state other than Alabama should consult with that state's teacher certification office early in their program of study to insure compliance with requirements. Many state directors of teacher credentialing have signed Interstate Agreements through NASDTEC that expedite the certification process.

UNIVERSITY OF WEST ALABAMA

College of Education
Teacher Education Program
UWA Station 8
Livingston, Alabama 35470
Phone: (205) 652-3421
Fax: (205) 652-3706
E-mail: admissions@univ.westal.edu
Internet: http://www.univ.westal.edu

Institution Description: The University of West Alabama, formerly named Livingston University, is a state institution. It was established and chartered as Livingston Female Academy 1835. It received a state grant, became Alabama Normal School, and offered first instruction at the postsecondary level in 1882. The name was changed to State Teachers College, Livingston, Alabama. After several other name changes, the current name was adopted in 1996.

The College of Education has as its primary objectives the training of competent teachers for school systems in Alabama, the promotion of improved instructional programs in elementary and secondary schools within the university service area and the other colleges within the university.

Institution Control: Public.

Calendar: Semester. Academic year August to May.

Official(s): Dr. Tom DeVaney, Dean.

Faculty: Full-time 11.

UNIVERSITY OF WEST ALABAMA—*cont'd*

Degrees Awarded: 69 baccalaureate; 128 master's.

Admission Requirements: *Undergraduate:* Graduation from an accredited secondary school or GED; minimum 2.0 GPA; College Board SAT or ACT composite. *Teacher education specific:* Acceptance to the teacher education program must be submitted after completion of general education requirements; faculty interview. *Graduate:* Baccalaureate degree from a regionally accredited institution; GRE; other tests/exams may be required; faculty interview. *Teacher education specific:* Completion of all required courses and internship in undergraduate field.

Fees and Expenses: Undergraduate: in-state $3,498 per academic year; out-of-state $6,558. Graduate: Tuition charged per credit hour. On-campus room and board: $2,958. Other expenses: $2,254. Books and supplies: $700.

Financial Aid: Resources specifically for eligible students enrolled in teacher education programs are awarded on the basis of financial need and academic merit. The institution has a Program Participation Agreement with the U.S. Department of Education for eligible students to receive Pell Grants and other federal aid. *Contact:* Federal Aid Office at (305) 652-3576.

Accreditation: *Regional:* SACS. *Professional:* NCATE. *Member of:* AACTE. *Approved by:* Alabama State Department of Education.

Undergraduate Programs: Undergraduate majors are offered in elementary education K-6 and collaborative teacher/special education K-6/6-12. All baccalaureate programs require the completion of 120 semester hours; exit proficiency exams; Alabama Initial Teacher Certification Test; and comprehensives in individual fields. Upon completion of 90 semester hours, students must submit an application for internship.

Graduate Programs: The Master of Arts in Teaching degree program is designed for those students who are already certified at the Class B level and wish to pursue a master's degree program and Alabama Class A certification. The program is also available to those students who hold a non-teaching bachelor's degree and are not seeking certification.

Students who complete requirements for the degree Master of Education and who meet all requirements specified by the Sate Board of Education may be recommended to teacher certification in one of the following areas as determined by the nature of their work: early childhood, elementary, high school, pre-school-grade twelve, school counseling, education administration, library media and special education.

Licensure/Reciprocity: Alabama. Students seeking teaching certification in a state other than Alabama should consult with that state's teacher certification office early in their program of study to insure compliance with requirements. Many state directors of teacher credentialing have signed Interstate Agreements through NASDTEC that expedite the certification process.

ALASKA

ALASKA PACIFIC UNIVERSITY

Education Department
Carr-Gottstein 211
4101 University Drive
Anchorage, Alaska 99508-4672
Phone: (907) 564-8378
Fax: (907) 564-8396
E-mail: eddept@alaskapacific.edu
Internet: http://www.alaskapacific.edu

Institution Description: Alaska Pacific University is a private institution affiliated with the United Methodist Church. The university was incorporated as Alaska Methodist University in 1957. The present name was adopted in 1978.

The Teacher Preparation Program carries out the holistic philosophy of the university which stresses a commitment to Alaska's intercultural and international heritage. Participants in the program may pursue study at either the undergraduate or graduate level. The undergraduate program includes a K-8 Education certificate for teacher aides.

Institution Control: Private.

Calendar: Semester. Academic year September to May.

Official(s): Theodore R. Munsch, Chair.

Faculty: Full-time 1; part-time 7.

Degrees Awarded: 10 baccalaureate; 14 master's.

Admission Requirements: *Undergraduate:* Either graduation from accredited secondary school or GED; minimum GPA 2.5; College Board SAT or ACT composite. Graduate: baccalaureate degree; before admittance to the Master of Arts in Teaching Program, students must complete all prerequisite courses with at least C or better; write a 304 page essay outlining educational philosophy and why a teaching career is desired; submit scores from the Miller Analogy Test or GRE; completion of PRAXIS I series of tests; interview with the Education Faculty.

Fees and Expenses: Undergraduate: in-state $12,300 per academic year; out-of-state $16,218. On-campus room and board: $1,200 to $1,500 per semester. Meal plan $1,550 per semester. Books and supplies: $840.

Financial Aid: Resources specifically for eligible students enrolled in teacher education programs are awarded on the basis of financial need and academic merit. *Contact:* Financial Aid Office: (907) 564-8342.

Accreditation: *Regional:* NASC. *Approved by:* Alaska Department of Education.

Undergraduate Programs: The Education Department offers a major in K-8 education that prepares students for a career in teaching. The program provides a strong background in the liberal arts as well as professional education courses. The program includes a K-8 education certificate. The degree requires completion of all required coursework with grades of C or better and a total of 128 credit hours.

Graduate Programs: The Masters of Arts in Teaching degree is specifically designed for people who have completed baccalaureate degrees from regionally accredited institutions in non-education disciplines but who are now interested in becoming teachers. At the present time the university offers a kindergarten through eighth grade certification with a master's degree. The program is primarily a sequential, school-based, daytime, 48 credit program.

Licensure/Reciprocity: Alaska. Students seeking teaching certification in a state other than Alaska should consult with that state's certification officer early in their program of study to insure compliance with requirements. Many state directors of teacher education credentialing have signed Interstate Agreements through NASDTEC that expedite the certification process.

SHELDON JACKSON COLLEGE

Department of Education
801 Lincoln
Sitka, Alaska 99835-7699
Phone: (907) 747-3666
Fax: (907) 747-5212
E-mail: yukonjohn@sj-alaska.edu
Internet: http://www.sj-alaska.edu

Institution Description: Sheldon Jackson College is a private, independent, nonprofit college affiliated with the United Presbyterian Church (U.S.A.). It was established in 1878 as Sitka Training School and moved to its present location in 1882. The present name was adopted in 1966.

The college offers programs in elementary and secondary education plus a teacher certification program for holders of baccalaureate degrees. Situated in southeast Alaska, the campus provides a unique multicultural environment for students. Field experience and student teaching provide opportunities for students to serve in rural communities throughout Alaska.

Institution Control: Private.

Calendar: Semester. Academic year August to May.

Official(s): Dr. Karen Packard, Chair

Faculty: Full-time 3; part-time 2.

Degrees Awarded: 6 baccalaureate.

Admission Requirements: *Undergraduate:* Rolling admission plan. Either graduation from secondary school or GED. Mature students may be accepted without GED or high school diploma upon favorable recommendations and demonstrated ability. *Teacher education specific:* In order to be admitted to the Teacher Preparation Program and to enroll in upper division education courses, students must submit a formal application. Applicants must have passed all section of PRAXIS I prior to admission into the program. *Graduate:* Student must hold a baccalaureate degree from an accredited institution; have a cumulative GPA of 2.5 or higher; get a passing score on the reading, writing, and mathematics portions exam and take the PRAXIS II exam in the appropriate area.

Fees and Expenses: $9,650 per academic year. On-campus room and board: $6,920. Books and supplies: $750.

Financial Aid: Resources specifically for eligible students enrolled in teacher education programs are awarded on the basis of financial need and academic merit. *Contact:* Financial Aid Office at (907) 747-5207.

Accreditation: *Regional:* NASC. *Approved by:* Alaska Department of Education.

Undergraduate Programs: The baccalaureate degree program in elementary education places an emphasis on preparing graduates to teach in the villages, towns, and rural communities of Alaska. The baccalaureate degree program in secondary educa-

SHELDON JACKSON COLLEGE—*cont'd*

tion places an emphasis upon preparing graduates to teach in the areas of language arts, mathematics/science, or social science. Successful completion of 130 credit hours are required.

Graduate Programs: The graduate teacher certification program for holders of baccalaureate degrees leads to endorsement by the State of Alaska in elementary or secondary education. Students must have a broad general education in their undergraduate work.

Licensure/Reciprocity: Alaska. Students seeking teaching certification in a state other than Alaska should consult with that state's certification officer early in their program of study to insure compliance with requirements. Many state directors of teacher education credentialing have signed Interstate Agreements through NASDTEC that expedite the certification process.

UNIVERSITY OF ALASKA ANCHORAGE

College of Education
3211 Providence Drive
Anchorage, Alaska 995080-8046
Phone: (907) 786-4401
Fax: (907) 786-4444
E-mail: aycoed@uaa.alaska.edu
Internet: http://www.alaska.edu

Institution Description: The University of Alaska, Anchorage (UAA) is comprised of a main and 4 community campuses (Kenai Peninsula College, Kodiak College, Matanuska-Susitna College, and Prince William Sound Community College). UAA is one of 3 major administrative units of the statewide system. The university was established, offered first instruction at the postsecondary level, and awarded its first degree in 1970.

All students desiring a degree, certification, or endorsement through an undergraduate or graduate program must apply for admission to the university and to the College of Education.

Institution Control: Public.

Calendar: Semester. Academic year June to May.

Official(s): Dr. Mary Snyder, Dean.

Faculty: Full-time 44.

Degrees Awarded: 89 baccalaureate; 78 master's.

Admission Requirements: *Undergraduate:* Rolling admission plan; either graduation from an accredited secondary school or GED; minimum GPA 2.5; College Board SAT or ACT composite; *Teacher education specific:* Student applicant must complete all departmental requirements including required tests. *Graduate:* Applications to the Master of Arts in Teaching (MAT) program and supporting documentation are due October 1. For information regarding the MAT program, contact the College of Education. *Teacher education specific:* Applicants must meet subject area requirements for a certification endorsement.

Fees and Expenses: Undergraduate: in-state $2,977 per academic year; out-of-state $8,197. On-campus room and board: $6,730. Books and supplies: $891.

Financial Aid: Resources specifically for eligible students enrolled in teacher education programs are awarded on the basis of financial need and merit. The institution has a Program Participation Agreement with the U.S. Department of Education for eligible students to receive Pell Grants and other federal aid. *Contact:* Financial Aid Office at (907) 786-1586.

Accreditation: *Regional:* NASC. *Professional:* NCATE. *Approved by:* Alaska Department of Education.

Undergraduate Programs: Baccalaureate degree programs are offered in the areas of early childhood, counseling and guidance, educational leadership, elementary education, and special education. Student must successfully complete 130 credit hours with a 2.0 GPA.

Graduate Programs: The Master of Arts in Teaching is an intensive experience for the exceptional graduate student who has both academic preparation in the content area taught in the

public schools and significant life experience. The program integrates coursework and field experiences to meet Alaska and national teacher education standards.

Licensure/Reciprocity: Alaska. Students seeking licensure in Alaska must successfully complete the School of Education's approved program as well as any additional requirements that may be initiated by the Alaska Department of Education and early Development. Students seeking teaching certification in a state other than Alaska should consult with that state's certification office early in their program of study to insure compliance with requirements. Many state directors of teacher education credentialing have signed Interstate Agreements through NASDTEC that expedite the certification process.

UNIVERSITY OF ALASKA FAIRBANKS

School of Education
P.O. Box 757480
Fairbanks, Alaska 99775-6480
Phone: (907) 474-1341
Fax: (907) 474-5451
E-mail: fysoed@uaf.edu
Internet: http://www.uaf.edu

Institution Description: The university was established in 1917 and offered awarded first degree at the postsecondary level in 1922.The present name was adopted in 1935.

University of Alaska Fairbanks education programs prepare educators to work in urban and rural Alaska and to work with multicultural and minority students, especially Alaska Native students.

Institution Control: Public.

Calendar: Semester. Academic year September to May.

Official(s): Dr. Roger Norris-Tull, Dean. Dr. Carol Barnhardt, Elementary Faculty Chair; Dr. Diane Noble, Secondary Faculty Chair; Dr. Alion Mooty, Graduate Faculty Chair.

Faculty: Full-time 22l; part-time 19,

Degrees Awarded: 31 baccalaureate; 19 master's.

Admission Requirements: *Undergraduate:* Rolling admissions plan. Either graduation from an accredited secondary school or GED; ACT/SAT scores; interview when appropriate. *Teacher education specific:* enrollment in professional internship; passing scores on PRAXIS I exams in reading, writing, and mathematics; 2 letters of recommendation; resume; 2 essays. *Graduate:* Baccalaureate degree from accredited university with GPA of 3.0; GRE scores letters of recommendation; passing scores on PRAXIS I exam in reading, writing, and mathematics. *Teacher education specific:* completed Alaska Department of Education and early childhood authorization packet.

Fees and Expenses: Undergraduate: in-state $90 to $102 per credit; out-of-state $281 to $293. Graduate: in-state $202 per credit; out-of-state $393 per credit. Required fees: $245 per semester. On-campus room: $2,510 to $2,670; board $2,660 to $32,500. health insurance $250.

Financial Aid: Resources specifically for eligible students enrolled in teacher education programs are awarded on the basis of financial need and academic merit. *Contact:* Financial Aid Office at (907) 474-7256 or fyfinaid@uaf.edu.

Accreditation: *Regional:* NASC. *Professional:* NCATE. *Member of:* AACTE. *Approved by:* Alaska Department of Education.

Undergraduate Programs: The Bachelor of Arts in elementary education is an interdisciplinary degree. Students will take courses in content areas that will prepare them for successful teaching at an elementary level. The components of this degree program include: completion of 127 credits; core/general university requirements; subject area coursework applicable to elementary teaching; education courses integrated withy classroom and community experiences; senior year internship experience following calendar of rural or urban school district; performance assessment and portfolio development.

Graduate Programs: Post-Baccalaureate Elementary Licensure Program is a graduate level, intensive, year-long program designed to provide students with the coursework and internship experience necessary to meet the Alaska Teacher Standards and be eligible for licensure as a elementary teacher in Alaska. The classroom-based program is built upon the principle of partnership that is a cooperative effort between interns, mentor teachers, and university faculty partners. A minimum of 27 credits is required.

The secondary post-baccalaureate program is an intensive, classroom-based secondary licensure program (33 credits) that prepares post-baccalaureate candidates to teach in multicultural settings in Alaska. A Master of Education degree is awarded upon completion of the program.

Licensure/Reciprocity: Alaska. Students seeking licensure in Alaska must successfully complete the School of Education's approved program as well as any additional requirements that may be initiated by the Alaska Department of Education and early Development. Students seeking teaching certification in a state other than Alaska should consult with that state's certification office early in their program of study to insure compliance with requirements. Many state directors of teacher education credentialing have signed Interstate Agreements through NASDTEC that expedite the certification process.

UNIVERSITY OF ALASKA SOUTHEAST
Center for Teacher Education
11120 Glacier Highway
Juneau, Alaska 99801-8699
Phone: (907) 465-6429
Fax: (907) 465-5159
E-mail: marilyn.taylor@uas.alaska.edu
Internet: http://www.uas.alaska.edu

Institution Description: The campus was established as University of Alaska, Juneau and offered first instruction at the postsecondary level in 1956. The present name was adopted in 1980.

The Center for Teacher Education offers various programs leading to teacher certification certificates that are transferable to all 50 states.

Institution Control: Public.

Calendar: Semester. Academic year July to May.

Official(s): Dr. Marilyn Taylor, Dean

Faculty: Full-time 21; part-time 15.

Degrees Awarded: 11 undergraduate; 53 master's.

Admission Requirements: *Undergraduate:* Graduation from an accredited high school with a GPA of at least 2.0; either SAT or ACT exam scores; have graduated with an associate degree from a regionally accredited institution or have completed at least 30 college semester credits with a GPA of at least 2.0. *Graduate:* Students must seek formal admission to graduate study; baccalaureate degree from an accredited institution with a GPA of 3.0 overall. *Teacher education specific:* official transcript; three recommendations; writing sample consisting of a state-

ment of professional objectives; a sample of academic, work-related or other writing, and an impromptu writing sample; official copy of PRAXIS I exam results. Applicant must also submit documentation of successful work with children in an elementary or early childhood school setting.

Fees and Expenses: Undergraduate: upper division in-state $102 per credit hour, lower division $90 per credit hour; upper division out-of-state $293 per credit hour; lower division $281 per credit hour. Graduate: in-state $202 per credit hour; $393 per credit hour out-of-state. On-campus room $1,500 double; meal plan $985. Books and supplies: $400 t0 $600.

Financial Aid: Resources specifically for eligible students enrolled in teacher education programs are awarded on the basis of academic merit and financial need. *Contact:* Barbara Burnett at (907) 465-6255 or e-mail barbara.burnett@uas.alaska.edu.

Accreditation: *Regional:* NASC. *Professional:* NCATE. *Member of:* AACTE. *Approved by:* Alaska Department of Education.

Undergraduate Programs: The Bachelor of Arts in elementary education is a four-year program. The degree requirements are interdisciplinary and provide breadth in the content areas necessary for successful teaching at the elementary level and depth in the opportunities to connect theory and practice in a variety of real classroom, school, and community contexts. The main components of this program include subject area coursework; addition subject area coursework; foundation courses in education with practical experiences in the schools, and a capstone year-long experience where the professional education courses are integrated with student teaching. The degree requires the completion of 130 credit hours.

Graduate Programs: The Master of Arts in Teaching (MAT) programs are designed for students who have completed a baccalaureate degree with content coursework appropriate to their teaching area and grade level and who are seeking a teaching certificate. Prior to completing the MAT program, prospective teachers must pass state mandated PRAXIS II content exams. The program requires the completion of 36 credit hours.

The Master of Education programs extend and develop classroom skills and abilities of practicing teachers in elementary and secondary education. The program requires the completion of 36 credit hours.

Licensure/Reciprocity: Alaska. Students seeking licensure in Alaska must successfully complete the School of Education's approved program as well as any additional requirements that may be initiated by the Alaska Department of Education and early Development. Students seeking teaching certification in a state other than Alaska should consult with that state's certification office early in their program of study to insure compliance with requirements. Many state directors of teacher education credentialing have signed Interstate Agreements through NASDTEC that expedite the certification process.

ARIZONA

ARIZONA STATE UNIVERSITY MAIN

College of Education
Division of Curriculum and Instruction
P.O. Box 870211
Tempe, Arizona 85287-0211
Phone: (480) 965-3306
Fax: (480) 965-9144
E-mail: cnigrad@asu.edu
Internet: http://www.asu.edu

Institution Description: Arizona State University Main, formerly named Arizona State University, is a state institution. It was established as Territorial Normal School in 1885, then chartered and offered first instruction at postsecondary level in 1886. Senior level was added and name was changed to Tempe State Teachers College in 1929. After several name changes, the present name was adopted in 1996.

The mission of the Division of Curriculum and Instruction is to promote scholarly inquiry and practice in teaching and teacher education. The division offers the Bachelor, Post-Baccalaureate, Master of Arts, Master of Education, and Doctor of Education degree programs.

Institution Control: Public.

Calendar: Semester. Academic year August to May.

Official(s): Dr. Eugene E. Garcia, Dean; Dr. Thomas Barone, Division Director.

Faculty: 200 tenured and untenured.

Degrees Awarded: 437 baccalaureate; 326 master's.

Admission Requirements: *Undergraduate:* Graduation from accredited secondary school with rank in the upper 25% of graduating class; minimum ACT composite of 22 for in-state students or 24 for out-of-state students; SAT combined score of 1040 for in-state students or 1110 for out-of-state students. GED test score of 50 or higher accepted. *Teacher education specific:* Students must seek admission to the professional Initial Teacher Certification Program. Admission is competitive. *Graduate:* Baccalaureate degree from a regionally accredited institution; 3.0 GPA. *Teacher education specific:* Contact the division for application deadline; scores from aptitude tests appropriate for the program to be pursued are required.

Fees and Expenses: Undergraduate: in-state $2,585 per academic year; out-of-state $11,105. Graduate: Tuition charged per credit hour. On-campus room and board: $5,866. Other expenses: $3,325. Books and supplies: $748.

Financial Aid: Resources specifically for eligible students enrolled in teacher education programs are awarded on the basis of academic merit and financial need. The institution has a Program Participation Agreement with the U.S. Department of Education for eligible students to receive Pell Grants and other federal aid. *Contact:* Financial Aid Office at (480) 965-3355.

Accreditation: *Regional:* NCA. *Professional:* NCATE. *Member of:* AACTE. *Approved by:* Arizona State Board of Education.

Undergraduate Programs: The College of Education offers five undergraduate degree programs in the following majors: early childhood education, elementary education, multilingual/multicultural education, secondary education, and special education. Within secondary education, the college collaborates with the College of Liberal Arts to offer 18 areas of specialization. Students interested in teacher certification in art, music, or dance are admitted to the College of Fine Arts, completing additional coursework through the College of Education.

Candidates for teacher certification must successfully complete the appropriate examinations within the Arizona Educator Proficiency Assessments (AEPA) program. All baccalaureate programs require the completion of 120 semester hours, 2.50 cumulative GPA, and 2.50 in the professional teacher preparation program with at least a C in each professional teacher preparation program course, directed field experience during each of 4 semesters of the program, including student teaching.

Graduate Programs: The College of Education offers 20 graduate degrees with many concentrations. Contact the division for university-wide requirements and application procedures.

Licensure/Reciprocity: Arizona. Students seeking teaching certification in a state other than Arizona should consult with that state's teacher certification office early in their program of study to insure compliance with requirements. Many state directors of teacher credentialing have signed Interstate Agreements through NASDTEC that expedite the certification process.

ARIZONA STATE UNIVERSITY WEST

College of Education
Professional Teacher Preparation Program
4701 West Thunderbird Road
P.O. Box 37100
Phoenix, Arizona 85069
Phone: (602) 543-6300
Fax: (602) 543-6250
E-mail: http://www.west.asu.edu
Internet: coe@west.asu.edu

Institution Description: Arizona State University West is a unit of the Arizona State University system. The unit was separately accredited by the NCA in 1992.

The College of Education offers undergraduate programs in elementary education, either a general program or optional concentrations in Bilingual/ESL or early childhood education, secondary education, and special education. An opportunity exists for all students pursuing the elementary and secondary streams to obtain a middle-school endorsement.

Institution Control: Public.

Calendar: Semester. Academic year August to May.

Official(s): Dr. Michael Awender, Dean.

Degrees Awarded: 314 baccalaureate; 74 master's.

Admission Requirements: *Undergraduate:* Graduation from accredited secondary school with rank in the upper 25% of graduating class; minimum ACT composite of 22 for in-state students or 24 for out-of-state students; SAT combined score of 1040 for in-state students or 1110 for out-of-state students. GED test score of 50 or higher accepted. *Teacher education specific:* Students must seek admission to the professional Initial Teacher Certification Program. Admission is competitive. *Graduate:* Baccalaureate degree from a regionally accredited institution; 3.0 GPA. *Teacher education specific:* An Arizona teaching certificate is a prerequisite for admission to the program. Contact the division for application deadline; scores from aptitude tests appropriate for the program to be pursued are required.

Fees and Expenses: Undergraduate: in-state $2,585 per academic year; out-of-state $11,505. Graduate: Tuition charged per credit hour. On-campus room and board: $7,236. Other expenses: $4,175. Books and supplies: $750.

Financial Aid: Resources specifically for eligible students enrolled in teacher education programs are awarded on the basis of financial need and academic merit. The institution has a Program Participation Agreement with the U.S. Department of Education for eligible students to receive Pell Grants and other federal aid. *Contact:* Financial Aid Office at (602) 543-8178.

Accreditation: *Regional:* NCA. *Professional:* NCATE. *Member of:* AACTE. *Approved by:* Arizona State Board of Education.

Undergraduate Programs: The elementary education program prepares student to develop and implement instructional programs for children from grades K-8. The program leads to eligibility for certification by the Arizona Department of Education. Students develop knowledge, skills and competencies necessary to teach children from diverse ethnic and cultural backgrounds.

The early childhood education program leads to eligibility for certification in grades K-8. The program prepares students to enact the professional roles that will be concerned with the developmental and education needs of children from birth through 8th grade.

A Bachelor of Arts in elementary education-bilingual education prepares individuals to teach in a bilingual environment. English as a Second Language option prepares student to teach in an elementary ESL environment. This option features field experiences in schools with ESL programs. Secondary education programs are offered that prepare students to become effective and reflective teachers of adolescents.

The Department of Special Education is committed to quality preparation for future teachers who educate students with disabilities. Graduates of the program receive a B.A. degree in special education with certification to teach K-12 special education. They receive a cross-categorical endorsement to teach students with mild disabilities in the categories of learning disabilities, behavior disorders, mental retardation, orthopedic impairments, and traumatic brain injury.

Graduate Programs: The College of Education Graduate Studies offers masters programs in educational administration, elementary education (with various concentrations), secondary education (with various concentrations), and special education with a concentration in infants and small children. All coursework must be completed within a six-year time limit. Following completion of coursework, each student pursuing the Master in Education degree will be required to complete a comprehensive exam or applied project.

Licensure/Reciprocity: Arizona. Students seeking teaching certification in a state other than Arizona should consult with that state's teacher certification office early in their program of study to insure compliance with requirements. Many state directors of teacher credentialing have signed Interstate Agreements through NASDTEC that expedite the certification process.

GRAND CANYON UNIVERSITY
College of Education
3300 West Camelback Road
Phoenix, Arizona 85017
Phone: (602) 589-2474
Fax: (602) 589-2447
E-mail: admissions@grand-canyon.edu
Internet: http://www.grand-canyon.edu

Institution Description: Grand Canyon University, formerly known as Grand Canyon College, is a private college owned and operated by the Arizona Southern Baptist Convention. The campus was established in Prescott, chartered, incorporated, and offered first instruction at the postsecondary level in 1949. The campus was moved to its present location in 1951 and the present name was adopted in 1994.

The College of Education provides a holistic approach to education, wherein the mind, body, and spirit are seen as essential partners on the learning process.

Institution Control: Private.
Calendar: Semester. Academic year August to May.
Official(s): Dr. Becky B. Clark, Dean.
Faculty: 21 tenured.
Degrees Awarded: 70 baccalaureate; 50 master's.
Admission Requirements: *Undergraduate:* Graduation from an accredited secondary school or GED; 3.0 GPA; top 25% of graduating class; College Board SAT score 1050 or ACT composite score 22. *Teacher education specific:* 2.5 GPA; three references; handbook agreement. *Graduate:* Baccalaureate degree with cumulative 2.0 GPA. *Teacher education specific:* 3.0 GPA; three references; interview with Director of Graduate Programs.
Fees and Expenses: Undergraduate $14,500 per academic year. Graduate: $7,080 per academic year. On-campus room and board: $7,200. Books and supplies: $815.
Financial Aid: Resources specifically for eligible students enrolled in teacher education programs are awarded on the basis of academic merit and financial need. *Contact:* Rosanna Short at (602) 589-2885 or rshort@grand-canyon.edu.
Accreditation: *Regional:* NCA. *Member of:* AACTE. *Approved by:* Arizona State Board of Education.
Undergraduate Programs: Degree programs are offered in the following areas: elementary (grades K-8); special education-learning disabilities/emotionally handicapped; secondary (grades 7-12) with subject area emphasis; teaching English as a second language endorsement; K-12 endorsement in the areas of art, music, and physical education. The field-based experience is the touchstone of a pre-service teacher's program in teacher education. Classroom experience begins as early as the sophomore year. The 129 field experience hours that are required in the classroom provide valuable knowledge prior to student teaching. Completion of a total of 128 credit hours are required for all baccalaureate degree programs.
Graduate Programs: Students with a bachelor's degree may enroll in the accelerated degree program culminating in a Master of Education degree. In the program, students may choose between an elementary or secondary education emphasis. Coursework varies by emphasis. Some prerequisite work may be needed. Secondary students must have a major in an area commonly taught in the public schools.
Licensure/Reciprocity: Arizona. Students seeking teaching certification in a state other than Arizona should consult with that state's teacher certification office early in their program of study to insure compliance with requirements. Many state directors of teacher credentialing have signed Interstate Agreements through NASDTEC that expedite the certification process.

NORTHERN ARIZONA UNIVERSITY
College of Education
Teaching and Learning
P.O. Box 5774
Flagstaff, Arizona 86011-5774
Phone: (928) 523-2611
Fax: (520) 523-5511
E-mail: admissions@nau.edu
Internet: http://www.nau.edu

Institution Description: Northern Arizona University is a state institution that was established as Northern Arizona Normal School in 1899. The name was changed to Northern Arizona State and Teachers College and became a 4-year institution in 1925. The present name was adopted in 1966.

The mission of the College of Education is to prepare education professionals to create the schools of tomorrow. This mission is based upon the fundamental beliefs in the dignity and inherent worth of all people and in the central role of education in a democratic society.

Institution Control: Public.
Calendar: Semester. Academic year August to May.
Official(s): Dr. Daniel L. Kain, Dean.
Faculty: Full-time 112; adjunct 4.

NORTHERN ARIZONA UNIVERSITY—*cont'd*

Degrees Awarded: 744 baccalaureate; 1,026 master's.

Admission Requirements: *Undergraduate:* Graduation from accredited secondary school with rank in the upper 25% of graduating class; minimum ACT composite of 22 for in-state students or 24 for out-of-state students; SAT combined score of 1040 for in-state students or 1110 for out-of-state students. GED test score of 50 or higher accepted. *Teacher education specific:* Students must seek admission to the professional Initial Teacher Certification Program. Admission is competitive. *Graduate:* Baccalaureate degree from a regionally accredited institution; 3.0 GPA. *Teacher education specific:* An Arizona teaching certificate is a prerequisite for admission to the program. Contact the division for application deadline; scores from aptitude tests appropriate for the program to be pursued are required.

Fees and Expenses: Undergraduate: in-state $2,585 per academic year; out-of-state $11,105. On-campus room and board: $5,866. Other expenses: $3,325. Books and supplies: $748.

Financial Aid: Resources specifically for eligible students enrolled in teacher education programs are awarded on the basis of academic merit and financial need. The institution has a Program Participation Agreement with the U.S. Department of Education for eligible students to receive Pell Grants and other federal aid. *Contact:* Financial Aid Office at (928) 523-4951.

Accreditation: *Regional:* NCA. *Professional:* NCATE. *Member of:* AACTE. *Approved by:* Arizona State Board of Education.

Undergraduate Programs: The College of Education offers courses in teacher preparation through instructional leadership (elementary education, secondary education, technology education, vocational education, and library science) and educational specialties (special education, bilingual/multicultural education, and educational technology). All baccalaureate programs required the completion of general education requirements, core education courses, and professional studies including student teaching. The programs require the completion of 120 semester hours and comprehensive exams in the subject area.

Graduate Programs: Graduate programs are offered that lead to a Master in Education in early childhood education, elementary education, or secondary education. The programs offer advanced courses in teaching methods, curriculum, and related areas.

An Ed.D. in Curriculum and Instruction is offered for doctoral students seeking advanced preparation in teaching and learning. Specific requirements exist for entrance into the master's and doctoral programs.

Licensure/Reciprocity: Arizona. Students seeking teaching certification in a state other than Arizona should consult with that state's teacher certification office early in their program of study to insure compliance with requirements. Many state directors of teacher credentialing have signed Interstate Agreements through NASDTEC that expedite the certification process.

PRESCOTT COLLEGE

Teacher Education Program
301 Grove Avenue
Prescott, Arizona 86301
Phone: (928) 778-2090
Fax: (928) 776-5137
E-mail: lplaut@prescott.edu
Internet: http://www.prescott.edu

Institution Description: Prescott College was established as Prescott Center College in 1965. It is a private, independent, nonprofit college. The current name was adopted in 1981.

The Teacher Education Program stresses experiential learning and self-direction within an interdisciplinary curriculum. The curriculum integrates philosophy, theory, and practice so that students synthesize knowledge and skills, confronting important value issues and making personal commitments.

Institution Control: Private.

Calendar: Quarter. Academic year September to May.

Official(s): Dr. Daniel E. Garvey, President; Dr. Steve Walters, Dean, Adult Degree Programs.

Faculty: Full-time 45.

Degrees Awarded: 98 baccalaureate; 14 master's.

Admission Requirements: *Undergraduate:* Graduation from secondary school or GED. *Teacher education specific:* Students who apply to the Teacher Education Program undergo a thorough admissions process including transcript evaluation, writing samples, letters of reference, and personal interviews.

Fees and Expenses: $13,550 per academic year. New student orientation fee $373; student activity fee $575. Off-campus housing and utilities: $4,966. Personal expenses: $1,438; transportation: $928; books and supplies: $485.

Financial Aid: Resources specifically for eligible students enrolled in teacher education programs are awarded on the basis of academic merit and financial need. The institution has a Program Participation Agreement with the U.S. Department of Education for eligible students to receive Pell Grants and other federal aid. *Contact:* Financial Aid Office at (800) 628-6365 or finaid@prescott.edu.

Accreditation: *Regional:* NCA. *Approved by:* Arizona State Board of Education.

Undergraduate Programs: Courses in the teacher education program emphasize current educational research and theory, as well as practical experience in the classroom. Students are expected to master educational principles and apply these in many problem-solving situations in courses and in their student teaching assignment. Most students take five years or one post-bachelor year to complete Arizona teacher certification. Programs include elementary education, secondary education, special education; Dual certification special and elementary education and endorsements in bilingual education and English as a second language.

Post-Baccalaureate Teacher Certification Programs are available. The Adult Degree Program features courses designed as independent mentored studies, a combination of a tutorial, independent research and experiential application. The Master of Arts Program is designed so that each student works with a graduate advisor who assists and guides the student in planning, carrying out, and evaluating all stages of graduate study. Students must complete their coursework in the Adult Degree Program before enrolling in the Master of Arts Program.

Licensure/Reciprocity: Arizona. Students seeking teaching certification in a state other than Arizona should consult with that state's teacher certification office early in their program of study to insure compliance with requirements. Many state directors of teacher credentialing have signed Interstate Agreements through NASDTEC that expedite the certification process.

UNIVERSITY OF ARIZONA

College of Education
Department Teaching and Teacher Education
P.O. Box 210069
Tucson, Arizona 85721-0069
Phone: (520) 621-1602
Fax: (520 621-7821
E-mail: tsollars@email.arizona.edu
Internet: http://www.arizona.edu

Institution Description: The University of Arizona is a state institution and land-grant college that was established and chartered in 1885.

The Department of Teaching and Teacher Education helps prepare undergraduate students for careers as elementary and secondary teachers. Graduates of these programs are eligible for State of Arizona teacher certification and will have completed most of the qualifications needed for certification in other U.S. states. As an upper-division college, the College of Education offers junior and senior courses to students who have completed the requirements for admission to the undergraduate teacher preparation program.

The College of Education also offers master's and doctoral programs leading to positions in school leadership, research and development, and teacher education.

Institution Control: Public.

Calendar: Semester. Academic year August to May.

Official(s): Dr. Ronald W. Marx, Dean.

Faculty: Full-time 14.

Degrees Awarded: 458 baccalaureate; 257 master's.

Admission Requirements: *Undergraduate:* Either graduation from secondary school with 16 units or GED; College Board SAT or ACT composite. *Teacher education specific:* Students should apply for admission into the Teacher Preparation Program early in the second semester of their sophomore year. *Graduate:* Baccalaureate degree in education or a related field from a regionally accredited institution. *Teacher education specific:* 3.0 GPA figured on the last 60 units; 15 units of previous coursework should be within preservice education; one year of teaching in a full-time instructional position within a school setting; faculty interview.

Fees and Expenses: Undergraduate: in-state $2,593 per academic year; out-of-state $11,113. Graduate: Tuition is charged per credit hour. On-campus room and board: $6,568. Other expenses: $2,815. Books and supplies: $735.

Financial Aid: Resources specifically for eligible students enrolled in teacher education programs are awarded on the basis of financial need and academic merit. The institution has a Program Participation Agreement with the U.S. Department of Education for eligible students to receive Pell Grants and other federal aid. Graduate students are eligible for assistantships and fellowships that provide financial aid and opportunities to work with faculty members on research and to participate in the preservice preparation of teachers. *Contact:* Financial Aid Office at (520) 621-1858.

Accreditation: *Regional:* NCA. *Professional:* NCATE. *Member of:* AACTE. *Approved by:* Arizona State Board of Education.

Undergraduate Programs: Students enrolled in the undergraduate program earn either the Bachelor of Arts in Education or the Bachelor of Science in Education. The program normally consists of three semesters of professional coursework (including field experience), and one semester of student teaching.

To qualify for teacher certification, people who already have a bachelor's degree in subject commonly taught in school may apply to the teacher preparation program as post-baccalaureate students. The program normally consists of two-three semesters of professional coursework and one semester of student teaching. Additional coursework may be needed to fulfill deficiencies.

The College of Education also offers courses to qualify teachers for a special endorsement on their teaching certificate for bilingual education (English/Spanish).

Graduate Programs: The Master of Arts degree program requires students to focus graduate coursework in one of two strands: education strand (focus on teaching and schooling); and subject matter strand (focus on the content knowledge of teaching). A minimum of 33 units of graduate courses are required (college core 3 units; major core 6 units; supporting coursework 24 units). Exit requirements include oral defense of thesis and the master's comprehensive examination.

The Doctor of Philosophy degree in Teaching and Teacher Education offers students the pursuit of a variety of concentrations and specializations, including teacher reflection and development; classroom processes and management; curriculum theory; social studies, mathematics and science education; environmental learning; educational foundations and policy studies; and technology applications. Contact the College of Education for specific requirements.

Licensure/Reciprocity: Arizona. Students seeking teaching certification in a state other than Arizona should consult with that state's teacher certification office in their program of study to insure compliance with requirements. Many state directors of teacher credentialing have signed Interstate Agreements through NASDTEC that expedite the certification process.

UNIVERSITY OF PHOENIX

Phoenix Campus

4615 East Elwood Street
Phoenix, Arizona 85040-1908
Phone: (480) 966-7400
Fax: (480) 921-8538
E-mail: PhilLundberg@apollogrp.edu
Internet: http://www.phoenix.edu/phoenix

Institution Description: The University of Phoenix (Institute for Professional Development until 1977) is a private institution primarily for working adults. It offers upper division and graduate study only. The university was established and incorporated as Institute for Professional Development in 1976. The present name was adopted in 1977.

The Phoenix Campus offers a wide selection of continuing education and professional growth courses specifically developed for educators. The university combines current, real-world education with class schedules that can accommodate the student's busy schedules.

Institution Control: Private.

Calendar: 5-, 6-, and 11-week sessions throughout the calendar year.

Official(s): Phil Lundberg, Vice President/Director, Phoenix Campus.

Faculty: Full-time 125 at the Phoenix Campus.

Degrees Awarded: 123 master's.

Admission Requirements: *Graduate:* Baccalaureate degree from a regionally accredited institution. *Teacher education specific:* Contact the university for specific admission requirements.

Fees and Expenses: $8,400 per academic year. Off-campus room and board: $1,175. Books and supplies: $750.

Financial Aid: Resources specifically for eligible students enrolled in teacher education programs are awarded on the basis of academic merit and financial need. The institution has a Program Participation Agreement with the U.S. Department of Education for eligible students to receive Pell Grants and other federal aid. *Contact:* Financial Aid Office at (480) 966-7400.

Accreditation: *Regional:* NCA. *Professional:* NCATE. *Member of:* AACTE. *Approved by:* Arizona State Board of Education.

Graduate Programs: The Master of Education degree may be pursued in the following areas of specialization: administration and supervision, adult education and distance learning, curriculum and instruction; curriculum and technology, educational counseling; special education/cross categorical; teacher education for elementary licensure; teacher education for secondary licensure. Contact the university for specific program coursework requirements.

Licensure/Reciprocity: Arizona. Students seeking teaching certification in a state other than Arizona should consult with that state's teacher certification office early in their program of study to insure compliance with requirements. Many state directors of teacher credentialing have signed Interstate Agreements through NASDTEC that expedite the certification process.

ARKANSAS

ARKANSAS STATE UNIVERSITY

College of Education

Department of Teacher Education

114 Cooley Education/Communications Building

P.O. Box 940

State University, Arkansas 72467

Phone: (870) 972-3059

Fax: (870) 910-8045

E-mail: COE@astate.edu

Internet: http://www.astate.edu

Institution Description: Arkansas State University (ASU) is a state institution located in Jonesboro, Arkansas. Arkansas State University developed from one of four state agricultural schools which were established in 1909 by the Arkansas General Assembly. The institution opened as a vocational high school in 1910; reorganized as a junior college 1918; name changed to State Agricultural and Mechanical College in 1925; became Arkansas State College in 1933. A graduate program leading to master of science in education was established in 1955 and university status granted 1967 and name became Arkansas State University.

The mission of the Department of Teacher Education encompasses three areas: teaching, service, and research. The major purpose of the department is teaching, which contributes significantly toward the accomplishment of the department's primary goals: preparing professionally emerging teachers and emerging professionals in the fields of early childhood education, elementary education, middle grades education, and reading. In addition, the department offers a graduate program in early childhood services.

Institution Control: Public.

Calendar: Semester. Academic year mid-August to early May.

Official(s): Dr. John Beineke, Dean, College of Education; Dr. Veda McClain, Chair, Department of Teacher Education.

Faculty: Full-time 26.

Degrees Awarded: 327 baccalaureate; 122 master's; 7 doctorate.

Admission Requirements: *Undergraduate:* Graduation from an accredited secondary school; ACT or SAT score; PRAXIS I test score. *Teacher education specific:* Application to the Department of Teacher Education after completion of the sophomore year. *Graduate:* Baccalaureate degree from an accredited institution; completion of PRAXIS II examinations in the students area of concentration. *Teacher education specific:* Students must have completed a minimum of 18 semester hours of professional education courses including the requirements for a valid teaching license based on a four-year teacher education program.

Fees and Expenses: Undergraduate: in-state $4,480 per academic year; out-of-state $10,090. On-campus room and board $4,060. Books and supplies $900.

Financial Aid: Resources specifically for eligible students enrolled in teacher education programs are awarded on the basis of financial need. *Contact:* Financial Aid Office at (870) 972-2310.

Accreditation: *Regional:* NCA. *Professional:* NCATE. *Member of:* AACTE. *Approved by:* Arkansas Department of Education.

Undergraduate Programs: Bachelor of Science in Education with a concentration in elementary childhood education requires the completion of general education requirements; specialty area requirements, major and professional studies requirements. The middle-level education program is designed to prepare teachers to teach in grades 4-8 as a mathematics and science specialist or as an English/language arts and social studies specialist, and in grades 4-8 as a self-contained generalist. The department offers three classes for secondary education: Introduction to Secondary Teaching, Performance-Based Instructional Design; Educational Measurement with Computer Applications. All baccalaureate programs require the completion of 124 credit hours with a 2.0 GPA.

Graduate Programs: The Department of Teacher Education offers the Master of Science in Education degree with majors in early childhood education, early childhood services, elementary education, and reading education.

Licensure/Reciprocity: Arkansas. Students seeking teaching certification in a state other than Arkansas should consult with that state's certification officer early in their program of study to insure compliance with requirements. Many state directors of teacher education credentialing have signed Interstate Agreements through NASDTEC that expedite the certification process.

ARKANSAS TECH UNIVERSITY

School of Education

Department of Curriculum and Instruction

Russellville, Arkansas 72801-2222

Phone: (501) 968-0350

Fax: (501) 964-0522

E-mail: dennis.fleniken@mail.atu.edu

Internet: http://www.atu.edu

Institution Description: Arkansas Tech University (Arkansas Polytechnic College until 1976) is a state institution. It was established as a Second District Agricultural School 1909 and offered first instruction at postsecondary level 1921. The college became Arkansas Polytechnic College, became 4-year institution, and awarded first degree (baccalaureate) in 1925. The present name was adopted in 1976.

The Department of Curriculum and Instruction offers three undergraduate programs leading to Arkansas teacher licensure: early childhood education, middle childhood/early adolescence, and secondary education.

Institution Control: Public.

Calendar: Semester. Academic year August to May.

Official(s): Dr. Dennis W. Fleniken, Dean, School of Education; Dr. David C. Bell, Head, Department of Curriculum and Instruction.

Faculty: Full-time 14.

Degrees Awarded: 154 baccalaureate; 108 master's.

Admission Requirements: *Undergraduate:* Completion of secondary school graduation requirements with a minimum 2.0 GPA from an Arkansas public secondary school; ACT or SAT score. *Teacher education specific:* Application filed with Department of Education. *Graduate:* Baccalaureate degree from an accredited institution *Teacher education specific:* Applicant must meet all required entrance requirements.

Fees and Expenses: Undergraduate: in-state $3,076 per academic year, out-of-state $6,152. On-campus room and board: $3,756. Books and supplies $800.

Financial Aid: Resources specifically for eligible students enrolled in teacher education programs are awarded on the basis of financial need. The university has a program participation agreement with the U.S. Department of Education for eligible students to receive Pell Grants and other federal aid. *Contact:* Financial Aid Office at (479) 968-0399.

Accreditation: *Regional:* NCA. *Professional:* NCATE. *Member of:* AACTE. *Approved by:* Arkansas Department of Education.

Undergraduate Programs: The early childhood education program leads to a B.S. degree. It is designed to prepare students to teach children pre-school through grade four.

The middle childhood/early adolescence program leads to a B.S. degree. It is designed to prepare students to work with children in grade four through grade seven. Students enrolled in this program may choose from one of two areas of interdisciplinary concentration: mathematics/science or language arts/social studies.

The secondary education program leads to the appropriate degree in the area of teaching (e.g., math education majors receive a B.S. in mathematics). Completion of the secondary program will provide the student with licensure in the teaching of grade seven through grade twelve. Completion of the art or music program will lead to licensure from pre-school through grade twelve.

Most of the programs at the baccalaureate level require the completion of 124 credit hours.

Graduate Programs: The department offers graduate programs aimed at improving the educational background of teachers. Graduate degrees are offered with the following majors: instructional technology, gifted and talented education, elementary education, secondary education, educational leadership, and instruction improvement. The graduate degree requires the completion of 36 credit hours.

Licensure/Reciprocity: Arkansas. Students seeking teaching certification in a state other than Arkansas should consult with that state's certification officer early in their program of study to insure compliance with requirements. Many state directors of teacher education credentialing have signed Interstate Agreements through NASDTEC that expedite the certification process.

HARDING UNIVERSITY

School of Education
Teacher Education Program
900 East Center
Searcy, Arkansas 72149
Phone: (501) 279-4050
Fax: (501) 279-4805
E-mail: education@harding.edu
Internet: http://www.@harding.edu

Institution Description: Harding University (Harding College until 1979) is a private university affiliated with the Church of Christ. It was chartered in Morrilton as Arkansas Christian College, a junior college, in 1919 and offered first instruction at postsecondary level 1922. The assets of Harper College (in Kansas, established 1915) were purchased and name to Harding College 1924. The campus moved to its present location 1934 and adopted present name in 1979.

The mission of the teacher education program is to prepare teachers who are scholarly, caring and nurturing, and who are self-directed facilitators of student learning. Graduates are expected to enter their professional careers as highly educated people in both the liberal arts and in the field of specialization with a sincere commitment to the teaching profession.

Institution Control: Private.

Calendar: Semester. Academic year August to May.

Official(s): Dr. Lewis Finley, Dean, School of Education; Dr. Jan Morgan, Chair, Teacher Education Program.

Faculty: Full-time 22; part-time 12.

Degrees Awarded: 97 baccalaureate; 113 master's.

Admission Requirements: *Undergraduate:* Either graduation from accredited secondary school with 15 academic units or GED; ACT or SAT score. *Teacher education specific:* All students who plan to teach must apply to the Teacher Education Program before the end of their sophomore year. Requirements include: recommendation by four faculty members; minimum cumulative GPA of 2.5 on a 4.0 scale in all education and prerequisite courses; admittance to the program before taking required professional education core courses; pass the PRAXIS I test. *Graduate:* Baccalaureate degree from an accredited institution. *Teacher education specific:* Students who did not certify to teach on the undergraduate level may do so while enrolled the graduate program.

Fees and Expenses: Undergraduate: $9,180 per academic year. On-campus room and board: $4,650. Books and supplies $500.

Financial Aid: Resources specifically for eligible students enrolled in teacher education programs are awarded on the basis of financial need and merit. The institution has a program participation agreement with the U.S. Department of Education for eligible students to receive Pell Grants and other federal aid. *Contact:* Financial Aid Office at (501) 279-4257.

Accreditation: *Regional:* NCA. *Professional:* NCATE. *Member of:* AACTE. *Approved by:* Arkansas Department of Education.

Undergraduate Programs: Undergraduate programs have been developed that lead to the Bachelor of Arts, Bachelor of Science, or Bachelor of Music in Education degree. All baccalaureate degrees require the completion of 128 credit hours with a 2.0 GPA.

Graduate Programs: The Master of Arts in Teaching degree is designed for the professional development of the K-12 classroom teacher. This program provides for the life long learner's enhancement of skills and knowledge, utilizing contemporary topics in curriculum and instruction.

The Master of Education degree is designed to give new as well as in-service teachers advanced training in subject matter fields and in professional education. The Master of Science in Education degree is planned to facilitate student attainment of vocational and personal goals without completing teacher certification requirements.

Licensure/Reciprocity: Arkansas. Students seeking teaching certification in a state other than Arkansas should consult with that state's certification officer early in their program of study to insure compliance with requirements. Many state directors of teacher education credentialing have signed Interstate Agreements through NASDTEC that expedite the certification process.

HENDERSON STATE UNIVERSITY

Teachers College
1100 Henderson Street
Arkadelphia, Arkansas 71999-0001
Phone: (870) 230-5427
Fax: (870) 230-5400
E-mail: harris@hsu.edu
Internet: http://www.hsu.edu

Institution Description: Henderson State University (Henderson State College until 1975) was established in 1890.

The university provides students the opportunity to prove their ability to become a licensed teacher in Arkansas. The Teacher Education Program offers experiences necessary to meet initial teacher license requirements and to have success as a beginning teacher.

Institution Control: Public.

Calendar: Semester. Academic year August to May.

Official(s): Dr. Judy Harrison, Director.

Faculty: Full-time 20; part-time 21.

Degrees Awarded: 77 baccalaureate; 67 master's.

Admission Requirements: *Undergraduate:* Graduation from an accredited high school; ACT score of 19; 2.5 GPA. *Teacher education specific:* Students are admitted to the program after successfully completing: application for admission; interview;

HENDERSON STATE UNIVERSITY—*cont'd*

personality inventory; PRAXIS I examination; GPA of 2.50 or higher. GRADUATE; Baccalaureate degree from an accredited institution; PRAXIS II II examinations in specialty area and principles of learning and teaching. Contact Teachers College, Henderson for further details.

Fees and Expenses: Undergraduate: in-state $3,252 per academic year; out-of-state $6,402. On-campus room and board: $3,368. Books and supplies $800.

Financial Aid: Resources specifically for eligible students enrolled in teacher education programs are awarded on the basis of merit and financial need. The institution has a program participation agreement with the U.S. Department of Education for eligible students to receive Pell Grants and other federal aid. *Contact:* Financial Aid Office at (870) 230-5148.

Accreditation: *Regional:* NCA. *Professional:* NCATE. *Member of:* AACTE. *Approved by:* Arkansas Department of Education.

Undergraduate Programs: The culminating experience of the Teacher Education Program, after completion of all required courses and other degree requirements, is the Professional Semester. A quality assurance factor is inherent in the university policy which requires a 2.5 GPA overall and in the major field for admission to teacher internship.

Graduate Programs: Graduate degree programs are available. Contact Teachers College, Henderson for detailed information.

Licensure/Reciprocity: Arkansas. Students seeking teaching certification in a state other than Arkansas should consult with that state's certification officer early in their program of study to insure compliance with requirements. Many state directors of teacher education credentialing have signed Interstate Agreements through NASDTEC that expedite the certification process.

HENDRIX COLLEGE

Department of Education
1600 Washington Avenue
Conway, Arkansas 72032-3080
Phone: (501) 329-6811
Fax: (501) 420-1200
E-mail: edu@hendrix.edu
Internet: http://www.hendrix.edu

Institution Description: Hendrix College is a private college affiliated with the United Methodist Church. The college was established in Altus as Central Collegiate Institute in 1876 and was purchased by Arkansas Methodist Conference and incorporated 1884. The college merged with Henderson-Brown College to become Hendrix-Henderson College in 1929. A further merger in 1933 with Galloway Women's College led to the adoption of the present name.

The Department of Education prepares early childhood, middle school, and secondary education teachers. Students participate in multicultural workshops, discipline conferences, and the classroom management program. The teacher certification programs provide a strong liberal arts education and give students in-depth experience and full certification.

Institution Control: Private.

Calendar: Semester. Academic year September to June.

Official(s): Dr. James M. Jessings, Department Head; Dr. Darlene G. Wills, Assistant Professor.

Faculty: Full-time 3.

Degrees Awarded: 5 baccalaureate.

Admission Requirements: *Undergraduate:* Graduation from an accredited secondary school or GED; College Board SAT or ACT composite score. *Teacher education specific:* All students interested in the Hendrix Teacher Education Licensure Program are urged to attend an annual meeting held at the beginning of each academic year to discuss completing a minor, or licensure in education at the early childhood, middle school, or secondary level. Students interested in teacher licensure should make application for admission to the program during the spring semester of the freshman year. Prospective teachers should take the PRAXIS I examination no later than January of the sophomore year.

Fees and Expenses: Undergraduate: $14,900 per academic year. On-campus room and board: $5,090. Books and supplies $700.

Financial Aid: Resources specifically for eligible students enrolled in teacher education programs are awarded on the basis of financial need and academic merit. The institution has a program participation agreement with the U.S. Department of Education for eligible students to receive Pell Grants and other federal aid. *Contact:* Financial Aid Office at (501) 450-1382.

Accreditation: *Regional:* NCA. *Professional:* NCATE. *Member of:* AACTE. *Approved by:* Arkansas Department of Education.

Undergraduate Programs: During the senior year, students enrolled in the Teacher Education Program must complete the specified early childhood, middle school, or secondary education courses including student teaching. After the completion of all degree requirements, the student may make application to the Hendrix Teacher Licensure Officer for approval.

Licensure/Reciprocity: Arkansas. Students seeking teaching certification in a state other than Arkansas should consult with that state's certification officer early in their program of study to insure compliance with requirements. Many state directors of teacher education credentialing have signed Interstate Agreements through NASDTEC that expedite the certification process.

JOHN BROWN UNIVERSITY

Division of Teacher Education
2000 West University Street
Siloam Springs, Arkansas 72761
Phone: (501) 524-9500
Fax: (501) 524-9548
E-mail: jbinfo@jbu.edu
Internet: http://www.jbu.edu

Institution Description: John Brown University is a private, independent, nonprofit Christian college established and incorporated as Southwestern Collegiate Institute, a junior college. The name was changed John E. Brown College 1920 and reorganized to comprise John E. Brown College, Siloam School of the Bible, and John E. Brown Vocational College. The present name was adopted in 1948.

The Division of Teacher Education prepares students to teach in public, private, or Christian schools. Students will spend hours in actual classrooms and at other school functions, getting experience with the students that will be taught.

Institution Control: Private.

Calendar: Semester. Academic year August to May.

Official(s): Dr. Sandra S. Van Thiel, Chair.

Faculty: Full-time 8.

Degrees Awarded: 24 baccalaureate.

Admission Requirements: *Undergraduate:* Graduation from an accredited high school or GED; 2.5 cumulative high school GPA; SAT or ACT composite score; two references. *Teacher education specific:* Completion of required English, math, and speech courses with a grade of C or better; PRAXIS I scores which meet the state minimum requirements in reading, writing, and mathematics; formal approval of the candidate's portfolio by the Teacher Education Division adviser.

Fees and Expenses: Undergraduate: $13,044 per academic year. On-campus room and board: $4,798. Books and supplies $700.

Financial Aid: Resources specifically for eligible students enrolled in teacher education programs are awarded on the basis of financial need and academic merit. The institution has a program participation agreement with the U.S. Department of Education for eligible students to receive Pell Grants and other federal aid. *Contact:* Financial Aid Office at (479) 524-7157.

Accreditation: *Regional:* NCA. *Professional:* NCATE. *Member of:* AACTE. *Approved by:* Arkansas Department of Education.

Undergraduate Programs: Degrees offered by the Division of Teacher Education include programs leading to preschool/early adolescence and adolescence/young adulthood (grades (7-12) licensure; programs leading to middle childhood/early adolescence licensure (grades 4-8); and programs leading to early childhood education (preschool-grade 4). All candidates for teacher education degrees are required to take PRAXIS II series consisting of a professional and a teacher field test in each area in which the candidate is seeking to be licensed. Eligibility for a teaching license requires the completion of all courses in the student's program; recommendation by the Division upon successful completion of an internship experience.

Licensure/Reciprocity: Arkansas. Students seeking teaching certification in a state other than Arkansas should consult with that state's certification officer early in their program of study to insure compliance with requirements. Many state directors of teacher education credentialing have signed Interstate Agreements through NASDTEC that expedite the certification process.

LYON COLLEGE

Teacher Education
2300 Highland Road
PO Box 2317
Batesville, Arkansas 72501
Phone: (870) 698-4373
Fax: (870) 698-4622
E-mail: whitfieldp@lyon.edu
Internet: http://www.lyon.edu

Institution Description: Lyon College, formerly known as Arkansas College, is a private, independent, nonprofit college affiliated with the Presbyterian Church (U.S.A.). Lyon College is the oldest private college in Arkansas still operating under its original charter. Since its founding as Arkansas College in 1872, the institution changed its name in 1994 to honor the service of the Frank Lyon, Sr. family of Little Rock.

The Teacher Education Program at Lyon College requires students to complete a major in one of the liberal arts disciplines offered by the college. Then, while finishing the major in the senior year, students in early childhood/elementary, middle school, or secondary education experience a year-long internship in one of the several local partnership school districts (Batesville, Southside, or Sulphur Rock).

Institution Control: Private.

Calendar: Semester. Academic year August to May.

Official(s): Dr. Patricia Whitfield, Department Chair; Dr. Tom Carpenter, Professor.

Faculty: Full-time 2; part-time 1.

Degrees Awarded: 12 baccalaureate.

Admission Requirements: *Undergraduate:* Graduation from an accredited high school or GED; applicants would ordinarily have taken a college preparatory curriculum; College Board SAT or ACT composite score. *Teacher education specific:* Students who are interested in the education concentration are encouraged to meet with an education faculty member during their sophomore year.

Fees and Expenses: Undergraduate: $11,990 per academic year. Required fees: $405. On-campus room and board: $5,600. Books and supplies $500.

Financial Aid: Resources specifically for eligible students enrolled in teacher education programs are awarded on the basis of financial need, academic merit, athletic ability. The institution has a program participation agreement with the U.S. Department of Education for eligible students to receive Pell Grants and other federal aid. *Contact:* Financial Aid Office at (870) 793-9813.

Accreditation: *Regional:* NCA. *Professional:* NCATE. *Member of:* AACTE. *Approved by:* Arkansas Department of Education.

Undergraduate Programs: The early childhood/elementary education concentration is designed to prepare students to be effective teachers on the early childhood level. Through a course of study grounded in the liberal arts, the concentration fosters intellectual skills, humane instincts, and an understanding of both the material to be taught and the developmental processes of children. The degree requires the successful completion of 120 credit hours of which 28 in the concentration.

Students pursuing the middle school education (grades 4-8) concentration may focus in the areas of English language srts/social studies or mathematics/science. The degree programs require the successful completion of 120 credit hours of which 24 credit hours of liberal ares requirements in each of the fields.

Through the secondary education concentration, the college assists students in the qualifying major who wish to teach at the secondary level. The curriculum offered adds professional training and classroom experience to a solid education in the liberal arts. Students wishing to pursue this concentration must be formally admitted by the Liberal Arts Teacher Education Committee. The degree program requires the successful completion of 120 credit hours which must include specified teaching field requirements as well as 22 credits in the concentration.

Licensure/Reciprocity: Arkansas. Students seeking teaching certification in a state other than Arkansas should consult with that state's certification officer early in their program of study to insure compliance with requirements. Many state directors of teacher education credentialing have signed Interstate Agreements through NASDTEC that expedite the certification process.

OUACHITA BAPTIST UNIVERSITY

School of Education
Department of Education
410 Ouachita Street
Arkadelphia, Arkansas 71998-0001
Phone: (870) 245-5154
Fax: (870) 245-5500
E-mail: educ@obu.edu
Internet: http://www.obu.edu

Institution Description: Ouachita Baptist University is a private institution affiliated with the Arkansas Baptist State Convention (Southern Baptist). It was established and chartered as Ouachita Baptist College in 1886.

The mission of the department is to provide the curriculum and environment that will produce future teachers who are student centered; possess the knowledge, skills and dispositions for being effective in the classroom; and who are lifelong learners involved in their disciplines and professional development.

Institution Control: Private.

Calendar: Semester. Academic year August to May.

Official(s): Dr. Jeanna Westmoreland, Dean, School of Education; Troy Garlin, Chair, Department of Education.

Faculty: Full-time 7.

Degrees Awarded: 32 baccalaureate.

Admission Requirements: *Undergraduate:* Rolling admissions plan. Graduation from an accredited high school or GED; completion of 16 units in college preparatory courses; College Board SAT or ACT composite score. *Teacher education specific:* Cumulative GPA of 2.5 or passing scores on all three parts of the PRAXIS exam; grade of C or better in grammar and rhetoric. Admission to the professional semester in the senior year has specific requirements. In addition to the 2.5 GPA requirements, the student must take and pass all the required PRAXIS II Subject Area Assessments in the student's teaching field.

Fees and Expenses: Undergraduate: $12,010 per academic year. On-campus room and board: $4,450. Books and supplies $800.

Financial Aid: Resources specifically for eligible students enrolled in teacher education programs are awarded on the basis of academic merit and financial need. The Institution has a program participation agreement with the U.S. Department of Education for eligible students to receive Pell Grants and other federal aid. *Contact:* Financial Aid Office at (870) 245-5570.

Accreditation: *Regional:* NCA. *Professional:* NCATE. *Member of:* AACTE. *Approved by:* Arkansas Department of Education.

OUACHITA BAPTIST UNIVERSITY—*cont'd*

Undergraduate Programs: The Department of Education offers programs leading to the degree of Bachelor of Science in Education. Early childhood majors are prepared to teach preschool through grade four. Middle school majors are prepared to teach grades four through eight. Students majoring in secondary education are prepared for various subject matter fields (grades 7-12). Each major has definite specified course requirements. The degree requires the completion of 128 credit hours.

Licensure/Reciprocity: Arkansas. Students seeking teaching certification in a state other than Arkansas should consult with that state's certification officer early in their program of study to insure compliance with requirements. Many state directors of teacher education credentialing have signed Interstate Agreements through NASDTEC that expedite the certification process.

PHILANDER SMITH COLLEGE

Division of Education
1 Trudie Kibbe Reed Drive
Little Rock, Arkansas 72202
Phone: (501) 370-5248
Fax: (501) 370-5247
E-mail: cugwe@philander.edu
Internet: http://www.philander.edu

Institution Description: Philander Smith College is an independent, nonprofit institution affiliated with the United Methodist Church. The college was established as Walden Seminary and adopted its present name in 1882.

The Division of Education offers teacher education programs in early childhood education, middle childhood/early adolescence education (language arts/social studies), as well as non-teaching/non-licensure programs in physical education and early childhood administration. Each program is built upon a sound liberal arts foundation and an appropriate content area foundation.

Institution Control: Private.

Calendar: Semester. Academic year August to May.

Official(s): Dr. Chime Uko Igwe, Division Chair.

Faculty: Full-time 7; part-time 1; adjunct 5.

Degrees Awarded: 9 baccalaureate.

Admission Requirements: *Undergraduate:* Rolling admissions plan; graduation from an accredited high school with a 2.5 GPA. Admission to the college does not automatically admit the candidate to the teacher education program. *Teacher education specific:* Application is due to the division by March 15 during the semester of the sophomore year. PRAXIS I, II, and III passing scores; entry interview.

Fees and Expenses: Undergraduate $5,200 per academic year. Required fees: $250. On-campus room and board: $3,000. Books and supplies $700.

Financial Aid: Resources specifically for eligible students enrolled in teacher education programs are awarded on the basis of academic merit and financial need. *Contact:* Betty Goodwin at (501) 375-9835 or bgoodwin@philander.edu.

Accreditation: *Regional:* NCA. *Professional:* NCATE. *Member of:* AACTE. *Approved by:* Arkansas Department of Education.

Undergraduate Programs: The licensure program in early childhood education leads to the Bachelor of Science degree. The components of the program include an in-depth study of young children's development and the implications for early childhood teachers; profession, content, and technology courses designed exclusively for prospective early childhood teachers; integrated content courses are designed and team-taught across the curriculum; and field practicum concurrently with the content courses. Completion of 127 credit hours is required for the degree.

Key components of the middle childhood/early adolescence licensure program include an in-depth study of young adolescent development and the implications for middle childhood teachers; professional, content and technology courses designed exclusively for prospective middle childhood teach-

ers; integrated content and methods courses are designed and team-taught across the curriculum; and field internships taken concurrently with the content courses. The program leads to the Bachelor of Science degree and require the completion of 127 credit hours.

Licensure/Reciprocity: Arkansas. Students seeking teaching certification in a state other than Arkansas should consult with that state's certification officer early in their program of study to insure compliance with requirements. Many state directors of teacher education credentialing have signed Interstate Agreements through NASDTEC that expedite the certification process.

SOUTHERN ARKANSAS UNIVERSITY

School of Graduate Studies
P.O. Box 9302
100 East University
Magnolia, Arkansas 71754
Phone: (870) 235-4150
Fax: (870) 235-5035
E-mail: gradstudies@saumag.edu
Internet: http://www.saumag.edu

Institution Description: Southern Arkansas University (formerly Southern State College) is a state institution with a branch campus in East Camden. It was established by the Arkansas Legislature as a secondary-level Third District Agricultural School and chartered 1909. The present name was adopted in 1976.

The basic purpose of the graduate program is to meet the advanced educational needs of students living in southwest Arkansas and neighboring areas. The program was begun in 1975 in response to the demands of many teachers working in schools within commuting distance of the university.

Institution Control: Public.

Calendar: Semester. Academic year August to mid-May.

Official(s): Dr. John R. Jones, Dean of Graduate Studies; Dr. Kim K. Bloss-Bernard, Chair, Department of Curriculum and Instruction.

Faculty: Full-time 4; part-time 4; adjunct 4.

Degrees Awarded: 48 master's.

Admission Requirements: *Graduate:* Baccalaureate degree from an accredited institution; a cumulative GPA of 2.75 or above on a 4.00 scale; GRE exam score of 900 or above. *Teacher education specific:* In addition to meeting the conditions required of all candidates for the master's degree, candidates for the degree in elementary education or secondary education must be qualified to hold a standard teaching certificate or license in their respective fields.

Fees and Expenses: Graduate: in-state $155 per credit hour; $220 per credit hour out-of-state; other required fees $118. Cost of books and supplies vary.

Financial Aid: Resources specifically for eligible students enrolled in teacher education programs are awarded on the basis of financial need. *Contact:* Bronwyn Sneed at bcsneed@saumag.edu or (310) 230-4023.

Accreditation: *Regional:* NCA. *Professional:* NCATE. *Member of:* AACTE. *Approved by:* Arkansas Department of Education.

Graduate Programs: The Master of Education programs in elementary education and secondary education are offered with the following specialties: general elementary, early childhood, reading education, special education, gifted/talented, and math/science. The programs require completion of 36 credit hours. All candidates are required to complete 18 semester hours of core courses, 18 semester hours of elementary or secondary education core courses, and 18 hours from an area of specialization.

The Master of Arts in Teaching is a program primarily for individuals who have an undergraduate degree from an accredited institution in a content area but who lack training in pedagogy. Students choose from one of the licensure areas for grades 7-12.

Licensure/Reciprocity: Arkansas. Students seeking teaching certification in a state other than Arkansas should consult with that state's certification officer early in their program of study to insure compliance with requirements. Many state directors of teacher education credentialing have signed Interstate Agreements through NASDTEC that expedite the certification process.

UNIVERSITY OF ARKANSAS AT FAYETTEVILLE
College of Education and Health Professions
Department of Curriculum and Instruction
201 Graduate Education Building
Fayetteville, Arkansas 72701
Phone: (479) 575-4212
Fax: (479) 575-8797
E-mail: cied@uark.edu
Internet: http://www.uark.edu

Institution Description: The university was established as Arkansas Industrial University in 1871. The first baccalaureate degree was awarded in 1876. The present name was adopted in 1899.

The Department of Curriculum and Instruction prepares students for careers in the field of education, offering concentrations in the areas of childhood education, middle level education, secondary education, education for students with mild disabilities and gifted and talented instruction. Students may graduate with a Bachelor of Science degree in Education or go on to earn the Master of Arts in teaching degree. A variety of subject concentrations are available to those students who choose the middle and secondary level program tracks.

Institution Control: Public.

Calendar: Semester. Academic year August to mid-May.

Official(s): Dr. Tom Smith, Department Head; Shirley Lefever-Davis, Coordinator of Graduate Programs.

Faculty: Full-time 24, part-time 8; adjunct 5.

Degrees Awarded: 191 baccalaureate; 202 master's.

Admission Requirements: *Undergraduate:* Either graduation from an accredited secondary school with a 3.0 GPA; ACT composite score of 20. All students admitted to the university are eligible for enrollment in the College of Education and health Professions. *Teacher education specific:* Students interested in majoring in curriculum and instruction should declare their major upon enrollment to begin meeting requirements as soon as possible. The PRAXIS I exam must be passed after completion of 45 or more program hours with a grade of C or better. *Graduate:* GPA of 2.7 for all coursework taken prior to receipt of baccalaureate degree or 3.0 GPA in last 60 hours of undergraduate study. Students who plan to study for an advanced degree in a subject field should consult with the head of the department concerning course requirements to begin graduate study. *Teacher education specific:* Specialization requirements for a Bachelor of Science degree in education may not be sufficient in every field to gain admission for graduate study.

Fees and Expenses: Undergraduate: in-state $3,810 per academic year; $10,560 out-of-state. Graduate: $2,016 in-state, out-of-state $4,770. Required fees: $960. On-campus room and board: $5,087. Books and supplies $850. Other fees: $1,170.

Financial Aid: Resources specifically for eligible students enrolled in teacher education programs are awarded on the basis of financial need and merit. *Contact:* Kelly Carter at kmcarte@uark.edu or (479) 575-4464.

Accreditation: *Regional:* NCA. *Professional:* NCATE. *Member of:* AACTE. *Approved by:* Arkansas Department of Education.

Undergraduate Programs: Initial teacher licensure programs in the areas of early childhood education, middle school education, and secondary education are offered by the Department of Curriculum and Instruction. The Bachelor of Science degree in education is awarded upon the completion of all required courses for a 128 to 131 credit hours.

Graduate Programs: The Master of Arts in Teaching degree program may be pursued in the areas of early childhood, middle level, and secondary education. The programs require the completion of 34 semester hours and all required program area specifics.

Licensure/Reciprocity: Arkansas. Students seeking teaching certification in a state other than Arkansas should consult with that state's certification officer early in their program of study to insure compliance with requirements. Many state directors of teacher education credentialing have signed Interstate Agreements through NASDTEC that expedite the certification process.

UNIVERSITY OF ARKANSAS AT LITTLE ROCK
College of Education
Department of Teacher Education
2801 South University
Little Rock, Arkansas 72204-1099
Phone: (501) 569-3124
Fax: (501) 569-3127
E-mail: kdirons@ualr.edu
Internet: http://www.ualr.edu

Institution Description: The university was established and incorporated as Little Rock Junior College in 1927. It became a 4-year institution and its name was changed to Little Rock University in 1957. It merged with the University of Arkansas and the present name was adopted in 1969.

The mission of the Department of Teacher Education is to provide balanced programs to embody institutional and college goals, the Arkansas Department licensure requirements, guidelines of learned societies, and to promote contemporary educational philosophies and practices.

Institution Control: Public.

Calendar: Semester. Academic year August to May.

Official(s): Dr. Shirley Freeman-Turner, Department Chair.

Faculty: Full-time 25.

Degrees Awarded: 46 baccalaureate; 95 master's.

Admission Requirements: *Undergraduate:* Rolling admissions plan. Graduation from an accredited high school with 15 units or GED; minimum 2.0 GPA; College Board SAT or ACT composite score. *Teacher education specific:* Applications are accepted from students who have completed specified courses in English, speech, and math with grades of C or better. Applicants must have completed a total of 30 hours with a cumulative GPA of 2.65 or better; completion of PRAXIS I exam. *Graduate:* Baccalaureate degree from a regionally accredited institution with a cumulative GPA of at least 2.75 on a 4.0 scale; *Teacher education specific:* Favorable recommendation from faculty;

Fees and Expenses: Undergraduate: in-state $2,850 per academic year; $7,344 out-of-state. On-campus room and board: $2,700. Books and supplies $750.

Financial Aid: Resources specifically for eligible students enrolled in teacher education programs are awarded on the basis of financial need. The institution has a program participation agreement with the U.S. Department of Education for eligible students to receive Pell Grants and other federal aid. *Contact:* Financial Aid Office at (501) 569-3130.

Accreditation: *Regional:* NCA. *Professional:* NCATE. *Member of:* AACTE. *Approved by:* Arkansas Department of Education.

Undergraduate Programs: The Department of Teacher Education offers two Bachelor of Science in Education degrees: early childhood education and middle childhood education which includes specialties in math/science and social studies/language arts. An undergraduate minor in secondary education is available for interested students. All programs require the completion of 129 credit hours.

Graduate Programs: The department offers Master of Education degrees in early childhood education, middle childhood education, reading, secondary education, and special education specialist degree in elementary education. The Master of Edu-

UNIVERSITY OF ARKANSAS AT LITTLE ROCK—*cont'd*

cation programs allow students to develop a plan of study to pursue their individual and career goals. The programs require the completion of 36 graduate credit hours including 18 core area hours.

Licensure/Reciprocity: Arkansas. Students seeking teaching certification in a state other than Arkansas should consult with that state's certification officer early in their program of study to insure compliance with requirements. Many state directors of teacher education credentialing have signed Interstate Agreements through NASDTEC that expedite the certification process.

UNIVERSITY OF ARKANSAS AT MONTICELLO

School of Education
P.O. Box 3596
Monticello, Arkansas 71655-3596
Phone: (870) 460-1062
Fax: (870) 460-1321
E-mail: Richard@uamont.edu
Internet: http://www.uamont.edu

Institution Description: The university was established as the Fourth District Agricultural School in 1909. The name was changed to Arkansas Agricultural and Mechanical College in 1925 and merged with University of Arkansas and adopted present name in 1971.

The School of Education is dedicated to providing excellence in education that reaches beyond the curricular offerings and programs to positively impact those students who will someday teach. The department places emphasis on learning, teaching, technology, and service learning provides the foundation for the innovative programs, all of which are grounded in the latest research and theory available.

Institution Control: Public.

Calendar: Semester. Academic year August to May.

Official(s): Dr. Rhonda Richards, Dean.

Faculty: Full-time 15.

Degrees Awarded: 39 baccalaureate; 1 master's.

Admission Requirements: *Undergraduate:* Rolling admissions plan. Graduation from approved high school; ACT composite score. *Teacher education specific:* Students must make application to the School of Education; PRAXIS I exam scores must be submitted; formal interview with faculty. *Graduate:* Bachelor of Arts or Bachelor of Science degree from a regionally accredited college; cumulative GPA of 3.0 in the last 60 hours; complete a criminal background check; submit official GRE score; passing scores on all parts of the PRAXIS I for reading, writing, and mathematics. *Teacher education specific:* All teacher candidates should pass the PRAXIS II Specialty Areas test prior to the internship experience.

Fees and Expenses: Undergraduate: in-state $3,175 per academic year; $6,415 out-of-state. On-campus room and board: $3,100. Books and supplies $800.

Financial Aid: Resources specifically for eligible students enrolled in teacher education programs are awarded on the basis of financial need and merit. The institution has a program participation agreement with the U.S. Department of Education for eligible students to receive Pell Grants and other federal aid. *Contact:* Financial Aid Office at (870) 460-1050.

Accreditation: *Regional:* NCA. *Professional:* NCATE. *Member of:* AACTE. *Approved by:* Arkansas Department of Education.

Undergraduate Programs: The School of Education offers programs in early childhood special education, middle Level Education, secondary education, and health and physical education. All baccalaureate programs require the completion of specific courses in the student's major area for a total of 124 credit hours.

Graduate Programs: The Master of Arts in Teaching (MAT) is available to students who have completed a baccalaureate degree that includes content areas coursework equivalent to the undergraduate licensure requirements at the university. Students who do not meet all requirements will be required to complete additional coursework. Students may elect one of the following areas of licensure at the 7-12 level: biology, English, mathematics, social studies, art, music, or physical education.

Licensure/Reciprocity: Arkansas. Students seeking teaching certification in a state other than Arkansas should consult with that state's certification officer early in their program of study to insure compliance with requirements. Many state directors of teacher education credentialing have signed Interstate Agreements through NASDTEC that expedite the certification process.

UNIVERSITY OF ARKANSAS AT PINE BLUFF

School of Education
Department of Elementary, Secondary and Special Education
1200 North University Drive
Mail Slot 4927
Pine Bluff, Arkansas 71611
Phone: (870) 575-8240
Fax: (870) 543-8484
E-mail: admissions@uapb.edu
Internet: http://www.uapb.edu

Institution Description: The university in Pine bluff was chartered in 1873 and established established as Branch Normal College. It became a junior college in 1885 and its name was changed to Arkansas Agricultural, Mechanical and Normal College in 1928. As a senior college it was merged with the University of Arkansas and adopted its present name in 1972.

The Department of Elementary, Secondary, and Special Education has as its major function the professional preparation of certifiable teachers at the early childhood, elementary, and secondary levels.

Institution Control: Public.

Calendar: Semester. Academic year August to May.

Official(s): Dr. Calvin Johnson, Dean, School of Education; Dr. George Herts, Chair, Department of Elementary, Secondary, and Special Education.

Faculty: Full-time 7.

Degrees Awarded: 19 baccalaureate; 18 master's.

Admission Requirements: *Undergraduate:* Graduation from an accredited secondary school with 16 units or GED; ACT composite score. *Teacher education specific:* PRAXIS I with passing scores; GPA of 2.5 in general education courses; personal interview; letter of recommendation from an academic advisor.

Fees and Expenses: Undergraduate: in-state $3,458 per academic year; $6,989 out-of-state. On-campus room and board: $4,282. Books and supplies $1,000. Other expenses: $3,110.

Financial Aid: Resources specifically for eligible students enrolled in teacher education programs are awarded on the basis of financial need and academic merit. The institution has a program participation agreement with the U.S. Department of Education for eligible students to receive Pell Grants and other federal aid. *Contact:* Financial Aid Office at (870) 575-8304.

Accreditation: *Regional:* NCA. *Professional:* NCATE. *Member of:* AACTE. *Approved by:* Arkansas Department of Education.

Undergraduate Programs: Students may pursue the Bachelor Science in Education degree in the following program areas: elementary education, elementary childhood education; reading endorsement, secondary education, special education (K-12) mildly handicapped; and vocational education. Programs in the secondary education teaching fields are: agriculture, art, biology, business, chemistry, English, home economics, mathematics, music, physical education, social studies, and trades and industrial education. Majors in these areas should confer with chairperson of the respective departments of the university as well as the secondary education advisor. All baccalaureate programs require the completion of specific course requirements and at least 120 credit hours with a GPA of 2.0.

Licensure/Reciprocity: Arkansas. Students seeking teaching certification in a state other than Arkansas should consult with that state's certification officer early in their program of study to insure compliance with requirements. Many state directors of teacher education credentialing have signed Interstate Agreements through NASDTEC that expedite the certification process.

UNIVERSITY OF CENTRAL ARKANSAS
College of Education-Professional Education Unit
Mashburn 100
201 Donaghey Avenue
Conway, Arkansas 72035
Phone: (501) 450-5175
Fax: (501) 450-5358
E-mail: aream@mail.uca.edu
Internet: http://www.uca.edu

Institution Description: The University of Central Arkansas is a state institution. Established and chartered as the Arkansas State Normal School 1907; offered first instruction at postsecondary level 1908; awarded first degree (baccalaureate) 1920; changed name to Arkansas State Teachers College 1925, State College of Arkansas 1967; adopted present name 1975.

The College of Education-Professional Education Unit offers teacher education programs at the undergraduate level leading to the baccalaureate degree with teacher certification and licensure. Graduate programs are offered that lead to advanced degree programs leading to licensure.

Institution Control: Public.

Calendar: Semesters. Academic year Aug. to mid-May.

Official(s): Dr. Jane McHaney, Dean; Ken Vaughn, Director of Admissions and Licensure.

Faculty: Full-time 42; part-time 25; adjunct 7.

Degrees Awarded: 93 baccalaureate; 508 master's.

Admission Requirements: *Undergraduate:* Secondary school cumulative GPA 2.75 or above; or rank in upper 40% of graduating class; or composite ACT score of 19 or above; or combined SAT score of 930 or above. *Teacher education specific:* 2.36 GPA or above, C or higher in identified general education courses; PRAXIS I passing scores; completion of 45 semester hours; 2 recommendations; writing samples; interview. *Graduate:* Baccalaureate degree from accredited institution; cumulative undergraduate GPA of 2.7 out of 4.0; minimum of 3.0 GPA on previous coursework; submit GRE or GMAT scores; meet other program requirements. *Teacher education specific:* letters of recommendations; interviews; teaching license.

Fees and Expenses: Undergraduate: in-state $3,770; out-of-state $7,082. Graduate: in-state $4,320; out-of-state $8,688. Required fees: $735 undergraduate, $663 graduate. On-campus room and board: $3,786. Books and supplies $1,000. Post office box $10; parking decal $40.

Financial Aid: Resources specifically for eligible students enrolled in teacher education programs are awarded on the basis of academic merit and financial need. Minority scholarships available. *Contact:* Cheryl Lyons, Director for Financial Aid; (301) 450-3140 or clyons@mail.uca.edu.

Accreditation: *Regional:* NCA. *Professional:* NCATE. *Member of:* AACTE. *Approved by:* Arkansas Department of Education.

Undergraduate Programs: All students may major in one of the following areas to receive licensure: early childhood or middle level education; secondary areas 7th to 12th grades (business technology, English, family and consumer sciences, marketing technology; mathematics; sciences (life science/earth science; physical science/earth science); social studies; oreschool-8th grades and 7th to 12th grades: art, French, kinesiology/physical education/health; Music (instrumental and vocal), Spanish.

Credit hours required range from 124 to 134 credit hours depending on program. Candidates are required to complete a general education core, major course requirements and internship experiences in the public schools.

Graduate Programs: The Professional Education Unit offers advanced degree programs that lead to licensure: Master's degree programs: library, media and information technologies, reading, school counseling; school leadership/management/administration; school psychology; special education (instructional specialist- birth to 8 years; grades 4-12). Credit hour requirements range from 30 to 47 credit hours depending on program. Specialist's degree program: educational leadership (37 credit hours); doctoral degree program: school psychology (120 credit hours).

Licensure/Reciprocity: Arkansas. Students seeking teaching certification in a state other than Arkansas should consult with that state's certification officer early in their program of study to insure compliance with requirements. Many state directors of teacher education credentialing have signed Interstate Agreements through NASDTEC that expedite the certification process.

UNIVERSITY OF THE OZARKS
Division of Education
Dr. Wiley Lin Jurie Teacher Education Center
415 North College Avenue
Clarksville, Arkansas 72830
Phone: (479) 979-1331
Fax: (479) 979-1328
E-mail: lpelts@ozarks.edu
Internet: http://www.ozarks.edu

Institution Description: The University of the Ozarks is a private, nonprofit college affiliated with the United Presbyterian Church (U.S.A.). It was established by Cumberland Presbyterians as Cane Hill College and offered first instruction at the postsecondary level 1834. The present name was adopted in 1987.

The Division of Education offers programs on the early childhood and secondary levels. A strong emphasis is placed on experience and on working with children of diverse backgrounds and special needs.

Institution Control: Private.

Calendar: Semester. Academic year July to June.

Official(s): Dr. George Stone, Department Head; Dr. Betty Robinson, Licensure Officer; Marsha Tindell, Director of Field Experiences.

Faculty: Full-time 5; variable part-time faculty.

Degrees Awarded: 14 baccalaureate.

Admission Requirements: *Undergraduate:* Graduation from secondary school with a 2.0 GPA; College Board SAT or ACT composite. *Teacher education specific:* Student must be classified as at least a sophomore; overall GPA of 2.75 or better; PRAXIS I score; interview with Teacher Education Council.

Fees and Expenses: $11,520 per academic year. Required fees: $360. On-campus room and board: $4,680. Books and supplies $800 (some courses require lab fees).

Financial Aid: Resources specifically for eligible students enrolled in teacher education programs are awarded on the basis of academic merit and financial need. *Contact:* Jana Hart at (479) 979-1221 or jhart@ozarks.edu.

Accreditation: *Regional:* NCA. *Professional:* NCATE. *Member of:* AACTE. *Approved by:* Arkansas Department of Education.

Undergraduate Programs: All early childhood education (P-4) students seeking licensure in Arkansas are required to take a course in Arkansas history. There are specific course requirements in professional education and specialty areas. The program requires the completion of 128 credit hours.

UNIVERSITY OF THE OZARKS—*cont'd*

The middle level education (P-4) offers options in math and science emphasis and language arts and social studies emphasis. Specific courses in professional education and specialty areas are required. Successful completion of 128 credit hours is required for the baccalaureate degree.

Licensure/Reciprocity: Arkansas. Students seeking teaching certification in a state other than Arkansas should consult with that state's certification officer early in their program of study to insure compliance with requirements. Many state directors of teacher education credentialing have signed Interstate Agreements through NASDTEC that expedite the certification process.

CALIFORNIA

AZUSA PACIFIC UNIVERSITY

School of Education
Department of Teacher Education
901 East Alosta Avenue
Azusa, California 91702-7000
Phone: (626) 969-3434
Fax: (626) 969-7180
E-mail: brashear@apu.edu
Internet: http://www.apu.edu

Institution Description: Azusa Pacific University (Azusa Pacific College until 1981) is a private, independent, nonprofit institution. It was established and chartered as Training School for Christian Workers and offered first instruction at the postsecondary level in 1899. The university merged with Los Angeles Pacific College and changed name to Azusa Pacific College in 1965. The present name was adopted in 1981.

The primary goal of the Department of Teacher Education is to provide the training and experience needed to qualify for California's multiple-subject, single-subject, and special education teaching credentials. The program was established in 1983.

Institution Control: Private.

Calendar: Semester. Academic year September to April.

Official(s): Dr. Terrence Cummings, Dean; Dr. Nancy Brashear, Chair, Department of Teacher Education.

Faculty: Full-time 17.

Degrees Awarded: 36 baccalaureate; 822 master's; 5 doctorate.

Admission Requirements: *Undergraduate:* Either graduation from a secondary school with a college preparatory curriculum or GED; College Board SAT or ACT composite. *Teacher education specific:* During the first two years of enrollment, it is suggested that prospective teacher complete university general education requirements and prerequisites to upper-division coursework; application may be submitted as early as the junior or senior year. *Graduate:* Baccalaureate degree from a regionally accredited institution; GRE. *Teacher education specific:* Professional qualification test/exams; faculty interview.

Fees and Expenses: $17,140 per academic year. On-campus room and board: $6,310. Other expenses: $2,465. Books and supplies: $1,210.

Financial Aid: Resources specifically for eligible students enrolled in teacher education programs are awarded on the basis of financial need and academic merit. The institution has a Program Participation Agreement with the U.S. Department of Education for eligible students to receive Pell Grants and other federal aid. *Contact:* Financial Aid Office at (626) 969-3434, ext. 3009.

Accreditation: *Regional:* WASC. *Professional:* NCATE. *Approved by:* California Commission on Teacher Credentialing.

Undergraduate Programs: An accelerated degree program, the Bachelor of Arts in Human Development, provides subject matter preparation for prospective elementary school teachers, along with a Bachelor of Arts in Liberal Studies for traditional undergraduate students. Each baccalaureate program requires the completion of 126 semester hours including a general education core and professional studies courses. Candidates for the degree are eligible to student teach after advancement to stu-

dent teaching status following successful clearance, which includes attending a mandatory student teaching information meeting.

Graduate Programs: Azusa Pacific offers 10 subject matter programs for students completing their bachelor degrees. When credential courses are combined with selected courses required for a Master of Arts in Education with an emphasis in teaching or special education, both the teaching credential and master's degree may be obtained.

Licensure/Reciprocity: California. Students seeking teaching certification in a state other than California should consult with that state's certification office arly in their program of study to insure compliance with requirements. Many state directors of teacher credentialing have signed Interstate Agreements through NASDTEC that expedite the certification process.

CALIFORNIA LUTHERAN UNIVERSITY

School of Education
60 West Olsen Road
Thousand Oaks, California 91360-2787
Phone: (805) 492-2411
Fax: (805) 492-3114
E-mail: cluadm@callutheran.edu
Internet: http://www.callutheran.edu

Institution Description: California Lutheran University is a private college affiliated with The Evangelical Lutheran Church in America. It was established in 1959 and offered first instruction at the postsecondary level in 1961.

Students preparing to teach in elementary schools complete an undergraduate major in liberal studies and a program of professional studies to qualify for the California Multiple Subjects (Elementary) teaching credential. Students in the secondary program complete an approved program or major in their subject area as undergraduates.

Institution Control: Private.

Calendar: Semester. Academic year September to May.

Official(s): Dr. Carol A. Bartell, Dean.

Faculty: Full-time 17.

Degrees Awarded: 47 baccalaureate; 137 master's.

Admission Requirements: *Undergraduate:* Graduation from secondary school or GED; College Board SAT or ACT composite. *Teacher education specific:* Students must complete specific requirements as dictated by the student's major; completion of general education coursework; faculty interview. *Graduate:* Baccalaureate degree from a regionally accredited institution. *Teacher education specific:* Complete all admission requirements and tests/exams; faculty interview.

Fees and Expenses: $19,050 per academic year. On-campus room and board: $6,920. Other expenses: $2,520. Books and supplies: $1,010.

Financial Aid: Resources specifically for eligible students enrolled in teacher education programs are awarded on the basis of academic merit and financial need. The institution has a Program Participation Agreement with the U.S. Department of Education for eligible students to receive Pell Grants and other federal aid. *Contact:* Financial Aid Office at (805) 493-3115.

Accreditation: *Regional:* WASC. *Member of:* AACTE. *Approved by:* California Commission on Teacher Credentialing.

CALIFORNIA LUTHERAN UNIVERSITY—
cont'd

Undergraduate Programs: Undergraduate majors in liberal studies (middle and high school teaching) have academic coursework augmented by fieldwork in public school classrooms where prospective teachers observe expert teachers and begin to apply what they are learning in their courses. The professional programs leading to the bachelor's degree cover a full range of elementary, secondary, bilingual, special education, administrative, and counseling disciplines. Bachelor's programs require the completion of 127 credit hours. All credential studies offer the option of earning a master's degree along with a credential.

Graduate Programs: Master of Arts programs are offered in curriculum and instruction with specialization areas in cross-cultural language and academic development (CLAD); curriculum coordination; elementary education; reading; secondary education; and subject area specialization. Also offered are programs leading to the Master of Science in counseling and guidance, Master of Arts in educational administration, Master of Education, and Master of Science in special education.

A Doctor of Education in educational leadership is also offered to qualified candidates.

Licensure/Reciprocity: California. Students seeking teaching certification in a state other than California should consult with that state's certification office early in their program of study to insure compliance with requirements. Many state directors of teacher credentialing have signed Interstate Agreements through NASDTEC that expedite the certification process.

CALIFORNIA POLYTECHNIC STATE UNIVERSITY, SAN LUIS OBISPO

University Center for Teacher Education
1 Grand Avenue
San Luis Obispo, California 93407
Phone: (805) 756-7380
Fax: (805) 756-7422
E-mail: bkonopak@calpoly.edu
Internet: http://www.calpoly.edu

Institution Description: The university was established as California Polytechnic School, a vocational secondary school in 1901. It became a junior college and offered first instruction at the postsecondary level in 1927. A third year was added in 1936 and a fourth year in 1940. The name was changed to California State Polytechnic College, San Luis Obispo in 1947. The present name was adopted in 1972.

The Liberal Studies Department offers three options of study to students. They may pursue a broadly based and interdisciplinary Bachelor of Arts program with their choice of an individualized course of study or an elementary education concentration.

Institution Control: Public.

Calendar: Quarter. Academic year June to May.

Official(s): Dr. Bonnie Konopak, Dean; Dr. Carl Brown, Associate Dean and Director of Teacher Education.

Faculty: Full-time 15; part-time 6; adjunct 20.

Degrees Awarded: 69 baccalaureate; 88 master's.

Admission Requirements: *Undergraduate:* High school graduation with college preparatory study; cumulative grade of C or better. *Teacher education specific:* Application by junior year; faculty interview.

Fees and Expenses: $2,900 in-state per academic year; $2,900 out-of-state plus $188 per unit. On-campus room and board: $6,850. Books and supplies: $1,500.

Financial Aid: Resources specifically for eligible students enrolled in teacher education programs are awarded on the basis of academic merit and financial need. *Contact:* John E. Anderson at (805) 756-5393 or anderson@calpoly.edu.

Accreditation: *Regional:* WASC. *Member of:* AACTE. *Approved by:* California Commission on Teacher Credentialing.

Undergraduate Programs: The Bachelor of Arts in Liberal Studies with elementary education concentration is intended primarily for students wishing to become elementary school teachers. Those students who do not meet the application criteria for the blended program may continue to pursue the BA degree and subsequently may enter the post-baccalaureate multiple subject credential programs. The concentration contains an area of emphasis that gives depth to the students' education in the subject matter of their choice and may enable the credential candidate to achieve a supplemental authorization to teach a specific content area at the middle school level. The program requires the completion of 186 quarter units.

The Bachelor of Science in liberal studies/multiple subject credential or special education credential program curriculum offers innovative coordination of subject matter with professional coursework, as well as a significant number of field experiences in elementary schools or special education settings. The program requires the completion of 196 quarter units.

Licensure/Reciprocity: California. Students seeking teaching certification in a state other than California should consult with that state's certification office early in their program of study to insure compliance with requirements. Many state directors of teacher credentialing have signed Interstate Agreements through NASDTEC that expedite the certification process.

CALIFORNIA STATE POLYTECHNIC UNIVERSITY, POMONA

College of Education and Integrative Skills
Department of Education
3801 West Temple Avenue
Pomona, California 91768
Fax: (909) 869-2300
E-mail: cppadmit@csupomona.edu
Internet: http://www.csupomona.edu

Institution Description: The university was established as the southern California branch of California State Polytechnic School in 1938. It became an independent state college in 1966 and the present name was adopted in 1972.

The Department of Education is solely a post-baccalaureate department, offering the teacher credential programs as well as a master's degree program in education.

Institution Control: Public.

Calendar: Quarter. Academic year June to May..

Official(s): Dr. Dr. Joan Bissell, Dean; Barbara E. Bromley, Chair, Department of Education.

Faculty: Full-time 22; adjunct 35.

Degrees Awarded: 53 master's.

Admission Requirements: *Graduate:* Completion of a four-year college course of study and a baccalaureate degree from a regionally accredited or internationally recognized institution; 3.0; *Teacher education specific:* Meet the professional, personal, scholastic, and other standards for graduate studies which may include qualifying examinations; teaching credential (multiple subject, single subject, education specialist).

Fees and Expenses: $1,795 in-state per academic year; out-of-state $10,255. On-campus room and board: $7,115. Other expenses: $2,050. Books and supplies: $1,140.

Financial Aid: Resources specifically for eligible students enrolled in teacher education programs are awarded on the basis of academic merit and financial need. The institution has a Program Participation Agreement with the U.S. Department of Education for eligible students to receive Pell Grants and other federal aid. *Contact:* Financial Aid Office at (909) 869-3700.

Accreditation: *Regional:* WASC. *Member of:* AACTE. *Approved by:* California Commission on Teacher Credentialing.

Graduate Programs: The Master of Arts in Education is an advanced degree with specific emphases available in bilingual education, curriculum and instruction, design-based learning, educational multimedia, heritage languages (literacy and leadership); language arts/literacy, and special education. A minimum of 45 quarter units of acceptable graduate-level work must be completed.

Licensure/Reciprocity: California. Students seeking teaching certification in a state other than California should consult with that state's certification office early in their program of study to insure compliance with requirements. Many state directors of teacher credentialing have signed Interstate Agreements through NASDTEC that expedite the certification process.

CALIFORNIA STATE UNIVERSITY, BAKERSFIELD
School of Education
Department of Teacher Education
9001 Stockdale Highway
Bakersfield, California 93311-1099
Phone: (805) 664-2011
Fax: (805) 664-3036
E-mail: admissions@csubak.edu
Internet: http://www.csubak.edu

Institution Description: The campus was established and chartered as California State College, Kern County in 1965. The name was changed to California State College, Bakersfield in 1967. University status was achieved in 1988.

The philosophy of the School of Education has as its basis confluent education which perceives learning as the merging of cognitive, affective, social, and psychomotor domains. This belief underscores the premise that education nurtures and promotes intellectual growth and the emotional, social, and physical well-being of all students with a special focus on diversity and equity.

Institution Control: Public.

Calendar: Quarter. Academic year September to June.

Official(s): Dr. Sheryl L. Santos, Dean; Michelle Zachlod, Chair, Department of Teacher Education.

Faculty: Full-time 27.

Degrees Awarded: 27 baccalaureate; 97 master's.

Admission Requirements: *Undergraduate:* High school graduation with completion of a 15-unit comprehensive pattern of college preparatory study with a grade of C or better; College Board SAT or ACT composite. *Teacher education specific:* Departmental approval; completion of courses are in the general education core plus a major field of study that is appropriate for the baccalaureate degree and future teacher credentialing. *Graduate:* Baccalaureate degree from a regionally accredited institution; specific professional tests; faculty interview. *Teacher education specific:* Graduates must pass California requirements for teacher credentials.

Fees and Expenses: Undergraduate in-state $814.75 per quarter; out-of-state: $188 per unit plus $786 state university fee (includes campus mandatory fees). Graduate in-state $884.75 per quarter; out-of-state $188 per unit plus $884.75 state university fee (includes campus mandatory fees). Per academic year: on-campus room and board: $6,545; other expenses: $2,625; books and supplies: $980.

Financial Aid: Resources specifically for eligible students enrolled in teacher education programs are awarded on the basis of financial need and academic merit. The institution has a Program Participation Agreement with the U.S. Department of Education for eligible students to receive Pell Grants and other federal aid. *Contact:* Financial Aid Office at (661) 664-3016.

Accreditation: *Regional:* WASC. *Professional:* NCATE. *Member of:* AACTE. *Approved by:* California Commission on Teacher Credentialing.

Undergraduate Programs: The Blended Baccalaureate for Excellence in Scholarship and Teaching is designed especially for undergraduate studies majors who wish to become teachers. Highly-motivated students can earn a Bachelor of Arts in liberal studies and multiple subjects credential in four years.

Graduate Programs: The Master of Arts and Master of Science in Education degrees are offered in the following concentrations: bilingual/multilingual education, counseling, curriculum and instruction, early childhood, educational administration, reading and language arts, and special education. All candidates for teaching credentials have coursework and fieldwork opportunities working with English language learners and also with students with disabilities.

Licensure/Reciprocity: California. Students seeking teaching certification in a state other than California should consult with that state's certification office early in their program of study to insure compliance with requirements. Many state directors of teacher credentialing have signed Interstate Agreements through NASDTEC that expedite the certification process.

CALIFORNIA STATE UNIVERSITY, CHICO
Department of Education
Modoc Hall 215
Chico, California 95929-0222
Phone: (530) 898-6421
Fax: (530) 898-6177
E-mail: mkotar@csuchico.edu
Internet: http://www.csuchico.edu/educ

Institution Description: The university was established as Chico Normal School in 1887 and offered first instruction at the postsecondary level in 1889. The name was changed to Chico State Teachers College in 1921, to Chico State College in 1935, to the present name in 1972.

The CSU, Chico professional education programs prepare educators to be informed decision-makers. Graduates develop a high level of competence consistent with the California Standards for the teaching profession.

Institution Control: Public.

Calendar: Semester. Academic year August to May.

Official(s): Dr. Michael Kotar, Chair.

Faculty: Full-time 18; part-time 30.

Degrees Awarded: 21 baccalaureate; 75 master's.

Admission Requirements: *Undergraduate:* Graduation from an approved secondary school; SAT or ACT scores are only required if high school GPA is less than 3.0. *Teacher education specific:* Departmental approval; completion of courses in the general education core plus a major field of study that is appropriate for the baccalaureate degree and future teacher credentialing. *Graduate:* Baccalaureate degree from a regionally accredited institution; overall GPA of 3.0 in the last 60 semester (90 quarter) units attempted; *Teacher education specific:* PRAXIS Multiple Subject Assessment for Teachers or California Examination for Teachers; basic teaching credential; an approved major; faculty interview.

Fees and Expenses: Undergraduate in-state $786 per semester; out-of-state $282 per unit plus $786 state university fee. Graduate in-state $867 per semester; out-of-state $282 per unit plus $867 state university fee. Required fees: $470 average per academic year. On-campus room and board: $6,545. Other expenses: $2,625. Books and supplies: $1,080.

Financial Aid: Resources specifically for eligible students enrolled in teacher education programs are awarded on the basis of financial need and academic merit. The institution has a Program Participation Agreement with the U.S. Department of Education for eligible students to receive Pell Grants and other federal aid. *Contact:* Financial Aid Office.

Accreditation: *Regional:* WASC. *Member of:* AACTE. *Approved by:* California Commission on Teacher Credentialing.

Undergraduate Programs: Subject matter preparation programs are offered in agriculture, art, English, health, languages, liberal studies, mathematics, music, physical education, science, social science, and history. Blended programs for the bachelor's degree and credential are available for multiple subject (elementary teaching) and physical education. Students who opt for the Blended Teacher Education Program select a liberal studies major credential. Students are encouraged to attend a program overview during the junior or senior year.

Graduate Programs: Multiple (elementary) and single (secondary) subject programs leading to California teaching credentials are available. Advanced credentialing for administrative services and library media teacher as well as the Master of Arts in Education are also offered.

CALIFORNIA STATE UNIVERSITY, CHICO—
cont'd

Licensure/Reciprocity: California. Students seeking teaching certification in a state other than California should consult with that state's certification office early in their program of study to insure compliance with requirements. Many state directors of teacher credentialing have signed Interstate Agreements through NASDTEC that expedite the certification process.

CALIFORNIA STATE UNIVERSITY, DOMINGUEZ HILLS

School of Education
Department of Teacher Education
1000 East Victoria Street
Carson, California 90747
Phone: (310) 243-3522
Fax: (310) 243-2800
E-mail: srussell@csudh.edu
Internet: http://www.csudh.edu

Institution Description: The campus was established as California State College, Dominguez Hills and was chartered in 1960. First instruction at the postsecondary level began in 1965. The present name was adopted in 1977.

The Graduate Education Program is designed to provide knowledge and understanding of the basic foundations and theories of education as well as advanced training in specific fields. The curriculum objectives seek to promote a blending of theory and practice to assist students who seek advancement within their chosen field in education, public service, or private industry.

Institution Control: Public.

Calendar: Semester. Academic year August to May.

Official(s): Dr. Sharon E. Russell, Chair.

Faculty: Full-time 35; part-time 108.

Degrees Awarded: 338 master's.

Admission Requirements: *Undergraduate:* Graduation from an approved secondary school; SAT or ACT scores are only required if high school GPA is less than 3.0. *Teacher education specific:* California law requires a subject area major; there are no undergraduate degree programs in education; passing score on the California Basic Skills Test. *Graduate:* Baccalaureate degree from a regionally accredited institution; overall GPA of 2.5 on previous academic and related work; *Teacher education specific:* PRAXIS Multiple Subject Assessment for Teachers or California Examination for Teachers; basic teaching credential; an approved major.

Fees and Expenses: Undergraduate in-state $786 per semester; out-of-state $282 per unit plus $786 state university fee. Graduate in-state $867 per semester; out-of-state $282 per unit plus $867 state university fee. Per academic year: required fees: $470 average; on-campus room and board: $6,545; other expenses: $2,625; books and supplies: $1,080.

Financial Aid: Resources specifically for eligible students enrolled in teacher education programs are awarded on the basis of financial need and academic merit. The institution has a Program Participation Agreement with the U.S. Department of Education for eligible students to receive Pell Grants and other federal aid. *Contact:* Financial Aid Office.

Accreditation: *Regional:* WASC. *Professional:* NCATE. *Member of;* AACTE. *Approved by:* California Commission on Teacher Credentialing.

Undergraduate Programs: The credential program offers multiple and single subject credential with two options: the University Intern option and the Student Teaching option. Students must complete a liberal studies major and should contact the Liberal Studies Coordinator upon entering the university.

Graduate Programs: The Master of Arts in Education is offered with options in counseling, educational administration, individualized program, multicultural program, physical education administration, teaching/curriculum, and technology based education.

The Master of Arts in special education offers options in early childhood, mild/moderate disabilities, and moderate/severe disabilities.

Both of the foregoing degree programs require the completion of 30 units of coursework with a minimum 3.0 GPA. A minimum of 21 semester units must be completed in residence.

Licensure/Reciprocity: California. Students seeking teaching certification in a state other than California should consult with that state's certification office early in their program of study to insure compliance with requirements. Many state directors of teacher credentialing have signed Interstate Agreements through NASDTEC that expedite the certification process.

CALIFORNIA STATE UNIVERSITY, FRESNO

Kremen School of Education and Human Development
Department of Curriculum and Instruction
5241 North Maple Avenue
Fresno, California 93740
Phone: (559) 278-0240
Fax: (559) 278-4812
E-mail: kremen@csufresno.edu
Internet: http://www.csufresno.edu

Institution Description: Established as Fresno State Normal School, the institution was chartered and offered first instruction at the postsecondary level in 1911. The name was changed to Fresno State Teachers College and became a 4-year institution in 1921. After a name change to Fresno State College in 1935, the present name was adopted in 1972.

The primary mission of the Department of Curriculum and Instruction is the preparation and continuing education of K-12 educators, The coursework offers students opportunities to develop and refine their understanding of the teaching/learning process while experiencing the best of the world of practice.

Institution Control: Public.

Calendar: Semester. Academic year August to May.

Official(s): Dr. Joan Henderson-Sparks, Chair.

Faculty: Full-time 5; part-time 28.

Degrees Awarded: 55 baccalaureate; 236 master's.

Admission Requirements: *Undergraduate:* Graduation from an approved secondary school; SAT or ACT scores are only required if high school GPA is less than 3.0. *Teacher education specific:* California law requires a subject area major; there are no undergraduate degree programs in education. *Graduate:* Baccalaureate degree from a regionally accredited institution; overall GPA of 2.5 on previous academic and related work; *Teacher education specific:* PRAXIS Multiple Subject Assessment for Teachers or California Examination for Teachers; basic teaching credential; an approved major.

Fees and Expenses: Undergraduate in-state $786 per semester; out-of-state $282 per unit plus $786 state university fee. Graduate in-state $867 per semester; out-of-state $282 per unit plus $867 state university fee. Per academic year: required fees: $470 average; on-campus room and board: $6,545; other expenses: $2,625; books and supplies: $1,080.

Financial Aid: Resources specifically for eligible students enrolled in teacher education programs are awarded on the basis of financial need and academic merit. The institution has a Program Participation Agreement with the U.S. Department of Education for eligible students to receive Pell Grants and other federal aid. *Contact:* Financial Aid Office.

Accreditation: *Regional:* WASC. *Professional:* NCATE. *Member of:* AACTE. *Approved by:* California Commission on Teacher Credentialing.

Undergraduate Programs: A basic teaching credential may be earned in conjunction with a baccalaureate degree or following completion of a fifth-year course of study. Undergraduate majors can be pursued in areas in which students wish to teach. Baccalaureate degree programs require the completion of a general education core plus a major program for a total of 124 semester hours.

Graduate Programs: The multiple subject credential holder is authorized to teach in self-contained classrooms from K-12. Programs include general; early childhood education; multiple subject - CLAD/BCLAD); multiple subject teacher in preparation internship program; and special education preliminary level I education specialist credential and dual certification program.

The Single Subject Credential holder is authorized to teach in the subject area of the credential in departmentalized classrooms typically found in middle school and senior high school settings. This credential is offered in :agriculture, art, business, English, English-speech, English-drama, English-ESL, foreign languages (French and Spanish), home economics, industrial technology, mathematics, music, physical education, science, and social science.

The Preliminary Level I Education Specialist program is offered through the Department of Counseling, Special Education, and Rehabilitation.

Licensure/Reciprocity: California. Students seeking teaching certification in a state other than California should consult with that state's certification office early in their program of study to insure compliance with requirements. Many state directors of teacher credentialing have signed Interstate Agreements through NASDTEC that expedite the certification process.

CALIFORNIA STATE UNIVERSITY, FULLERTON

School of Education
Department of Elementary and Bilingual Education
800 North State College Boulevard
Fullerton, California 92634-9480
Phone: (714) 278-2011
Fax: (714) 278-3456
E-mail: info@csufullerton.edu
Internet: http:www.hdcs.csufullerton.edu/eled

Institution Description: California State University, Fullerton is a state institution. It was established and chartered as Orange County State College in 1957. The name was changed to Orange State College in 1962, to California State College at Fullerton in 1964; and to the present name in 1972.

The Professional Teacher Preparation Program prepares individuals to teach in self-contained classrooms at the elementary or middle school level where multiple subjects are taught.

Institution Control: Public.

Calendar: Semester. Academic year August to June.

Official(s): Dr. L.Y. Hollis, Dean, School of Education; Carmen Zuniga Dunlap, Chair, Department of Elementary and Bilingual Education.

Faculty: Full-time ; part-time ; adjunct.

Degrees Awarded: 372 baccalaureate; 351 master's.

Admission Requirements: *Undergraduate:* Graduation from an accredited secondary school or GED. *Teacher education specific:* Freshmen may opt to simultaneously pursue an undergraduate major and a teacher credential through the Blended Teacher Education Program. This leads to a subject credential or to a basic education specialist credential. California law requires an academic major; there is no major in education. *Graduate:* Baccalaureate degree from a regionally accredited institution; overall GPA of 2.5 on previous academic and related work; *Teacher education specific:* PRAXIS Multiple Subject Assessment for Teachers or California Examination for Teachers; basic teaching credential; an approved major.

Fees and Expenses: Undergraduate in-state $786 per semester; out-of-state $282 per unit plus $786 state university fee. Graduate in-state $867 per semester; out-of-state $282 per unit plus $867 state university fee. Per academic year: required fees: $470 average; on-campus room and board: $6,545; other expenses: $2,625; books and supplies: $1,080.

Financial Aid: Resources specifically for eligible students enrolled in teacher education programs are awarded on the basis of financial need and academic merit. The institution has a

Program Participation Agreement with the U.S. Department of Education for eligible students to receive Pell Grants and other federal aid. *Contact:* Financial Aid Office at $714) 278-3125.

Accreditation: *Regional:* WASC. *Professional:* NCATE. *Member of:* AACTE. *Approved by:* California Commission on Teacher Credentialing.

Undergraduate Programs: Students who opt for the Blended Teacher Education Program select a liberal studies major credential through the Blended Teacher Education Program. Majors in the social sciences, humanities, or natural sciences provide an excellent background for careers in elementary school teaching. Individuals interested in working as bilingual teachers may consider a major in a non-English language. Students are encouraged to attend a program overview during the junior or senior year.

Graduate Programs: The Master of Science in Education with a bilingual/bicultural education concentration is designed to develop instructors who can work as classroom or resource teachers to help individuals teach others how to provide experiences in the cultural heritage of the target population. The program will also help individuals to interpret and implement research related to bilingual/bicultural children.

The Master of Science in Education with a concentration in educational technology is designed to help classroom teachers upgrade their skills and knowledge of new educational technologies and their role in the classroom. The program also prepares them for technology leadership roles in public and private schools.

The Master of Science in Education with elementary curriculum and instruction concentration is designed to help career classroom teachers upgrade their skills and become informed about new ideas in elementary teaching. A minimum of adviser-approved 30 units is required for the degree.

Licensure/Reciprocity: California. Students seeking teaching certification in a state other than California should consult with that state's certification office early in their program of study to insure compliance with requirements. Many state directors of teacher credentialing have signed Interstate Agreements through NASDTEC that expedite the certification process.

CALIFORNIA STATE UNIVERSITY, HAYWARD

College of Education and Allied Studies
Department of Teacher Education
25800 Carlos Bee Boulevard
Hayward, California 94542-3011
Phone: (510) 885-3027
Fax: (510) 885-4632
E-mail: curen@csuhayward.edu
Internet: http://www.csuhayward.edu

Institution Description: The university was established as Alameda County State College in 1957. The name was changed to California State College at Hayward in 1963, to California State College, Hayward in 1968, and to the present name in 1972.

The Department of Teacher Education offers primarily post-baccalaureate and graduate courses.

Institution Control: Public.

Calendar: Quarter. Academic year September to June.

Official(s): Dr. Phillip E. Curen, Chair, Department of Teacher Education.

Faculty: Full-time 24; 50-60 part-time.

Degrees Awarded: 207 master's.

Admission Requirements: *Undergraduate:* Graduation from an approved secondary school; SAT or ACT scores are only required if high school GPA is less than 3.0. *Teacher education specific:* California law requires a subject area major; there are no undergraduate degree programs in education. *Graduate:* Baccalaureate degree from a regionally accredited institution. *Teacher education specific:* Subject matter competency; prior field experience and letters of recommendation; California Basic Educational Skills Examination; admission interview.

CALIFORNIA STATE UNIVERSITY, HAYWARD—cont'd

Fees and Expenses: Undergraduate in-state $814.75 per quarter; out-of-state $188 per unit plus $786 state university fee (includes campus mandatory fees). Graduate in-state $884.75 per quarter; out-of-state $188 per unit plus $884.75 state university fee (includes campus mandatory fees). Per academic year: on-campus room and board: $6,545; other expenses: $2,625; books and supplies: $900.

Financial Aid: Resources specifically for eligible students enrolled in teacher education programs are awarded on the basis of financial need and academic merit. The institution has a Program Participation Agreement with the U.S. Department of Education for eligible students to receive Pell Grants and other federal aid. *Contact:* Financial Aid Office at (510) 885-3018.

Accreditation: *Regional:* WASC. *Professional:* NCATE. *Member of:* AACTE. *Approved by:* California Commission on Teacher Credentialing.

Graduate Programs: The Master of Science in Education degree programs are offered in the areas of curriculum (children's literature and reading; elementary education; environmental education; mathematics education; science and health education; individualized program); reading; urban teacher leadership; and educational technology leadership. Teaching credential preparation programs are available in multiple subject, single subject, and reading specialist.

Licensure/Reciprocity: California. Students seeking teaching certification in a state other than California should consult with that state's certification office early in their program of study to insure compliance with requirements. Many state directors of teacher credentialing have signed Interstate Agreements through NASDTEC that expedite the certification process.

CALIFORNIA STATE UNIVERSITY, LONG BEACH

Department of Teacher Education
ED1-13
1250 Bellflower Boulevard
Long Beach, California 90840
Phone: (562) 985-9259
Fax: (562) 985-5733
E-mail: tcheduc@csulb.edu
Internet: http://www.csulb.edu

Institution Description: The university was established as Los Angeles-Orange County State College and offered first instruction at the postsecondary level in 1949. The name was changed to Long Beach State College in 1950, to California State College, Long Beach in 1968, and to the present name in 1972.

The central mission of the university's relationship to K-12 schools is to improve the quality of preparation programs for school personnel and to insure that scholarly, pedagogical, and technological expertise be made available to students on an ongoing basis.

Institution Control: Public.

Calendar: Semester. Academic year August to May.

Official(s): Dr. Catherine DuCharme, Chair.

Faculty: Full-time 35; part-time 75.

Degrees Awarded: 332 baccalaureate; 147 master's.

Admission Requirements: *Undergraduate:* Graduation from an approved secondary school or GED; College Board SAT or ACT composite. *Teacher education specific:* Faculty interview; approval for academic major in the field in which the student plans to teach. *Graduate:* Baccalaureate degree from a regionally accredited institution. *Teacher education specific:* Students must submit a program application, official transcripts, test scores; and fulfill any additional program requirements to the College of Education.

Fees and Expenses: Undergraduate in-state $786 per semester; out-of-state $282 per unit plus $786 state university fee. Graduate in-state $867 per semester; out-of-state $282 per unit plus $867 state university fee. Per academic year: required fees: $470 average; on-campus room and board: $6,545; other expenses: $2,625; books and supplies: $1,080.

Financial Aid: The institution has a Program Participation Agreement with the U.S. Department of Education for eligible students to receive Pell Grants and other federal aid. *Contact:* Financial Aid Office at (562) 985-5574.

Accreditation: *Regional:* WASC. *Professional:* NCATE. *Member of:* AACTE. *Approved by:* California Commission on Teacher Credentialing.

Undergraduate Programs: The Bachelor of Arts in Liberal Studies provides a crossdisciplinary liberal arts program of study. There are three programs in the major: the Integrated Teacher Education Program for students intending to become teachers and who wish to combine subject matter preparation for elementary teaching with coursework leading to a multiple subject teacher credential; a program for students who seek subject matter preparation for elementary teaching as preparation for a postbaccalaureate credential program; a program for students with more varied professional or career goals who prefer a sound generalist program.

Graduate Programs: The Master of Arts in Education programs are designed for teachers holding their teaching credential who desire to continue formal studies. Programs for elementary teachers include curriculum and instruction, early childhood education, middle school emphasis, and reading and language arts. Programs for secondary teachers include curriculum and instruction and reading and language arts. Those desiring to become secondary teachers (high school or junior high level) earn a single cubject credential.

Licensure/Reciprocity: California. Students seeking teaching certification in a state other than California should consult with that state's certification office early in their program of study to insure compliance with requirements. Many state directors of teacher credentialing have signed Interstate Agreements through NASDTEC that expedite the certification process.

CALIFORNIA STATE UNIVERSITY, LOS ANGELES

Charter College of Education
Division of Curriculum and Instruction
King Hall C2097
5151 State University Drive
Los Angeles, California 90032
Phone: (323) 343-4350
Fax: (323) 343-6469
E-mail: chawley@calstatela.edu
Internet: http://www.calstatela.edu

Institution Description: Established as Los Angeles State College, the campus was chartered and offered first instruction at the postsecondary level in 1947. The name was changed to Los Angeles State College of Applied Arts and Sciences in 1949, to California State College at Los Angeles in 1964, to California State College, Los Angeles in 1968. The present name was adopted in 1972.

The Division of Curriculum and Instruction offers program advisement for master's degree programs approved by the California Commission on Teacher Credentialing.

Institution Control: Public.

Calendar: Quarter. Academic year September to June.

Official(s): Dr. Cherie Hawley, Chair.

Faculty: Full-time 20; emeriti 29.

Degrees Awarded: 386 baccalaureate; 405 master's.

Admission Requirements: *Undergraduate:* Graduation from an approved secondary school or GED; College Board SAT or ACT composite. *Teacher education specific:* Faculty interview; approval for liberal studies major in the field for which the student plans to teach. *Graduate:* Baccalaureate degree from a regionally accredited institution. *Teacher education specific:* Students must submit a program application, official transcripts, test scores; and fulfill any additional program requirements to the College of Education.

Fees and Expenses: Undergraduate in-state $814.75 per quarter; out-of-state $188 per unit plus $786 state university fee (includes campus mandatory fees). Graduate in-state $884.75 per quarter; out-of-state $188 per unit plus $884.75 state university fee (includes campus mandatory fees). Per academic year: on-campus room and board: $6,545; other expenses: $2,625; books and supplies: $980.

Financial Aid: Resources specifically for eligible students enrolled in teacher education programs are awarded on the basis of financial need and academic merit. The institution has a Program Participation Agreement with the U.S. Department of Education for eligible students to receive Pell Grants and other federal aid. *Contact:* Financial Aid Office at (323) 343-1784.

Accreditation: *Regional:* WASC. *Professional:* NCATE. *Member of:* AACTE. *Approved by:* California Commission on Teacher Credentialing.

Undergraduate Programs: California law requires a subject area major. There are no undergraduate degree programs in education. Students must have a passing score on the California Basic Skills Test.

Graduate Programs: The Master of Arts in Education degree is offered with options in bilingual/multicultural education in the elementary classroom; curriculum and instruction in the urban elementary school; early childhood education; mathemtics education; reading and language arts education in the elementary classroom; and science education.

The Master of Arts in Education option in middle and secondary curriculum and instruction is offered with a variety of concentrations.

Licensure/Reciprocity: California. Students seeking teaching certification in a state other than California should consult with that state's certification office early in their program of study to insure compliance with requirements. Many state directors of teacher credentialing have signed Interstate Agreements through NASDTEC that expedite the certification process.

CALIFORNIA STATE UNIVERSITY, MONTEREY BAY

College of Professional Studies
Department of Teacher Education
100 Campus Center
Seaside, California 93955
Phone: (831) 582-3518
Fax: (831) 582-3783
E-mail: greenfield@csumb.edu
Internet: http://www.csumb.edu

Institution Description: California State University, Monterey Bay is part of the California State University System. The university was established in 1994 on the former Fort Ord Army Base and opened for classes in 1995.

The Department of Teacher Education offers a curriculum that reflects a high degree of integration between theory and practice. Collaborative program development between public schools, the community and the university has created a hands-on learning environment that prepares students to teach linguistically and culturally diverse student groups.

Institution Control: Public.

Calendar: Semester. Academic year August to May.

Official(s): Dr. Dorothy Lloyd, Dean, College of Professional Studies.

Faculty: Not reported.

Degrees Awarded: 11 master's.

Admission Requirements: *Undergraduate:* Graduation from an approved secondary school; SAT or ACT scores are only required if high school GPA is less than 3.0. *Teacher education specific:* California law requires a subject area major; there are no undergraduate degree programs in education. *Graduate:* Baccalaureate degree from a regionally accredited institution; GRE; overall GPA of 2.75 on undergraduate academic and related work; *Teacher education specific:* Basic teaching credential; an approved major; three letters of recommendation; two years of successful teaching experience.

Fees and Expenses: Undergraduate in-state $786 per semester; out-of-state $282 per unit plus $786 state university fee. Graduate in-state $867 per semester; out-of-state $282 per unit plus $867 state university fee. Per academic year: required fees: $470 average; on-campus room and board: $6,620; other expenses: $2,680; books and supplies: $1,280.

Financial Aid: Resources specifically for eligible students enrolled in teacher education programs are awarded on the basis of financial need and academic merit. The institution has a Program Participation Agreement with the U.S. Department of Education for eligible students to receive Pell Grants and other federal aid. *Contact:* Financial Aid Office at (831-582-3518.

Accreditation: *Regional:* WASC. *Professional:* NCATE. *Member of:* AACTE. *Approved by:* California Commission on Teacher Credentialing.

Graduate Programs: The Master of Arts in Education program consists of eight graduate courses, including completion of a thesis. The program is designed as a sequel for those who have already completed a teacher credential program. The coursework and educational experiences are intentionally structured to help teachers become effective teachers of the culturally and linguistically divers students in the schools of the region.

Licensure/Reciprocity: California. Students seeking teaching certification in a state other than California should consult with that state's certification office early in their program of study to insure compliance with requirements. Many state directors of teacher credentialing have signed Interstate Agreements through NASDTEC that expedite the certification process.

CALIFORNIA STATE UNIVERSITY, NORTHRIDGE

Michael D. Eisner College of Education
18111 Nordhoff Street
Northridge, California 91330
Phone: (818) 677-1230
Fax: (818) 677-1200
E-mail: coe@.csun.edu
Internet: http://www.csun.edu

Institution Description: The university was established as San Fernando Valley Campus of Los Angeles State College of Applied Arts and Sciences in 1956. It was chartered as a separate institution and changed name to San Fernando Valley State College in 1958. The present name was adopted in 1972.

The mission of the College of Education is to prepare teachers, counselors, administrators, and other professionals to serve the diverse educational needs of the region.

Institution Control: Public.

Calendar: Semester. Academic year August to May.

Official(s): Dr. Philip J. Rusche, Dean; Dr. Bonnie Ericson, Chair, Secondary Education.

Faculty: Full-time 36.

Degrees Awarded: 58 undergraduate; 267 master's.

Admission Requirements: *Undergraduate:* Graduation from an approved secondary school; Overall GPA 3.0. College Board SAT or ACT composite. *Teacher education specific:* California law requires a subject area major; there are three integrated teacher education programs for undergraduates who intend to become teachers. *Graduate:* Baccalaureate degree from a regionally accredited institution; overall GPA of 3.0 on previous academic and related work; *Teacher education specific:* GRE or Miller Analogies Test with passing score required for GPAs less than 3.0; basic teaching credential; an approved major.

Fees and Expenses: Undergraduate in-state $786 per semester; out-of-state $282 per unit plus $786 state university fee. Graduate in-state $867 per semester; out-of-state $282 per unit plus $867 state university fee. Per academic year: required fees: $470 average; on-campus room and board: $7,700; other expenses: $2,625; books and supplies: $1,280.

Financial Aid: Resources specifically for eligible students enrolled in teacher education programs are awarded on the basis of financial need and academic merit. The institution has a

CALIFORNIA STATE UNIVERSITY, NORTHRIDGE—*cont'd*

Program Participation Agreement with the U.S. Department of Education for eligible students to receive Pell Grants and other federal aid. *Contact:* Financial Aid Office at (818) 677-2085.

Accreditation: *Regional:* WASC. *Professional:* NCATE. *Member of:* AACTE. *Approved by:* California Commission on Teacher Credentialing.

Undergraduate Programs: There are three undergraduate programs for students intending to become teachers. The Integrated Teacher Education Program (freshman option) is a program for obtaining a baccalaureate degree and multiple subject teaching credential concurrently. The Integrated Teacher Program (junior option) is also a program for obtaining a bachelor's degree and multiple subject teaching credential concurrently. The Four-Year Integrated (freshman only) is a program for obtaining a bachelor's degree and single subject teaching credential in the area of English or mathematics simultaneously.

Graduate Programs: The Master of Arts in Education program is offered with specializations in curriculum and instruction, language and literacy, and multilingual/multicultural education. This program is offered through the Department of Elementary Education and requires the completion of 30 units (School of Education core courses, specialization area courses, and Elementary Department courses).

The Master of Arts in Education program is offered with specialization in secondary education. The program requires the completion of a total of 30 units made up of core requirements, departmental requirements, and program options. This program is designed to prepare the secondary teacher for advancement as master teacher, supervising teacher, subject matter teaching specialist, or department chairperson.

Licensure/Reciprocity: California. Students seeking teaching certification in a state other than California should consult with that state's certification office early in their program of study to insure compliance with requirements. Many state directors of teacher credentialing have signed Interstate Agreements through NASDTEC that expedite the certification process.

CALIFORNIA STATE UNIVERSITY, SACRAMENTO

College of Education
Department of Teacher Education

6000 J Street
Sacramento, California 95819-6079
Phone: (916) 278-6403
Fax: (916) 278-61755290
E-mail: admissions@csus.edu
Internet: http://www.csus.edu

Institution Description: The university was chartered and offered first instruction at the postsecondary level in 1947.

The Department of Teacher Education offers programs that enable students to pursue an academic subject area agenda combined with a teacher preparation program.

Institution Control: Public.

Calendar: Semester. Academic year September to May.

Official(s): Dr. Robert Pritchard, Department Chair.

Faculty: Full-time 33; part-time 56.

Degrees Awarded: 221 baccalaureate; 344 master's.

Admission Requirements: *Undergraduate:* High school graduation; qualifying eligibility index (combination of high school GPA and SAT *or* ACT); completion with a minimum grade of C for each of the courses in the comprehensive pattern of college preparatory subject matter requirements. *Teacher education specific:* Minimum 2.67 GPA; successful completion of all three sections of California Basic Education Skills Test; verification of two approved 40-hour field experiences; two letters of recommendation. *Graduate:* Baccalaureate degree from a regionally accredited institution; 2.5 GPA in the last 60 semester units attempted. *Teacher education specific:* Successful completion of all

sections of California Basic Education Skills Test; writing proficiency; minimum 2.67 GPA; field experiences; two letters of recommendation; faculty interview.

Fees and Expenses: Undergraduate in-state $786 per semester; out-of-state $282 per unit plus $786 state university fee. Graduate in-state $867 per semester; out-of-state $282 per unit plus $867 state university fee. Per academic year: required fees: $470 average; on-campus room and board: $6,545; other expenses: $2,625; books and supplies: $1,080.

Financial Aid: Resources specifically for eligible students enrolled in teacher education programs are awarded on the basis of financial need and academic merit. The institution has a Program Participation Agreement with the U.S. Department of Education for eligible students to receive Pell Grants and other federal aid. *Contact:* Suzy Lunstead at (916) 278-5088 or alcalde@csus.

Accreditation: *Regional:* WASC. *Member of:* AACTE. *Approved by:* California Commission on Teacher Credentialing.

Undergraduate Programs: The College of Education offers three undergraduate blended programs which enable students to blend or combine the completion of a baccalaureate degree in an academic field with a teacher preparation program. These blended programs include liberal studies, mathematics, and physical education. The programs require the completion of 135 credit units.

Graduate Programs: Advanced degree programs of student in education for individuals already certified at the baccalaureate level are offered through three departments within the College of Education: Department of Teacher Education, Department of Bilingual/Multicultural Education, and the Department of Special Education. In general, the masters options consist of a 30-unit program that includes a culminating experience consisting of one of the following: thesis, project, or exam. In addition to a baccalaureate degree requirement, the majority of program options require that candidates possess a valid teaching credential.

Licensure/Reciprocity: California. Students seeking teaching certification in a state other than California should consult with that state's certification office early in their program of study to insure compliance with requirements. Many state directors of teacher credentialing have signed Interstate Agreements through NASDTEC that expedite the certification process.

CALIFORNIA STATE UNIVERSITY, SAN BERNARDINO

College of Education

5500 State College Parkway
San Bernardino, California 92407-2397
Phone: (909) 880-5000
E-mail: coe@csusb.edu
Internet: http://www.csusb.edu

Institution Description: The university was established in 1960 and offered first instruction at the postsecondary level in 1965. The first baccalaureate degree was awarded in 1967.

The mission of the College of Education is to prepare education and human service professionals through the development of curriculum and programs that transform individuals and community.

Institution Control: Public.

Calendar: Quarter. Academic year September to June.

Official(s): Dr. Patricia Arlen, Dean.

Faculty: Full-time 97.

Degrees Awarded: 11 baccalaureate; 327 master's.

Admission Requirements: *Undergraduate:* Graduation from an approved secondary school; SAT or ACT scores are only required if high school GPA is less than 3.0. *Teacher education specific:* California law requires a subject area major; there are no undergraduate degree programs in education. *Graduate:* Baccalaureate degree from a regionally accredited institution; overall GPA of 2.5 on previous academic and related work; *Teacher* *education specific:* PRAXIS Multiple Subject Assessment for Teachers or California Examination for Teachers; basic teaching credential; an approved major.

Fees and Expenses: Undergraduate: in-state $1,931 per academic year; out-of-state $10,391. On-campus room and board: $8,610. Other expenses: $2,470. Books and supplies: $1,300.

Financial Aid: Resources specifically for eligible students enrolled in teacher education programs are awarded on the basis of financial need and academic merit. The institution has a Program Participation Agreement with the U.S. Department of Education for eligible students to receive Pell Grants and other federal aid. *Contact:* Financial Aid Office at (909) 880-7800.

Accreditation: *Regional:* WASC. *Professional:* NCATE. *Member of:* AACTE. *Approved by:* California Commission on Teacher Credentialing.

Graduate Programs: The Master of Arts in Education degree program offers options in bilingual/crosscultural education; career and technical education; curriculum and instruction; environmental education; instructional technology; kinesiology; English, history, and Spanish (for secondary teachers), reading/language arts; science education; special education; and teaching English to speakers of other languages.

The college also offers credential programs designed to prepare students to teach in a variety of settings. In addition to the multiple, single, and designated subjects credentials, specialist and services credential programs are also available.

Licensure/Reciprocity: California. Students seeking teaching certification in a state other than California should consult with that state's certification office early in their program of study to insure compliance with requirements. Many state directors of teacher credentialing have signed Interstate Agreements through NASDTEC that expedite the certification process.

CALIFORNIA STATE UNIVERSITY, SAN MARCOS

College of Education
University Hall
333 South Twin Oaks Valley Road
San Marcos, California 92096
Phone: (760) 750-4300
Fax: (760) 750-3352
E-mail: apply@csusm.edu
Internet: http://www.csusm.edu

Institution Description: California State University, San Marcos, began enrollments in 1990.

The mission of the College of Education is to collaboratively transform public education by preparing thoughtful educators and advancing professional practices.

Institution Control: Public.

Calendar: Semester. Academic year August to May.

Official(s): Dr. Steve Lilly, Dean.

Faculty: Full-time 36.

Degrees Awarded: 35 master's.

Admission Requirements: *Undergraduate:* Graduation from an approved secondary school; SAT or ACT scores are only required if high school GPA is less than 3.0. *Teacher education specific:* California law requires a subject area major; there are no undergraduate degree programs in education. Students normally enroll in a liberal studies program. *Graduate:* Baccalaureate degree from a regionally accredited institution; overall GPA of 2.67 on previous academic and related work; *Teacher education specific:* PRAXIS Multiple Subject Assessment for Teachers or California Examination for Teachers; basic teaching credential; an approved major.

Fees and Expenses: Undergraduate in-state $786 per semester; out-of-state $282 per unit plus $786 state university fee. Graduate in-state $867 per semester; out-of-state $282 per unit plus $867 state university fee. Per academic year: required fees: $470 average; on-campus room and board: $8,206; other expenses: $2,788; books and supplies: $1,080.

Financial Aid: Resources specifically for eligible students enrolled in teacher education programs are awarded on the basis of financial need and academic merit. The institution has a Program Participation Agreement with the U.S. Department of Education for eligible students to receive Pell Grants and other federal aid. *Contact:* Financial Aid Office at (760) 750-4850.

Accreditation: *Regional:* WASC. *Professional:* NCATE. *Member of:* AACTE. *Approved by:* California Commission on Teacher Credentialing.

Undergraduate Programs: The Integrated Credential Program is designed for teacher candidates who decide early in their academic career to become an elementary teacher. Including the program prerequisites, students are enrolled in the program for 6 semesters in a cohort configuration. Candidates pursue a degree major and have two practicum experiences early in the program.

Graduate Programs: Teacher credential programs are offered in: multiple subject (elementary), integrated credential program, middle school, single subject (secondary), special education, and bilingual education (BCLAD).

The Master of Arts in Education for K-12 is designed for classroom teachers, administrators, and other educators who wish to extend or refine their knowledge beyond the level attained in their previous studies. Options for the degree program include educational administration, life science, math and technology for diverse learners, special education, and teaching-learning and leadership.

Licensure/Reciprocity: California. Students seeking teaching certification in a state other than California should consult with that state's certification office early in their program of study to insure compliance with requirements. Many state directors of teacher credentialing have signed Interstate Agreements through NASDTEC that expedite the certification process.

CALIFORNIA STATE UNIVERSITY, STANISLAUS

College of Education
Department of Teacher Education
330 Demergann Bava Hall
801 West Monte Vista Avenue
Turlock, California 95382
Phone: (209) 667-3357
Fax: (209) 667-3788
E-mail: mggordon@csustan.edu
Internet: http://www.csustan.edu/TeacherEd/

Institution Description: Established by the state legislature in 1957 and chartered as Stanislaus State College. It offered first instruction at the postsecondary level in 1960. The present name was adopted in 1985.

The Department of Teacher Education offers professional programs to prepare candidates for credentials in elementary and secondary school teaching, bilingual emphasis teaching, and reading.

Institution Control: Public.

Calendar: Semester. Academic year September to May.

Official(s): Dr. Irma Guxman Wagner, Dean, College of Education; Dr. Juan M. Flores, Chair, Department of Teacher Education.

Faculty: Full-time ; part-time ; adjunct.

Degrees Awarded: 13 undergraduate; 35 master's.

Admission Requirements: *Undergraduate:* Graduation from an approved secondary school; SAT or ACT scores are only required if high school GPA is less than 3.0. *Teacher education specific:* California law requires a subject area major; there are no undergraduate degree programs in education. Students interested in becoming teachers may enroll in the Liberal Studies and Blended Program. *Graduate:* Baccalaureate degree from a regionally accredited institution; overall GPA of 2.67 on previous academic and related work; *Teacher education specific:* PRAXIS Multiple Subject Assessment for Teachers or California Examination for Teachers; basic teaching credential; an approved major.

CALIFORNIA STATE UNIVERSITY, STANISLAUS—cont'd

Fees and Expenses: Undergraduate in-state $786 per semester; out-of-state $282 per unit plus $786 state university fee. Graduate in-state $867 per semester; out-of-state $282 per unit plus $867 state university fee. Per academic year: required fees: $470 average; on-campus room and board: $7,375; other expenses: $2,110; books and supplies: $920.

Financial Aid: Resources specifically for eligible students enrolled in teacher education programs are awarded on the basis of financial need and academic merit. The institution has a Program Participation Agreement with the U.S. Department of Education for eligible students to receive Pell Grants and other federal aid. *Contact:* Financial Aid Office at (209) 667-3336.

Accreditation: *Regional:* WASC. *Professional:* NCATE. *Member of:* AACTE. *Approved by:* California Commission on Teacher Credentialing.

Undergraduate Programs: The Bachelor of Arts in liberal studies provides a rigorous crossdisciplinary liberal arts program of study. Students intending to become teachers combine subject matter preparation with integrated teacher education courses.

Graduate Programs: Credential programs are offered in multiple subjects, single subject, and reading/language arts specialist. Graduate programs leading to a Master of Arts in Education are available in curriculum and instruction with concentration in elementary, multilingual education, reading, or secondary education.

Licensure/Reciprocity: California. Students seeking teaching certification in a state other than California should consult with that state's certification office early in their program of study to insure compliance with requirements. Many state directors of teacher credentialing have signed Interstate Agreements through NASDTEC that expedite the certification process.

HOLY NAMES COLLEGE

Education Department
3500 Mountain Boulevard
Oakland, California 94619-1699
Phone: (510) 436-1515
Fax: (510) 436-1199
E-mail: yee@hnc.edu
Internet: http://www.hnc.edu

Institution Description: Holy Names College is a private, independent, nonprofit Catholic college sponsored by the Sisters of the Holy Names of Jesus and Mary. It was established as Convent of Our Lady of the Sacred Heart in 1868, chartered 1880, and became Convent and College of the Holy Names in 1908. Graduates received California teaching credentials beginning in 1930. The campus moved from Lake Merritt, Oakland, in 1957. The school became completely coeducational and the present name was adopted in 1971.

The Education Department focuses on preparing qualified and committed educators for the urban schools of Oakland and nearby city schools.

Institution Control: Private.

Calendar: Semester. Academic year August to May.

Official(s): Dr. Gary Yee, Department Chair.

Faculty: Full-time 4; part-time 1; adjunct 6.

Degrees Awarded: 13 master's.

Admission Requirements: *Graduate:* Baccalaureate degree from an accredited institution; *Teacher education specific:* CBEST exam; 3.0 GPA; subject matter preparation; letters of recommendation; faculty interview.

Fees and Expenses: $480 per credit hour. On-campus room: $3,900 per academic year. Board: $3,800 per academic year.

Financial Aid: Resources specifically for eligible students enrolled in teacher education programs are awarded on the basis of financial need and academic merit. The institution has a Program Participation Agreement with the U.S. Department of Education for eligible students to receive Pell Grants and other federal aid. *Contact:* Loretta William at (510) 436-1315.

Accreditation: *Regional:* WASC. *Approved by:* California Commission on Teacher Credentialing.

Graduate Programs: The Teacher Education curriculum for each program is designed to satisfy current CCTC competencies. Thee are two practicum options: student teaching and intern teaching. Every curriculum includes 9 units in education and theory courses. The multiple subject curriculum (elementary through middle school) includes 11 units in curriculum and instruction courses and 11 units in fieldwork/teaching courses. The single subject curriculum (middle school through high school) includes 6 units in curriculum and instruction courses and 13 units in one content area course in the student's teaching major and fieldwork/teaching courses.

The Master of Education degree is designed to provide the necessary coursework in human learning theory, instructional design, educational assessment, research and advanced study in an area of concentration (special education, Urban Education, Advanced Studies in Curriculum and Instruction). The degree requires the completion of 30 units.

Licensure/Reciprocity: California. Students seeking teaching certification in a state other than California should consult with that state's certification office early in their program of study to insure compliance with requirements. Many state directors of teacher credentialing have signed Interstate Agreements through NASDTEC that expedite the certification process.

HUMBOLDT STATE UNIVERSITY

Department of Education
1 Harpst Street
Arcata, California 95521-8299
Phone: (707) 826-5867
Fax: (707) 826-5868
E-mail: hsuinfo@laurel.humboldt.edu
Internet: http://www.humboldt.edu

Institution Description: The university was established and chartered as Humboldt State Normal School in 1913. The name was changed to Humboldt State Teachers College in 1921, to Humboldt State College in 1935, and to California State University, Humboldt in 1972. The present name was adopted in 1974.

The credentials program of the Department of Education include administrative services, elementary education, secondary education, and special education.

Institution Control: Public.

Calendar: Semester. Academic year August to May.

Official(s): Dr. Sally Botzler, Department Chair.

Faculty: Full-time 36.

Degrees Awarded: 188 baccalaureate (liberal arts and sciences).

Admission Requirements: *Undergraduate:* Graduation from an approved secondary school; SAT or ACT scores are only required if high school GPA is less than 3.0. *Teacher education specific:* California law requires a subject area major; there are no undergraduate degree programs in education. Students interested in becoming teachers may enroll in the minor in Education Program. *Graduate:* Baccalaureate degree from a regionally accredited institution; overall GPA of 2.67 on previous academic and related work; *Teacher education specific:* PRAXIS Multiple Subject Assessment for Teachers or California Basic Education Skills Test examination for teachers; basic teaching credential; an approved major; faculty interview.

Fees and Expenses: Undergraduate in-state $786 per semester; out-of-state $282 per unit plus $786 state university fee. Graduate in-state $867 per semester; out-of-state $282 per unit plus $867 state university fee. Required fees: $470 average per academic year. On-campus room and board: $6,70. Other expenses: $2,390. Books and supplies: $1,030.

Financial Aid: Resources specifically for eligible students enrolled in teacher education programs are awarded on the basis of financial need and academic merit. The institution has a Program Participation Agreement with the U.S. Department of Education for eligible students to receive Pell Grants and other federal aid. *Contact:* Financial Aid Office at: (707) 826-3011.

Accreditation: *Regional:* WASC. *Approved by:* California Commission on Teacher Credentialing.

Undergraduate Programs: The minor in education provides an overview of the field and offers students opportunities to learn more about teaching and other education careers during their undergraduate years. Those who have already chosen teaching as a career find that the minor provides a strong background in many contemporary issues.

Graduate Programs: The Master of Arts in Education program requirements include core courses and special emphases areas (administrative services, curriculum and instruction, special education, and special studies). Students must maintain an overall 3.0 GPA in the program.

The secondary education or the elementary education credential programs are one-year programs that begin in the fall of each year. These programs are typically begun after the completion of the bachelor's degree. After completion of the credential requirements, students may receive the multiple subject credential for the elementary level or the single subject credential for teaching at the secondary level.

Licensure/Reciprocity: California. Students seeking teaching certification in a state other than California should consult with that state's certification office early in their program of study to insure compliance with requirements. Many state directors of teacher credentialing have signed Interstate Agreements through NASDTEC that expedite the certification process.

LOYOLA MARYMOUNT UNIVERSITY
School of Education
Teacher Education Division
One LMU Drive
Los Angeles, California 90045-2659
Phone: (310) 338-2700
Fax: (310) 338-2797
E-mail: education@lmu.edu
Internet: http://www.lmu.edu

Institution Description: Loyola Marymount University (Loyola University of Los Angeles and Marymount College until 1973) is a private institution conducted by the Society of Jesus, Religious of the Sacred Heart of Mary, and the Sisters of St. Joseph of Orange, Roman Catholic Church.

The university offers a variety of programs that lead to master's degree, teaching credentials, and/or certificates for service in diverse educational settings. Faculty across the university work together to carry out the Jesuit and Marymount traditions of educating youth.

Institution Control: Private.

Calendar: Semester. Academic year August to May.

Official(s): Dr. Albert P. Koppes, Dean, School of Education.

Faculty: Full-time 3.

Degrees Awarded: 200 master's.

Admission Requirements: *Graduate:* Baccalaureate degree and cumulative undergraduate GPA of 2.8 or a 2.85 in the last 60 semester hours. *Teacher education specific:* California Basic Educational Skills Test score report; Multiple Subject Assessment for Teachers scores for those who did not major in liberal studies; recommendations; faculty interview.

Fees and Expenses: $21,644 per academic year. On-campus room and board: $6,930. Other expenses: $1,900. Books and supplies: $800.

Financial Aid: Resources specifically for eligible students enrolled in teacher education programs are awarded on the basis of financial need and academic merit. The institution has a Program Participation Agreement with the U.S. Department of Education for eligible students to receive Pell Grants and other federal aid. *Contact:* Financial Aid Office at: (310) 338-2753.

Accreditation: *Regional:* WASC. *Professional:* NCATE. *Member of:* AACTE. *Approved by:* California Commission on Teacher Credentialing.

Graduate Programs: Teaching credential programs are offered in elementary (multiple subject) CLAD or BCLAD credential; secondary (single subject) CLAD or BCLAD) credential; and special education (mild/moderate disabilities) credential.

The Master of Arts degree programs include elementary education, secondary education, special education, Catholic inclusive education, general education, child and adolescent literacy, literacy and language arts.

Licensure/Reciprocity: California. Students seeking teaching certification in a state other than California should consult with that state's certification office early in their program of study to insure compliance with requirements. Many state directors of teacher credentialing have signed Interstate Agreements through NASDTEC that expedite the certification process.

NATIONAL UNIVERSITY
School of Education
Teacher Education Program
11255 North Torrey Pines Road
La Jolla, California 92037
Phone: (858) 642-8358
Fax: (858) 642-8724
E-mail: treynolds@nu.edu
Internet: http://www.nu.edu

Institution Description: National University is a private, independent, nonprofit institution focused on the working adult. The school was founded in 1971 to serve the nontraditional student. Fifteen learning centers are located throughout San Diego County. Regional academic and learning centers are also located in Costa Mesa, Sacramento, Redding, San Jose, Stockton, Fresno, Bakersfield, San Bernardino, Los Angeles, Sherman Oaks, Orange, and Twentynine Palms.

The Department of Teacher Education within the School of Education recommends more teachers for credentials than any other single institution in California and holds more K-12 teacher training contracts with elementary and secondary school districts than any other university in the state.

Institution Control: Private.

Calendar: Quarter. Academic year July to June.

Official(s): Dr. Thomas Reynolds, Chair, Department of Teacher Education.

Faculty: Full-time 49.

Degrees Awarded: 510 baccalaureate; 1,379 post-baccalaureate certificates.

Admission Requirements: *Graduate:* Baccalaureate degree from a regionally accredited institution; GPA of 2.5 or better. *Teacher education specific:* Students with a GPA of 2.0 to 2.49 may be admitted if they have achieved a satisfactory score on the GMAT, GRE, Miller Analogies Test, or an approved standardized specific program exam; official transcripts of prior education.

Fees and Expenses: Graduate/post-baccalaureate $237.77 per quarter unit. Other fees may apply.

Financial Aid: Resources specifically for students enrolled in teacher education programs are awarded on the basis of financial need and academic merit. The institution has a Program Participation Agreement with the U.S. Department of Education for eligible students to receive Pell Grants and other federal aid. *Contact:* Financial Aid at (858) 842-8512.

Accreditation: *Regional:* WASC. *Member of:* AACTE. *Approved by:* California Commission on Teacher Credentialing.

Graduate Programs: The Master of Arts in Teaching and the Master of Education Crosscultural Teaching degrees are offered by the Department of Teacher Education. Master of Science in Education degree programs are available online.

NATIONAL UNIVERSITY—*cont'd*

Students may choose from fifteen post-baccalaureate certificate programs including Preliminary Multiple Subject (TED); Fifth Year Program; Professional Clear Single Subject (BCLAD); Preliminary Multiple Subject (TED); Preliminary Single Subject (TED); Professional Clear Multiple Subject (TED and BCLAD); Preliminary Single Subject (BCLAD).

Licensure/Reciprocity: California. Students seeking certification in a state other than California should consult with that state's certification office early in their program of study to insure compliance with requirements. Many state directors of teacher credentialing have signed Interstate Agreements through NASDTEC that expedite the certification process.

PACIFIC OAKS COLLEGE

Teacher Education Program

5 Westmoreland Place
Pasadena, California 91103
Phone: (626) 397-1331
Fax: (626) 397-1399
E-mail: cgrutrik@pacificoaks.edu
Internet: http://www.pacificoaks.edu

Institution Description: Pacific Oaks College is a Quaker-initiated upper division and graduate college, focused on human development and early childhood education. The college maintains sites in Pasadena, Seattle, and Oakland. The college was established as Pacific Oaks Friends School in 1945. The present name was adopted in 1961.

The mission of the Teacher Education Program is to prepare professional educators who understand diversity, are grounded in human development, and value children.

Institution Control: Private.

Calendar: Semester. Academic year September to May.

Official(s): Dr. Cindy Grutrik, Chair, Teacher Education Program.

Faculty: Full-time 4; adjunct 8.

Degrees Awarded: Not reported.

Admission Requirements: *Graduate:* Baccalaureate degree from a regionally accredited institution; must be able to critically analyze literature and situations at a graduate level; possess strong oral and written expression skills. *Teacher education specific:* Students must pass the California Basic Educational Skills Test; faculty interview.

Fees and Expenses: $16,200 per academic year. Required fees: $30 per semester.

Financial Aid: Resources specifically for eligible students enrolled in teacher education programs are awarded on the basis of financial need and academic merit. The institution has a Program Participation Agreement with the U.S. Department of Education for eligible students to receive Pell Grants and other federal aid. *Contact:* Tracie Matthews, Director of Financial Aid at (626) 397-1346 or e-mail at tmatthews@pacificoaks.edu.

Accreditation: *Regional:* WASC. *Approved by:* California Commission on Teacher Credentialing.

Graduate Programs: The Preliminary Multiple Subject English Learner Teaching Credential is the first level of a two-level credential. Candidates complete the second level through an Induction program in their district of employment. The Preliminary credential qualifies candidates to teach K-12 multiple subjects in self-contained classrooms. Pacific Oaks also offers Preliminary Level I and Professional Level II Education Specialist Credential which qualifies candidates to teach students with mild to moderate disabilities in grades K-12.

Licensure/Reciprocity: California. Students seeking teaching certification in a state other than California should consult with that state's certification office early in their program of study to insure compliance with requirements. Many state directors of teacher credentialing have signed Interstate Agreements through NASDTEC that expedite the certification process.

PACIFIC UNION COLLEGE

Education Department

One Angwin Way
Angwin, California 94508-9707
Phone: (707) 965-7265
Fax: (707) 965-6645
E-mail: jbuller@puc.edu
Internet: http://www.puc.edu

Institution Description: Pacific Union College is a private college affiliated with the Seventh-day Adventist Church. It was established as Healdsburg College in 1882. The present name was adopted in 1906.

The Department of Education offers courses examining the relationship between teachers, their colleagues, students, and communities and how to improve these relationships.

Institution Control: Private.

Calendar: Semester. Academic year September to April.

Official(s): Dr. Jean Buller, Chair, Education Department.

Faculty: Full-time 5, part-time 2.

Degrees Awarded: 125 baccalaureate; 73 master's.

Admission Requirements: *Undergraduate:* Either graduation from a secondary school or equivalent; 2.3 cumulative GPA. *Teacher education specific:* Chair interview; California Basic Education Skills Test; completion of educational foundation courses. *Graduate:* Baccalaureate degree from a regionally accredited institution; GRE; 3.0 cumulative GPA; 2 recommendations; 2 interviews; teaching credential.

Fees and Expenses: $17,115 per academic year. Required fees: $120. On-campus room and board: $4,950.

Financial Aid: Resources specifically for eligible students enrolled in teacher education programs are awarded on the basis of financial need and academic merit. The institution has a Program Participation Agreement with the U.S. Department of Education for eligible students to receive Pell Grants and other federal aid. *Contact:* Glen Bobst, Director of Student Finance at (707) 965-7200 or e-mail at gbobst@puc.edu.

Accreditation: *Regional:* WASC. *Approved by:* California Commission on Teacher Credentialing.

Undergraduate Programs: Individuals desiring certification at the elementary level complete a state-approved bachelor's degree in Liberal Studies, while those desiring secondary certification complete a state-approved bachelor's degree in the content area of their credential. In addition to the degree, candidates must complete a teacher education program that includes coursework and field experience. The degree and teacher education can be completed simultaneously at the undergraduate level, or the degree may be completed first and then the teacher training at the post-baccalaureate level.

Graduate Programs: The Master of Education degree in Instructional Leadership centers on developing leadership skills, technological proficiency, and innovative teaching techniques. The program requires a minimum of 45 quarter hours of upper-division and graduate classes. Specific requirements include 26 hours of professional education core classes, 12 hours approved support area, and 7 hours of graduate project. Coursework in the subject area is based on the student's professional goals and will be determined by the student's advisor.

Licensure/Reciprocity: California. Students seeking teaching certification in a state other than California should consult with that state's certification office early in their program of study to insure compliance with requirements. Many state directors of teacher credentialing have signed Interstate Agreements through NASDTEC that expedite the certification process.

PATTEN COLLEGE

Education Division

2433 Coolidge Avenue
Oakland, California 94601
Phone: (510) 261-8500
Fax: (510) 535-0491
E-mail: ensorkar@patten.edu
Internet: http://www.patten.edu

Institution Description: Patten College (Patten Bible College and Theological Seminary, until 1980) is an independent Christian college dedicated to providing a liberal arts education with a strong biblical studies emphasis. It was established as Oakland Bible Institute in 1944. The present name was adopted in 1980.

The Master of Arts in Education program is designed for those who want advanced preparation in the foundations of human learning, effective instructional design and assessment, education of culturally and linguistically divers students, and strong educational leadership.

Institution Control: Private.

Calendar: Semester. Academic year September to May.

Official(s): Dr. Karen Ensor, Division Chair.

Faculty: Full-time 11 part-time 13; adjunct 4.

Degrees Awarded: 65 master's.

Admission Requirements: *Graduate:* Baccalaureate degree from an accredited institution with GPA 2.5 or higher; GPA of 3.0 or higher in all applicable postbaccalaureate work. *Teacher education specific:* California Basic Educational Skills Test; 3 letters of recommendation; demonstrate academic writing skills.

Fees and Expenses: $9,840 per academic year. On-campus room and board: $5,800. Books and supplies: $700.

Financial Aid: Resources specifically for eligible students enrolled in teacher education programs are awarded on the basis of financial need and academic merit. The institution has a Program Participation Agreement with the U.S. Department of Education for eligible students to receive Pell Grants and other federal aid. *Contact:* Robert Olivera at 510) 261-8500, ext. 783 or e-mail at oliverrob@patternedu.

Accreditation: *Regional:* WASC. *Approved by:* California Commission on Teacher Credentialing.

Graduate Programs: The Master of Arts in Education program is a two-year, full-time sequence of courses leading to an M.A. in Education with optional teaching credential. The program requires a minimum of 34 units, among which 16 units are core courses, at least 12 units in the area of concentration choice, and 6 elective units in the field of education. Concentrations are available in organizational leadership, teaching English as a second language, and curriculum design. A thesis/project culminates all requirements. The candidate produces a comprehensive, approved research document in the area of concentration.

The Teaching Credential Programs are designed to include all requirements of CCTC and the special emphases of Patten University. The programs offer preparation for the multiple and single subject credentials through sequenced coursework and fieldwork experiences that will enable them to teach all students in California classrooms. The first semester includes twelve semester units of professional coursework including a three-semester unit course in the teaching of reading, prior to the second semester student teaching/intern practicum. The second semester program includes ten semester units of full-time student teaching, along with advanced professional education courses closely linked to the student teaching.

Licensure/Reciprocity: California. Students seeking teaching certification in a state other than California should consult with that state's certification office early in their program of study to insure compliance with requirements. Many state directors of teacher credentialing have signed Interstate Agreements through NASDTEC that expedite the certification process.

PEPPERDINE UNIVERSITY
Graduate School of Education and Psychology
6100 Center Drive
Los Angeles, California 90045
Phone: (310) 568-5600
Fax: (310) 568-5775
E-mail: gsep@pepperdine.edu
Internet: http://www.pepperdine.edu

Institution Description: Pepperdine University is a private, independent, nonprofit institution affiliated with the Church of Christ. It was established and incorporated as George Pepperdine College and offered first instruction at the postsecondary level in 1937. The name was changed to Pepperdine College in 1962. The present name was adopted in 1979.

The Graduate School of Education and Psychology was created in 1982 when the education and psychology divisions were combined. The school offers programs that prepare teachers and administrators to make a difference as a classroom teacher or other educational facilitator.

Institution Control: Private.

Calendar: Quarter. Academic year August to May.

Official(s): Dr. Margaret J. Weber, Dean; Cheryl D. Lampe, Program Director.

Faculty: Full-time 15; part-time 21 adjunct 40.

Degrees Awarded: 396 master's.

Admission Requirements: *Graduate:* Baccalaureate degree from a regionally accredited institution; two professional recommendations. *Teacher education specific:* Current teaching credential; California Basic Education Skills Test.

Fees and Expenses: $675 per unit.

Financial Aid: Resources specifically for eligible students enrolled in teacher education programs are awarded on the basis of academic merit and financial need. *Contact:* Robin Bailey-Chen at (310) 568-5735 or e-mail at robin.bailey-chen@pepperdine.edu.

Accreditation: *Regional:* WASC. *Member of:* AACTE. *Approved by:* California Commission on Teacher Credentialing.

Graduate Programs: The Master of Arts in Education and Teaching Credential Program requires the completion of 47 units of coursework/student teaching with a CLAD teaching credential. The academic year consists of three terms. The primary focus of the program configuration is to provide a content-based pedagogy to expand the depth and quality of curricular methods courses offered for students who are seeking either the multiple or single subject credential. Beginning in the fall of 2003, the program incorporated an induction phase where teachers work in a school district under their preliminary credential for a period of time before receiving the professional credential. The induction phase allows the application of theory and teaching methods learned in the university teacher preparation program.

Licensure/Reciprocity: California. Students seeking teaching certification in a state other than California should consult with that state's certification office early in their program of study to insure compliance with requirements. Many state directors of teacher credentialing have signed Interstate Agreements through NASDTEC that expedite the certification process.

POINT LOMA NAZARENE UNIVERSITY
Department of Teacher Education
3900 Lomaland Drive
San Diego, California 92106
Phone: (619) 849-7064
Fax: (619) 849-2579
E-mail: discover@ptloma.edu
Internet: http://www.ptloma.edu

Institution Description: Point Loma Nazarene University is a private college affiliated with the Church of the Nazarene. The campus was established in Los Angeles as Pacific Bible College in 1902 and moved to Pasadena, changed name to Pasadena University, and offered first instruction at the postsecondary level in 1910. The campus was moved to its present location in San Diego and changed name to Point Loma College in 1973. The present name was adopted in 1998.

The Department of Teacher Education offers selected credential and degree programs. The department is committed to prepare thoughtful, culturally sensitive, scholarly professional educators who utilize the latest research and exemplary methods to insure learning and achievement.

Institution Control: Private.

POINT LOMA NAZARENE UNIVERSITY—
cont'd

Calendar: Semester. Academic year August to May.

Official(s): Dr. Charles Downing, Chair.

Faculty: Full-time 5.

Degrees Awarded: 6 baccalaureate; 87 master's.

Admission Requirements: *Undergraduate:* Graduation from an accredited secondary school or GED; College Board SAT or ACT composite. *Teacher education specific:* The liberal studies major should apply to the department as early as possible with intent to pursue a teaching career. *Graduate:* Baccalaureate from an accredited institution. *Teacher education specific:* Teaching credential; California Basic Educational Skills Test; faculty interview.

Fees and Expenses: $15,760 per academic year. On-campus room and board: $6,380. Other expenses: $3,270. Books and supplies: $1,210.

Financial Aid: Resources specifically for eligible students enrolled in teacher education programs are awarded on the basis of financial need and academic merit. The institution has a Program Participation Agreement with the U.S. Department of Education for eligible students to receive Pell Grants and other federal aid. *Contact:* Financial Aid Office at: (619) 849-2296.

Accreditation: *Regional:* WASC. *Member of:* AACTE. *Approved by:* California Commission on Teacher Credentialing.

Undergraduate Programs: The liberal studies major must complete the general education requirements. The major should be in the area in which the student intends to teach. The liberal studies curriculum includes courses in education fundamentals.

Graduate Programs: A Multiple Subject Teaching Credential enables a person to teach in a self-contained (K-12) classroom. Point Loma prepares liberal studies majors as well as other students who have completed a bachelor's program for the teaching professions. Students receive coursework in educational research and theory as well as methodology in reading, language arts, science, social studies and mathematics.

Individuals who plan to teach at the secondary level need to pursue the single subject credential in an approved discipline of their choice. Point Loma offer single subject programs in the: art and design, music, physical education, English, social science, home economics, mathematics, and biology.

Licensure/Reciprocity: California. Students seeking teaching certification in a state other than California should consult with that state's certification office early in their program of study to insure compliance with requirements. Many state directors of teacher credentialing have signed Interstate Agreements through NASDTEC that expedite the certification process.

SAINT MARY'S COLLEGE OF CALIFORNIA

School of Education
1928 St. Mary's Road
Moraga, California 94556
Phone: (510) 631-4000
Fax: (510) 376-7193
E-mail: smcadmit@stmarys-ca.edu
Internet: http://www.stmarys-ca.edu

Institution Description: Saint Mary's College of California is a private institution affiliated with the Institute of the Brothers of the Christian Schools. It was established as Saint Mary's College by the Archbishop of San Francisco in 1863. The present name was adopted in 1938.

The School of Education offers programs leading to teacher certification in California. Undergraduate programs are preliminary preparation for teaching careers.

Institution Control: Private.

Calendar: Semester. Academic year September to May.

Official(s): Dr. Nancy Sorenson, Dean, School of Education.

Faculty: Full-time 32; adjunct 4.

Degrees Awarded: 61 master's.

Admission Requirements: *Undergraduate:* Graduation with 15 units from an accredited secondary school or GED; College Board SAT or ACT composite. *Teacher education specific:* Undergraduate courses in education are offered to students who plan to teach. Students should consult with the School of Education advisor early in their undergraduate years. *Graduate:* Baccalaureate degree from an accredited institution; GPA of 3.0 or better; demonstration of graduate-level writing proficiency. *Teacher education specific:* Approval of program Director.

Fees and Expenses: $20,750 per academic year. On-campus room and board: $8,550. Other expenses: $2,646. Books and supplies: $845.

Financial Aid: Resources specifically for eligible students enrolled in teacher education programs are awarded on the basis of financial need and academic merit. The institution has a Program Participation Agreement with the U.S. Department of Education for eligible students to receive Pell Grants and other federal aid. *Contact:* Financial Aid Office at: (925) 631-4370 or via e-mail at finaid@stmarys-ca.edu.

Accreditation: *Regional:* WASC. *Member of:* AACTE. *Approved by:* California Commission on Teacher Credentialing.

Undergraduate Programs: The School of Education offers undergraduate courses in education as preliminary preparation for a career in teaching and as part of a liberal education. The prospective elementary teacher ordinarily majors in liberal and civic studies or the integral program. The prospective secondary teacher generally majors in a field in which he/she plans to teach. The college currently offers approved teaching majors in art, biology, English, French, government, history, mathematics, physical education, and Spanish.

Graduate Programs: The Master of Arts degree programs are offered in the areas of counseling, early childhood education, educational administration, reading leadership, and special education. Students who wish to pursue the Master's degree without a specialist or services Credential should consult the director of the program within their area of interest. A proposal for a special in interdisciplinary course of study may be presented to the appropriate director and the Dean for approval.

The Master of Education degree is built upon completion of a basic teaching credential program. The basic credential programs (multiple subject and single subject) include courses in education and supervised teaching.

Licensure/Reciprocity: California. Students seeking teaching certification in a state other than California should consult with that state's certification office early in their program of study to insure compliance with requirements. Many state directors of teacher credentialing have signed Interstate Agreements through NASDTEC that expedite the certification process.

SAN DIEGO STATE UNIVERSITY

College of Education
School of Teacher Education
5500 Campanile Drive
San Diego, California 92182
Phone: (619) 594-6544
Fax: (619) 594-7089
E-mail: admission@sdsu.edu
Internet: http://www.sdsu.edu

Institution Description: The university was established as San Diego State Normal School in 1987. The name was changed to San Diego State Teachers College in 1921 and to San Diego State College in 1935. The present name was adopted in 1971.

The purpose of the School of Teacher Education is to provide systemic professional development for teachers throughout their careers, so that they may provide quality education to the diverse student population of California.

Institution Control: Public.

Calendar: Semester. Academic year August to May.

Official(s): Dr. Lionel R. Meno, Dean, College of Education.

Faculty: Not reported.

Degrees Awarded: 255 baccalaureate; 401 master's.

Admission Requirements: *Undergraduate:* Graduation from an approved secondary school; SAT or ACT scores are only required if high school GPA is less than 3.0. *Teacher education specific:* Departmental approval; completion of courses in the general education core plus a major field of study that is appropriate for the baccalaureate degree and future teacher credentialing. *Graduate:* Baccalaureate degree from a regionally accredited institution; overall GPA of 2.5 on previous academic and related work; *Teacher education specific:* PRAXIS Multiple Subject Assessment for Teachers or California Examination for Teachers; basic teaching credential; an approved major.

Fees and Expenses: Undergraduate in-state $786 per semester; out-of-state $282 per unit plus $786 state university fee. Graduate in-state $867 per semester; out-of-state $282 per unit plus $867 state university fee. Per academic year: required fees: $470 average; on-campus room and board: $6,545; other expenses: $2,625; books and supplies: $1,080.

Financial Aid: Resources specifically for eligible students enrolled in teacher education programs are awarded on the basis of financial need and academic merit. The institution has a Program Participation Agreement with the U.S. Department of Education for eligible students to receive Pell Grants and other federal aid. *Contact:* Financial Aid Office at (619) 594-6323.

Accreditation: *Regional:* WASC. *Professional:* NCATE. *Member of:* AACTE. *Approved by:* California Commission on Teacher Credentialing.

Undergraduate Programs: Undergraduate students acquire the baccalaureate degree in the liberal arts/sciences with concentration in the area in which they plan to teach.

Graduate Programs: The Master of Arts degree programs are designed to promote and support learning and the development through scholarly reading, study, and exchange of ideas. Graduate study involves work at the classroom, school, and district levels.

Programs are available for the Master of Arts in elementary or secondary curriculum and instruction. Programs are offered also with special attention to social studies, science education, and K-8 mathematics education.

Licensure/Reciprocity: California. Students seeking teaching certification in a state other than California should consult with that state's certification office early in their program of study to insure compliance with requirements. Many state directors of teacher credentialing have signed Interstate Agreements through NASDTEC that expedite the certification process.

SAN FRANCISCO STATE UNIVERSITY
College of Education
1600 Holloway Avenue
San Francisco, California 94132
Phone: (415) 338-1201
Fax: (415) 338-7238
E-mail: ugadmit@sfsu.edu
Internet: http://www.sfsu.edu

Institution Description: San Francisco State University is a multipurpose institution of higher education. It was established as San Francisco Normal School in 1899. The name was changed to San Francisco State Teachers' College in 1921 and added upper division programs in 1923. The present name was adopted in 1974.

The College of Education develops and maintains rigorous professional preparation in the pedagogical and clinical skills that professionals are required to use in providing effective services to individuals and their families, especially for those residing in ethnically and racially diverse communities.

Institution Control: Public.

Calendar: Semester. Academic year August to May.

Official(s): Dr. Jacob E. Perea, Dean, College of Education; Dr. Laureen Chew, Chair, Department of Elementary Education; Dr. Nathan Avani, Chair, Department of Secondary Education.

Faculty: Full-time 64 (Secondary Education), 42 (Elementary Education).

Degrees Awarded: 181 baccalaureate; 67 master's.

Admission Requirements: *Undergraduate:* Graduation from an approved secondary school; SAT or ACT scores are only required if high school GPA is less than 3.0. *Teacher education specific:* Departmental approval; completion of courses in the general education core plus a major field of study that is appropriate for the baccalaureate degree and future teacher credentialing.

Fees and Expenses: Undergraduate in-state $786 per semester; out-of-state $282 per unit plus $786 state university fee. Graduate in-state $867 per semester; out-of-state $282 per unit plus $867 state university fee. Per academic year: required fees $470 average; on-campus room and board: $9,570; other expenses: $3,500; books and supplies: $1,200.

Financial Aid: Resources specifically for eligible students enrolled in teacher education programs are awarded on the basis of financial need and academic merit. The institution has a Program Participation Agreement with the U.S. Department of Education for eligible students to receive Pell Grants and other federal aid. *Contact:* Financial Aid Office at: (415) 338-2582.

Accreditation: *Regional:* WASC. *Professional:* NCATE. *Member of:* AACTE. *Approved by:* California Commission on Teacher Credentialing.

Undergraduate Programs: All baccalaureate degrees require the completion of 124 to 132 units and major requirements as designated by the program pursued.

Graduate Programs: The Department of Elementary Education offers four Master of Arts programs: early childhood education; elementary education; language and literacy; mathematics education.

The Department of Secondary Education offers a Master of Arts program that affords teachers to pursue special interests such as urban education, multicultural education, middle school education, mathematics education, science education, and alternative education.

Licensure/Reciprocity: California. Students seeking teaching certification in a state other than California should consult with that state's certification office early in their program of study to insure compliance with requirements. Many state directors of teacher credentialing have signed Interstate Agreements through NASDTEC that expedite the certification process.

SAN JOSE STATE UNIVERSITY
College of Education
One Washington Square
San Jose, California 95192-0071
Phone: (408) 924-3600
E-mail: coe@sjsu.edu
Internet: http://www.sjsu.edu

Institution Description: The school was established as Minns' Evening Normal School, a department of the San Francisco School System in 1857. It became a state institution and changed name to California State Normal School in 1862. The name was changed to San Jose State Teachers College in 1921. After several name changes, the present name was adopted in 1974.

The mission of the College of Education is to prepare educators who have the knowledge, skills, dispositions and ethics that insure equity and excellence for students in a culturally diverse, technologically complex, global community.

Institution Control: Public.

Calendar: Semester. Academic year August to May.

Official(s): Dr. Susan Meyers, Dean, College of Education.

Faculty: Full-time 21 (Department of Elementary Education), 5 (Department of Secondary Education).

Degrees Awarded: 128 baccalaureate; 387 master's.

Admission Requirements: *Undergraduate:* Graduation from an approved secondary school; SAT or ACT scores are only required if high school GPA is less than 3.0. *Teacher education specific:* Departmental approval; completion of courses in the general education core plus a major field of study that is appropriate for the baccalaureate degree and future teacher credentialing. *Graduate:* Baccalaureate degree from a regionally

SAN JOSE STATE UNIVERSITY—*cont'd*

accredited institution; overall GPA of 3.0 in the last 60 semester (90 quarter) units attempted; *Teacher education specific:* PRAXIS Multiple Subject Assessment for Teachers or California Examination for Teachers; basic teaching credential; an approved major; faculty interview.

Fees and Expenses: Undergraduate in-state $786 per semester; out-of-state $282 per unit plus $786 state university fee. Graduate in-state $867 per semester; out-of-state $282 per unit plus $867 state university fee. Per academic year: required fees $470 average; on-campus room and board: $8,135; other expenses: $2,070; books and supplies: $885.

Financial Aid: Resources specifically for eligible students enrolled in teacher education programs are awarded on the basis of financial need and academic merit. The institution has a Program Participation Agreement with the U.S. Department of Education for eligible students to receive Pell Grants and other federal aid. *Contact:* Financial Aid Office at: (408) 283-7500.

Accreditation: *Regional:* WASC. *Professional:* NCATE. *Member of:* AACTE. *Approved by:* California Commission on Teacher Credentialing.

Undergraduate Programs: All baccalaureate degrees require the completion of 124 to 132 units and major requirements as designated by the program pursued. Students who desire to teach in elementary school must complete a multiple subjects matter Preparation program or pass MSAT. For middle school teaching, the student must complete requirements for secondary teaching with a supplementary authorization. For high school teaching, students must complete a single subject matter preparation program or pass PRAXIS.

Graduate Programs: The Department of Elementary Education offers the Master of Arts in Education with three emphases: Literacy Across the Curriculum for an Equitable Society; Science and Technology; and Critical Research. Each emphasis has a 30-semester unit program. Students are required to take at least one advanced course in each of the following: curriculum, educational foundations, and educational research. In addition a thesis or special project is required.

Licensure/Reciprocity: California. Students seeking teaching certification in a state other than California should consult with that state's certification office early in their program of study to insure compliance with requirements. Many state directors of teacher credentialing have signed Interstate Agreements through NASDTEC that expedite the certification process.

SANTA CLARA UNIVERSITY

Department of Education
500 El Camino Real
Santa Clara, California 95053
Phone: (408) 554-6801
Fax: (408) 554-2392
E-mail: tosavage@scu.edu
Internet: http://www.scu.edu

Institution Description: Santa Clara University is a private, independent, nonprofit institution affiliated with the Society of Jesus, Roman Catholic Church. It was established as Santa Clara College and offered first instruction at the postsecondary level in 1851. The name was changed to University of Santa Clara in 1912. The present name was adopted recently.

The Department of Education offers fifth-year programs leading to the master's degree.

Institution Control: Private.

Calendar: Quarter. Academic year September to June.

Official(s): Dr. Thomas Savage, Dean.

Faculty: Full-time 9; part-time 3; adjunct 9.

Degrees Awarded: 58 master's.

Admission Requirements: *Graduate:* Baccalaureate degree from a regionally accredited institution. *Teacher education specific:* 3.0 GPA; three letters of recommendation.

Fees and Expenses: $383 per unit. Required fees: $230. Books and supplies: $1,000.

Financial Aid: Resources specifically for eligible students enrolled in teacher education programs are awarded on the basis of financial need and academic merit. The institution has a Program Participation Agreement with the U.S. Department of Education for eligible students to receive Pell Grants and other federal aid. *Contact:* Helen Valine at (408) 554-4656 or e-mail at hvaline@scu.edu.

Accreditation: *Regional:* WASC. *Approved by:* California Commission on Teacher Credentialing.

Graduate Programs: The Department of Education offers credentials for elementary (multiple subjects), secondary (single subjects), special education, and educational administration. The Master of Arts degrees are offered in reading, instructional technology, curriculum and instruction, high education administration, special education, and educational administration.

Licensure/Reciprocity: California. Students seeking teaching certification in a state other than California should consult with that state's teacher certification office early in their program of study to insure compliance with requirements. Many state directors of teacher credentialing have signed Interstate Agreements through NASDTEC that expedite the certification process.

SONOMA STATE UNIVERSITY

School of Education
Stevenson Hall
1801 East Cotati Avenue
Rohnert Park, California 94928-3609
Phone: (707) 664-3115
Fax: (707) 664-2060
E-mail: admitme@sonoma.edu
Internet: http://www.sonoma.edu

Institution Description: Sonoma State University is a unit of the California State University System. It was established as Sonoma State College in 1960 and became California State College, Sonoma in 1972. The present name was adopted in 1978.

Institution Control: Public.

Calendar: Semester. Academic August to May.

Official(s): Dr. Phyllis Fernlund, Dean; Dr. Perry M. Marker, Chair, Department of Curriculum Studies and Secondary Education; Dr. Mary Ann Nickel, Department of Literacy Studies and Elementary Education.

Faculty: Full-time 8 (Curriculum Studies and Secondary Education), 6 (Early Childhood and Elementary Education).

Degrees Awarded: 40 baccalaureate; 37 master's.

Admission Requirements: *Undergraduate:* Graduation from an approved secondary school; SAT or ACT scores are only required if high school GPA is less than 3.0. *Teacher education specific:* Departmental approval; completion of courses in the general education core plus a major field of study that is appropriate for the baccalaureate degree and future teacher credentialing. *Graduate:* Baccalaureate degree from a regionally accredited institution; overall GPA of 3.0 in the last 60 semester (90 quarter) units attempted; *Teacher education specific:* PRAXIS Multiple Subject Assessment for Teachers or California Examination for Teachers; basic teaching credential; an approved major; faculty interview.

Fees and Expenses: Undergraduate in-state $786 per semester; out-of-state $282 per unit plus $786 state university fee. Graduate in-state $867 per semester; out-of-state $282 per unit plus $867 state university fee. Per academic year: required fees: $470 average; on-campus room and board: $7,540; other expenses: $2,625; books and supplies: $1,210 per academic year.

Financial Aid: Resources specifically for eligible students enrolled in teacher education programs are awarded on the basis of financial need and academic merit. The institution has a Program Participation Agreement with the U.S. Department of Education for eligible students to receive Pell Grants and other federal aid. *Contact:* Financial Aid Office at: (707) 664-2389.

Accreditation: *Regional:* WASC. *Member of:* AACTE. *Approved by:* California Commission on Teacher Credentialing.

Undergraduate Programs: All baccalaureate degrees require the completion of 124 to 132 units and major requirements as designated by the program pursued. Students who desire to teach in elementary school must complete a multiple subjects matter preparation program or pass MSAT. For middle school teaching, the student must complete requirements for secondary teaching with a supplementary authorization. For high school teaching, students must complete a single subject matter preparation program or pass PRAXIS.

Graduate Programs: In addition to teaching credential programs (multiple subject and secondary education), students can pursue the Master of Arts in Curriculum Teaching and Learning, applicable to a wide variety of nonteaching positions in education, government, and the corporate sector. Students may design their own program of study (area of emphasis), or select an area of emphasis in Educational Technology specifically designed for those interested in technology applications in the public or private sectors.

Licensure/Reciprocity: California. Students seeking teaching certification in a state other than California should consult with that state's certification office early in their program of study to insure compliance with requirements. Many state directors of teacher credentialing have signed Interstate Agreements through NASDTEC that expedite the certification process.

STANFORD UNIVERSITY
School of Education
Teacher Education Program
Stanford, California 94305-2060
Phone: (650) 723-2300
E-mail: edudept@stanford.edu
Internet: http://www.stanford.edu

Institution Description: Stanford University is a private, independent, nonprofit institution. The university was established and chartered as Leland Stanford Junior University in 1885.

The School of Education focuses on graduate education and research training and does not offer an undergraduate major. However, an honors program permits interested undergraduates to build on the training acquired in their major field of study by pursuing additional courses and a research or practicum project in the area of education.

Institution Control: Private.

Calendar: Quarter. Academic year September to June.

Official(s): Dr. Deborah J. Stipek, Dean.

Faculty: Full-time 14 (Curriculum Studies and Teacher Education).

Degrees Awarded: 309 baccalaureate; 488 master's.

Admission Requirements: *Undergraduate:* Graduation from an accredited secondary school or GED; College Board SAT or ACT composite. *Teacher education specific:* Students should apply for entry into the Honors Program during their junior year; faculty interview. *Graduate:* Baccalaureate from an accredited institution; letters of recommendation. *Teacher education specific:* Passing scores on required tests/exam; faculty interview.

Fees and Expenses: $27,204 per academic year. On-campus room and board: $8,880. Other expenses: $1,725. Books and supplies: $1,155.

Financial Aid: Resources specifically for eligible students enrolled in teacher education programs are awarded on the basis of financial need and academic merit. The institution has a Program Participation Agreement with the U.S. Department of Education for eligible students to receive Pell Grants and other federal aid. *Contact:* Financial Aid Office at: (650) 723-3058.

Accreditation: *Regional:* WASC. *Professional:* NCATE. *Member of:* AACTE. *Approved by:* California Commission on Teacher Credentialing.

Undergraduate Programs: The School of Education offers courses and programs to undergraduates interested in developing educationally oriented skills while pursuing a major course of study. The baccalaureate degree is awarded by other departments in the liberal arts and sciences.

Graduate Programs: The Stanford Teacher Education Program leads to the Master of Arts degree and teaching credential in the areas of English, languages (French, German, Japanese, Spanish), mathematics, science (biology, chemistry, physics), history/social science, coterminal degree-secondary, and coterminal degree-elementary.

The Curriculum Studies and Teacher Education Program offers a Master of Arts degree program with specializations in English, literacy, general curriculum, mathematics; and science teacher education.

Licensure/Reciprocity: California. Students seeking teaching certification in a state other than California should consult with that state's certification office early in their program of study to insure compliance with requirements. Many state directors of teacher credentialing have signed Interstate Agreements through NASDTEC that expedite the certification process.

UNIVERSITY OF CALIFORNIA, BERKELEY
Graduate School of Education
Berkeley, California 94720-5800
Phone: (510) 642-6000
Fax: (510) 642-7333
E-mail: ouars@uclink.berkeley.edu
Internet: http://www.berkeley.edu

Institution Description: The university was incorporated as College of California, a private institution in 1855. It offered first instruction at postsecondary level in 1860. Control was transferred to the state and name was changed to University of California in 1868.

The Graduate School of Education offers programs leading to the Master of Arts degree in Developmental Teacher Education and Multicultural Master's and Credential Program. An undergraduate minor in education program is also housed in the Graduate School of Education.

Institution Control: Public.

Calendar: Semester. Academic year August to May.

Official(s): Dr. P. David Pearson, Dean.

Faculty: Full-time 55.

Degrees Awarded: 131 master's; 39 doctorate.

Admission Requirements: *Undergraduate:* Graduation with 16 academic units from an accredited secondary school; College Board SAT or ACT composite. *Teacher education specific:* Application for admission to the program; faculty interview. *Graduate:* Baccalaureate degree from a regionally accredited institution. *Teacher education specific:* Letters of recommendation; faculty interview; teaching credential. Candidates must take the GRE and CBEST exams.

Fees and Expenses: Total resident undergraduate fees per semester: $2,928.95, nonresident $10,033.95. Graduate fees per semester: resident $3,084.45; nonresident $9,329.95. On-campus room and board: $10,610. Books and supplies: $1,110.

Financial Aid: The institution has a Program Participation Agreement with the U.S. Department of Education for eligible students to receive Pell Grants and other federal aid. Numerous programs provide ways to finance the cost of graduate school. Some are administered by the Graduate School of Education and others are administered by the Financial Aid Office (510) 642-0485.

Accreditation: *Regional:* WASC. *Approved by:* California Commission on Teacher Credentialing.

Undergraduate Programs: The undergraduate minor in education enables students to gain a critical understanding of the correlations between education and the development of societies and individuals. The courses include field work that provides students with experiences in their surrounding communities in K-12 classrooms, co-teaching, tutoring, mentoring, assisting with an environmental education course, or participating in a vast array of educational activities.

Graduate Programs: The Developmental Teacher Program includes a two-year, full-time sequence of courses and student teaching leading to a Master of Arts degree and a multiple subject credential. The program allows time for a gradual introduc-

UNIVERSITY OF CALIFORNIA, BERKELEY—
cont'd

tion to teaching in five student teaching placements that span the elementary school grades. Both coursework and placements emphasize teaching strategies geared to California's multicultural and multilingual classrooms.

The Multicultural Urban Secondary English Master's and Credential Program is a two-year program that prepares candidates to teach secondary English to both native speakers of English and second-language learners. At the end of the fist year, candidates receive a teaching credential to teach classes in grades six through twelve. During the second year, candidates take an seminar in which they complete a project that involves them in teacher research and reflection on their teaching.

The Master of Arts in Language, Literacy, and Culture is offered with courses that cover the basic concepts and theories in language and literacy learning as well as courses in their area of specialization or teaching credential. The degree program includes a number of specializations such as reading, writing, literature, education of language minority students, and the study of athletes and academic achievement.

Licensure/Reciprocity: California. Students seeking teaching certification in a state other than California should consult with that state's certification office early in their program of study to insure compliance with requirements. Many state directors of teacher credentialing have signed Interstate Agreements through NASDTEC that expedite the certification process.

UNIVERSITY OF CALIFORNIA, DAVIS

School of Education
One Shields Avenue
Davis, California 95616-8678
Phone: (530) 752-1011
Fax: (530) 752-6363
E-mail: inkucd@ucdavis.edu
Internet: http://www.ucdavis.edu

Institution Description: The school was established as University Farm, a 3-year institution in 1905. It became a 4-year degree-granting institution and changed name to College of Agriculture in 1923. The present name was adopted in 1959.

Through the graduate programs offered by the School of Education, students are prepare to take leadership roles in strengthening schools. advancing research and scholarship, and improving education policy.

Institution Control: Public.

Calendar: Quarter. Academic year September to June.

Official(s): Dr. Harold Levine, Dean, School of Education.

Faculty: Full-time 28.

Degrees Awarded: Not reported.

Admission Requirements: *Undergraduate:* Graduation from an accredited secondary school; College Board SAT or ACT composite score. *Teacher education specific:* Acceptance into the program; faculty interview. *Graduate:* Baccalaureate degree from a regionally accredited institution; overall GPA of 3.0 in the last 90 quarter units attempted; *Teacher education specific:* PRAXIS Multiple Subject Assessment for Teachers or California Examination for Teachers; basic teaching credential; an approved major; faculty interview.

Fees and Expenses: Undergraduate: in-state $4,300 per academic year; out-of-state $16,574. Graduate: in-state $2,371 per quarter; out-of-state $6,535.78 (tuition reduction plans available to eligible students). On-campus room and board: $8,765. Other expenses: $2,075. Books and supplies: $1,165.

Financial Aid: Resources specifically for eligible students enrolled in teacher education programs are awarded on the basis of financial need and academic merit. The institution has a Program Participation Agreement with the U.S. Department of Education for eligible students to receive Pell Grants and other federal aid. *Contact:* Financial Aid Office at: (530) 752-2390.

Accreditation: *Regional:* WASC. *Approved by:* California Commission on Teacher Credentialing.

Undergraduate Programs: The education minor is open to all UC Davis undergraduates. The minor offers an introduction to educational theory, research, and practice. It also gives students the opportunity to engage in fieldwork in local schools. Twenty units are required for the program and at least 12 units of the 20-unit minimum must be in education courses.

Graduate Programs: Teaching Credential/Master of Arts program offers an opportunity for qualified students to obtain both a Master of Arts in Education degree and a multiple subject or single subject credential. The program is offered as a full-time, five-quarter program. It provides coursework that incorporates a theoretical approach to the teaching-learning process and it encourages close interactions among teacher candidate and teacher education faculty.

Licensure/Reciprocity: California. Students seeking teaching certification in a state other than California should consult with that state's certification office early in their program of study to insure compliance with requirements. Many state directors of teacher credentialing have signed Interstate Agreements through NASDTEC that expedite the certification process.

UNIVERSITY OF CALIFORNIA, IRVINE

Department of Education
2001 Berkeley Place
Irvine, California 92697-5500
Phone: (949) 824-5117
Fax: (949) 824-2965
E-mail: educate@uci.edu
Internet: http://www.uci.edu

Institution Description: The Irvine campus was established in 1961 and first offered instruction in 1965. The first degree (baccalaureate) was awarded in 1968.

The Department of Education offers both multiple subject and single subject teaching credential programs. An undergraduate minor in educational studies is also offered to students who want to explore the field of education during their four-year curriculum.

Institution Control: Public.

Calendar: Quarter. Academic year September to June.

Official(s): Dr. David Brant, Chair, Department of Education.

Faculty: Full-time 33; adjunct 5.

Degrees Awarded: 72 master's; 1 doctorate.

Admission Requirements: *Undergraduate:* Graduation from an accredited secondary school; College Board SAT or ACT composite score. *Teacher education specific:* Acceptance into the program; faculty interview. *Graduate:* Baccalaureate degree from a regionally accredited institution; overall GPA of 3.0 in the last 90 quarter units attempted; *Teacher education specific:* PRAXIS Multiple Subject Assessment for Teachers or California Examination for Teachers; basic teaching credential; an approved major; faculty interview.

Fees and Expenses: Undergraduate: in-state $4,427 per academic year; out-of-state $16,983. Graduate: in-state $2,439.50 per quarter; out-of-state $6,602.58 (tuition reduction plans available to eligible students). On-campus room and board: $8,601. Other expenses: $2,455. Books and supplies: $1,355.

Financial Aid: Resources specifically for eligible students enrolled in teacher education programs are awarded on the basis of financial need and academic merit. The institution has a Program Participation Agreement with the U.S. Department of Education for eligible students to receive Pell Grants and other federal aid. *Contact:* Financial Aid Office at: (949) 824-6261.

Accreditation: *Regional:* WASC. *Approved by:* California Commission on Teacher Credentialing.

Undergraduate Programs: The undergraduate minor in educational studies is designed to allow students to explore a broad range of issues in the field of education as well as to provide a foundation for becoming a teacher in grades K-12. The program consists of a coordinated set of courses that include an introductory-level course and several advanced courses in the field of education. A number of the minor's elective courses are offered by other academic units.

Graduate Programs: The Master of Arts in Teaching in elementary and secondary education programs integrate the two teacher credential programs with an advanced degree program in a 15-month sequence of full-time study and student teaching. The program places special emphasis on the preparation of new teachers for leadership, and provides them with the knowledge, skills, and confidence needed to be successful in California's schools serving cultural and linguistically diverse student populations. The Cross Cultural Language and Academic Development (CLAD) emphasis is embedded in both credential programs.

Licensure/Reciprocity: California. Students seeking teaching certification in a state other than California should consult with that state's certification office early in their program of study to insure compliance with requirements. Many state directors of teacher credentialing have signed Interstate Agreements through NASDTEC that expedite the certification process.

UNIVERSITY OF CALIFORNIA, LOS ANGELES

Graduate School of Education and Information Studies
Teacher Education Program
405 Hilgard Avenue
Los Angeles, California 90095
Phone: (310) 825-8326
Fax: (310) 206-6293
E-mail: info@gseis.ucla.edu
Internet: http://www.centerx.gseis.ucla.edu/tep

Institution Description: The Southern Branch of the University of California opened in 1919 offering a 2-year program in undergraduate instruction in letters and science and in the Teachers College. A 4-year Teachers College curriculum was begun in 1922. The institution was renamed the University of California at Los Angeles in 1927, soon to be known as UCLA. The present name was adopted in 1958.

The Teacher Education Program offers an undergraduate preparation program as well as a two-year program leading to the Master of Education degree.

Institution Control: Public.

Calendar: Quarter. Academic year September to June.

Official(s): Dr. Aimee Dorr, Dean; Dr. Eloise Metcalfe, Director of Teacher Education Program.

Faculty: Full-time 49; part-time 20; adjunct 20.

Degrees Awarded: 258 master's; 55 doctorate.

Admission Requirements: *Undergraduate:* Graduation from an accredited secondary school; specific course requirements; SAT I; 3 SAT exams. *Teacher education specific:* Open only to seniors in last year of math, science, and music degree programs; 3 letters of recommendation; faculty interview. *Graduate:* Baccalaureate degree from a regionally accredited institution; 3.0 GPA in junior and senior high school years; 3 letters of recommendation; two official undergraduate transcripts. *Teacher education specific:* CBEST score report; Subject Matter score report *or* subject matter waiver letter; scholarship essay; interview workshop.

Fees and Expenses: Undergraduate: in-state $4,427 per academic year; out-of-state $16,684. Graduate: in-state $2,439.50 per quarter; out-of-state $6,602.58 (tuition reduction plans available to eligible students). On-campus room and board: $7,969 to $11,529. Other expenses: $2,455. Books and supplies: $1,000.

Financial Aid: Resources specifically for eligible students enrolled in teacher education programs are awarded on the basis of financial need and academic merit. The institution has a Program Participation Agreement with the U.S. Department of Education for eligible students to receive Pell Grants and other federal aid. *Contact:* Ron Rothstein at: $310) 825-8328 or rothstein@gseis.ucla.edu.

Accreditation: *Regional:* WASC. *Approved by:* California Commission on Teacher Credentialing.

Undergraduate Programs: An undergraduate program in mathematics and science has been developed collaboratively with the UCLA Department of Mathematics and the UCLA Science Departments. Students complete a bachelor's degree while simultaneously beginning to fulfill California teaching credential requirements. During year two in the program, they are full-time teachers on an intern credential in urban schools. Students complete the program with a Master of Education and a single subject credential in mathematics or science with an option BCLAD emphasis. Students who enroll in the Spanish BCLAD take additional language and culture-specific coursework.

Through a partnership with the UCLA music department, undergraduate music majors take education courses and do fieldwork while completing their bachelor's degree and credential requirements.

Graduate Programs: The graduate two-year program begins in year one with a comprehensive academic sequence comprised of the basic requirements for the credential and the master's degree. Additionally, students participate in student teaching at schools with racially, culturally, and linguistically diverse low-income student populations. In the second year of the program, students participate in a paid residency assignment at low-income, urban schools while simultaneously completing their final program coursework and portfolio for the Master of Education degree.

Licensure/Reciprocity: California. Students seeking teaching certification in a state other than California should consult with that state's certification office early in their program of study to insure compliance with requirements. Many state directors of teacher credentialing have signed Interstate Agreements through NASDTEC that expedite the certification process.

UNIVERSITY OF CALIFORNIA, RIVERSIDE

Graduate School of Education
Division of Teacher Education
Sproul Hall 1207
1900 University Avenue
Riverside, California 92521-0128
Phone: (909) 787-5225
Fax: (909) 787-3942
E-mail: education@ucr.edu/teach
Internet: http://www.ucr.edu

Institution Description: In 1954 the College of Letters and Sciences was founded as a small undergraduate college. In 1961, the Graduate Division founded.

The Graduate School of Education offers opportunities for teachers, administrators, and other professionals to pursue high quality and professionally relevant advanced degree programs. The several master's degree programs are specifically designed to assist school practitioners in developing their professional skills.

Institution Control: Public.

Calendar: Quarter. Academic year September to June.

Official(s): Dr. Robert C. Calfee, Dean, Graduate School of Education; Dr. Athena Waite, Director of Teacher Education.

Faculty: Full-time 24; part-time 3; adjunct 2.

Degrees Awarded: 75 master's; 13 doctorate.

Admission Requirements: *Undergraduate:* Graduation from an approved secondary school; SAT or ACT scores are only required if high school GPA is less than 3.0. *Teacher education specific:* Departmental approval; completion of courses in the general education core plus a major field of study that is appropriate for the baccalaureate degree and future teacher credentialing. *Graduate:* Baccalaureate degree from a regionally accredited institution; overall GPA of 3.0 in the last 90 quarter units attempted; *Teacher education specific:* PRAXIS Multiple Subject Assessment for Teachers or California Examination for Teachers; basic teaching credential; an approved major; faculty interview.

UNIVERSITY OF CALIFORNIA, RIVERSIDE—
cont'd

Fees and Expenses: Undergraduate: in-state $4,427 per academic year; out-of-state $16,806. Graduate: in-state $2,371 per quarter; out-of-state $6,535.78 (tuition reduction plans available to eligible students). On-campus room and board: $8,700. Other expenses: $2,600. Books and supplies: $1,350.

Financial Aid: Resources specifically for eligible students enrolled in teacher education programs are awarded on the basis of financial need and academic merit. The institution has a Program Participation Agreement with the U.S. Department of Education for eligible students to receive Pell Grants and other federal aid. *Contact:* Financial Aid Office at: (909) 787-3878.

Accreditation: *Regional:* WASC. *Approved by:* California Commission on Teacher Credentialing.

Undergraduate Programs: The undergraduate minor in education enables students to gain a critical understanding of the correlations between education and the development of societies and individuals. The courses include field work that provides students with experiences in their surrounding communities in K-12 classrooms, co-teaching, tutoring, mentoring, assisting with an environmental education course, or participating in a vast array of educational activities.

Graduate Programs: The Master of Education and a teaching credential may be earned in four terms (summer, fall, winter, spring). The program is ideally suited to UC Riverside graduates who have taken prerequisite courses as undergraduates.

The Master of Arts in Education degree is available with specializations within three general areas and there is also the possibility of combining some programs such as Reading Specialist or Administrative Services. The specific number of courses varies among programs, but 40 quarter units are required in most specializations.

Licensure/Reciprocity: California. Students seeking teaching certification in a state other than California should consult with that state's certification office early in their program of study to insure compliance with requirements. Many state directors of teacher credentialing have signed Interstate Agreements through NASDTEC that expedite the certification process.

UNIVERSITY OF CALIFORNIA, SAN DIEGO

Teacher Education Program
900 Gilman Drive
La Jolla, California 92093
Phone: (619) 534-3120
E-mail: tepinfo@ucsd.edu
Internet: http://www.admissions.ucsd.edu

Institution Description: The university was established as Marine Biological Station of San Diego in 1903. It joined the University of California system as Scripps Institution of Biological Research in 1912. The name was changed to University of California Scripps Institution of Oceanography in 1925. The institution became a general campus of the University of California in 1958 and adopted the present name in 1960.

The Teacher Education Program offers several programs for those interested in teacher training and educational professional development.

Institution Control: Public.

Calendar: Quarter. Academic year September to June.

Official(s): Dr. Randall J. Souviney, Director.

Faculty: Full-time 8.

Degrees Awarded: 80 master's.

Admission Requirements: *Undergraduate:* Graduation from an accredited secondary school; College Board SAT or ACT composite score; three SAT II Subject Tests (writing, math, and optional subject. *Teacher education specific:* Application to the teacher education program; faculty interview. *Graduate:* Baccalaureate degree from a regionally accredited institution; references; faculty interview. *Teacher education specific:* Teaching credential.

Fees and Expenses: Undergraduate: in-state $4,363 per academic year; out-of-state $16,872. Graduate: in-state $2,371 per quarter; out-of-state $6,535.78 (tuition reduction plans available to eligible students). On-campus room and board: $8,065. Books and supplies: $1,225.

Financial Aid: The institution has a Program Participation Agreement with the U.S. Department of Education for eligible students to receive Pell Grants and other federal aid. *Contact:* Financial Aid Office at: (858) 534-4430.

Accreditation: *Regional:* WASC. *Approved by:* California Commission on Teacher Credentialing.

Undergraduate Programs: Undergraduate students from any major or college are eligible for the minor in teacher education. The minor consists of a minimum of 28 units.

Graduate Programs: The Master of Education Degree/Credential Program is for those seeking the California multiple subject teaching credential for elementary school teachers. The program is for a 21-month study consisting of educational foundations coursework, professional preparation coursework, and the preparation of a teaching performance assessment portfolio.

The Master in Education single subject credential program for secondary school teachers is available with concentration in the areas of: biology, chemistry, geoscience, English, mathematics, and physics.

Licensure/Reciprocity: California. Students seeking teaching certification in a state other than California should consult with that state's certification office early in their program of study to insure compliance with requirements. Many state directors of teacher credentialing have signed Interstate Agreements through NASDTEC that expedite the certification process.

UNIVERSITY OF CALIFORNIA, SANTA BARBARA

Gevirtz Graduate School of Education
Department of Teacher Education
Santa Barbara, California 93106
Phone: (805) 893-2084
Fax: (805) 893-2676
E-mail: gevirtz@sa.ucsb.edu
Internet: http://www.ucsb.edu

Institution Description: The university was established as Anna S. C. Blake Manual Training School, a private school, in 1891. Control was transferred to the city of Santa Barbara in 1892 then came under state jurisdiction as Santa Barbara Normal School of Manual Arts and Home Economics in 1909. The name was changed to Santa Barbara Normal School in 1919 then became Santa Barbara in 1921. The institution became part of the university system as Santa Barbara College in 1944. The present name was adopted in 1958.

The Teacher Education Program provides future teachers with a solid theoretical foundation as well as field work.

Institution Control: Public.

Calendar: Quarter. Academic year September to Jane..

Official(s): Dr. Charles Bazerman, Chair, Department of Education; Dr. Ralph Nair, Director, Teacher Education Program.

Faculty: Full-time 47.

Degrees Awarded: 145 master's; 19 doctorate.

Admission Requirements: *Graduate:* Baccalaureate degree from a regionally accredited institution; letters of recommendation; faculty interview; teaching credential. Candidates must take the GRE and CBEST exams.

Fees and Expenses: Undergraduate: in-state $4,363 per academic year; out-of-state $16,535.78. Graduate: in-state $2,371 per quarter; out-of-state $6,535.78 (tuition reduction plans available to eligible students). On-campus room and board: $8,835. Other expenses: $2,130. Books and supplies: $1,225.

Financial Aid: The institution has a Program Participation Agreement with the U.S. Department of Education for eligible students to receive Pell Grants and other federal aid. *Contact:* Financial Aid Office at: (805) 893-2432.

Accreditation: *Regional:* WASC. *Approved by:* California Commission on Teacher Credentialing.

Graduate Programs: The Teacher Education Program leads to both a California State teaching credential and a Master of Arts in Education degree. The multiple subject credential program (for elementary) and the single subject credential program (secondary) are offered and include a summer session (begins the first week in August, a fall quarter, winter and spring terms, and a post-summer session.

Licensure/Reciprocity: California. Students seeking teaching certification in a state other than California should consult with that state's certification office early in their program of study to insure compliance with requirements. Many state directors of teacher credentialing have signed Interstate Agreements through NASDTEC that expedite the certification process.

UNIVERSITY OF CALIFORNIA, SANTA CRUZ

Education Department
212 Crown College
1156 High Street
Santa Cruz, California 95064
Phone: (831) 459-2889
Fax: (831) 459-4452
E-mail: education@ucsc.edu
Internet: http://www.ucsc.edu

Institution Description: The University of California, Santa Cruz is a public research institution established in 1962. It offered first instruction at the postsecondary level in 1965.

The purpose of the Education Department's instructional programs is to prepare all students to engage in the analysis and integration of educational theory, research, and practice for a multilingual, multicultural society.

Institution Control: Public.

Calendar: Quarter. Academic year September to June.

Official(s): Dr. Rodney T. Ogawa, Department Chair.

Faculty: Full-time 24.

Degrees Awarded: 111 master's.

Admission Requirements: *Undergraduate:* Graduation from an accredited secondary school; College Board SAT or ACT composite score; three SAT II Subject Tests (writing, math, and optional subject. *Teacher education specific:* Application to the Department; faculty interview. High school students who plan to pursue a career in education should take the course required for UC admission and complete any courses recommended as background for their intended major. *Graduate:* Baccalaureate degree from a regionally accredited institution; references/recommendations. *Teacher education specific:* Teaching credential; specific tests/exams.

Fees and Expenses: Undergraduate: in-state $4,427 per academic year; out-of-state $16, 806. Graduate: in-state $2,455 per quarter; out-of-state $6,619 (tuition reduction plans available to eligible students). On-campus room and board: $11,265. Other expenses: $2,600. Books and supplies: $1,205.

Financial Aid: Resources specifically for eligible students enrolled in teacher education programs are awarded on the basis of financial need and academic merit. The institution has a Program Participation Agreement with the U.S. Department of Education for eligible students to receive Pell Grants and other federal aid. *Contact:* Financial Aid Office at: (831) 459-2963.

Accreditation: *Regional:* WASC. *Approved by:* California Commission on Teacher Credentialing.

Undergraduate Programs: The minor in education is an undergraduate course of study that explores the history of educational thought and philosophy, the politics and economics of education, theories of cognition, learning and pedagogy, and issues of cultural and linguistic diversity in education. The minor is designed to be useful to both liberal arts study generally and as a foundation for students planning to become teachers. Baccalaureate degree programs require the completion of 180 units.

Graduate Programs: The Master of Arts in Education: Teaching offers the CLAD and BCLAD [bilingual] Crosscultural, Language and Academic Development) emphasis teaching credentials. These emphases provide the training necessary to teach English-speaking and limited-English-proficient students, while providing and understanding of the cultural and linguistic diversity in the California public Schools. The BCLAD language of emphasis in Spanish.

The preliminary multiple subjects teaching credential for elementary school teachers and the preliminary single subject teaching credential for secondary teachers are available. The single subject program offers the following subject areas: mathematics, English, social sciences, and science.

Licensure/Reciprocity: California. Students seeking teaching certification in a state other than California should consult with that state's certification office early in their program of study to insure compliance with requirements. Many state directors of teacher credentialing have signed Interstate Agreements through NASDTEC that expedite the certification process.

UNIVERSITY OF THE PACIFIC

Benerd School of Education
3601 Pacific Avenue
Stockton, California 95211-0197
Phone: (209) 946-2211
Fax: (209) 946-2413
E-mail: jnagle@pacific.edu
Internet: http://www.pacific.edu

Institution Description: The University of the Pacific is a private, nonsectarian institution formerly affiliated with the United Methodist Church. It was established and chartered as California Wesleyan University in 1851. The name was changed to University of the Pacific in 1852 and to College of the Pacific in 1911. The present name was readopted in 1961.

The Benerd School of Education provides a program that provides a sequenced program that allows completion of a degree in four years and a preliminary credential in four or four and a half years concurrent with the degree program. It is committed to a philosophy of combining professional theory with practical fieldwork and utilizes the diversity of Stockton-area schools for teacher preparation.

Institution Control: Private.

Calendar: Semester. Academic year August to May.

Official(s): Dr. John M. Nagle, Dean, Benerd School of Education; Dr. Marilyn Draheim, Chair, Department of Curriculum and Instruction.

Faculty: Full-time 25; part-time 15.

Degrees Awarded: 49 baccalaureate; 59 master's.

Admission Requirements: *Undergraduate:* Either graduation from an accredited secondary school or GED; College Board SAT preferred, ACT composite accepted. *Teacher education specific:* Acceptance by the Benerd School of Education with a diversified major in liberal studies. *Graduate:* Baccalaureate degree from a regionally accredited institution; letters of recommendation; approved major. *Teacher education specific:* California Basic Education Skills Test; faculty interview; teaching credential.

Fees and Expenses: $23,180 per academic year. Required fees: $520 per academic year. On-campus room and board: $7,490.

Financial Aid: Resources specifically for eligible students enrolled in teacher education programs are awarded on the basis of financial need and academic merit. The institution has a Program Participation Agreement with the U.S. Department of Education for eligible students to receive Pell Grants and other federal aid. *Contact:* Financial Aid Office at: (209) 946-2421.

Accreditation: *Regional:* WASC. *Professional:* NCATE. *Member of:* AACTE. *Approved by:* California Commission on Teacher Credentialing.

Undergraduate Programs: Students interested in secondary school teaching should choose a major in the Arts and Science Division or in the Conservatory of Music. These students will

UNIVERSITY OF THE PACIFIC—*cont'd*

work toward a single subject teaching credential in English, mathematics, music, physical education, sciences, social science, Spanish, teaching English as a second language.

Students who want to become elementary or middle school teachers enroll directly in the Bernerd School of Education and earn a Bachelor of Arts degree with a diversified major. The major automatically satisfies three of the four academic areas needed to earn an preliminary multiple subjects credential: general education. Student teaching is completed in the junior and senior years.

Graduate Programs: The Master of Arts in Education degree requires the completion of 30 to 32 units of graduate work depending on Plan A (thesis), Plan B (seminars), or Plan C (projects. Specialized program are also available that provide opportunity for courses offers to be linked with other schools and departments.

The Master of Education degree program is designed for students who desire to obtain an initial teaching credential concurrently with a master's degree. The program requires the completion of at least 38 units.

The Master of Education in music education is administered by the Conservatory of Music. It requires completion of at least 38 units.

Licensure/Reciprocity: California. Students seeking teaching certification in a state other than California should consult with that state's certification office early in their program of study to insure compliance with requirements. Many state directors of teacher credentialing have signed Interstate Agreements through NASDTEC that expedite the certification process.

UNIVERSITY OF SAN DIEGO

School of Education
5998 Alcala Park
San Diego, California 92110-2492
Phone: (619) 260-4540
Fax: (619) 260-4695
E-mail: cgetz@.sandiego.edu
Internet: http://www.sandiego.edu

Institution Description: The University of San Diego is a private, independent, nonprofit institution affiliated with the Roman Catholic Church. It was established and chartered as San Diego College for Women in 1949. The college merged with the University of San Diego College for Men and adopted its present name in 1972.

The School of Education offers programs leading to the Master of Education and Master of Arts degree for students who are already credentials or who are concurrently enrolled in a graduate credential program.

Institution Control: Private.

Calendar: Semester. Academic year begins September to May.

Official(s): Dr. Steven Gelb, Program Director.

Faculty: Full-time 18; adjunct 15.

Degrees Awarded: 98 master's; 25 doctorate.

Admission Requirements: *Undergraduate:* Graduation for an approved secondary school; recommendation from high school faculty; personal essay. *Teacher education specific:* overall 2.75 GPA; letter of reference; previous experience working with children; interview with faculty. *Graduate:* Baccalaureate degree from a regionally accredited institution with overall 2.75 GPA; 3 letters of reference; previous experience working with children; faculty interview.

Fees and Expenses: Undergraduate: $760 per unit; graduate: $825 per unit. Required fees: $110. On-campus room and board: $3,700 to $5,000 per semester. Books and supplies: $200 to $200 per semester.

Financial Aid: Resources specifically for eligible students enrolled in teacher education programs are awarded on the basis of financial need and academic merit. *Contact:* Lorena Meza at (619) 260-7585 or e-mail at meza@sandiego.edu.

Accreditation: *Regional:* WASC. *Member of:* AACTE. *Approved by:* California Commission on Teacher Credentialing.

Undergraduate Programs: Students may graduate in four years with a Bachelor of Arts degree and a teaching credential in multiple or single subject or in special education. The Level I Educational Specialist degree is offered in the areas of early childhood special education, mild/moderate disabilities, and severe/profound disabilities. Multiple subject and special education credential students major in a diversified liberal arts program consisting of 96 units, 30 units in education, including a semester of student teaching. Single subject candidates major in the area in which they plan to teach and the requirements differ by subject matter area.

Graduate Programs: There are five specialization areas in the Master of Education program, all of which require 30 units of study (character education, curriculum and teaching, literacy, special education, and teaching English as a second language).

Master of Arts in Teaching programs are offered in four teaching fields (history, international relations, social science, and bilingual/Spanish).

Licensure/Reciprocity: California. Students seeking teaching certification in a state other than California should consult with that state's certification office early in their program of study to insure compliance with requirements. Many state directors of teacher credentialing have signed Interstate Agreements through NASDTEC that expedite the certification process.

UNIVERSITY OF SOUTHERN CALIFORNIA

Rossier School of Education
University Park
Los Angeles, California 90089-1455
Phone: (213) 740-2311
Fax: (213) 740-6364
E-mail: admission@usc.edu
Internet: http://www.usc.edu

Institution Description: The University of Southern California is a private, independent, nonprofit institution. It was established and incorporated under Methodist sponsorship and offered first instruction at the postsecondary level in 1880. The religious affiliation ended in 1929.

The Rossier School of Education is committed to preparing teachers, researchers, counselors, administrators, and curricular specialists for leadership positions.

Institution Control: Private.

Calendar: Semester. Academic year September to May.

Official(s): Dr. Karen Symms Gallagher, Dean.

Faculty: Full-time 46.

Degrees Awarded: 45 baccalaureate; 151 master's; 91 doctorate.

Admission Requirements: *Undergraduate:* Graduation from an accredited secondary school; minimum GPA 2.7; College Board SAT preferred; ACT composite accepted. *Teacher education specific:* Faculty interview with major department. *Graduate:* Baccalaureate degree or its equivalent from an accredited institution; GPA of 3.0 is usually expected; satisfactory test scores on the GRE; three letters of recommendation. *Teacher education specific:* Complete all admission requirements and tests/exams for the program to be pursued; personal statement; faculty interview.

Fees and Expenses: Undergraduate: $26,956 per academic year. On-campus room and board: $8,512. Other expenses: $2,210. Books and supplies: $630.

Financial Aid: Resources specifically for eligible students enrolled in teacher education programs are awarded on the basis of financial need and academic merit. The institution has a Program Participation Agreement with the U.S. Department of Education for eligible students to receive Pell Grants and other federal aid. *Contact:* Financial Aid Office at: (213) 740-1111.

Accreditation: *Regional:* WASC. *Member of:* AACTE. *Approved by:* California Commission on Teacher Credentialing.

Undergraduate Programs: The Bachelor of Science in General Studies is designed for students who plan to become elementary classroom teachers. This program offers coursework toward the multiple subject teaching credential. This credential authorized graduates to teach kindergarten through 8th grades.

Students wishing to obtain a single subject credential should pursue a baccalaureate program in the areas of their choice. These students enroll in the College of Liberal Arts and Sciences programs in English, foreign languages, science, mathematics or in music with the School of Music.

Graduate Programs: The School of Education offers the following graduate degree teacher preparation programs: Master of Science in Education and the Master of Science in Teaching English to Speakers of Other Languages. A minimum of 20 graduate units earned in residence at USC is required for the master's degree.

Licensure/Reciprocity: California. Students seeking teaching certification in a state other than California should consult with that state's certification office early in their program of study to insure compliance with requirements. Many state directors of teacher credentialing have signed Interstate Agreements through NASDTEC that expedite the certification process.

WESTMONT COLLEGE

Department of Education
955 La Paz Road
Santa Barbara, California 93108
Phone: (805) 565-6165
Fax: (805) 565-7101
E-mail: lmeister@westmont.edu
Internet: http://www.westmont.edu

Institution Description: Westmont College is a private, nonprofit, interdenominational Christian college. It was established in 1937 and awarded its first baccalaureate degree in 1941.

The Department of Education offers programs leading to the baccalaureate degree with teaching credential and a postbaccalaureate program for teaching candidates.

Institution Control: Private.

Calendar: Semester. Academic year August to May.

Official(s): Dr. Andrew Mullen, Chair, Department of Education.

Faculty: Full-time 3; part-time 4.

Degrees Awarded: 29 baccalaureate; 14 master's.

Admission Requirements. *Undergraduate.* Either graduation from accredited secondary school or GED; evaluation is based on cumulative grade point average; results of either SAT I or ACT composite; assessment of several personal areas (activi-

ties, leadership, and a desire to support the values of Westmont College. *Teacher education specific:* Acceptance into an undergraduate program major in Liberal Studies; 2.85 GPA or 2.75 GPA and passing score on California Basic Education Skills Test (CBEST); personal recommendations; faculty interview. *Graduate:* Baccalaureate degree from a regionally accredited institution. *Teacher education specific:* Personal interview, 2.85 GPA or 2.75 GPA and passing score on CBEST.

Fees and Expenses: Undergraduate $24,244 per academic year; graduate: $17,563. Required fees: $666. On-campus room and board: $8,378 per academic year.

Financial Aid: Resources specifically for eligible students enrolled in teacher education programs are awarded on the basis of financial need and academic merit. The institution has a Program Participation Agreement with the U.S. Department of Education for eligible students to receive Pell Grants and other federal aid. *Contact:* Diane Horvath at (805) 565-6061 or e-mail at dhorvath@westmont.edu.

Accreditation: *Regional:* WASC. *Approved by:* California Commission on Teacher Credentialing.

Undergraduate Programs: Students intending to teach at the elementary level normally pursue a major in liberal studies, fulfilling California requirements for multiple subject credential. Students intending to teach at the secondary level pursue an undergraduate major in the subject they wish to teach, fulfilling California requirements for single subject credential. Westmont has state-approved single subject programs in English, mathematics, history/social science, art, and kinesiology/physical education. With careful planning, it is possible for students to complete both the undergraduate major and the "fifth" year in four years of study.

Graduate Programs: The Department of Education offers a fifth year of postbaccalaureate study for teaching candidates at the elementary and secondary levels. In both cases, the program leads to an initial California teaching credential. The fifth year consists of 30 units of professional study.

Licensure/Reciprocity: California. Students seeking teaching certification in a state other than California should consult with that state's certification office early in their program of study to insure compliance with requirements. Many state directors of teacher credentialing have signed Interstate Agreements through NASDTEC that expedite the certification process.

COLORADO

ADAMS STATE COLLEGE

School of Education and Graduate Studies
Department of Teacher Education
208 Edgemont Boulevard
Alamosa, Colorado 81102
Phone: (719) 587-7776
Fax: (719) 587-7873
E-mail: asced@adams.edu
Internet: http://www.adams.edu

Institution Description: Adams State College was established as State Normal School at Alamosa in 1921. The name was changed to Adams State Normal School in 1923 and to Adams State Teachers College of Southern Colorado in 1929. The present name was adopted in 1945.

Programs of graduate study at Adams State College are based on a model of teachers as reflective decision-makers who demonstrate leadership in a professional manner.

Institution Control: Public.

Calendar: Semester. Academic year August to May.

Official(s): Dr. Barbara M. Medina, Department Chair.

Faculty: Full-time 12; adjunct 6.

Degrees Awarded: 187 master's.

Admission Requirements: *Undergraduate:* Graduation from an accredited secondary school with an overall 2.0 GPA; College Board SAT or ACT composite. *Teacher education specific:* Teacher candidates must successfully pass the appropriate content area exam prior to student teaching. *Graduate:* Baccalaureate degree from a regionally accredited institution; faculty interview. *Teacher education specific:* Completion of all licensure exam requirements; faculty interview; recommendations.

Fees and Expenses: In-state $2,384 per academic year; out-of-state $7,424. Other expenses: $1,775. On-campus room and board: $6,184. Books and supplies: $1,100.

Financial Aid: Resources specifically for eligible students enrolled in teacher education programs are awarded on the basis of financial need and academic merit. The institution has a Program Participation Agreement with the U.S. Department of Education for eligible students to receive Pell Grants and other federal aid. *Contact:* Financial Aid Office at: (719) 587-7306.

Accreditation: *Regional:* NCA. *Professional:* NCATE. *Member of:* AACTE. *Approved by:* Colorado Department of Education.

Undergraduate Programs: Initial licensure may be obtained in elementary, secondary, and K-12 programs. Adams State College has developed specific programs of study for each licensure area and several emphasis areas (elementary licensure), and content areas (secondary and K-12 licensure). The programs of study include the Bachelor of Arts interdisciplinary studies major and licensure courses for secondary education, K-12, and early childhood education. All baccalaureate programs require the completion of 120 semester hours.

Graduate Programs: Master of Arts programs are offered with areas of emphasis that include: literacy language and culture; educational leadership, special education, Masters PLUS, and literacy.

Licensure/Reciprocity: Colorado. Students seeking teaching certification in a state other than Colorado should consult with that state's certification office early in their program of study to insure compliance with requirements. Many state directors of teacher credentialing have signed Interstate Agreements through NASDTEC that expedite the certification process.

COLORADO COLLEGE

Education Department
14 East Cache La Poudre Street
Colorado Springs, Colorado 80903
Phone: (719) 389-6472
Fax: (719) 389-6473
E-mail: mendoza@coloradocollege.edu
Internet: http://www.coloradocollege.edu

Institution Description: Colorado College is a private, independent, nonprofit college. It was established, chartered, and offered first instruction at the postsecondary level in 1874.

Teacher education programs are offered at the undergraduate and graduate levels.

Institution Control: Private.

Calendar: Semester. Academic year September to May. Graduate students follow the block plan whereby each class is 3-1/2 weeks in length (equivalent to 4 semester hours).

Official(s): Dr. Charlotte Mendoza, Chair, Education Department.

Faculty: Full-time 3; part-time 6; adjunct 15.

Degrees Awarded: 57 master's.

Admission Requirements: *Undergraduate:* Graduation from an accredited secondary school with 16 academic units or GED; College Board SAT or ACT composite. *Teacher education specific:* 80 hours of observation and participation in local public schools; recommendation from two classroom teachers with whom the student has worked and from the department chair in the major; cumulative GPA of at least 2.5. *Graduate:* Baccalaureate degree from a regionally accredited institution; GRE; GPA of at least 2.7 in the major. *Teacher education specific:* Teacher endorsement; field experience; liberal arts background; academic recommendations.

Fees and Expenses: Undergraduate: $25,968 per academic year. Graduate: $18,546. health insurance: $895. On-campus room and board: $6,336 to $8,480. Books and supplies: $800 to $1,000. Teacher licensure fee and tests: $250.

Financial Aid: Resources specifically for eligible students enrolled in teacher education programs are awarded on the basis of financial need and academic merit. The institution has a Program Participation Agreement with the U.S. Department of Education for eligible students to receive Pell Grants and other federal aid. *Contact:* Marsh Unruh at (719) 389-6472.

Accreditation: *Regional:* NCA. *Member of:* AACTE. *Approved by:* Colorado Department of Education.

Undergraduate Programs: As an undergraduate at Colorado College, a student cannot major in education. If the student wishes to each secondary school, enrollment in a major in the area of interest is recommended and completion of the secondary teacher program. If elementary teaching is sought, a major in any liberal arts discipline should be pursued while completing the elementary teacher program.

Graduate Programs: The Master of Arts in Teaching (MAT) program is fourteen months of full-time enrollment. Furing the first summer of the secondary MAT program, the student completes his/her content background courses and writes an extended research paper. The first semester is devoted to reading and secondary school teaching methods and student teaching, then a full-time internship in a local school for a semester. During the second summer, additional education coursework is completed.

For the Elementary MAT program, the student will enroll during the first summer in social studies and language arts, science and health, and expressive arts teaching methods. One research paper is accomplished. The first semester is devoted to mathematics and reading methods courses and student teaching after which a full-time internship semester in a local school. During the second summer, additional coursework is completed.

Licensure/Reciprocity: Colorado. Students seeking teaching certification in a state other than Colorado should consult with that state's certification office early in their program of study to insure compliance with requirements. Many state directors of teacher credentialing have signed Interstate Agreements through NASDTEC that expedite the certification process.

COLORADO STATE UNIVERSITY

School of Education/Educator Licensing Program
111 Education
Fort Collins, Colorado 80523-2632
Phone: (970) 491-5292
Fax: (970) 491-2632
E-mail: teachinfo@cahs.colostate.edu
Internet: http://www.soe.cahs.colostate.edu

Institution Description: Colorado State University is a state institution and land-grant college. It was established as Agricultural College of Colorado in 1870. The name was changed to The Colorado State College of Agriculture and Mechanic Arts in 1935, to Colorado Agricultural and Mechanical College in 1951, and to its present name in 1957.

Teacher preparation programs at Colorado State serve the needs of individuals preparing to teach in academic areas (middle school, junior high, and high school) with additional specialty areas for grades K-12. The university is presently the only institution in Colorado designated to provide vocational credentialing programs.

Institution Control: Public.

Calendar: Semester. Academic year August to May.

Official(s): Dr. Rick Ginsberg, Director; Dr. Jean Lehmann, Associate Director, Graduate Programs; Dr. Dave Whaley, Associate Director, Educator Licensing.

Faculty: Full-time 38; part-time 28.

Degrees Awarded: 178 master's.

Admission Requirements: *Undergraduate:* Graduation from an accredited secondary school with 15 academic units; College Board SAT or ACT composite. *Teacher education specific:* Cumulative GPA of 2.75; basic skills proficiency; computer proficiency; documented work experience with school-age children; passing score on the PLACE Content Exam; recommendation from a key education adviser. *Graduate:* Baccalaureate degree from a regionally accredited institution; 3.0 GPA. *Teacher education specific:* Fulfill specific departmental exam/test requirements; faculty interview; letters of recommendation.

Fees and Expenses: Undergraduate in-state $1,453.95 per semester, out-of-state $6,689.88. Graduate in-state $1,674.82 per semester, out-of-state $6,977.70. Required fees: $418.20 per semester. On-campus room and board: $6,180. Books and supplies: $1,180.

Financial Aid: Resources specifically for eligible students enrolled in teacher education programs are awarded on the basis of financial need and academic merit. The institution has a Program Participation Agreement with the U.S. Department of Education for eligible students to receive Pell Grants and other federal aid. *Contact:* Financial Aid Office at: (970) 491-6321.

Accreditation: *Regional:* NCA. *Professional:* NCATE. *Member of:* AACTE. *Approved by:* Colorado Commission on Higher Education.

Undergraduate Programs: Professional education delivers twelve initial programs in secondary education, two K-12 programs in art and music, and a program in early childhood education. Teacher candidates attain a thorough level of academic competence in the theory and practice of their respective disciplines. Candidates enrolled in the initial program must complete an approved academic major. Most undergraduate degrees are restricted to a maximum of 120 credits.

The department provides teacher licensing and credentialing programs for career and technical education. Programs include agricultural education, business education, distributive education, home economics, and industrial arts.

Graduate Programs: Teacher candidates who have previous baccalaureate degrees, work experience, coursework compatible with a licensure area may pursue Project Promise, a 10-month teacher preparation program that provides intensive coursework integrated with multiple field experiences. The Teacher Education and Masters (TEAM) Program provides an opportunity for people who have a bachelor's degree and an interest in education to become instructional leaders while obtaining both a teaching license and a master's degree.

Licensure/Reciprocity: Colorado. Students seeking teaching certification in a state other than Colorado should consult with that state's certification office early in their program of study to insure compliance with requirements. Many state directors of teacher credentialing have signed Interstate Agreements through NASDTEC that expedite the certification process.

COLORADO STATE UNIVERSITY - PUEBLO

College of Education, Engineering, and Professional Studies
Teacher Education Program
2200 Bonforte Boulevard
Pueblo, Colorado 81001-4901
Phone: (719) 549-2039
Fax: (719) 549-2419
E-mail: info@uscolo.edu
Internet: http://www.uscolo.edu

Institution Description: Colorado State University - Pueblo, formerly University of Southern Colorado was established as the Southern Colorado Junior College and offered first instruction at the postsecondary level in 1933. The name was changed to Pueblo Junior College in 1937. In 1975, the Colorado General Assembly granted the institution university status and the name University of Southern Colorado was adopted. The present name became official in 2003.

The teacher education program is a university-wide responsibility. Content area experts participate in teacher training and contribute to the department's program.

Institution Control: Public.

Calendar: Semester. Academic year August to May.

Official(s): Dr. Victoria Marqueson, Director, Teacher Education.

Faculty: Full-time 6.

Degrees Awarded: 179 master's.

Admission Requirements: *Undergraduate:* Graduation from an accredited secondary school with GPA averages and SAT or ACT composite scores that place the student in the upper two thirds of graduating seniors. *Teacher education specific:* Application after 45 college hours; The Program for Licensing Assessment for Colorado Educators (PLACE) must be successfully completed before student teaching assignment. *Graduate:* Baccalaureate degree from a regionally accredited institution; *Teacher education specific:* pass all required departmental exams/tests; letters of recommendation; approved major; faculty interview.

Fees and Expenses: Undergraduate in-state $1,453.95 per semester, out-of-state $6,689.88. Graduate in-state $1,674.82 per semester, out-of-state $6,977.70. Required fees: $418.20 per semester. On-campus room and board: $6,184 per semester. Books and supplies: $1,180.

COLORADO STATE UNIVERSITY - PUEBLO—*cont'd*

Financial Aid: Resources specifically for eligible students enrolled in teacher education programs are awarded on the basis of financial need and academic merit. The institution has a Program Participation Agreement with the U.S. Department of Education for eligible students to receive Pell Grants and other federal aid. *Contact:* Financial Aid Office at: (719) 549-2753.

Accreditation: *Regional:* NCA. *Member of:* AACTE. *Approved by:* Colorado Department of Education.

Undergraduate Programs: In Colorado, students cannot major in education. Instead, they complete an academic major in the area in which they wish to teach. These programs include elementary education where teachers major in liberal studies preparing them to teach all subjects and minor in education. Secondary teachers (middle school and high school) major in English, mathematics, biology, chemistry, physics, history, political science, or Spanish. K-12 teachers can major in music education, art (teaching emphasis) or K-12 physical education (teaching emphasis).

The Teacher Education Program is responsible for managing and facilitating initial teacher licensure programs. A minor in Reading is offered that is intended for students in any licensure area who wish to have a recognized strength in the teaching of reading and other language arts.

Graduate Programs: There are currently cohort master's degree programs being offered on the CSU-Pueblo campus through Colorado State University. One program is designed to prepared educators for administrative licensure.

Licensure/Reciprocity: Colorado. Students seeking teaching certification in a state other than Colorado should consult with that state's certification office early in their program of study to insure compliance with requirements. Many state directors of teacher credentialing have signed Interstate Agreements through NASDTEC that expedite the certification process.

FORT LEWIS COLLEGE

School of Education
Teacher Education Department
1000 Rim Drive
Durango, Colorado 81301
Phone: (970) 247-7280
Fax: (970) 247-7184
E-mail: kennedy_j@fortlewis.edu
Internet: http://www.fortlewis.edu

Institution Description: Fort Lewis University was established as Fort Lewis School and chartered in 1911. It became Fort Lewis A&M College in 1948 and adopted its present name in 1964.

The Teacher Education Department offers baccalaureate programs leading to the teaching credential.

Institution Control: Public.

Calendar: Trimester. Academic year September to May.

Official(s): Dr. Ginny Engman, Dean, School of Education; Dr. Joe Lounge, Chair, Teacher Education Department.

Faculty: Full-time 8; part-time 3.

Degrees Awarded: 76 baccalaureate.

Admission Requirements: *Undergraduate:* Graduation from an accredited secondary school with 15 units or GED. *Teacher education specific:* 2.5 GPA; proof of working with children; completion of 30 hours of core courses; Program for Licensing Assessment for Colorado Educators (PLACE) must be successfully completed before student teaching assignment; faculty interview.

Fees and Expenses: Undergraduate: in-state $1,010 per term; out-of-state $5,280. Required fees: $384.25 per term. On-campus room: $1,507 to $2,600 per term; board: $487 to $1,325 per term. Books and supplies: $425 per term.

Financial Aid: Resources specifically for eligible students enrolled in teacher education programs are awarded on the basis of financial need and academic merit. The institution has a Program Participation Agreement with the U.S. Department of Education for eligible students to receive Pell Grants and other federal aid. *Contact:* Financial Aid Office at: 970 247-7184.

Accreditation: *Regional:* NCA. *Member of:* AACTE. *Approved by:* Colorado Department of Education.

Undergraduate Programs: Students seeking licensure in the early childhood (preschool, grades K-3) and Elementary (grades K-6) levels complete a baccalaureate degree and the required licensing sequence. Early childhood and elementary students are required to select the interdisciplinary studies major. Students have the option of adding English as a Second language or bilingual endorsements to this licensure.

Secondary and K-12 teachers concentrate on specific subject areas. They are also expected to participate in extracurricular activities such as coaching and advising the various clubs and organizations. Students seeking licensing with the secondary program (grades 7-12) or K-12 level, must complete a baccalaureate degree in an approved major with the required professional sequence with Colorado Department of Education endorsement standards. Endorsement in the secondary program are offered in biology, chemistry, English, geology, mathematics, physics, social studies, and Spanish. Students may earn add-on endorsement in bilingual education or English as a second language.

Licensure/Reciprocity: Colorado. Students seeking teaching certification in a state other than Colorado should consult with that state's certification office early in their program of study to insure compliance with requirements. Many state directors of teacher credentialing have signed Interstate Agreements through NASDTEC that expedite the certification process.

METROPOLITAN STATE COLLEGE OF DENVER

School of Professional Studies
Teacher Education Department
1006 Eleventh Street
P.O. Box 173362
Denver, Colorado 80217-3362
Phone: (303) 556-6228
Fax: (303) 556-6345
E-mail: tapiam@mscd.edu
Internet: http://www.mscd.edu

Institution Description: Metropolitan State College of Denver is a state institution that shares a campus and facilities with the Community College of Denver-Auraria Campus and the University of Colorado at Denver. It was established in 1963.

The Teacher Education programs integrate recent research, theory, and the practice. They are designed to meet the educational needs of school districts and they are coordinated with other academic departments, state educational agencies, and professional and learned societies.

Institution Control: Public.

Calendar: Semester. Academic year August to May.

Official(s): Dr. Larry Bettermann, Chair, Teacher Education Department.

Faculty: Full-time 30. part-time 25.

Degrees Awarded: 208 baccalaureate.

Admission Requirements: *Undergraduate:* Open enrollment. *Teacher education specific:* 2.5 GPA; basic skills in writing, mathematics, and oral communication; must have taken college-level math; Program for Licensing Assessment for Colorado Educators (PLACE) must be successfully completed before student teaching assignment.

Fees and Expenses: Undergraduate: in-state $3,315 per academic year, out-of-state $9,665. Other expenses: $1,775. On-campus room and board: $7,875. Books and supplies: $1,145.

Financial Aid: Resources specifically for eligible students enrolled in teacher education programs are awarded on the basis of financial need and academic merit. The institution has a Program Participation Agreement with the U.S. Department of Education for eligible students to receive Pell Grants and other federal aid. *Contact:* Cindy Hejl at (303) 556-4029.

Accreditation: *Regional:* NCA. *Professional:* NCATE. *Member of:* AACTE. *Approved by:* Colorado Department of Education.

Undergraduate Programs: The Teacher Education Department offers programs leading to the baccalaureate degree and licensure in early childhood, elementary education, secondary education, K-12 education, reading, special education, and bilingual education. All baccalaureate degrees require the completion of 120 to 130 semester hours and a 2.0 GPA.

Licensure/Reciprocity: Colorado. Students seeking teaching certification in a state other than Colorado should consult with that state's certification office early in their program of study to insure compliance with requirements. Many state directors of teacher credentialing have signed Interstate Agreements through NASDTEC that expedite the certification process.

REGIS UNIVERSITY
Education Department
Teacher Education Program
3333 Regis Boulevard
Denver, Colorado 80221-1099
Phone: (303) 458-4136
Fax: (303) 964-5534
E-mail: cross@regis.edu
Internet: http://www.regis.edu

Institution Description: Regis University is a nonprofit institution affiliated with the Society of Jesus. It was established as Las Vegas College in the New Mexico Territory in 1877 and in 1884 moved to Colorado as the College of the Sacred Heart. The name was changed to Regis College in 1921. The present name was adopted in 1991.

The teacher education program at Regis College is part of the Jesuit tradition that provides a value-centered liberal arts education.

Institution Control: Private.

Calendar: Semester. Academic year August to May.

Official(s): Dr. John Cross, Chair, Teacher Education Program.

Faculty: Full-time 0.

Degrees Awarded: 10 baccalaureate; 102 master's.

Admission Requirements: *Undergraduate:* Graduation from an accredited secondary school with 15 academic units or GED; College Board SAT or ACT composite. *Teacher education specific:* Minimum 2.5 GPA for prior college work; completion of specified education courses; faculty interview. Students must complete a major in an academic content area The Program for Licensing Assessment for Colorado Educators (PLACE) must be successfully completed before student teaching assignment. *Graduate:* Baccalaureate degree from a regionally accredited institution; approved major. *Teacher education specific:* Pass all required departmental exams/tests; teaching credential; letters of recommendation; faculty interview.

Fees and Expenses: Undergraduate: $20,700 per academic year; graduate $330 per credit hour. *Other expenses: $1,775. On-campus room and board: $7,600. Books and supplies: $1,145.*

Financial Aid: Resources specifically for eligible students enrolled in teacher education programs are awarded on the basis of financial need and academic merit. The institution has a Program Participation Agreement with the U.S. Department of Education for eligible students to receive Pell Grants and other federal aid. *Contact:* Financial Aid Office at: (303) 458-4066.

Accreditation: *Regional:* NCA. *Member of:* AACTE. *Approved by:* Colorado Department of Education.

Undergraduate Programs: Because all students must complete a major in an academic content area, students do not major in education at Regis University. All students successfully completing the teacher education program may be recommended for licensure at the appropriate grade levels. The programs leading to recommendation for licensure contain their own specific requirements. All baccalaureate degrees require the completion of 128 credit hours.

Graduate Programs: The Master of Arts in Education: Learning and Teaching program actively engages teachers in collaborative, reflective, and challenging learning experiences. The program requires completion of 30 hours.

The Master of Education is offered with many options for both aspiring and experienced educators who are seeking either a licensure or who already have a degree and wish to become licensed. In addition, options are available for teachers who wish to upgrade their skills and credentials.

Licensure/Reciprocity: Colorado. Students seeking teaching certification in a state other than Colorado should consult with that state's certification office early in their program of study to insure compliance with requirements. Many state directors of teacher credentialing have signed Interstate Agreements through NASDTEC that expedite the certification process.

UNIVERSITY OF COLORADO AT BOULDER
School of Education
UCB 249
Boulder, Colorado 80309-0030
Phone: (303) 492-6937
Fax: (303) 492-7115
E-mail: edadvise@colorado.edu
Internet: http://www.colorado.edu/education

Institution Description: The university was established and chartered in 1876 and offered first instruction at the postsecondary level in 1877.

The School of Education offers undergraduate licensure programs and graduate programs leading to the master of arts degrees in the areas within the Curriculum and Instruction Department.

Institution Control: Public.

Calendar: Semester. Academic year August to May.

Official(s): Dr. Lorrie A. Shepard, Dean; Dr. Jennie Whitcomb, Assistant Dean.

Faculty: Full-time 33; part-time 1; adjunct 40.

Degrees Awarded: 17 baccalaureate; 135 master's.

Admission Requirements: *Undergraduate:* High school diploma or equivalent; College Board SAT or ACT composite. *Teacher education specific:* 2.5 GPA; 56 hours completed or in progress; 25 hours of youth experience; math and verbal basic skills. *Graduate:* Baccalaureate degree; 2.75 GPA; academic preparation for advanced study. *Teacher education specific:* 2.75 overall GPA; 3.0 post-baccalaureate GPA; four references. The Program for Licensing Assessment for Colorado Educators (PLACE) must be successfully completed before student teaching assignment.

Fees and Expenses: Undergraduate: in-state $2,776 per academic year, $18,120 out-of-state. Graduate: $3,690 in-state, $18,120 out-of-state. Required fees: $791. On-campus room and board: $6,272. Books and supplies: $1,142. Other fees may apply.

Financial Aid: Resources specifically for eligible students enrolled in teacher education programs are awarded on the basis of financial need and academic merit. The institution has a Program Participation Agreement with the U.S. Department of Education for eligible students to receive Pell Grants and other federal aid. *Contact:* Sara McDonald at (303) 492-6937 or e-mail at sara.mcdonald@colorado.edu.

Accreditation: *Regional:* NCA. *Professional:* NCATE. *Member of:* AACTE. *Approved by:* Colorado Department of Education.

Undergraduate Programs: Undergraduate students may pursue a bachelor's degree by selecting a major that supports the teaching field and level to be sought. Majors in the elementary education track are: anthropology, astronomy, communications, distributed studies (biology, chemistry, geology), economics, English, geography, geology, history, humanities, linguistics, mathematics, political science, physics, psychology, and Spanish. The secondary education track includes English (communications, English, linguistics, Spanish); foreign language (French, German, Italian, Japanese, Latin, Russian, Spanish); mathematics; social studies; K-12 music. All licensure programs are

UNIVERSITY OF COLORADO AT BOULDER—*cont'd*

designed to provide committed and qualified students solid preparation in the liberal arts, an academic discipline, and education. Coursework and field experiences prepare the student for teaching in a diverse society.

Graduate Programs: The School of Education offers graduate study in four degree areas. Two of these are broad enough that they are further subdivided into specialized programs. In the Instruction and Curriculum program area it is possible to work on both a Masters degree and teacher certification in specified Masters Plus programs. In two of the program areas, Literacy and Educational and Cultural Diversity, it is possible to earn advanced teaching endorsements concurrent with work on the Masters degree.

The programs in Instruction and Curriculum focus most directly on the practice of teaching. Emphases in elementary education leading to the Master of Arts degree include elementary education, elementary mathematics education; bilingual/ESL education, and bilingual special education. The emphases in secondary education leading to the Master of Arts degree include alternative/experiential education, English education, mathematics education, science education, and social studies education. The Master of Arts Plus program in these areas include initial teacher certification (elementary or secondary).

Other master's programs include Social, Multicultural/Bilingual Foundations and Education/Psychology.

Licensure/Reciprocity: Colorado. Students seeking teaching certification in a state other than Colorado should consult with that state's certification office early in their program of study to insure compliance with requirements. Many state directors of teacher credentialing have signed Interstate Agreements through NASDTEC that expedite the certification process.

UNIVERSITY OF COLORADO AT COLORADO SPRINGS

College of Education
Teacher Education Program
1420 Austin Bluffs Parkway
P.O. Box 7150
Colorado Springs, Colorado 80933-7150
Phone: (719) 262-4111
Fax: (719) 262-4110
E-mail: dnelson@uccs.edu
Internet: http://www.uccs.edu

Institution Description: University of Colorado at Colorado Springs is a state institution. It was established, chartered, offered first instruction at the postsecondary level in 1965. The campus was known as the University of Colorado - Colorado Springs Center until 1972 when the present name was adopted.

Central features of the Teacher Education Program are the integration of education courses with field experiences. The program is based on a decision-making model of teaching by providing students with knowledge and experiences that will assist them in making their decisions as teachers. The program requires student to have experiences with diverse populations and in diverse settings.

Institution Control: Public.

Calendar: Semester. Academic year August to May.

Official(s): Dr. David Nelson, Department Chair.

Faculty: Full-time 40; part-time 60 (College of Education).

Degrees Awarded: 126 baccalaureate; 176 master's.

Admission Requirements: *Undergraduate:* Graduation with 16 units from an approved secondary school or GED; College Board SAT or ACT composite. *Teacher education specific:* Completion of PRAXIS I and II; content area major; oral interview. *Graduate:* Baccalaureate degree from a regionally accredited institution; GRE and MAT exam scores. *Teacher education specific:* Program for Licensing Assessment for Colorado Educators (PLACE) must be successfully completed,

Fees and Expenses: Undergraduate: in-state $2,776 per academic year, $18,120 out-of-state. Graduate: $3,690 in-state, $18,120 out-of-state. Required fees: $100. On-campus room and board: $6,272. Books and supplies: $800. Other fees may apply.

Financial Aid: Resources specifically for eligible students enrolled in teacher education programs are awarded on the basis of financial need and academic merit. The institution has a Program Participation Agreement with the U.S. Department of Education for eligible students to receive Pell Grants and other federal aid. *Contact:* Lee Ingles-Noble at (303) 262-3000 or e-mail at inoble@uccs.edu.

Accreditation: *Regional:* NCA. *Professional:* NCATE. *Member of:* AACTE. *Approved by:* Colorado Department of Education.

Undergraduate Programs: The undergraduate Teacher Education Program includes a one-year intensive, full-time program that leads to recommendation for licensure from the State of Colorado. The program consists of a total of 35 semester hours for secondary and 38 hours for elementary. The program consists of a combination of professional coursework that includes foundations of education, educational psychology, curriculum and methodology, and field experiences of over 800 hours in area partner schools and professional development school sites.

Graduate Programs: The Alternative Licensure Program (ALP) is a 12-month program of three semesters. The Elementary ALP requires 30 credit hours to complete the licensure portion; the secondary ALP requires 27 credit hours to complete the licensure portion. Licensure training is offered in the endorsement areas of: elementary K-6, secondary 7-12, English, mathematics, science, Spanish, social studies. The programs consist of professional coursework and resident teaching for an entire school year.

A Master of Arts in Curriculum and Instruction includes the coursework for the ALP and additional courses for the elementary or secondary track.

Licensure/Reciprocity: Colorado. Students seeking teaching certification in a state other than Colorado should consult with that state's certification office early in their program of study to insure compliance with requirements. Many state directors of teacher credentialing have signed Interstate Agreements through NASDTEC that expedite the certification process.

UNIVERSITY OF COLORADO AT DENVER

School of Education
CB 106, P.O. Box 173364
1250 14th Street
Denver, Colorado 80217-3364
Phone: (303) 556-2844
Fax: (303) 556-4479
E-mail: kim.pham@cudenver.edu
Internet: http://www.cudenver.edu

Institution Description: University of Colorado at Denver shares a campus and facilities with the Community College of Denver and Metropolitan State College of Denver. It was established and offered first instruction at the postsecondary level in 1912. The present name was adopted in 1972.

The School of Education in conjunction with the College of Liberal Arts and Sciences offers a collaborative program leading to the Bachelor of Arts degree and teacher licensure. Master's degree program in seven areas are also offered by the School of Education.

Institution Control: Public.

Calendar: Semester. Academic year June to May.

Official(s): Dr. Lynn K. Rhodes, Dean; Elizabeth Lozleski, Associate Dean.

Faculty: Full-time 50; part-time 85; adjunct 11.

Degrees Awarded: 255 baccalaureate; 381 master's.

Admission Requirements: *Undergraduate:* High School graduate or GED; College Board SAT or ACT composite. *Teacher education specific:* Students must with advisor; completion of at lest their core curriculum and 12 hours of major courses; 2.75 GPA; The Program for Licensing Assessment for Colorado Educators (PLACE) must be successfully completed before student teaching assignment. *Graduate:* GPA of 2.5 or better; standardized examinations; prior professional experience; portfolio. *Teacher education specific:* Applicant must meet specific departmental requirements; must be licensed teachers; faculty review.

Fees and Expenses: Undergraduate: in-state $1,514 per semester, $7,328 out-of-state. Graduate: $2,258 in-state, $8,537 out-of-state. Other fees apply depending on number of credits enrolled. No campus housing. Books and supplies: $300 to $400 per semester. Parking $3.25 per day.

Financial Aid: Resources specifically for eligible students enrolled in teacher education programs are awarded on the basis of financial need and academic merit. The institution has a Program Participation Agreement with the U.S. Department of Education for eligible students to receive Pell Grants and other federal aid. *Contact:* Ellie Miller at (303) 556-2886 or e-mail at ellie.miller@cudenver.edu.

Accreditation: *Regional:* NCA. *Professional:* NCATE. *Member of:* AACTE. *Approved by:* Colorado Department of Education.

Undergraduate Programs: The Initial Professional Teacher Education Program (IPTE) prepares elementary and secondary teachers for a variety of school settings through academic work, professional studies, classroom teaching experiences, and community field experiences. The program is a collaborative effort with the College of Liberal Arts and Sciences. A Bachelor of Arts degree is earned and leads to teacher licensure in elementary education (individual structured major); secondary social studies (history or political science major); secondary English (English major) and secondary math (math major).

Graduate Programs: The School of Education offers a doctoral program in Educational Leadership and Innovation, two Educational Specialist degrees, and master's degrees in seven program areas. Students in these degree programs may pursue a variety of state licenses for teaching and school administration, or may elect to earn these licenses with pursuing a graduate degree.

Licensure/Reciprocity: Colorado. Students seeking teaching certification in a state other than Colorado should consult with that state's certification office early in their program of study to insure compliance with requirements. Many state directors of teacher credentialing have signed Interstate Agreements through NASDTEC that expedite the certification process.

UNIVERSITY OF DENVER
College of Education
Teacher Education Program
2135 East Wesley Avenue
Denver, Colorado 80208
Phone: (303) 871-2503
Fax: (303) 871-3422
E-mail: ccmcconne@du.edu
Internet: http://www.du.edu

Institution Description: University of Denver is a private, independent, nonprofit institution. It was established and chartered as Colorado Seminary in 1864. The school closed in 1867 and reopened, offered first instruction at the postsecondary level, and adopted its present name in 1880.

The Teacher Education Program is a practice-oriented, integrated educational experience that prepares individuals to become classroom leaders who help all children learn at high levels.

Institution Control: Private.

Calendar: Quarter. Academic year September to June.

Official(s): Dr. Virginia Maloney, Dean.

Faculty: Full-time 20,

Degrees Awarded: 81 baccalaureate; 62 master's.

Admission Requirements: *Undergraduate:* Graduation from an accredited high school or GED; College Board SAT or ACT composite. *Teacher education specific:* Qualified undergraduate are eligible for the program after completion of a 40 credit hour elementary or secondary education minor. The Program for Licensing Assessment for Colorado Educators (PLACE) must

be successfully completed before student teaching assignment. *Graduate:* Baccalaureate degree from a regionally accredited institution; faculty interview; approved major.

Fees and Expenses: $23,250 per academic year. On-campus room and board: $6,987. Other expenses: $1,010. Books and supplies: $900.

Financial Aid: Resources specifically for eligible students enrolled in teacher education programs are awarded on the basis of financial need and academic merit. The institution has a Program Participation Agreement with the U.S. Department of Education for eligible students to receive Pell Grants and other federal aid. *Contact:* Financial Aid Office at: (303) 871-4900.

Accreditation: *Regional:* NCA. *Approved by:* Colorado Department of Education.

Undergraduate Programs: The Teacher Education Program is an intensive, 40 quarter credit hour, nine-month academic experience designed for individuals who already hold a bachelor's degree and seek a Colorado teaching license. Undergraduate students complete a 40 credit hour elementary or secondary minor. Licensure programs are offered for: elementary education (grades K-6); secondary education (grades 7-12); art education (grades K-12); and music education (grades K-12).

Graduate Programs: The Combined Licensure and Master's Program is a 52 quarter credit course of study that prepares individuals to teach in public schools while working toward a master's degree with an emphasis in teaching. The program is comprised of the Teacher Education Program described above, followed by 6 credits in curriculum leadership and 6 credits in one area of concentration (strand). Strand areas include aesthetic education, literacy, technology, urban education, and specialization in various content areas.

The Curriculum and Instruction Program prepares students to design and deliver quality education in formal and informal learning settings. Programs are offered through this program for students interested in a teaching license, an MA, or a PhD.

Licensure/Reciprocity: Colorado. Students seeking teaching certification in a state other than Colorado should consult with that state's certification office early in their program of study to insure compliance with requirements. Many state directors of teacher credentialing have signed Interstate Agreements through NASDTEC that expedite the certification process.

UNIVERSITY OF NORTHERN COLORADO
College of Education
Greeley, Colorado 80639
Phone: (970) 351-2817
Fax: (970) 351-2312
E-mail: marsha.stewart@unco.edu
Internet: http://www.unco.edu/coe

Institution Description: University of Northern Colorado is a state institution. It was established as State Normal School and offered first instruction at the postsecondary level 1889. The name was changed to Colorado State Teachers College in 1911, to Colorado State College of Education in 1935, to Colorado State College in 1957, and to its present name in 1970.

The College of Education offers Professional Teacher Preparation Programs that are designed to prepare teacher education candidates for licensure in Colorado.

Institution Control: Public.

Calendar: Semester. Academic year August to May.

Official(s): Dr. Eugene Sheean, Dean.

Faculty: Full-time 74; 8 adjunct full-time; 12 adjunct part-time.

Degrees Awarded: 17 baccalaureate; 216 master's.

Admission Requirements: *Undergraduate:* Admission is based upon academic criteria including the secondary school academic record, rank in class, standardized test scores (College Board SAT or ACT composite), and the academic record from all previous colleges the student may have attended. *Teacher education specific:* Sophomore status at time of application; completion of all prerequisite education courses; Program for Licensing Assessment for Colorado Educators (PLACE) must be successfully completed before student teaching assignment.

UNIVERSITY OF NORTHERN COLORADO—
cont'd

*Graduate:*Baccalaureate from a regionally accredited institution; GRE results; three letters of recommendation. *Teacher education specific:* Teaching credential; approved major; current resume that summarizes academic and professional experiences, activities, publications, and other pertinent information; written statement of career goals.

Fees and Expenses: Undergraduate in-state $1,145 per semester, out-of-state $5,292. Graduate in-state $1,554 per semester, out-of-state $5,634. Required fees: $418 per semester. On-campus room and board: $2,980 per semester. Books and supplies: $875.

Financial Aid: Resources specifically for eligible students enrolled in teacher education programs are awarded on the basis of financial need and academic merit. The institution has a Program Participation Agreement with the U.S. Department of Education for eligible students to receive Pell Grants and other federal aid. *Contact:* Sherril Bostron at (970 351-2502 or e-mail at sherrill.bostron@unco.edu.

Accreditation: *Regional:* NCA. *Professional:* NCATE. *Member of:* AACTE. *Approved by:* Colorado Department of Education.

Undergraduate Programs: The Professional Teacher Education Programs (PTEP) prepare teacher education candidates for the following Colorado State Board of Education approved licensure/endorsement: early childhood professional teacher education program; elementary professional teacher education program-interdisciplinary studies; middle grades professional teacher education program, 5-9—English, mathematics, social science, Spanish; secondary professional teacher education program, 7-12—biological sciences, chemistry, communication, earth sciences, English, foreign languages, geography, history, mathematics, physical science, physics, social science, theatre arts; K-12 professional teacher education program.

Licensure programs are offered in music education (K-12), physical education (K-12), theatre arts (secondary), and visual arts education (art, K-12). Credits required for the programs vary from 120 to 169 credit hours.

Graduate Programs: The Elementary Education Post-Baccalaureate Licensure Program is offered through the Graduate School. The program requires the completion of 48 credit hours of specified courses. The Colorado PLACE Test for elementary education must be passed prior to admission to the program.

Students seeking an added endorsement to teach at the elementary school level and wishing to count licensure hours toward a Master of Arts Teaching degree in elementary education must apply to the Graduate School for admission into the Master of Arts in Teaching degree program at the same time he/she applies to the Post-Baccalaureate Licensure program in elementary education.

The Principals' Licensure Program (non-degree) is designed according to the Standards for Principals through the Colorado Department of Education and State Board of Education. Program requirements include 27 semester hours of coursework including a field experience.

Licensure/Reciprocity: Colorado Students seeking teaching certification in a state other than Colorado should consult with that state's certification office early in their program of study to insure compliance with requirements. Many state directors of teacher credentialing have signed Interstate Agreements through NASDTEC that expedite the certification process.

CONNECTICUT

CENTRAL CONNECTICUT STATE UNIVERSITY

School of Education and Professional Studies
Department of Teacher Education

Barnard Hall
1615 Stanley Street
New Britain, Connecticut 06050
Phone: (860) 832-2110
Fax: (860) 832-2109
E-mail: hoffmann@ccsu.edu
Internet: http://www.ccsu.edu

Institution Description: Central Connecticut State University was established as New Britain Normal School in 1849. It became a 4-year institution and changed name to Teachers College of Connecticut in 1933. The name was changed to Central Connecticut State College in 1959 and the present name was adopted in 1983.

The aim of programs in the School of Education and Professional Studies is to prepare individuals who are both liberally educated and in command of the requisite professional knowledge to be able to provided exemplary practice in their chosen field.

Institution Control: Public.

Calendar: Semester. Academic year August to May.

Official(s): Dr. Nancy Hoffman, Chair, Department of Teacher Education.

Faculty: Full-time 17.

Degrees Awarded: 200 baccalaureate; 511 master's.

Admission Requirements: *Undergraduate:* Either graduation with at least 13 units of college preparatory work; GED will be considered; College Board SAT or ACT composite. *Teacher education specific:* Student must choose an undergraduate major compatible with the field in which he/she wishes to teach. *Graduate:* Baccalaureate degree from a regionally accredited institution; completion of all required tests/examinations; GRE. *Teacher education specific:* Letters of recommendation; faculty interview.

Fees and Expenses: In-state $5,960 per academic year required fees; out-of-state $12,918. On-campus room: $3,918; board: $3,132. Books and supplies: $800 per semester.

Financial Aid: Resources specifically for eligible students enrolled in teacher education programs are awarded on the basis of financial need and academic merit. The institution has a Program Participation Agreement with the U.S. Department of Education for eligible students to receive Pell Grants and other federal aid. *Contact:* Financial Aid Office at: (860) 832-2200.

Accreditation: *Regional:* NEASC. *Professional:* NCATE. *Member of:* AACTE. *Approved by:* Connecticut Department of Education.

Undergraduate Programs: Undergraduate Programs are offered with concentration in the areas of early childhood, elementary education, and secondary education (PK-12 teachers in special subject fields). All baccalaureate degree programs require the completion of core courses, a major, and required courses in education. A total of 122 to 130 credit hours is required depending on program pursued. Students who complete a teacher education program and complete a certification application may be recommended by the university's certification office but the final decision is that of the Connecticut Department of Education, Bureau of Certification and Professional Development.

Graduate Programs: Graduate programs leading to the Master of Teaching in Education degree are offered in the areas of early childhood education, elementary education, secondary education, and educational foundations. Each program has their own specific course requirements.

The Department also offers post-baccalaureate students a Summer-through-Summer program that results in initial elementary education teacher certification and 21 hours toward a master's degree.

Licensure/Reciprocity: Connecticut. Students seeking teaching certification in a state other than Connecticut should consult with that state's certification office early in their program of study to insure compliance with requirements. Many state directors of teacher credentialing have signed Interstate Agreements through NASDTEC that expedite the certification process.

EASTERN CONNECTICUT STATE UNIVERSITY

School of Education and Professional Studies
Education Department

Charles R. Webb Hall 164
83 Windham Street
Willimantic, Connecticut 06226
Phone: (860) 465-4530
Fax: (860) 465-4485
E-mail: Coopert@easternct.edu
Internet: http://www.easternct.edu

Institution Description: Eastern Connecticut State University was established as Willimantic Normal School in 1889. The name was changed to Willimantic State Teachers College in 1937. The name was changed to Willimantic State College in 1959 and to its present name in 1982.

The Education Department offers certification programs in the areas of early childhood education, elementary education, secondary education. A physical education program is offered through the Health and Physical Education Department.

Institution Control: Public.

Calendar: Semester. Academic year August to May.

Official(s): Dr. Patricia A. Kleine, Dean; Dr. Tuesday L. Cooper, Associate Dean; Dr. David L. Stoloff, Chair, Education Department.

Faculty: Full-time 27, adjunct 31.

Degrees Awarded: 47 baccalaureate; 64 master's.

Admission Requirements: *Undergraduate:* Graduation from an accredited secondary school or GED; College Board SAT or ACT composite. *Teacher education specific:* All undergraduate students must complete an undergraduate major besides education. *Graduate:* Baccalaureate from an accredited institution in an approved major. *Teacher education specific:* Undergraduate GPA of at least 2.70; passing of the Praxis I Test; essay on teaching and professional commitment; 3 letters of reference; faculty interview.

EASTERN CONNECTICUT STATE UNIVERSITY—*cont'd*

Fees and Expenses: In-state $5,960 per academic year including required fees; out-of-state $12,918. On-campus room: $3,918; board: $3,132. Books and supplies: $800 per semester.

Financial Aid: Resources specifically for eligible students enrolled in teacher education programs are awarded on the basis of financial need and academic merit. The institution has a Program Participation Agreement with the U.S. Department of Education for eligible students to receive Pell Grants and other federal aid. *Contact:* Kenneth Briggs, Financial Aid Office, Unit Supervisor at: (860) 405-4432.

Accreditation: *Regional:* NEASC. *Member of:* AACTE. *Approved by:* Connecticut Department of Education.

Undergraduate Programs: All undergraduate students seeking teacher certification must complete an academic major besides education, a minimum of 39 credits in general academic courses, a United States history survey course, and a health course. Certification programs are usually three or four semesters in length. There are specific program prerequisites that must be completed in the programs for early childhood education, middle level education and secondary education in the areas of mathematics, general sciences, biology, environmental earth science, history/social studies, and English. All baccalaureate degree programs require the completion of a minimum of 120 semester hours.

Graduate Programs: The Education Department offers two certification programs at the graduate level to meet the changing needs of Connecticut schools. The early childhood education certification/Master of Science program is designed for people interested in advanced studies in early childhood education and in teaching in preschool programs and in grades K-3. The elementary education certification/Master of Science in education program is designed for individuals interested in a program in graduate studies and intensive field experiences leading to certification for grades 1-6.

The Master of Science in secondary education program is designed to include a strong core of graduate education courses. The program also includes studies in curricular topics, reflecting the practitioner-orientation. The program, with or without certification, is offered in the subject areas of mathematics, history/social studies, English, biology, and earth science.

Licensure/Reciprocity: Connecticut. Students seeking teaching certification in a state other than Connecticut should consult with that state's certification office early in their program of study to insure compliance with requirements. Many state directors of teacher credentialing have signed Interstate Agreements through NASDTEC that expedite the certification process.

FAIRFIELD UNIVERSITY

Graduate School of Education and Allied Professions
1073 North Benson Road
Fairfield, Connecticut 06824-5195
Phone: (203) 254-4000
Fax: (203) 254-4199
E-mail: admis@fairfield.edu
Internet: http://www.fairfield.edu

Institution Description: Fairfield University is a private, non-profit Jesuit institution. It was founded as Fairfield University with a preparatory school in 1942.

The Graduate School of Education and Allied Professions offers undergraduates, graduate students, and continuing education students a well-rounded education distinguished by real-world opportunities within and beyond the classroom.

Institution Control: Private.

Calendar: Semester. Academic year September to May.

Official(s): Dr. Margaret Deigman, Dean.

Faculty: Full-time 18.

Degrees Awarded: 132 master's.

Admission Requirements: *Undergraduate:* Graduation from an accredited secondary school with 15 academic units; College Board SAT or ACT composite. *Teacher education specific:* Students pursue an academic major in liberal studies. *Graduate:* Baccalaureate degree from a regionally accredited institution; GRE. *Teacher education specific:* Successful completion of PRAXIS I Test; letters of recommendation; faculty interview.

Fees and Expenses: Undergraduate: $25,560 per academic year; graduate: $410 per credit hour. On-campus room and board: $8,560. Other expenses: $2,000. Books and supplies: $800.

Financial Aid: Resources specifically for eligible students enrolled in teacher education programs are awarded on the basis of financial need and academic merit. The institution has a Program Participation Agreement with the U.S. Department of Education for eligible students to receive Pell Grants and other federal aid. *Contact:* Financial Aid Office at: (203) 254-4125.

Accreditation: *Regional:* NEASC. *Member of:* AACTE. *Approved by:* Connecticut Department of Education.

Undergraduate Programs: The undergraduate program in education is conducted in collaboration with the Graduate School of Education and Allied Professions and affords undergraduates the opportunity to seek an initial teaching certificate at the secondary school level (grades 7-12). Students pursue a liberal arts major and a minor in education. Through this program, students may be certified in one of the following areas: English, history/social studies, natural sciences, mathematics, or languages (modern or ancient). All baccalaureate degree programs require completion of 120 credit hours including general education courses, core courses, and major/minor courses.

Graduate Programs: Master of Arts degree programs with teacher certification are offered in the areas of bilingual education, elementary education, secondary education, special education, English as a second language. Most programs require the completion of 33 credit hours.

Licensure/Reciprocity: Connecticut. Students seeking teaching certification in a state other than Connecticut should consult with that state's certification office early in their program of study to insure compliance with requirements. Many state directors of teacher credentialing have signed Interstate Agreements through NASDTEC that expedite the certification process.

MITCHELL COLLEGE

Education Department
437 Pequot Avenue
New Haven, Connecticut 06320
Phone: (860) 701-5153
Fax: (860) 701-5706
E-mail: strader_w@mitchell.edu
Internet: http://www.mitchell.edu

Institution Description: Mitchell College was founded in 1938 as New London Junior College on the waterfront estate of Alfred Mitchell. In 1950 the name of the college was changed to Mitchell College to honor the Mitchell family. The college is now a four-year institution offering associate and baccalaureate programs.

The college offers degree programs in the field of education leading to the bachelor of science degree.

Institution Control: Private.

Calendar: Semester. Academic year August to May.

Official(s): Dr. William H. Strader, Department Chair.

Faculty: Full-time 3; adjunct 6.

Degrees Awarded: 3 baccalaureate.

Admission Requirements: *Undergraduate:* Graduation from an accredited high school or GED; College Board SAT or ACT composite. *Teacher education specific:* Letters of recommendation; faculty interview.

Fees and Expenses: Full-time resident comprehensive fee $25,141; commuter student $17,266.

Financial Aid: Resources specifically for eligible students enrolled in teacher education programs are awarded on the basis of financial need and academic merit. The institution has a

Program Participation Agreement with the U.S. Department of Education for eligible students to receive Pell Grants and other federal aid. *Contact:* : Jachlyn Stolz at (860) 701-5040 or e-mail at stolz_j@mitchell.edu.

Accreditation: *Regional:* NEASC. *Approved by:* Connecticut Department of Education.

Undergraduate Programs: The early childhood education program combines theory, research, and practice with a strong liberal arts background in addition to specialized courses in child development. The baccalaureate program with emphasis in Human Development and Family Studies is a four-year program culminating in the Observation and Student Teaching I (N-K) and II (1st-3rd grade) where students are students are conducting their full-time student teaching experiences. Total credits for graduation with a Bachelor of Science degree range from 122 to 128 credit hours.

The baccalaureate program with emphasis in psychology requires completion of 128 credit hours and leads to the Bachelor of Science degree with teaching credential. The PRAXIS Pre-Professional Skills Test is required for all teacher certification candidates.

Licensure/Reciprocity: Connecticut. Students seeking teaching certification in a state other than Connecticut should consult with that state's certification office early in their program of study to insure compliance with requirements. Many state directors of teacher credentialing have signed Interstate Agreements through NASDTEC that expedite the certification process.

QUINNIPIAC UNIVERSITY

Division of Education
275 Mount Carmel Avenue
Hamden, Connecticut 06518-0569
Phone: (203) 582-8200
Fax: (203) 582-8201
E-mail: Anne.Dichele@quinnipiac.edu
Internet: http://www.quinnipiac.edu

Institution Description: Quinnipiac University is a private, independent, nonprofit college. It was incorporated as Connecticut College of Commerce in New Haven and offered first instruction at the postsecondary level in 1929. The present name was adopted in 1951 and the college merged with Larson College in 1952. The campus was moved to its present location in 1966.

The purpose of division's five-year program is to prepare graduates with the perspectives, knowledge and skills to become master educators.

Institution Control: Private.

Calendar: Semester. Academic year August to May.

Official(s): Dr. Cynthia Dubea, Dean; Dr. Anne M. Dichele, Director, Elementary/MA Program; Dr. Gloria Holmes, Director, Middle-Secondary/MA Program.

Faculty: Full-time 6; adjunct 30.

Degrees Awarded: 77 master's.

Admission Requirements: *Undergraduate:* Graduation with 16 units from an accredited secondary school or equivalent; College Board SAT or ACT composite. *Teacher education specific:* Students choose an appropriate liberal arts major in the area in which they wish to teach. *Graduate:* Baccalaureate degree from a regionally accredited institution. *Teacher education specific:* Students holding a baccalaureate degree may enter the fifth-year program that leads to the teaching credential and the Master of Arts degree; letters of recommendation; faculty interview.

Fees and Expenses: $20,200 per academic year. Required fees: $920. On-campus room and board: $9,450. Other expenses: $1,325. Books and supplies: $600.

Financial Aid: Resources specifically for eligible students enrolled in teacher education programs are awarded on the basis of financial need and academic merit. The institution has a Program Participation Agreement with the U.S. Department of Education for eligible students to receive Pell Grants and other

federal aid. Master of Arts in Teaching students may choose paid internships which greatly reduce their overall costs. *Contact:* Financial Aid Office at: (205) 582-8750.

Accreditation: *Regional:* NEASC. *Member of:* AACTE. *Approved by:* Connecticut Department of Education.

Undergraduate Programs: The Five-Year BA/MAT Program offers students a bachelor's degree in an academic major and a Master of Arts in Teaching degree leading to certification through the Connecticut State Department of Education. The program is divided into a two-year pre-professional component and a three-year professional component that begins in the fall semester of their junior year. Supervised fieldwork includes undergraduate observation and fieldwork, a graduate internship, and student teaching. Following completion of the fourth year of study, students receive a Bachelor of Arts degree in their academic major.

Graduate Programs: The Master of Arts in Teaching degree is awarded upon completion of the fifth-year of the Five-Year BA/MAT Program. Students may concentrate in elementary education, middle school education, or secondary education. Specific requirements must be completed in the various program areas. The teaching credential is awarded by the Connecticut State Department of Education.

Licensure/Reciprocity: Connecticut. Students seeking teaching certification in a state other than Connecticut should consult with that state's certification office early in their program of study to insure compliance with requirements. Many state directors of teacher credentialing have signed Interstate Agreements through NASDTEC that expedite the certification process.

SOUTHERN CONNECTICUT STATE UNIVERSITY

School of Education
Davis Hall 103
501 Crescent Street
New Haven, Connecticut 06515-1355
Phone: (203) 392-5900
Fax: (203) 392-5908
E-mail: garfieldj@southernct.edu
Internet: http://www.southernct.edu

Institution Description: Southern Connecticut State University is a public institution. It was established and chartered as New Haven Normal School and offered first instruction at the postsecondary level in 1893. It became New Haven State Teachers College, a four-year college, in 1937. The present name was adopted in 1959.

Institution Control: Public.

Calendar: Semester. Academic year August to May.

Official(s): Dr. James Garfield, Dean

Faculty: Full-time 13 (Graduate Studies, Education).

Degrees Awarded: 184 baccalaureate; 410 master's.

Admission Requirements: *Undergraduate:* Graduation with 16 units from an accredited secondary school or GED; minimum 2.7 GPA; College Board SAT. *Teacher education specific:* Pass PRAXIS I; letters of recommendation; entry portfolio; essay; faculty interview. *Graduate:* Baccalaureate degree from a regionally accredited institution; undergraduate GPA 2.5. *Teacher education specific:* Pass PRAXIS I; letters of recommendation; entry portfolio; essay; faculty interview.

Fees and Expenses: In-state $5,960 per academic year including required fees; out-of-state $12,918. On-campus room: $3,918; board: $3,132. Books and supplies: $800 per semester.

Financial Aid: Resources specifically for eligible students enrolled in teacher education programs are awarded on the basis of financial need and academic merit. The institution has a Program Participation Agreement with the U.S. Department of Education for eligible students to receive Pell Grants and other federal aid. *Contact:* Avon Dennis at (203) 392-5222.

Accreditation: *Regional:* NEASC. *Professional:* NCATE. *Member of:* AACTE. *Approved by:* Connecticut Department of Education.

SOUTHERN CONNECTICUT STATE UNIVERSITY—cont'd

Undergraduate Programs: Rather than pursue a traditional major, the highly focused students in the Liberal Studies Program combine a number of established minors to create a unique educational experience that meets their academic, personal, and career goals. Students majoring in elementary education and elementary/special education may choose Liberal Studies as a subject-area major. Minors may be pursued in any subject areas except those offered by the School of Education. Students complete two eight-week student teaching experiences. All baccalaureate degree programs required the completion of 122 credit hours.

Graduate Programs: The School of Education offers certification programs and graduate degrees in early childhood education, elementary education, and cross endorsement courses for middle grades education. Programs are offered leading to certification in early childhood and elementary education for those holding a bachelors degree and who wish to become certified teachers in Connecticut.

The Departments of Education and Special Education jointly offer the collaborative early childhood teacher certification program at the graduate level. Students may specialize in either birth to kindergarten or nursery to grade 3.

A Master of Science degree with a specialization for regular classroom teachers is offered to those who are already certified and hold a bachelor's degree.

Licensure/Reciprocity: Connecticut. Students seeking teaching certification in a state other than Connecticut should consult with that state's certification office early in their program of study to insure compliance with requirements. Many state directors of teacher credentialing have signed Interstate Agreements through NASDTEC that expedite the certification process.

UNIVERSITY OF CONNECTICUT

Neag School of Education
Teacher Education Program

249 Glenbrook Road
Storms, Connecticut 06269
Phone: (860) 486-0287
Fax: (860) 486-0210
E-mail: education@uconn.edu
Internet: http://www.uconn.edu

Institution Description: The University of Connecticut was established and chartered as Storrs Agricultural School and offered first instruction at the postsecondary level in 1881. The present name was adopted in 1939.

The Neag School of Education offers integrated baccalaureate and master's teacher preparation programs. These curricula integrate coursework, school-based clinical experiences, and university and K-12 faculty in the preparation of pre-service teachers.

Institution Control: Public.

Calendar: Semester. Academic year September to May.

Official(s): Dr. Richard Schwab, Dean; Dr. Thomas DeFranco, Associate Dean; Dr. Jean McGivney-Burrelle, Director of Teacher Education Program.

Faculty: Full-time 18.

Degrees Awarded: 114 baccalaureate; 211 master's.

Admission Requirements: *Undergraduate:* Graduation from an accredited high school; College Board SAT 1 or ACT composite; residency affidavit. *Teacher education specific:* Sufficient credits to be eligible; Connecticut testing requirement; experience working with children; written essays; recommendations; competitive GPA. *Graduate:* Baccalaureate from a regionally accredited college; official transcripts; GPA 3.0; GRE test scores; three letters of reference. *Teacher education specific:* PRAXIS I test results; personal statement; faculty interview; three references.

Fees and Expenses: Undergraduate: in-state $5,260 per academic year; out-of-state $16,044. Graduate: in-state $6,478 per academic year; out-of-state $16,830. On-campus room and board: $7,000 (average) per academic year. Books and supplies: $800.

Financial Aid: Resources specifically for eligible students enrolled in teacher education programs are awarded on the basis of financial need and academic merit. The institution has a Program Participation Agreement with the U.S. Department of Education for eligible students to receive Pell Grants and other federal aid. *Contact:* Jean Main, Director, Financial Aid at (860) 486-6231.

Accreditation: *Regional:* NEASC. *Professional:* NCATE. *Member of:* AACTE. *Approved by:* Connecticut Department of Education.

Undergraduate Programs: The Integrated Bachelor's/Master's (IB/M) Teacher Preparation Program is a five-year comprehensive teacher preparation program. Students enter the IB/M program in their junior year and are enrolled in the program for three years, earning both a bachelor's and a master's degree. Students who complete the requirements and also successfully complete Connecticut's essential skills and subject knowledge testing requirements qualify for the university's recommendation to teach in Connecticut and elsewhere. Available subject areas include: elementary (grades 1-6), special education (grades K-12), English (grades 7-12), history/social studies (grades 7-12), mathematics (grades 7-12), science (grades 7-12), agriculture (pre K-12), foreign language (pre K-12), and music (pre K-12).

Graduate Programs: The Teacher Certification Program for College Graduates (TCPCG) is one of two teacher certification programs offered. The program is offered at the Stamford and Hartford Branches only. TCPCG students enter the program after obtaining a bachelor's degree in an appropriate area. Program subject areas include: agriculture education (K-12), English education (grades 7-12), foreign language (grades K-12 in French, German, Italian, Latin, Spanish), history/social studies (grades 7-12), mathematics education (grades 7-12); science education (grades 7-12 in biology, chemistry, earth science, general science, physics), special education (grades K-12).

Licensure/Reciprocity: Connecticut. Students seeking teaching certification in a state other than Connecticut should consult with that state's certification office early in their program of study to insure compliance with requirements. Many state directors of teacher credentialing have signed Interstate Agreements through NASDTEC that expedite the certification process.

UNIVERSITY OF HARTFORD

College of Education, Nursing, and Health Professions
Division of Education

Hillyer Hall 252
200 Bloomfield Avenue
West Hartford, Connecticut 06117
Phone: (860) 768-4520
Fax: (860) 768-5197
E-mail: remiller@hartford.edu
Internet: http://www.hartford.edu

Institution Description: The University of Hartford is a private, independent, nonprofit institution. It was chartered as the University of Hartford by the union of Hartford Art School (established 1877), Hillyer College (established 1879), and Hartt College of Music (established 1920).

The Division of Education offers both undergraduate and graduate teacher education programs.

Institution Control: Private.

Calendar: Semester. Academic year September to May.

Official(s): Dr. Regina Miller, Division Chair.

Faculty: Full-time 17; adjunct 21.

Degrees Awarded: 69 baccalaureate; 112 master's.

Admission Requirements: *Undergraduate:* Graduation from an accredited secondary school or GED; College Board SAT or ACT composite. *Teacher education specific:* 2.67 GPA; pass PRAXIS I; letters of recommendation. *Graduate:* Baccalaureate degree from an accredited institution; approved major. *Teacher education specific:* 2.67 GPA; pass PRAXIS I; letters of recommendation; faculty interview.

Fees and Expenses: $20,410 per academic year. Required fees: $741. On-campus room and board: $8,200 to $10,000. Books and supplies: $1,600.

Financial Aid: Resources specifically for eligible students enrolled in teacher education programs are awarded on the basis of financial need and academic merit. The institution has a Program Participation Agreement with the U.S. Department of Education for eligible students to receive Pell Grants and other federal aid. *Contact:* Financial Aid Office at: (860) 708-4296 or e-mail at finaid@hartford.edu.

Accreditation: *Regional:* NEASC. *Professional:* NCATE. *Member of:* AACTE. *Approved by:* Connecticut Department of Education.

Undergraduate Programs: The Early Education Program includes a study of the theoretical and practical aspects of the physical, intellectual, language, social/emotional, and creative needs of young children. Students participate in a placement with children in nursery school or kindergarten and complete another placement in either birth to age 3 or grades 1, 2, and 3.

Students in the Elementary Education Program complete a subject major in any discipline offered by the university or an interdisciplinary behavioral studies major. The professional core comprises two full semesters of integrated professional practicum experience and one full semester of student teaching in public school settings. Students have the option to enroll in a program that integrates a special education core and leads to a dual certificate.

The Integrated Elementary Education and Special Education Program is a professional preparation program that gives an in-depth understanding of disabilities in addition to knowledge of the developmental, academic, and social needs of all children of elementary school age. The program features a planned sequence of coursework, independent study, field observations, student teaching, conferences, lectures, and other educational experiences. Upon successful completion of coursework and specified PRAXIS II examinations, a recommendation of the university leads to teacher certification in special education (grades 1-12) and elementary education (grades 1-6).

The secondary education teaching endorsement area in English is possible for students who complete the program in secondary education. The core of the program features a full semester of integrated instruction and experience in an urban or suburban public school setting.

Graduate Programs: The Elementary Education Program is designed to prepare teachers at the graduate level to work with students in elementary schools. The program focuses on the content of elementary education as well as the pedagogy of teaching students in this age group. Upon completion of coursework, a comprehensive exam and the PRAXIS II exam(s), candidates are recommended for certification in their area.

The Early Childhood Education Program is designed to prepare teachers at the graduate level to work in school settings with all children between birth and kindergarten and/or nursery and third grade. The program focuses on an inclusion model and prepares the student to work with families, provide for the integration of children and services, and to collaborate with other professionals. Upon completion of coursework and a comprehensive exam, candidates will be recommended for certification in their programs of study.

Licensure/Reciprocity: Connecticut. Students seeking teaching certification in a state other than Connecticut should consult with that state's certification office early in their program of study to insure compliance with requirements. Many state directors of teacher credentialing have signed Interstate Agreements through NASDTEC that expedite the certification process.

WESTERN CONNECTICUT STATE UNIVERSITY

School of Professional Studies
Education and Educational Psychology Department
West Side Campus, Room 249
181 White Street
Danbury, Connecticut 06810-6860
Phone: (203) 837-8510
Fax: (203) 837-8413
E-mail: cordy@wcsu.edu
Internet: http://www.wcsu.edu

Institution Description: Western Connecticut State University was established as Danbury State Normal School in 1903. It became Danbury State Teachers College in 1937 and its name was changed name to Danbury State College in 1959. It was named Western Connecticut State College in 1967 and attained university status and its present name in 1983.

The Education and Educational Psychology Department offers teacher education programs in elementary education and secondary education.

Institution Control: Public.

Calendar: Semester. Academic year September to May.

Official(s): Dr. Thomas Cordy, Dean, Education and Educational Psychology Department.

Faculty: Full-time 9.

Degrees Awarded: 47 baccalaureate; 64 master's.

Admission Requirements: *Undergraduate:* Graduation with 14 units from an accredited secondary school or GED; College Board SAT or ACT composite. *Teacher education specific:* Application to the teacher education programs as early in the students undergraduate study and upon determining that teaching is the career goal. *Graduate:* Baccalaureate degree from a regionally accredited institution. *Teacher education specific:* Approved undergraduate major; letters of recommendation; essay; faculty interview.

Fees and Expenses: In-state $5,960 per academic year including required fees; out of state $12,918. On campus room: $3,910, board: $3,132. Books and supplies: $800 per semester.

Financial Aid: Resources specifically for eligible students enrolled in teacher education programs are awarded on the basis of financial need and academic merit. The institution has a Program Participation Agreement with the U.S. Department of Education for eligible students to receive Pell Grants and other federal aid. *Contact:* Financial Aid Office at: (203) 837-8580.

Accreditation: *Regional:* NEASC. *Member of:* AACTE. *Approved by:* Connecticut Department of Education.

Undergraduate Programs: The baccalaureate program in elementary education includes subject areas in American studies, anthropology/sociology, biology, communication, English, English-writing option, history, mathematics, political science, psychology, social sciences, and Spanish. Students must complete a specified curriculum that includes core courses, professional preparation courses, and student teaching assignment. All baccalaureate degrees require the completion of 120 to 123 semester hours.

Graduate Programs: The Master of Science in Education Program is offered with concentrations in English and mathematics. Options are available in curriculum, instructional technology, reading (non-certification) and special education.

Graduate level Teacher Certification Only Programs are designed for individuals holding a bachelor's degree from an accredited institution and who are seeking to earn initial teacher certification in Connecticut or New York.

Licensure/Reciprocity: Connecticut. Students seeking teaching certification in a state other than Connecticut should consult with that state's certification office early in their program of study to insure compliance with requirements. Many state directors of teacher credentialing have signed Interstate Agreements through NASDTEC that expedite the certification process.

DELAWARE

DELAWARE STATE UNIVERSITY

College of Education and Human Performance
Education and Humanities Building 245
1200 North DuPont Highway
Dover, Delaware 19901
Phone: (302) 857-6720
Fax: (302) 857-6722
E-mail: dwooledg@dsc.edu
Internet: http://www.dsc.edu

Institution Description: Delaware State University, formerly named Delaware State College, is a state institution founded in 1891. It offered first instruction at the postsecondary level in 1892 and awarded its first degree in 1893.

The Education Department provides teacher education curricula for teacher preparation programs at the undergraduate and graduate levels.

Institution Control: Public.

Calendar: Semester. Academic year September to May.

Official(s): Dr. Doris E. Wooledge, Dean; Dr. Joseph Falodun, Chair.

Faculty: Full-time 16.

Degrees Awarded: 31 baccalaureate; 10 master's.

Admission Requirements: *Undergraduate:* Either graduation with 15 units from an accredited secondary school or GED. *Teacher education specific:* Student should make application for the Education Department by the end of the sophomore year; must pass PRAXIS I test. *Graduate:* Baccalaureate degree from a regionally accredited institution; GRE. *Teacher education specific:* Must pass all departmental/state tests/examinations; teaching credential; faculty interview.

Fees and Expenses: $3,956 in-state per academic year; $8,752 out-of-state. On-campus room and board: $6,178. Other expenses: $3,806. Books and supplies: $1,050.

Financial Aid: Resources specifically for eligible students enrolled in teacher education programs are awarded on the basis of financial need and academic merit. The institution has a Program Participation Agreement with the U.S. Department of Education for eligible students to receive Pell Grants and other federal aid. *Contact:* Financial Aid Office at: (302) 857-6250.

Accreditation: *Regional:* MSA. *Professional:* NCATE. *Member of:* AACTE. *Approved by:* Delaware State Department of Education.

Undergraduate Programs: The undergraduate programs leading to the bachelor's degree and teacher certification are offered in the areas of early care and education (N-K), primary education (K-4), middle level education, early care and education/exceptional (grades 3-6), elementary special education (grades 7-12), science education (earth science/physical science, general science). Field experiences are assigned to assist the student in connecting professional and pedagogical theories to classroom teaching.

Graduate Programs: Graduate programs are offered in curriculum and instruction, special education, science education, and adult literacy. These programs lead to the master's degree.

Licensure/Reciprocity: Delaware. Students seeking teaching certification in a state other than Delaware should consult with that state's teacher certification office early in their program of study to insure compliance with requirements. Many state directors of teacher credentialing have signed Interstate Agreements through NASDTEC that expedite the certification process.

UNIVERSITY OF DELAWARE

College of Human Services, Education, and Public Policy
School of Education
113 Willard Hall
Newark, Delaware 19716
Phone: (302) 831-3334
Fax: (302) 831-
E-mail: cmclark@udel.edu
Internet: http://www.udel.edu

Institution Description: The University of Delaware is a privately-controlled, state-assisted institution. It was founded in 1743 and chartered as Newark College. It became a land-grant college and changed name to Delaware College in 1876. The present name was adopted in 1921.

Responsibility for the professional teacher education programs rests with the University Council on Teacher Education. Programs aim to develop teachers who are reflective practitioners serving diverse communities of learners and scholars, problem solvers, and partners. The undergraduate teacher education programs are located in four colleges: Agriculture and Natural Resources, Arts and Sciences, Health and Nursing Science, and Human Services, Education, and Public Policy. Prospective students should contact the colleges to review curriculum requirements in their teacher education programs. Programs of the School of Education are described below.

Institution Control: Private.

Calendar: Semester. Academic year September to May.

Official(s): Dr. Tim Banekov, Dean; Dr. Chris Clark, Director, School of Education.

Faculty: Full-time 62.

Degrees Awarded: 418 baccalaureate; 100 master's; 16 doctorate.

Admission Requirements: *Undergraduate:* Graduation with 16 academic units from an accredited secondary school; College Board SAT or ACT composite. *Teacher education specific:* Students must be accepted into a program in one of the four colleges in the university. *Graduate:* Baccalaureate degree from a regionally accredited institution. *Teacher education specific:* Student must pass all exam/test requirements for admission into a program; teaching credential; faculty interview.

Fees and Expenses: $5,890 in-state per academic year; $15,420 out-of-state. On-campus room and board: $5,822. *Other expenses: $1,500. Books and supplies: $800.*

Financial Aid: Resources specifically for eligible students enrolled in teacher education programs are awarded on the basis of financial need and academic merit. The institution has a Program Participation Agreement with the U.S. Department of Education for eligible students to receive Pell Grants and other federal aid. *Contact:* Financial Aid Office at: (302) 831-6761.

Accreditation: *Regional:* MSA. *Professional:* NCATE. *Member of:* AACTE. *Approved by:* Delaware State Department of Education.

Undergraduate Programs: The early childhood development and education program is for students who plan to work with young children and their families in schools, child care programs, and early intervention settings. Students may receive certification as teachers of children from birth to kindergarten or they may be certified in early childhood special education.

The elementary teacher education program is designed to prepare students for careers as teachers of exceptional children and/or regular elementary education (K-4, 5-8) with additional endorsements in middle school mathematics, middle school science, bilingual education, or teaching English as a second language.

Graduate Programs: The Master of Arts in Education degree program offers specializations in cognition and instruction, educational policy, English as a second language/bilingualism, exceptional children and youth, and measurement/statistics/evaluation.

The Master of Education degree program is offered with specializations in college counseling, curriculum and instruction, educational leadership, educational technology, exceptional children and youth, school counseling, and secondary education.

Doctoral programs are also available in educational leadership, applied human development, cognition and instruction, curriculum and instruction, and educational policy.

Licensure/Reciprocity: Delaware. Students seeking teaching certification in a state other than Delaware should consult with that state's teacher certification office early in their program of study to insure compliance with requirements. Many state directors of teacher credentialing have signed Interstate Agreements through NASDTEC that expedite the certification process.

WESLEY COLLEGE

School of Education
120 North State Street
Dover, Delaware 19901-3875
Phone: (302) 736-2300
Fax: (302) 736-2301
E-mail: info@wesley.edu
Internet: http://www.wesley.edu

Institution Description: Wesley College is a private college affiliated with the United Methodist Church. It was established and chartered as Wilmington Conference Academy in 1873 and rechartered as Wesley Collegiate Institute in 1918. The college closed in 1932 and reopened as Wesley Junior College in 1942. The present name was adopted in 1958.

The Education Department offers teacher education programs at both the baccalaureate and graduate levels. Focus of the programs is placed on reflective thinking and action research.

Institution Control: Private.

Calendar: Semester. Academic year August to May.

Official(s): Dr. J. Thomas Sturgis, Chair; Dr. Patricia B. Patterson, Professor of Education.

Faculty: Full-time 17.

Degrees Awarded: 43 baccalaureate; 9 master's.

Admission Requirements: *Undergraduate:* Graduation with 16 academic units from an approved secondary school; College Board SAT or ACT composite. *Teacher education specific:* Acceptance by the Education Department; program approval; pass all departmental exam/test requirements. *Graduate:* Baccalaureate from a regionally accredited institution. *Teacher education specific:* Faculty interview; teaching credential; completion of all departmental and state tests/exams; faculty interview.

Fees and Expenses: Undergraduate: $13,000 per academic year. Graduate: $285 per credit hour. Required fees: $705. On-campus room: $2,100 to $6,500; board: $3,100. Approximate total expenses per academic year: $19,905.

Financial Aid: Resources specifically for eligible students enrolled in teacher education programs are awarded on the basis of financial need and academic merit. The institution has a

Program Participation Agreement with the U.S. Department of Education for eligible students to receive Pell Grants and other federal aid. *Contact:* Financial Aid Office at: (302) 736-2338.

Accreditation: *Regional:* MSA. *Professional:* NCATE. *Member of:* AACTE. *Approved by:* Delaware State Department of Education.

Undergraduate Programs: The elementary/middle school education program provides for K-8 certification. Preparation includes coursework in child and young adolescent development; learning theories; classroom management; language arts, mathematics, science, and social studies curricula. the program requires that each teacher candidate complete two content area concentrations selected from: life science, earth science, English, social science, mathematics. Secondary certification in a fifth-year program is possible for students who major in English, biology, or social studies. Upon completion of the undergraduate degree program, candidates enroll in the secondary education with initial certification program that leads to a Master of Arts in Teaching degree.

Graduate Programs: The Master of Arts in Teaching degree program is designed to provide individuals who hold a bachelor's degree in an academic discipline with the professional education courses required for secondary certification. Coursework includes a fourteen-week student teaching experience.

The Master of Education or Master of Arts in Education degree programs are designed to provide certified teachers with advanced study. Coursework focuses on the professional dimensions of teaching as well as current research and effective practice. Fifteen credit hours of core coursework is required. Students elect from a variety of concentrations (literacy, middle school, focused content area) and may elect to complete a thesis or choose a non-thesis option.

Licensure/Reciprocity: Delaware. Students seeking teaching certification in a state other than Delaware should consult with that state's teacher certification office early in their program of study to insure compliance with requirements. Many state directors of teacher credentialing have signed Interstate Agreements through NASDTEC that expedite the certification process.

WILMINGTON COLLEGE

Division of Education
320 DuPont Highway
New Castle, Delaware 19720
Phone: (302) 328-9401
Fax: (302) 328-8907
E-mail: admissions@wilmcoll.edu
Internet: http://www.wilmcoll.edu

Institution Description: Wilmington College is a private, independent, nonprofit college. It was established in 1965 and offered first instruction at the postsecondary level in 1968.

The Division of Education prepares students for careers as professional educators. Coursework and supervised field experiences stress the creation of effective and appropriate learning environments.

Institution Control: Private.

Calendar: Semester. Academic year September to June.

Official(s): Dr. Barbara M. Raetsch, Division Chair.

Faculty: Full-time 18.

Degrees Awarded: 86 baccalaureate; 355 master's.

Admission Requirements: *Undergraduate:* Graduation from an accredited secondary school or GED; College Board SAT or ACT composite. *Teacher education specific:* Acceptance by the Division of Education; pass all Delaware's PRAXIS I: PPST testing requirements prior to admission to the first methods course; faculty interview. *Graduate:* Baccalaureate from a regionally accredited institution; GRE. *Teacher education specific:* Departmental interview; pass all departmental and/or state required tests; two letters of recommendation; departmental interview.

Fees and Expenses: Undergraduate $231 per credit hour. Graduate $284 per credit hour. On-campus room and board: $5,900. Other expenses: $4,500. Books and supplies: $750.

WILMINGTON COLLEGE—cont'd

Financial Aid: Resources specifically for eligible students enrolled in teacher education programs are awarded on the basis of financial need and academic merit. The institution has a Program Participation Agreement with the U.S. Department of Education for eligible students to receive Pell Grants and other federal aid. *Contact:* Financial Aid Office at: (802) 328-9401.

Accreditation: *Regional:* MSA. *Approved by:* Delaware State Department of Education.

Undergraduate Programs: The Bachelor of Science in Education degree prepares students for teaching positions from birth to grade 8. Students choose a teaching concentration that leads to certification in either early care and education (birth through kindergarten), primary education (grades K-4), or middle level education (grades 5-8). Supervised field experiences are an integral part of the teacher preparation program. The baccalaureate program requires the completion of 120 semester hours.

Graduate Programs: The Master of Education degree programs include concentrations in the areas of: school leadership, instruction, literacy, school counseling, elementary studies, elementary special education, reading, applied technology in education. All programs have specific course requirements.

Licensure/Reciprocity: Delaware. Students seeking teaching certification in a state other than Delaware should consult with that state's teacher certification office early in their program of study to insure compliance with requirements. Many state directors of teacher credentialing have signed Interstate Agreements through NASDTEC that expedite the certification process.

DISTRICT OF COLUMBIA

AMERICAN UNIVERSITY

School of Education
4400 Massachusetts Avenue, N.W.
Washington, District of Columbia 20016
Phone: (202) 885-1000
Fax: (202) 885-6014
E-mail: tesconi@american.edu
Internet: http://www.american.edu

Institution Description: American University is a private institution affiliated with the United Methodist Church. It was established as graduate school, chartered, and incorporated in 1893. The undergraduate level was added in 1925.

The School of Education offers programs that prepare teachers, educational leaders and managers, education specialists, and researchers. Degree programs can be completed on a full- or part-time basis.

Institution Control: Private.

Calendar: Semester. Academic year September to May.

Official(s): Dr. Charles Tesconi, Dean.

Faculty: Full-time 8.

Degrees Awarded: 20 baccalaureate; 80 master's; 13 doctorate.

Admission Requirements: *Undergraduate:* Either graduation with 16 units from an approved secondary school or GED; College Board SAT or ACT composite. *Teacher education specific:* Students must consult with an adviser from the School of Education as early as possible to discuss the coordination of general education requirements with certification requirements. *Graduate:* Baccalaureate degree from a regionally accredited institution; satisfactory score on the Miller Analogies Test or GRE; faculty interview. *Teacher education specific:* All coursework must be approved by the director of the program pursued; successful field performance.

Fees and Expenses: Undergraduate: $769 per credit hour. Graduate: $827 per credit hour. On-campus room and board: $9,488 per academic year. Other expenses: $1,300. Books and supplies: $600.

Financial Aid: Resources specifically for eligible students enrolled in teacher education programs are awarded on the basis of financial need and academic merit. The institution has a Program Participation Agreement with the U.S. Department of Education for eligible students to receive Pell Grants and other federal aid. *Contact:* Financial Aid Office at: (202) 885-6100.

Accreditation: *Regional:* MSA. *Professional:* NCATE. *Member of:* AACTE. *Approved by:* District of Columbia Educational Credentialing and Standards.

Undergraduate Programs: The Bachelor of Arts in elementary education requires completion of a total of 120 credit hours. A total of 58 credit hours of major course requirements with grades of C or better.

The program in secondary education is designed for students who wish to obtain teaching credentials in secondary education while completing their majors in the humanities, arts, natural and social sciences. A total of 36 credit hours in secondary course requirements must be completed with grades of C or better.

A minor in educational studies requires a total of 21 credit hours and at least 12 credit hours unique to the minor.

The minor in special education requires 18 credit hours with grades of C or better and at least 12 credit hours unique to the minor.

Graduate Programs: The School of Education offers programs that lead to K-12 certification. Students interested in teaching in elementary or secondary schools or in programs for English for speakers of other languages enroll in the Masters of Arts in Teaching (M.A.T.) Concentrations available include elementary education, secondary education, English for speakers of other languages; graduate certificate in all level secondary teaching.

The Master of Arts in Education programs offers concentrations in: specialized studies, educational leadership, special education, learning disabilities, and educational technology.

Licensure/Reciprocity: District of Columbia. Students seeking teaching certification in other states should consult with that state's teacher certification office early in their program of study to insure compliance with requirements. Many state directors of teacher credentialing have signed Interstate Agreements through NASDTEC that expedite the certification process.

THE CATHOLIC UNIVERSITY OF AMERICA

Department of Education
Teacher Education Program
O'Boyle Hall, Room 218
620 Michigan Avenue, N.E.
Washington, District of Columbia 20064
Phone: (202) 319-5200
Fax: (202) 319-4441
E-mail: admissions@cua.edu
Internet: http://www.cua.edu

Institution Description: The Catholic University of America is a private, independent institution affiliated with the Roman Catholic Church. It was established as a graduate institution in 1887 and offered first instruction at the postsecondary level in 1889. Undergraduate instruction was begun in 1904.

The emphasis in the Teacher Education Program is on providing the candidate with the professional education coursework needed for licensure in early childhood, elementary, or secondary education. Each of the programs presents teaching as reflective practice.

Institution Control: Private.

Calendar: Semester. Academic year August to May.

Official(s): Dr. Shavarum M. Wall, Chair.

Faculty: Full-time 15, 5 part-time, 6 adjunct.

Degrees Awarded: 29 baccalaureate; 17 master's; 3 doctorate.

Admission Requirements: *Undergraduate:* Graduation with 17 units from an approved secondary school or GED; College Board SAT or ACT composite. *Teacher education specific:* Students should consult with an advisor early in their undergraduate career regarding degree track. *Graduate:* Baccalaureate from a regionally accredited institution; official score on the Miller Analogies Test or GRE. *Teacher education specific:* Three letters of recommendations; statement of goals; faculty interview.

Fees and Expenses: Undergraduate and graduate: $22,0000 per academic year full-time; part-time $850 per credit hour. On-campus room and board: $8,632. Other expenses: $2,350. Books and supplies: $870.

THE CATHOLIC UNIVERSITY OF AMERICA—*cont'd*

Financial Aid: Resources specifically for eligible students enrolled in teacher education programs are awarded on the basis of financial need and academic merit. The institution has a Program Participation Agreement with the U.S. Department of Education for eligible students to receive Pell Grants and other federal aid. Various other financial packages are available. The department of education has a limited number of financial aid awards for graduate students. *Contact:* Financial Aid Office at: (202) 319-5307.

Accreditation: *Regional:* MSA. *Professional:* NCATE. *Member of:* AACTE. *Approved by:* District of Columbia Educational Credentialing and Standards.

Undergraduate Programs: The early childhood, elementary, and secondary education programs offer candidates the opportunity to acquire essential knowledge skills and dispositions for beginning teachers. Candidates who plan to teach grades 1 - 6 should major in early childhood education. Candidates who plan to teach in a departmentalized setting in a middle, junior, or senior high school (grades 7 - 12) have a joint major in education and another Arts and Sciences department. Joint programs in secondary education are offered in the departments of art, biology, chemistry, drama, English, Greek, Latin, history, mathematics, and modern languages.

Graduate Programs: The Master of Arts in Teacher Education programs are offered for early childhood, elementary education, and secondary education. The teacher certification program provides students with knowledge of the teaching and schooling processes, including learning theory and teaching methodology; interpersonal skills required in the teaching/learning process; knowledge of curriculum theory and design based on individual assessments; competency in the development and use of instructional materials; and opportunities to apply theory through directed practicum experience.

Licensure/Reciprocity: District of Columbia. Students seeking teaching certification in other states should consult with that state's teacher certification office early in their program of study to insure compliance with requirements. Many state directors of teacher credentialing have signed Interstate Agreements through NASDTEC that expedite the certification process.

GALLAUDET UNIVERSITY

Department of Education
800 Florida Avenue, N.E.
Washington, District of Columbia 20002
Phone: (202) 651-5750
Fax: (202) 651-5744
E-mail: education.department@gallaudet.edu
Internet: http://www.gallaudet.edu

Institution Description: Gallaudet University is a private, independent, nonprofit college for the deaf that was established as Kendall School in 1856 and incorporated as Columbia Institution for the Instruction of the Deaf and Dumb and Blind in 1857. The name was changed to National Deaf Mute College in 1864, to Columbia Institution for the Instruction of the Deaf and Dumb in 1865, and became Gallaudet College 1954. The present name was adopted in 1986.

The Department of Education has prepared over 1,800 teachers of deaf and hard of hearing children and youth.

Institution Control: Private.

Calendar: Semester. Academic year September to May.

Official(s): Dr. Richard R. Lytle, Chair, Department of Education.

Faculty: Full-time 16.

Degrees Awarded: 5 baccalaureate; 52 master's.

Admission Requirements: *Undergraduate:* Graduation from an approved secondary school (recommend college preparatory units) or GED; College Board SAT or ACT composite. *Teacher education specific:* Gallaudet examination. *Graduate:* Bac-calaureate degree from a regionally accredited institution. *Teacher education specific:* GRE score; sign language requirements (vary by program); letters of recommendation; faculty interview.

Fees and Expenses: $9,115 per academic year. On-campus room and board: $7,800. Other expenses: $3,000. Books and supplies: $750.

Financial Aid: Resources specifically for eligible students enrolled in teacher education programs are awarded on the basis of financial need and academic merit. The institution has a Program Participation Agreement with the U.S. Department of Education for eligible students to receive Pell Grants and other federal aid. Financial aid for qualified graduate students include tuition waivers, tuition stipends, scholarships, loan programs, and work-study programs. *Contact:* Financial Aid Office at: (202) 651-5290.

Accreditation: *Regional:* MSA. *Professional:* NCATE. *Member of:* AACTE. *Approved by:* District of Columbia Educational Credentialing and Standards.

Undergraduate Programs: The program leading to the Bachelor of Arts degree is a regular education program requiring completion of a general education core and specified courses in the major area. All undergraduate courses are conducted in sigh language. Students who fulfill prerequisites at Gallaudet are strongly encouraged to do so only if they possess adequate sign language skills. It is strongly recommended that applicants complete prerequisites before entering the M.A. teacher preparation program.

Graduate Programs: The Master of Arts teacher preparation program prepares entry-level educators seeking state licensure in the area of deaf and hard of hearing and CED certification in the education of deaf and hard of hearing students. Students may follow a course of study in one of four areas of specialization: family-centered early education, multiple disabilities, elementary education, secondary education. The program is designed to develop students' abilities to communicate, collaborate, and to become reflective teachers. Areas developed include a commitment to the importance of sign language in deaf education, collaborations with other professionals, consistent attention to fostering self-esteem in deaf and hard of hearing students, and respect and understanding of the cultural context of those students' experiences.

Licensure/Reciprocity: District of Columbia. Students seeking teaching certification in other states should consult with that state's teacher certification office early in their program of study to insure compliance with requirements. Many state directors of teacher credentialing have signed Interstate Agreements through NASDTEC that expedite the certification process.

GEORGE WASHINGTON UNIVERSITY

Graduate School of Education and Human Development
Department of Teacher Preparation and Special Education
2121 I Street, N.W.
Washington, District of Columbia 20052
Phone: (202) 994-6170
Fax: (202) 994-0325
E-mail: jshotel@gwu.edu
Internet: http://www.gwu.edu

Institution Description: George Washington University is a private, independent, nonprofit institution that was chartered as The Columbian College in the District of Columbia in 1821. The name was changed to Columbian University in 1873 and adopted the present name in 1904.

The Graduate School of Education and Human development is committed to providing the highest quality education to its students.

Institution Control: Private.

Calendar: Semester. Academic year August to May.

Official(s): Dr. Mary Hatwood Futrell, Dean; Dr. Jay r. Shotel, Chair, Department of Teacher Preparation.

Faculty: Full-time 26.

Degrees Awarded: 333 master's; 33 doctorate.

Admission Requirements: *Graduate:* Baccalaureate degree from a regionally accredited institution. *Teacher education specific:* Two recommendations; teaching certificate (if applicable); statement of purpose essay; program faculty interview; GRE or Miller Analogies Test; transcript analysis form (secondary education applicants only); sample of scholarly work (elementary education applicants only).

Fees and Expenses: $810 per credit hour. On-campus room and board: $9,110. Other expenses: $1,800. Books and supplies: $850.

Financial Aid: Resources specifically for eligible students enrolled in teacher education programs are awarded on the basis of financial need and academic merit. The institution has a Program Participation Agreement with the U.S. Department of Education for eligible students to receive Pell Grants and other federal aid. *Contact:* Financial Aid Office at: (202) 994-6620.

Accreditation: *Regional:* MSA. *Professional:* NCATE. *Member of:* AACTE. *Approved by:* District of Columbia Educational Credentialing and Standards.

Graduate Programs: The Department of Teacher Preparation offers the following programs leading to the Master of Arts in Education degree: curriculum and instruction, early childhood special education; infant special education; special education for adolescents with emotional and behavioral disabilities; transition special education.

The Master of Education degree programs include elementary education and secondary education.

The department has partnerships or professional development school initiatives with the District of Columbia, Fairfax County (Virginia), Montgomery County (Maryland), the city of Falls Church, the city of Alexandria, and the Prince George's County (Maryland) public schools.

Licensure/Reciprocity: District of Columbia. Students seeking teaching certification in other states should consult with that state's teacher certification office early in their program of study to insure compliance with requirements. Many state directors of teacher credentialing have signed Interstate Agreements through NASDTEC that expedite the certification process.

HOWARD UNIVERSITY

School of Education
Department of Curriculum and Instruction
2400 Sixth Street, N.W.
Washington, District of Columbia 20059
Phone: (202) 806-7343
Fax: (202) 806-5297
E-mail: mirving@howard.edu
Internet: http://www.howard.edu

Institution Description: Howard University is a private, independent, nonprofit institution. The university was established, chartered, and offered first instruction at the postsecondary level in 1867.

The School of Education offers teacher education programs at the baccalaureate and graduate levels.

Institution Control: Private.

Calendar: Semester. Academic year August to May.

Official(s): Dr. Marilyn M. Irving, Department Head.

Faculty: Full-time 10, adjunct 8.

Degrees Awarded: 7 baccalaureate; 28 master's.

Admission Requirements: *Undergraduate:* Either graduation with 16 units from a secondary school or GED; College Board SAT or ACT composite. *Teacher education specific:* Application to the department at least by the sophomore year. *Graduate:* GRE scores; three letters of recommendation from professors or educators; statement of interest; autobiographical sketch. *Teacher education specific:* All of the above; GRE required only for the Master of Arts program.

Fees and Expenses: $10,320 per academic year. On-campus room and board: $5,170. Other expenses; $2,985. Books and supplies: $1,070.

Financial Aid: Resources specifically for eligible students enrolled in teacher education programs are awarded on the basis of financial need and academic merit. The institution has a Program Participation Agreement with the U.S. Department of Education for eligible students to receive Pell Grants and other federal aid. *Contact:* Financial Aid Office at: (202) 806-2820.

Accreditation: *Regional:* MSA. *Professional:* NCATE. *Member of:* AACTE. *Approved by:* District of Columbia Educational Credentialing and Standards.

Undergraduate Programs: Students may receive teacher certification at the secondary level by combining a major in an academic filed with the secondary professional minor that includes 30 credits of coursework and work/student teaching.

Graduate Programs: The Department of Curriculum and Instruction offers a 5-year program for students seeking teacher certification in early childhood and elementary education. Students in the 5-year Early childhood program major in Human Development. During the 5th year, students pursue the Master of Education degree that provides for their certification. Students in the 5-year elementary education program major in English, mathematics, history, and Afro-American studies. During their 5th year, Students pursue the Master of Education degree that provides teacher certification.

The department also offers the following degree programs: Early Childhood-Master of Arts in Teaching (M.A.T.), Master of Education (M.Ed.), Master of Arts (M.A.), and the Certificate of Advanced Graduate Study (C.A.G.S.); Elementary Curriculum and Teaching-M.Ed.); Secondary Curriculum and Teaching-M.A.T., M.Ed., M.A., and C.A.G.S.; Reading-M.A.T., M.Ed., M.A., C.A.G.; Special Education-M.Ed., M.A. C.A.G.S.

Licensure/Reciprocity: District of Columbia. Students seeking teaching certification in other states should consult with that state's teacher certification office early in their program of study to insure compliance with requirements. Many state directors of teacher credentialing have signed Interstate Agreements through NASDTEC that expedite the certification process.

TRINITY COLLEGE

School of Education
Teacher Education Programs
125 Michigan Avenue, N.E.
Washington, District of Columbia 20017-1094
Phone: (202) 884-9000
Fax: (202) 884-9229
E-mail: admissions@trinitydc.edu
Internet: http://www.trinitydc.edu

Institution Description: Trinity College is a private college conducted by the Sisters of Notre Dame de Namur, Roman Catholic Church. It was established, chartered, and incorporated in 1897.

Teacher preparation at Trinity College emphasizes field-based instruction that includes a series of integrated field experiences and practicum experiences at different grade/age levels in a variety of school settings.

Institution Control: Private.

Calendar: Semester. Academic year September to May.

Official(s): Dr. Roberta Dorr, Director of Teacher Education Programs.

Faculty: Full-time 4.

Degrees Awarded: 3 baccalaureate; 155 master's.

Admission Requirements: *Undergraduate:* Graduation from secondary school with 16 academic units; College board SAT or ACT composite. *Teacher education specific:* Students considering any academic program in the field of education should officially switch to a faculty advisor in the School of Education. *Graduate:* Baccalaureate degree from a regionally accredited

TRINITY COLLEGE—*cont'd*

institution. *Teacher education specific:* Completion of required exams/tests; letters of recommendation; statement of goals; faculty interview.

Fees and Expenses: Undergraduate $450 per credit; graduate: $12,400 per academic year. On-campus room and board: $6,970. Other expenses: $2,000. Books and supplies: $600.

Financial Aid: Resources specifically for eligible students enrolled in teacher education programs are awarded on the basis of financial need and academic merit. The institution has a Program Participation Agreement with the U.S. Department of Education for eligible students to receive Pell Grants and other federal aid. *Contact:* Financial Aid Office at: (202) 884-9530.

Accreditation: *Regional:* MSA. *Member of:* AACTE. *Approved by:* District of Columbia Educational Credentialing and Standards.

Undergraduate Programs: The School of Education offers an undergraduate major in education in conjunction with the College of Arts and Sciences, an education minor in education, and a Bachelor of Arts/Master of Arts (B.A./M.A.T.) in Teaching Program. The former two programs require completion of a major subject area. The major in education and the B.A./M.A.T. Program require a on-semester full-time internship of supervised student teaching after the successful completion of all education coursework.

Graduate Programs: Graduate programs for teacher certification are offered as well as degree programs in counseling, teacher education, curriculum and instruction, and educational administration. Courses stress current issues, trends, and the application of contemporary research. Teacher education programs include the Master of Arts in Teaching with concentrations in early childhood education, elementary education, and secondary education (English, Math, Science, Social Studies).

The Master of Education degree program is offered in curriculum and instruction with specializations in: teaching reading, teaching English to speakers of other languages (TESOL); education for democracy, diversity, and social justice.

Licensure/Reciprocity: District of Columbia. Students seeking teaching certification in other states should consult with that state's teacher certification office early in their program of study to insure compliance with requirements. Many state directors of teacher credentialing have signed Interstate Agreements through NASDTEC that expedite the certification process.

UNIVERSITY OF THE DISTRICT OF COLUMBIA
College of Arts and Sciences
Department of Education
4200 Connecticut Avenue, N.W.
Washington, District of Columbia 20008
Phone: (202) 282-5210
Fax: (202) 274-6180
E-mail: info@udc.edu
Internet: http://www.udc.edu

Institution Description: The University of the District of Columbia is a federal institution and land-grant college. It was established in 1975 as a merger of District of Columbia Teachers College (established 1851), Federal City College (established 1966), and Washington Technical College (established 1966).

The Department of Education administers both pre-service and in-service professional programs. The department seeks to prepare certified teachers and other professionals in a variety of curricular offerings.

Institution Control: Public.

Calendar: Semester. Academic year August to May.

Official(s): Dr. William Lawrence Pollard, President.

Faculty: Full-time 17.

Degrees Awarded: 8 baccalaureate; 13 master's.

Admission Requirements: *Undergraduate:* Open admissions for graduates of approved high schools or GED. *Teacher education specific:* Completion of a minimum of 45 credit hours of college-level work; cumulative GPA! 2.5 or better; autobiographical sketch; PRAXIS I exams; two recommendations; interview with Admissions Committee of the Teacher Education Program. *Graduate:* Baccalaureate degree from a regionally accredited institution. *Teacher education specific:* Same as for undergraduate admission.

Fees and Expenses: Undergraduate: in-district $2,070, out-of-district $4,710. Off-campus room and board: $6,500. Other expenses: $2,100. Books and supplies: $400.

Financial Aid: Resources specifically for eligible students enrolled in teacher education programs are awarded on the basis of financial need and academic merit. The institution has a Program Participation Agreement with the U.S. Department of Education for eligible students to receive Pell Grants and other federal aid. *Contact:* Financial Aid Office at: (202) 274-5060.

Accreditation: *Regional:* MSA. *Member of:* AACTE. *Approved by:* District of Columbia Educational Credentialing and Standards.

Undergraduate Programs: The Department of Education offers degree programs leading to the Bachelor of Arts in: early childhood education; elementary education, and special education.

In addition, the department offers certification courses for teachers in the areas of business, foreign languages, art, music, mathematics, science, social studies, health and physical education, English, special education, and adult education.

Graduate Programs: At the graduate level, the department offers a Master of Arts degree in early childhood education and a Master of Arts degree in special education.

Licensure/Reciprocity: District of Columbia. Students seeking teaching certification in other states should consult with that state's teacher certification office early in their program of study to insure compliance with requirements. Many state directors of teacher credentialing have signed Interstate Agreements through NASDTEC that expedite the certification process.

FLORIDA

BETHUNE-COOKMAN COLLEGE

Division of Education
640 Dr. Mary McLeod Bethune Drive
Daytona Beach, Florida 32114-3099
Phone: (386) 481-2000
Fax: (386) 481-2001
E-mail: byrdw@cookman.edu
Internet: http://www.cookman.edu

Institution Description: Bethune-Cookman College is a private college related to the United Methodist Church. The college was established and chartered in 1923 as Daytona-Cookman Collegiate Institute through a merger of Cookman Institution (established 1872) and Daytona Normal and Industrial Institute for Girls (established 1904). The present name was adopted in 1931.

The Division of Education offers the Bachelor of Science degree in four areas and teacher certification in selected areas from four other divisions of the college.

Institution Control: Private.

Calendar: Semester. Academic year August to April.

Official(s): Dr. Oswald P. Bronson, Sr., President.

Faculty: Full-time 14, part-time 5.

Degrees Awarded: 41 baccalaureate.

Admission Requirements: *Undergraduate:* Graduation from an approved secondary school or GED; College Board SAT or ACT composite. *Teacher education specific:* Complete all exit requirements of the General Studies Division; GPA of at least 2.5; College Level Academic Skills Test (CLAST); document involvement in community service projects.

Fees and Expenses: $10,106 per academic year. On-campus room and board: $6,252. Other expenses: $2,200. Books and supplies: $730.

Financial Aid: Resources specifically for eligible students enrolled in teacher education programs are awarded on the basis of financial need and academic merit. The institution has a Program Participation Agreement with the U.S. Department of Education for eligible students to receive Pell Grants and other federal aid. *Contact:* Financial Aid Office at: (386) 481-2620.

Accreditation: *Regional:* SACS. *Professional:* NCATE. *Member of:* AACTE. *Approved by:* Florida Department of Education.

Undergraduate Programs: The Bachelor of Science degree programs are offered in the areas of: elementary education; exceptional student education (specific learning disabilities, varying exceptionalities, endorsement in pre-kindergarten handicapped); physical education (K-6, K-12), or recreation (without teacher certification); recreation and leisure studies.

Teacher certification in the following areas in conjunction with degrees offered by other divisions in the areas of biology, business, chemistry, English, music, physics, social science.

The Bachelor of Science in elementary education is designed to prepare teachers for elementary schools, grades 1-6. This program of study is comprised of the general education curriculum, specialized and professional curriculum, and student teaching. The Department of Exceptional Student Education offers Bachelor of Science degrees in specific learning disabilities and varying exceptionalities, as well as endorsement in pre-kindergarten handicapped. The Department of Physical Educa-

tion offers programs leading to the Bachelor of Science in physical education with teacher certification at K-8 or 6-12 levels with nonteaching concentration in recreation.

Licensure/Reciprocity: Florida. Students seeking teaching certification in a state other than Florida should consult with that state's teacher certification office early in their program of study to insure compliance with requirements. Many state directors of teacher credentialing have signed Interstate Agreements through NASDTEC that expedite the certification process.

All students completing a Florida State-approved Teacher Education Program must pass all portions of the Florida Teacher Certification Examination (FTCE).

FLORIDA AGRICULTURAL AND MECHANICAL UNIVERSITY

College of Education
Center for Teacher Preparation and Career Development
Gore Education Center-B, Room 200
Tallahassee, Florida 32307-4900
Phone: (850) 599-3619
Fax: (850) 561-2211
E-mail: donald.mcbride@famu.edu
Internet: http://www.famu.edu

Institution Description: Florida Agricultural and Mechanical University was established as The State Normal College for Colored Students in 1887. It became a land-grant college in 1890 and offered first instruction at the postsecondary level in 1905. The name was changed to Florida Agricultural and Mechanical College in 1909. The present name was adopted in 1953.

The College of Education has identified the Center for Teacher Preparation as the resource facility to assist the preparation of undergraduate teacher majors for entry into the teaching profession for elementary and secondary schools in Florida.

Institution Control: Public.

Calendar: Semester. Academic year May to May.

Official(s): Dr. John A. middleton, Dean, College of Education; Donald L. McBride, Director, Center for Teacher Preparation and Career Development.

Faculty: Full-time 13.

Degrees Awarded: 166 baccalaureate; 78 master's.

Admission Requirements: *Undergraduate:* Either graduation from an approved secondary school or GED; College Board SAT combined score of 800: ACT composite score of 17. *Teacher education specific:* GPA of 2.5 or higher for the general education component of undergraduate studies; completion of all the required courses taken as part of the Center for Teacher Education Preparation Program. *Graduate:* Baccalaureate from a regionally accredited institution; combined score of 1000 on the verbal and quantitative sections of the GRE or a 3.0 GPA covering the last 60 hours of the undergraduate preparation. *Teacher education specific:* Two letters of recommendation; eligibility for or possess a Florida educator's teaching certificate,

Fees and Expenses: Undergraduate in-state $90.42 per credit hour, out-of-state $458.02. Graduate in-state $196.27 per credit hour, out-of-state $730.80, Other expenses: $4,000. On-campus room and board: $5,000. Books and supplies: $1,400.

FLORIDA AGRICULTURAL AND MECHANICAL UNIVERSITY—*cont'd*

Financial Aid: Resources specifically for eligible students enrolled in teacher education programs are awarded on the basis of financial need and academic merit. The institution has a Program Participation Agreement with the U.S. Department of Education for eligible students to receive Pell Grants and other federal aid. *Contact:* Financial Aid Office at: (850) 599-3730.

Accreditation: *Regional:* SACS. *Professional:* NCATE. *Member of:* AACTE. *Approved by:* Florida Department of Education.

Undergraduate Programs: The major purpose of the elementary education program is to provide carefully planned experiences that will result in the development of competent teachers. the curriculum is organized to provide approximately two years of general education courses. The two years consists of professional and specialized preparation. The program leads to a Bachelor of Science in elementary education with certification in varying exceptionalities and reading.

Undergraduate degrees in secondary education (through the College of Arts and Sciences) can be pursued in the concentrations of art, biology, English, French, history, math, music, physics, political science, Spanish, and theatre. Certification is offered in these areas.

Graduate Programs: The Department of Secondary Education and Foundations offers the Master of Science or Master of Education in secondary education with concentrations in the following areas: biology, chemistry, English, history, mathematics, and physics.

The Master in Education and Master of Science in elementary education programs are offered with certification in varying exceptionalities and reading.

Licensure/Reciprocity: Florida. Students seeking teaching certification in a state other than Florida should consult with that state's teacher certification office early in their program of study to insure compliance with requirements. Many state directors of teacher credentialing have signed Interstate Agreements through NASDTEC that expedite the certification process.

All students completing a Florida State-approved Teacher Education Program must pass all portions of the Florida Teacher Certification Examination (FTCE).

FLORIDA ATLANTIC UNIVERSITY

College of Education
Department of Teacher Education
ED47, Room 494
777 Glades Road
Boca Raton, Florida 33431-0991
Phone: (954) 236-1046
Fax: (954) 236-1049
E-mail: fritzer@fau.edu
Internet: http://www.fau.edu

Institution Description: Florida Atlantic University is a state institution that was established in 1961. It offered first instruction at the postsecondary level in 1964 and awarded its first degree (baccalaureate) in 1965.

The broad range of graduate and undergraduate professional programs offered by the Department of Teacher Education promotes collaboration among faculty, students, and school personnel.

Institution Control: Public.

Calendar: Semester. Academic year August to May.

Official(s): Dr. Gail Burnaford, Chair, Department of Teacher Education.

Faculty: Full-time 38.

Degrees Awarded: 473 baccalaureate; 281 master's.

Admission Requirements: *Undergraduate:* Graduation from an accredited secondary school or GED; admission is based primarily on high school GPA and SAT/ACT score. *Teacher education specific:* Faculty interview. *Graduate:* Baccalaureate degree from a regionally accredited institution. *Teacher education specific:* Completion of all required state/department exams/tests; letters of recommendation; faculty interview.

Fees and Expenses: Undergraduate: resident $98.09 per credit hour; nonresident $465.17 per credit hour. Graduate: resident $209.82 per credit hour; nonresident $775.15. On-campus room and board: $5,600. Other expenses: $2,815. Books and supplies: $660.

Financial Aid: Resources specifically for eligible students enrolled in teacher education programs are awarded on the basis of financial need and academic merit. The institution has a Program Participation Agreement with the U.S. Department of Education for eligible students to receive Pell Grants and other federal aid. *Contact:* Financial Aid Office at: (954) 297-3530.

Accreditation: *Regional:* SACS. *Professional:* NCATE. *Member of:* AACTE. *Approved by:* Florida Department of Education.

Undergraduate Programs: The Department of Education offers undergraduate degree programs leading to the Bachelor of Arts and the Bachelor of Arts in in the following areas: elementary education, exceptional student education, English education, social science education, math education, science education (biology, chemistry, physics).

The department also provides the secondary education teacher certification component to the following majors offered in the Dorothy F. Schmidt College of Arts and Letters: art, French, German, Spanish.

Graduate Programs: Graduate Programs are offered to qualified persons who have had sufficient and satisfactory undergraduate preparation. The programs in curriculum and instruction include art (K-12), elementary education (1-6) English/language arts (6-12) environmental science education, drama (6-12) foreign language (French, Spanish, K-12), Holocaust and Judaic studies, mathematics, reading, science (biology, chemistry, earth science, physics 6-12), social science (6-12), initial certification in pre-kindergarten/primary education (age 3 - grade 3), and initial certification in secondary education.

The program in elementary education is for certified teachers and a program for initial certification in elementary education is offered. The program for exceptional student education and varying exceptionalities is offered for initial certification.

Licensure/Reciprocity: Florida. Students seeking teaching certification in a state other than Florida should consult with that state's teacher certification office early in their program of study to insure compliance with requirements. Many state directors of teacher credentialing have signed Interstate Agreements through NASDTEC that expedite the certification process.

All students completing a Florida State-approved Teacher Education Program must pass all portions of the Florida Teacher Certification Examination (FTCE).

FLORIDA GULF COAST UNIVERSITY

College of Education
10501 FGCU Boulevard, South
Fort Myers, Florida 33965-6565
Phone: (239) 590-1000
Fax: (239) 590-1004
E-mail: oar@fgcu.edu
Internet: http://www.fgcu.edu

Institution Description: Florida Gulf Coast University is a member institution of the Florida State University System. The university was founded in 1991 and is located in southwestern Lee County.

The College of Education offers undergraduate and graduate programs in teacher education preparation programs.

Institution Control: Public.

Calendar: Semester. Academic year August to May.

Official(s): Dr. Larry Byrnes, Dean, College of Education.

Faculty: Full-time 30.

Degrees Awarded: 121 baccalaureate; 86 master's.

Admission Requirements: *Undergraduate:* Graduation from an accredited secondary school or GED; College Board SAT or ACT composite. *Teacher education specific:* Overall 2.5 GPA; pass all subsections of the College Level Academic Skills Test (CLAST); satisfaction of Gordon Rule and general education requirements; satisfaction of applicable common prerequisite requirements. *Graduate:* Baccalaureate degree from a regionally accredited institution. *Teacher education specific:* Combined score of 1000 or higher on the GRE; GRE or Miller Analogies Test score; three professional recommendations.

Fees and Expenses: Undergraduate resident $94.57 per credit hour; nonresident $439,73. Graduate resident $196.22 per credit hour, nonresident $730.75. On-campus room and board: $7,000 per academic year. Other expenses: $1,400. Books and supplies: $700.

Financial Aid: Resources specifically for eligible students enrolled in teacher education programs are awarded on the basis of financial need and academic merit. The institution has a Program Participation Agreement with the U.S. Department of Education for eligible students to receive Pell Grants and other federal aid. *Contact:* Financial Aid Office at: (239) 590-7920.

Accreditation: *Regional:* SACS. *Member of:* AACTE. *Approved by:* Florida Department of Education.

Undergraduate Programs: The Bachelor of Arts in early childhood education is designed to prepare students for certification for preschool (birth to age 4) and pre-kindergarten/primary (age 3 to grade 3) and as pre-kindergarten/disabilities endorsement. The program consists of 129 credit hours and includes ESOL endorsement.

The Bachelor of Arts in elementary education is designed to prepare students for teaching in Florida's elementary schools and for certification as elementary school teachers (kindergarten through grade 6). The program includes coursework and field experience in elementary school setters throughout the university's five county area of service to enable students to integrate teaching practice. The program consists of 126 credit hours and includes ESOL endorsement.

The Bachelor of Arts in special education consists of 126 credit hours and includes ESOL endorsement. Students attain certification in Exceptional Student Education. K-12 grades covers teaching children with emotional behavioral disabilities/mental retardation, specific learning disabilities, and physical disabilities. Field experiences are central to the program and commence in the first semester.

Graduate Programs: The Master of Education elementary degree program is designed to provide focused graduate study in an area of specialization for teachers currently certified to teach in the elementary grades.

The Master of Arts in elementary education (initial certification) enables students with a BS/BA in another field without elementary certification to meet requirements for both elementary certification and the master's degree.

The Master of Art in Teaching program provides opportunities for individuals with baccalaureate degrees in biology, English, history, mathematics, social sciences, or related field to gain initial secondary certification along with a graduate degree in education.

Licensure/Reciprocity: Florida. Students seeking teaching certification in a state other than Florida should consult with that state's teacher certification office early in their program of study to insure compliance with requirements. Many state directors of teacher credentialing have signed Interstate Agreements through NASDTEC that expedite the certification process.

All students completing a Florida State-approved Teacher Education Program must pass all portions of the Florida Teacher Certification Examination (FTCE).

FLORIDA INTERNATIONAL UNIVERSITY
College of Education
ZEB 320
11200 SW 8th Street
Miami, Florida 33199-0001
Phone: (305) 348-3202
Fax: (305) 348-3205
E-mail: Linda.Blanton@fiu.edu
Internet: http://www.fiu.edu

Institution Description: Florida International University is a state institution that primarily provides upper division and graduate study. The university was established and chartered in 1965. The present name was adopted in 1969. A limited lower division program was begun in 1981.

The College of Education offers initial teacher preparation programs at the upper division undergraduate level and master's degree programs.

Institution Control: Public.

Calendar: Semester. Academic year August to May.

Official(s): Dr. Linda P. Blanton,Dean.

Faculty: Full-time 87, part-time 2, adjunct 128.

Degrees Awarded: 387 baccalaureate; 128 master's.

Admission Requirements: *Undergraduate:* Upper division standing, 2.0 GPA. *Teacher education specific:* Passing scores on the College Level Academic Skills Test (CLAST). *Graduate:* Bachelor's degree from a regionally accredited institution; 3.0 GPA for last 60 semester hours of undergraduate work and/or a GRE score of 1000. *Teacher education specific:* art, reading, special education, counselor education, and school psychology programs have eliminated GRE requirement to reflect institutional change.

Fees and Expenses: Undergraduate: in-state $83.72 per semester hour, out-of-state $399.23. Graduate: in-state $117.05 per semester hour, out-of-state $685.64. Room and board: $6,500 per academic year. Books and supplies: $540 per semester.

Financial Aid: Resources specifically for eligible students enrolled in teacher education programs are awarded on the basis of financial need and academic merit. The institution has a Program Participation Agreement with the U.S. Department of Education for eligible students to receive Pell Grants and other federal aid. *Contact:* Ana Sarasti at (305) 348-2489 or e-mail at Ana.Sarasti@fiu.edu.

Accreditation: *Regional:* SACS. *Professional:* NCATE. *Member of:* AACTE. *Approved by:* Florida Department of Education.

Undergraduate Programs: The College of Education offers initial teacher preparation programs in most major liberal arts subject areas. Students choose a major and receive certification in an appropriate content area, e.g. elementary education 1-6, art education K-12, mathematics education 6-12). All programs are over 120 semester hours in length. Students must fulfill general education core courses, foreign language requirement, common prerequisites for teacher education, professional education requirements, and content area courses.

Graduate Programs: The Master of Art in Teaching initial teacher preparation programs are offered in art, biology, chemistry, English, French, mathematics, physics, social studies, Spanish, varying exceptionalities. The program is designed for candidates with a baccalaureate degree appropriate to the certification area but without certification and are seeking entry into the teaching professions. The program includes courses that provide the necessary background in professional education together with the master's level academic coursework. The program requires the completion of 45-48 semester hours depending on each student's previous academic preparation.

Licensure/Reciprocity: Florida. Students seeking teaching certification in a state other than Florida should consult with that state's teacher certification office early in their program of study to insure compliance with requirements. Many state directors of teacher credentialing have signed Interstate Agreements through NASDTEC that expedite the certification process.

FLORIDA INTERNATIONAL UNIVERSITY—
cont'd

All students completing a Florida State-approved Teacher Education Program must pass all portions of the Florida Teacher Certification Examination (FTCE).

FLORIDA MEMORIAL COLLEGE

Division of Education
15800 N.W. 42nd Avenue
Miami, Florida 33054-6199
Phone: (305) 623-4279
Fax: (305) 626-3600
E-mail: mberry@fmc.edu
Internet: http://www.fmc.edu

Institution Description: Florida Memorial College is a private college affiliated with the Baptist Church. It was established in 1917 as Florida Baptist Academy through a merger of Florida Baptist Institute for Negroes and Florida Normal and Industrial School. In 1918 the name was changed to Florida Normal and Industrial Institute and in 1950 to Florida Normal and Industrial Memorial College. The present name was adopted in 1963.

The Bachelor of Science degree programs along with teacher education curriculum prepare students for a professional teaching career in their respective content areas.

Institution Control: Private.

Calendar: Semester. Academic year August to May.

Official(s): Dr. Mildred Berry, Chairperson.

Faculty: Full-time 11.

Degrees Awarded: 46 baccalaureate.

Admission Requirements: *Undergraduate:* Either graduation from accredited secondary school or GED; minimum GPA 2.0. *Teacher education specific:* Application early in the undergraduate program; meet with adviser to determine program direction.

Fees and Expenses: $4,473.50 per semester. General fees: $743. Room $1,213. Board $1,060.50.

Financial Aid: Resources specifically for eligible students enrolled in teacher education programs are awarded on the basis of financial need and academic merit. The institution has a Program Participation Agreement with the U.S. Department of Education for eligible students to receive Pell Grants and other federal aid. *Contact:* Brian Phillip, Director of Financial Aid at (305) 626-3745 or e-mail at bphillip@fmc.edu.

Accreditation: *Regional:* SACS. *Professional:* NCATE. *Approved by:* Florida Department of Education.

Undergraduate Programs: The Division of Education offers majors in eleven teacher education programs: biology (with certification); elementary education; exceptional student education (K-12); middle grades English, general sciences, and mathematics; music education (K-12), physical education (K-8 and 6-12), secondary education English and mathematics. The Bachelor of Science degree is offered in these specialized fields.

The Professional Education Program provides teacher trainees with the skills and competencies necessary to be effective educators by emphasizing such areas as methodologies of instruction, classroom management, curriculum, assessment, field activities, and internship experience.

Licensure/Reciprocity: Florida. Students seeking teaching certification in a state other than Florida should consult with that state's teacher certification office early in their program of study to insure compliance with requirements. Many state directors of teacher credentialing have signed Interstate Agreements through NASDTEC that expedite the certification process.

All students completing a Florida State-approved Teacher Education Program must pass all portions of the Florida Teacher Certification Examination (FTCE).

FLORIDA STATE UNIVERSITY

College of Education
Teacher Education Unit
Tallahassee, Florida 32306-1037
Phone: (850) 644-6885
Fax: (850) 644-2725
E-mail: info@coe.fsu.edu
Internet: http://www.fsu.edu

Institution Description: Florida State University is a state institution that was established as Seminary West of the Suwanee in 1851. It became a state college for women in 1905. The college became coeducational and adopted the present name in 1947.

The College of Education includes six academic departments and offers undergraduate and graduate degrees in 27 fields of study.

Institution Control: Public.

Calendar: Semester. Academic year August to April.

Official(s): Dr. Richard Kunckel, Dean, College of Education.

Faculty: College of Education: full-time 76, part-time 34.

Degrees Awarded: 505 baccalaureate; 381 master's.

Admission Requirements: *Undergraduate:* Either graduation from an approved secondary school or GED; College Board SAT or ACT composite. *Teacher education specific:* GPA of 2.5 or higher for the general education component of undergraduate studies. *Graduate:* Baccalaureate from a regionally accredited institution; combined score of 1000 on the verbal and quantitative sections of the GRE Or a 3.0 GPA covering the last 60 hours of the undergraduate preparation. *Teacher education specific:* Two letters of recommendation; eligibility for or possess a Florida educator's teaching certificate,

Fees and Expenses: Undergraduate in-state $90.42 per credit hour, out-of-state $458.02. Graduate in-state $196.27 per credit hour, out-of-state $730.80, Other expenses: $1,905. On-campus room and board: $6,450. Books and supplies: $725.

Financial Aid: Resources specifically for eligible students enrolled in teacher education programs are awarded on the basis of financial need and academic merit. The institution has a Program Participation Agreement with the U.S. Department of Education for eligible students to receive Pell Grants and other federal aid. *Contact:* Financial Aid Office at: (850) 644-5871.

Accreditation: *Regional:* SACS. *Professional:* NCATE. *Member of:* AACTE. *Approved by:* Florida Department of Education.

Undergraduate Programs: The undergraduate programs in the College of Education prepare teachers for a wide range of educational careers. Students are provided with experiences that enable them to acquire professional competencies required in each field. The college believes that all students should acquire a solid grounding in the liberal arts and an understanding of human learning and behavior.

The Department of Elementary and Early Childhood Education prepares students for careers in teaching, research and service in universities, public and private schools, government, educational agencies, and other human service professions. The program of study is tailored to complement each student's experience so that the individual may realize current educational needs and achieve desired professional goals. Programs lead to the bachelor's degree.

The middle and secondary education programs include English education, health education, mathematics education, multilingual/multicultural education, science education, and social science education. These programs lead to the Master of Arts in Teaching and the Master in Education degrees with the teaching credential.

The Department of Special Education and Rehabilitation Counseling Services offers programs for teachers who specialize in serving students with disabilities.

Graduate Programs: Graduate programs are available in all of the areas described above for undergraduate study. Programs lead to the Master of Education, Master of Arts in Teaching, and the Master of Science degrees. Contact the various departments for specific course and field work requirements.

Licensure/Reciprocity: Florida. Students seeking teaching certification in a state other than Florida should consult with that state's teacher certification office early in their program of study to insure compliance with requirements. Many state directors of teacher credentialing have signed Interstate Agreements through NASDTEC that expedite the certification process.

All students completing a Florida State-approved Teacher Education Program must pass all portions of the Florida Teacher Certification Examination (FTCE).

NOVA SOUTHEASTERN UNIVERSITY

Fischler Graduate School of Education and Human Services

National Graduate Teacher Online Program

3301 College Avenue
Fort Lauderdale, Florida 33314
Phone: (800) 541-6682
E-mail: gtepinfo@nova.edu
Internet: http://www.nova.edu

Institution Description: Nova Southeastern University is a private, independent, nonprofit institution. It was established and chartered as Nova University of Advanced Technology in 1964. The present name was adopted in 1994 after a merger with the Southeastern University of the health Sciences.

The Graduate Teacher Education Online Program is a program leading to Master of Science and Education Specialist degrees. The purpose of the program is to provide distance education through utilization of research, guided activities, and practical experience to a diverse population of professional educators.

Institution Control: Private.

Calendar: Semester. Academic year August to May.

Official(s): Ray Ferrero, Jr., President.

Faculty: Full-time 24.

Degrees Awarded: 192 baccalaureate; 1,426 master's; 60 doctorate.

Admission Requirements: *Graduate: Teacher education specific:* Must have passed the College Level Academic Skills Test; meet GTEP Academic Performance Benchmarks.

Fees and Expenses: $340 per credit. Students must obtain access to the Internet via a commercial carrier.

Financial Aid: Resources specifically for eligible students enrolled in teacher education programs are awarded on the basis of financial need and academic merit. The institution has a Program Participation Agreement with the U.S. Department of Education for eligible students to receive Pell Grants and other federal aid. *Contact:* Financial Aid Office at: (954) 262-3380.

Accreditation: *Regional:* SACS. *Member of:* AACTE. *Approved by:* Florida Department of Education.

Graduate Programs: Students admitted to the online program are assigned to a cluster. They follow a clearly established program of study for their specialization (major) and must comply with program requirements for degree candidacy and completion. Clusters begin in fall, winter, or summer. Student will complete their program in 3 terms. The Master of Science in Education is offered with concentrations in curriculum instruction and technology; education of young children; education - teaching and learning; educational technology, elementary curriculum and instruction; environmental education; management and administration of educational programs; special studies education; special education. The Education Specialist degree online program is offered with concentration in curriculum/instruction management and administration and technology management and administration.

Types of students enrolling in programs include those seeking a graduate degree and initial certification within an approved program; those seeking a graduate degree and new preparation certification within an approved program or within a secondary education areas; graduate students not seeking certification or licensure; non degree and non-certification or licensure students.

Online courses are conducted through the Internet, allowing students to receive and submit coursework and interact with participants and professors via a computer and Internet connection. Participants log into the course management system (WebCT) each week to complete activities and assignments and to interact with the professor and other students in the class. All registration, correspondence, and course participation are conducted electronically.

Licensure/Reciprocity: Students seeking teaching certification should consult with the certification office of the state of interest early before pursuing their program of study to insure compliance with requirements.

ROLLINS COLLEGE

Department of Education

Teacher Education

1000 Holt Avenue
Winter Park, Florida 32789-4499
Phone: (407) 646-2242
Fax: (407) 646-2545
E-mail: jhewit@@rollins.edu
Internet: http://www.rollins.edu

Institution Description: Rollins College is a private, independent, nonprofit college. It was established and incorporated by thirteen Congregational churches and offered first instruction at the postsecondary level in 1885.

The Department of Education offers state-approved academic and field experiences that prepare students to enter the teaching profession.

Institution Control: Private.

Calendar: Semester. Academic year August to May.

Official(s): Dr. Alden Moe, Dean; Dr. Scott Hewit, Director of Teacher Education.

Faculty: Full-time 6; adjunct 12.

Degrees Awarded: 30 baccalaureate; 7 master's.

Admission Requirements: *Undergraduate:* Graduation from an accredited secondary school; College Board SAT or ACT composite. *Teacher education specific:* Application should be made as soon as student declares an elementary major or decides to seek certification in a secondary area; 2.5 GPA; passing score on the College Level Academic Skills Test (CLAST). *Graduate:* Baccalaureate degree from a regionally accredited institution. *Teacher education specific:* Passing score on CLAST, 3.0 GPA; essay; faculty interview.

Fees and Expenses: Undergraduate: $26,250 per academic year. Graduate: $700 per 3-credit course. On-campus room and board: $8,050. Books and supplies: $538.

Financial Aid: Resources specifically for eligible students enrolled in teacher education programs are awarded on the basis of financial need and academic merit. The institution has a Program Participation Agreement with the U.S. Department of Education for eligible students to receive Pell Grants and other federal aid. *Contact:* Phil Asbury at (407) 646-2395 or e-mail at pasbury@rollins.edu.

Accreditation: *Regional:* SACS. *Approved by:* Florida Department of Education.

Undergraduate Programs: Students can major in elementary education (grades K-6) or obtain certification to teach in secondary schools (grades 6-12) by completing selected majors in the intended teaching area and the education certification course sequence. Major requirements include foundation courses in professional education, elementary of secondary course sequence, and clinical experience including student teaching.

Graduate Programs: The Master of Arts in Teaching is a program designed to prepare individuals who have obtained the bachelor's degree for careers in elementary education. The curriculum combines strong academics with intensive practical experiences in the classroom. Students complete the required courses, including a one-semester internship at an area elementary school.

ROLLINS COLLEGE—*cont'd*

The Master of Education in elementary education is a program designed for certified elementary teachers. The program offers courses in practical areas to expand proficiency of experienced classroom teachers. Written and oral comprehensive examinations are required for graduation.

Licensure/Reciprocity: Florida. Students seeking teaching certification in a state other than Florida should consult with that state's teacher certification office early in their program of study to insure compliance with requirements. Many state directors of teacher credentialing have signed Interstate Agreements through NASDTEC that expedite the certification process.

All students completing a Florida State-approved Teacher Education Program must pass all portions of the Florida Teacher Certification Examination (FTCE).

STETSON UNIVERSITY

Department of Teacher Education
Davis Hall
421 North Woodland Boulevard
Deland, Florida 32723
Phone: (386) 822-7000
Fax: (386) 822-9387
E-mail: eheins@stetson.edu
Internet: http://www.stetson.edu

Institution Description: Stetson University is a private institution affiliated with the Florida Baptist Convention of the Southern Baptist Convention. It was established as Deland Academy in 1883. After several name changes over the years. the present name was adopted in 1993.

The Department of Teacher Education, in collaboration with the schools and community, stresses a holistic program of individual development perceiving students as active inquirers and participants in their own growth.

Institution Control: Private.

Calendar: Semester. Academic year August to May.

Official(s): Dr. Elizabeth D. Heins, Chair, Department of Teacher Education.

Faculty: Full-time 12.

Degrees Awarded: 37 baccalaureate; 38 master's.

Admission Requirements: *Undergraduate:* Graduation from an approved secondary school or GED; College Board SAT or ACT composite. *Teacher education specific:* 2.5 GPA; passing score on all areas of the College Level Academic Skills Test (CLAST) or PRAXIS I; recommendations from three professors; faculty review; computer competency.

Fees and Expenses: $20,475. On-campus room and board: $6,650. Other expenses: $2,920. Books and supplies: $1,620.

Financial Aid: Resources specifically for eligible students enrolled in teacher education programs are awarded on the basis of financial need and academic merit. The institution has a Program Participation Agreement with the U.S. Department of Education for eligible students to receive Pell Grants and other federal aid. *Contact:* Financial Aid Office at: (386) 822-7120.

Accreditation: *Regional:* SACS. *Professional:* NCATE. *Member of:* AACTE. *Approved by:* Florida Department of Education.

Undergraduate Programs: The elementary education program is designed as an initial teaching certification program. Teacher education candidates are placed early in their program in field experiences. These field experiences culminate with a traditional full-time internship. Candidates are trained to work effectively with children that use English as a second language (ESOL). All Stetson teacher education candidates graduate endorsed to teach ESOL and general education students in K-6 classrooms.

Students seeking a degree in secondary education must complete a major in their content area and the professional core in education. Content ares include: biology, chemistry, English, foreign language (German, French, Spanish), mathematics, music, and social sciences.

Licensure/Reciprocity: Florida. Students seeking teaching certification in a state other than Florida should consult with that state's teacher certification office early in their program of study to insure compliance with requirements. Many state directors of teacher credentialing have signed Interstate Agreements through NASDTEC that expedite the certification process.

All students completing a Florida State-approved Teacher Education Program must pass all portions of the Florida Teacher Certification Examination (FTCE).

UNIVERSITY OF CENTRAL FLORIDA

College of Education
4000 Central Florida Boulevard
Orlando, Florida 32816-1992
Phone: (407) 823-2153
Fax: (407) 823-5135
E-mail: martin@mail.ucf.edu
Internet: http://www.ucf.edu

Institution Description: The University of Central Florida (Florida Technological University until 1978) is a member of the State University System of Florida. It offered first instruction at the postsecondary level in 1968. The present name was adopted in 1978.

The College of Education offers undergraduate and graduate programs for teaching in all levels of elementary and secondary education.

Institution Control: Public.

Calendar: Semester. Academic year August to April.

Official(s): Dr. Sandra Robinson, Dean.

Faculty: Full-time 125; part-time 9; adjunct 90.

Degrees Awarded: 668 baccalaureate; 325 master's.

Admission Requirements: *Undergraduate:* Graduation from secondary school or GED; College Board SAT or ACT composite. *Teacher education specific:* University general education requirements or an associate in arts degree; 3.5 GPA; pass all four parts of College Level Academic Skills Test (CLAST); complete program prerequisites. *Graduate:* Baccalaureate degree from a regionally accredited institution. *Teacher education specific:* Undergraduate GPA of 3.0 on last 60 hours attempted; minimum 1000 on GRE; at least 3 years of full-time teaching.

Fees and Expenses: Undergraduate: in-state $58.45 per credit; out-of-state $58.45 per credit hour $300.49 fee. Graduate: in-state $147.34 per credit hour; out-of-state $147.34 per credit hour plus $465.33 fee. Other required fees: $23.56 in-state undergraduate, $29.36 graduate; $42.71 out-of-state undergraduate, $54. graduate. On-campus room and board: $4,056. Books and supplies: $800.

Financial Aid: Resources specifically for eligible students enrolled in teacher education programs are awarded on the basis of financial need and academic merit. The institution has a Program Participation Agreement with the U.S. Department of Education for eligible students to receive Pell Grants and other federal aid. *Contact:* Financial Aid Office at: (407) 823-2827.

Accreditation: *Regional:* SACS. *Professional:* NCATE. *Member of:* AACTE. *Approved by:* Florida Department of Education.

Undergraduate Programs: The role of the College of Education at the undergraduate level is to prepare students for careers as early childhood, elementary, secondary, exception, physical, vocational education teachers. The baccalaureate degree programs include area of concentration in art, early childhood, elementary, English language arts, exceptional student, foreign language, mathematics, physical education, science, social science, and vocational education and industry training. Credit requirements range from 122 to 128 semester hours depending on program pursued.

Graduate Programs: Graduate degree programs are offered at the doctoral and master's levels. Doctoral programs are offered in curriculum and instruction, educational leadership, and education (counselor, elementary, exceptional, instructional, mathematics).

Master's programs are offered in art education, counselor education, curriculum and instruction, early childhood, educational leadership, elementary, English language arts, exceptional education, instructional technology, mathematics, music, physical education, reading, science, and vocational education.

Licensure/Reciprocity: Florida. Students seeking teaching certification in a state other than Florida should consult with that state's teacher certification office early in their program of study to insure compliance with requirements. Many state directors of teacher credentialing have signed Interstate Agreements through NASDTEC that expedite the certification process.

All students completing a Florida State-approved Teacher Education Program must pass all portions of the Florida Teacher Certification Examination (FTCE).

UNIVERSITY OF FLORIDA
School of Teaching and Learning
Gainesville, Florida 32611-7048
Phone: (352) 392-9191
Fax: (352) 392-8774
E-mail: tdana@ufl.edu
Internet: http://www.ufl.edu

Institution Description: The University of Florida is a state institution and land-grant college. It was established as East Florida Seminary and offered first instruction at the postsecondary level in 1853. The present name was adopted in 1903.

The faculty of the School of Teaching and Learning offers a broad range of programs in curriculum and teaching.

Institution Control: Public.

Calendar: Semester. Academic year August to August.

Official(s): Dr. Tom Dana, Director, School of Teaching and Learning.

Faculty: Full-time 34.

Degrees Awarded: 250 baccalaureate; 387 master's; 35 doctorate.

Admission Requirements: *Undergraduate:* Admission is selective and offered only to those applicants whose credentials are academically sound and whose interests and aptitude reflect a well-rounded secondary school experience; College Board SAT or ACT composite. *Teacher education specific:* Application as early as possible during lower-level general education course achievement; faculty interview; demonstrate academic qualification; passing College Level Academic Skills Test (CLAST) or PRAXIS I. *Graduate:* Baccalaureate degree from a regionally accredited institution; 3.0 GPA for all upper-division work; GRE score of 1000. *Teacher education specific:* Three letters of recommendation; teaching credential; faculty interview.

Fees and Expenses: Undergraduate resident $92.68 per credit hour, nonresident $460.28. Graduate resident $205.26 per credit hour, nonresident $774.53. Other expenses: $2,715. On-campus room and board: $5,640. Books and supplies: $780.

Financial Aid: Resources specifically for eligible students enrolled in teacher education programs are awarded on the basis of financial need and academic merit. The institution has a Program Participation Agreement with the U.S. Department of Education for eligible students to receive Pell Grants and other federal aid. *Contact:* Financial Aid Office at: (352) 392-1275.

Accreditation: *Regional:* SACS. *Professional:* NCATE. *Member of:* AACTE. *Approved by:* Florida Department of Education.

Undergraduate Programs: The faculty of the School of Teaching and Learning offers teacher preparation programs in elementary and secondary education known as PROTEACH. These rigorous programs consist of five years of intensive study in the arts and sciences and professional education culminating in the Master of Education degree and state certification as a classroom teacher.

Graduate Programs: In addition to the above initial teacher preparation programs, the department offers four advanced degree programs (traditional master's, Education Specialist, Doctor of Education, and Doctor of Philosophy. Areas of concentration are: curriculum, teaching and teacher education;

early childhood education; educational psychology; English education; English for speakers of other languages/bilingual education; language arts and literature; mathematics education; reading education; science and environmental education; social studies education.

Licensure/Reciprocity: Florida. Students seeking teaching certification in a state other than Florida should consult with that state's teacher certification office early in their program of study to insure compliance with requirements. Many state directors of teacher credentialing have signed Interstate Agreements through NASDTEC that expedite the certification process.

All students completing a Florida State-approved Teacher Education Program must pass all portions of the Florida Teacher Certification Examination (FTCE).

UNIVERSITY OF MIAMI
School of Education
Department of Teaching and Learning
312 Merrick Building
5202 University Drive
Coral Gables, Florida 33124-2040
Phone: (305) 284-3505
Fax: (305) 284-3003
E-mail: syarger@miami.edu
Internet: http://www.education.miami.edu

Institution Description: The University of Miami is a private, independent, nonprofit institution. It was established in 1925 and offered first instruction at the postsecondary level in 1926.

The Department of Teaching and Learning offers undergraduate and graduate programs in the areas of elementary education, special education, secondary education, and music education.

Institution Control: Private.

Calendar: Semester. Academic year August to May.

Official(s): Dr. Sam J. Yarger, Dean; Dr. Liz Rothlein, Associate Dean.

Faculty: Full-time 47; part-time 7; adjunct 44.

Degrees Awarded: 59 baccalaureate; 153 master's.

Admission Requirements: *Undergraduate:* Graduation from an approved secondary school or GED; College Board SAT. *Teacher education specific:* Counselor evaluation; College Level Academic Skills Test; essay. *Graduate:* Baccalaureate from a regionally accredited institution. *Teacher education specific:* GRE scores; three letters or recommendation; acceptable GPA; English competency requirement; interview.

Fees and Expenses: Undergraduate $24,380 per academic year. Graduate $1,010 per credit hour. Required fees: $215.75 (activity, athletic, gym). On-campus room and board: $8.020. Books and supplies: $600.

Financial Aid: Resources specifically for eligible students enrolled in teacher education programs are awarded on the basis of financial need and academic merit. The institution has a Program Participation Agreement with the U.S. Department of Education for eligible students to receive Pell Grants and other federal aid. *Contact:* Office of Financial Assistance at: (305) 284-5214 or e-mail at ofas@miami.edu.

Accreditation: *Regional:* SACS. *Professional:* NCATE. *Member of:* AACTE. *Approved by:* Florida Department of Education.

Undergraduate Programs: All education students enrolled in teacher certification programs choose a major field of student in the College of Arts and Sciences and either a major or a minor in the field of education. An education student can acquire a major in arts and sciences with an education minor within a traditional four-year 120-credit hour program. Field experiences and associate teaching placements are achieved in a variety of schools in the Miami area. Programs are offered for elementary education (grades K-6), special education (grades K-12), secondary education (grades 6-12), and music education. The programs lead to a Bachelor of Science in Education (B.S.Ed.) degree.

UNIVERSITY OF MIAMI—*cont'd*

Graduate Programs: The School of Education offers 18 programs leading to a Master of Science in Education (M.S.Ed.), a Specialist in Education (Ed.S.), or a Doctor of Philosophy (Ph.D.).

Licensure/Reciprocity: Florida. Students seeking teaching certification in a state other than Florida should consult with that state's teacher certification office early in their program of study to insure compliance with requirements. Many state directors of teacher credentialing have signed Interstate Agreements through NASDTEC that expedite the certification process.

All students completing a Florida State-approved Teacher Education Program must pass all portions of the Florida Teacher Certification Examination (FTCE).

UNIVERSITY OF NORTH FLORIDA

College of Education and Human Services

4567 St. Johns Bluff Road, South
Jacksonville, Florida 32224-2645
Phone: (904) 620-2520
E-mail: kkastern@unf.edu
Internet: http://www.unf.edu

Institution Description: The University of North Florida is a state university providing full undergraduate and graduate programs of study. It was established in 1965 and offered first instruction at the postsecondary level in 1972.

Students in the College of Education and Human Services may choose career paths in teaching in the K-12 school setters or careers in sports leadership.

Institution Control: Public.

Calendar: Semester. Academic year May to April.

Official(s): Dr. Katherine Kasten, Dean.

Faculty: Not reported.

Degrees Awarded: 279 baccalaureate; 397 master's; 12 doctorate.

Admission Requirements: *Undergraduate:* Graduation from an approved secondary school or GED; College Board SAT or ACT composite. *Teacher education specific:* Acceptance into the teacher education program; pass all sections of the College Level Academic Skills Test (CLAST). *Graduate:* Baccalaureate from a regionally accredited institution. *Teacher education specific:* Letters of recommendation; faculty interview; GRE scores; pass all required tests/examinations.

Fees and Expenses: Undergraduate: in-state $2,913 per academic year; out-of-state $13,268.10 out-of-state. Graduate: in-state $208.44 per credit hour; out-of-state $742.97. On-campus room and board: $5,486. Other expenses: $847. Books and supplies: $600.

Financial Aid: Resources specifically for eligible students enrolled in teacher education programs are awarded on the basis of financial need and academic merit. The institution has a Program Participation Agreement with the U.S. Department of Education for eligible students to receive Pell Grants and other federal aid. *Contact:* Financial Aid Office at: (904) 620-2604.

Accreditation: *Regional:* SACS. *Professional:* NCATE. *Member of:* AACTE. *Approved by:* Florida Department of Education.

Undergraduate Programs: Undergraduate programs leading to the Bachelor of Arts in Education degree have as their primary objective the preparation of educators with broad foundations in various competencies. Programs are offered in elementary education, pre-K/primary education, middle school education, secondary education, physical education, sport leadership, and K-12 programs in art and music.

Graduate Programs: Programs for uncertified post-baccalaureate students leading to initial certification and the master's degree are offered in elementary education and secondary education.

The Master of Education degree majors include elementary education, secondary education, mathematics teacher education, music education, science education, special education, counselor education, and educational leadership.

Doctor of Education degree programs are available.

Licensure/Reciprocity: Florida. Students seeking teaching certification in a state other than Florida should consult with that state's teacher certification office early in their program of study to insure compliance with requirements. Many state directors of teacher credentialing have signed Interstate Agreements through NASDTEC that expedite the certification process.

All students completing a Florida State-approved Teacher Education Program must pass all portions of the Florida Teacher Certification Examination (FTCE).

UNIVERSITY OF SOUTH FLORIDA

College of Education

4202 East Fowler Avenue
Tampa, Florida 33620-9951
Phone: (813) 974-2011
Fax: (813) 974-9689
E-mail: bullseye@admin.usf.edu
Internet: http://usf.edu

Institution Description: The University of South Florida is a state institution with campuses in Lakeland, Sarasota, St. Petersburg, and Tampa. It was established in 1956.

The College of Education is a comprehensive metropolitan unit that was created in 1960.

Institution Control: Public.

Calendar: Semester. Academic year August to May.

Official(s): Chairpersons: Dr. W.R. Sullins, Adult, Career, and Higher Education; Dr. M. Mann, Childhood/Language Arts/Reading Education; Dr. M.J. Steward, Physical Education, Wellness and Sports Studies; Dr. C. Hines, Psychological and Social Foundations; Dr. J. F. Kaywell, Secondary Education; Dr. D. Thomas, Special Education.

Faculty: Total instructional faculty 194 (all sites).

Degrees Awarded: 696 baccalaureate; 566 master's; 31 doctorate.

Admission Requirements: *Undergraduate:* Graduation from an approved secondary school or GED; College Board SAT or ACT composite. *Teacher education specific:* Acceptance into the teacher education program after completion of the university's liberal arts freshman and sophomore requirements and state-mandated common prerequisites; pass all sections of the College Level Academic Skills Test (CLAST). *Graduate:* Baccalaureate from a regionally accredited institution. *Teacher education specific:* Letters of recommendation; faculty interview; GRE scores; pass all required tests/examinations.

Fees and Expenses: Undergraduate: in-state $2,913 per academic year; out-of-state $13,268.10 out-of-state. Graduate: in-state $208.44 per credit hour; out-of-state $742.97. On-campus room and board: $6,110. Books and supplies: $700.

Financial Aid: Resources specifically for eligible students enrolled in teacher education programs are awarded on the basis of financial need and academic merit. The institution has a Program Participation Agreement with the U.S. Department of Education for eligible students to receive Pell Grants and other federal aid. *Contact:* Financial Aid Office at: (813) 620-4700.

Accreditation: *Regional:* SACS. *Professional:* NCATE. *Member of:* AACTE. *Approved by:* Florida Department of Education.

Undergraduate Programs: The College of Education offers baccalaureate programs in childhood/language arts/reading education, early childhood education: pre-kindergarten/primary, elementary education, secondary education, and English education. All programs have specific requirements. Field experiences and student teaching assignments must be successfully completed before applying for teacher certification.

Graduate Programs: Graduate programs are offered leading to the Master of Arts in Teaching and the Master of Education degrees. These graduate programs are advanced tracks in the areas of childhood/language arts/reading education, early childhood education: pre-kindergarten/primary, elementary education, secondary education, and English education. All programs have specific requirements.

Doctoral programs in various areas are also available.

Licensure/Reciprocity: Florida. Students seeking teaching certification in a state other than Florida should consult with that state's teacher certification office early in their program of study to insure compliance with requirements. Many state directors of teacher credentialing have signed Interstate Agreements through NASDTEC that expedite the certification process.

All students completing a Florida State-approved Teacher Education Program must pass all portions of the Florida Teacher Certification Examination (FTCE).

UNIVERSITY OF WEST FLORIDA

Division of Teacher Education

11000 University Parkway
Pensacola, Florida 32514-5750
Phone: (850) 474-2893
Fax: (850) 474-2856
E-mail: sdow@uwf.edu
Internet: http://www.uwf.edu

Institution Description: The University of West Florida is a state institution offering undergraduate and graduate study. It was established in 1963.

The Division of Teacher Education offers a variety of teacher preparation programs on both the undergraduate and graduate levels.

Institution Control: Public.

Calendar: Semester. Academic year August to August.

Official(s): Dr. Joseph Peters, Chair, Division of Teacher Education.

Faculty: Full-time 30; adjunct 30.

Degrees Awarded: 127 baccalaureate; 167 master's; 29 doctorate.

Admission Requirements: *Undergraduate:* Graduation from an approved secondary school or GED; College Board SAT or ACT composite. *Teacher education specific:* Minimum 2.5 GPA; pass all sections of the College Level Academic Skills Test (CLAST) or PRAXIS I; autobiographical sketch; essay on career goals; faculty interview. *Graduate:* Baccalaureate from a regionally accredited institution; 3.0 GPA in the last 60 hours of coursework to meet the bachelor's degree requirements. *Teacher education specific:* GRE scores; pass all sections of CLAST or PRAXIS I; letters of recommendation; faculty interview.

Fees and Expenses: Undergraduate: in-state $2,913 per academic year; out-of-state $13,268.10. Graduate: in-state $208.44 per credit hour; out-of-state $742.97. On-campus room and board: $6,110. Books and supplies: $700.

Financial Aid: Resources specifically for eligible students enrolled in teacher education programs are awarded on the basis of financial need and academic merit. The institution has a Program Participation Agreement with the U.S. Department of Education for eligible students to receive Pell Grants and other federal aid. *Contact:* Cathy Brown at: (850) 474-3145 or e-mail at fawned@uwf.edu.

Accreditation: *Regional:* SACS. *Professional:* NCATE. *Member of:* AACTE. *Approved by:* Florida Department of Education.

Undergraduate Programs: The Division of Teacher Education offers five bachelor of arts programs. The B.A. program in pre-kindergarten/primary education will prepare graduates to teach preschool through third grade.

The division offers two specializations leading to the B.A. degree: the NCATE/DOE approved specialization leads directly to Florida teacher certification and the second prepares students to work in private settings or agencies that do not require graduation from an initial certification program.

The B.A. program in middle school education is designed to prepare students who plan to teach in grades 5-9.

The B.A. program in special education is designed to prepared students who plan to teach children and youth who are mentally handicapped, learning disabled, or emotionally handicapped.

Graduate Programs: Various divisions within the College of Professional Studies offer master's degree specializations leading to the M.Ed. degree in curriculum and instruction.

The doctoral degree in curriculum and instruction is designed to meet the educational needs of regional place bound, full-time employed professionals who will be selected from a wide range of educational backgrounds.

Licensure/Reciprocity: Florida. Students seeking teaching certification in a state other than Florida should consult with that state's teacher certification office early in their program of study to insure compliance with requirements. Many state directors of teacher credentialing have signed Interstate Agreements through NASDTEC that expedite the certification process.

All students completing a Florida State-approved Teacher Education Program must pass all portions of the Florida Teacher Certification Examination (FTCE).

WARNER SOUTHERN COLLEGE

Teacher Education Department

5301 Highway 27 South
Lake Wales, Florida 33859
Phone: (863) 638-7243
Fax: (863) 638-7125
E-mail: faselt@@warner.edu
Internet: http://www.warner.edu

Institution Description: Warner Southern College is an independent, nonprofit institution affiliated with the Church of God. It was established and offered first instruction at the post-secondary level in 1968.

The Teacher Education Department offers undergraduate programs leading to the baccalaureate degree.

Institution Control: Private.

Calendar: Semester. Academic year August to May.

Official(s): Dr. Terry Fasel, Dean.

Faculty: Full-time 5; part-time 5; adjunct 3.

Degrees Awarded: 31 baccalaureate.

Admission Requirements: *Undergraduate:* Graduation from an approved secondary school or GED; College Board SAT or ACT composite. *Teacher education specific:* Junior level status; 2.5 GPA; background check; recommendations and references; passing scores on all scores of the College Level Academic Skills Test (CLAST).

Fees and Expenses: $11,286 per academic year. Required fees: $45. On-campus room and board: $4,952. Books and supplies: $400.

Financial Aid: Resources specifically for eligible students enrolled in teacher education programs are awarded on the basis of financial need and academic merit. The institution has a Program Participation Agreement with the U.S. Department of Education for eligible students to receive Pell Grants and other federal aid. *Contact:* Lori White at: (863) 638-7203.

Accreditation: *Regional:* SACS. *Approved by:* Florida Department of Education.

Undergraduate Programs: Students in the Teacher Education Program must have all the general education requirements as other majors plus required courses in English/communication, science, math, social science, and humanities. All students must take courses in the foundational core and professional semester. The major in elementary education (grades K-6) requires an additional 30 credit hours of specialization courses.

The major in exceptional student education consists of the foundational core and professional semester plus 36 credit hours of specialization courses.

WARNER SOUTHERN COLLEGE—cont'd

Students majoring in English education, music education, physical education teaching, science education, science and math education, and social science education must complete the major in the department of specialization.

Licensure/Reciprocity: Florida. Students seeking teaching certification in a state other than Florida should consult with that state's teacher certification office early in their program of study to insure compliance with requirements. Many state directors of teacher credentialing have signed Interstate Agreements through NASDTEC that expedite the certification process.

All students completing a Florida State-approved Teacher Education Program must pass all portions of the Florida Teacher Certification Examination (FTCE).

GEORGIA

ALBANY STATE UNIVERSITY

College of Education

Department of Teacher Education

504 College Drive

Albany, Georgia 31705

Phone: (229) 430-4715

Fax: (229) 430-4993

E-mail: abeard@asurams.edu

Internet: http:/www.asurams.edu

Institution Description: Albany State University, formerly named Albany State College, is a state institution. It was established as Albany Bible and Manual Training Institute in 1903. It became Albany State College in 1943 and achieved university status in 1996.

Students in the teacher education programs are given opportunities to observe, serve, and work with students in schools and other educational settings to conceptualize and apply theory and practice in an authentic setting.

Institution Control: Public.

Calendar: Semester. Academic year August to July.

Official(s): Dr. Barbara Holmes, Dean, College of Education; Dr. A. Beard, Chair, Department of Teacher Education.

Faculty: Full-time 11.

Degrees Awarded: 51 baccalaureate; 92 master's.

Admission Requirements: *Undergraduate:* Graduation from an approved secondary school or GED; College Board SAT or ACT composite. *Teacher education specific:* Completion of a minimum of 36 semester hours of general education core; 2.5 GPA or above; successful completion of PRAXIS I and Regents' Examination; computer proficiency; satisfaction of unique requirements of the specific program applied to and faculty approval. *Graduate:* Baccalaureate degree from a regionally accredited institution. *Teacher education specific:* Undergraduate GPA 2.5 or better; score of 800 on the GRE; teacher certification; approval by the Department Chairperson and the Dean of the College of Education.

Fees and Expenses: Undergraduate: in-state $1,296 per semester (including fees); out-of-state $4,614. Graduate in-state $1,517 per semester (including fees); out-of-state $5,498. Room and board: $7,120 per academic year. Other expenses: $1,758. Books and supplies: $800.

Financial Aid: Resources specifically for eligible students enrolled in teacher education programs are awarded on the basis of financial need and academic merit. The institution has a Program Participation Agreement with the U.S. Department of Education for eligible students to receive Pell Grants and other federal aid. *Contact:* Financial Aid Office at: (229) 430-4650.

Accreditation: *Regional:* SACS. *Professional:* NCATE. *Member of:* AACTE. *Approved by:* Georgia Professional Standards Commission.

Undergraduate Programs: The College of Education offers the Bachelor of Science degree in early childhood education. The program requires the minimum of 120 semester hours. Student teaching is the culminating experience of the entry level baccalaureate programs and is provided in selected public schools. Successful completion of this program leads to certification by the Georgia Professional Standards Commission.

The Bachelor of Science degree program in middle grades education (grades 4-8) requires a minimum of 122 semester hours including student teaching. Formal admission to the teacher education program is required before students are permitted to register for upper level courses. Successful completion leads to certification by the Georgia Professional Standards Commission.

Graduate Programs: The Master of Education Degree in early childhood education requires successful completion of a minimum of 36 semester hours. The 36-semester hour program leads to the 1-5 certification in early childhood education and is designed to prepare teachers to work with children in grades P-5. Completion of the program leads to certification by the Georgia Professional Standards Commission.

Licensure/Reciprocity: Georgia. Students seeking teaching certification in a state other than Georgia should consult with that state's teacher certification office early in their program of study to insure compliance with requirements. Many state directors of teacher credentialing have signed Interstate Agreements through NASDTEC that expedite the certification process.

ARMSTRONG ATLANTIC STATE UNIVERSITY

College of Education

Teacher Education Programs

11935 Abercorn Street

Savannah, Georgia 31419-1997

Phone: (912) 927-5398

Fax: (912) 921-7925

E-mail: coe@armstrong.edu

Internet: http://www.armstrong.edu

Institution Description: Armstrong Atlantic State University, formerly Armstrong State College, is a public institution. It was established as Armstrong College of Savannah in 1935 and was incorporated into the University of Georgia System in 1959. The present name was adopted in 1995.

The College of Education through its teacher education programs offers undergraduate and graduate programs leading to certification in various areas.

Institution Control: Public.

Calendar: Semester. Academic year September to June.

Official(s): Dr. Evelyn Dandy, Dean; Dr. Patti Brandt, Assistant Dean.

Faculty: Full-time 40; part-time 42.

Degrees Awarded: 102 baccalaureate; 136 master's.

Admission Requirements: *Undergraduate:* Graduation from an approved secondary school or GED; College Board SAT or ACT composite. *Teacher education specific:* Education majors are required to complete 40 semester hours of college credit with a 2.5 GPA; pass Regents' Test; complete 10 hours of educational community service; pass all sections of the PRAXIS I Test. *Graduate:* Baccalaureate degree from a regionally accredited institution. *Teacher education specific:* Student must have completed a teacher certification program; transcript evaluation; completion of 10 hours of educational community service; pass all sections of PRAXIS I.

ARMSTRONG ATLANTIC STATE UNIVERSITY—cont'd

Fees and Expenses: Undergraduate: in-state $1,296 per semester (including fees); out-of-state $4,614. Graduate in-state $1,517 per semester (including fees); out-of-state $5,498. Room and board: $4,500 per academic year. Other expenses: $1,758. Books and supplies: $800.

Financial Aid: Resources specifically for eligible students enrolled in teacher education programs are awarded on the basis of financial need and academic merit. The institution has a Program Participation Agreement with the U.S. Department of Education for eligible students to receive Pell Grants and other federal aid. *Contact:* Lee Ann Kirkland at: (912) 929-5272 or e-mail at kirklale@mail.armstrong.edu.

Accreditation: *Regional:* SACS. *Professional:* NCATE. *Member of:* AACTE. *Approved by:* Georgia Professional Standards Commission.

Undergraduate Programs: The Department of Early Childhood Education offers the Bachelor of Science in early childhood education as well as teacher certification. The baccalaureate in art education is offered in conjunction with the Department of Art, Music, and Theatre. Majors and minors in library media are available (the major in library media is only available as part of a double major.

The Department of middle grades and secondary education offers the Bachelor of Science in Education in middle grades education. In conjunction with the College of Arts and Sciences, the Bachelor of Arts in English, history, or political science are offered with teacher certification. The Bachelor of Science degree is offered with concentrations in biology, chemistry, and mathematical sciences, all with teacher certification.

Graduate Programs: The Master of Education degree is offered in adult education, middle grades education, and secondary education (English, mathematics, broadfield science, and broadfield social science),

The Post-Baccalaureate Teacher Preparation Program is for those holding a baccalaureate or higher degree from an accredited college or university but not yet eligible for a license to teach.

Licensure/Reciprocity: Georgia. Students seeking teacher certification in a state other than Georgia should consult with that state's teacher certification office early in their program of study to insure compliance with requirements. Many state directors of teacher credentialing have signed Interstate Agreements through NASDTEC that expedite the certification process.

ATLANTA CHRISTIAN COLLEGE

Department of Education
Teacher Education Program
2605 Ben Hill Road
East Point, Georgia 30344
Phone: (404) 761-8861
Fax: (404) 669-2024
E-mail: doe@acc.edu
Internet: http://www.acc.edu

Institution Description: Atlanta Christian College is a private, independent, nonprofit Christian college related to the Christian Churches and Churches of Christ. It was established and chartered in 1928.

The Department of Education offers a baccalaureate program leading to teacher certification in early childhood education.

Institution Control: Private.

Calendar: Semester. Academic year August to May.

Official(s): Dr. William L. Russell, Chair, Department of Education.

Faculty: Full-time 2; adjunct 6.

Degrees Awarded: 9 baccalaureate.

Admission Requirements: *Undergraduate:* Graduation from an approved secondary school or GED; College Board SAT or ACT Composite. *Teacher education specific:* Faculty interview; completion of general education core; pass all required test/examinations.

Fees and Expenses: $9,950 per academic year. On-campus room and board: $3,950. Other expenses: $5,160. Books and supplies: $700.

Financial Aid: Resources specifically for eligible students enrolled in teacher education programs are awarded on the basis of financial need and academic merit. The institution has a Program Participation Agreement with the U.S. Department of Education for eligible students to receive Pell Grants and other federal aid. *Contact:* Financial Aid Office at: (404) 761-8861.

Accreditation: *Regional:* SACS. *Professional:* NCATE. *Approved by:* Georgia Professional Standards Commission.

Undergraduate Programs: The Bachelor of Science Degree in early childhood education is designed to prepare teachers to work with children in preschool through fifth grade. The major requires 63 semester hours of education courses. The student progresses from general studies courses and foundational education courses into the teacher education program. The program is three semesters of teacher education courses and the student teaching experience in local elementary schools.

The degree program also has a minor in biblical studies that requires completion of specific courses.

Licensure/Reciprocity: Georgia. Students seeking teaching certification in a state other than Georgia should consult with that state's teacher certification office early in their program of study to insure compliance with requirements. Many state directors of teacher credentialing have signed Interstate Agreements through NASDTEC that expedite the certification process.

AUGUSTA STATE UNIVERSITY

College of Education
Department of Teacher Development
2500 Walton Way
Augusta, Georgia 30904-2200
Phone: (706) 737-1401
Fax: (706) 667-4353
E-mail: coe@aug.edu
Internet: http://www.aug.edu

Institution Description: Augusta State University, formerly Augusta College, is a state-supported institution that was established as the Junior College of Augusta in 1925. It became Augusta College, a unit of the University System of Georgia, in 1958 and became a 4-year institution in 1963. The present name was adopted in 1996.

The Department of Teacher Development prepares educators with the knowledge and skills required to bring students of diverse backgrounds to high levels of academic achievement.

Institution Control: Public.

Calendar: Semester. Academic year August to May.

Official(s): Dr. Richard Harrison, Dean, College of Education; Dr. Mark Warner, Chair, Department of Teacher Development.

Faculty: Full-time 10 (Teacher Development).

Degrees Awarded: 77 baccalaureate; 60 master's.

Admission Requirements: *Undergraduate:* Graduation with 16 academic units from an approved secondary school or GED; College Board SAT. *Teacher education specific:* Cumulative GPA 2.5 or above; successful performance on all portions of the Regents' Examination; pass PRAXIS I test; faculty recommendation. *Graduate:* Baccalaureate degree from a regionally accredited institution. *Teacher education specific:* Teaching credential; completion of all Georgia required tests/examinations; GPA 2.5 or better; letters of recommendation; faculty interview

Fees and Expenses: Undergraduate: in-state $1,296 per semester (including fees); out-of-state $4,614. Graduate in-state $1,517 per semester (including fees); out-of-state $5,498. Room and board: $6,986 per academic year. Books and supplies: $832.

Financial Aid: Resources specifically for eligible students enrolled in teacher education programs are awarded on the basis of financial need and academic merit. The institution has a Program Participation Agreement with the U.S. Department of Education for eligible students to receive Pell Grants and other federal aid. *Contact:* Financial Aid Office at: (706) 737-1431.

Accreditation: *Regional:* SACS. *Professional:* NCATE. *Member of:* AACTE. *Approved by:* Georgia Professional Standards Commission.

Undergraduate Programs: The College of Education offers undergraduate programs in early childhood Education, middle grades education, secondary education (French, history, mathematics, political science, science, social studies, Spanish.

P-12 Programs are offered in health and physical education, music education, and special education (intellectual disorders).

Endorsement Programs are available in gifted, pre-school handicapped, and teacher support specialist.

Graduate Programs: Graduate programs are offered in the following areas: early childhood education (M.Ed., Ed.S.); middle grades education (M.Ed., Ed.S.), secondary education (M.Ed., Ed.S.) in English, history, mathematics, social studies; special education (M.Ed.) in behavior disorders, intellectual disorders, interrelated special education, and learning disabilities.

Licensure/Reciprocity: Georgia. Students seeking teaching certification in a state other than Georgia should consult with that state's teacher certification office early in their program of study to insure compliance with requirements. Many state directors of teacher credentialing have signed Interstate Agreements through NASDTEC that expedite the certification process.

BERRY COLLEGE
Charter School of Education and Human Sciences
Teacher Education
2277 Martha Berry Highway
Mount Berry, Georgia 30149
Phone: 706) 232-5374
Fax: (706) 236-2248
E-mail: admissions@berry.edu
Internet: http://www.berry.edu

Institution Description: Berry College is a private, independent, nonprofit college. It was established in 1903 as The Boy's Industrial School. The name was changed to The Berry College in 1908 and The Martha Berry School for Girls was founded in 1909. Both institutions were incorporated as The Berry Schools in 1917 and became The Berry Schools and College in 1930. The present name was adopted in 1983.

The mission of the Charter School is to prepare and develop individuals for the teaching profession through academically challenging and field-based experiences.

Institution Control: Private.

Calendar: Semester. Academic year August to May.

Official(s): Dr. Jackie McDowell, Dean, Charter School of Education and Human Sciences.

Faculty: Full-time 20, part-time 37.

Degrees Awarded: 56 baccalaureate; 58 master's.

Admission Requirements: *Undergraduate:* Graduation with 20 academic units from an approved secondary school or GED; College Board SAT or ACT composite. *Teacher education specific:* Completion of two semesters of college work; 2.5 GPA or better; pass the PRAXIS I test; two letters of recommendation; faculty interview. *Graduate:* Baccalaureate degree from a regionally accredited institution. *Teacher education specific:* Pass the PRAXIS II tests in the area of preparation; teaching credential when appropriate; letters of recommendation; faculty interview.

Fees and Expenses: $14,260 per academic year. On-campus room and board: $5,624. Other expenses: $2,246. Books and supplies: $800.

Financial Aid: Resources specifically for eligible students enrolled in teacher education programs are awarded on the basis of financial need and academic merit. The institution has a

Program Participation Agreement with the U.S. Department of Education for eligible students to receive Pell Grants and other federal aid. *Contact:* Financial Aid Office at: (706) 236-1714.

Accreditation: *Regional:* SACS. *Professional:* NCATE. *Member of:* AACTE. *Approved by:* Georgia Professional Standards Commission.

Undergraduate Programs: The early childhood education major leads to the Bachelor of Science degree and prepares teachers for certification in preschool through grade 5.

The middle grades education major (4-8) leads to the Bachelor of Science degree and leads to certification in grades 4-8. The middle grades teacher must have a broad general education in addition to a knowledge of the techniques and materials needed to teach middle grades subjects.

The secondary education ninor leads to certification for grades 7-12. Certification is available in English, mathematics, biology, chemistry, physics, history, government, or social sciences.

Graduate Programs: Graduate programs and postbaccalaureate certification programs are offered in early childhood education (P-5), middle grades education (4-8), secondary education (art, foreign language, health and physical education, music) and for grades 7-12 in English, mathematics, science (biology, chemistry, physics), social science, history, and political science.

Licensure/Reciprocity: Georgia. Students seeking teaching certification in a state other than Georgia should consult with that state's teacher certification office early in their program of study to insure compliance with requirements. Many state directors of teacher credentialing have signed Interstate Agreements through NASDTEC that expedite the certification process.

BRENAU UNIVERSITY
School of Education
Department of Teacher Education
One Centennial Circle
Gainesville, Georgia 30501
Phone: (770) 534-6220
Fax: (770) 534-6221
E-mail: bware@lib.brenau.edu
Internet: http://www.brenau.edu

Institution Description: Brenau University is a private, independent, nonprofit institution. It was established as Georgia Baptist Female Seminary in 1878. The present name was adopted in 1900.

The School of Education offers both undergraduate and graduate programs leading to teacher certification in Georgia.

Institution Control: Private.

Calendar: Semester. Academic year September to June.

Official(s): Dr. William B. Ware, Dean, School of Education.

Faculty: Full-time 16; part-time 3; adjunct 53.

Degrees Awarded: 88 baccalaureate; 142 master's.

Admission Requirements: *Undergraduate:* Graduation with 16 units from an accredited secondary school or GED; College Board SAT or ACT composite. *Teacher education specific:* Completion of 10 hours in a major; 2.5 GPA; passing score on PRAXIS I; statement of career goals; pass all Brenau University required tests/exams. *Graduate:* Baccalaureate degree from a regionally accredited institution; undergraduate GPA of 3.0; GRE. *Teacher education specific:* Faculty interview and recommendation; specific admission requirements may be applicable to some programs.

Fees and Expenses: $21,800 comprehensive fee per academic year.

Financial Aid: Resources specifically for eligible students enrolled in teacher education programs are awarded on the basis of financial need and academic merit. The institution has a Program Participation Agreement with the U.S. Department of Education for eligible students to receive Pell Grants and other federal aid. *Contact:* Pam Barrett at (770-534-6142 or e-mail at barrett@lib.brenau.edu.

BRENAU UNIVERSITY—cont'd

Accreditation: *Regional:* SACS. *Member of:* AACTE. *Approved by:* Georgia Professional Standards Commission.

Undergraduate Programs: The Department of Undergraduate Teacher Education offers majors in early childhood education (Bachelor of Arts, Bachelor of Science). A concentration in early childhood education leads to Georgia certification for pre-school through grade five. In the field experiences and appropriate professional courses, attention is given to the education of the growing child.

A major in middle grades education leads to certification for grades four through eight. The major in middle grades education has two areas of content concentration. The primary and secondary concentrations may be selected from language arts, mathematics, science or social studies.

Special education-intellectual disabilities programs lead to the B.A. and B.S. degrees. The programs are offered for those who will teach in a public school classroom for students P-12 who have intellectual disabilities.

Graduate Programs: The School of Education offers graduate programs leading to the Master of Arts in Teaching and the Master of Education degrees.

Licensure/Reciprocity: Georgia. Students seeking teaching certification in a state other than Georgia should consult with that state's teacher certification office early in their program of study to insure compliance with requirements. Many state directors of teacher credentialing have signed Interstate Agreements through NASDTEC that expedite the certification process.

BREWTON-PARKER COLLEGE

Teacher Education Unit
Division of Education
  Highway 280
  Mt. Vernon, Georgia 30445
  Phone: (912) 583-2241
  Fax: (912) 583-4498
  E-mail: info@bpc.edu
  Internet: http://www.bpc.edu

Institution Description: Brewton-Parker College is a private college offering programs in business, education, liberal arts, and religion. It is affiliated with the Baptist Church. It was established as Union Baptist Institute in 1904.

The mission of the Teacher Education Unit is that the professional teachers produced through the programs will acquire a strong foundation of research-based knowledge, strengthen philosophical attitudes and values, and demonstrate sound pedagogical practices.

Institution Control: Private.

Calendar: Semester. Academic year September to June.

Official(s): Dr. Laurey Jossey, Chair, Education Division.

Faculty: Full-time 9.

Degrees Awarded: 60 baccalaureate.

Admission Requirements: *Undergraduate:* Graduation from an approved secondary school or GED; College Board SAT or ACT composite. *Teacher education specific:* Student must meet all requirements for pre-admission including PRAXIS I Test; minimum GPA of 2.5 or higher; portfolio assessment; pass PRAXIS II.

Fees and Expenses: $8,950 per academic year. On-campus room and board: $4,600. Other expenses: $2,400. Books and supplies: $1,000.

Financial Aid: Resources specifically for eligible students enrolled in teacher education programs are awarded on the basis of financial need and academic merit. The institution has a Program Participation Agreement with the U.S. Department of Education for eligible students to receive Pell Grants and other federal aid. *Contact:* Financial Aid Office at:(912) 483-3215.

Accreditation: *Regional:* SACS. *Member of:* AACTE. *Approved by:* Georgia Professional Standards Commission.

Undergraduate Programs: Early childhood education (preK-5) candidates plan their course of study with their academic advisors. The program leads to the Bachelor of Science degree.

The major in middle grades education (grades 4-8) chooses two areas of concentration from social studies, mathematics, science, or language arts. The areas of concentration will affect the choice of some courses in the college core curriculum.

Secondary education majors (grades 7-12) are advised by the Arts and Sciences faculty in their content area.

Licensure/Reciprocity: Georgia. Students seeking teaching certification in a state other than Georgia should consult with that state's teacher certification office early in their program of study to insure compliance with requirements. Many state directors of teacher credentialing have signed Interstate Agreements through NASDTEC that expedite the certification process.

CLARK ATLANTA UNIVERSITY

School of Education
Department of Curriculum
  223 James P. Brawley Drive
  Atlanta, Georgia 30314
  Phone: (404) 880-6334
  Fax: (404) 880-6997
  E-mail: info@cau.edu
  Internet: http://www.cau.edu

Institution Description: Clark Atlanta University is a private institution affiliated with the United Methodist Church. It was founded in 1988 upon the merger of Clark College and Atlanta University.

The objective of the Curriculum Department's undergraduate programs are to provide pre-service education for prospective teachers and a background in the principles of education for students preparing for general and social service areas of education.

Institution Control: Private.

Calendar: Semester. Academic year September to May.

Official(s): Dr. Janet Fisher, Chair, Department of Curriculum.

Faculty: Full-time 15; adjunct 6.

Degrees Awarded: 25 baccalaureate; 61 master's; 14 doctorate.

Admission Requirements: *Undergraduate:* Graduation from an accredited secondary school or GED; College Board SAT or ACT composite; 500-word essay. *Teacher education specific:* Passing score on PRAXIS I Test; 2.5 GPA or better; 2 appraisal forms; faculty interview.

Fees and Expenses: $12,312 per academic year. Required fees: $550. On-campus room and board: $6,440.

Financial Aid: Resources specifically for eligible students enrolled in teacher education programs are awarded on the basis of financial need and academic merit. The institution has a Program Participation Agreement with the U.S. Department of Education for eligible students to receive Pell Grants and other federal aid. *Contact:* Financial Aid Office at: (404) 880-8992.

Accreditation: *Regional:* SACS. *Professional:* NCATE. *Member of:* AACTE. *Approved by:* Georgia Professional Standards Commission.

Undergraduate Programs: The early childhood education program (grades 4-8) leads to the Bachelor of Arts and prepares instructional personnel to direct the education of young children to age ten (pre-school-grade five).

The middle grades education program leads to a Bachelor of Arts and is designed to provide the knowledge, skills, and instructional strategies needed to facilitate effectively the academic achievement and affective development of young adolescents. The core curriculum credit hours are incorporated into the total program requirements of 124-126 credit hours.

Licensure/Reciprocity: Georgia. Students seeking teaching certification in a state other than Georgia should consult with that state's teacher certification office early in their program of study to insure compliance with requirements. Many state

directors of teacher credentialing have signed Interstate Agreements through NASDTEC that expedite the certification process.

CLAYTON COLLEGE AND STATE UNIVERSITY

Teacher Education

Office G-205
5900 North Lee Street
Morrow, Georgia 30260-1250
Phone: (770) 961-3578
Fax: (770) 961-4335
E-mail: marygracesurma@mail.clayton.edu
Internet: http://www.clayton.edu

Institution Description: Clayton College and State University, formerly known as Clayton State College, is a public institution. It was established in 1969 as Clayton Junior College and became a senior college in 1986.

The Teacher Education program has partnerships with middle schools in six local counties (Clayton, Fayette, Fulton, Henry, Rockdale, Griffin-Spalding).

Institution Control: Public.

Calendar: Semester. Academic year September to June.

Official(s): Dr. Larnell Flannagan, Coordinator for Middle Level Education.

Faculty: Full-time 4.

Degrees Awarded: 16 baccalaureate.

Admission Requirements: *Undergraduate:* Graduation from an accredited secondary school or GED; College Board SAT or ACT composite. *Teacher education specific:* Regents' Testing Program; minimum competence in computers; GPA of 2.5; completion of at least 45 semester hours of college work; writing assessment

Fees and Expenses: Undergraduate: in-state $1,296 per semester (including fees); out-of-state $4,614. Graduate in-state $1,517 per semester (including fees); out-of-state $5,498. Room and board: $6,050 per academic year. Other expenses: $2,274. Books and supplies: $850.

Financial Aid: Resources specifically for eligible students enrolled in teacher education programs are awarded on the basis of financial need and academic merit. The institution has a Program Participation Agreement with the U.S. Department of Education for eligible students to receive Pell Grants and other federal aid. *Contact:* Financial Aid Office at: (770) 961-3511.

Accreditation: *Regional:* SACS. *Professional:* NCATE. *Member of:* AACTE. *Approved by:* Georgia Professional Standards Commission.

Undergraduate Programs: The middle level education program (grades 4-8) leading to a Bachelor of Arts degree is committed to the idea that the best place to learn about teaching middle school students is in the middle schools. Upon completion of the program, students have developed a high competency in using computers and other technology in the classroom. The program requires the completion of a general education core, major area course requirements, and field experience in local area middle schools.

Licensure/Reciprocity: Georgia. Students seeking teaching certification in a state other than Georgia should consult with that state's teacher certification office early in their program of study to insure compliance with requirements. Many state directors of teacher credentialing have signed Interstate Agreements through NASDTEC that expedite the certification process.

COLUMBUS STATE UNIVERSITY

College of Education
Department of Teacher Education

4225 University Avenue
Columbus, Georgia 31909-5645
Phone: (706) 568-2255
Fax: (706) 568-2462
E-mail: tbutcher@colstate.edu
Internet: http://www.colstate.edu

Institution Description: Columbus State University was formerly known as Columbus College. It was established as a junior college in 1958. An upper-division program was added in 1966. The institution attained university status and the present name was adopted in 1996.

The College of Education overall mission is to guide individuals in the process of becoming skillful, competent, knowledgeable, and reflective professionals.

Institution Control: Public.

Calendar: Semester. Academic year August to June.

Official(s): Dr. Thomas Harrison, Dean, College of Education; Dr. Tina Butcher, Chair, Department of Teacher Education.

Faculty: Full-time 16.

Degrees Awarded: 88 baccalaureate; 117 master's.

Admission Requirements: *Undergraduate:* Graduation from an approved secondary school or GED; College Board SAT or ACT composite. *Teacher education specific:* Completion of two semesters of college work; 2.5 GPA or better; pass the PRAXIS I test; two letters of recommendation; faculty interview. *Graduate:* Baccalaureate degree from a regionally accredited institution. *Teacher education specific:* Pass the PRAXIS II tests in the area of preparation; teaching credential where appropriate; letters of recommendation; faculty interview.

Fees and Expenses: Undergraduate: in-state $1,338 per semester (including fees); out-of-state $4,656. Graduate in-state $1,589 per semester (including fees); out-of-state $5,540. Room and board: $7,120 per academic year. Other expenses: $2,505. Books and supplies: $800.

Financial Aid: Resources specifically for eligible students enrolled in teacher education programs are awarded on the basis of financial need and academic merit. The institution has a Program Participation Agreement with the U.S. Department of Education for eligible students to receive Pell Grants and other federal aid. *Contact:* Financial Aid Office at: (706) 568-2036.

Accreditation: *Regional:* SACS. *Professional:* NCATE. *Member of:* AACTE. *Approved by:* Georgia Professional Standards Commission.

Undergraduate Programs: Baccalaureate programs are offered in early childhood education, middle grades education (language arts/social studies, math/science), secondary education with concentrations in English language arts, mathematics, history, biology, chemistry, earth/space, and the Bachelor of Arts in French or Spanish with certification.

Graduate Programs: Graduate programs include: early childhood education (M.Ed., Ed.S.); fast track master's teaching program (M.Ed.); Intern teaching team program (M.Ed.); health and physical education (M.Ed.); instructional technology (M.S.); middle grades education (language arts/social studies and math/science (M.Ed., Ed.S.), secondary education (M.Ed., Ed.S.) in English language arts, mathematics, history, biology, chemistry; special education (M.Ed.) in behavioral disorders, learning disabilities, mental retardation.

Licensure/Reciprocity: Georgia. Students seeking teaching certification in a state other than Georgia should consult with that state's teacher certification office early in their program of study to insure compliance with requirements. Many state directors of teacher credentialing have signed Interstate Agreements through NASDTEC that expedite the certification process.

EMMANUEL COLLEGE

School of Education

181 Springs Street
Franklin Springs, Georgia 30639
Phone: (706) 245-2834
Fax: (706) 245-4424
E-mail: hollinshead@emmanuelcollege.edu
Internet: http://www.emmanuelcollege.edu

Institution Description: Emmanuel College is a private four-year college affiliated with the Pentecostal Holiness Church. It was established as Franklin Springs Institute in 1919 and the present name was adopted in 1939.

The School of Education offers undergraduate programs with various areas of concentration that lead to Georgia teacher certification.

Institution Control: Private.

Calendar: Semester. Academic year August to May.

Official(s): Dr. Vicki Hollinshead, Dean.

Faculty: Full-time 6; part-time 6.

Degrees Awarded: 33 baccalaureate.

Admission Requirements: *Undergraduate:* High school graduation or GED; College Board SAT or ACT composite. *Teacher education specific:* Pass PRAXIS I Test; 2.5 GPA; portfolio evaluation; philosophy of education paper; recommendations.

Fees and Expenses: $8,801 per academic year. Required fees: $270. On-campus room and board: $4,136. Books and supplies: $600.

Financial Aid: Resources specifically for eligible students enrolled in teacher education programs are awarded on the basis of financial need and academic merit. The institution has a Program Participation Agreement with the U.S. Department of Education for eligible students to receive Pell Grants and other federal aid. *Contact:* Mary Beadles at: (706) 245-7226.

Accreditation: *Regional:* SACS. *Approved by:* Georgia Professional Standards Commission.

Undergraduate Programs: Early childhood education majors complete 125 hours with a 2.5 GPA and successful completion of student teaching. This degree leads to certification in grades PreK-5.

Middle grades education majors complete 124-131 hours depending on the areas of primary and secondary concentration. A 2.5 GPA and successful completion of student teaching is required. The degree leads to certification in grades 4-8.

Social science education majors complete 124 hours and leads to certification in social science in grades 7-12. math education majors complete 121 hours that lead to certification in math education in grades 7-12.

Other baccalaureate programs are offered in business education (130 hours), English education (126 hours), and music education (137 hours).

Licensure/Reciprocity: Georgia. Students seeking teacher certification in a state other than Georgia should consult with that state's teacher certification office early in their program of study to insure compliance with requirements. Many state directors of teacher credentialing have signed Interstate Agreements through NASDTEC that expedite the certification process.

EMORY UNIVERSITY

Division of Educational Studies

240 North Decatur Building
1784 North Decatur Road
Atlanta, Georgia 30030
Phone: (404) 727-6468
Fax: (404) 727-2799
E-mail: gavant@emory.edu
Internet: http://www.emory.edu

Institution Description: Emory University is a private institution affiliated with the United Methodist Church. It was established in Oxford as Emory College and offered first instruction at postsecondary level in 1836. It was chartered under the present name and the campus moved to Atlanta in 1915.

The Division of Educational Studies offers graduate programs only.

Institution Control: Private.

Calendar: Semester. Academic year August to May.

Official(s): Dr. Eleanor C. Main, Chair, Division of Educational Studies.

Faculty: Full-time 11; adjunct 20.

Degrees Awarded: 7 baccalaureate; 7 master's; 2 doctorate.

Admission Requirements: *Graduate:* GPA 3.0; GRE in 50th %ile or better; 3 recommendations; purpose statement; faculty interview. *Teacher education specific:* Pass all required departmental/state tests/exams.

Fees and Expenses: $12,885 per semester. Required fees: $170. On-campus room and board: $13,000 per academic year. Books and supplies: $1,000.

Financial Aid: All Master of Arts in Teaching students receive 75% discount on billing because they are preparing to be teachers. *Contact:* Glen R. Avant at (404) 727-0612 or gavant@emory.edu.

Accreditation: *Regional:* SACS. *Professional:* NCATE. *Member of:* AACTE. *Approved by:* Georgia Professional Standards Commission.

Graduate Programs: The Master of Arts in Teaching programs are designed to develop knowledge and skill in instruction and competence in subject matter. Internships are provided in urban middle and secondary schools with diverse student populations. If certification requirements are followed and successfully complete, graduates become eligible for the appropriate professional teaching certification. The degree leads to certification in either middle grades (4-8) or secondary education (7-12). Coursework for the degrees requires a minimum of 36 semester hours.

The Master of Education degree is designed for experienced teachers who want to develop advanced breadth and depth in the subject matter and research of their teaching field. A planned program is developed to include a specialization in such areas as middle grades and secondary education in the content fields of English, mathematics, science, and social studies. Admission requires a minimum of two years teaching experience. The degree requires completion of a minimum of 36 semester hours.

The Doctor of Philosophy program is for the student who aspires to a career in educational research. The program is designed to develop a high level of knowledge in the foundation and processes of instruction.

Licensure/Reciprocity: Georgia. Students seeking teaching certification in a state other than Georgia should consult with that state's teacher certification office early in their program of study to insure compliance with requirements. Many state directors of teacher credentialing have signed Interstate Agreements through NASDTEC that expedite the certification process.

FORT VALLEY STATE UNIVERSITY

College of Arts, Sciences, and Education
Department of Curriculum and Instruction

William Merida Hubbard Education Building
1005 State College Drive
Fort Valley, Georgia 31030-4313
Phone: (478) 825-6365
E-mail: strange@fvsu.edu
Internet: http://www.fvsu.edu

Institution Description: Fort Valley State University, formerly named Fort Valley State College, is a public land-grant college. It was established as Fort Valley High and Industrial School in 1895. It merged with State Teachers and Agriculture College at Forsyth and became Fort Valley State College in 1939. The present name was adopted in 1995.

The Department of Curriculum and Instruction offers undergraduate and graduate programs leading to teacher certification.

Institution Control: Public.

Calendar: Semester. Academic year September to June.

Official(s): Dr. Julius Scipio, Dean; Dr. Anthony Strange, Chair, Department of Curriculum and Instruction.

Faculty: Full-time 8.

Degrees Awarded: 47 baccalaureate; 42 master's.

Admission Requirements: *Undergraduate:* Graduation from an approved secondary school or GED; College Board SAT or ACT composite. *Teacher education specific:* Completion of two semesters of college work; 2.5 GPA or better; pass the PRAXIS I test; two letters of recommendation; faculty interview. *Graduate:* Baccalaureate degree from a regionally accredited institution. *Teacher education specific:* Pass the PRAXIS II tests in the area of preparation; teaching credential where appropriate; letters of recommendation; faculty interview.

Fees and Expenses: Undergraduate: in-state $1,296 per semester (including fees); out-of-state $4,614. Graduate in-state $1,517 per semester (including fees); out-of-state $5,498. Room and board: $4,078 per academic year. Other expenses: $3,250. Books and supplies: $1,200.

Financial Aid: Resources specifically for eligible students enrolled in teacher education programs are awarded on the basis of financial need and academic merit. The institution has a Program Participation Agreement with the U.S. Department of Education for eligible students to receive Pell Grants and other federal aid. *Contact:* Financial Aid Office at: (478) 825-6363.

Accreditation: *Regional:* SACS. *Professional:* NCATE. *Member of:* AACTE. *Approved by:* Georgia Professional Standards Commission.

Undergraduate Programs: The Department of Curriculum and Instruction offers programs leading to the Bachelor of Science in early childhood education and middle grades education with teacher certification. The programs require the completion of a minimum of 120 semester hours, including field experiences and student teaching.

Graduate Programs: The graduate programs offered by the department include the Master of Science in early childhood education and the Bachelor of Science in middle grades education.

A Montesorri Certification Program is also available.

Licensure/Reciprocity: Georgia. Students seeking teaching certification in a state other than Georgia should consult with that state's teacher certification office early in their program of study to insure compliance with requirements. Many state directors of teacher credentialing have signed Interstate Agreements through NASDTEC that expedite the certification process.

GEORGIA COLLEGE AND STATE UNIVERSITY

The John H. Lounsbury School of Education

231 West Hancock Street

Milledgeville, Georgia 31061

Phone: (478) 453-5004

Fax: (478) 445-1914

E-mail: gcsuadmit@mail.gcsu.edu

Internet: http://www.gscu.edu

Institution Description: Georgia College and State University is a comprehensive state institution. It was established and chartered as Georgia Normal and Industrial College in 1889. The name was changed to Georgia State College for Women in 1922 and became The Women's College of Georgia in 1961. The institution became coeducational in 1971 and the present name was adopted in 1996.

The John H. Lounsbury School of Education offers certification and career development programs and maintains partnerships with community schools, their districts, other academic institutions, and professional education agencies.

Institution Control: Public.

Calendar: Semester. Academic year August to May.

Official(s): Dr. Rosemary DePaola, President.

Faculty: Full-time 25; part-time 13; adjunct 2.

Degrees Awarded: 124 baccalaureate; 164 master's.

Admission Requirements: *Undergraduate:* Graduation from an approved secondary school or GED; College Board SAT or ACT composite. *Teacher education specific:* Completion of two semesters of college work; 2.5 GPA or better; pass the PRAXIS I test; two letters of recommendation; faculty interview. *Graduate:* Baccalaureate degree from a regionally accredited institution. *Teacher education specific:* Pass the PRAXIS II tests in the area of preparation; teaching credential where appropriate; letters of recommendation; faculty interview.

Fees and Expenses: Undergraduate: in-state $1,338 per semester (including fees); out-of-state $4,656. Graduate in-state $1,559 per semester (including fees); out-of-state $5,540. Room and board: $4,620 per academic year. Other expenses: $1,692. Books and supplies: $968.

Financial Aid: Resources specifically for eligible students enrolled in teacher education programs are awarded on the basis of financial need and academic merit. The institution has a Program Participation Agreement with the U.S. Department of Education for eligible students to receive Pell Grants and other federal aid. *Contact:* Financial Aid Office at: (478) 445-5149.

Accreditation: *Regional:* SACS. *Professional:* NCATE. *Member of:* AACTE. *Approved by:* Georgia Professional Standards Commission.

Undergraduate Programs: The undergraduate programs of the Department of Early Childhood and Middle Grades Education are field-based, combining supervised experience in the public schools with university coursework. The early childhood program leads toward the completion of certification requirements for teachers of pre-kindergarten through grade five. The middle grades program leads toward certification in grades four through eight.

Graduate Programs: The Department of Early Childhood offers the following graduate degree programs: Master of Education in early childhood education and the Master of Education in middle grades education.

The Specialist in Education programs are offered in early childhood education and middle grades education.

The Department of Foundations and Secondary Education offers several graduate degree programs. The Master of Arts in Teaching degree prepares candidates for initial Georgia certification in secondary teaching fields. The Master of Education degree in secondary education is offered with specializations in English, mathematics, social sciences, natural sciences, French, and Spanish. The Department also provides core foundations and instructional technology courses for other teacher education programs.

Licensure/Reciprocity: Georgia. Students seeking teaching certification in a state other than Georgia should consult with that state's teacher certification office early in their program of study to insure compliance with requirements. Many state directors of teacher credentialing have signed Interstate Agreements through NASDTEC that expedite the certification process.

GEORGIA SOUTHERN UNIVERSITY

College of Education

Teacher Education Program

Highway 301, South

P.O. Box 8033

Statesboro, Georgia 30460-8033

Phone: (912) 681-0698

Fax: (912) 681-5514

E-mail: coe@gasou.edu

Internet: http://www.gasou.edu

Institution Description: Georgia Southern University is a regional state university. It was established as First District Agricultural and Mechanical High School and chartered in 1906. Georgia Southern's status was changed in 1990 from a Type II (4-year senior college) to a Type 1 (regional university) with a change in name to Georgia Southern University.

The Teacher Education Program offers a variety of degree pursuits leading to teacher certification in Georgia.

GEORGIA SOUTHERN UNIVERSITY—*cont'd*

Institution Control: Public.

Calendar: Semester. Academic year September to June.

Official(s): Dr. Nicholas L. Henry, President.

Faculty: Full-time ; part-time ; adjunct.

Degrees Awarded: 188 baccalaureate; 157 master's; 23 doctorate.

Admission Requirements: *Undergraduate:* Graduation from an approved secondary school or GED; College Board SAT or ACT composite. *Teacher education specific:* Completion of at least two semesters of college work; 2.5 GPA or better; pass the PRAXIS I test; two letters of recommendation; faculty interview. *Graduate:* Baccalaureate degree from a regionally accredited institution. *Teacher education specific:* Pass the PRAXIS II tests in the area of preparation; teaching credential where appropriate; letters of recommendation; faculty interview.

Fees and Expenses: Undergraduate: in-state $1,338 per semester (including fees); out-of-state $4,656. Graduate in-state $1,559 per semester (including fees); out-of-state $5,540. Room and board: $4,620 per academic year. Other expenses: $1,692. Books and supplies: $968.

Financial Aid: Resources specifically for eligible students enrolled in teacher education programs are awarded on the basis of financial need and academic merit. The institution has a Program Participation Agreement with the U.S. Department of Education for eligible students to receive Pell Grants and other federal aid. *Contact:* Financial Aid Office at: (912) 661-5413.

Accreditation: *Regional:* SACS. *Professional:* NCATE. *Member of:* AACTE. *Approved by:* Georgia Professional Standards Commission.

Undergraduate Programs: The Bachelor of Science in Education programs are offered for early childhood education, middle grades education, secondary and P-12 education, and special education. The pre-professional block (PPB) of courses (nine hours) are taken concurrently during the fourth semester at Georgia Southern. Prior to enrolling in the PPB, students should have all other requirements for admission to the Teacher Education Program satisfied in order to progress in the program.

Graduate Programs: The Master of Education degree programs are offered in early childhood, middle grades, secondary and P-12, special education, instructional technology, reading education, counselor education educational leadership, higher education, and school psychology.

Doctoral programs include the Ed.D. in curriculum studies, Ed.S. in teaching and learning, Ed.S. in counselor education, Ed.S. in school psychology, and the Ed.D. in educational administration.

Licensure/Reciprocity: Georgia. Students seeking teaching certification in a state other than Georgia should consult with that state's teacher certification office early in their program of study to insure compliance with requirements. Many state directors of teacher credentialing have signed Interstate Agreements through NASDTEC that expedite the certification process.

GEORGIA SOUTHWESTERN STATE UNIVERSITY

School of Education
800 Wheatley Street
Americus, Georgia 31709-4693
Phone: (229) 931-2145
Fax: (229) 931-2163
E-mail: gswapps@canes.gsw.edu
Internet: http://www.gsw.edu

Institution Description: Georgia Southwestern State University, formerly named Georgia Southwestern College, is a member institution of the University of Georgia System. It was established in 1906 as Third District Agricultural and Mechanical School. The present name was adopted in 1996.

The mission of the School of Education is the preparation and continuous development of candidates from diverse populations to high levels of achievement.

Institution Control: Public.

Calendar: Semester. Academic year August to May.

Official(s): Dr. Mary Gendermalik Cooper, Dean, School of Education; Dr. Leslie J. Walford, Chair, Department of Middle grades and Secondary Education; Dr. Judith W.Spann, Chair, Department of Special Education, Reading, and Early Childhood education.

Faculty: Full-time 16; part-time 24.

Degrees Awarded: 76 baccalaureate; 122 master's.

Admission Requirements: *Undergraduate:* Graduation from an approved secondary school or GED; College Board SAT or ACT composite. *Teacher education specific:* Completion of two semesters of college work; 2.5 GPA or better; pass the PRAXIS I test; two letters of recommendation; faculty interview. *Graduate:* Baccalaureate degree from a regionally accredited institution. *Teacher education specific:* Pass the PRAXIS II tests in the area of preparation; teaching credential where appropriate; letters of recommendation; faculty interview.

Fees and Expenses: Undergraduate: resident $1,399 per semester (including fees); nonresident $4,717. Graduate resident $1,620 per semester (including fees); nonresident $5,601. Room and board: $3,926 per academic year. Other expenses: $4,004. Books and supplies: $850.

Financial Aid: Resources specifically for eligible students enrolled in teacher education programs are awarded on the basis of financial need and academic merit. The institution has a Program Participation Agreement with the U.S. Department of Education for eligible students to receive Pell Grants and other federal aid. *Contact:* Financial Aid Office at: (229) 928-1378.

Accreditation: *Regional:* SACS. *Professional:* NCATE. *Member of:* AACTE. *Approved by:* Georgia Professional Standards Commission.

Undergraduate Programs: The School of Education offers undergraduate degree programs leading to the Bachelor of Arts and teacher certification in art, English, and music. The Bachelor of Science in Education programs are offered in early childhood education, exercise science, health and physical education, intellectual disabilities, learning disabilities, middle grades education, and recreation. All programs require the completion of a general education core, subject area major, field experiences, and student teaching.

Graduate Programs: The Master in Education degree program include: early childhood, middle grades education, reading, secondary education (biology, chemistry, English, health and physical education, history, math, science, social science), and special education (behavior disorders, intellectual disabilities, learning disabilities). All programs require the completion of specific courses.

Licensure/Reciprocity: Georgia. Students seeking teaching certification in a state other than Georgia should consult with that state's teacher certification office early in their program of study to insure compliance with requirements. Many state directors of teacher credentialing have signed Interstate Agreements through NASDTEC that expedite the certification process.

GEORGIA STATE UNIVERSITY

College of Education
University Plaza
33 Gilmer Street S.E.
Atlanta, Georgia 30303-3083
Phone: (404) 651-2000
E-mail: coe@gsu.edu
Internet: http://www.gsu.edu

Institution Description: Georgia State University was established as Georgia Institute of Technology, Evening School of Commerce, and offered first instruction at the postsecondary level in 1913. The present name was adopted in 1969.

The College of Education offers comprehensive programs in all areas of teacher education to its students at the Instructional Technology Center in downtown Atlanta.

Institution Control: Public.

Calendar: Semester. Academic year September to June.

Official(s): Dr. Ron Colarusso, Dean, College of Education.

Faculty: Full-time 87; part-time 29.

Degrees Awarded: 169 baccalaureate; 528 master's; 30 doctorate.

Admission Requirements: *Undergraduate:* Graduation from an approved secondary school or GED; College Board SAT or ACT composite. *Teacher education specific:* Completion of at least two semesters of college work; 2.5 GPA or better; pass the PRAXIS I test; two letters of recommendation; faculty interview. *Graduate:* Baccalaureate degree from a regionally accredited institution. *Teacher education specific:* Pass the PRAXIS II tests in the area of preparation; teaching credential where appropriate; letters of recommendation; faculty interview.

Fees and Expenses: Undergraduate: in-state $1,338 per semester (including fees); out-of-state $4,656. Graduate in-state $1,559 per semester (including fees); out-of-state $5,540. Room and board: $7,948 per academic year. Other expenses: $2,978. Books and supplies: $1,320.

Financial Aid: Resources specifically for eligible students enrolled in teacher education programs are awarded on the basis of financial need and academic merit. The institution has a Program Participation Agreement with the U.S. Department of Education for eligible students to receive Pell Grants and other federal aid. *Contact:* Financial Aid Office at: (404) 651-2227.

Accreditation: *Regional:* SACS. *Professional:* NCATE. *Member of:* AACTE. *Approved by:* Georgia Professional Standards Commission.

Undergraduate Programs: The Bachelor of Science in Education degree programs include early childhood education and middle childhood education. The early childhood program prepares teachers to work with young children in pre-K through fifth-grade classrooms.

The middle childhood education program prepares educators who can meet the needs of young adolescents. Graduates develop content knowledge in two teaching fields (language arts, mathematics, science, social science). Successful completion of the program leads to a recommendation for licensure for grades 4-8.

Graduate Programs: The Master of Education degree programs include majors in behavior/learning disabilities, communication disorders, early childhood education, early childhood education - alternative preparation program, leadership, English education - alternative preparation program, and health and physical education .

Licensure/Reciprocity: Georgia. Students seeking teaching certification in a state other than Georgia should consult with that state's teacher certification office early in their program of study to insure compliance with requirements. Many state directors of teacher credentialing have signed Interstate Agreements through NASDTEC that expedite the certification process.

KENNESAW STATE UNIVERSITY
Bagwell College of Education
Professional Teacher Education Unit
Kennesaw Hall, Room 3018
1000 Chastain Road
Marietta, Georgia 30144-5591
Phone: (770) 423-6117
Fax: (770) 423-6527
E-mail: bcoe@kennesaw.edu
Internet: http://www.kennesaw.edu

Institution Description: Kennesaw State University is a four-year institution of the University System of Georgia. It was established 1965 as Kennesaw Junior College. The first baccalaureate degree was awarded in 1980. The institution became Kennesaw State College in 1988 and Kennesaw State University in 1996.

The Professional Teacher Education Unit prepares professional learning facilitators to understand their disciplines and principles of pedagogy and who will reflect that knowledge through instructional decisions that foster the success of all learners.

Institution Control: Public.

Calendar: Quarter. Academic year August to May.

Official(s): Dr. Betty L. Siegel, President.

Faculty: Not reported.

Degrees Awarded: 362 baccalaureate; 68 master's.

Admission Requirements: *Undergraduate:* Graduation from an approved secondary school or GED; College Board SAT or ACT composite. *Teacher education specific:* Completion of two semesters of college work; 2.5 GPA or better; pass the PRAXIS I test; two letters of recommendation; faculty interview. *Graduate:* Baccalaureate degree from a regionally accredited institution. *Teacher education specific:* Pass the PRAXIS II tests in the area of preparation; teaching credential where appropriate; letters of recommendation; faculty interview.

Fees and Expenses: Undergraduate: in-state $1,338 per semester (including fees); out-of-state $4,656. Graduate in-state $1,589 per semester (including fees); out-of-state $5,540. Room and board: $7,120 per academic year. Other expenses: $2,505. Books and supplies: $800.

Financial Aid: Resources specifically for eligible students enrolled in teacher education programs are awarded on the basis of financial need and academic merit. The institution has a Program Participation Agreement with the U.S. Department of Education for eligible students to receive Pell Grants and other federal aid. *Contact:* Financial Aid Office at: (770) 423-6074.

Accreditation: *Regional:* SACS. *Professional:* NCATE. *Member of:* AACTE. *Approved by:* Georgia Professional Standards Commission.

Undergraduate Programs: The programs leading to a baccalaureate degree and teaching certification include majors in: early childhood, middle grades, secondary education (English, mathematics, science [biology, chemistry, or physics], social science, art (P-12 programs) foreign language (French, Spanish), music, health/physical education /sport science (teacher education P-12 track). All programs require the completion of a general education core, professional studies, content area, field experiences, and student teaching.

Graduate Programs: Graduate program offerings include Master of Education in adolescent education, early childhood education, educational leadership, and special education.

Licensure/Reciprocity: Georgia. Students seeking teaching certification in a state other than Georgia should consult with that state's teacher certification office early in their program of study to insure compliance with requirements. Many state directors of teacher credentialing have signed Interstate Agreements through NASDTEC that expedite the certification process.

LAGRANGE COLLEGE
Department of Education
601 Broad Street
LaGrange, Georgia 30230
Phone: (706) 880-8202
Fax: (706) 880-8319
E-mail: jharrison@lgc.edu
Internet: http://www.lgc.edu

Institution Description: LaGrange College is a private, independent, nonprofit college affiliated with the North Georgia Annual Conference of the United Methodist Church. The college was established as LaGrange Female Academy in 1831. The present name was adopted in 1934 and the school became coeducational in 1953.

The Department of Education offers both undergraduate and graduate programs for teacher preparation.

LAGRANGE COLLEGE—*cont'd*

Institution Control: Private.

Calendar: Semester. Academic year September to May.

Official(s): Dr. Jennifer S. Harrison, Chair, Department of Education.

Faculty: Full-time 5; adjunct 5.

Degrees Awarded: 13 baccalaureate; 14 master's.

Admission Requirements: *Undergraduate:* Graduation from an accredited secondary school or GED; College Board SAT or ACT composite. *Teacher education specific:* Completion of core curriculum; PRAXIS I; GPA of 2.5 or better; faculty interview; background check. *Graduate:* Baccalaureate degree from a regionally accredited institution. *Teacher education specific:* Miller Analogy Test or GRE; three letters of recommendation; teaching certificate.

Fees and Expenses: $14,482 per academic year. On-campus room and board: $6,128. Books and supplies: $1,000.

Financial Aid: Resources specifically for eligible students enrolled in teacher education programs are awarded on the basis of financial need and academic merit. The institution has a Program Participation Agreement with the U.S. Department of Education for eligible students to receive Pell Grants and other federal aid. *Contact:* Sylvia Smith at: (706) 880-8241 or e-mail at ssmith@lagrange.edu.

Accreditation: *Regional:* SACS. *Member of:* AACTE. *Approved by:* Georgia Professional Standards Commission.

Undergraduate Programs: The early childhood education program prepares professionals to teach in a variety of subjects in Pre-K through fifth grades. Candidates spend at least 7 hours every week in supervised field experiences each semester prior to student teaching. In addition to the general education core requirements, students earn 63 semester hours in required coursework.

The middle grades pre-service teachers will have a broad academic background in each of the areas of concentration. Sequential coursework begins in the junior year with an in-depth study of the nature and needs of early adolescents. The program requires a minimum of 7 jhours of supervised field experience prior to student teaching.

Graduate Programs: The Master of Education in curriculum and instruction is designed to develop teachers as instructional leaders of their schools by increasing their knowledge and experience. The program may be completed in six consecutive terms. A total of 30 semester hours is required for the degree.

The Master of Arts in Teaching program is designed for those with a four-year degree who wish to become teachers in either high schools or middle schools. The primary objective of the program is for those with bachelor's degrees in areas of middle grades and secondary certification to receive their initial teaching preparation at the master's level.

Licensure/Reciprocity: Georgia. Students seeking teaching certification in a state other than Georgia should consult with that state's teacher certification office early in their program of study to insure compliance with requirements. Many state directors of teacher credentialing have signed Interstate Agreements through NASDTEC that expedite the certification process.

MERCER UNIVERSITY

Tift College of Education
Department of Teacher Education
1400 Coleman Avenue
Macon, Georgia 31207
Phone: (478) 301-2700
Fax: (478) 301-2655
E-mail: admissions@mercer.edu
Internet: http://www.mercer.edu

Institution Description: Mercer University is comprised of schools located in Macon and Atlanta and offers programs at the baccalaureate, master's, doctorate, and first-professional levels. The university is a private institution affiliated with the Georgia Baptist Convention. It was established as Mercer Institute in 1833.

The College of Education prepares teachers in the foundations of the education profession, in content bases for curricula, and the characteristics of diverse learners.

Institution Control: Private.

Calendar: Semester. Academic year August to May.

Official(s): Dr. Carl R. Martray, Dean; Dr. Margaret Rainey Morris, Chair, Department of Teacher Education.

Faculty: Full-time 33.

Degrees Awarded: 168 baccalaureate; 74 master's.

Admission Requirements: *Undergraduate:* Either graduation with 16 units from an approved secondary school or GED; College Board SAT or ACT composite. *Teacher education specific:* PRAXIS I; completion of general education requirements; career goal essay; faculty interview. *Graduate:* Baccalaureate degree from a regionally accredited institution. *Teacher education specific:* Completion of all required department tests/exams; GRE; faculty interview; teaching credential.

Fees and Expenses: $20,791 per academic year. On-campus room and board: $6,720. Other expenses: $1,215. Books and supplies: $850.

Financial Aid: Resources specifically for eligible students enrolled in teacher education programs are awarded on the basis of financial need and academic merit. The institution has a Program Participation Agreement with the U.S. Department of Education for eligible students to receive Pell Grants and other federal aid. *Contact:* Financial Aid Office at: (478) 301-2670.

Accreditation: *Regional:* SACS. *Member of:* AACTE. *Approved by:* Georgia Professional Standards Commission.

Undergraduate Programs: The early childhood program provides a learning-centered curriculum that promotes inquiry and understanding of the physical, social, emotional, and cognitive development of young children. A minimum of 128 semester hours must be completed, including the general education core, subject area major, field experiences, and student teaching. The program leads to the Bachelor of Science degree and Georgia teacher certification.

The Holistic Child program is a four-year program of study in which the student will experience varied field and life experience within the culture and diverse school and community populations. The program leads to the Bachelor of Science degree. The program requires the completion of 127 semester hours of specified courses.

The middle grades education teacher certification program works in collaboration with other academic departments to help achieve appreciation for and competence in the core knowledge areas. The Bachelor of Science degree requires the completion of 128 semester hours of specified courses.

The secondary (7-12) and special subjects (P-12) programs have the overall objective of supporting and complementing the student's major in a content areas. Students must meet the requirements for the degree from both the College of Liberal Arts and the Tift College of Education.

Graduate Programs: Graduate programs include the Master of Education in early childhood, middle grades, reading, and secondary education with concentrations in the areas of English, history, math, broadfield science, and broadfield social science.

Licensure/Reciprocity: Georgia. Students seeking teaching certification in a state other than Georgia should consult with that state's teacher certification office early in their program of study to insure compliance with requirements. Many state directors of teacher credentialing have signed Interstate Agreements through NASDTEC that expedite the certification process.

NORTH GEORGIA COLLEGE AND STATE UNIVERSITY

Department of Education

Teacher Education Program

College Avenue
Dahlonega, Georgia 30597-1001
Phone: (706) 864-1800
Fax: (706) 864-1478
E-mail: tdavis@ngcsu.edu
Internet: http://www.ngcsu.edu

Institution Description: North Georgia College and State University was established in 1872. The present name was adopted in 1996.

The Department of Education offers undergraduate and graduate programs and prepares students for teacher certification.

Institution Control: Public.

Calendar: Semester. Academic year August to May.

Official(s): Dr. Robert Michael, Dean, Department of Education; Dr. Susan Gannentry, Chair, Teacher Education.

Faculty: Full-time 22.

Degrees Awarded: 138 baccalaureate; 107 master's.

Admission Requirements: *Undergraduate:* Graduation from an approved secondary school or GED; College Board SAT or ACT composite. *Teacher education specific:* Completion of two semesters of college work; 2.75 GPA or better; pass the PRAXIS I test; two letters of recommendation; faculty interview. *Graduate:* Baccalaureate degree from a regionally accredited institution. *Teacher education specific:* Pass the PRAXIS II tests in the area of preparation; teaching credential where appropriate; letters of recommendation; faculty interview.

Fees and Expenses: Undergraduate: in-state $1,404 per semester (including fees); out-of-state $4,722. Graduate in-state $1,625 per semester (including fees); out-of-state $5,606. Room and board: $4,016 per academic year. Other expenses: $2,980. Books and supplies: $750.

Financial Aid: Resources specifically for eligible students enrolled in teacher education programs are awarded on the basis of financial need and academic merit. The institution has a Program Participation Agreement with the U.S. Department of Education for eligible students to receive Pell Grants and other federal aid. *Contact:* Financial Aid Office at: (706) 854-1412.

Accreditation: *Regional:* SACS. *Professional:* NCATE. *Member of:* AACTE. *Approved by:* Georgia Professional Standards Commission.

Undergraduate Programs: Undergraduate programs are offered in early childhood, middle grades, special education, secondary education (English, math, science) social science, music, art, foreign language (French, Spanish), and physical education. Field experience (student teaching) is accomplished in schools with a 30-mile radius of Dahlonega. The programs lead to the baccalaureate degree and Georgia teacher certification.

Graduate Programs: Master in Education programs are offered in early childhood, middle grades, special education, secondary education, and art. Specific requirements for each program must be completed.

Licensure/Reciprocity: Georgia. Students seeking teaching certification in a state other than Georgia should consult with that state's teacher certification office early in their program of study to insure compliance with requirements. Many state directors of teacher credentialing have signed Interstate Agreements through NASDTEC that expedite the certification process.

OGLETHORPE UNIVERSITY

Division of Education

4484 Peachtree Road, N.E.
Atlanta, Georgia 30319
Phone: (404) 364-8387
Fax: (404) 364-8534
E-mail: broberts@oglethorpe.edu
Internet: http://www.oglethorpe.edu

Institution Description: Oglethorpe University is a private, independent, nonprofit institution. It was established as Oglethorpe University in 1835. The name was changed to Oglethorpe College in 1964. The present name was readopted in 1971.

The Division of Education offers only graduate programs in teacher education.

Institution Control: Private.

Calendar: Semester. Academic year August to May.

Official(s): Dr. Beth Roberts, Division Head.

Faculty: Full-time 57; part-time 25.

Degrees Awarded: 12 baccalaureate; 6 master's.

Admission Requirements: *Graduate:* Baccalaureate degree from a regionally accredited institution. *Teacher education specific:* Undergraduate GPA 2.8; GRE 1000; passing scores on PRAXIS I; career goal essay; three recommendations.

Fees and Expenses: $6,000 per academic year. On-campus room and board: $6,300. Books and supplies: $800.

Financial Aid: Resources specifically for eligible students enrolled in teacher education programs are awarded on the basis of financial need and academic merit. The institution has a Program Participation Agreement with the U.S. Department of Education for eligible students to receive Pell Grants and other federal aid. *Contact:* Patrick Bononnes at (404) 364-8366 or e-mail at pbonnones@oglethrope.edu.

Accreditation: *Regional:* SACS. *Approved by:* George Professional Standards Commission.

Graduate Programs: The Master of Arts in Teaching early childhood education program is based on a broad liberal arts background. The program emphasizes strong academic preparation and the role of teacher as leaner. The program offers the degree and initial certification for early childhood educators. Candidates must complete 50 hours of field experience and pass PRAXIS II tests. A cumulative GPA of 3.0 or higher must be maintained. Student teaching, a supervised internship in a diverse elementary public school classroom, is the capstone experience in the program.

Licensure/Reciprocity: Georgia. Students seeking teaching certification in a state other than Georgia should consult with that state's teacher certification office early in their program of study to insure compliance with requirements. Many state directors of teacher credentialing have signed Interstate Agreements through NASDTEC that expedite the certification process.

PAINE COLLEGE

Teacher Education Unit

1235 Fifteenth Street
Augusta, Georgia 30901-3182
Phone: (706) 432-0727
Fax: (706) 432-0897
E-mail: watersm@mail.paine.edu
Internet: http://www.paine.edu

Institution Description: Paine College is a private college affiliated with the Christian Methodist Episcopal Church and the United Methodist Church. It was established as Paine Institute in 1882. The present name was adopted in 1903.

The Teacher Education Unit offers teacher preparation programs leading to Georgia teacher certification.

Institution Control: Private.

Calendar: Semester. Academic year August to May.

Official(s): Dr. Margie Waters, Unit Chairman.

Faculty: Full-time 7; part-time 4; adjunct 1.

PAINE COLLEGE—cont'd

Degrees Awarded: 12 baccalaureate.

Admission Requirements: *Undergraduate:* Graduation from an accredited secondary school or GED; minimum 2.0 GPA; College Board SAT or ACT composite. *Teacher education specific:* Pass the PRAXIS I Test; pass college-wide Sophomore Proficiency Examination in English; provide proof of membership in a professional education organization; pass background check; faculty interview.

Fees and Expenses: $8,448 per academic year. On-campus room and board: $3,940. Books and supplies: $800.

Financial Aid: Resources specifically for eligible students enrolled in teacher education programs are awarded on the basis of financial need and academic merit. The institution has a Program Participation Agreement with the U.S. Department of Education for eligible students to receive Pell Grants and other federal aid. College grants and scholarship awards are available to qualified applicants. *Contact:* Gerri Bogan at (706) 821-8222 or bogang@mail.paine.edu.

Accreditation: *Regional:* SACS. *Approved by:* Georgia Professional Standards Commission.

Undergraduate Programs: The Division of Education provides programs of study that lead to teacher certification in the areas of early childhood education and middle grades education. Secondary programs are offered in biology, English, history, and math These programs require that students complete the major in the discipline in either the Division of Humanities, Division of Natural Sciences and Mathematics, or the Division of Social Sciences. Students then complete coursework required to be eligible for initial certification by taking courses within the Division of Education.

Licensure/Reciprocity: Georgia. Students seeking teaching certification in a state other than Georgia should consult with that state's teacher certification office early in their program of study to insure compliance with requirements. Many state directors of teacher credentialing have signed Interstate Agreements through NASDTEC that expedite the certification process.

SPELMAN COLLEGE

Department of Education
Giles Hall, Suite 5
350 Spelman Lane, S.W.
Atlanta, Georgia 30314-4399
Phone: (706) 864-1998
Fax: (706) 864-1886
E-mail: doe@spelman.edu
Internet: http://www.spelman.edu

Institution Description: Spelman College is a private, independent, nonprofit college for women. It was established as Atlanta Baptist Female Seminary in 1881. The name was changed to Spelman Seminary in 1884 and the present name was adopted in 1924.

The goal of the teacher education program is to develop teachers who are committed to education in urban, multicultural, and international communities.

Institution Control: Private.

Calendar: Semester. Academic year August to May.

Official(s): Dr. Marshlita Sims Peterson, Chair, Department of Education.

Faculty: Full-time 11.

Degrees Awarded: 17 baccalaureate.

Admission Requirements: *Undergraduate:* Graduation from an approved secondary school or GED; minimum 2.0 GPA; College Board SAT or ACT composite. *Teacher education specific:* Passing score on PRAXIS I; GRE score of 1000; three recommendations; career goal essay; faculty interview.

Fees and Expenses: $12,575 per academic year. On-campus room and board: $7,300. Other expenses: $3,382. Books and supplies: $1,610.

Financial Aid: Resources specifically for eligible students enrolled in teacher education programs are awarded on the basis of financial need and academic merit. The institution has a Program Participation Agreement with the U.S. Department of Education for eligible students to receive Pell Grants and other federal aid. *Contact:* Financial Aid Office at: (404) 215-7809.

Accreditation: *Regional:* SACS. *Professional:* NCATE. *Member of:* AACTE. *Approved by:* Georgia Professional Standards Commission.

Undergraduate Programs: The preparation program in early childhood education is a part of the child development major program. It requires the completion of general education and core requirements plus a major program in child development that offers a certifiable teaching field in early childhood education.

The secondary teacher preparation program is offered as a minor program to be combined with major programs in other departments. A student seeking certification to teach at the secondary level (grades 7-12) must complete the general education and core requirements, a major program that offers a certifiable teaching field, i.e. chemistry, biology, physics, mathematics, English, economics, history, and political science and the professional sequence in secondary education.

A preparation program is offered as a minor program to be combined with major programs in French, Spanish, and music. A student seeking certification in these fields to teach in grades P-12 must complete the general education core requirements, a major program that offers a certifiable teaching field in music, French, or Spanish and the professional sequence in Preschool through 12th grade education.

Licensure/Reciprocity: Georgia. Students seeking teaching certification in a state other than Georgia should consult with that state's teacher certification office early in their program of study to insure compliance with requirements. Many state directors of teacher credentialing have signed Interstate Agreements through NASDTEC that expedite the certification process.

STATE UNIVERSITY OF WEST GEORGIA

College of Education
Department of Curriculum and Instruction
1600 Maple Street
Carrollton, Georgia 30118-0001
Phone: (770) 836-6500
Fax: (770) 836-6720
E-mail: coe@westga.edu
Internet: http://www.westga.edu

Institution Description: The State University of West Georgia, formerly known as West Georgia College, is a coeducational, liberal arts, residential institution. It was established as 4th District Agricultural and Mechanical School in 1906. The present name was adopted in 1933. The school became a 4-year institution in 1957 and became a state university in 1996.

The mission of the College of Education is to provide excellence in the initial and advanced preparation of professionals for a variety of settings.

Institution Control: Public.

Calendar: Semester. Academic year September to June.

Official(s): Dr. Diane Boothe, Chair, Department of Curriculum and Instruction.

Faculty: Full-time 45.

Degrees Awarded: 164 baccalaureate; 298 master's.

Admission Requirements: *Undergraduate:* Graduation from an approved secondary school or GED; College Board SAT or ACT composite. *Teacher education specific:* Completion of at least two semesters of college work; 2.5 GPA or better; pass the PRAXIS I test; two letters of recommendation; faculty interview. *Graduate:* Baccalaureate degree from a regionally accredited institution. *Teacher education specific:* Pass the PRAXIS II tests in the area of preparation; teaching credential where appropriate; letters of recommendation; faculty interview.

Fees and Expenses: Undergraduate: in-state $1,338 per semester (including fees); out-of-state $4,656. Graduate in-state $1,559 per semester (including fees); out-of-state $5,540. Room and board: $7,948 per academic year. Other expenses: $2,978. Books and supplies: $1,320.

Financial Aid: Resources specifically for eligible students enrolled in teacher education programs are awarded on the basis of financial need and academic merit. The institution has a Program Participation Agreement with the U.S. Department of Education for eligible students to receive Pell Grants and other federal aid. *Contact:* Financial Aid Office at: (404) 651-2227.

Accreditation: *Regional:* SACS. *Professional:* NCATE. *Approved by:* Georgia Professional Standards Commission.

Undergraduate Programs: Undergraduate programs leading to a baccalaureate degree and teacher certification include: early childhood/elementary education; middle grades education; P-12 education; reading; and secondary education. All programs require completion of general education requirements, core courses, major subject area(s), field experiences, and student teaching.

Graduate Programs: Graduate programs leading to the Master in Education degree are offered in early childhood/elementary education, middle grades education, P-12 education, and reading. Master in Education programs are offered in secondary education with concentrations in English, math, science, social studies, and French.

Education Specialist programs are offered with concentrations in English, science, and social studies. All graduate programs require the completion of specific courses.

Licensure/Reciprocity: Georgia. Students seeking teaching certification in a state other than Georgia should consult with that state's teacher certification office early in their program of study to insure compliance with requirements. Many state directors of teacher credentialing have signed Interstate Agreements through NASDTEC that expedite the certification process.

UNIVERSITY OF GEORGIA

College of Education
School of Teacher Education
G-3 Aderhold Hall
Athens, Georgia 30602-7122
Phone: (706) 542-4244
Fax: (706) 542-4277
E-mail: info@coe.uga.edu
Internet: http://www.coe.uga.edu

Institution Description: The University of Georgia is a state institution and land-grant college. It was established and chartered in 1785.

The College of Education offers undergraduate and graduate programs for teacher preparation and Georgia certification.

Institution Control: Public.

Calendar: Semester. Academic year August to May.

Official(s): Dr. Laurie Hart, Department Head, Elementary Education.

Faculty: Full-time 214.

Degrees Awarded: 611 baccalaureate; 397 master's; 111 doctorate.

Admission Requirements: *Undergraduate:* Graduation from an approved secondary school or GED; College Board SAT or ACT composite. *Teacher education specific:* Completion of at least two semesters of college work; 2.5 GPA or better; pass the PRAXIS I test; two letters of recommendation; faculty interview. *Graduate:* Baccalaureate degree from a regionally accredited institution. *Teacher education specific:* Pass the PRAXIS II tests in the area of preparation; teaching credential where appropriate; letters of recommendation; faculty interview.

Fees and Expenses: Undergraduate: in-state $1,338 per semester (including fees); out-of-state $4,656. Graduate in-state $1,559 per semester (including fees); out-of-state $5,540. Room and board: $7,948 per academic year. Other expenses: $2,978. Books and supplies: $1,320.

Financial Aid: Resources specifically for eligible students enrolled in teacher education programs are awarded on the basis of financial need and academic merit. The institution has a Program Participation Agreement with the U.S. Department of Education for eligible students to receive Pell Grants and other federal aid. *Contact:* Financial Aid Office at: (706) 542-6147.

Accreditation: *Regional:* SACS. *Professional:* NCATE. *Member of:* AACTE. *Approved by:* Georgia Professional Standards Commission.

Undergraduate Programs: The Department of Elementary Education offers programs leading to the baccalaureate degree in early childhood, pre-kindergarten to second grade, and middle school. These programs require the completion of general education courses, core requirements, field experiences, and student teaching.

Other baccalaureate programs are offered in science education, social science education, language education (English, foreign language, TESOL), mathematics education, communication science and disorders, occupational studies, physical education and sport studies, recreation and leisure studies. All programs have specific course requirements.

Graduate Programs: Master in Education degree programs are offered in the areas of early childhood, middle school, and elementary education. The Master in Education programs emphasize broad professional development for elementary (prekindergarten-grade 5 and middle schools (grades 4-8) teachers. The specialist programs are terminal degree programs that emphasize advanced studies and action research.

The doctoral programs assist educators in developing research and teaching skills, engaging in intensive studies of educational issues, and conducting and disseminating original educational research.

Licensure/Reciprocity: Georgia. Students seeking teaching certification in a state other than Georgia should consult with that state's teacher certification office early in their program of study to insure compliance with requirements. Many state directors of teacher credentialing have signed Interstate Agreements through NASDTEC that expedite the certification process.

VALDOSTA STATE UNIVERSITY

College of Education
1500 North Patterson Street
Valdosta, Georgia 31698
Phone: (229) 245-6424
Fax: (229) 333-7167
E-mail: dryals@valdosta.edu
Internet: http://www.valdosta.edu

Institution Description: Valdosta State University was established by the state legislature in 1906. It became South Georgia Normal College and offered first instruction at the postsecondary level as a two-year institution for women in 1913. The name was changed to Georgia State Woman's College and became a four-year institution in 1922. The school became coeducational and the present name was adopted in 1950. In 1993 it became a regional university of the University System of Georgia.

The College of Education offers undergraduate and graduate programs leading to teacher preparation and certification.

Institution Control: Public.

Calendar: Semester. Academic year August to May.

Official(s): Dr. Philip Gunter, Dean.

Faculty: Full-time 120, part-time 30.

Degrees Awarded: 316 baccalaureate; 187 master's; 11 doctorate.

Admission Requirements: *Undergraduate:* Graduation from an approved secondary school or GED; College Board SAT or ACT composite. *Teacher education specific:* Completion of at least two semesters of college work; 2.5 GPA or better; pass the PRAXIS I test; two letters of recommendation; faculty interview. *Graduate:* Baccalaureate degree from a regionally accred-

VALDOSTA STATE UNIVERSITY—cont'd

ited institution. *Teacher education specific:* Pass the PRAXIS II tests in the area of preparation; teaching credential where appropriate; letters of recommendation; faculty interview.

Fees and Expenses: Undergraduate: in-state $122 per semester hour; out-of-state $373. Graduate in-state $139 per semester hour, out-of-state $440. Room and board: $1,278 per semester. Books and supplies: $300 per semester.

Financial Aid: Resources specifically for eligible students enrolled in teacher education programs are awarded on the basis of financial need and academic merit. The institution has a Program Participation Agreement with the U.S. Department of Education for eligible students to receive Pell Grants and other federal aid. *Contact:* Douglas Tanner at: (229) 333-5935 or e-mail at dtanner@valdosta.edu.

Accreditation: *Regional:* SACS. *Professional:* NCATE. *Member of:* AACTE. *Approved by:* Georgia Professional Standards Commission.

Undergraduate Programs: Students can major in and receive certification in early childhood education, middle grades education, secondary education (English, math, biology, chemistry, earth/space, physics, history, political science), foreign language education (French, Spanish), business education, music education, health and physical education, special education, communication disorders, technical trade and industrial education, and art education. Generally, 126 semester hours are required for graduation, including field experiences and student teaching.

Graduate Programs: The Master of Education degree is offered in business education, curriculum and instructional technology, early childhood and reading education, educational leadership, kinesiology and physical education, middle grades and secondary education, psychology and counseling, and special education and communication disorders. All programs require the completion of specific course requirements.

The Doctor of Education (Ed.D.) is an advanced program of study offered in adult and career education, curriculum and instruction, and educational leadership.

Licensure/Reciprocity: Georgia. Students seeking teaching certification in a state other than Georgia should consult with that state's teacher certification office early in their program of study to insure compliance with requirements. Many state directors of teacher credentialing have signed Interstate Agreements through NASDTEC that expedite the certification process.

HAWAII

BRIGHAM YOUNG UNIVERSITY - HAWAII CAMPUS

School of Education
Teacher Education Programs
55-220 Kulanui Street
Laie, Oahu, Hawaii 96762-1294
Phone: (808) 283-3885
Fax: (808) 293-3988
E-mail: admissions@byuh.edu
Internet: http://www.byuh.edu

Institution Description: Brigham Young University-Hawaii Campus (Church College of Hawaii until 1974) is a private institution affiliated with The Church of Jesus Christ of Latter-Day Saints. It was established as the Church College of Hawaii and offered first instruction at the postsecondary level in 1955. The present name was adopted in 1974.

The Teacher Education Programs present teaching skills in an orderly sequence providing students opportunities to develop into teachers prepared to serve in various educational communities and environments.

Institution Control: Private.

Calendar: Semester. Academic year August to April.

Official(s): Dr. Roy Winstead, Dean, School of Education.

Faculty: Full-time 6; part-time 4, adjunct 10.

Degrees Awarded: 50 baccalaureate.

Admission Requirements: *Undergraduate:* Graduation from an approved secondary school or GED; College Board SAT or ACT composite. *Teacher education specific:* Cumulative GPA of 2.0 or higher; passing scores on PRAXIS I; successful completion of required tests/exams; graduation plan. POST-BACCALAUREATE: Bachelor's degree from an accredited institution; GPA of 2.0 or higher. *Teacher education specific:* Passing scores on the PRAXIS I and II; complete School of Education admissions packet.

Fees and Expenses: Undergraduate: $2,490 per academic year. On-campus room and board: $4,520. Other expenses: $1,654. Books and supplies: $910.

Financial Aid: Resources specifically for eligible students enrolled in teacher education programs are awarded on the basis of financial need and academic merit. The institution has a Program Participation Agreement with the U.S. Department of Education for eligible students to receive Pell Grants and other federal aid. *Contact:* Financial Aid Office at: (808) 293-3530.

Accreditation: *Regional:* WASC. *Member of:* AACTE. *Approved by:* Hawaii Department of Education.

Undergraduate Programs: The Teacher Education Programs include elementary education, secondary education, special education, dual licensing, basic teacher license, alternative licensing program, international teacher education program. Master of subject area content and teaching skills are measured during the courses taken as well as during the supervision in public school classroom activities. Standards set by the School of Education and those of the Hawaii State Department of Education must be met before the student will be recommended for teacher certification.

Graduate Programs: Hawaii residents with an earned baccalaureate degree from a accredited institution who desire to teach in the public schools but do not have initial basic teacher license may apply for admission to the Professional Diploma Program (5th year). The programs include specialization in elementary, secondary, or special education.

Licensure/Reciprocity: Hawaii. Students seeking teaching certification in a state other than Hawaii should consult with that state's teacher certification office early in their program of study to insure compliance with requirements. Many state directors of teacher credentialing have signed Interstate Agreements through NASDTEC that expedite the certification process.

UNIVERSITY OF HAWAII AT HILO

Education Department
Teacher Education Program
200 West Kawili Street
Hilo, Hawaii 96720-4091
Phone: (808) 974-7311
Fax: (808) 974-7622
E-mail: sehna@uhh.hawaii.edu
Internet: http://uhh.hawaii.edu

Institution Description: The school was established as Extension Division of University of Hawaii and offered first instruction at the postsecondary level in 1947. It became a 4-year institution and the name was changed to Hilo College in 1970. The present name was adopted in 1979.

The Teacher Education Program is a post-baccalaureate program designed to qualify teacher candidates for a license issued by the Hawaii Department of Education.

Institution Control: Public.

Calendar: Semester. Academic year August to May.

Official(s): Dr. Rose Tseng, Chair, Teacher Education Program.

Faculty: Full-time 6.

Degrees Awarded: 15 master's.

Admission Requirements: *Graduate:* Baccalaureate degree from a regionally accredited institution; minimum GPA of 2.75 for last 60 hours of undergraduate work. *Teacher education specific:* Passing scores on PRAXIS I II; interview with Education Department faculty.

Fees and Expenses: In-state $1,658 per academic year; out-of-state $7,274. On-campus room and board: $6,043. Other expenses: $1,409. Books and supplies: $1,020.

Financial Aid: Resources specifically for eligible students enrolled in teacher education programs are awarded on the basis of financial need and academic merit. The institution has a Program Participation Agreement with the U.S. Department of Education for eligible students to receive Pell Grants and other federal aid. *Contact:* Financial Aid Office at: (808) 974-7324.

Accreditation: *Regional:* WASC. *Approved by:* Hawaii Department of Education.

Graduate Programs: The Teacher Education Program prepares students to teach at either the elementary (grades K-6) or secondary (grades 7-12) level. Prospective elementary teachers are required to take specific supplemental coursework which may also be used to fulfill some general education requirements of their undergraduate degree. Prospective secondary teachers are required to major in academic disciplines related to the areas of licensure identified by the State of Hawaii. Some majors and/or

UNIVERSITY OF HAWAII AT HILO—*cont'd*

licensure areas require additional supplemental coursework which must be taken prior to admission to the Teacher Education Program.

The Master of Education degree program is a 33-credit hour cohort program. It is a generalist degree. Admission is based upon previous preparation and requires completion of a baccalaureate degree.

Licensure/Reciprocity: Hawaii. Students seeking teaching certification in a state other than Hawaii should consult with that state's teacher certification office early in their program of study to insure compliance with requirements. Many state directors of teacher credentialing have signed Interstate Agreements through NASDTEC that expedite the certification process.

UNIVERSITY OF HAWAII AT MANOA

College of Education
Wisk Annex 2-128
1776 University Avenue
Honolulu, Hawaii 96822
Phone: (808) 956-7703
Fax: (808) 956-3106
E-mail: coe_info@uhm.hawaii.edu
Internet: http://www.uhm.hawaii.edu

Institution Description: The university was established and chartered as College of Hawaii in 1907. The present name was adopted in 1972.

The College of Education is an upper division college and graduate professional school that prepares teachers, administrators, school counselors, and other education personnel.

Institution Control: Public.

Calendar: Semester. Academic year August to May.

Official(s): Dr. Randy Hitz, Dean.

Faculty: Full-time 55.

Degrees Awarded: 197 baccalaureate; 228 master's; 14 doctorate.

Admission Requirements: *Graduate:* Baccalaureate degree from a regionally accredited institution; minimum GPA of 2.75 for last 60 hours of undergraduate work. *Teacher education specific:* Passing scores on PRAXIS I II; interview with Education Department faculty.

Fees and Expenses: Undergraduate: resident $1,656 per semester, nonresident $4,896. Graduate: resident $2,232 per semester, nonresident $5,304. On-campus room and board: $6,043. Other expenses: $1,410. Books and supplies: $1,020.

Financial Aid: Resources specifically for eligible students enrolled in teacher education programs are awarded on the basis of financial need and academic merit. The institution has a Program Participation Agreement with the U.S. Department of Education for eligible students to receive Pell Grants and other federal aid. *Contact:* Financial Aid Office at: (808) 956-7251.

Accreditation: *Regional:* WASC. *Professional:* NCATE. *Member of:* AACTE. *Approved by:* Hawaii Department of Education.

Graduate Programs: The College of Education offers Master of Education degrees in counseling and guidance, curriculum studies, early childhood education, educational administration, educational foundations, educational psychology, educational technology, special education, and teaching.

The Master of Education in Teaching, a two-year interdisciplinary, field-based program, is designed for students who have earned baccalaureate degrees in fields other than education. Graduates are qualified for state teacher certification in either elementary or secondary education at the professional certificate level. Students must be registered full-time and progress through the program in cohorts.

The Doctor of Philosophy in Education is a college-wide degree awarded for academic preparation for professional practice and research in the field of education.

Licensure/Reciprocity: Hawaii. Students seeking teaching certification in a state other than Hawaii should consult with that state's teacher certification office early in their program of study to insure compliance with requirements. Many state directors of teacher credentialing have signed Interstate Agreements through NASDTEC that expedite the certification process.

IDAHO

BOISE STATE UNIVERSITY

College of Education

Teacher Education Academic Degree Programs

Education Building
1910 University Drive
Boise, Idaho 83725-1700
Phone: (208) 426-1134
Fax: (208) 426-4365
E-mail: bsuinfor@boisestate.edu
Internet: http://www.boisestate.edu

Institution Description: Boise State University was established as Boise Junior College in 1932. It became a four-year institution and the name was changed to Boise College in 1965. The college became part of the state system of higher education and the name was changed to Boise State College in 1969. The current name was adopted in 1974.

The mission of the College of Education is to prepare professionals using models that incorporate integrated teaching and learning practices to insure high level of knowledge and skill, commitment to democratic values, and the ability to work with a diverse population.

Institution Control: Public.

Calendar: Semester. Academic year August to May.

Official(s): Dr. Joyce Lynn Garrett, Dean; Dr. Glenn R. Potter, Associate Dean; Dr. Michael Heikkinen, Chair, Teacher Education Academic Degree Programs.

Faculty: Full-time 12.

Degrees Awarded: 340 baccalaureate; 172 master's; 6 doctorate.

Admission Requirements: *Undergraduate:* Graduation from an approved secondary school with a 2.0 GPA or GED; College Board SAT or ACT composite for students under 21 years of age. *Teacher education specific:* Advising for teacher education is accomplished by program coordinators and faculty in College of Arts and Science and College of Education. *Graduate:* Baccalaureate from a regionally accredited institution. *Teacher education specific:* Pass all departmental-required tests/exams; recommendations; faculty interview.

Fees and Expenses: Undergraduate: resident $3,251 per year; nonresident $9,971. Graduate: resident $3,929 per year; nonresident $10,649. Required fees: $737 health insurance fee per year (can be waive if student has comparable insurance. On-campus room and board: $4,258. Other expenses: $3,228. Books and supplies: $920.

Financial Aid: Resources specifically for eligible students enrolled in teacher education programs are awarded on the basis of financial need and academic merit. The institution has a Program Participation Agreement with the U.S. Department of Education for eligible students to receive Pell Grants and other federal aid. *Contact:* David Tolman, Director, Financial Aid at: (208) 426-1540.

Accreditation: *Regional:* NASC. *Professional:* NCATE. *Member of:* AACTE. *Approved by:* Idaho State Department of Education.

Undergraduate Programs: Undergraduate baccalaureate programs include bilingual education, blended early childhood education/ECE special education, elementary education, and subject area full endorsements.

The secondary education program is offered through the Department of Curriculum Instruction and other departments in the College of Arts and Science. Programs includes specialization in the subject areas of anthropology, art, biology, chemistry, communication, earth science/geography, economics, English, French, German, history, physical education/health education, mathematics, music, physics, political science, sociology/social sciences, Spanish, theatre arts.

Graduate Programs: Master's degree programs offered through the Department of Curriculum and Instruction include: bilingual education/English as a second language, physical education, secondary certification, early childhood, reading, and special education.

A second master's degree may be earned in any area of emphasis offered at Boise State.

A Master in Education is offered outside the College of Education in the areas of: art, music, mathematics, history, economics, earth science, English, and social work.

A doctoral program in curriculum and instruction leads to the Doctor of Education degree.

Licensure/Reciprocity: Idaho. Students seeking teaching certification in a state other than Idaho should consult with that state's teacher certification office early in their program of study to insure compliance with requirements. Many state directors of teacher credentialing have signed Interstate Agreements through NASDTEC that expedite the certification process.

IDAHO STATE UNIVERSITY

College of Education

Division of Teacher Education

Box 8059
741 South 7th Avenue
Pocatello, Idaho 83209
Phone: (208) 282-3259
Fax: (208) 282-4697
E-mail: harris@isu.edu
Internet: http://www.isu.edu

Institution Description: The school was incorporated as The Academy of Idaho, a secondary school, in 1901. It became the Southern Branch of the University of Idaho and offered first instruction at the postsecondary level in 1927. In 1947 the college became an independent institution and was named Idaho State College. The present name was adopted in 1963.

The College of Education prepares students who will enter the profession of education. All programs are experiential, collaborative, problem-centered, standards-based, research-guided, and technologically supported.

Institution Control: Public.

Calendar: Semester. Academic year August to May.

Official(s): Dr. Larry B. Harris, Dean.

Faculty: Full-time 55; part-time 1120; adjunct 6.

Degrees Awarded: 250 baccalaureate; 93 master's; 17 doctorate.

Admission Requirements: *Undergraduate:* Graduation from an approved secondary school or GED; College Board SAT or ACT composite. *Teacher education specific:* Application is made to the College of Education following the completion of at least 26 credit hours of college work; 2.75 overall GPA; recommendations; completion of required education courses; faculty inter-

IDAHO STATE UNIVERSITY—cont'd

view. *Graduate:* Baccalaureate degree from a regionally accredited institution; GPA of 3.0 or higher for all subject division credits taken at the undergraduate level. *Teacher education specific:* GRE or Miller Analogies Test; one year of pre-K-12 teaching experience.

Fees and Expenses: Undergraduate: resident $3,251 per year; nonresident $9,971. Graduate: resident $3,929 per year; nonresident $10,649. Required fees: $737 health insurance fee per year (can be waive if student has comparable insurance. On-campus room and board: $4,300. Other expenses: $3,000. Books and supplies: $900.

Financial Aid: Resources specifically for eligible students enrolled in teacher education programs are awarded on the basis of financial need and academic merit. The institution has a Program Participation Agreement with the U.S. Department of Education for eligible students to receive Pell Grants and other federal aid. *Contact:* Doug Severs at: (208) 282-2921 or seve-doug@isu.edu.

Accreditation: *Regional:* NASC. *Professional:* NCATE. *Member of:* AACTE. *Approved by:* Idaho State Department of Education.

Undergraduate Programs: All students pursuing a bachelor's degree in the College of Education must fulfill the university's general education requirements. Bachelor's degrees in teacher education are: Bachelor of Arts in early childhood education; Bachelor of Arts and Bachelor of Science in elementary education, physical education, and secondary education; Bachelor of Music Education. Course requirements are distributed within the areas of professional foundations, content specialization, and research and evaluation. Field experience and student teaching requirements must also be met.

Graduate Programs: Graduate degrees include Master of Education, Master of Physical Education, Educational Specialist, and Doctor of Education Leadership. Programs at the master's level include child and family studies (options in family studies, early childhood education, and early childhood special education). A planned fifth-year option is available in teacher education.

Sixth-year special degrees are offered in special education, school psychology, and education administration.

The program leading to Doctor of Education Leadership is also offered.

Licensure/Reciprocity: Idaho. Students seeking teaching certification in a state other than Idaho should consult with that state's teacher certification office early in their program of study to insure compliance with requirements. Many state directors of teacher credentialing have signed Interstate Agreements through NASDTEC that expedite the certification process.

LEWIS-CLARK STATE COLLEGE

Education Division
Teacher Education Program
500 8th Avenue
Lewiston, Idaho 83501-2698
Phone: (208) 799-5272
Fax: (209) 799-2063
E-mail: moff@lcsc.edu
Internet: http://www.lcsc.edu

Institution Description: Lewis-Clark State College was established as Lewis-Clark Normal School and offered first instruction at the postsecondary level in 1893. The present name was adopted in 1971.

The Teacher Education Program is offered in a learning environment where students obtain solid experience to become teachers.

Institution Control: Public.

Calendar: Semester. August to May.

Official(s): Dr. Jeanette Hill, Division Chair.

Faculty: Full-time 17.

Degrees Awarded: 35 baccalaureate.

Admission Requirements: *Undergraduate:* Graduation from an approved secondary school or GED; College Board SAT or ACT composite. *Teacher education specific:* After completing the course Principles of Education, all college core and prerequisite courses and an entrance exam, students with a GPA of 2.75 or better may apply for entry into the Teacher Education Program.

Fees and Expenses: Undergraduate: resident $3,250 per year; nonresident $9,970. On-campus room and board: $3,880. Other expenses: $3,230. Books and supplies: $1,500. .

Financial Aid: Resources specifically for eligible students enrolled in teacher education programs are awarded on the basis of financial need and academic merit. The institution has a Program Participation Agreement with the U.S. Department of Education for eligible students to receive Pell Grants and other federal aid. *Contact:* Financial Aid Office at: (208) 792-2224.

Accreditation: *Regional:* NASC. *Professional:* NCATE. *Member of:* AACTE. *Approved by:* Idaho State Department of Education.

Undergraduate Programs: Programs at the baccalaureate level are offered with majors in: elementary education (grades K-8), general studies, interdisciplinary studies, kinesiology, (also with health and physical education endorsement for grades K-12; psychology, and secondary education content majors with professional teaching certification program (grades 6-12).

Content areas in which majors or minors may be pursued to support the teacher education program offerings to secondary certification include: art, biology, chemistry, drama, English, foreign language, journalism, music, speech, earth science, history, mathematics, natural science, political science, and social science.

Candidates for the bachelor's degree in the teacher education program must complete a minimum of 128 semester credits, have an overall GPA of 2.75, receive passing scores are all division-required exams.

Licensure/Reciprocity: Idaho. Students seeking teaching certification in a state other than Idaho should consult with that state's teacher certification office early in their program of study to insure compliance with requirements. Many state directors of teacher credentialing have signed Interstate Agreements through NASDTEC that expedite the certification process.

NORTHWEST NAZARENE UNIVERSITY

Education Department
Teacher Education Program
623 Holly Street
Nampa, Idaho 83686
Phone: (208) 467-8258
Fax: (208) 467-8562
E-mail: dcartwright@nnu.edu
Internet: http://www.nnu.edu

Institution Description: Northwest Nazarene University is a private institution affiliated with the Church of the Nazarene. It was established in 1913. University status was attained and the present name adopted in 1999.

The purpose of the teacher education program is to improve the world of practice in the field of education. This purpose is carried out through programs and projects that stress the following: the preparation of beginning elementary, middle school, and secondary teachers; continuing involvement in planning, evaluation, and inservice for educational institutions from kindergarten through higher education.

Institution Control: Private.

Calendar: Semester. Academic year September to June.

Official(s): Dr. Dennis Cartwright, Dean; Karen Blacklock, Chair, Teacher Education Program.

Faculty: Full-time 7; part-time 4; adjunct 20.

Degrees Awarded: 38 baccalaureate; 83 master's.

Admission Requirements: *Undergraduate:* Graduation from an approved high school with a 2.5 GPA or GED; College Board SAT or ACT composite. *Teacher education specific:* Application for internship program. *Graduate:* Baccalaureate from a regionally accredited institution. *Teacher education specific:* Subject area competence; completion with passing scores on all departmental-required tests/exams; teaching credential; recommendations; faculty interview.

Fees and Expenses: $15,330 per year. Required fees: $590 per year. Graduate tuition charged per semester hour. On-campus room and board: $4,440 per year. Other expenses: $1,700. Books and supplies: $760.

Financial Aid: Resources specifically for eligible students enrolled in teacher education programs are awarded on the basis of financial need and academic merit. The institution has a Program Participation Agreement with the U.S. Department of Education for eligible students to receive Pell Grants and other federal aid. Scholarships with specific criteria for an award are available to qualified students. *Contact:* Financial Aid Office at: (208) 467-8638.

Accreditation: *Regional:* NACS. *Professional:* NCATE. *Member of:* AACTE. *Approved by:* Idaho State Department of Education.

Undergraduate Programs: The program that prepares elementary teachers features a year-long internship that combines university coursework integrated with K-6 classroom experience. Majors spend a year in one of six Professional Development Schools. During the year the candidates examine classroom management strategies and teaching methods first-hand. Students must complete general education requirements and core courses.

Secondary education programs require a teaching area or a first and second teaching fields. Areas available include art, biology, English, mathematics, music, kinesiology, and social science. Approved teaching major areas require 67 semester credits.

Graduate Programs: The Master of Education in curriculum and instruction is for the professional educator desiring to improve classroom teaching skills and or to specialize in leadership roles. The program focuses on research and its application and utilizes the reflection process in the curriculum and learning environment. The program consists of required courses for a total of 34 semester hours.

The Master of Education in the exceptional child program is for classroom teachers who hold elementary, secondary, or special education certification and who desire further expertise and/or become certified to teach exceptional children.

Licensure/Reciprocity: Idaho. Students seeking teaching certification in a state other than Idaho should consult with that state's teacher certification office early in their program of study to insure compliance with requirements. Many state directors of teacher credentialing have signed Interstate Agreements through NASDTEC that expedite the certification process.

UNIVERSITY OF IDAHO
College of Education
Division of Teaching, Learning, and Leadership
875 Perimeter Drive
Moscow, Idaho 83844-2282
Phone: (208) 885-6772
Fax: (208) 885-6558
E-mail: admappl@uidaho.edu
Internet: http://www.uidaho.edu

Institution Description: The University of Idaho is a state institution and land-grant college that was chartered in 1890.

The Division of Teaching, Learning, and Leadership provides undergraduate and graduate programs for the preparation of personnel who teach in and lead schools in Idaho, the region, and nation.

Institution Control: Public.

Calendar: Semester. Academic year August to May.

Official(s): Dr. Jeanne Christiansen, Dean, College of Education.

Faculty: Not reported.

Degrees Awarded: 212 baccalaureate; 228 master's; 29 doctorate.

Admission Requirements: *Undergraduate:* Graduation from an accredited secondary school or GED; College Board SAT or ACT composite. *Teacher education specific:* Applicant must complete the Idaho Comprehensive Literary Assessment; departmental approval. *Graduate:* Baccalaureate degree from a regionally accredited institution; GPA of 3.0 or higher for all subject division credits taken at the undergraduate level. *Teacher education specific:* GRE or Miller Analogies Test; one year of pre-K-12 teaching experience.

Fees and Expenses: Undergraduate: resident $12,850 total costs per academic year; nonresident $20,042. Graduate: resident $16,080; nonresident $23,472. On-campus room and board: $4,580. Books and supplies: $1,190.

Financial Aid: Resources specifically for eligible students enrolled in teacher education programs are awarded on the basis of financial need and academic merit. The institution has a Program Participation Agreement with the U.S. Department of Education for eligible students to receive Pell Grants and other federal aid. *Contact:* Financial Aid Office at: (208) 885-6312.

Accreditation: *Regional:* NASC. *Professional:* NCATE. *Member of:* AACTE. *Approved by:* Idaho State Department of Education.

Undergraduate Programs: Programs offered on the Moscow and Coeur d'Alene campuses include the Bachelor of Science in Education degree in elementary education, secondary education, special education, and early childhood education. A reading endorsement is also offered. Students will have an Idaho teaching certificate in their field at graduation.

Students who have degrees in a teaching field or are getting a degree in a teaching field but have not yet graduated may take classes to be certified in education.

Graduate Programs: Degrees available include: Master in Education, Master of Science in Education, Education Specialist, Doctorate in Education, Doctorate of Philosophy in Education. Program emphases include: curriculum and instruction, educational leadership-administration, principalship, superintendency-special education and higher education administration. Online master's courses are available.

Licensure/Reciprocity: Idaho. Students seeking teaching certification in a state other than Idaho should consult with that state's teacher certification office early in their program of study to insure compliance with requirements. Many state directors of teacher credentialing have signed Interstate Agreements through NASDTEC that expedite the certification process.

ILLINOIS

AUGUSTANA COLLEGE

Department of Education
Teacher Education
639 Thirty-eighth Street
Rock Island, Illinois 61201-2296
Phone: (309) 794-7000
Fax: (309) 794-7431
E-mail: admissions@augustana.edu
Internet: http://www.augustana.edu

Institution Description: Augustana College is a private, undergraduate college affiliated with the Evangelical Lutheran Church in America. It was established as Augustana Seminary in 1860. The name was changed to Augustana College Theological Seminary in 1865. The present name was adopted in 1948.

The teacher education program offers students an education based on specialized professional instruction and the liberal arts.

Institution Control: Private.

Calendar: Semester. Academic year September to May.

Official(s): Dr. Charles Hyser, Chair, Education Department.

Faculty: Full-time 5; part-time 2.

Degrees Awarded: 28 baccalaureate.

Admission Requirements: *Undergraduate:* Graduation from an approved secondary school or GED; College Board SAT or ACT composite. *Teacher education specific:* Minimum 2.5 GPA; pass Illinois Basic Skills Test; faculty interview.

Fees and Expenses: $19,608 per academic year. On-campus room and board: $5,586. Other expenses: $1,200. Books and supplies: $675.

Financial Aid: Resources specifically for eligible students enrolled in teacher education programs are awarded on the basis of financial need and academic merit. The institution has a Program Participation Agreement with the U.S. Department of Education for eligible students to receive Pell Grants and other federal aid. *Contact:* Financial Aid Office at: (309) 794-7207.

Accreditation: *Regional:* NCA. *Professional:* NCATE. *Approved by:* Illinois State Board of Education.

Undergraduate Programs: Augustana's education majors develop a thorough knowledge of teaching theory in a context that includes a wide range of practical experience. Annual planning and assessment meetings with local educators insure that the teacher education program provides prospective teachers with the skills necessary to meet the complete spectrum of classroom challenges. Clinical experience begins with the first course in the education sequence and is incorporated throughout the entire curriculum. Students are supervised by experienced education faculty and typically exceed the 100 hours of classroom work required by the Illinois State Board of Education. Majors are offered for teaching in both elementary and secondary education. The department offers coursework for emphases in art education, music education, and physical education. The baccalaureate degrees require the completion of 123 semester credits.

Licensure/Reciprocity: Illinois. Students seeking teaching certification in a state other than Illinois should consult with that state's teacher certification office early in their program of study to insure compliance with requirements. Many state directors of teacher credentialing have signed Interstate Agreements through NASDTEC that expedite the certification process.

AURORA UNIVERSITY

College of Education
347 South Gladstone Avenue
Aurora, Illinois 60506-4892
Phone: (630) 844-1542
Fax: (630) 844-5530
E-mail: mdlewis@aurora.edu
Internet: http://www.aurora.edu

Institution Description: Aurora University is a private, independent, nonprofit liberal arts college founded by the Advent Christian Church in 1893 as Mendota College. The college adopted the name Aurora College and moved to its resent location in 1912. The present name was adopted in 1985.

The College of Education prepares future teachers by means of a collaborative relationship model in a developmental teacher education program located on-site in K-12 schools.

Institution Control: Private.

Calendar: Quarter. Academic year September to June.

Official(s): Dr. Mary Daly Lewis, Dean.

Faculty: Full-time 5; adjunct 28.

Degrees Awarded: 50 baccalaureate; 450 master's; 15 doctorate.

Admission Requirements: *Undergraduate:* Entering freshman must be in upper 60% of graduating class; ACT 19 or better; SAT score 910 or better; 16 academic units or equivalent. *Teacher education specific:* Competency in written and oral communications; 2.75 GPA; pass Illinois Basic Skills Test; submit criminal background check form. *Graduate:* Baccalaureate degree from a regionally accredited institution; 2.75 GPA; 3 letters of recommendation; official transcripts. *Teacher education specific:* Pass Illinois Basic Skills Test; submit criminal background check form; written writing sample; faculty interview.

Fees and Expenses: Undergraduate: $15,250 per academic year; graduate $17,640. On-campus room and board: $5,514. Books and supplies: $200.

Financial Aid: Resources specifically for eligible students enrolled in teacher education programs are awarded on the basis of financial need and academic merit. The institution has a Program Participation Agreement with the U.S. Department of Education for eligible students to receive Pell Grants and other federal aid. *Contact:* Heather Gutierrez, Office of Financial Aid at: (630) 844-5533 or e-mail at admission@aurora.edu.

Accreditation: *Regional:* NCA. *Approved by:* Illinois State Board of Education.

Undergraduate Programs: Aurora University offers baccalaureate programs approved by the Illinois State Board of Education in the following teaching areas: biology (6-12), computer science (6-12), elementary education (K-9), English (6-12), mathematics (6-12), physical education (K-12 and 6-12), social studies (6-12). When a student meets the Aurora University graduation requirements, completes one or more of the above areas of concentration, meets the required performance outcomes by taking the required professional education and general education courses, and passes the required state tests, he/she will be recommended for Illinois certification. The Bachelor of Arts degree is awarded upon completion of all coursework and student teaching.

Graduate Programs: The Master of Arts in Teaching - Certification Program has two options: elementary and secondary education. The program offers students the opportunity to earn both a master's degree and a standard elementary or secondary education certificate. The program is intended for students who have already obtained a bachelor's degree.

Licensure/Reciprocity: Illinois. Students seeking teaching certification in a state other than Illinois should consult with that state's teacher certification office early in their program of study to insure compliance with requirements. Many state directors of teacher credentialing have signed Interstate Agreements through NASDTEC that expedite the certification process. Reciprocity agreement also through the Central States Teacher Exchange Agreement.

BRADLEY UNIVERSITY
College of Education and health Sciences
Department of Teacher Education
1501 West Bradley Avenue
Peoria, Illinois 61625-0001
Phone: (309) 676-7611
E-mail: wsf@bradley.edu
Internet: http://www.bradley.edu

Institution Description: Bradley University is a private, independent, nonprofit institution. It was established and incorporated as Bradley Polytechnic Institute in 1897. The present name was adopted in 1946.

Institution Control: Private.

Calendar: Semester. Academic year August to May.

Official(s): Dr. Jean Marie Grant, Chair, Department of Teacher Education.

Faculty: Full-time 15.

Degrees Awarded: 132 baccalaureate; 53 master's.

Admission Requirements: *Undergraduate:* Graduation from an approved secondary school or GED; College Board SAT or ACT composite. *Teacher education specific:* Application for entry into the program as early as sophomore year; pass Illinois Basic Skills Test; faculty interview. *Graduate:* Baccalaureate degree from a regionally accredited institution. *Teacher education specific:* Pass Illinois Basic Skills Test and content area subject matter test; recommendations; faculty interview.

Fees and Expenses: Undergraduate: $16,800 per academic year. Graduate: Tuition charged by credit hour (contact the university for current rate). On-campus room and board: $5,980 per academic year. Required fees: $130. Other expenses: $2,100. Books and supplies: $600.

Financial Aid: Resources specifically for eligible students enrolled in teacher education programs are awarded on the basis of financial need and academic merit. The institution has a Program Participation Agreement with the U.S. Department of Education for eligible students to receive Pell Grants and other federal aid. *Contact:* Financial Aid Office at: (309) 677-3089.

Accreditation: *Regional:* NCA. *Professional:* NCATE. *Approved by:* Illinois State Board of Education.

Undergraduate Programs: The Bachelor of Arts or Bachelor of Science in early childhood education programs prepare students to work with children from birth through third grade. The major also requires a second major in liberal arts and can be chosen from a concentration in social studies, general science or humanities.

The Bachelor of Arts or Bachelor of Science in elementary education degree program qualifies students to teach any grade from kindergarten to grade six. The student also earns a second major in the liberal arts (social studies, general science, or humanities).

The Bachelor of Arts or Bachelor of Science in special education emphasizes teaching children and you who possess learning disabilities and emotional disorders from kindergarten through 12th grade.

Graduate Programs: The graduate program leads to a Master of Arts degree in curriculum and instruction. The program is designed to prepare kindergarten through 12th-grade teachers for greater responsibility in their role as educational leaders and informed decision makers. The program provides a mix of theory with practical application and offers enough flexibility that students can tailor their program to fit their needs.

Licensure/Reciprocity: Illinois. Students seeking teaching certification in a state other than Illinois should consult with that state's teacher certification office early in their program of study to insure compliance with requirements. Many state directors of teacher credentialing have signed Interstate Agreements through NASDTEC that expedite the certification process.

CHICAGO STATE UNIVERSITY
College of Education
330 Education Building
9501 South King Drive
Chicago, Illinois 60628-1598
Phone: (773) 995-2472
Fax: (773) 995-3762
E-mail: S-Westbrooks@csu.edu
Internet: http://www.csu.edu

Institution Description: Chicago State University is an urban, nonresidential state institution. It was established as Cook County Normal School in 1867. The present name was adopted in 1971.

Undergraduate and graduate teacher education programs are offered leading to Illinois certification.

Institution Control: Public.

Calendar: Semester. Academic year August to May.

Official(s): Dr. Sandra Westrooks, Dean.

Faculty: Not reported.

Degrees Awarded: 82 baccalaureate; 270 master's.

Admission Requirements: *Undergraduate:* Graduation from an accredited secondary school or GED; College Board SAT or ACT composite. *Teacher education specific:* Application by the sophomore year; pass Illinois Basic Skills Test; faculty interview. *Graduate:* Baccalaureate degree from a regionally accredited institution. *Teacher education specific:* Pass Illinois Basic Skills Test and content area subject matter test; recommendations; teacher credential; faculty interview.

Fees and Expenses: Undergraduate: in-state $3,774 per academic year; out-of-state $9,239. Graduate: Tuition is charged on a per credit hour basis. Other expenses: $2,800. Books and supplies: $1,400.

Financial Aid: Resources specifically for eligible students enrolled in teacher education programs are awarded on the basis of financial need and academic merit. The institution has a Program Participation Agreement with the U.S. Department of Education for eligible students to receive Pell Grants and other federal aid. *Contact:* Financial Aid Office at: (312) 995-2034.

Accreditation: *Regional:* NCA. *Professional:* NCATE. *Approved by:* Illinois State Board of Education.

Undergraduate Programs: The Bachelor of Science in Education degree in early childhood education has two options: early childhood education and child studies. The Bachelor of Science in elementary education offers eight areas of concentration: computer science, English and language arts, science, literacy and reading, mathematics, social studies, and Spanish. The Bachelor of Science in Education degree in bilingual elementary education leads to Illinois certification. All baccalaureate programs require completion of general education requirements, core education courses, and subject area competence. All degrees require the completion of 120 semester hours.

Graduate Programs: The Master of Arts in Teaching in secondary education, Master of Arts in Teaching in early childhood education, and the Master of Science in Education in curriculum and instruction are offered with various options. A Master of Science in bilingual education program is also offered.

CHICAGO STATE UNIVERSITY—*cont'd*

The Teachers for ChicagoLand Program is a two year master's/intern program offered through a partnership between Chicago State University and the Consortium of South Triad School Districts. The program enables college graduates to complete teacher certification requirements and earn a master's degree while interning in a school as a full-time resident teacher under the direct supervision of a teacher/mentor and a university clinical supervisor.

Licensure/Reciprocity: Illinois. Students seeking teaching certification in a state other than Illinois should consult with that state's teacher certification office early in their program of study to insure compliance with requirements. Many state directors of teacher credentialing have signed Interstate Agreements through NASDTEC that expedite the certification process.

CONCORDIA UNIVERSITY

College of Education
Teacher Education

7400 Augusta Street
River Forest, Illinois 60305-1499
Phone: (708) 771-8300
Fax: (708) 209-3176
E-mail: crfadmis@curf.edu
Internet: http://www.curf.edu

Institution Description: Concordia University is a private institution affiliated with the Lutheran Church-Missouri Synod. It was established as Concordia Teachers College in 1864. It became Concordia College in 1978 and attained university status in 1988.

The College of Education prepares teachers and Directors of Christian Education to meet the demands of church and society with preprofessional studies and practice.

Institution Control: Private.

Calendar: Semester. Academic year August to May.

Official(s): Dr. Cynthia L. Kuck, Dean, College of Education.

Faculty: Not reported.

Degrees Awarded: 88 baccalaureate; 162 master's; 1 doctorate.

Admission Requirements: *Undergraduate:* Graduation from an accredited secondary school or GED; College Board SAT or ACT composite. *Teacher education specific:* Application to Teacher Education program by the sophomore year; pass Illinois Basic Skills Test; faculty interview. *Graduate:* Baccalaureate degree from a regionally accredited institution. *Teacher education specific:* Pass Illinois Basic Skills Test and content area subject matter test; recommendations; faculty interview.

Fees and Expenses: Undergraduate: $16,900 per academic year. Graduate: $530 per credit hour. On-campus room and board: $5,000. Other expenses: $100. Books and supplies: $600.

Financial Aid: Resources specifically for eligible students enrolled in teacher education programs are awarded on the basis of financial need and academic merit. The institution has a Program Participation Agreement with the U.S. Department of Education for eligible students to receive Pell Grants and other federal aid. *Contact:* Financial Aid Office at: (708) 209-3115.

Accreditation: *Regional:* NCA. *Professional:* NCATE. *Approved by:* Illinois State Board of Education.

Undergraduate Programs: Baccalaureate degree programs include the Bachelor of Arts in early childhood education, elementary education, secondary education, director of Christian education, pre-seminary program, music education, and director of parish music. All bachelor's degree programs require completion of general education courses, core education courses, subject area concentration, field experience, and student teaching. A total of 128 to 149 semester hours is required for the various degree programs.

Graduate Programs: The Master of Teaching degree is offered in early childhood education, elementary education, and secondary education. The Master of Arts in Education degree is offered in early childhood education, reading education, school leadership, school counseling, and urban teaching.

Doctoral degree programs are offered in early childhood education, public educational leadership, and non-public educational leadership.

Licensure/Reciprocity: Illinois. Students seeking teaching certification in a state other than Illinois should consult with that state's teacher certification office early in their program of study to insure compliance with requirements. Many state directors of teacher credentialing have signed Interstate Agreements through NASDTEC that expedite the certification process.

DEPAUL UNIVERSITY

School of Education
1 East Jackson Boulevard
Chicago, Illinois 60614
Phone: (773) 325-7740
Fax: (773) 362-3222
E-mail: edadmissions@depaul.edu
Internet: http://www.depaul.edu

Institution Description: DePaul University is a private institution affiliated with Congregation of the Mission, Roman Catholic Church. It was established as Vincent's College in 1898. The present name was adopted in 1907.

The Teacher Education Department prepares urban professional multicultural educators through integrated theory and practice programs of courses and field experiences.

Institution Control: Private.

Calendar: Quarter. Academic year September to June.

Official(s): Rev. John P. Minogue, C.M., President.

Faculty: Full-time 38; part-time 60.

Degrees Awarded: 142 baccalaureate; 382 master's; 7 doctorate.

Admission Requirements: *Undergraduate:* Graduation from an accredited secondary school or GED; College Board SAT or ACT composite. *Teacher education specific:* Students must pass the Basic Skills Test offered by the Illinois Certification Testing System; minimum 2.75 GPA. *Graduate:* Baccalaureate degree from a regionally accredited institution. *Teacher education specific:* Previous GPA of 2.75 or above; two letters of recommendation from professors or supervisors; official transcripts; written statement of purpose; faculty interview.

Fees and Expenses: $18,750 undergraduate full-time. Graduate: $860 per credit hour. On-campus room and board: $7,905. Other expenses: $200. Books and supplies: $900.

Financial Aid: Resources specifically for eligible students enrolled in teacher education programs are awarded on the basis of financial need and academic merit. The institution has a Program Participation Agreement with the U.S. Department of Education for eligible students to receive Pell Grants and other federal aid. *Contact:* Financial Aid Office at: (773) 362-8091.

Accreditation: *Regional:* NCA. *Professional:* NCATE. *Approved by:* Illinois State Board of Education.

Undergraduate Programs: Undergraduate program concentrations include elementary education, secondary education, and special education. For each major, there are liberal studies requirements as well clinical/field experiences, student teaching, and state certification tests. Future teachers are required to spend a minimum of 100 hours during the day in schools interacting with students and learning about schools. Teacher candidates complete a period of student teaching which is a full 10 week commitment. A total of 188 quarter hours are required for the baccalaureate degrees.

Graduate Programs: The Teaching and Learning Program which leads to the Master of Arts or Master of Education was designed for students who hold a bachelor's degree and would like to enter the teaching profession. The program prepares individuals for teaching careers in early childhood (ages birth through 8 years or third grade), elementary (grades K-9), or secondary (grades 6-12. Students may also pursue the Middle School Management Program which leads to an endorsement. To complete the program, the student must complete general education requirements and concentration requirements. Teacher candidates must pass state certification test and complete clinical/field experiences and student teaching. All program elements and concentrations are offered at the Lincoln Park campus. elementary education and secondary education are offered at the Barat campus.

Licensure/Reciprocity: Illinois. Students seeking teaching certification in a state other than Illinois should consult with that state's teacher certification office early in their program of study to insure compliance with requirements. Many state directors of teacher credentialing have signed Interstate Agreements through NASDTEC that expedite the certification process.

EASTERN ILLINOIS UNIVERSITY

College of Education and Professional Studies
Teacher Education Programs
Buzzard Hall - Room 1420
Charleston, Illinois 61920-3099
Phone: (217) 581-2524
Fax: (217) 581-2518
E-mail: ceps@eiu.edu
Internet: http://www.eiu.edu

Institution Description: Eastern Illinois University is a comprehensive state institution. It was established as Eastern Illinois State Normal School in 1895. The name was changed to Eastern Illinois State Teachers College in 1921. It became Eastern Illinois State College in 1947 and the present name was adopted in 1957.

The goal of the College of Education and Professional Studies is to prepare professionals who will advance the intellectual, physical, psychological, and social well-being of our society.

Institution Control: Public.

Calendar: Semester. Academic year August to May.

Official(s): Dr. Charles Rohn, Dean; Dr. Maribeth Brunning, Chair, Department of Early Childhood, Elementary and Middle Level Education; Dr. Mahmood Butt, Chair, Department of Secondary Education and Foundations.

Faculty: Full-time 38.

Degrees Awarded: 520 baccalaureate; 227 master's.

Admission Requirements: *Undergraduate:* Graduation from an approved secondary school or GED; ACT composite. *Teacher education specific:* Basic Skills Test; 2.65 GPA; students must pass the Content Area/Subject Matter Knowledge Test in order to receive credit for student teaching. *Graduate:* Baccalaureate degree from a regionally accredited institution. *Teacher education specific:* Letters of recommendation; Illinois teaching credential; faculty interview.

Fees and Expenses: Undergraduate: in-state $118.75 per semester hour, out-of-state $356.25 Graduate: in-state $125 per semester hour, out-of-state $375. Required fees: $674.15 per semester. On-campus room and board: $6,000 per academic year. Other expenses: $2,130. Books and supplies: $120.

Financial Aid: Resources specifically for eligible students enrolled in teacher education programs are awarded on the basis of financial need and academic merit. The institution has a Program Participation Agreement with the U.S. Department of Education for eligible students to receive Pell Grants and other federal aid. *Contact:* Financial Aid Office at: (217) 581-3713.

Accreditation: *Regional:* NCA. *Professional:* NCATE. *Approved by:* Illinois State Board of Education.

Undergraduate Programs: Undergraduate programs lead to the Bachelor of Science in elementary education and middle level education. The elementary program is offered with either a middle school option or a general option. The Bachelor of Science in special education is offered with a standard special option and certifications in elementary, special, and secondary education.

The Bachelor of Science in secondary education is offered with subject area concentrations, professional education requirements, an alternate secondary education program (competency-based) and an adult education minor. All baccalaureate programs require general education courses, core courses, subject area majors, field experiences, and student teaching.

Graduate Programs: Graduate programs are offered in elementary education (M.S. in Ed.), special education (M.S. in Ed.) and educational administration (M.S. in Ed., Ed.S.). Teacher certification programs for the post-baccalaureate student are also available.

Licensure/Reciprocity: Illinois. Students seeking teaching certification in a state other than Illinois should consult with that state's teacher certification office early in their program of study to insure compliance with requirements. Many state directors of teacher credentialing have signed Interstate Agreements through NASDTEC that expedite the certification process.

ELMHURST COLLEGE

Department of Education
Teacher Preparation Program
190 Prospect
Elmhurst, Illinois 60126-3096
Phone: (630) 617-3400
Fax: (630) 617-5501
E-mail: admit@elmhurst.edu
Internet: http://www.elmhurst.edu

Institution Description: Elmhurst College is a private, independent, nonprofit college affiliated with the United Church of Christ. It was established as Elmhurst Pro-Seminary and Academy in 1871. The school was reorganized into Elmhurst Academy and Junior College in 1919 and the present name was adopted in 1924. It became coeducational in 1930.

The Department of Education offers programs that include a mix of general and professional knowledge, specialized content area knowledge, and clinical experiences,

Institution Control: Private.

Calendar: Semester. Academic year August to May.

Official(s): Dr. Mary J. Selke, Chair, Teacher Education.

Degrees Awarded: 97 baccalaureate; 8 master's.

Admission Requirements: *Undergraduate:* Graduation from an approved secondary school or GED; College Board SAT or ACT composite; minimum 2.75 GPA. *Teacher education specific:* Completion of at least 28 semester hours of college-level work; cumulative GPA of 2.5; passing scores on all sections of the Illinois Basic Skills Test. *Graduate:* Baccalaureate from an regionally accredited institution. *Teacher education specific:* Program is designed for teachers who are currently working in the public schools in primary or early childhood classrooms.

Fees and Expenses: Undergraduate: $17,500 per academic year. Graduate: $590 per credit hour. On-campus room and board: $5,796. Other expenses: $1,100. Books and supplies: $650.

Financial Aid: Resources specifically for eligible students enrolled in teacher education programs are awarded on the basis of financial need and academic merit. The institution has a Program Participation Agreement with the U.S. Department of Education for eligible students to receive Pell Grants and other federal aid. *Contact:* Financial Aid Office at: (630) 617-3079.

Accreditation: *Regional:* NCA. *Professional:* NCATE. *Approved by:* Illinois State Board of Education.

Undergraduate Programs: The Teacher Preparation Curriculum requires baccalaureate-seeking students to meet requirements in three categories: general education, professional courses; and courses in subject area preparation. Certification as a teacher is allowable only after all of the requirements have been met, including passing scores on the state's basic skills and subject specialty exams. Elmhurst College requires a minimum of 100 clock hours of field experiences for all degree candidates.

ELMHURST COLLEGE—*cont'd*

Graduate Programs: The Master of Education in early childhood special education is an interdisciplinary program designed to prepare professionals to work with young children with disabilities. The program involves a two-year, part-time program of study during which coursework and field experiences are closely interwoven. The focus of the program is on strategies that promote interdisciplinary collaboration, family-oriented services, and personnel sensitive to cultural diversity.

Licensure/Reciprocity: Illinois. Students seeking teaching certification in a state other than Illinois should consult with that state's teacher certification office early in their program of study to insure compliance with requirements. Many state directors of teacher credentialing have signed Interstate Agreements through NASDTEC that expedite the certification process.

EUREKA COLLEGE

Teacher Education

300 East College Avenue
Eureka, Illinois 61530
Phone: (309) 467-6330
Fax: (309) 467-6304
E-mail: snafziger@eureka.edu
Internet: http://www.eureka.edu

Institution Description: Eureka College is a private college affiliated with the Christian Church (Disciples of Christ). It was established as Walnut Grove Academy in 1848. The present name was adopted in 1855.

The college offers undergraduate programs in teacher education.

Institution Control: Private.

Calendar: Semester. Academic year September to May.

Official(s): Dr. Shelli Nafziger, Chair, Teacher Education.

Faculty: Full-time 1; part-time 2; adjunct 4.

Degrees Awarded: 15 baccalaureate.

Admission Requirements: *Undergraduate:* Graduation with 16 academic units from an approved secondary school or GED; ACT composite. *Teacher education specific:* Pass Illinois Basic Skills Test; pass college writing exam; 2.5 GPA.

Fees and Expenses: $18,700 per academic year. Required fees: $400. On-campus room and board: $5,880. Books and supplies: $750.

Financial Aid: Resources specifically for eligible students enrolled in teacher education programs are awarded on the basis of financial need and academic merit. The institution has a Program Participation Agreement with the U.S. Department of Education for eligible students to receive Pell Grants and other federal aid. *Contact:* Ellen Rigsby at: (309) 467-6311 or e-mail at erigsby@eureka.edu.

Accreditation: *Regional:* NCA. *Approved by:* Illinois State Board of Education.

Undergraduate Programs: Students can major in elementary education, vocal music (K-12), and gain secondary certification (6-12) in biology, English, mathematics, history, physical education, physical science. The professional education course sequence plus 100 hours of in-school clinical experiences must be completed in order to student teach for 11 weeks.

Licensure/Reciprocity: Illinois. Students seeking teaching certification in a state other than Illinois should consult with that state's teacher certification office early in their program of study to insure compliance with requirements. Many state directors of teacher credentialing have signed Interstate Agreements through NASDTEC that expedite the certification process.

GOVERNORS STATE UNIVERSITY

College of Education
Division of Education

1 University Parkway
University Park, Illinois 60466-0975
Phone: (708) 534-4050
Fax: (708) 534-8451
E-mail: info@gsuteach.com
Internet: http://www.govst.edu

Institution Description: Governors State University is a state institution providing upper division and graduate study only. The university was established in 1969.

Institution Control: Public.

Calendar: Trimester. Academic year September to August.

Official(s): Dr. Roger V. Bennett, Dean, College of Education; Dr. David Blood, Chair, Division of Education.

Faculty: Full-time 73; part-time 3; adjunct 61.

Degrees Awarded: 99 baccalaureate; 475 master's.

Admission Requirements: *Undergraduate:* Student must have completed 60 credit hours with a a 2.0 GPA. *Teacher education specific:* 2.5 GPA. *Graduate:* Baccalaureate degree from a regionally accredited institution. *Teacher education specific:* 2.75 GPA; 3.0 GPA in any attempted graduate coursework.

Fees and Expenses: Undergraduate: in-state $2,832 per academic year, out-of-state $3,120. Graduate: in-state $8,496 per academic year, out-of-state $9,360. Required fees: $231.

Financial Aid: Resources specifically for eligible students enrolled in teacher education programs are awarded on the basis of financial need and academic merit. The institution has a Program Participation Agreement with the U.S. Department of Education for eligible students to receive Pell Grants and other federal aid. *Contact:* Freda Whisenton-Comer at (708) 534-4481 or e-mail at f-comer@govst.edu.

Accreditation: *Regional:* NCA. *Professional:* NCATE. *Approved by:* Illinois State Board of Education.

Undergraduate Programs: Students may major in early childhood, elementary, or secondary education. secondary education students may enroll in the following majors: biology, chemistry, or English with additional education courses incorporated into their programs. Credit hour requirements range from 125 to 133 hours.

Graduate Programs: Initial certification programs are offered in early childhood (M.A.) and elementary education (nondegree alternative certification program at the post-baccalaureate level).

Advanced programs for teacher certification are offered in reading, multicategorical special education, and communication disorders. School service certification are offered through M.A. programs in school counseling, school psychology, and communication disorders. Administrative certifications (general administrative and school business official) are ordered through the M.A. in educational administration.

Licensure/Reciprocity: Illinois. Students seeking teaching certification in a state other than Illinois should consult with that state's teacher certification office early in their program of study to insure compliance with requirements. Many state directors of teacher credentialing have signed Interstate Agreements through NASDTEC that expedite the certification process. Reciprocity agreement also through the Central States Teacher Exchange Agreement.

GREENVILLE COLLEGE

Education Department
Teacher Education Program

315 East College Avenue
Greenville, Illinois 62246-0159
Phone: (618) 664-2800
Fax: (618) 664-1373
E-mail: eblue@greenville.edu
Internet: http://www.greenville.edu

Institution Description: Greenville College is a private, non-profit college affiliated with the Free Methodist Church of North America. It was established in 1892.

The Teacher Education Program includes undergraduate and graduate degree programs that prepare teachers to serve in a culturally diverse world.

Institution Control: Private.

Calendar: Semester. Academic year September to May.

Official(s): Dr. Ed Blue, Director, Teacher Education Program.

Faculty: Full-time 14.

Degrees Awarded: 55 baccalaureate.

Admission Requirements: *Undergraduate:* Graduation from an accredited high school or GED; College Board SAT or ACT composite. *Teacher education specific:* Passing scores on Illinois Basic Skills Test; apply to program by sophomore year; interview by Teacher Education Program faculty. *Graduate:* Baccalaureate degree from a regionally accredited institution. *Teacher education specific:* Test results reflecting a passing score on the Illinois Basic Skills Test or GRE; official transcripts; background check; faculty interview.

Fees and Expenses: Undergraduate $15,666 per academic year. Graduate: $302 per credit hour. On-campus room: $2,634 to $3,520. On-campus board: $2,932. Other expenses: $1,850. Books and supplies: $800. Other fees may apply. Traditional tuition/room/board/fees $21,342 per academic year.

Financial Aid: Resources specifically for eligible students enrolled in teacher education programs are awarded on the basis of financial need and academic merit. The institution has a Program Participation Agreement with the U.S. Department of Education for eligible students to receive Pell Grants and other federal aid. *Contact:* Financial Aid Office at: (618) 664-7111.

Accreditation: *Regional:* NCA. *Member of:* AACTE. *Approved by:* Illinois State Board of Education.

Undergraduate Programs: An early childhood education major requires 48 hours of general education courses, 29 hours of professional studies courses, 37 hours of early childhood specialization courses, and 8 additional credits.

The elementary education major requires 48 hours of general education courses, 28 hours of professional studies courses, and 24 hours of elementary education courses. A middle school endorsement requires 18 hours per area.

A student majoring in secondary education (grades 6-12) may seek certification in the areas of: biology, chemistry, English language arts, mathematics, music, physical education, physics, history, Spanish. Additional teaching endorsements may be earned in many areas of study.

A special education major requires 48 hours of general education courses, 29 hours of professional studies courses, and 44 hours of special education Specialization courses.

Graduate Programs: The Master of Arts in Teaching degree program requires the completion of the 42-semester hour program. Both elementary and secondary certification is offered. Courses include state-mandated field experiences in addition to the regular coursework. Student teaching follows coursework, field experience, and required Illinois testing.

The Master of Arts in Education is a 32 semester hour program that can be completed in approximately 22 months. The coursework schedule is tailored to working adults.

Licensure/Reciprocity: Illinois. Students seeking teaching certification in a state other than Illinois should consult with that state's teacher certification office early in their program of study to insure compliance with requirements. Many state directors of teacher credentialing have signed Interstate Agreements through NASDTEC that expedite the certification process. Reciprocity agreement also through the Central States Teacher Exchange Agreement.

ILLINOIS STATE UNIVERSITY
College of Education
Teacher Education Program
Campus Box 5300
North and School Streets
Normal, Illinois 61790
Phone: (309) 438-5415
Fax: (309) 438-3813
E-mail: coe@ilstu.edu
Internet: http://www.ilstu.edu

Institution Description: Illinois State University was begun as Illinois State Normal University in 1857. The present name was adopted in 1964.

Undergraduate and graduate teacher education programs are offered through the College of Education and other colleges across the university.

Institution Control: Public.

Calendar: Semester. Academic year August to May.

Official(s): Dr. Dianne E. Ashby, Dean, College of Education.

Faculty: Full-time 207; part-time 145.

Degrees Awarded: 1,015 baccalaureate; 235 master's; 43 doctorate.

Admission Requirements: *Undergraduate:* Graduation from an approved secondary school or GED; College Board SAT or ACT composite. *Graduate:* Admission decision is made in specific department.

Fees and Expenses: Undergraduate: in-state $4,397 per academic year; out-of-state $9,166. Graduate: $4,429 in-state per academic year; out-of-state $9,299. Required fees: $1,298. On-campus room and board: $4,864.

Financial Aid: Resources specifically for eligible students enrolled in teacher education programs are awarded on the basis of financial need and academic merit. The institution has a Program Participation Agreement with the U.S. Department of Education for eligible students to receive Pell Grants and other federal aid. *Contact:* Dr. Charles Boudreau at: (309) 438-2231 or e-mail at caboudr@ilstu.edu.

Accreditation: *Regional:* NCA. *Professional:* NCATE. *Approved by:* Illinois State Board of Education.

Undergraduate Programs: Undergraduate teacher education programs are offered in five colleges across the university: College of Education (early childhood, elementary, middle level, and special education); College of Arts and Sciences (biology, chemistry, English language arts, history/social sciences/geography, and mathematics; College of Fine Arts (art, music, theatre/dance); College of Applied Science and Technology (agriculture, family and consumer sciences, health sciences, technology education, and physical education); College of Business (business education).

Graduate Programs: Graduate professional education programs are offered in: reading, special education, speech pathology and audiology, school psychology, and education administration (principalship, superintendency, chief school business official). Each program requires an internship with focused research an/or instructional activity. Requirements for admission to programs and for recommendation for certification are program specific.

Licensure/Reciprocity: Illinois. Students seeking teaching certification in a state other than Illinois should consult with that state's teacher certification office early in their program of study to insure compliance with requirements. Many state directors of teacher credentialing have signed Interstate Agreements through NASDTEC that expedite the certification process. Reciprocity agreement also through the Central States Teacher Exchange Agreement.

LEWIS UNIVERSITY

College of Education

One University Parkway
Romeoville, Illinois 60446-2298
Phone: (815) 838-0500
Fax: (815) 838-9456
E-mail: minesj@lewisu.edu
Internet: http://www.lewisu.edu

Institution Description: Lewis University is a private institution conducted by the Brothers of the Christian Schools, a Roman Catholic teaching order. It was established as Holy Name Technical School in 1932. The present name was adopted in 1973.

The College of Education offers a curriculum designed to prepare teachers, supervisors, and administrators for public, Catholic, and other private elementary schools, middle schools, and secondary schools.

Institution Control: Private.

Calendar: Semester. Academic year August to May.

Official(s): Dr. Jeanette Mines, Dean, College of Education.

Faculty: Full-time 15.

Degrees Awarded: 46 baccalaureate; 101 master's.

Admission Requirements: *Undergraduate:* Graduation with 15 academic units from an approved secondary school or GED; ACT composite preferred, College Board SAT accepted. *Teacher education specific:* Acceptance into the program by sophomore year; passing scores on Illinois Basic Skills Test; personal interview. *Graduate:* Baccalaureate degree from a regionally accredited institution. *Teacher education specific:* Teaching credential if not seeking certification; personal goal statement; passing scores on all departmental/state required tests; maintain and undergraduate GPA of at least 2.75 in the last 60 hours of coursework; three letters of recommendation; acceptance by the Graduate Council of the College of Arts and Sciences; satisfactory completion of the Graduate Entrance Writing Examination.

Fees and Expenses: Undergraduate: $7,975 per semester; graduate $540 per credit hour. Room: $1,975 to $2,275 per semester. Board: $950 to $1,350 depending on meal plan selected. Residential amenities fee: $650 per semester. Other fees may apply.

Financial Aid: Resources specifically for eligible students enrolled in teacher education programs are awarded on the basis of financial need and academic merit. The institution has a Program Participation Agreement with the U.S. Department of Education for eligible students to receive Pell Grants and other federal aid. *Contact:* Financial Aid Office at: (815) 838-0500, ext. 5263.

Accreditation: *Regional:* NCA. *Professional:* NCATE. *Member of:* AACTE. *Approved by:* Illinois State Board of Education.

Undergraduate Programs: The Bachelor of Arts degree program in elementary education requires the completion of a total of 128 semester hours including sequences in general education, professional education, major area of concentration (47 hours), and field experiences.

The Bachelor of Arts in secondary education program include approved areas as follows: biology, chemistry, computer science, English, mathematics, physics, psychology, history, speech/education. Completion of all programs entitles students to apply for the Initial High School Certificate. A total of 128 semester hours is required for the degree.

Graduate Programs: The Master of Arts in Education program offers programs leading to certification in the following specializations: reading and literacy, school administration, special education, secondary certification.

The Master of Education degree is offered in curriculum and instruction with specializations in reading and literacy, school administration, special education, and teaching and learning.

Candidates who already possess a master's degree and all prerequisites may complete the requirements for the Type 10 Standard Special Certificate in reading, special education (K-12).

Licensure/Reciprocity: Illinois. Students seeking teaching certification in a state other than Illinois should consult with that state's teacher certification office early in their program of study to insure compliance with requirements. Many state directors of teacher credentialing have signed Interstate Agreements through NASDTEC that expedite the certification process. Reciprocity agreement also through the Central States Teacher Exchange Agreement.

LOYOLA UNIVERSITY OF CHICAGO

School of Education
Teacher Education Program

820 North Michigan Avenue
Chicago, Illinois 60611
Phone: (312) 915-6899
Fax: (312) 915-6660
E-mail: education@luc.edu
Internet: http://www.luc.edu

Institution Description: Loyola University of Chicago is a private, independent, nonprofit Jesuit institution affiliated with the Roman Catholic Church. It was established as St. Ignatius College in 1870. The present name was adopted in 1909.

The School of Education provides programs that develop professional skills and knowledge both for the classroom and for diverse urban environments. The School of Education maintains partnerships with the Chicago Public Schools and the Chicago Archdiocese Schools

Institution Control: Private.

Calendar: Semester. Academic year August to April.

Official(s): Dr. David Prasse, Chairperson, Department of Curriculum, Instruction, and Educational Psychology.

Faculty: Full-time 22.

Degrees Awarded: 48 baccalaureate; 144 master's; 88 doctorate.

Admission Requirements: *Undergraduate:* Graduation with 15 academic units from an approved secondary school or GED; College Board SAT or ACT composite. *Teacher education specific:* Acceptance as an education teacher candidate by the sophomore year; passing scores on the Illinois Basic Skills Test; personal goal statement. *Graduate:* Baccalaureate degree from a regionally accredited institution. *Teacher education specific:* Faculty interview; successful completion of all required departmental/state tests/exams.

Fees and Expenses: Undergraduate: $19,472 per academic year; graduate: $384 per semester hour in 300 level courses; $548 in 400-500 level courses. On-campus room and board: $7,430 per academic year. Other expenses: $1,600. Books and supplies: $800.

Financial Aid: Resources specifically for eligible students enrolled in teacher education programs are awarded on the basis of financial need and academic merit. The institution has a Program Participation Agreement with the U.S. Department of Education for eligible students to receive Pell Grants and other federal aid. *Contact:* Financial Aid Office at: (312) 508-3155.

Accreditation: *Regional:* NCA. *Member of:* AACTE. *Approved by:* Illinois State Board of Education.

Undergraduate Programs: The School of Education offers teacher certification programs for elementary and secondary education. Students interested in elementary education (grades K-9) are admitted to the School of Education and major in elementary education. Students interested in secondary education (grades 6-12) are admitted to the College of Arts and Science and major in the specific content area and complete the minor in the specific content area and complete the minor in Professional Studies in Education with eligibility for certification. Content areas available include art, biology, chemistry, English, French, history, Italian, Latin, mathematics, political science, psychology, Spanish, and theatre. All programs lead to the bachelor's degree.

Graduate Programs: Teacher education programs at the graduate level include: curriculum and instruction with elementary certification (M.Ed.); curriculum and instruction with secondary certification (M.Ed.); curriculum and instruction (M.A.

without certification); curriculum and instruction (M.Ed.) without certification in the strands of reading, technology, classroom assessment, school improvement, subject matter; curriculum and instruction with certification (M.Ed.); and instructional leadership (M.Ed.).

Licensure/Reciprocity: Illinois. Students seeking teaching certification in a state other than Illinois should consult with that state's teacher certification office early in their program of study to insure compliance with requirements. Many state directors of teacher credentialing have signed Interstate Agreements through NASDTEC that expedite the certification process.

MACMURRAY COLLEGE

Division of Education
447 East College Avenue
Jacksonville, Illinois 62650
Phone: (217) 479-7224
Fax: (217) 479-7177
E-mail: education@mac.edu
Internet: http://www.mac.edu

Institution Description: MacMurray College is a private college affiliated with the United Methodist Church. The college was established as Illinois Conference Female Academy in 1846. The present name was adopted in 1953 and the college merged with MacMurray College for Men (established 1955) in 1969.

The Division of Education offers baccalaureate programs in teacher education.

Institution Control: Private.

Calendar: Semester. Academic year August to May.

Official(s): Dr. Ellen Crowe, Dean, Education Department.

Faculty: Full-time 9; part-time 13.

Degrees Awarded: 32 baccalaureate.

Admission Requirements: *Undergraduate:* Graduation from an approved secondary school or GED; ACT score of 23 or higher; top 25% of graduation class. *Teacher education specific:* 2.5 GPA; pass Illinois Basic Skills Test; B or better in field experience and C or better in education courses.

Fees and Expenses: $14,500 per academic year. Room: $2,310 to $2,515. Board: $2,550 to $2,990. Books and supplies: $775.

Financial Aid: Resources specifically for eligible students enrolled in teacher education programs are awarded on the basis of financial need and academic merit. The institution has a Program Participation Agreement with the U.S. Department of Education for eligible students to receive Pell Grants and other federal aid. *Contact:* Rhonda Cors at: (217) 479-7041 or e-mail at rhonda@mac.edu.

Accreditation: *Regional:* NCA. *Approved by:* Illinois State Board of Education.

Undergraduate Programs: The Division of Education offers programs in six areas: deaf and hard of hearing, elementary education, secondary education, special education, physical education, and music education. These programs offer courses for the professional preparation of teachers in each of these categories. The courses are offered within the framework of the liberal arts, a combination that is designed to produce teachers who are educated in the major fields of learning and at the same time are practitioners in the school classroom.

Preparation for teaching in secondary schools is also offered in the fields of biology, English, history, mathematics, and Spanish. Students major in the academic field in which they plan to teach. In a major field, 33 hours are required.

An assessment system with six checkpoints is used to admit students to the Teacher Education Program and to monitor their progress on a regular basis.

Licensure/Reciprocity: Illinois. Students seeking teaching certification in a state other than Illinois should consult with that state's teacher certification office early in their program of study to insure compliance with requirements. Many state directors of teacher credentialing have signed Interstate Agreements through NASDTEC that expedite the certification process.

MILLIKIN UNIVERSITY

School of Education
Teacher Education Programs
Shilling 307
1184 West Main Street
Decatur, Illinois 62522-2084
Phone: (217) 424-6244
Fax: (217) 425-3993
E-mail: jkupper@millikin.edu
Internet: http://www.millikin.edu

Institution Description: Millikin University is a private, independent, nonprofit institution affiliated with The Presbyterian Church in the United States of America. It was established and chartered in 1901. The present name was adopted in 1953.

Teacher Education Programs at Millikin draw heavily on offerings of the colleges and schools that comprise the university. The programs are overseen by the Committee on Teacher Education Programs.

Institution Control: Private.

Calendar: Semester. Academic year August to May.

Official(s): Dr. Jodi Kipper, Director, School of Education; Dr. Darlene Hoffman, Chair, Education Department; Dr. Mary Eddy, Director, Teacher Education Programs.

Faculty: Full-time 6; part-time 1; adjunct 14.

Degrees Awarded: 82 baccalaureate.

Admission Requirements: *Undergraduate:* Graduation with 15 academic units from an approved secondary school or GED; ACT score of 20; class rank in top 50%; job experience/extracurricular activities. *Teacher education specific:* 2.5 GPA; pass Illinois Basic Skills Test, C+ in composition courses; exploratory portfolio.

Fees and Expenses: $18,334 per academic year. On-campus room and board: $6,125. Required fees: $400 (activity, technology). Books and supplies: $600.

Financial Aid: Resources specifically for eligible students enrolled in teacher education programs are awarded on the basis of financial need and academic merit. The institution has a Program Participation Agreement with the U.S. Department of Education for eligible students to receive Pell Grants and other federal aid. *Contact:* Jeanne Puckett, Director of Financial Aid at (217) 424-6343 or e-mail at jpuckett@mail.millikin.edu.

Accreditation: *Regional:* NCA. *Member of:* AACTE. *Approved by:* Illinois State Board of Education.

Undergraduate Programs: Teacher education programs leading to the bachelor's degree are: elementary education (grades K-9); biology education (grades 6-12); chemistry education (grades 6-12); English, French, Spanish (grades 6-12); mathematics (grades 6-12); social science (6-12); physical education-secondary education (grades 6-12); physical education-secondary and specialist (grades K-12); art education (grades K-12); music education (grades K-12); social nurse certificate-school service personnel (grades K-12). All programs require the completion of general education courses, professional program courses, and major requirements. All programs require the successful completion of a minimum of 100 clock hours of pre-teaching experiences in school classroom. Student teaching must be completed for graduation. The Bachelor of Arts or the Bachelor of Science degrees are awarded upon successful completion of all teacher education program requirements.

Licensure/Reciprocity: Illinois. Students seeking teaching certification in a state other than Illinois should consult with that state's teacher certification office early in their program of study to insure compliance with requirements. Many state directors of teacher credentialing have signed Interstate Agreements through NASDTEC that expedite the certification process. Reciprocity agreement also through the Central States Teacher Exchange Agreement.

NATIONAL-LOUIS UNIVERSITY

College of Education
122 South Michigan Avenue
Chicago, Illinois 60603
Phone: (800) 658-8632
Fax: (312) 261-3247
E-mail: info@nl.edu
Internet: http://www.nl.edu

Institution Description: National-Louis University, formerly the National College of Education, is a private institution with branch campuses in Chicago, Wheeling (IL), Wheaton (IL), and centers in St. Louis, Atlanta, Milwaukee, Elgin (IL), Tampa/Orlando, northern Virginia/Washington, D.C., and Heidelberg, Germany. The university was established as Chicago Training School in 1886. It became a four-year institution and renamed National College of Education in 1930. The present name was adopted in 1989.

Institution Control: Private.

Calendar: Quarter. Academic year September to June.

Official(s): Dr. Elizabeth M. Hawthorne, Dean.

Faculty: Full-time 170.

Degrees Awarded: 135 baccalaureate; 1,474 master's; 19 doctorate.

Admission Requirements: *Undergraduate:* Graduation from an approved secondary school or GED; College Board SAT or ACT composite. *Teacher education specific:* Passing scores on Illinois Basic Skills Test; acceptance into teacher education program by end of sophomore year; faculty interview. *Graduate:* Baccalaureate degree from a regionally accredited institution. *Teacher education specific:* Passing scores on Illinois Basic Skills Test or GRE; letters of recommendation; faculty interview.

Fees and Expenses: Undergraduate: $14,715 per academic year; graduate: $513 per credit hour. On-campus room and board: $5,913. Other expenses: $1,806. Books and supplies: $936. Other fees may apply.

Financial Aid: Resources specifically for eligible students enrolled in teacher education programs are awarded on the basis of financial need and academic merit. The institution has a Program Participation Agreement with the U.S. Department of Education for eligible students to receive Pell Grants and other federal aid. *Contact:* Rebecca Babel Financial Aid Office at: (847) 475-5770 or e-mail @rbabel.nl.edu.

Accreditation: *Regional:* NCA. *Professional:* NCATE. *Member of:* AACTE. *Approved by:* Illinois State Board of Education.

Undergraduate Programs: The Bachelor of Arts in early childhood education and the Bachelor of Arts in elementary education degrees lead to certification in the stae of Illinois. The B.A. in early childhood is designed for individuals who wish to teach children, birth through age 8. The B.A. in elementary education is designed for individuals who wish to teach children, kindergarten through grade 9. Both programs require the completion of general education courses, professional studies courses, field experiences, and student teaching.

Graduate Programs: The Master of Arts in Teaching degree will lead to certification in Illinois. It is designed for individuals with undergraduate degrees in fields other than education. The Master of Education degree is for teachers seeking professional growth in the classroom. The Master of Science in Education is for exceptionally qualified teachers aspiring to leadership positions and further graduate study.

Within the master's degree programs, Illinois entitlement certification is available in: administration and supervision; early childhood education; elementary education; school nurse; behavior disorders; learning disabilities; reading specialist; secondary education.

Licensure/Reciprocity: Illinois. Students seeking teaching certification in a state other than Illinois should consult with that state's teacher certification office early in their program of study to insure compliance with requirements. Many state directors of teacher credentialing have signed Interstate Agreements through NASDTEC that expedite the certification process.

NORTH PARK UNIVERSITY

School of Education
Box 29
3225 West Foster Avenue
Chicago, Illinois 60625
Phone: (773) 244-5730
Fax: (773) 244-4952
E-mail: hernandez-azcoitia@@northpark.edu
Internet: http://www.northpark.edu

Institution Description: North Park University, formerly known as North Park College and Theological Seminary, is a private institution affiliated with the Evangelical Covenant Church of America. It was established as a two-year institution in 1891 and became a four-year college in 1958. The present name was adopted in 1997.

The Teacher Education Program aims to prepare teachers for educational leadership through a background in liberal arts.

Institution Control: Private.

Calendar: Semester. Academic year September to May.

Official(s): Dr. Diana Hernandez-Azcoitia, Dean.

Faculty: Full-time 9; part-time 1; adjunct 12.

Degrees Awarded: 20 baccalaureate; 65 master's.

Admission Requirements: *Undergraduate:* Graduation from an approved secondary school or GED; College Board SAT or ACT composite. *Teacher education specific:* Passing scores on the Illinois Basic Skills Test; successful completion of professional term. *Graduate:* Baccalaureate degree from a regionally accredited institution; transcripts with a 2.5 or above GPA. *Teacher education specific:* Three letters of recommendation; if seeking certification, passing scores on the Illinois Basic Skills Test; faculty interview.

Fees and Expenses: Undergraduate $19,470 per academic year. Graduate: $10,800. On-campus room and board: $3,500.

Financial Aid: Resources specifically for eligible students enrolled in teacher education programs are awarded on the basis of financial need and academic merit. The institution has a Program Participation Agreement with the U.S. Department of Education for eligible students to receive Pell Grants and other federal aid. "Serving the City" scholarships for full-time teachers in Chicago schools. *Contact:* Annette Miley at (773) 244-5525 or e-mail at financial aid@northpark.edu.

Accreditation: *Regional:* NCA. *Member of:* AACTE. *Approved by:* Illinois State Board of Education.

Undergraduate Programs: The following undergraduate programs are offered: early childhood; elementary education; secondary education with concentrations in biology, English, French, general science, history, mathematics, physical education, physics, social studies, Spanish, and speech; special K-12; art; music; and physical education . All programs require the completion of general education courses, professional education courses, major subject area, field experiences, and student teaching.

Graduate Programs: The Master of Education Teacher Leadership Program is designed for those who wish to improve personal practice and to influence others as models of good practice and leaders in their schools. The program offers coursework in the most current theories and practice in a wide variety of areas. The program requires the completion of 32 semester hours including core courses, two hours of electives, and all candidates are required to design and implement a master's level project. The project must be approved by the assigned facilitator and chair, approved in accordance with university policy, and presented to an outside professional group.

Licensure/Reciprocity: Illinois. Students seeking teaching certification in a state other than Illinois should consult with that state's teacher certification office early in their program of study to insure compliance with requirements. Many state directors of teacher credentialing have signed Interstate Agreements through NASDTEC that expedite the certification process. Reciprocity agreement also through the Central States Teacher Exchange Agreement.

NORTHEASTERN ILLINOIS UNIVERSITY
College of Education
Department of Teacher Education
5500 North St. Louis Avenue
Chicago, Illinois 60625-4699
Phone: (773) 583-4050
Fax: (773) 794-6246
E-mail: N-Giblin@neiu.edu
Internet: http://www.neiu.edu

Institution Description: Northeastern Illinois University, a state institution, was established as Cook County Normal School in 1867. After numerous name changes over the years, the present name was adopted in 1971.

The Department of Teacher Education encompasses seven programs of study in preservice and inservice teacher preparation.

Institution Control: Public.

Calendar: Semester. Academic year August to May.

Official(s): Dr. Nan J. Giblin, Dean, College of Education.

Faculty: Full-time 25; part-time 5.

Degrees Awarded: 251 baccalaureate; 365 master's.

Admission Requirements: *Undergraduate:* Graduation from an approved secondary school or GED; ACT composite. *Teacher education specific:* Basic Skills Test; 2.65 GPA; students must pass the Content Area/Subject Matter Knowledge Test in order to receive credit for student teaching. *Graduate:* Baccalaureate degree from a regionally accredited institution. *Teacher education specific:* Letters of recommendation; Illinois teaching credential; faculty interview.

Fees and Expenses: Undergraduate: in-state $3,000 per academic year, out-of-state $8,018 out-of-state. Graduate: Tuition is charged per credit hour. On-campus room and board: $6,894. Other expenses: $4,212. Books and supplies: $960.

Financial Aid: Resources specifically for eligible students enrolled in teacher education programs are awarded on the basis of financial need and academic merit. The institution has a Program Participation Agreement with the U.S. Department of Education for eligible students to receive Pell Grants and other federal aid. *Contact:* Financial Aid Office at: (773) 442-5000.

Accreditation: *Regional:* NCA. *Professional:* NCATE. *Member of:* AACTE. *Approved by:* Illinois State Board of Education.

Undergraduate Programs: Each undergraduate program of study involves coursework in educational history and philosophy, equational psychology, and pedagogy, as well as extensive field-based experiences at public and parochial schools located in the Chicago metropolitan area.

The early childhood education program prepares teachers of children from birth to 8 years of age for all areas of the curriculum. The elementary education program prepares teachers of children from kindergarten to ninth grade for all areas of the elementary curriculum. In the bilingual/bicultural education program, teacher candidates complete a major in bilingual/bicultural education along with a major in elementary education.

The secondary education program prepares teachers of children in grades 6-12. Majors are offered in: art, biology, English, history, mathematics, music (K-12), physical education, and Spanish.

Graduate Programs: The bilingual/bicultural program involves graduate study leading to a master's degree for both preservice (Master of Arts in Teaching) and inservice teachers (Master of Science in Instruction) without certification.

The program in language arts offers coursework leading to a master's degree in the area of literacy and English acquisition.

The reading program leads to a reading specialist certification for teachers of children in grades K-12.

The teacher certification program for post-baccalaureate students is designed for returning students with degrees in fields other that education who wish to obtain teaching certification in early childhood education, elementary education, secondary education (art, biology, English, history, mathematics, physical education, Spanish) and music education with standard special entitlement (grades K-12).

Licensure/Reciprocity: Illinois. Students seeking teaching certification in a state other than Illinois should consult with that state's teacher certification office early in their program of study to insure compliance with requirements. Many state directors of teacher credentialing have signed Interstate Agreements through NASDTEC that expedite the certification process. Reciprocity agreement also through the Central States Teacher Exchange Agreement.

NORTHERN ILLINOIS UNIVERSITY
College of Education
Teacher Certification Programs
Provost's Office
DeKalb, Illinois 60115
Phone: (815) 753-0494
Fax: (815) 753-0701
E-mail: eseaver@niu.edu
Internet: http://www.niu.edu

Institution Description: Northern Illinois University was established as Northern Illinois State Normal School in 1895. The name was changed to Northern Illinois State Teachers College and became a four-year institution in 1921. The current name was adopted in 1957.

Teacher Certification Programs are offered through the various academic departments of the university.

Institution Control: Public.

Calendar: Semester. Academic year August to May.

Official(s): Dr. C. Sorensen, Dean, College of Education.

Faculty: Full-time 192; part-time 93.

Degrees Awarded: 529 baccalaureate; 531 master's; 59 doctorate.

Admission Requirements: *Undergraduate:* Graduation from an approved secondary school or GED; requires college preparatory curriculum; ACT composite score of 19; upper 50% class rank. *Teacher education specific:* Pass Illinois Basic Skills Test; background check; faculty interview. *Graduate:* Baccalaureate degree from a regionally accredited institution. *Teacher education specific:* 2.75 minimum GPA; GRE.

Fees and Expenses: Undergraduate: in-state $3,741.12; out-of-state $7,482.24. Graduate: in-state $7482.24; out-of-state $7,086. Required fees: $1,230 undergraduate; $1,216.56 graduate. On-campus room and board: $4,352 - $7,780. Books and supplies: $900.

Financial Aid: Resources specifically for eligible students enrolled in teacher education programs are awarded on the basis of financial need and academic merit. The institution has a Program Participation Agreement with the U.S. Department of Education for eligible students to receive Pell Grants and other federal aid. *Contact:* Kathleen Brunson at (815) 753-1300.

Accreditation: *Regional:* NCA. *Professional:* NCATE. *Member of:* AACTE. *Approved by:* Illinois State Board of Education.

Undergraduate Programs: Initial teacher certification entitlement programs include: early childhood certificate (birth through grade 3); standard elementary certificate (K-9); standard high school certificate (6-12) with concentrations in biological science, chemistry, English, family and consumer sciences, French, general science, German, health education, history, mathematics, physical education, physical science, physics, social science, Spanish); standard special certificate (K-12) with concentrations in art, blind and partially seeing, learning behavior specialist, music, and physical education.

Upon satisfactory completion of one or more of the above initial certification programs, students must have an overall GPA of 2.5 or above in all coursework taken. Courses include general education requirements and professional preparation courses. Students must successfully complete as minimum of 100 clock hours of clinical experience prior to student teaching.

NORTHERN ILLINOIS UNIVERSITY—*cont'd*

Graduate Programs: Certification programs are offered to those students with a baccalaureate degree who have not had previous teaching experience. Those with the bachelor's degree will be considered as having completed the general education requirements as described for undergraduate programs. All other requirements must be met.

Licensure/Reciprocity: Illinois. Students seeking teaching certification in a state other than Illinois should consult with that state's teacher certification office early in their program of study to insure compliance with requirements. Many state directors of teacher credentialing have signed Interstate Agreements through NASDTEC that expedite the certification process. Reciprocity agreement also through the Central States Teacher Exchange Agreement.

NORTHWESTERN UNIVERSITY

School of Education and Social Policy

Annenberg Hall 117
2120 Campus Drive
Evanston, Illinois 60208
Phone: (847) 467-1999
E-mail: sesp@northwestern.edu
Internet: http://www.northwestern.edu

Institution Description: Northwestern University is a private, independent, nonprofit institution established in 1850. The university has campuses in Evanston and Chicago.

The School of Education and Social Policy offers undergraduate and graduate programs secondary teacher education.

Institution Control: Private.

Calendar: Quarter. Academic year September to June.

Official(s): Dr. Sophie Harouturian-Gordon, Director, Education Program.

Faculty: Full-time 35.

Degrees Awarded: 16 baccalaureate; 101 master's; 8 doctorate.

Admission Requirements: *Undergraduate:* Graduation from an approved secondary school or GED; College Board SAT or ACT composite. *Teacher education specific:* Acceptance into the program by sophomore year; passing scores on Illinois Basic Skills Test; personal goal statement; faculty interview. *Graduate:* Baccalaureate degree from a regionally accredited institution. *Teacher education specific:* Passing scores on Illinois Basic Skills Test or GRE; Academic Content Areas Test; pass all other departmental/state tests/exams; faculty interview.

Fees and Expenses: Undergraduate: $27,228. Graduate: Tuition charged per credit hour. On-campus room and board: $8,446. Other expenses: $2,03. Books and supplies: $1,266.

Financial Aid: Resources specifically for eligible students enrolled in teacher education programs are awarded on the basis of financial need and academic merit. The institution has a Program Participation Agreement with the U.S. Department of Education for eligible students to receive Pell Grants and other federal aid. *Contact:* Financial Aid Office at: (847) 491-7400.

Accreditation: *Regional:* NCA. *Approved by:* Illinois State Board of Education.

Undergraduate Programs: The secondary teaching program combines coursework in the liberal arts with professional education courses. Students earn a Bachelor of Science in education and social policy as well as earning a recommendation for certification through entitlement for secondary teaching (grades 6-12). Forty-five courses are required for the degree. Illinois certification can be earned in a wide range of majors within the Weinberg College of Arts and Sciences, including art, English, history, economics with history, political science with history, sociology with history, mathematics, biology, chemistry, physics, French, German, Latin, or Spanish.

Graduate Programs: The Master of Science in Education program seeks to prepare professionals who are dedicated to and skilled at helping individuals of all ages improve themselves through education in the contexts of school, family, community, and work. Students in the program pursue one of five concentrations: elementary teaching. middle school teaching, secondary teaching, advanced teaching, higher education administration and policy.

Licensure/Reciprocity: Illinois. Students seeking teaching certification in a state other than Illinois should consult with that state's teacher certification office early in their program of study to insure compliance with requirements. Many state directors of teacher credentialing have signed Interstate Agreements through NASDTEC that expedite the certification process. Reciprocity agreement also through the Central States Teacher Exchange Agreement.

ROOSEVELT UNIVERSITY

College of Education

430 South Michigan Avenue
Chicago, Illinois 60605
Phone: (312) 341-3700
Fax: (312) 341-4326
E-mail: education@roosevelt.edu
Internet: http://www.roosevelt.edu

Institution Description: Roosevelt University is a private, independent, nonprofit institution. It was established as Roosevelt College of Chicago in 1945. The present name was adopted in 1954.

The College of Education offers undergraduate and graduate teacher preparation programs.

Institution Control: Private.

Calendar: Semester. Academic year August to May.

Official(s): Dr. George Lowery, Dean.

Faculty: Full-time 32; adjunct 54.

Degrees Awarded: 59 baccalaureate; 221 master's.

Admission Requirements: *Undergraduate:* Graduation with 15 academic units from an approved secondary school or GED; College Board SAT, ACT composite, or Roosevelt University Assessment Test required. *Teacher education specific:* Completion of English and math requirements with grades of C or better; passing score on Illinois Basic Skills Test; completion of 6 hours of education coursework with grades of C or better. *Graduate:* Baccalaureate degree from a regionally accredited institution. *Teacher education specific:* GPA of 2.7 in last half of undergraduate work.

Fees and Expenses: Undergraduate: $482 per credit hour; graduate: $578 per credit hour. On-campus room and board: $6,500.

Financial Aid: Resources specifically for eligible students enrolled in teacher education programs are awarded on the basis of financial need and academic merit. The institution has a Program Participation Agreement with the U.S. Department of Education for eligible students to receive Pell Grants and other federal aid. *Contact:* Walter O'Neill, Director of Financial Aid at: (312) 341-2195.

Accreditation: *Regional:* NCA. *Professional:* NCATE. *Member of:* AACTE. *Approved by:* Illinois State Board of Education.

Undergraduate Programs: Undergraduates can major in elementary education or early childhood education and receive teacher certification. Candidates seeking secondary certification combine their major in an academic field with 36 hours of education coursework. Secondary certification is offered in business education, English, general science, social studies, Spanish, or theater arts. Final certification requires successful completion of state exams.

Graduate Programs: For candidates who have earned a bachelor's degree, the College of Education offers initial certification programs leading to the M.A. in early childhood education, elementary education, and secondary education (in the areas of business education, English, general science, social studies, Spanish, or theater arts). For candidates who have achieved teacher certification at the baccalaureate level, the Master of Arts in teacher leadership, the Master of Arts and Doctor of Education in educational leadership and organizational change are offered.

Licensure/Reciprocity: Illinois. Students seeking teaching certification in a state other than Illinois should consult with that state's teacher certification office early in their program of study to insure compliance with requirements. Many state directors of teacher credentialing have signed Interstate Agreements through NASDTEC that expedite the certification process. Reciprocity agreement also through the Central States Teacher Exchange Agreement.

SAINT XAVIER UNIVERSITY
School of Education
Teacher Preparation Program
3700 West 103rd Street
Chicago, Illinois 60655
Phone: (773) 298-3200
Fax: (773) 779-9061
E-mail: education@sxu.edu
Internet: http://www.sxu.edu

Institution Description: Saint Xavier University is a private college affiliated with the Sisters of Mercy—Chicago Province, Roman Catholic Church. It was chartered as Saint Francis Xavier Academy for Females in 1847. The academy Saint Xavier College in 1956 became coeducational in 1969. The present name was adopted in 1989.

The School of Education offers the Bachelor of Science in Education degree through undergraduate programs of study that prepare students to assume teaching responsibilities in early childhood, elementary and secondary schools settings.

Calendar: Semester. Academic year September to May.

Official(s): Dr. B. Gulley, Dean, School of Education.

Faculty: Full-time 35.

Degrees Awarded: 145 baccalaureate; 678 master's.

Admission Requirements: *Undergraduate:* Graduation with 16 academic units from an approved secondary school or GED; College Board SAT or ACT composite. *Teacher education specific:* Official admittance to the program by sophomore year; declaration of major and minor; passing scores on Illinois Basic Skills Test; faculty interview; personal goal statement. *Graduate:* Baccalaureate degree from a regionally accredited institution. *Teacher education specific:* Passing scores on Illinois Basic Skills Test and Academic Subject Area Test; faculty interview; teaching credential where applicable; letters of recommendation.

Fees and Expenses: Undergraduate $16,500 per academic year; graduate $550 per semester hour. On-campus room and board: $6,484. Other expenses: $1,239. Books and supplies: $900.

Financial Aid: Resources specifically for eligible students enrolled in teacher education programs are awarded on the basis of financial need and academic merit. The institution has a Program Participation Agreement with the U.S. Department of Education for eligible students to receive Pell Grants and other federal aid. *Contact:* Financial Aid Office at: (773) 298-3070.

Accreditation: *Regional:* NCA. *Professional:* NCATE. *Member of:* AACTE. *Approved by:* Illinois State Board of Education.

Undergraduate Programs: The early childhood education program prepares students to teach children from birth through grade three. The program requires the completion of 120 semester hours including general education courses, professional studies courses, field experiences, and student teaching.

The elementary education program prepares candidates to teach children from kindergarten through grade 6, or through grade 8 in schools organized in a K-8 model. The program requires the completion of 120 semester hours including general education courses, professional studies courses, field experiences, and student teaching.

The secondary education program prepares candidates to teach students in grades 9 through 12. Students major in an academic area within the School of Arts and Sciences and minor in education. The program requires the successful completion of 120 semester hours including general education courses, professional studies courses, field experiences, and student teaching.

The English as a second language (ESL) and bilingual approval program prepares certified teachers to design and deliver effective instruction for culturally and linguistically diverse students.

Graduate Programs: The Master of Arts in Education is offered through the following areas of concentration: educational/administration and supervision, curriculum and instruction, multicultural special education, reading, individualized program. Students selecting the individualized program may pursue an initial teaching certificate in early childhood education, elementary education, or secondary education.

Licensure/Reciprocity: Illinois. Students seeking teaching certification in a state other than Illinois should consult with that state's teacher certification office early in their program of study to insure compliance with requirements. Many state directors of teacher credentialing have signed Interstate Agreements through NASDTEC that expedite the certification process.

SOUTHERN ILLINOIS UNIVERSITY AT CARBONDALE
College of Education and Human Services
Department of Curriculum and Instruction
MC4624
Carbondale, Illinois 62901
Phone: (618) 453-2415
Fax: (618) 453-1646
E-mail: johnm@@siu.edu
Internet: http://www.siu.edu

Institution Description: Southern Illinois University at Carbondale is a comprehensive public university. It was established in 1869. The present name was adopted in 1947.

The College of Education and Human Services offers programs leading to the bachelor's degree in various concentrations. Graduate degrees are offered through the Graduate School.

Institution Control: Public.

Calendar: Semester. Academic year August to May.

Official(s): Dr. Keith Hillkirk, Dean.

Faculty: Full-time 42 Curriculum and Instruction).

Degrees Awarded: 1,078 baccalaureate; 250 master's; 28 doctorate.

Admission Requirements: *Undergraduate:* High school graduation in upper 50% of graduating class; ACT 21 or SAT 930 or better. *Teacher education specific:* Passing scores on Illinois Basic Skills Test; overall 2.75 GPA; must have completed 30 semester hour of coursework. *Graduate:* Baccalaureate from a regionally accredited institution. institution. *Teacher education specific:* Overall undergraduate GPA of at least 3.0; applicants must be approved for admission by the graduate program in which they intend to pursue a degree and must meet any requirements established by the program in addition to those of the Graduate School; successful completion of all department/state tests/exams.

Fees and Expenses: Undergraduate: in-state $3,660 per academic year; out-of-state $7,320. Graduate: in-state $3,696 per academic year; out-of-state $7,392. Required fees: $1,199.

Financial Aid: Resources specifically for eligible students enrolled in teacher education programs are awarded on the basis of financial need and academic merit. The institution has a Program Participation Agreement with the U.S. Department of Education for eligible students to receive Pell Grants and other federal aid. *Contact:* Daniel R. Mann at: (618) 453-4334.

Accreditation: *Regional:* NCA. *Professional:* NCATE. *Member of:* AACTE. *Approved by:* Illinois State Board of Education.

Undergraduate Programs: The School of Education grants the Bachelor of Science degree with majors in early childhood education, elementary education, health education, physical education, and special education. The Bachelor of Science degrees with majors in psychology and speech pathology and audiol-

SOUTHERN ILLINOIS UNIVERSITY AT CARBONDALE—*cont'd*

ogy also are offered. Students taking degrees in other majors may qualify for a secondary teaching certificate by completing an approved program in teacher education.

Secondary certificate programs include subject area concentrations in art, biology, chemistry, English, French, general science, German, health education, history, mathematics, physical education, physics, and Spanish.

A minimum of 100 clock hours of pre-student teaching clinical experiences is required in the area for which a student seeks certification. Student teaching requires full-day involvement in a public school.

Graduate Programs: The Department of Curriculum and Instruction offers a professional development sequence in early childhood special education in order to enhance the knowledge base and working practices of professionals in the Southern Illinois region who are serving young children with disabilities and their families.

The department also offers a course of study leading to the Master of Science in Education degree with a major in secondary education and a concentration in any one of 11 teaching fields. The program is designed for professional educators who hold teaching positions in middle schools, junior and senior high schools, community colleges, or adult education agencies. The approved teaching fields are art, biology, chemistry, English, foreign languages, history, mathematics, physics, reading, science, and speech communication.

Doctoral programs are pursued through the Graduate School.

Licensure/Reciprocity: Illinois. Students seeking teaching certification in a state other than Illinois should consult with that state's teacher certification office early in their program of study to insure compliance with requirements. Many state directors of teacher credentialing have signed Interstate Agreements through NASDTEC that expedite the certification process. Reciprocity agreement also through the Central States Teacher Exchange Agreement.

SOUTHERN ILLINOIS UNIVERSITY AT EDWARDSVILLE

School of Education
Department of Curriculum and Instruction
Box 1049, SIUE
Edwardsville, Illinois 62026
Phone: (618) 650-3350
Fax: (618) 650-3359
E-mail: ldetoye@siue.edu
Internet: http://www.siue.edu

Institution Description: Southern Illinois University at Edwardsville was established as a branch of the Carbondale campus in 1957.

The School of Education offers undergraduate programs in professional education. Professional education programs prepare students for teaching positions in early childhood, elementary, health education, secondary, special, and physical education.

Institution Control: Public.

Calendar: Semester. Academic year August to May.

Official(s): Dr. Elliott Lessen, Dean; Dr. Lela M. Detoye, Associate Dean.

Faculty: Full-time 18.

Degrees Awarded: 240 baccalaureate; 209 master's.

Admission Requirements: *Undergraduate:* Graduation from an approved secondary school or GED; high school course requirements also considered; College Board SAT or ACT composite. *Teacher education specific:* Students must be officially admitted to a program in the designated department to secure a student teaching assignment, be graduated in teacher education, and qualify for a teaching certificate; Illinois Basic Skills Test. *Graduate:* Baccalaureate from a regionally accredited institution. *Teacher education specific:* Overall undergraduate GPA of

at least 3.0; applicants must be approved for admission by the graduate program in which they intend to pursue a degree and must meet any requirements established by the program in addition to those of the Graduate School; successful completion of all department/state tests/exams.

Fees and Expenses: Undergraduate: in-state $476.60 including fees per three-semester hour course; $791.60. Graduate: in-state $517.10 including fees per three-semester hour course, out-of-state $892.10.

Financial Aid: Resources specifically for eligible students enrolled in teacher education programs are awarded on the basis of financial need and academic merit. The institution has a Program Participation Agreement with the U.S. Department of Education for eligible students to receive Pell Grants and other federal aid. *Contact:* Sharon Berry at: (618) 650-3871 or e-mail at shaberr@siue.edu.

Accreditation: *Regional:* NCA. *Professional:* NCATE. *Member of:* AACTE. *Approved by:* Illinois State Board of Education.

Undergraduate Programs: The School of Education grants the Bachelor of Science degree with majors in early childhood education, elementary education, health education, physical education, and special education. The Bachelor of Science degrees with majors in psychology and speech pathology and audiology also are offered. Students taking degrees in other majors may qualify for a secondary teaching certificate by completing an approved program in teacher education.

Secondary certificate programs include subject area concentrations in art, biology, chemistry, English, French, general science, German, health education, history, mathematics, physical education, physics, and Spanish.

A minimum of 100 clock hours of pre-student teaching clinical experiences is required in the area for which a student seeks certification. Student teaching requires full-day involvement in a public school.

Graduate Programs: The Department of Curriculum and Instruction offers a professional development sequence in early childhood special education in order to enhance the knowledge base and working practices of professionals in the Southern Illinois region who are serving young children with disabilities and their families.

The department also offers a course of study leading to the Master of Science in Education degree with a major in secondary education and a concentration in any one of 11 teaching fields. The program is designed for professional educators who hold teaching positions in middle schools, junior and senior high schools, community colleges, or adult education agencies. The approved teaching fields are art, biology, chemistry, English, foreign languages, history, mathematics, physics, reading, science, and speech communication.

Licensure/Reciprocity: Illinois. Students seeking teaching certification in a state other than Illinois should consult with that state's teacher certification office early in their program of study to insure compliance with requirements. Many state directors of teacher credentialing have signed Interstate Agreements through NASDTEC that expedite the certification process. Reciprocity agreement also through the Central States Teacher Exchange Agreement.

UNIVERSITY OF ILLINOIS AT CHICAGO

College of Education
1040 West Harrison Street
Chicago, Illinois 60607
Phone: (312) 996-5641
Fax: (312) 996-6400
E-mail: bgates@uic.edu
Internet: http://www.uic.edu

Institution Description: The University of Illinois at Chicago is a state institution. The present name was adopted in 1982 after consolidation of the two Chicago campuses formerly known as the University of Illinois at the Medical Center and the University of Illinois at Chicago Circle.

The College of Education offers programs at the undergraduate and graduate levels.

Institution Control: Public.

Calendar: Semester. Academic year August to May.

Official(s): Dr. Victoria Chou, Dean, College of Education.

Faculty: Full-time 61; part-time 29; adjunct 6.

Degrees Awarded: 149 baccalaureate; 187 master's; 17 doctorate.

Admission Requirements: *Undergraduate:* Graduation from an approved secondary school or GED; ACT composite. *Teacher education specific:* Basic Skills Test; 2.65 GPA; students must pass the Content Area/Subject Matter Knowledge Test in order to receive credit for student teaching. *Graduate:* Baccalaureate degree from a regionally accredited institution. *Teacher education specific:* Letters of recommendation; Illinois teaching credential; faculty interview.

Fees and Expenses: Undergraduate: resident $3,399 including fees per semester; nonresident $7,247. Graduate: resident $3,774 including fees per semester; nonresident $8,965.

Financial Aid: Resources specifically for eligible students enrolled in teacher education programs are awarded on the basis of financial need and academic merit. The institution has a Program Participation Agreement with the U.S. Department of Education for eligible students to receive Pell Grants and other federal aid.

Accreditation: *Regional:* NCA. *Member of:* AACTE. *Approved by:* Illinois State Board of Education.

Undergraduate Programs: The programs offered by the College of Education are overseen by the Council on Teacher Education which consists of deans from the colleges that sponsor professional education programs leading to teacher, administrator, and school service personnel certificates.

The Bachelor of Arts in elementary education requires the completion of general education courses, subject area major, professional studies, field experiences, and student teaching.

Graduate Programs: The Master of Education programs are offered in the areas of curriculum and instruction; early childhood education; elementary education; leadership and administration; literacy, language, and culture; secondary education, a self-designed degree program, and special education.

Endorsements/approvals available through graduate level courses include bilingual approval, English as a new language approval, and the middle school endorsement.

Doctoral programs (Ph.D.) are available in curriculum and instruction, educational psychology, policy studies in urban education, and special education.

Licensure/Reciprocity: Illinois. Students seeking teaching certification in a state other than Illinois should consult with that state's teacher certification office early in their program of study to insure compliance with requirements. Many state directors of teacher credentialing have signed Interstate Agreements through NASDTEC that expedite the certification process. Reciprocity agreement also through the Central States Teacher Exchange Agreement.

UNIVERSITY OF ILLINOIS AT SPRINGFIELD

School of Education and Human Services
Department of Teacher Education
Shepherd Road
Springfield, Illinois 62794-9243
Phone: (217) 206-4817
Fax: (217) 206-7188
E-mail: admissions@uis.edu
Internet: http://www.uis.edu

Institution Description: University of Illinois at Springfield, formerly known as Sangamon State University. is a public institution providing upper division and graduate study only. It was established in 1969 and the present name was adopted in 1995.

The Department of Teacher Education offers a variety of opportunities for both pre-service and experienced teachers.

Institution Control: Public.

Calendar: Semester. Academic year begins August to May.

Official(s): Dr. Larry Stonecipher, Dean.

Faculty: Full-time 8.

Degrees Awarded: 33 master's.

Admission Requirements: *Undergraduate:* High school record of scholastic achievement; College Board SAT or ACT composite. *Teacher education specific:* Passing scores on Illinois Basic Skills Test; overall 2.5 GPA; background check; personal goal statement; faculty interview. *Graduate:* Baccalaureate degree from a regionally accredited institution. *Teacher education specific:* Passing scores on all department/state required tests/exams; field experiences; faculty interview.

Fees and Expenses: Undergraduate: in-state $4,309 per academic year; out-of-state $10,879. Graduate: $540 per semester hour. On-campus room and board: $6,370. Books and supplies: $1,000.

Financial Aid: Resources specifically for eligible students enrolled in teacher education programs are awarded on the basis of financial need and academic merit. The institution has a Program Participation Agreement with the U.S. Department of Education for eligible students to receive Pell Grants and other federal aid. *Contact:* David Pardieck, Financial Aid Office at:(217) 206-6724.

Accreditation: *Regional:* NCA. *Member of:* AACTE. *Approved by:* Illinois State Board of Education.

Undergraduate Programs: The teacher education minor provides coursework that leads to Illinois initial certification at the elementary or secondary level when combined with an appropriate academic major and fulfillment of general education and campus requirements. The minimum number of hours for graduation is 120 semester hours, 60 hours of which are earned at the University of Illinois at Springfield. The baccalaureate programs require the completion of general education courses, professional studies, field experiences, and student teaching. The Bachelor of Arts or Bachelor of Science degree is awarded upon successful completion of all requirements.

Graduate Programs: Graduate programs for experienced teachers leading to the master's and doctorate degrees are offered in a variety of disciplines and are obtained through the Graduate School.

Licensure/Reciprocity: Illinois. Students seeking teaching certification in a state other than Illinois should consult with that state's teacher certification office early in their program of study to insure compliance with requirements. Many state directors of teacher credentialing have signed Interstate Agreements through NASDTEC that expedite the certification process. Reciprocity agreement also through the Central States Teacher Exchange Agreement.

UNIVERSITY OF ILLINOIS AT URBANA-CHAMPAIGN

College of Education
1310 South Sixth Street
Champaign, Illinois 61820
Phone: (217) 333-2800
Fax: (217) 244-3647
E-mail: bmclvngr@uiuc.edu
Internet: http://www.uiuc.edu

Institution Description: The university was chartered in 1867 as the Illinois Industrial University. The first baccalaureate degree was conferred in 1878.

The programs offered by the College of Education are overseen by the Council on Teacher Education which consists of deans from the six colleges that sponsor professional education programs leading to teacher, administrator, and school service personnel certificates.

Institution Control: Public.

Calendar: Semester. Academic year September to May.

Official(s): Dr. Susan Fowler, Dean; James A. Leach, Associate Dean of Academic Affairs.

Faculty: Full-time 103; adjunct 33.

UNIVERSITY OF ILLINOIS AT URBANA-CHAMPAIGN—*cont'd*

Degrees Awarded: 263 baccalaureate; 311 master's; 55 doctorate.

Admission Requirements: *Undergraduate:* Graduation with 15 academic units from an approved secondary school or GED; College Board SAT or ACT composite. *Teacher education specific:* Minimum 2.5 GPA; passing scores on Illinois Basic Skills Test. *Graduate:* Baccalaureate degree from a regionally accredited institution. *Teacher education specific:* Passing scores on all Illinois Certification Testing System exams; letters of recommendation; faculty interview.

Fees and Expenses: Undergraduate: in-state $4,302 to $5,878, out-of-state $12,906 to $14,482. Graduate: in-state $4,900 to $6,476; out-of-state $13,574 to $15,150. Required fees: $1,402. On-campus room and board: $6,188 to $8,394. Books and supplies: $782 to $1,004. Other fees may apply.

Financial Aid: Resources specifically for eligible students enrolled in teacher education programs are awarded on the basis of financial need and academic merit. The institution has a Program Participation Agreement with the U.S. Department of Education for eligible students to receive Pell Grants and other federal aid. *Contact:* Office Financial Aid at: (217) 333-0100.

Accreditation: *Regional:* NCA. *Member of:* AACTE. *Approved by:* Illinois State Board of Education.

Undergraduate Programs: Undergraduate programs leading to the baccalaureate degree include early childhood education; elementary education (K-9); secondary education (6-12) with concentrations in agricultural education, biology, chemistry, earth science, English, French, German, Latin, mathematics, physics, Russian, social studies, Spanish); special education (K-12) in art, music, and physical education. All programs require the completion of general education courses, professional studies, academic major, field experiences, and student teaching.

Graduate Programs: Graduate level secondary (6-12) certification programs are offered in agricultural education, biology, chemistry, earth science, English, mathematics, physics, social studies, and Spanish. These programs require passage of the appropriate content area test for admission.

Other programs leading to the master's degree include early childhood education, elementary education, and special education (K-12).

Licensure/Reciprocity: Illinois. Students seeking teaching certification in a state other than Illinois should consult with that state's teacher certification office early in their program of study to insure compliance with requirements. Many state directors of teacher credentialing have signed Interstate Agreements through NASDTEC that expedite the certification process. Reciprocity agreement also through the Central States Teacher Exchange Agreement.

UNIVERSITY OF ST. FRANCIS

College of Education

500 North Wilcox Street
Joliet, Illinois 60435
Phone: (815) 740-3376
Fax: (815) 740-42264
E-mail: education@stfrancis.edu
Internet: http://www.stfrancis.edu

Institution Description: The University of St. Francis, formerly the College of St. Francis, is a Catholic, Franciscan private institution. It was founded in 1920.

The College of Education prepares its students with a broad base of general and professional studies combined with observation and participation in a variety of classrooms.

Institution Control: Private.

Calendar: Semester. Academic year August to May.

Official(s): Dr. John Gambro, Dean; Dr. Michele Anders, Associate Dean.

Faculty: Full-time 12.

Degrees Awarded: 60 baccalaureate; 56 master's.

Admission Requirements: *Undergraduate:* Graduation from an accredited high school or GED; College Board SAT or ACT composite. *Teacher education specific:* Passing scores on the Illinois Basic Skills Test; apply to program by sophomore year; faculty interview. *Graduate:* Baccalaureate degree from a regionally accredited institution. *Teacher education specific:* 2.75 GPA; computer competency; two letters of recommendation; faculty interview; passing scores on the Illinois Certification Testing System exams.

Fees and Expenses: Undergraduate: $7,885 per academic year. Graduate: $350 per credit hour. On-campus room and board: $2,900.

Financial Aid: Resources specifically for eligible students enrolled in teacher education programs are awarded on the basis of financial need and academic merit. Teacher Shortage Scholarships are available to qualifying students. The institution has a Program Participation Agreement with the U.S. Department of Education for eligible students to receive Pell Grants and other federal aid. *Contact:* Mary Shaw, Financial Aid Office at: (815) 740-3996 or e-mail at mshaw@stfrancis.edu.

Accreditation: *Regional:* NCA. *Member of:* AACTE. *Approved by:* Illinois State Board of Education.

Undergraduate Programs: Elementary education majors prepare to teach in kindergarten through ninth-grade classroom. An intensive semester of professional experience in an area school plus an advanced student teaching experience bring the theory and practice of education together. During student teaching, candidates participate in a professional seminary that helps them prepare for job interviews and certification procedures.

Secondary education students major in one of four major teaching areas of the contemporary high school: science, social science, English/language arts, or mathematics. Secondary education teacher candidates take classes in middle school psychology and curriculum to earn middle school endorsements.

Special Education students receive preparation to earn Learning Behavior Specialist I Certification. Specialized coursework and four separate field experiences lead to certification in pre-kindergarten through 12th grades.

All programs require the completion of general education courses, professional studies, field experiences, and student teaching.

Graduate Programs: The Master of Education with Certification provides student the opportunity to earn a master's degree in education at the same time they earn an initial Illinois elementary (K-9) or secondary (6-12) teaching certificate. Secondary certification is offered in the subject areas of science, English/language arts, social science, and Mathematics.

The Master of Science in Education degree programs are designed to provide educators with a relevant course of study that will increase their understanding of current educational theories and practice. The field-based program emphasize the application of learning theory in instruction, curriculum development, and educational leadership. Concentrations are offered in reading, middle school, administration, technology, elementary (K-5) curriculum and instruction, differentiated instruction, and English as a second language.

Licensure/Reciprocity: Illinois. Students seeking teaching certification in a state other than Illinois should consult with that state's teacher certification office early in their program of study to insure compliance with requirements. Many state directors of teacher credentialing have signed Interstate Agreements through NASDTEC that expedite the certification process.

WESTERN ILLINOIS UNIVERSITY
College of Education and Human Services
Teacher Education Program
Harrison Hall
One University Circle
Macomb, Illinois 61455-1390
Phone: (309) 298-1690
Fax: (309) 298-3111
E-mail: education@wiu.edu
Internet: http://www.wiu.edu

Institution Description: Western Illinois University is a state institution. It was established as Western Illinois State Normal School in 1899. The name was changed to Western Illinois State Teachers College in 1921, to Western Illinois State College in 1947, and to its current name in 1957.

The Teacher Education Program provides over twenty areas of certification and involves all colleges of the university.

Institution Control: Public.

Calendar: Semester. Academic year August to May.

Official(s): Dr. Kathy Barclay, Chairperson, Curriculum and Instruction.

Faculty: Not reported.

Degrees Awarded: 445 baccalaureate; 461 master's.

Admission Requirements: *Undergraduate:* Graduation from an approved secondary school or GED; ACT composite. *Teacher education specific:* Basic Skills Test; 2.65 GPA; students must pass the Content Area/Subject Matter Knowledge Test in order to receive credit for student teaching. *Graduate:* Baccalaureate degree from a regionally accredited institution. *Teacher education specific:* Letters of recommendation; Illinois teaching credential; faculty interview.

Fees and Expenses: Undergraduate: in-state $4,498 per academic year; out-of-state $7,963. Graduate: in-state $125 per semester hour; out-of-state $375. Required fees: $674.15 per semester. On-campus room and board: $5,082 per academic year. Other expenses: $2,234. Books and supplies: $800.

Financial Aid: Resources specifically for eligible students enrolled in teacher education programs are awarded on the basis of financial need and academic merit. The institution has a Program Participation Agreement with the U.S. Department of Education for eligible students to receive Pell Grants and other federal aid. *Contact:* Financial Aid Office at: (309) 298-2446.

Accreditation: *Regional:* NCA. *Professional:* NCATE. *Approved by:* Illinois State Board of Education.

Undergraduate Programs: Undergraduate programs lead to the Bachelor of Science in early childhood education and elementary education. The elementary program is offered with either a middle school option or a general option. The Bachelor of Science in special education is offered with a standard special option and certifications in elementary, special, and secondary education.

The Bachelor of Science in secondary education is offered with subject area concentrations in agriculture education, biology, chemistry, English, French, history, mathematics, physical education, physics, and Spanish. A baccalaureate program in bilingual education is also offered.

All candidates seeking teacher certification must complete supervised preclinical field experiences totaling at least 100 clock hours. General education courses, professional studies, subject area major, and student teaching are must be successfully completed.

Graduate Programs: Graduate level secondary (6-12) certification programs are offered in agricultural education, biology, chemistry, earth science, English, mathematics, physics, social studies, and Spanish. These programs require passage of the appropriate content area test for admission.

Other programs leading to the Master of Arts in Teaching degree include elementary education, education and interdisciplinary studies, reading, and special education.

Licensure/Reciprocity: Illinois. Students seeking teaching certification in a state other than Illinois should consult with that state's teacher certification office early in their program of study to insure compliance with requirements. Many state directors of teacher credentialing have signed Interstate Agreements through NASDTEC that expedite the certification process.

WHEATON COLLEGE
Department of Education
501 East College Avenue
Wheaton, Illinois 60187
Phone: (630) 752-5041
Fax: (630) 752-5555
E-mail: Andrew.Bruelle@@wheaton.edu
Internet: http://www.wheaton.edu

Institution Description: Wheaton College is a private, nondenominational college committed to Christian liberal arts education. The college was established in 1860.

The Teacher Education Program is an experience-oriented program based on the liberal arts. Students in teacher education are encouraged to explore biblical teachings and perspectives as they related to the role of the teacher in the typical classroom.

Institution Control: Private.

Calendar: Semester. Academic year September to May.

Official(s): Dr. Andrew Brulle, Dean.

Faculty: Full-time 6; adjunct 7.

Degrees Awarded: 45 baccalaureate; 40 master's.

Admission Requirements: *Undergraduate:* Graduation with 18 units from secondary school or GED; College Board SAT or ACT composite. *Teacher education specific:* 2.5 GPA in preliminary education classes; acceptable performance in practice, portfolio; passing scores on Illinois Basic Skills Test; faculty interview. *Graduate:* Baccalaureate from a regionally accredited institution. *Teacher education specific:* Christian commitment; 2.8 undergraduate GPA; GRE; passing scores on all Illinois Certification Testing System required exams; faculty interview.

Fees and Expenses: Undergraduate: $9,250 per semester. Graduate: $464 per semester hour. Required fees: $1,265. On-campus room and board: $3,050 per semester.

Financial Aid: Resources specifically for eligible students enrolled in teacher education programs are awarded on the basis of financial need and academic merit. The institution has a Program Participation Agreement with the U.S. Department of Education for eligible students to receive Pell Grants and other federal aid. *Contact:* Financial Aid Office e-mail at: finaid@wheaton.edu.

Accreditation: *Regional:* NCA. *Professional:* NCATE. *Member of:* AACTE. *Approved by:* Illinois State Board of Education.

Undergraduate Programs: The Initial Elementary Certificate program is offered for elementary education majors for kindergarten through grade 9. The program requires the completion of general education courses, professional studies, field experiences, subject area major, and student teaching.

The Initial Secondary Certificate program is offered for secondary education students from grades 6-12. Students must complete a program in an approved major field of specialization. Currently majors are: biology, communications, English, French, German, history, mathematics, physical science, psychology, social science, and Spanish. Majors in communications, political science, and psychology require a second teaching field. The certificate can be earned as a traditional undergraduate student in conjunction with the Master of Arts in Teaching.

Middle grade endorsements are offered for art, biological science, French, general science, German, language arts, math, music, physical education, social science, Spanish, speech, and speech/theater. Presently Illinois does not require a separate teaching certificate for middle schools. A middle grade endorsement can be added to any of the initial certificates listed above.

WHEATON COLLEGE—*cont'd*

Graduate Programs: The Maser of Arts in Teaching is a fifth-year program designed for those students with a baccalaureate degree but require a teaching certificate in their area of expertise.

Licensure/Reciprocity: Illinois. Students seeking teaching certification in a state other than Illinois should consult with that state's teacher certification office early in their program of study to insure compliance with requirements. Many state directors of teacher credentialing have signed Interstate Agreements through NASDTEC that expedite the certification process. Reciprocity agreement also through the Central States Teacher Exchange Agreement.

INDIANA

ANDERSON UNIVERSITY

School of Education
Teacher Education Program
1100 East Fifth Street
Anderson, Indiana 46012-3495
Phone: (765) 649-9071
Fax: (765) 641-3851
E-mail: info@anderson.edu
Internet: http://www.anderson.edu

Institution Description: Anderson University is a private institution affiliated with the Church of God. It was established as Anderson Bible Training School in 1917. The name was changed to Anderson College and Theological Seminary in 1929, to Anderson College in 1964, and to the present name in 1987.

The mission of the Teacher Education Program is to provide opportunities for the development of qualified and knowledgeable emerging teachers to assume professional positions in public, private, and international educational institutions.

Institution Control: Private.

Calendar: Semester. Academic year September to May.

Official(s): Dr. Diana Ross, Chair, School of Education.

Faculty: Full-time 8.

Degrees Awarded: 91 baccalaureate; 11 master's.

Admission Requirements: *Undergraduate:* Graduation from an accredited high school or GED; College Board SAT or ACT composite. *Teacher education specific:* Majors must apply before enrolling in EDUC 3200; 2.50 overall GPA; favorable recommendations from education faculty; completion of assessment of written and oral communication; acceptable scores on the PRAXIS I test; background check. *Graduate:* Baccalaureate degree from a regionally accredited institution. *Teacher education specific:* Completion of all required department/state tests/exams; letters of recommendation; faculty interview.

Fees and Expenses: $17,050 per academic year. Graduate: tuition is charges per credit hour. On-campus room $3,330 per academic year; board $2,230 (basic meal plan). Other expenses: $1,800. Books and supplies: $700.

Financial Aid: Resources specifically for eligible students enrolled in teacher education programs are awarded on the basis of financial need and academic merit. The institution has a Program Participation Agreement with the U.S. Department of Education for eligible students to receive Pell Grants and other federal aid. *Contact:* Financial Aid Office at: (765) 641-4182.

Accreditation: *Regional:* NCA. *Professional:* NCATE. *Member of:* AACTE. *Approved by:* Indiana Professional Studies Board.

Undergraduate Programs: The School of Education offers undergraduate professional education in courses leading to licensing in early and middle childhood, adolescence, and adolescence/young adult. Students may also receive a major in elementary education and licensing in special education through a partnership with Ball State University.

Majors are available in elementary education (primary and intermediate, K-12) and senior high/middle school grades (5-12). Majors and minors available include: English, French, Spanish, health and safety, journalism (5-12 minor only), mathematics, music (K-12 area major only), music (5-12 minor only), choral, instrument, general, physical education (K-12 area major only; 5-12 major and minor), science. chemistry, physics, social studies, economics, government, psychology, sociology, history, world civilization, theater arts, visual arts (K-12 major only; 5-12 major and minor).

Graduate Programs: The Master of Education degree is designed around the cohort model whereby 18 to 22 practicing teachers pursue the program together. The core courses are composed of 24 graduate semester hours taken in sequence over four terms. Six hours of electives are offered during the summer.

Licensure/Reciprocity: Indiana. Students seeking teaching certification in a state other than Indiana should consult with that state's teacher certification office early in their program of study to insure compliance with requirements. Many state directors of teacher credentialing have signed Interstate Agreements through NASDTEC that expedite the certification process.

BALL STATE UNIVERSITY

Teachers College
2000 University Avenue
Muncie, Indiana 47306
Phone: (765) 265-8560
Fax: (765) 265-8793
E-mail: ackuo@wp.bou.edu
Internet: http://www.bsu.edu

Institution Description: Ball State University was established as Indiana State Normal School, Eastern Division in 1918. It became known as Ball State Teachers College in 1929 and the present name was adopted in 1965.

The undergraduate and graduate programs offered by the college include the baccalaureate, master's, and doctorate.

Institution Control: Public.

Calendar: Semester. Academic year August to May.

Official(s): Dr. Roya A. Weaver, Dean; Dr. Lawrence L. Smith, Chairman, Division of Elementary Education.

Faculty: Full-time 32.

Degrees Awarded: 445 baccalaureate; 291 master's; 23 doctorate.

Admission Requirements: *Undergraduate:* Graduation from an accredited secondary school or GED; College Board SAT or ACT composite. *Teacher education specific:* Acceptance into the teacher education program by sophomore year; passing score on the PRAXIS I test; faculty interview. *Graduate:* Baccalaureate degree from a regionally accredited institution. *Teacher education specific:* bPassing scores on both PRAXIS I and II; letters of recommendation; faculty interview.

Fees and Expenses: Undergraduate: in-state $4,700 per academic year; out-of-state $12,480. Graduate: tuition charged per credit hour. On-campus room and board: $5,546. Other expenses: $2,015. Books and supplies: $840.

Financial Aid: Resources specifically for eligible students enrolled in teacher education programs are awarded on the basis of financial need and academic merit. The institution has a Program Participation Agreement with the U.S. Department of Education for eligible students to receive Pell Grants and other federal aid. *Contact:* Financial Aid Office at: (765) 285-5800.

BALL STATE UNIVERSITY—cont'd

Accreditation: *Regional:* NCA. *Professional:* NCATE. *Member of:* AACTE. *Approved by:* Indiana Professional Standards Board.

Undergraduate Programs: The elementary education undergraduate program requires the student to complete fifteen semester hours in the specialized content concentration areas. These areas include: English as a second language, fine arts, home/school/community relations, language arts, mathematics, foreign language, psychology and counseling, science, state/world connections, technology, and wellness. All programs require the completion of at least 126 semester hours including general education core, professional studies, field experiences, and student teaching.

Graduate Programs: The Master of Arts in Education in elementary education is designed to provide expertise for the master teacher in a 9-12 semester hour focus area of the candidate's choice. The degree does **not** meet all standards for an initial teaching license. Inservice elementary teachers may select focus areas in reading, early childhood, or elementary education. The degree program requires the completion of 30 to 33 semester hours.

Postgraduate students who have already completed a Bachelor of Arts degree or a Bachelor of Science degree at an accredited institution may choose to pursue a licensure program in elementary education, early childhood education, or may choose to apply for the Transition to Teaching Licensure Program.

The Doctor of Education in elementary education offers advanced development for public school professionals and others who seek future leadership and service to the profession. The program requires a minimum of 90 hours of graduate credit.

The Doctor of Philosophy in elementary education is designed for graduate students who are interested in a career as a college or university professor. The program requires a minimum of 90 hours of graduate credit.

Licensure/Reciprocity: Indiana. Students seeking teaching certification in a state other than Indiana should consult with that state's teacher certification office early in their program of study to insure compliance with requirements. Many state directors of teacher credentialing have signed Interstate Agreements through NASDTEC that expedite the certification process. Reciprocity agreement also through the Central States Teacher Exchange Agreement.

BETHEL COLLEGE

Division of Education

1001 West McKinley Avenue
Mishawaka, Indiana 46545
Phone: (219) 259-8511
Internet: http://www.bethelcollege.edu

Institution Description: Bethel College is a private college affiliated with the Missionary Church. It was established and offered first instruction at the postsecondary level in 1947.

The mission of the Division of Education is the undergraduate preparation of elementary, middle school/junior high, and high school teachers for both public and private schools.

Institution Control: Private.

Calendar: Semester. Academic year August to May.

Official(s): Dr. Jeffrey Beck, Chair.

Faculty: Full-time 8, part-time 1, adjunct 3.

Degrees Awarded: 52 baccalaureate.

Admission Requirements: *Undergraduate:* Graduation from an accredited secondary school or GED; College Board SAT or ACT composite. *Teacher education specific:* Acceptance into the teacher education program by sophomore year; passing score on the PRAXIS I test; faculty interview; PRAXIS II tests are required for most content areas.

Fees and Expenses: $13,900 per academic year. On-campus room and board: $4,500. Other expenses: $100. Books and supplies: $1,000.

Financial Aid: Resources specifically for eligible students enrolled in teacher education programs are awarded on the basis of financial need and academic merit. The institution has a Program Participation Agreement with the U.S. Department of Education for eligible students to receive Pell Grants and other federal aid. *Contact:* Financial Aid Office at: (219) 257-3316.

Accreditation: *Regional:* NCA. *Professional:* NCATE. *Member of:* AACTE. *Approved by:* Indiana Professional Standards Board.

Undergraduate Programs: Bethel College education programs include the elementary education major (K-6), secondary and all grades majors (business education, English, mathematics, music education, physical education, science, and social studies). Concentrations, endorsements, and other programs include: coaching endorsement, driver and traffic safety education endorsement, elementary music endorsement, health education minor, kindergarten endorsement, early childhood education major, sport studies major. All baccalaureate programs require the completion of at least 124 semester hours and include general education core, professional studies, subject area major, field experiences, and student teaching.

Licensure/Reciprocity: Indiana. Students seeking teaching certification in a state other than Indiana should consult with that state's teacher certification office early in their program of study to insure compliance with requirements. Many state directors of teacher credentialing have signed Interstate Agreements through NASDTEC that expedite the certification process. Reciprocity agreement also through the Central States Teacher Exchange Agreement.

BUTLER UNIVERSITY

College of Education
Teacher Preparation Program

4600 Sunset Avenue
Indianapolis, Indiana 46208
Phone: (317) 940-9501
Fax: (317) 940-9930
E-mail: educ@butler.edu
Internet: http://www.butler.edu

Institution Description: Butler University is a private, independent, nonprofit institution. It was chartered as North Western Christian University in 1850. The present name was adopted in 1877.

The College of Education is dedicated to preparing teachers, administrators, school counselors, and professionals in health-related professions. A special feature of the teacher preparation programs involves an early introduction to the profession of teaching.

Institution Control: Private.

Calendar: Semester. Academic year August to May.

Official(s): Dr. Robert Rider, Dean, College of Education.

Faculty: Full-time 17, part-time 26.

Degrees Awarded: 111 baccalaureate; 83 master's.

Admission Requirements: *Undergraduate:* Graduation from an accredited secondary school or GED; College Board SAT or ACT composite. *Teacher education specific:* Acceptance into the teacher education program by sophomore year; passing score on the PRAXIS I test; faculty interview. *Graduate:* Baccalaureate degree from a regionally accredited institution. *Teacher education specific:* Passing scores on both PRAXIS I and II; letters of recommendation; faculty interview.

Fees and Expenses: Undergraduate $19,990. Graduate: Tuition charged per credit hour. On-campus room and board: $6,710. Other expenses: $1,750. Books and supplies: $750.

Financial Aid: Resources specifically for eligible students enrolled in teacher education programs are awarded on the basis of financial need and academic merit. The institution has a Program Participation Agreement with the U.S. Department of Education for eligible students to receive Pell Grants and other federal aid. *Contact:* Financial Aid Office at: (877) 940-2000.

Accreditation: *Regional:* NCA. *Professional:* NCATE. *Member of:* AACTE. *Approved by:* Indiana Professional Standards Board.

Undergraduate Programs: In addition to a comprehensive liberal arts background, the early and middle childhood education program prepares students for teaching and instructional leadership in elementary schools. By completing the program requirements (general education core, major subject area, professional studies, field experiences, student teaching), Early and middle childhood education majors earn the baccalaureate degree. Graduating seniors meet state course requirements for licensure in early childhood (beginning with kindergarten) and middle school settings.

The middle/secondary program enables students to combine the strength of in-depth preparation in an academic content area with the professional teacher education skills necesary for success in the classroom. Extensive clinical experiences are provided to student teaching in a variety of school settings. A middle school program (grades 5-9), a middle school/secondary program (grades 5-12) and a secondary program (grades 9-12) may have content area major (36 to 52 hours) in: English, foreign language, mathematics, science, and social studies.

Graduate Programs: Graduate programs are offered leading to the Master of Science in Education (educational administration, effective teaching) and the Master of Science in school counseling.

Licensure/Reciprocity: Indiana. Students seeking teaching certification in a state other than Indiana should consult with that state's teacher certification office early in their program of study to insure compliance with requirements. Many state directors of teacher credentialing have signed Interstate Agreements through NASDTEC that expedite the certification process. Reciprocity agreement also through the Central States Teacher Exchange Agreement.

DEPAUW UNIVERSITY
Education Department
313 South Locust Street
Greencastle, Indiana 46135
Phone: (765) 658-4800
Fax: (765) 658-4007
E-mail: education@depauw.edu
Internet: http://www.depauw.edu

Institution Description: DePauw University is a private, non-profit institution affiliated with the United Methodist Church. It was established in 1837. Women were first admitted in 1867. The present name was adopted in 1884.

The Education Department offers baccalaureate programs leading to teaching licensure in Indiana.

Institution Control: Private.

Calendar: Semester. Academic year August to May.

Official(s): Dr. Marcelle McVerran, Chairperson.

Faculty: Full-time 9.

Degrees Awarded: 12 baccalaureate.

Admission Requirements: *Undergraduate:* Graduation from an accredited secondary school or GED; College Board SAT or ACT composite. *Teacher education specific:* Acceptance into the teacher education program by sophomore year; passing score on the PRAXIS I test; faculty interview. *Graduate:* Baccalaureate degree from a regionally accredited institution. *Teacher education specific:* Passing scores on both PRAXIS I and II; letters of recommendation; faculty interview.

Fees and Expenses: Undergraduate: $22,400. Graduate: Tuition charged per credit hour. On-campus room and board: $6,800. Other expenses: $950. Books and supplies: $600.

Financial Aid: Resources specifically for eligible students enrolled in teacher education programs are awarded on the basis of financial need and academic merit. The institution has a Program Participation Agreement with the U.S. Department of Education for eligible students to receive Pell Grants and other federal aid. *Contact:* Financial Aid Office at: (765) 658-4030.

Accreditation: *Regional:* NCA. *Professional:* NCATE. *Member of:* AACTE. *Approved by:* Indiana Professional Standards Board.

Undergraduate Programs: The elementary education program includes an sequences as follows: introductory, learning theories, methods, and professional. There are general studies courses and general education requirements (English, history, social studies, science, mathematics, fine arts, psychology) and proficiency in written and oral expression. The program leads to the baccalaureate degree.

Requirements for a minor in education (secondary teaching) requires completion of a major in a subject area other than education. It focuses on student teaching . In addition to the general studies courses, students may choose a major in: English, foreign language, math, music, physical education, science (life sciences, earth/space, physical, chemistry, physics), social studies (economics, geographical perspectives, government, psychology, sociology), language arts, theater arts, visual arts.

Licensure/Reciprocity: Indiana. Students seeking teaching certification in a state other than Indiana should consult with that state's teacher certification office early in their program of study to insure compliance with requirements. Many state directors of teacher credentialing have signed Interstate Agreements through NASDTEC that expedite the certification process. Reciprocity agreement also through the Central States Teacher Exchange Agreement.

FRANKLIN COLLEGE OF INDIANA
Education Department
Teacher Education Program
501 East Monroe Street
Franklin, Indiana 46131-2598
Phone: (800) 852-0232
Fax: (317) 738-8000
E-mail: devins@Franklin college.edu.edu
Internet: http://www.franklincollege.edu

Institution Description: Franklin College of Indiana is a private college affiliated with Indiana Baptist Convention of the American Baptist Churches in the U.S.A. It was established as Indiana Baptist Manual Labor Institute in 1834.

A variety of teacher education programs are offered by the Education Department leading to elementary and secondary teaching certification and licensure.

Institution Control: Private.

Calendar: Semester. Academic year September to May.

Official(s): Dr. Barbara J. Devins, Chair/Director of Teacher Education.

Faculty: Full-time 6.

Degrees Awarded: 43 baccalaureate.

Admission Requirements: *Undergraduate:* Graduation from an accredited secondary school or GED; College Board SAT or ACT composite. *Teacher education specific:* Acceptance into the teacher education program by sophomore year; passing score on the PRAXIS I test; faculty interview.

Fees and Expenses: $15,635 per academic year. On-campus room and board: $5,280. Other expenses: $1,600. Books and supplies: $800.

Financial Aid: Resources specifically for eligible students enrolled in teacher education programs are awarded on the basis of financial need and academic merit. The institution has a Program Participation Agreement with the U.S. Department of Education for eligible students to receive Pell Grants and other federal aid. *Contact:* Financial Aid Office at: (317) 738-8075.

Accreditation: *Regional:* NCA. *Professional:* NCATE. *Member of:* AACTE. *Approved by:* Indiana Professional Standards Board.

Undergraduate Programs: Elementary education majors are eligible to receive an initial teaching license that qualifies a teacher to teach in an elementary school, primary, or intermediate setting, including kindergarten. All coursework and field experience align with the state board's developmental standards and generalist content standards for early childhood and middle childhood. The program requires the completion of a general education core, professional studies, field experiences, and student teaching. The baccalaureate program requires completion of 128 semester hours.

FRANKLIN COLLEGE OF INDIANA—*cont'd*

Students who enroll in the secondary education teacher education program leads to initial Indiana certification to teach in a middle school, junior high school, or high school setting. All coursework and field experiences align with the Indiana development standards for early adolescence and adolescence/young adulthood. In addition, coursework, field experiences, and student teaching must be completed. the available content areas include: foreign languages (Spanish or French) language arts (English), mathematics, science (life sciences or physical science), physical education, and social studies (economics, government and citizenship, historical perspectives, psychology, or sociology). The baccalaureate program requires the completion of 128 semester hours.

Licensure/Reciprocity: Indiana. Students seeking teaching certification in a state other than Indiana should consult with that state's teacher certification office early in their program of study to insure compliance with requirements. Many state directors of teacher credentialing have signed Interstate Agreements through NASDTEC that expedite the certification process. Reciprocity agreement also through the Central States Teacher Exchange Agreement.

GOSHEN COLLEGE

Education Department
Teacher Education
1700 South Main Street
Goshen, Indiana 46526
Phone: (574) 535-7440
Fax: (574) 535-7445
E-mail: margam@goshen.edu
Internet: http://www.goshen.edu

Institution Description: Goshen College is a private college affiliated with the Mennonite Church. It was established as Elkhart Institute in 1894.

The Education Department prepares teachers to be lifelong learners who also professionally active. They also invite preservice teachers to put their faith into practice in all aspects of teaching and learning.

Institution Control: Private.

Calendar: Semester. Academic year August to May.

Official(s): Dr. K. Meyer Reimer, Chair, Education Department; Dr. Marg Mast, Director of Teacher Education.

Faculty: Full-time 4; adjunct 3.

Degrees Awarded: 23 baccalaureate.

Admission Requirements: *Undergraduate:* Graduation from an accredited secondary school or GED; College Board SAT or ACT composite. *Teacher education specific:* Acceptance into the teacher education program by sophomore year; successful performance in early fieldwork experiences; references from former teachers; demonstrated experience with children or youth, written essay; passing score on the PRAXIS I test; faculty interview.

Fees and Expenses: $16,320 per academic year. Required fees: $330. On-campus room and board: $2,800. Books and supplies: $700.

Financial Aid: Resources specifically for eligible students enrolled in teacher education programs are awarded on the basis of financial need and academic merit. The institution has a Program Participation Agreement with the U.S. Department of Education for eligible students to receive Pell Grants and other federal aid. *Contact:* E-mail Financial Aid Office at: finaid@goshen.edu.

Accreditation: *Regional:* NCA. *Professional:* NCATE. *Member of:* AACTE. *Approved by:* Indiana Professional Standards Board.

Undergraduate Programs: Upon completion of a major in elementary education, students are eligible to be certified to teach kindergarten through sixth grade. Fieldwork takes place in a variety of classroom settings where students learn to teach language arts, math, social studies, science, art, physical education, and music. Students also explore approaches to classroom man-

agement, discipline, and education. The program requires the completion of a general education core, professional studies, field experiences, and student teaching for a total of 120 credit hours.

Students can be certified to teach fifth through eighth graders upon completion of teacher education requirements for teachers of early adolescents and content requirements in the chosen teaching field. Certification for grades 5-8 may be a stand-alone certification or may be done in conjunction with certification to teach high school with an elementary education major. The program requires the successful completion of 120 credit hours.

Students can be certified to teach fifth through 12th graders upon completion of teacher education requirements for teachers of early adolescence and young adults and content requirements in the chose field of instruction. Goshen offers teaching majors in business, English, English as a second language, health, Spanish, mathematics, music, physical education, science, social studies, theater arts and visual arts. The baccalaureate program requires the completion of a general education core, professional studies, subject area major, field experiences, and student teaching for a total of 120 credit hours.

Licensure/Reciprocity: Indiana. Students seeking teaching certification in a state other than Indiana should consult with that state's teacher certification office early in their program of study to insure compliance with requirements. Many state directors of teacher credentialing have signed Interstate Agreements through NASDTEC that expedite the certification process. Reciprocity agreement also through the Central States Teacher Exchange Agreement.

HUNTINGTON COLLEGE

Education Department
Teacher Education
2303 College Avenue
Huntington, Indiana 46750
Phone: (260) 359-4231
Fax: (260) 356-9448
E-mail: jpaff@huntington.edu
Internet: http://www.huntington.edu

Institution Description: Huntington College is a private, Christian liberal arts college affiliated with Church of the United Brethren in Christ. It was established as Central College at Huntington in 1897. The present name was adopted in 1917.

The Education Department offers programs to students who desire to become teachers at the elementary of secondary level. Teacher education programs include a planned series of courses, a series of field experiences, and student teaching during the senior year.

Institution Control: Private.

Calendar: Semester. Academic year September to May.

Official(s): Dr. Terrell M. Peace, Department Chair and Director of Teacher Education.

Faculty: Full-time 6.

Degrees Awarded: 60 baccalaureate.

Admission Requirements: *Undergraduate:* Graduation from an accredited secondary school or GED; College Board SAT or ACT composite. *Teacher education specific:* Acceptance into the teacher education program by sophomore year; passing score on the PRAXIS I test; faculty interview.

Fees and Expenses: $15,920 per academic year. On-campus room and board: $5,680. Other expenses: $1,100. Books and supplies: $700.

Financial Aid: Resources specifically for eligible students enrolled in teacher education programs are awarded on the basis of financial need and academic merit. The institution has a Program Participation Agreement with the U.S. Department of Education for eligible students to receive Pell Grants and other federal aid. *Contact:* Financial Aid Office at: (260) 359-4015.

Accreditation: *Regional:* NCA. *Professional:* NCATE. *Member of:* AACTE. *Approved by:* Indiana Professional Standards Board.

Undergraduate Programs: Teacher education programs lead to the baccalaureate degree and licensure. In addition to student teaching, students in both the elementary and secondary Programs complete a teaching practicum. This three-week, full-day experience takes place in multicultural settings in Fort Wayne. The elementary program includes an eight-week field experience during the junior year.

Elementary majors may also take an integrated curriculum course during the senior year that teaches strategies for integrating computers and thematic units into the general curriculum.

All baccalaureate programs require the completion of a general education core, subject area major (secondary program), professional studies, field experiences, and student teaching for a total of 128 credit hours.

A special education minor prepares students to provide mild intervention in grades K-6. All-grade majors are available in art, music, and physical education. Secondary education majors can be certified to teach middle school and high school subjects (art, business, English, mathematics, science, or social studies.

Licensure/Reciprocity: Indiana. Students seeking teaching certification in a state other than Indiana should consult with that state's teacher certification office early in their program of study to insure compliance with requirements. Many state directors of teacher credentialing have signed Interstate Agreements through NASDTEC that expedite the certification process. Reciprocity agreement also through the Central States Teacher Exchange Agreement.

INDIANA STATE UNIVERSITY

School of Education
210 North 7th Street
Terre Haute, Indiana 47809
Phone: (812) 237-2919
Fax: (812) 237-4348
E-mail: ess@isugw.indstate.edu
Internet: http://www.indstate.edu

Institution Description: Indiana State University is a comprehensive, residential, state-assisted institution of higher education serving the community, state and nation through undergraduate and graduate instruction, research and public service. It was established as Indiana State Normal School in 1865. The name was changed to Indiana State Teachers College in 1929, to Indiana State College in 1961, and to its present name in 1965.

The Department of Curriculum and Instruction offers professional courses needed in the preparation of all grade, junior high/middle school, and senior high teachers.

Institution Control: Public.

Calendar: Semester. Academic year August to May.

Official(s): Dr. C. Jack Maynard, Dean, School of Education.

Faculty: Full-time 68; part-time 1; adjunct 18.

Degrees Awarded: 228 baccalaureate; 115 master's; 39 doctorate.

Admission Requirements: *Undergraduate:* Graduation from an accredited secondary school or GED; College Board SAT or ACT composite. *Teacher education specific:* Acceptance into the teacher education program by sophomore year; passing score on the PRAXIS I test; faculty interview. *Graduate:* Baccalaureate degree from a regionally accredited institution. *Teacher education specific:* Passing scores on both PRAXIS I and II; letters of recommendation; faculty interview.

Fees and Expenses: Undergraduate: in-state $2,661 per academic years, out-of-state $5,895. Graduate: in-state $242 in-state per credit hour, out-of-state $481. Required fees: $50 technology fee per semester. On-campus room and board: $3,648 per semester. Books and supplies: $750.

Financial Aid: Resources specifically for eligible students enrolled in teacher education programs are awarded on the basis of financial need and academic merit. The institution has a Program Participation Agreement with the U.S. Department of Education for eligible students to receive Pell Grants and other federal aid. *Contact:* Norman Hayes at: (800) 841-4744.

Accreditation: *Regional:* NCA. *Professional:* NCATE. *Member of:* AACTE. *Approved by:* Indiana Professional Standards Board.

Undergraduate Programs: The Department of Elementary and Early Childhood Education offers Bachelor of Science or the Bachelor of Arts degree programs. The programs require the completion of 124 semester hours including a general education core, professional studies, field experiences, and student teaching. The early childhood special education minor (38-39 hours) leads to eligibility to teach infants, toddlers, and preschool children with special needs. The minor can be added to the Indiana Standard Teaching License in early childhood or all grade education with a special education major.

Students with academic majors are required to complete at least 47 hours of general education coursework. Professional education coursework is required for the junior high/middle high school program and the all-grade program. As students progress through each program, they are assessed on the basis of standards created by the Interstate New Teacher Assessment and Support Consortium. Subject content areas include: English, English as a new language, family and consumer sciences, foreign languages, mathematics, music, and science The baccalaureate degree requires the completion of a minimum of 124 semester hours in a general education core, subject area major, professional studies, field experiences, and student teaching.

Graduate Programs: The Master of Education in early childhood education (32 semester hours minimum) program qualifies the student for licensure provided that the students holds a Standard License and has completed five years of appropriate teaching experience. The kindergarten-primary and elementary with kindergarten endorsement license may also be professionalized with this degree program with the completion of prescribed courses in related studies and appropriate teaching experience.

The Master of Education Degree in curriculum and instruction serves the needs of individuals who are seeking to develop leadership skills in educational settings. The program requires a minimum of 32 semester hours of which 18 hours must be completed in either professional education or in an area of endorsement. Individual programs may be mutually conceptualized by the student and the advisor.

Licensure/Reciprocity: Indiana. Students seeking teaching certification in a state other than Indiana should consult with that state's teacher certification office early in their program of study to insure compliance with requirements. Many state directors of teacher credentialing have signed Interstate Agreements through NASDTEC that expedite the certification process. Reciprocity agreement also through the Central States Teacher Exchange Agreement.

INDIANA UNIVERSITY BLOOMINGTON

School of Education
Teacher Education Program
201 North Rose Avenue
Bloomington, Indiana 47405
Phone: (812) 856-8500
Fax: (812) 856-8518
E-mail: kinman@indiana.edu
Internet: http://www.indiana.edu

Institution Description: The university was established as Indiana State Seminary in 1820. The present name was adopted in 1838.

The School of Education offers both undergraduate and graduate programs for teacher preparation and licensure in Indiana.

Institution Control: Public.

Calendar: Semester. Academic year September to May.

Official(s): Address inquiries to Associate Dean for Teacher Education.

Faculty: Full-time 106; part-time 15; adjunct 45.

Degrees Awarded: 990 baccalaureate; 304 master's; 72 doctorate.

INDIANA UNIVERSITY BLOOMINGTON—
cont'd

Admission Requirements: *Undergraduate:* Graduation from an accredited secondary school or GED; an academic honors diploma is strongly recommended; a minimum of 26 semesters of college preparatory courses; rank in upper half of high school graduating class; College Board SAT or ACT composite. *Teacher education specific:* Acceptance into the teacher education program by sophomore year; passing score on the PRAXIS I test; faculty interview. *Graduate:* Baccalaureate degree from a regionally accredited institution. *Teacher education specific:* Passing scores on both PRAXIS I and II; personal goal statement; minimum 3.0 GPA in last 60 hours of undergraduate coursework; teaching credential where appropriate; letters of recommendation; faculty interview.

Fees and Expenses: Undergraduate: in-state $142.75 per credit hour; out-of-state $474.50. Graduate: in-state $196.65 per credit hour; out-of-state $572.85. On-campus room and board: $1,848 to $5,200 per semester. Books and supplies: $300 per semester.

Financial Aid: Resources specifically for eligible students enrolled in teacher education programs are awarded on the basis of financial need and academic merit. The institution has a Program Participation Agreement with the U.S. Department of Education for eligible students to receive Pell Grants and other federal aid. *Contact:* Office of Financial Assistance at: (812) 855-0321.

Accreditation: *Regional:* NCA. *Professional:* NCATE. *Member of:* AACTE. *Approved by:* Indiana Professional Standards Board.

Undergraduate Programs: The teacher education undergraduate program includes those majors traditionally associated with licensure guidelines found throughout the U.S. Programs in childhood education, elementary education, exceptional needs education, and secondary education are available. All programs require at least 124 semester hours of credit including a general education core, subject major, professional studies, field experiences, and student teaching. Academic programs have been revised to incorporate a standards-based, performance-driven curriculum developed by the Interstate New Teacher Assessment and Support Consortium. The professional education component includes 47 credit hours including student teaching.

Graduate Programs: Graduate educational programs may be found in five academic departments that include: Instructional Systems Technology, Language Education, Curriculum and Instruction, Counseling and Educational Psychology, and Educational Leadership and Policy Studies. These departments offer majors leading to the Master of Science degree, Specialist in Education, Doctor of Education, and Doctor of Philosophy.

Licensure/Reciprocity: Indiana. Students seeking teaching certification in a state other than Indiana should consult with that state's teacher certification office early in their program of study to insure compliance with requirements. Many state directors of teacher credentialing have signed Interstate Agreements through NASDTEC that expedite the certification process. Reciprocity agreement also through the Central States Teacher Exchange Agreement.

INDIANA UNIVERSITY EAST

Division of Education
2325 Chester Boulevard
Richmond, Indiana 47374
Phone: (765) 973-8208
Fax: (765) 973-8288
E-mail: mwatkins@iue.edu
Internet: http://www.iue.edu

Institution Description: In 1946 Earlham College and Indiana University established the Eastern Indiana Center, which was originally administered as a cooperative program to give adults in the community an opportunity to pursue college-level study as part-time students. In 1970, Indiana University assumed complete administrative control and began working toward the development of a new campus that opened in 1975.

The mission of the Division of Education is to prepare teachers who are reflective scholars, instructional leaders, and global citizens to serve the community by promoting and facilitating practice in education.

Institution Control: Public.

Calendar: Semester. Academic year August to May.

Official(s): Dr. Marilyn S. Watkins, Chairperson, Division of Education.

Faculty: Full-time 12.

Degrees Awarded: 26 baccalaureate.

Admission Requirements: *Undergraduate:* Graduation from an accredited secondary school or GED; College Board SAT or ACT composite. *Teacher education specific:* Acceptance into the teacher education program by sophomore year; passing score on the PRAXIS I test; faculty interview. *Graduate:* Baccalaureate degree from a regionally accredited institution. *Teacher education specific:* Passing scores on both PRAXIS I and II; letters of recommendation; faculty interview.

Fees and Expenses: Undergraduate: in-state $142.75 per credit hour; out-of-state $474.50. Graduate: in-state $196.65 per credit hour; out-of-state $572.85. On-campus room and board: $6,900. Other expenses: $3,100. Books and supplies: $800.

Financial Aid: Resources specifically for eligible students enrolled in teacher education programs are awarded on the basis of financial need and academic merit. The institution has a Program Participation Agreement with the U.S. Department of Education for eligible students to receive Pell Grants and other federal aid. *Contact:* Financial Aid Office at: (765) 973-8206.

Accreditation: *Regional:* NCA. *Professional:* NCATE. *Member of:* AACTE. *Approved by:* Indiana Professional Standards Board.

Undergraduate Programs: Programs offered by the Division of Education include: elementary grades 1-6, 7&8 nondepartmentalized; kindergarten junior high/middle school (additions to elementary license) in language arts, mathematics, science, social studies; secondary education with subject areas in English, mathematics, science (biology, chemistry, earth/space, general); Science (physical), social studies.

Most of the professional education courses in both elementary and secondary programs include corequisite field experiences. These experiences provide students with increasing amounts of responsibility in school settings and serve as preparation for full-time student teaching. Students are assigned to a variety of schools and grade levels throughout their programs including placements in urban, suburban, and rural school environments.

All baccalaureate programs require the completion of a general education core, subject major, professional studies, field experiences, and student teaching for a minimum of 120 credit hours.

Licensure/Reciprocity: Indiana. Students seeking teaching certification in a state other than Indiana should consult with that state's teacher certification office early in their program of study to insure compliance with requirements. Many state directors of teacher credentialing have signed Interstate Agreements through NASDTEC that expedite the certification process. Reciprocity agreement also through the Central States Teacher Exchange Agreement.

INDIANA UNIVERSITY KOKOMO

Division of Education
2300 South Washington Street
Kokomo, Indiana 46904
Phone: (765) 455-9367
Fax: (765) 455-9587
E-mail: lhenry@iuk.edu
Internet: http://www.iuk.edu

Institution Description: The institution was established as Kokomo Center of Indiana University in 1945. The present name was adopted in 1968.

Graduates of the teacher education program meet state requirements for teaching certification. Reciprocal agreements have been accomplished with 40 other states.

Institution Control: Public.

Calendar: Semester. Academic year August to May.

Official(s): Dr. Loren Henry, Chair, Division of Education.

Faculty: Full-time 9.

Degrees Awarded: 52 baccalaureate; 1 master's.

Admission Requirements: *Undergraduate:* Graduation from an accredited secondary school or GED; College Board SAT or ACT composite. *Teacher education specific:* Acceptance into the teacher education program by sophomore year; passing score on the PRAXIS I test; faculty interview. *Graduate:* Baccalaureate degree from a regionally accredited institution. *Teacher education specific:* Passing scores on both PRAXIS I and II; letters of recommendation; faculty interview.

Fees and Expenses: Undergraduate: in-state $142.75 per credit hour; out-of-state $474.50. Graduate: in-state $196.65 per credit hour; out-of-state $572.85. On-campus room and board: $6,190. Other expenses: $2,110. Books and supplies: $1,050.

Financial Aid: Resources specifically for eligible students enrolled in teacher education programs are awarded on the basis of financial need and academic merit. The institution has a Program Participation Agreement with the U.S. Department of Education for eligible students to receive Pell Grants and other federal aid. *Contact:* Financial Aid Office at: (765) 455-9216.

Accreditation: *Regional:* NCA. *Professional:* NCATE. *Member of:* AACTE. *Approved by:* Indiana Professional Standards Board.

Undergraduate Programs: The teacher education undergraduate program includes those majors traditionally associated with licensure guidelines found throughout the U.S. Programs in elementary education and secondary education are available. All programs require at least 120 to 124 semester hours of credit including a general education core, subject major, professional studies, field experiences, and student teaching. Academic programs have been revised to incorporate a standards-based, performance-driven curriculum developed by the Interstate New Teacher Assessment and Support Consortium. The professional education component includes 47 credit hours including student teaching.

Graduate Programs: Graduate educational programs offered include a Master of Science in elementary education and a Master of Science in secondary education. Secondary licensure programs are also offered as a fifth-year program for those baccalaureate graduates without a teaching certification.

Licensure/Reciprocity: Indiana. Students seeking teaching certification in a state other than Indiana should consult with that state's teacher certification office early in their program of study to insure compliance with requirements. Many state directors of teacher credentialing have signed Interstate Agreements through NASDTEC that expedite the certification process. Reciprocity agreement also through the Central States Teacher Exchange Agreement.

INDIANA UNIVERSITY NORTHWEST

Division of Education
3400 Broadway
Gary, Indiana 46408
Phone: (219) 980-6989
Fax: (219) 981-4208
E-mail: swigle@iunhaw1.iun.indiana.edu
Internet: http://www.iun.edu

Institution Description: The university was established in 1922 but discontinued operation in 1933. It assumed control of Gary College (established 1933) and made it an extension center in 1948. It then joined with Calumet Center to form Indiana University Northwest in 1963.

The mission of the Division of Education is to prepare professional educators who have knowledge, skills, and dispositions essential for becoming reflective professionals and master educators.

Institution Control: Public.

Calendar: Semester. Academic year August to May.

Official(s): Dr. Stan Wigle, Dean, Division of Education.

Faculty: Full-time 14.

Degrees Awarded: 36 baccalaureate; 27 master's.

Admission Requirements: *Undergraduate:* Graduation from an accredited secondary school or GED; College Board SAT or ACT composite. *Teacher education specific:* Acceptance into the teacher education program by sophomore year; passing score on the PRAXIS I test; faculty interview. *Graduate:* Baccalaureate degree from a regionally accredited institution. *Teacher education specific:* Passing scores on both PRAXIS I and II; letters of recommendation; faculty interview.

Fees and Expenses: Undergraduate: in-state $142.75 per credit hour; out-of-state $474.50. Graduate: in-state $196.65 per credit hour; out-of-state $572.85. On-campus room and board: $6,400. Other expenses: $2,110. Books and supplies: $750.

Financial Aid: Resources specifically for eligible students enrolled in teacher education programs are awarded on the basis of financial need and academic merit. The institution has a Program Participation Agreement with the U.S. Department of Education for eligible students to receive Pell Grants and other federal aid. *Contact:* Financial Aid Office at: (219) 980-6877.

Accreditation: *Regional:* NCA. *Professional:* NCATE. *Member of:* AACTE. *Approved by:* Indiana Professional Standards Board.

Undergraduate Programs: The teacher education undergraduate program includes those majors traditionally associated with licensure guidelines found throughout the U.S. Programs in childhood education, elementary education, exceptional needs education, and secondary education are available. All programs require at least 124 semester hours of credit including a general education core, subject major, professional studies, field experiences, and student teaching. Academic programs have been revised to incorporate a standards-based, performance-driven curriculum developed by the Interstate New Teacher Assessment and Support Consortium. The professional education component includes 47 credit hours including student teaching.

Graduate Programs: The master's degree in elementary education is for individuals who want to develop competencies necessary to function as a master teacher and to professionalize a standard teacher's license. The degree focuses on educational inquiry throughout the required course offerings culminating with an exit course that requires a research document and its oral defense. The courses deal in depth at the foundation areas of educational research, philosophy, psychology, and evaluation that are prerequisites to the advanced educational methods courses in language arts, mathematics, reading, science, and social studies.

The master's degree in secondary education is for individuals who want to develop competencies necessary to function as a master teacher and to professionalize a standard teacher's license. The degree focuses on educational inquiry throughout the required course offerings culminating with an exit course that requires a research document and its oral defense.

Licensure/Reciprocity: Indiana. Students seeking teaching certification in a state other than Indiana should consult with that state's teacher certification office early in their program of study to insure compliance with requirements. Many state directors of teacher credentialing have signed Interstate Agreements through NASDTEC that expedite the certification process. Reciprocity agreement also through the Central States Teacher Exchange Agreement.

INDIANA UNIVERSITY - PURDUE UNIVERSITY FORT WAYNE

School of Education
Neff Hall
2101 East Coliseum Boulevard
Fort Wayne, Indiana 46805-1499
Phone: (260) 481-6441
Fax: (219) 481-6880
E-mail: bkanpool@ipfw.edu
Internet: http://www.ipfw.edu

INDIANA UNIVERSITY - PURDUE UNIVERSITY FORT WAYNE—cont'd

Institution Description: The school was established as Fort Wayne Center of Indiana University in 1917. Purdue University established a campus in Fort Wayne in 1941 and initiated a cooperative arrangement with Indiana University in 1964. The present name was adopted in 1968.

Institution Control: Public.

Calendar: Semester. Academic year August to May.

Official(s): Dr. Barry Kanpool, Dean, School of Education.

Faculty: Full-time 27.

Degrees Awarded: 157 baccalaureate; 107 master's.

Admission Requirements: *Undergraduate:* Graduation from an accredited secondary school or GED; College Board SAT or ACT composite. *Teacher education specific:* Acceptance into the teacher education program by sophomore year; passing score on the PRAXIS I test; faculty interview. *Graduate:* Baccalaureate degree from a regionally accredited institution. *Teacher education specific:* Passing scores on both PRAXIS I and II; letters of recommendation; faculty interview.

Fees and Expenses: Undergraduate: in-state $142.75 per credit hour; out-of-state $474.50. Graduate: in-state $196.65 per credit hour; out-of-state $572.85. On-campus room and board: $5,574. Other expenses: $2,748. Books and supplies: $800.

Financial Aid: Resources specifically for eligible students enrolled in teacher education programs are awarded on the basis of financial need and academic merit. The institution has a Program Participation Agreement with the U.S. Department of Education for eligible students to receive Pell Grants and other federal aid. *Contact:* Financial Aid Office at: (260) 481-6820.

Accreditation: *Regional:* NCA. *Professional:* NCATE. *Member of:* AACTE. *Approved by:* Indiana Professional Standards Board.

Undergraduate Programs: The Bachelor of Science in elementary education program leads to the Indiana Standard License. The student will complete 40 credits of professional education training and a well-balanced core of liberal arts courses. The Field Experience Program is a four-part series of methods courses and supervised practical experiences that may start as early as the freshman year. In the senior year a student spends 12 weeks to an entire semester in full-time student teaching in local elementary schools.

The Bachelor of Science in Education with a secondary focus is intended to prepare students for successful careers as teachers of children in junior and high school classroom settings. With additional coursework and field experiences, students may also add additional content and grade level teaching specialty areas to their license. Teaching majors are available in: English/language arts, foreign language, mathematics, science (biology, chemistry, earth/space science, general science, physics, physical science), social studies, communications, and theater.

Graduate Programs: The master's degree in elementary education is for individuals who want to develop competencies necessary to function as a master teacher and to professionalize a standard teacher's license. The courses required deal in depth at the foundation areas of educational research, philosophy, psychology, and evaluation .

The master's degree in secondary education is for individuals who want to develop competencies necessary to function as a master teacher and to professionalize a standard teacher's license. The degree focuses on educational inquiry throughout the required course offerings culminating with an exit course that requires a research document and its oral defense.

Licensure/Reciprocity: Indiana. Students seeking teaching certification in a state other than Indiana should consult with that state's teacher certification office early in their program of study to insure compliance with requirements. Many state directors of teacher credentialing have signed Interstate Agreements through NASDTEC that expedite the certification process. Reciprocity agreement also through the Central States Teacher Exchange Agreement.

INDIANA UNIVERSITY SOUTH BEND
School of Education
Teacher Education Program
Greenlawn Hall 101
1700 Mishawaka Avenue
South Bend, Indiana 46634-7111
Phone: (574) 237-4845
Fax: (574) 237-4550
E-mail: alane@iusb.edu
Internet: http://www.iusb.edu

Institution Description: Indiana University at South Bend was established in 1940. The present name was adopted in 1968.

The mission of the School of Education is to prepare students to serve as effective teachers and members of related professions and to assist students in meeting Indiana certification requirements for public school personnel. The programs leading to licensing are designed to meet the standards of the Interstate New Teacher Assessment and Support Consortium.

Institution Control: Public.

Calendar: Semester. Academic year August to May.

Official(s): Dr. Gwendolyn Mettetal, Dean, School of Education.

Faculty: Full-time 23, emeriti 9.

Degrees Awarded: 131 baccalaureate; 124 master's.

Admission Requirements: *Undergraduate:* Graduation from an accredited secondary school or GED; College Board SAT or ACT composite. *Teacher education specific:* Acceptance into the teacher education program by sophomore year; passing score on the PRAXIS I test; faculty interview. *Graduate:* Baccalaureate degree from a regionally accredited institution. *Teacher education specific:* Passing scores on both PRAXIS I and II; educational foundation courses; letters of recommendation; faculty interview.

Fees and Expenses: Undergraduate: in-state $120.60 per credit hour; out-of-state $318,95 out-of-state. Graduate: in-state $157,45 per credit hour; out-of-state $360.15. On-campus room and board: $5,600. Other expenses: $2,500. Books and supplies: $800.

Financial Aid: Resources specifically for eligible students enrolled in teacher education programs are awarded on the basis of financial need and academic merit. The institution has a Program Participation Agreement with the U.S. Department of Education for eligible students to receive Pell Grants and other federal aid. *Contact:* Bev Cooper or Cindy Lang at: (574) 237-4357 or e-mail at finaid@iusb.edu.

Accreditation: *Regional:* NCA. *Professional:* NCATE. *Member of:* AACTE. *Approved by:* Indiana Professional Standards Board.

Undergraduate Programs: The Bachelor of Science in Education degree programs are offered in elementary education, secondary education (English, mathematics, social studies, science). Students may add certification areas to the license by completing certain requirements in addition to the elementary or secondary degree requirements.

Most programs in education have very few electives and consist of several components: general education, education foundation courses, education pedagogy courses, content course (secondary education majors take the courses for their content area), student teaching. All candidates must take the National Teachers Examination prior to applying for an Indiana teaching license.

Graduate Programs: The School of Education offers graduate courses required for the Master of Science in elementary or secondary education with standard certification in school administration. The master's degree in secondary education candidate will require a minimum of 36 credit hours of graduate courses in the content area, in professional education, and in research, including a capstone research project during their last two semesters.

Students who have already completed a bachelor's degree in a field outside of education and who then decide that they want to enter the field of teaching must complete a number of education courses.

Graduate students may also complete a Master of Science in special education degree by completing at least 36 hours of coursework.

Licensure/Reciprocity: Indiana. Students seeking teaching certification in a state other than Indiana should consult with that state's teacher certification office early in their program of study to insure compliance with requirements. Many state directors of teacher credentialing have signed Interstate Agreements through NASDTEC that expedite the certification process. Reciprocity agreement also through the Central States Teacher Exchange Agreement.

INDIANA UNIVERSITY SOUTHEAST

School of Education
Hillside Hall 0020
4201 Grant Line Road
New Albany, Indiana 47150-6405
Phone: (812) 941-2385
Fax: (812) 941-2667
E-mail: seeinfo@ius.edu
Internet: http://www.ius.edu

Institution Description: The university was established as Falls City Center in 1941. The present name was adopted in 1968.

The mission of the School of Education is to develop high-quality caring professionals who will stimulate the continuous renewal of schools within a multicultural society.

Institution Control: Public.

Calendar: Semester. Academic year August to May.

Official(s): Dr. Gloria J. Murray, Dean, School of Education.

Faculty: Full-time 28; 20 adjunct.

Degrees Awarded: 169 baccalaureate; 150 master's.

Admission Requirements: *Undergraduate:* Graduation from an accredited secondary school or GED; College Board SAT or ACT composite. *Teacher education specific:* Acceptance into the teacher education program by sophomore year; passing score on the PRAXIS I test; faculty interview. *Graduate:* Baccalaureate degree from a regionally accredited institution. *Teacher education specific:* Passing scores on both PRAXIS I and II; letters of recommendation; faculty interview.

Fees and Expenses: Undergraduate: in-state $120.60 per credit hour; out-of-state $318,95. Graduate: in-state $157,45 per credit hour; out-of-state $360.15. On-campus room and board: $5,600. Other expenses: $2,500. Books and supplies: $800.

Financial Aid: Resources specifically for eligible students enrolled in teacher education programs are awarded on the basis of financial need and academic merit. The institution has a Program Participation Agreement with the U.S. Department of Education for eligible students to receive Pell Grants and other federal aid. *Contact:* Financial Aid Office at: (812) 941-2246 or e-mail at FiancialAid@ius.edu.

Accreditation: *Regional:* NCA. *Professional:* NCATE. *Member of:* AACTE. *Approved by:* Indiana Professional Standards Board.

Undergraduate Programs: The School of Education offers a program leading to the Bachelor of Science in elementary education or special education. Students in the elementary program may add certification through an endorsement for teaching junior and middle school class in language arts, mathematics, science, and social studies. Endorsements are also available in kindergarten and in special education. Additional specialities in health education, music, physical education, visual arts, language arts, mathematics, recreation, science, and social studies are available.

The school offers a program in secondary education leading to the Bachelor of Science in secondary education with teaching majors in English, mathematics, science, and social studies. Students who have completed a major may also minor in anthropology, biology, chemistry, earth/space science, economics, English, French, German, physical science, physics, political science, psychology, reading, sociology, Spanish, special education, speech communication and theater, U.S. history, visual arts, or world civilization.

A major in special education can be completed with specialization in emotional handicaps or mild disabilities. Endorsements in kindergarten and junior high/middle school may be added to this major.

Graduate Programs: The Master of Science in Education degree programs are offered with majors in elementary education, secondary education, and counseling. The school offers graduate certification programs in reading, certain areas of special education, kindergarten, junior high/middle school education, and educational leadership (principal's certification for Indiana Elementary, Indiana Secondary, and Kentucky K-12).

Licensure/Reciprocity: Indiana. Students seeking teaching certification in a state other than Indiana should consult with that state's teacher certification office early in their program of study to insure compliance with requirements. Many state directors of teacher credentialing have signed Interstate Agreements through NASDTEC that expedite the certification process. Reciprocity agreement also through the Central States Teacher Exchange Agreement.

INDIANA WESLEYAN UNIVERSITY

Division of Education
Teacher Education Program
4201 South Washington Street
Marion, Indiana 46953
Phone: (785) 674-6901
Fax: jfreemyer(785) 677-2333
E-mail: jelsberry@indwes.edu
Internet: http://www.indwes.edu

Institution Description: Indiana Wesleyan University, formerly Marion College, is a private, independent, nonprofit college affiliated with The Wesleyan Church. It was established in 1919.

The Teacher Education Program is a blend of liberal arts education, content-specific coursework, and clinical field placements.

Institution Control: Private.

Calendar: Semester. Academic year September to May.

Official(s): Dr. James S. Elsberry, Chair, Teacher Education Program.

Faculty: Full-time 11.

Degrees Awarded: 89 baccalaureate; 510 master's.

Admission Requirements: *Undergraduate:* Graduation with 16 units from an approved secondary school or GED; College Board SAT or ACT composite. *Teacher education specific:* Apply to the program by sophomore year; PRAXIS I test scores; letters of recommendation; faculty interview. *Graduate:* Baccalaureate degree from a regionally accredited institution. *Teacher education specific:* GPA of 2.75 in all previous undergraduate work; National Teachers Examination, GRE, or Miller Analogies Test score; two letters of recommendation; one year teaching experience; valid teacher's license.

Fees and Expenses: Undergraduate: $14,496 per academic year. Graduate: Tuition charged per credit hour. On-campus room and board: $5,158. Other expenses: $1,575. Books and supplies: $800.

Financial Aid: Resources specifically for eligible students enrolled in teacher education programs are awarded on the basis of financial need and academic merit. The institution has a Program Participation Agreement with the U.S. Department of Education for eligible students to receive Pell Grants and other federal aid. *Contact:* Financial Aid Office at:(765) 677-2116.

Accreditation: *Regional:* NCA. *Professional:* NCATE. *Member of:* AACTE. *Approved by:* Indiana Professional Standards Board.

Undergraduate Programs: Baccalaureate programs include elementary education, all grade certification, senior high/junior high/middle school certification, and special education. All programs require completion of a general education core, professional studies, subject area major (secondary education), field experiences, and student teaching. A total of a minimum of 124 semester hours must be successfully completed.

INDIANA WESLEYAN UNIVERSITY—*cont'd*

Graduate Programs: The Master of Education degree program in curriculum and instruction is designed to further develop the skills of classroom teachers. Development of practical approaches to educational challenges is a major goal of the program. Completion of 36 semester hours at the graduate level is required for graduation. A core program consisting of 10 courses and 30 semester hours is offered in sequence to cohorts of professionals.

Licensure/Reciprocity: Indiana. Students seeking teaching certification in a state other than Indiana should consult with that state's teacher certification office early in their program of study to insure compliance with requirements. Many state directors of teacher credentialing have signed Interstate Agreements through NASDTEC that expedite the certification process.

MANCHESTER COLLEGE

Department of Education
Teacher Education Program
604 East College Avenue
North Manchester, Indiana 46962
Phone: (219) 982-5000
Fax: (219) 982-5043
E-mail: admitinfo@manchester.edu
Internet: http://www.manchester.edu

Institution Description: Manchester College is a private college affiliated with the Church of the Brethren. It was established as Manchester College and Bible School in 1889. The present name was adopted in 1902.

The Teacher Education Program embraces the college's liberal arts program as well as the State of Indiana's requirements for licensing.

Institution Control: Private.

Calendar: Semester. Academic year September to May.

Official(s): Dr. Lindan Hill, Chair, Division of Teacher Education.

Faculty: Full-time 5.

Degrees Awarded: 52 baccalaureate.

Admission Requirements: *Undergraduate:* Graduation from an approved secondary school or GED; College Board SAT preferred, ACT composite accepted. *Teacher education specific:* Cumulative GPA 2.5; attendance at a Celebrating Diversity Workshop with a satisfactory reflection paper based on the experience; three faculty member references.

Fees and Expenses: $26,090 per academic year. On-campus room and board: $5,990. Other expenses: $1,450. Books and supplies: $550.

Financial Aid: Resources specifically for eligible students enrolled in teacher education programs are awarded on the basis of financial need and academic merit. The institution has a Program Participation Agreement with the U.S. Department of Education for eligible students to receive Pell Grants and other federal aid. *Contact:* Financial Aid Office at: (260) 982-5055.

Accreditation: *Regional:* NCA. *Professional:* NCATE. *Member of:* AACTE. *Approved by:* Indiana Professional Studies Board.

Undergraduate Programs: The baccalaureate program major in elementary education includes endorsements in coaching, French, German, health and safety, language arts, mathematics, science, social studies, kindergarten, physical education (grades 1-6), Spanish, special education, and visual arts (grades 1-6).

The senior high-junior high/middle school program offers majors in English, French, German, mathematics, physical education, Spanish, speech communication and theater, visual arts.

The secondary education program offers majors in English, French, German, mathematics, physical education, Spanish, speech communication and theater arts, and visual arts.

All grade education (K-12) programs are offered with majors in music (vocal and instrumental), music choral), physical education, and visual arts.

All programs require the completion of a general education core, professional studies, field experiences, and student teaching for a total of 128 semester hours.

Licensure/Reciprocity: Indiana. Students seeking teaching certification in a state other than Indiana should consult with that state's teacher certification office early in their program of study to insure compliance with requirements. Many state directors of teacher credentialing have signed Interstate Agreements through NASDTEC that expedite the certification process. Reciprocity agreement also through the Central States Teacher Exchange Agreement.

MARIAN COLLEGE

Education Department
Teacher Education Program
3200 Cold Spring Road
Indianapolis, Indiana 46222-1997
Phone: (317) 955-6089
Fax: (317) 955-6406
E-mail: jmwitcher@marian.edu
Internet: http://www.marian.edu

Institution Description: Marian College is a coeducational, comprehensive liberal arts college developed by the Sisters of Saint Francis, Oldenburg, Indiana, Roman Catholic Church. It was established at Oldenburg, Indiana as Saint Francis Normal School for Women in 1851. It merged with Immaculate Conception Junior College (founded 1924) and the present name was adopted in 1936. The college was moved to its present site in 1937 and became coeducational in 1954.

As part of a Franciscan college, the Education Department integrates core values into the program: the dignity of the individual, stewardship, reconciliation, and peace and justice.

Institution Control: Private.

Calendar: Semester. Academic August to May.

Official(s): Dr. Susan Blackwell, Chair.

Faculty: Full-time 8; part-time 2; 4 adjunct.

Degrees Awarded: 34 baccalaureate; 13 master's.

Admission Requirements: *Undergraduate:* Graduation from an approved secondary school or GED; 2.0 GPA; 880 SAT score or 19 ACT composite. *Teacher education specific:* 2.5 GPA in education courses; PRAXIS I test; 30 credits completed; faculty interview. *Graduate:* Baccalaureate degree from a regionally accredited institution; *Teacher education specific:* 2.75 GPA; PRAXIS I and II tests; content area experience; background check; experience working with children.

Fees and Expenses: $16,800 per academic year. Graduate: $12,000 per academic year. Required fees: $660. On-campus room and board: $5,900. Books and supplies: $700.

Financial Aid: Resources specifically for eligible students enrolled in teacher education programs are awarded on the basis of financial need and academic merit. The institution has a Program Participation Agreement with the U.S. Department of Education for eligible students to receive Pell Grants and other federal aid. *Contact:* John E. Shelton at: (317) 955-6040 or e-mail at jshelton@marian.edu.

Accreditation: *Regional:* NCA. *Professional:* NCATE. *Approved by:* Indiana Professional Standards Board.

Undergraduate Programs: The Education Department supports the development of beginning teachers in four programs: elementary generalist (K-5), exceptional needs (K-5, added to the elementary generalist; middle school licensing [6-8, added on to K-6 and/or 9-12]; and secondary licensing (9-12). All students complete a liberal arts core focused on moral reasoning, scientific and quantitative reasoning, individual and social awareness, effective communication and cultural awareness (65-73 credits). This core provides the needed foundation in the liberal arts to ensure that the beginning teaches are well-grounded in their subject knowledge. Students must successfully complete a multiple phase assessment program in order to be recommended for an Indiana license.

Graduate Programs: The Master of Arts in Teaching degree program is for post-baccalaureate individuals. The program is a "Transition to Teaching" program that provides a pathway to become licensed elementary teachers in Indiana. Completion of the program leads to licensure for primary and intermediate grades. This is a full-time program that organizes participants in cohorts that complete intensive internship experiences with trained mentors in elementary schools. It includes a concentration in second language learning to ensure that graduates have critical knowledge and skills necessary to meet the needs of all learners.

Licensure/Reciprocity: Indiana. Students seeking teaching certification in a state other than Indiana should consult with that state's teacher certification office early in their program of study to insure compliance with requirements. Many state directors of teacher credentialing have signed Interstate Agreements through NASDTEC that expedite the certification process. Reciprocity agreement also through the Central States Teacher Exchange Agreement.

OAKLAND CITY UNIVERSITY

School of Education
140 North Lucretia
Oakland City, Indiana 47660
Phone: (812) 749-4781
Fax: (812) 749-1233
E-mail: pswails@oak.edu
Internet: http://www.oak.edu

Institution Description: Oakland City University, formerly named Oakland City College, is a private college affiliated with the General Association of General Baptists.

The School of Education is the officially designated unit for the design, approval, and continuous evaluation and development of teacher education programs at Oakland City University.

Institution Control: Private.

Calendar: Semester. Academic year August to May.

Official(s): Dr. Patricia A. Swails, Dean.

Faculty: Full-time 12; part-time 4; adjunct 18.

Degrees Awarded: 52 baccalaureate.

Admission Requirements: *Undergraduate:* Graduation from an approved secondary school or GED; College Board SAT or ACT composite; letter of recommendation. *Teacher education specific:* 2.5 GPA; completion of foundations of education course; English competency exam; PRAXIS I with passing score; interview; portfolio defense; faculty recommendations. *Graduate:* Undergraduate GPA 3.0; GRE or Miller Analogies Test. *Teacher education specific:* Two letters of recommendation; passing scores on PRAXIS I; interview; valid teaching license for nonlicensure candidates.

Fees and Expenses: Undergraduate $383 per credit hour; graduate $275 per credit hour. Required fees: $250 per semester. On-campus room and board: $4,330. Books and supplies: $200 to $500 per semester.

Financial Aid: Resources specifically for eligible students enrolled in teacher education programs are awarded on the basis of financial need and academic merit. The institution has a Program Participation Agreement with the U.S. Department of Education for eligible students to receive Pell Grants and other federal aid. Performance scholarships (art, music, athletics) available to qualified applicants *Contact:* Caren Richeson at (812) 749-4781, ext. 224 or e-mail at cricheson @oak.edu.

Accreditation: *Regional:* NCA. *Professional:* NCATE. *Member of:* AACTE. *Approved by:* Indiana Professional Studies Board.

Undergraduate Programs: The School of Education offers baccalaureate programs in elementary education (early childhood, middle childhood), reading, and professional education for secondary education majors (early adolescence, adolescence/ young adults) in business education, vocational business, industrial technology, English, mathematics, health, physical education, science, and social science. Professional education courses are also taught for the all-grade education programs in health, music, visual arts, physical education, and special education (early childhood and mildly handicapped). The university's general studies core requirement of 41 semester hours must be successfully completed for all education degree programs as well as professional studies, field experiences, and student teaching. All baccalaureate programs require successful completion of 128 semester hours.

Graduate Programs: The Master of Arts for Teaching Option I program is designed for persons who have already acquired a baccalaureate degree in a content area, nonteaching, and have decided that they want to change to a career in teaching. The emphasis of the program is placed on meeting the entrance requirements to the teaching professional. Professional study is combined with practical classroom experience. The Option II program is designed for persons who have completed a baccalaureate degree in a teaching field. It is designed to be an induction model for new teachers and a continuing professional education model for experienced educators.

Both options include requirements for directed observation and pre-planned classroom experiences.

Licensure/Reciprocity: Indiana. Students seeking teaching certification in a state other than Indiana should consult with that state's teacher certification office early in their program of study to insure compliance with requirements. Many state directors of teacher credentialing have signed Interstate Agreements through NASDTEC that expedite the certification process.

PURDUE UNIVERSITY

School of Education
Teacher Education Program
100 North University Street
West Lafayette, Indiana 47907-2098
Phone: (765) 494-2341
Fax: (765) 494-5832
E-mail: info@soe.purdue.edu
Internet: http://www.soe.purdue.edu

Institution Description: Purdue University is a state university and land-grant college. Classes began in 1874.

The Teacher Education Program standards, curricula, assessments, and licensure are in accord with regulations promulgated by the Indiana Professional Standards Board.

Institution Control: Public.

Calendar: Semester. Academic year September to May.

Official(s): Dr. George Hynd, Dean.

Faculty: Full-time 74; part-time 54; adjunct 9.

Degrees Awarded: 467 baccalaureate; 192 master's; 35 doctorate.

Admission Requirements: *Undergraduate:* Graduation from an accredited secondary school or GED; College Board SAT or ACT composite. *Teacher education specific:* Acceptance into the teacher education program by sophomore year; passing score on the PRAXIS I test; faculty interview. *Graduate:* Baccalaureate degree from a regionally accredited institution. *Teacher education specific:* Passing scores on both PRAXIS I and II; educational foundation courses; letters of recommendation; faculty interview.

Fees and Expenses: Undergraduate/graduate: $5,860 per academic year. On-campus room and board: $6,700. Books and supplies: $890.

Financial Aid: Resources specifically for eligible students enrolled in teacher education programs are awarded on the basis of financial need and academic merit. The institution has a Program Participation Agreement with the U.S. Department of Education for eligible students to receive Pell Grants and other federal aid. *Contact:* Joyce Hall, Director, Financial Aid at: (765) 494-0998 or e-mail at facontact@purdue.edu.

Accreditation: *Regional:* NCA. *Professional:* NCATE. *Member of:* AACTE. *Approved by:* Indiana Professional Standards Board.

Undergraduate Programs: The Teacher Education Program offers baccalaureate programs in early childhood, middle childhood (elementary education), early adolescence (junior high/

PURDUE UNIVERSITY—cont'd

middle school), adolescence/young adulthood (secondary), and exceptional needs (special education. Requirements of these performance-based programs vary by content areas. Students must complete a general education core, professional studies, subject area major (secondary education), field experiences, and student teaching.

A person who already holds a bachelor's degree may complete a teacher education program as an "undergraduate for licensing only" student.

Graduate Programs: Graduate programs leading to the master's degree are offered in early childhood, middle childhood (elementary education), early adolescence (junior high/middle school), adolescence/young adulthood (secondary), and exceptional needs (special education. Requirements of these performance-based programs vary by content areas. Official performance-based program guidelines are available via the School of Education Office of Professional Preparation and Licensure.

Licensure/Reciprocity: Indiana. Students seeking teaching certification in a state other than Indiana should consult with that state's teacher certification office early in their program of study to insure compliance with requirements. Many state directors of teacher credentialing have signed Interstate Agreements through NASDTEC that expedite the certification process. Reciprocity agreement also through the Central States Teacher Exchange Agreement.

PURDUE UNIVERSITY CALUMET

School of Education
Teacher Education Programs
2200 169th Street
Hammond, Indiana 46323
Phone: (219) 989-2335
Fax: (219) 989-3215
E-mail: huscj@calumet.purdue.edu
Internet: http://www.calumet.purdue.edu

Institution Description: The campus was established as Purdue University Center, Hammond in 1946. The name was changed to Purdue University, Calumet Center in 1959, to Purdue University-Calumet Campus in 1962, and to the present name in 1978.

The School of Education faculty is committed to providing the human and technological resources necessary to enable students to construct knowledge, develop practices, and foster relationships.

Institution Control: Public.

Calendar: Semester. Academic year August to May.

Official(s): Dr. Robert H. Rivers, Dean, School of Education; Dr. Robert Colon, Chair, Graduate Studies in Education.

Faculty: Full-time 22; part-time 2.

Degrees Awarded: 62 baccalaureate; 75 master's.

Admission Requirements: *Undergraduate:* Graduation from an accredited secondary school or GED; College Board SAT or ACT composite. *Teacher education specific:* Acceptance into the teacher education program by sophomore year; passing score on the PRAXIS I test; faculty interview. *Graduate:* Baccalaureate degree from a regionally accredited institution. *Teacher education specific:* Passing scores on both PRAXIS I and II; educational foundation courses; letters of recommendation; faculty interview.

Fees and Expenses: Undergraduate: in-state $109 per credit hour; $274 out-of-state. Graduate: in-state $141.70 per credit hour; $321.95 out-of-state. Required fees: $10.60 per credit hour. Books and supplies: $300 to $500 per semester.

Financial Aid: Resources specifically for eligible students enrolled in teacher education programs are awarded on the basis of financial need and academic merit. The institution has a Program Participation Agreement with the U.S. Department of Education for eligible students to receive Pell Grants and other federal aid. *Contact:* Mary Ann Bishel at (219) 989-2301 or e-mail at bishelm@calumet.purdue.edu.

Accreditation: *Regional:* NCA. *Professional:* NCATE. *Member of:* AACTE. *Approved by:* Indiana Professional Standards Board.

Undergraduate Programs: Undergraduate baccalaureate degree programs offered by the School of Education include: Bachelor of Arts in elementary education (grades 1-6) with endorsements in junior high/middle school, kindergarten, learning disabilities, mildly mentally handicapped, seriously emotionally handicapped, and reading. The Bachelor of Arts or Bachelor of Science in secondary education (grades 5-12) with majors in biology, chemistry, economics, English, French, German, government, mathematics, physics, psychology, sociology, Spanish, U.S. history, and world civilization. Minors are available in English, French, German, Spanish, learning disabilities, mathematics, computers, mildly mentally handicapped, seriously emotionally handicapped, reading, chemistry, general science, physics, economics, government, psychology, sociology, U.S. history, and world civilization.

Graduate Programs: The School of Education offers a variety of master's degrees and license programs through the Graduate Studies in Education. Programs include: Master of Science, elementary education (33 credits); Master of Science, elementary education /special education Emphasis (33 credits); Master of Science, elementary science education (33 credits); Master of Science, elementary mathematics education (33 credits); Master of Science, secondary Education (33 credits); Master of Science, school counseling or mental health counseling (60 credits); Master of Science, instructional design (33 credit); Master of Science, educational administration: elementary (33 credit). All programs require the completion of required core courses and specific area courses such as foundations, counseling, curriculum, special education, and administration.

Licensure/Reciprocity: Indiana. Students seeking teaching certification in a state other than Indiana should consult with that state's teacher certification office early in their program of study to insure compliance with requirements. Many state directors of teacher credentialing have signed Interstate Agreements through NASDTEC that expedite the certification process. Reciprocity agreement also through the Central States Teacher Exchange Agreement.

SAINT JOSEPH'S COLLEGE

Education Department
P.O. Box 935
Rensselaer, Indiana 47978
Phone: (219) 866-6384
Fax: (219) 866-6300
E-mail: education@saintjoe.edu
Internet: http://www.saintjoe.edu

Institution Description: Saint Joseph's College is a private, independent, nonprofit college sponsored by the Missionaries of the Precious Blood, Roman Catholic Church. The college was established in 1889 and became a four-year institution in 1936. The college became coeducational in 1968.

The Education Department offers baccalaureate programs leading to Indiana licensure.

Institution Control: Private.

Calendar: Semester. Academic year August to April.

Official(s): Dr. Jennifer Barce, Dean.

Faculty: Full-time 54; part-time 24.

Degrees Awarded: 16 baccalaureate.

Admission Requirements: *Undergraduate:* Graduation with 15 academic units from an accredited secondary school or GED; College Board SAT or ACT composite. *Teacher education specific:* Acceptance into program by sophomore year; PRAXIS I scores; personal goal statement; faculty interview.

Fees and Expenses: $17,900 per academic year. Required fees: $160. On-campus room and board: $6,190. Other expenses: $1,050. Books and supplies: $700.

Financial Aid: Resources specifically for eligible students enrolled in teacher education programs are awarded on the basis of financial need and academic merit. The institution has a Program Participation Agreement with the U.S. Department of

Education for eligible students to receive Pell Grants and other federal aid. Minority Leadership Scholarship available to qualified applicant. *Contact:* Dianne Mickey at (219) 866-6163 or e-mail at financialaid@saintjoe.edu.

Accreditation: *Regional:* NCA. *Professional:* NCATE. *Member of:* AACTE. *Approved by:* Indiana Professional Standards Board.

Undergraduate Programs: The elementary education major leads to licensure in preschool, kindergarten, elementary, or middle school settings. The student will be in the classroom from day one, participating in field placements in both public and private school settings located near the college. The program requires the completion of a general education core, professional studies, field experiences, and student teaching for a total of 120 semester hours.

The secondary Education major concentrates in one of the college's major subject areas. The student will participate in field placements in both public and private school settings. The program requires completion of a subject content area in the liberal arts curriculum, general education core, field experiences, and student teaching for a total of 120 semester hours.

Licensure/Reciprocity: Indiana. Students seeking teaching certification in a state other than Indiana should consult with that state's teacher certification office early in their program of study to insure compliance with requirements. Many state directors of teacher credentialing have signed Interstate Agreements through NASDTEC that expedite the certification process. Reciprocity agreement also through the Central States Teacher Exchange Agreement.

SAINT MARY-OF-THE-WOODS COLLEGE

Department of Education
Teacher Education Program
  Hulman Hall
  Saint Mary-of-the-Woods, Indiana 47876
  Phone: (812) 535-5151
  Fax: (812) 535-4613
  E-mail: smeier@@smwc.edu
  Internet: http://www.smuc.edu

Institution Description: Saint Mary-of-the-Woods College is a private women's college affiliated with the Roman Catholic Church. The college was established in 1841.

The mission of the Department of Education is to prepare competent, caring, professional teachers who are able to meet the needs of a diverse society.

Institution Control: Private.

Calendar: Semester. Academic year July to June.

Official(s): Dr. Christine Bahr, Dean. Department of Education.

Faculty: Full-time 8; part-time 16.

Degrees Awarded: 39 baccalaureate.

Admission Requirements: *Undergraduate:* Graduation with 16 academic units from an approved secondary school or GED; College Board SAT or ACT composite. *Teacher education specific:* Personal goal statement; 2.5 GPA; faculty interview; PRAXIS I test scores.

Fees and Expenses: $16,530 per academic year. Required fees: $500. On-campus room and board: $6,250. Books and supplies: $500.

Financial Aid: Resources specifically for eligible students enrolled in teacher education programs are awarded on the basis of financial need and academic merit. The institution has a Program Participation Agreement with the U.S. Department of Education for eligible students to receive Pell Grants and other federal aid. *Contact:* Jan Benton at (812) 535-5109 or e-mail at jbenton@smwc.edu.

Accreditation: *Regional:* NCA. *Professional:* NCATE. *Member of:* AACTE. *Approved by:* Indiana Professional Standards Board.

Undergraduate Programs: Students choose from nine majors including middle school/high school specializations. A total of 125 credits is required for the Bachelor of Science degree with 2.5 GPA and no education courses with a grade lower than C. A series of field experiences is required with a culminating semester of student teaching.

An accelerated licensure program is available for students who hold a bachelor's degree (higher admission standards apply).

Licensure/Reciprocity: Indiana. Students seeking teaching certification in a state other than Indiana should consult with that state's teacher certification office early in their program of study to insure compliance with requirements. Many state directors of teacher credentialing have signed Interstate Agreements through NASDTEC that expedite the certification process.

SAINT MARY'S COLLEGE

Education Department
  Madeleva Hall, Room 321
  Notre Dame, Indiana 46556-5001
  Phone: (574) 284-4485
  Fax: (574) 284-4878
  E-mail: dhanks@saintmarys.edu
  Internet: http://www.saintmarys.edu

Institution Description: Saint Mary's College is a private women's college affiliated with the Congregation of the Sisters of the Holy Cross, Roman Catholic Church. Men are admitted as special students. The college was established in 1844.

The Education Department offers teacher preparation programs leading to licensure in elementary and secondary education.

Institution Control: Private.

Calendar: Semester. Academic year August to May.

Official(s): Dr. Dale A. Banks, Department Head.

Faculty: Full-time 6; part-time 1; adjunct 15.

Degrees Awarded: 33 baccalaureate.

Admission Requirements: *Undergraduate:* Graduation from an approved secondary school or GED; minimum 2.5 GPA; lowest acceptable secondary school class standing 66th %ile; College Board SAT or ACT composite. *Teacher education specific:* GPA 2.5; completion of the course "Teaching in a Multicultural Society"; recommendations from two faculty members; completion of National Teachers Examinations, advanced writing proficiency.

Fees and Expenses: $20,400 per academic year. On-campus room and board: $4,100. Other expenses: $1,850. Books and supplies: $1,000.

Financial Aid: Resources specifically for eligible students enrolled in teacher education programs are awarded on the basis of financial need and academic merit. The institution has a Program Participation Agreement with the U.S. Department of Education for eligible students to receive Pell Grants and other federal aid. *Contact:* Financial Aid Office at: (574) 284-4557.

Accreditation: *Regional:* NCA. *Member of:* AACTE. *Approved by:* Indiana Professional Standards Board.

Undergraduate Programs: The baccalaureate program leading to licensure in elementary education is organized into three tiers. Each tier is concerned with the conceptual framework of multicultural education, the utilization of instruction in ongoing field experience/practicum placements, and incremental teaching periods. The curriculum includes general studies, content studies, pedagogical and professional integrative studies for initial teacher preparation. A total of 128 semester hours must be successfully completed.

The secondary education program prepares students to teach senior high and junior high/middle school. A subject major concentration consists of 36 to 52 semester hours. Students must develop and submit for evaluation three portfolios during their course of study and involves making an oral presentation about the contents of the portfolio. The program requires the completion of a general education core, subject area major, professional studies, field experiences, and student teaching for a total of 128 semester hours.

Licensure/Reciprocity: Indiana. Students seeking teaching certification in a state other than Indiana should consult with that state's teacher certification office early in their program of study to insure compliance with requirements. Many state

SAINT MARY'S COLLEGE—*cont'd*

directors of teacher credentialing have signed Interstate Agreements through NASDTEC that expedite the certification process.

TAYLOR UNIVERSITY

Department of Education
Teacher Education Program
500 West Reade Avenue
Upland, Indiana 46989
Phone: (765) 998-5134
Fax: (765) 998-4925
E-mail: nrbenjamin@tayloru.edu
Internet: http://www.tayloru.edu

Institution Description: Taylor University is a private, independent, nonprofit, evangelical Christian college. It was established by the Methodist Episcopal Church in 1846. The present name was adopted in 1890.

The Department of Education provides students with professional preparation in the areas of elementary and secondary education. The comprehensive liberal arts curriculum structured within the general education requirements provides the foundation for subject-matter competence as well as lifelong learning, leadership, and continued growth in the teaching profession.

Institution Control: Private.

Calendar: Semester. Academic year September to May.

Official(s): Dr. Carl Siler, Director of Teacher Education.

Faculty: Full-time 8.

Degrees Awarded: 86 baccalaureate.

Admission Requirements: *Undergraduate:* Graduation from an approved secondary school or GED; College board SAT or ACT composite. *Teacher education specific:* Application to the Teacher Education Committee by first term of sophomore year; formal admission after completing three terms of college work; portfolio requirements; faculty interview.

Fees and Expenses: $17,490 per academic year. On-campus room and board: $4,130. Other expenses: $1,500. Books and supplies: $700.

Financial Aid: Resources specifically for eligible students enrolled in teacher education programs are awarded on the basis of financial need and academic merit. The institution has a Program Participation Agreement with the U.S. Department of Education for eligible students to receive Pell Grants and other federal aid. *Contact:* Financial Aid Office at: (765) 998-5125.

Accreditation: *Regional:* NCA. *Professional:* NCATE. *Member of:* AACTE. *Approved by:* Indiana Professional Standards Board.

Undergraduate Programs: The elementary education (first through sixth grades) baccalaureate program includes general education courses, directed electives, free choice electives, and professional education courses. Certification minors and endorsements may be added to the elementary license: computer endorsement, junior high/middle school endorsement (language arts, mathematics, science, social studies), kindergarten endorsement, and music minor.

The all-grade education (kindergarten through twelfth grades) baccalaureate program is offers for all-grade education in music (instrumental, choral, and general), physical education, and visual arts. The same minors and endorsements listed above may be added.

The senior high, junior high and middle school education (fifth through twelfth grades) and secondary education (ninth through twelfth grades) is offered a variety of majors and minors. The student preparing to teach in the secondary schools should select a teaching and to select a minor or endorsement.

All baccalaureate programs require the completion of 128 semester hours including a general education core, professional studies, subject area major (secondary education students), field experiences, and student teaching.

Licensure/Reciprocity: Indiana. Students seeking teaching certification in a state other than Indiana should consult with that state's teacher certification office early in their program of study to insure compliance with requirements. Many state directors of teacher credentialing have signed Interstate Agreements through NASDTEC that expedite the certification process. Reciprocity agreement also through the Central States Teacher Exchange Agreement.

UNIVERSITY OF EVANSVILLE

School of Education
Teacher Education Program
1800 Lincoln Avenue
Evansville, Indiana 47722
Phone: (812) 479-2004
Fax: (812) 471-6998
E-mail: education@evansville.edu
Internet: http://www.evansville.edu

Institution Description: University of Evansville is a private institution affiliated with The United Methodist Church. It was established as Moore's Hill Male and Female Collegiate Institute in 1854. The name was changed to Moore's Hill College in 1887, to Evansville College in 1919, and to the current name in 1967.

The School of Education offers undergraduate education programs leading to a baccalaureate degree and Indiana licensure.

Institution Control: Private.

Calendar: Semester. Academic year August to May.

Official(s): Dr. Charles Watson, Dean.

Faculty: Full-time 8; part-time 8.

Degrees Awarded: 75 baccalaureate.

Admission Requirements: *Undergraduate:* Graduation from an approved secondary school or GED; 2.5 GPA recommended; lowest acceptable secondary school class standing 40th %ile; College Board SAT or ACT composite; counselor essay recommendation; involvement in extracurricular activities. *Teacher education specific:* PRAXIS I test scores; 2.6 GPA; faculty interview.

Fees and Expenses: $17,900 per academic year. Required fees: $270 activity fees; $60 health and wellness. On-campus room: $2,780; meal plan $2,940.

Financial Aid: Resources specifically for eligible students enrolled in teacher education programs are awarded on the basis of financial need and academic merit. The institution has a Program Participation Agreement with the U.S. Department of Education for eligible students to receive Pell Grants and other federal aid. *Contact:* Joann Laugel at: (812) 479-2150 or e-mail at j125@evansville.edu.

Accreditation: *Regional:* NCA. *Professional:* NCATE. *Member of:* AACTE. *Approved by:* Indiana Professional Standards Board.

Undergraduate Programs: The Bachelor of Science degree and teacher licensure program is offered with majors in elementary education, senior high, junior high and mdddle school education, and all-grade education. The programs must include at least one teaching major and may include one or more teaching minors or teaching endorsements. All programs require the completion of a general education core, professional studies, subject area major (secondary education), field experiences, and student teaching. All baccalaureate programs require the successful completion of 124 semester hours.

Licensure/Reciprocity: Indiana. Students seeking teaching certification in a state other than Indiana should consult with that state's teacher certification office early in their program of study to insure compliance with requirements. Many state directors of teacher credentialing have signed Interstate Agreements through NASDTEC that expedite the certification process.

UNIVERSITY OF INDIANAPOLIS

Department of Teacher Education
1400 East Hanna Avenue
Indianapolis, Indiana 46227-3697
Phone: (317) 788-3285
Fax: (317) 788-3300
E-mail: breitsma@uindy.edu
Internet: http://www.uindy.edu

Institution Description: University of Indianapolis is a private, independent, nonprofit institution affiliated with the United Methodist Church. It was established as Indiana Central University in 1902.

The Department of Teacher Education offers programs at the bachelor's and master's levels.

Institution Control: Private.

Calendar: Semester. Academic year August to April.

Official(s): Dr. Beverly A. Reitsma, Chair; Dr. Kathy Moran, Associate Dean.

Faculty: Full-time 14; part-time 1; adjunct 12.

Degrees Awarded: 65 baccalaureate; 44 master's.

Admission Requirements: *Undergraduate:* Graduation from an approved high school or GED; College Board SAT or ACT composite. *Teacher education specific:* Application to the department by beginning of sophomore year; PRAXIS I test; National Teachers Examination; personal goal essay; faculty interview. *Graduate:* Baccalaureate degree from a regionally accredited institution with a minimum cumulative GPA of 2.5. *Teacher education specific:* Teaching license; three letters of recommendation; passing scores on the PRAXIS I test; National Teachers Examination; faculty interview.

Fees and Expenses: Undergraduate $8,310 per semester; graduate $285 per credit hour. Required fees: $50 student activity fee. On-campus room: $1,485 per semester; board: $1,445 per semester.

Financial Aid: Resources specifically for eligible students enrolled in teacher education programs are awarded on the basis of financial need and academic merit. The institution has a Program Participation Agreement with the U.S. Department of Education for eligible students to receive Pell Grants and other federal aid. *Contact:* Rita Hankley at (317) 788-3347 or e-mail at hankley@uindy.edu.

Accreditation: *Regional:* NCA. *Professional:* NCATE. *Member of:* AACTE. *Approved by:* Indian Professional Standards Board.

Undergraduate Programs: The elementary education program prepares teacher candidates to teach in grades kindergarten to sixth. Features of the program include classes taught on-site at area elementary schools, field experiences at all elementary grade levels, and multiple opportunities to practice instructional and assessment strategies under the guidance of mentor teachers. The program integrates literacy and special needs instruction throughout the curriculum.

The middle level education program prepares teacher candidates to meet the development needs of students in 5th through 8th grades. Candidates in this program choose two subject concentrations from English/language arts, mathematics, or social studies. Candidates learn how to work as a member of an instructional team and implement an integrated curriculum in literacy and methods classes taught on-site at local middle schools.

The middle level/high school education program leading to licensure will allow the graduate to teach at the early adolescent and adolescent levels (5-12). License programs are offered in foreign language, science, English/language arts, mathematics, social studies, theater arts, and business education.

The all-grade program allows the licensee to teach in any grade (K-12) in music teaching, health/physical education, and visual arts. With a minimum of coursework, candidates have the option of adding mild interventions (special education) to their licenses.

Graduate Programs: The Master of Arts in Curriculum and Instruction requires 36 credit hours including 12 hours of core requirements and 12 hours of focused study in a specific content area. The remaining 12 hours may be in elective courses or 6 hours of electives or 6 hours doing a project. The program offers instruction in: literacy education, organizing a curriculum, applying technology, meeting special needs, educational research, effective teaching strategies, classroom management, critical thinking, distance education.

Licensure/Reciprocity: Indiana. Students seeking teaching certification in a state other than Indiana should consult with that state's teacher certification office early in their program of study to insure compliance with requirements. Many state directors of teacher credentialing have signed Interstate Agreements through NASDTEC that expedite the certification process. Reciprocity agreement also through the Central States Teacher Exchange Agreement.

UNIVERSITY OF NOTRE DAME

Institute for Educational Initiatives
154 I.E.I.
Notre Dame, Indiana 46556
Phone: (574) 631-3430
Fax: (574) 631-7729
E-mail: Johnstone.3@nd.edu
Internet: http://www.ace/nd.edu

Institution Description: The University of Notre Dame is a private, independent, nonprofit institution affiliated with the Congregation of Holy Cross, Indiana Province of Priests, Roman Catholic Church. The university was established in 1842 under its present official name, University of Notre Dame du Lac.

The Alliance for Catholic Education is a two-year service program offering college graduates the opportunity to serve as full-time teachers in under-resourced Catholic schools across the southern United States.

Institution Control: Private.

Calendar: Semester. Academic year August to May.

Official(s): Dr. Joyce V. Johnstone, Director.

Faculty: Full-time 29; part-time 9; adjunct 20.

Degrees Awarded: 76 master's.

Admission Requirements: *Graduate:* Baccalaureate degree from a regionally accredited institution. *Teacher education specific:* 3.0 GPA; GRE scores (500 verbal, 500 mathematical); interview; personal essay; recommendations.

Fees and Expenses: No fees or tuition.

Financial Aid: Students receive a stipend from participating schools.

Accreditation: *Regional:* NCA. *Professional:* NCATE. *Approved by:* Indiana Professional Studies Board.

Graduate Programs: ACE teachers spend two summers (June-July) studying in the Master of Education program at Notre Dame and two school years (August to May) teaching in under-resources Catholic schools across the country. While teaching, participants live in small communities of 4-7 members and together share the many challenges and rewards of beginning teaching. ACE participants are encouraged to share with one another the journey of becoming committed Catholic school teachers.

Students receive a modest living stipend, usually about $11,000. The student is required to pay about $200 per month and to share utilities for housing. The M.Ed. program during the summer is cost-free.

Licensure/Reciprocity: Indiana. Students seeking teaching certification in a state other than Indiana should consult with that state's teacher certification office early in their program of study to insure compliance with requirements. Many state directors of teacher credentialing have signed Interstate Agreements through NASDTEC that expedite the certification process.

UNIVERSITY OF SOUTHERN INDIANA
School of Education and Human Services
Department of Teacher Education
8600 University Boulevard
Evansville, Indiana 47712
Phone: (812) 464-1939
E-mail: cprice@usi.edu
Internet: http://www.usi.edu

Institution Description: The university was established as the Evansville regional campus of Indiana State University (Terre Haute) in 1971. It was made a separate state university in 1985 when the present name was adopted.

The Mission of the Department of Teacher Education is to graduate students who are prepared to contribute to the educational processes in today's schools. The programs offered provide a strong academic background in general education.

Institution Control: Public.

Calendar: Semester. Academic year August to May.

Official(s): Dr. Charles Price, Chairman, Department of Teacher Education.

Faculty: Full-time 15.

Degrees Awarded: 165 baccalaureate; 37 master's.

Admission Requirements: *Undergraduate:* Graduation from an approved secondary school or GED; College Board SAT or ACT composite. *Teacher education specific:* Application to the program by the first term of the sophomore year; National Teacher Examination; PRAXIS I test; faculty interview. *Graduate:* Baccalaureate degree from a regionally accredited institution. *Teacher education specified:* Candidacy application to be completed after 18 semester hours of coursework; PRAXIS I and II tests; teaching credential.

Fees and Expenses: Undergraduate: in-state $3,231 per academic year; out-of-state $7,632. Graduate: Tuition charged per credit hour. On-campus room and board: $4,940. Other expenses: $2,456. Books and supplies: $800.

Financial Aid: Resources specifically for eligible students enrolled in teacher education programs are awarded on the basis of financial need and academic merit. The institution has a Program Participation Agreement with the U.S. Department of Education for eligible students to receive Pell Grants and other federal aid. *Contact:* Financial Aid Office at: (812) 464-1767.

Accreditation: *Regional:* NCA. *Professional:* NCATE. *Member of:* AACTE. *Approved by:* Indiana Professional Studies Board.

Undergraduate Programs: The Bachelor of Science in elementary education degree leads to licensure to teach all subjects in grades one to six. The program includes a general education core, subject major, professional studies, field experiences, and student teaching.

The secondary and all-grade baccalaureate program (grades 9-12) may qualify for a license to teach junior high/middle school (grades 5-12). The program requires the completion of a general education core, subject content area courses, professional studies, field experiences, and student teaching.

The special education program is offered for those seeking a standard Indiana license in exceptional needs, and mild intervention. The program leads to the Bachelor of Science degree.

All programs require the successful completion of 124 semester hours including the appropriate foreign language requirement.

Graduate Programs: The Master of Science in Education degree programs involve advanced study designed to enhance the knowledge and skills of teachers in elementary, middle, junior high, and senior high schools. Programs are offered in elementary and secondary education. The programs blend studies of educational theory with analysis of current theories and practice in teaching. The programs require the completion of 33 semester hours of coursework.

Licensure/Reciprocity: Indiana. Students seeking teaching certification in a state other than Indiana should consult with that state's teacher certification office early in their program of study to insure compliance with requirements. Many state directors of teacher credentialing have signed Interstate Agreements through NASDTEC that expedite the certification process. Reciprocity agreement also through the Central States Teacher Exchange Agreement.

VALPARAISO UNIVERSITY
Department of Education
Huegli Hall 110
U.S. Highway 30
Valparaiso, Indiana 46383
Phone: (219) 464-5314
Fax: (219) 464-5381
E-mail: Albert.Trost@valpo.edu
Internet: http://www.valpo.edu

Institution Description: Valparaiso University is a private institution affiliated with the Lutheran Church-Missouri Synod. The school was established as Valparaiso Male and Female Academy in 1859. It closed in 1869 and reopened as Northern Indiana Normal School and Business Institute in 1873. The name was changed to Valparaiso College and the present name adopted in 1907.

The mission of the Department of Education is to prepare teachers who effectively carry out their roles through the application of their professional knowledge, dispositions and performances, and the implementation of relevant research findings.

Institution Control: Private.

Calendar: Semester. Academic year August to May.

Official(s): Dr. Albert R. Trost, Dean.

Faculty: Full-time 10; part-time 7.

Degrees Awarded: 52 baccalaureate; 26 master's.

Admission Requirements: *Undergraduate:* Graduation from an approved secondary school or GED; College Board SAT or ACT composite. *Teacher education specific:* Application to the program by sophomore year; PRAXIS I scores; faculty interview. *Graduate:* Baccalaureate degree from a regionally accredited institution. *Teacher education specific:* PRAXIS I and II; GRE or Miller Analogies Tests; reflective essay that states personal career goals; letters of recommendation.

Fees and Expenses: Undergraduate: $19,632 per academic year. Graduate: $410 per credit hour. On-campus room and board: $3,570. Other expenses: $1,370. Books and supplies: $600.

Financial Aid: Resources specifically for eligible students enrolled in teacher education programs are awarded on the basis of financial need and academic merit. The institution has a Program Participation Agreement with the U.S. Department of Education for eligible students to receive Pell Grants and other federal aid. *Contact:* Financial Aid Office at:(219) 464-5015.

Accreditation: *Regional:* NCA. *Professional:* NCATE. *Member of:* AACTE. *Approved by:* Indiana Professional Studies Board.

Undergraduate Programs: The department offers a program of study leading to certification for teaching in an elementary classroom. In addition, the teacher candidate may add a specialization in reading or special education (learning disabilities). A junior high/middle level endorsement may be added to the elementary education certificate. The programs require the completion of a general education core, professional studies, field experiences, and student teaching. The Bachelor of Science in Education is awarded upon successful completion of all requirements.

The Bachelor of Arts in elementary education (with a secondary education complementary major) leading to secondary education certification is available in: art, biology, coaching, chemistry, earth/space science, economics, English, French, geography, German, health and safety, history, journalism, Latin, mathematics, music, physical education, physics, psychology, reading, science, Spanish, special education, speech, theater.

Graduate Programs: Programs of study are offered leading to the following degrees: Master of Education with a concentration in teaching and learning; Master of Education with a concentration in special education (learning disabled, mild mentally handicapped, mild disabilities, emotionally handicapped); Master of Science in special education and a Master of Arts with a concentration in school psychology.

Licensure/Reciprocity: Indiana. Students seeking teaching certification in a state other than Indiana should consult with that state's teacher certification office early in their program of study to insure compliance with requirements. Many state directors of teacher credentialing have signed Interstate Agreements through NASDTEC that expedite the certification process.

WABASH COLLEGE

Teacher Education Area of Concentration

P.O. Box 352
301 West Wabash Avenue
Crawfordsville, Indiana 47933-0352
Phone: (765) 361-4338
Fax: (765) 361-6070
E-mail: teachered@wabash.edu
Internet: http://www.wabash.edu

Institution Description: Wabash College is a private, independent college. It was established as Wabash Manual Labor College and Teachers Seminary in 1832. The present name was adopted in 1851.

The Teacher Education Program offers undergraduate preparation for teaching certification in Indiana.

Institution Control: Private.

Calendar: Semester. Academic year August to May.

Official(s): Dr. Deborah A. Butler, Director, Teacher Education Area of Concentration.

Faculty: Full-time 6.

Degrees Awarded: Not reported.

Admission Requirements: *Undergraduate:* Graduation from an approved secondary school or GED; College Board SAT or ACT composite. *Teacher education specific:* Application to the program by sophomore year; personal essay stating career goals; PRAXIS I scores; faculty interview.

Fees and Expenses: $19,837 per academic year. On-campus room and board: $6,397. Other expenses: $2,400. Books and supplies: $600.

Financial Aid: Resources specifically for eligible students enrolled in teacher education programs are awarded on the basis of financial need and academic merit. The institution has a Program Participation Agreement with the U.S. Department of Education for eligible students to receive Pell Grants and other federal aid. *Contact:* Financial Aid Office at: (765) 361-6370.

Accreditation: *Regional:* NCA. *Professional:* NCATE. *Member of:* AACTE. *Approved by:* Indiana Professional Studies Board.

Undergraduate Programs: The teacher education program prepares students to teach English, French, German, Latin, Spanish, mathematics, biology, chemistry, physics, speech, theater, history, political science, economics or psychology. The baccalaureate program requires the completion of a general education core, subject major in the liberal arts and sciences, professional studies, and field experiences. A 10-week student teaching program is offered in a variety of schools during the senior year in urban, rural, and suburban settings. Students seeking a teaching license often participate in national and international study programs in their major during the junior year.

Licensure/Reciprocity: Indiana. Students seeking teaching certification in a state other than Indiana should consult with that state's teacher certification office early in their program of study to insure compliance with requirements. Many state directors of teacher credentialing have signed Interstate Agreements through NASDTEC that expedite the certification process.

IOWA

BRIAR CLIFF COLLEGE
Department of Education
3303 Rebecca Street
Sioux City, Iowa 51104
Phone: (712) 279-5132
Fax: (712) 279-5410
E-mail: admissions@briar-cliff.edu
Internet: http://www.briar-cliff.edu

Institution Description: Briar Cliff College is a private, independent, nonprofit college affiliated with the Franciscan Order of the Catholic Church. It was established as a junior college for women, in 1930. The college became a 4-year institution in 1956 and coeducational in 1966.

Briar Cliff College offers undergraduate programs leading to the baccalaureate degree in elementary, secondary, and special education.

Institution Control: Private.

Calendar: Modified 3-3 plan. Academic year September to May.

Official(s): Dr. Kenneth Berg, Chair, Department of Education.

Faculty: Full-time 4.

Admission Requirements: *Undergraduate:* Graduation with 16 academic units from an approved secondary school; ACT composite. *Teacher education specific:* Application by the first term of the sophomore year; PRAXIS I test; declaration of subject major; faculty interview. *Graduate:* Baccalaureate degree from an accredited institution; teaching credential; faculty interview.

Fees and Expenses: Undergraduate $15,540 per academic year. Graduate: $229 per credit hour. On-campus room and board: $5,106. Other expenses: $2,385. Books and supplies: $675.

Financial Aid: Resources specifically for eligible students enrolled in teacher education programs are awarded on the basis of financial need and academic merit. The institution has a Program Participation Agreement with the U.S. Department of Education for eligible students to receive Pell Grants and other federal aid. *Contact:* Financial Aid Office at: (712)279-1814.

Accreditation: *Regional:* NCA. *Member of:* AACTE. *Approved by:* Iowa Department of Education.

Undergraduate Programs: The elementary education major requires completion of a general education core, required education foundation courses, professional studies, field experiences, and student teaching. A total of 120 credit hours is required for the baccalaureate degree.

The secondary education major also requires the completion of a general education core, subject area major, professional studies, field experiences, and student teaching. The baccalaureate degree program requires the successful completion of 120 credit hours.

The special education major is an option for students in either the elementary or secondary education programs.

Graduate Programs: The Master of Arts in Education is a 34-hour non-thesis interdisciplinary program designed for those who teach in the elementary, middle, or secondary levels in either the public or non-public school systems.

Licensure/Reciprocity: Iowa. Students seeking teaching certification in a state other than Iowa should consult with that state's teacher certification office early in their program of study to insure compliance with requirements. Many state directors of teacher credentialing have signed Interstate Agreements through NASDTEC that expedite the certification process.

BUENA VISTA UNIVERSITY
School of Education and Exercise Science
Teacher Education Program
610 West Fourth
Storm Lake, Iowa 50588
Phone: (712) 749-2275
Fax: (712) 749-1468
E-mail: finneganj@bvu.edu
Internet: http://www.bvu.edu

Institution Description: Buena Vista University is a private, independent, nonprofit institution affiliated with the United Presbyterian Church U.S.A. It was established incorporated in 1891.

The Teacher Education Program offers both baccalaureate and master's degree programs.

Institution Control: Private.

Calendar: Semester. Academic year August to May.

Official(s): Dr. Kline Capps, Dean, School of Education and Exercise Science.

Faculty: Full-time 20; part-time 52.

Degrees Awarded: 235 baccalaureate; 26 master's.

Admission Requirements: *Undergraduate:* Each applicant is reviewed individually; taking into consideration are: GPA, ACT scores, and high school standing. *Teacher education specific:* Apply to Teacher Education Program by the sophomore year; personal goal statement; PRAXIS I test score; faculty interview. *Graduate:* Baccalaureate degree from a regionally accredited institution. *Teacher education specific:* Must complete all required departmental tests/exams; GPA 2.75; GRE; 3 letters of recommendation; academic autobiography; faculty interview.

Fees and Expenses: Undergraduate $13,738 per academic year. Graduate: $233 per credit hour. On-campus room and board: $5,230. Books and supplies: $250 per semester.

Financial Aid: Resources specifically for eligible students enrolled in teacher education programs are awarded on the basis of financial need and academic merit. The institution has a Program Participation Agreement with the U.S. Department of Education for eligible students to receive Pell Grants and other federal aid. *Contact:* Leanne Valentine, Director of Financial Assistance at: (712) 749-2164.

Accreditation: *Regional:* NCA. *Approved by:* Iowa Department of Education.

Undergraduate Programs: Students can major in elementary education and receive certification as an elementary school teacher or receive certification at the secondary level by combining a major in an academic field with a core of education courses. A total of 128 credit hours with 2.5 GPA is required for graduation.

Graduate Programs: The Master of Science in Education program is designed to prepare students for the role of professional school counselor. The program is organized into three phases: preparation for graduate study, study and preparation, and a capstone activity.

Licensure/Reciprocity: Iowa. Students seeking teaching certification in a state other than Iowa should consult with that state's teacher certification office early in their program of study to insure compliance with requirements. Many state directors of teacher credentialing have signed Interstate Agreements through NASDTEC that expedite the certification process.

CENTRAL COLLEGE
Applied Arts Division
Education Department
812 University
Pella, Iowa 50219
Phone: (641) 628-5116
Fax: (641) 628-5316
E-mail: admission@central.edu
Internet: http://www.central.edu

Institution Description: Central College, formerly known as Central University of Iowa, is a private institution affiliated with the Reformed Church in America. It was established by the Iowa Baptist Convention in 1853.

The Education Department offers undergraduate programs leading to a baccalaureate degree and teacher credential.

Institution Control: Private.

Calendar: Semester. Academic year August to May.

Official(s): Dr. Philip George, Education Department Chairperson.

Faculty: Full-time 7.

Degrees Awarded: 54 baccalaureate.

Admission Requirements: *Undergraduate:* Each applicant is reviewed individually; taking into consideration are: GPA, ACT scores, and high school standing. *Teacher education specific:* Apply to Teacher Education Program by the sophomore year; personal goal statement; PRAXIS I test score; faculty interview.

Fees and Expenses: $16,612 per academic year. On-campus room and board: $5,796. Other expenses: $1,500. Books and supplies: $750.

Financial Aid: Resources specifically for eligible students enrolled in teacher education programs are awarded on the basis of financial need and academic merit. The institution has a Program Participation Agreement with the U.S. Department of Education for eligible students to receive Pell Grants and other federal aid. *Contact:* Financial Aid Office at: (641) 628-5268.

Accreditation: *Regional:* NCA. *Member of:* AACTE. *Approved by:* Iowa Department of Education.

Undergraduate Programs: A fundamental graduation requirement for all students is the completion of an academic major. By the end of the sophomore year, students should file a "declaration of major" with the academic records office. In addition, the baccalaureate programs in elementary and secondary education require the completion of a general education core, professional studies, field experiences, and student teaching. A total of 120 semester hours must be successfully completed for graduation.

Licensure/Reciprocity: Iowa. Students seeking teaching certification in a state other than Iowa should consult with that state's teacher certification office early in their program of study to insure compliance with requirements. Many state directors of teacher credentialing have signed Interstate Agreements through NASDTEC that expedite the certification process.

CLARKE COLLEGE
Education Department
MS 1733
1550 Clarke Drive
Dubuque, Iowa 52001
Phone: (563) 588-6331
Fax: (563) 588-8604
E-mail: mfanderson@clarke.edu
Internet: http://www.clarke.edu

Institution Description: Clarke College is a private college affiliated with the Sisters of Charity of the Blessed Virgin Mary, Roman Catholic Church. It was established as St. Mary's Academy in 1843.

The Education Department offers teacher preparation programs for the elementary and secondary grades.

Institution Control: Private.

Calendar: Semester. Academic year August to May.

Official(s): Dr. Michael F. Anderson, Dean.

Faculty: Full-time 12; part-time 3; adjunct 6.

Degrees Awarded: 25 baccalaureate; 16 master's.

Admission Requirements: *Undergraduate:* High school transcripts; graduation with 16 academic units; College Board SAT or ACT composite. *Teacher education specific:* Apply to Teacher Education Program by the sophomore year; personal goal statement; PRAXIS I test; faculty interview. *Graduate:* Baccalaureate from a regionally accredited institution. *Teacher education specific:* Undergraduate GPA 2.75; teaching credential or eligibility for teacher licensure; two recommendations.

Fees and Expenses: Undergraduate/graduate: $16,580 per academic year. On-campus room $2,970; board: $2,970. Books and supplies: $700.

Financial Aid: Resources specifically for eligible students enrolled in teacher education programs are awarded on the basis of financial need and academic merit. The institution has a Program Participation Agreement with the U.S. Department of Education for eligible students to receive Pell Grants and other federal aid. *Contact:* Michael Pope at: (563) 588-6327 or e-mail at mike.page@clarke.edu.

Accreditation: *Regional:* NCA. *Professional:* NCATE. *Member of:* AACTE. *Approved by:* Iowa Department of Education.

Undergraduate Programs: The elementary education major must complete general education requirements; a professional studies core, field experiences, and student teaching. All elementary education majors must have an approved 24 semester hour concentration of specialization in a single liberal arts discipline or an interdisciplinary program of 12 semester hours in each field of an approved academic major outside of education or a concentration in special education.

Students seeking licensure at the secondary level and/or K-12 level must complete a 30-semester hour teaching major in an approved teaching major field and required general education core, professional studies, field experiences, and student teaching. Middle school, reading, and Catholic schools endorsements are available.

Graduate Programs: A Master of Education degree program is available for an individual who wishes to pursue a teaching license and holds a bachelor's degree from a regionally accredited institution.

Licensure/Reciprocity: Iowa. Students seeking teaching certification in a state other than Iowa should consult with that state's teacher certification office early in their program of study to insure compliance with requirements. Many state directors of teacher credentialing have signed Interstate Agreements through NASDTEC that expedite the certification process.

COE COLLEGE
Teacher Education
1220 First Avenue N.E.
Cedar Rapids, Iowa 52402
Phone: (319) 399-8000
Fax: (319) 399-8830
E-mail: o-admissions@coe.edu
Internet: http://www.coe.edu

Institution Description: Coe College is a private institution affiliated with the United Presbyterian Church in the United States of America. It was established as Cedar Rapids Collegiate Institute and offered first instruction at the postsecondary level 1851. Leander Clark College was absorbed in 1919.

The Teacher Education Department combines a liberal arts education with courses in the theory and practice of teaching.

Institution Control: Private.

COE COLLEGE—cont'd

Calendar: Semester. Academic year August to May.

Official(s): Dr. McNabb, Chair, Teacher Education.

Degrees Awarded: 27 baccalaureate; 9 master's.

Admission Requirements: *Undergraduate:* Graduation from an approved secondary school or GED; College Board SAT or ACT composite. *Teacher education specific:* Application for admission after completion of the course in Educational Foundations; 2.5 GPA; student essay; PRAXIS I test; faculty interview.

Fees and Expenses: $20,540 per academic year. On-campus room and board: $5,610. Other expenses: $1,600. Books and supplies: $800.

Financial Aid: Resources specifically for eligible students enrolled in teacher education programs are awarded on the basis of financial need and academic merit. The institution has a Program Participation Agreement with the U.S. Department of Education for eligible students to receive Pell Grants and other federal aid. *Contact:* Financial Aid Office at: (319) 399-8540.

Accreditation: *Regional:* NCA. *Member of:* AACTE. *Approved by:* Iowa Department of Education.

Undergraduate Programs: The Bachelor of Arts in elementary education and liberal studies requires 10 course credits in liberal arts, a general education core; professional studies, special methods courses, and student teaching. elementary endorsements (grades K-6) include art, English/language arts, French, German, Spanish, health, history, math, music, physical education, science, social studies, and reading.

The Bachelor of Arts in secondary education requires the completion of a subject area major, a general education core, professional studies, and student teaching (in middle school, junior high school, or senior high school).

Licensure/Reciprocity: Iowa. Students seeking teaching certification in a state other than Iowa should consult with that state's teacher certification office early in their program of study to insure compliance with requirements. Many state directors of teacher credentialing have signed Interstate Agreements through NASDTEC that expedite the certification process.

DRAKE UNIVERSITY

School of Education
Teaching and Learning
2507 University Avenue
Des Moines, Iowa 50311
Phone: (515) 271-3911
Fax: (515) 271-2831
E-mail: salina.shrofel@drake.edu
Internet: http://www.drake.edu

Institution Description: Drake University is a private, independent, nonprofit institution. It was founded by the Disciples of Christ through transfer of faculty of Oskaloosa College in 1881.

The School of Education offers undergraduate and master degree programs leading to elementary or secondary licensure with a variety of specialties and endorsements.

Institution Control: Private.

Calendar: Semester. Academic year August to May.

Official(s): Dr. Salina Shrofel, Dean, School of Education; Dr. Eunice Merideth, Chair, Teaching and Learning.

Faculty: Full-time 23.

Degrees Awarded: 57 baccalaureate; 20 master's; 10 doctorate.

Admission Requirements: *Undergraduate:* Graduation from an approved high school or GED; minimum 2.5 GPA; College Board SAT or ACT composite. *Teacher education specific:* Application to Teaching and Learning by sophomore year; declaration of major; PRAXIS I test; faculty interview. *Graduate:* Baccalaureate degree from a regionally accredited institution. *Teacher education specific:* PRAXIS I and II tests; GRE; goal statement; faculty interview.

Fees and Expenses: Undergraduate: $18,390 per academic year. Graduate: Tuition charged per credit hour. On-campus room and board: $5,490. Other expenses: $1,975. Books and supplies: $700.

Financial Aid: Resources specifically for eligible students enrolled in teacher education programs are awarded on the basis of financial need and academic merit. The institution has a Program Participation Agreement with the U.S. Department of Education for eligible students to receive Pell Grants and other federal aid. The School of Education offers approximately $30,000 in scholarships each year for students who exhibit academic excellence and good character. The state of Iowa also offers forgivable loans for teachers in areas of need. *Contact:* Financial Aid Office at: (515) 271-2905.

Accreditation: *Regional:* NCA. *Member of:* AACTE. *Approved by:* Iowa Department of Education.

Undergraduate Programs: The School of Education offers a strong professional program with a solid foundation in the arts and sciences, providing knowledge and perspective for disciplines taught in elementary schools. The Drake curriculum requires first-year seminars that foster development of critical thinking and written and oral communication skills through a topical focus, and a senior capstone.

The school supports subject endorsements at the elementary level (K-6) in art, early childhood, English/language arts, health, mathematics, reading, history, science, theater and communication studies, social studies, and unified (early childhood with emphasis on special education). The program leads to the Bachelor of Science in Education.

The secondary education endorsements include middle school, special education, reading, early childhood, and united early childhood. The program leads to the Bachelor of Science in Education.

Graduate Programs: The Master of Arts in Teaching degree is offered and leads to secondary certification. The Master of Science in Teaching leads to elementary certification. Master's programs for currently certified teachers includes the Master of Education in early childhood; the Master of Special Education, and the Master of Science in effective teaching, learning, and leadership.

Licensure/Reciprocity: Iowa. Students seeking teaching certification in a state other than Iowa should consult with that state's teacher certification office early in their program of study to insure compliance with requirements. Many state directors of teacher credentialing have signed Interstate Agreements through NASDTEC that expedite the certification process.

GRACELAND UNIVERSITY

School of Education
Teacher Education Program
700 College Avenue
Lamoni, Iowa 50140
Phone: (641) 784-5000
Fax: (515) 784-5453
E-mail: education@graceland.edu
Internet: http://www.graceland.edu

Institution Description: Graceland University, formerly Graceland College, is a private institution affiliated with Reorganized Church of Jesus Christ of Latter Day Saints. The school was reorganized as junior college 1920 and reestablished at the senior level 1960. It became Graceland University in 2000.

The Teacher Education Program offers programs leading to the bachelor's degree.

Institution Control: Private.

Calendar: Semester. Academic year August to May.

Official(s): Dr. William L. Armstrong, Dean.

Faculty: Full-time 15; emeriti 5.

Degrees Awarded: 117 baccalaureate; 46 master's.

Admission Requirements: *Undergraduate:* Graduation from an approved secondary school or GED; 2.0 GPA; College Board SAT combined score of 960 or ACT composite score of 21.

Teacher education specific: Acceptance into the program by the sophomore year; declaration of major; personal goal statement; PRAXIS I test; faculty interview.

Fees and Expenses: $13,750 per academic year. On-campus room and board: $4,530. Other expenses: $1,210. Books and supplies: $750.

Financial Aid: Resources specifically for eligible students enrolled in teacher education programs are awarded on the basis of financial need and academic merit. The institution has a Program Participation Agreement with the U.S. Department of Education for eligible students to receive Pell Grants and other federal aid. *Contact:* Financial Aid Office at: (641) 784-5140.

Accreditation: *Regional:* NCA. *Professional:* NCATE. *Approved by:* Iowa Department of Education.

Undergraduate Programs: Students working toward the Bachelor of Arts degree with an elementary education major (K-6 grade level) must complete in addition to the general education requirements, major requirements, and one approved concentration. Concentrations are available in art, English/language arts, foreign language, health, mathematics, music, physical education, reading, social science/history, social science/social studies, speech communication/theater. Student teaching begins in the senior year.

The Bachelor of Arts degree with a major in secondary education (7-12 grade level) must complete, in addition to the general education requirements, a secondary teaching major in the following endorsements: art, biology, chemistry, English, German, health, history, mathematics, music, physical education, Spanish, speech communication, theater.

A secondary education student majoring in art, music, or physical education may also complete a modified teacher education program adding an elementary level endorsement in the same field (e.g., secondary and elementary music).

Licensure/Reciprocity: Iowa. Students seeking teaching certification in a state other than Iowa should consult with that state's teacher certification office early in their program of study to insure compliance with requirements. Many state directors of teacher credentialing have signed Interstate Agreements through NASDTEC that expedite the certification process.

GRAND VIEW COLLEGE
Education Department
Teacher Education Program
1200 Grandview Avenue
Des Moines, Iowa 50316
Phone: (515) 263-2800
Fax: (515) 263-6095
E-mail: admissions@gvc.edu
Internet: http://www.gvc.edu

Institution Description: Grand View College is a private college affiliated with the Evangelical Lutheran Church in America. It was established and chartered in 1896.

The Teacher Education Program is committed to the preparation of teachers within the liberal arts tradition.

Institution Control: Private.

Calendar: Semester. Academic year August to April.

Official(s): Dr. Robin Trimble White, Chair, Education Department and Director of Teacher Education Program.

Faculty: Full-time 7; adjunct 4.

Degrees Awarded: 48 baccalaureate.

Admission Requirements: *Undergraduate:* Graduation from an approved secondary school or GED; College Board SAT or ACT composite. *Teacher education specific:* 2.5 GPA in pre-education curriculum; successful completion of College English proficiency requirement; passing score on PRAXIS I; satisfactory references.

Fees and Expenses: $14,194 per academic year. On-campus room and board: $4,798. Other expenses: $3,214. Books and supplies: $600.

Financial Aid: Resources specifically for eligible students enrolled in teacher education programs are awarded on the basis of financial need and academic merit. The institution has a

Program Participation Agreement with the U.S. Department of Education for eligible students to receive Pell Grants and other federal aid. *Contact:* Financial Aid Office at: (515) 263-2820.

Accreditation: *Regional:* NCA. *Member of:* AACTE. *Approved by:* Iowa Department of Education.

Undergraduate Programs: The elementary education program aims to prepare students to be teachers in public and private elementary schools. It combines a strong liberal arts background with rigorous professional development, The apprenticeship model requires extensive practical experience in public and private school classrooms in preparation for the final semester of student teaching. Students must select at least one endorsement. The curriculum requires the completion of 130 credit hours.

The secondary education program requires the completion of 130 credit hours including a general education core and major in one of the following majors: art, biology, business, English, general science, mathematics, music, social science. secondary endorsements are also offered. In-school experiences are available at locations in Des Moines and the surrounding suburban and small community school districts.

Licensure/Reciprocity: Iowa. Students seeking teaching certification in a state other than Iowa should consult with that state's teacher certification office early in their program of study to insure compliance with requirements. Many state directors of teacher credentialing have signed Interstate Agreements through NASDTEC that expedite the certification process.

GRINNELL COLLEGE
Department of Education
Grinnell, Iowa 50112
Phone: (641) 269-4871
Fax: (641) 269-4414
E-mail: ketter@grinnell.edu
Internet: http://www.grinnell.edu

Institution Description: Grinnell College is a private, independent institution that was established in 1846.

The Department of Education is a member of the Division of Social Studies. The department seeks to develop each student's ability to analyze problems in education, to evaluate proposed solutions, and to act upon the results of that analysis in ethical ways.

Institution Control: Private.

Calendar: Semester. Academic year August to May.

Official(s): Dr. Jean Ketter, Dean.

Degrees Awarded: 11 baccalaureate.

Admission Requirements: *Undergraduate:* Graduation with 16 academic units from an approved secondary school. College Board SAT or ACT composite. *Teacher education specific:* Students seeking licensure must apply to enter the Practitioner Preparation Program no later than the deadline for declaring a major, usually in the second semester of the sophomore year; PRAXIS I; faculty interview.

Fees and Expenses: $22,900 per academic year. On-campus room and board: $6,330. Required fees: $630. Books and supplies: $700 per year.

Financial Aid: Resources specifically for eligible students enrolled in teacher education programs are awarded on the basis of financial need and academic merit. The institution has a Program Participation Agreement with the U.S. Department of Education for eligible students to receive Pell Grants and other federal aid. *Contact:* Arnold Woods at (641) 269-3250 or e-mail at woods@grinnell.edu.

Accreditation: *Regional:* NCA. *Member of:* AACTE. *Approved by:* Iowa Department of Education.

Undergraduate Programs: Baccalaureate programs leading to secondary licensure are available in the areas of: American history, anthropology, art, biology, chemistry, economics, English, French, German, general science, Latin, mathematics, physics, psychology, Russian, Spanish, sociology, and world history. A

GRINNELL COLLEGE—cont'd

total of 124 credit hours must be completed including a general education core, field experiences, subject area major, and student teaching.

Programs leading to elementary licensure include a general education core, professional studies, an approved major, and an approved course in each: mathematics, humanities, American history, coursework in both a biological and physical science. The completion of 124 credit hours also includes field experiences and student teaching.

Licensure/Reciprocity: Iowa. Students seeking teaching certification in a state other than Iowa should consult with that state's teacher certification office early in their program of study to insure compliance with requirements. Many state directors of teacher credentialing have signed Interstate Agreements through NASDTEC that expedite the certification process.

IOWA STATE UNIVERSITY

College of Education
Teacher Education Program

Ames, Iowa 50011
Phone: (806) 262-3810
Fax: (806) 294-2592
E-mail: coe@iastate.edu
Internet: http://www.iastate.edu

Institution Description: Iowa State University is a public institution. It was established and incorporated as Iowa Agricultural College in 1858. The present name was adopted in 1959.

The Teacher Education Program leads to licensure to teach at the elementary or secondary level.

Institution Control: Public.

Calendar: Semester. Academic year August to May.

Official(s): Dr. Thomas Andre, Chair, Curriculum and Instruction.

Faculty: Full-time and part-time 126.

Degrees Awarded: 359 baccalaureate; 142 master's; 32 doctorate.

Admission Requirements: *Undergraduate:* Graduation from an approved secondary school or GED; College Board SAT or ACT composite. *Teacher education specific:* Student must be accepted by a selection committee; factors considered include scholarship, interest in teaching, character, and physical and mental health. *Graduate:* Baccalaureate degree from a regionally accredited institution. *Teacher education specific:* PRAXIS I and II; consultation with a coordinator in the area in which the student desires to teach; faculty interview.

Fees and Expenses: Undergraduate: in-state $4,110 per academic year; out-of-state $12,802. Graduate: Tuition is charged per credit hour. Other expenses: $2,385. On-campus room and board: $5,020. Books and supplies: $754.

Financial Aid: Resources specifically for eligible students enrolled in teacher education programs are awarded on the basis of financial need and academic merit. The institution has a Program Participation Agreement with the U.S. Department of Education for eligible students to receive Pell Grants and other federal aid. *Contact:* Financial Aid Office at: (515) 294-2223.

Accreditation: *Regional:* NCA. *Member of:* AACTE. *Approved by:* Iowa Department of Education.

Undergraduate Programs: All prospective teachers are required to complete a program in general education which is integrated with their professional training and extends through the undergraduate curriculum. A professional teacher education requirement includes certain studies related directly to the profession of teaching. The areas of specialization available include: agricultural sciences and agribusiness, biology, chemistry, coaching interscholastic athletics, curriculum and instruction, early childhood education, earth sciences, elementary education, English, English as a second language, family and consumer sciences, foreign language and literatures; general science, health education, human development and family studies, mathematics, music, physical education, physical sciences, physics, reading, special education, speech communication. A total of 122 to 134 credit hours is required for the baccalaureate degree including field experiences and student teaching.

Graduate Programs: Master's degree and doctoral programs are also offered with emphases in the areas described above.

Licensure/Reciprocity: Iowa. Students seeking teaching certification in a state other than Iowa should consult with that state's teacher certification office early in their program of study to insure compliance with requirements. Many state directors of teacher credentialing have signed Interstate Agreements through NASDTEC that expedite the certification process.

LORAS COLLEGE

Department of Education
Teacher Licensure Programs

1450 Alta Vista Street
Dubuque, Iowa 52001
Phone: (563) 588-7836
Fax: (563) 588-7964
E-mail: David_Salyer@loras.edu
Internet: http://www.loras.edu

Institution Description: Loras College is a private college affiliated with the Archdiocese of Dubuque, Roman Catholic Church. It was established as Saint Raphael's Seminary for men in 1839. After several name changes over the years, the present name was adopted in 1939. Women were admitted in 1971.

The Department of Education offers a variety of programs with 50 licensure and endorsement programs including Teachers for Catholic Schools.

Institution Control: Private.

Calendar: Semester. Academic year August to May.

Official(s): Dr. David M. Salyer, Chair, Department of Education.

Faculty: Full-time 10.

Degrees Awarded: 65 baccalaureate; 12 master's.

Admission Requirements: *Undergraduate:* Graduation from an accredited secondary school or GED; College Board SAT or ACT composite. *Teacher education specific:* Student must make application to the Department of Education during the sophomore year; 2.5 GPA in all coursework attempted; declaration of major with the Office of Academic Affairs; completed required education courses; faculty interview.

Fees and Expenses: $17,949 per academic year. Other expenses: $1,000. On-campus room and board: $5,895. Books and supplies: $1,100.

Financial Aid: Resources specifically for eligible students enrolled in teacher education programs are awarded on the basis of financial need and academic merit. The institution has a Program Participation Agreement with the U.S. Department of Education for eligible students to receive Pell Grants and other federal aid. *Contact:* Financial Aid Office at: (563) 588-7136.

Accreditation: *Regional:* NCA. *Member of:* AACTE. *Approved by:* Iowa Department of Education.

Undergraduate Programs: All students enrolled in teaching licensure programs must complete a general education core, professional studies, area major, field experiences, and student teaching. All baccalaureate degrees require the completion of 120 semester hours. Majors are offered in elementary education; unified early childhood education; behavioral disorders, K-6, special education; behavioral disorders, 7-12, special education; mental disabilities, K-6, special education.

Students seeking licensure at the secondary and/or K-12 level must have an academic major outside of education in an approved teaching major field in addition to their teacher education major. Secondary programs include: secondary education, 7-12; art, K-12; music, K-12; physical education, K-12.

Licensure/Reciprocity: Iowa. Students seeking teaching certification in a state other than Iowa should consult with that state's teacher certification office early in their program of study to insure compliance with requirements. Many state directors of teacher credentialing have signed Interstate Agreements through NASDTEC that expedite the certification process.

LUTHER COLLEGE

Education Department
Koren Hall
700 College Drive
Decorah, Iowa 52101-1045
Phone: (563) 387-2000
Fax: (563) 387-1107
E-mail: nyejudy@luther.edu
Internet: http://www.luther.edu

Institution Description: Luther College is a private institution affiliated with The Evangelical Lutheran Church in America. It was established as a college for men in 1861. It became coeducational in 1936.

The Education Department believes that a strong liberal arts background prepares the student for specialization in the educational program.

Institution Control: Private.

Calendar: Semester. Academic year September to May.

Official(s): Dr, Judith Bowstead Nye, Chair, Department of Education.

Faculty: Full-time 12.

Degrees Awarded: 57 baccalaureate.

Admission Requirements: *Undergraduate:* Graduation from an approved secondary school or GED; lowest acceptable high school standing 50th %ile; College Board SAT or ACT composite. *Teacher education specific:* Application to teacher education program in sophomore year; completion of basic education courses; PRAXIS I; declaration of major field; faculty interview.

Fees and Expenses: $20,310 per academic year. On-campus room and board: $4,040. Other expenses: $2,255. Books and supplies: $710.

Financial Aid: Resources specifically for eligible students enrolled in teacher education programs are awarded on the basis of financial need and academic merit. The institution has a Program Participation Agreement with the U.S. Department of Education for eligible students to receive Pell Grants and other federal aid. *Contact:* Financial Aid Office at: (563) 387-1018.

Accreditation: *Regional:* NCA. *Professional:* NCATE. *Member of:* AACTE. *Approved by:* Iowa Department of Education.

Undergraduate Programs: The Bachelor of Arts in Education leading to licensure for secondary school teaching requires the completion of a general education core, professional studies, subject area major, field experiences, and student teaching. Major areas include: American government, American history, anthropology, art, biology, business, chemistry, coaching, economics, English/language arts, German, Latin, Spanish, French, health, mathematics, music, physical education, science, psychology, world history, sociology, speech communication/theater.

The baccalaureate program leading to licensure for elementary school teaching includes endorsements in art (K-6); English/language arts K-6; health academic endorsement (K-6); music (K-6); physical education (K-6); science (K-6); social studies (K-6); Spanish (K-6); speech communications (K-6). Other endorsements include: early childhood, middle school, learning disabilities, English as a second language, multicategorical resource endorsement-mild, and reading. The baccalaureate programs require the completion of general education core, professional studies, major area, field experiences, and student teaching for a total of 128 credit hours.

Licensure/Reciprocity: Iowa. Students seeking teaching certification in a state other than Iowa should consult with that state's teacher certification office early in their program of study to insure compliance with requirements. Many state directors of teacher credentialing have signed Interstate Agreements through NASDTEC that expedite the certification process.

MORNINGSIDE COLLEGE

Education Department
Teacher Education Program
1501 Morningside Avenue
Sioux City, Iowa 51106
Phone: (712) 274-5000
Fax: (712) 274-5101
E-mail: cutler@morningside.edu
Internet: http://www.morningside.edu

Institution Description: Morningside College is a private institution affiliated with The United Methodist Church. It was established as the University of the Northwest in 1889 under the auspices of the Northwest Town Conference of the Methodist Episcopal Church. The present name was adopted in 1894 and absorbed Charles City College in 1914.

The Education Department offers programs leading to professional teaching credentials in elementary and secondary education.

Institution Control: Private.

Calendar: Semester. Academic year August to May.

Official(s): Dr. Susan K. Cutler, Dean, Teacher Education Program.

Faculty: Full-time 6.

Degrees Awarded: 45 baccalaureate; 66 master's.

Admission Requirements: *Undergraduate:* Graduation from an approved secondary school or GED; College Board SAT or ACT composite. *Teacher education specific:* Application to teacher education program by sophomore year; PRAXIS I; personal goal statement; declaration of major; faculty interview.

Fees and Expenses: Undergraduate: $15,400 per academic year. Graduate: Tuition charge per credit hour. General fee: $900. On-campus room: $2,750; board $2,510. Books and supplies: $800.

Financial Aid: Resources specifically for eligible students enrolled in teacher education programs are awarded on the basis of financial need and academic merit. The institution has a Program Participation Agreement with the U.S. Department of Education for eligible students to receive Pell Grants and other federal aid. *Contact:* Financial Aid Office at: (712) 274-5159.

Accreditation: *Regional:* NCA. *Professional:* NCATE. *Member of:* AACTE. *Approved by:* Iowa Department of Education.

Undergraduate Programs: Programs leading to the bachelor's degree and state licensure include programs in elementary education (dual major with special education) and secondary education. All programs require the completion of a general education core, professional studies, subject major, field experiences, and student teaching for a total of 124 credit hours. The secondary education program includes areas of concentration in: art, biology, business education, chemistry, English, history, mathematics, music, physics, political science, psychology, social studies, Spanish.

Graduate Programs: A Master of Arts in Teaching degree is offered through the Department of Graduate Studies. For particulars of this program, contact Dr. Glenna Tevis at (712) 274-5269.

Licensure/Reciprocity: Iowa. Students seeking teaching certification in a state other than Iowa should consult with that state's teacher certification office early in their program of study to insure compliance with requirements. Many state directors of teacher credentialing have signed Interstate Agreements through NASDTEC that expedite the certification process.

NORTHWESTERN COLLEGE

Education Department
101 7th Street, S.W.
Orange City, Iowa 51041-1996
Phone: (712) 707-7002
Fax: (712) 707-7037
E-mail: Schulte@nwciowa.edu
Internet: http://www.nwciowa.edu

NORTHWESTERN COLLEGE—cont'd

Institution Description: Northwestern College is a private Christian liberal arts college affiliated with the Reformed Church in America. It was established as Northwestern Classical Academy in 1882. The school became a four-year college and the present name was adopted in 1957.

The Teacher Education Program commits itself to a Christ-centered holistic development of teachers to serve society in diverse classroom settings.

Institution Control: Private.

Calendar: Semester. Academic year August to May.

Official(s): Dr. Ed Starkenburg, Dean.

Faculty: Full-time 5; part-time 2; adjunct 1.

Degrees Awarded: 65 baccalaureate.

Admission Requirements: *Undergraduate:* Graduation from an accredited secondary school or GED; College Board SAT or ACT composite; minimum 2.0; lowest secondary class standing 50th %ile. *Teacher education specific:* Passing scores on PRAXIS I; written recommendation from the department of the student's major subject field; completion of an entrance portfolio; cumulative 2.5 GPA; faculty interview.

Fees and Expenses: $15,290 per academic year. On-campus room and board: $4,350. Books and supplies: $500 per year.

Financial Aid: Resources specifically for eligible students enrolled in teacher education programs are awarded on the basis of financial need and academic merit. The institution has a Program Participation Agreement with the U.S. Department of Education for eligible students to receive Pell Grants and other federal aid. *Contact:* Gena Schmidt, Financial Aid Assistant at:(712) 707-7130 or e-mail at gena@nwciowa.edu.

Accreditation: *Regional:* NCA. *Professional:* NCATE. *Member of:* AACTE. *Approved by:* Iowa Department of Education.

Undergraduate Programs: The School of Education offers the following basic programs leading to the bachelor's degree and licensure: elementary endorsement (K-6), secondary endorsement (7-12) that also requires an approved major; coaching authorization. Other specialized programs include endorsements in: unified early childhood education, early childhood education; instructional strategist (K-6, K-12); reading (K-6); middle school (5-8); English as a second language (K-12). All programs require the completion of a general education core, professional studies, subject major, field experiences, and student teaching for a total of 124 credit hours.

Licensure/Reciprocity: Iowa. Students seeking teaching certification in a state other than Iowa should consult with that state's teacher certification office early in their program of study to insure compliance with requirements. Many state directors of teacher credentialing have signed Interstate Agreements through NASDTEC that expedite the certification process.

ST. AMBROSE UNIVERSITY

College of Education and Health Sciences
Teacher Education Program

518 West Locust Street
Davenport, Iowa 52803-2898
Phone: (563) 333-6115
Fax: (563) 333-6799
E-mail: education@sau.edu
Internet: http://www.sau.edu

Institution Description: St. Ambrose University, formerly St. Ambrose College, is a private, nonprofit institution affiliated with the Roman Catholic Church. It was established as St. Ambrose Seminary in 1882. The school adopted the St. Ambrose College name in 1928 and that was officially changed to St. Ambrose University in 1987.

The Practitioner Preparation (Teacher Education) Program at St. Ambrose University includes areas of study necessary to prepare highly professional classroom teachers, and enables the student to receive an initial license to teach in Iowa agencies and schools.

Institution Control: Private.

Calendar: Semester. Academic year August to May.

Official(s): Dr. Robert S. Risbow, Dean; Dr. Dean Marple, Chair, Department of Secondary Education; Dr. Rachel Serianz, Chair, Elementary Science; Dr. William Hitchings, Dean, Special Education.

Faculty: Full-time 13; part-time 5; adjunct 10.

Degrees Awarded: 79 baccalaureate; 19 master's.

Admission Requirements: *Undergraduate:* Graduation from an approved secondary school or GED; 2.5 minimum GPA and either high school rank in the upper 50% or ACT composite score of 21. *Teacher education specific:* Maintain a 2.7 cumulative GPA; 3.0 GPA in education; 3.0 GPA in major field (for early childhood and secondary majors); pass C-BASE examination; complete 70 field hours in EDUC 205; faculty evaluation.

Fees and Expenses: Undergraduate $8,325 per academic year. On-campus room: $1,350 to $2,160; board: $1,300 to $1,640.

Financial Aid: Resources specifically for eligible students enrolled in teacher education programs are awarded on the basis of financial need and academic merit. The institution has a Program Participation Agreement with the U.S. Department of Education for eligible students to receive Pell Grants and other federal aid. *Contact:* Julie Huack at: (563) 333-6314 or e=mail at huackjulie@sau;.edu.

Accreditation: *Regional:* NCA. *Approved by:* Iowa Department of Education.

Undergraduate Programs: The Education Department offers a variety of programs, all of which require the completion of a general education core, professional studies, field experiences, and student teaching for a total of 120 semester hours.

The department offers an endorsement in early childhood education. This endorsement allows individuals to be licensed to teach children from birth to third grade in a variety of settings such as preschools and primary elementary classes. Teachers in this specialty are equipped to address the needs of all children,

The elementary education major allows a student to teach in a self-contained classroom for grades kindergarten through sixth. In addition, each elementary major also completes additional courses which add an endorsement to the elementary license in areas of: English/language arts, mathematics, reading, science, social studies, and special education.

A secondary teaching license in Iowa allows the license holder to teach in grades 7 through 12. Each secondary license also includes an endorsement teaching area. Endorsements are offered in the areas of: American government, art (K-12), biology, business education, chemistry, economics, English, French, general science, German, health, history, mathematics, music (K-12), physical education (K-12), physics, psychology, reading, sociology, Spanish, speech communication/theater.

Licensure/Reciprocity: Iowa. Students seeking teaching certification in a state other than Iowa should consult with that state's teacher certification office early in their program of study to insure compliance with requirements. Many state directors of teacher credentialing have signed Interstate Agreements through NASDTEC that expedite the certification process.

UNIVERSITY OF IOWA

College of Education
Department of Curriculum and Instruction

N549 Lindquist Center
Iowa City, Iowa 52242
Phone: (319) 335-5359
Fax: (319) 335-5364
E-mail: coe-tess@uiowa.edu
Internet: http//www.uiowa.edu

Institution Description: The University of Iowa is a state institution. The university was chartered in 1847 under its present official name, State University of Iowa.

The Office of Teacher Education and Student Services coordinates the programs at both the undergraduate and graduate levels.

Institution Control: Public.

Calendar: Semester. Academic year August to May.

Official(s): Dr. Sandra Damico, Dean.

Faculty: Full-time 98; part-time 3; adjunct 14.

Degrees Awarded: 192 baccalaureate; 147 master's; 49 doctorate.

Admission Requirements: *Undergraduate:* Graduation from an approved secondary school; applicants must have completed a prescribed set of high school courses; College Board SAT or ACT composite. *Teacher education specific:* Student must have attained sophomore standing; 2.70 GPA of all college coursework; completed the 10-hour volunteer experience; PRAXIS I test scores; faculty interview. *Graduate:* Baccalaureate degree from a regionally accredited institution. *Teacher education specific:* Application to the Graduate College must be filed; letters of recommendation; faculty interview; pass all required departmental tests/exams.

Fees and Expenses: Undergraduate: resident $4,993 including fees per academic year; nonresident $12,285. On-campus room and board: $5,930. Books and supplies: $840.

Financial Aid: Resources specifically for eligible students enrolled in teacher education programs are awarded on the basis of financial need and academic merit. The institution has a Program Participation Agreement with the U.S. Department of Education for eligible students to receive Pell Grants and other federal aid. *Contact:* Mark Warner at: (319) 335-1450 or e-mail at financial-aid@uiowa.edu.

Accreditation: *Regional:* NCA. *Member of:* AACTE. *Approved by:* Iowa Department of Education.

Undergraduate Programs: Teacher Education Programs prepare students to teach in early childhood, elementary, and secondary schools. Undergraduate students seeking secondary school licensure/certification are degree candidates in the College of Liberal Arts and Sciences and must complete the requirements for the Bachelor of Arts, Bachelor of Science, or Bachelor of Music degrees. Before taking required professional education courses, undergraduate students must be admitted to the Teacher Education Program. All undergraduate degree programs required the completion of 120 credit hours including a general education core, program major, professional studies, and student teaching.

Graduate Programs: The Master of Arts program in early childhood education is designed to prepare individuals to administer programs and/or deliver education and care to children from infancy through early primary grades in private or public settings. The Master of Arts in elementary education is designed to prepare candidates to serve as team leaders, grade level or subject area supervisors, curriculum consultants, or master teachers.

Advanced degree programs are offered and jointly administered with departments in the College of Liberal Arts in the following fields of professional interest: art education, communication studies education, curriculum and supervisions, developmental reading, English education, foreign language education, mathematics education, music education, physical education, science education, social studies education, and special education. Completion of the programs lead to the Master of Arts degree.

Licensure/Reciprocity: Iowa. Students seeking teaching certification in a state other than Iowa should consult with that state's teacher certification office early in their program of study to insure compliance with requirements. Many state directors of teacher credentialing have signed Interstate Agreements through NASDTEC that expedite the certification process.

UNIVERSITY OF NORTHERN IOWA
College of Education
Department of Curriculum and Instruction
612 Schindler Education Center
1227 West 27th Street
Cedar Falls, Iowa 50614-0606
Phone: (319) 273-2167
Fax: (319) 273-5886
E-mail: Rick.Traw@uni.edu
Internet: http://www.uni.edu

Institution Description: The University of Northern Iowa is a state institution. It was established as Iowa State Normal School in 1876. The name was changed to Iowa State Teachers College in 1909, to State College of Iowa in 1961, and the present name was adopted in 1967.

The Department of Curriculum and instruction administers the teacher education program. The department's mission is to prepare professionals who demonstrate capable performance and insightful leadership for entry level and senior positions.

Institution Control: Public.

Calendar: Semester. Academic year August to May.

Official(s): Dr. Rick Traw, Department Head; Dr. Jerri Schroeder, Chair, Teaching Program.

Faculty: Full-time 43 (College of Education).

Degrees Awarded: 582 baccalaureate; 165 master's; 10 doctorate.

Admission Requirements: *Undergraduate:* Graduation from an approved secondary school or GED; College Board SAT or ACT composite. *Teacher education specific:* Application to teaching program by sophomore year; declaration of major in which student desires to teach; PRAXIS series scores; faculty interview. *Graduate:* Baccalaureate degree from a regionally accredited institution. *Teacher education specific:* Completion of all departmental tests/exams; personal goal statement; recommendations; faculty interview.

Fees and Expenses: Undergraduate: in-state $4,118 per academic year; $10,426 out-of-state. On-campus room and board: $4,540. Other expenses: $2,945. Books and supplies: $800.

Financial Aid: Resources specifically for eligible students enrolled in teacher education programs are awarded on the basis of financial need and academic merit. The institution has a Program Participation Agreement with the U.S. Department of Education for eligible students to receive Pell Grants and other federal aid. *Contact:* Financial Aid Office at: (319) 273-2700.

Accreditation: *Regional:* NCA. *Member of:* AACTE. *Approved by:* Iowa Department of Education.

Undergraduate Programs: The Bachelor of Arts - Teaching Program requires the completion of 130 semester hours. On this program, students are prepared as teachers of art, business education, communications, geography, English, foreign languages, health, industrial arts, mathematics, physical education, science, social science subjects (economics, history, political science), and speech. Also, a program in special education for teachers of art, industrial arts, music, physical education, special education, and speech correction. There are also program in early childhood and elementary education (kindergarten through sixth grade) and middle eevel education in various areas of instruction. The programs require completion of a general education core, subject area major, field experiences, and student teaching.

Graduate Programs: The Master of Arts in Education requires the completion of a minimum of 30 semester hours. The degree is designed for students whose work is primarily in professional education. Majors are available in curriculum and instruction, early childhood education, educational psychology; educational technology, postsecondary education (student affairs), principalship, school counseling, and special education.

UNIVERSITY OF NORTHERN IOWA—*cont'd*

The Master of Arts requires the minimum of 30 semester hours. Programs are available for advanced preparation of elementary and secondary teachers, for college teaching, including programs for Iowa Public Junior College licensure, and for graduate study without reference to teaching.

Licensure/Reciprocity: Iowa. Students seeking teaching certification in a state other than Iowa should consult with that state's teacher certification office early in their program of study to insure compliance with requirements. Many state directors of teacher credentialing have signed Interstate Agreements through NASDTEC that expedite the certification process.

WARTBURG COLLEGE

Education Department

100 Wartburg Boulevard
Waverly, Iowa 50677
Phone: (319) 352-4226
Fax: (319) 352-8583
E-mail: Cheryl.budlong@wartburg.edu
Internet: http://www.wartburg.edu

Institution Description: Wartburg College is a private institution affiliated with The Evangelical Lutheran Church in America. It was chartered as Wartburg Normal School in 1852. The name was changed to Wartburg Normal College in 1920. The school merged with four other Lutheran colleges and the present name was adopted in 1935.

The Education Department offers undergraduate teacher preparation programs.

Institution Control: Private.

Calendar: Semester (4-4-1 plan). Academic year September to May.

Official(s): Dr. Cheryl Budlong, Department Head.

Faculty: Full-time 6; adjunct 5.

Degrees Awarded: 78 baccalaureate.

Admission Requirements: *Undergraduate:* Graduation from an approved secondary school or GED; College Board SAT or ACT composite. *Teacher education specific:* Admittance to teacher program by sophomore year; declaration of a subject area major; PRAXIS I score of 174; adviser recommendation. faculty interview.

Fees and Expenses: $17,150 per academic year. On-campus room and board: $4,800. Required fees: $380 per term.

Financial Aid: Resources specifically for eligible students enrolled in teacher education programs are awarded on the basis of financial need and academic merit. The institution has a Program Participation Agreement with the U.S. Department of Education for eligible students to receive Pell Grants and other federal aid. *Contact:* Jennifer Sassman at: (319) 352-8262.

Accreditation: *Regional:* NCA. *Professional:* NCATE. *Member of:* AACTE. *Approved by:* Iowa Department of Education.

Undergraduate Programs: Education programs are based on a solid liberal arts background. As early as the first year, prospective teachers may become involved in teaching activities. Throughout the program, one-on-one tutoring and small- and large-group presentations are components of practicum experiences. Methods courses emphasize instructional planning, a variety of teaching strategies, and technology integration. Before graduation, all teacher education students must complete a 25 hour experience in a cultural setting significantly different from their own. The culminating experience is student teaching, integrating preparation with practice.

Licensure/Reciprocity: Iowa. Students seeking teaching certification in a state other than Iowa should consult with that state's teacher certification office early in their program of study to insure compliance with requirements. Many state directors of teacher credentialing have signed Interstate Agreements through NASDTEC that expedite the certification process.

KANSAS

BAKER UNIVERSITY
Department of Education
Teacher Education Program
Eighth Street
Baldwin City, Kansas 66006-0065
Phone: (785) 594-8992
Fax: (785) 594-8363
E-mail: peggy.harris@baker.edu
Internet: http://www.baker.edu

Institution Description: Baker University is a private, independent, nonprofit institution affiliated with the United Methodist Church.

The mission of the Department of Education is to develop highly effective professional educators.

Institution Control: Private.

Calendar: Semester. Academic year September to May.

Official(s): Dr. Peggy Harris, Chair, Department of Education; Dr. Bill Neuerswander, Director of Teacher Education.

Faculty: Full-time 5; adjunct 3.

Degrees Awarded: 16 undergraduate.

Admission Requirements: *Undergraduate:* Graduation from an approved secondary school or GED; College Board SAT or ACT composite. *Teacher education specific:* Application to program by sophomore year and after completion of educational foundations course; personal goal statement; PRAXIS I test score; declaration of major subject area; faculty interview.

Fees and Expenses: $13,670 per academic year. On-campus room and board: $5,170. Other expenses: $2,760. Books and supplies: $900.

Financial Aid: Resources specifically for eligible students enrolled in teacher education programs are awarded on the basis of financial need and academic merit. The institution has a Program Participation Agreement with the U.S. Department of Education for eligible students to receive Pell Grants and other federal aid. *Contact:* Jeanne Mott at: (785) 594-64395 or e-mail at jeanne.mott@bakeru.edu.

Accreditation: *Regional:* NCA. *Professional:* NCATE. *Member of:* AACTE. *Approved by:* Kansas State Department of Education.

Undergraduate Programs: The elementary education program is built upon a strong tradition of combining theory and practice to achieve its major goal of preparing effective teachers. Majors must complete the university general education component, 37 professional education hours, and 39 hours of required elementary education courses.

The secondary education program requires the completion of a general education component, professional studies courses, a subject area major, and field experiences.

All programs lead to the baccalaureate degree and required student teaching in area schools.

Licensure/Reciprocity: Kansas. Students seeking teaching certification in a state other than Kansas should consult with that state's teacher certification office early in their program of study to insure compliance with requirements. Many state directors of teacher credentialing have signed Interstate Agreements through NASDTEC that expedite the certification process.

BENEDICTINE COLLEGE
Education Department
1020 North 2nd Street
Atchison, Kansas 66002
Phone: (913) 367-5340
Fax: (913) 367-5462
E-mail: bcadmiss@benedictine.edu
Internet: http://www.benedictine.edu

Institution Description: Benedictine College is a private, nonprofit college affiliated with the Roman Catholic Church. Saint Benedict's College wasw established to train men for the priesthood in 1859. Saint Scholastica's Academy for women was established in 1863. Saint Benedict's College merged with Mount Saint Scholastica College to form Benedictine College in 1971.

The Education Department programs call for future teachers and administrators to perceive their roles in education as developers of community.

Institution Control: Private.

Calendar: Semester. Academic year August to May.

Official(s): Dr. Dianna Henderson and Dr. Charles Osborn, Co-Chairs, Education Department.

Faculty: Full-time 56; part-time 3.

Degrees Awarded: 33 baccalaureate; 15 master's.

Admission Requirements: *Undergraduate:* Graduation from an approved secondary school or GED; College Board SAT or ACT composite. *Teacher education specific:* Application to the program by sophomore year; passing scores on PRAXIS I; declaration of major; personal goal statement; faculty interview. *Graduate:* Baccalaureate degree from a regionally accredited institution. *Teacher education specific:* Completion of all required departmental tests/exams; teaching credential where required; faculty interview.

Fees and Expenses: Undergraduate: $13,400 per academic year; graduate $240 per credit hour. On-campus room and board: $5,630. Other expenses: $2,000. Books and supplies: $900.

Financial Aid: Resources specifically for eligible students enrolled in teacher education programs are awarded on the basis of financial need and academic merit. The institution has a Program Participation Agreement with the U.S. Department of Education for eligible students to receive Pell Grants and other federal aid. *Contact:* Keith Jaloma at: (800) 467-5340 or e-mail at kjaloma@benedictine.edu.

Accreditation: *Regional:* NCA. *Professional:* NCATE. *Member of:* AACTE. *Approved:* by Kansas State Department of Education.

Undergraduate Programs: The education program is grounded in a Benedictine, liberal arts tradition and advocates that the goals and means of the educative process are complementary. The department offers both a major and minor in education. The baccalaureate programs offered include elementary, special, and secondary education with concentrations in liberal arts, foreign language, health and physical education, English, mathematics, mass communication, computer studies, natural and/or biological science, psychology, religious studies, social science, and special education. The programs require the completion of a general education core, professional studies, field experiences, subject are major, and student teaching. A minimum of 128 credit hours is required. Comprehensive exams are required in the individual fields of study.

BENEDICTINE COLLEGE—cont'd

Graduate Programs: The master's programs offered by the Education Department lead to various career options in administration, research, and teaching.

Licensure/Reciprocity: Kansas. Students seeking teaching certification in a state other than Kansas should consult with that state's teacher certification office early in their program of study to insure compliance with requirements. Many state directors of teacher credentialing have signed Interstate Agreements through NASDTEC that expedite the certification process.

BETHANY COLLEGE

Education Department
421 North First Street
Lindsborg, Kansas 67456-1897
Phone: (785) 227-3380
Fax: (785) 227-2004
E-mail: admissions@bethany1b.edu
Internet: http://www.bethanylb.edu

Institution Description: Bethany College is a private college affiliated with the Central State Synod of the Evangelical Lutheran Church in America. It was established as Bethany Academy in 1881. The present name was adopted in 1886.

The Education Department offers programs in in the areas of elementary education, pre-kindergarten to 12th grade, and secondary education.

Institution Control: Private.

Calendar: Semester. Academic year September to May.

Official(s): Dr. Marlysue Holmquist, Department Chair.

Faculty: Full-time 4.

Degrees Awarded: 30 baccalaureate.

Admission Requirements: *Undergraduate:* Graduation from an approved high school or GED; College Board SAT or ACT composite. *Teacher education specific:* Application to program by sophomore year and after completion of educational foundations course; personal goal statement; PRAXIS I test score; declaration of major subject area; faculty interview.

Fees and Expenses: $13,590 per academic year. On-campus room and board: $3,850. Other expenses: $1,810. Books and supplies: $800.

Financial Aid: Resources specifically for eligible students enrolled in teacher education programs are awarded on the basis of financial need and academic merit. The institution has a Program Participation Agreement with the U.S. Department of Education for eligible students to receive Pell Grants and other federal aid. *Contact:* Financial Aid Office at: (800) 826-2281, ext. 8114.

Accreditation: *Regional:* NCA. *Professional:* NCATE. *Member of:* AACTE. *Approved by:* Kansas State Department of Education.

Undergraduate Programs: Teaching majors are offered in the following areas with grade levels: art (preK-12); biology (6-12); business (6-12); chemistry (6-12); elementary education (K-5); English (6-12); health and physical education (preK-12); mathematics (6-12); music (preK-12); social studies (6-12). The following endorsements are available to supplement the teaching major: computer science (6-12); economics (6-12); health and physical education (6-12); history (5-8); language arts (5-8); general mathematics (6-12); mathematics (5-8); physics (5-12); psychology (6-12); general science (5-8); social studies (5-9); early childhood special education (K-6); interrelated special education (K-6 and 6-12); speech and theater (6-12).

All programs require the completion of a general education core, professional studies, subject area major, field experiences, and student teaching for a total of 128 semester hours.

Licensure/Reciprocity: Kansas. Students seeking teaching certification in a state other than Kansas should consult with that state's teacher certification office early in their program of study to insure compliance with requirements. Many state directors of teacher credentialing have signed Interstate Agreements through NASDTEC that expedite the certification process.

EMPORIA STATE UNIVERSITY

Department of Teacher Education
1200 Commercial Street
Campus Box 4036
Emporia, Kansas 66801
Phone: (620) 341-5367
Fax: (316) 341-5785
E-mail: mehringt@emporia.edu
Internet: http://www.emporia.edu

Institution Description: Emporia State University (formerly Emporia Kansas State College) is a public institution. It was established as Kansas State Normal School in 1863. The name was changed to Kansas State Teachers College in 1923, to Emporia Kansas State College in 1974, and to the current name in 1977.

Baccalaureate and graduate programs are offered by the Department of Teacher Education in a variety of subject areas.

Institution Control: Public.

Calendar: Semester. Academic year September to May.

Official(s): Dr. Teresa A. Mehring, Dean; Dr. Phillip Bennett, Associate Dean.

Faculty: Full-time 67; part-time 6.

Degrees Awarded: 229 baccalaureate; 198 master's.

Admission Requirements: *Undergraduate:* Graduation from an approved secondary school; 21 ACT or GPA of 2.0 on core curriculum or rank in top one-third of graduating class. *Teacher education specific:* Minimum 2.75 GPA in core general education courses; PRAXIS test scores of 172 in writing, 173 in reading, 174 in math; grade of C or better in selected courses. *Graduate:* Baccalaureate degree from a regionally accredited institution. *Teacher education specific:* GRE or Miller Analogies Test scores; baccalaureate degree with 2.75 GPA or better.

Fees and Expenses: Undergraduate: in-state $2,200 per academic year; out-of-state $8,338. Graduate: $2,640 in-state $8,454 out-of-state Required fees: $576. On-campus room and board: $4,222. Books and supplies: $750.

Financial Aid: Resources specifically for eligible students enrolled in teacher education programs are awarded on the basis of financial need and academic merit. The institution has a Program Participation Agreement with the U.S. Department of Education for eligible students to receive Pell Grants and other federal aid. *Contact:* Wilma Kasnic at: (620) 341-5457 or e-mail at kasnicwi@emporia.edu.

Accreditation: *Regional:* NCA. *Professional:* NCATE. *Member of:* AACTE. *Approved by:* Kansas State Department of Education.

Undergraduate Programs: All elementary education majors must complete a language arts area of concentration and then choose a second area of concentration from the areas of; art, bicultural education, coaching, early childhood education, early childhood special education, English, English as a second language, ethnic/gender studies, health education, instructional technology, mathematics, music, natural sciences, psychology, social sciences, special education, or theater/drama. The program leads to the Bachelor of Science in Education.

The Bachelor of Science in Education with a secondary education major is available to students. The program is a joint responsibility of the Department of Teacher Education and other departments of the university offering teaching field programs.

All programs require the completion of a general education core, subject area major, professional studies, field experiences, and student teaching.

Graduate Programs: The Master of Science degree in early childhood education offers areas of concentration in early childhood curriculum and instruction and early childhood special education. Certification is also available in early childhood and early childhood special education.

The Master Teacher Program is for the teaching practitioner in settings from early childhood through adolescence and young childhood. The student learns to deal more effectively with diverse student teachers and move from theory to best practice in the field.

Other graduate programs are offered by in a variety of fields and concentrations. Contact the the Department of Teacher Education for details or search their web site at http://www.emporia.edu/sleme/cima.htm.

Licensure/Reciprocity: Kansas. Students seeking teaching certification in a state other than Kansas should consult with that state's teacher certification office early in their program of study to insure compliance with requirements. Many state directors of teacher credentialing have signed Interstate Agreements through NASDTEC that expedite the certification process.

FORT HAYS STATE UNIVERSITY
College of Education and Technology
Teacher Education Department
600 Park Street
Hays, Kansas 67601-4099
Phone: (785) 628-4204
Fax: (785) 628-4140
E-mail: teachered@fhsu.edu
Internet: http://www.fhsu.edu

Institution Description: Fort Hays State University (Fort Hays Kansas State College until 1977) is a land-grant college. It was established as the Western Branch of Kansas Normal School of Emporia in 1902. The name was changed to Fort Hays Kansas State Normal School in 1914, to Kansas State Teachers College of Hays in 1923, to Fort Hays Kansas State College in 1931, and to the present name in 1977.

The primary objective of the Teacher Education Department is the preparation of teachers for grades K-6.

Institution Control: Public.

Calendar: Semester. Academic year August to May.

Official(s): Dr. Edward H. Hammon, Dean; Dr. Tom Newton, Chair, Teacher Education Department.

Faculty: Full-time 13.

Degrees Awarded: 174 baccalaureate; 100 master's.

Admission Requirements: *Undergraduate:* Graduation from an approved secondary school or GED; high school GPA 3,0; minimum ACT composite score of 24 or higher or minimum SAT score of 970. *Teacher education specific:* PRAXIS I with passing scores in minimum of two areas; two letters of recommendation from educators; faculty interview. *Graduate:* Baccalaureate from a regionally accredited institution. *Teacher education specific:* Minimum 3.0 on the last 60 hours of college coursework; official transcripts; evidence of teaching licensure; brief statement of professional goals.

Fees and Expenses: Undergraduate: $2,328 in-state per academic year; $7,488 out-of-state. Graduate: $247 per credit hour. On-campus room and board: $4,256. Other expenses: $2,750. Books and supplies: $750.

Financial Aid: Resources specifically for eligible students enrolled in teacher education programs are awarded on the basis of financial need and academic merit. The institution has a Program Participation Agreement with the U.S. Department of Education for eligible students to receive Pell Grants and other federal aid. *Contact:* Financial Aid Office at:(785) 628-4408.

Accreditation: *Regional:* NCA. *Professional:* NCATE. *Member of:* AACTE. *Approved by:* Kansas State Department of Education.

Undergraduate Programs: The elementary education program is designed to focus on themes that provide links between general education, professional education, and the practical application of field experience. The Bachelor of Science in Education is awarded upon completion of a general education core, subject area major, professional studies, and student teaching. A minimum of 124 credit hours is required for graduation.

The secondary education program leading to licensure requires the completion of required courses in a subject area offered through the liberal arts component of the university and under the advisement of the Department of Teacher Education. The program requires the completion of a minimum of 124 credit hours and includes the general education core, subject area major, professional studies, field experiences, and student teaching. The Bachelor of Science in Education award upon successful completion of all requirements.

Other options to the programs in the Teacher Education Department are available upon faculty advisement.

Graduate Programs: The Master of Science in elementary education requires a minimum of 35 graduate hours of core courses and a 12-hour specialization component (reading, English as a second language, library media, or content areas outside the Department of Teacher Education).

The Master of Science in secondary education requires a minimum of 30 graduate hours in an approved program. The student must meet all departmental and Graduate School degree requirements.

Licensure/Reciprocity: Kansas. Students seeking teaching certification in a state other than Kansas should consult with that state's teacher certification office early in their program of study to insure compliance with requirements. Many state directors of teacher credentialing have signed Interstate Agreements through NASDTEC that expedite the certification process.

FRIENDS UNIVERSITY
College of Arts and Sciences
Division of Education
116 Davis Hall
2100 University Street
Wichita, Kansas 67213-3397
Phone: (316) 295-5825
Fax: (316) 262-5027
E-mail: ppenn@friends.edu
Internet: http://www.friends.edu

Institution Description: Friends University is a private, independent, nonprofit institution. It was established in 1898 and awarded its first baccalaureate degree in 1901.

The Division of Education works closely with all kinds of schools, public and private. Over eleven majors are offered within the division.

Institution Control: Private.

Calendar: Semester. Academic year August to May.

Official(s): Dr. Patricia Penn, Division Chair.

Faculty: Full-time 4.

Degrees Awarded: 39 baccalaureate; 31 master's.

Admission Requirements: *Undergraduate:* Graduation from an approved secondary school or GED; College Board SAT or ACT composite. *Teacher education specific:* Passing scores on PRAXIS I test; application to program by sophomore year with declaration of subject area in which the student desires to teach; faculty interview. *Graduate:*Baccalaureate degree from a regionally accredited institution. *Teacher education specific:* Official transcripts; 3.0 GPA or higher in the major field of study; current teaching certificate; Miller Analogies Test score of 30 or above preferred or GRE combined score of 850 or above; minimum of one year teaching experience; two letters of recommendation; program director interview.

Fees and Expenses: $12,835 per academic year. Graduate: $599 per credit hour. On-campus room and board: $6,200. Other expenses: $3,260. Books and supplies: $900.

Financial Aid: Resources specifically for eligible students enrolled in teacher education programs are awarded on the basis of financial need and academic merit. The institution has a Program Participation Agreement with the U.S. Department of Education for eligible students to receive Pell Grants and other federal aid. *Contact:* Financial Aid Office at: (316) 295-5200.

Accreditation: *Regional:* NCA. *Professional:* NCATE. *Approved by:* Kansas State Department f Education.

FRIENDS UNIVERSITY—cont'd

Undergraduate Programs: The baccalaureate programs lead to licensure in Kansas and require the completion of a general education core, subject area major, professional studies, field experiences, and student teaching. Students major in a liberal arts and science subject area under the advisement of the Division of Education. The programs require the completion of 124 credit hours and including exit competency examinations.

Graduate Programs: The Master of Arts in Teaching at the university is an 18-month, 30 credit hour degree program. It is designed to provide elementary and secondary teachers with an interdisciplinary, field-based study of teaching and the learning process. The focus is on the practical application of learning-teaching skills in the classroom where theory and practice coverage. The student, in cooperation with a faculty advisor, designs an individualized plan for an action research study.

Licensure/Reciprocity: Kansas. Students seeking teaching certification in a state other than Kansas should consult with that state's teacher certification office early in their program of study to insure compliance with requirements. Many state directors of teacher credentialing have signed Interstate Agreements through NASDTEC that expedite the certification process.

KANSAS STATE UNIVERSITY

College of Education
6 Bluemont Hall
1100 Midcampus Drive
Manhattan, Kansas 66506
Phone: (785) 532-5525
Fax: (785) 532-7304
E-mail: edcoll@ksu.edu
Internet: http://www.ksu.edu

Institution Description: Kansas State University is a land-grant institution established as Kansas State Agricultural College in 1858. The name was changed to Kansas State College of Agriculture and Applied Science in 1931. The present name was adopted in 1959.

The College of Education programs prepare individuals for the broad spectrum of educational positions. Primary consideration is given to preparing education students for the various positions in elementary, secondary, and vocation programs.

Institution Control: Public.

Calendar: Semester. Academic year August to May.

Official(s): Dr. Michael C. Holen, Dean; Dr. Janice R. Wissman, Associate Dean.

Faculty: Full-time 77; part-time 20.

Degrees Awarded: 364 baccalaureate; 209 master's; 25 doctorate.

Admission Requirements: *Undergraduate:* ACT score 21 or above or SAT score 980 or above; rank in top third of graduation class or complete Regents' precollege curriculum. *Teacher education specific:* Passing scores on PRAXIS I; expository writing I and II and public speaking with grade of C or higher; minimum of 50 credit hours; 2.5 GPA. Secondary education teaching specialty requires specified early field experiences and a core GPA of 2.75 in general education courses. *Graduate:* Baccalaureate degree from a regionally accredited institution. *Teacher education specific:* Student must be admitted to the Graduate School of the university; 3.0 GPA or higher in last 60 hours of undergraduate work; completion of all required department tests/exams; follow a study plan under advisement with the department within the College of Education.

Fees and Expenses: Undergraduate: in-state $86 per credit hour; out-of-state $328. Graduate: in-state $126.85 per credit hour; out-of-state $380.75. Other required fees include technology and privilege fees. On-campus room and board: $4,500. Books and supplies: $600-$1,000 per academic year.

Financial Aid: Resources specifically for eligible students enrolled in teacher education programs are awarded on the basis of financial need and academic merit. The institution has a Program Participation Agreement with the U.S. Department of Education for eligible students to receive Pell Grants and other federal aid. *Contact:* Lawrence E. Moeder, Director of Student Financial Assistance at: (785) 532-6420 or e-mail at larrym@ksu.edu.

Accreditation: *Regional:* NCA. *Professional:* NCATE. *Member of:* AACTE. *Approved by:* Kansas State Department of Education.

Undergraduate Programs: All students admitted to the College of Education are assigned a pre-professional advisor from the Center for Student and Professional Services. When students are admitted to the professional program, generally late in their sophomore year or early in their junior year, they are assigned a faculty advisor from the teaching field of study which the students have chosen. All programs require a general education core, professional studies, subject area major, field experiences, and student teaching. Baccalaureate programs lead to licensure for elementary and secondary teachers.

Graduate Programs: Graduate programs are designed for students who require advanced levels of education and advanced degrees for their desired roles in the field of education. Programs are offered in curriculum and instruction. administration and leadership, educational psychology, elementary education, secondary education, special education, and student counseling and personnel services. Programs leading to the Master of Science, Doctor of Philosophy, and Doctor of Education are available. Emphasis is placed on elementary, secondary, post-secondary, occupational, and vocational programs.

Licensure/Reciprocity: Kansas. Students seeking teaching certification in a state other than Kansas should consult with that state's teacher certification office early in their program of study to insure compliance with requirements. Many state directors of teacher credentialing have signed Interstate Agreements through NASDTEC that expedite the certification process.

KANSAS WESLEYAN UNIVERSITY

Teacher Education Department
East Claflin
Salina, Kansas 67401
Phone: (800) 874-1154
Fax: (785) 827-0927
E-mail: pkramer@kwu.edu
Internet: http://www.kwu.edu

Institution Description: Kansas Wesleyan University is a private institution affiliated with the United Methodist Church. It was chartered in 1885.

The Teacher Education Program is based on the foundation of liberal studies and complemented by a comprehensive study in the teaching field.

Institution Control: Private.

Calendar: Semester. Academic year August to May.

Official(s): Dr. Phyllis Kearns-Cramer, Chair, Teacher Education Department.

Faculty: Full-time 2; adjunct 3.

Degrees Awarded: 13 baccalaureate.

Admission Requirements: *Undergraduate:* Graduation from an approved secondary school or GED; minimum 2.5 GPA; ACT composite. *Teacher education specific:* Acceptance into program by sophomore year; declaration of major; personal goal statement; PRAXIS I test scores; faculty interview.

Fees and Expenses: $13,400 per academic year. On-campus room and board: $4,600. Other expenses: $4,350. Books and supplies: $650.

Financial Aid: Resources specifically for eligible students enrolled in teacher education programs are awarded on the basis of financial need and academic merit. The institution has a Program Participation Agreement with the U.S. Department of Education for eligible students to receive Pell Grants and other federal aid. *Contact:* Financial Aid Office at: (785) 827-5541, ext. 1130.

Accreditation: *Regional:* NCA. *Professional:* NCATE. *Approved by:* Kansas State Department of Education.

Undergraduate Programs: The Bachelor of Arts Degree in elementary education requires the completion of a general education core of 27 credit hours and 29 to 33 credits in professional studies. Admission to the Teacher Education program is required before candidates may take 300 and 400 level professional education courses. The secondary education minor requirements include core requirements and an appropriate major in a content area. Students may also adopt an early childhood minor and a special education program. A minimum of 123 credit hours is required.

Licensure/Reciprocity: Kansas. Students seeking teaching certification in a state other than Kansas should consult with that state's teacher certification office early in their program of study to insure compliance with requirements. Many state directors of teacher credentialing have signed Interstate Agreements through NASDTEC that expedite the certification process.

MCPHERSON COLLEGE
Department of Curriculum and Instruction
Teacher Education Program
1600 East Euclid Street
McPherson, Kansas 67460
Phone: (620) 241-0731
Fax: (620) 241-8443
E-mail: admiss@mcpherson.edu
Internet: http://www.mcpherson.edu

Institution Description: McPherson College is a private college affiliated with the Church of the Brethren. It was established as McPherson College and Industrial Institute in 1887. The present name was adopted in 1898.

The primary focus of the Department of Curriculum and Instruction is on the preparation of education professionals. The Teacher Education Program offers preparation for careers in elementary education, secondary education, and special education.

Institution Control: Private.

Calendar: Semester. Academic year September to May.

Official(s): Dr. Marilyn Kimbrell, Director, Teacher Education Program.

Faculty: Full-time 3.

Degrees Awarded: 10 baccalaureate.

Admission Requirements: *Undergraduate:* Graduation from an approved secondary school or GED; minimum 2.5 GPA; College Board SAT or ACT composite. *Teacher education specific:* Acceptance into program by sophomore year; declaration of major; personal goal statement; PRAXIS I test scores; passing required sections of the College BASE with a score of 235; faculty interview.

Fees and Expenses: $13,345 per academic year. On-campus room and board: $6,200. Other expenses: $3,235. Books and supplies: $720.

Financial Aid: Resources specifically for eligible students enrolled in teacher education programs are awarded on the basis of financial need and academic merit. The institution has a Program Participation Agreement with the U.S. Department of Education for eligible students to receive Pell Grants and other federal aid. *Contact:* Financial Aid Office at: (620) 241-0731.

Accreditation: *Regional:* NCA. *Professional:* NCATE. *Approved by:* Kansas State Department of Education.

Undergraduate Programs: Programs leading to certification and endorsement include: K-6 certification with endorsements in elementary education, English as a second language, and special education; 7-12 certification with endorsements in biology, chemistry, computer studies, English, English as a second language, foreign language (Spanish), general industrial technology, general science, mathematics, psychology, social studies, special education, speech communication/drama; K-12 certification with endorsements in art, health, music, physical education, special education. All programs leading to certification require the completion of a general education core, the subject area major, professional studies, field experiences, and student teaching. The bachelor degree programs require the completion of 124 credit hours.

Licensure/Reciprocity: Kansas. Students seeking teaching certification in a state other than Kansas should consult with that state's teacher certification office early in their program of study to insure compliance with requirements. Many state directors of teacher credentialing have signed Interstate Agreements through NASDTEC that expedite the certification process.

MIDAMERICA NAZARENE COLLEGE
Division of Education
2030 East College Way
Olathe, Kansas 66062
Phone: (913) 782-3792
Fax: (913) 791-3290
E-mail: sdrake@mnu.edu
Internet: http://www.mnu.edu

Institution Description: MidAmerica Nazarene College is a private institution affiliated with the International Church of the Nazarene. It was established in 1966.

The Division of Education offers both undergraduate and graduate programs.

Institution Control: Private.

Calendar: Semester. Academic year September to May.

Official(s): Dr. Brad King, Chair, Division of Education.

Faculty: Full-time 5.part-time ; adjunct.

Degrees Awarded: 45 baccalaureate; 92 master's.

Admission Requirements: *Undergraduate:* Graduation with 15 academic units from an approved secondary school or GED; ACT composite required. *Teacher education specific:* Acceptance into program by sophomore year; PRAXIS I test scores; declaration of major; personal goal statement; faculty interview. *Graduate:* Baccalaureate degree from a regionally accredited institution. *Teacher education specific:* Completion of all required departmental exams/tests; faculty interview.

Fees and Expenses: Undergraduate: $12,280 per academic year. Graduate: $7,860 including tuition, books, and fees. On-campus room and board: $5,535.

Financial Aid: Resources specifically for eligible students enrolled in teacher education programs are awarded on the basis of financial need and academic merit. The institution has a Program Participation Agreement with the U.S. Department of Education for eligible students to receive Pell Grants and other federal aid. *Contact:* Financial Aid Office at: (913) 791-3298.

Accreditation: *Regional:* NCA. *Member of:* AACTE. *Approved by:* Kansas State Department of Education.

Undergraduate Programs: Students entering the baccalaureate programs offered by the Division of Education may choose from two majors: elementary education (kindergarten through sixth grade) or secondary education (sixth through twelfth grade). Students who plan to teach in the secondary grades are advised to major in the academic field of their choice. The following academic programs are offered: biology (6-12); business (6-12); elementary education (K-6); English language arts (6-12); history and government (K-6); music (P-12); physical education (P-12); Spanish (P-12), speech/theater (6-12); sport management (non-teaching). The baccalaureate programs require the completion of a general education core, professional studies, subject area major, field experiences, and student teaching for a total of 126 credit hours.

Graduate Programs: The Master of Education degree program is a 14-month program that emphasizes professional and personal development, as well as teacher leaders. It focuses on the practical application of new learning.

MIDAMERICA NAZARENE COLLEGE—*cont'd*

Licensure/Reciprocity: Kansas. Students seeking teaching certification in a state other than Kansas should consult with that state's teacher certification office early in their program of study to insure compliance with requirements. Many state directors of teacher credentialing have signed Interstate Agreements through NASDTEC that expedite the certification process.

OTTAWA UNIVERSITY

Teacher Education Program
    1001 South Cedar Street
    Ottawa, Kansas 66067
    Phone: (785) 242-5200
    Fax: (785) 229-1007
    E-mail: education@ottawa.edu
    Internet: http://www.ottawa.edu

Institution Description: Ottawa University is a private institution affiliated with the American Baptist Church. It was established in 1865.

The Teacher Education Program plays a coordinating role among all departments of the university for a variety of certification programs that are approved by the State of Kansas.

Institution Control: Private.

Calendar: Semester. Academic year August to May.

Official(s): Dr. Merilee Queen, Teacher Education Coordinator.

Faculty: Faculty is drawn various departments on the university of which there are 51 members.

Degrees Awarded: 9 baccalaureate.

Admission Requirements: *Undergraduate:* Graduation from an approved secondary school or GED; College Board SAT or ACT composite. *Teacher education specific:* 2.5 GPA; 2.75 GPA in professional education and content area; PRAXIS I test scores; declaration of major; two recommendations; current health certificate.

Fees and Expenses: $12,450 per academic year. On-campus room and board: $4,160. Other expenses: $2,960. Books and supplies: $750.

Financial Aid: Resources specifically for eligible students enrolled in teacher education programs are awarded on the basis of financial need and academic merit. The institution has a Program Participation Agreement with the U.S. Department of Education for eligible students to receive Pell Grants and other federal aid. *Contact:* Financial Aid Office at: (785) 242-5200, ext. 5570.

Accreditation: *Regional:* NCA. *Professional:* NCATE. *Member of:* AACTE. *Approved by:* Kansas State Department of Education.

Undergraduate Programs: Certification programs leading to a baccalaureate degree include: pre-K, early childhood; K-6 elementary education; K-12 physical education; music, and art. Secondary education concentration areas include: biology, drama, English, health, mathematics, U.S. history/government/world history; psychology. Programs leading to licensure and the Bachelor of Arts degree require the completion of a general education core, professional studies, subject area major, field experiences, and student teaching. All baccalaureate programs require the completion of a minimum of 124 credit hours.

Licensure/Reciprocity: Kansas. Students seeking teaching certification in a state other than Kansas should consult with that state's teacher certification office early in their program of study to insure compliance with requirements. Many state directors of teacher credentialing have signed Interstate Agreements through NASDTEC that expedite the certification process.

PITTSBURG STATE UNIVERSITY

College of Education
Department of Curriculum and Instruction
    201 Hughes Hall1
    1701 South Broadway
    Pittsburg, Kansas 66762-7551
    Phone: (620) 235-4508
    Fax: (620) 235-4520
    E-mail: psucoe@pittstate.edu
    Internet: http://www.pittstate.edu

Institution Description: Pittsburg State University was established and chartered as Kansas State Manual Training Normal School in 1903. The name was changed to Kansas State Teachers College of Pittsburg in 1925, to Kansas State College of Pittsburg in 1959, and to its present name in 1978.

The mission of the Department of Curriculum and Instruction is to provide professional teacher preparation from early childhood through secondary education in a multicultural society.

Institution Control: Public.

Calendar: Semester. Academic year August to May.

Official(s): Dr. Sandra Greer, Chair, Department of Curriculum and Instruction.

Faculty: Full-time 14.

Degrees Awarded: 172 baccalaureate; 25 master's.

Admission Requirements: *Undergraduate:* Graduate from an approved secondary school or GED; ACT composite. *Teacher education specific:* Application to teacher education program during sophomore year; three references; PRAXIS I test scores; completion of general education core with 2.75 GPA. *Graduate:* Baccalaureate degree from a regionally accredited institution. *Teacher education specific:* Student must be admitted to the Graduate School of the university; 3.0 GPA or higher in last 60 hours of undergraduate work; completion of all required department tests/exams; follow a study plan under advisement with the department within the College of Education.

Fees and Expenses: Undergraduate: in-state $2,534 per academic year, $7,496 out-of-state. Graduate: $114 in-state per credit hour, $285. On-campus room and board: $3,538. Other expenses: $2404. Books and supplies: $600.

Financial Aid: Resources specifically for eligible students enrolled in teacher education programs are awarded on the basis of financial need and academic merit. The institution has a Program Participation Agreement with the U.S. Department of Education for eligible students to receive Pell Grants and other federal aid. *Contact:* Financial Aid Office at: (620) 235-4240.

Accreditation: *Regional:* NCA. *Professional:* NCATE. *Member of:* AACTE. *Approved by:* Kansas State Department of Education.

Undergraduate Programs: An undergraduate major in elementary education leads to the Bachelor of Science in Education degree. The Department of Curriculum and Instruction provides a sequence of courses in professional education. Including is an entire semester devoted to professional coursework, related laboratory experiences, and off-campus student teaching. The fields of concentration can be satisfied by completing the elementary education program: English, speech, literature field of history and social science, science and mathematics. Secondary teaching fields include computer studies, early childhood education, middle level education, multicultural education, special education, or K-9 certification in French and Spanish for the elementary teacher. All programs require the completion of 124 to 127 credit hours.

Graduate Programs: The Master of Science Degree in Teaching course of study can be pursued with a major in teaching and an emphasis in early childhood, elementary, or secondary. For those students who have already completed elementary education certification, the early childhood emphasis meets the requirements for an additional endorsement for early childhood certification. Students may choose from two different plans: Option I which requires a minimum of 30 hours including a thesis; Option II requires a minimum of 33 hours.

The Master of Science Degree in reading is offered with two emphases: reading specialist certification or classroom reading teacher (no certification included).

Licensure/Reciprocity: Kansas. Students seeking teaching certification in a state other than Kansas should consult with that state's teacher certification office early in their program of study to insure compliance with requirements. Many state directors of teacher credentialing have signed Interstate Agreements through NASDTEC that expedite the certification process.

UNIVERSITY OF KANSAS
School of Education
Department of Teaching and Leadership
421 J.R. Pearson Hall
1122 West Campus Road
Lawrence, Kansas 66045
Phone: (785) 864-3726
Fax: (785) 864-7030
E-mail: fredrod@ku.edu
Internet: http://www.soe.ku.edu

Institution Description: The University of Kansas is a multi-campus state institution. It was established and chartered in 1864.

The School of Education offers an undergraduate professional teacher education program and graduate programs in curriculum and instruction and educational policy and leadership.

Institution Control: Public.

Calendar: Semester. Academic year August to May.

Official(s): Dr. John Rury, Chair, Teaching and Leadership; Dr. Fred Rodriguez, Associate Dean.

Faculty: Full-time 31. part-time 15; adjunct 30.

Degrees Awarded: 164 baccalaureate; 267 master's; 42 doctorate.

Admission Requirements: *Undergraduate:* Graduation from an accredited secondary school; top 25% of graduating class; ACT composite. *Teacher education specific:* 2.75 cumulative GPA; essay, two letters of reference, Pre-Professional Skills Test scores. *Graduate:* Baccalaureate degree from a regionally accredited institution; 3.0 GPA; GRE. *Teacher education specific:* 3.5 minimum GPA; letters of reference; faculty interviews.

Fees and Expenses: Undergraduate: in-state $117.55 per credit hour, $366.75 out-of-state; graduate in-state $256.05 per credit hour; $419.80 out-of-state. On-campus room $2,500 per academic year; board cost varies by meal plan. Various required fees. Books and supplies: $1,000 to $1,500.

Financial Aid: Resources specifically for eligible students enrolled in teacher education programs are awarded on the basis of financial need and academic merit. The institution has a Program Participation Agreement with the U.S. Department of Education for eligible students to receive Pell Grants and other federal aid. Need-based scholarships are available for qualified students. *Contact:* Brenda Maigaard at: (785) 864-5491.

Accreditation: *Regional:* NCA. *Professional:* NCATE. *Member of:* AACTE. *Approved by:* Kansas State Department of Education.

Undergraduate Programs: The Bachelor of Science in Education degree program offered by the Department of Teaching and Leadership is an extended five-year program. After the fourth year, students earn the Bachelor of Science in Education, The degree program requires a generous sampling of courses in the humanities, language arts, social sciences, and mathematics. Students also take a significant number of courses in the majors and minors they select for teacher licensure and in courses that prepare them to be professional educators. During the fifth year, students enroll in graduate courses and complete an internship and student teaching. At completion, students will have earned 15 hours toward a master's degree.

Graduate Programs: The Master of Science in Education and Master of Arts degrees are designed to produce graduates who possess expertise in contemporary theories, procedures, and research. Optional areas of specialization are reading, mathematics, science, language arts, social studies, foreign language, economics, middle level, educational communication and technology, teaching English as a second language, and multicultural education. The Master of Arts degree also stresses a high level of subject area knowledge. Students may select a 30-hour program including a thesis or project or a 36-hour nonthesis program.

Licensed teacher can add endorsement fields, with or without completing a master's degree in English as a second language, reading, and gifted education. A Graduate Licensure Program allows student who have completed a bachelor's degree with substantial coursework in a major in the sciences, mathematics, or foreign language an opportunity to gain licensure to teach in those fields.

Licensure/Reciprocity: Kansas. Students seeking teaching certification in a state other than Kansas should consult with that state's teacher certification office early in their program of study to insure compliance with requirements. Many state directors of teacher credentialing have signed Interstate Agreements through NASDTEC that expedite the certification process.

UNIVERSITY OF SAINT MARY
Department of Education
Teacher Education Program
4100 South Fourth Street Trafficway
Leavenworth, Kansas 66048
Phone: (913) 682-5151
Fax: (913) 758-6118
E-mail: juliano@stmary.edu
Internet: http://www.stmary.edu

Institution Description: The University of Saint Mary, formerly Saint Mary College is a private, liberal arts, coeducational college founded and sponsored by the Sisters of Charity of Leavenworth, Roman Catholic. It was established in 1860.

The Department of Education is dedicated to liberal professional preparation for teaching. The education program standards promote teacher candidate outcomes based upon national standards for beginning teachers.

Institution Control: Private.

Calendar: Semester. Academic year August to May.

Official(s): Sr. Francis Juliano, Head, Department of Education.

Faculty: Full-time 7.

Degrees Awarded: 22 baccalaureate.

Admission Requirements: *Undergraduate:* Graduation with 16 units from an accredited secondary school or GED; College Board SAT or ACT composite. *Teacher education specific:* Application to the Teacher Education Program by September 1 of junior year; cumulative GPA of 2.75; passing scores on the PRAXIS I test. *Graduate:* baccalaureate degree from a regionally accredited institution. *Teacher education specific:* Teaching credential; references; faculty interview.

Fees and Expenses: $13,128 per academic year. Graduate tuition charged per credit hour. On-campus room and board: $5,122. Other expenses: $1,530. Books and supplies: $800.

Financial Aid: Resources specifically for eligible students enrolled in teacher education programs are awarded on the basis of financial need and academic merit. The institution has a Program Participation Agreement with the U.S. Department of Education for eligible students to receive Pell Grants and other federal aid. *Contact:* Financial Aid Office at: (913) 758-6449.

Accreditation: *Regional:* NCA. *Professional:* NCATE. *Approved by:* Kansas State Department of Education.

Undergraduate Programs: The Bachelor of Science in elementary education program requires junior status. The general education core is completed during the first two years of enrollment. The major requires a professional education foundations core and a curriculum core; field core experience, and student teaching in the final semester. Areas of concentration for 15 hours is recommended in one of the arts and sciences. A minimum of 128 hours is required for graduation.

UNIVERSITY OF SAINT MARY—cont'd

The Bachelor of Science in child development education is a program designed to prepare graduates for service in pre-schools, childcare centers, and related areas. Competencies pertaining to child development, teaching, and program development within this major build a foundation for those seeking a career in the field of early childcare and education. A minimum of 128 hours is required for graduation including a general education core, professional studies, subject area major, field experiences, and student teaching.

Students preparing for secondary teaching acquire a major one of the following: biology, chemistry, English, history, mathematics, or theatre. Major requirements are completed under advisement of various departments of the university. The Bachelor of Science in secondary education requires completion of a general education core, subject area major, professional studies, and student teaching for a minimum of 128 credit hours.

Graduate Programs: A thirty credit-hour Master of Arts degree in the area of education is offered to educators interested in the study of education and society. The program invites professional practitioners seeking advancement and improved practice to enhance personal growth and strengthen organizational performance.

Licensure/Reciprocity: Kansas. Students seeking teaching certification in a state other than Kansas should consult with that state's teacher certification office early in their program of study to insure compliance with requirements. Many state directors of teacher credentialing have signed Interstate Agreements through NASDTEC that expedite the certification process.

WASHBURN UNIVERSITY

Department of Education
Teacher Education Program
1700 SW College Avenue
Topeka, Kansas 66621
Phone: (785) 231-1010, x427
Fax: (785) 231-1089
E-mail: admissions@washburn.edu
Internet: http://www.washburn.edu

Institution Description: Washburn University of Topeka is a public urban institution. It was established by the Congregational Church in 1865 and became Washburn Municipal University of Topeka in 1941. The present name was adopted in 1952.

The teacher education programs are offered at both the undergraduate and graduate levels.

Institution Control: Public.

Calendar: Semester. Academic year August to May.

Official(s): Dr. Sandra Winn Tetwiler, Chair, Teacher Education Program.

Faculty: Full-time 15,

Degrees Awarded: 50 baccalaureate; 20 master's.

Admission Requirements: *Undergraduate:* Graduation from an accredited secondary school or GED; ACT composite. *Teacher education specific:* Candidates must apply to the program by their junior year; completion of general education core with 2.75 GPA and the professional course sequence; recommendations; Pre-Professional Skills Test or PRAXIS I scores; declaration of major. *Graduate:* Baccalaureate degree from a regionally accredited institution. *Teacher education specific:* Teaching credential for most programs; GRE or Miller Analogies Test; faculty interview; recommendations.

Fees and Expenses: Undergraduate: resident $3,656 per academic year, nonresident $8,186. Graduate: resident $150 per credit hour, nonresident $307. On-campus room and board: $4,686. Other expenses: $2,840. Books and supplies: $800.

Financial Aid: Resources specifically for eligible students enrolled in teacher education programs are awarded on the basis of financial need and academic merit. The institution has a Program Participation Agreement with the U.S. Department of Education for eligible students to receive Pell Grants and other federal aid. *Contact:* Financial Aid Office at: (765) 231-1010, x1151.

Accreditation: *Regional:* NCA. *Professional:* NCATE. *Member of:* AACTE. *Approved by:* Kansas State Department of Education.

Undergraduate Programs: All students seeking an initial license complete a well-rounded sequence of general education courses delivered by arts and sciences departments and complete a professional sequence of courses delivered through the Department of Education. The elementary education teacher candidates pursuing a K-6 license complete appropriate specialty courses and receive a Bachelor of Education upon completion of required courses and clinical experiences. In the process of completing the K-6 program, teacher candidates choose one of five complementary options, four of which lead to a second teaching license. Candidates may choose to pursue a program of study leading to a birth through grade three license or a middle school (5-8) license in English/language arts, social studies, or mathematics. The middle school license is delivered collaboratively between the Department of Education and the appropriate departments offering content for the 5-8 subject area.

The Secondary Licensure Program (6-12) leads to the Bachelor of Arts or Bachelor of Science degree. Subject area concentrations are offered in biology (BA or BS), chemistry (BA), English/language arts (BA), history/government (BA), mathematics (BA). Candidates in the P-12 Licensure Program complete a major in their teaching disciplines and receive a Bachelor of Arts or Bachelor of Science in their subject major.

Graduate Programs: The Department of Education offers graduate courses and where appropriate, clinical experiences and internships for teachers wishing to pursue the Master in Education degree. Teachers may also enroll in graduate courses to work toward additional teaching endorsements, licensure renewal, or professional development. Coursework is offered in educational leadership, special education, reading, adaptive special education, building leadership, district leadership, and reading specialist.

Licensure/Reciprocity: Kansas. Students seeking teaching certification in a state other than Kansas should consult with that state's teacher certification office early in their program of study to insure compliance with requirements. Many state directors of teacher credentialing have signed Interstate Agreements through NASDTEC that expedite the certification process.

WICHITA STATE UNIVERSITY

Teacher Education Program
Department of Curriculum and Instruction
151 Corbin
1845 Fairmount
Wichita, Kansas 67260
Phone: (316) 978-3456
Fax: (316) 978-3085
E-mail: jon.engelhardt@wichita.edu
Internet: http://www.wichita.edu

Institution Description: The school was Incorporated as Fairmount College in 1887 and was established by the Congregational Church as Fairmount Institute in 1892. It became a municipal institution and changed name to Municipal University of Wichita in 1926. The name was changed to the University of Wichita in 1956. The university became part of the state system and became Wichita State University in 1964.

The College of Education offers a four-semester Teacher Education Program that is outcome-based with accompanying field experiences each semester.

Institution Control: Public.

Calendar: Semester. Academic year August to May.

Official(s): Dr. Jon Engelhardt, Dean, College of Education.

Faculty: Full-time 55; part-time 1.

Degrees Awarded: 207 baccalaureate; 221 master's; 3 doctorate.

Admission Requirements: Graduation from an approved secondary school or GED; ACT composite. *Teacher education specific:* Overall 2.5 GPA and completion of general education coursework with at least 2.75 GPA; Pre-Professional Skills test scores; faculty interview. *Graduate:* Baccalaureate from a regionally accredited institution. *Teacher education specific:* GRE general test; teaching credential where appropriate; completion of all departmental tests/exams; recommendations; faculty interview.

Fees and Expenses: Undergraduate: in-state $3,055 per academic year; $9,832 out-of-state. Graduate: in-state $105 per credit hour; out-of-state $341. On-campus room and board: $4.420. Other expenses: $3,260. Books and supplies: $850.

Financial Aid: Resources specifically for eligible students enrolled in teacher education programs are awarded on the basis of financial need and academic merit. The institution has a Program Participation Agreement with the U.S. Department of Education for eligible students to receive Pell Grants and other federal aid. *Contact:* Financial Aid Office at: (316) 978-3430.

Accreditation: *Regional:* NCA. *Professional:* NCATE. *Member of:* AACTE. *Approved by:* Kansas State Department of Education.

Undergraduate Programs: Undergraduate teacher education in Curriculum and Instruction is a five-stage competency-based program beginning with an introduction to teaching and concluding with reflections on an extended student teaching experience. The program includes extensive field experiences and the on-going development of a professional portfolio. Baccalaureate programs at the elementary and secondary levels require the completion of 124 to 143 credit hours.

Graduate Programs: The College of Education offers programs leading to the Master of Arts in communicative disorders and sciences; the Master of Education in counseling, curriculum and instruction, educational administration, educational psychology, physical education, the Specialist in Education (Ed.S.) in school psychology, the Doctor of Education (Ed.D.) in educational administration, and the Doctor of Philosophy (Ph.D.) in communicative disorders and sciences.

Licensure/Reciprocity: Kansas. Students seeking teaching certification in a state other than Kansas should consult with that state's teacher certification office early in their program of study to insure compliance with requirements. Many state directors of teacher credentialing have signed Interstate Agreements through NASDTEC that expedite the certification process. Reciprocity agreement also through the Central States Teacher Exchange Agreement.

KENTUCKY

ASBURY COLLEGE

Education Department

1 Macklem Drive
Wilmore, Kentucky 40390
Phone: (859) 858-3511
Fax: (859) 858-3921
E-mail: verna.lowe@asbury.edu
Internet: http://asbury.edu

Institution Description: Asbury College is a private, independent, nonprofit college. It was established and offered first instruction at postsecondary level in 1890.

The objective of the Education Department is to provide a strong academic program to prepare quality teachers who are committed to professional excellence.

Institution Control: Private.

Calendar: Semester. Academic year August to May.

Official(s): Dr. Verna J. Lowe, Chair, Education Department.

Faculty: Full-time 7; part-time 5.

Degrees Awarded: 43 baccalaureate; 9 master's.

Admission Requirements: *Undergraduate:* Graduation from an approved secondary school or GED; SAT score of 1100 or ACT composite score of 24. *Teacher education specific:* Minimum of 30 semester hours of college credit; cumulative GPA of 2.75; portfolio review; faculty interview. *Graduate:* Baccalaureate degree from a regionally accredited institution. *Teacher education specific:* Official transcripts of all college/university coursework; minimum 2.75 GPA; valid provisional or Standard Kentucky Teaching Certificate or statement of eligibility; GRE minimum score of 850 or passing score on PRAXIS tests.

Fees and Expenses: Undergraduate: $16,352 per academic year. Graduate: $274 per credit hour. Required fees: $148. On-campus room and board: $3,000. Books and supplies: $1,000 per year.

Financial Aid: Resources specifically for eligible students enrolled in teacher education programs are awarded on the basis of financial need and academic merit. The institution has a Program Participation Agreement with the U.S. Department of Education for eligible students to receive Pell Grants and other federal aid. Kentucky Teacher Scholarships available to qualifying students. *Contact:* Financial Aid Office at: (859) 858-3511.

Accreditation: *Regional:* SACS. *Professional:* NCATE. *Member of:* AACTE. *Approved by:* Kentucky Educational Professional Standards Board.

Undergraduate Programs: The Kentucky Department of Education mandates four levels of certification requirements which include elementary (P-5), middle school (5-9), secondary (8-12), and all grade level (P-12). Students must meet the requirements of one of the prescribed certification programs.

Students preparing to teach in the elementary school grades (P-5) must complete 89 hours in the major and 39 in general education. The middle grades (5-9) program requires the completion of 61-64 hours in the major and 48 general education and electives. The secondary education (8-12) student must follow the curriculum as outlined by the departments offering majors in education. The program requires 48 hours of general education courses, 34-37 hours of professional courses, and a teaching major of 36-56 hours.

Students preparing to teach at all levels must follow the curriculum as outlined by the departments offering P-12 majors. These majors must complete 46-48 hours in general education, professional courses of 28-34 hours, and a P-12 teaching major of 34-56 hours.

Graduate Programs: The graduate program offers the Master of Arts degree with the opportunity for study in the areas of: English as a second language, instructional media, and learning and behavior disorders.

Licensure/Reciprocity: Kentucky. Students seeking teaching certification in a state other than Kentucky should consult with that state's teacher certification office early in their program of study to insure compliance with requirements. Many state directors of teacher credentialing have signed Interstate Agreements through NASDTEC that expedite the certification process.

BELLARMINE COLLEGE

School of Education

Miles Hall 120
2001 Newburg Road
Louisville, Kentucky 40205
Phone: (502) 452-8191
Fax: (502) 452-8002
E-mail: admissions@ballarmine.edu
Internet: http://www.bellarmine.educ

Institution Description: Bellarmine College is a private college affiliated with the Roman Catholic Church. It was established as a men's college in 1950. It merged with Ursuline College, a women's college, and the name was changed to Bellarmine-Ursuline College in 1968. The present name was was adopted in 1971.

The School of Education offers undergraduate teacher education programs leading to eligibility for Provisional Certification in Kentucky.

Institution Control: Private.

Calendar: Semester. Academic year August to May.

Official(s): Dr. Maureen R. Norris, Dean, School of Education.

Faculty: Full-time 10.

Degrees Awarded: 24 baccalaureate; 126 master's.

Admission Requirements: *Undergraduate:* Graduation with 16 academic units from an approved secondary school or GED; College Board SAT or ACT composite. *Teacher education specific:* Cumulative GPA 2.5; evidence of specific competency levels in oral and written communication, reading, writing, and computation; successful review of student portfolio; recommendations from instructors. *Graduate:* Baccalaureate degree from a regionally accredited institution. *Teacher education specific:* Overall all 2.75 GPA; 3.0 GPA in student's major; GRE; two recommendations from former professors or current employers; professional goal statement; PRAXIS scores (middle/secondary applicants only).

Fees and Expenses: $17,010 per academic year. Graduate tuition charged per credit hour. On-campus room and board: $5,530. Other expenses: $1,700. Books and supplies: $700.

Financial Aid: Resources specifically for eligible students enrolled in teacher education programs are awarded on the basis of financial need and academic merit. The institution has a

Program Participation Agreement with the U.S. Department of Education for eligible students to receive Pell Grants and other federal aid. Kentucky Teacher Scholarships available to qualifying students. *Contact:* Financial Aid Office at: (502) 452-8126.

Accreditation: *Regional:* SACS. *Professional:* NCATE. *Member of:* AACTE. *Approved by:* Kentucky Educational Professional Standards Board.

Degrees Offered: Baccalaureate, Master's.

Undergraduate Programs: The School of Education offers programs leading to teacher certification in elementary (grades (P-5), middle school (5-9), secondary (8-12), and special education, learning and behavior disorders (P-12). All graduates from these programs, which can be completed in four years, will have two teaching certifications, one in regular education and one in special education.

The secondary education program offers teaching certification for grades 8-12 in the following content areas: art, biology, chemistry, English, mathematics, music, social studies, and a computer science endorsement. Secondary education majors graduate with a content major in the subject area and teacher education certification in that area.

All baccalaureate programs require the completion of general education, subject are major, professional studies, field experiences, and student teaching. Completion of a total 126 credit hours is required.

Graduate Programs: The Master of Arts programs include early elementary education, grades 1-5; middle school education, grades 5-9; and learning and behavior disorders, grades P-12. The programs require the completion of a minimum of 36 hours of graduate coursework; cumulative 3.0 GPA through the program of studies; either a Performance Assessment Experience or a Master's thesis in education.

The Master of Arts in Teaching programs are available in early elementary education, grades P-5; middle school education, grades 5-9; and secondary school education, grades 9-12. These programs are accelerated programs that meet evenings and multiple Saturdays per semester.

Licensure/Reciprocity: Kentucky. Students seeking teaching certification in a state other than Kentucky should consult with that state's teacher certification office early in their program of study to insure compliance with requirements. Many state directors of teacher credentialing have signed Interstate Agreements through NASDTEC that expedite the certification process.

BEREA COLLEGE
Education Studies Department
Chestnut Street
Berea, Kentucky 40404
Phone: (839) 985-3077
Fax: (839) 985-3164
E-mail: admissions@berea.edu
Internet: http://www.berea.edu

Institution Description: Berea College is a private, independent, nonprofit, nondenominational Christian college. It was established in 1855.

All departments in Berea College contribute in some way to the teacher preparation programs offered through the Education Studies Department.

Institution Control: Private.

Calendar: Semester. Academic year September to May.

Official(s): Dr. Kathryn Akural, Chairpersons, Education Studies Department.

Faculty: Full-time 6; part-time 9.

Degrees Awarded: 30 baccalaureate.

Admission Requirements: *Undergraduate:* Graduation from an approved secondary school, completion of home school curriculum, or GED. *Teacher education specific:* Minimum of 30 semester hours of college credit; cumulative GPA of 2.75; portfolio review; faculty interview.

Fees and Expenses: $507 per academic year. On-campus room and board: $4,303. Other expenses: $1,415. Books and supplies: $675.

Financial Aid: Resources specifically for eligible students enrolled in teacher education programs are awarded on the basis of financial need and academic merit. The institution has a Program Participation Agreement with the U.S. Department of Education for eligible students to receive Pell Grants and other federal aid. Kentucky Teacher Scholarships available to qualifying students. The college has a commitment to provide an educational opportunity primarily for students from Appalachia. *Contact:*Financial Aid Office at: (859) 885-3310.

Accreditation: *Regional:* SACS. *Professional:* NCATE. *Member of:* AACTE. *Approved by:* Kentucky Educational Professional Standards Board.

Undergraduate Programs: The general education program is central both to the fulfillment of the college's commitments and to the attainment of the mission and goals of Berea's Teacher Education Program. The general education program emphasizes concepts, ideas, and ways of thinking that are essential to the preparation of all P-12 teachers. The baccalaureate program includes the general education core, professional studies, subject area major, field experiences, and student teaching.

Licensure/Reciprocity: Kentucky. Students seeking teaching certification in a state other than Kentucky should consult with that state's teacher certification office early in their program of study to insure compliance with requirements. Many state directors of teacher credentialing have signed Interstate Agreements through NASDTEC that expedite the certification process.

BRESCIA UNIVERSITY
Division of Educational Studies
717 Frederica Street
Owensboro, Kentucky 42301
Phone: (270) 685-3131
Fax: (270) 686-4266
E-mail: admissions@brescia.edu
Internet: http://www.brescia.edu

Institution Description: Brescia University, formerly Brescia College, is a private institution affiliated with the Roman Catholic Church. It was established as Mount Saint Joseph Junior College in 1925. It became a four-year college and was renamed Brescia College in 1950. University status was acquired in 1998.

The Division of Educational Studies offers programs for the certification of elementary, middle and secondary school teachers, and teachers in the field of special education.

Institution Control: Private.

Calendar: Semester. Academic year August to May.

Official(s): Dr. Sharon Sullivan, Chair, Division of Educational Studies.

Faculty: Full-time 5.

Degrees Awarded: 18 baccalaureate; 4 master's.

Admission Requirements: *Undergraduate:* Graduation from an approved secondary school or GED; College Board SAT or ACT composite. *Teacher education specific:* Admission to the program prior to beginning upper division courses; PRAXIS I test scores; department interview; background check; 2.5 cumulative GPA. *Graduate:* Baccalaureate degree from a regionally accredited institution. *Teacher education specific:* portfolio presentation; references; teaching credential; faculty interview.

Fees and Expenses: Undergraduate: $10,130 per academic year. Graduate: Tuition charged per credit hour. On-campus room and board: $ 5,020. Other expenses: $1,800. Books and supplies: $1,000.

Financial Aid: Resources specifically for eligible students enrolled in teacher education programs are awarded on the basis of financial need and academic merit. The institution has a Program Participation Agreement with the U.S. Department of Education for eligible students to receive Pell Grants and other federal aid. Kentucky Teacher Scholarships available to qualifying students. *Contact:* Financial Aid Office at: (685) 685-4290.

BRESCIA UNIVERSITY—cont'd

Accreditation: *Regional:* SACS. *Member of:* AACTE. *Approved by:* Kentucky Educational Professional Standards Board.

Undergraduate Programs: The Educational Studies Programs include: Bachelor of Science degree in elementary education with P-5 certification; the Bachelor of Science degree in middle school education with 5-9 certification; and the Bachelor of Science or Arts degree in secondary education with 8-12 certification in biological science, English, mathematics, physical science, and social studies; the Bachelor of of Arts degree in P-12 certification in art education or Spanish; the Bachelor of Science degree in special education with P-12 certification.

All baccalaureate programs require the completion of a general education core, professional studies, subject area major, field experiences, and student teaching. Completion of 128 credit hours is required for all programs.

Graduate Programs: The Master of Science in curriculum and instruction is offered to teachers to enhance and refine their classroom management and instructional skills. the class calendar is structured to allow complete the program within a two-year framework.

Licensure/Reciprocity: Kentucky. Students seeking teaching certification in a state other than Kentucky should consult with that state's teacher certification office early in their program of study to insure compliance with requirements. Many state directors of teacher credentialing have signed Interstate Agreements through NASDTEC that expedite the certification process.

CENTRE COLLEGE

Division of Social Studies
Education Program
600 West Walnut Street
Danville, Kentucky 40422-1394
Phone: (859) 238-5307
Fax: (859) 236-7925
E-mail: nystrom@centre.edu
Internet: http://www.centre.edu

Institution Description: Centre College is a private, independent, nonprofit institution. It was established and chartered in 1819. It merged with Central University of Richmond in 1901, then merged with Kentucky College for Women in 1926. The name Centre College was adopted in 1982.

The purpose of the Education Program is to provide study for undergraduate students in the methods and theories of effective teaching and to give students practical experiences in classroom settings.

Institution Control: Private.

Calendar: Semester (4-1-4 plan). Academic year September to May.

Official(s): Dr. Bradley Nystrom, Chair, Education Program.

Faculty: Full-time 5; part-time 2; adjunct 3.

Degrees Awarded: 6 baccalaureate.

Admission Requirements: *Undergraduate:* Graduation from an approved secondary school or GED; College Board SAT or ACT composite. *Teacher education specific:* ACT 21 composite score; 2.5 GPA; PRAXIS I test scores; faculty interview.

Fees and Expenses: $20,400 per academic year. On-campus room and board: $6,400. Books and supplies: $1,700.

Financial Aid: Resources specifically for eligible students enrolled in teacher education programs are awarded on the basis of financial need and academic merit. The institution has a Program Participation Agreement with the U.S. Department of Education for eligible students to receive Pell Grants and other federal aid. Kentucky Teacher Scholarships available to qualifying students. *Contact:* Financial Aid Office at: (800 423-6236 or e-mail at finaid@centre.edu.

Accreditation: *Regional:* SACS. *Member of:* AACTE. *Approved by:* Kentucky Educational Professional Standards Board.

Undergraduate Programs: Centre College offers teacher certification programs in elementary education K-5, secondary education 8-12 (biological sciences, chemistry, English, mathematics, physics, social studies); and K-12 certification in art, French, German, and Spanish.

All baccalaureate programs require the completion of an academic emphasis component, related studies courses, professional preparation courses, field experiences, and student teaching.

Licensure/Reciprocity: Kentucky. Students seeking teaching certification in a state other than Kentucky should consult with that state's teacher certification office early in their program of study to insure compliance with requirements. Many state directors of teacher credentialing have signed Interstate Agreements through NASDTEC that expedite the certification process.

CUMBERLAND COLLEGE

Education Department
6178 College Station Drive
Williamsburg, Kentucky 40769
Phone: (606) 539-4433
Fax: (609) 539-4303
E-mail: pprewitt@cumberlandcollege.edu
Internet: http://www.cumberlandcollege.edu

Institution Description: Cumberland College is a private institution affiliated with the Southern Baptist Church. It was established as Williamsburg Institute in 1889 and the current name was adopted in 1913.

The college is dedicated to provided training for future teachers by offering a curriculum that combines theory with practical experience, set within the framework of a liberal arts program.

Institution Control: Private.

Calendar: Semester. Academic year August to May.

Official(s): Dr. John Farris, Chair, Education Department.

Faculty: Full-time 10.

Degrees Awarded: 40 baccalaureate; 43 master's.

Admission Requirements: *Undergraduate:* Graduation from an approved secondary school or GED; College Board SAT or ACT composite. *Teacher education specific:* Minimum of 30 semester hours of college credit; cumulative GPA of 2.75; portfolio review; faculty interview. *Graduate:* Baccalaureate degree from a regionally accredited institution. *Teacher education specific:* Official transcripts of all college/university coursework; minimum 2.75 GPA; valid provisional or Standard Kentucky Teaching Certificate or statement of eligibility; GRE or passing score on PRAXIS tests.

Fees and Expenses: Undergraduate: $10,958 per academic year. Graduate: $180 per credit hour. On-campus room and board: $4,676. Other expenses: $2,330. Books and supplies: $800.

Financial Aid: Resources specifically for eligible students enrolled in teacher education programs are awarded on the basis of financial need and academic merit. The institution has a Program Participation Agreement with the U.S. Department of Education for eligible students to receive Pell Grants and other federal aid. Kentucky Teacher Scholarships available to qualifying students. *Contact:* Financial Aid Office at: (606) 549-2200, ext. 4220.

Accreditation: *Regional:* SACS. *Member of:* AACTE. *Approved by:* Kentucky Educational Professional Standards Board.

Undergraduate Programs: From their first entry into the program, students are encouraged to begin thinking of themselves as apprentice teachers. Through the building of their portfolios, they learn to think critically, analyzing how selected work from each course functions as vital to their professional preparation. Field experience and supervised student teaching in the classroom gives them practical experience. The curriculum combines theory with practical experience, set within the framework of a liberal arts program. All baccalaureate programs require completion of 128 credit hours.

Graduate Programs: The graduate program in teacher education was established in 1981 primarily to aid in-service teachers in the mid-Appalachian region who wanted to advance their professional careers. Students may apply for candidacy in programs leading to a Master of Arts in Education or a Master of Arts in instructional leadership. Courses are offered in the evenings, on weekends, and during the summer.

Licensure/Reciprocity: Kentucky. Students seeking teaching certification in a state other than Kentucky should consult with that state's teacher certification office early in their program of study to insure compliance with requirements. Many state directors of teacher credentialing have signed Interstate Agreements through NASDTEC that expedite the certification process.

EASTERN KENTUCKY UNIVERSITY
College of Education
521 Lancaster Avenue
Richmond, Kentucky 40475
Phone: (859) 622-1000
Fax: (859) 622-1020
E-mail: mark.wasicsko@eku.edu
Internet: http://www.eku.edu

Institution Description: Eastern Kentucky University is a state institution. It was established as Eastern Kentucky State Normal School in 1906. The name was changed to Eastern Kentucky State Teachers College in 1930 and the present name was adopted in 1966.

The College of Education offers undergraduate programs leading to teacher certification and graduate programs for teacher career enhancement.

Institution Control: Public.

Calendar: Semester. Academic year August to May.

Official(s): Dr. Mark Wasicsko, Dean, College of Education.

Faculty: Full-time 29.

Degrees Awarded: 281 baccalaureate; 259 master's.

Admission Requirements: *Undergraduate:* Graduation from an approved secondary school or GED, ACT composite score of 18 or higher. *Teacher education specific:* Minimum of 30 semester hours of college credit; cumulative GPA of 2.75; portfolio review; faculty interview. *Graduate:* Baccalaureate degree from a regionally accredited institution. *Teacher education specific:* Official transcripts of all college/university coursework; minimum 2.75 GPA; valid provisional or Standard Kentucky Teaching Certificate or statement of eligibility; GRE minimum score of 850 or passing score on PRAXIS tests.

Fees and Expenses: Undergraduate: in-state $2,928 per academic year; out-of-state $8.040. Graduate: in-state $1,468 or $165 per credit hour. On-campus room and board: $4,146. Other expenses: $1,350. Books and supplies: $800.

Financial Aid: Resources specifically for eligible students enrolled in teacher education programs are awarded on the basis of financial need and academic merit. The institution has a Program Participation Agreement with the U.S. Department of Education for eligible students to receive Pell Grants and other federal aid. Kentucky Teacher Scholarships available to qualifying students. *Contact:* Financial Aid Office at: (859) 622-2361.

Accreditation: *Regional:* SACS. *Professional:* NCATE. *Member of:* AACTE. *Approved by:* Kentucky Educational Professional Standards Board.

Undergraduate Programs: The baccalaureate programs include undergraduate majors in communication disorders, elementary education, middle grade education, secondary education, and special education (concentrations in deaf and hard of hearing, interdisciplinary early childhood education, interpreting for deaf individuals, learning and behavior disorders, moderate and severe disabilities). Undergraduate minors are available in special education and secondary education.,

Undergraduate endorsements and certificates are offered in: driver education, English as a second language, and physical education. All baccalaureate programs require the completion

of 136 credit hours including a general education core, professional studies, subject area courses, field experiences, and student teaching.

Graduate Programs: The Specialist in Education degree is a professional degree designed for position s that call for a level of study and specialization beyond the master's degree. The 30-hour minimum requirement is structure and unified-program oriented toward the student's professional objectives.

The Master of Arts in Education is offered with concentration in school counseling, curriculum and instruction, special education, library science, and reading. The Master of Arts degree is offered in mental health counseling and student personnel services in high education. Other graduate endorsements and certificates are also offered.

Licensure/Reciprocity: Kentucky. Students seeking teaching certification in a state other than Kentucky should consult with that state's teacher certification office early in their program of study to insure compliance with requirements. Many state directors of teacher credentialing have signed Interstate Agreements through NASDTEC that expedite the certification process.

KENTUCKY CHRISTIAN COLLEGE
Keeran School of Education
100 Academic Parkway
Grayson, Kentucky 41143-1199
Phone: (606) 474-3267
Fax: (606) 474-3155
E-mail: kruffner@email.kcc.edu
Internet: http://www.kcc.edu

Institution Description: Kentucky Christian College is a private college offering programs designed to prepare students for Christian leadership and service in the church and in professions throughout the world. The college was founded in 1919 and has maintained an affiliation with the Churches of Christ and Christian Churches.

The Keeran School of Education offers baccalaureate programs in the various liberal arts disciplines.

Institution Control: Private.

Calendar: Semester. Academic year August to May.

Official(s): Dr. Kail D. Ruffner, Dean, Keeran School of Education.

Faculty: Full-time 4; part-time 2.

Degrees Awarded: 23 baccalaureate.

Admission Requirements: *Undergraduate:* Graduation with 16 academic units from an approved secondary school or GED; College Board SAT or ACT composite. *Teacher education specific:* Minimum of 30 semester hours of college credit; cumulative GPA of 2.75; portfolio review; faculty interview.

Fees and Expenses: $4,320 per academic year. Fees and books: $3,222. On-campus room and board: $4,298.

Financial Aid: Resources specifically for eligible students enrolled in teacher education programs are awarded on the basis of financial need and academic merit. The institution has a Program Participation Agreement with the U.S. Department of Education for eligible students to receive Pell Grants and other federal aid. Kentucky Teacher Scholarships available to qualifying students. *Contact:* Jennie Bender at: (606) 474-3226 or e-mail at jbender@email.kcc.edu.

Accreditation: *Regional:* SACS. *Approved by:* Kentucky Educational Professional Standards Board.

Undergraduate Programs: All programs require a major in teacher education: the Bachelor of Science degree is offered with concentrations primary through grade 5; middle school grades 5-9, and music (all grades).

The Bachelor of Arts degree is offered with concentrations for primary through grade 5; middle school grades 5-9, and music (all grades).

All baccalaureate programs require the completion of a general education core, professional studies, subject area courses, field experiences, and student teaching. Student teaching place-

KENTUCKY CHRISTIAN COLLEGE—*cont'd*
ments are made within a 45 mile driving distance from the college campus. All student teachers must complete 60 days in their student teaching assignment.

Licensure/Reciprocity: Kentucky. Students seeking teaching certification in a state other than Kentucky should consult with that state's teacher certification office early in their program of study to insure compliance with requirements. Many state directors of teacher credentialing have signed Interstate Agreements through NASDTEC that expedite the certification process.

KENTUCKY STATE UNIVERSITY
Division of Education and Human Services
Area of Teacher Education
Hathaway Hall 215
400 East Main Street
Frankfort, Kentucky 40601
Phone: (502) 597-5919
Fax: (502) 597-5917
E-mail: lyates@gwmail.kysu.edu
Internet: http://www.kysu.edu

Institution Description: Kentucky State University is a state-assisted public institution. It was established as Kentucky Normal Institute in 1886. The present name was adopted in 1972.

The primary purpose of the Area of Teacher Education is to coordinate and administer all programs leading to teaching certification at the university.

Institution Control: Public.

Calendar: Semester. Academic year August to May.

Official(s): Dr. Lucian Yates III, Chair, Area of Teacher Education.

Faculty: Full-time 12; part-time 9; adjunct 5.

Degrees Awarded: 26 baccalaureate.

Admission Requirements: *Undergraduate:* Graduation from an approved high school with a per-college curriculum; ACT of 21. *Teacher education specific:* GPA 2.75; competency in written and oral communication; faculty interview.

Fees and Expenses: Undergraduate: in-state $3,450 per academic year; out-of-state $9,224. Required fees: $556. On-campus room and board: $3,172.

Financial Aid: Resources specifically for eligible students enrolled in teacher education programs are awarded on the basis of financial need and academic merit. The institution has a Program Participation Agreement with the U.S. Department of Education for eligible students to receive Pell Grants and other federal aid. Kentucky Teacher Scholarships available to qualifying students. *Contact:* Donna Miller at: (502 597-5919 or e-mail at dmiller@gwmail.kysu.edu.

Accreditation: *Regional:* SACS. *Professional:* NCATE. *Member of:* AACTE. *Approved by:* Kentucky Educational Professional Standards Board.

Undergraduate Programs: The Area of Teacher Education offers baccalaureate degree programs leading to teacher certification in art education, biology education, birth to primary education, elementary education, English education, mathematics education, music education, physical education, and social studies education. Teaching minors are available in English, history, mathematics, and sociology. Endorsement for teaching computer science is available. All programs lead to the bachelor's degree and require successful completion of a general education core, professional studies, subject area major, field experiences, and student teaching.

Licensure/Reciprocity: Kentucky. Students seeking teaching certification in a state other than Kentucky should consult with that state's teacher certification office early in their program of study to insure compliance with requirements. Many state directors of teacher credentialing have signed Interstate Agreements through NASDTEC that expedite the certification process.

MOREHEAD STATE UNIVERSITY
College of Education
Teacher Education Program
University Boulevard
Morehead, Kentucky 40351
Phone: (606) 783-2221
Fax: (606) 783-5038
E-mail: coe@moreheadstate.edu
Internet: http://www.moreheadstate.edu

Institution Description: Morehead State University was chartered as Morehead State Normal School in 1922. The name was changed to Morehead State Normal School and Teachers College in 1926, to Morehead State Teachers College in 1930, to Morehead State College 1948. The present name was adopted in 1966.

Teacher education is a field-based program that provides extensive laboratory experiences with student teaching in area schools.

Institution Control: Public.

Calendar: Semester. Academic year August to May.

Official(s): Dr. Dan H. Branham, Dean, Teacher Education Program.

Faculty: Full-time 11.

Degrees Awarded: 190 baccalaureate; 271 master's.

Admission Requirements: *Undergraduate:* Graduation from an approved secondary school or GED; College Board SAT or ACT composite. *Teacher education specific:* Minimum of 45 semester hours of college credit; GRE or PRAXIS test scores; faculty interview.

Fees and Expenses: Undergraduate: in-state $2,926 per academic year; out-of-state $7,780. On-campus room and board: $4,000. Other expenses: $1,200. Books and supplies: $600.

Financial Aid: Resources specifically for eligible students enrolled in teacher education programs are awarded on the basis of financial need and academic merit. The institution has a Program Participation Agreement with the U.S. Department of Education for eligible students to receive Pell Grants and other federal aid. Kentucky Teacher Scholarships available to qualifying students. *Contact:* Financial Aid Office at: (606) 783-2011.

Accreditation: *Regional:* SACS. *Professional:* NCATE. *Member of:* AACTE. *Approved by:* Kentucky Educational Professional Standards Board.

Undergraduate Programs: Students in elementary and middle grades education must select an area of concentration either elementary (teaching certification in grades P-5) or middle grades (teaching certification in grades 5-8). Students seeking initial secondary certification are required to complete a bachelor's degree and concentration in the following preparation programs; English, mathematics, social studies, biological science, agriculture, business and marketing education, human sciences, industrial education, art, French, health, physical education, or music.

All programs require the completion of a general education core, professional studies, subject area major, field experiences, and student teaching. A total of 128 credit hours is required for the bachelor's degree.

Licensure/Reciprocity: Kentucky. Students seeking teaching certification in a state other than Kentucky should consult with that state's teacher certification office early in their program of study to insure compliance with requirements. Many state directors of teacher credentialing have signed Interstate Agreements through NASDTEC that expedite the certification process.

MURRAY STATE UNIVERSITY

College of Education
Teacher Education Program
2101 Alexander Hall
15th and Main
Murray, Kentucky 42071
Phone: (270) 762-2054
Fax: (270) 762-3073
E-mail: jhooks@murraystate.edu
Internet: http://www.murraystate.edu

Institution Description: Murray State University is a public institution. It was established and chartered as Murray Normal School in 1922. The name was changed to Murray Normal School and Teachers College in 1926, to Murray State Teachers College in 1930, and to Murray State College in 1948. The present name was adopted in 1966.

The College of Education prepares professionals in early childhood, elementary, middle and secondary education.

Institution Control: Public.

Calendar: Semester. Academic year August to May.

Official(s): Dr. Russ Wall, Dean, College of Education; Dr. Janice Hooks, Assistant Dean.

Faculty: Full-time 18.

Degrees Awarded: 222 baccalaureate; 190 master's.

Admission Requirements: *Undergraduate:* Graduation from an accredited secondary school or GED; College Board SAT or ACT composite. *Teacher education specific:* Minimum of 30 semester hours of college credit; cumulative GPA of 2.75; portfolio review; faculty interview. *Graduate:* Baccalaureate degree from a regionally accredited institution. *Teacher education specific:* Official transcripts of all college/university coursework; valid provisional or Standard Kentucky Teaching Certificate or statement of eligibility.

Fees and Expenses: Undergraduate: in-state $3,032 per academic year; out-of-state Graduate: in-state $1,440 per academic year; out-of-state $4,004. On-campus room and board: $4,420. Other expenses: $1,140. Books and supplies: $700.

Financial Aid. Resources specifically for eligible students enrolled in teacher education programs are awarded on the basis of financial need and academic merit. The institution has a Program Participation Agreement with the U.S. Department of Education for eligible students to receive Pell Grants and other federal aid. Kentucky Teacher Scholarships available to qualifying students. *Contact:* Financial Aid Office at: (270) 762-2546.

Accreditation: *Regional:* SACS. *Professional:* NCATE. *Member of:* AACTE. *Approved by:* Kentucky Educational Professional Standards Board.

Undergraduate Programs: Undergraduate programs leading to the bachelor's degree and certification include the fields of: agricultural education, art, biological science, career and teaching education, chemistry, earth science, elementary education, English, health and physical education, interdisciplinary early childhood education, learning and behavior disorders, math education, middle school education, modern languages, music education, physics, secondary school education. All programs require completion of a general education core, professional studies, subject area major, field experiences, and student teaching. Completion of 128 credit hours is required for all baccalaureate degree programs.

Graduate Programs: The master's level programs include: advanced studies in learning and behavior disorders, agricultural education, career and technical education, early elementary education and school counseling; interdisciplinary early childhood education, and industrial education.

Licensure/Reciprocity: Kentucky. Students seeking teaching certification in a state other than Kentucky should consult with that state's teacher certification office early in their program of study to insure compliance with requirements. Many state directors of teacher credentialing have signed Interstate Agreements through NASDTEC that expedite the certification process.

NORTHERN KENTUCKY UNIVERSITY

College of Education
BEP Building
Nunn Drive
Highland Heights, Kentucky 40199
Phone: (859) 572-5229
Fax: (859) 572-6623
E-mail: bruno@nku.edu
Internet: http://www.nku.edu

Institution Description: Northern Kentucky University is a state institution. It was established as Northern Kentucky State College in 1968. The present name was adopted in 1976.

The faculty of the College of Education is committed to developing a teacher education program that sets a standard of excellence in pre-service education of teachers.

Institution Control: Public.

Calendar: Semester. Academic year August to May.

Official(s): Dr. Rachelle Bruno, Dean, Dr. Lynne Smith, Associate Dean.

Faculty: Full-time 40. part-time 6 adjunct 32.

Degrees Awarded: 203 baccalaureate; 170 master's.

Admission Requirements: *Undergraduate:* Open enrollment. *Teacher education specific:* GPA 2.5; meet minimum requirements of ACT 21 or SAT 990. *Graduate:* Baccalaureate degree from a regionally accredited institution. *Teacher education specific:* Teaching certificate for advanced programs; GRE; faculty interview.

Fees and Expenses: Undergraduate: in-state $3,744; out-of-state $7,992. Graduate: in-state $210 per credit hour; out-of-state $483 per credit hour. On-campus room and board: $4,388. Books and supplies: $500 per year.

Financial Aid: Resources specifically for eligible students enrolled in teacher education programs are awarded on the basis of financial need and academic merit. The institution has a Program Participation Agreement with the U.S. Department of Education for eligible students to receive Pell Grants and other federal aid. Kentucky Teacher Scholarships available to qualifying students. *Contact:* Financial Aid Office at: (859) 572-5229.

Accreditation: *Regional:* SACS. *Professional:* NCATE. *Member of:* AACTE. *Approved by:* Kentucky Educational Professional Standards Board.

Undergraduate Programs: The elementary education (P-5) program leads to the degree of Bachelor of Arts. The program requires the completion of a general studies core, professional education courses, related courses, and at least one emphasis area (English/communications, mathematics, science, social studies, special education).

Students who wish to complete the P-12 preparation program in special education must also complete certification requirements for teaching certificates at the P-5 elementary program, the middle grades program with an endorsement for teaching special education, or a content major and the complete certification sequence in secondary education.

Successful completion of the middle grades program (5-9) leads to the Bachelor of Arts degree. The program requirements include general studies, professional studies, related coursework, and teaching field specifications.

The secondary education program leads to a bachelor's degree and certification. Students major in secondary education and receive the bachelor's degree from their content area department.

Graduate Programs: The College of Education offers graduate programs leading to the Master of Arts in Education, Master of Arts in Teaching, a non-degree fifth year program, and a non-degree Rank I program.

Licensure/Reciprocity: Kentucky. Students seeking teaching certification in a state other than Kentucky should consult with that state's teacher certification office early in their program of study to insure compliance with requirements. Many state directors of teacher credentialing have signed Interstate Agreements through NASDTEC that expedite the certification process.

SPALDING UNIVERSITY
School of Education
851 South Fourth Street
Louisville, Kentucky 40203-2118
Phone: (502) 585-7121
Fax: (502) 585-7123
E-mail: blindsey@spalding.edu
Internet: http://www.spalding.edu

Institution Description: Spalding University is a private independent institution affiliated with the Sisters of Charity of Nazareth, Roman Catholic Church. It was established in Louisville in 1920 as Nazareth College, a branch campus of Nazareth Academy in Nazareth. The name was changed to Catherine Spalding College in 1963. The college merged with Nazareth Academy, became coeducational, and the name was changed to Spalding College in 1969. It became Spalding University in 1984.

The mission of the School of Education is the preparation of educators who possess intellectual understanding, holistic perspective, and professional skills to lead others to the maximum use of their potential for lifelong learning in a multicultural society.

Institution Control: Private.

Calendar: Semester. Academic year August to May.

Official(s): Dr. Betty Lindsey, Dean.

Faculty: Full-time 12; part-time 1; adjunct 30.

Degrees Awarded: 21 baccalaureate; 79 master's; 28 doctorate.

Admission Requirements: *Undergraduate:* Graduation from an approved secondary school or GED; College Board SAT or ACT composite. *Teacher education specific:* 21 ACT of 990 SAT or specified scores on PRAXIS I test; GPA 2.5; recommendations; writing sample; health screening; interview. *Graduate:* Baccalaureate degree from a regionally accredited institution. *Teacher education specific:* Official transcripts of all college/university coursework; GRE or Miller Analogies Test; 2.5 GPA; recommendations; writing sample; interview.

Fees and Expenses: Undergraduate $6,425 per academic year. Graduate: $420 per credit hour. Graduate fees $4.00 per credit hour. On-campus room: $1,660 single, $2,290 double. Books and supplies: $35 per course.

Financial Aid: Resources specifically for eligible students enrolled in teacher education programs are awarded on the basis of financial need and academic merit. The institution has a Program Participation Agreement with the U.S. Department of Education for eligible students to receive Pell Grants and other federal aid. *Contact:* Melissa Beam at: (502) 589-9911, ext. 2359 or e-mail at mbeam@spalding. edu.

Accreditation: *Regional:* SACS. *Professional:* NCATE. *Member of:* AACTE. *Approved by:* Kentucky Educational Professional Standards Board.

Undergraduate Programs: The School of Education offers preparation programs leading to the initial professional certificate/license. Programs include: Bachelor of Science in early elementary (grades P-5); middle school (grades 5-9), learning behavior disorders (grades P-12). The programs require the completion of a general education core, professional studies, subject area major, field experiences, and student teaching for a total of 128 credit hours.

Graduate Programs: The Master of Arts in Teaching is offered in the program areas of: early elementary (grades P-5); middle school (grades 5-9); high school (grades 8-12); art (grades P-12); business and marketing (grades 5-12); and learning and behavior disorders (grades P-12).

Advanced degree programs include a Master of Arts in Education for professional enhancement, Master of Arts - school administrator; and a doctorate in leadership education (open to persons who hold a master's degree in any discipline).

Licensure/Reciprocity: Kentucky. Students seeking teaching certification in a state other than Kentucky should consult with that state's teacher certification office early in their program of study to insure compliance with requirements. Many state directors of teacher credentialing have signed Interstate Agreements through NASDTEC that expedite the certification process.

TRANSYLVANIA UNIVERSITY
Education Program
300 North Broadway
Lexington, Kentucky 40508-1797
Phone: (859) 233-8174
Fax: (859) 233-8749
E-mail: ahurley@transy.edu
Internet: http://www.transy.edu

Institution Description: Transylvania University is a private independent institution affiliated with the Christian Church (Disciples of Christ). It was established and chartered as Transylvania Seminary in 1780. The name was changed to Transylvania University in 1799. The name was changed to Kentucky University in 1865 but readopted the name Transylvania in 1908.

The Education Program offers teacher education programs in elementary, middle, and secondary school levels.

Institution Control: Private.

Calendar: Semester (4-4-1 plan). Academic year September to May.

Official(s): Dr. Angela Hurley, Division Chair; Dr. Kathy Edher, Program Chair.

Faculty: Full-time 4; part-time 1; adjunct 1.

Degrees Awarded: 8 baccalaureate.

Admission Requirements: *Undergraduate:* Graduation from an approved secondary school or GED; College Board SAT or ACT composite; admission selective based on SAT or ACT scores and high school class standing. *Teacher education specific:* Minimum ACT of 21; minimum 2.75 GPA overall and in major; writing sample; recommendations from college faculty; interview.

Fees and Expenses: $17,660 per academic year. On-campus room and board: $6,120.

Financial Aid: Resources specifically for eligible students enrolled in teacher education programs are awarded on the basis of financial need and academic merit. The institution has a Program Participation Agreement with the U.S. Department of Education for eligible students to receive Pell Grants and other federal aid. Kentucky Teacher Scholarships available to qualifying students. *Contact:* David Cecil at e-mail dcecil@transy.edu.

Accreditation: *Regional:* SACS. *Professional:* NCATE. *Member of:* AACTE. *Approved by:* Kentucky Educational Professional Standards Board.

Undergraduate Programs: The Education Program is embedded liberal arts environment and stresses a foundation in theory and philosophy combined with practice in school settings for every course. Students can receive a degree in elementary or middle grades education; K-12 certification for music, art, French, Spanish, and physical education; or secondary certification by combining either a major in English, biology, chemistry, mathematics, physics, or history with a minor in education. Graduation requirements include the successful completion of at least 36 units with a 2.75 GPA overall in education and in the area of specialization. All students must complete a program portfolio of assigned materials.

Licensure/Reciprocity: Kentucky. Students seeking teaching certification in a state other than Kentucky should consult with that state's teacher certification office early in their program of study to insure compliance with requirements. Many state directors of teacher credentialing have signed Interstate Agreements through NASDTEC that expedite the certification process.

UNION COLLEGE

Department of Educational Studies
Teacher Education Program

310 College Street
Barbourville, Kentucky 40906
Phone: (606) 546-4151
Fax: (606) 546-1663
E-mail: enroll@unionky.edu
Internet: http://www.unionky.edu

Institution Description: Union College is a private college affiliated with the United Methodist Church. It was established, chartered, and incorporated in 1879.

The undergraduate programs in Educational Studies have as their primary objective the preparation of well-educated teachers for public and private schools in Kentucky and the nation.

Institution Control: Private.

Calendar: Semester. Academic year August to May.

Official(s): Dr.Robert Swanson, Professor, Graduate Studies.

Faculty: Full-time 10; adjunct 8.

Degrees Awarded: 14 baccalaureate; 109 master's.

Admission Requirements: *Undergraduate:* Graduation from an approved secondary school or GED; College Board SAT or ACT composite. *Teacher education specific:* Minimum of 30 semester hours of college credit; cumulative GPA of 2.75; portfolio review; faculty interview. *Graduate:* Baccalaureate degree from a regionally accredited institution. *Teacher education specific:* Official transcripts of all college/university coursework; minimum 2.75 GPA; valid provisional or Standard Kentucky Teaching Certificate or statement of eligibility; passing scores on PRAXIS tests.

Fees and Expenses: $12,430 per academic year. Graduate: $225 per credit hour. On-campus room and board: $4,500. Other expenses: $1,500. Books and supplies: $550.

Financial Aid: Resources specifically for eligible students enrolled in teacher education programs are awarded on the basis of financial need and academic merit. The institution has a Program Participation Agreement with the U.S. Department of Education for eligible students to receive Pell Grants and other federal aid. Kentucky Teacher Scholarships available to qualifying students. *Contact:* Financial Aid Office at: (606) 546-1223.

Accreditation: *Regional:* SACS. *Member of:* AACTE. *Approved by:* Kentucky Educational Professional Standards Board.

Undergraduate Programs: The Educational Studies curriculum includes majors in elementary education, middle grades education, secondary education, and special education. All programs require the completion of a liberal education core, multicultural studies, pre-professional courses, professional studies, major subject concentration, field experiences, and student teaching. Baccalaureate programs require the completion of 128 credit hours.

Graduate Programs: The graduate program is dedicated to serving area educators by enhancing their ability to work effectively with students, parents, educators, and community leaders. Through the Master of Arts in Education, the fifth-year non-degree and Rank I programs, graduate students can enhance their initial preparation as classroom teachers. Rank I programs include elementary school, middle school, and secondary school education. Rank II programs include similar fields of study with specialization in language arts, science, and social studies.

Licensure/Reciprocity: Kentucky. Students seeking teaching certification in a state other than Kentucky should consult with that state's teacher certification office early in their program of study to insure compliance with requirements. Many state directors of teacher credentialing have signed Interstate Agreements through NASDTEC that expedite the certification process.

UNIVERSITY OF KENTUCKY

College of Education

103 Dickey Hall
Lexington, Kentucky 40506-0017
Phone: (859) 257-6076
Fax: (859) 257-9000
E-mail: sandidg@uky.edu
Internet: http://www.uky.edu

Institution Description: University of Kentucky is a state institution and land-grant college. It was established as Agricultural and Mechanical College of Kentucky University and chartered in 1865. The present name was adopted in 1916.

The College of Education prepares students for professional careers in the field of education and human services.

Institution Control: Public.

Calendar: Semester. Academic year August to May.

Official(s): Dr. James G. Cibulka, Dean; Dr. Rosetta F. Sandidge, Associate Dean.

Faculty: Full-time 91; part-time 47; adjunct 2.

Degrees Awarded: 238 baccalaureate; 179 master's; 24 doctorate.

Admission Requirements: *Undergraduate:* Graduation from an approved secondary school or GED; college preparatory curriculum; minimum 2.0 GPA. *Teacher education specific:* Student must have completed 60 semester hours; must certify their knowledge of Kentucky Professional Code of Ethics; admissions portfolio; ACT composite score of 21 or SAT 990. PRAXIS I test scores; faculty interview. *Graduate:* Baccalaureate degree from a regionally accredited institution. *Teacher education specific:* Overall 2.75 GPA; GRE; official transcripts for previous college coursework; teaching credential required for certain programs; recommendations; faculty interview.

Fees and Expenses: Undergraduate: in-state $4,546.50 per academic year; out-of-state $11,226.50. Graduate: in-state $4,974.50 per academic year; $12,314.50. Required fees: $544.50. On-campus room and board: $4,285. Books and supplies: $200 up per semester.

Financial Aid: Resources specifically for eligible students enrolled in teacher education programs are awarded on the basis of financial need and academic merit. The institution has a Program Participation Agreement with the U.S. Department of Education for eligible students to receive Pell Grants and other federal aid. Kentucky Teacher Scholarships available to qualifying students. *Contact:* Lynda S. George at: (859) 257-3172.

Accreditation: *Regional:* SACS. *Professional:* NCATE. *Member of:* AACTE. *Approved by:* Kentucky Educational Professional Standards Board.

Undergraduate Programs: Students pursuing one of the following majors earn the Bachelor of Arts in Education degree: elementary education, health promotion, kinesiology (teacher certification, business, exercise science), middle school education, secondary education, or special education (learning and behavior disorders).

The major in secondary education leading to the Bachelor of Arts in Education is offered with specializations in English, foreign language (French, German, Latin, Spanish, Russian) mathematics, science, (biology, chemistry, earth science, physical science, or physics), or social studies.

Students pursuing special education (moderate and severe disabilities) earn the Bachelor of Science degree

All programs require the completion of a general education core, professional studies, subject area major, field experiences, and student teaching for a minimum of 120 semester hours.

Graduate Programs: The following graduate level initial education certification programs are available at the University of Kentucky: stand-alone certification in special education/learning and behavior disorders, grades P-12; Master of Science program leading to certification in moderate/sever disabilities, grades P-12; Master of Arts in Education with initial certification in secondary education, grades 8-12, English, mathematics, science (biology, chemistry earth science, physical science or physics), social studies; Master of Arts in Education with initial certification in foreign language education, grades P-12); Mas-

UNIVERSITY OF KENTUCKY—*cont'd*

ters of Arts in education with initial certification, grades 5-12 in business and marketing education; Master of Science in vocational education with initial certification, grades 5-12; Master of Science in communication disorders with initial certification, grades P-12; and certification program in school psychology, grades P-12.

The university also offers programs leading to the Doctor of Education (Ed.D.) and Doctor of Philosophy (Ph.D.).

Licensure/Reciprocity: Kentucky. Students seeking teaching certification in a state other than Kentucky should consult with that state's teacher certification office early in their program of study to insure compliance with requirements. Many state directors of teacher credentialing have signed Interstate Agreements through NASDTEC that expedite the certification process.

UNIVERSITY OF LOUISVILLE

College of Education and Human Development
Department of Teaching and Learning

2301 South Third Street
Louisville, Kentucky 40292-0001
Phone: (502) 852-6431
Fax: (502) 852-6431
E-mail: karen@louisville.edu
Internet: http://www.louisville.edu

Institution Description: The University of Louisville is a state institution that was established as Jefferson Seminary in 1837. The present name was adopted in 1846.

Through its academic programs, the Department of Teaching and Learning, prepares educators to work in early childhood, elementary, middle, secondary, and special education.

Institution Control: Public.

Calendar: Semester. Academic year June to May.

Official(s): Dr. Karen Karp, Chair, Department of Teaching and Learning.

Faculty: Full-time 37.

Degrees Awarded: 70 baccalaureate; 350 master's; 24 doctorate.

Admission Requirements: *Undergraduate:* Graduation from an approved secondary school or GED; SAT or ACT composite. *Teacher education specific:* Minimum of 30 semester hours of college credit; cumulative GPA of 2.75; portfolio review; faculty interview. *Graduate:* Baccalaureate degree from a regionally accredited institution. *Teacher education specific:* Official transcripts of all college/university coursework; minimum 2.75 GPA; valid provisional or Standard Kentucky Teaching Certificate or statement of eligibility; passing scores on PRAXIS tests.

Fees and Expenses: Undergraduate: in-state $4,082 per academic year; out-of-state $11,162. Graduate: Tuition charged per credit hour. On-campus room and board: $7,744. Other expenses: $3,348. Books and supplies: $700.

Financial Aid: Resources specifically for eligible students enrolled in teacher education programs are awarded on the basis of financial need and academic merit. The institution has a Program Participation Agreement with the U.S. Department of Education for eligible students to receive Pell Grants and other federal aid. Kentucky Teacher Scholarships available to qualifying students. *Contact:* Financial Aid Office at: (502) 852-5511.

Accreditation: *Regional:* SACS. *Professional:* NCATE. *Member of:* AACTE. *Approved by:* Kentucky Educational Professional Standards Board.

Undergraduate Programs: The College of Education and Human Development offers certification at the bachelor's level in early elementary education. Students can choose from two concentrations, either interdisciplinary early childhood education which leads to birth through kindergarten certification, or certification in grades P-5 combined with certification in grades P-12 learning and behavior disorders. The certification program in occupational education at the bachelor's level is for vocational education teachers to further their education and rank level.

The teacher education programs are delivered in concert with practitioners in the schools and community agencies. Courses and experiences with students occur at the schools where teachers, staff, and students participating actively in them.

Graduate Programs: Certification programs are offered through the Master of Arts in Teaching program. Based on the belief that teachers must have a strong grounding in the liberal arts and sciences, the programs require that applicants earn a bachelor's degree first. The MAT programs blend instruction in pedagogy and curriculum development with opportunities for action research and service learning projects. The MAT is offered in the areas of: early elementary, middle or secondary school teaching as well as art, foreign language, music, and physical education.

The Master of Education degree is offered in interdisciplinary early childhood education, learning and behavior disorders, and moderate and severe disabilities.

Licensure/Reciprocity: Kentucky. Students seeking teaching certification in a state other than Kentucky should consult with that state's teacher certification office early in their program of study to insure compliance with requirements. Many state directors of teacher credentialing have signed Interstate Agreements through NASDTEC that expedite the certification process.

WESTERN KENTUCKY UNIVERSITY

College of Education and Behavioral Sciences

201 Tate Page Hall
1 Big Red Way
Bowling Green, Kentucky 42101-3576
Phone: (270) 745-4662
Fax: (270) 745-6474
E-mail: cebs.college@wku.edu
Internet: http://www.wku.edu

Institution Description: Western Kentucky University is a state institution. It was established as Western Kentucky State Normal School in 1906. The name was changed to Western Kentucky State Normal School and Teachers College in 1922, to Western Kentucky State Teachers College in 1930, to Western Kentucky State College in 1948, and to its present name in 1966.

The College of Education and Behavioral Sciences offers undergraduate programs leading to teaching certification and graduate programs to further enhance professional achievement.

Institution Control: Public.

Calendar: Semester. Academic year August to May.

Official(s): Dr. Sam Evans, Dean, College of Education and Behavioral Sciences.

Faculty: Full-time 65; part-time 14; adjunct 39.

Degrees Awarded: 322 baccalaureate; 323 master's.

Admission Requirements: *Undergraduate:* Graduation from an approved secondary school or GED; SAT or ACT composite. *Teacher education specific:* Minimum of 30 semester hours of college credit; cumulative GPA of 2.75; portfolio review; faculty interview. *Graduate:* Baccalaureate degree from a regionally accredited institution. *Teacher education specific:* Official transcripts of all college/university coursework; minimum 2.75 GPA; valid provisional or Standard Kentucky Teaching Certificate or statement of eligibility (where required for certain programs; GRE; passing scores on PRAXIS tests; faculty interview.

Fees and Expenses: Undergraduate: in-state $1,825 per semester; out-of-state $4,248. Graduate: in-state $1,999 per semester; out-of-state $2,179. On-campus room and board: $2,200 per semester. Books and supplies: $1,000.

Financial Aid: Resources specifically for eligible students enrolled in teacher education programs are awarded on the basis of financial need and academic merit. The institution has a Program Participation Agreement with the U.S. Department of Education for eligible students to receive Pell Grants and other

federal aid. Kentucky Teacher Scholarships available to qualifying students. *Contact:* Pam Jukes at: (270) 745-2157 or e-mail at pam.jukes@wku.edu.

Accreditation: *Regional:* SACS. *Professional:* NCATE. *Member of:* AACTE. *Approved by:* Kentucky Educational Professional Standards Board.

Undergraduate Programs: The university offers degree programs leading to initial certification in early childhood education, elementary education, middle grades education, learning and behavioral disorders, and in content specific disciplines. All content specific programs are housed in the department of the majors, i.e., mathematics, English, Music. All programs are standards-based with all candidates completing a Teacher Work Sample documenting their performance relative to state teacher standards and ability to impact P-12 student learning during their student teaching experience. All programs require completion of a general education core, professional studies, subject content area (secondary education), field experiences, and student teaching for a minimum of 128 semester hours.

Graduate Programs: In addition to the Master of Arts in Education programs, students may pursue advanced certification in selected MA and MS degree programs, i.e., English, agriculture, mathematics, physical education. Advanced certification is also available in elementary education, library media, school counseling, educational administration, and school psychology. Alternate route to certification programs are currently available in school principalship, special education, middle grades education, and secondary education. All of the program include employment by a school district during enrollment in the program.

Licensure/Reciprocity: Kentucky. Students seeking teaching certification in a state other than Kentucky should consult with that state's teacher certification office early in their program of study to insure compliance with requirements. Many state directors of teacher credentialing have signed Interstate Agreements through NASDTEC that expedite the certification process.

LOUISIANA

CENTENARY COLLEGE OF LOUISIANA

Department of Education
2911 Centenary Boulevard
Shreveport, Louisiana 71104
Phone: (318) 869-5011
Fax: (318) 869-5026
E-mail: admissions@centenary.edu
Internet: http://www.centenary.edu

Institution Description: Centenary College of Louisiana is a private college affiliated with the United Methodist Church. It was established and chartered in Jackson as the College of Louisiana in 1825. It merged with Centenary College (established 1839) and the present name was adopted in 1845. The campus moved to its present location 1908.

The Department of Education seeks to help students develop a strong, professional foundation for teaching in the elementary or secondary schools.

Institution Control: Private.

Calendar: Semester. Academic year August to May.

Official(s): Dr. Sue Hernandez, Chair, Department of Education.

Faculty: Full-time 4; part-time 8.

Degrees Awarded: 13 baccalaureate; 16 master's.

Admission Requirements: *Undergraduate:* Graduation with 15 academic units from an approved secondary school or GED; College Board SAT or ACT composite. *Teacher education specific:* Acceptance into the teacher preparation program by the sophomore year; PRAXIS I test scores; declaration of major area; personal goal statement; faculty interview. *Graduate:* Baccalaureate from a regionally accredited institution. *Teacher education specific:* Maintain a 2.5 GPA; teaching credential where appropriate; recommendations and faculty interview.

Fees and Expenses: Undergraduate: $16,500 per academic year. Graduate: $430 per credit hour. On-campus room and board: $5,550. Other expenses: $2,300. Books and supplies: $100.

Financial Aid: Resources specifically for eligible students enrolled in teacher education programs are awarded on the basis of financial need and academic merit. The institution has a Program Participation Agreement with the U.S. Department of Education for eligible students to receive Pell Grants and other federal aid. Teacher Scholarships available to qualifying students. *Contact:* Financial Aid Office at: (318) 869-5137.

Accreditation: *Regional:* SACS. *Member of:* AACTE. *Approved by:* Louisiana Department of Education.

Degrees Offered: Baccalaureate; Master's.

Undergraduate Programs: The Department of Education offers programs leading to the Bachelor of Arts or Bachelor of Science in elementary education (grades 1-6); the Bachelor of Music in music education (instrumental and vocal, grades K-12); and the Bachelor of Science in health/physical education. Certification in grades 7-12 are offered with majors in biology, business, chemistry, earth science, English, environmental science, French, general science, German, Latin, mathematics, physics, and Spanish.

All pre-service teachers take courses in the foundation of education, educational psychology, human growth and development, and special needs children. Elementary pre-service teachers take additional courses in reading, language arts, social studies, and science methods of teaching. Secondary candidates take courses in secondary methods and content area reading. All programs require the completion of a minimum of 124 credit hours.

Graduate Programs: The Master of Education in school administration is for those who wish to be school principals at the elementary or secondary level. The Master of Education in supervision of instruction is designed for those who wish to be instructional coordinators at the school level or supervisors of instruction at the parish level.

The Master of Arts in Teaching (elementary and secondary) are designed for those who are not certified to teach upon entry into the program and who wish to seek certification as they pursue the master's degree. The degree programs require the completion of 36 hours, not including student teaching.

Licensure/Reciprocity: Louisiana. Students seeking teaching certification in a state other than Louisiana should consult with that state's teacher certification office early in their program of study to insure compliance with requirements. Many state directors of teacher credentialing have signed Interstate Agreements through NASDTEC that expedite the certification process.

DILLARD UNIVERSITY

Division of Educational and Psychological Studies
2601 Gentilly Boulevard
New Orleans, Louisiana 70122
Phone: (504) 283-8822
Fax: (504) 286-4668
E-mail: education@dillard.edu
Internet: http://www.dillard.edu

Institution Description: Dillard University is a private institution affiliated with the United Methodist Church and the United Church of Christ. It was established in 1930 through a merger of New Orleans University and Straight College (both established 1869).

Educational Studies is the newest major offered in the Division of Educational and Psychological Studies. It was designed to capture the best of a liberal arts education combined with the study of education.

Institution Control: Private.

Calendar: Semester. Academic year August to May.

Official(s): Dr. Kassie Freeman, Dean, Educational Studies.

Degrees Awarded: 9 baccalaureate.

Admission Requirements: *Undergraduate:* Graduation from an approved secondary school or GED; College Board SAT or ACT composite. *Teacher education specific:* GPA of 2.0 or higher after first year of study; personal goal statement; involvement in academic and extracurricular activities; declaration of major area; faculty interview.

Fees and Expenses: $11,109 per academic year. On-campus room and board: $6,908. Other expenses: $2,757. Books and supplies: $1,000.

Financial Aid: Resources specifically for eligible students enrolled in teacher education programs are awarded on the basis of financial need and academic merit. The institution has a Program Participation Agreement with the U.S. Department of

Education for eligible students to receive Pell Grants and other federal aid. Teacher Scholarships available to qualifying students. *Contact:* Financial Aid Office at: (504) 816-4677.

Accreditation: *Regional:* SACS. *Professional:* NCATE. *Member of:* AACTE. *Approved by:* Louisiana Department of Education.

Degrees Offered: Baccalaureate.

Undergraduate Programs: Students in Educational Studies are required to complete in-depth coursework in foreign language, demonstrate proficiency in writing, and exhibit strong analytical and problem-solving skills. Graduates of the program will be thoroughly grounded in methods of inquiry, culturally relevant pedagogy, and state-of-the art technology. Students are prepared for positions in educational settings that do not require teacher certification. Students must complete 20 hours in community service each semester for a total of 120 hours. The baccalaureate degree program requires the completion of a total of 125 semester hours.

Licensure/Reciprocity: Louisiana. Students seeking teaching certification in a state other than Louisiana should consult with that state's teacher certification office early in their program of study to insure compliance with requirements. Many state directors of teacher credentialing have signed Interstate Agreements through NASDTEC that expedite the certification process.

GRAMBLING STATE UNIVERSITY
College of Education
Department Teacher Education
100 Main Street
Grambling, Louisiana 71245
Phone: (318) 274-3881
Fax: (318) 274-2398
E-mail: coe@gram.edu
Internet: http://www.gram.edu

Institution Description: Grambling State University (Grambling College until 1974) was established in 1901.

The Department of Teacher Education offers undergraduate, graduate, and post-baccalaureate alternate certification programs.

Institution Control: Public.

Calendar: Semester. Academic year August to May.

Official(s): Dr. Loretta Jaggers, Chair, Teacher Education.

Faculty: Full-time 9.

Degrees Awarded: 450 baccalaureate candidates.

Admission Requirements: *Undergraduate:* Graduation from an approved secondary school or GED; College Board SAT or ACT composite. *Teacher education education specific:* Minimum of 30 semester hours of college credit; cumulative GPA of 2.75; portfolio review; faculty interview. *Graduate:* Baccalaureate degree from a regionally accredited institution. *Teacher education specific:* Official transcripts of all college/university coursework; minimum 2.75 GPA; passing scores on PRAXIS tests; faculty interview.

Fees and Expenses: Undergraduate: in-state $2,740 per academic year; out-of-state $8,286. Graduate: Tuition charged per credit hour. Other expenses: $23265. On-campus room and board: $2,912. Other expenses: $2,526. Books and supplies: $1,000.

Financial Aid: Resources specifically for eligible students enrolled in teacher education programs are awarded on the basis of financial need and academic merit. The institution has a Program Participation Agreement with the U.S. Department of Education for eligible students to receive Pell Grants and other federal aid. Teacher Scholarships available to qualifying students. *Contact:* Financial Aid Office at: (318) 274-6056.

Accreditation: *Regional:* SACS. *Professional:* NCATE. *Member of:* AACTE. *Approved by:* Louisiana Department Board of Education.

Degrees Offered: Baccalaureate; Master's.

Undergraduate Programs: The elementary education curriculum prepares classroom teachers for grades 1-6. The student may elect to add courses in special education with the aim of certification in both the regular elementary classroom and the special education classroom.

The elementary and secondary education programs are for students choosing to teach fine arts, French, or health and physical education in elementary or high schools. Curricula leading to certification in secondary classroom teaching are offered in the content areas of: biology, chemistry, English, mathematics, physics, and social studies. Students may enhance their degrees by earning additional certification endorsement, second degrees, or with two majors.

All baccalaureate programs require the completion of a general education core, professional studies, content area major (secondary education), field experiences, and student teaching. The department has collaborative relationships with the Colleges of Liberal Arts, Science, and Technology. A minimum of 128 semester hours must be completed for the degree award.

Graduate Programs: The Master of Education is a professional graduate degree designed to enrich a student's academic and professional background. The program is tailored to meet the individual needs of the student. Teacher certification is not required to enter the program.

Licensure/Reciprocity: Louisiana. Students seeking teaching certification in a state other than Louisiana should consult with that state's teacher certification office early in their program of study to insure compliance with requirements. Many state directors of teacher credentialing have signed Interstate Agreements through NASDTEC that expedite the certification process.

LOUISIANA STATE UNIVERSITY
College of Education
Teacher Education Programs
221 Peabody Hall
Baton Rouge, Louisiana 70803
Phone: (225) 578-1258
Fax: (225) 578-2267
E-mail: fuhrma@lsu.edu
Internet: http://www.lsu.edu

Institution Description: The institution was established as Louisiana State Seminary of Learning and Military Academy in 1853. The name was changed to Louisiana State University in 1870. The present name was adopted in 1877.

The teacher preparation programs have resulted from collaboration among faculty from the College of Education, the College of Arts and Sciences, the College of Basic Sciences, the College of Agriculture, and local school partners.

Institution Control: Public.

Calendar: Semester. Academic year August to May.

Official(s): Dr. Barbara S. Fuhrmann, Dean, College of Education.

Faculty: Full-time 74l part-time 9.

Degrees Awarded: 467 baccalaureate; 171 master's; 29 doctorate.

Admission Requirements: *Undergraduate:* Graduation from an approved high school or GED; ACT composite score of 21. *Teacher education specific:* 2.5 GPA; passing scores on PRAXIS I; declaration of major; faculty interview. *Graduate:* Baccalaureate degree from a regionally accredited institution. *Teacher education specific:* GPA 3.0; GRE score of 1000 (verbal and quantitative); completion of all departmental tests/exams; recommendations; faculty interview.

Fees and Expenses: Undergraduate: in-state $1,832 per semester; out-of-state $4,452. Graduate: in-state $1,838 per semester; out-of-state $4,488.

Financial Aid: Resources specifically for eligible students enrolled in teacher education programs are awarded on the basis of financial need and academic merit. The institution has a Program Participation Agreement with the U.S. Department of Education for eligible students to receive Pell Grants and other

LOUISIANA STATE UNIVERSITY—*cont'd*

federal aid. Teacher Scholarships available to qualifying students. *Contact:* Office of Student Aid and Scholarships at: (225) 578-3103 or e-mail at financialaid@lsu.edu.

Accreditation: *Regional:* SACS. *Professional:* NCATE. *Member of:* AACTE. *Approved by:* Louisiana Department of Education.

Degrees Offered: Baccalaureate; Master's.

Undergraduate Programs: The early childhood grades PK-5 program is an integrated, collaborative program designed to produce PK-5 educators. Candidates are introduced to the field of early childhood education as early as their freshman year. During the junior year, students earn nine of their credits each semester in field-based professional blocks in two different professional development school settings. The each semester of the senior year incorporates field-based student teaching.

The program for elementary grades 1-6 is offered with two concentrations: four-year teacher certification and five-year certification leading to the master's degree. Both of these concentrations incorporate field experience in a varied socioeconomic and cultural settings.

The secondary grades 7-12 program is offered through the content-area colleges (arts and sciences, basic sciences) in close partnership with the College of Education. This model centers on an introductory course exploring contemporary educational issues followed by an sequence of four professional practice seminars integrated into the academic program. Students matriculate through the program in cohorts, thus establishing an identify as members of a learning community.

All programs require the general education core, subject area major (secondary education), professional courses, field experiences, and student teaching for a minimum of 120 semester hours. Certification programs in agricultural, business, home economics, and industrial education are undergoing redesign by the College of Agriculture.

Graduate Programs: The Master of Education degree is a full-year of graduate-level professional preparation. Students earn a master's degree in education and Louisiana Teacher Certification by completing 37-43 credit hours beyond a bachelor's degree in elementary education or secondary education and successfully completing the PRAXIS requirements. The program feature extended experiences in diverse school settings.

The Master of Arts in Education is designed for students with undergraduate degrees in education fields who seek graduate level studies to extend their studies by taking coursework in several areas in curriculum and instruction. The student can take 30 hours of coursework with a written comprehensive examination or take 30 hours of coursework and six hours of thesis with an oral examination.

Licensure/Reciprocity: Louisiana. Students seeking teaching certification in a state other than Louisiana should consult with that state's teacher certification office early in their program of study to insure compliance with requirements. Many state directors of teacher credentialing have signed Interstate Agreements through NASDTEC that expedite the certification process.

LOUISIANA STATE UNIVERSITY IN SHREVEPORT

College of Education and Human Development
One University Place
Shreveport, Louisiana 71115
Phone: (318) 797-5000
Fax: (318) 797-5286
E-mail: coehd@lsus.edu
Internet: http://www.lsus.edu

Institution Description: The university is a state institution that was established and chartered in 1965.

The Department of Education offers undergraduate, graduate, and post-baccalaureate alternate certification programs.

Institution Control: Public.

Calendar: Semester. Academic year August to May.

Official(s): Dr. Gale W. Bridger, Dean.

Faculty: Full-time 28; adjunct 2.

Degrees Awarded: 63 baccalaureate; 33 master's.

Admission Requirements: *Undergraduate:* Graduation from an approved secondary school or GED; College Board SAT or ACT composite. *Teacher education education specific:* Minimum of 30 semester hours of college credit; cumulative GPA of 2.75; portfolio review; faculty interview. *Graduate:* Baccalaureate degree from a regionally accredited institution. *Teacher education specific:* Official transcripts of all college/university coursework; minimum 2.75 GPA; passing scores on PRAXIS tests; faculty interview.

Fees and Expenses: Undergraduate: in-state $2,368 per academic year; out-of-state $6,598. Graduate: in-state $105 per credit hour; out-of-state $175. Other expenses: $2,585. On-campus room and board: $6,403. Books and supplies: $900.

Financial Aid: Resources specifically for eligible students enrolled in teacher education programs are awarded on the basis of financial need and academic merit. The institution has a Program Participation Agreement with the U.S. Department of Education for eligible students to receive Pell Grants and other federal aid. Teacher Scholarships available to qualifying students. *Contact:* Financial Aid Office at: (318) 797-5363.

Accreditation: *Regional:* SACS. *Professional:* NCATE. *Member of:* AACTE. *Approved by:* Louisiana Department Board of Education.

Degrees Offered: Baccalaureate; Master's.

Undergraduate Programs: The elementary education curriculum prepares classroom teachers for grades 1-6. The student may elect to add courses in special education with the aim of certification in both the regular elementary classroom and the special education classroom.

The elementary and secondary education program is for students choosing to teach fine arts, French, or health and physical education in elementary or high schools. Curricula leading to certification in secondary classroom teaching are offered in the content areas of: biology, chemistry, English, mathematics, physics, and social studies. Students may enhance their degrees by earning additional certification endorsement, second degrees, or with two majors.

All baccalaureate programs require the completion of a general education core, professional studies, content area major (secondary education), field experiences, and student teaching. A minimum of 128 semester hours must be completed for the degree award.

Graduate Programs: The Master of Education is a professional graduate degree designed to enrich a student's academic and professional background. The program is tailored to meet the individual needs of the student. Teacher certification is not required to enter the program.

Licensure/Reciprocity: Louisiana. Students seeking teaching certification in a state other than Louisiana should consult with that state's teacher certification office early in their program of study to insure compliance with requirements. Many state directors of teacher credentialing have signed Interstate Agreements through NASDTEC that expedite the certification process.

LOUISIANA TECH UNIVERSITY

College of Education
Box 3163, Tech Station
Ruston, Louisiana 71272
Phone: (318) 257-3712
Fax: (318) 257-2957
E-mail: claborde@latech.edu
Internet: http://www.latech.edu

Institution Description: Louisiana Tech University is a state institution. It was established as Industrial Institute and College of Louisiana in 1894. The name was changed to Louisiana Polytechnic Institute in 1920 and the present name was adopted 1970.

The mission of The College of Education is to provide high quality educational experiences for current and prospective professionals from baccalaureate to doctoral levels.

Institution Control: Public.

Calendar: Quarter. Academic year September to May.

Official(s): Dr. JoAnn Dauzat, Dean, College of Education.

Faculty: Full-time 19; part-time 12; adjunct 8.

Degrees Awarded: 92 baccalaureate; 135 master's; 10 doctorate.

Admission Requirements: *Undergraduate:* Graduation with 15 academic units from an approved secondary school; ACT composite preferred. *Teacher education specific:* Applicant must have earned at least 46 semester hours of credit; 2.2 GPA; speech and hearing test; satisfactory scores on PRAXIS I; faculty interview. *Graduate:* Baccalaureate degree from a regionally accredited institution. *Teacher education specific:* Teaching certificate where required; 2.75 GPA on the last 60 hours of coursework; GRE; faculty interview.

Fees and Expenses: Undergraduate and graduate in-state $3,099 per academic year; out-of-state $6,847. Various required fees. Books and supplies: $600 to $1,000 per year.

Financial Aid: Resources specifically for eligible students enrolled in teacher education programs are awarded on the basis of financial need and academic merit. The institution has a Program Participation Agreement with the U.S. Department of Education for eligible students to receive Pell Grants and other federal aid. Teacher Scholarships available to qualifying students. *Contact:* Roger Vick at: (318) 257-2641 or e-mail at techaid@ltfa.latech.edu.

Accreditation: *Regional:* SACS. *Professional:* NCATE. *Member of:* AACTE. *Approved by:* Louisiana Department of Education.

Degrees Offered: Baccalaureate; Master's.

Undergraduate Programs: The teacher education curriculum prepares student to function as teachers in a variety of field and situations. Programs are organized as elementary, middle, secondary, and all-level. Generally, elementary teachers are in charge of teaching children between the grades of preschool to 6th grade. Middle school teachers address the needs of children mostly in grades 4-8 with secondary teachers in charge of students in grades 7-12. Various school organizations may have different configurations of these grades, All baccalaureate programs require the completion of a general education core, professional studies, content area major (secondary education), field experiences, and student teaching. A minimum of 122 credit hours is required for most baccalaureate programs.

Graduate Programs: The Master of Education Fifth-Year Program is designed for liberal arts and sciences graduates who seek initial certification in a teaching area and a master's degree. Certification areas include: art, business, elementary education, English, foreign languages, health and physical education, mathematics, music, science, social studies, speech, and vocational agriculture.

The Master of Science in curriculum and instruction will be required to earn a minimum of 36 credit hours which may include 6 hours credit for a thesis. An approved plan of study must be submitted during the first quarter of enrollment.

The Master of Education program is offered with concentrations available in: early childhood (K-3), elementary education (1-6), middle school (4-8), special education mild/moderate (1-12), and secondary education (7-12).

All programs are offered in the Department of Curriculum Instruction, and Leadership.

Licensure/Reciprocity: Louisiana. Students seeking teaching certification in a state other than Louisiana should consult with that state's teacher certification office early in their program of study to insure compliance with requirements. Many state directors of teacher credentialing have signed Interstate Agreements through NASDTEC that expedite the certification process.

LOYOLA UNIVERSITY NEW ORLEANS
Department of Education and Counseling
6363 St. Charles Avenue
New Orleans, Louisiana 70118
Phone: (504) 865-2011
Fax: (504) 865-3383
E-mail: madoyle@loyno.edu
Internet: http://www.loyno.edu

Institution Description: Loyola University New Orleans is a private institution affiliated with the Society of Jesus, Roman Catholic Church. It was established as Preparatory College of Immaculate Conception in 1847. The name was changed to Loyola College in 1904 and to its present name in 1912.

The Department of Education and Counseling offers a practice-oriented curriculum where students spend a large amount of time in actual school settings.

Institution Control: Private.

Calendar: Semester. Academic year August to May.

Official(s): Dr. Mary Ann Doyle, Director of Undergraduate Programs; Dr. Janet Melancon, Graduate Education Director.

Faculty: Full-time 10.

Degrees Awarded: 31 baccalaureate; 25 master's.

Admission Requirements: *Undergraduate:* Graduation from an accredited secondary school or GED; College Board SAT or ACT composite. *Teacher education specific:* Application to the department by sophomore year; declaration of major; PRAXIS I test scores; faculty interview. *Graduate:* Baccalaureate degree from a regionally accredited institution. *Teacher education specific:* Miller Analogies Test or GRE; official transcripts of undergraduate work; writing sample; three recommendations; personal interview.

Fees and Expenses: Undergraduate: $19,362 per academic year. Graduate: $312 per credit hour. On-campus room and board: $7,633. Other expenses: $1,476. Books and supplies: $1,000.

Financial Aid: Resources specifically for eligible students enrolled in teacher education programs are awarded on the basis of financial need and academic merit. The institution has a Program Participation Agreement with the U.S. Department of Education for eligible students to receive Pell Grants and other federal aid. Teacher Scholarships available to qualifying students. *Contact:* Financial Aid Office at: (504) 865-3231.

Accreditation: *Regional:* SACS. *Member of:* AACTE. *Approved by:* Louisiana Department of Education.

Degrees Offered: Baccalaureate; Master's.

Undergraduate Programs: The department offers certification to elementary majors in grades 1-8 and early childhood (preschool and kindergarten). Prospective secondary education teachers may be certified in English, social studies, mathematics, sciences, foreign languages, journalism, and art. All baccalaureate programs require the completion of a general education core, professional studies, subject area major (secondary education), field experiences, and student teaching. A minimum of 124 semester hours must be completed for each program.

Graduate Programs: The Master of Science in Education offered at Loyola may be earned in reading, elementary education, or secondary education. These programs offer close working relationships among faculty and students in a dynamic learning community that values strong theoretical foundations and opportunities for teaching practice.

Licensure/Reciprocity: Louisiana. Students seeking teaching certification in a state other than Louisiana should consult with that state's teacher certification office early in their program of study to insure compliance with requirements. Many state directors of teacher credentialing have signed Interstate Agreements through NASDTEC that expedite the certification process.

MCNEESE STATE UNIVERSITY
Burton College of Education
Department of Teacher Education
4100 Ryan Street
Lake Charles, Louisiana 70609
Phone: (337) 475-5424
Fax: (337) 475-5012
E-mail: admissions@mcneese.edu
Internet: http://www.mcneese.edu

Institution Description: McNeese State University was established as Lake Charles Junior College, a division of Louisiana State University in 1939. It became a four-year institution, separated from Louisiana State, and the name was changed to McNeese State College in 1950. The present name was adopted in 1970.

Programs in the Burton College of Education contribute to the student's liberal and professional education. The purpose of the Department of Teacher Education is to prepare students to fulfill their role in the teaching profession.

Institution Control: Public.

Calendar: Semester. Academic year August to May.

Official(s): Dr. Wayne Fetter, Department Head.

Faculty: Full-time 12.

Degrees Awarded: 176 baccalaureate; 106 master's.

Admission Requirements: *Undergraduate:* Graduation from an accredited secondary school or GED; ACT composite for placement. *Teacher education specific:* Satisfactory completion of required education courses; complete 30 semester hours with a minimum 2.5 GPA; minimum scores on PRAXIS I or minimum scores on the National Teacher Examinations; submit two letters of recommendations; autobiography. *Graduate:* Baccalaureate from a regionally accredited institution. *Teacher education specific:* Teaching credential where required by the program pursued; completion of all departmental required tests/exams; faculty interview.

Fees and Expenses: Undergraduate: in-state $2,544 per academic year; out-of-state $8,684. Graduate: Tuition is charged per credit hour. On-campus room and board: $2,720. Other expenses: $2,326. Books and supplies: $1,000.

Financial Aid: Resources specifically for eligible students enrolled in teacher education programs are awarded on the basis of financial need and academic merit. The institution has a Program Participation Agreement with the U.S. Department of Education for eligible students to receive Pell Grants and other federal aid. Teacher Scholarships available to qualifying students. *Contact:* Financial Aid Office at: (337) 474-5065.

Accreditation: *Regional:* SACS. *Professional:* NCATE. *Member of:* AACTE. *Approved by:* Louisiana Department Board of Education.

Degrees Offered: Baccalaureate; Master's.

Undergraduate Programs: The Department of Teacher Education offers a curriculum leading to the Bachelor of Arts degree in early childhood education designed to meet the needs of students preparing to teach nursery through grade eight.

The Bachelor of Arts degree in elementary education is designed to meet the needs of students preparing to teach grades 1-8.

A curriculum leading to the Bachelor of Science degree in secondary education is designed to meet the needs of students preparing to teach in the following subject areas: art, biology, business, chemistry, English, foreign language, mathematics, social studies, and speech.

The Bachelor of Arts degree in special education (general) is offered with various concentrations.

All baccalaureate programs require the completion of a general education core, professional studies, subject area major (secondary education), field experiences, and student teaching for a minimum of 124 credit hours.

Graduate Programs: The Master of Arts in Education degree programs include early childhood education, elementary education, secondary education in subject specializations, and special education.

Licensure/Reciprocity: Louisiana. Students seeking teaching certification in a state other than Louisiana should consult with that state's teacher certification office early in their program of study to insure compliance with requirements. Many state directors of teacher credentialing have signed Interstate Agreements through NASDTEC that expedite the certification process.

NICHOLLS STATE UNIVERSITY
College of Education
Department of Teacher Education
220 Polk Hall
University Station, Louisiana Highway 1
Thibodaux, Louisiana 70310
Phone: (985) 448-4314
Fax: (985) 448-4926
E-mail: admissions@nich.edu
Internet: http://www.nich.edu

Institution Description: Nicholls State University was established as Francis T. Nicholls Junior College of Louisiana State University in 1948. It became an independent institution, added upper division, and the name was changed to Francis T. Nicholls State College in 1956. The present name was adopted in 1970.

The Department of Teacher Education offers programs of study leading to bachelor's degrees in elementary and secondary education.

Institution Control: Public.

Calendar: Semester. Academic year August to May.

Official(s): Dr. Rodriguez-Landry, Department Head.

Faculty: Full-time 18.

Degrees Awarded: 142 baccalaureate; 58 master's.

Admission Requirements: *Undergraduate:* Graduation from an accredited secondary school or GED; ACT composite. *Teacher education specific:* PRAXIS I passing test scores; 2.5 GPA; personal goal statement; required educational foundations and professional courses; faculty interview.

Fees and Expenses: Undergraduate: in-state $2,448 per academic year. out-of-state $7, On-campus room and board: .$3,252. Other expenses: $2,326. Books and supplies: $1,000.

Financial Aid: Resources specifically for eligible students enrolled in teacher education programs are awarded on the basis of financial need and academic merit. The institution has a Program Participation Agreement with the U.S. Department of Education for eligible students to receive Pell Grants and other federal aid. Teacher Scholarships available to qualifying students. *Contact:* Financial Aid Office at: (504) 448-4048.

Accreditation: *Regional:* SACS. *Professional:* NCATE. *Member of:* AACTE. *Approved by:* Louisiana Department of Education.

Degrees Offered: Baccalaureate.

Undergraduate Programs: The Department of Teacher Education offers programs of study leading to the following baccalaureate degrees: Bachelor of Arts in elementary education, Bachelor of Arts in special education, Bachelor of Arts or Bachelor of Science in secondary education, and a Bachelor of Music Education degree.

The Bachelor of Arts in elementary education has certification pathways for PK-3, 1-6, and 4-8. Within the Bachelor of Arts and Bachelor of Science in secondary education the following primary certification pathways are offered: art, business, English, French, social studies, health and physical education, mathematics, general science.

All programs require the completion of a general education core, professional studies, field experiences, and student teaching. A minimum of 130 semester hours is required for the degree awards.

Licensure/Reciprocity: Louisiana. Students seeking teaching certification in a state other than Louisiana should consult with that state's teacher certification office early in their program of study to insure compliance with requirements. Many state

directors of teacher credentialing have signed Interstate Agreements through NASDTEC that expedite the certification process.

NORTHWESTERN STATE UNIVERSITY
College of Education
Teacher Education Center
College Avenue
Natchitoches, Louisiana 71497
Phone: (318) 357-6288
Fax: (318) 357-6275
E-mail: tollett@nsula.edu
Internet: http://www.nsula.edu

Institution Description: Northwestern State University of Louisiana is land-grant college. It was established as Louisiana Normal School in 1884. It became a four-year institution and the name was changed to Louisiana State Normal College in 1918, to Northwestern State College of Louisiana in 1944, and to its present name in 1970.

Programs and degrees in teacher education are offered through the College of Education at the undergraduate and graduate levels.

Institution Control: Public.

Calendar: Semester. Academic year August to May.

Official(s): Dr. John R. Tollett, Dean, College of Education.

Faculty: Full-time 26; part-time 7; adjunct 16.

Degrees Awarded: 118 baccalaureate; 189 master's; 1 doctorate.

Admission Requirements: *Undergraduate:* Graduation from an accredited secondary school or GED; ACT composite. *Teacher education specific:* PRAXIS I passing scores; 2.5 GPA; completion of 30 hours of coursework; faculty interview. *Graduate:* Baccalaureate from a regionally accredited institution. *Teacher education specific:* Teaching credential where required by program pursued; GRE score 800 or above; recommendations; faculty interview.

Fees and Expenses: Undergraduate: in-state $,084 per academic year; out-of-state $6,078. Graduate: in-state and out-of-state $3,036. Required fees: Parking $25, health $25. On-campus room and board: $3,700. Books and supplies: $400.

Financial Aid: Resources specifically for eligible students enrolled in teacher education programs are awarded on the basis of financial need and academic merit. The institution has a Program Participation Agreement with the U.S. Department of Education for eligible students to receive Pell Grants and other federal aid. Teacher Scholarships available to qualifying students. *Contact:* Misty Chelette at: (318) 357-5961 or e-mail at chelettem@nsula.edu.

Accreditation: *Regional:* SACS. *Professional:* NCATE. *Member of:* AACTE. *Approved by:* Louisiana Department of Education.

Degrees Offered: Baccalaureate; Master's.

Undergraduate Programs: A student in the College of Education may select a degree program that will lead to initial teacher certification in one of the following areas: Pre-K to 3rd grade, elementary grades 1-6, middle grades 4-8, secondary education grades 7-12, and music education and physical education K-12. Add-on certifications are available in: school librarian, special education mild/moderate special education severe/profound, and special education early intervention. All baccalaureate programs require the completion of a general education core, professional studies, field experiences, and student teaching for a minimum of 128 credit hours.

Graduate Programs: Master's and/or Educational Specialist degrees can be earned in such areas as education technology, adult education, school administration, student personnel services, early childhood education, school counseling, and special education. These options permit students to personalize their degree plans according to their interests.

Licensure/Reciprocity: Louisiana. Students seeking teaching certification in a state other than Louisiana should consult with that state's teacher certification office early in their program of

study to insure compliance with requirements. Many state directors of teacher credentialing have signed Interstate Agreements through NASDTEC that expedite the certification process.

SOUTHEASTERN LOUISIANA UNIVERSITY
Division of Education and Human Development
Department of Teaching and Learning
2004 Charles E. Cate Teacher Education Center
University Station
Hammond, Louisiana 70402
Phone: (905) 549-2221
Fax: (905) 549-5009
E-mail: admissions@selu.edu
Internet: http://www.selu.edu

Institution Description: The institution was established and chartered as Hammond Junior College in 1925. It became a four-year institution and the name was changed to Southeastern Louisiana College in 1928. The present name was adopted in 1970.

The Department of Teaching and Learning provides professional courses for all majors in Education and special education curricula.

Institution Control: Public.

Calendar: Semester. Academic year June to May.

Official(s): Dr. Martha Head, Dean.

Faculty: Full-time 38.

Degrees Awarded: 304 baccalaureate; 124 master's.

Admission Requirements: *Undergraduate:* Graduation from an accredited secondary school or GED; ACT composite. *Teacher education specific:* PRAXIS I passing scores; 2.5 GPA; completion of 30 hours of coursework; faculty interview. *Graduate:* Baccalaureate from a regionally accredited institution. *Teacher education specific:* Teaching credential where required by program pursued; GRE score 800 or above; recommendations; faculty interview.

Fees and Expenses: Undergraduate: in-state $2,618 per academic year; out-of-state $7,946. Graduate: Tuition charged per credit hour. Other expenses: $2,326. On-campus room and board: $4,074. Books and supplies: $1,000.

Financial Aid: Resources specifically for eligible students enrolled in teacher education programs are awarded on the basis of financial need and academic merit. The institution has a Program Participation Agreement with the U.S. Department of Education for eligible students to receive Pell Grants and other federal aid. Teacher Scholarships available to qualifying students. *Contact:* Financial Aid Office at: (985) 549-2245.

Accreditation: *Regional:* SACS. *Professional:* NCATE. *Member of:* AACTE. *Approved by:* Louisiana Department of Education.

Degrees Offered: Baccalaureate; Master's.

Undergraduate Programs: Baccalaureate programs are offered in elementary and special education mild/moderate disabilities. Students with majors in these areas must complete a general education core, professional studies, field experiences, and student teaching. The programs require the completion of a minimum of 119 credit hours.

Graduate Programs: The Master of Education in curriculum and instruction program is offered with areas of concentration in: kindergarten, elementary, secondary, adult education, reading specialist (elementary and secondary) gifted education (elementary and secondary), English as a Second Language, and educational technology.

The Master of Education in special education program is offered with concentrations in: early childhood, educational diagnostician, supervisor/director of special education, mild/moderate disabilities, and severe/profound disabilities.

Licensure/Reciprocity: Louisiana. Students seeking teaching certification in a state other than Louisiana should consult with that state's teacher certification office early in their program of study to insure compliance with requirements. Many state

SOUTHEASTERN LOUISIANA
UNIVERSITY—cont'd

directors of teacher credentialing have signed Interstate Agreements through NASDTEC that expedite the certification process.

SOUTHERN UNIVERSITY AND AGRICULTURAL AND MECHANICAL COLLEGE AT BATON ROUGE

College of Education
Department of Curriculum and Instruction

Southern University Branch Post Office
Baton Rouge, Louisiana 70813
Phone: (225) 771-4500
Fax: (225) 771-2123
E-mail: admissions@subr.edu
Internet: http://www.subr.edu

Institution Description: The institution was established as Southern University in New Orleans in 1880. The present name was adopted in 1890. The school was recognized as a land-grant college in 1892.

The mission of the College of Education is to provide leadership and guidance for the professional preparation of various school and clinical personnel.

Institution Control: Public.

Calendar: Semester. Academic year August to May.

Official(s): Dr. Ivory Toldson, Dean.

Faculty: Full-time 45; part-time 11.

Degrees Awarded: 84 baccalaureate; 124 master's; 1 doctorate.

Admission Requirements: *Undergraduate:* Graduation from an accredited secondary school or GED; ACT composite. *Teacher education specific:* PRAXIS I passing scores; 2.5 GPA; completion of 30 hours of coursework; faculty interview. *Graduate:* Baccalaureate from a regionally accredited institution. *Teacher education specific:* Teaching credential where required by program pursued; GRE; recommendations; faculty interview.

Fees and Expenses: Undergraduate: in-state $2,702 per academic year; out-of-state $6,494. Graduate tuition charged per credit. On-campus room and board: $4,306. Books and supplies: $1,200.

Financial Aid: Resources specifically for eligible students enrolled in teacher education programs are awarded on the basis of financial need and academic merit. The institution has a Program Participation Agreement with the U.S. Department of Education for eligible students to receive Pell Grants and other federal aid. Teacher Scholarships available to qualifying students. *Contact:* Financial Aid Office at: (225) 771-2790.

Accreditation: *Regional:* SACS. *Professional:* NCATE. *Member of:* AACTE. *Approved by:* Louisiana Department of Education.

Degrees Offered: Baccalaureate; Master's.

Undergraduate Programs: The Department of Curriculum and Instruction offers programs leading to the Bachelor of Arts degree and teaching licensure in elementary education, music education, and special education. The Bachelor of Science degree program is offered in secondary education. All programs require the completion of a general education core, professional studies, subject area major (secondary education), field experiences, and student teaching. A minimum of 124 semester hours must be completed for degree awards.

Graduate Programs: The Master of Education in elementary education, Master of Education in secondary education, and Master of Education in special education programs are offered through the Departments of Curriculum and Instruction and Special Education.

A Doctor of Philosophy in special education program is also offered through the Department of Special Education.

Licensure/Reciprocity: Louisiana. Students seeking teaching certification in a state other than Louisiana should consult with that state's teacher certification office early in their program of study to insure compliance with requirements. Many state directors of teacher credentialing have signed Interstate Agreements through NASDTEC that expedite the certification process.

TULANE UNIVERSITY

Teacher Education Program

421 Newcomb Hall
6823 St. Charles Avenue
New Orleans, Louisiana 70118
Phone: (504) 865-5342
Fax: (504) 862-8715
E-mail: admission@tulane.edu
Internet: http://www.tulane.edu

Institution Description: Tulane University is a private independent institution that includes Tulane College for Men and Newcomb College for Women. The school was established as Medical College of Louisiana in 1834. It became part of the University of Louisiana in 1847 but reverted to private control and adopted its present official name, Tulane University of Louisiana, in 1887.

Tulane's teacher preparation and certification programs have an articulation agreement with Loyola University New Orleans for certain education courses.

Institution Control: Private.

Calendar: Semester. Academic year August to May.

Official(s): Dr. Teri C. Davis, Director.

Faculty: Full-time 7; part-time 5.

Degrees Awarded: 13 baccalaureate.

Admission Requirements: *Undergraduate:* Graduation from an accredited secondary school or GED; College Board SAT or ACT composite. *Teacher education specific:* PRAXIS I and II test scores; declaration of subject major; completion of required coursework in education during first year; faculty interview.

Fees and Expenses: Undergraduate: $20,310 per academic year. On-campus room and board: $7,642. Other expenses: $7,642. Books and supplies: $800.

Financial Aid: Resources specifically for eligible students enrolled in teacher education programs are awarded on the basis of financial need and academic merit. The institution has a Program Participation Agreement with the U.S. Department of Education for eligible students to receive Pell Grants and other federal aid. Teacher Scholarships available to qualifying students. *Contact:* Financial Aid Office at: (504) 825-5723.

Accreditation: *Regional:* SACS. *Approved by:* Louisiana Department of Education.

Degrees Offered: Baccalaureate.

Undergraduate Programs: A major in early childhood education/psychology will allow a student to prepare for a career working with young children from birth to age eight. This coordinate major in psychology lays a foundation for a future in careers such as private school teaching, nursery school administration/teaching, child psychology, and child legal advocacy. The bachelor's degree program requires the completion of a general education core, professional studies, field experiences, and student teaching. A minimum of 128 credit hours must be completed for the degree award.

The secondary education program leading to certification includes a total of 34 hours of education courses. Six courses are taken at Tulane and five additional courses are taken at Loyola University. The Successful completion of the program offers students the opportunity for licensure and teaching at the secondary level (grades 7-12). The program requires the completion of a general education core, professional studies, subject area major, field experiences, and student teaching. A minimum of 128 credit hours must be completed.

Licensure/Reciprocity: Louisiana. Students seeking teaching certification in a state other than Louisiana should consult with that state's teacher certification office early in their program of study to insure compliance with requirements. Many state directors of teacher credentialing have signed Interstate Agreements through NASDTEC that expedite the certification process.

UNIVERSITY OF LOUISIANA AT LAFAYETTE

College of Education
Department of Curriculum and Instruction
104 University Circle
Lafayette, Louisiana 70503
Phone: (337) 482-1000
Fax: (337) 482-6195
E-mail: coe@louisiana.edu
Internet: http://www.louisiana.edu

Institution Description: University of Louisiana at Lafayette, formerly named University of Southwestern Louisiana, is a state institution. It was established as a junior college in 1916. The current name was adopted in 1999.

The College of Education offers undergraduate programs leading to the baccalaureate degree and teacher certification as well as graduate programs to educators for professional career enhancement.

Institution Control: Public.

Calendar: Semester. Academic year August to May.

Official(s): Dr. Gerald Carson, Dean, College of Education; Dr. Mary Jane Ford, Head, Department of Curriculum and Instruction.

Faculty: Not reported.

Degrees Awarded: 273 baccalaureate; 64 master's.

Admission Requirements: *Undergraduate:* Graduation from an accredited secondary school or GED; ACT composite. *Teacher education specific:* PRAXIS I passing scores; 2.5 GPA; completion of 30 hours of coursework; faculty interview. *Graduate:* Baccalaureate from a regionally accredited institution. *Teacher education specific:* Teaching credential where required by program pursued; GRE score 800 or above; recommendations; faculty interview.

Fees and Expenses: Undergraduate: in-state $2,388 per academic year; out-of-state $8,858. Graduate: in-state $79 per credit hour; out-of-state $369. On-campus room and board: $2,896. Other expenses: $2,650. Books and supplies: $1,000.

Financial Aid: Resources specifically for eligible students enrolled in teacher education programs are awarded on the basis of financial need and academic merit. The institution has a Program Participation Agreement with the U.S. Department of Education for eligible students to receive Pell Grants and other federal aid. Teacher Scholarships available to qualifying students. *Contact:* Financial Aid Office at: (377) 482-6506.

Accreditation: *Regional:* SACS. *Professional:* NCATE. *Member of:* AACTE. *Approved by:* Louisiana Department of Education.

Degrees Offered: Baccalaureate; Master's.

Undergraduate Programs: The Department of Curriculum and Instruction offers programs leading to licensure and the Bachelor of Arts degree in early childhood education (PreK-3), elementary education (1-6), and middle school education (4-8). Students preparing for certification to teach in grades 7-12 must select both a primary major and a secondary minor teaching area. Concentrations for the Bachelor of Science in secondary education include: agriculture, biology, business, chemistry, earth science, English, family and consumer science, general science, industrial arts, mathematics, modern language (French, German, Spanish), physics, social studies, and speech.

Other Bachelor of Science degree programs are offered in kinesiology, art education, music education, special education (early intervention), and special education (mild/moderate).

All baccalaureate programs required the completion of a general education core, professional studies, field experiences, and student teaching. A minimum of 124 credit hours must be completed for the degree award.

Graduate Programs: Graduate degree programs are offered leading to the Master of Education in administration and supervision and the Master of Education in curriculum and instruction. Contact the Office of Graduate Studies for specific program requirements.

Licensure/Reciprocity: Louisiana. Students seeking teaching certification in a state other than Louisiana should consult with that state's teacher certification office early in their program of study to insure compliance with requirements. Many state directors of teacher credentialing have signed Interstate Agreements through NASDTEC that expedite the certification process.

UNIVERSITY OF LOUISIANA AT MONROE

College of Education and Human Development
Strauss Hall
700 University Avenue
Monroe, Louisiana 71209
Phone: (318) 342-1235
Fax: (318) 342-1240
E-mail: coe@ulm.edu
Internet: http://www.ulm.edu

Institution Description: The institution was established as Louisiana State University in New Orleans in 1956. The present name was adopted in 1974.

The College of Education and Human Development is dedicated to preparing learning facilitators by involving students in the interaction of general education, professional studies, and specialty studies with appropriate clinical and field experiences.

Institution Control: Public.

Calendar: Semester. Academic year August to May.

Official(s): Dr. Beverly Flowers-Gibson, Director, Office of Field Experiences and Teacher Education.

Faculty: Full-time 78; part-time 30.

Degrees Awarded: 87 baccalaureate; 59 master's.

Admission Requirements: *Undergraduate:* Graduation from an accredited secondary school or GED; ACT composite. *Teacher education specific:* PRAXIS I passing scores; 2.5 GPA; completion of 30 hours of coursework; faculty interview. *Graduate:* Baccalaureate from a regionally accredited institution. *Teacher education specific:* Teaching credential where required by program pursued; GRE score 800 or above; recommendations; faculty interview.

Fees and Expenses: Undergraduate: in-state $2,452 per academic year; out-of-state $8,858. Graduate: in-state $79 per credit hour; out-of-state $369. On-campus room and board: $2,896. Other expenses: $2,650. Books and supplies: $1,000.

Financial Aid: Resources specifically for eligible students enrolled in teacher education programs are awarded on the basis of financial need and academic merit. The institution has a Program Participation Agreement with the U.S. Department of Education for eligible students to receive Pell Grants and other federal aid. Teacher Scholarships available to qualifying students. *Contact:* Financial Aid Office at: (318) 342-5320.

Accreditation: *Regional:* SACS. *Professional:* NCATE. *Member of:* AACTE. *Approved by:* Louisiana Department of Education.

Degrees Offered: Baccalaureate; Master's.

Undergraduate Programs: Undergraduate degree programs include the Bachelor of Arts in art, elementary education, English, foreign language, social studies, special education, speech, and psychology. Students must select both a major and a secondary minor. Bachelor of Science degree programs include mathematics, science, health and physical education, and physical education (general). Students also must select a major and secondary minor.

All programs require the completion of a general education core, professional studies, and student teaching. The field experiences include over 100 hours of site-based experiences that culminate in an all-day, full semester of student teaching. A minimum of 124 credit hours must be completed for the degree award.

Graduate Programs: Graduate degree programs include the Master of Education and Doctor of Education programs in curriculum and instruction; Master of Education and Educational Specialist in elementary or secondary education; Master of Education in reading; Master of Education in special education.

UNIVERSITY OF LOUISIANA AT MONROE—
cont'd

Licensure/Reciprocity: Louisiana. Students seeking teaching certification in a state other than Louisiana should consult with that state's teacher certification office early in their program of study to insure compliance with requirements. Many state directors of teacher credentialing have signed Interstate Agreements through NASDTEC that expedite the certification process.

UNIVERSITY OF NEW ORLEANS
College of Education
Department of Curriculum and Instruction
Lake Front
New Orleans, Louisiana 70148
Phone: (504) 280-6000
Fax: (504) 280-7393
E-mail: admissions@uno.edu
Internet: http://www.uno.edu

Institution Description: The institution was established as Louisiana State University in New Orleans in 1956. The present name was adopted in 1974.

The Department of Curriculum and Instruction recognizes its mission as serving a culturally diverse community through collaboration and partnerships with both public and private educational institutions.

Institution Control: Public.

Calendar: Semester. Academic year August to May.

Official(s): Dr. Renee Carbergue, Chair, Department of Curriculum and Instruction.

Faculty: Full-time 17.

Degrees Awarded: 137 baccalaureate; 234 master's; 29 doctorate.

Admission Requirements: *Undergraduate:* Graduation from an accredited secondary school or GED; minimum ACT composite score of 20. *Teacher education specific:* PRAXIS I passing scores; 2.5 GPA; completion of 30 hours of coursework; faculty interview. *Graduate:* Baccalaureate from a regionally accredited institution. *Teacher education specific:* Teaching credential where required by program pursued; GRE; recommendations; faculty interview.

Fees and Expenses: Undergraduate: in-state $2,832 per academic year; out-of-state $9,676. Graduate: in-state $2,748 per academic year; out-of-state $9,792. On-campus room and board: $3,630. Other expenses: $2,000. Books and supplies: $1,000.

Financial Aid: Resources specifically for eligible students enrolled in teacher education programs are awarded on the basis of financial need and academic merit. The institution has a Program Participation Agreement with the U.S. Department of Education for eligible students to receive Pell Grants and other federal aid. Teacher Scholarships available to qualifying students. *Contact:* Financial Aid Office at: (504) 280-6603.

Accreditation: *Regional:* SACS. *Professional:* NCATE. *Member of:* AACTE. *Approved by:* Louisiana Department of Education.

Degrees Offered: Baccalaureate; Master's; Doctorate.

Undergraduate Programs: Undergraduate programs leading to the Bachelor of Arts degree and certification include: elementary education; secondary education with concentrations in English, French, German, Spanish, social studies, vocal music, instrumental music. The Bachelor of Science degree programs include secondary education with concentrations in biology, chemistry, geology, and mathematics.

All programs require the completion of a general education core, professional studies, field experiences, and student teaching. A minimum of 128 credit hours is required.

Graduate Programs: The minimum requirement for the Master of Arts degree in curriculum and instruction is 33 semester hours, including research methods, and a minimum of 6 semester hours in a minor or related field outside the major department. Students entering the department for secondary education master's programs in English, science, social studies, and math are required to complete a minimum of 9 semester hours from courses in cognate areas. Each candidate is required to pass a written and/or oral comprehensive examination.

Licensure/Reciprocity: Louisiana. Students seeking teaching certification in a state other than Louisiana should consult with that state's teacher certification office early in their program of study to insure compliance with requirements. Many state directors of teacher credentialing have signed Interstate Agreements through NASDTEC that expedite the certification process.

XAVIER UNIVERSITY OF LOUISIANA
College of Arts and Sciences
Division of Education
7325 Palmetto Street
New Orleans, Louisiana 70125
Phone: (504) 520-7386
Fax: (504) 520-7909
E-mail: doe@xula.edu
Internet: http://www.xula.edu

Institution Description: Xavier University of Louisiana is a private institution affiliated with the Sisters of the Blessed Sacrament, Roman Catholic Church. It was established as Xavier University, a secondary school, in 1915 and became a two-year normal school in 1917. It became a four-year college in 1925.

The Division of Education combines professional abilities with a liberal arts education to prepare its graduates for a careers as educators.

Institution Control: Private.

Calendar: Semester. Academic year August to May.

Official(s): Dr. Ken Butte, Dean; Dr. Rosalind Pijeaux-Hale, Chair, Division of Education.

Faculty: Full-time 19.

Degrees Awarded: 6 baccalaureate; 53 master's.

Admission Requirements: *Undergraduate:* Graduation from an accredited secondary school or GED; College SAT or ACT composite. *Teacher education specific:* PRAXIS I passing scores; 2.5 GPA; completion of 30 hours of coursework; faculty interview. *Graduate:* Baccalaureate from a regionally accredited institution. *Teacher education specific:* Teaching credential where required by program pursued; GRE; recommendations; faculty interview.

Fees and Expenses: Undergraduate: $10,100 per academic year. Graduate: Tuition charged per credit hour. On-campus room and board: $6,000. Other expenses: $1,475. Books and supplies: $1,000.

Financial Aid: Resources specifically for eligible students enrolled in teacher education programs are awarded on the basis of financial need and academic merit. The institution has a Program Participation Agreement with the U.S. Department of Education for eligible students to receive Pell Grants and other federal aid. Teacher Scholarships available to qualifying students. *Contact:* Financial Aid Office at: (504) 483-7517.

Accreditation: *Regional:* SACS. *Professional:* NCATE. *Member of:* AACTE. *Approved by:* Louisiana Department of Education.

Degrees Offered: Baccalaureate; Master's.

Undergraduate Programs: The Bachelor of Arts and Bachelor of Science degrees are offered in the following areas of concentration: art, biology, chemistry, pre-K to 3rd grade, English, health and physical education, foreign language, mathematics, music, social studies, special education (mild/moderate), speech pathology, and middle school. The programs require the completion of a minimum of 128 credit hours including a general education core, professional studies, subject major, field experiences, and student teaching.

Graduate Programs: The Master of Arts degrees are offered in: administration and supervision (school principalship, supervision of instruction); curriculum and instruction (early childhood, elementary education, reading specialist, secondary education, and counseling).

For those students who do not choose education as a career path until late in their degree program can become certified teachers through alternate degree programs. The Teacher Practitioner program consists of 18 hours of master level classes leading to a practitioner license and teacher certification. It is for teachers employed or with a commitment from a school district for a position.

The Master of Arts in Teaching program leads to certification and requires 33 hours of coursework.

Licensure/Reciprocity: Louisiana. Students seeking teaching certification in a state other than Louisiana should consult with that state's teacher certification office early in their program of study to insure compliance with requirements. Many state directors of teacher credentialing have signed Interstate Agreements through NASDTEC that expedite the certification process.

MAINE

UNIVERSITY OF MAINE

College of Education and Human Development

5713 Chaibourne Hall
Orono, Maine 04469-5713
Phone: (207) 581-1561
Fax: (207) 581-1213
E-mail: coehd@umaine.edu
Internet: http://www.umaine.edu

Institution Description: The University of Maine was established and incorporated as State College of Agriculture and Mechanic Arts in 1865. The name was changed to University of Maine in 1897.

The College of Education and Human Development provides and extensive liberal arts selection, a thorough grounding in theory and practice, exposure to the latest research and trends, and internships and field experiences.

Institution Control: Public.

Calendar: Semester. Academic year September to May.

Official(s): Dr. Robert Cobb, Dean.

Faculty: Full-time 48.

Degrees Awarded: 228 baccalaureate; 179 master's; 4 doctorate.

Admission Requirements: *Undergraduate:* Graduation from an accredited secondary school or GED; College Board SAT or ACT composite. *Teacher education specific:* PRAXIS I test scores; application to the program by sophomore year; declaration of major; faculty interview. *Graduate:* Baccalaureate from a regionally accredited institution. *Teacher education specific:* Passing scores on all required department/state tests/exams; recommendations; faculty interview.

Fees and Expenses: Undergraduate: in-state $5,550 per academic year; out-of-state $13,620. Graduate: in-state $210 per credit hour; out-of-state $599. On-campus room and board: $5,928. Other expenses: $1,600. Books and supplies: $700.

Financial Aid: Resources specifically for eligible students enrolled in teacher education programs are awarded on the basis of financial need and academic merit. The institution has a Program Participation Agreement with the U.S. Department of Education for eligible students to receive Pell Grants and other federal aid. Maine Teacher Scholarships available to qualifying students. *Contact:* Financial Aid Office at: (581-1324.

Accreditation: *Regional:* NEASC. *Professional:* NCATE. *Member of:* AACTE. *Approved by:* Maine Department of Education.

Undergraduate Programs: The college offers bachelor's degrees in the areas of early childhood education, elementary education, secondary education, child development and family relations, kinesiology and physical education, and athletic training. All programs require completion of a general education core, professional studies, subject area major, field experiences, and student teaching. Students successfully completing the programs are eligible for either a Bachelor of Science in Education or a Bachelor of Science in Child Development and Family Relations. A minimum of 120 credit hours of required college work is necessary for graduation.

Graduate Programs: The Master of Arts in Teaching and the Master of Science degrees require a thesis. The Master of Education is a non-thesis program. A number of specialty areas or concentrations are available for each degree program. Graduate students plan their programs based on Graduate School and College requirements, certification guidelines, professional association recommendations, and individual goals.

Licensure/Reciprocity: Maine. Students seeking teaching certification in a state other than Maine should consult with that state's teacher certification office early in their program of study to insure compliance with requirements. Many state directors of teacher credentialing have signed Interstate Agreements through NASDTEC that expedite the certification process.

UNIVERSITY OF MAINE AT FARMINGTON

College of Education, Health, and Rehabilitation

252 Main Street
Farmington, Maine 04938
Phone: (207) 778-7171
Fax: (207) 778-7157
E-mail: annlynch@umf.maine.edu
Internet: http://www.umf.maine.edu

Institution Description: The institution was established as Western Maine Normal School in 1863. After several name changes over the years, the present name was adopted in 1970.

Students in the teacher preparation programs get experience in the classroom as early as the sophomore year. They also do practicums and internships to fine-tune their skills and build a foundation for their future careers.

Institution Control: Public.

Calendar: Semester. Academic year September to May.

Official(s): Dr. Kathy Yardley, Dean.

Faculty: Full-time 44; part-time 22.

Degrees Awarded: 175 baccalaureate.

Admission Requirements: *Undergraduate:* Graduation from an accredited secondary school or GED; College Board SAT or ACT composite. *Teacher education specific:* Application to the program by sophomore year; PRAXIS I test scores; declaration of major; personal goal statement; faculty interview.

Fees and Expenses: Undergraduate: in-state $4,290 per academic year; out-of-state $10,470. Required fees: $590. On-campus room and board: $5 318. Books and supplies: Varies by program.

Financial Aid: Resources specifically for eligible students enrolled in teacher education programs are awarded on the basis of financial need and academic merit. The institution has a Program Participation Agreement with the U.S. Department of Education for eligible students to receive Pell Grants and other federal aid. Maine Teacher Scholarships available to qualifying students. *Contact:* Ronald Miliken at: (707) 778-7100 or e-mail at umfinaid@umf.maine.edu.

Accreditation: *Regional:* NEASC. *Professional:* NCATE. *Member of:* AACTE. *Approved by:* Maine Department of Education.

Undergraduate Programs: The Department of Early Childhood and Elementary Education offers majors in early childhood education and elementary education. The Department of Middle/Secondary Education offers majors with concentrations in English/language arts, mathematics and computer sciences, science, and social science. The Department of Special Education and Rehabilitation Services offers programs preparing teachers of children and youth who have mild to moderate disabilities in the areas of emotional disturbance, learning disabilities, and mental retardation.

All programs require the completion of a general education core, professional studies, program area subject major, field experiences, and student teaching. A minimum of 120 semesters hours must be successfully completed.

Licensure/Reciprocity: Maine. Students seeking teaching certification in a state other than Maine should consult with that state's teacher certification office early in their program of study to insure compliance with requirements. Many state directors of teacher credentialing have signed Interstate Agreements through NASDTEC that expedite the certification process.

UNIVERSITY OF MAINE AT PRESQUE ISLE

College of Education
Department of Education

181 Main Street
Presque Isle, Maine 04769-2888
Phone: (207) 768-9400
Fax: (207) 768-9534
E-mail: janesco@umpi.maine.edu
Internet: http://www.umpi.maine.edu

Institution Description: The institution was established as Aroostook State Normal School in 1903. The name was changed to Aroostook State Teachers College in 1952, to Aroostook State College in 1965, to Aroostook State College of the University of Maine in 1968, and to its present name in 1970.

The Department of Education offers programs leading to the bachelor's degree and teacher certification.

Institution Control: Public.

Calendar: Semester. Academic year August to May.

Official(s): Dr. Gary Janesco, Department of Field Experiences and Certification.

Faculty: Full-time 7.

Degrees Awarded: 24 baccalaureate.

Admission Requirements: *Undergraduate:* Graduation from an accredited secondary school or GED; College Board SAT or ACT composite. *Teacher education specific:* Application to the program by sophomore year; PRAXIS I test scores; declaration of major; personal goal statement; faculty interview.

Fees and Expenses: Undergraduate: in-state $4,290 per academic year; out-of-state $10,470. On-campus room and board: $4,494. Other expenses: $2,200. Books and supplies: $650.

Financial Aid: Resources specifically for eligible students enrolled in teacher education programs are awarded on the basis of financial need and academic merit. The institution has a Program Participation Agreement with the U.S. Department of Education for eligible students to receive Pell Grants and other federal aid. Maine Teacher Scholarships available to qualifying students. *Contact:* Financial Aid Office at: (207) 768-9513.

Accreditation: *Regional:* NEASC. *Member of:* AACTE. *Approved by:* Maine Department of Education.

Undergraduate Programs: The elementary education major leads to the Bachelor of Science degree. All candidates must complete the general education core, professional education courses, subject area major, field experiences, and student teaching.

The Bachelor of Arts in art education is a four-year program intended to prepare students to teach the visual arts in the public school system. The program includes instruction in the studio art subjects, and art education studies in addition to the general core curriculum. A minimum of 121 credit hours is required for graduation.

The Bachelor of Science degree in health education is a four-year program. It emphasizes the acquisition of knowledge and skills in cognitive, affective, and behavioral aspects of health education. Students must complete a general education core, a professional education sequence, and concentration requirements for a total of 128 hours.

The teaching degree in physical education is designed specifically for those students who wish to become a certified physical education teacher. A student must complete the general education core, professional education sequence, and physical education major requirements.

The secondary education major leads to the Bachelor of Science degree. Students must complete the general education core, the professional education sequence, and the subject area requirements for a total of 128 credit hours.

Licensure/Reciprocity: Maine. Students seeking teaching certification in a state other than Maine should consult with that state's teacher certification office early in their program of study to insure compliance with requirements. Many state directors of teacher credentialing have signed Interstate Agreements through NASDTEC that expedite the certification process.

UNIVERSITY OF SOUTHERN MAINE

College of Education and Human Development
Teacher Education Department

96 Falmouth Street
Portland, Maine 04103
Phone: (207) 780-4141
Fax: (207) 780-5215
E-mail: usmadm@usm.maine.edu
Internet: http://www.usm.maine.edu

Institution Description: The institution was established as Western Maine Normal School in 1879. The name was changed to Gorham State Teachers College in 1945, to Gorham State College in 1965, and to Gorham State College of the University of Maine in 1968. The school merged with the University of Maine in Portland and the name was changed to University of Maine at Portland-Gorham in 1970. The present name was adopted in 1978.

Students in the teacher education programs are trained in the literature and research of their disciplines and have extensive field-based experiences.

Institution Control: Public.

Calendar: Semester. Academic year September to May.

Official(s): Dr. Kenneth Jones, Director, Teacher Education Department.

Faculty: Full-time 11.

Degrees Awarded: 43 baccalaureate; 187 master's.

Admission Requirements: *Undergraduate:* Graduation from an accredited secondary school or GED; College Board SAT or ACT composite. *Teacher education specific:* Application to the program by sophomore year; PRAXIS I test scores; declaration of major; personal goal statement; faculty interview.

Fees and Expenses: Undergraduate: in-state $4,796 per academic year; out-of-state $10,470. Required fees: $590. On-campus room and board: $5 958. Books and supplies: $660.

Financial Aid: Resources specifically for eligible students enrolled in teacher education programs are awarded on the basis of financial need and academic merit. The institution has a Program Participation Agreement with the U.S. Department of Education for eligible students to receive Pell Grants and other federal aid. Maine Teacher Scholarships available to qualifying students. *Contact:* Financial Aid Office at: (207) 780-5250.

Accreditation: *Regional:* NEASC. *Professional:* NCATE. *Member of:* AACTE. *Approved by:* Maine Department of Education.

Undergraduate Programs: The Teachers for Elementary and Middle Schools (TEAMS) Program is a 4-1/2 year teacher certification program designed for undergraduate students with a strong interest in teaching at the elementary or middle school level. Students participate in school-based field experiences every year of the program. Students also pursue a major in an academic subject other than education. Graduate credit is earned in the first half of the fifth year. The program leads to a bachelor's degree and teacher licensure by the Maine Department of Education.

UNIVERSITY OF SOUTHERN MAINE—*cont'd*

Graduate Programs: The Extended Teacher Education Program (ETEP) is for individuals who already hold a bachelor's degree. It is designed for those interested in teaching: elementary and middle school, grades K-8, general education; special education, grades K-8; secondary school, grades 7-12: English, language arts, life science, mathematics, physical science, social studies; foreign language, K-12: French, German, Spanish. ETEP is a graduate level program consisting of two distinct phases: the internship year and the master's degree for beginning teachers. The internship year provides all of the courses and experiences required for state certification. Upon successful completion of the internship and placement in a teaching position, interns can earn a master's degree for an additional 13 credits of part-time study.

Licensure/Reciprocity: Maine. Students seeking teaching certification in a state other than Maine should consult with that state's teacher certification office early in their program of study to insure compliance with requirements. Many state directors of teacher credentialing have signed Interstate Agreements through NASDTEC that expedite the certification process.

MARYLAND

BOWIE STATE UNIVERSITY

School of Education
Teacher Education Program
14000 Jericho Park Road
Bowie, Maryland 20715
Phone: (301) 860-3130
Fax: (301) 860-3415
E-mail: admissions@bowiestate.edu
Internet: http://www.bowiestate.edu

Institution Description: Bowie State University was established as Industrial School for Colored Youth in 1865 and was renamed Normal School No. 3 in 1908. It became Normal and Industrial School for the Training of Colored Youth in 1925. The name was changed to Maryland State Teachers College in 1935 and became Bowie State College in 1963. The present name was adopted and the institution joined the University System of Maryland in 1988.

The School of Education, established in 2001 as the first professional school within the university, has the primary responsibility for coordinating university efforts designed to prepare individuals to assume positions of teaching, counseling, and leadership in the P-12 school setting.

Institution Control: Public.

Calendar: Semester. Academic year September to May.

Official(s): Dr. Vernon C. Polite, Dean; Dr. Lola De Cousite, Chair, Teacher Education Program.

Faculty: Full-time 18.

Degrees Awarded: Not reported.

Admission Requirements: *Undergraduate:* Graduation from an approved secondary school or GED; minimum ACT score of 19. *Teacher education specific:* Application to the program after completion of a minimum of 32 semester hours; autobiography; faculty evaluation from two faculty members; formal interview; passing scores on PRAXIS I. *Graduate:* Baccalaureate degree from a regionally accredited institution. *Teacher education specific:* Teaching credential as required by a program; passing scores on any departmental required tests/exams; recommendations; faculty interview.

Fees and Expenses: Undergraduate: in-state $3,344 per academic year; out-of-state $10,360. Graduate: Tuition charged per credit hour. Other expenses $1,970. On-campus room and board: $5,673. Books and supplies: $1,205.

Financial Aid: Resources specifically for eligible students enrolled in teacher education programs are awarded on the basis of financial need and academic merit. The institution has a Program Participation Agreement with the U.S. Department of Education for eligible students to receive Pell Grants and other federal aid. Maryland Teacher Scholarships available to qualifying students. *Contact:* Financial Aid Office at: (301) 860-3540.

Accreditation: *Regional:* MSA. *Professional:* NCATE. *Member of:* AACTE. *Approved by:* Maryland State Department of Education.

Undergraduate Programs: The early childhood/special education program is organized to provide prospective teachers with essential competencies needed to effectively meet the intellectual, emotional, and social needs of young children. The program leads to the Bachelor of Science and requires the comple-

tion of 143 semester house of coursework including a general education core, subject major, field experiences, and student teaching.

Students in the elementary education program must complete a comprehensive multidisciplinary program of study and a sequence of professional courses in education, theory, and a method of elementary teaching. Students earn a Bachelor of Science degree after the completion of 140 semester hours of coursework including a professional core of 63 semester hours.

The secondary education track is for students enrolled in departments with state-approved programs and with courses in the methods of teaching the major subject. All students pursing the degree in secondary education must complete 51 semester hours of coursework in education as well as meet the requirements of the major department.

Students who hold a baccalaureate degree who wish to become certified teachers must enroll as second degree students.

Graduate Programs: The university offers graduate programs leading to the Master of Education with concentrations in elementary education, guidance and counseling, reading, school administration and supervision; secondary education (academic content field, curriculum specialist, mathematics specialist; and special education. A Doctor of Education in educational leadership may also be pursued.

Licensure/Reciprocity: Maryland. Students seeking teaching certification in a state other than Maryland should consult with that state's teacher certification office early in their program of study to insure compliance with requirements. Many state directors of teacher credentialing have signed Interstate Agreements through NASDTEC that expedite the certification process.

COLLEGE OF NOTRE DAME OF MARYLAND

Education Department
4701 North Charles Street
Baltimore, Maryland 21210-2476
Phone: (410) 532-5349
Fax: (410) 532-5330
E-mail: dschessler@ndm.edu
Internet: http://www.ndm.edu

Institution Description: The College of Notre Dame of Maryland is a private college primarily for women. It is affiliated with the Roman Catholic Church. The college was established as Notre Dame of Maryland Collegiate Institute for Young Ladies in 1873. It was chartered as four-year college and the present name was adopted in 1896.

The Education Department seeks to develop educators who are visionary leaders and decision-makers. Programs are holistic, personal, and charged with ethical and moral thinking.

Institution Control: Private.

Calendar: Semester. Academic year September to May.

Official(s): Dr. Sharon Slear, Chair, Education Department.

Faculty: Full-time 18.

Degrees Awarded: 28 baccalaureate; 206 master's.

Admission Requirements: *Undergraduate:* Graduation with 18 academic units from an approved secondary school or GED; College Board SAT. *Teacher education specific:* Students are encouraged to declare the major by the spring semester of their

COLLEGE OF NOTRE DAME OF MARYLAND—cont'd

freshman year; PRAXIS I test scores; faculty interview. *Graduate:* Baccalaureate degree from a regionally accredited institution. *Teacher education specific:* Teaching experience where required by the program pursued; recommendations; faculty interview; PRAXIS I and II; 3.0 cumulative GPA.

Fees and Expenses: Undergraduate: $17,925 per academic year. Graduate: $350 per credit hour. Other expenses: $1,000. On-campus room and board: $7,400. Books and supplies: $600.

Financial Aid: Resources specifically for eligible students enrolled in teacher education programs are awarded on the basis of financial need and academic merit. The institution has a Program Participation Agreement with the U.S. Department of Education for eligible students to receive Pell Grants and other federal aid. Maryland Teacher Scholarships available to qualifying students. *Contact:* Financial Aid Office at: (410) 532-5369.

Accreditation: *Regional:* MSA. *Professional:* NCATE. *Member of:* AACTE. *Approved by:* Maryland State Board of Education.

Undergraduate Programs: The four-year liberal studies/elementary education major provides an integrated and balanced sequence of liberal studies and professional courses that include practical field experiences and culminate in an extended teaching internship in the senior year.

The four-year secondary education program requires the completion of a full academic major in one of the following fields: art, biology, chemistry, English, history/social studies, foreign languages, mathematics, or music. Students can also complete a balanced sequence of educational studies culminating in an extended teaching internship in the senior year.

Graduate Programs: The five-year BA/MAT students complete the liberal arts major at the undergraduate level and then enter the master of arts in teaching program. The BA/MAT program includes the teaching internship in the fifth year.

The college offers a variety of graduate programs designed for post-baccalaureate studies: Certificate of Advanced Study in Education; Master of Arts in teaching English to speakers of other languages; Master of Arts in Teaching; Master of Arts in leadership in teaching; advanced certification for teaching.

Licensure/Reciprocity: Maryland. Students seeking teaching certification in a state other than Maryland should consult with that state's teacher certification office early in their program of study to insure compliance with requirements. Many state directors of teacher credentialing have signed Interstate Agreements through NASDTEC that expedite the certification process.

COPPIN STATE COLLEGE

Division of Education
Teacher Education Programs
2500 West North Avenue
Baltimore, Maryland 21216-3698
Phone: (410) 951-3000
Fax: (410) 951-3600
E-mail: jchampan@coppin.edu
Internet: http://www.coppin.edu

Institution Description: Coppin State College is a member institution of the University of Maryland System. It was established as a teacher training program housed in Douglas High School in 1900. It became Fannie Jackson Coppin Normal School in 1926 and became four-year college in 1930. The name was changed to Coppin State Teachers College in 1950 and the present name was adopted in 1967.

The Teacher Education Programs are specifically designed to prepare teachers and represent a cooperative effort by all departments involved in the preparation of teachers.

Institution Control: Public.

Calendar: Semester. Academic year September to May.

Official(s): Dr. Julius Chapman, Dean, Division of Education.

Faculty: 14 full-time.

Degrees Awarded: 13 baccalaureate; 118 master's.

Admission Requirements: *Undergraduate:* Graduation from an approved secondary school or GED; College Board SAT. *Teacher education specific:* Application to the program after completion of a minimum of 30 semester hours; declaration of a major; complete Phase I of the Undergraduate Performance-Based Assessment Portfolio; faculty evaluation from two faculty members; formal interview; passing scores on PRAXIS I.

Fees and Expenses: Undergraduate: in-state $4,104 academic year; out-of-state $9,513. Other expenses $2,785. On-campus room and board: $6,115. Books and supplies: $700.

Financial Aid: Resources specifically for eligible students enrolled in teacher education programs are awarded on the basis of financial need and academic merit. The institution has a Program Participation Agreement with the U.S. Department of Education for eligible students to receive Pell Grants and other federal aid. Maryland Teacher Scholarships available to qualifying students. *Contact:* Financial Aid Office at: (410) 951-3636.

Accreditation: *Regional:* MSA. *Professional:* NCATE. *Member of:* AACTE. *Approved by:* Maryland State Department of Education.

Undergraduate Programs: The Division of Education offers undergraduate majors for the preparation of teachers in the areas of early childhood, elementary and special education and majors leading to certification in secondary education in English, mathematics, history/social studies, biology, and chemistry. Students earn the baccalaureate degree after completing the general education requirements, professional education courses, including a sequence of clinical experiences and student teaching, and an academic specialization appropriate to the generally accepted philosophy and objectives of the respective programs. A minimum of 128 semester hours is required for all baccalaureate degrees.

Licensure/Reciprocity: Maryland. Students seeking teaching certification in a state other than Maryland should consult with that state's teacher certification office early in their program of study to insure compliance with requirements. Many state directors of teacher credentialing have signed Interstate Agreements through NASDTEC that expedite the certification process.

FROSTBURG STATE UNIVERSITY

College of Education
Educational Professions Department
101 Braddock Road
Frostburg, Maryland 21532-1099
Phone: (301) 687-4759
Fax: (301) 687-7798
E-mail: sarisman@frostburg.edu
Internet: http://www.frostburg.edu

Institution Description: Frostburg State University was established as State Normal School at Frostburg in 1898. The name was changed to State Teachers College at Frostburg in 1935 and to Frostburg State College in 1963. The present name was adopted in 1987.

The teacher education programs are committed to preparing professionals who are able to provide quality instruction, service, and leadership.

Institution Control: Public.

Calendar: Semester. Academic year September to May.

Official(s): Dr. Susan Arisman, Dean, College of Education; Dr. Kenneth Witmer, Department Chair.

Faculty: Full-time 48; part-time 20.

Degrees Awarded: 93 baccalaureate; 126 master's.

Admission Requirements: *Undergraduate:* Graduation from an accredited secondary school or GED; College Board SAT. *Teacher education specific:* Completion of at least 60 credit hours (junior standing); cumulative 2.5 GPA; grade of C or better on required courses; advisor recommendation; PRAXIS I test scores. *Graduate: Teacher education specific:* Baccalaureate degree from a regionally accredited institution. *Teacher education specific:* Minimum grade of C in advanced writing course; completion of college-level mathematics and literature course; minimum 3.0 GPA; passing grade on PRAXIS I; student must be admitted to the Graduate School.

Fees and Expenses: Undergraduate: in-state $3,814 per academic year; out-of-state $9,910. Graduate: in-state $1,863, out-of-state $3,906 or $217 per credit hour. Required fees: $986 undergraduate plus $41 per credit hour. On-campus room and board: $5,616. Books and supplies: $800.

Financial Aid: Resources specifically for eligible students enrolled in teacher education programs are awarded on the basis of financial need. The institution has a Program Participation Agreement with the U.S. Department of Education for eligible students to receive Pell Grants and other federal aid. *Contact:* Angela Hovatter at: (301) 687-4301 or e-mail at ahovatter@frostburg.edu.

Accreditation: *Regional:* MSA. *Professional:* NCATE. *Member of:* AACTE. *Approved by:* Maryland State Board of Education.

Undergraduate Programs: The Educational Professions Department offers an early childhood/elementary major leading to eligibility for certification in nursery school through grade 6 and middle school. Also offered is an elementary education major leading to eligibility for certification in grades 1-6 and middle school. A business education major leading to certification in grades 7-12 is offered in cooperation with the Business Education Department. All programs require the completion of general education core, professional studies, subject area major, field experiences, and student teaching. A minimum of 120 semester hours is required for the baccalaureate degrees.

The department also offers approved teacher education programs leading to eligibility for certification secondary education (biology, business education, chemistry, English, foreign languages, earth science, mathematics, physics, social studies) for grades 7-12 as well as middle school depending on subject area, and K-12 education (art, music, health, physical education) for grades kindergarten-12. All programs require completion of a general education core, professional studies, subject major, field experiences, and student teaching.

Graduate Programs: The Master of Arts in Teaching program is designed to provide qualified individuals with a master's degree and initial certification in the area of elementary education or a secondary education content specialization by providing study of the knowledge, skills, and dispositions necessary for effective teachers. the program contains extensive field work in professional development school settings and anticipates the full-time enrollment of the candidate.

Licensure/Reciprocity: Maryland. Students seeking teaching certification in a state other than Maryland should consult with that state's teacher certification office early in their program of study to insure compliance with requirements. Many state directors of teacher credentialing have signed Interstate Agreements through NASDTEC that expedite the certification process.

JOHNS HOPKINS UNIVERSITY
Graduate Division of Education
Department of Teacher Preparation
3400 North Charles Street
Baltimore, Maryland 21218-2680
Phone: (410) 516-8273
Fax: (410) 516-3323
E-mail: stotko@jhu.edu
Internet: http://www.jhu.edu

Institution Description: Johns Hopkins University is an independent institution. It was incorporated in 1867 and offered first instruction at the postsecondary level in 1876.

Teacher education programs are offered only at the graduate level.

Institution Control: Private.

Calendar: Semester. Academic year September to May.

Official(s): Dr. Edward Pajak, Director, Graduate Division of Education; Dr. Elaine Stotko, Chair, Department of Teacher Education.

Faculty: Full-time 34; adjunct 140.

Degrees Awarded: 490 master's; 1 doctorate.

Admission Requirements: *Graduate:* Baccalaureate degree from a regionally accredited institution. *Teacher education specific:* PRAXIS I test scores; 3.0 GPA; transcripts of all previous coursework; recommendations; faculty interview.

Fees and Expenses: Graduate: $345 per credit hour. Other fees may apply.

Financial Aid: Resources specifically for eligible students enrolled in teacher education programs are awarded on the basis of financial need and academic merit. *Contact:* Laura Donnelly, Director, Financial Aid at: (410) 872-1230.

Accreditation: *Regional:* MSA. *Professional:* NCATE. *Member of:* AACTE. *Approved by:* Maryland State Board of Education.

Graduate Programs: The Master of Arts in Teaching program is designed to meet the needs of recent graduates of bachelor or graduate degree programs in appropriate content areas, as well as mid-career professionals working in business, industry, engineering, or the military who desire to make a career change into teaching. The program emphasizes the integration of a solid foundation of subject matter expertise with the most current knowledge base on teaching and learning. Students participate in a variety of field placements in school settings. The program is delivered in several formats. Each format includes 39 credits of the program, but provides candidates options for part-time study, full-time study and immersion in schools, or immersion in the profession with part-time study. Teacher certification areas are offered in elementary and secondary education.

Additional graduate programs are available in the areas of school administration, reading, technology for educators, school counseling, and special education.

Licensure/Reciprocity: Maryland. Students seeking teaching certification in a state other than Maryland should consult with that state's teacher certification office early in their program of study to insure compliance with requirements. Many state directors of teacher credentialing have signed Interstate Agreements through NASDTEC that expedite the certification process.

LOYOLA COLLEGE IN MARYLAND
Education Department
Beatty Hall, Room 104
4501 North Charles Street
Baltimore, Maryland 21210
Phone: (410) 617-5095
Fax: (410) 617-2176
E-mail: admissions@loyola.edu
Internet: http://www.loyola.edu

Institution Description: Loyola College in Maryland is affiliated with the Society of Jesus, Roman Catholic Church. It was established as a men's college in 1852. The college merged with Mount Saint Agnes College for Women in 1971.

The Education Department promotes leadership and scholarship in the development of teachers, counselors, administrators, and other educators.

Institution Control: Private.

Calendar: Semester. Academic year September to August.

Official(s): Dr. Victor R. Delclos, Chair, Education Department.

Faculty: Full-time 16.

Degrees Awarded: 48 baccalaureate; 300 master's.

Admission Requirements: *Undergraduate:* Graduation with 16 academic units from an approved secondary school or GED; College Board SAT. *Teacher education specific:* Students are encouraged to declare the major by the spring semester of their freshman year; PRAXIS I test scores; faculty interview. *Graduate:* Baccalaureate degree from a regionally accredited institution. *Teacher education specific:* Teaching experience where required by the program pursued; recommendations; faculty interview; PRAXIS I; 3.0 cumulative GPA.

Fees and Expenses: $24,310 per academic year. Graduate: $244 per credit hour. On-campus room and board: $7,720. Other expenses: $1,270. Books and supplies: $740.

LOYOLA COLLEGE IN MARYLAND—*cont'd*

Financial Aid: Resources specifically for eligible students enrolled in teacher education programs are awarded on the basis of financial need and academic merit. The institution has a Program Participation Agreement with the U.S. Department of Education for eligible students to receive Pell Grants and other federal aid. Maryland Teacher Scholarships available to qualifying students. *Contact:* Financial Aid Office at: (410) 617-2576.

Accreditation: *Regional:* MSA. *Professional:* NCATE. *Member of:* AACTE. *Approved by:* Maryland State Board of Education.

Undergraduate Programs: Elementary education majors are prepared for teaching through a program that blends theory with practice. Students completing the program satisfy course requirements for certification in Maryland. To enable education majors to respond to the needs of exceptional children, courses in special education are required. The Bachelor of Arts degree is awarded upon completion of a general education core, professional studies, field experiences, and student teaching. A minimum of 120 semester hours must be completed.

The department offers a minor in special education that provides students with a basic understanding of special education, the diverse learner, and assessment and instructional strategies for children with special needs.

A program minor in secondary education allows students from other disciplines to complete degree requirements for their major while taking education courses required for certification.

Graduate Programs: Programs are offered by the department leading to a Master of Arts, Master of Education, the Certificate of Advanced Study in School Management, and the Certificate of Advanced Study in Education. Degree programs are offered in the areas of administration and supervision, curriculum and instruction, educational technology, school counseling, Montessori education, reading, special education, and teacher education.

Licensure/Reciprocity: Maryland. Students seeking teaching certification in a state other than Maryland should consult with that state's teacher certification office early in their program of study to insure compliance with requirements. Many state directors of teacher credentialing have signed Interstate Agreements through NASDTEC that expedite the certification process.

MCDANIEL COLLEGE

Education Department
Thompson Hall
2 College Hill
Westminster, Maryland 21157-4390
Phone: (410) 857-2501
Fax: (410) 857-2515
E-mail: admission@mcdaniel.edu
Internet: http://www.mcdaniel.edu

Institution Description: McDaniel College, formerly known as Western Maryland College, is a four-year college of liberal arts and sciences. It was established in 1867 and was named for the Western Maryland Railroad. The current name was adopted recently.

The Education Department offers students programs that feature a minor in elementary or secondary education.

Institution Control: Private.

Calendar: Semester. Academic year August to May.

Official(s): Dr. Joan Develin Coley, President.

Faculty: Full-time 18.

Degrees Awarded: 22 baccalaureate; 362 master's.

Admission Requirements: *Undergraduate:* Graduation with 16 academic units from an accredited secondary school or GED; College Board SAT. *Teacher education specific:* PRAXIS I test scores; faculty interview.

Fees and Expenses: $21,780 per academic year. On-campus room and board: $5,280. Other expenses: $1,070. Books and supplies: $1,070.

Financial Aid: Resources specifically for eligible students enrolled in teacher education programs are awarded on the basis of financial need and academic merit. The institution has a Program Participation Agreement with the U.S. Department of Education for eligible students to receive Pell Grants and other federal aid. Maryland Teacher Scholarships available to qualifying students. *Contact:* Financial Aid Office at: (410) 857-2233.

Accreditation: *Regional:* MSA. *Professional:* NCATE. *Member of:* AACTE. *Approved by:* Maryland State Board of Education.

Undergraduate Programs: Teaching certification is provided at both the elementary and secondary levels. The McDaniel program prepares students for certification in elementary education and the following secondary education fields: art, biology, chemistry, English, French, German, mathematics, music, physical education, physics, social studies and Spanish. All education courses provide students with actual classroom experience through observation, tutoring, and an extensive student teaching experience in a professional development school setting. The physical education, music, and art programs offer K-12 certification option. Students combine a minor in elementary or secondary education with a major in another department of the college to complete their programs. All baccalaureate programs require the completion of 128 credit hours.

Licensure/Reciprocity: Maryland. Students seeking teaching certification in a state other than Maryland should consult with that state's teacher certification office early in their program of study to insure compliance with requirements. Many state directors of teacher credentialing have signed Interstate Agreements through NASDTEC that expedite the certification process.

MORGAN STATE UNIVERSITY

Department of Teacher Education and Administration
1700 East Cold Spring Lane
Baltimore, Maryland 21251
Phone: (443) 885-3333
Fax: (443) 885-3684
E-mail: jwaller@morgan.edu
Internet: http://www.morgan.edu

Institution Description: Morgan State University was chartered as Centenary Bible Institute in 1867 and became Morgan College in 1890. The name was changed to Morgan State College in 1939 and the present name was adopted in 1975.

The teacher education program at Morgan State University is designed to complement the historical liberal arts character of the institution.

Institution Control: Public.

Calendar: Semester. Academic year September to May.

Official(s): Dr. Patricia L. Morris-Welch, Dean; Professor Iola Ragins Smith, Chairperson.

Faculty: Full-time 15.

Degrees Awarded: 66 baccalaureate; 13 master's; 13 doctorate.

Admission Requirements: *Undergraduate:* Graduation from an approved secondary school or GED; College Board SAT or ACT composite. *Teacher education specific:* Completion of education foundations course; completion of a minimum of 60 semester credits; PRAXIS I test scores; completion of the university's speech and writing proficiency requirements; must meet state qualifying score on PRAXIS II prior to graduation. *Graduate:* Baccalaureate degree from a regionally accredited institution. *Teacher education specific:* Teaching experience where required by the program pursued; recommendations; faculty interview; PRAXIS I; 3.0 cumulative GPA.

Fees and Expenses: Undergraduate: in-state $4,698 per academic year; out-of-state $11,118. Graduate: in-state $193 per credit hour; out-of-state $364. Required fees: $40 per credit. On-campus room and board: $6,360. Other expenses: $2,650. Books and supplies: $1,000.

Financial Aid: Resources specifically for eligible students enrolled in teacher education programs are awarded on the basis of financial need and academic merit. The institution has a Program Participation Agreement with the U.S. Department of

Education for eligible students to receive Pell Grants and other federal aid. Maryland Teacher Scholarships available to qualifying students. *Contact:* Financial Aid Office at: (443) 885-3170.

Accreditation: *Regional:* MSA. *Professional:* NCATE. *Member of:* AACTE. *Approved by:* Maryland State Board of Education.

Undergraduate Programs: The elementary education certification program offers courses and learning experiences designed to prepare students for an elementary school teaching career. The program includes the broad base of liberal arts courses required of all university students. Specific requirements of the program include academic courses, professional education courses, professional methods courses, and student teaching. Students must register and sit for the PRAXIS I tests by the end of their sophomore year. Successful completion of the appropriate PRAXIS II assessments prior to graduation is mandatory.

The secondary education certification program offers courses and learning experiences for preparation of secondary school teachers in: art, biology chemistry, English, history, mathematics, music, physical education, and physics. Specific requirements of the program include: academic courses in an appropriate teaching field as prescribed by the department or school in which the major is pursued; professional education courses; professional methods courses and student teaching. PRAXIS I tests (3) must be passed by the end of the sophomore year; qualifying score on PRAXIS II must be achieved prior to graduation.

Graduate Programs: The Master of Arts in Teaching and the Master of Science in elementary or middle school education programs are offered through the Graduate School of the university. Each program has specific objectives and required courses. Contact the Department of Teacher Education (Dr. Iola Regins Smith, Chairperson) for detailed information.

Licensure/Reciprocity: Maryland. Students seeking teaching certification in a state other than Maryland should consult with that state's teacher certification office early in their program of study to insure compliance with requirements. Many state directors of teacher credentialing have signed Interstate Agreements through NASDTEC that expedite the certification process.

MOUNT SAINT MARY'S COLLEGE

Education Department
Teacher Education Programs
16300 Old Emmitsburg Road
Emmitsburg, Maryland 21727
Phone: (301) 447-6122
Fax: (301) 447-5755
E-mail: admissions@msmary.edu
Internet: http://www.msmary.edu

Institution Description: Mount Saint Mary's College is a private independent institution affiliated with the Roman Catholic Church. It was established in 1808.

The Education Department is committed to a broad and integrated liberal arts core as a foundation for teachers at all levels.

Institution Control: Private.

Calendar: Semester. Academic year August to May.

Official(s): Dr. Christopher Blake, Department Chair and Director of Teacher Education.

Faculty: Full-time 10.

Degrees Awarded: 51 baccalaureate; 24 master's.

Admission Requirements: *Undergraduate:* Graduation with 16 academic units from an approved secondary school or GED; College Board SAT. *Teacher education specific:* Submit application no later than the second semester of the sophomore year; declaration of major; must satisfy the college's writing competency; interview; PRAXIS I exam before entering the program in the junior year. *Graduate:* Baccalaureate degree from a regionally accredited institution. *Teacher education specific:* Teaching credential where required by the program pursued; recommendations; faculty interview.

Fees and Expenses: $19,700 per academic year. Graduate: $260 per credit. On-campus room and board: $7,300. Other expenses: $1,450. Books and supplies: $800.

Financial Aid: Resources specifically for eligible students enrolled in teacher education programs are awarded on the basis of financial need and academic merit. The institution has a Program Participation Agreement with the U.S. Department of Education for eligible students to receive Pell Grants and other federal aid. Maryland Teacher Scholarships available to qualifying students. *Contact:* Financial Aid Office at: (301) 447-5207.

Accreditation: *Regional:* MSA. *Member of:* AACTE. *Approved by:* Maryland State Board of Education.

Undergraduate Programs: Any student in good academic standing at the college may minor in education (18 credits).

The elementary education program is designed to prepare students to teach at the elementary school level, grades 1-6, as well as middle school. The elementary education and special education (dual major) is a four-year program that follows the requirements for the elementary major and includes additional courses for certification in generic special education (grades 1-6 plus middle school).

The program in art education prepares students to be certified in art (pre-K through grade 12). Students complete a major in fine arts with certification to teach.

The programs in secondary education are designed to prepare students to teach at the secondary level in English, social studies, or mathematics. Each student must have a major in an academic subject field.

All baccalaureate programs require completion of a general education core, professional studies, field experiences, and student teaching. A minimum of 120 semester hours.

Graduate Programs: The Master of Education program is designed for certified teachers seeking a graduate degree in elementary education, instructional technology, or reading specialist.

The Master of Arts in Teaching degree program is designed for those who seek an initial Maryland teaching certificate and a graduate degree. The programs offered include: MAT degree with initial certification in elementary education (grades 1-6); MAT degree with dual certification in elementary and special education (grades 1-6); MAT degree with certification in secondary teaching (grades 5-12); Master of Arts in Teaching with initial certification in art education (grades k-12).

Licensure/Reciprocity: Maryland. Students seeking teaching certification in a state other than Maryland should consult with that state's teacher certification office early in their program of study to insure compliance with requirements. Many state directors of teacher credentialing have signed Interstate Agreements through NASDTEC that expedite the certification process.

SALISBURY STATE UNIVERSITY

School of Education and Professional Studies
Department of Education
1101 Camden Avenue
Salisbury, Maryland 21801
Phone: (410) 543-6000
Fax: (410) 548-6160
E-mail: education@ssu.edu
Internet: http://www.ssu.edu

Institution Description: Salisbury State University was established as Maryland State Normal School at Salisbury, a two-year institution, in 1925. It became a four-year college and renamed State Teacher's College at Salisbury in 1935. The name was changed to Salisbury State College in 1963 and the present name was adopted in 1988.

The Department of Education offers programs leading to the bachelor's and master's degrees.

Institution Control: Public.

Calendar: Semester. Academic year September to May.

Official(s): Dr. Dorsey Hammond, Chair, Department of Education.

Faculty: Full-time 30.

SALISBURY STATE UNIVERSITY—*cont'd*

Degrees Awarded: 231 baccalaureate; 95 master's.

Admission Requirements: *Undergraduate:* Graduation from an approved secondary school or GED; College Board SAT or ACT composite. *Teacher education specific:* Completion of education foundations course; completion of a minimum of 60 semester credits; PRAXIS I test scores; must meet state qualifying score on PRAXIS II prior to graduation. *Graduate:* Baccalaureate degree from a regionally accredited institution. *Teacher education specific:* Teaching credential where required by the program pursued; recommendations; faculty interview.

Fees and Expenses: Undergraduate: in-state $4,804 per academic year; out-of-state $10,568. Graduate: in-state $124 per credit hour; out-of-state $364. On-campus room and board: $6,380. Other expenses: $2,150. Books and supplies: $675.

Financial Aid: Resources specifically for eligible students enrolled in teacher education programs are awarded on the basis of financial need and academic merit. The institution has a Program Participation Agreement with the U.S. Department of Education for eligible students to receive Pell Grants and other federal aid. Funding for prospective and current teachers in various awards is available for qualifying students. *Contact:* Financial Aid Office at: (410) 543-6165.

Accreditation: *Regional:* MSA. *Professional:* NCATE. *Member of:* AACTE. *Approved by:* Maryland State Board of Education.

Undergraduate Programs: The Department of Education offers bachelor's degrees leading to teacher certification in the following areas (subject areas in italic have been designated Critical Shortage Areas in Maryland): early childhood education (pre-K-3), elementary education, health education (7-12), and physical education (K-12). Secondary and K-12 education programs include concentrations in *biology, chemistry,* English, French, history/social studies, *mathematics,* music (K-12), *physics,* and *Spanish.*

All programs require the completion of a general education core, professional studies, subject concentration (secondary education), field experiences, and student teaching. A minimum of 120 credit hours must be completed for the degree award.

Graduate Programs: Graduate education programs include the Master of Arts in Teaching and Master of Arts in English: teaching of English to speakers of other languages for secondary/K-12 certification. Advanced certification for currently certified teachers includes the Master of Education: reading specialist and Master of Education: public school administration.

Professional development programs for currently certified teachers not leading to teacher certification include the Master of Education in the fields of early childhood, elementary, middle/secondary, postsecondary, and teaching and learning with technology.

Licensure/Reciprocity: Maryland. Students seeking teaching certification in a state other than Maryland should consult with that state's teacher certification office early in their program of study to insure compliance with requirements. Many state directors of teacher credentialing have signed Interstate Agreements through NASDTEC that expedite the certification process.

TOWSON UNIVERSITY

College of Education
Teacher Education Unit
Hawkins Hall, room 301
8000 York Road
Towson, Maryland 21252-0001
Phone: (410) 704-2570
Fax: (410) 704-2733
E-mail: coe@towson.edu
Internet: http://www.towson.edu

Institution Description: Towson University is an institutional member of the University of Maryland System. It was established and chartered as Maryland State Normal School in 1866.

The name was changed to State Teachers College at Towson in 1935 and to Towson State College in 1963. The present name was adopted in 1976.

As the first teacher-training institution in Maryland, Towson University has been preparing men and women for teaching careers for over 135 years. Programs of study lead to the baccalaureate degree in education with certification in early childhood, elementary, and special education.

Institution Control: Public.

Calendar: Semester. Academic year August to May.

Official(s): Dr. Thomas Proffitt, Dean.

Faculty: Full-time 74.

Degrees Awarded: 310 baccalaureate; 320 master's.

Admission Requirements: *Undergraduate:* Graduation from an approved secondary school or GED; College Board SAT or ACT composite. *Teacher education specific:* Completion of education foundations course; completion of a minimum of 60 semester credits; PRAXIS I test scores; must meet state qualifying score on PRAXIS II prior to graduation. *Graduate:* Baccalaureate degree from a regionally accredited institution. *Teacher education specific:* Teaching credential where required by the program pursued; recommendations; faculty interview.

Fees and Expenses: Undergraduate: in-state $3,956 per academic year; out-of-state $11,602. On-campus room and board: $6,322. Other expenses: $2,150. Books and supplies: $675.

Financial Aid: Resources specifically for eligible students enrolled in teacher education programs are awarded on the basis of financial need and academic merit. The institution has a Program Participation Agreement with the U.S. Department of Education for eligible students to receive Pell Grants and other federal aid. Funding for prospective and current teachers in various awards is available for qualifying students. *Contact:* Vince Pecora at (410) 704-4286 or e-mail at vpecora@towson.edu.

Accreditation: *Regional:* MSA. *Professional:* NCATE. *Member of:* AACTE. *Approved by:* Maryland State Board of Education.

Undergraduate Programs: The Department of Early Childhood Education offers programs of study that include: early childhood education, the major in elementary education with eligibility for early childhood education certification. The programs require completion of a general education core, professional studies, field experiences, and student teaching. A minimum of 120 semester hours must be completed for the degree award.

The Department of Elementary Education offers the major in elementary education, the major with eligibility for early childhood certification, the integrated elementary education-special education major, and the elementary education major with a minor in selected disciplines.

The Department of Reading, Special Education, and Instructional Technology is responsible for courses that are not limited to a single teacher education program. The programs include a major in special education, the major in integrated elementary education-special education.

The Department of Secondary Education offers 13 certification programs in the secondary subject areas of biology, chemistry, earth-space science, English, French, geography, German, school health, history, mathematics, physics, social science, and Spanish. The programs of education for junior, middle, and high school teachers are designed to bring about close integration between teaching methods and the practical experience of student teaching.

Graduate Programs: Master's degree programs are offered in the areas of early childhood education, elementary education, instructional technology, reading, secondary education, and special education.

The Doctor of Education degree program in instructional technology focuses on the development of instructional expertise to meet the present and future needs of technology integration in instruction across the education spectrum.

Licensure/Reciprocity: Maryland. Students seeking teaching certification in a state other than Maryland should consult with that state's teacher certification office early in their program of study to insure compliance with requirements. Many state

directors of teacher credentialing have signed Interstate Agreements through NASDTEC that expedite the certification process.

UNIVERSITY OF MARYLAND BALTIMORE COUNTY

Department of Education
Teacher Education Programs
1000 Hilltop Circle
Baltimore, Maryland 21250
Phone: (410) 455-2465
Fax: (410) 455-1880
E-mail: rivkin@umbc.edu
Internet: http://www.umbc.edu

Institution Description: The university was established in 1963 and offered first instruction at the postsecondary level in 1966.

The Department of Education offers students the opportunity to combine an academic major in their subject area of interest with teaching training programs leading to certification.

Institution Control: Public.

Calendar: Semester. Academic year September to May.

Official(s): Dr. Mary S. Rivkin, Chair.

Faculty: Full-time 16.

Degrees Awarded: 34 baccalaureate; 124 master's.

Admission Requirements: *Undergraduate:* Graduation from an approved secondary school or GED; College Board SAT or ACT composite. *Teacher education specific:* Completion of education foundations course; completion of a minimum of 45 semester credits; PRAXIS I test scores; must meet state qualifying score on PRAXIS II prior to graduation. *Graduate:* Baccalaureate degree from a regionally accredited institution. *Teacher education specific:* Minimum grade of C in advanced writing course; completion of college-level mathematics and literature course; minimum 3.0 GPA; passing grade on PRAXIS I; student must be admitted to the Graduate School.

Fees and Expenses: Undergraduate: in-state $4,804 per academic year; out-of-state $10,568. Graduate: in-state $124 per credit hour; out-of-state $364. On-campus room and board: $6,400. Other expenses: $2,150. Books and supplies: $675.

Financial Aid: Resources specifically for eligible students enrolled in teacher education programs are awarded on the basis of financial need and academic merit. The institution has a Program Participation Agreement with the U.S. Department of Education for eligible students to receive Pell Grants and other federal aid. Funding for prospective and current teachers in various awards is available for qualifying students. *Contact:* Financial Aid Office at: (410) 706-7347.

Accreditation: *Regional:* MSA. *Professional:* NCATE. *Member of:* AACTE. *Approved by:* Maryland State Board of Education.

Undergraduate Programs: The Department of Education confers the degrees of Bachelor of Arts or Bachelor of Science depending on the amount of liberal arts study included in a particular degree program. Minimum requirements are 120 semester hours. In addition to the general education requirements and specific requirements for each curriculum, the college requires that all majors complete a Foundations of Education course.

Graduate Programs: Master's degree requirements vary according to the area of concentration and the type of degree. Programs typically require 30 to 36 semester hours, a six-hour comprehensive examination, and one to two seminary papers. The Master of Arts and the Master of Education programs are available.

The Doctor of Education is offered in all areas of specialization. The doctorate requires 60 semester hours beyond the master's degree, a doctoral dissertation, and an oral examination in defense of the dissertation is required.

Licensure/Reciprocity: Maryland. Students seeking teaching certification in a state other than Maryland should consult with that state's teacher certification office early in their program of study to insure compliance with requirements. Many state

directors of teacher credentialing have signed Interstate Agreements through NASDTEC that expedite the certification process.

UNIVERSITY OF MARYLAND COLLEGE PARK

College of Education
Teacher Education
3119 Benjamin Building
College Park, Maryland 20742
Phone: (301) 405-2358
Fax: (301) 314-9890
E-mail: education@umd.edu
Internet: http://www.umd.edu

Institution Description: The campus was established as Maryland Agricultural College in 1856. The name was changed to Maryland State College of Agriculture in 1916 and the present name was adopted in 1920.

Teacher Education in the College of Education is committed to providing future teachers with preparation programs that foster the development of critical knowledge and skills needed to effectively teach all children and young people in our diverse society.

Institution Control: Public.

Calendar: Semester. Academic year September to May.

Official(s): Dr. Edna Mora Szmanski, Dean; Dr. Stephen Kaziol, Chair.

Faculty: Full-time 103.

Degrees Awarded: 317 baccalaureate; 243 master's; 50 doctorate.

Admission Requirements: *Undergraduate:* Graduation from an accredited secondary school; College Board SAT or ACT composite. *Teacher education specific:* PRAXIS I; 2.5 GPA; English and math fundamental studies; completion of 45 credits; goal statement; list of experiences with children; 3 letters of recommendation. *Graduate:* Baccalaureate degree from an accredited institution; minimum 3.0 GPA; letters of recommendation; scores on national standardized exams. *Teacher education specific:* Relevant content portion of PRAXIS II; goal statement; portfolio of creative works; faculty interview.

Fees and Expenses: Undergraduate: $5,727 in-state per academic year; $14,587 out-of-state. Graduate: in-state $301 per credit hour; $466 out-of-state. On-campus room and board: $3,930 per semester. Books and supplies: $500 per semester.

Financial Aid: Resources specifically for eligible students enrolled in teacher education programs are awarded on the basis of financial need and academic merit. The institution has a Program Participation Agreement with the U.S. Department of Education for eligible students to receive Pell Grants and other federal aid. Teacher scholarships available to qualifying students. *Contact:* Kathy Angelletti, Assistant Dean at: (301) 405-2358 or e-mail at: Kangel@umd.edu.

Accreditation: *Regional:* MSA. *Professional:* NCATE. *Member of:* AACTE. *Approved by:* Pennsylvania Department of Education.

Degrees Offered: Baccalaureate; Master's; Doctorate.

Undergraduate Programs: The College of Education confers the degrees of Bachelor of Arts or Bachelor of Science depending on the amount of liberal arts study included in a particular degree program. The programs available include elementary education, English education, foreign language education: Spanish/French/Russian/German; art education; English/speech education; English/theatre education; mathematics education; science education: physics/chemistry/biology; social studies education: geography/history/government. All programs required the completion of 120 semester hours including general education, professional studies, field experiences, and student teaching.

Graduate Programs: The Masters of Arts with thesis is offered by all departmental programs except teaching of English to speakers of other languages. The Master of Education Degree is offered by all departmental programs except art education. Individual programs may require additional coursework

UNIVERSITY OF MARYLAND COLLEGE PARK—*cont'd*

beyond the college's minimum 30 hour requirement. Also required is a six-hour comprehensive examination and one or two seminary papers. Requirements for master's degree vary according to the area of concentration and the type of degree.

The Doctor of Philosophy is offered by all areas of specialization and requires a minimum of 12 dissertation credit hours. The Doctor of Education is offered by most areas of specialization. The doctorate requires a planned sequence of 60 semester hours beyond the master's degree.

Licensure/Reciprocity: Maryland. Students seeking teaching certification in a state other than Maryland should consult with that state's teacher certification office early in their program of study to insure compliance with requirements. Many state directors of teacher credentialing have signed Interstate Agreements through NASDTEC that expedite the certification process.

UNIVERSITY OF MARYLAND EASTERN SHORE

School of Arts and Professions
Department of Education/Teacher Education Program
Backbone Road
Princess Anne, Maryland 21853-1299
Phone: (410) 651-6410
Fax: (410) 651-7922
E-mail: admissions@umes.umd.edu
Internet: http://www.umes.umd.edu

Institution Description: The institution was established as Princess Anne of the Delaware Conference Academy in 1886. It became a division of the University of Maryland and the name was changed to Maryland State College in 1948. The present name was adopted in 1970.

The Department of Education offers undergraduate and graduate programs. Emphasis is placed on preparing minority and rural educators.

Institution Control: Public.

Calendar: Semester. Academic year August to May.

Official(s): Dr. Karen Verbeke, Chair and Director of Teacher Education.

Faculty: Full-time 10.

Degrees Awarded: 22 baccalaureate; 27 master's.

Admission Requirements: *Undergraduate:* Graduation from an approved secondary school or GED; College Board SAT or ACT composite. *Teacher education specific:* Completion of education foundations course; completion of a minimum of 45 semester credits; PRAXIS I test scores; must meet state qualifying score on PRAXIS II prior to graduation. *Graduate:*Baccalaureate degree from a regionally accredited institution. *Teacher education specific:* Minimum grade of C in advanced writing course; completion of college-level mathematics and literature course; minimum 3.0 GPA; passing grade on PRAXIS I; student must be admitted to the Graduate School.

Fees and Expenses: Undergraduate: in-state $4,804 per academic year; out-of-state $10,568. Graduate: in-state $124 per credit hour; out-of-state $364. On-campus room and board: $6,380. Other expenses: $2,150. Books and supplies: $675.

Financial Aid: Resources specifically for eligible students enrolled in teacher education programs are awarded on the basis of financial need and academic merit. The institution has a Program Participation Agreement with the U.S. Department of Education for eligible students to receive Pell Grants and other federal aid. Funding for prospective and current teachers in various awards is available for qualifying students. *Contact:* Financial Aid Office at: (410) 651-5174.

Accreditation: *Regional:* MSA. *Member of:* AACTE. *Approved by:* Maryland State Board of Education.

Undergraduate Programs: The Department of Education directs a variety of undergraduate programs in the field of teacher education. The department is organized into two primary program areas: specialty education and secondary education. Every education major selects either the specialty or secondary program area. All education majors also choose a specific area of specialization within their general program area.

The Specialty Education program offers specialized areas of art education (pre-K-12), music education (pre-K-12), and special education (1-8, 6-12). The secondary education program offers concentrations in the areas of: agriculture, biology, business, chemistry, English, family and consumer science, mathematics, social studies, and technology. All students must complete a general education core, professional studies, field experiences, and student teaching. A minimum of 120 semester hours must be completed for the baccalaureate degree.

Graduate Programs: The Master of Arts in Teaching and a graduate guidance and counseling program are offered by the department through the Graduate School.

Licensure/Reciprocity: Maryland. Students seeking teaching certification in a state other than Maryland should consult with that state's teacher certification office early in their program of study to insure compliance with requirements. Many state directors of teacher credentialing have signed Interstate Agreements through NASDTEC that expedite the certification process.

VILLA JULIE COLLEGE

Department of Education
1525 Greenspring Valley Road
Stevenson, Maryland 21153-0641
Phone: (410) 486-7000
Fax: (410) 486-3552
E-mail: admissions@vjc.edu
Internet: http://www.vjc.edu

Institution Description: Villa Julie College is a private, independent, nonprofit institution. It was founded in 1947 by Sisters of Notre Dame de Namur as a two-year institution. It became a four-year in 1988.

Villa Julie College offers a variety of options for students interested in working with children. A program is offered that leads to teacher certification and an other that leads to leadership positions in non-public settings for very young children.

Institution Control: Private.

Calendar: Semester. Academic year August to May.

Official(s): Dr. Paul D. Lack, Academic Dean.

Faculty: Full-time 14; part-time 10.

Degrees Awarded: 36 baccalaureate.

Admission Requirements: *Undergraduate:* Graduation from an approved secondary school or GED; College Board SAT or ACT composite. *Teacher education specific:* Completion of education foundations course; completion of a minimum of 60 semester credits; PRAXIS I test scores; must meet state qualifying score on PRAXIS II prior to graduation.

Fees and Expenses: $12,798 per academic year. On-campus room and board: $6,300. Other expenses: $2,780. Books and supplies: $1,000.

Financial Aid: Resources specifically for eligible students enrolled in teacher education programs are awarded on the basis of financial need and academic merit. The institution has a Program Participation Agreement with the U.S. Department of Education for eligible students to receive Pell Grants and other federal aid. Maryland Teacher Scholarships available to qualifying students. *Contact:* Financial Aid Office at: (410) 486-7001.

Accreditation: *Regional:* MSA. *Member of:* AACTE. *Approved by:* Maryland State Board of Education.

Undergraduate Programs: The early childhood education: liberal arts and technology program is offered and leads to the baccalaureate degree. Teacher candidates complete an education course sequence in their selected area of certification. The education courses are designed to help teacher candidates develop the competencies and dispositions necessary for successful teaching and lifelong learning. The program leads to certification and requires the completion of the general education core, professional studies, field experiences, and student teaching. Technology is an integral part of the curriculum. A minimum of 120 semester hours is required for the baccalaureate degree.

Early childhood leadership program is designed to prepare students to assume leadership position s in child care, Head Start programs, nonpublic school settings, and agencies that support those settings. The program includes a strong foundation in child development, a variety of field experiences, the integration of theory and practice, and electives in either administration or classroom leadership. Graduates of the program are **not** eligible for teacher certification. A minimum of 120 semester hours is required for the baccalaureate degree.

Licensure/Reciprocity: Maryland. Students seeking teaching certification in a state other than Maryland should consult with that state's teacher certification office early in their program of study to insure compliance with requirements. Many state directors of teacher credentialing have signed Interstate Agreements through NASDTEC that expedite the certification process.

MASSACHUSETTS

BAY PATH COLLEGE

Education Department

588 Longmeadow Street
Longmeadow, Massachusetts 01106
Phone: (413) 565-1227
Fax: (413) 565-1116
E-mail: eleavitt@baypath.edu
Internet: http://www.baypath.edu

Institution Description: Bay Path College is an independent four-year college for women. It was founded in 1897 as Bay Path Institute in Springfield. The campus was moved to its present location in 1945 and the present name was adopted in 1988. Men are admitted for the graduate study. >r<Programs are offered by the Education Department leading to the baccalaureate degree and teacher licensure.

Institution Control: Private.

Calendar: Semester. Academic year September to May.

Official(s): Dr. Estelle Leavitt, Department Chairperson.

Faculty: Full-time 2; adjunct 6.

Degrees Awarded: 54 baccalaureate.

Admission Requirements: *Undergraduate:* Graduation from an approved secondary school or GED; 2.5 GPA or greater; minimum SAT verbal of 450 or greater and a total SAT score of 900 or greater. *Teacher education specific:* Must major in liberal studies; maintain a 3.0 GPA; pass the communication and Literacy exam of the Massachusetts Tests for Educator Licensure (MTEL) pass early childhood or elementary education exam **and** the Foundations of Reading exam of the MTEL.

Fees and Expenses: $16,890 per academic year. On-campus room and board: $8,020. Books and supplies: $750.

Financial Aid: Resources specifically for eligible students enrolled in teacher education programs are awarded on the basis of financial need and academic merit. The institution has a Program Participation Agreement with the U.S. Department of Education for eligible students to receive Pell Grants and other federal aid. Teacher Scholarships available to qualifying students. *Contact:* Stephanie King, Director of Financial Aid at: (413) 565-1345 or sking@baypath.edu.

Accreditation: *Regional:* NEASC. *Member of:* AACTE. *Approved by:* Massachusetts Department of Education.

Undergraduate Programs: Students can major in either early childhood education or elementary education within the bachelor of arts degree program in liberal studies. Both education majors lead toward initial licensure as a public school teacher with the Massachusetts Department of Education. The liberal studies degree program helps prepare the student in subjects that she will teach, including English, history, mathematics, science, government, and geography. In addition, the student elects a sequence of education courses that prepares her to teach using the Massachusetts Curriculum Frameworks. In the last year of study, the student enters the senior year experience in education that consists of two intensive field experiences: pre-practicum and practicum (student teaching). A minimum cumulative of 3.0 GPA is required to begin the practicum. Graduation requirements include the completion of 122-124 credits with a final GPA of at least 3.0.

Licensure/Reciprocity: Massachusetts. Students seeking teaching certification in a state other than Massachusetts should consult with that state's teacher certification office early in their program of study to insure compliance with requirements. Many state directors of teacher credentialing have signed Interstate Agreements through NASDTEC that expedite the certification process.

BOSTON COLLEGE

Lynch School of Education
Teacher Education Department

Campion Hall
140 Commonwealth Avenue
Chestnut Hill, Massachusetts 02467
Phone: (617) 552-4200
Fax: (617) 552-0812
E-mail: murphygp@bc.edu
Internet: http://www.bc.edu

Institution Description: Boston College is an independent institution affiliated with the Society of Jesus, Roman Catholic Church. It was established in 1863.

Programs within the Teacher Education Department offer degrees at both the undergraduate and graduate levels.

Institution Control: Private.

Calendar: Semester. Academic year September to May.

Official(s): Dr. Mary M. Brabeck, Dean; Dr. Joseph M. O'Keefe, Associate Dean.

Faculty: Full-time 60; part-time 38.

Degrees Awarded: 184 baccalaureate; 247 master's; 49 doctorate.

Admission Requirements: *Undergraduate:* Graduation from an accredited secondary school or GED; College Board SAT or ACT composite. *Teacher education specific:* Admission to the Teacher Education program with submission of all required supporting materials; MTEL tests. *Graduate:* Baccalaureate degree from a regionally accredited institution. *Teacher education specific:* Teaching credential where required by program pursued; MTEL tests; recommendations; faculty interview.

Fees and Expenses: $27,080 per academic year. On-campus room and board: $8,250.

Financial Aid: Resources specifically for eligible students enrolled in teacher education programs are awarded on the basis of financial need and academic merit. The institution has a Program Participation Agreement with the U.S. Department of Education for eligible students to receive Pell Grants and other federal aid. Teacher scholarships available to qualifying students. *Contact:* Robert Carpenter at: (617) 552-3300.

Accreditation: *Regional:* NEASC. *Professional:* NCATE. *Member of:* AACTE. *Approved by:* Massachusetts Department of Education.

Undergraduate Programs: At the undergraduate level, all students pursuing an education major leading to licensure are required to complete a second major in Arts and Sciences or an interdisciplinary major. Students may choose a major in early childhood education, elementary education, and secondary education.

Curriculum requirements for students majoring in early childhood education include coursework in the following areas: child development and learning including their applications to the classroom; curriculum and models in early education, teaching diverse learners and children with special needs, the subject matter of reading, language arts and literature, mathematics, science, social studies, the arts, health and physical education; evaluation procedures, methods for teaching problem solving and critical thinking skills.

The major in elementary education prepares students for teaching children without disabilities and children with mild disabilities in regular classrooms, grades one through six. The major requirements include foundation and professional courses.

The major in secondary education prepares students for teaching in senior high schools, grades 9-12. Requirements include: courses in child and adolescent development; theory and instruction in teaching diverse populations and meeting the special needs of children; teaching reading, writing, and specific subject methods courses; classroom assessment. The program also includes three pre-practicum experiences beginning in the sophomore year. The full practicum is completed in the senior year.

Graduate Programs: The Master of Education program in teaching prepares students for licensure as early childhood, elementary, or secondary teachers in either regular or special education. The program in reading/literacy leads to K-12 licensure as a reading specialist for teachers who are already certified and have one year of teaching experience.

The Master of Arts in Teaching and the Master of Science in Teaching programs prepare students to teach at the secondary level in English, history, biology, chemistry, geology, physics, mathematics, French, Spanish, Latin, and classical humanities.

The Master of Education and Certificate of Advanced Educational Specialization are offered to experienced teachers who wish to develop a curriculum specialty in mathematics, science, technology, literacy, English, or history, or who wish to earn a general Master's degree in curriculum and teaching.

The Juris Doctor/Master of Education program is for students interested in serving the legal and educational needs of students, families, and communities. Dual degree candidates file separate applications and are admitted by both the Lynch School of Education and the Boston College of Law.

The Doctor of Philosophy program in curriculum and instruction readies students to assume leadership roles in curriculum, instruction and teacher education in schools, school systems, or other related instructional environments, or to enter the professorate in curriculum and instruction.

Licensure/Reciprocity: Massachusetts. Students seeking teaching certification in a state other than Massachusetts should consult with that state's teacher certification office early in their program of study to insure compliance with requirements. Many state directors of teacher credentialing have signed Interstate Agreements through NASDTEC that expedite the certification process.

BOSTON UNIVERSITY
School of Education
Two Sherborn Street
Boston, Massachusetts 02215
Phone: (617) 353-3212
Fax: (617) 353-6156
E-mail: jdee@bu.edu
Internet: http://www.bu.edu

Institution Description: Boston University is an independent institution that was established as Methodist General Biblical Institute in Newbury, Vermont. The campus was moved to Boston and the name was changed to Boston Theological Seminary in 1867. The present name was adopted when the institution achieved university status.

The Boston University School of Education provides comprehensive teacher preparation to students in more than 20 concentrations.

Institution Control: Private.

Calendar: Semester. Academic year September to May.

Official(s): Dr. Douglas Sears, Dean.

Faculty: Full-time 35; part-time 45; adjunct 1.

Degrees Awarded: 113 baccalaureate; 307 master's; 21 doctorate.

Admission Requirements: *Undergraduate:* Graduation from an accredited secondary school or GED; College Board SAT or ACT composite. *Teacher education specific:* Application to the program by sophomore year; MTEL tests; declaration of major; School of Education Literacy Test must be taken during the first semester; faculty interview. *Graduate:* Baccalaureate from a regionally accredited institution. *Teacher education specific:* Teaching credential when required by the program pursued; recommendations; faculty interview.

Fees and Expenses: Undergraduate and graduate $27,042 per academic year. On-campus room and board: $7,500.

Financial Aid: Resources specifically for eligible students enrolled in teacher education programs are awarded on the basis of financial need and academic merit. The institution has a Program Participation Agreement with the U.S. Department of Education for eligible students to receive Pell Grants and other federal aid. Teacher scholarships available to qualifying students. *Contact:* Financial Assistance Office at: (617) 353-2965.

Accreditation: *Regional:* NEASC. *Member of:* AACTE. *Approved by:* Massachusetts Department of Education.

Undergraduate Programs: Undergraduate studies are designed to help prepare students to become competent professional educators in any one of several related fields. Competency is developed in four kinds of courses: general studies in the liberal arts and sciences; specialized knowledge based on concentration in a discipline or field; professional studies in instructional design, human development, communications, and evaluation; and practical skills acquired through guided and supervised field experiences. The Bachelor of Science degree is awarded upon the completion of a minimum of 128 semester hours.

College of Arts and Sciences students have the option to complete teacher licensure programs in secondary education by completing the required courses as a specialization through the University Collaborative Degree Program.

Graduate Programs: The School of Education offers the Master of Education degree, the Master of Arts in Teaching degree, the Certificate of Advanced Graduate Study, and the Doctor of Education degree in most areas of study. Although programs are grouped within academic departments that reflect the chief teaching and research interests of the faculty, coursework and projects often extend across departmental lines into other areas of the school and university.

Licensure/Reciprocity: Massachusetts. Students seeking teaching certification in a state other than Massachusetts should consult with that state's teacher certification office early in their program of study to insure compliance with requirements. Many state directors of teacher credentialing have signed Interstate Agreements through NASDTEC that expedite the certification process.

BRIDGEWATER STATE COLLEGE
School of Education and Allied Studies
Teacher Education Program
Bridgewater, Massachusetts 02325
Phone: (508) 697-1200
Fax: (508) 697-1707
E-mail: admission@bridgew.edu
Internet: http://www.bridgew.edu

Institution Description: Bridgewater State College is a public institution. It was established as Bridgewater Normal School in 1840. The name was changed to Bridgewater State Teachers College in 1932, to State College at Bridgewater in 1960, and to its present name in 1968.

BRIDGEWATER STATE COLLEGE—*cont'd*

All programs offered by the school are devoted to developing professionals who are committed to excellence, understand best practices and research, and work collaboratively in their chosen areas.

Institution Control: Public.

Calendar: Semester. Academic year September to May.

Official(s): Dr. Anna Bradfield, Dean, School of Education and Allied Studies.

Faculty: Full-time 14.

Degrees Awarded: 176 baccalaureate; 195 master's.

Admission Requirements: *Undergraduate:* Graduation from an approved secondary school or GED; College Board SAT. *Teacher education specific:* Minimum of 40 contact hours (20 hours for secondary and middle school) working with children or youth; 2.8 GPA; MTEL portion on Communication and Literacy Skills. two faculty recommendations; faculty interview. interview. *Graduate:* Baccalaureate degree from a regionally accredited institution. *Teacher education specific:* teacher credential if required for program pursued; recommendations; faculty interview; MTEL tests required for graduation and application for licensure.

Fees and Expenses: Undergraduate: in-state $3,745 per academic year; out-of-state $9,875. Graduate: Tuition charged per credit hour. On-campus room and board: $5,366. Other expenses: $1,836. Books and supplies: $600.

Financial Aid: Resources specifically for eligible students enrolled in teacher education programs are awarded on the basis of financial need and academic merit. The institution has a Program Participation Agreement with the U.S. Department of Education for eligible students to receive Pell Grants and other federal aid. Teacher scholarships available to qualifying students. *Contact:* Financial Aid Office at: (508) 531-1341.

Accreditation: *Regional:* NEASC. *Professional:* NCATE. *Member of:* AACTE. *Approved by:* Massachusetts Department of Education.

Undergraduate Programs: Majors are offered in early childhood education, elementary education, health education, physical education, and special education. Minors are available in: communication disorders, coaching, dance, exercise physiology, health promotion; health resources management, instructional media, and special education. The secondary education minor (high school, middle school education or PreK-12 specialist licenses) with major concentrations in: biology, chemistry, dance, earth sciences, English, foreign language-Spanish (5-12), history, mathematics, music, physics, theater, visual arts (PreK-8 and 5-12). All programs lead to the baccalaureate degree and require the completion of a minimum of 120 semester hours.

Graduate Programs: Graduate curricula leading to the master's degree and Certificate of Advanced Graduate Study are offered in the following fields: Master of Arts in Teaching (secondary education) and professional programs in conjunction with several of the departments in the School of Arts and Sciences; Master of Education in: counseling, early childhood, educational leadership, health promotion, instructional technology, reading, and special education; Master of Science in: physical education and Post Master's Programs toward a Certificate of Advanced Graduate Study with concentrations in counseling, educational leadership, and reading.

Licensure/Reciprocity: Massachusetts. Students seeking teaching certification in a state other than Massachusetts should consult with that state's teacher certification office early in their program of study to insure compliance with requirements. Many state directors of teacher credentialing have signed Interstate Agreements through NASDTEC that expedite the certification process.

COLLEGE OF OUR LADY OF THE ELMS

Education Division
Marian Hall
291 Springfield Street
Chicopee, Massachusetts 01013-2839
Phone: (413) 594-2761
Fax: (413) 592-4871
E-mail: hukowicze@elms.edu
Internet: http://www.elms.edu

Institution Description: College of Our Lady of the Elms is a private coeducational college affiliated with the Roman Catholic Church. It was established, chartered, and offered first instruction at the postsecondary level in 1928.

The goal of the Division of Education is to educate students to make a distinctive contribution to American education and society.

Institution Control: Private.

Calendar: Semester. Academic year September to May.

Official(s): Dr. Elizabeth Hukowicz, Division Chair.

Degrees Awarded: 16 baccalaureate; 61 master's.

Admission Requirements: *Undergraduate:* Graduation from an approved secondary school or GED; College Board SAT; *Teacher education specific:* Successful completion of pre-education coursework; completion of Communication and Literacy portion of the MTEL; two faculty endorsements.

Fees and Expenses: $16,490 per academic year. On-campus room and board: $6,490. Other expenses: $1,450. Books and supplies: $600.

Financial Aid: Resources specifically for eligible students enrolled in teacher education programs are awarded on the basis of financial need and academic merit. The institution has a Program Participation Agreement with the U.S. Department of Education for eligible students to receive Pell Grants and other federal aid. Teacher scholarships available to qualifying students. *Contact:* Financial Aid Office at: (413) 594-2761.

Accreditation: *Regional:* NEASC. *Member of:* AACTE. *Approved by:* Massachusetts Department of Education.

Undergraduate Programs: Students seeking initial licensure must fulfill requirements for either an arts/sciences major or a liberal arts major in addition to their professional preparation major in education. Students preparing to teach biology, chemistry, English, Spanish, history, or mathematics at the secondary level must major in their academic disciplines. Students pursuing licensure in early childhood, elementary education, English language learner, or teacher of students with moderate disabilities will major in English, history, mathematics, or science. The recommended major is a combined English/history liberal arts major.

Licensure/Reciprocity: Massachusetts. Students seeking teaching certification in a state other than Massachusetts should consult with that state's teacher certification office early in their program of study to insure compliance with requirements. Many state directors of teacher credentialing have signed Interstate Agreements through NASDTEC that expedite the certification process.

EASTERN NAZARENE COLLEGE

Department of Education
Teacher Education Programs
23 East Elm Avenue
Quincy, Massachusetts 02170-2999
Phone: (617) 745-3000
Fax: (617) 745-3915
E-mail: nfiacco@enc.edu
Internet: http://www.enc.edu

Institution Description: Eastern Nazarene College is a private Christian liberal arts college. It was established and incorporated in 1918.

The Department of Education is committed to preparing teachers to serve all levels including early childhood, elementary, middle school, high school, and special needs.

Institution Control: Private.

Calendar: Semester. Academic year September to May.

Official(s): Dr. Noreen Pfautz Fiacco, Chair, Department of Teacher Education.

Faculty: Full-time 5.

Degrees Awarded: 10 baccalaureate; 36 master's.

Admission Requirements: *Undergraduate:* Graduation with 16 academic units from an approved secondary school or GED. *Teacher education specific:* Minimum of 30 semester hours of college credit; cumulative GPA of 2.75; portfolio review; completion of Communication and Literacy portion of the MTEL; faculty interview. *Graduate:* Baccalaureate degree from a regionally accredited institution. *Teacher education specific:* Official transcripts of all college/university coursework; minimum 2.75 GPA; valid provisional or teacher licensure depending on program pursued; MTEL tests.

Fees and Expenses: Undergraduate: in-state $15,365 per academic year. Graduate: Tuition charged per credit hour. Other expenses: $1,600. On-campus room and board: $5,215. Books and supplies: $1,000.

Financial Aid: Resources specifically for eligible students enrolled in teacher education programs are awarded on the basis of financial need and academic merit. The institution has a Program Participation Agreement with the U.S. Department of Education for eligible students to receive Pell Grants and other federal aid. Teacher Scholarships available to qualifying students. *Contact:* Financial Aid Office at: (617) 745-3712.

Accreditation: *Regional:* NEASC. *Member of:* AACTE. *Approved by:* Massachusetts Department of Education.

Undergraduate Programs: Programs leading to the baccalaureate degree and certification include: early childhood, elementary, middle school, secondary, movement arts (physical education), and music. All programs require the completion of a general education core, professional studies, subject major, field experiences, and student teaching. A minimum of 130 semester hours must be completed for the degree.

Graduate Programs: Graduate programs leading to the master's degree are offered in the following: administration, early childhood, educational technology, elementary education, teaching English as a second language, middle school education, secondary education, special needs, teaching of reading, program development (non-certification).

Licensure/Reciprocity: Massachusetts. Students seeking teaching certification in a state other than Massachusetts should consult with that state's teacher certification office early in their program of study to insure compliance with requirements. Many state directors of teacher credentialing have signed Interstate Agreements through NASDTEC that expedite the certification process.

ENDICOTT COLLEGE

Education Department
376 Hale Street
Beverly, Massachusetts 01915
Phone: (918) 232-2323
Fax: (918) 232-3100
E-mail: lehart@endicott.cdu
Internet: http://www.endicott.edu

Institution Description: Endicott College is situated in the residential section of Beverly on the north shore of Massachusetts Bay. It was established in 1939 by a group of civic leaders as a two-year college. It became a four year institution in 1952.

The college offers programs leading to Massachusetts licensure and the baccalaureate and graduate degrees.

Institution Control: Private.

Calendar: Semester. Academic year August to May.

Official(s): Dr. Sara Ouay, Dean of Education.

Faculty: Full-time 3.

Degrees Awarded: 13 baccalaureate; 178 master's.

Admission Requirements: *Undergraduate:* Graduation from an accredited high school or GED; College Board SAT. *Teacher education specific:* Combined score of 1000 on the SAT. *Graduate:* Baccalaureate degree from a regionally accredited institution, *Teacher education specific:* GRE or Miller Analogies Test; Communication and Literacy Test on the MTEL.

Fees and Expenses: Undergraduate: $16,744 per academic year. Graduate: $254 per credit hour. Required fees: $604. On-campus room and board: $8,858.

Financial Aid: Resources specifically for eligible students enrolled in teacher education programs are awarded on the basis of financial need and academic merit. The institution has a Program Participation Agreement with the U.S. Department of Education for eligible students to receive Pell Grants and other federal aid. Teacher scholarships available to qualifying students. *Contact:* Thomas Redman at: (978 232-2005).

Accreditation: *Regional:* NEASC. *Member of:* AACTE. *Approved by:* Massachusetts Department of Education.

Undergraduate Programs: The early childhood education (preK-grade 2) program leads to the Bachelor of Arts in Liberal Studies. Through coursework that includes art, history, literature, math, science, geography, economics, and politics, the liberal studies major provides the interdisciplinary background needed to meet the minimum requirements of the early childhood curriculum. Through internships and practica, participation in the classroom occurs during each year of the education program. A total of 128 credit hours is required for the degree.

The elementary education (grade 1-6) major program leads to the Bachelor of Arts in Liberal Studies. The program follows a similar track as described above and includes a general education core, professional studies, subject major, field experiences and student teaching. A total of 128 credit hours must be completed for the degree award.

Graduate Programs: Graduate programs in education build upon the baccalaureate degree in the areas of early childhood and elementary education. Programs for students with a baccalaureate degree but no licensure may elect a master's degree program that will qualify them for Massachusetts certification. Students must meet all requirements including the Massachusetts Tests for Educator Licensure (MTEL.)

Licensure/Reciprocity: Massachusetts. Students seeking teaching certification in a state other than Massachusetts should consult with that state's teacher certification office early in their program of study to insure compliance with requirements. Many state directors of teacher credentialing have signed Interstate Agreements through NASDTEC that expedite the certification process.

FITCHBURG STATE COLLEGE

Education Unit
Teacher Education
160 Pearl Street
Fitchburg, Massachusetts 01420-2697
Phone: (978) 665-3501
Fax: (978) 665-3509
E-mail: efrancis@fsc.edu
Internet: http://www.fsc.edu

Institution Description: Fitchburg State College is a public institution that was established in 1895. The name was changed to State Teachers College in 1932. The college became State College at Fitchburg in 1960 and the present name was adopted in 1967.

Housed in two education departments and several liberal arts and sciences departments, faculty across the college are engaged in a concerted effort to enhance and expand undergraduate, post-baccalaureate, and graduate licensure programs.

Institution Control: Public.

Calendar: Semester. Academic year September to May.

Official(s): Dr. Elaine Francis, Dean.

Faculty: Full-time 33.

Degrees Awarded: 85 baccalaureate; 298 master's.

FITCHBURG STATE COLLEGE—*cont'd*

Admission Requirements: *Undergraduate:* Graduation with 16 academic units from an accredited secondary school or GED; College Board SAT. *Teacher education specific:* Minimum of 40 contact hours (20 hours for secondary and middle school) working with children or youth; 3.0 GPA; MTEL portion on Communication and Literacy Skills. faculty recommendations; faculty interview. *Graduate:* Baccalaureate degree from a regionally accredited institution. *Teacher education specific:* Teacher credential if required for program pursued; recommendations; faculty interview; MTEL tests required for graduation and application for licensure.

Fees and Expenses: Undergraduate: in-state $3,688 per academic year; out-of-state $9,768. Graduate: Tuition charged per credit hour. On-campus room and board: $6,124. Other expenses: $1,850. Books and supplies: $600.

Financial Aid: Resources specifically for eligible students enrolled in teacher education programs are awarded on the basis of financial need and academic merit. The institution has a Program Participation Agreement with the U.S. Department of Education for eligible students to receive Pell Grants and other federal aid. Teacher scholarships available to qualifying students. *Contact:* Financial Aid Office at: (978) 665-3156.

Accreditation: *Regional:* NEASC. *Professional:* NCATE. *Member of:* AACTE. *Approved by:* Massachusetts Department of Education.

Undergraduate Programs: All undergraduate programs in teacher education are grounded in the liberal arts and sciences with a comprehensive foundation in pedagogy. All teacher education majors graduate with a dual major in education and in the liberal arts and sciences that is required of all future teachers by the Commonwealth of Massachusetts and Fitchburg State College. Licensure programs are offered in early childhood, elementary and middle school; special education, and secondary education. Secondary licensure programs are offered for students seeking initial licensure in six different areas for grades 8-12 (biology, earth science, English, history, mathematics and grades 5-6 in technology education). The programs leading Bachelor of Science degree require completion of a general education core, professional studies, subject major, field experiences, and student teaching. Degree requirements include 120 to 127 semester hours.

Graduate Programs: Graduate programs are offered in the following areas: early childhood; elementary; middle school education; special education; and secondary education. The college offers both licensure and non-licensure options in the degree programs leading to the Master of Arts in Teaching degree and the Master of Arts in Education degree.

Licensure/Reciprocity: Massachusetts. Students seeking teaching certification in a state other than Massachusetts should consult with that state's teacher certification office early in their program of study to insure compliance with requirements. Many state directors of teacher credentialing have signed Interstate Agreements through NASDTEC that expedite the certification process.

FRAMINGHAM STATE COLLEGE

Education Department
Teacher Education
  100 State Street
  P.O. Box 9101
  Framingham, Massachusetts 01701-9101
  Phone: (508) 620-1220
  Fax: (508) 626-4592
  E-mail: education@framingham.edu
  Internet: http://www.framingham.edu

Institution Description: Framingham State College is a member of Massachusetts Board of of Higher Education. It was established and chartered in 1939 in Lexington as State Normal School, a women's institution. The school was moved to West Newton in 1844 and to its present location in 1853.

The college was the first public college in America to offer a teacher preparation program . The teacher education program utilizes modern technology to enhance student advancement. All students use wireless laptop computers and participate in technology-enhanced courses.

Institution Control: Public.

Calendar: Semester. Academic year September to May.

Official(s): Dr. Cathleen Baydoso, Chair, Education Department.

Faculty: Full-time 9; adjunct 7.

Degrees Awarded: 32 baccalaureate; 544 master's.

Admission Requirements: *Undergraduate:* Graduation with 16 academic units from an accredited secondary school or GED; College Board SAT. *Teacher education specific:* Completion of basic education foundations courses; 3.0 GPA; MTEL portion on Communication and Literacy Skills. faculty recommendations; faculty interview. *Graduate:* Baccalaureate degree from a regionally accredited institution. *Teacher education specific:* Teacher credential if required for program pursued; 2 letters of recommendation; GRE or Miller Analogies Test; statement of purpose; faculty interview; MTEL tests required for graduation and application for licensure.

Fees and Expenses: Undergraduate: in-state $3,937 per academic year; out-of-state $10,077. Graduate: Tuition charged per credit hour. On-campus room and board: $4,651. Other expenses: $3,250. Books and supplies: $700.

Financial Aid: Resources specifically for eligible students enrolled in teacher education programs are awarded on the basis of financial need and academic merit. The institution has a Program Participation Agreement with the U.S. Department of Education for eligible students to receive Pell Grants and other federal aid. Teacher scholarships available to qualifying students. *Contact:* Financial Aid Office at: (508) 625-4534.

Accreditation: *Regional:* NEASC. *Member of:* AACTE. *Approved by:* Massachusetts Department of Education.

Undergraduate Programs: Students must meet the requirements for initial licensure in early childhood teacher (preK-2) or elementary teacher (1-6) through completion of a coordinate major in education. secondary education students minoring in education obtain an initial license in the following fields: studio art, biology, chemistry, English, history, mathematics, Spanish, and world languages. Students may obtain middle school licensure in earth science (5-9) or in the secondary subjects listed above.

Students may also obtain the health/family and consumer sciences teacher initial license (all levels), and teacher of visual art (preK-12) by arrangement with the Art and Music Department.

Graduate Programs: The Post-Baccalaureate Teacher Licensure Program leads to the initial teacher license for those persons holding a bachelor's degree. Concentrations available include early childhood, elementary education, and secondary education.

Graduate programs leading to the master's degree including the Master of Arts degree (educational leadership) and the Master of Education. The M.Ed. degree is offered with concentrations in art, biology, curriculum and instructional technology, elementary education, early childhood education, English, English history, literacy and language, mathematics, Spanish, special education, teachers in American Schools Overseas.

Licensure/Reciprocity: Massachusetts. Students seeking teaching certification in a state other than Massachusetts should consult with that state's teacher certification office early in their program of study to insure compliance with requirements. Many state directors of teacher credentialing have signed Interstate Agreements through NASDTEC that expedite the certification process.

GORDON COLLEGE
Division of Education
255 Grapevine Road
Wenham, Massachusetts 01984
Phone: (978) 867-4322
Fax: (978) 867-3704
E-mail: lwells@gordon.edu
Internet: http://www.gordon.edu

Institution Description: Gordon College is a private, independent, nonprofit, Christian college. It was established as the Boston Missionary Training Institute in 1889. After several name changes, it became Gordon Bible College in 1916. The present name was adopted in 1985 when Barrington College of Rhode Island merged with the college in 1985.

Programs at Gordon College are built on a Christian philosophy of education that challenge students to integrate their faith, learning, and teaching.

Institution Control: Private.

Calendar: Semester. Academic year August to May.

Official(s): Dr. Malcolm L. Patterson, Department Head; Dr. Janet Arndt, Licensure Officer.

Faculty: Full-time 6; part-time 4; adjunct 4.

Degrees Awarded: 6 baccalaureate; 30 master's.

Admission Requirements: *Undergraduate:* Graduation from an accredited secondary school or GED; College Board SAT or ACT composite; strong academic promise and strong Christian commitment; college preparatory coursework. *Teacher education specific:* 2.7 GPA; complete core curriculum as well as a liberal arts major. *Graduate:* Three references; two essays; official transcripts. *Teacher education specific:* MTEL test; GRE or Miller Analogies Test; 3.0 GPA; successful completion of at least one graduate-level course.

Fees and Expenses: Undergraduate: $26,000 per academic year. Graduate: $840 per semester course. On-campus room and board: $6,500. (No graduate housing available). Books and supplies: $1,000.

Financial Aid: Resources specifically for eligible students enrolled in teacher education programs are awarded on the basis of financial need and academic merit. The institution has a Program Participation Agreement with the U.S. Department of Education for eligible students to receive Pell Grants and other federal aid. Teacher scholarships available to qualifying students. No graduate financial aid available. *Contact:* Barbara Layne at (978) 867-4035.

Accreditation: *Regional:* NEASC. *Member of:* AACTE. *Approved by:* Massachusetts Department of Education.

Undergraduate Programs: All students desiring to complete an undergraduate education program leading to licensure must be approved by the division for acceptance, complete an appropriate liberal arts major or sequence, maintain a 2.70 GPA and pass the required MTEL tests.

Students preparing to teach in middle school must minor with a focus in two of four areas (English, history, science, mathematics) and choose an appropriate arts major and a second minor.

Students preparing to teach in secondary schools may select from a variety of teaching majors with a secondary education minor in: biology, chemistry, English, history, mathematics, physics, social studies, French, and Spanish. An English major may also complete a certificate program for teaching English as a second language. Any secondary minor may also prepare to be a bilingual teacher in addition to the regular teaching area. The Department of Early Childhood, Elementary, and Special Education offers programs leading baccalaureate degrees in those areas.

All programs leading to the baccalaureate degree require completion of a general education core, professional studies, field experiences, and student teaching with a minimum of 124 semester hours.

Graduate Programs: The Master of Education, Curriculum and Instruction is designed for students who have no prior teaching experience and/or teaching license. Programs are offered in: early childhood (preK-2), elementary (1-6), students with moderate disabilities (preK-8 and 5-12), middle school and secondary (5-8 and 5-12).

The program in the Master of Arts in Teaching, Curriculum and Instruction is designed for students who possess a Massachusetts licensure or its equivalent and wish to pursue the professional license through the completion of the appropriate master's degree program.

A Master of Music Education program is also offered through the Education Division and the Department of Arts and Music.

Licensure/Reciprocity: Massachusetts. Students seeking teaching certification in a state other than Massachusetts should consult with that state's teacher certification office early in their program of study to insure compliance with requirements. Many state directors of teacher credentialing have signed Interstate Agreements through NASDTEC that expedite the certification process.

HARVARD UNIVERSITY
Graduate School of Education
Teacher Education Program
310A Longfellow Hall
13 Appian Way
Cambridge, Massachusetts 02138
Phone: (617) 495-1551
Fax: (617) 495-8821
E-mail: Orin_Gutlerner@gsu.harvard.edu
Internet: http://www.harvard.edu

Institution Description: Harvard University is a private, independent, nonprofit institution. The undergraduate program at Harvard College includes Radcliffe College. The university was established in 1636.

The Undergraduate Teacher Program (UTEP) at Harvard was established in 1985 by the faculties of Arts and Sciences and the Graduate School of Education.

Institution Control: Private.

Calendar: Semester. Academic year September to May.

Official(s): Dr. Ellen Condiffe Lagemann, Dean, Graduate School of Education.

Faculty: Full-time 27; part-time 80.

Degrees Awarded: Not reported.

Admission Requirements: *Undergraduate:* Graduation from an approved secondary school; College Board SAT or ACT composite; high academic achievement. *Teacher education specific:* Personal statement; demonstrated commitment to public service; current transcript; two letters of recommendation; resumeé ; plan of study must explicitly detail how the applicant's coursework in the Faculty of Arts and Sciences will fulfill the relevant subject matter knowledge requirements of the Commonwealth of Massachusetts. *Graduate:* Baccalaureate degree from a regionally accredited institution. *Teacher education specific:* Statement of purpose; recommendations; pass MTEL tests; faculty interview.

Fees and Expenses: Undergraduate: $27,448 per academic year. Graduate: Tuition charged per credit hour. On-campus room and board: $8,500. Other expenses: $1,550. Books and supplies: $950.

Financial Aid: Resources specifically for eligible students enrolled in teacher education programs are awarded on the basis of financial need and academic merit. The institution has a Program Participation Agreement with the U.S. Department of Education for eligible students to receive Pell Grants and other federal aid. Teacher scholarships available to qualifying students. *Contact:* Financial Aid Office at: (617) 495-1581.

Accreditation: *Regional:* NEASC. *Member of:* AACTE. *Approved by:* Massachusetts Department of Education.

Undergraduate Programs: The Undergraduate Teacher Education Program (UTEP) seeks academically strong and service-oriented students who are interested in public school teaching and committed to the challenges of education. This elective program combines coursework in the Graduate School of Educa-

HARVARD UNIVERSITY—cont'd

tion and field work in Boston area public schools. Successful completion of the program requirements and a passing score on the MTEL enable graduates to receive educator licensure at the middle or high school level. All students must complete education coursework, field work (pre-practicum and student teaching).

Graduate Programs: The Harvard Graduate School of Education's Teacher Education Program (TEP) prepares individual to become middle or secondary school classroom teachers in urban setting. This intensive eleven-month masters program combines classwork and fieldwork to bring together theory and practice. The program leads to licensure at the secondary level.

There are two components of TEP: the MidCareer Math and Science program and the Teaching and Curriculum program. The former prepares math and science professionals who want to become secondary math and science teachers. The latter program prepares all other candidates, i.e., recent and not-so-recent college graduates, liberal arts concentrators, and mid-career humanities candidates.

Licensure/Reciprocity: Massachusetts. Students seeking teaching certification in a state other than Massachusetts should consult with that state's teacher certification office early in their program of study to insure compliance with requirements. Many state directors of teacher credentialing have signed Interstate Agreements through NASDTEC that expedite the certification process.

LESLEY COLLEGE

School of Education
29 Everett Street
Cambridge, Massachusetts 02138-2790
Phone: (617) 868-9600
Fax: (617) 349-8599
E-mail: jwu@lesley.edu
Internet: http://www.lesley.edu

Institution Description: Lesley College is a private, independent, nonprofit college offering programs in education, human services, liberal studies, and management. It was established as Lesley Normal School in 1909. The present name was adopted in 1943.

The instructional coursework for the education programs are designed to prepare students for teaching in a multicultural society and are based upon a process or clinical approach.

Institution Control: Private.

Calendar: Semester. Academic year September to May.

Official(s): Joseph Cronin, Dean, School of Education.

Faculty: Full-time 125; part-time 34.

Degrees Awarded: 48 baccalaureate; 2,091 master's; 9 doctorate.

Admission Requirements: *Undergraduate:* Graduation from an approved secondary school; College Board SAT or ACT composite; recommendations. *Teacher education specific:* Students must meet certain academic criteria before receiving full acceptance into teacher education programs. *Graduate:* Transcripts; two professional recommendations; essay. *Teacher education specific:* Portfolio (art education only); Miller Analogies Test (school counseling only); GRE or MAT; writing sample, resumé ; faculty interview.

Fees and Expenses: Undergraduate: $18,300 per academic year. Graduate: $12,600. Required fees: $175 (undergraduate). On-campus room and board: $8,300. Books and supplies: $700.

Financial Aid: Resources specifically for eligible students enrolled in teacher education programs are awarded on the basis of financial need and academic merit. The institution has a Program Participation Agreement with the U.S. Department of Education for eligible students to receive Pell Grants and other federal aid. Teacher scholarships available to qualifying students. Certain scholarships target specific teaching fields, e.g., special education, math/science, literacy. *Contact:* Paul Henderson, Director of Financial Aid at: (617) 349-8710 or e-mail @finaid@mail.lesley.edu.

Accreditation: *Regional:* . *Member of:* AACTE. *Approved by:* Massachusetts Department of Education.

Undergraduate Programs: The early childhood education major leads to certification as an early childhood teacher, grades 1-6. Students in the major must choose a liberal arts major to complement their professional study. The program requires during the junior year A 150-hour practicum in a preschool or kindergarten setting. The senior practicum will be a semester experience in either grade one or two.

The elementary education major leads to certification as an elementary teacher, grades 1-6.The senior practicum will be a semester experience at the level within the 106 grade range. Students in this major must choose a liberal arts major to complement their professional study.

The middle school major leads to certification as a middle school teacher, grades 5-8. The senior practicum will be a semester experience in one setting within the 5-8 range. Coursework within grades 5-8 gives the student experience with children of different ages and to a variety of curricula, organizations studies, and grouping strategies characteristic of the middle school.

The day care leadership major prepares the student for teaching and leadership roles in preschool and day care settings. This program does **not** lead to a teaching certificate since there is currently no Massachusetts certificate for day care.

Accelerated bachelor's/master's programs are offered in the above specializations of early childhood, elementary, middle school, and special education.

Graduate Programs: Master's programs leading to licensure include the Master of Education in early childhood, elementary, middle school, art, special education, and technology in education. Other programs include consulting teacher of reading, creative arts in learning, curriculum and instruction, educational leadership, and science in education (online).

Licensure/Reciprocity: Massachusetts. Students seeking teaching certification in a state other than Massachusetts should consult with that state's teacher certification office early in their program of study to insure compliance with requirements. Many state directors of teacher credentialing have signed Interstate Agreements through NASDTEC that expedite the certification process.

NORTHEASTERN UNIVERSITY

College of Arts and Sciences
School of Education
50 Nightingale Hall
360 Huntington Avenue
Boston, Massachusetts 02115
Phone: (617) 373-4216
Fax: (617) 373-8934
E-mail: soe@neu.edu
Internet: http://www.neu.edu

Institution Description: Northeastern University is a private, independent, nonprofit institution that was established as Northeastern College of the Boston Young Men's Christian Association in 1898. The present name was adopted in 1936.

The School of Education prepares community-dedicated educators who foster the academic achievement and personal success of children and youth in diverse urban settings.

Institution Control: Private.

Calendar: Semester. Academic year September to June.

Official(s): Dr. James W. Fraser, Dean, School of Education; Dr. Linda J. Foreier, Chair, Teacher Education.

Faculty: Full-time 15.

Degrees Awarded: 26 baccalaureate; 70 master's.

Admission Requirements: *Undergraduate:* Graduation from an approved secondary school or GED; College Board SAT or ACT composite required. *Teacher education specific:* Must be enrolled in an appropriate College of Arts and Sciences major; complete introductory education courses; achieve a 2.75 GPA. *Graduate:* Baccalaureate degree from a regionally accredited institution. *Teacher education specific:* Personal statement; official transcripts; GRE scores; three letters of recommendation.

Fees and Expenses: $24,467 per academic year. Graduate: Tuition charged per credit. On-campus room and board: $9,660. Other expenses: $1,695. Books and supplies: $900.

Financial Aid: Resources specifically for eligible students enrolled in teacher education programs are awarded on the basis of financial need and academic merit. The institution has a Program Participation Agreement with the U.S. Department of Education for eligible students to receive Pell Grants and other federal aid. Teacher scholarships available to qualifying students. *Contact:* Financial Aid Office at: (617) 373-3190.

Accreditation: *Regional:* NEASC. *Member of:* AACTE. *Approved by:* Massachusetts Department of Education.

Undergraduate Programs: The School of Education offers an approved program for elementary education. Students may also obtain an additional license in special education or early childhood by completing the appropriate additional coursework and half practicum. Students may earn a license as an elementary education teacher (grades 1-6) in either the BA or BS/MAT model or path BA or BS only. Early childhood or special education additional licensers are only possible in the 5-year BA or BS/MAT model.

Students completing the program in early childhood education may achieve a second license with elementary education. Early childhood licensure qualifies students to teach pre-K to grade 2 students with or without disabilities. Additional courses to the elementary program of study include special education, pre-K curriculum, and language development.

The program in secondary education is offered for teaching secondary education grades 8-12. Students may also obtain an additional license in special education (grades 5-12) or middle school (grades 5-8) by completing the appropriate additional coursework and half practicum.

All baccalaureate programs require the completion of a general education core, professional studies, field experiences, and student teaching for a total of 176 quarter hours.

Graduate Programs: The graduate programs are offered leading to a Master of Arts in Teaching degree to prepare or further develop the skills of elementary and secondary school teachers. Students are prepared to understand their subject area and who have the ability to connect and educate children in diverse urban communities.

Licensure/Reciprocity: Massachusetts. Students seeking teaching certification in a state other than Massachusetts should consult with that state's teacher certification office early in their program of study to insure compliance with requirements. Many state directors of teacher credentialing have signed Interstate Agreements through NASDTEC that expedite the certification process.

SALEM STATE COLLEGE

School of Education
Education Building 303, North Campus
352 Lafayette Street
Salem, Massachusetts 01970-5353
Phone: (978) 542-6266
Fax: (978) 542-6126
E-mail: soe@salemstate.edu
Internet: http://www.salemstate.edu

Institution Description: Salem State College (within the Massachusetts State College System until 1981) is a member of Massachusetts Board of Regents of Higher Education. It was established as Salem Normal School in 1854.

The School of Education offers an array of undergraduate and graduate programs that prepare the student for licensure.

Institution Control: Public.

Calendar: Semester. Academic year September to May.

Official(s): Dr. Vicky Gallagher, Chairperson.

Faculty: Full-time 21.

Degrees Awarded: 180 baccalaureate; 239 master's.

Admission Requirements: *Undergraduate:* Graduation with 16 academic units from an approved secondary school or GED; College Board SAT. *Teacher education specific:* Completion of basic education foundations courses; 3.0 GPA; MTEL portion on Communication and Literacy Skills; faculty recommendations; faculty interview. *Graduate:* Baccalaureate degree from a regionally accredited institution. *Teacher education specific:* Teacher credential if required for program pursued; letters of recommendation; GRE or Miller Analogies Test; statement of purpose; faculty interview; MTEL tests required for graduation and application for licensure.

Fees and Expenses: Undergraduate: in-state $3,937 per academic year; out-of-state $10,077. Graduate: Tuition charged per credit hour. On-campus room and board: $5,428. Other expenses: $1,440. Books and supplies: $800.

Financial Aid: Resources specifically for eligible students enrolled in teacher education programs are awarded on the basis of financial need and academic merit. The institution has a Program Participation Agreement with the U.S. Department of Education for eligible students to receive Pell Grants and other federal aid. Teacher scholarships available to qualifying students. *Contact:* Financial Aid Office at: (978) 542-6112.

Accreditation: *Regional:* NEASC. *Professional:* NCATE. *Member of:* AACTE. *Approved by:* Massachusetts Department of Education.

Undergraduate Programs: The secondary education minor prepares Arts and Sciences majors in the discipline they seek to acquire secondary school licensure. Majors include: art, biology, chemistry, English, geography, geology, history, mathematics, and theatre arts. The minor in education requires the completion of specified courses. An education major is also available that requires the completion of a general education core, professional courses, field experiences, and student teaching. A minimum of 122 credit hours is required for the baccalaureate degree.

Graduate Programs: Graduate programs in education include the of Master of Arts in Teaching degree is available in the following concentrations: art, biology, chemistry, English, English as a second language, history, mathematics, and Spanish. The Master of Education is offered in bilingual education, early childhood, educational leadership, elementary education, middle school education initial licensure, reading secondary education, and special education.

Licensure/Reciprocity: Massachusetts. Students seeking teaching certification in a state other than Massachusetts should consult with that state's teacher certification office early in their program of study to insure compliance with requirements. Many state directors of teacher credentialing have signed Interstate Agreements through NASDTEC that expedite the certification process.

TUFTS UNIVERSITY

Department of Education
Teacher Licensure Programs
Medford, Massachusetts 02155-5555
Phone: (617) 628-5000
Fax: (617) 627-3536
E-mail: education@tufts.edu
Internet: http://www.tufts.edu

Institution Description: Tufts University is a private, independent, nonprofit institution. It was established and chartered as Tufts College under control of Universalist Church of America in 1852. The present name was adopted in 1955.

The Department of Education offers courses in educational theory, practice, and research.

Institution Control: Private.

Calendar: Semester. Academic year August to May.

Official(s): Dr. Kathleen Weiler, Chair.

Faculty: Full-time 13; part-time 16.

Degrees Awarded: 62 baccalaureate; 110 master's; 2 doctorate.

Admission Requirements: *Undergraduate:* Graduation from an approved secondary school or GED; College Board SAT with 3 achievements or ACT composite. *Teacher education specific:* Students must begin taking required courses by the spring semester of their sophomore year; MTEL portion on Communi-

TUFTS UNIVERSITY—*cont'd*

cation and Literacy Skills; faculty recommendations. *Graduate:* Baccalaureate degree from a regionally accredited institution. *Teacher education specific:* Teacher credential if required for program pursued; 3 letters of recommendation; statement of purpose; faculty interview; MTEL tests required for graduation and application for licensure.

Fees and Expenses: $28,155 per academic year. Graduate tuition charged per credit hour. On-campus room and board: $8,310. Other expenses: $1,135. Books and supplies: $800.

Financial Aid: Resources specifically for eligible students enrolled in teacher education programs are awarded on the basis of financial need and academic merit. The institution has a Program Participation Agreement with the U.S. Department of Education for eligible students to receive Pell Grants and other federal aid. Teacher scholarships available to qualifying students. *Contact:* Financial Aid Office at: (617) 627-2000.

Accreditation: *Regional:* NEASC. *Professional:* NCATE. *Member of:* AACTE. *Approved by:* Massachusetts Department of Education.

Undergraduate Programs: The Department of Education does not have an undergraduate major, but offers a number of courses for undergraduate students interested in exploring the field of education. The department offers undergraduate licensure in only two programs; art education and elementary education.

Graduate Programs: The department offers graduate programs that prepare candidates for licensure as elementary school teachers and as middle and high school teachers of English, political science, political philosophy, history, mathematics, general science, earth science, biology, chemistry, physics, French, Spanish, German, Japanese, Latin, and classical humanities, and visual art. The department also offers a graduate-degree program in preparation for state licensure and national certification as school psychologists.

The Master of Arts in educational studies provides an opportunity for graduate students to pursue an individual courses of study. The Master of Arts in museum education prepares students for courses in museum setting. The department also offers M.S. and Ph.D. programs in mathematics, science, technology, and engineering in education.

Licensure/Reciprocity: Massachusetts. Students seeking teaching certification in a state other than Massachusetts should consult with that state's teacher certification office early in their program of study to insure compliance with requirements. Many state directors of teacher credentialing have signed Interstate Agreements through NASDTEC that expedite the certification process.

UNIVERSITY OF MASSACHUSETTS AMHERST

School of Education
Department of Teacher Education and Curriculum Studies

Furcolo Hall, Room 103
Amherst, Massachusetts 01003-8370
Phone: (413) 545-2336
E-mail: admissions@umass.edu
Internet: http://www.umass.edu

Institution Description: University of Massachusetts Amherst is a Research I public land-grant institution. It was established as Massachusetts Agricultural College in 1863. The name was changed to Massachusetts State College in 1931 and to its present name in 1947.

The Department of Teacher Education and Curriculum Studies seeks to improve public education through the planning, delivery, and continuous improvement of N-12 teacher education programs at the undergraduate and master's levels.

Institution Control: Public.

Calendar: Semester. Academic year September to May.

Official(s): Dr. Andrew Effrat, Dean.

Faculty: Full-time 40; part-time 11.

Degrees Awarded: 9 baccalaureate; 211 master's; 42 doctorate.

Admission Requirements: *Undergraduate:* Graduation from an approved secondary school or GED; College Board SAT or ACT composite. *Teacher education specific:* Completion of education foundations courses; MTEL portion on Communication and Literacy Skills; faculty recommendations. *Graduate:* Baccalaureate degree from a regionally accredited institution. *Teacher education specific:* Teacher credential if required for program pursued; letters of recommendation; GRE or Miller Analogies Test; statement of purpose; faculty interview; MTEL tests required for graduation and application for licensure.

Fees and Expenses: Undergraduate: in-state $6,660 per academic year; out-of-state $15,513. Graduate: Tuition charged per credit hour. On-campus room and board: $5,473. Other expenses: $1,400. Books and supplies: $500.

Financial Aid: Resources specifically for eligible students enrolled in teacher education programs are awarded on the basis of financial need and academic merit. The institution has a Program Participation Agreement with the U.S. Department of Education for eligible students to receive Pell Grants and other federal aid. Teacher scholarships available to qualifying students. *Contact:* Financial Aid Office at: (413) 545-0801.

Accreditation: *Regional:* NEASC. *Professional:* NCATE. *Member of:* AACTE. *Approved by:* Massachusetts Department of Education.

Undergraduate Programs: Pre-K-12 teacher preparation programs are offered with concentrations in art, bilingual education, English as a second language, music education, and special education.

The secondary teacher program provides courses, field experiences, and clinical experiences leading to licensure at the middle and high school levels in the following fields; English education, political science/political philosophy, Latin and classical humanities (5-12), mathematics, science, French, Italian, Spanish, Portuguese, and Chinese.

The Education Specialist Preparation Programs include the areas of administration, reading, school guidance counselor, school psychologist, and speech/language/hearing disorders.

All baccalaureate programs require the completion of a general education core, professional studies, field experiences, and student teaching for a minimum of 120 credit hours.

Graduate Programs: The Master of Education degree programs are offered in bilingual education, child study and early education, educational technology, elementary teacher education, reading and writing, and secondary teacher education.

Doctoral programs (Ed.D.) are offered in the following areas: child and family studies, language/literature and culture, mathematics and science education; and teacher education and school improvement.

Licensure/Reciprocity: Massachusetts. Students seeking teaching certification in a state other than Massachusetts should consult with that state's teacher certification office early in their program of study to insure compliance with requirements. Many state directors of teacher credentialing have signed Interstate Agreements through NASDTEC that expedite the certification process.

UNIVERSITY OF MASSACHUSETTS BOSTON

Graduate College of Education

100 Morrissey Boulevard
Boston, Massachusetts 02125
Phone: (617) 287-7600
Fax: (617) 287-7664
E-mail: coe@umb.edu
Internet: http://www.umb.edu

Institution Description: The university was founded as a coeducational institution in 1964.

The Graduate College of Education offers both undergraduate and graduate programs in teacher preparation. An experimental program, Teach Next Year, is offered to qualified students.

Institution Control: Public.

Calendar: Semester. Academic year September to May.

Official(s): Dr. Denise Patmon, Chair; Lee Hart, Associate Chair.

Faculty: Full-time 38; part-time 47.

Degrees Awarded: 25 baccalaureate; 243 master's; 12 doctorate.

Admission Requirements: *Undergraduate:* Graduation from an approved secondary school; College Board SAT. *Teacher education specific:* Students are eligible to apply to the Teacher Certification Program during the semesters in which they are approaching the first half of the degree requirements (60 credits); minimum 3.0 GPA; evidence of taking Communications and Literacy portion of the MTEL. *Graduate:* Baccalaureate degree from a regionally accredited institution. *Teacher education specific:* Official transcript of all college work; GRE, MAT, or MTEL scores as required by the program to which the applicant is seeking admission; three letters of recommendation; statement of interests and intent; faculty interview.

Fees and Expenses: Undergraduate: resident $5,215 per academic year; nonresident $14,550. Graduate: resident $108 per credit; nonresident $406.50. Mandatory fees per semester: resident $1,760; nonresident $2,333.

Financial Aid: Resources specifically for eligible students enrolled in teacher education programs are awarded on the basis of financial need and academic merit. The institution has a Program Participation Agreement with the U.S. Department of Education for eligible students to receive Pell Grants and other federal aid. A variety of scholarships from private donors, alumni, and family foundations are available to qualifying students. *Contact:* Judy Keyes at (617) 287-6300 or e-mail @ judy.keyes@umb.edu.

Accreditation: *Regional:* NEASC. *Professional:* NCATE. *Member of:* AACTE. *Approved by:* Massachusetts Department of Education.

Undergraduate Programs: The Bachelor of Science or Bachelor of Arts degree with a major in one of the liberal arts or science is offered. The program in secondary or middle school teaching requires that the student major in the subject area in which he/she desires to teach. Those who wish to teach in high school social studies departments can major in history, American studies, or political science. Students interested in elementary School Teaching can select any of the majors offered by the college. All programs require completion of a general education core, professional studies, subject major, field experiences, and student teaching.

Graduate Programs: The Teacher Education Master of Education program is housed in the Graduate College of Education's Department of School Organization, Curriculum, and Instruction. It is an interdisciplinary program involving appropriate disciplines in the liberal arts and education. The program offers three tracks, each of which provides option at the early childhood, elementary, middle school, and secondary level. Track A if for individuals who wish to earn the M.Ed. without certification. Track B is for those seeking the M.Ed. and initial licensure in Massachusetts. Students in this track wish to become certified as well as earning the M.Ed. Track C is for those who have earned initial licensure while undergraduates and who wish to earn professional licensure and the M.Ed.

Licensure/Reciprocity: Massachusetts. Students seeking teaching certification in a state other than Massachusetts should consult with that state's teacher certification office early in their program of study to insure compliance with requirements. Many state directors of teacher credentialing have signed Interstate Agreements through NASDTEC that expedite the certification process.

UNIVERSITY OF MASSACHUSETTS LOWELL

School of Education
Professional Preparation Programs for Educators
One University Avenue
Lowell, Massachusetts 01854-5104
Phone: (978) 934-4000
Fax: (978) 934-3000
E-mail: admissions@uml.edu
Internet: http://www.uml.edu

Institution Description: University of Massachusetts Lowell, formerly known as the University of Lowell, is a public institution. It was formed in 1975 by a merger with Lowell State College (chartered in 1894).

The School of Education offers preparation programs in undergraduate and graduate study.

Institution Control: Public.

Calendar: Semester. Academic year September to May.

Official(s): Dr. Michelle Scribner-MacLean, Chair, Curriculum and Instruction.

Faculty: Full-time 19.

Degrees Awarded: 20 baccalaureate; 84 master's; 17 doctorate.

Admission Requirements: *Undergraduate:* Graduation with 16 academic units from an accredited secondary school or GED; College Board SAT. *Teacher education specific:* Completion of education foundations courses; MTEL portion on Communication and Literacy Skills; faculty recommendations. *Graduate:* Baccalaureate degree from a regionally accredited institution. *Teacher education specific:* Teacher credential if required for program pursued; three letters of recommendation; academic test scores specified for various degree programs; statement of purpose; faculty interview; MTEL tests required for graduation and application for licensure.

Fees and Expenses: Undergraduate: in-state $5,215 per academic year; out-of-state $14,650. Graduate: Tuition charged per credit hour. On-campus room and board: $5,465. Other expenses: $1,100. Books and supplies: $500.

Financial Aid: Resources specifically for eligible students enrolled in teacher education programs are awarded on the basis of financial need and academic merit. The institution has a Program Participation Agreement with the U.S. Department of Education for eligible students to receive Pell Grants and other federal aid. Teacher scholarships available to qualifying students. *Contact:* Financial Aid Office at: (978) 834-4220.

Accreditation: *Regional:* NEASC. *Professional:* NCATE. *Member of:* AACTE. *Approved by:* Massachusetts Department of Education.

Undergraduate Programs: Pre-K-12 teacher preparation programs are offered with concentrations in art, bilingual education, English as a second language, music education, and special education.

The secondary teacher program provides courses, field experiences, and clinical experiences leading to licensure at the middle and high school levels in the following fields; English education, political science/political philosophy, Latin and classical humanities (5-12), mathematics, science, French, Italian, Spanish, Portuguese, and Chinese.

The specialist preparation programs include the areas of administration, reading, school guidance counselor, school psychologist, and speech/language/hearing disorders.

All baccalaureate programs require the completion of a general education core, professional studies, field experiences, and student teaching for a minimum of 120 credit hours.

Graduate Programs: The Master of Education degree is offered in curriculum and instruction (initial license), educational administration, reading and language. The Certificate of Advanced Study program is offered in: curriculum and instruction, educational administration, planning and policy, and reading and language.

UNIVERSITY OF MASSACHUSETTS
LOWELL—*cont'd*

An online Master's Degree Program in educational administration is designed primarily to meet the needs and challenges of individuals planning careers as educational leaders in elementary and secondary schools.

The Doctor of Education degree offers specialization in mathematics and science education, leadership in schooling, and language arts and literacy.

Licensure/Reciprocity: Massachusetts. Students seeking teaching certification in a state other than Massachusetts should consult with that state's teacher certification office early in their program of study to insure compliance with requirements. Many state directors of teacher credentialing have signed Interstate Agreements through NASDTEC that expedite the certification process.

WESTFIELD STATE COLLEGE

Education Department

577 Western Avenue
Westfield, Massachusetts 01086-1630
Phone: (413) 572-5315
Fax: (413) 562-3613
E-mail: vmillen@wsc.ma.edu
Internet: http://www.wsc.ma.edu

Institution Description: Westfield State College is a public institution that was established as Barre Normal School in 1838. The name was changed to Westfield Normal School in 1844, to State Teachers College at Westfield in 1932. The present name was adopted in 1968.

The Education Department offers undergraduate and graduate programs to prepare students for teaching careers.

Institution Control: Public.

Calendar: Semester. Academic year September to May.

Official(s): Dr. Martin Henley, Dean.

Faculty: Full-time 21.

Degrees Awarded: 169 baccalaureate; 68 master's.

Admission Requirements: *Undergraduate:* Graduation with 16 academic units from an approved secondary school or GED; College Board SAT. *Teacher education specific:* Completion of education foundations courses; MTEL portion on Communication and Literacy Skills; faculty recommendations. *Graduate:* Baccalaureate degree from a regionally accredited institution. *Teacher education specific:* Teacher credential if required for program pursued; letters of recommendation; academic test scores specified for various degree programs; statement of purpose; faculty interview; MTEL tests required for graduation and application for licensure.

Fees and Expenses: Undergraduate: in-state $3,755 per academic year; out-of-state: $9,835. Graduate: Tuition is charged per credit. On-campus room and board: $5,100. Books and supplies: $650.

Financial Aid: Resources specifically for eligible students enrolled in teacher education programs are awarded on the basis of financial need and academic merit. The institution has a Program Participation Agreement with the U.S. Department of Education for eligible students to receive Pell Grants and other federal aid. Teacher scholarships available to qualifying students. *Contact:* Financial Aid Office at: (413) 572-5218.

Accreditation: *Regional:* NEASC. *Professional:* NCATE. *Member of:* AACTE. *Approved by:* Massachusetts Department of Education.

Undergraduate Programs: Students in the elementary education programs leading to the Bachelor of Science degree may choose either early childhood (grades PreK-2) or elementary education (grades 1-6) as their major field. All students majoring in education or completing a licensure program must also complete a liberal arts, sciences, or interdisciplinary major. To meet licensure requirements within four years, the department encourages liberal studies or general science as the second major.

Students in the special education program may choose to major or complete the licensure program sequence to prepare as a teacher of children with moderate to severe disabilities. Students seeking either licensure program in special education must complete a second major in liberal arts or sciences, or an interdisciplinary major.

Graduate Programs: Graduate programs leading to the master's degree include instructional technology, elementary education, reading, secondary education (biology, chemistry, general science, history, mathematics), and special education. All programs lead to professional licensure. Students are required to successfully complete a written comprehensive examination to demonstrate mastery of knowledge gained in coursework and to related concepts across the curriculum.

Licensure/Reciprocity: Massachusetts. Students seeking teaching certification in a state other than Massachusetts should consult with that state's teacher certification office early in their program of study to insure compliance with requirements. Many state directors of teacher credentialing have signed Interstate Agreements through NASDTEC that expedite the certification process.

WHEELOCK COLLEGE

Education Division

200 The Riverway
Boston, Massachusetts 02215-4176
Phone: (617) 879-2167
Fax: (617) 879 7795
E-mail: dlevin@wheelock.edu
Internet: http://www.wheelock.edu

Institution Description: Wheelock College is a private, independent, nonprofit college. It was established as Wheelock School in 1888 and became a four-year institution in 1941. The present name was adopted in 1941.

The Education Division offers undergraduate and graduate programs plus professional certificates in the teacher education field.

Institution Control: Private.

Calendar: Semester. Academic year September to May.

Official(s): Dr. Diane E. Levin, Chair.

Faculty: Full-time 2.

Degrees Awarded: 53 baccalaureate; 125 master's.

Admission Requirements: *Undergraduate:* Graduation from an approved secondary school or GED; College Board SAT. *Teacher education specific:* Commitment to Early Childhood; completion of education foundations courses; MTEL portion on Communication and Literacy Skills; faculty recommendations. *Graduate:* Baccalaureate degree from a regionally accredited institution. *Teacher education specific:* Teacher credential if required for program pursued; letters of recommendation; academic test scores specified for various degree programs; statement of purpose; faculty interview; MTEL tests required for graduation and application for licensure.

Fees and Expenses: Undergraduate $18,925 per academic year. Graduate: Tuition charged per credit hour. On-campus room and board: $2,250. Other expenses: $2,530. Books and supplies: $450.

Financial Aid: Resources specifically for eligible students enrolled in teacher education programs are awarded on the basis of financial need and academic merit. The institution has a Program Participation Agreement with the U.S. Department of Education for eligible students to receive Pell Grants and other federal aid. Teacher scholarships available to qualifying students. *Contact:* Financial Aid Office at: (617) 879-2267.

Accreditation: *Regional:* NEASC. *Professional:* NCATE. *Member of:* AACTE. *Approved by:* Massachusetts Department of Education.

Undergraduate Programs: The Early Childhood Care and Education Program focuses on comprehensive care and education of chilfen from birth to 8-years old, and professional interactions with their families and communities. Emphasis is placed on responding to the developmental, cultural, and racial uniqueness of each child as students learn to design, implement, and evaluate learning environments and curricula activities. Each student completes two practica in public or private early childhood settings.

The child care specialist concentration provides a variety of options for students interested in working with children in early child care settings. Students may work toward Office of Child Care Services leading to teaching certification.

The elementary education concentration prepares students to become teachers of elementary age children (grades 1 through 6) in public and private schools. Students study the foundations of elementary theories and methods of teaching in inclusive classrooms, and curriculum development.

All programs require the completion of a general education core, professional studies, field experiences, and student teaching.

Graduate Programs: On campus graduate programs include: early childhood education (preK-2); elementary education (grades 1-6); elementary teacher initial licensure (grades 1-6); language and literacy; leadership, policy, and administration in early care and education; teacher of students with moderate learning; disabilities initial licensure (teaching and learning; teaching students with special needs program); preK-8 (urban teacher program, elementary grades 1-6).

Licensure/Reciprocity: Massachusetts. Students seeking teaching certification in a state other than Massachusetts should consult with that state's teacher certification office early in their program of study to insure compliance with requirements. Many state directors of teacher credentialing have signed Interstate Agreements through NASDTEC that expedite the certification process.

MICHIGAN

ADRIAN COLLEGE

Teacher Education Program
110 South Madison Street
Adrian, Michigan 49221-2575
Phone: (517) 265-5161
Fax: (517) 264-3331
E-mail: admissions@adrian.edu
Internet: http://www.adrian.edu

Institution Description: Adrian College is a private college affiliated with the United Methodist Church. It was established in 1859 and assimilated West Lafayette College (OH) in 1916.

The Adrian College Teacher Education Program is designed to enable students to meet the Michigan certification requirements.

Institution Control: Private.

Calendar: Semester. Academic year August to May.

Official(s): Dr. George Shirk, Chair, Teacher Education.

Faculty: Full-time 7.

Degrees Awarded: 7 baccalaureate.

Admission Requirements: *Undergraduate:* Graduation with 15 academic units from an approved secondary school or GED; College Board SAT or ACT composite. *Teacher education specific:* Candidates in teacher education must seek major and minor departmental guidance before beginning their sophomore year; overall GPA of 2.7; must pass the Basic Skills Test of the Michigan Tests for Teacher Certification; faculty approval.

Fees and Expenses: $15,660 per academic year. On-campus room and board: $5,080. Other expenses: $1,575. Books and supplies: $400.

Financial Aid: Resources specifically for eligible students enrolled in teacher education programs are awarded on the basis of financial need and academic merit. The institution has a Program Participation Agreement with the U.S. Department of Education for eligible students to receive Pell Grants and other federal aid. Teacher scholarships available to qualifying students. *Contact:* Financial Aid Office at: (517) 265-5161, ext. 4523.

Accreditation: *Regional:* NCA. *Member of:* AACTE. *Approved by:* Michigan Department of Education.

Undergraduate Programs: The teacher education program will qualify the student to meet the certification requirements for elementary and secondary school education in Michigan. Certification is offered in conjunction with Bachelor of Arts, Bachelor of Science, or Bachelor of Music Education degrees.

Teacher certification is available in the following curricula: art, bilingual education (Spanish), biology, business administration, chemistry, communication arts and sciences, early childhood education, earth science, economics, elementary education, English, family life studies, French, German, health education, health/physical education/recreation, history, mathematics, music, natural science, political science, psychology, religion (academic study), social studies, sociology, and Spanish.

All baccalaureate programs require completion of a general education core, professional studies, subject area major/minor (secondary education), field experiences, and student teaching. A minimum of 124 semester hours is required for the degree award.

Licensure/Reciprocity: Michigan. Students seeking teaching certification in a state other than Michigan should consult with that state's teacher certification office early in their program of study to insure compliance with requirements. Many state directors of teacher credentialing have signed Interstate Agreements through NASDTEC that expedite the certification process.

ALMA COLLEGE

Department of Education
Teacher Education Program
614 West Superior Street
Alma, Michigan 48801-1599
Phone: (517) 463-7111
Fax: (517) 463-7277
E-mail: admissions@alma.edu
Internet: http://www.alma.edu

Institution Description: Alma College is a private, independent, nonprofit college associated with the Presbyterian Church (U.S.A.). It was established in 1886.

Almas's Teacher Education Program is designed to help students become skillful, reflective, and ethical professionals through a combination of classroom study and classroom experience.

Institution Control: Public.

Calendar: Semester. Academic year September to May.

Official(s): Dr. Anthony Rikard, Department Chair.

Faculty: Full-time 7.

Degrees Awarded: 43 baccalaureate.

Admission Requirements: *Undergraduate:* Graduation with 16 academic units from an approved secondary school; minimum 3.0 GPA; College Board SAT preferred; ACT composite accepted. *Teacher education specific:* Application to the program by the sophomore year; must pass the Basic Skills of the Michigan Tests for Teacher Certification; faculty interview.

Fees and Expenses: $17,582 per academic year. On-campus room and board: $6,335. Other expenses: $1,500. Books and supplies: $750.

Financial Aid: Resources specifically for eligible students enrolled in teacher education programs are awarded on the basis of financial need and academic merit. The institution has a Program Participation Agreement with the U.S. Department of Education for eligible students to receive Pell Grants and other federal aid. Teacher scholarships available to qualifying students. *Contact:* Financial Aid Office at: (517) 463-7347.

Accreditation: *Regional:* NCA. *Member of:* AACTE. *Approved by:* Michigan Department of Education.

Undergraduate Programs: The early childhood education program is designed for students interested in working with children from birth through age 8. It includes kindergarten through 2nd grade, as well as preschool and child care programs.

The elementary education program is for students who desire to teach at the elementary level, which includes K-5 in all subjects and K-8 for a self-contained classroom, as well as K-8 in a content area major or minor.

The secondary teacher education program is for students who desire to teach in grades 7-12. Secondary education students do not carry an education major, but rather a major and a minor in the two subject areas that the student would like to teach.

All students may seek either secondary or elementary certification. The programs lead to the baccalaureate degree and require completion of a general education core, professional studies, field experiences, and student teaching for a minimum of 126 credit hours.

Licensure/Reciprocity: Michigan. Students seeking teaching certification in a state other than Michigan should consult with that state's teacher certification office early in their program of study to insure compliance with requirements. Many state directors of teacher credentialing have signed Interstate Agreements through NASDTEC that expedite the certification process.

ANDREWS UNIVERSITY

School of Education
Teaching, Learning, and Curriculum
Bell Hall 014
Berrien Springs, Michigan 49104-1500
Phone: (269) 471-6719
Fax: (269) 471-6374
E-mail: hellingc@andrews.edu
Internet: http://www.andrews.edu

Institution Description: Andrews University is a private institution affiliated with the Seventh-day Adventist Church. It was established as Battle Creek College in 1874. The campus was moved to Berrien Springs and the name was changed to Emmanuel Missionary College in 1901. The college merged with Seventh-day Adventist Theological Seminary (established 1934) and Potomac University (established 1958) in 1960. The present name was adopted at the time of the merger.

The Department of Teaching, Learning, and Curriculum offers undergraduate degrees, graduate degrees, and teacher certification.

Institution Control: Private.

Calendar: Semester. Academic year September to May.

Official(s): Dr. Candice Hollingsead, Chairperson.

Faculty: Full-time 20; part-time 4; adjunct 50.

Degrees Awarded: 22 baccalaureate; 32 master's; 24 doctorate.

Admission Requirements: *Undergraduate:* Graduation from an approved secondary school or GED; College Board SAT or ACT composite. *Teacher education specific:* Application to the program by sophomore year; two evaluation forms; the Basic Skills portion of the Michigan Test for Teacher Certification; faculty interview. *Graduate:* Baccalaureate degree from a regionally accredited institution. *Teacher education specific:* 500 word statement of purpose; professional experience, GRE scores; pass all required tests/exams; faculty interview.

Fees and Expenses: Undergraduate: $7,100 per academic year. Graduate: $585 per credit hour (M.A.); $685 (Doctorate). On-campus room and board: $2,590 per year. Books and supplies: $200.

Financial Aid: Resources specifically for eligible students enrolled in teacher education programs are awarded on the basis of financial need and academic merit. The institution has a Program Participation Agreement with the U.S. Department of Education for eligible students to receive Pell Grants and other federal aid. Teacher scholarships available to qualifying students. *Contact:* Jerri Gifford at: (269) 471-0750.

Accreditation: *Regional:* NCA. *Professional:* NCATE. *Member of:* AACTE. *Approved by:* Michigan Department of Education.

Undergraduate Programs: The Bachelor of Science in elementary education degree is a professional degree with emphasis in the curriculum and methodology of teaching in the elementary school. Students must include a planned program minor and one subject content major or two minors. Students may choose the Bachelor of Arts degree with elementary certification.

Students preparing for teaching in secondary schools (grades 7-12) may choose from either the Bachelor of Arts or the Bachelor of science degree programs. These degrees are offered by the College of Arts and Sciences, School of Education, and College of Technology.

All programs require completion of a general education core, professional studies, content area subject(s), field experiences, and student teaching.

Graduate Programs: The Master of Arts in Teaching program is an interdepartmental curriculum for teachers who desire a combination of professional preparation and subject-matter specialization.

The Master of Arts program is a one- or two-year program beyond the bachelor's degree and is offered in all three departments of the School of Education.

The Educational Specialist program builds upon the master's degree in providing a more focused program of study, generally taking a minimum of one year beyond the master's level.

The Doctor of Education and the Doctor of Philosophy degree programs consist of coursework and a dissertation, usually taking a minimum of two years of work beyond the master's level.

Licensure/Reciprocity: Michigan. Students seeking teaching certification in a state other than Michigan should consult with that state's teacher certification office early in their program of study to insure compliance with requirements. Many state directors of teacher credentialing have signed Interstate Agreements through NASDTEC that expedite the certification process.

CALVIN COLLEGE

Education Department
Teacher Education Program
3201 Burton Street S.E.
Grand Rapids, Michigan 49546
Phone: (616) 526-6201
Fax: (616) 526-6505
E-mail: educdept@calvin.edu
Internet: http://www.calvin.edu

Institution Description: Calvin College is a four-year liberal arts college owned and operated by the Christian Reformed Church in North America. It was established in 1876. It became a four-year college in 1908 and the present name was adopted in 1921.

Teacher education programs are offered on the undergraduate and graduate levels.

Institution Control: Private.

Calendar: Semester. Academic year September to May.

Official(s): Dr. Thomas B. Hoeksema, Dean; Dr. Susan S. Hasseler, Director of Teacher Education.

Faculty: Full-time 15; part-time 6.

Degrees Awarded: 83 baccalaureate; 11 master's.

Admission Requirements: *Undergraduate:* Graduation with 15 academic units from an approved secondary school; College Board SAT or ACT composite; 2.5 GPA. *Teacher education specific:* Application to the program by sophomore year; the Basic Skills portion of the Michigan Test for Teacher Certification; multiple performance assessments; completion of two introductory education courses; faculty interview. *Graduate:* Baccalaureate degree from a regionally accredited institution. *Teacher education specific:* Admission essay; professional experience where required by program pursued; GRE scores; pass all required tests/exams; professional recommendations; faculty interview.

Fees and Expenses: Undergraduate: $15,750 per academic year. Graduate: $370 per semester hour. On-campus room and board: $5,485. Books and supplies: $500.

Financial Aid: Resources specifically for eligible students enrolled in teacher education programs are awarded on the basis of financial need and academic merit. The institution has a Program Participation Agreement with the U.S. Department of Education for eligible students to receive Pell Grants and other

CALVIN COLLEGE—*cont'd*

federal aid. Teacher scholarships available to qualifying students. *Contact:* Edward Keresty at: (616) 526-6137 or ekerestl@calvin.edu.

Accreditation: *Regional:* NCA. *Professional:* NCATE. *Member of:* AACTE. *Approved by:* Michigan Department of Education.

Undergraduate Programs: In Michigan, teachers are generally certified to teach at the elementary (K-8) or secondary level (7-12) level. There are a few specialty areas in which students can be certified to teach in grades K-12 (e.g., art, foreign languages, music, physical education, and special education. All teacher education students are required to complete the liberal arts core and a series of professional course. In addition, students are required to complete a major and minor or multiple minors in disciplinary specialty area. Students who wish to teach at the middle school level are advised to follow the elementary teacher education core requirements, choose two minors that they would like to teach in a middle school level, and take the professional courses that are geared toward middle school students.

Graduate Programs: The Master of Education program serves elementary and secondary teachers and administrators who wish advanced professional training and who need to satisfy the requirements for continuing certification or additional endorsements. All programs must include a minimum of 32 semester hours. Degree programs offered include: M.Ed. in curriculum and instruction; M.Ed. in curriculum and instruction with concentrations in educational leadership, literacy/reading, and learning disabilities.

The Post-Baccalaureate Non-degree Teacher Education Program is for those who have a bachelor's degree from an accredited institution but have not obtained a teacher certificate.

Licensure/Reciprocity: Michigan. Students seeking teaching certification in a state other than Michigan should consult with that state's teacher certification office early in their program of study to insure compliance with requirements. Many state directors of teacher credentialing have signed Interstate Agreements through NASDTEC that expedite the certification process.

CENTRAL MICHIGAN UNIVERSITY

College of Education and Human Services

Ronan 307
Mount Pleasant, Michigan 48859
Phone: (989) 774-8995
Fax: (989) 774-1999
E-mail: ehs@cmich.edu
Internet: http://www.cmich.edu

Institution Description: Central Michigan University is a state institution that was established in 1902. After numerous name changes, the present name was adopted in 1959.

Central Michigan teacher preparation programs prepares students for the classroom. The programs are concept- and knowledge-driven that encourage students to become critical thinkers and problem solvers.

Institution Control: Public.

Calendar: Semester. Academic year August to May.

Official(s): Dr. Karen K. Adams, Dean.

Faculty: Regular 91; temporary 86.

Degrees Awarded: 585 baccalaureate; 577 master's; 11 doctorate.

Admission Requirements: *Undergraduate:* Graduation from an accredited secondary school or GED; ACT composite. *Teacher education specific:* Completion of 60 credit hours; 2.7 GPA; Michigan Basic Skills Test; declaration of major and minor; interview. *Graduate:* Baccalaureate degree from a regionally accredited institution. *Teacher education specific:* Statement of purpose; professional experience, GRE scores; pass all required tests/exams; faculty interview.

Fees and Expenses: Undergraduate: in-state $4,240 per academic year; out-of-state $10,171. Graduate: in-state $5,290, out-of-state $10,102. On-campus room and board: $5,220. Books and supplies: $750.

Financial Aid: Resources specifically for eligible students enrolled in teacher education programs are awarded on the basis of financial need and academic merit. The institution has a Program Participation Agreement with the U.S. Department of Education for eligible students to receive Pell Grants and other federal aid. Teacher scholarships available to qualifying students. *Contact:* Terry Uran at: (989) 774-7428.

Accreditation: *Regional:* NCA. *Professional:* NCATE. *Member of:* AACTE. *Approved by:* Michigan Department of Education.

Undergraduate Programs: The elementary education option prepares the candidate to work with students in grades kindergarten through eight. Candidates choose courses in language arts, humanities, science, social sciences, cultural and human diversity, mathematics, computer and technology education, health and physical education, and art and music education. To satisfy state certification requirements, three minors or one major and one minor must be selected.

The secondary education option enables the candidate to teach in grades seven through 12. The program requires the completion of a a major and minor that will represent a subject field in which the candidate will be certified to teach.

In both the elementary and secondary programs, students may choose from a variety of majors and minors in the arts, sciences, languages, and other areas. In addition to general curriculum areas, the college offers programs in bilingual/bicultural education, child development, middle level education, reading education, and special education.

All programs leading to the baccalaureate degree require the completion of a general education core, professional studies, content area courses, field experiences, and student teaching.

Graduate Programs: The Master of Education program serves elementary and secondary teachers and administrators who wish advanced professional training and who need to satisfy the requirements for continuing certification or additional endorsements. The Master of Arts in Teaching program leading to the master's degree include the Master of Arts in Teaching program requires the completion of specific requirements as dictated by the area chosen by the student.

Licensure/Reciprocity: Michigan. Students seeking teaching certification in a state other than Michigan should consult with that state's teacher certification office early in their program of study to insure compliance with requirements. Many state directors of teacher credentialing have signed Interstate Agreements through NASDTEC that expedite the certification process.

CONCORDIA COLLEGE

School of Education

4090 Geddes Road
Ann Arbor, Michigan 48105
Phone: (734) 995-7392
Fax: (734) 995-7405
E-mail: frustt@cuaa.edu
Internet: http://www.cuaa.edu

Institution Description: Concordia College (Concordia Lutheran Junior College until 1976) is a private college affiliated with The Lutheran Church-Missouri Synod. It was established in 1962 and the present name was adopted in 1976.

Concordia's School of Education curriculum has been developed to be consistent and in compliance with all standards and requirements established by the Michigan Department of Education.

Institution Control: Private.

Calendar: Semester. Academic year September to May.

Official(s): Dr. Timothy Frusti, Chairman; Dr. Janice Nelson, Secondary Education Coordinator; Dr. Carolyn Hannum, Elementary Education Coordinator.

Faculty: Full-time 3; part-time 7; adjunct 9.

Degrees Awarded: 3 baccalaureate.

Admission Requirements: *Undergraduate:* Graduation from an accredited secondary school or GED; ACT composite. *Teacher education specific:* 2.5 GPA; minimum 80 hours of field experience; pass the Basic Skills portion of the Michigan Test for Teacher Certification; interview; two positive letters of recommendation.

Fees and Expenses: $17,250 per academic year. On-campus room and board: $6,745. Books and supplies: $600.

Financial Aid: Resources specifically for eligible students enrolled in teacher education programs are awarded on the basis of financial need and academic merit. The institution has a Program Participation Agreement with the U.S. Department of Education for eligible students to receive Pell Grants and other federal aid. Teacher scholarships available to qualifying students. *Contact:* Sandra Tarbox at: (754) 995-7408 or e-mail at sandra.tarbox@cuaa.edu.

Accreditation: *Regional:* NCA. *Member of:* AACTE. *Approved by:* Michigan Department of Education.

Undergraduate Programs: The elementary education program consists of three components: general studies, professional education studies, and specialty studies (a major or two minors). Completion of a fourth component, the Lutheran Teacher Diploma requirements, certifies the student to serve in the teaching ministry of the Lutheran Church - Missouri Synod. Completion of the program leads to certification to teach all subjects in grades kindergarten to fifth and all subject in grades 6 to 8 in self-contained classrooms. Passing the MTTC content area test also qualifies to teach in a departmentalized program (grades 6 to 8) in the area(s) of specialization (majors or minors). A minimum of 132 semester hours are required for the degree.

The secondary education program consists of the same four components as described above for elementary education and leads to certification to teach grades seven through twelve in the areas of the student's specialized studies. A minimum of 127 semester hours must be completed for the degree award.

Licensure/Reciprocity: Michigan. Students seeking teaching certification in a state other than Michigan should consult with that state's teacher certification office early in their program of study to insure compliance with requirements. Many state directors of teacher credentialing have signed Interstate Agreements through NASDTEC that expedite the certification process.

EASTERN MICHIGAN UNIVERSITY

College of Education
Department of Teacher Education
204 Porter Building
Ypsilanti, Michigan 48197
Phone: (734) 487-1416
Fax: (734) 487-3060
E-mail: undergraduate.admissions@emich.edu
Internet: http://www.emich.edu

Institution Description: Eastern Michigan University is a state institution that was established as Michigan State Normal School in 1849. After several name changes, the present name was adopted in 1959.

The Department of Teacher Education provides graduate and undergraduate courses.

Institution Control: Public.

Calendar: Semester. Academic year September to April.

Official(s): Dr. Jerry Robbins, Dean, College of Education; Dr. Alane D. Starko, Chair, Department of Teacher Education.

Faculty: Full-time 48.

Degrees Awarded: 790 baccalaureate; 329 master's; 17 doctorate.

Admission Requirements: *Undergraduate:* Graduation from an approved secondary school or GED; College Board SAT of ACT composite. *Teacher education specific:* Completion of 56 credit hours with overall GPA 2.5; Michigan Basic Skills Test; declaration of major and minor; interview. *Graduate:* Baccalau-

reate degree from a regionally accredited institution. *Teacher education specific:* Statement of purpose; professional experience, GRE scores; pass all required tests/exams; faculty interview.

Fees and Expenses: Undergraduate: in-state $5,030 per academic year; out-of-state $13,760. Graduate: Tuition is charged per credit hour. On-campus room and board: $5,600. Other expenses: $2,300. Books and supplies: $900.

Financial Aid: Resources specifically for eligible students enrolled in teacher education programs are awarded on the basis of financial need and academic merit. The institution has a Program Participation Agreement with the U.S. Department of Education for eligible students to receive Pell Grants and other federal aid. Teacher scholarships available to qualifying students. *Contact:* Financial Aid Office at: (754) 487-0455.

Accreditation: *Regional:* NCA. *Professional:* NCATE. *Member of:* AACTE. *Approved by:* Michigan Department of Education.

Undergraduate Programs: The curricula for the elementary education programs leading to the bachelor's degree consist of courses in general education, a major and minor (or three minors), and a required group of professional education courses. If the student wishes to be endorsed in a subject field, an additional minor from the approved list will be required. A variation of this program is available for those who wish to be prepared as early childhood teachers. Ordinarily, the degree earned is the bachelor of science. The Bachelor of Arts degree requires the completion of 75 hours in the liberal arts and one year of college credit in foreign language.

The curricula for the secondary/K-12 teacher education programs consist of an appropriately selected group of courses in general education, a chosen major and minor, and a required group of professional education courses. Approved majors include: biology, business services and technology education, chemistry, communication, computer science, earth science, economics, French, general science, geography, German, history, vocational education, language/literature/and writing, marketing, mathematics, physics, political science, psychology, social studies, sociology, and Spanish.

Graduate Programs: Post-baccalaureate students may pursue programs leading to Michigan certification to teach at the elementary and secondary levels. Applicants must pass all three parts of the Basic Skills test (Michigan Test for Teacher Certification). Specific details regarding these programs may be found http://www.emich.edu/coe/newhome.

Licensure/Reciprocity: Michigan. Students seeking teaching certification in a state other than Michigan should consult with that state's teacher certification office early in their program of study to insure compliance with requirements. Many state directors of teacher credentialing have signed Interstate Agreements through NASDTEC that expedite the certification process.

GRAND VALLEY STATE UNIVERSITY

School of Education
1133 Mackinac Hall
1 Campus Drive
Allendale, Michigan 49401
Phone: (616) 331-2094
Fax: (616) 331-2330
E-mail: go2gvsu@gvsu.edu
Internet: http://www.gvsu.edu

Institution Description: Grand Valley State University, formerly Grand Valley State College, is a state institution offering liberal arts and professional programs. It was chartered in 1960.

The School of Education enrolls over 2,000 students per year. Classes are scheduled so that students benefit from educators across the state.

Institution Control: Public.

Calendar: Semester. Academic year August to May.

Official(s): Dr. Linda McCrea, Department Chair.

Faculty: Full-time 30.

Degrees Awarded: 151 baccalaureate; 416 master's.

GRAND VALLEY STATE UNIVERSITY—*cont'd*

Admission Requirements: *Undergraduate:* Graduation from an approved secondary school or GED; College Board SAT or ACT composite; 2.7 GPA. *Teacher education specific:* Must pass the Basic Skills portion of the Michigan Test for Teacher Certification; declaration of major. *Graduate:* Baccalaureate from a regionally accredited institution. *Teacher education specific:* Teaching licensure where required by the program; pass all required tests/exams; faculty interview.

Fees and Expenses: Undergraduate: in-state $5,100 per academic year; out-of-state $10,940. Graduate: Tuition charged per credit hour. On-campus room and board: $5,660. Other expenses $1,680. Books and supplies: $800.

Financial Aid: Resources specifically for eligible students enrolled in teacher education programs are awarded on the basis of financial need and academic merit. The institution has a Program Participation Agreement with the U.S. Department of Education for eligible students to receive Pell Grants and other federal aid. Teacher scholarships available to qualifying students. *Contact:* Financial Aid Office at: (616) 321-3234.

Accreditation: *Regional:* NCA. *Professional:* NCATE. *Member of:* AACTE. *Approved by:* Michigan Department of Education.

Undergraduate Programs: In conjunction with other departments and programs, the undergraduate program prepares students for certification in elementary and secondary education and in three areas of special education. Faculty from the undergraduate program and from subject area concentrations teach courses and seminars in educational philosophy and psychology, methods and materials, and school organization and management.

The elementary teaching major and the secondary teaching major programs are offered in various fields of study in the arts and humanities, science and math, and social sciences. The programs lead to the baccalaureate degree and require the completion of a general education core, professional studies, field experiences, and student teaching for a minimum of 120 semester hours.

Graduate Programs: Graduate Teacher Certification is available to selected candidates who already possess a bachelor's degree and teachable major. Upon completion of certification requirements, they may continue coursework toward the master's degree in elementary or secondary education.

The Master of Education in general education is offered with emphases in early childhood, educational leadership, educational technology, elementary, gifted and talented, teaching English as a second language, secondary, adult and higher education or middle and high school education with concentrations in English, mathematics, biology, physics, history, or college student affairs leadership.

The Master of Education with emphasis in reading/language arts and the Master of Education in special education are also offered. Other endorsement and approval programs are available,

Licensure/Reciprocity: Michigan. Students seeking teaching certification in a state other than Michigan should consult with that state's teacher certification office early in their program of study to insure compliance with requirements. Many state directors of teacher credentialing have signed Interstate Agreements through NASDTEC that expedite the certification process.

HOPE COLLEGE
Education Department
Teacher Education Program
141 East 12th Street
Holland, Michigan 49423
Phone: (616) 395-7000
Fax: (616) 395-7922
E-mail: admissions@hope.edu
Internet: http://www.hope.edu

Institution Description: Hope College is a private, independent, nonprofit college affiliated with the Reformed Church in America. It was established in 1862.

The Education Department prepares students to teach in elementary and secondary schools.

Institution Control: Private.

Calendar: Semester. Academic year August to May.

Official(s): Dr. Leslie Wessman, Chairperson.

Faculty: Full-time 15.

Degrees Awarded: 109 baccalaureate.

Admission Requirements: *Undergraduate:* Graduation with 16 academic units from an approved secondary school or GED; ACT composite preferred; College Board SAT accepted. *Teacher education specific:* Application should be made during the sophomore year or following completion of the introductory courses and field placements; faculty interview; must pass the Basic Skills portion of the Michigan Test for Teacher Certification.

Fees and Expenses: $18,270 per academic year. On-campus room and board: $5,690. Other expenses: $1,335. Books and supplies: $640.

Financial Aid: Resources specifically for eligible students enrolled in teacher education programs are awarded on the basis of financial need and academic merit. The institution has a Program Participation Agreement with the U.S. Department of Education for eligible students to receive Pell Grants and other federal aid. Teacher scholarships available to qualifying students. *Contact:* Financial Aid Office at: (616) 395-7765.

Accreditation: *Regional:* NCA. *Professional:* NCATE. *Member of:* AACTE. *Approved by:* Michigan Department of Education.

Undergraduate Programs: Upon graduation and being granted provisional certification, individuals seeking elementary teaching certification in the State of Michigan are able to teach in all subject areas, kindergarten through 5th grade. They may teach all subjects in the 6th through 8th grades if classes are self-contained or in their major or minor subjects and the individual has received endorsements in those subject areas. Besides completing coursework in the general education liberal arts curriculum and a declared academic or composite major, elementary education students also fulfill requirements for a minor. Student must also successfully complete coursework in the professional education sequence and meet criteria to student teach. Student teaching most often takes place during the first or second semester of the senior year.

Licensure/Reciprocity: Michigan. Students seeking teaching certification in a state other than Michigan should consult with that state's teacher certification office early in their program of study to insure compliance with requirements. Many state directors of teacher credentialing have signed Interstate Agreements through NASDTEC that expedite the certification process.

MADONNA UNIVERSITY
Teacher Education Program
36600 Schoolcraft Road
Livonia, Michigan 48150-1173
Phone: (734) 432-5339
Fax: (734) 432-5393
E-mail: muinfo@madonna.edu
Internet: http://www.madonna.edu

Institution Description: Madonna University, formerly Madonna College, is a private, independent, nonprofit college sponsored by the Felician Sisters, Roman Catholic Church. It was established in 1937 and became a four-year college in 1947 when the present name was adopted.

The Teacher Education Program prepares students to provide caring, competent, and professional service to children in K-12 educational settings.

Institution Control: Private.

Calendar: Semester. Academic year July to June.

Official(s): Dr. Robert Kean, Dean; Nancy Cross, Advisor.

Faculty: Student/faculty ration 5 to 1.

Degrees Awarded: 22 baccalaureate; 50 master's.

Admission Requirements: *Undergraduate:* Graduation with 15 academic units from an approved secondary school or GED; ACT composite required. *Teacher education specific:* Declaration of intention to prepare for the profession of teaching at the elementary or secondary level; application to program by end of sophomore year; 2.75 GPA; Michigan Basic Skills Test and the Teacher Education Program Basic Skills Test; two recommendations. *Graduate:* Baccalaureate degree from a regionally accredited institution. *Teacher education specific:* Statement of purpose; professional experience, GRE scores; pass all required tests/exams; faculty interview.

Fees and Expenses: $8,350 per academic year. Graduate: Tuition charged per credit hour. On-campus room and board: $5,252. Other expenses: $2,010. Books and supplies: $900.

Financial Aid: Resources specifically for eligible students enrolled in teacher education programs are awarded on the basis of financial need and academic merit. The institution has a Program Participation Agreement with the U.S. Department of Education for eligible students to receive Pell Grants and other federal aid. Teacher scholarships available to qualifying students. *Contact:* Financial Aid Office at: (734) 432-5663.

Accreditation: *Regional:* NCA. *Professional:* NCATE. *Member of:* AACTE. *Approved by:* Michigan Department of Education.

Undergraduate Programs: The child development program offers a major and minor. The major may be combined with another major, such as psychology or social work. The early childhood education is a minor offered for elementary teacher certification. The program leads to a bachelor's degree. The early childhood endorsement program is offered at the undergraduate and post-bachelor levels.

The family and consumer sciences program prepares students to teach life management education and family and consumer science. The major may be used for elementary and secondary teaching certificates. A secondary teacher vocational authorization is also available.

Teaching certificates can be earned in the following majors; art, biology, chemistry, communication arts, computer science (secondary only), English, English/Journalism, English/Speech, general science (elementary only), history, family and consumer science (home economics), Japanese, mathematics, music education, natural science, social studies, sociology, Spanish, and vocational trades.

All baccalaureate programs require the completion of a general education core, professional studies, field experiences, and student teaching.

Graduate Programs: The College of Education offers graduate programs for teachers: Master of Arts in Teaching with a specialization in learning disabilities or literacy education; Master of Science in Administration with specialties in Catholic school leadership or educational leadership offered for part-time students with a full-time work commitment; Master of Arts in teaching English to speakers of other language designed to educate and train teachers and offer foundations in theoretical and applied linguistics, educational theory and practice, as well as cultural aspects of language learning, teaching, and assessment.

Licensure/Reciprocity: Michigan. Students seeking teaching certification in a state other than Michigan should consult with that state's teacher certification office early in their program of study to insure compliance with requirements. Many state directors of teacher credentialing have signed Interstate Agreements through NASDTEC that expedite the certification process.

MARYGROVE COLLEGE
Education Unit
Teacher Certification Program
Madame Cadillac Building, Room 223
8425 West McNichols Road
Detroit, Michigan 48221-2599
Phone: (313) 927-1457
Fax: (313) 927-1345
E-mail: gncfedries@marygrove.edu
Internet: http://www.marygrove.edu

Institution Description: Marygrove College is a private college affiliated with the Sisters Servants of the Immaculate Heart of Mary, Roman Catholic Church. It was established in 1905. The present name was adopted in 1925.

The education programs at Marygrove College seek to combine technical skill and knowledge with guided experiences that will foster the goals of educational professionalism.

Institution Control: Private.

Calendar: Semester. Academic year September to May.

Official(s): Dr. J. Rivard, Chair; Gale McFedries, Teacher Certification contact.

Faculty: Full-time 14.

Degrees Awarded: 7 baccalaureate; 2,960 master's.

Admission Requirements: *Undergraduate:* Graduation with 16 units from an approved secondary school or GED; College Board SAT or ACT composite. *Teacher education specific:* 2.7 GPA; completion of all developmental education foundation courses; passing score on the Michigan Teacher Certification Basic Skills Test; faculty interview. *Graduate:* Baccalaureate degree from a regionally accredited institution. *Teacher education specific:* Statement of purpose; professional experience, GRE scores; pass all required tests/exams; faculty interview.

Fees and Expenses: $11,250 per academic year. Graduate: Tuition charged per credit hour. On-campus room and board: $6,000. Other expenses: $1,815. Books and supplies: $725.

Financial Aid: Resources specifically for eligible students enrolled in teacher education programs are awarded on the basis of financial need and academic merit. The institution has a Program Participation Agreement with the U.S. Department of Education for eligible students to receive Pell Grants and other federal aid. Teacher scholarships available to qualifying students. *Contact:* Financial Aid Office at: (313) 927-1250.

Accreditation: *Regional:* NCA. *Professional:* NCATE. *Member of:* AACTE. *Approved by:* Michigan Department of Education.

Undergraduate Programs: The Education Unit, in cooperation withy other academic units, prepares students for teaching at the preschool, elementary, and secondary levels. After successfully completing the general education requirements, the coursework for teacher certification, the major and minor, and passing the appropriate Michigan Tests for Teacher Certification, the student will be eligible for recommendation for a provisional teaching certificate from the State of Michigan. Two specific majors are offered in the education unit: early childhood education and special education. Specific departments in the college offer all other teaching majors. All programs lead to the baccalaureate degree and require a minimum 128 credit hours including the general education core, professional studies, field experiences, and student teaching.

Graduate Programs: Graduate programs in the education unit combine technical skills, knowledge and experiences to help students achieve the highest levels of educational professionalism. The programs include the Master of Arts in Teaching, Teacher Certification, the Griots Program-a teacher certification program leading to the Master of Education degree for African American males interested in changing careers, the Master of Education in reading, and the Master of Arts in educational administration.

Licensure/Reciprocity: Michigan. Students seeking teaching certification in a state other than Michigan should consult with that state's teacher certification office early in their program of study to insure compliance with requirements. Many state

MARYGROVE COLLEGE—cont'd

directors of teacher credentialing have signed Interstate Agreements through NASDTEC that expedite the certification process.

MICHIGAN STATE UNIVERSITY

College of Education
Department of Teacher Education

313 Erickson Hall
East Lansing, Michigan 48824
Phone: (517) 353-5091
Fax: (517) 353-5092
E-mail: coe@msu.edu
Internet: http://www.msu.edu

Institution Description: Michigan State University is the nation's pioneer land-grant college. It was established as Agricultural College of State of Michigan in 1855. After several name changes, the present name was adopted in 1964.

The Department of Teacher Education offers students the opportunity to study teaching, learning, curriculum, and educational policy at all levels.

Institution Control: Public.

Calendar: Semester. Academic year August to May.

Official(s): Dr. Mary Lindeberg, Chair, Department of Teacher Education.

Faculty: Full-time 54.

Degrees Awarded: 287 baccalaureate; 536 master's; 44 doctorate.

Admission Requirements: *Undergraduate:* Graduation from an approved secondary school with four years of college preparatory courses; College Board SAT or ACT composite. *Teacher education specific:* Must pass the Basic Skills portion of the Michigan Test for Teacher Certification; declaration of major; faculty interview. *Graduate:* Baccalaureate from a regionally accredited institution. *Teacher education specific:* Teaching licensure where required by the program; pass all required tests/exams; faculty interview.

Fees and Expenses: Undergraduate: in-state $6,100; out-of-state $15,170. Graduate: Tuition charged per credit hour. On-campus room and board: $4,890. Other expenses: $1,360. Books and supplies: $800.

Financial Aid: Resources specifically for eligible students enrolled in teacher education programs are awarded on the basis of financial need and academic merit. The institution has a Program Participation Agreement with the U.S. Department of Education for eligible students to receive Pell Grants and other federal aid. Teacher scholarships available to qualifying students. *Contact:* Financial Aid Office at: (517) 353-5940.

Accreditation: *Regional:* NCA. *Member of:* AACTE. *Approved by:* Michigan Department of Education.

Undergraduate Programs: Baccalaureate programs are offered in elementary and secondary education. These programs combine a baccalaureate degree, a teaching major and/or minor concentrations and teaching certification courses, followed by a full-year teaching internship in a public school. The special education program combines regular elementary teaching certification and K-12 endorsement in one of two areas in special education: learning disabilities or deaf education. Both certification and endorsement are awarded only after completion of a fifth-year internship experience. The program leads to a Bachelor of Arts degree.

Graduate Programs: The Post Bachelor Certification Program provides an integrated baccalaureate/post-baccalaureate internship program. The program combines a baccalaureate degree in a disciplinary major and minor concentrations with teacher certification courses followed by a year-long internship in the school. Students in the internship year combine teaching with graduate-level professional study courses, some of which may apply to a master's degree program.

The Master of Arts in curriculum and teaching is designed to facilitate the professional and personal growth of experienced educators. The program requires active learning and field-based inquiry.

The Master of Arts in literacy and language instruction program is designed for competent and dedicated teachers in K-12 classrooms. The program provides a balance of theory, research, and practice toward developing literacy leaders at the school and district levels, as well as for government, business, and private settings where literacy is a primary concern.

Other teacher education master's degree programs and doctoral programs are offered. The doctoral program in curriculum, teaching, and educational policy is of particular note. Contact the College of Education for further information.

Licensure/Reciprocity: Michigan. Students seeking teaching certification in a state other than Michigan should consult with that state's teacher certification office early in their program of study to insure compliance with requirements. Many state directors of teacher credentialing have signed Interstate Agreements through NASDTEC that expedite the certification process.

NORTHERN MICHIGAN UNIVERSITY

School of Education
Teacher Education Certification Programs

Whitman Hall, Room 104
1401 Presque Isle Avenue
Marquette, Michigan 49855
Phone: (906) 227-2728
Fax: (906) 227-2764
E-mail: soe@nmu.edu
Internet: http://www.nmu.edu

Institution Description: Northern Michigan University is a state institution. It was established as Northern Michigan Normal School in 1899. The present name was adopted in 1963.

The School of Education offers undergraduate and graduate programs leading to baccalaureate and master's degrees.

Institution Control: Public.

Calendar: Semester. Academic year September to May.

Official(s): Dr. Debra Thatcher, Director, Teacher Education Certification Programs.

Faculty: Full-time 4 (teacher education).

Degrees Awarded: 171 baccalaureate; 76 master's.

Admission Requirements: *Undergraduate:* Graduation from an approved secondary school or GED; ACT composite score of 19. *Teacher education specific:* Must pass the Basic Skills portion of the Michigan Test for Teacher Certification; declaration of major. *Graduate:* Baccalaureate from a regionally accredited institution. *Teacher education specific:* Teaching licensure where required by the program; pass all required tests/exams; faculty interview.

Fees and Expenses: Undergraduate: in-state $4,780; out-of-state $7,732. Graduate: Post-degree and graduate study tuition and fees for college graduates who would like to obtain a teaching certificate are charged at the undergraduate rate. On-campus room and board: $5,500. Other expenses: $1,410. Books and supplies: $600.

Financial Aid: Resources specifically for eligible students enrolled in teacher education programs are awarded on the basis of financial need and academic merit. The institution has a Program Participation Agreement with the U.S. Department of Education for eligible students to receive Pell Grants and other federal aid. Teacher scholarships available to qualifying students. *Contact:* Financial Aid Office at: (906) 227-2327.

Accreditation: *Regional:* NCA. *Professional:* NCATE. *Member of:* AACTE. *Approved by:* Michigan Department of Education.

Undergraduate Programs: Elementary education certification allows the student to teach all subjects in grades K-5 as well as the subject areas of the major or minor for grades 6-8. Teaching concentration options are English, French, geography, German, history, language arts, mathematics, physical education, science, social studies, or Spanish.

The secondary education certification allows the student to teach grades 7-12 and some areas of specialty for K-12. The university offers 22 major and minor fields, including art and design, biology, business education, chemistry, earth science, economics, English, French, general science, geography, German, health education, history, industrial technology, mathematics, music education, physical education, PE/coaching, physics, political science, social studies, and Spanish.

Special education majors are endorsed to teach grades K-12 in either emotional impairment or cognitive impairment. Students also complete either the elementary or secondary program.

All programs require the completion of a general education core, professional studies, field experiences, and student teaching.

Graduate Programs: The Master of Arts in Education degree programs offer six basic curricula: elementary education, educational administration, learning disabilities, instructional leadership, secondary education, and school guidance counseling. Each program follows course requirements in all four areas: foundations of education, research, cognates, and area of concentration. These programs require the completion of 34 to 41 semester hours.

An Education Specialist program is also offered by the School of Education.

Licensure/Reciprocity: Michigan. Students seeking teaching certification in a state other than Michigan should consult with that state's teacher certification office early in their program of study to insure compliance with requirements. Many state directors of teacher credentialing have signed Interstate Agreements through NASDTEC that expedite the certification process.

OAKLAND UNIVERSITY

School of Education and Human Services
Department of Curriculum, Instruction, and Leadership
544 O'Dowd Hall
Rochester, Michigan 48309-4401
Phone: (248) 370-3050
Fax: (248) 370-4202
E-mail: wiggins@oakland.edu
Internet: http://www.oakland.edu

Institution Description: Oakland University is a state institution. It was established as Michigan State University at Oakland in 1957. The present name was adopted in 1963.

The educational programs for undergraduate and graduate study provide a strong theoretical knowledge base plus experiential learning opportunities.

Institution Control: Public.

Calendar: Semester. Academic year September to April.

Official(s): Dr. Mary L. Otto, Dean, School of Education and Human Services; Dr. Robert Wiggins, Associate Dean.

Faculty: Full-time 68; part-time 96.

Degrees Awarded: 281 baccalaureate; 359 master's; 9 doctorate.

Admission Requirements: *Undergraduate:* Graduation from an approved secondary school or GED; ACT composite. *Teacher education specific:* Must pass the Basic Skills portion of the Michigan Test for Teacher Certification; declaration of major. *Graduate:* Baccalaureate from a regionally accredited institution. *Teacher education specific:* Teaching licensure where required by the program; pass all required tests/exams; faculty interview.

Fees and Expenses: Undergraduate: in-state $5,530 per academic year; out-of-state $15,170. Graduate: in-state $7,610; out-of-state contact the university for current rate. On-campus room: $5,232 per academic year; board: various meal plans available.

Financial Aid: Resources specifically for eligible students enrolled in teacher education programs are awarded on the basis of financial need and academic merit. The institution has a Program Participation Agreement with the U.S. Department of

Education for eligible students to receive Pell Grants and other federal aid. Teacher scholarships available to qualifying students. *Contact:* Financial Aid Advisor at: (248) 370-2550.

Accreditation: *Regional:* NCA. *Professional:* NCATE. *Member of:* AACTE. *Approved by:* Michigan Department of Education.

Undergraduate Programs: The School of Education and Human Services offers programs designed to prepare students for careers in teaching and related human service activities. The programs include a Bachelor of Science in elementary education, a five-year secondary education program leading to teaching certification for selected majors, and a Bachelor of Science in human resource development. Minors in human resource development and in labor and employment studies are also available. All baccalaureate programs require completion of a general education core, professional studies, field experiences, and student teaching. A minimum of 124 credit hours is required for the baccalaureate degree.

Graduate Programs: Programs leading to the Doctor of Philosophy in reading, counseling, early childhood education, educational leadership, and music education are offered. Other master's level programs include the Master of Arts in counseling, the Master of Arts in Teaching in reading and language arts, and the Master of Education in three areas: early childhood; curriculum, instruction, and leadership; special education. A Master of Training and Development Program is also offered.

Licensure/Reciprocity: Michigan. Students seeking teaching certification in a state other than Michigan should consult with that state's teacher certification office early in their program of study to insure compliance with requirements. Many state directors of teacher credentialing have signed Interstate Agreements through NASDTEC that expedite the certification process.

SAGINAW VALLEY STATE UNIVERSITY

College of Education
Teacher Education Program
7400 Bay Road
University Center, Michigan 48710-0001
Phone: (989) 964-4057
Fax: (989) 790-0180
E-mail: coe-dean@.svsu.edu
Internet: http://www.svsu.edu

Institution Description: Saginaw Valley State College (Saginaw Valley College until 1975) is a state institution that was established in 1963. The present name was adopted in 1987.

The mission of the Teacher Education Program is to prepare pre-service teacher education students in basic and advanced programs.

Institution Control: Public.

Calendar: Semester. Academic year August to August.

Official(s): Dr. Steve Barbus, Dean.

Faculty: Full-time 26.

Degrees Awarded: 306 baccalaureate; 431 master's.

Admission Requirements: *Undergraduate:* Graduation from an approved secondary school or GED; ACT composite preferred; College Board SAT accepted. *Teacher education specific:* Achieve university basic skills requirements; general education requirements; two content area minors; pass Michigan Tests for Teacher Certification. *Graduate:* Baccalaureate degree from a regionally accredited institution. *Teacher education specific:* Must complete two content area minors; professional studies coursework; Michigan Tests for Teacher Certification.

Fees and Expenses: Undergraduate: in-state, $4,365 per academic year; out-of-state $9,290. Graduate: Tuition charged per credit hour. On-campus room and board: $5,485. Other expenses: $2,500. Books and supplies: $800.

Financial Aid: Resources specifically for eligible students enrolled in teacher education programs are awarded on the basis of financial need and academic merit. The institution has a Program Participation Agreement with the U.S. Department of

SAGINAW VALLEY STATE UNIVERSITY—
cont'd
Education for eligible students to receive Pell Grants and other federal aid. Teacher scholarships available to qualifying students. *Contact:* Financial Aid Office at: (989) 964-4103.

Accreditation: *Regional:* NCA. *Professional:* NCATE. *Member of:* AACTE. *Approved by:* Michigan Department of Education.

Undergraduate Programs: Basic programs offered in the Teacher Education Program include: elementary education, secondary education, special education (emotionally impaired adn learning disabilities), and bilingual education. Undergraduate teacher certification candidates also have the option of adding an additional endorsement to their initial teaching certificate. The early childhood endorsement is often required to teach kindergarten, first or second grade, and is required to teach in Michigan's four-year old Readiness Program. Interested candidates must be accepted into the elementary teacher education program before they can begin to take courses for the endorsement. In relation to the two content area minors and planned program minor for elementary education program, the endorsement would be considered a third minor and require successful completion of 20 credit hours.

All baccalaureate programs require the completion of a general education core, professional studies, field experiences, and student teaching. A minimum of 124 semester hours must be successfully completed for the degree award.

Graduate Programs: The Master of Arts in Teaching program provides opportunities for academic preparation and professional renewal for practicing educators. The program increases elementary and secondary teachers' knowledge and understanding of th learning process and their teaching methods and skills. It also offers teachers the opportunity to increase their competence in various subject area specializations.

Licensure/Reciprocity: Michigan. Students seeking teaching certification in a state other than Michigan should consult with that state's teacher certification office early in their program of study to insure compliance with requirements. Many state directors of teacher credentialing have signed Interstate Agreements through NASDTEC that expedite the certification process.

SPRING ARBOR UNIVERSITY
School of Education
Teacher Certification Programs
106 East Main
Spring Arbor, Michigan 49283-9799
Phone: (800) 968-9103
Fax: (517) 750-1536
E-mail: soe@arbor.edu
Internet: http://www.arbor.edu

Institution Description: Spring Arbor University, formerly Spring Arbor College, is a private four-year institution affiliated with the Free Methodist Church. It was established in 1873.

The Teacher Certification Program seeks to give its students a group of key concepts and skills of teaching, based on psychological and sociological principles applied to the theory and practice of educational techniques.

Institution Control: Private.

Calendar: Semester. Academic year September to May.

Official(s): Dr. David G. Hamilton, Dean.

Faculty: Full-time 15.

Degrees Awarded: 63 baccalaureate; 74 master's.

Admission Requirements: *Undergraduate:* Graduation from an approved secondary school or GED; enhanced ACT composite score of 20 recommended. *Teacher education specific:* Completion of all developmental education foundation courses; passing score on the Michigan Teacher Certification Basic Skills Test; faculty interview. *Graduate:* Baccalaureate degree from a regionally accredited institution. *Teacher education specific:* Statement of purpose; professional experience, GRE scores; pass all required tests/exams; faculty interview.

Fees and Expenses: Undergraduate $13,900 per academic year. Graduate: Tuition charged per credit hour. On-campus room and board: $5,330. Other expenses: $1,375. Books and supplies: $600.

Financial Aid: Resources specifically for eligible students enrolled in teacher education programs are awarded on the basis of financial need and academic merit. The institution has a Program Participation Agreement with the U.S. Department of Education for eligible students to receive Pell Grants and other federal aid. *Contact:* Financial Aid Office at: (517) 750-6468.

Accreditation: *Regional:* NCA. *Professional:* NCATE. *Member of:* AACTE. *Approved by:* Michigan Department of Education.

Undergraduate Programs: The professional education programs offered at Spring Arbor University include: elementary certification that cover K-5 for all subjects and grades 6, 7, and 8 in the candidate's major or minor disciplines. The secondary certification program covers grades 7-12 in the candidate's major and minor disciplines. K-12 endorsement for both elementary and secondary candidates is available for majors in art, music, and exercise and sport science.

All baccalaureate programs require the completion of a general education core, content area major/minor, professional studies, field experiences, and student teaching. A minimum of 124 credit hours must be successfully completed for the degree award.

Graduate Programs: The graduate program is designed not only for those who wish to obtain a master's degree but also for those who wish to meet certification requirements in additional areas, who wish to meet provisional or professional education certificate requirements, or who wish to broaden or refresh their knowledge in areas of professional education.

The Master of Arts in Education program is designed for certified teachers who wish to obtain a master's degree with a concentration area in instruction and curriculum. Individual who are not certified teachers may also enroll in selected courses in the Post-Baccalaureate (Non-Degree) Program to explore their interest in education.

Licensure/Reciprocity: Michigan. Students seeking teaching certification in a state other than Michigan should consult with that state's teacher certification office early in their program of study to insure compliance with requirements. Many state directors of teacher credentialing have signed Interstate Agreements through NASDTEC that expedite the certification process.

UNIVERSITY OF DETROIT MERCY
College of Liberal Arts and Education
Teacher Education Program
4001 West McNichols Road
Detroit, Michigan 48221
Phone: (313) 993-1287
Fax: (313) 993-1166
E-mail: stoecka@udmercy.edu
Internet: http://www.udmercy.edu

Institution Description: The University of Detroit Mercy is a private, independent, nonprofit institution affiliated with the Jesuit order and Sisters of Mercy of the Roman Catholic Church. It was established as Detroit College in 1877. The college became University of Detroit Mercy upon the merger with Mercy College of Detroit in 1990.

The university offers both undergraduate and graduate programs leading to teacher certification.

Institution Control: Private.

Calendar: Semester. Academic year September to May.

Official(s): Fr. John Staudenmaier, S.J., Dean.

Faculty: Full-time 10; part-time 2; adjunct 14.

Degrees Awarded: 41 baccalaureate; 70 master's.

Admission Requirements: *Undergraduate:* Graduation from an approved secondary school or GED; College Board SAT or ACT composite. *Teacher education specific:* Pass all three subtests of the Michigan Basic Skills Test; overall GPA 2.5; completion of 12 credits in major with 2.7 GPA and 9 credits in minor with 2.7

GPA; two recommendations from professional educators; faculty interview. *Graduate:* Baccalaureate degree from a regionally accredited institution. *Teacher education specific:* Statement of purpose; professional experience; GRE scores; pass all required tests/exams; faculty interview.

Fees and Expenses: Undergraduate: $9,875 per academic year. Graduate: $640 per credit. On-campus room and board: $6,538.

Financial Aid: Resources specifically for eligible students enrolled in teacher education programs are awarded on the basis of financial need and academic merit. The institution has a Program Participation Agreement with the U.S. Department of Education for eligible students to receive Pell Grants and other federal aid. Teacher scholarships available to qualifying students. *Contact:* Sandra Ross at: (313) 993-3350.

Accreditation: *Regional:* NCA. *Member of:* AACTE. *Approved by:* Michigan Department of Education.

Undergraduate Programs: The College of Liberal Arts and Education offers programs leading to the Bachelor of Arts degree with elementary certification. The college also offers a Bachelor of Arts degree with secondary education for selected majors: social studies and science. The Bachelor of Science in Education is offered in the teacher certification program in special education. Students who wish to complete the requirements for a secondary teaching certificate do so in conjunction with the College of Liberal Arts or the College of Engineering Science. They pursue the degree program in their respective areas and are recommended for a teaching certificate when all requirements are completed.

Students preparing to teach in the elementary school pursue the Bachelor of Arts degree with a teaching major and a teaching minor in an academic subject area in addition to the university core curriculum requirements and the professional education sequence.

Graduate Programs: The college offers a teacher certification program for those individuals who possess a baccalaureate degree. Master's degree programs are offered in curriculum and instruction, early childhood education, special education, and secondary teacher certification.

The Master of Arts in Teaching Mathematics and the Master of Arts in School Counseling are offered outside the Arts and Education Department.

Licensure/Reciprocity: Michigan. Students seeking teaching certification in a state other than Michigan should consult with that state's teacher certification office early in their program of study to insure compliance with requirements. Many state directors of teacher credentialing have signed Interstate Agreements through NASDTEC that expedite the certification process.

UNIVERSITY OF MICHIGAN
School of Education
Educational Studies
610 East University Avenue
Ann Arbor, Michigan 48109-1259
Phone: (734) 764-1817
E-mail: soe@umich.edu
Internet: http://www.umich.edu

Institution Description: The University of Michigan is a state institution that was established in 1837. It awarded its first baccalaureate degree in 1845.

The goal of Educational Studies is to prepare scholars and educators who have the appropriate knowledge, skills, and habits of mind to provide leadership in tackling the educational issues of the 21st century.

Institution Control: Public.

Calendar: Trimester. Academic year September to May.

Official(s): Dr. Karen Wixson, Dean.

Faculty: Full-time 58.

Degrees Awarded: 151 baccalaureate; 169 master's; 30 doctorate.

Admission Requirements: *Undergraduate:* Graduation from an approved secondary school or GED; College Board SAT or ACT composite. *Teacher education specific:* Must pass the Basic Skills portion of the Michigan Test for Teacher Certification; declaration of major. *Graduate:* Baccalaureate from a regionally accredited institution. *Teacher education specific:* Teaching licensure where required by the program; pass all required tests/exams; faculty interview.

Fees and Expenses: Undergraduate: in-state $7,485 per academic year; out-of-state $23,365. Graduate: Tuition charged per credit hour. On-campus room and board: $6,375. Other expenses: $2,100. Books and supplies: $750.

Financial Aid: Resources specifically for eligible students enrolled in teacher education programs are awarded on the basis of financial need and academic merit. The institution has a Program Participation Agreement with the U.S. Department of Education for eligible students to receive Pell Grants and other federal aid. Teacher scholarships available to qualifying students. *Contact:* Financial Aid Office at: (734) 763-6600.

Accreditation: *Regional:* NCA. *Member of:* AACTE. *Approved by:* Michigan Department of Education.

Undergraduate Programs: The undergraduate elementary teacher education program prepares the student to teach in: grades K-8 in self-contained classrooms; grades 6-8 in subject area classes corresponding to the student's major and/or minor. The Bachelor of Arts or a Bachelor of Science will be awarded upon successful completion of the program. Candidates will have satisfied requirements in each of the following areas: subject matter preparation, professional and pedagogical preparation, other program requirements for certification, licensure in Michigan.

Graduate Programs: The Master's/Certification programs have been developed for students who have a B.A./B.S. degree in an area that is relevant for teaching. The certification programs include undergraduate elementary, undergraduate secondary, elementary master's, and secondary master's certification.

The Master of Arts specializations include: curriculum development, English, social studies, early childhood, educational administration and policy, educational foundations and policy, learning technologies, literacy/language and culture, mathematics, and science.

The Ph.D. specializations include: early childhood, educational administration and policy, educational foundations and policy, learning technologies, literacy/language and culture, mathematics, science, special education, teaching and teacher education, and quantitative methods in education.

Licensure/Reciprocity: Michigan. Students seeking teaching certification in a state other than Michigan should consult with that state's teacher certification office early in their program of study to insure compliance with requirements. Many state directors of teacher credentialing have signed Interstate Agreements through NASDTEC that expedite the certification process.

UNIVERSITY OF MICHIGAN - DEARBORN
School of Education
4901 Evergreen Road
Dearborn, Michigan 48128-1491
Phone: (313) 593-5090
Fax: (313) 593-9961
E-mail: Joanno@umd.umich.edu
Internet: http://www.umd.umich.edu

Institution Description: The university was established and chartered as an upper division branch campus of the University of Michigan in 1959. It became a four-year institution in 1971.

Students admitted to any of the education program are provided with an academic and professional background for teaching in multicultural society.

Institution Control: Public.

Calendar: Trimester. Academic year September to August.

Official(s): Dr. John Poster, Dean; Dr. Bonnie Beyer, Associate Dean.

UNIVERSITY OF MICHIGAN - DEARBORN—
cont'd

Faculty: Full-time 27; part-time 2; adjunct 45.

Degrees Awarded: 130 baccalaureate; 110 master's.

Admission Requirements: *Undergraduate:* Graduation with 15 academic units from an approved secondary school or GED; College Board SAT or ACT composite. *Teacher education specific:* Must pass the Basic Skills portion of the Michigan Test for Teacher Certification; declaration of major; 2.7 GPA. *Graduate:* Baccalaureate from a regionally accredited institution. *Teacher education specific:* Teaching licensure where required by the program; 3.0 GPA; pass all required tests/exams; faculty interview.

Fees and Expenses: Undergraduate: in-state $222.60 per credit hour; out-of-state $505.30. Graduate: in-state $259.95 per credit hour; out-of-state $820.50. Books and supplies: $600.

Financial Aid: Resources specifically for eligible students enrolled in teacher education programs are awarded on the basis of financial need and academic merit. The institution has a Program Participation Agreement with the U.S. Department of Education for eligible students to receive Pell Grants and other federal aid. Teacher scholarships available to qualifying students. *Contact:* John Mason at: (313) 593-5300 or e-mail at JAMason@umd.umich.edu.

Accreditation: *Regional:* NCA. *Member of:* AACTE. *Approved by:* Michigan Department of Education.

Undergraduate Programs: The elementary school certification program has been developed for those students intending to teach in either the elementary or middle school. It permits students to meet the requirements for both a bachelor's degree and the Michigan Elementary Provisional Certificate. The curriculum includes academic study and profession preparation studies. Students are required to complete all distribution requirement as well as those for the selected major and minor. Academic majors/minors may be selected from: language arts, social studies, science, or mathematics.

Secondary school certification students are endorsed to teach in their major and minor subjects. The content areas include: biology, chemistry, computer science, earth science, economics, English, English as a second language, environmental studies, French, general science, German, history, mathematics, physical science, physics, political science, psychology, social studies, sociology, Spanish, speech.

All baccalaureate programs require the completion of a general education core, professional studies, field experiences, and student teaching.

Graduate Programs: A graduate program in special education - K-12 endorsement: learning disabilities or emotional impairment requires the completion of 30 credit hours. Prior teacher certification is required. Contact the School of Education for information regarding other graduate programs offered.

Licensure/Reciprocity: Michigan. Students seeking teaching certification in a state other than Michigan should consult with that state's teacher certification office early in their program of study to insure compliance with requirements. Many state directors of teacher credentialing have signed Interstate Agreements through NASDTEC that expedite the certification process.

UNIVERSITY OF MICHIGAN - FLINT
School of Education and Human Services
Education Department
   430 David M. French Hall
   Flint, Michigan 48502-1950
   Phone: (810) 762-3260
   Fax: (810) 762-3102
   E-mail: edu@flint.umich.edu
   Internet: http://www.flint.umich.edu

Institution Description: The university was established as Flint College of the University of Michigan in 1956. The present name was adopted in 1971.

The Department of Education is the basic teacher education unit at the university. Program offerings are designed to assist prospective elementary and secondary teachers in acquiring the skills and abilities necessary for teaching in a multicultural society.

Institution Control: Public.

Calendar: Semester. Academic year July to June.

Official(s): Dr. Eric Worch, Chair, Department of Education.

Faculty: Full-time 13; emeriti 6.

Degrees Awarded: 200 baccalaureate; 27 master's.

Admission Requirements: *Undergraduate:* Graduation from an approved secondary school or GED; ACT composite. *Teacher education specific:* Completion of at least 55 semester hours of coursework; 2.75 GPA or better; pass the Basic Skills portion of the Michigan Test for Teacher Certification; declaration of major. *Graduate:* Baccalaureate from a regionally accredited institution. *Teacher education specific:* Teaching licensure where required by the program; pass all required tests/exams; faculty interview.

Fees and Expenses: Undergraduate: in-state $4,494 per academic year; out-of-state $8,990. Graduate: Tuition charged per semester hour. On-campus room and board: $5,995. Other expenses: $2,274. Books and supplies: $770.

Financial Aid: Resources specifically for eligible students enrolled in teacher education programs are awarded on the basis of financial need and academic merit. The institution has a Program Participation Agreement with the U.S. Department of Education for eligible students to receive Pell Grants and other federal aid. Teacher scholarships available to qualifying students. *Contact:* Financial Aid Office at: (810) 762-3444.

Accreditation: *Regional:* NCA. *Member of:* AACTE. *Approved by:* Michigan Department of Education.

Undergraduate Programs: Six baccalaureate programs in teacher education are available: general program for elementary teacher certification (Bachelor of Science), Bachelor of Music Education, Bachelor of Science in art education, Honors Program in elementary education (Bachelor of Science), general program for secondary teacher certification (Bachelor of Arts or Bachelor of Science). In addition, a specialization is offered in early childhood education. All baccalaureate programs require the completion of a general education core, professional studies, field experiences, and student teaching. Students are required to complete a minimum of fourteen weeks of supervised student teaching as part of the culminating program requirement.

Graduate Programs: The Education Department offers graduate programs in early childhood education; elementary education with certification, literacy (K-12); and urban/multicultural education. In addition, a graduate program in educational administration is offered in collaboration with the university's Program in Public Administration.

Licensure/Reciprocity: Michigan. Students seeking teaching certification in a state other than Michigan should consult with that state's teacher certification office early in their program of study to insure compliance with requirements. Many state directors of teacher credentialing have signed Interstate Agreements through NASDTEC that expedite the certification process.

WAYNE STATE UNIVERSITY
College of Education
Teacher Education Division
   4200 Faculty/Administration Building
   5050 Cass Avenue
   Detroit, Michigan 48202
   Phone: (313) 577-0902
   Fax: (313) 577-3200
   E-mail: admissions@wayne.edu
   Internet: http://www.wayne.edu

Institution Description: Wayne State University was established in 1933 as the Colleges of the City of Detroit through a merger of The Detroit Medical College (established 1868), Detroit Teachers College (established as Detroit Normal Training School 1881), and the College of the City of Detroit (established as a Detroit Junior College 1917). The school became a state institution and the present name was adopted in 1956.

The Teacher Education Division offers certification programs in elementary, secondary, and K-12 endorsements.

Institution Control: Public.

Calendar: Semester. Academic year August to August.

Official(s): Dr. Paula C. Wood, Dean; Dr. Sharon Elliott, Assistant Dean, Teacher Education Division.

Faculty: Full-time 51.

Degrees Awarded: 344 baccalaureate; 548 master's; 34 doctorate.

Admission Requirements: *Undergraduate:* Graduation from an approved secondary school or GED; ACT composite. *Teacher education specific:* Must pass the Basic Skills portion of the Michigan Test for Teacher Certification; declaration of major. *Graduate:* Baccalaureate from a regionally accredited institution. *Teacher education specific:* Teaching licensure where required by the program; pass all required tests/exams; faculty interview.

Fees and Expenses: Undergraduate: in-state $3,675 per academic year; out-of-state $8,260. Graduate: Tuition charged per credit hour. On-campus room and board: $6,630. Other expenses: $3,300. Books and supplies: $675.

Financial Aid: Resources specifically for eligible students enrolled in teacher education programs are awarded on the basis of financial need and academic merit. The institution has a Program Participation Agreement with the U.S. Department of Education for eligible students to receive Pell Grants and other federal aid. Teacher scholarships available to qualifying students. *Contact:* Financial Aid Office at: (313) 577-3378.

Accreditation: *Regional:* NCA. *Member of:* AACTE. *Approved by:* Michigan Department of Education.

Undergraduate Programs: The Teacher Education Division offers certification programs in elementary, secondary, and K-12 Endorsements in the areas of: art, bilingual/bicultural education, career and technical education, early childhood, English, mathematics, middle level education, reading, science, social studies, and speech. The elementary education program qualifies the holder to teach all subjects in kindergarten through grade five. Additionally, the major and minor subjects may be taught in the sixth through eighth grades. Students select a teaching major and minor or three minors.

The secondary education curriculum qualifies the holder to teach grades 7-12. Students elect an academic major and minor.

Teacher certification can be obtained as part a bachelor's degree in education, a post-bachelor's program, or a Master of Arts in Teaching. Students also have the option of earning certification in conjunction with a bachelor's degree from the College of Liberal Arts, College of Science, College of Fine/Performing;Communication Arts.

Graduate Programs: Graduate programs at the master's level are also offered in the above listed areas. At the Education Specialist level (30 hours beyond the master's) there are programs in curriculum and instruction (with a specific area of focus), special education, and reading/language/literature.

Licensure/Reciprocity: Michigan. Students seeking teaching certification in a state other than Michigan should consult with that state's teacher certification office early in their program of study to insure compliance with requirements. Many state directors of teacher credentialing have signed Interstate Agreements through NASDTEC that expedite the certification process.

WESTERN MICHIGAN UNIVERSITY

College of Education
Teaching, Learning, and Leadership

2306 Sangren Hall
1903 West Michigan Avenue
Kalamazoo, Michigan 49008-5167
Phone: (269) 387-3530
Fax: (269) 387-2096
E-mail: ask-wmu@wmich.edu
Internet: http://www.wmich.edu

Institution Description: Western Michigan University is a state institution. It was established as Western State Normal School in 1903. The name was changed to Western State Teachers College in 1927, to Western Michigan College of Education in 1941, to Western Michigan College in 1955, and to its present name in 1957.

The Department of Teaching, Learning, and Leadership is engaged in research and other activities that produce new knowledge, develop, model and provide leadership in the development of improved educational policy at all levels.

Institution Control: Public.

Calendar: Trimester. Academic year August to April.

Official(s): Dr. Van Cooley, Chair, Department of Teaching, Learning, and Leadership.

Faculty: Full-time 42; part-time 29.

Degrees Awarded: 847 baccalaureate; 488 master's; 20 doctorate.

Admission Requirements: *Undergraduate:* Graduation from an approved secondary school or GED; ACT composite. *Teacher education specific:* Must pass the Basic Skills portion of the Michigan Test for Teacher Certification; declaration of major. *Graduate:* Baccalaureate from a regionally accredited institution. *Teacher education specific:* Teaching licensure where required by the program; pass all required tests/exams; faculty interview.

Fees and Expenses: Undergraduate: in-state $4,925 per academic year; out-of-state $11,610. Graduate: Tuition charged per credit hour. On-campus room and board: $6,130. Books and supplies: $810.

Financial Aid: Resources specifically for eligible students enrolled in teacher education programs are awarded on the basis of financial need and academic merit. The institution has a Program Participation Agreement with the U.S. Department of Education for eligible students to receive Pell Grants and other federal aid. Teacher scholarships available to qualifying students. *Contact:* Financial Aid Office at: (289) 387-6000.

Accreditation: *Regional:* NCA. *Professional:* NCATE. *Member of:* AACTE. *Approved by:* Michigan Department of Education.

Undergraduate Programs: The Department of Teaching, Learning, and Leadership offers certification programs in elementary, secondary, early childhood, special education (options I and II). The elementary education program qualifies the holder to teach all subjects in kindergarten through grade five. Additionally, the major and minor subjects may be taught in the sixth through eighth grades. Students select a teaching major and minor or three minors.

The secondary education curriculum qualifies the holder to teach grades 7-12. Students elect an academic major and minor.

Teacher certification can be obtained as part a bachelor's degree in education, a post-bachelor's program, or a Master of Arts in Teaching.

All baccalaureate programs require the completion of a general education core, professional studies, field experiences, content area major/minor), and student teaching.

Graduate Programs: The Master of Arts in Educational and Professional Development offers program options in: early childhood education, reading, elementary school teaching and learning, teaching in the middle school.

WESTERN MICHIGAN UNIVERSITY—*cont'd*

Other graduate programs include the Master of Arts in educational leadership and the Education Specialist in educational leadership. Doctor of Education and Doctor of Philosophy programs in educational leadership are also offered.

Licensure/Reciprocity: Michigan. Students seeking teaching certification in a state other than Michigan should consult with that state's teacher certification office early in their program of study to insure compliance with requirements. Many state directors of teacher credentialing have signed Interstate Agreements through NASDTEC that expedite the certification process.

AUGSBURG COLLEGE

Education Department

2211 Riverside
Minneapolis, Minnesota 55454
Phone: (612) 330-1130
Fax: (612) 330-1339
E-mail: olsonv@augsburg.edu
Internet: http://www.augsburg.edu

Institution Description: Augsburg College is a private college affiliated with the Evangelical Lutheran Church in America. It was established in Wisconsin as Augsburg Seminary in 1869 and was moved to its present location in 1872. The present name was adopted in 1963.

Augsburg's Education Department offers both undergraduate and graduate programs. Their Weekend College offers the opportunity to obtain education licensure in classes that meet every other weekend and limited weekday evenings.

Institution Control: Private.

Calendar: Semester. Academic year September to May.

Official(s): Dr. Vicki Olson, Chair.

Faculty: Full-time 13; part-time 4' adjunct 23.

Degrees Awarded: 55 baccalaureate.

Admission Requirements: *Undergraduate:* Graduation from an accredited secondary school or GED; College board SAT or ACT composite. *Teacher education specific:* Minimum 2.5 GPA; letters of recommendation; PRAXIS I test scores. *Graduate:* Baccalaureate degree from a regionally accredited institution. *Teacher education specific:* 3.0 cumulative GPA; PRAXIS I and II scores; letters of recommendation; faculty interview.

Fees and Expenses: Undergraduate day $17,825 per academic year; weekend $1,440 per course. Graduate weekend $1,500 per course. On-campus room and board: $6,000 per academic year. Books and supplies: $800.

Financial Aid: Resources specifically for eligible students enrolled in teacher education programs are awarded on the basis of financial need and academic merit. The institution has a Program Participation Agreement with the U.S. Department of Education for eligible students to receive Pell Grants and other federal aid. Teacher scholarships available to qualifying students. *Contact:* Paul Terrio at: (612) 330-1049 or e-mail at terriop@augsburg.edu.

Accreditation: *Regional:* NCA. *Professional:* NCATE. *Member of:* AACTE. *Approved by:* Minnesota Board of Teaching.

Undergraduate Programs: The program in elementary education (day and weekend classes) offer specialty areas in communication arts and social studies. Specialty areas in mathematics and science are also available. The K-6 elementary with a middle school specialty license allows the graduate to teach in grades k-6 and in the specialty area of math, science, social studies, or language arts in middle school. The Weekend College offers this license to people who already hold a bachelor's degree and meet admission requirements, as well as to people seeking a bachelor's degree. The number of supporting liberal arts courses required for licensure depends upon the courses taken previously as part of the bachelor's degree.

K-12 and 5-12 licensures in secondary education for several content areas are offered in Weekend College through a combination of graduate and undergraduate coursework. The equivalent of a major in a content area is required. Majors offered in the Weekend College include: communication arts, literature, history, economics, psychology, sociology, studio arts. Majors offered primarily through the weekday program include: biology, chemistry, physics, health/physical education, theatre/dance, mathematics.

Graduate Programs: Graduate coursework completed as part of the licensure program forms the core of the education master's degree program. Up to six graduate licensure courses can be carried into the master's program. The masters' degree is attained through successful completion of a minimum of three additional graduate-level courses.

Licensure/Reciprocity: Minnesota. Students seeking teaching certification in a state other than Minnesota should consult with that state's teacher certification office early in their program of study to insure compliance with requirements. Many state directors of teacher credentialing have signed Interstate Agreements through NASDTEC that expedite the certification process.

BEMIDJI STATE UNIVERSITY

College of Professional Studies
Department of Professional Education

Education Art Building
1500 Birchmont Drive N.E.
Bemidji, Minnesota 56601-2699
Phone: (218) 755-3734
Fax: (218) 755-4048
E-mail: admissions@bemidji.msus.edu
Internet: http://www.bemidji.msus.edu

Institution Description: Bemidji State University is a public institution. It was established as Bemidji State Normal School in 1913. The name was changed to Bemidji State Teachers College in 1921 and to Bemidji State College in 1957. The present name was adopted in 1976.

The Department of Professional Education is committed to high-quality graduate education for pre-K-12 and post-secondary teachers.

Institution Control: Public.

Calendar: Quarter. Academic year September to May.

Official(s): Dr. Jack Reynolds, Chair.

Faculty: Full-time 25.

Degrees Awarded: 289 baccalaureate; 34 master's.

Admission Requirements: *Undergraduate:* Graduation from an accredited secondary school or GED; College board SAT or ACT composite. *Teacher education specific:* Minimum 2.5 GPA; letters of recommendation; PRAXIS I test scores. *Graduate:* Baccalaureate degree from a regionally accredited institution. *Teacher education specific:* 3.0 cumulative GPA; PRAXIS I and II scores; letters of recommendation; faculty interview.

Fees and Expenses: Undergraduate: in-state $5,170 per academic year; out-of-state $9,410. Graduate: Tuition charged per credit hour. On-campus room and board: $4,360. Other expenses: $700. Books and supplies: $850.

Financial Aid: Resources specifically for eligible students enrolled in teacher education programs are awarded on the basis of financial need and academic merit. The institution has a Program Participation Agreement with the U.S. Department of

BEMIDJI STATE UNIVERSITY—*cont'd*

Education for eligible students to receive Pell Grants and other federal aid. Teacher scholarships available to qualifying students. *Contact:* Financial Aid Office at: (218) 755-2034.

Accreditation: *Regional:* NCA. *Member of:* AACTE. *Approved by:* Minnesota Board of Teaching.

Undergraduate Programs: The undergraduate areas of study offered by the Department of Professional Studies include the Bachelor of Science in early childhood education, Bachelor of Science in elementary education, Bachelor of Science in secondary education, all leading to teacher licensure. The programs require the completion of a general education core, professional studies, field experiences, content area major/minor, and student teaching. Other baccalaureate programs are offered in the field of special education. A minimum of 192 quarter hours must be successfully completed for the degree award.

Graduate Programs: The Master of Science-Education degree program promotes the scholarly development of professional teachers who directly influence the learning process of preschool through post-secondary students. The program requires the completion of core courses (19 credits); electives (14-19 credits), and research (2-4 credits).

The educational/information communications and technology field of emphasis provides advanced studies in educational technology for in-service P-12 and post-secondary teachers. It is primarily an online program and is a collaborative emphasis with Minnesota State University Moorhead.

Licensure/Reciprocity: Minnesota. Students seeking teaching certification in a state other than Minnesota should consult with that state's teacher certification office early in their program of study to insure compliance with requirements. Many state directors of teacher credentialing have signed Interstate Agreements through NASDTEC that expedite the certification process.

BETHEL COLLEGE

Education Department
Box 14
3900 Bethel Drive
St. Paul, Minnesota 55112-6999
Phone: (651) 638-6339
Fax: (651) 635-8647
E-mail: bcoll-admit@bethel.edu
Internet: http://www.bethel.edu

Institution Description: Bethel College is a private college affiliated with the Baptist General Conference. It was established as Scandinavian Department of Baptist Union Theological Seminary of the University of Chicago in 1871. After several name changes, the present name was adopted in 1947. The college became a four-year institution in 1949.

Bethel College offers undergraduate and graduate programs leading to teacher certification.

Institution Control: Private.

Calendar: Semester. Academic year August to May.

Official(s): Dr. Sandi Horn, Chairman; Dr. Joy Rasmussen, Director of Graduate Programs.

Faculty: Full-time 19; part-time 16; adjunct 12.

Degrees Awarded: 95 baccalaureate; 56 master's.

Admission Requirements: *Undergraduate:* Graduation from accredited secondary school or GED; College Board SAT, ACT composite, or PSAT. *Teacher education specific:* Minimum 2.5 GPA; personal autobiographical statement; letters of recommendation; PRAXIS I test scores. *Graduate:* Baccalaureate degree from a regionally accredited institution. *Teacher education specific:* 3.0 cumulative GPA; PRAXIS I and II scores; letters of recommendation; faculty interview.

Fees and Expenses: Undergraduate $18,700 per academic year. Graduate: $325 per credit. On-campus room and board: $6,300. Books and supplies: $1,500.

Financial Aid: Resources specifically for eligible students enrolled in teacher education programs are awarded on the basis of financial need and academic merit. The institution has a

Program Participation Agreement with the U.S. Department of Education for eligible students to receive Pell Grants and other federal aid. Teacher scholarships available to qualifying students. *Contact:* Jeff Olson or Dan Nelson at: 651 638-6241.

Accreditation: *Regional:* NCA. *Member of:* AACTE. *Approved by:* Minnesota Board of Teaching.

Undergraduate Programs: The Education Department offers teacher preparation programs for elementary, secondary, and special education licensure. All programs lead to the baccalaureate degree and Minnesota licensure and require completion of general education core, professional studies, field experiences, content area major/minor, and student teaching. A minimum of 122 semester hours is required for the degree award.

Graduate Programs: The Master of Arts in Teaching is designed for college graduates who aspire to teach at the secondary level (grades 5-12). The program is a student-centered, standards-driven collaboration between students, college professors, and local school districts.

The Master of education programs include instructional leadership: K-12 and special education. The goal of these programs is to enhance the knowledge, competencies, and attitudes of experienced teachers.

The college offers graduate-level licensure options that include emotional/behavioral disorders, learning disabilities, and secondary education (grades 5-12) in communication arts and literature; general science with an emphasis in chemistry, life science, and/or physical science; mathematics, social studies, or health.

Licensure/Reciprocity: Minnesota. Students seeking teaching certification in a state other than Minnesota should consult with that state's teacher certification office early in their program of study to insure compliance with requirements. Many state directors of teacher credentialing have signed Interstate Agreements through NASDTEC that expedite the certification process.

COLLEGE OF SAINT BENEDICT

Education Department
Teacher Education Program
37 South College Avenue
St. Joseph, Minnesota 56374
Phone: (320) 363-5709
Fax: (320) 363-5136
E-mail: mopitz@csbsju.edu
Internet: http://www.csbsju.edu

Institution Description: College of St. Benedict is a private college affiliated with the Sisters of the Order of St. Benedict, Roman Catholic Church. The college was chartered as St. Benedict's College and Academy in 1887.

The Education Department, working with the other academic departments of the College of Arts and Science, builds upon the core curriculum of a liberal arts program to prepare undergraduate students to become teachers.

Institution Control: Private.

Calendar: Semester. Academic year September to May.

Official(s): Dr. Doug Mullin, Department Chair.

Faculty: Full-time 17; part-time 11.

Degrees Awarded: 58 baccalaureate.

Admission Requirements: *Undergraduate:* Graduation from an accredited secondary school or GED; College Board SAT, ACT composite, or PSAT. *Teacher education specific:* Minimum 2.5 GPA; letters of recommendation; PRAXIS I test scores.

Fees and Expenses: $18,920 per academic year. On-campus room and board: $5,790. Other expenses: $700. Books and supplies: $800.

Financial Aid: Resources specifically for eligible students enrolled in teacher education programs are awarded on the basis of financial need and academic merit. The institution has a Program Participation Agreement with the U.S. Department of Education for eligible students to receive Pell Grants and other federal aid. Teacher scholarships available to qualifying students. *Contact:* Financial Aid Office at: (320) 363-5388.

Accreditation: *Regional:* NCA. *Member of:* AACTE. *Approved by:* Minnesota Board of Teaching.

Undergraduate Programs: Programs offered include a major in elementary education, as well as various secondary and K-12 education programs. A major in elementary education leads to general teacher licensure for grades K-6 and requires a supportive content specialty leading to middle level licensure for grades 5-8. Content specialties include communication arts/literature, mathematics, science, social science, and world languages (French, German, and Spanish). A minor in secondary education leads to teacher licensure for grades 5-12 and supports a content/teaching major in communication arts/literature, mathematics, science, or social science. A minor in secondary education also supports a non-licensed content/teaching major for teaching theology for grades 5-12. K-12 licensure programs are available for content/teaching majors in music and world languages (French, German, and Spanish).

Licensure/Reciprocity: Minnesota. Students seeking teaching certification in a state other than Minnesota should consult with that state's teacher certification office early in their program of study to insure compliance with requirements. Many state directors of teacher credentialing have signed Interstate Agreements through NASDTEC that expedite the certification process.

COLLEGE OF ST. CATHERINE

Education Department
Mendel Hall, Room 201
2004 Randolph Avenue
St. Paul, Minnesota 55105
Phone: (651) 690-6000
Fax: (651) 690-8651
E-mail: education@stkate.edu
Internet: http://www.stkate.edu

Institution Description: College of St. Catherine is a private women's college affiliated with the Sisters of St. Joseph of Carondelet, Roman Catholic Church. It was established in 1905.

The Education Department is committed to developing teachers who are prepared to enter today's classroom.

Institution Control: Private.

Calendar: Semester. Academic year September to May.

Official(s): Dr. Linda Distad, Associate Dean.

Faculty: Full-time 12.

Degrees Awarded: 46 baccalaureate; 133 master's.

Admission Requirements: *Undergraduate:* Graduation from an accredited secondary school or GED; College board SAT or ACT composite. *Teacher education specific:* Minimum 2.5 GPA; letters of recommendation; PRAXIS I test scores. *Graduate:* Baccalaureate degree from a regionally accredited institution. *Teacher education specific:* 3.0 cumulative GPA; PRAXIS I and II scores; letters of recommendation; faculty interview.

Fees and Expenses: $18,250 per academic year. Graduate: Tuition charged per credit hour. On-campus room and board: $5,170. Other expenses: $550. Books and supplies: $600.

Financial Aid: Resources specifically for eligible students enrolled in teacher education programs are awarded on the basis of financial need and academic merit. The institution has a Program Participation Agreement with the U.S. Department of Education for eligible students to receive Pell Grants and other federal aid. Teacher scholarships available to qualifying students. *Contact:* Financial Aid Office at: (651) 690-6540.

Accreditation: *Regional:* NCA. *Member of:* AACTE. *Approved by:* Minnesota Board of Teaching.

Undergraduate Programs: The undergraduate education program prepares students for teaching at the elementary, secondary, and K-12 levels. Students receive either a B.A. or B.S. in elementary education and a teaching license with either a preprimary or middle level specialty. A teacher licensure program for secondary education offers students either a B.A. or B.S. in a content area and a teaching license in either secondary or kindergarten-grade 12. The content areas include: communication arts/literature, chemistry, family and consumer science,

life sciences, mathematics, and social studies. Majors for the kindergarten-grade 12 include: dance and theatre arts, music, physical education, visual arts, world languages and culture (French and Spanish).

Graduate Programs: The Master of Arts in Education program offers options in elementary with preprimary specialty (ages 3 - grade 6); elementary and middle level specialty (K-8); secondary (grades 5-12). and kindergarten - grade 12.

Teachers with valid Minnesota teaching licenses who want to add a new area(s) to their current license can do so through the Graduate Education Certificate Program. Certificates for new areas of licensure are offered at the elementary, middle school, K-12, and 5-12 levels.

Licensure/Reciprocity: Minnesota. Students seeking teaching certification in a state other than Minnesota should consult with that state's teacher certification office early in their program of study to insure compliance with requirements. Many state directors of teacher credentialing have signed Interstate Agreements through NASDTEC that expedite the certification process.

COLLEGE OF ST. SCHOLASTICA

Education Department
Office Tower Hall
1200 Kenwood Avenue
Duluth, Minnesota 55811
Phone: (218) 723-5971
Fax: (218) 723-6290
E-mail: admissions@css.edu
Internet: http://www.css.edu

Institution Description: The College of St. Scholastica is a private, independent college sponsored by the Duluth Benedictine Sisters (Roman Catholic). The college was established in 1912 and became a four-year institution with its present name in 1924.

The education program emphasizes reflective practice, student-centered learning, integration of curricular areas, and effective use of technology.

Institution Control: Private.

Calendar: Semester. Academic year September to May.

Official(s): Dr. Betty Preus, Department Chair.

Faculty: Full-time 18.

Degrees Awarded: 18 baccalaureate; 63 master's.

Admission Requirements: *Undergraduate:* Graduation from an accredited secondary school or GED; College board SAT, PSAT, or ACT. composite. *Teacher education specific:* Documentation of experiences working with children; application essay; overall 2.8 GPA; letters of recommendation; PRAXIS I test scores. *Graduate:* Baccalaureate degree from a regionally accredited institution. *Teacher education specific:* 3.0 cumulative GPA; PRAXIS I and II scores; letters of recommendation; faculty interview.

Fees and Expenses: Undergraduate: $18,216 per academic year. Graduate: Tuition charged per credit hour. On-campus room and board: $5410. Other expenses: $1,100. Books and supplies: $700.

Financial Aid: Resources specifically for eligible students enrolled in teacher education programs are awarded on the basis of financial need and academic merit. The institution has a Program Participation Agreement with the U.S. Department of Education for eligible students to receive Pell Grants and other federal aid. Teacher scholarships available to qualifying students. *Contact:* Financial Aid Office at: (218) 723-6047.

Accreditation: *Regional:* NCA. *Member of:* AACTE. *Approved by:* Minnesota Board of Teaching.

Undergraduate Programs: The Education Department prepares students to teach at the elementary/middle (K-8) and middle/secondary levels (grades 5-12). Licensure programs are also available in K-12 library media specialist, music education, and school social work. A program in Ojibwe language and culture prepares individuals to teach American Indian students. Courses to prepare individuals for coaching are also available.

COLLEGE OF ST. SCHOLASTICA—*cont'd*

Middle/secondary licensure programs are available in communication arts and literature, social studies, mathematics, life science (biology), and chemistry.

Graduate Programs: The Master of Education in curriculum and instruction provides access to graduate education through an online format. The program challenges students to examine their practice from an analytical and reflective viewpoint. Core courses are designed to provide students with a solid foundation in effective teaching practices. These courses include an emphasis on student learning, diversity issues, and authentic assessment. The curriculum and instruction program can be completed in two years with two courses per semester.

Licensure/Reciprocity: Minnesota. Students seeking teaching certification in a state other than Minnesota should consult with that state's teacher certification office early in their program of study to insure compliance with requirements. Many state directors of teacher credentialing have signed Interstate Agreements through NASDTEC that expedite the certification process.

CONCORDIA COLLEGE AT MOORHEAD

Department of Education

901 Eighth Street South
Moorhead, Minnesota 56562
Phone: (218) 299-3622
Fax: (218) 299-3947
E-mail: reinhill@cord.edu
Internet: http://www.cord.edu

Institution Description: Concordia College is a private liberal arts college affiliated with the Evangelical Lutheran Church of America. It was established in 1912.

The purpose of the Department of Education is to prepare caring, competent, and qualified teachers who act in the best interests of the students they will serve.

Institution Control: Private.

Calendar: Semester. Academic year August to May.

Official(s): Dr.Noell Reinhiller, Chair, Department of Education.

Faculty: Full-time 15.

Degrees Awarded: 106 baccalaureate.

Admission Requirements: *Undergraduate:* Graduation from an approved secondary school or GED; College Board SAT, PSAT, or ACT composite. *Teacher education specific:* Application essay; declaration of major; faculty interview; letters of recommendation; PRAXIS test scores.

Fees and Expenses: $15,635 per academic year. On-campus room and board: $4,310. Other expenses: $900. Books and supplies: $700.

Financial Aid: Resources specifically for eligible students enrolled in teacher education programs are awarded on the basis of financial need and academic merit. The institution has a Program Participation Agreement with the U.S. Department of Education for eligible students to receive Pell Grants and other federal aid. Teacher scholarships available to qualifying students. *Contact:* Financial Aid Office at: (218) 299-3010.

Accreditation: *Regional:* NCA. *Professional:* NCATE. *Member of:* AACTE. *Approved by:* Minnesota Board of Teaching.

Undergraduate Programs: Licensure programs offered by the Department of Education include elementary and secondary education. Concentrations available include: biology, business education, chemistry, communication arts/literature, French, German (major and minor), health, Latin (major and minor), mathematics, music, Norwegian (major and minor), parent education, physical education, physics, Russian, social studies, Spanish (major and minor), visual art. All programs require completion of a general education core, professional studies, field experiences, content area, and student teaching. A total of 126 semester hours with a 2.0 GPA is required for the degree.

Licensure/Reciprocity: Minnesota. Students seeking teaching certification in a state other than Minnesota should consult with that state's teacher certification office early in their program of study to insure compliance with requirements. Many state directors of teacher credentialing have signed Interstate Agreements through NASDTEC that expedite the certification process.

CONCORDIA UNIVERSITY AT ST. PAUL

College of Education
Teacher Education Professional Program

275 Syndicate Street North
St. Paul, Minnesota 55104-5494
Phone: (651) 641-8230
Fax: (651) 659-0207
E-mail: admiss@csp.edu
Internet: http://www.csp.edu

Institution Description: Concordia University at St. Paul is a private college affiliated with the Lutheran Church-Missouri Synod. It was established in 1893.

The College of Education prepares professionals in a Lutheran liberal arts environment for life-long learning and service in teaching, research, and leadership in a global community.

Institution Control: Private.

Calendar: Quarter. Academic year September to May.

Official(s): Dr. Lorrn Maly, Dean, College of Education.

Faculty: Full-time 11.

Degrees Awarded: 85 baccalaureate; 81 master's.

Admission Requirements: *Undergraduate:* Graduation from an accredited secondary school or GED; ACT composite. *Teacher education specific:* Accumulate 48 semester credits with a GPA of 2.5 or higher; PRAXIS I test; program portfolio; faculty interview. *Graduate:* Baccalaureate degree from a regionally accredited institution. *Teacher education specific:* 3.0 cumulative GPA; PRAXIS I and II scores; letters of recommendation; faculty interview.

Fees and Expenses: Undergraduate: $18,225 per academic year. Graduate: Tuition charged per credit hour On-campus room and board: $4,530. Other expenses: $1,000. Books and supplies: $500.

Financial Aid: Resources specifically for eligible students enrolled in teacher education programs are awarded on the basis of financial need and academic merit. The institution has a Program Participation Agreement with the U.S. Department of Education for eligible students to receive Pell Grants and other federal aid. Teacher scholarships available to qualifying students. *Contact:* Financial Aid Office at: (651) 641-8204.

Accreditation: *Regional:* NCA. *Professional:* NCATE. *Member of:* AACTE. *Approved by:* Minnesota Board of Teaching.

Undergraduate Programs: The College of Education offers Minnesota state-approved teaching licenses in the following areas: birth through grade 3; pre-kindergarten through grade 6; kindergarten through grade 8 (with specialties in communication arts/literature, mathematics, science, or social studies); mathematics in grades 5-12; life science in grades 9-12; visual arts—kindergarten through grade 12; English as a second language—kindergarten through grade 12; vocal and/or instrumental music—kindergarten through grade 12; physical education (grades K-12) and health (grades 5-12); parent education; special education—learning disabilities and/or emotional and behavioral disorders; bilingual education (an add-on to any of the above).

All baccalaureate programs require the completion of a general education core, professional studies, field experiences, content area major/minor, and student teaching.

The preparation of educators for Lutheran schools and churches is a collaboration between the College eof Education and the College of Vocation and Ministry.

Graduate Programs: The College of Education and the College of Graduate and Continuing Studies jointly offer a graduate program leading to a Master of Arts in Education with emphasis in early childhood education.

Licensure/Reciprocity: Minnesota. Students seeking teaching certification in a state other than Minnesota should consult with that state's teacher certification office early in their program of study to insure compliance with requirements. Many state directors of teacher credentialing have signed Interstate Agreements through NASDTEC that expedite the certification process.

GUSTAVUS ADOLPHUS COLLEGE

Education Department
800 West College Avenue
St. Peter, Minnesota 56082
Phone: (507) 933-7457
Fax: (507) 933-6020
E-mail: dpitton@gac.edu
Internet: http://www.gac.edu

Institution Description: Gustavus Adolphus College is a private college affiliated with the Evangelical Lutheran Church in America. It was established in 1862. The present name was adopted in 1876.

The Education Department offers baccalaureate programs leading to licensure in all areas from kindergarten to secondary education.

Institution Control: Private.

Calendar: Semester. Academic year September to June.

Official(s): Dr. Debra Pitton, Department Head.

Faculty: Full-time 7; part-time 1; adjunct 1.

Degrees Awarded: 36 baccalaureate.

Admission Requirements: *Undergraduate:* Graduation with at least 12 academic units from an approved secondary school or GED; College Board SAT or ACT composite. *Teacher education specific:* 2.75 overall GPA; interview; writing assessment; sophomore status; PRAXIS test.

Fees and Expenses: $18,940 per academic year. Required fees: $365. On-campus room and board: $4,900. Books and supplies: $500.

Financial Aid: Resources specifically for eligible students enrolled in teacher education programs are awarded on the basis of financial need and academic merit. The institution has a Program Participation Agreement with the U.S. Department of Education for eligible students to receive Pell Grants and other federal aid. Teacher scholarships available to qualifying students. *Contact:* Robert Helgeson at: (507) 933-7527 or rhelgeson@gac.edu.

Accreditation: *Regional:* NCA. *Professional:* NCATE. *Member of:* AACTE. *Approved by:* Minnesota Board of Teaching.

Undergraduate Programs: The Department of Education provides programs in teacher education that lead to licensure in teaching kindergarten, elementary school, middle school, and secondary school. Students in the elementary education program must complete all college requirements for the Bachelor of Arts degree; complete specified education courses, completion of multicultural and special needs field experiences; completion of requirements of one concentration area (communication arts/literature, science, social studies, mathematics) or a major in a foreign language.

A Bachelor of Arts degree with a teaching major is required to complete the secondary education program. Approved teaching majors are art, biology, chemistry, communication arts/literature, earth science, French, German, health, mathematics, music, physical education, physics, social studies, and Spanish.

Students in the elementary and secondary education programs may qualify for head coaching by completing the course requirements for a coaching major as outlined by the Department of Health and Exercise Science.

Licensure/Reciprocity: Minnesota. Students seeking teaching certification in a state other than Minnesota should consult with that state's teacher certification office early in their program of study to insure compliance with requirements. Many state directors of teacher credentialing have signed Interstate Agreements through NASDTEC that expedite the certification process.

HAMLINE UNIVERSITY

Department of Education
1536 Hewitt Avenue
St. Paul, Minnesota 55104-1284
Phone: (651) 523-2800
Fax: (651) 523-2458
E-mail: admis@hamline.edu
Internet: http://www.hamline.edu

Institution Description: Hamline University is a private, nonprofit university affiliated with the United Methodist Church. It was established in 1854.

The education program at Hamline University serves as a bridge to teaching in urban, rural, suburban, and international educational environments.

Institution Control: Private.

Calendar: Semester. Academic year September to May.

Official(s): Dr. Therese J. Riley, Chair, Education Department.

Faculty: Full-time 12.

Degrees Awarded: 212 master's; 6 doctorate.

Admission Requirements: *Undergraduate:* Graduation with 16 academic units from an accredited secondary school or GED; College Board SAT or ACT composite. *Teacher education specific:* Sophomore standing; completion of basic education course with a 2.5 GPA or above; PRAXIS tests; approval by faculty. *Graduate:* Baccalaureate degree from a regionally accredited institution. *Teacher education specific:* 3.0 cumulative GPA; PRAXIS I and II scores; letters of recommendation; faculty interview.

Fees and Expenses: $18,970 per academic year. On-campus room and board: $5,000. Other expenses: $650. Books and supplies: $1,350.

Financial Aid: Resources specifically for eligible students enrolled in teacher education programs are awarded on the basis of financial need and academic merit. The institution has a Program Participation Agreement with the U.S. Department of Education for eligible students to receive Pell Grants and other federal aid. Teacher scholarships available to qualifying students. *Contact:* Financial Aid Office at: (651) 523-2280.

Accreditation: *Regional:* NCA. *Professional:* NCATE. *Member of:* AACTE. *Approved by:* Minnesota Board of Teaching.

Undergraduate Programs: Hamline students do not major in education, but complete a full liberal arts major in the field of their choice. Completion of the professional education sequence, taken in addition to the major, leads to a Minnesota teaching license.

The Department of Education offers an elementary education major, with kindergarten through grade 1 licensure. General licensure is for grades K-6 with a middle school area of concentration for teaching grades 5-6. The secondary Licensure in grades 5 through 12 accompanies an area major. Licensure for grades Kindergarten through 12 is also offered for selected majors. Students who complete the selected teacher education program receive a Bachelor of Arts degree.

Graduate Programs: Hamline University offers instruction with a blend of theory into practice throughout all of its education programs: Master of Arts in Teaching; Master of Arts in Education; Master of Arts in English as a Second Language; Master of Arts in Education: Natural Science and Environmental Education. A Doctorate in Education may also be pursued at Hamline.

The Master of Arts in Teaching program provides initial licensure for those seeking a first teaching license (elementary, secondary, or K-12). Programs are also available for those who already hold a valid teaching license and desire an additional license in another content area.

Licensure/Reciprocity: Minnesota. Students seeking teaching certification in a state other than Minnesota should consult with that state's teacher certification office early in their program of

HAMLINE UNIVERSITY—*cont'd*

study to insure compliance with requirements. Many state directors of teacher credentialing have signed Interstate Agreements through NASDTEC that expedite the certification process.

MACALESTER COLLEGE
Educational Studies
1600 Grand Avenue
St. Paul, Minnesota 55105
Phone: (651) 696-6302
Fax: (651) 696-6033
E-mail: hughes@macalester.edu
Internet: http://www.macalester.edu

Institution Description: Macalester College is a private college affiliated with the Presbyterian Church (U.S.A.).

Macalester teacher education programs prepare students to become effective teachers across eight subject matter areas on the secondary level.

Institution Control: Private.

Calendar: Semester. Academic year September to May.

Official(s): Dr. Ruthanne Kurth-Schai, Chair.

Faculty: Full-time 1; adjunct 5.

Degrees Awarded: 4 baccalaureate.

Admission Requirements: *Undergraduate:* Graduation from an approved secondary school or GED; College Board SAT or ACT composite. *Teacher education specific:* Sophomore standing; statement of purpose; declaration of major; PRAXIS tests; approval by faculty.

Fees and Expenses: $23,775 per academic year. On-campus room and board: $6,516. Other expenses: $700. Books and supplies: $750.

Financial Aid: Resources specifically for eligible students enrolled in teacher education programs are awarded on the basis of financial need and academic merit. The institution has a Program Participation Agreement with the U.S. Department of Education for eligible students to receive Pell Grants and other federal aid. Teacher scholarships available to qualifying students. *Contact:* Financial Aid Office at: (651) 696-6214.

Accreditation: *Regional:* NCA. *Member of:* AACTE. *Approved by:* Minnesota Board of Teaching.

Undergraduate Programs: Licensure programs are offered in the following areas for secondary education (grades 5-12): social studies, communication arts and literature, mathematics, biology, chemistry, physics, earth and space science. Students usually choose major concentrations relevant to their area of licensure. The teacher education curriculum consists of four requirement categories: foundation courses; curriculum and pedagogy; student teaching and seminar, and a course in developmental psychology. The minor concentration in educational studies is designed to provide structured opportunities for students to engage in the study of education as an interdisciplinary field of social inquiry and advocacy.

Licensure/Reciprocity: Minnesota. Students seeking teaching certification in a state other than Minnesota should consult with that state's teacher certification office early in their program of study to insure compliance with requirements. Many state directors of teacher credentialing have signed Interstate Agreements through NASDTEC that expedite the certification process.

MINNESOTA STATE UNIVERSITY, MANKATO
College of Education
Department of Teacher Education
118 Armstrong Hall
Mankato, Minnesota 56001
Phone: (507) 389-5445
Fax: (507) 389-2566
E-mail: coled@mnsu.edu
Internet: http://www.mnsu.edu

Institution Description: Minnesota State University, Mankato was formerly named Mankato State University. It was established in 1868.

The College of Education offers programs in early childhood, elementary, secondary, and professional education.

Institution Control: Public.

Calendar: Semester. Academic year September to May.

Official(s): Dr. Michael A. Miller, Dean; Dr. Maureen Prenn, Coordinator of Professional Education.

Faculty: Full-time 52.

Degrees Awarded: 320 baccalaureate; 174 master's.

Admission Requirements: *Undergraduate:* Graduation from an accredited secondary school or GED; ACT composite required. *Teacher education specific:* 2.5 GPA (2.75 for elementary and early childhood programs); 30 semester credits; PRAXIS test scores; courses in human relations and introduction to education; faculty recommendations. *Graduate:* Baccalaureate degree from a regionally accredited institution. *Teacher education specific:* 3.0 GPA; GRE or Miller Analogies Test; recommendations.

Fees and Expenses: Undergraduate: in-state $4,506 per academic year; out-of-state $8,775. Graduate: in-state $6,617.50; out-of-state $10,700. On-campus room and board: $4,297.

Financial Aid: Resources specifically for eligible students enrolled in teacher education programs are awarded on the basis of financial need and academic merit. The institution has a Program Participation Agreement with the U.S. Department of Education for eligible students to receive Pell Grants and other federal aid. Teacher scholarships available to qualifying students. *Contact:* Cheryl Kalakian at: (507) 389-1215 or cheryl.kalakian@mnsu.edu.

Accreditation: *Regional:* NCA. *Professional:* NCATE. *Member of:* AACTE. *Approved by:* Minnesota Board of Teaching.

Undergraduate Programs: The Department of Educational Studies provides professional education for early childhood and elementary teachers. The general goals of the program are to develop the dispositions, knowledge, and skills of candidates for licensure; to make available pre-professional clinical experiences in order to introduce students to the total school context; to provide the direct experience of classroom teaching under supervision; to develop understanding of curriculum design in its theory and process of formulation.

The K-12 and secondary programs department prepares undergraduate and graduate students for initial licensure as professional educators in K-12, middle and high school classrooms. Concentrations available include: business education, communication arts and literature; dance and theatre; developmental adapted physical education; English as a second language; family consumer science; health sciences; instrumental and vocal music; mathematics; physical education; science; social studies; visual arts; and world languages and culture.

Graduate Programs: Master's programs are offered in the following areas: elementary and early childhood, educational technology, teaching and learning, library media education, educational leadership, experiential education. The Master of Arts in Teaching is also offered.

Educational Specialist programs include: educational administration; educational leadership; curriculum and instruction; library media education.

Licensure/Reciprocity: Minnesota. Students seeking teaching certification in a state other than Minnesota should consult with that state's teacher certification office early in their program of study to insure compliance with requirements. Many state directors of teacher credentialing have signed Interstate Agreements through NASDTEC that expedite the certification process.

MINNESOTA STATE UNIVERSITY, MOORHEAD

College of Education and Human Services
Teacher Education
1104 7th Avenue South
Moorhead, Minnesota 56563
Phone: (218) 236-2011
Fax: (218) 236-2168
E-mail: coehs@moorhead.edu
Internet: http://www.moorhead.edu

Institution Description: The school was established as Moorhead Normal School and chartered in 1885. It became a four-year institution and the name was changed to Moorhead State Teachers College in 1921. The name Moorhead State College was adopted in 1957 and the present name in 1975.

The Teacher Education program provides baccalaureate and graduate tracks leading to teaching licensure in Minnesota.

Institution Control: Public.

Calendar: Semester. Academic year August to May.

Official(s): Dr. Dorothy M. Suomala, Dean; Dr. Bobbe Shreve, Director, Teacher Education.

Faculty: Full-time 57.

Degrees Awarded: 286 baccalaureate; 43 master's.

Admission Requirements: *Undergraduate:* Graduation from an accredited secondary school or GED; College Board SAT or ACT composite. *Teacher education specific:* 2.5 GPA 30 semester credits; PRAXIS test scores; courses educational foundations; faculty recommendations. *Graduate:* Baccalaureate degree from a regionally accredited institution. *Teacher education specific:* 3.0 GPA; GRE or Miller Analogies Test; recommendations.

Fees and Expenses: Undergraduate: in-state $4,506 per academic year; out-of-state $8,775. Graduate: in-state $6,618; out-of-state $10,700. On-campus room and board: $4,300.

Financial Aid: Resources specifically for eligible students enrolled in teacher education programs are awarded on the basis of financial need and academic merit. The institution has a Program Participation Agreement with the U.S. Department of Education for eligible students to receive Pell Grants and other federal aid. Teacher scholarships available to qualifying students. *Contact:* Financial Aid Office at: (218) 236-2251.

Accreditation: *Regional:* NCA. *Professional:* NCATE. *Member of:* AACTE. *Approved by:* Minnesota Board of Teaching.

Undergraduate Programs: The Bachelor of Arts degree represents a general liberal arts degree with a major in liberal arts or fine/performing arts areas. The Bachelor of Science degree represents a degree with a major in professional areas other than liberal or fine/performing arts. Programs available include: art education, biology, early childhood, elementary education, English, chemistry, health education, mathematics, music, physical education, physics, social studies, Spanish, special education. All baccalaureate programs require the completion of a general education core, professional studies, field experiences, content area major/minor, and student teaching. Semester hours required range from 120 to 128.

Graduate Programs: A master's degree may be awarded to a holder of a baccalaureate degree and successful completion of 30 to 54 semester credits in a coherent program indicating mastery of specified knowledge and skills.

The Master of Science degree represents completion of a course of graduate studies in science, business, industry, nursing, education, or studies in the liberal or fine arts that include a professional component. Graduate programs are also offered in: counseling and student affairs; curriculum and instruction; educational leadership; reading; special education.

Licensure/Reciprocity: Minnesota. Students seeking teaching certification in a state other than Minnesota should consult with that state's teacher certification office early in their program of study to insure compliance with requirements. Many state directors of teacher credentialing have signed Interstate Agreements through NASDTEC that expedite the certification process.

ST. CLOUD STATE UNIVERSITY

College of Education
Department of Teacher Development
A132 Education Building
720 Fourth Avenue South
St. Cloud, Minnesota 56301-4498
Phone: (320) 255-5007
Fax: (320) 255-2933
E-mail: coe@stcloudstate.edu
Internet: http://www.stcloudstate.edu

Institution Description: The college was established as Third State Normal School in 1869. The name was changed to St. Cloud State Normal School in 1869, to St. Cloud State Teachers College in 1921, to St. Cloud State College in 1957, and to its present name in 1975.

The College of Education is committed to the preparation of teachers, administrators, counselors, education scholars, and other school and community professionals.

Institution Control: Public.

Calendar: Semester. Academic year September to May.

Official(s): Dr. Joanne W. McKay, Dean; Dr. Stephen Hornstein, Chair, Teacher Development.

Faculty: Full-time 24,

Degrees Awarded: 471 baccalaureate; 92 master's.

Admission Requirements: *Undergraduate:* Graduation from an approved secondary school or GED; College Board SAT, PSAT, or ACT composite. *Teacher education specific:* Admission to major program; PRAXIS tests; faculty interview and approval. *Graduate:* Baccalaureate degree from an accredited institution. *Teacher education specific:* Completion of all departmental required tests/exams; recommendations; faculty interview.

Fees and Expenses: Undergraduate: in-state $4,506 per academic year; out-of-state $8,775. Graduate: in-state $6,617.50; out-of-state $10,700. On-campus room and board: $3,788. Other expenses: $2,550. Books and supplies: $800.

Financial Aid: Resources specifically for eligible students enrolled in teacher education programs are awarded on the basis of financial need and academic merit. The institution has a Program Participation Agreement with the U.S. Department of Education for eligible students to receive Pell Grants and other federal aid. Teacher scholarships available to qualifying students. *Contact:* Financial Aid Office at: (320) 255-2047.

Accreditation: *Regional:* NCA. *Professional:* NCATE. *Member of:* AACTE. *Approved by:* Minnesota Board of Teaching.

Undergraduate Programs: The Department of Teacher Development offers an elementary education major leading to licensure for grades K-8, and the professional licensure component for students seeking subject area teaching certification in grades 5-12 and students seeking teaching certification in art, music, or physical education for grades K-12. The programs lead to the Bachelor of Science degree. All programs require the completion of a general education core, professional studies, field experiences, content area major/minor, and student teaching.

Graduate Programs: The Master of Science in curriculum and instruction is offered to applicants who have completed an undergraduate teacher education program from an accredited teacher preparation institution. The program is designed for both full-time and part-time students. Courses are offered evenings during the academic year and during the daytime in the summer.

Licensure/Reciprocity: Minnesota. Students seeking teaching certification in a state other than Minnesota should consult with that state's teacher certification office early in their program of study to insure compliance with requirements. Many state directors of teacher credentialing have signed Interstate Agreements through NASDTEC that expedite the certification process.

ST. OLAF COLLEGE
Education Department
Teacher Education Program
1520 St. Olaf Avenue
Northfield, Minnesota 55057
Phone: (507) 646-3245
Fax: (507) 646-3246
E-mail: solid@stolaf.edu
Internet: http://www.stolaf.edu

Institution Description: St. Olaf College is a private liberal arts college affiliated with Evangelical Lutheran Church in America. It was established in 1874.

The Teacher Education Program leads to teaching licensure in elementary, middle and secondary levels, and special education.

Institution Control: Private.

Calendar: Semester. Academic year September to May.

Official(s): Dr. Mark Schelske. Dean.

Faculty: Full-time 7; part-time 7; adjunct 3.

Degrees Awarded: 25 baccalaureate.

Admission Requirements: *Undergraduate:* Graduation with 15 academic units from an approved secondary school; upper 25% of graduating class; College Board SAT or ACT composite. *Teacher education specific:* Application by sophomore year; acceptable GPA; statement of purpose; faculty interview.

Fees and Expenses: Comprehensive fee $28,500 (includes tuition, fees, room and board).

Financial Aid: Resources specifically for eligible students enrolled in teacher education programs are awarded on the basis of financial need and academic merit. The institution has a Program Participation Agreement with the U.S. Department of Education for eligible students to receive Pell Grants and other federal aid. Teacher scholarships available to qualifying students. *Contact:* Katharine Ruby, Director, Financial Aid Office at: (507) 646-3019 or e-mail at ruby@stolaf.edu.

Accreditation: *Regional:* NCA. *Professional:* NCATE. *Member of:* AACTE. *Approved by:* Minnesota Board of Teaching.

Undergraduate Programs: By combining liberal arts and a major in an academic field with courses and experiences in professional education, students can meet the requirements for licensure in secondary and middle level grades (5-12) in: communications arts and literature; mathematics; science (life science, physics, chemistry); social studies; K-12 grades in world languages (French, German, Latin, Spanish); visual art, music (vocal, instrumental, classroom) and dance/theatre. Opportunities are also available for license preparation in English as a second language, special education, and elementary education K-6/5-8. The college's 4-1-4 calendar makes off-campus studies available including three programs during January and full semesters of student teaching abroad, primarily in Asia.

Licensure/Reciprocity: Minnesota. Students seeking teaching certification in a state other than Minnesota should consult with that state's teacher certification office early in their program of study to insure compliance with requirements. Many state directors of teacher credentialing have signed Interstate Agreements through NASDTEC that expedite the certification process.

SOUTHWEST MINNESOTA STATE UNIVERSITY
Department of Education
1501 State Street
Marshall, Minnesota 56258
Phone: (507) 537-7115
Fax: (507) 537-6153
E-mail: personj@southwestmsu.edu
Internet: http://www.southwestmsu.edu

Institution Description: Southwest Minnesota State University was established in 1963. The present name was adopted in 1976.

The Department of Education offers programs leading to licensure in various teaching specialties.

Institution Control: Public.

Calendar: Quarter. Academic year September to May.

Official(s): Eileen VanWie, Accreditation Coordinator.

Faculty: Full-time 11.

Degrees Awarded: 105 baccalaureate; 272 master's.

Admission Requirements: *Undergraduate:* Graduation from an approved secondary school or GED; College Board SAT or ACT composite. *Teacher education specific:* Completion of 45 semester credits; minimum 2.8 GPA; completion of foundation of education courses; PRAXIS test scores; statement of purpose; faculty interview. *Graduate:* Baccalaureate degree from a regionally accredited institution. *Teacher education specific:* Completion of all departmental required tests/exams; recommendations; faculty interview.

Fees and Expenses: Undergraduate: in-state $4,506 per academic year; out-of-state $8,775. Graduate: in-state $6,618l out-of-state $10,700. On-campus room and board: $4,265. Other expenses: $1,800. Books and supplies: $800.

Financial Aid: Resources specifically for eligible students enrolled in teacher education programs are awarded on the basis of financial need and academic merit. The institution has a Program Participation Agreement with the U.S. Department of Education for eligible students to receive Pell Grants and other federal aid. Teacher scholarships available to qualifying students. *Contact:* Financial Aid Office at: (507) 537-8281.

Accreditation: *Regional:* NCA. *Member of:* AACTE. *Approved by:* Minnesota Board of Teaching.

Undergraduate Programs: The Department of Education provides teacher licensure programs in a variety of areas: early childhood education (birth-grade 3); K-6 elementary education with specializations (preprimary education, ages 3-5; communication arts/literature grades 5-8; mathematics grades 5-8; science grades 5-8; science grades 5-8; social science grades 5-8; social science grades 5-8; world languages and cultures: Spanish K-8).

The secondary education program includes the areas of: communication arts/literature grades 5-12; health grades 5-12; mathematics grades 5-12; social science grades 5-12; science grades 5-8; biology grades 9-12; chemistry grades 9-12.

The K-12 program offers concentration in the areas of: art; music: instrumental, vocal; physical education; world languages and cultures: Spanish; developmental adaptive physical education.

All baccalaureate programs require the completion of a general education core, professional studies, field experiences, content area major/minor, and student teaching.

Graduate Programs: The Master of Science in Special Education and the Master of Science in Education (non-licensure) are provided as on-campus programs.

Licensure/Reciprocity: Minnesota. Students seeking teaching certification in a state other than Minnesota should consult with that state's teacher certification office early in their program of study to insure compliance with requirements. Many state directors of teacher credentialing have signed Interstate Agreements through NASDTEC that expedite the certification process.

UNIVERSITY OF MINNESOTA - DULUTH
College of Education and Human Service Professions
Department of Education
125 Bohannon Hall
Duluth, Minnesota 55812-3012
Phone: (218) 726-7233
Fax: (218) 726-7008
E-mail: educ@d.umn.edu
Internet: http://www.d.umn.edu

Institution Description: The institution was chartered as State Normal School in 1895. The name was changed to Duluth State Normal School in 1905, to Duluth State Teachers College in 1927, and in 1947 joined the university system and the present name was adopted.

The mission of the Department of Education is to prepare learner-sensitive educators with the knowledge, skills, and dispositions to contribute to a better society.

Institution Control: Public.

Calendar: Semester. Academic year September to May.

Official(s): Dr. Paul N. Deputy, Dean; Dr. Frank Guldbrandsen, Chair, Department of Education.

Faculty: Full-time 42.

Degrees Awarded: 212 baccalaureate; 52 master's.

Admission Requirements: UNDERGRADUATE; Open admission to students in top 35% of their secondary school graduating class; College Board SAT or ACT composite. *Teacher education specific:* Completion of 20 or more credits; 2.0 minimum GPA; PRAXIS test scores; faculty interview. *Graduate:* Baccalaureate degree from a regionally accredited institution. *Teacher education specific:* Completion of all department required tests/exams; teaching licensure if required by program pursued; 2.8 GPA; faculty interview; recommendations.

Fees and Expenses: Undergraduate: in-state $6,046 per academic year; out-of-state $17,150. Graduate: in-state $2,921 per academic year; out-of-state $5,843. Required fees: $722 per semester. On-campus room and board: $2,645 per semester. Books and supplies: $400 per semester.

Financial Aid: Resources specifically for eligible students enrolled in teacher education programs are awarded on the basis of financial need and academic merit. The institution has a Program Participation Agreement with the U.S. Department of Education for eligible students to receive Pell Grants and other federal aid. Teacher scholarships available to qualifying students. *Contact:* Brenda Herzig at: (218) 726-8000.

Accreditation: *Regional:* NCA. *Professional:* NCATE. *Member of:* AACTE. *Approved by:* Minnesota Board of Teaching.

Undergraduate Programs: The Bachelor of Applied Arts prepares students to teach in selected secondary education fields. Majors include teaching: communication arts/literature, French, German, social studies (concentrations in anthropology, economics, geography, history, political science, psychology, sociology, Spanish, women's studies. Majors in art education K-12 for the B.F.A. degree and in music education K-12 for the B.M. degree are available through the School of Fine Arts.

The Bachelor of Applied Science degree program prepares students to work with young children or teach in elementary and selected secondary education fields and offers the non-teaching field of athletic training, communication sciences and disorders, community health education, exercise science, psychology, and recreation.

Graduate Programs: The Master of Education Program for Professional Development is for those in education or human service professions. The two-year program uses the cohort model and combines traditional classroom experience and distance education delivery systems. The program requires a minimum of 30 credits.

The Master of Education in Environmental Education is designed for college graduates who plan to work as environmental educators in diverse settings such as public and private schools, institutions of higher education, nature centers, outdoor educational programs; parks and recreations programs, and independent environmental organizations.

The Master of Special Education is designed for licensed special education teachers and offers advanced training in behavior intervention planning, administration and supervision, research, and program evaluation.

A Doctor of Education degree program is offered in collaboration with the University of Minnesota-Twin Cities.

Licensure/Reciprocity: Minnesota. Students seeking teaching certification in a state other than Minnesota should consult with that state's teacher certification office early in their program of study to insure compliance with requirements. Many state directors of teacher credentialing have signed Interstate Agreements through NASDTEC that expedite the certification process.

UNIVERSITY OF MINNESOTA - MORRIS
Division of Education
600 East 4th Street
Morris, Minnesota 56267-2132
Phone: (320) 589-6800
Fax: (320) 589-6401
E-mail: jkuechle@mrs.umn.edu
Internet: http://www.mrs.umn.edu

Institution Description: The school was established in 1959 and awarded its first baccalaureate degree in 1964.

Teacher education is part of the lifelong development of an effective teacher that includes an individual's study of liberal arts disciplines and pedagogy, teaching, and other life experiences.

Institution Control: Public.

Calendar: Quarter. Academic year September to June.

Official(s): Dr. Judy Kuechle, Chair.

Faculty: Full-time 7; part-time 1; adjunct 6.

Degrees Awarded: 33 baccalaureate.

Admission Requirements: *Undergraduate:* UMM is a selective institution that considers SAT or ACT scores, class rank, GPA, course selection, community involvement, and an essay in its admission decisions. Average ACT score is 25 and 80% of students are in the top 20% of their graduating class. *Teacher education specific:* PRAXIS I; 2.5 GPA; 60 credits by sophomore year; education foundation course; interview; recommendations; faculty approval.

Fees and Expenses: Undergraduate/graduate $231 per credit. On-campus room and board: $4,500. Required fees: $600. Books and supplies: $650.

Financial Aid: Resources specifically for eligible students enrolled in teacher education programs are awarded on the basis of financial need and academic merit. The institution has a Program Participation Agreement with the U.S. Department of Education for eligible students to receive Pell Grants and other federal aid. Teacher scholarships available to qualifying students. *Contact:* Pam Engebretson at: (320) 589-6055 or e-mail at engebrpj@mrs.umn.edu.

Accreditation: *Regional:* NCA. *Professional:* NCATE. *Member of:* AACTE. *Approved by:* Minnesota Board of Teaching.

Undergraduate Programs: The elementary education major leads to licensure as a teacher for grades K-6. Students obtaining a K-6 license must also be licensed in a specialty area. The five areas offered are: preprimary, middle level communication arts/literature, middle level mathematics, middle level science, and middle level social studies.

Students seeking licensure for secondary education must have a major in one of the following fields: chemistry (9-12), communication arts and literature (9-12) dance and theatre arts (K-12), earth and space science (9-12), French (K-12), general science (5-9), German (K-12), instrumental music (K-12), life science (9-12), mathematics (5-12), physics (9-12), social studies (5-12), Spanish (K-12), visual arts (K-12), and vocal music (K-12).

All baccalaureate programs require the completion of a general education core, professional studies, field experiences, content area major/minor, and student teaching.

Licensure/Reciprocity: Minnesota. Students seeking teaching certification in a state other than Minnesota should consult with that state's teacher certification office early in their program of study to insure compliance with requirements. Many state directors of teacher credentialing have signed Interstate Agreements through NASDTEC that expedite the certification process.

UNIVERSITY OF MINNESOTA - TWIN CITIES

College of Education and Human Development
Department of Curriculum and Instruction

145 Peik Hall
178 Pillsbury Drive SE
Minneapolis, Minnesota 55455
Phone: (612) 625-6806
Fax: (612) 626-7496
E-mail: coehd@tc.umn.edu
Internet: http://www.umn.edu/tc/

Institution Description: University of Minnesota - Twin Cities is a state institution. It was established and chartered in 1851.

The Department of Curriculum and Instruction prepares teachers and educational leaders, supports the local education community through outreach programs, and is actively involved in research that provides the teaching community with valuable guidance and support.

Institution Control: Public.

Calendar: Semester. Academic year September to May.

Official(s): Dr. Steven Yussen, Dean, College of Education and Human Development; Dr. Deborah Dillon, Chair, Department of Curriculum and Instruction.

Faculty: Full-time 36 (Curriculum and Instruction).

Degrees Awarded: 194 baccalaureate; 561 master's; 67 doctorate.

Admission Requirements: *Undergraduate:* Graduation from an approved secondary school or GED; College Board SAT or ACT composite. *Teacher education specific:* Almost all licensure programs are offered at the graduate level. Undergraduate juniors or seniors who plan to teach in public schools may have preferred admission to an M.Ed./initial licensure program. *Graduate:* Baccalaureate degree from a regionally accredited institution. *Teacher education specific:* Completion of all department required tests/exams (PRAXIS I and II); teaching licensure if required by program pursued; faculty interview; recommendations.

Fees and Expenses: Undergraduate: in-state $6,280 per academic year; out-of-state $17,150. Graduate: in-state $2,921 per academic year; out-of-state $7,230. Required fees: On-campus room and board: $5,896. Other expenses: $1,745. Books and supplies: $750.

Financial Aid: Resources specifically for eligible students enrolled in teacher education programs are awarded on the basis of financial need and academic merit. The institution has a Program Participation Agreement with the U.S. Department of Education for eligible students to receive Pell Grants and other federal aid. Teacher scholarships available to qualifying students. Numerous resources for financial aid within the college, university, and elsewhere are available for qualifying students. *Contact:* Financial Aid Office at: (612) 624-1665.

Accreditation: *Regional:* NCA. *Professional:* NCATE. *Member of:* AACTE. *Approved by:* Minnesota Board of Teaching.

Undergraduate Programs: Almost all licensure programs are offered at the graduate level. Current undergraduate students and working professionals can apply. Students must have a solid grounding in their content area (the subject matter they hope to teach) whether it is biology, algebra, Spanish, geography, art, or any subject.

Graduate Programs: Teacher licensure programs (PreK-12) offered at the graduate level and leading to the master's degree in the areas of education include: agricultural education, art, business and industry, early childhood/early childhood special education, elementary, English, family, mathematics, music, physical, science, second languages and cultures, social studies, and technology.

Additional licensure programs include: adult basic education, agricultural (grades 5-12), business (grades 5-12), communication arts and literature (grades 5-12), developmental/adapted physical education (grades preK-12), English as a second language (grades K-12), kindergarten, mathematics educa-

tion (grades 5-12), middle level (grades 5-8), parent education, reading (grades K-12), science (grades 9-12), social studies (grades 5-12), special education, world languages and cultures (grades K-8 or K-12).

The Master of Education/Professional Studies program in special education includes: deaf or hard of hearing (birth-grade 12), developmental disabilities (grades K-12), learning disabilities (grades K-12).

A Doctor of Education degree program is offered in collaboration with the University of Minnesota-Duluth.

Licensure/Reciprocity: Minnesota. Students seeking teaching certification in a state other than Minnesota should consult with that state's teacher certification office early in their program of study to insure compliance with requirements. Many state directors of teacher credentialing have signed Interstate Agreements through NASDTEC that expedite the certification process.

UNIVERSITY OF ST. THOMAS

School of Education
Teacher Education

MOH 217
1000 LaSalle Avenue
Minneapolis, Minnesota 55403
Phone: (651) 962-4420
Fax: (651) 962-6160
E-mail: kjneary@stthomas.edu
Internet: http://www.stthomas.edu

Institution Description: The University of St. Thomas is a private institution affiliated with the Archdiocese of St. Paul and Minneapolis, Roman Catholic Church. It was established in 1885 and became the College of St. Thomas in 1894. The present name was adopted in 1989.

The School of Education offers both undergraduate and graduate teacher education programs leading to teaching licensure.

Institution Control: Private.

Calendar: Semester. Academic year September to May.

Official(s): Dr. David Iigoni, Chair.

Faculty: Full-time 8; adjunct 10.

Degrees Awarded: 55 baccalaureate; 336 master's; 28 doctorate.

Admission Requirements: *Undergraduate:* Graduation from an approved secondary school or GED; College Board SAT, PSAT, or ACT composite. *Teacher education specific:* Admission to major program; PRAXIS tests; faculty interview and approval. *Graduate:* Baccalaureate degree from an accredited institution. *Teacher education specific:* Completion of all departmental required tests/exams; recommendations; faculty interview.

Fees and Expenses: Undergraduate: $19,470 per academic year. Graduate: Tuition charged per credit hour. On-campus room and board: $5,860. Other expenses: $2,530. Books and supplies: $800.

Financial Aid: Resources specifically for eligible students enrolled in teacher education programs are awarded on the basis of financial need and academic merit. The institution has a Program Participation Agreement with the U.S. Department of Education for eligible students to receive Pell Grants and other federal aid. Teacher scholarships available to qualifying students. *Contact:* Financial Aid Office at: (651) 962-6550.

Accreditation: *Regional:* NCA. *Professional:* NCATE. *Member of:* AACTE. *Approved by:* Minnesota Board of Teaching.

Undergraduate Programs: The coursework in the elementary education major features an interdisciplinary approach to learning with team teaching and block scheduling of some classes. All students observe and participate in two clinical experiences in school settings for 130 hours prior to their student teaching semester. Students are also required to complete an experience in a cultural setting different from their own.

St. Thomas students interested in becoming high school teachers (grades 7-12) may earn a minor in secondary education. The program enables students to major in a specific academic discipline they would like to teach and to minor in secondary education.

The Science and Math for Elementary Education Program focuses on math and science as a discipline and includes courses in mathematics, computers in elementary education, general biology, chemistry, geology, and physics.

All baccalaureate programs require the completion of a general education core, professional studies, field experiences, and student teaching.

Graduate Programs:

Teacher Education offers a program designed to provide professional preparation of teachers for various levels of grades K-12 for post-baccalaureate initial licensure and the Master of Arts in Teaching. The elementary (K-8) program is geared toward people who have satisfactorily completed a baccalaureate degree in a field other than education, or educators who wish to add a kindergarten-elementary-middle school endorsement.

The Collaborative Urban Educator program is intended for persons who have completed a bachelor's degree in a field other than education or who already have a teaching license in something other than special education.

Licensure/Reciprocity: Minnesota. Students seeking teaching certification in a state other than Minnesota should consult with that state's teacher certification office early in their program of study to insure compliance with requirements. Many state directors of teacher credentialing have signed Interstate Agreements through NASDTEC that expedite the certification process.

WINONA STATE UNIVERSITY

College of Education
Teacher License Programs
8th and Johnson Street
Winona, Minnesota 55987-5838
Phone: (507) 457-5000
Fax: (507) 457-5620
E-mail: coe@winona.msus.edu
Internet: http://www.winona.msus.edu

Institution Description: The institution was established as First State Normal School at Winona in 1860. After several name changes over the years, the present name was adopted in 1976.

Teacher license programs are offered at the undergraduate and graduate levels.

Institution Control: Public.

Calendar: Semester. Academic year September to May.

Official(s): Dr. Jean Leicester, Chair.

Faculty: Full-time 19.

Degrees Awarded: 259 baccalaureate; 101 master's.

Admission Requirements: *Undergraduate:* Graduation from an approved secondary school or GED; College Board SAT or ACT composite. *Teacher education specific:* Declaration of a major as soon as possible; must pass writing clearance exam; completion of 30 semester hours; minimum 2.75 GPA or better; PRAXIS test scores; background experience essay; faculty interview. *Graduate:* Baccalaureate degree from a regionally accredited institution. *Teacher education specific:* Completion of all departmental required tests/exams; recommendations; faculty interview.

Fees and Expenses: Undergraduate: in-state $4,506 per academic year; out-of-state $8,775. Graduate: in-state $6,618; out-of-state $10,700. On-campus room and board: $4,180. Other expenses: $1,710. Books and supplies: $800.

Financial Aid: Resources specifically for eligible students enrolled in teacher education programs are awarded on the basis of financial need and academic merit. The institution has a Program Participation Agreement with the U.S. Department of Education for eligible students to receive Pell Grants and other federal aid. Teacher scholarships available to qualifying students. *Contact:* Financial Aid Office at: (507) 457-5090.

Accreditation: *Regional:* NCA. *Professional:* NCATE. *Member of:* AACTE. *Approved by:* Minnesota Board of Teaching.

Undergraduate Programs: The Bachelor of Arts degree represents a general liberal arts degree with a major in liberal arts or fine/performing arts areas. The Bachelor of Science degree represents a degree with a major in professional areas other than liberal or fine/performing arts. Programs available include: art education, biology, early childhood, elementary education, English, chemistry, health education, mathematics, music, physical education, physics, social studies, Spanish, special education. All baccalaureate programs require the completion of a general education core, professional studies, field experiences, content area major/minor, and student teaching. Semester hours required range from 120 to 128.

Graduate Programs: A master's degree may be awarded to a holder of a baccalaureate degree and successful completion of 30 to 54 semester credits in a coherent program indicating mastery of specified knowledge and skills.

The Master of Science degree represents completion of a course of graduate studies in science, business, industry, nursing, education, or studies in the liberal or fine arts that include a professional component. Graduate programs are also offered in: counseling and student affairs; curriculum and instruction; educational leadership; reading; special education.

Licensure/Reciprocity: Minnesota. Students seeking teaching certification in a state other than Minnesota should consult with that state's teacher certification office early in their program of study to insure compliance with requirements. Many state directors of teacher credentialing have signed Interstate Agreements through NASDTEC that expedite the certification process.

MISSISSIPPI

ALCORN STATE UNIVERSITY

School of Education and Psychology
Department of Teacher Education
Administration Building 216
1000 ASU Drive 480
Lorman, Mississippi 39096-7500
Phone: (601) 877-6200
Fax: (601) 877-3867
E-mail: ebarnes@alcorn.edu
Internet: http://www.alcorn.edu

Institution Description: Alcorn State University is a state institution and land-grant college. The present name was adopted in 1974.

The Department of Education offers teacher education programs leading to the baccalaureate and master's degrees.

Institution Control: Public.

Calendar: Semester. Academic year August to May.

Official(s): Dr. Levie T. Robinson, Chairperson, Department of Teacher Education.

Faculty: Full-time 10.

Degrees Awarded: 30 baccalaureate; 104 master's.

Admission Requirements: *Undergraduate:* Graduation with 15 academic units from an approved secondary school or GED; ACT composite. *Teacher education specific:* Student must successfully pass PRAXIS I; 2.5 GPA on 44 semester hours of core courses; must pass English Proficiency Examination; recommendations by two faculty members. *Graduate:* Baccalaureate degree from a regionally accredited institution. *Teacher education specific:* Teaching licensure where required by the program pursued; PRAXIS II passing score; faculty interview; recommendations.

Fees and Expenses: Undergraduate: in-state $3,460 per academic year; out-of-state $7,970. Graduate: Tuition is charged by the credit hour. On-campus room and board: $3,550. Other expenses: $3,000. Books and supplies: $1,000.

Financial Aid: Resources specifically for eligible students enrolled in teacher education programs are awarded on the basis of financial need and academic merit. The institution has a Program Participation Agreement with the U.S. Department of Education for eligible students to receive Pell Grants and other federal aid. Teacher scholarships available to qualifying students. *Contact:* Financial Aid Office at: (601) 877-6190.

Accreditation: *Regional:* SACS. *Professional:* NCATE. *Member of:* AACTE. *Approved by:* Mississippi State Department of Education.

Undergraduate Programs: The Department of Education is concerned with the preparation of all prospective teachers by the provision of professional education courses for those preparing to teach in elementary education (K-8), special education, and psychology/sociology. The department administers a curriculum for majors in elementary education and offers courses in secondary education.

Bachelor of Science degree programs are awarded upon the completion of a general education core, professional studies, field experiences, content area major/minor (secondary education program), and student teaching.

The special education curriculum leads to a non-categorical degree in the mildly and moderately handicapped. Areas of handicapping condition included are children with learning disabilities, mildly emotionally disturbed, mentally retarded, and severely and profoundly handicapped. Students who complete the special education curriculum are certified to teach exceptional children in both elementary and secondary schools.

Graduate Programs: The Master of Science in Education and the Educational Specialist degrees are offered in elementary education.

Licensure/Reciprocity: Mississippi. Students seeking teaching certification in a state other than Mississippi should consult with that state's teacher certification office early in their program of study to insure compliance with requirements. Many state directors of teacher credentialing have signed Interstate Agreements through NASDTEC that expedite the certification process.

DELTA STATE UNIVERSITY

College of Education
Division of Curriculum, Instruction, Leadership, and Research
215 W.M. Kethley Hall
Highway 8 West
Cleveland, Mississippi 38733
Phone: (662) 846-4100
Fax: (662) 846-4016
E-mail: coe@deltast.edu
Internet: http://www.deltast.edu

Institution Description: Delta State University was established as Delta State Teachers College in 1924. The present name was adopted in 1974.

The College of Education offers undergraduate and graduate programs leading to teacher certification.

Institution Control: Public.

Calendar: Semester. Academic year August to May.

Official(s): Dr. E.E. Caston, Dean, College of Education.

Faculty: Full-time 50.

Degrees Awarded: 195 baccalaureate; 82 master's; 1 doctorate.

Admission Requirements: *Undergraduate:* Graduation with 15 academic units from an approved secondary school or GED; ACT composite. *Teacher education specific:* Student must successfully pass PRAXIS I; 2.5 GPA on 44 semester hours of core courses; must pass English Proficiency Examination; recommendations by two faculty members. *Graduate:* Baccalaureate degree from a regionally accredited institution. *Teacher education specific:* GRE or Miller Analogies Test; teaching licensure where required by the program pursued; PRAXIS II passing score; faculty interview; recommendations.

Fees and Expenses: Undergraduate: in-state $3,548 per academic year; out-of-state $7,970. Graduate: Tuition is charged by the credit hour. On-campus room and board: $3,180. Other expenses: $3,000. Books and supplies: $700.

Financial Aid: Resources specifically for eligible students enrolled in teacher education programs are awarded on the basis of financial need and academic merit. The institution has a Program Participation Agreement with the U.S. Department of

Education for eligible students to receive Pell Grants and other federal aid. Teacher scholarships available to qualifying students. *Contact:* Financial Aid Office at: (662) 846-4670.

Accreditation: *Regional:* SACS. *Professional:* NCATE. *Member of:* AACTE. *Approved by:* Mississippi State Department of Education.

Undergraduate Programs: The Bachelor of Science in Education degree in elementary education (K-8) and secondary education programs are offered. secondary education subject majors include art, biology, business education, chemistry education, language and literature, mathematics, music, and social sciences education. All baccalaureate programs require the completion of a general education core, professional studies, field experiences, and student teaching. A minimum of 128 semester hours is required for the degree.

Graduate Programs: A candidate for the Master of Education degree must complete a minimum of 33 to 36 semester hours of graduate work consisting of core courses, major field hours and elective hours as specified. An oral and/or written examination in the candidate's major field is administered by a committee appointed by the division chair.

The Doctor of Education Degree in Professional Studies is designed to prepare educators of personal and professional stature to assume the duties and responsibilities of teaching and various types of service and leadership roles.

Licensure/Reciprocity: Mississippi. Students seeking teaching certification in a state other than Mississippi should consult with that state's teacher certification office early in their program of study to insure compliance with requirements. Many state directors of teacher credentialing have signed Interstate Agreements through NASDTEC that expedite the certification process.

JACKSON STATE UNIVERSITY

College of Education and Human Development
School of Education

Joseph H. Jackson School of Education Building
1300 John R. Lynch Street
Jackson, Mississippi 39217
Phone: (601) 979-3415
Fax: (601) 979-7048
E-mail: ivory.phillips@jsums.edu
Internet: http://www.jsums.edu

Institution Description: Jackson State University (Jackson State College until 1974) was established by the American Baptist Home Mission Society in 1877. After several name changes, the present name was adopted in 1974.

The School of Education has as its primary purpose and responsibility the development, administration, supervision, and evaluation of programs in teacher education and other related human services which support the teaching profession nnd the mission of the university.

Institution Control: Public.

Calendar: Semester. Academic year August to May.

Official(s): Dr. Ivory Phillips, Dean, College of Education and Human Development; Dr. Evelyn White, Dean, School of Education.

Faculty: Full-time 53.

Degrees Awarded: 168 baccalaureate; 119 master's; 21 doctorate.

Admission Requirements: *Undergraduate:* Graduation with 16-17 academic units from an approved secondary school or GED; College Board SAT or ACT composite. *Teacher education specific:* Completion of 44 hours of prescribed coursework; minimum 2.5 GPA; PRAXIS I examination by end of freshman year; two recommendations. *Graduate:* Baccalaureate degree from a regionally accredited institution. *Teacher education specific:* GRE or Miller Analogies Test; teaching licensure where required by the program pursued; PRAXIS II passing score; faculty interview; recommendations.

Fees and Expenses: Undergraduate: in-state $1,806 per semester; out-of-state $4,058. Graduate: in-state/out-of-state $4,058 per semester, On-campus room $333 to $665 per semester; board $234 to $268 per semester. Additional designated fees apply.

Financial Aid: Resources specifically for eligible students enrolled in teacher education programs are awarded on the basis of financial need and academic merit. The institution has a Program Participation Agreement with the U.S. Department of Education for eligible students to receive Pell Grants and other federal aid. Teacher scholarships available to qualifying students. *Contact:* Financial Aid Office at (609) 979-3415.

Accreditation: *Regional:* SACS. *Professional:* NCATE. *Member of:* AACTE. *Approved by:* Mississippi State Department of Education.

Undergraduate Programs: The School of Education offers a variety of programs leading to the Bachelor of Science and Bachelor of Science in Education degrees. Degree programs leading to teacher certification include: elementary education (K-4 and 4-8); special education; social science education; health/physical education/recreation (with concentrations in either health or physical education; content areas for secondary school. All baccalaureate programs require the completion of a general education core, professional studies, content area major/minor, field experiences, and student teaching. The programs require the completion of a minimum of 128 semester hours.

Other programs that lead to the Bachelor of Science degree but **not** to teacher certification include: child care and family education; educational technology; ethnic studies; recreation; therapeutic recreation; special education (non-teaching).

Graduate Programs: The master-level programs in elementary and early childhood education and reading allow students to develop a mastery of structure, skills, concepts, ideas, values, facts, and method of inquiry that constitute their field of specialization. The programs require the completion of 36 semester hours if the candidate does not complete a scholarly paper or thesis.

The Master of Arts in Teaching-elementary education or secondary education are alternate route programs for persons already holding bachelor non-education degrees. A minimum of 33 hours must be completed for each degree.

The Specialist in Elementary Education Program is for those persons holding a master's degree from an accredited college or university. The program objectives embrace experiences that incorporate multicultural and global perspectives that help education students understand and apply appropriate strategies for individual learning needs.

A Doctorate in early childhood education is also offered by the School of Education.

Licensure/Reciprocity: Mississippi. Students seeking teaching certification in a state other than Mississippi should consult with that state's teacher certification office early in their program of study to insure compliance with requirements. Many state directors of teacher credentialing have signed Interstate Agreements through NASDTEC that expedite the certification process.

MILLSAPS COLLEGE

Education Department
Teacher Education Program

1701 North State Street
Jackson, Mississippi 39210
Phone: (601) 974-1050
Fax: (601) 974-1059
E-mail: education@millsaps.edu
Internet: http://www.millsaps.edu

Institution Description: Millsaps College is a private college affiliated with the United Methodist Church. It was established in 1890.

The Teacher Program emphasizes leadership and scholarship and utilizes a research-as-service model.

Institution Control: Private.

MILLSAPS COLLEGE—*cont'd*

Calendar: Semester. Academic year August to May.

Official(s): Dr. Connie S. Schimmel, Chairperson.

Degrees Awarded: 14 baccalaureate.

Admission Requirements: *Undergraduate:* Graduation with 14 academic units from an approved secondary school or GED; College Board SAT or ACT composite. *Teacher education specific:* Completion of 44 hours of prescribed coursework; minimum 2.5 GPA; PRAXIS I examination by end of freshman year; PRAXIS II before graduation; two recommendations.

Fees and Expenses: $17,375 per academic year. On-campus room and board: $6,365. Other expenses: $3,850. Books and supplies: $800.

Financial Aid: Resources specifically for eligible students enrolled in teacher education programs are awarded on the basis of financial need and academic merit. The institution has a Program Participation Agreement with the U.S. Department of Education for eligible students to receive Pell Grants and other federal aid. Teacher scholarships available to qualifying students. *Contact:* Financial Aid Office at: (601) 974-1220.

Accreditation: *Regional:* SACS. *Professional:* NCATE. *Member of:* AACTE. *Approved by:* Mississippi Department of Education.

Undergraduate Programs: The teacher education program allows undergraduates to explore teaching as a career option and to become fully prepared and licensed to teach successfully at the elementary or secondary level within the regular framework of a Bachelor of Arts or Bachelor of Science degree. Participants can major in an academic subject and earn secondary and/or middle school licensure in: art, biology, chemistry, general science, English, drama, social studies, mathematics, music education (instrumental or vocal), physics, psychology, sciences, theatre, and world languages including French, Latin, Spanish, and German. Students may major in elementary education and receive licensure at the elementary school level. Students may also minor in education. Supplemental licensure is available in mild/moderate disability and gifted. All baccalaureate programs require completion of a general education core, professional studies, content area major, field experiences. and student teaching for a minimum of 128 semester hours.

Licensure/Reciprocity: Mississippi. Students seeking teaching certification in a state other than Mississippi should consult with that state's teacher certification office early in their program of study to insure compliance with requirements. Many state directors of teacher credentialing have signed Interstate Agreements through NASDTEC that expedite the certification process.

MISSISSIPPI COLLEGE

Department of Teacher Education and Leadership

College P.O. Box 4009
200 West College Street
Clinton, Mississippi 39058
Phone: (601) 925-3226
Fax: (601) 925-3804
E-mail: education@mc.edu
Internet: http://www.mc.edu

Institution Description: Mississippi College is a private college affiliated with the Mississippi Baptist Convention (Southern Baptist). It was established in 1826 and adapted the present name in 1830. It became a men's men's institution in 1850 and absorbed Hillman College, a women's institution in 1942.

The Teacher Education programs at Mississippi College lead to certification and licensure for elementary and secondary school teaching.

Institution Control: Private.

Calendar: Semester. Academic year August to May.

Official(s): Dr. Tom Williams, Chairman, Department of Teaching Education and Leadership.

Faculty: Full-time 11; part-time 1; adjunct 3.

Degrees Awarded: 84 baccalaureate; 55 master's.

Admission Requirements: *Undergraduate:* Graduation with 15 academic units from an approved secondary school or GED; College Board SAT or ACT Composite. *Teacher education specific:* ACT score of 18; personal essay; 2.5 in content area; C or better in professional courses; PRAXIS I test; writing exam; faculty interview. *Graduate:* Baccalaureate degree from a regionally accredited institution. *Teacher education specific:* GRE; PRAXIS II before graduation; teaching licensure if required by program pursued; letters of recommendation; faculty interview.

Fees and Expenses: Undergraduate: $10,888 per academic year. Graduate: $268 per credit hour. Fixed fee: $219. On-campus room and board: $5,225.

Financial Aid: Resources specifically for eligible students enrolled in teacher education programs are awarded on the basis of financial need and academic merit. The institution has a Program Participation Agreement with the U.S. Department of Education for eligible students to receive Pell Grants and other federal aid. Teacher scholarships available to qualifying students. *Contact:* Mary Giuhan at: (601) 925-3212 or e-mail at giuhan@mc.edu.

Accreditation: *Regional:* SACS. *Professional:* NCATE. *Member of:* AACTE. *Approved by:* Mississippi State Department of Education.

Undergraduate Programs: Students can major in elementary education and receive certification as an elementary school teacher or receive certification at the secondary level (English, social studies, biology, chemistry, music, art, French, Spanish, physical education, computer science, special education, mathematics) by combining a major in an academic field with a series of professional education courses. All baccalaureate programs require the completion of a general education core, professional studies, content area major, field experiences, and student teaching. A minimum of 130 credit hours must be completed for the degree award.

Graduate Programs: The Department of Teacher Education offers the Master of Education degree for elementary and secondary teachers. The degrees offered include school counseling, teaching arts, and educational leadership. The Master of Science in Education is offered in art education (K-12) and in music (K-12) in coordination with the major area departments.

Licensure/Reciprocity: Mississippi. Students seeking teaching certification in a state other than Mississippi should consult with that state's teacher certification office early in their program of study to insure compliance with requirements. Many state directors of teacher credentialing have signed Interstate Agreements through NASDTEC that expedite the certification process.

MISSISSIPPI STATE UNIVERSITY

College of Education
Department of Curriculum and Instruction

P.O. Box 6305
Mississippi State, Mississippi 39762
Phone: (662) 325-3717
Fax: (662) 325-8784
E-mail: coe@.msstate.edu
Internet: http://www.msstate.edu

Institution Description: Mississippi State University is a state institution and land-grant college. It was established as Mississippi Agricultural and Mechanical College in 1878, The name was changed to Mississippi State College in 1932 and the present name was adopted in 1958.

The Department of Curriculum and Instruction offers programs designed to prepare teachers for K-12 classrooms.

Institution Control: Public.

Calendar: Semester. Academic year August to May.

Official(s): Dr. Roy Ruby, Dean, College of Education.

Faculty: Full-time 26 (Curriculum and Instruction).

Degrees Awarded: 488 baccalaureate; 256 master's; 27 doctorate.

Admission Requirements: *Undergraduate:* Graduation from an approved secondary school or GED; ACT score of 15; may submit SAT of 720 in lieu of ACT, *Teacher education specific:* Completion of 44 hours of prescribed coursework; minimum 2.5 GPA; PRAXIS I examination by end of freshman year; two recommendations. *Graduate:* Baccalaureate degree from a regionally accredited institution. *Teacher education specific:* GRE; teaching certificate; statement of purpose; writing sample; PRAXIS II passing score; three letters of recommendation; faculty interview.

Fees and Expenses: Undergraduate: in-state $3,875 per academic year; out-of-state $8,790. Graduate: Tuition charged per credit hour. On-campus room and board: $5,200. Other expenses: $1,800. Books and supplies: $750.

Financial Aid: Resources specifically for eligible students enrolled in teacher education programs are awarded on the basis of financial need and academic merit. The institution has a Program Participation Agreement with the U.S. Department of Education for eligible students to receive Pell Grants and other federal aid. Teacher scholarships available to qualifying students. *Contact:* Financial Aid Office at: (662) 325-2450.

Accreditation: *Regional:* SACS. *Professional:* NCATE. *Member of:* AACTE. *Approved by:* Mississippi State Department of Education.

Undergraduate Programs: The Department of Curriculum and Instruction offers undergraduate study in elementary, secondary, and special education. secondary education is offered with concentrations in: biology, chemistry, physics, English/language arts, foreign language, mathematics, social studies, speech communications. All baccalaureate programs require the completion of a general education core, professional studies, content area major, field experiences, and student teaching. A minimum of 128 credit hours must be completed for the degree award.

Graduate Programs: The master-level programs in elementary, secondary, and curriculum and instruction program allow students to develop a mastery of structure, skills, concepts, ideas, values, facts, and method of inquiry that constitute their field of specialization. The programs require the completion of 36 semester hours if the candidate does not complete a scholarly paper or thesis.

The Master of Arts in Teaching-elementary education or secondary education are alternate route programs for persons already holding bachelor non-education degrees. A minimum of 33 hours must be completed for each degree.

The Education Specialist in elementary education program is for those persons holding a master's degree from an accredited college or university. The program objectives embrace experiences that incorporate multicultural and global perspectives that help education students understand and apply appropriate strategies for individual learning needs.

A doctorate in early childhood education is also offered by the Department of Curriculum and Instruction.

Licensure/Reciprocity: Mississippi. Students seeking teaching certification in a state other than Mississippi should consult with that state's teacher certification office early in their program of study to insure compliance with requirements. Many state directors of teacher credentialing have signed Interstate Agreements through NASDTEC that expedite the certification process.

MISSISSIPPI UNIVERSITY FOR WOMEN
Division of Education and Human Services
W-Box 1637
College Street
Columbus, Mississippi 39701
Phone: (662) 329-7175
Fax: (662) 329-8515
E-mail: hjenkins@muw.edu
Internet: http://www.muw.edu

Institution Description: Mississippi University for Women is a state institution. It was established in 1884, The present name was adopted in 1974.

The Department of Education and Human Services offers undergraduate and graduate programs leading to teaching licensure.

Institution Control: Public.

Calendar: Semester. Academic year August to May.

Official(s): Dr. Hal E. Jenkins, II, Division Head.

Faculty: Full-time 26; part-time 2; adjunct 10.

Degrees Awarded: 54 baccalaureate; 22 master's.

Admission Requirements: *Undergraduate:* Graduation with 15-1/2 units from an approved secondary school or GED; ACT minimum composite score of 16. *Teacher education specific:* 2.5 overall GPA; passage of PRAXIS I; faculty interview. *Graduate:* Baccalaureate from a regionally accredited institution. *Teacher education specific:* GRE; 3.0 GPA; recommendations; PRAXIS II exam prior to graduation.

Fees and Expenses: Undergraduate/graduate: in-state $3,298 per academic year; out-of-state $7,965. On-campus room and board: $3,230. Books and supplies: $1,000.

Financial Aid: Resources specifically for eligible students enrolled in teacher education programs are awarded on the basis of financial need and academic merit. The institution has a Program Participation Agreement with the U.S. Department of Education for eligible students to receive Pell Grants and other federal aid. Teacher scholarships available to qualifying students. *Contact:* Don Rainer at: (662) 329-7114 or e-mail at drainer@muw.edu.

Accreditation: *Regional:* SACS. *Professional:* NCATE. *Member of:* AACTE. *Approved by:* Mississippi State Department of Education.

Undergraduate Programs: All students preparing to teach should follow the appropriate program including: elementary education K-8; special subject area-grades K-12 (art, music, and physical education) and the various subject areas of secondary education grades 7-12 (chemistry, physical science, English, family and consumer sciences, biology, general science, mathematics, social studies). All baccalaureate programs require the completion of a general education core, professional studies, content area major, field experiences, and student teaching. A minimum of 128-133 credit hours must be completed for the degree award.

Graduate Programs: The university awards six graduate degrees: Master of Arts in Teaching, Master of Education in gifted studies, Master of Education in instructional management, Master of Science in health education, Master of Education in reading/literacy, and the Master of Science in speech-language pathology.

Licensure/Reciprocity: Mississippi. Students seeking teaching certification in a state other than Mississippi should consult with that state's teacher certification office early in their program of study to insure compliance with requirements. Many state directors of teacher credentialing have signed Interstate Agreements through NASDTEC that expedite the certification process.

MISSISSIPPI VALLEY STATE UNIVERSITY
College of Education
Department of Teacher Education
14000 Highway 82 West
Itta Bena, Mississippi 38941-1400
Phone: (601) 254-9041
Fax: (601) 254-7900
E-mail: admissions@mvsu.edu
Internet: http://www.mvsu.edu

Institution Description: Mississippi Valley State University (Mississippi Valley State College until 1974) is a state institution. It was established as Mississippi Vocational College in 1946. The present name was adopted in 1974.

The core mission of the College of Education is to prepare competent pre service and in-service teachers and other personnel for the schools of the Mississippi Delta region, the state of Mississippi, the nation, and beyond.

Institution Control: Public.

MISSISSIPPI VALLEY STATE UNIVERSITY—
cont'd

Calendar: Semester. Academic year August to May.

Official(s): Dr. Burnette Joiner, Dean, College of Education.

Faculty: Full-time 17.

Degrees Awarded: 70 baccalaureate; 50 master's.

Admission Requirements: *Undergraduate:* Graduation from an approved secondary school or GED; College Board SAT or ACT composite. *Teacher education specific:* Minimum of 45 semester hours of college credit; cumulative GPA of 2.5; portfolio review; PRAXIS I passing score; English Proficiency Examination; faculty interview. *Graduate:* Baccalaureate degree from a regionally accredited institution. *Teacher education specific:* Teacher certification in the proposed major field; 2.5 GPA; PRAXIS scores that meet Mississippi Certification requirements; GRE; demonstration of writing ability; faculty interview.

Fees and Expenses: Undergraduate in-state $3,415 per academic year; out-of-state $7,965. Graduate: Tuition charged per credit hour. On-campus room and board: $4,150. Books and supplies: $700.

Financial Aid: Resources specifically for eligible students enrolled in teacher education programs are awarded on the basis of financial need and academic merit. The institution has a Program Participation Agreement with the U.S. Department of Education for eligible students to receive Pell Grants and other federal aid. Teacher scholarships available to qualifying students. *Contact:* Financial Aid Office at: (601) 254-3338.

Accreditation: *Regional:* SACS. *Professional:* NCATE. *Member of:* AACTE. *Approved by:* Mississippi State Department of Education.

Undergraduate Programs: Undergraduate programs offered in the Teacher Education Program include elementary education and childhood education. Add-on certification/endorsement are available in speech communications, computer applications, music education instrumental, and early childhood education. All baccalaureate programs require the completion of a general education core, professional studies, content area major, field experiences, and student teaching. A minimum of 124 credit hours must be completed for the degree award.

Graduate Programs: The Master of Science in elementary education and the Master of Science in special education programs are designed to prepare graduates to accept professional responsibilities at the elementary school level and to increase their leadership role as community change agents. A minimum of 36 credit hours must be completed for the degree award.

The Master of Arts in Teaching program is for individuals matriculating from non-teacher education programs. A minimum of 33 semester hours must be completed for the degree award.

Licensure/Reciprocity: Mississippi. Students seeking teaching certification in a state other than Mississippi should consult with that state's teacher certification office early in their program of study to insure compliance with requirements. Many state directors of teacher credentialing have signed Interstate Agreements through NASDTEC that expedite the certification process.

UNIVERSITY OF MISSISSIPPI

School of Education
Department of Curriculum and Instruction
University, Mississippi 38677-1848
Phone: (662) 915-7350
Fax: (662) 915-6718
E-mail: soe@olemiss.edu
Internet: http://www.olemiss.edu

Institution Description: The University of Mississippi is a state institution. It was chartered in 1844.

The School of Education is dedicated to the preparation of professionals for the near and distant future. Its mission is to prepare skilled professionals who positively and effectively interact with all persons.

Institution Control: Public.

Calendar: Semester. Academic year August to May.

Official(s): Dr. Fannye Love, Department Chair.

Faculty: Full-time 27.

Degrees Awarded: 206 baccalaureate; 163 master's; 27 doctorate.

Admission Requirements: *Undergraduate:* Graduation with 15-1/2 units from an approved secondary school or GED; ACT minimum composite score of 18 or SAT 840. *Teacher education specific:* 2.5 overall GPA; passage of PRAXIS I; faculty interview. *Graduate:* Baccalaureate from a regionally accredited institution. *Teacher education specific:* GRE; 3.0 GPA; recommendations; PRAXIS II exam prior to graduation.

Fees and Expenses: Undergraduate: in-state $3,916 per academic year; out-of-state $8,826. Graduate: Tuition charged per credit hour. On-campus room and board: $5,200. Other expenses: $2,800. Books and supplies: $800.

Financial Aid: Resources specifically for eligible students enrolled in teacher education programs are awarded on the basis of financial need and academic merit. The institution has a Program Participation Agreement with the U.S. Department of Education for eligible students to receive Pell Grants and other federal aid. Teacher scholarships available to qualifying students. *Contact:* Financial Aid Office at: (662) 915-7175.

Accreditation: *Regional:* SACS. *Professional:* NCATE. *Member of:* AACTE. *Approved by:* Mississippi State Department of Education.

Undergraduate Programs: The elementary education curriculum includes a liberal arts core curriculum of 45 hours, courses in general education, and 41 hours of specialized professional education.

The secondary education degree programs include the areas of science, mathematics, English, foreign languages, and social studies.

The programs and services that exceptional children are provided through special education include: placement in regular or special schools; special assistance in regular and special classrooms; clinical services in psychology; remedial education, speech, and other related services.

A minimum of 131 hours must be completed for the degree award.

Graduate Programs: Graduate teacher education programs prepare professionals in three areas: elementary, secondary, and special education. These programs offer a variety of learning experiences that promote the acquisition of knowledge, skills, and dispositions that facilitate lifelong learning in an interactive and diverse society.

The Master of Education, Doctor of Education, and Doctor of Philosophy degrees are awarded upon successful completion of all requirements for the program pursued.

Licensure/Reciprocity: Mississippi. Students seeking teaching certification in a state other than Mississippi should consult with that state's teacher certification office early in their program of study to insure compliance with requirements. Many state directors of teacher credentialing have signed Interstate Agreements through NASDTEC that expedite the certification process.

UNIVERSITY OF SOUTHERN MISSISSIPPI

College of Education and Psychology
Department of Curriculum, Instruction, and Special Education
2901 Hardy
Southern Station P.O. Box 5001
Hattiesburg, Mississippi 39406-5001
Phone: (601) 266-4568
Fax: (601) 266-4062
E-mail: admissions@usm.edu
Internet: http://www.usm.edu

Institution Description: The University of Southern Mississippi is a state institution with a branch campus in Long Beach. It was chartered as Mississippi Normal College in 1910. The name was changed to State Teachers College in 1924, to Mississippi Southern College in 1940, and to its present name in 1962.

The Department of Curriculum, Instruction, and Special Education offers undergraduate and graduate programs leading to teacher certification.

Institution Control: Public.

Calendar: Semester. Academic year August to May.

Official(s): Dr. W. Lee Pierce, Dean, College of Education and Psychology; Dr. Dana Thames, Chairperson, Curriculum and Instruction.

Faculty: Full-time 17. part-time 1; adjunct 5.

Degrees Awarded: 390 baccalaureate; 226 master's; 46 doctorate.

Admission Requirements: *Undergraduate:* Graduation from an approved secondary school or GED; ACT composite minimum score of 15 required. *Teacher education specific:* 2.5 overall GPA; passage of PRAXIS I; faculty interview. *Graduate:* Baccalaureate from a regionally accredited institution. *Teacher education specific:* GRE; 3.0 GPA; recommendations; PRAXIS II exam prior to graduation; recommendations; faculty interview.

Fees and Expenses: Undergraduate: in-state $3,785 per academic year; out-of-state $8,660. Graduate: Tuition charged per credit hour. On-campus room and board: $4,450. Other expenses: $2,500. Books and supplies: $750.

Financial Aid: Resources specifically for eligible students enrolled in teacher education programs are awarded on the basis of financial need and academic merit. The institution has a Program Participation Agreement with the U.S. Department of Education for eligible students to receive Pell Grants and other federal aid. Teacher scholarships available to qualifying students. *Contact:* Financial Aid Office at: (601) 266-4774.

Accreditation: *Regional:* SACS. *Professional:* NCATE. *Member of:* AACTE. *Approved by:* Mississippi State Department of Education.

Undergraduate Programs: The Bachelor of Science degree in elementary education K-8 has areas of concentration in: English language, foreign language, reading instruction, science, and social studies. The Bachelor of Science degree in elementary education K-4 includes educational methodologies specific to kindergarten students and continuing through the early primary grades. The Bachelor of Science degree in special education K-12 prepares individuals to teach in several areas of exceptionality. All baccalaureate programs require the completion of a general education core, professional studies, content area major, field experiences, and student teaching. A minimum of 128 credit hours must be completed for the degree award.

Graduate Programs: The Department of Curriculum, Instruction, and Special Education offers graduate degrees in the areas of elementary education, early childhood education, reading instruction, secondary education, and special education. secondary areas of emphasis include: art, biology, chemistry, English, foreign language, mathematics, music education, physical education, physics, science, social studies, and speech communication. Special education offers emphasis in: behavior disorders, gifted education, learning disabilities, mental retardation (mild/moderate, severe/profound).

The Master of Science degree is offered with areas of emphasis in reading and secondary education. secondary areas of emphasis include: art, biology, chemistry, English, foreign language, mathematics, music education, physical education, physics, science, social studies, and speech communication.

Also offered by the department are the Education Specialist, Doctor of Education, and Doctor of Philosophy degree programs.

Licensure/Reciprocity: Mississippi. Students seeking teaching certification in a state other than Mississippi should consult with that state's teacher certification office early in their program of study to insure compliance with requirements. Many state directors of teacher credentialing have signed Interstate Agreements through NASDTEC that expedite the certification process.

MISSOURI

AVILA COLLEGE

Department of Education
Teacher Education Programs
11901 Wornall Road
Kansas City, Missouri 64145
Phone: (816) 942-8400
Fax: (816) 942-3362
E-mail: admissions@mail.avila.edu
Internet: http://www.avila.edu

Institution Description: Avila College is a private college affiliated with the Roman Catholic Church. It was established as College of St. Teresa, a women's college, in 1916. The present name was adopted in 1963 and the college became coeducational in 1969.

The Department of Education offers teacher certification programs at the undergraduate and graduate levels.

Institution Control: Private.

Calendar: Semester. Academic year August to July.

Official(s): Dr. Deanna Angotti, Director.

Faculty: Full-time 9; part-time 23.

Degrees Awarded: 15 baccalaureate; 59 master's.

Admission Requirements: *Undergraduate:* Graduation with 16 units from an approved secondary school or GED; College Board SAT or ACT composite. *Teacher education specific:* College Basic Academic Subjects Examination (C-BASE); completion of at least 60 semester hours of college work; professional education courses; 2.5 GPA; recommendations. *Graduate:* Baccalaureate degree from a regionally accredited institution. *Teacher education specific:* 2.5 GPA; PRAXIS Specialty Examination; faculty interview.

Fees and Expenses: Undergraduate: $14,160 per academic year. Graduate: Tuition charged per credit hour. On-campus room and board: $6,300. Other expenses: $4,150. Books and supplies; $800.

Financial Aid: Resources specifically for eligible students enrolled in teacher education programs are awarded on the basis of financial need and academic merit. The institution has a Program Participation Agreement with the U.S. Department of Education for eligible students to receive Pell Grants and other federal aid. Teacher scholarships available to qualifying students. *Contact:* Financial Aid Office at: (816) 501-3600.

Accreditation: *Regional:* NCA. *Member of:* AACTE. *Approved by:* Missouri State Department of Elementary and Secondary Education.

Undergraduate Programs: Programs for state-approved teacher education leading to licensure and the baccalaureate degree include: elementary 1-6, special education K-12, mild/moderate class categorical, middle school 5-9; secondary School 9-12 (biology, business, chemistry, English, general science, mathematics, music education, social studies, speech/theater, unified science [biology or chemistry endorsement must be specified]).

All baccalaureate programs require the completion of a general education core, professional studies, field experiences, content area major, and student teaching. A total of 128 semester hours is required for the degree.

Graduate Programs: The Graduate Level Education Certification Program is designed for the adult who has completed a baccalaureate degree and wishes to pursue teaching certification. The education courses required for the 9-12 high school teaching certificate are offered in an intensive format. Courses for elementary, special education, and middle school are also offered at a graduate level.

Licensure/Reciprocity: Missouri. Students seeking teaching certification in a state other than Missouri should consult with that state's teacher certification office early in their program of study to insure compliance with requirements. Many state directors of teacher credentialing have signed Interstate Agreements through NASDTEC that expedite the certification process.

CENTRAL MISSOURI STATE UNIVERSITY

College of Education and Human Services
Department of Curriculum and Instruction
Levinger Building 2190
Warrensburg, Missouri 64093
Phone: (660) 543-4272
Fax: (660) 543-4167
E-mail: admit@cmsu1.cmsu.edu
Internet: http://www.cmsu.edu

Institution Description: Central Missouri State University was established as State Normal School for Second National District of Missouri in 1871. The name was changed to Central Missouri State Teachers College in 1919, to Central Missouri State in 1946, and to the present name in 1972.

The Department of Curriculum and Instruction offers undergraduate and graduate programs leading to teaching licensure in Missouri.

Institution Control: Public.

Calendar: Semester. Academic year August to May.

Official(s): Ann Pearce, Special Assistant to the President.

Faculty: Full-time 23.

Degrees Awarded: 338 baccalaureate; 124 master's.

Admission Requirements: *Undergraduate:* Applicant must have placed in the upper two/thirds of graduating class; ACT composite score of 20; completion of the core high school curriculum. *Teacher education specific:* Pass all sections of the Missouri C-BASE Test; hand written autobiography; 2.75 GPA in all coursework; faculty interview. *Graduate:* Baccalaureate degree from a regionally accredited institution. *Teacher education specific:* 2.5 GPA; PRAXIS Specialty Examination; faculty interview.

Fees and Expenses: Undergraduate: in-state $3,240 per academic year; out-of-state $6,247. On-campus room and board: $4,630. Other expenses: $2,300. Books and supplies: $450.

Financial Aid: Resources specifically for eligible students enrolled in teacher education programs are awarded on the basis of financial need and academic merit. The institution has a Program Participation Agreement with the U.S. Department of Education for eligible students to receive Pell Grants and other federal aid. Teacher scholarships available to qualifying students. *Contact:* Financial Aid Office at: (660) 543-4040

Accreditation: *Regional:* NCA. *Professional:* NCATE. *Member of:* AACTE. *Approved by:* Missouri Department of Elementary and Secondary Education.

Undergraduate Programs: Undergraduate programs leading to Missouri licensure and the baccalaureate degree include early childhood, elementary, early childhood/elementary double major, middle school, and child and family development. All programs require the completion of a general education core, professional studies, content area major, field experiences, and student teaching. A total of 124 semester hours must be successfully completed for the degree award.

Graduate Programs: The Master of Science in Education degree is awarded upon completion of a minimum of 32 hours. Areas of concentration include elementary education, secondary education, and literacy education.

The Master of Arts in Teaching is an alternative-certification program designed to provide pedagogical instruction and didactics training for post-baccalaureate students interested in the teaching profession. This degree program is intensive and cohort structured.

Licensure/Reciprocity: Missouri. Students seeking teaching certification in a state other than Missouri should consult with that state's teacher certification office early in their program of study to insure compliance with requirements. Many state directors of teacher credentialing have signed Interstate Agreements through NASDTEC that expedite the certification process.

COLLEGE OF THE OZARKS
Education Department
Teacher Education Program
P.O. Box 17
Point Lookout, Missouri 65726
Phone: (417) 334-6411
Fax: (417) 348-1432
E-mail: drapinchuk@cofo.edu
Internet: http://www.cofo.edu

Institution Description: The College of the Ozarks, formerly School of the Ozarks, is a private, independent, nonprofit college related by covenant to the Presbyterian Church (U.S.A.). It was established in 1956 and became a four-year institution in 1965.

Professional educational programs are designed to help graduates be reflective decision makers and effective teachers.

Institution Control: Private.

Calendar: Semester. Academic year August to May.

Official(s): Dr. Dana Mcmahon, Director, Teacher Education.

Faculty: Full-time 4; adjunct 1.

Degrees Awarded: 45 baccalaureate.

Admission Requirements: *Undergraduate:* Graduation from an accredited secondary school or GED; ACT composite score of 20 or better. *Teacher education specific:* GPA 2.5 with 30 semester hours completed; C-BASE minimum score for each portion of the test; successful completion of PRAXIS.

Fees and Expenses: Undergraduate: Full-time students work 15 hours per week on campus in exchange for free tuition; part-time students charged at $250 per semester hour. Required fees: $175. On-campus room and board: $3,550.

Financial Aid: Resources specifically for eligible students enrolled in teacher education programs are awarded on the basis of financial need and academic merit. The institution has a Program Participation Agreement with the U.S. Department of Education for eligible students to receive Pell Grants and other federal aid. Teacher scholarships available to qualifying students. *Contact:* Kyle McCarty at: (417) 336-6411.

Accreditation: *Regional:* NCA. *Member of:* AACTE. *Approved by:* Missouri Department of Elementary and Secondary Education.

Undergraduate Programs: Undergraduate programs in teacher education lead to the Bachelor of Arts or Bachelor of Science degrees and licensure to teach in Missouri schools. Each graduate of the education program will demonstrate satisfactory knowledge and understanding of: significant content in the liberal arts core complement of the program; a variety of teaching methods and their application to the teaching-learning process; a variety of evaluation techniques essential to effective assessment of student learning; the profession of teaching as documented in current research; the specialized areas of study.

Majors are offered in elementary education and secondary education with certification endorsements available in art, French, physical education, Spanish, health, early childhood and middle school (language arts, mathematics, science, social studies, business education family and consumer sciences, agriculture). All programs require the completion of a minimum of 124 semester hours.

Licensure/Reciprocity: Missouri. Reciprocity with Arkansas. Students seeking teaching certification in other states should consult with that state's teacher certification office early in their program of study to insure compliance with requirements. Many state directors of teacher credentialing have signed Interstate Agreements through NASDTEC that expedite the certification process.

CULVER-STOCKTON COLLEGE
Division of Education
One College Hill
Canton, Missouri 63435
Phone: (217) 231-6000
Fax: (217) 231-6611
E-mail: sabegglen@culver.edu
Internet: http://www.culver.edu

Institution Description: Culver-Stockton College is a private college affiliated with the Christian Church (Disciples of Christ). It was established in 1853. The present name was adopted in 1918.

The Teacher Education Program at Culver-Stockton College prepares teacher candidates to become successful, caring, reflective practitioners in public and private PreK-12 classrooms.

Institution Control: Private.

Calendar: Semester. Academic year August to May.

Official(s): Dr. Sue R. Abegglen, Chair.

Faculty: Full-time 4; part-time 17; adjunct 4.

Degrees Awarded: 21 baccalaureate.

Admission Requirements: *Undergraduate:* Graduation from an approved secondary school or GED; College Board SAT or ACT composite. *Teacher education specific:* GPA 2.5 with 30 semester hours completed; C-BASE minimum score for each portion of the test; successful completion of PRAXIS; faculty interview.

Fees and Expenses: $11,800 per academic year. On-campus room and board: $5,200. Other expenses: $1,610. Books and supplies: $600.

Financial Aid: Resources specifically for eligible students enrolled in teacher education programs are awarded on the basis of financial need and academic merit. The institution has a Program Participation Agreement with the U.S. Department of Education for eligible students to receive Pell Grants and other federal aid. Teacher scholarships available to qualifying students. *Contact:* Karyn Bishoff at: (217) 231-6468.

Accreditation: *Regional:* NCA. *Member of* AACTE. *Approved by:* Missouri Department of Elementary and Secondary Education.

Undergraduate Programs: Certification programs offered by the Division of Education include: early education (infants and toddlers to third graders); elementary education (grades 1-6); middle school; secondary education (high school 9-12); special education.

To become certified to teach middle school or secondary school, students must choose an area of concentration (language arts, mathematics, science, social studies). secondary education majors must choose from the areas of certification in: art (k-12), biology, English, history/political science, mathematics (K-12), music (K-12), physical education (K-12), speech, theatre (K-12).

All programs require the completion of a general education core, professional education studies, content area major, field experiences, and student teaching. A minimum of 124 credit hours must be completed for the degree award.

CULVER-STOCKTON COLLEGE—*cont'd*

Licensure/Reciprocity: Missouri. Reciprocity with Illinois, Iowa, Kansas, Nebraska, South Dakota. Students seeking teaching certification in other states should consult with that state's teacher certification office early in their program of study to insure compliance with requirements. Many state directors of teacher credentialing have signed Interstate Agreements through NASDTEC that expedite the certification process.

DRURY UNIVERSITY

School of Education

Teacher Preparation Program

900 North Benton
Springfield, Missouri 65802
Phone: (417) 873-7171
Fax: (417) 873-7269
E-mail: dbeach@drury.edu
Internet: http://www.drury.edu

Institution Description: Drury University is a private, independent, nonprofit institution affiliated with the United Church of Christ and the Christian Church (Disciples of Christ). It was established as Drury College in 1873. The present name was adopted in 2000.

The mission of the teacher preparation program is to develop liberally educated professionals with a disposition to make reflective decisions, help others learn, and add value to the live of children in a global society.

Institution Control: Private.

Calendar: Semester (4-1-4 plan). Academic year August to May.

Official(s): Dr. Daniel Beach, Director, School of Education and Child Development; Dr. Terry Hudson, Director, Graduate Education Program.

Faculty: Not reported.

Degrees Awarded: 95 baccalaureate; 76 master's.

Admission Requirements: *Undergraduate:* Graduation from an approved secondary school or GED; College Board SAT or ACT composite score. *Teacher education specific:* Minimum of 30 semester hours of college credit; cumulative GPA of 2.75; C-BASE test scores; portfolio review; faculty interview. *Graduate:* Baccalaureate degree from a regionally accredited institution. *Teacher education specific:* Official transcripts of all college/university coursework; minimum 2.75 GPA; teaching licensure when required by program pursued; GRE or Miller Analogies Test; PRAXIS test before graduation.

Fees and Expenses: Undergraduate: $12,565 per academic year. Graduate: Tuition charged per academic year. On-campus room and board: $4,520. Other expenses: $3,100. Books and supplies: $1,000.

Financial Aid: Resources specifically for eligible students enrolled in teacher education programs are awarded on the basis of financial need and academic merit. The institution has a Program Participation Agreement with the U.S. Department of Education for eligible students to receive Pell Grants and other federal aid. Teacher scholarships available to qualifying students. *Contact:* Financial Aid Office at: (417) 873-7319.

Accreditation: *Regional:* NCA. *Professional:* NCATE. *Member of:* AACTE. *Approved by:* Missouri Department of Elementary and Secondary Education.

Undergraduate Programs: The university offers programs for the preparation of both elementary and secondary teachers. The professional preparation is grounded not only in the academic disciplines, but also in partnership with the public. Students participate in a series of clinical experiences that may begin as early as the freshman year and conclude in the senior year. Clinical experiences include teaching students in the public schools, field experiences related to areas of specialization, practica, and student teaching. Baccalaureate degrees conferred include elementary education, middle school education (endorsement), and secondary education. A minimum of 124 credit hours is required for the degree award.

Graduate Programs: The Master in Education degree requires successful completion of 36 semester hours. Emphasis areas include: elementary; middle school (humanities, science, or social science); secondary (humanities, science, or social science), secondary (physical education); gifted education (elementary and secondary teachers); human services; instructional technology.

Licensure/Reciprocity: Missouri. Students seeking teaching certification in a state other than Missouri should consult with that state's teacher certification office early in their program of study to insure compliance with requirements. Many state directors of teacher credentialing have signed Interstate Agreements through NASDTEC that expedite the certification process.

EVANGEL COLLEGE

Education Department

1111 North Glenstone Avenue
Springfield, Missouri 65802
Phone: (417) 865-2815
Fax: (417) 865-9599
E-mail: huechtemanb@evangel.edu
Internet: http://evangel.edu

Institution Description: Evangel College is a private college of arts and sciences affiliated with the Assemblies of God. It was established, chartered, and offered first instruction at the post-secondary level in 1955.

The Education Department, in cooperation with other departments and through its own curriculum development, implements professional career preparation programs in teaching.

Institution Control: Private.

Calendar: Semester. Academic year September to May.

Official(s): Dr. Becky Huechteman, Chair.

Faculty: Full-time (from other departments); part-time 8; adjunct 5.

Degrees Awarded: 71 baccalaureate.

Admission Requirements: *Undergraduate:* Graduation from an approved secondary school or GED; ACT composite. *Teacher education specific:* 2.5 GPA; passing of C-BASE test; minimum C grade in English composition and math course. *Graduate:* Baccalaureate degree from a regionally accredited institution. *Teacher education specific:* Official transcripts of all college/university coursework; minimum 3.0 GPA; GRE or Miller Analogies Test; letters of reference; PRAXIS test before graduation.

Fees and Expenses: Undergraduate: $9,920 per academic year. Graduate: $190 per credit hour. Required fees: $715. On-campus room and board: $1,980 to $2,980 per semester. Books and supplies: $500.

Financial Aid: Resources specifically for eligible students enrolled in teacher education programs are awarded on the basis of financial need and academic merit. The institution has a Program Participation Agreement with the U.S. Department of Education for eligible students to receive Pell Grants and other federal aid. Teacher scholarships available to qualifying students. *Contact:* Kathy White at: (417) 865-2815 or e-mail at whitek@evangel.edu.

Accreditation: *Regional:* NCA. *Professional:* NCATE. *Member of:* AACTE. *Approved by:* Missouri Department of Elementary and Secondary Education.

Undergraduate Programs: The Education Department offers teacher preparation programs leading to certification in the following areas: early childhood education (birth to grade 6); elementary education (grades 1-6); special education; middle school education (grades 5-9); secondary education (grades 9-12). All programs require the completion of a general education core, professional studies, content area major, field experiences, and student teaching. At least 135 credits are required for the degree, depending on the area.

Graduate Programs: The Master of Elementary Education program is designed for the teacher whose career goal is to remain in the classroom as a master teacher. The program provides a unique opportunity to integrate study, research, and practical experience. A total of 35 credits is required for the degree

The Master of Reading Education program is designed to prepare educational leaders in the field of reading as teachers, clinicians, supervisors, directors, and coordinators of reading programs. Coursework enables students to explore trends and issues, improve assessment, and develop effective methods and strategies for reading instruction. The degree requires the completion of 35 credit hours (38 credit hours if seeking certification).

Licensure/Reciprocity: Missouri. Students seeking teaching certification in a state other than Missouri should consult with that state's teacher certification office early in their program of study to insure compliance with requirements. Many state directors of teacher credentialing have signed Interstate Agreements through NASDTEC that expedite the certification process.

FONTBONNE COLLEGE
Division of Education
Teacher Certification Programs
6800 Wydown Boulevard
St. Louis, Missouri 63105
Phone: (314) 862-3456
Fax: (314) 889-1451
E-mail: education@fontbonne.edu
Internet: http://www.fontbonne.edu

Institution Description: Fontbonne College is a private, independent, nonprofit college sponsored by the Sisters of St. Joseph of Carondelet, Roman Catholic Church. It was established in 1917.

The Division of Education offers teacher certification programs at the undergraduate and graduate levels.

Institution Control: Private.

Calendar: Semester. Academic year August to May.

Official(s): Dr. William Freeman, Dean.

Faculty: Full-time 10.

Degrees Awarded: 83 baccalaureate; 54 master's.

Admission Requirements: *Undergraduate:* Graduation with 16 academic units from an approved secondary school or GED; College Board SAT or ACT composite. *Teacher education specific:* Completion of C-BASE test; 30 semester hours of college credit; cumulative GPA of 2.5; portfolio review; faculty interview. *Graduate:* Baccalaureate degree from a regionally accredited institution. *Teacher education specific:* Official transcripts of all college/university coursework; minimum 2.75; teaching licensure when required by program pursued; PRAXIS II tests before graduation.

Fees and Expenses: $13,714 per academic year. Graduate: Tuition charged per credit hour. On-campus room and board: $6,535. Other expenses: $3,170. Books and supplies: $700.

Financial Aid: Resources specifically for eligible students enrolled in teacher education programs are awarded on the basis of financial need and academic merit. The institution has a Program Participation Agreement with the U.S. Department of Education for eligible students to receive Pell Grants and other federal aid. Teacher scholarships available to qualifying students. *Contact:* Financial Aid Office at: (314) 889-1414.

Accreditation: *Regional:* NCA. *Member of:* AACTE. *Approved by:* Missouri Department of Elementary and Secondary Education.

Undergraduate Programs: Undergraduate teacher certification programs are available in elementary education, middle school education, special education, and secondary education. All programs lead to the Bachelor of Arts degree and require the completion of a general education core, professional requirements/teaching methods, professional courses required from other departments, and clinical experience. A minimum of 128 credit hours must be successfully completed.

Graduate Programs: Graduate program certifications offered include reading specialist (K-12), special education: mild and moderate disabilities cross-categorical (K-12, speech-language specialist (K-12), and family and consumer sciences (5-12). The Master of Arts degree is awarded for completion of the program.

Licensure/Reciprocity: Missouri. Students seeking teaching certification in a state other than Missouri should consult with that state's teacher certification office early in their program of study to insure compliance with requirements. Many state directors of teacher credentialing have signed Interstate Agreements through NASDTEC that expedite the certification process.

HARRIS-STOWE STATE COLLEGE
Department of Teacher Education
3026 Laclede Avenue
St. Louis, Missouri 63103
Phone: (314) 340-3661
Fax: (314) 340-3690
E-mail: kempl@hssc.edu
Internet: http://www.hssc.edu

Institution Description: Harris-Stowe State College is a four-year state institution. It was established in 1857 as St. Louis Normal School for women. The college became coeducational in 1940; and merged with Stowe Teachers College in 1954. The current name was adopted in 1979.

The Department of Teacher Education offers a professional curriculum that provides for the systematic exposure of students to a variety of instructional approaches.

Institution Control: Private.

Calendar: Semester. Academic year August to May.

Official(s): Dr. Larry Kemp, Department Head.

Faculty: Full-time 18.

Degrees Awarded: 52 baccalaureate.

Admission Requirements: *Undergraduate:* Graduation from an approved secondary school or GED; ACT composite score of 20 or higher. *Teacher education specific:* Completion of C-BASE test; 48 semester hours of college credit; cumulative GPA of 2.5; portfolio review; faculty interview.

Fees and Expenses: Undergraduate: in-state $2,980 per academic year; out-of-state $5,755. On-campus room and board: $6,300. Other expenses: $2,810. Books and supplies: $720.

Financial Aid: Resources specifically for eligible students enrolled in teacher education programs are awarded on the basis of financial need and academic merit. The institution has a Program Participation Agreement with the U.S. Department of Education for eligible students to receive Pell Grants and other federal aid. Teacher scholarships available to qualifying students. *Contact:* Financial Aid Office at: (314) 340-3500.

Accreditation: *Regional:* NCA. *Professional:* NCATE. *Member of:* AACTE. *Approved by:* Missouri Department of Elementary and Secondary Education.

Undergraduate Programs: The Department of Teacher Education offers four degree programs. The degrees and accompanying certification are offered in: early childhood education, elementary education, middle school education, and secondary school education. Each program consists of four major components: general education, covering the first two years of college work in basic disciplines; specialty studies including options in major and minor subject matter; professional teacher education, covering the final two years of professional studies; and field-based experiences including introductory experiences, practica, and a full semester teaching apprenticeship. The Bachelor of Science degree is awarded upon successful completion of all program requirements.

Licensure/Reciprocity: Missouri. Students seeking teaching certification in a state other than Missouri should consult with that state's teacher certification office early in their program of study to insure compliance with requirements. Many state

HARRIS-STOWE STATE COLLEGE—*cont'd*

directors of teacher credentialing have signed Interstate Agreements through NASDTEC that expedite the certification process.

LINCOLN UNIVERSITY

College of Liberal Arts, Education, and Journalism
Division of Education
820 Chestnut Street
Jefferson City, Missouri 65101
Phone: (573) 681-5000
E-mail: henryp@lincoln.edu
Internet: http://www.lincoln.edu

Institution Description: Lincoln University is a state institution. It was founded as Lincoln Institute in 1866 as a private institution. It became a state institution in 1879. The present name was adopted in 1921.

The Division of Education offers undergraduate and graduate programs leading to teaching certification in Missouri.

Institution Control: Public.

Calendar: Semester. Academic year August to May.

Official(s): Dr. Patrick Henry, Chair, Division of Education.

Faculty: Full-time 7.

Degrees Awarded: 53 baccalaureate; 42 master's.

Admission Requirements: *Undergraduate:* Graduation from an approved secondary school or GED; ACT composite required. *Teacher education specific:* C-BASE test score; 30 semester hours of college credit; cumulative GPA of 2.75; portfolio review; faculty interview. *Graduate:* Baccalaureate degree from a regionally accredited institution. *Teacher education specific:* 2.5 GPA; PRAXIS Specialty Examination; faculty interview.

Fees and Expenses: Undergraduate: in-state $3,260 per academic year; out-of-state $6,895. Graduate: Tuition is charged per credit hour. On-campus room and board: $3,790. Other expenses: $1,745. Books and supplies: $800.

Financial Aid: Resources specifically for eligible students enrolled in teacher education programs are awarded on the basis of financial need and academic merit. The institution has a Program Participation Agreement with the U.S. Department of Education for eligible students to receive Pell Grants and other federal aid. Teacher scholarships available to qualifying students. *Contact:* Financial Aid Office at: (573) 681-6156.

Accreditation: *Regional:* NCA. *Professional:* NCATE. *Member of:* AACTE. *Approved by:* Missouri Department of Elementary and Secondary Education.

Undergraduate Programs: The Bachelor of Science in Education programs offered include majors in the areas of: art, biology, business, chemistry, elementary education, English, music (instrumental and vocal), mathematics, middle school education, physical education, physics, social science, special and elementary education, special education. All programs require the completion of a general education core, professional studies, subject/content area, field experiences, and student teaching. A minimum of 124 credit hours is required for the degree award.

Education program minors include concentration areas in: instructional technology, music, and elementary education in special education.

Graduate Programs: The Master in Education degree requires successful completion of 36 semester hours. Emphasis areas include: elementary; middle school; secondary education; special education, and instructional technology.

Licensure/Reciprocity: Missouri. Students seeking teaching certification in a state other than Missouri should consult with that state's teacher certification office early in their program of study to insure compliance with requirements. Many state directors of teacher credentialing have signed Interstate Agreements through NASDTEC that expedite the certification process.

LINDENWOOD UNIVERSITY

Division of Education
Teacher Education Programs
209 South Kings Highway
St. Charles, Missouri 63301
Phone: (636) 949-2000
Fax: (636) 949-4910
E-mail: admissions@lindenwood.edu
Internet: http://www.lindenwood.edu

Institution Description: Lindenwood University, formerly Lindenwood College, offers a liberal arts program, an evening division, and a college for individualized education. The institution is a private, independent, nonprofit college informally affiliated with The Presbyterian Church (U.S.A.).

The Division of Education offers undergraduate and graduate programs leading to teaching certification in Missouri.

Institution Control: Private.

Calendar: Semester. Academic year August to May.

Official(s): Dr. Richard A. Boyle, Dean.

Faculty: Full-time 18.

Degrees Awarded: 106 baccalaureate; 423 master's.

Admission Requirements: *Undergraduate:* Graduation with 16 academic units from an approved secondary school or GED; College Board SAT or ACT composite. *Teacher education specific:* C-BASE test; portfolio review; faculty interview. *Graduate:* Baccalaureate degree from a regionally accredited institution. *Teacher education specific:* Official transcripts of all college/university coursework; minimum 2.75; teaching licensure when required by program pursued; PRAXIS II tests before student teaching.

Fees and Expenses: Undergraduate $11,200 per academic year. Graduate: Tuition charged per credit hour. On-campus room and board: $5,800. Other expenses: $5,275. Books and supplies: $2,250.

Financial Aid: Resources specifically for eligible students enrolled in teacher education programs are awarded on the basis of financial need and academic merit. The institution has a Program Participation Agreement with the U.S. Department of Education for eligible students to receive Pell Grants and other federal aid. Teacher scholarships available to qualifying students. *Contact:* Financial Aid Office at: (646) 949-4923.

Accreditation: *Regional:* NCA. *Member of:* AACTE. *Approved by:* Missouri Department of Elementary and Secondary Education.

Undergraduate Programs: Education Certification Programs include: early childhood and special education; early childhood (birth through grade 3); elementary (1-6); elementary/special education (grades K-12); middle school (grades 5-9 in mathematics, science, social studies, English, business, speech/theatre); secondary (9-12 in business, English, health, industrial technology, mathematics, marketing education, unified science, social studies, speech/theatre); special education (K-12 in learning disabilities, behaviorally disordered, mentally handicapped, cross-categorical); K-12 certification in art, foreign language (French, Spanish), music (instrumental, vocal), physical education. The baccalaureate degree is awarded upon completion of the general education core, professional studies, subject/content area, professional studies, field experiences, and student teaching.

Graduate Programs: The graduate programs offered by the Division of Education include the Master of Arts in Teaching, Master of Arts in educational administration, Master of Arts in education specialist, Master of Arts in character education, and the Master of Arts in library media. The various programs provide teachers the opportunity to enroll in graduate studies in their teaching field. The Advanced Program Certification areas include: counselor K-12, school psychological examiner, special reading, educational administration (elementary, middle, secondary), special education administrator, special education, library media specialist, educational specialist.

Licensure/Reciprocity: Missouri. Students seeking teaching certification in a state other than Missouri should consult with that state's teacher certification office early in their program of study to insure compliance with requirements. Many state directors of teacher credentialing have signed Interstate Agreements through NASDTEC that expedite the certification process.

MARYVILLE UNIVERSITY OF SAINT LOUIS

School of Education
Teacher Education Programs
13550 Conway Road
St. Louis, Missouri 63141-7299
Phone: (314) 529-9466
Fax: (314) 542-9085
E-mail: teachered@maryville.edu
Internet: http://www.maryville.edu

Institution Description: Maryville University of Saint Louis is a private, independent, nonprofit institution. It was established in 1872 by the Society of the Sacred Heart as Maryville Academy as a school for women, It became four-year college in 1923. The present name was adopted in 1991.

The School of Education in conjunction with the facilities of the School of Liberal Arts and Professional Programs and partner schools is committed to working toward the simultaneous renewal of schools and the preparation of educational leaders.

Institution Control: Private.

Calendar: Semester. Academic year August to May.

Official(s): Dr. Katharine Rasch, Dean.

Faculty: Full-time 14.

Degrees Awarded: 30 baccalaureate; 74 master's.

Admission Requirements: *Undergraduate:* Graduation from an approved secondary school or GED; College Board SAT or ACT composite. *Teacher education specific:* C-BASE score; 30 semester hours of college credit; cumulative GPA of 2.75; portfolio review; faculty interview. *Graduate:* Baccalaureate degree from a regionally accredited institution. *Teacher education specific:* Official transcripts of all college/university coursework; minimum 2.75; teaching licensure when required by program pursued; PRAXIS II test completion.

Fees and Expenses: Undergraduate: $14,400 per academic year. Graduate: Tuition charged per credit hour. On-campus room and board: $7,100. Other expenses: $4,100. Books and supplies: $850.

Financial Aid: Resources specifically for eligible students enrolled in teacher education programs are awarded on the basis of financial need and academic merit. The institution has a Program Participation Agreement with the U.S. Department of Education for eligible students to receive Pell Grants and other federal aid. Teacher scholarships available to qualifying students. *Contact:* Financial Aid Office at: (800) 627-9855, ext. 9360.

Accreditation: *Regional:* NCA. *Professional:* NCATE. *Member of:* AACTE. *Approved by:* Missouri Department of Elementary and Secondary Education.

Undergraduate Programs: The Department of Teacher Education offers the Bachelor of Arts programs in elementary education, middle level education, English (secondary English licensure), history (secondary social studies licensure), and art education. The Bachelor of Science programs include biology (secondary unified science licensure, and chemistry (secondary unified science licensure). All programs require the completion of a general education core, professional studies, subject/content area. field experiences, and student teaching. A minimum of 128 semester hours must be successfully completed.

Graduate Programs: The Master of Arts in Education degree programs include: early childhood licensure, educational leadership, gifted education endorsement, elementary education/psychology, elementary education/English, and secondary teaching and inquiry (secondary mathematics, English, unified science).

Licensure/Reciprocity: Missouri. Students seeking teaching certification in a state other than Missouri should consult with that state's teacher certification office early in their program of study to insure compliance with requirements. Many state

MISSOURI BAPTIST COLLEGE

Division of Education
Teacher Education Program
One College Park Drive
St. Louis, Missouri 63141-8698
Phone: (314) 434-2334
Fax: (314) 434-7596
E-mail: admissions@mobap.edu
Internet: http://www.mobap.edu

Institution Description: Missouri Baptist College is a private college affiliated with the Missouri Baptist Convention (Southern Baptist). It was established as an extension center of Hannibal-LaGrange College in 1957 and was chartered as Missouri Baptist College of St. Louis, a two-year institution, in 1963. The college merged with Hannibal-LaGrange College, adopted the present name in 1967, and became a four-year institution in 1972.

The Division of Education offers both undergraduate and graduate programs leading to teacher certification in Missouri.

Institution Control: Private.

Calendar: Semester. Academic year August to April.

Official(s): Dr. James French, Director, Teacher Education Certification.

Faculty: Full-time 10.

Degrees Awarded: 60 baccalaureate; 95 master's.

Admission Requirements: *Undergraduate:* Graduation from an approved secondary school or GED; ACT composite. *Teacher education specific:* C-BASE test; 30 semester hours of college credit; cumulative GPA of 2.5 portfolio review; faculty interview. *Graduate:* Baccalaureate degree from a regionally accredited institution. *Teacher education specific:* Official transcripts of all college/university coursework; minimum 2.75; teaching licensure when required by program pursued; PRAXIS tests before graduation.

Fees and Expenses: Undergraduate: $11,310 per academic year. Graduate: Tuition is charged per credit hour. On-campus room and board: $6,600. Books and supplies: $1,600.

Financial Aid: Resources specifically for eligible students enrolled in teacher education programs are awarded on the basis of financial need and academic merit. The institution has a Program Participation Agreement with the U.S. Department of Education for eligible students to receive Pell Grants and other federal aid. Teacher scholarships available to qualifying students. *Contact:* Financial Aid Office at: (314) 392-2368.

Accreditation: *Regional:* NCA. *Member of:* AACTE. *Approved by:* Missouri Department of Elementary and Secondary Education.

Undergraduate Programs: The Teacher Education Program prepares professional educators for certification in both public and private educational settings at the following levels: early childhood (birth-grade 3); early childhood special education (birth-grade 3); elementary (grades 1-6); middle school (grades 5-9); secondary (grades (9-12); cross-categorical disabilities (kindergarten-grade 12 special education); driver education (grades 9-12); library media specialist (kindergarten-grade 12); reading specialist (kindergarten-grade 12).

All programs lead to the baccalaureate degree and require the completion of a general education core, professional studies, subject/content area, field experiences, and student teaching. A minimum of 128 credit hours must be successfully completed.

Graduate Programs: The Education Division and Graduate Studies offers the following graduate programs: Master of Science in Education: Classroom Teaching (available with a variety of certification); Master of Science in Education: Counseling Education K-12 (with certification and courses leading to licensure).

MISSOURI BAPTIST COLLEGE—*cont'd*

Licensure/Reciprocity: Missouri. Students seeking teaching certification in a state other than Missouri should consult with that state's teacher certification office early in their program of study to insure compliance with requirements. Many state directors of teacher credentialing have signed Interstate Agreements through NASDTEC that expedite the certification process.

MISSOURI SOUTHERN STATE COLLEGE

School of Education
3950 East Newman Road
Joplin, Missouri 64801-1595
Phone: (417) 625-9314
Fax: (417) 659-9771
E-mail: horvath-m@mail.mssc.edu
Internet: http://www.mssc.edu

Institution Description: Missouri Southern State College is a public institution. It was established as Joplin Junior College in 1937 and began an upper division curriculum in 1967.

The School of Education offers undergraduate and graduate programs leading to teacher certification in Missouri.

Institution Control: Private.

Calendar: Semester. Academic year August to May.

Official(s): Dr. Michael Horvath, Dean, School of Education; Dr. Deborah Pulliam, Chair.

Faculty: Full-time 13; adjunct 6.

Degrees Awarded: 132 baccalaureate.

Admission Requirements: *Undergraduate:* Graduation from an approved secondary school or GED; ACT composite. *Teacher education specific:* Pass all sections of the Missouri C-BASE test; ACT enhanced score of 20 or SAT of 800; 35 semester hours of college credit; handwritten autobiography; cumulative GPA of 2.75; faculty interview.

Fees and Expenses: Undergraduate: in-state $127 per credit; out-of-state $234 per credit. Required fees: $65. On-campus room and board: $2,240-$2,440 per semester. Other fees may apply where appropriate.

Financial Aid: Resources specifically for eligible students enrolled in teacher education programs are awarded on the basis of financial need and academic merit. The institution has a Program Participation Agreement with the U.S. Department of Education for eligible students to receive Pell Grants and other federal aid. Teacher scholarships available to qualifying students. *Contact:* James Gilbert at: (417) 625-9325 or e-mail at gilbert-j@mssu.edu.

Accreditation: *Regional:* NCA. *Professional:* NCATE. *Member of:* AACTE. *Approved by:* Missouri Department of Elementary and Secondary Education.

Undergraduate Programs: The Bachelor of Science in Education programs include: elementary education; elementary education/early childhood; elementary education/special education; elementary education/TESOL; middle school education; secondary education (9-12); K-12 Education. All programs require the completion of a general education core, professional studies, subject/content area, field experiences, and student teaching. A minimum of 124 credit hours must be successfully completed for the degree award.

Licensure/Reciprocity: Missouri. Students seeking teaching certification in a state other than Missouri should consult with that state's teacher certification office early in their program of study to insure compliance with requirements. Many state directors of teacher credentialing have signed Interstate Agreements through NASDTEC that expedite the certification process.

MISSOURI WESTERN STATE COLLEGE

School of Professional Studies
Department of Education
JGM Building, Room 111
4525 Downs Drive
St. Joseph, Missouri 64507
Phone: (816) 271-4232
Fax: (816) 271-4525
E-mail: porr@mwsc.edu
Internet: http://www.mwsc.edu

Institution Description: Missouri Western State College was established in 1915 as St. Joseph Junior College and was transformed into a four-year college in 1969. The college became a full member of the state of Missouri system in 1977.

The Department of Education is concerned with the total process of helping individuals become teachers.

Institution Control: Public.

Calendar: Semester. Academic year August to May.

Official(s): Dr. Richard Porr, Chairperson.

Faculty: Full-time 11.

Degrees Awarded: 94 baccalaureate.

Admission Requirements: *Undergraduate:* Graduation from an approved secondary school or GED; ACT composite. *Teacher education specific:* Pass all sections of the Missouri C-BASE test; ACT composite of 22 or higher or SAT combined score of 1030 or higher; cumulative GPA 2.5; satisfactory completion of education foundation courses; faculty interview.

Fees and Expenses: Undergraduate: in-state $4,065 per academic year; out-of-state $7,370. On-campus room and board: $3,804. Other expenses: $2,100. Books and supplies: $700.

Financial Aid: Resources specifically for eligible students enrolled in teacher education programs are awarded on the basis of financial need and academic merit. The institution has a Program Participation Agreement with the U.S. Department of Education for eligible students to receive Pell Grants and other federal aid. Teacher scholarships available to qualifying students. *Contact:* Financial Aid Office at: (816) 271-4301.

Accreditation: *Regional:* NCA. *Professional:* NCATE. *Member of:* AACTE. *Approved by:* Missouri Department of Elementary and Secondary Education.

Undergraduate Programs: The elementary education major must select one area of academic subject concentration from a possible set of fifteen areas. Four of the concentration areas also yield additional teaching endorsements: early childhood education (grade pre-kindergarten to grade 3); early childhood-special education; mild-moderate cross categorical disabilities, and middle school education (grades 5-9). Other subject areas of concentration include English, Spanish, French, German, mathematics, reading, general science, and social science.

A Bachelor of Science in Education with a major in middle school education is offered. The middle school major must select two areas of concentration from the following core set of subjects: social studies, language arts, mathematics, and science.

Secondary teacher certification is available for grades 9-12 in most academic fields. In art, music, physical education, and foreign languages, certification is available for kindergarten to grade 12.

All programs require the completion of a general education core, professional studies, subject/content area, field experiences, and student teaching. A minimum of 124 credit hours must be successfully completed for the degree award.

Licensure/Reciprocity: Missouri. Students seeking teaching certification in a state other than Missouri should consult with that state's teacher certification office early in their program of study to insure compliance with requirements. Many state directors of teacher credentialing have signed Interstate Agreements through NASDTEC that expedite the certification process.

NORTHWEST MISSOURI STATE UNIVERSITY

College of Education and Human Services
Teacher Education Unit
264 Administration Building
800 University Drive
Maryville, Missouri 64468-6001
Phone: (660) 562-1778
Fax: (660) 562-1212
E-mail: admissions@nwmissouri.edu
Internet: http://www.nwmissouri.edu

Institution Description: Northwest Missouri State University was established in 1905. The name became Northwest Missouri State Teachers College in 1919, Northwest Missouri State College in 1949, and the present name in 1972.

The Teacher Education Unit is made up of two main departments: Curriculum and Instruction and Education Leadership. These two departments work closely together to provide a comprehensive learning environment for all teacher education candidates.

Institution Control: Public.

Calendar: Semester. Academic year August to May.

Official(s): Dr. Max Ruhl, Dean.

Faculty: Full-time 34.

Degrees Awarded: 190 baccalaureate; 130 master's.

Admission Requirements: *Undergraduate:* Graduation from an approved secondary school or GED; College Board SAT or ACT composite. *Teacher education specific:* Pass all sections of the Missouri C-BASE test; 35 semester hours of college credit; cumulative GPA of 2.75; portfolio review; faculty interview. *Graduate:* Baccalaureate degree from a regionally accredited institution. *Teacher education specific:* Official transcripts of all college/university coursework; minimum 2.75; teaching licensure when required by program pursued; PRAXIS tests before graduation.

Fees and Expenses: Undergraduate: in-state $4,410 per academic year; out-of-state $7,255. Graduate: Tuition charged per credit hour. On-campus room and board: $4,560. Other expenses: $2,050. Books and supplies: $400.

Financial Aid: Resources specifically for eligible students enrolled in teacher education programs are awarded on the basis of financial need and academic merit. The institution has a Program Participation Agreement with the U.S. Department of Education for eligible students to receive Pell Grants and other federal aid. Teacher scholarships available to qualifying students. *Contact:* Financial Aid Office at: (660) 562-1363.

Accreditation: *Regional:* NCA. *Professional:* NCATE. *Member of:* AACTE. *Approved by:* Missouri Department of Elementary and Secondary Education.

Undergraduate Programs: The Teacher Education Unit offers undergraduate programs leading to the bachelor's degree and certification. These programs include: elementary education, middle school education (subject area concentrations required), special education, art, music, modern languages, business, communications/theatre arts, English, family and consumer science, physical education, mathematics, science, social studies, vocational agriculture.

All programs require the completion of a general education core, professional studies, subject/content area, field experiences, and student teaching. A minimum of 124 credit hours must be successfully completed for the degree award.

Graduate Programs: The Master of Science in Education offers the following areas of concentration: educational leadership; English; guidance and counseling; health and physical education; special education; reading; science; teaching: agriculture, English, early childhood, instructional technology, elementary, mathematics, middle school, music, history; teaching and learning: elementary online degree.

Licensure/Reciprocity: Missouri. Students seeking teaching certification in a state other than Missouri should consult with that state's teacher certification office early in their program of study to insure compliance with requirements. Many state directors of teacher credentialing have signed Interstate Agreements through NASDTEC that expedite the certification process.

PARK UNIVERSITY

School of Education
8700 NW River Park Drive
Parkville, Missouri 64152-3795
Phone: (816) 585-6335
Fax: (816) 741-4371
E-mail: eddept@mail.park.edu
Internet: http://www.park.edu

Institution Description: Park University is a private institution affiliated with the Reorganized Church of Jesus Christ of Latter Day Saints. It was established in 1875.

The School of Education offers graduate and undergraduate programs leading to teaching certification.

Institution Control: Private.

Calendar: Semester. Academic year August to May.

Official(s): Dr. Patricia Hutchens McCleellan, Associate Dean.

Faculty: Full-time 10; part-time 22.

Degrees Awarded: 49 baccalaureate; 23 master's.

Admission Requirements: *Undergraduate:* Graduation from an approved secondary school or GED; ACT composite score of 21; top 50% of graduating class. *Teacher education specific:* 2.75 GPA; pass all sections of Missouri C-BASE test; interview. *Graduate:* Baccalaureate degree from a regionally accredited institution. *Teacher education specific:* Official transcripts of all college/university coursework; minimum 2.75; teaching licensure when required by program pursued; PRAXIS tests before graduation.

Fees and Expenses: Undergraduate: $200 per credit hour. Graduate: $270 per credit hour. On-campus room and board: $5,500 per academic year. Books and supplies: $800.

Financial Aid: Resources specifically for eligible students enrolled in teacher education programs are awarded on the basis of financial need and academic merit. The institution has a Program Participation Agreement with the U.S. Department of Education for eligible students to receive Pell Grants and other federal aid. Teacher scholarships available to qualifying students. *Contact:* Financial Aid Office.

Accreditation: *Regional:* NCA. *Approved by:* Missouri Department of Elementary and Secondary Education.

Undergraduate Programs: The School of Education offers four certification programs: early childhood, elementary, middle and secondary (English, math, social studies, unified science, Spanish K-12, art K-12. Also offered is a child and family studies degree that does not lead to certification.

All programs require the completion of a general education core, professional studies, subject/content area, field experiences, and student teaching. A minimum of 120 semester hours must be successfully completed for the degree award.

Graduate Programs: Four graduate programs are offered: Master of Education (no thesis), Master of Education in educational administration (principal certification), Master of Education in special education (advanced certification), and Master of Arts in Teaching (leads to certification in middle or secondary).

Licensure/Reciprocity: Missouri. Students seeking teaching certification in a state other than Missouri should consult with that state's teacher certification office early in their program of study to insure compliance with requirements. Many state directors of teacher credentialing have signed Interstate Agreements through NASDTEC that expedite the certification process.

ROCKHURST UNIVERSITY

Department of Education
VanAckerman Hall
1100 Rockhurst Road
Kansas City, Missouri 64110-2561
Phone: (816) 501-4140
Fax: (816) 501-4169
E-mail: mary.lewis@.rockhurst.edu
Internet: http://www.rockhurst.edu

Institution Description: Rockhurst University is a private, independent, nonprofit Jesuit institution affiliated with the Roman Catholic Church. It was founded in 1910. University status was achieved in 1998.

The central focus of the Department of Education is to prepare teachers who have a solid background in their chosen fields of study.

Institution Control: Private.

Calendar: Semester. Academic year August to May.

Official(s): Dr. Debra A. Pellegrino, Department Head.

Faculty: Full-time 7; adjunct 5.

Degrees Awarded: 13 baccalaureate; 25 master's.

Admission Requirements: *Undergraduate:* Graduation from an approved secondary school or GED; College Board SAT or ACT composite. *Teacher education specific:* Passing scores on all sections of the Missouri C-BASE test; cumulative GPA of 2.5; portfolio review; faculty interview. *Graduate:* Baccalaureate degree from a regionally accredited institution. *Teacher education specific:* Official transcripts of all college/university coursework; minimum 2.5 GPA; essay describing professional goals; two letters of recommendations; faculty interview; PRAXIS tests before graduation.

Fees and Expenses: Undergraduate: $575 per credit hour. Graduate: $280 per credit hour. On-campus room and board: $2,675 to $3,575 per semester. Books and supplies: $150 per semester.

Financial Aid: Resources specifically for eligible students enrolled in teacher education programs are awarded on the basis of financial need and academic merit. The institution has a Program Participation Agreement with the U.S. Department of Education for eligible students to receive Pell Grants and other federal aid. Teacher scholarships available to qualifying students. *Contact:* Carla Boren at: (816 501-4100 or carla.boren@rockhurst.edu.

Accreditation: *Regional:* NCA. *Approved by:* Missouri Department of Elementary and Secondary Education.

Undergraduate Programs: The Department of Education offers programs in elementary and secondary school education. Students seeking a secondary school certification in a particular content area must complete a major in that area as well as in education. Students seeking elementary certification receive the generalist background provided by a major in elementary education as well as specialist knowledge acquired by coursework in a particular concentration area. All programs lead to the baccalaureate degree and require the completion of a general education core, professional studies, subject/content area, field experiences, and student teaching. A minimum of 120 semester hours is required for the degree award.

Graduate Programs: The aim of Rockhurst's Master in Education program is to develop educational leaders who are actively engaged in educational matters and who will be well prepared to assume a variety of educational roles in K-12 schools. The program calls upon students to analyze alternatives in curriculum, teaching methodology, and assessment and to consider the implications of such alternatives for a multicultural society. Master of Education students may enroll in one of three tracks: initial teacher certification in secondary education, literacy studies, integrated humanities.

Licensure/Reciprocity: Missouri. Students seeking teaching certification in a state other than Missouri should consult with that state's teacher certification office early in their program of study to insure compliance with requirements. Many state directors of teacher credentialing have signed Interstate Agreements through NASDTEC that expedite the certification process.

SAINT LOUIS UNIVERSITY

Department of Educational Studies
221 North Grand Boulevard
St. Louis, Missouri 63103
Phone: (314) 977-2500
Fax: (314) 977-2136
E-mail: admitme@slu.edu
Internet: http://www.slu.edu

Institution Description: Saint Louis University is a private institution affiliated with the Society of Jesus, Roman Catholic Church. It was established as Saint Louis Academy in 1818.

The aim of Educational Studies is to prepare teachers who have leadership qualities including risk-taking, civic responsibility, and ethical character.

Institution Control: Private.

Calendar: Semester. Academic year August to May.

Official(s): Dr. Ann M. Rule, Chairperson.

Faculty: Full-time 12.

Degrees Awarded: 43 baccalaureate; 34 master's; 79 doctorate.

Admission Requirements: *Undergraduate:* Graduation from an accredited secondary school. College Board SAT or ACT composite. *Teacher education specific:* Passing scores on all sections of the Missouri C-BASE test; cumulative GPA of 2.5; portfolio review; faculty interview. *Graduate:* Baccalaureate degree from a regionally accredited institution. *Teacher education specific:* Official transcripts of all college/university coursework; minimum 2.5 GPA; essay describing professional goals; two letters of recommendations; faculty interview; PRAXIS tests before graduation.

Fees and Expenses: Undergraduate: $22,050 per academic year. Graduate: $650 per credit hour. On-campus room and board: room (double occupancy) $3,540 - $7,250; board $3,330 (8 meal plan). Other expenses: $8,625. Books and supplies: $1,050.

Financial Aid: Resources specifically for eligible students enrolled in teacher education programs are awarded on the basis of financial need and academic merit. The institution has a Program Participation Agreement with the U.S. Department of Education for eligible students to receive Pell Grants and other federal aid. Teacher scholarships available to qualifying students. *Contact:* Financial Aid Office at: (314) 977-2350.

Accreditation: *Regional:* NCA. *Professional:* NCATE. *Member of:* AACTE. *Approved by:* Missouri Department of Elementary and Secondary Education.

Undergraduate Programs: There are two distinct programs in the undergraduate portion of teacher education. The first program prepares students for a Bachelor of Arts degree in Education and certification to teach. Students in this program can pursue one of the following certifications: early childhood, elementary, secondary, middle school, special education, or early childhood special education. The second program prepares students for a bachelor's degree in education, but it does not prepare the student for teaching in the schools, instead this degree is often used in preparation for other professions that may require teaching or training skills. The pre-teaching laboratory course is a response to the need for teacher candidates to observe and participate in the teaching process early in their career.

Graduate Programs: Graduate work in the Department of Educational Studies is designed for those interested in pursuing the Master of Arts in curriculum and instruction, educational foundations, or special education. All 32-hour Master of Arts programs must include at least six hours of research. At the end of the program, the student will prepare a theme paper on a topic related to the student's coursework.

The Master of Arts in Teaching is designed for classroom teachers interested in professional and personal growth. Courses are determined in consultation with the advisor.

The Doctor of Education is intended to prepare professionals for leadership positions in educational institutions through a practical, problem-oriented program. Students may choose an area of concentration in either curriculum and instruction or educational foundations.

Licensure/Reciprocity: Missouri. Students seeking teaching certification in a state other than Missouri should consult with that state's teacher certification office early in their program of study to insure compliance with requirements. Many state directors of teacher credentialing have signed Interstate Agreements through NASDTEC that expedite the certification process.

SOUTHEAST MISSOURI STATE UNIVERSITY

College of Education
Department of Middle and Secondary Education
1 University Plaza
Cape Girardeau, Missouri 63701
Phone: (573) 651-2408
Fax: (573) 651-2410
E-mail: coe@semo.edu
Internet: http://www.semo.edu

Institution Description: Southeast Missouri State University is a public institution. It was established as the Southeast Missouri Normal School in 1873. The name was changed to Southeast Missouri State Teachers College in 1919 and to Southeast Missouri State College in 1946. The present name was adopted in 1972.

The Department of Middle and Secondary Education prepares students for teaching responsibilities in secondary and middle level classrooms and assists in the preparation of school administrators and superintendents.

Institution Control: Public.

Calendar: Semester. Academic year August to May.

Official(s): Dr. I. Sue Sheppard, Dean; Dr. Fred Yeo, Chairperson.

Faculty: Full-time 6; part-time 2.

Degrees Awarded: 294 baccalaureate, 78 master's.

Admission Requirements: *Undergraduate:* Graduation from an approved secondary school or GED; College Board SAT or ACT composite. *Teacher education specific:* Pass all sections of the Missouri C-BASE test; 35 semester hours of college credit; cumulative GPA of 2.5; portfolio review; faculty interview. *Graduate:* Baccalaureate degree from a regionally accredited institution. *Teacher education specific:* Official transcripts of all college/university coursework; minimum 2.75; teaching licensure when required by program pursued; PRAXIS II before graduation.

Fees and Expenses: Undergraduate: in-state $4,035 per academic year. Graduate: $7,110. On-campus room and board: $4,938. Other expenses: $2,650. Books and supplies: $350.

Financial Aid: Resources specifically for eligible students enrolled in teacher education programs are awarded on the basis of financial need and academic merit. The institution has a Program Participation Agreement with the U.S. Department of Education for eligible students to receive Pell Grants and other federal aid. Teacher scholarships available to qualifying students. *Contact:* Financial Aid Office at: (573) 651-2253.

Accreditation: *Regional:* NCA. *Professional:* NCATE. *Member of:* AACTE. *Approved by:* Missouri Department of Elementary and Secondary Education.

Undergraduate Programs: The undergraduate teacher preparation program includes joint responsibility with the appropriate academic department for 9-12 programs leading to secondary certification in mathematics, unified science, English, social studies, industrial technology, foreign language, family and consumer science, business, and speech/theatre education, as well as K-12 certification in physical education, art, and music.

The middle school program leads to both a degree in middle level education and certification in areas of concentration including science, mathematics, language arts, and social stud-ies. All programs are extensively field-based with opportunities for early and continuing experience in actual classroom circumstances.

Students must also complete a general education core, professional studies, subject/content area, and student teaching.

Graduate Programs: The department offers a Master of Arts degree with a major in secondary education with several emphases and participates in certifications in teaching English to speakers of other languages (TESOL), adult basic education, and speech and language specialist (K-12).

The department coordinates Southeast's Alternative Certification Program helping districts and students from all over Missouri facilitate career changes into secondary teaching.

Licensure/Reciprocity: Missouri. Students seeking teaching certification in a state other than Missouri should consult with that state's teacher certification office early in their program of study to insure compliance with requirements. Many state directors of teacher credentialing have signed Interstate Agreements through NASDTEC that expedite the certification process.

SOUTHWEST BAPTIST UNIVERSITY

Department of Education
Teacher Education Program
SBU/Gott Educational Center
1600 University Avenue
Missouri 65613
Phone: (417) 328-1717
Fax: (417) 328-2045
E-mail: jbryant@sbuniv.edu
Internet: http://www.sbuniv.edu

Institution Description: Southwest Baptist University (Southwest Baptist College until 1981) is a private institution supported by the Missouri Baptist Convention (Southern Baptist).

The Department of Education is a learning community preparing teachers to be caring, effective practitioners in todays' schools.

Institution Control: Private.

Calendar: Semester. Academic year August to May.

Official(s): Dr. Judy Bryant, Chair, Director of Teacher Education; Dr. Tom Hollis, Director of Graduate Studies in Education.

Faculty: Full-time 8; part-time 5; adjunct 2.

Degrees Awarded: 62 baccalaureate; 356 master's.

Admission Requirements: *Undergraduate:* Graduation from an approved secondary school or GED; College Board SAT or ACT composite. *Teacher education specific:* Pass all sections of Missouri C-BASE test; complete teacher education file; cumulative GPA of 2.5; faculty interview. *Graduate:* Baccalaureate degree from a regionally accredited institution. *Teacher education specific:* Official transcripts of all college/university coursework; proof of passing scores on PRAXIS II or GRE.

Fees and Expenses: Undergraduate: $10,600 per academic year. Graduate: $135 per credit hour. Required fees: $466. On-campus room and board: $3,180.

Financial Aid: Resources specifically for eligible students enrolled in teacher education programs are awarded on the basis of financial need and academic merit. The institution has a Program Participation Agreement with the U.S. Department of Education for eligible students to receive Pell Grants and other federal aid. Teacher scholarships available to qualifying students. *Contact:* Brad Gamle at: (417) 328-1823 or e-mail at bgamble@sbuniv.edu.

Accreditation: *Regional:* NCA. *Member of:* AACTE. *Approved by:* Missouri Department of Elementary and Secondary Education.

Undergraduate Programs: The elementary education major (grades 1-6) program offers second areas of certification in: early childhood (birth-grade 3); art K-9, health K-9, physical education K-9, Spanish K-9, and middle school education 5-9.

Middle school majors must complete a minimum of 21 semester hours in two areas of concentration: language arts 5-9, mathematics 5-9, science 5-9, social science 5-9, Spanish K-9, speech 5-9.

SOUTHWEST BAPTIST UNIVERSITY—*cont'd*

Certification in secondary education consists of the completion of an academic major in which initial certification is sought. A second area of certification is suggested in: art, biology, chemistry, English, mathematics, music (instrumental, vocal), physical education, social science, speech/theatre, united science.

Graduate Programs: The purpose of the graduate program in education is to provide learning experiences that will assist teachers to improve their capability to teach in elementary, middle, and secondary schools. The Master of Science in Education degree program has two options: a program consisting of 36 semester hours that include a professional core and electives **or** a program consisting of 39 semester hours and includes four core courses. Six hours of approved courses may be substituted for the master's project.

Licensure/Reciprocity: Missouri. Students seeking teaching certification in a state other than Missouri should consult with that state's teacher certification office early in their program of study to insure compliance with requirements. Many state directors of teacher credentialing have signed Interstate Agreements through NASDTEC that expedite the certification process.

SOUTHWEST MISSOURI STATE UNIVERSITY

School of Teacher Education
Hill Hall 207D
901 South National Avenue
Springfield, Missouri 65804
Phone: (417) 836-6759
Fax: (417) 836-6252
E-mail: fhg565f@smsu.edu
Internet: http://www.smsu.edu

Institution Description: Southwest Missouri State University is a state-assisted multipurpose university with a branch campus at West Plains and a research campus in Mountain Grove, Missouri. It was established in 1905.

The goal of the School of Teacher Education is to prepare reflective teachers, specialists, and administrators who are committed to the education of children and the ideals of scholarship, leadership, lifelong learning, and service to society.

Institution Control: Public.

Calendar: Semester. Academic year August to May.

Official(s): Dr. Fred H. Groves, Director.

Faculty: Full-time 41.

Degrees Awarded: 410 baccalaureate; 242 master's.

Admission Requirements: *Undergraduate:* Graduation from an approved secondary school or GED; College Board SAT or ACT composite. *Teacher education specific:* Pass all sections of the Missouri C-BASE test; 35 semester hours of college credit; cumulative GPA of 2.75; portfolio review; faculty interview. *Graduate:* Baccalaureate degree from a regionally accredited institution. *Teacher education specific:* Official transcripts of all college/university coursework; minimum 2.75; teaching licensure when required by program pursued; PRAXIS II before graduation.

Fees and Expenses: Undergraduate: in-state $4,275 per academic year; out-of-state: $8,114. Graduate: $7,110. On-campus room and board: $4,950. Books and supplies: $800.

Financial Aid: Resources specifically for eligible students enrolled in teacher education programs are awarded on the basis of financial need and academic merit. The institution has a Program Participation Agreement with the U.S. Department of Education for eligible students to receive Pell Grants and other federal aid. Teacher scholarships available to qualifying students. *Contact:* Financial Aid Office at: (417) 836-5262.

Accreditation: *Regional:* NCA. *Professional:* NCATE. *Member of:* AACTE. *Approved by:* Missouri Department of Elementary and Secondary Education.

Undergraduate Programs: The School of Teacher Education offers programs in early childhood education, elementary education, middle school education, and secondary education. These programs lead to the Bachelor of Science in Education degree and carry with them an initial professional certificate to teach in Missouri. All programs require the completion of a general education core, professional studies, field experiences, subject/content area, and student teaching.

The majors for K-12 grades and secondary education include: art, agriculture, education, business education, English, foreign language (French, German, Latin, Spanish), industrial technology, mathematics, music, physical education, unified science, social science, speech and theatre, vocation family and consumer science.

Graduate Programs: The Master of Science in elementary education and the Master of Science: secondary education are offered in cooperation with the Graduate School. The Master of Science in secondary education includes concentrations in agriculture, art, biology, business, chemistry, earth science, English, geography, history, home economics, industrial education, mathematics, music, natural science, physical education, physics, political science, social science, speech and theatre.

Licensure/Reciprocity: Missouri. Students seeking teaching certification in a state other than Missouri should consult with that state's teacher certification office early in their program of study to insure compliance with requirements. Many state directors of teacher credentialing have signed Interstate Agreements through NASDTEC that expedite the certification process.

TRUMAN STATE UNIVERSITY

Division of Education
100 East Normal
205 McClain Hall
Kirksville, Missouri 63501-9980
Phone: (660) 785-4000
Fax: (660) 785-4181
E-mail: admissions@truman.edu
Internet: http://www.truman.edu

Institution Description: Formerly named Northeast Missouri State University, Truman State University was established in 1867. The institution was designated as the official statewide public liberal arts and sciences university by the Missouri legislature in 1986.

The Master of Arts in Education is the only teacher certification program offered at Truman State University.

Institution Control: Public.

Calendar: Semester. Academic year August to May.

Official(s): Dr. Sam Minner, Division Head.

Faculty: Full-time 24.

Degrees Awarded: 91 master's.

Admission Requirements: *Graduate:* Baccalaureate degree from a regionally accredited institution. *Teacher education specific:* GRE score; minimum 2.75 GPA; references.

Fees and Expenses: Graduate: $7,110 per academic year. On-campus room and board: $4,928. Other expenses: $3,800. Books and supplies: $600.

Financial Aid: Resources specifically for eligible students enrolled in teacher education programs are awarded on the basis of financial need and academic merit. The institution has a Program Participation Agreement with the U.S. Department of Education for eligible students to receive Pell Grants and other federal aid. Teacher scholarships available to qualifying students. *Contact:* Financial Aid Office at: (860) 785-4130.

Accreditation: *Regional:* NCA. *Professional:* NCATE. *Member of:* AACTE. *Approved by:* Missouri Department of Elementary and Secondary Education.

Graduate Programs: The Master of Education program, designed in 1986, is the first extended teacher preparation program in Missouri. Students admitted into the program must first complete a bachelor of science or bachelor of arts degree in a liberal arts and sciences field. Enrollment begins either in spring or fall. During the spring or fall semester following completion of the baccalaureate degree, students enroll in pedagogical coursework and the specialty area coursework, The internship experience can be either an unpaid one-semester option or a paid year-long internship. In the year-long internship, the student is hired as a teacher of record by a public school. The student signs a contract and is paid by the public school to fill a full-time teaching position and while completing the internship requirement. The program encourages internship and placements in diverse settings that include schools in the St. Louis and Kansas City regions. Internships may also be arranged in rural school settings.

Licensure/Reciprocity: Missouri. Students seeking teaching certification in a state other than Missouri should consult with that state's teacher certification office early in their program of study to insure compliance with requirements. Many state directors of teacher credentialing have signed Interstate Agreements through NASDTEC that expedite the certification process.

UNIVERSITY OF MISSOURI - COLUMBIA

College of Education
118 Hill Hall
Columbia, Missouri 65211
Phone: (573) 882-7831
Fax: (573) 882-4024
E-mail: tiger.coe@missouri.edu
Internet: http://www.missouri.edu

Institution Description: The university was established and chartered in 1839.

The College of Education offers undergraduate and graduate programs leading to teaching certification.

Institution Control: Public.

Calendar: Semester. Academic year August to May.

Official(s): Dr. Richard Andrews, Dean; Dr. Deborah Carr, Assistant Dean, Undergraduate Studies and Teacher Development; Dr. Richard Robinson, Director, Graduate Studies.

Faculty: Full-time 87; part-time 11; adjunct 39.

Degrees Awarded: 229 baccalaureate; 417 master's; 73 doctorate.

Admission Requirements: *Undergraduate:* Graduation from an accredited secondary school; College Board SAT or ACT composite. *Teacher education specific:* 2.5 GPA; attainment of junior status (60 hours); passing scores in all segments of the Missouri C-BASE examination; faculty interview. *Graduate:* Baccalaureate degree from a regionally accredited institution with satisfactory academic record. *Teacher education specific:* GRE or Miller Analogies Test required for Counseling Program; minimum 2.75 GPA; faculty review.

Fees and Expenses: Undergraduate: in-state $219.55 per credit; out-of-state $554.45. Graduate: in-state $261.55 per credit hour; out-of-state $663.95. On-campus room and board: $5,374 (average), varies by hall and meal plan. Books and supplies: $860.

Financial Aid: Resources specifically for eligible students enrolled in teacher education programs are awarded on the basis of financial need and academic merit. The institution has a Program Participation Agreement with the U.S. Department of Education for eligible students to receive Pell Grants and other federal aid. Teacher scholarships available to qualifying students. *Contact:* Joe Camille, Director at: (573) 882-7506 or e-mail @finaid@missouri.edu.

Accreditation: *Regional:* NCA. *Professional:* NCATE. *Member of:* AACTE. *Approved by:* Missouri Department of Elementary and Secondary Education.

Undergraduate Programs: Degree programs are offered by the Department of Early Childhood and Elementary Education in the following areas: early childhood, elementary, literacy, art, mathematics, science, social studies, early childhood special education, special education: general, cross categorical, learning disabilities, behavioral disorders, mental retardation, gifted education.

Undergraduate programs are offered by the Department of Learning, Teaching, and Curriculum in the areas of: art, music education, agriculture, business and marketing, career and technical education, English, foreign languages, literacy/reading education, mathematics, science, social studies.

All baccalaureate programs require the completion of a general education core, professional studies, subject/content area, field experiences, and student teaching. A minimum of 120 semester hours is required for the degree award.

Graduate Programs: Graduate degree programs leading to the Master of Science in Education include the following concentrations: art, music, business and marketing, career and technical education, family and consumer science;, English, literacy/reading, mathematics, science, social studies.

A student may concurrently pursue certification with the master's degree program. All graduate students who seek teaching certification will need to be admitted to Professional Standing.

Licensure/Reciprocity: Missouri. Students seeking teaching certification in a state other than Missouri should consult with that state's teacher certification office early in their program of study to insure compliance with requirements. Many state directors of teacher credentialing have signed Interstate Agreements through NASDTEC that expedite the certification process.

UNIVERSITY OF MISSOURI - KANSAS CITY

School of Education
Division of Curriculum and Instructional Leadership
5100 Rockhill Road
Kansas City, Missouri 64110-2499
Phone: (816) 235-2231
Fax: (816) 235-5270
E-mail: education@umkc.edu
Internet: http://www.umkc.edu

Institution Description: The institution was established and chartered as University of Kansas City in 1929 and became part of University of Missouri system in 1963.

The Division of Curriculum and Instructional Leadership is committed to the urban mission of the university. A special emphasis is placed on developing professionals prepared to function in our culturally pluralistic society.

Institution Control: Public.

Calendar: Semester. Academic year August to May.

Official(s): Dr. John Cleek, Dean; Dr. Susan Adler, Teacher Education Program Head.

Faculty: Full-time 50; adjunct 94.

Degrees Awarded: 96 baccalaureate; 283 master's; 4 doctorate.

Admission Requirements: *Undergraduate:* Graduation from an accredited secondary school; College Board SAT or ACT composite. *Teacher education specific:* 2.5 GPA; attainment of junior status (60 hours); passing scores in all segments of the Missouri C-BASE examination; faculty interview. *Graduate:* Baccalaureate degree from a regionally accredited institution with satisfactory academic record. *Teacher education specific:* GRE or Miller Analogies Test required for Counseling Program; minimum 2.75 GPA; faculty review.

Fees and Expenses: Undergraduate: in-state $219.55 per credit; out-of-state $554.45. Graduate: in-state $261.55 per credit hour; out-of-state $663.95. Required fees: $30 building fee; $115 Student Center Fee required each term. On-campus room and board: $5,635. Books and supplies: $500-$1000 per term. Parking $120 per year.

Financial Aid: Resources specifically for eligible students enrolled in teacher education programs are awarded on the basis of financial need and academic merit. The institution has a Program Participation Agreement with the U.S. Department of Education for eligible students to receive Pell Grants and other federal aid. Teacher scholarships available to qualifying students. *Contact:* Carol Rotach at: (816) 235-1154 or e-mail at finaid.umkc.edu.

UNIVERSITY OF MISSOURI - KANSAS CITY—cont'd

Accreditation: *Regional:* NCA. *Professional:* NCATE. *Member of:* AACTE. *Approved by:* Missouri Department of Elementary and Secondary Education.

Undergraduate Programs: The Division of Curriculum and Instructional Leadership offers degree programs leading to the Bachelor of Arts degree in: early childhood education, elementary education, middle school education, and secondary education. All programs require the completion of a general education core, professional studies, subject/content area, field experiences, and student teaching. The various programs require a minimum of 120 semester hours.

Graduate Programs: The Department of Special Education offers the Master of Arts in behavior disorders and Master of Arts in learning disabilities. Each of the two areas offers 15 hours n area-specific studies with an additional 25 hours offered in general education studies.

The "career change option" allows students who hold undergraduate degrees in areas outside of education to concurrently complete basic education courses and special education training. Students from fields as varied as sociology, business, landscape design, and dentistry have been able to pursue teaching certification and directly impact special education teacher shortages in the greater Kansas City area as well as across Missouri and Kansas.

The Teaching English as a Second Language (TESOL) Program offers a Master of Arts in curriculum and instruction and K-12 endorsement ESL teachers with current teaching credentials.

Licensure/Reciprocity: Missouri. Reciprocity with Kansas, Iowa, Nebraska, North Dakota. Students seeking teaching certification in other states should consult with that state's teacher certification office early in their program of study to insure compliance with requirements. Many state directors of teacher credentialing have signed Interstate Agreements through NASDTEC that expedite the certification process.

UNIVERSITY OF MISSOURI - ST. LOUIS

College of Education
Division of Teaching and Learning
135 Marillac Hall
8001 Natural Bridge Road
St. Louis, Missouri 63121-4499
Phone: (314) 516-5937
Fax: (314) 516-5310
E-mail: coe@ccmail.umsl.edu
Internet: http://www.umsl.edu

Institution Description: The University of Missouri - St. Louis is a public, state-supported institution. It was established in 1960.

The Division of Teaching and Learning offers undergraduate and graduate degree programs.

Institution Control: Public.

Calendar: Semester. Academic year to May.

Official(s): Dr. Charles Schlitz, Dean.

Faculty: Full-time 56, part-time 76.

Degrees Awarded: 281 baccalaureate; 253 master's; 20 doctorate.

Admission Requirements: *Undergraduate:* Graduation from an accredited secondary school; College Board SAT or ACT composite. *Teacher education specific:* 2.5 GPA; attainment of junior status (60 hours); passing scores in all segments of the Missouri C-BASE examination; faculty interview. *Graduate:* Baccalaureate degree from a regionally accredited institution with satisfactory academic record. *Teacher education specific:* GRE or Miller Analogies Test required for Counseling Program; minimum 2.75 GPA; faculty review.

Fees and Expenses: Undergraduate: in-state $5,470 per academic year; out-of-state $14,012. Graduate: Tuition is charged per credit hour. On-campus room and board: $8,762. Other expenses: $4,720. Books and supplies: $625.

Financial Aid: Resources specifically for eligible students enrolled in teacher education programs are awarded on the basis of financial need and academic merit. The institution has a Program Participation Agreement with the U.S. Department of Education for eligible students to receive Pell Grants and other federal aid. Teacher scholarships available to qualifying students. *Contact:* Financial Aid Office at: (313) 516-5526.

Accreditation: *Regional:* NCA. *Professional:* NCATE. *Member of:* AACTE. *Approved by:* Missouri Department of Elementary and Secondary Education.

Undergraduate Programs: The Division of Teaching and Learning offers programs leading to the Bachelor of Education degree and teacher certification in: early childhood-birth to 3rd grade; elementary education 1-6; middle school 5-9; physical education K-9 or K-12; special education-learning disabilities K-12; special education-behavioral disorders; special education-mentally handicapped. Secondary education programs are offered in the areas of biology 9-12, chemistry 9-12, English 9-12, foreign languages K-12 (French, German, Spanish), mathematics 9-12, physics 9-12, social studies 9-12.

All programs require the completion of a general education core, professional studies, subject/content area, field experiences, and student teaching. Semester hours required for the degree award range from 120 to 132.

Graduate Programs: The Graduate School offers a variety of programs leading to the Master of Education degree. Included are the areas and emphases for elementary education (early childhood, reading specialization, physical education); secondary education (curriculum and instruction, reading specialization, adult education, higher education, physical education, educational technology, foreign language); special education (early childhood, learning disabilities, developmental disabilities, emotional/behavior disorder); educational administration; counseling (school counseling, community counseling). Requirements vary among the emphases offered in the areas listed.

The Doctor of Education and Doctor of Philosophy programs with emphasis in counseling are offered by the Graduate School.

Licensure/Reciprocity: Missouri. Students seeking teaching certification in a state other than Missouri should consult with that state's teacher certification office early in their program of study to insure compliance with requirements. Many state directors of teacher credentialing have signed Interstate Agreements through NASDTEC that expedite the certification process.

WASHINGTON UNIVERSITY IN ST. LOUIS

Department of Education
Box 1183
One Brooking Drive
St. Louis, Missouri 63130-4899
Phone: (314) 935-6776
Fax: (314) 935-4982
E-mail: mriesehn@artsci.edu
Internet: http://www.wustl.edu

Institution Description: Washington University is a private, independent, nonprofit institution that was established and chartered in 1853. The present name was adopted in 1857.

The elementary and secondary teacher education programs are designed to produce teachers who take an inquiry-oriented approach to education.

Institution Control: Private.

Calendar: Semester. Academic year August to May.

Official(s): Dr. William Tate, Department Head; Dr. Margaret Finders, Director of Teacher Education.

Faculty: Full-time 12; adjunct 10.

Degrees Awarded: 10 baccalaureate; 15 master's.

Admission Requirements: *Undergraduate:* Graduation from an approved secondary school or GED; College Board SAT or ACT composite. *Teacher education specific:* Passing scores on all sections of the Missouri C-BASE exam; cumulative GPA of 2.75; portfolio review; faculty interview. *Graduate:* Baccalaureate degree from a regionally accredited institution. *Teacher education specific:* Official transcripts of all college/university coursework; minimum 2.75; teaching licensure when required by program pursued; PRAXIS II tests before graduation.

Fees and Expenses: Undergraduate: $27,620 per academic year. Graduate: Tuition charged per credit hour. On-campus room and board: $8,627. Other expenses: $1,590. Books and supplies: $950.

Financial Aid: Resources specifically for eligible students enrolled in teacher education programs are awarded on the basis of financial need and academic merit. The institution has a Program Participation Agreement with the U.S. Department of Education for eligible students to receive Pell Grants and other federal aid. Teacher scholarships available to qualifying students. *Contact:* Financial Aid Office at: (888 547-6670.

Accreditation: *Regional:* NCA. *Member of:* AACTE. *Approved by:* Missouri Department of Elementary and Secondary Education.

Undergraduate Programs: The Elementary Teacher Preparation Program prepares students to teach grades 1-6 and requires coursework in three areas: general education, professional education, and a second academic major. Forty-nine credit hours of professional education coursework are required for elementary certification. The second academic major is decided upon by the student in consultation with higher education advisor.

The Middle School Teacher Preparation Program prepares students to teach grades 5-9 and requires coursework in general education, professional education, and in one or two subject areas. A 21-credit concentration in the subject area is also required in a core content field.

The Secondary Teacher Preparation Program is offered in the areas of: art, Asian and Near Eastern languages and literatures, biology, chemistry, classics, earth and planetary sciences, English, Germanic languages and literature, history, mathematics, physics, political science, Romance languages and literatures.

All teacher education programs involve experience working in school settings, culminating in a semester of field experience on-site at a local public school.

Graduate Programs: Graduate programs offered include the Master of Arts in Teaching that provides students with graduate study in their own field, preparation in education, and a sustained clinical experience.

The Master of Arts in Education-Instruction Process offers four options or stands of study: professional development, elementary/middle school science education, English as a second language, or education in a diverse society.

The Master of Arts in Education is offered to liberal arts graduates who are interested in pursuing an elementary school teaching career. The program prepares students to teach grades 1-6 and requires student teaching and coursework in foundations of education and curriculum and instruction.

The Post-Baccalaureate Teacher Certification Program is designed for those with a baccalaureate degree in a subject area that is taught in the secondary schools. The program leads to teacher certification only; no degree is granted through this program.

The doctoral program offers opportunities for examining educational processes and problems from sociocultural and interdisciplinary perspectives. The program leads to the Doctor of Philosophy degree.

Licensure/Reciprocity: Missouri. Students seeking teaching certification in a state other than Missouri should consult with that state's teacher certification office early in their program of study to insure compliance with requirements. Many state directors of teacher credentialing have signed Interstate Agreements through NASDTEC that expedite the certification process.

WEBSTER UNIVERSITY
School of Education
Learning and Communication Arts
470 East Lockwood Avenue
St. Louis, Missouri 63119
Phone: (314) 968-7940
Fax: (314) 968-7718
E-mail: admit@webster.edu
Internet: http://www.webster.edu

Institution Description: Webster University is a private, independent, multicampus, nonprofit institution. It was founded as Loretto College by the Sisters of Loretto, Roman Catholic Church in 1915. The institution became secular in 1967 and a university in 1983.

The School of Education offers undergraduate and graduate programs leading to teacher certification. The school also includes the Beatrice and David Kornblum Institute for Teaching Excellence.

Institution Control: Private.

Calendar: Semester. Academic year August to May.

Official(s): Dr. Phyllis Eilinson, Chair, Learning and Communication Arts.

Faculty: Full-time 10.

Degrees Awarded: 46 baccalaureate; 320 master's.

Admission Requirements: *Undergraduate:* Graduation from an approved secondary school or GED; College Board SAT or ACT composite. *Teacher education specific:* Pass all sections of the Missouri C-BASE exam; cumulative GPA of 2.5; portfolio review; faculty interview. *Graduate:* Baccalaureate degree from a regionally accredited institution. *Teacher education specific:* Official transcripts of all college/university coursework; minimum 2.75; teaching licensure when required by program pursued; PRAXIS II results.

Fees and Expenses: Undergraduate: $14,600 per academic year. Graduate: Tuition charged per credit hour. On campus room and board: $8,626. Other expenses: $2,800. Books and supplies: $1,300.

Financial Aid: Resources specifically for eligible students enrolled in teacher education programs are awarded on the basis of financial need and academic merit. The institution has a Program Participation Agreement with the U.S. Department of Education for eligible students to receive Pell Grants and other federal aid. Teacher scholarships available to qualifying students. *Contact:* Financial Aid Office at: (314) 968-6992.

Accreditation: *Regional:* NCA. *Member of:* AACTE. *Approved by:* Missouri Department of Elementary and Secondary Education.

Undergraduate Programs: The Department of Learning and Communication Arts offers programs leading to the Bachelor of Arts in Education with teacher certification in: early childhood education, (birth-3); early childhood special education (birth-3); elementary (1-6); middle school education (5-9); secondary education (art K-12, English 9-12, foreign language K-12, mathematics 9-12, music K-12, social studies 9-12, unified science 9-12); special education K-12 mild/moderate cross-categorical. Students seeking secondary education certification choose a major in their specialty area. All programs require the completion of a general education core, professional studies, subject/content area, field experiences, and student teaching.

Graduate Programs: The Master of Arts in Teaching is offered in the areas of communications (including options for emphases in teaching English as a foreign language and teaching English as a second language); early childhood education; educational technology; mathematics; science; social sciences; special education.

The Education Specialist program is offered in administrative leadership.

WEBSTER UNIVERSITY—*cont'd*

Licensure/Reciprocity: Missouri. Students seeking teaching certification in a state other than Missouri should consult with that state's teacher certification office early in their program of study to insure compliance with requirements. Many state directors of teacher credentialing have signed Interstate Agreements through NASDTEC that expedite the certification process.

WESTMINSTER COLLEGE

Education Department

Teacher Education Program

501 Westminster Avenue

Fulton, Missouri 65203

Phone: (573) 592-5201

Fax: (573) 592-5217

E-mail: aulgurl@jaynet.wcmo.edu

Internet: http://www.wcmo.edu

Institution Description: Westminster College is a private, independent, nonprofit college. It was established as Fulton College in 1851 and adopted the present name in 1853.

The Teacher Education Program is designed to provide the academic and professional knowledge necessary for successful beginning teaching.

Institution Control: Private.

Calendar: Semester. Academic year August to May.

Official(s): Dr. Linda M. Aulgur, Chairman.

Faculty: Full-time 3; part-time 2; adjunct 2.

Degrees Awarded: 18 baccalaureate.

Admission Requirements: *Undergraduate:* Graduation from an accredited high school or GED; combination of ACT/SAT scores. *Teacher education specific:* Pass all sections of the Missouri C-Base exam; overall 2.5 GPA; background check; PRAXIS II exam before graduation.

Fees and Expenses: $12,300 per academic year. On-campus room and board: $5,430. Required fees: $370. Books and supplies: $1,000.

Financial Aid: Resources specifically for eligible students enrolled in teacher education programs are awarded on the basis of financial need and academic merit. The institution has a Program Participation Agreement with the U.S. Department of Education for eligible students to receive Pell Grants and other federal aid. Teacher scholarships available to qualifying students. *Contact:* Amy Bristol at: (573) 592-5364 or e-mail at Bristol@jaynet.ucmo.edu.

Accreditation: *Regional:* NCA. *Approved by:* Missouri Department of Elementary and Secondary Education.

Undergraduate Programs: Certification areas that lead to the baccalaureate degree are offered in: elementary education (early childhood endorsement); middle school education; secondary school education with concentrations in language arts, social science, mathematics, science, physical education, and business education. In addition to a major in education, students are expected to have at least one area of academic concentration. In addition to the academic requirements, preparation in teacher education includes action research, observation, demonstration, and participation in local school settings. A minimum of 122 semester hours is required for the degree award.

Licensure/Reciprocity: Missouri. Students seeking teaching certification in a state other than Missouri should consult with that state's teacher certification office early in their program of study to insure compliance with requirements. Many state directors of teacher credentialing have signed Interstate Agreements through NASDTEC that expedite the certification process.

WILLIAM JEWELL COLLEGE

Department of Education

Teacher Education Programs

500 College Hill

Liberty, Missouri 64068-1896

Phone: (816) 781-7700

Fax: (816) 415-5024

E-mail: Gardner@william.jewell.edu

Internet: http://www.william.jewell.edu

Institution Description: William Jewell College is a private college affiliated with the Baptist Church. It was established as a men's college in 1849 and became coeducational in 1921.

Teacher Education Programs are offered that lead to the baccalaureate degree and teacher certification.

Institution Control: Private.

Calendar: Semester. Academic year August to May.

Official(s): Dr. Donna Gardner, Chair.

Faculty: Full-time 4; part-time 2.

Degrees Awarded: 17 baccalaureate.

Admission Requirements: *Undergraduate:* Graduation from an accredited secondary school or GED; College Board SAT or ACT composite; writing sample; one recommendation. *Teacher education specific:* Completion of 45 semester hours; overall GPA of at least 2.5; pass all sections of the Missouri C-BASE exam; recommendation from a full-time faculty member; PRAXIS II before graduation.

Fees and Expenses: $16,500 per academic year. On-campus room and board: $5,650. Books and supplies: $600. Student Teaching fee: $200. education programs are awarded on the basis of financial need and academic merit. The institution has a Program Participation Agreement with the U.S. Department of Education for eligible students to receive Pell Grants and other federal aid. Teacher scholarships available to qualifying students. *Contact:* Sue Armstrong, Director, Financial Aid; e-mail armstrong@william.jewell.edu.

Accreditation: *Regional:* NCA. *Member of:* AACTE. *Approved by:* Missouri Department of Elementary and Secondary Education.

Undergraduate Programs: The Teacher Education Programs offered by the Department of Education include elementary education and secondary education. Courses that must be taken at William Jewell College include Instructional Methodology; Student Teaching in the Middle School; Student Teaching in the Secondary School; All-Level Student Teaching. The programs require the completion of a general education core, professional studies, subject/content area, and professional studies.

Post-Baccalaureate Teacher Education Programs are offered for elementary 1-6, secondary 9-12, and all level K-12. Specific courses must be taken in residence.

Alternative Certification Education Programs (secondary 9-12 and all level K-12) are also available for persons holding a bachelor's degree with a major in: art, English, social studies, mathematics, social studies, music, biology, chemistry, Spanish, French, speech/theatre.

Licensure/Reciprocity: Missouri. Students seeking teaching certification in a state other than Missouri should consult with that state's teacher certification office early in their program of study to insure compliance with requirements. Many state directors of teacher credentialing have signed Interstate Agreements through NASDTEC that expedite the certification process.

WILLIAM WOODS UNIVERSITY

Education Division

Teacher Education Program

One University Avenue

Fulton, Missouri 65251-1098

Phone: (573) 592-4348

Fax: (573) 592-1146

E-mail: lewing@williammwoods.edu

Internet: http://www.williamwoods.edu

Institution Description: William Woods University is an independent institution. It was chartered in northwestern Missouri as Female Orphans School of the Christian Church of Missouri in 1870 and the campus was moved to Fulton in 1890. University status was achieved in 1993 and the school became coeducational in 1996.

The Education Division offers programs leading to the baccalaureate degree and teacher certification.

Institution Control: Private.

Calendar: Semester. Academic year August to May.

Official(s): Dr. Tom Frankman, Division Chair.

Faculty: Full-time 9.

Degrees Awarded: 10 baccalaureate; 291 master's.

Admission Requirements: *Undergraduate:* Graduation from an accredited secondary school or GED; College Board SAT or ACT composite; writing sample; one recommendation. *Teacher education specific:* Completion of 45 semester hours; overall GPA of at least 2.5; pass all sections of the Missouri C-BASE exam; recommendation from a full-time faculty member; PRAXIS II before graduation.

Fees and Expenses: $13,750 per academic year. On-campus room and board: $5,700. Other expenses: $290. Books and supplies: $700.

Financial Aid: Resources specifically for eligible students enrolled in teacher education programs are awarded on the basis of financial need and academic merit. The institution has a Program Participation Agreement with the U.S. Department of Education for eligible students to receive Pell Grants and other federal aid. Teacher scholarships available to qualifying students. *Contact:* Financial Aid Office at: (573) 592-4232.

Accreditation: *Regional:* NCA. *Member of:* AACTE. *Approved by:* Missouri Department of Elementary and Secondary Education.

Undergraduate Programs: The Teacher Education Programs leading to the baccalaureate degree and teacher certification include: elementary education, middle school, and special education. An early childhood endorsement program is available, as are secondary certifications in art, English, history (social science), mathematics, physical education, and speech/theatre. The Bachelor of Science degree is awarded upon successful completion of the general education core, professional studies, subject/content area, field experiences, and student teaching. A minimum of 122 credit hours must be successfully completed for the degree award.

Licensure/Reciprocity: Missouri. Students seeking teaching certification in a state other than Missouri should consult with that state's teacher certification office early in their program of study to insure compliance with requirements. Many state directors of teacher credentialing have signed Interstate Agreements through NASDTEC that expedite the certification process.

MONTANA

MONTANA STATE UNIVERSITY - BILLINGS

College of Education and Human Services
Department of Curriculum and Instruction

1500 North 30th Street
Billings, Montana 59101-0298
Phone: (406) 657-2158
Fax: (406) 657-2299
E-mail: wmiller@msubillings.edu
Internet: http://www.msubillings.edu

Institution Description: Montana State University - Billings, formerly known as Eastern Montana College, is a public institution. It was founded in 1927.

The Department of Curriculum and Instruction offers undergraduate and graduate programs leading to licensure to teach at the elementary and secondary levels.

Institution Control: Public.

Calendar: Semester. Academic year September to May.

Official(s): Dr. Kenneth W. Miller, Department Chairperson.

Faculty: Full-time 17.

Degrees Awarded: 129 baccalaureate; 66 master's.

Admission Requirements: *Undergraduate:* Graduation from an accredited secondary school in upper half of graduating class; ACT composite score of 22 or a combined score of 1030 on SAT. *Teacher education specific:* Cumulative 2.5 SPA; Pre-Professional Skills Test (PPST) scores; passing score on writing exam; documentation of experience with children or adolescents. *Graduate:* Baccalaureate degree from a regionally accredited institution. *Teacher education specific:* Cumulative 3.0 GPA; minimum GRE score; recommendations; faculty interview.

Fees and Expenses: Undergraduate: in-state $4,070 per academic year; out-of-state $12,460. Graduate: in-state $235 per credit hour; out-of-state $592. Required fees: $572 for insurance. On-campus room and board: $5,370. Books and supplies: $1,000. Other expenses: $2,420.

Financial Aid: Resources specifically for eligible students enrolled in teacher education programs are awarded on the basis of financial need and academic merit. The institution has a Program Participation Agreement with the U.S. Department of Education for eligible students to receive Pell Grants and other federal aid. Teacher scholarships available to qualifying students. *Contact:* Financial Aid Office at: (406) 657-2188.

Accreditation: *Regional:* NASC. *Professional:* NCATE. *Member of:* AACTE. *Approved by:* Montana State Board of Education.

Undergraduate Programs: The Department of Curriculum and Instruction offers a program in elementary education leading to the Bachelor of Science in Education degree and certification with the broadfield major in elementary education. The special education program is offered with elementary and secondary options.

The Bachelor of Science or Bachelor of Arts degree with teaching certificate option is available with concentrations in the areas of: art (K-12), biology, chemistry, English history, mathematics, music (K-12), social science.

All baccalaureate programs require the completion of the general education core, professional studies, field experiences, subject/content area, and student teaching. A minimum of 128 credits must be earned for the degree award.

Graduate Programs: The Master of Education in Curriculum and Instruction provides professional development and scholarship for educators with diverse professional backgrounds. Options in the degree program include curriculum and instruction (K-8), educational technology, and interdisciplinary studies (teacher certification, elementary (K-8), secondary (5-12).

A Post-Baccalaureate program is a nondegree program leading to initial teacher certification and/or subject area endorsements.

Licensure/Reciprocity: Montana. Reciprocity with Utah, Idaho, California. Students seeking teaching certification in other states should consult with that state's teacher certification office early in their program of study to insure compliance with requirements. Many state directors of teacher credentialing have signed Interstate Agreements through NASDTEC that expedite the certification process.

MONTANA STATE UNIVERSITY - BOZEMAN

College of Education, Health, and Human Development
Department of Education

215 Reid Hall
Bozeman, Montana 59717
Phone: (406) 994-6670
Fax: (406) 994-3261
E-mail: uedrc@montana.edu
Internet: http://www.montana.edu

Institution Description: Montana State University - Bozeman is a public institution and land-grant college. It was chartered in 1893.

The Department of Education offers undergraduate and graduate programs leading to teacher certification in Montana.

Institution Control: Public.

Calendar: Semester. Academic year September to May.

Official(s): Dr. Robert Carson, Dean.

Faculty: Full-time 25; part-time 1; adjunct 23.

Degrees Awarded: 162 baccalaureate; 46 master's; 13 doctorate.

Admission Requirements: *Undergraduate:* Graduation from an accredited secondary school in upper half of graduating class; ACT composite score of 22 or a combined score of 1030 on SAT. *Teacher education specific:* Cumulative 2.5 SPA; Pre-Professional Skills Test (PPST) scores; passing score on writing exam; documentation of experience with children or adolescents. *Graduate:* Baccalaureate degree from a regionally accredited institution. *Teacher education specific:* Cumulative 3.0 GPA; minimum GRE score; recommendations; faculty interview.

Fees and Expenses: Undergraduate: in-state $4,070 per academic year; out-of-state $12,460. Graduate: in-state $235 per credit hour; out-of-state $592. Required fees: $572 for insurance. On-campus room and board: $5,370. Books and supplies: $1,000. Other expenses: $2,420.

Financial Aid: Resources specifically for eligible students enrolled in teacher education programs are awarded on the basis of financial need and academic merit. The institution has a Program Participation Agreement with the U.S. Department of

Education for eligible students to receive Pell Grants and other federal aid. Teacher scholarships available to qualifying students. *Contact:* Dr. Larry Baker at: (406) 994-4133.

Accreditation: *Regional:* NASC. *Professional:* NCATE. *Member of:* AACTE. *Approved by:* Montana State Board of Education.

Undergraduate Programs: Students majoring in elementary education must successfully complete a minimum of 128 credits to earn certification as an elementary school teacher. Options include early childhood education, library media K-12, mathematics, reading, and science education.

Secondary education students must earn a major in an academic field and complete 32-34 credits in education courses to be certified to teach grades 5-12. Multiple options are offered. All professional education courses must be passed with a 2.0 GPA or better.

Graduate Programs: The Master of Education in Curriculum and Instruction program provides academic preparation for prospective and in-service teachers who seek higher education in order to become master teachers, scholars, researchers, or curriculum coordinators in schools, districts, and in private and public educational agencies. The program is structured to allow full-time working professionals to continue their jobs while working toward an advanced degree. Four strands of the program include: practitioner for practicing educators; National Board Certification - for K-12 educators who want NBPTS certification while earning a master's degree; research - for those who want to pursue a doctoral degree; and master's plus certification - for individuals who already have a bachelor's degree and now want to become a teacher.

Licensure/Reciprocity: Montana. Reciprocity with Utah, Idaho, California. Students seeking teaching certification in other states should consult with that state's teacher certification office early in their program of study to insure compliance with requirements. Many state directors of teacher credentialing have signed Interstate Agreements through NASDTEC that expedite the certification process.

MONTANA STATE UNIVERSITY - NORTHERN

College of Education
Teacher Education Program
300 West 11th Street
Havre, Montana 59501
Phone: (406) 265-3700
Fax: (406) 265-3777
E-mail: msunadmit@msun.edu
Internet: http://msun.edu

Institution Description: Montana State University - Northern, formerly known as Northern Montana College, is a public institution. It was founded as Northern Montana Agriculture and Manual Training School in 1913 and became Northern Montana School in 1929. The present name was adopted in 1931.

Preparing students to become competent and productive educators is the primary goal of the Teacher Education Program.

Institution Control: Public.

Calendar: Semester. Academic year August to May.

Official(s): Dr. Darlene Sellers, Chair/Dean.

Faculty: Full-time 18.

Degrees Awarded: 61 baccalaureate; 75 master's.

Admission Requirements: *Undergraduate:* Graduation from an accredited secondary school or GED; ACT Composite. *Teacher education specific:* Completion of 34 semester credits of coursework with a 2.5 GPA; completion of basic education foundation courses; demonstrate verbal communication skills; two faculty recommendations. *Graduate:* Baccalaureate degree from a regionally accredited institution. *Teacher education specific:* Cumulative 3.0 GPA; GRE; recommendations; faculty interview;

Fees and Expenses: Undergraduate: in-state $3,800 per academic year; out-of-state $10,400. Graduate: Tuition charged per credit hour. On-campus room and board: $5,600. Other expenses: $1,400. Books and supplies: $1,000.

Financial Aid: Resources specifically for eligible students enrolled in teacher education programs are awarded on the basis of financial need and academic merit. The institution has a Program Participation Agreement with the U.S. Department of Education for eligible students to receive Pell Grants and other federal aid. Teacher scholarships available to qualifying students. *Contact:* Financial Aid Office at: (406) 265-3787.

Accreditation: *Regional:* NASC. *Professional:* NCATE. *Member of:* AACTE. *Approved by:* Montana State Board of Education.

Undergraduate Programs: Bachelor's degree programs include the elementary education program that leads to a teaching certificate to teach kindergarten through grade eight. Students completing one of the secondary education programs will lead to certification to teach in their subject area in grades 5-12 or K-12 in specific areas identified. Secondary education students who complete a regular major and a minor will be endorsed to teach in the two areas. Areas of concentration include: art, biology, early childhood, English, general science, health and physical education, history and social science, mathematics, music, physical science, reading, and science. All programs require the completion of a general education core, professional studies, field experiences, and student teaching.

Graduate Programs: The Master of Education degree is offered with options in counselor education or general science. The Master of Science in Education is offered with an option in learning development.

Licensure/Reciprocity: Montana. Students seeking teaching certification in a state other than Montana should consult with that state's teacher certification office early in their program of study to insure compliance with requirements. Many state directors of teacher credentialing have signed Interstate Agreements through NASDTEC that expedite the certification process.

UNIVERSITY OF GREAT FALLS

College of Education and Professional Studies
Education Department
1301 20th Street South
Great Falls, Montana 59405-4996
Phone: (406) 791-8210
Fax: (406) 791-5209
E-mail: enroll@ugf.edu
Internet: http://www.ugf.edu

Institution Description: University of Great Falls, formerly named College of Great Falls, is a private college affiliated with the Sisters of Providence, Roman Catholic Church. It was founded in 1932.

The Education Department offers undergraduate and graduate programs leading to teacher certification in Montana.

Institution Control: Private.

Calendar: Semester. Academic year August to May.

Official(s): Dr. Joe Fontana, Dean.

Faculty: Full-time 20.

Degrees Awarded: 54 baccalaureate; 3 master's.

Admission Requirements: *Undergraduate:* Graduation from an approved secondary school or GED; placement test required of all undergraduate students. *Teacher education specific:* Cumulative 2.5 SPA; Pre-Professional Skills Test (PPST) scores; evidence of writing ability by means of a brief essay; appropriate experience with youth; supportive recommendations; faculty interview. *Graduate:* Baccalaureate degree from a regionally accredited institution. *Teacher education specific:* Cumulative 3.0 GPA; minimum GRE score; recommendations; faculty interview.

Fees and Expenses: Undergraduate: $10,980 per academic year. Graduate: Tuition charged per credit hour. On-campus room and board: $5,100. Other expenses: $900. Books and supplies: $750.

UNIVERSITY OF GREAT FALLS—*cont'd*

Accreditation: *Regional:* NASC. *Member of:* AACTE. *Approved by:* Montana State Board of Education.

Undergraduate Programs: The elementary education program prepares prospective elementary teachers for successful teaching at all grade levels by providing thorough and balanced training in both teaching methods and content knowledge. Concentrations areas include: communication arts; early childhood; gifted and talented education, health and physical education; library/media services; mathematics; reading, science, social science, special education.

The secondary education major must be combined with an approved major and minor (or concentration. Approved majors include art, biology, English, general science, health and physical education, history, mathematics, social science, sociology, and special education.

The special education major must be combined with a major in elementary or secondary education. Special education teachers provide the most specialized diagnostic and prescriptive teaching available for children age three through twenty-one.

All programs lead to the Bachelor of Arts degree and include a general education core, professional studies, subject/content area, field experiences, and student teaching. A minimum of 128 semester hours is required for the degree award.

Graduate Programs: The graduate program includes coursework leading to the Master of Education degree, the Master of Arts in secondary teaching, and the Master of Science in counseling. A program leading to certification in elementary school administration is also available.

Licensure/Reciprocity: Montana. Students seeking teaching certification in a state other than Montana should consult with that state's teacher certification office early in their program of study to insure compliance with requirements. Many state directors of teacher credentialing have signed Interstate Agreements through NASDTEC that expedite the certification process.

UNIVERSITY OF MONTANA - MISSOULA

School of Education
Teacher Education Program
32 Campus Drive
Missoula, Montana 59812
Phone: (406) 243-4911
Fax: (406) 243-6757
E-mail: soe@.umt.edu
Internet: http://www.umt.edu

Institution Description: The University of Montana is a state institution that was founded in 1893.

The School of Education offers undergraduate and post-baccalaureate programs leading to Montana teaching licensure.

Institution Control: Public.

Calendar: Semester. Academic year August to May.

Official(s): Dr. Paul Rowland, Dean.

Faculty: Full-time 24.

Degrees Awarded: 142 baccalaureate; 86 master's; 9 doctorate.

Admission Requirements: *Undergraduate:* Graduation from an accredited secondary school in upper half of graduating class; ACT composite score of 22 or a combined score of 1030 on SAT. *Teacher education specific:* Cumulative 2.7 SPA; completion of 30 semester credits; Pre-Professional Skills Test (PPST) scores; evidence of writing ability by means of a brief essay; appropriate experience with youth; supportive recommendations from at least two faculty members. *Graduate:* Baccalaureate degree from a regionally accredited institution. *Teacher education specific:* Cumulative 3.0 GPA; minimum GRE score; recommendations; faculty interview.

Fees and Expenses: Undergraduate: in-state $3,960 per academic year; out-of-state $10,745. Graduate: Tuition charged per credit hour. On-campus room and board: $5,150. Other expenses: $2,800. Books and supplies: $760.

Financial Aid: Resources specifically for eligible students enrolled in teacher education programs are awarded on the basis of financial need and academic merit. The institution has a Program Participation Agreement with the U.S. Department of Education for eligible students to receive Pell Grants and other federal aid. Teacher scholarships available to qualifying students. *Contact:* Financial Aid Office at: (406) 243-5373.

Accreditation: *Regional:* NASC. *Professional:* NCATE. *Member of:* AACTE. *Approved by:* Montana State Board of Education.

Undergraduate Programs: The elementary education major prepares students to teach children K-8. The degree program includes a foundation in the liberal arts and sciences and one area of concentration.

Completion of requirements fro secondary teaching certificate/licensure prepares students to teach in middle and high schools, grades 5-12. Students major in the subject area they wish to teach.

All baccalaureate programs require the completion of a general education core, professional studies, subject/content area, field experiences, and student teaching. A minimum of 130 semester hours must be successfully completed for the degree award.

Graduate Programs: A combined Master's Degree/Certification in elementary or secondary education is a post-baccalaureate program offered through the Graduate Program in the Department of Curriculum and Instruction. Students complete a Master of Education in curriculum studies while earning the elementary or secondary certificate.

Licensure/Reciprocity: Montana. Students seeking teaching certification in a state other than Montana should consult with that state's teacher certification office early in their program of study to insure compliance with requirements. Many state directors of teacher credentialing have signed Interstate Agreements through NASDTEC that expedite the certification process.

UNIVERSITY OF MONTANA - WESTERN

Education Department
Teacher Education Program
710 South Atlantic Street
Dillon, Montana 59725-3598
Phone: (406) 683-7011
Fax: (406) 683-7493
E-mail: education@umwester.edu
Internet: http://www.umwestern.edu

Institution Description: The University of Montana - Western, formerly named Western Montana College, is a land-grant college. It was established in 1893.

The mission of the Education Department is the preparation of of teacher education candidates who exhibit content-knowledge, critical thinking, reflection, advocacy for children and a passion toward their profession.

Institution Control: Public.

Calendar: Semester. Academic year August to May.

Official(s): Dr. Cheri Jimeno, Dean.

Faculty: Full-time 24.

Degrees Awarded: 101 baccalaureate.

Admission Requirements: *Undergraduate:* Graduation from an accredited secondary school or GED; College Board SAT or ACT composite. *Teacher education specific:* Cumulative 2.7 SPA; completion of 30 semester credits; Pre-Professional Skills Test (PPST) scores; evidence of writing ability by means of a brief essay; appropriate experience with youth; supportive recommendations from at least two faculty members.:

Fees and Expenses: Undergraduate: in-state $3,240 per academic year; out-of-state: $8,885. On-campus room and board: $4,300. Other expenses: $2,995. Books and supplies: $675.

Financial Aid: Resources specifically for eligible students enrolled in teacher education programs are awarded on the basis of financial need and academic merit. The institution has a Program Participation Agreement with the U.S. Department of

Education for eligible students to receive Pell Grants and other federal aid. Teacher scholarships available to qualifying students. *Contact:* Financial Aid Office at: (406) 683-7511.

Accreditation: *Regional:* NASC. *Professional:* NCATE. *Member of:* AACTE. *Approved by:* Montana State Board of Education.

Undergraduate Programs: The Bachelor of Science in secondary education offers the following majors/minors that lead to secondary education or K-12 certificate endorsement: art, business education, biology, English, chemistry, computer science, dram, earth science, general science, health and physical education K-12, history, industrial technology, library K-12, mathematics, music K-12, physical science, reading K-12, social science, special education K-12.

The Bachelor of Science in elementary education (K-8) program must include specified courses. Students will be assigned an advisor upon acceptance into the teacher education program.

All bachelor degree programs require the completion of a general education core, professional studies, field experiences, subject/content area, and student teaching. A minimum of 120 semester hours must be successfully completed for the degree award.

Licensure/Reciprocity: Montana. Students seeking teaching certification in a state other than Montana should consult with that state's teacher certification office early in their program of study to insure compliance with requirements. Many state directors of teacher credentialing have signed Interstate Agreements through NASDTEC that expedite the certification process.

NEBRASKA

CHADRON STATE COLLEGE

Department of Education

1000 Main Street
Chadron, Nebraska 69337
Phone: (308) 432-6000
Fax: (308) 432-6464
E-mail: inquire@csc.edu
Internet: http://www.csc.edu

Institution Description: Chadron State College was established as Nebraska State Normal College in 1911. The name was changed to Nebraska State Teachers College in 1943 and the present name was adopted in 1960.

The Department of Education offers undergraduate and graduate programs leading to teacher certification in Nebraska.

Institution Control: Public.

Calendar: Semester. Academic year August to May.

Official(s): Dr. Patricia Cruzeiro, Chairperson.

Faculty: Full-time 11.

Degrees Awarded: 112 baccalaureate; 29 master's.

Admission Requirements: *Undergraduate:* Graduation from an accredited secondary school or GED; ACT/SAT not required if high school graduation 3 or more years prior to enrollment. *Teacher education specific:* 2.75 GPA; must pass PRAXIS I reading, writing, math exams. *Graduate:* Baccalaureate degree from a regionally accredited institution. *Teacher education specific:* GRE; PRAXIS II; 3.25 GPA on 12 credit hours; faculty interview; recommendations.

Fees and Expenses: Undergraduate: in-state $2,610 per academic year; out-of-state $5,220. Graduate: in-state $1,980; out-of-state $3,960. Required fees: $316. On-campus room and board: $3,654. Books and supplies: $600.

Financial Aid: Resources specifically for eligible students enrolled in teacher education programs are awarded on the basis of financial need and academic merit. The institution has a Program Participation Agreement with the U.S. Department of Education for eligible students to receive Pell Grants and other federal aid. Teacher scholarships available to qualifying students. *Contact:* Sherry Douglas at: (308) 432-6230 or e-mail at: sdouglas@csc.edu.

Accreditation: *Regional:* NCA. *Professional:* NCATE. *Member of:* AACTE. *Approved by:* Nebraska Department of Education.

Undergraduate Programs: Students can major in elementary education and receive certification as an elementary school teacher. A total of 120 credit hours with a 2.5 GPA in all areas is required for graduation. Ninety hours in residence and comprehensives in individual fields of study are also required.

Students can major in middle grades education with two content areas of specialization, and received certification as a middle school teacher. A total of 138 credit hours with a 2.5 GPA in all areas is required for graduation.

Students can major in secondary education and received certification as a secondary teacher. A total of 121 to 159 credit hours with a 2.5 GPA in all areas is required for graduation.

All programs lead to the baccalaureate degree and include a general education core, professional studies, subject/content area, field experiences, and student teaching.

Graduate Programs: The Department of Education offers advanced degree programs of study for teachers already certified at the baccalaureate level: Master of Science in Education (elementary,, secondary, school counseling). A Master of Science degree is offered in school administration with a focus on elementary or secondary school principal.

A Master of Arts in Education degree is offered in community counseling and with options in the following areas: language arts, humanities, fine arts, history, science/mathematics.

The Specialist in Education is offered with options for elementary principal, secondary principal, and school district superintendent.

Licensure/Reciprocity: Nebraska. Students seeking teaching certification in a state other than Nebraska should consult with that state's teacher certification office early in their program of study to insure compliance with requirements. Many state directors of teacher credentialing have signed Interstate Agreements through NASDTEC that expedite the certification process.

COLLEGE OF SAINT MARY

Education Department

1901 South 72nd Street
Omaha, Nebraska 68124
Phone: (402) 399-2432
Fax: (402) 399-2671
E-mail: mschulz@csm.edu
Internet: http://www.csm.edu

Institution Description: College of Saint Mary is a private, independent, nonprofit women's college founded in 1873 by the Sisters of Mercy, Roman Catholic Church.

The Education Department offers baccalaureate programs in teacher preparation leading to licensure in Nebraska.

Institution Control: Private.

Calendar: Semester. Academic year August to May.

Official(s): Dr. Merryellen Towey Schulz, Department Head.

Faculty: Full-time 3; part-time 1; adjunct 10.

Degrees Awarded: 9 baccalaureate.

Admission Requirements: *Undergraduate:* Graduation with 16 academic units from an accredited secondary school or GED; ACT composite preferred; College Board SAT accepted. *Teacher education specific:* Pass PRAXIS I reading writing, math exams; 2.5 GPA; legal clearance; digital portfolio; satisfactory performance in initial practica.

Fees and Expenses: Undergraduate: $15,770 per academic year. Required fees: $10 per credit technology fee; $50 matriculation fee. On-campus room and board: $6,000. Books and supplies: $500.

Financial Aid: Resources specifically for eligible students enrolled in teacher education programs are awarded on the basis of financial need and academic merit. The institution has a Program Participation Agreement with the U.S. Department of Education for eligible students to receive Pell Grants and other federal aid. Teacher scholarships available to qualifying students. *Contact:* Jenny Mosher at: (402) 399-2415 or e-mail at: jmosher@csm.edu.

Accreditation: *Regional:* NCA. *Approved by:* Nebraska Department of Education.

Undergraduate Programs: The Education Department offers a Bachelor of Arts or Bachelor of Science program for teachers at elementary levels (K-6). Students in the B.S. degree program major in elementary education and secure additional minors or majors in other certification programs. Students in the B.A. degree program major in both elementary education and an academic area.

The bachelor's degree program in early childhood education prepares the student for certification for teaching in pre-kindergarten through third grades. Graduates are prepared to assume greater responsibilities in professional settings.

Students with the special education endorsement may teach children and youth who are mildly and/or moderately disabled. Persons with this endorsement may also teach verified children and youth who are placed in multi-categorical programs.

The department offers endorsement in the following areas in secondary education: biology, chemistry, English, language arts, mathematics, natural science, general science.

All baccalaureate programs require the completion of a general education core, professional studies, subject/content area, field experiences, and student teaching.

Licensure/Reciprocity: Nebraska. Students seeking teaching certification in a state other than Nebraska should consult with that state's teacher certification office early in their program of study to insure compliance with requirements. Many state directors of teacher credentialing have signed Interstate Agreements through NASDTEC that expedite the certification process.

CONCORDIA UNIVERSITY NEBRASKA

800 North Columbia Avenue
College of Education
Seward, Nebraska 68434
Phone: (402) 643-3651
Fax: (402) 643-4073
E-mail: rbork@seward.cune.edu
Internet: http://www.cune.edu

Institution Description: Concordia University Nebraska is a private institution affiliated with the Lutheran Church-Missouri Synod. It was founded in 1894.

The university's mission in teacher education is to empower students as teachers, coaches, leaders, and learners for effective Christ-centered ministry and service to the church and the world.

Institution Control: Private.

Calendar: Semester. Academic year August to May.

Official(s): Dr. Ron Bork, Dean.

Faculty: Full-time 9; part-time 15; adjunct 4.

Degrees Awarded: 105 baccalaureate; 10 master's.

Admission Requirements: *Undergraduate:* Graduation with 16 academic units from an approved secondary school or GED; College Board SAT or ACT composite. *Teacher education specific:* 2.67 GPA; pass PRAXIS I reading, writing, math exams; portfolio; faculty interview.

Fees and Expenses: Undergraduate: $16,000 per academic year. Graduate: Tuition charged per credit hour. On-campus room and board: $5,000.

Financial Aid: Resources specifically for eligible students enrolled in teacher education programs are awarded on the basis of financial need and academic merit. The institution has a Program Participation Agreement with the U.S. Department of Education for eligible students to receive Pell Grants and other federal aid. Teacher scholarships available to qualifying students. *Contact:* Glo Hennig at: (402) 643-7270 or e-mail at: ghennig@seward.cune.edu.

Accreditation: *Regional:* NCA. *Professional:* NCATE. *Member of:* AACTE. *Approved by:* Nebraska Department of Education.

Undergraduate Programs: The elementary teacher education program consists of the general education component, the elementary education major, and a school subject concentration and electives. The program leads to the Bachelor of Science in Education degree and teacher certification.

Middle level content teaching areas include art, business education, foreign language, health and human performance, language arts, mathematics, natural sciences, and social sciences.

The secondary teacher education program consists of the general education component, professional education courses, and field endorsement, comprehensive subject major, or two subject endorsements and selected electives. Secondary field endorsements include: art K-12, business education, family and consumer sciences, industrial technology education, language arts, mathematics, music, health and physical education K-12, natural science, physical science, social science. Secondary subject endorsements include: biology, basic business, chemistry, English,geography, health, history, mathematics, music, physical education, physics, Spanish, speech/dram, theology.

Licensure/Reciprocity: Nebraska. Students seeking teaching certification in a state other than Nebraska should consult with that state's teacher certification office early in their program of study to insure compliance with requirements. Many state directors of teacher credentialing have signed Interstate Agreements through NASDTEC that expedite the certification process.

CREIGHTON UNIVERSITY

Education Department
2500 California Plaza
Omaha, Nebraska 68178
Phone: (402) 280-2820
Fax: (402) 280-1117
E-mail: sspencer@creighton.edu
Internet: http://www.creighton.edu

Institution Description: Creighton University is a private, independent, nonprofit institution. It was established as Creighton College in 1878.

The Education Department strives to produce teacher leaders who service public, Catholic, and other private schools in local and global diverse communities.

Institution Control: Private.

Calendar: Semester. Academic year August to August.

Official(s): Dr. Debra Ponce, Department Head; Dr Sharon Ishii-Jordan, Chair.

Faculty: Full-time 12; part-time 1; adjunct 13.

Degrees Awarded: 16 baccalaureate; 10 master's.

Admission Requirements: *Undergraduate:* Graduation from an accredited secondary school or GED; preference given to students with 2.5 GPA and class ranking in top 50th percentile; College Board SAT or ACT composite. *Teacher education specific:* Passing scores on writing, reading, and math exams on PRAXIS I test; completion of two college semesters; recommendations. *Graduate:* Baccalaureate degree from a regionally accredited institution. *Teacher education specific:* Minimum 3.0 GPA; passing scores on PRAXIS II before graduation; faculty interview.

Fees and Expenses: Undergraduate: $18,000 per academic year. Graduate: $507 per credit hour. Required fees: university fee $241 per semester. On-campus room and board: $6,440.

Financial Aid: Resources specifically for eligible students enrolled in teacher education programs are awarded on the basis of financial need and academic merit. Other awards based on leadership, ethnicity, alumni child. The institution has a Program Participation Agreement with the U.S. Department of Education for eligible students to receive Pell Grants and other federal aid. Teacher scholarships available to qualifying students. *Contact:* Robert Walker, Director of Financial Aid at: (800) 282-5835 or e-mail at: finaid@creighton.edu.

Accreditation: *Regional:* NCA. *Professional:* NCATE. *Member of:* AACTE. *Approved by:* Nebraska Department of Education.

CREIGHTON UNIVERSITY—*cont'd*

Undergraduate Programs: Students can major in elementary education and receive certification as an elementary school teacher. Students with prior undergraduate degrees are required to take only education classes for certification. Secondary students with prior degrees also take only education classes for certification. In some cases students must also take subject area classes to meet Nebraska certification requirements. All baccalaureate programs require the completion of a general education core, professional studies, subject/content area, field experiences, and student teaching. A GPA of 2.5 must be maintained throughout a program and no grade lower than C is acceptable. A minimum of 128 semester hours is required for the degree award.

Graduate Programs: The Department of Education offers secondary (7-12) initial teaching endorsements in the following subjects: art (K-12), biology, chemistry, English, French, German, history, journalism, language arts, Latin, mathematics, natural science, physical science, physics, political science, psychology, religious education (K-12), social science, sociology, Spanish, speech, theatre. Supplemental endorsements are offered in: computer science (7-12), English as a second language (K-12), and mild/moderate disabilities (7-12).

Licensure/Reciprocity: Nebraska. Students seeking teaching certification in a state other than Nebraska should consult with that state's teacher certification office early in their program of study to insure compliance with requirements. Many state directors of teacher credentialing have signed Interstate Agreements through NASDTEC that expedite the certification process.

DANA COLLEGE

Teacher Education Department
2848 College Drive
Blair, Nebraska 68008-1099
Phone: (402) 426-7337
Fax: (402) 426-7386
E-mail: admissions@dana.edu
Internet: http://www.dana.edu

Institution Description: Dana College is a private college affiliated with the Evangelical Lutheran Church in America. It was established as Trinity Seminary in 1884 and became Trinity Seminary and Blair College in 1885. The was name changed to Dana College and Trinity Seminary in 1903. Dana College became a separate entity in 1960.

The Teacher Education Program prepares students who want to become elementary, secondary, or special education teachers. The programs provide hands-on learning experiences and personalized advising and supervision.

Institution Control: Private.
Calendar: Semester. Academic year August to May.
Official(s): Dr. Ray Ferguson, Chair.
Faculty: Full-time 4.
Degrees Awarded: 18 baccalaureate.

Admission Requirements: *Undergraduate:* Graduation from an accredited secondary school or GED; ACT composite preferred, College Board SAT accepted. *Teacher education specific:* Declaration of an elementary or special education major or majoring in an area in which Dana certifies teachers at the secondary or K-12 level; passing scores on PRAXIS I test in reading, writing, and math exams; faculty interview.

Fees and Expenses: Undergraduate: $14,750 per academic year. On-campus room and board: $3,000. Other expenses: $1,620. Books and supplies: $600.

Financial Aid: Resources specifically for eligible students enrolled in teacher education programs are awarded on the basis of financial need and academic merit. The institution has a Program Participation Agreement with the U.S. Department of Education for eligible students to receive Pell Grants and other federal aid. Teacher scholarships available to qualifying students. *Contact:* Financial Aid Office at: (402) 426-1225.

Accreditation: *Regional:* NCA. *Professional:* NCATE. *Member of:* AACTE. *Approved by:* Nebraska Department of Education.

Undergraduate Programs: Those students who wish to graduate with a major in education must complete all program requirements (general education core, professional studies, subject/content area, field experiences, and student teaching) so that they are eligible for teacher certification in Nebraska. Teaching fields include: art (K-12), elementary education (K-6), mathematics (7-12), music (K-12), social science (7-12), special education (K-12). Teaching subjects 7-12 include: biology, business, chemistry, English, history, modern foreign language(German or Spanish). Teaching subjects K-12 include: instrumental music, physical education, vocal music.

Licensure/Reciprocity: Nebraska. Students seeking teaching certification in a state other than Nebraska should consult with that state's teacher certification office early in their program of study to insure compliance with requirements. Many state directors of teacher credentialing have signed Interstate Agreements through NASDTEC that expedite the certification process.

DOANE COLLEGE

Education Department
Teacher Education
1014 Boswell
Crete, Nebraska 68333
Phone: (402) 826-2161
Fax: (402) 826-8600
E-mail: admission@doane.edu
Internet: http://www.doane.edu

Institution Description: Doane College is a private, independent, nonprofit, liberal arts college affiliated with the United Church of Christ. It was established in 1858.

The Education Department is primarily responsible for the preparation of teachers and administrators in the K-12 schools.

Institution Control: Private.
Calendar: Semester (4-1-4 plan). Academic year August to May.
Official(s): Dr. Lyn C. Forester, Chair, Education Department.
Faculty: Full-time 12.
Degrees Awarded: 50 baccalaureate; 188 master's.

Admission Requirements: *Undergraduate:* Graduation with 16 academic units from an approved secondary school or GED; College Board SAT or ACT composite. *Teacher education specific:* 2.67 GPA; pass PRAXIS I reading, writing, math exams; portfolio; faculty interview. *Graduate:* Baccalaureate degree from a regionally accredited institution. *Teacher education specific:* PRAXIS II before graduation; GRE; recommendations; faculty interview.

Fees and Expenses: Undergraduate: $13,960 per academic year. Graduate: Tuition charged per credit hour. On-campus room and board: $4,300. Other expenses: $1,600. Books and supplies: $700.

Financial Aid: Resources specifically for eligible students enrolled in teacher education programs are awarded on the basis of financial need and academic merit. The institution has a Program Participation Agreement with the U.S. Department of Education for eligible students to receive Pell Grants and other federal aid. Teacher scholarships available to qualifying students. *Contact:* Financial Aid Office at: (402) 826-8260.

Accreditation: *Regional:* NCA. *Professional:* NCATE. *Member of:* AACTE. *Approved by:* Nebraska Department of Education.

Undergraduate Programs: Undergraduate majors include elementary education, special education, and secondary education (all students desiring secondary education certification major in the areas in which certification is sought). Areas include: art, biology, business principles, chemistry, English, English/language arts, French, German, history, mathematics, music, natural science, physical education, physical science, physics, political science, social science, Spanish, speech communication, theatre. Endorsements available include: middle school, early childhood, coaching, computer science, English as a second language. All baccalaureate programs require the completion of a minimum of 132 credit hours including a general education core, professional studies, subject/content area, field experiences, and student teaching.

Graduate Programs: The Master of Education in Curriculum and Instruction recognizes three broad categories of graduate student: degree-seeking, nondegree seeking, and endorsement seeking in the Accelerated Program (initial certification only for 7-12 programs). Thirty-six hours are required for the degree. Five courses are required; the remaining courses are electives that are selected by the graduate student in consultation with the academic advisor to best meet the professional goals of the student.

Licensure/Reciprocity: Nebraska. Students seeking teaching certification in a state other than Nebraska should consult with that state's teacher certification office early in their program of study to insure compliance with requirements. Many state directors of teacher credentialing have signed Interstate Agreements through NASDTEC that expedite the certification process.

HASTINGS COLLEGE

Department of Teacher Education
800 North Turner Avenue
Hastings, Nebraska 68901
Phone: (402) 463-2402
Fax: (402) 461-7490
E-mail: fcondos@hastings.edu
Internet: http://www.hastings.edu

Institution Description: Hastings College is a private, nonprofit college affiliated with the Presbyterian Church (USA). It was established in 1882.

The Teacher Education Department has a commitment to multicultural education, human relations, and successful living in a pluralistic society.

Institution Control: Private.

Calendar: Semester (4-1-4 plan). Academic year August to May.

Official(s): Dr. Fred J. Condos, Chair.

Faculty: Full-time 7.

Degrees Awarded: 48 baccalaureate; 17 master's.

Admission Requirements: *Undergraduate:* Graduation from an accredited secondary school or GED; College Board SAT or ACT composite. *Teacher education specific: Teacher education specific:* 2.5 GPA; pass PRAXIS I reading, writing, math exams; portfolio; faculty interview. *Graduate:* Baccalaureate degree from a regionally accredited institution. *Teacher education specific:* PRAXIS II before graduation; official transcripts for all previously attended colleges/universities; 2.5 overall GPA; two references from school administrators or college professors; faculty interview.

Fees and Expenses: Undergraduate: $14,554 per academic year. Graduate: Tuition charged per academic year. On-campus room and board: $4,000. Other expenses: $2,550. Books and supplies: $650.

Financial Aid: Resources specifically for eligible students enrolled in teacher education programs are awarded on the basis of financial need and academic merit. The institution has a Program Participation Agreement with the U.S. Department of Education for eligible students to receive Pell Grants and other federal aid. Teacher scholarships available to qualifying students. *Contact:* Financial Aid Office at: (402) 461-7391.

Accreditation: *Regional:* NCA. *Professional:* NCATE. *Member of:* AACTE. *Approved by:* Nebraska Department of Education.

Undergraduate Programs: Candidates for certification will be recommended for endorsement only in areas in which they have completed a successful student teaching experience. Field endorsements (at least one required for certification) include: art (K-12, general K-6); early childhood education (preK-3); elementary (K-8); language arts (7-12); mathematics (712); music-general (K-12); natural science (7-12); physical science (7-12), social science (7-12), special education mild/moderate (K-6, 7-12, K-12).

Subject endorsements include: basic business (7-12); biology (7-12); chemistry (7-12); coaching (7-12); English as a second language (K-12); German (7-12); history (7-12); music-instrumental (K-6, 7-12, K-12); physical education (K-6, 7-12, 12); physics (7-12); psychology (7-12); Spanish (7-12); theater (7-12); computer science; journalism and mass communication.

Graduate Programs: The Master of Arts in Teaching is offered to students who have a baccalaureate degree but no professional education and are seeking licensure to teach. Additionally, the program services certified and practicing teachers who are inclined to return to college to enhance their professional skills and add an endorsement area or to renew their certificate. The program requires 33 semesters of graduate credit.

Licensure/Reciprocity: Nebraska. Students seeking teaching certification in a state other than Nebraska should consult with that state's teacher certification office early in their program of study to insure compliance with requirements. Many state directors of teacher credentialing have signed Interstate Agreements through NASDTEC that expedite the certification process.

MIDLAND LUTHERAN COLLEGE

Teacher Education Program
900 North Clarkson
Fremont, Nebraska 68025
Phone: (800) 642-8382
Fax: (402) 721-0250
E-mail: admin@.mlc.edu
Internet: http://www.mlc.edu

Institution Description: Midland Lutheran College is a private college affiliated with the Nebraska and Rocky Mountain Synods of the Evangelical Lutheran Church in America. It was founded in 1888. The present name was adopted in 1962.

The Teacher Education Department faculty work in partnership with the campus community and area schools to provide students with academic coursework and field-based experiences in elementary, early childhood, and secondary settings.

Institution Control: Private.

Calendar: Semester (4-1-4 plan). Academic year September to May.

Official(s): Dr. Lori Moseman, Teacher Education Coordinator.

Faculty: Full-time 3.

Degrees Awarded: 26 baccalaureate.

Admission Requirements: *Undergraduate:* Graduation from an approved secondary school or GED; ACT composite. *Teacher education specific:* 2.5 GPA; pass PRAXIS I reading, writing, math exams; portfolio; faculty interview.

Fees and Expenses: Undergraduate: $15,400 per academic year. On-campus room and board: $4,300. Other expenses: $1,630. Books and supplies: $600.

Financial Aid: Resources specifically for eligible students enrolled in teacher education programs are awarded on the basis of financial need and academic merit. The institution has a Program Participation Agreement with the U.S. Department of Education for eligible students to receive Pell Grants and other federal aid. Teacher scholarships available to qualifying students. *Contact:* Financial Aid Office at: (402) 721-5480.

Accreditation: *Regional:* NCA. *Member of:* AACTE. *Approved by:* Nebraska Department of Education.

Undergraduate Programs: Programs are offered in early childhood, elementary, and secondary education leading to the Bachelor of Arts degree with a major in teacher education. Field endorsements include: art K-12, elementary K-8, mathematics 7-12, music K-12, natural science 7-12, physical science 7-12, social science 7-12, physical science K-6, physical education 7-12, speech/dram 7-12. Supplemental endorsements include coaching 7-12 and computer science 7-12.

Subject endorsements include: basic business 7-12, biology 7-12, chemistry 7-12, early childhood B-3, earth science 7-12, English 7-12, history 7-12.

MIDLAND LUTHERAN COLLEGE—*cont'd*

All programs require the completion of a general education core, professional studies, subject/content area, field experiences, and student teaching. A minimum of 128 credit hours is required for the degree award.

Licensure/Reciprocity: Nebraska. Students seeking teaching certification in a state other than Nebraska should consult with that state's teacher certification office early in their program of study to insure compliance with requirements. Many state directors of teacher credentialing have signed Interstate Agreements through NASDTEC that expedite the certification process.

NEBRASKA WESLEYAN UNIVERSITY
Department of Education
5000 St. Paul Avenue
Lincoln, Nebraska 68504-2796
Phone: (402) 466-2371
Fax: (402) 465-2179
E-mail: admissions@nebrwesleyan.edu
Internet: http://www.nebrwesleyan.edu

Institution Description: Nebraska Wesleyan University is a private, liberal arts institution affiliated with the United Methodist Church. It was established in 1887.

The Department of Education offers baccalaureate programs leading to teacher certification in Nebraska.

Institution Control: Private.

Calendar: Semester. Academic year August to May.

Official(s): Dr. Timothy Anderson, Department Chair.

Faculty: Full-time 4; part-time 3.

Degrees Awarded: 31 baccalaureate.

Admission Requirements: *Undergraduate:* Graduation from an accredited secondary school or GED; ACT composite. *Teacher education specific:* 2.5 GPA; pass PRAXIS I reading, writing, math exams; portfolio; faculty interview.

Fees and Expenses: Undergraduate: $15,645 per academic year. On-campus room and board: $4,446. Other expenses: $2,200. Books and supplies: $600.

Financial Aid: Resources specifically for eligible students enrolled in teacher education programs are awarded on the basis of financial need and academic merit. The institution has a Program Participation Agreement with the U.S. Department of Education for eligible students to receive Pell Grants and other federal aid. Teacher scholarships available to qualifying students. *Contact:* Financial Aid Office at: (402) 465-2212.

Accreditation: *Regional:* NCA. *Professional:* NCATE. *Member of:* AACTE. *Approved by:* Nebraska Department of Education.

Undergraduate Programs: The Bachelor of Arts and Bachelor of Science degree programs are offered in elementary education, middle grades education, and special education (mildly/moderately handicapped). Students seeking 7-12 certification receive a degree in their desired subject are. Students majoring in music receive a Bachelor of Music degree. Each education student receives a schedule from the department outlining the classes needed to reach his/her educational objective. In following the schedule, students graduate with a major and teaching certification in their field of interest. Students can also receive an endorsement in coaching or a field endorsement for general areas such as social sciences or language arts.

All programs require the completion of 126 credit hours including a general education core, professional studies, subject/content area, field experiences, and student teaching.

Licensure/Reciprocity: Nebraska. Students seeking teaching certification in a state other than Nebraska should consult with that state's teacher certification office early in their program of study to insure compliance with requirements. Many state directors of teacher credentialing have signed Interstate Agreements through NASDTEC that expedite the certification process.

PERU STATE COLLEGE
School of Education and Graduate Studies
Teacher Education Unit
P.O. Box 10
Peru, Nebraska 68421-9751
Phone: (402) 872-2244
Fax: (402) 872-2414
E-mail: ktande@oakmail.peru.edu
Internet: http://www.peru.edu

Institution Description: Peru State College was established as Mount Vernon College in 1865. The present name was adopted in 1963.

The Teacher Education Unit offers baccalaureate programs leading to teacher certification and preparation of teachers for the region, state, and the nation.

Institution Control: Public.

Calendar: Semester. Academic year August to May.

Official(s): Dr. Korinne Tande, Dean.

Faculty: Full-time 14; adjunct 10.

Degrees Awarded: 104 baccalaureate; 71 master's.

Admission Requirements: *Undergraduate:* Graduation from an accredited secondary school or GED; ACT composite. *Teacher education specific:* 2.5 GPA; pass PRAXIS I reading, writing, math exams; portfolio; faculty interview.

Fees and Expenses: Undergraduate: resident $87 per credit; nonresident $174. Graduate: resident $110 per credit; nonresident $220. On-campus room: $1,048 to $3,444 per academic year. Meal plans: $1,994 to $2,550 per academic year.

Financial Aid: Resources specifically for eligible students enrolled in teacher education programs are awarded on the basis of financial need and academic merit. The institution has a Program Participation Agreement with the U.S. Department of Education for eligible students to receive Pell Grants and other federal aid. Teacher scholarships available to qualifying students. *Contact:* Diana Lind at: (402) 872-2228 or e-mail at: dlind@oakmail.peru.edu.

Accreditation: *Regional:* NCA. *Professional:* NCATE. *Member of:* AACTE. *Approved by:* Nebraska Department of Education.

Undergraduate Programs: Baccalaureate programs available that lead to teacher certification are offered in the teaching fields of: art K-12, early childhood PreK-3, elementary K-8, language arts 7-12, mathematics 7-12, music K-12, middle grades education 4-9, natural science 7-12, physical science 7-12, social science 7-12, special education K-9/K-12 (mild/moderately handicapped). Supplemental endorsements include coaching 7-12 and computer science 7-12. Teaching subjects include: biology 7-12, basic business 7-12, chemistry 7-12, English 7-12, history 7-12, physical education K-6/7-12), preschool handicapped preK-K, vocal music K-6.

All programs require the completion of a general education core, professional studies, subject/content area, field experiences, and student teaching. A minimum of 125 credit hours are required for the degree award.

Licensure/Reciprocity: Nebraska. Students seeking teaching certification in a state other than Nebraska should consult with that state's teacher certification office early in their program of study to insure compliance with requirements. Many state directors of teacher credentialing have signed Interstate Agreements through NASDTEC that expedite the certification process.

UNION COLLEGE
Division of Human Development
3800 South 48th Street
Lincoln, Nebraska 68506
Phone: (402) 486-2331
Fax: (402) 486-2895
E-mail: ucenroll@ucollege.edu
Internet: http://www.ucollege.edu

Institution Description: Union College is a private liberal arts college affiliated with the Seventh-day Adventist Church. It was established in 1891.

The Division of Human Development offers degree programs in elementary and secondary education.

Institution Control: Private.

Calendar: Semester. Academic year August to May.

Official(s): Dr. Joe Allison, Division Chair.

Faculty: Full-time 12.

Degrees Awarded: 21 baccalaureate.

Admission Requirements: *Undergraduate:* Graduation from an accredited secondary school or GED; ACT composite. *Teacher education specific:* 2.5 GPA; pass PRAXIS I reading, writing, math exams; portfolio; faculty interview.

Fees and Expenses: Undergraduate: $12,158 per academic year. On-campus room and board: $3,390. Other expenses: $2,800. Books and supplies: $750.

Financial Aid: Resources specifically for eligible students enrolled in teacher education programs are awarded on the basis of financial need and academic merit. The institution has a Program Participation Agreement with the U.S. Department of Education for eligible students to receive Pell Grants and other federal aid. Teacher scholarships available to qualifying students. *Contact:* Financial Aid Office at: (402) 486-2505.

Accreditation: *Regional:* NCA. *Professional:* NCATE. *Member of:* AACTE. *Approved by:* Nebraska Department of Education.

Undergraduate Programs: The Bachelor of Science in elementary education is offered and requires 56 hours in the major. The student must complete the general education core, professional studies, field experiences, and student teaching.

The Bachelor of Science in secondary education requires the completion of 39 hours of professional education courses and 12 hours of special general education requirements plus the major area. Field endorsements include: art education K-12, language arts 7-12, mathematics 7-12, music education K-12, social science education 7-12. Subject endorsements include: art education K-6, biology 7-12, business education 7-12, computer education 7-12, English 7-12, history 7-12, music K-6/K-12, physical science 7-12, physics 7-12, religious education 7-12.

Licensure/Reciprocity: Nebraska. Students seeking teaching certification in a state other than Nebraska should consult with that state's teacher certification office early in their program of study to insure compliance with requirements. Many state directors of teacher credentialing have signed Interstate Agreements through NASDTEC that expedite the certification process.

UNIVERSITY OF NEBRASKA AT KEARNEY

College of Education
Teacher Education Program
COE Building - Room 117
1816 West 24th Street
Kearney, Nebraska 68849
Phone: (308) 865-8513
Fax: (308) 865-8987
E-mail: admissionsug@unk.edu
Internet: http://www.unk.edu

Institution Description: The University of Nebraska at Kearney (formerly Kearney State College) is a state institution. It was established in 1903.

The Professional Teacher Education Program administers the professional education component of all undergraduate and graduate teaching programs.

Institution Control: Public.

Calendar: Semester. Academic year August to May.

Official(s): Dr. Dennis Potthofff, Department Chair.

Faculty: Full-time 33.

Degrees Awarded: 158 baccalaureate; 165 master's.

Admission Requirements: *Undergraduate:* Graduation with 16 academic units from an accredited secondary school or GED; ACT composite recommended; College Board SAT accepted.

Teacher education specific: 2.5 GPA; pass PRAXIS I reading, writing, math exams; portfolio; faculty interview. *Graduate:* Baccalaureate degree from a regionally accredited institution. *Teacher education specific:* GRE combined score of 750 or better; current teaching endorsement where required by the program pursued.

Fees and Expenses: Undergraduate: in-state $3,610 per academic year; out-of-state $10,720. Graduate: Tuition charged per credit hour. On-campus room and board: $4,100. Other expenses: $2,780. Books and supplies: $720.

Financial Aid: Resources specifically for eligible students enrolled in teacher education programs are awarded on the basis of financial need and academic merit. The institution has a Program Participation Agreement with the U.S. Department of Education for eligible students to receive Pell Grants and other federal aid. Teacher scholarships available to qualifying students. *Contact:* Financial Aid Office at: (308) 865-8520.

Accreditation: *Regional:* NCA. *Professional:* NCATE. *Member of:* AACTE. *Approved by:* Nebraska Department of Education.

Undergraduate Programs: Undergraduate programs in teacher education leading to the Bachelor of Arts degree and teacher certification include: English as a second language; mild/moderate disabilities; early childhood special education; elementary education; middle grades teaching; early childhood education; minor in early childhood education. All baccalaureate programs require the completion of a general education core, professional studies, subject/content area, field experiences, and student teaching. A minimum of 125 credit hours must be successfully completed for the degree award.

Graduate Programs: The Master of Arts in Education - Curriculum and Instruction is a program designed for the professional educator. It requires thirty-six hours of coursework or thirty hours of coursework with six additional hours awarded for completion of a thesis. Both options culminate with a comprehensive examination over the curriculum, instructional, and foundations program components.

The Master of Science in Education Instructional Technology prepares graduates for careers in either business or education. The Master of Arts in Education degree program is offered with elementary education specialization; early childhood education; and reading specialization (K-6, 7-12, K-12). A Master of Science in Education: Middle School is also offered by the department.

Licensure/Reciprocity: Nebraska. Students seeking teaching certification in a state other than Nebraska should consult with that state's teacher certification office early in their program of study to insure compliance with requirements. Many state directors of teacher credentialing have signed Interstate Agreements through NASDTEC that expedite the certification process.

UNIVERSITY OF NEBRASKA AT OMAHA

College of Education
Teacher Education Department
Kayser Hall 314
60th and Dodge Street
Omaha, Nebraska 68182
Phone: (402) 554-3666
Fax: (402) 554-2023
E-mail: Danielson@mail.unomaha.edu
Internet: http://www.unomaha.edu

Institution Description: The campus was established as the University of Omaha in 1908. It became a campus of the University of Nebraska and the present name was adopted in 1968.

The Teacher Education Department offers undergraduate and graduate programs leading to teacher certification in elementary, middle level, and secondary education.

Institution Control: Public.

Calendar: Semester. Academic year August to May.

Official(s): Dr. Lana Danielson, Chair, Teacher Education Department.

Faculty: Full-time 66 (College of Education).

Degrees Awarded: 235 baccalaureate; 256 master's; 6 doctorate.

UNIVERSITY OF NEBRASKA AT OMAHA—
cont'd

Admission Requirements: *Undergraduate:* Graduation from an accredited secondary school or GED; College Board SAT or ACT composite. *Teacher education specific:* 2.5 GPA; pass PRAXIS I reading, writing, math exams; portfolio; faculty interview. *Graduate:* Baccalaureate degree from a regionally accredited institution. *Teacher education specific:* GRE; autobiographical statement; three letters of recommendation.

Fees and Expenses: Undergraduate: in-state $4,125 per academic year; out-of-state $10,720. Graduate: Tuition charged per credit hour. On-campus room and board: $5,840. Other expenses: $2,700. Books and supplies: $650.

Financial Aid: Resources specifically for eligible students enrolled in teacher education programs are awarded on the basis of financial need and academic merit. The institution has a Program Participation Agreement with the U.S. Department of Education for eligible students to receive Pell Grants and other federal aid. Teacher scholarships available to qualifying students. *Contact:* Financial Aid Office at: (402) 554-2327.

Accreditation: *Regional:* NCA. *Professional:* NCATE. *Member of:* AACTE. *Approved by:* Nebraska Department of Education.

Undergraduate Programs: The elementary education major is designed to prepare students to meet Nebraska requirements for an elementary (K-8) level teaching certificate. A minimum of 125 hours and a minimum cumulative GPA of 2.5 are required for completion of the degree and certification. The required coursework for the program is divided into four component areas: general education, professional core, professional major, and professional specialization.

The middle grades education program is designed to prepare students for Nebraska certification. The range of student may be from grades 4-9, depending on the organization of the individual district. The coursework for middle grades divided into five sections: general education, professional core, professional major, and two teaching areas. The academic teaching areas available at the middle grades level include: mathematics, science, language arts, and social science. One of the choices for the middle grades area must be mathematics or science.

The secondary education program is designed to prepare students for a secondary (7-12) level teaching certificate or a K-12 teaching or special services certificate. The required coursework is divided into three areas: general education, professional coursework, and the academic coursework for one field endorsement or two subject endorsements.

Graduate Programs: Teacher Education graduate programs include: Master of Arts in elementary or secondary education and the Master of Science in elementary education, reading, or secondary education. During the last semester or after completion of the coursework, students apply for comprehensive exams if they are not completing a thesis or a portfolio as part of their program.

Graduate Certificate Programs include: Instruction in Urban Schools and Instructional Technology.

Licensure/Reciprocity: Nebraska. Students seeking teaching certification in a state other than Nebraska should consult with that state's teacher certification office early in their program of study to insure compliance with requirements. Many state directors of teacher credentialing have signed Interstate Agreements through NASDTEC that expedite the certification process.

UNIVERSITY OF NEBRASKA - LINCOLN
College of Education and Human Services
Fourteenth and R Streets
Lincoln, Nebraska 68588
Phone: (402) 472-0889
Fax: (402) 472-6670
E-mail: jbofeldt@unl.edu
Internet: http://www.unl.edu

Institution Description: The institution was established and chartered in 1869.

The College of Education offers undergraduate and graduate programs leading to teaching and licensure in Nebraska.

Institution Control: Public.

Calendar: Semester. Academic year August to May.

Official(s): Dr. Marjorie Kostelnik, Dean.

Faculty: Full-time 37.

Degrees Awarded: 279 baccalaureate; 186 master's; 53 doctorate.

Admission Requirements: *Undergraduate:* Graduation with 16 academic units from an accredited secondary school or GED; ACT composite recommended; College Board SAT accepted. *Teacher education specific:* 2.5 GPA; pass PRAXIS I reading, writing, math exams; portfolio; faculty interview. *Graduate:* Baccalaureate degree from a regionally accredited institution. *Teacher education specific:* GRE; short autobiographical statement; three letters of recommendation.

Fees and Expenses: Undergraduate: in-state $4,125 per academic year; out-of-state $10,720. Graduate: Tuition charged per credit hour. On-campus room and board: $4,875. Other expenses: $2,420. Books and supplies: $760.

Financial Aid: Resources specifically for eligible students enrolled in teacher education programs are awarded on the basis of financial need and academic merit. The institution has a Program Participation Agreement with the U.S. Department of Education for eligible students to receive Pell Grants and other federal aid. Teacher scholarships available to qualifying students. *Contact:* Financial Aid Office at: (402) 472-2030.

Accreditation: *Regional:* NCA. *Professional:* NCATE. *Member of:* AACTE. *Approved by:* Nebraska Department of Education.

Undergraduate Programs: The elementary education program combines a solid foundation of courses in humanities, communication, mathematics, science, and social sciences with professional education courses. Professional courses include the foundations of education, child growth and development, multicultural education, instructional technology, and the principles of teaching all subject areas.

The middle level teacher education program allows students to become certified to teach in three special areas chosen from: mathematics, industrial technology, communications, world civilization, natural sciences, agriculture, art, family and consumer science, language arts, history, and social sciences.

The secondary education program includes the development of skills, dispositions, and understandings that must be evidenced in teaching/learning practices. Student teaching is the culminating experience and enables the student to integrate theory and practice, to refine teaching skills,and to gain valuable professional experience.

All programs require the completion of 124 semester hours.

Graduate Programs: The Master of Education program in teaching, learning, and teacher education requires core courses and courses in an approved focus area of study plus other course requirements. The degree program is offered both on-campus and as online courses.

Licensure/Reciprocity: Nebraska. Students seeking teaching certification in a state other than Nebraska should consult with that state's teacher certification office early in their program of study to insure compliance with requirements. Many state directors of teacher credentialing have signed Interstate Agreements through NASDTEC that expedite the certification process.

WAYNE STATE COLLEGE
School of Education and Counseling
Department of Teacher Education
1111 Main Street
Wayne, Nebraska 68787
Phone: (402) 375-7389
Fax: (402) 375-7204
E-mail: wscadmit@wscgate.wsc.edu
Internet: http://www.wsc.edu

Institution Description: Wayne State College is a unit of the Nebraska State College System. It was established in 1909.

The School of Education and Counseling offers undergraduate and graduate programs leading to teaching certification in Nebraska.

Institution Control: Public.

Calendar: Semester. Academic year August to May.

Official(s): Dr. Robert Sweetland, Department Chair.

Faculty: Full-time 13; part-time 11.

Degrees Awarded: 114 baccalaureate; 77 master's.

Admission Requirements: *Undergraduate:* Graduation with 16 academic units from an approved secondary school or GED; College Board SAT or ACT composite. *Teacher education specific:* 2.5 GPA; pass PRAXIS I reading, writing, math exams; portfolio; faculty interview. *Graduate:* Baccalaureate degree from a regionally accredited institution. *Teacher education specific:* GRE; autobiographical statement; letters of recommendation.

Fees and Expenses: Undergraduate: in-state $3,014 per academic year; out-of-state $5,300. Graduate: Tuition charged per credit hour. On-campus room and board: $3,760. Other expenses: $1,575. Books and supplies: $700.

Financial Aid: Resources specifically for eligible students enrolled in teacher education programs are awarded on the basis of financial need and academic merit. The institution has a Program Participation Agreement with the U.S. Department of Education for eligible students to receive Pell Grants and other federal aid. Teacher scholarships available to qualifying students. *Contact:* Financial Aid Office at: (402) 375-7230.

Accreditation: *Regional:* NCA. *Professional:* NCATE. *Member of:* AACTE. *Approved by:* Nebraska Department of Education.

Undergraduate Programs: Elementary education and elementary education with early childhood endorsement are available. Students may choose to add several endorsements to their basic elementary education program. The early childhood endorsement requires 30 hours and prepares students to work specifically with children from birth to age eight. Supplemental endorsements in English as second language (15 hours) and coaching (18 hours) are also available.

Programs are available for students who are planning to teach secondary grades 7-12. Students may prepare to teach music, art, or physical education in grades K-12. A supplemental endorsement in coaching (18 hours) is also available. All programs require completion of a general education core, professional studies, field experiences, and student teaching. A minimum of 125 credit hours is required for the degree award.

Graduate Programs: The Master in Education degree program in curriculum and instruction is designed primarily for K-12 teachers who wish to remain in the classroom and combine a teaching enhancement program with leadership and curriculum development skills. A typical program of study requires the completion of 36 credit hours (professional core courses-15 hours; content area of concentration-15 hours; plus an additional 6 hours of research application or thesis or electives).

Licensure/Reciprocity: Nebraska. Students seeking teaching certification in a state other than Nebraska should consult with that state's teacher certification office early in their program of study to insure compliance with requirements. Many state directors of teacher credentialing have signed Interstate Agreements through NASDTEC that expedite the certification process.

YORK COLLEGE
Education Department
1125 East 8th Street
York, Nebraska 68467-2699
Phone: (402) 363-5696
Fax: (402) 363-5699
E-mail: enroll@yc.ne.edu
Internet: http://www.yc.ne.edu

Institution Description: York College is a private liberal arts college affiliated with the Churches of Christ. The college was established in 1890.

The mission of York College is to provide a liberal arts education leading to an understanding of and philosophy of life consistent with Christian ideals.

Institution Control: Private.

Calendar: Semester. Academic year August to May.

Official(s): Dr. Kathleen B. Wheeler, Dean.

Faculty: Full-time 4; part-time 2.

Degrees Awarded: 27 baccalaureate.

Admission Requirements: *Undergraduate:* Graduation from an accredited secondary school; College Board SAT or ACT composite. *Teacher education specific:* Completion of 60 semester hour with a 2.5 GPA; PRAXIS I reading, writing, math exam scores; recommendations from three faculty members; freshman year portfolio; faculty interview.

Fees and Expenses: Undergraduate: $14,500 per academic year including tuition and fees, room, and meal plan.

Financial Aid: Resources specifically for eligible students enrolled in teacher education programs are awarded on the basis of academic merit. The institution has a Program Participation Agreement with the U.S. Department of Education for eligible students to receive Pell Grants and other federal aid. Teacher scholarships available to qualifying students. *Contact:* Deb Lowry at: (402) 363-5674 or e-mail at: dlowry@york.edu.

Accreditation: *Regional:* NCA. *Approved by:* Nebraska Department of Education.

Undergraduate Programs: Bachelor of Arts degree programs are available with field endorsement in: art K-12, elementary education, middle grades, religious education K-12, secondary: mathematics, natural science, physical science, speech/theatre, social science). Subject endorsements include: elementary general art K-6, physical education K-12, secondary: basic business, biology, English, history, psychology, reading and writing). A supplemental endorsement is offered in coaching 7-12.

All programs require the completion of a minimum of 128 semester hours including a general education core, professional studies, subject/content area, field experiences, and student teaching.

Licensure/Reciprocity: Nebraska. Students seeking teaching certification in a state other than Nebraska should consult with that state's teacher certification office early in their program of study to insure compliance with requirements. Many state directors of teacher credentialing have signed Interstate Agreements through NASDTEC that expedite the certification process.

NEVADA

SIERRA NEVADA COLLEGE

Teacher Education Program
999 Tahoe Boulevard
Incline Village, Nevada 89450-4269
Phone: (775) 831-1314
Fax: (775) 831-1347
E-mail: admissions@sierranevada.edu
Internet: http://www.sierranevada.edu

Institution Description: Sierra Nevada College is a private, independent, nonprofit college. It was established, chartered, and offered first instruction at the postsecondary level in 1969.

The mission of the Teacher Education Program is to provide the student with the knowledge and training to make him/her a successful teacher.

Institution Control: Private.

Calendar: Semester. Academic year September to May.

Official(s): Dr. Mary Peterson, Director.

Faculty: Full-time 27.

Degrees Awarded: 18 baccalaureate.

Admission Requirements: Certification programs: Baccalaureate degree from a regionally accredited institution. *Teacher education specific:* Transcripts from all postsecondary institutions attended; 3.0 GPA; 250-word essay (goal statement); PRAXIS reading, writing, math exam scores; minimum of 40 clock hours work with children.

Fees and Expenses: Contact the college for current fees and expenses.

Financial Aid: Resources specifically for eligible students enrolled in teacher education programs are awarded on the basis of financial need and academic merit. The institution has a Program Participation Agreement with the U.S. Department of Education for eligible students to receive Pell Grants and other federal aid. Teacher scholarships available to qualifying students. *Contact:* Financial Aid Office at: (775) 831-1314, ext. 4066.

Accreditation: *Regional:* NASC. *Member of:* AACTE. *Approved by:* Nevada Department of Education.

Graduate Programs: The "Fast-Track" program schedules the first and second semester coursework on weekends and evening. There are three program modules: Module One, Educational Foundations: The student will learn about learning and will be introduced to the sociological and psychological aspects of education. Module Two, Teaching Methods: The student will learn time-tested learning methods and classroom theory and style. Module Three: Student Teaching. Teaching experience in a public school where the student puts to use in an actual classroom setting what has been learned in the previous two modules. Concentrations are offered in the elementary and secondary levels.

The recertification program is designed for those licensed to teach in Nevada to grow professionally and renew their teaching licenses.

Licensure/Reciprocity: Nevada. Students seeking teaching certification in a state other than Nevada should consult with that state's teacher certification office early in their program of study to insure compliance with requirements. Many state directors of teacher credentialing have signed Interstate Agreements through NASDTEC that expedite the certification process.

UNIVERSITY OF NEVADA, LAS VEGAS

College of Education
Department of Curriculum and Instruction
CEB 354
4505 Maryland Parkway
Las Vegas, Nevada 89154-3001
Phone: (702) 895-3375
Fax: (702) 895-4068
E-mail: coe@unlv.edu
Internet: http://www.unlv.edu

Institution Description: The university was established as the Southern Regional Branch of the University of Nevada in 1951 and became a division in 1957. The name was changed to Nevada Southern University in 1965. The campus became autonomous in 1968 and the present name was adopted in 1969.

The Department of Curriculum and Instruction holds as its central mission the preparation and development of educators at all levels.

Institution Control: Public.

Calendar: Semester. Academic year August to May.

Official(s): Dr. Gregory A. Levett, Department Chairman.

Faculty: Full-time 40.

Degrees Awarded: 486 baccalaureate; 400 master's; 27 doctorate.

Admission Requirements: *Undergraduate:* Graduation from an accredited secondary school with a 3.0 GPA; College Board SAT or ACT composite. *Teacher education specific:* Completion of 24 hours of university core requirements with a 2.5 GPA; passing scores on the PRAXIS I reading, writing, and math exams; faculty interview. *Graduate:* Baccalaureate degree from a regionally accredited institution. *Teacher education specific:* Minimum of 18 hours of coursework in professional education; teaching license where appropriate for the program pursued; professional goal statement; faculty interview; recommendations.

Fees and Expenses: Undergraduate: in-state $2,626 per academic year; out-of-state $11,315. Graduate: Tuition is charged per credit hour. On-campus room and board: $6,940. Other expenses: $2,410. Books and supplies; $850.

Financial Aid: Resources specifically for eligible students enrolled in teacher education programs are awarded on the basis of financial need and academic merit. The institution has a Program Participation Agreement with the U.S. Department of Education for eligible students to receive Pell Grants and other federal aid. Teacher scholarships available to qualifying students. *Contact:* Judy Belanger at: (702) 895-3697.

Accreditation: *Regional:* NASC. *Professional:* NCATE. *Member of:* AACTE. *Approved by:* Nevada Department of Education.

Undergraduate Programs: Elementary education majors have the option to study in depth one subject area normally included in the elementary school curriculum (i.e. the major may select one of th approved areas of concentration. These areas include: art, early childhood education, English and literature, foreign language, health, mathematics, music, physical education, reading and language arts, social science, science, special education.

Secondary education majors must select from the fields available, a major (first) teaching field (one of the secondary areas of concentration) in which they wish to be licensed. Areas of concentration include: art, biological science, business education, chemistry, speech communication, earth science, English literature/American literature, English, French, general science, German, health, history, journalism, mathematics, physical science, physics, political science, social science, Spanish, theatre arts.

All programs include a general education core, professional studies, subject/content area, field experiences, and student teaching. The requirements for each of the Bachelor of Arts in Education degrees are identical to the Bachelor of Science in Education degrees in each of the fields with the exception that for the Bachelor of Arts students must successfully complete two courses in the same foreign language.

Graduate Programs: The Department of Curriculum and Instruction offers the Master of Education and the Master of Science degrees. Both degrees require a minimum of 36 semester hours of study. Students in the Master of Science program must complete a core of six semester hours in research and three semester hours in foundations. Students in the Master of Education program may take a comprehensive examination or complete a professional paper/project as the culminating activity for this degree. A thesis and its defense is the culminating activity for the Master of Science program.

Licensure/Reciprocity: Nevada. Students seeking teaching certification in a state other than Nevada should consult with that state's teacher certification office early in their program of study to insure compliance with requirements. Many state directors of teacher credentialing have signed Interstate Agreements through NASDTEC that expedite the certification process.

UNIVERSITY OF NEVADA, RENO
Department of Curriculum, Teaching, and Learning
Teacher Preparation Programs
College of Education Building - Room 2005
Mail Stop 280
Reno, Nevada 89557
Phone: (702) 775-4961
Fax: (702) 775-5220
E-mail: asknevada@unr.edu
Internet: http://www.unr.edu

Institution Description: The school was chartered as a preparatory school in 1864 and then established as Nevada State University in Elko in 1874. The campus was moved to Reno and the name changed to University of Nevada in 1885. The present name was adopted in 1969.

The Teacher Education Programs include an elementary and secondary curriculum leading to teaching licensure in Nevada.

Institution Control: Public.

Calendar: Semester. Academic year August to May.

Official(s): Dr. Vernon Luft, Associate Dean.

Faculty: Full-time 12.

Degrees Awarded: 202 baccalaureate; 105 master's; 18 doctorate.

Admission Requirements: *Undergraduate:* Graduation from an accredited secondary school with a 3.0 GPA; College Board SAT or ACT composite. *Teacher education specific:* Completion of 30 hours of university core requirements with a 2.5 GPA; passing scores on the PRAXIS I reading, writing, and math exams; faculty interview. *Graduate:* Baccalaureate degree from a regionally accredited institution. *Teacher education specific:* Minimum of 18 hours of coursework in professional education; teaching license where appropriate for the program pursued; professional goal statement; faculty interview; recommendations.

Fees and Expenses: Undergraduate: in-state $2,626 per academic year; out-of-state $11,315. Graduate: Tuition is charged per credit hour. On-campus room and board: $6,99. Other expenses: $4,895. Books and supplies; $1,000.

Financial Aid: Resources specifically for eligible students enrolled in teacher education programs are awarded on the basis of financial need and academic merit. The institution has a Program Participation Agreement with the U.S. Department of Education for eligible students to receive Pell Grants and other federal aid. Teacher scholarships available to qualifying students. *Contact:* Financial Aid Office at: (775) 784-4666.

Accreditation: *Regional:* NASC. *Professional:* NCATE. *Member of:* AACTE. *Approved by:* Nebraska Department of Education.

Undergraduate Programs: At the undergraduate level, bachelor's degree programs are offered in elementary and secondary education. The Bachelor of Science in Education with an elementary major prepares students to be eligible for licensure in Nevada as an elementary teacher for grades K-8. The Bachelor of Science/Arts in Education with a secondary education major prepares students for licensure in Nevada as a secondary teacher for grades 7-12. Students must complete requirements in a teaching major in areas such as English, science, math, or social studies.

The bachelor's degree programs require the completion of a general education core, professional studies, subject/content area, field experiences, and student teaching. A minimum of 124 semester credits is required for the degree award.

Graduate Programs: Master's degree programs are offered in a variety of concentrations for elementary and secondary teachers. Also, a post-baccalaureate program is offered for persons who have completed a bachelor's degree outside of education and are interested in becoming classroom teachers in secondary education.

Licensure/Reciprocity: Nevada. Students seeking teaching certification in a state other than Nevada should consult with that state's teacher certification office early in their program of study to insure compliance with requirements. Many state directors of teacher credentialing have signed Interstate Agreements through NASDTEC that expedite the certification process.

NEW HAMPSHIRE

COLBY-SAWYER COLLEGE
Department of Social Sciences and Education
541 Main Street
New London, New Hampshire 03257
Phone: (603) 526-3660
Fax: (603) 526-3452
E-mail: jewing@colby-sawyer.edu
Internet: http://www.colby-sawyer.edu

Institution Description: Colby-Sawyer College (Colby Junior College until 1975) is a private, independent college. It was established and incorporated as New London Academy in 1837. The present name was adopted in 1975.

The education programs offered at Colby-Sawyer College provide the opportunity for motivated students to prepare for careers as teachers in public and private schools.

Institution Control: Private.

Calendar: Semester. Academic year September to May.

Official(s): Dr. Janice K. Ewing, Department Head.

Faculty: Full-time 20; part-time 1; adjunct 9.

Degrees Awarded: 16 baccalaureate.

Admission Requirements: *Undergraduate:* Graduation with 15 academic units from an approved secondary school or GED; College Board SAT or ACT composite. *Teacher education specific:* Official high school transcript; two academic recommendations; PRAXIS I reading, writing, math test scores.

Fees and Expenses: $22,500 per academic year. On-campus room and board: $8,520. Other fees: $900. Books and supplies: $750.

Financial Aid: Resources specifically for eligible students are awarded on the basis of financial need and academic merit. The institution has a Program Participation Agreement with the U.S. Department of Education for eligible students to receive Pell Grants and other federal aid. *Contact:* Financial Aid Office at: (603) 526-3717 or e-mail at: cscfinaid@colby-sawyer.edu.

Accreditation: *Regional:* NEASC. *Approved by:* New Hampshire State Department of Education.

Undergraduate Programs: The early childhood certification program leads to certification in grades K-3. Students must meet the requirements for certification by completing the major requirements for the Bachelor of Science degree in the child development program supplemented by a core of required courses in education, including a teaching internship.

The content area education program provides teachers with a substantial study in a disciplinary area, a solid background in the liberal arts and sciences, and a practical grounding in educational issues and methods. Art education (K-12), biology secondary education (7-12), English language arts, and social studies education (K-12) certifications can be earned. Students in these programs major in art (fine and performing), biology, English, history, society and culture respectively and complete a required group of education courses include the student teaching internship. A minimum of 120 semester credits must be completed for the degree award.

Licensure/Reciprocity: New Hampshire. Students seeking teaching certification in a state other than New Hampshire should consult with that state's teacher certification office early in their program of study to insure compliance with require-

ments. Many state directors of teacher credentialing have signed Interstate Agreements through NASDTEC that expedite the certification process.

KEENE STATE COLLEGE
Teacher Education/Certification Programs
229 Main Street
Keene, New Hampshire 03435-1506
Phone: (603) 352-1909
Fax: (603) 358-2767
E-mail: admissions@keene.edu
Internet: http://www.keene.edu

Institution Description: Keene State College is a part of the University System of New Hampshire. It was established as Keene Normal School in 1909 and became a four-year institution in 1939 known as Keene Teachers College. The college became a division of University System of New Hampshire in 1939.

Education coursework focuses on the development of an understanding of the teaching profession, diversity of learners, and effective teaching practices with a series of supervised pre-professional experiences.

Institution Control: Public.

Calendar: Semester. Academic year August to May.

Official(s): Dr. Dottie Bauer, Department Chair.

Faculty: Full-time 29.

Degrees Awarded: 171 baccalaureate; 47 master's.

Admission Requirements: *Undergraduate:* Graduation from an approved secondary school with college preparatory program or GED; College Board SAT. *Teacher education specific:* Completion of PRAXIS I reading, writing, and math test scores; completion of 36 credits with 2.5 GPA; two references; completion of education foundation courses. *Graduate:* Baccalaureate degree from a regionally accredited institution. *Teacher education specific:* A minimum of one year's full-time teaching experience; faculty interview.

Fees and Expenses: Undergraduate: in-state $6,510 per academic year; out-of-state $12,560. Graduate: Tuition is charged per credit hour. On-campus room and board: $5,700. Other expenses: $2,050. Books and supplies: $600.

Financial Aid: Resources specifically for eligible students enrolled in teacher education programs are awarded on the basis of financial need and academic merit. The institution has a Program Participation Agreement with the U.S. Department of Education for eligible students to receive Pell Grants and other federal aid. Teacher scholarships available to qualifying students. *Contact:* Financial Aid Office at: (603) 358-2280.

Accreditation: *Regional:* NCA. *Professional:* NCATE. *Member of:* AACTE. *Approved by:* New Hampshire State Department of Education.

Undergraduate Programs: Teacher certification programs are offered with three options: early childhood (birth through age 8); elementary education (kindergarten through grade 6/8); elementary/special education; middle-junior high school mathematics; secondary/special education; secondary education teacher certification in the areas of biology, chemistry, chemistry-physics, earth sciences, social studies, English, French, mathematics, Spanish, technology education; K-12 certification in music, physical education. All options require the completion of a general education core, professional studies, subject/content area, field experiences, and student teaching. A minimum of 126 credit hours must be successfully completed for the degree award.

Graduate Programs: The Master of Education is offered with four options: special education, school counselor, educational leadership, and curriculum and instruction. The latter option is for the development and enhancement of teaching competencies and strategies for regular classroom teachers. The option is offered in two tracks. The first is designed for education professionals with experience in working in regular classrooms. The second track is designed for student with experiences that have led them to want to obtain an initial teaching certificate in childhood education, elementary education, middle school mathematics, physical education, or music education.

Licensure/Reciprocity: New Hampshire. Students seeking teaching certification in a state other than New Hampshire should consult with that state's teacher certification office early in their program of study to insure compliance with requirements. Many state directors of teacher credentialing have signed Interstate Agreements through NASDTEC that expedite the certification process.

PLYMOUTH STATE UNIVERSITY

Teacher Education Programs

MSC 38, Education Department
17 High Street
Plymouth, New Hampshire 03264-1595
Phone: (603) 535-2285
Fax: (603) 535-2879
E-mail: pcantor@mail.plymouth.edu
Internet: http://www.plymouth.edu

Institution Description: Plymouth State College is a member of the University System of New Hampshire. It was established in 1871.

The Council of Teacher Education is accountable for the development, administration, revision, and evaluation of all teacher education programs offered by Plymouth State University.

Institution Control: Public.

Calendar: Semester. Academic year September to May.

Official(s): Dr. Patricia Cantor, Department Head.

Faculty: Full-time 18; adjunct 2.

Degrees Awarded: 102 baccalaureate; 343 master's.

Admission Requirements: *Undergraduate:* Graduation from an approved secondary school with college preparatory program or GED; College Board SAT. *Teacher education specific:* Completion of PRAXIS I reading, writing, and math test scores; completion of 36 credits with 2.5 GPA; two references; completion of education foundation courses. *Graduate:* Baccalaureate degree from a regionally accredited institution. *Teacher education specific:* A minimum of one year's full-time teaching experience; faculty interview.

Fees and Expenses: Undergraduate: in-state $4,450 per academic year; out-of-state $10,110. Graduate: in-state $288 per credit hour; out-of-state $316. Required fees: $1,571. On-campus room and board: room $3,870 double; board $1,898 (meal plan).

Financial Aid: Resources specifically for eligible students enrolled in teacher education programs are awarded on the basis of financial need and academic merit. The institution has a Program Participation Agreement with the U.S. Department of Education for eligible students to receive Pell Grants and other federal aid. Teacher scholarships available to qualifying students. *Contact:* Financial Aid Office at: (603) 358-2280.

Accreditation: *Regional:* NCA. *Professional:* NCATE. *Member of:* AACTE. *Approved by:* New Hampshire State Department of Education.

Undergraduate Programs: The following programs are offered by the Teacher Education Department: art education (K-12); biological science education (7-12); childhood studies with an option in teacher certification (K-12); early childhood studies with an option in teacher certification (N-3); early childhood studies with an option in general special education (K-12); English with an option in teacher certification (5-12); French with an option in teacher certification (K-12); health education with an option in school health (K-12); mathematics with options in middle school teacher certification (K-8) and secondary teacher certification (7-12); music education (K-12); physical science education (7-12) with option sin chemistry and physical science; social science with an option in social studies teacher certification (5-12); Spanish with an option in teacher certification (K-12). All programs require the completion of a general education core, professional studies, subject/content area, field experiences, and student teaching. A minimum of 122 credit hours must be completed for the degree award.

Graduate Programs: The post-baccalaureate conversion program is an individually designed, competency-based program of study leading to the recommendation for New Hampshire teacher certification for those individuals who already hold a bachelor's degree. Certification is available in all areas covered by the college's teacher education program. The Master of Education degree and teacher certification can be accomplished in N-3, K-8, and K-12, 5-8, and 7-12 discipline areas.

Licensure/Reciprocity: New Hampshire. Students seeking teaching certification in a state other than New Hampshire should consult with that state's teacher certification office early in their program of study to insure compliance with requirements. Many state directors of teacher credentialing have signed Interstate Agreements through NASDTEC that expedite the certification process.

SOUTHERN NEW HAMPSHIRE UNIVERSITY

Teacher Education Program

2500 River Road
Manchester, New Hampshire 03106
Phone: (603) 668-2211
Fax: (603) 645-9665
E-mail: lpelletier@snhu.edu
Internet: http://www.snhu.edu

Institution Description: Established as New Hampshire College in 1932, the institution offered its first postsecondary degree in 1966. The present name was adopted in 1969.

Education at Southern New Hampshire University is a growing area with a diverse array of programs at the undergraduate and graduate level. The programs provide opportunities for professional growth and acquisition of the increased knowledge necessary for teachers and educational administrators in today's modern society.

Institution Control: Private.

Calendar: Semester. Academic year September to May.

Official(s): Dr. Laurence Pelletier, Director, Business Teacher Education.

Faculty: Full-time 12.

Degrees Awarded: 10 baccalaureate; 55 master's.

Admission Requirements: *Undergraduate:* Graduation from an accredited secondary school or GED; essay; College Board SAT. *Teacher education specific:* PRAXIS reading, writing, and math exam scores; 2.5 GPA; recommendations; faculty interview. *Graduate:* Baccalaureate degree from a regionally accredited institution.

Fees and Expenses: Undergraduate: $18,264 per academic year. Graduate: Tuition is charged per credit hour. On-campus room and board: $6.924. Other expenses: $1,250. Books and supplies: $700.

Financial Aid: Resources specifically for eligible students enrolled in teacher education programs are awarded on the basis of financial need and academic merit. The institution has a Program Participation Agreement with the U.S. Department of Education for eligible students to receive Pell Grants and other federal aid. Teacher scholarships available to qualifying students. *Contact:* Financial Aid Office at: (603) 668-2211.

Accreditation: *Regional:* NEASC. *Member of:* AACTE. *Approved by:* New Hampshire State Department of Education.

SOUTHERN NEW HAMPSHIRE
UNIVERSITY—cont'd

Undergraduate Programs: The undergraduate programs include: business teacher education, early childhood, elementary and general special education, English teacher education, marketing teacher education; social studies teacher education. All programs lead to the baccalaureate degree and require the completion of a general education core, professional studies, subject/content area, field experiences, and student teaching. A minimum of 120 semester hours must be successfully completed for the degree award.

Graduate Programs: Graduate programs offered include: Master of Education in curriculum and instruction; elementary teacher with general special education; secondary teacher with general special education.

The Master of Science in business education and teaching English as a second language are also offered at the Manchester Campus. Graduate certificates are available in: advanced study in education; computer technology educator; professional study in education; training and development. New Hampshire certification programs include: elementary teacher in general special education; secondary teacher with general special education; English as a special language.

Licensure/Reciprocity: New Hampshire. Students seeking teaching certification in a state other than New Hampshire should consult with that state's teacher certification office early in their program of study to insure compliance with requirements. Many state directors of teacher credentialing have signed Interstate Agreements through NASDTEC that expedite the certification process.

UNIVERSITY OF NEW HAMPSHIRE

Department of Education

105 Main Street
Durham, New Hampshire 03824
Phone: (603) 862-1234
Fax: (603) 862-0077
E-mail: admissions@unh.edu
Internet: http://www.unh.edu

Institution Description: University of New Hampshire is a state institution and land-grant, sea-grant, and space-grant institution. It was established in 1866.

The Department of Education prepares students for professional roles in public and private schools, higher education, research institutions, and human service organizations.

Institution Control: Public.

Calendar: Semester. Academic year August to May.

Official(s): Dr. Todd DeMitchell, Dean, Department of Education.

Faculty: Full-time 39.

Degrees Awarded: 96 baccalaureate; 201 master's; 8 doctorate.

Admission Requirements: *Undergraduate:* Admission based primarily upon successful completion of college preparatory coursework; GED accepted; College Board SAT. *Teacher education specific:* PRAXIS I reading, writing, and math exam scores; 2.5 GPA; completion education foundation courses; faculty interview. *Graduate:* Baccalaureate degree from a regionally accredited institution. *Teacher education specific:* Teaching licensure where required by program pursued; faculty interview; recommendations.

Fees and Expenses: Undergraduate: in-state $8,554 per academic year; out-of-state $19,024. Graduate: Tuition charged per credit hour. On-campus room and board: $6,235. Other expenses: $2,302. Books and supplies: $1,200.

Financial Aid: Resources specifically for eligible students enrolled in teacher education programs are awarded on the basis of financial need and academic merit. The institution has a Program Participation Agreement with the U.S. Department of Education for eligible students to receive Pell Grants and other federal aid. Teacher scholarships available to qualifying students. *Contact:* Financial Aid Office at: (603) 862-3600.

Accreditation: *Regional:* NCA. *Member of:* AACTE. *Approved by:* New Hampshire State Department of Education.

Undergraduate Programs: The basic program in teacher education is the five-year program in which students begin preparation for teaching at the undergraduate level with a semester of field experience and professional coursework in education. Students complete a baccalaureate degree outside of education and move into a fifth year of study and full-year internship which lead to either the Master of Arts in Teaching or the Master of Education degree and licensure for teaching. Students in music, mathematics, nursery school/kindergarten have the option of choosing a basic four-year undergraduate program for licensure.

Graduate Programs: The Department of Education offers three levels of professional graduate degrees: The Master of Arts in Teaching and Master of Education with specializations in administration, counseling, early childhood, elementary and secondary teacher education, reading, and special education; the Certificate of Advanced Graduate Studies in administration; the doctorate with a Ph.D. in education and a Ph.D. in Literacy and Schooling.

Licensure/Reciprocity: New Hampshire. Students seeking teaching certification in a state other than New Hampshire should consult with that state's teacher certification office early in their program of study to insure compliance with requirements. Many state directors of teacher credentialing have signed Interstate Agreements through NASDTEC that expedite the certification process.

NEW JERSEY

COLLEGE OF NEW JERSEY

School of Education
Forcing Hall 158
200 Bennington Road
Ewing, New Jersey 08628-0718
Phone: (609) 771-2100
Fax: (609) 637-5117
E-mail: educate@tcnj.edu
Internet: http://www.tcnj.edu

Institution Description: The College of New Jersey, formerly named Trenton State College, is a public institution. It was chartered as New Jersey State Normal and Model Schools in 1855.

The mission of the School of Education is to create professionals prepared to enrich the lives of the people of New Jersey through education.

Institution Control: Public.

Calendar: Semester. Academic year September to May.

Official(s): Dr. Terence O'Connor, Dean; Dr. Susan Hydro, Assistant Dean.

Faculty: Full-time 70; part-time 4; adjunct 97.

Degrees Awarded: 352 baccalaureate; 233 master's.

Admission Requirements: *Undergraduate:* High school graduation reflecting appropriate challenging curriculum; SAT/ACT scores; two letters of recommendation. *Teacher education specific:* There are performance requirements for students to progress through programs of professional education; PRAXIS I tests. *Graduate:* Baccalaureate degree from a regionally accredited institution. *Teacher education specific:* 2.75 GPA; letters of recommendation; standardized tests appropriate to discipline; personal interview. Praxis II before graduation.

Fees and Expenses: Undergraduate: in-state $6,131 per academic year; out-of-state $10,706. Graduate: in-state $422.80 per credit hour; out-of-state $591.90. Required fees: $2,070. On-campus room and board: $7,744 basic plan. Books and supplies: $500 to $1,000 per academic year.

Financial Aid: Resources specifically for eligible students enrolled in teacher education programs are awarded on the basis of financial need and academic merit. The institution has a Program Participation Agreement with the U.S. Department of Education for eligible students to receive Pell Grants and other federal aid. Teacher scholarships available to qualifying students. *Contact:* Jamie Hightower, Director of Student Financial Assistance at $609) 721-2211 or e-mail at osfa@tenj.edu.

Accreditation: *Regional:* MSA. *Professional:* NCATE. *Member of:* AACTE. *Approved by:* New Jersey State Department of Education.

Undergraduate Programs: Students seeking certification to teach at the secondary level enroll in one of the following academic majors in another school at the college: biology, chemistry, physics, English, history, mathematics, Spanish. Courses in pedagogy and field experiences are coordinated through the School of Education.

Students pursuing elementary and early childhood education are enrolled in either major and are required to select a second major (art, biology, English, history, mathematics, music, psychology, sociology, Spanish, math/science/technology).

A program in special education, language and literacy is also offered.

All baccalaureate programs require the completion of a general education core, professional studies, field experiences, and student teaching.

Graduate Programs: A five-year undergraduate/graduate program leads to the Master of Arts degree and certification. The Master of Education degree is also offered.

Licensure/Reciprocity: New Jersey. Students seeking teaching certification in a state other than New Jersey should consult with that state's teacher certification office early in their program of study to insure compliance with requirements. Many state directors of teacher credentialing have signed Interstate Agreements through NASDTEC that expedite the certification process.

COLLEGE OF SAINT ELIZABETH

Education Department
2 Convent Road
Morristown, New Jersey 07960-6989
Phone: (973) 290-4000
Fax: (973) 290-4710
E-mail: apply@liza.st-elizabeth.edu
Internet: http://www.st-elizabeth.edu

Institution Description: College of Saint Elizabeth is a private women's college affiliated with the Sisters of Charity of Saint Elizabeth, Roman Catholic Church. The college was established and offered first instruction at the postsecondary level in 1899. The mission of programs in the Education Department is to prepare students to be reflective practitioners.

Institution Control: Private.

Calendar: Semester. Academic year September to May.

Official(s): Dr. Harriet Sepinwall, Dean.

Faculty: Full-time 8.

Degrees Awarded: 20 baccalaureate; 23 master's.

Admission Requirements: *Undergraduate:* Graduation from an accredited secondary school or GED; College Board SAT. *Teacher education specific:* 2.5 GPA; application to program by sophomore year; PRAXIS I; personal statement; faculty interview. *Graduate:* Baccalaureate degree from a regionally accredited institution. *Teacher education specific:* PRAXIS II before graduation; letters of recommendation; faculty interview.

Fees and Expenses: Undergraduate $16,450 per academic year. Graduate: Tuition charged per credit hour. On-campus room and board: $8,130. Other expenses: $2,250. Books and supplies: $1,000.

Financial Aid: Resources specifically for eligible students enrolled in teacher education programs are awarded on the basis of financial need and academic merit. The institution has a Program Participation Agreement with the U.S. Department of Education for eligible students to receive Pell Grants and other federal aid. Teacher scholarships available to qualifying students. *Contact:* Financial Aid Office at: (973) 290-4445.

Accreditation: *Regional:* MSA. *Member of:* AACTE. *Approved by:* New Jersey State Department of Education.

Undergraduate Programs: The college offers a program leading to the Bachelor of Arts in elementary education with a minor in secondary education. A Teacher of the Handicapped Certifica-

COLLEGE OF SAINT ELIZABETH—*cont'd*

tion program is also offered. The baccalaureate programs require the completion of a general education core, professional studies, field experiences, and student teaching.

Graduate Programs: The Master of Arts in Education program has been designed to prepare professional educators to assume leadership roles in meeting the challenges educational and human service settings represent as a result of current cultural, social, technological, economic, learning and health factors, and global concerns.

Licensure/Reciprocity: New Jersey. Students seeking teaching certification in a state other than New Jersey should consult with that state's teacher certification office early in their program of study to insure compliance with requirements. Many state directors of teacher credentialing have signed Interstate Agreements through NASDTEC that expedite the certification process.

FAIRLEIGH DICKINSON UNIVERSITY

Peter Sammartino School of Education
Mail Code T-BH@-01
1000 River Road
Teaneck, New Jersey 07666-1996
Phone: (201) 692-2834
Fax: (201) 692-2603
E-mail: schoolofed@fdu.edu
Internet: http://www.fdu.edu

Institution Description: Fairleigh Dickinson University is a private, independent, nonprofit institution with campuses in Madison and Teaneck. It was founded in 1942.

The School of Education offers teacher education programs at the Metropolitan Campus in Teaneck, NJ and the Florham Campus in Madison, NJ.

Institution Control: Private.

Calendar: Semester. Academic year September to May.

Official(s): Dr. Mary Farrell, Chair.

Faculty: Full-time 20; adjunct 25.

Degrees Awarded: 112 baccalaureate; 84 master's.

Admission Requirements: *Undergraduate:* Graduation from an accredited secondary school with 16 academic units in college preparatory courses; College Board SAT or ACT composite; GED accepted. *Teacher education specific:* Students must maintain a 3.0 or better GPA; PRAXIS I. *Graduate:* Baccalaureate degree from a regionally accredited institution. *Teacher education specific:* 2.75 GPA or better; PRAXIS II before graduation; two letters of recommendation; faculty interview.

Fees and Expenses: Undergraduate: $18,654 per academic year. Graduate: $681 per credit hour. Other fees apply. On-campus room and board: $3,86 to $10,188 depending on choices. Books and supplies: $560 to $625 per year.

Financial Aid: Resources specifically for eligible students enrolled in teacher education programs are awarded on the basis of financial need and academic merit. The institution has a Program Participation Agreement with the U.S. Department of Education for eligible students to receive Pell Grants and other federal aid. Teacher scholarships available to qualifying students. *Contact:* Financial Aid Office at: (201) 692-2505.

Accreditation: *Regional:* MSA. *Approved by:* New Jersey State Department of Education.

Undergraduate Programs: The QUEST Teacher Preparation Program is a five year accelerated, combined degree (B.A./B.S.-M.A.T.) program that provides students the opportunity to pursue professional studies for teacher preparation leading to state licensure while earning a bachelor's degree in a liberal arts major and a Master of Arts in Teaching degree. Students may obtain state certification in elementary or secondary education in English social studies, mathematics, biological and/or physical science, or world languages.

Graduate Programs: The Master of Arts in Teaching is a graduate program in teacher preparation for individuals who have a baccalaureate degree in the liberal arts and desire to enter the teaching profession. It requires completion of 36 credits of which 22 meet the eligibility requirements for a New Jersey teacher certification and 14 credits of required and elective courses. Programs are available in elementary and secondary education and teaching English as second language.

The Master of Arts in Education for certified teachers is designed to address the knowledge and competencies required for teachers to meet the professional demands in today's schools. The program requires the completion of 36 credits of which 18 are in core courses and 18 in the various certificate programs available.

The Master of Arts in educational leadership is offered as a two-year sequence of courses and field experiences. A total of 36 credits must be completed for the degree award.

A Master of Arts in learning disabilities with certification as a teacher of the handicapped is also offered as well as a dyslexia specialist certificate program.

Licensure/Reciprocity: New Jersey. Students seeking teaching certification in a state other than New Jersey should consult with that state's teacher certification office early in their program of study to insure compliance with requirements. Many state directors of teacher credentialing have signed Interstate Agreements through NASDTEC that expedite the certification process.

FELICIAN COLLEGE

Department of Education
Teacher Education Division
262 South Main Street
Lodi, New Jersey 07644
Phone: (201) 559-6131
Fax: (201) 559-6188
E-mail: admissions@felician.edu
Internet: http://www.felician.edu

Institution Description: Felician College is an independent, four-year, coeducational Catholic College sponsored by the Felician Sisters of the Lodi, New Jersey Province. It was established in 1923.

The college offers undergraduate and graduate programs leading to teacher certification.

Institution Control: Private.

Calendar: Semester. Academic year September to May.

Official(s): Dr. Donna Basson, Dean, Teacher Education Division.

Faculty: Full-time 24.

Degrees Awarded: 36 baccalaureate; 6 master's.

Admission Requirements: *Undergraduate:* Graduation from an accredited secondary school with 16 academic units or GED; College Board SAT or ACT composite. *Teacher education specific:* Personal goal statement; application to program by sophomore year; PRAXIS I; faculty interview. *Graduate:* Baccalaureate degree from a regionally accredited institution. *Teacher education specific:* PRAXIS II before graduation; letters of recommendation; faculty interview.

Fees and Expenses: Undergraduate: $14,500 per academic year. Graduate: Tuition is charged per credit hour.On-campus room and board: $7,200. Other expenses: $3,500. Books and supplies: $2,000.

Financial Aid: Resources specifically for eligible students enrolled in teacher education programs are awarded on the basis of financial need and academic merit. The institution has a Program Participation Agreement with the U.S. Department of Education for eligible students to receive Pell Grants and other federal aid. Teacher scholarships available to qualifying students. *Contact:* Financial Aid Office at: (201) 559-6010.

Accreditation: *Regional:* MSA. *Member of:* AACTE. *Approved by:* New Jersey State Department of Education.

Undergraduate Programs: Felician College offers undergraduates three state-approved programs. elementary education qualifies graduates for an elementary school certificate to teach kindergarten through 8th grade. The early childhood education program qualifies graduates for an elementary school certificate to teach pre-school through 3rd grade. The special education program qualifies graduates for the teacher of handicapped certificate to teach nursery through 12th grade. Teacher candidates must have a second major (e.g., art, biology, computer science, English, history, mathematics, religious studies, social/behavioral sciences).

Graduate Programs: The Master of Arts program is designed to prepare certified teachers to become instructional leaders in elementary education, special education, or supervision. The program consists of 33 credits for the elementary strand, 39 credits for the special education strand, and 33 credits for the supervisory strand.

The Teacher Education Certification program is for persons holding a baccalaureate degree who desire to become teachers. The programs leads to certification in elementary education N-8, early childhood P-3, or special education N-12.

Licensure/Reciprocity: New Jersey. Students seeking teaching certification in a state other than New Jersey should consult with that state's teacher certification office early in their program of study to insure compliance with requirements. Many state directors of teacher credentialing have signed Interstate Agreements through NASDTEC that expedite the certification process.

GEORGIAN COURT COLLEGE
School of Education
900 Lakewood Avenue
Lakewood, New Jersey 08701-2697
Phone: (732) 364-2200
Fax: (732) 367-3920
E-mail: admissions-ugrad@georgian.edu
Internet: http://www.georgian.edu

Institution Description: Georgian Court College is a private women's college affiliated with and owned by the Sisters of Mercy, Roman Catholic Church. It was incorporated in 1905.

The School of Education offers undergraduate and graduate programs leading to teaching licensure.

Institution Control: Private.

Calendar: Semester. Academic year August to May.

Official(s): Dr. John Groves, Dean.

Faculty: Full-time 19.

Degrees Awarded: 36 baccalaureate; 187 master's.

Admission Requirements: *Undergraduate:* Graduation from an approved secondary school or GED; College Board SAT or ACT composite. *Teacher education specific:* Completion of Basic Skills PRAXIS I exams; 60 credits (elementary or secondary) or 50 credits (special education; GPA 2.5 or higher for first two years of college. *Graduate:* Baccalaureate degree from a regionally accredited institution. *Teacher education specific:* Official transcripts of all college/university course work; minimum 2.75; teaching licensure where required; faculty interview; may take up to 6 credits before matriculating.

Fees and Expenses: Undergraduate: $16,272 per academic year. Graduate: Tuition charged per credit hour. On-campus room and board: $6,600. Other expenses: $2,500. Books and supplies: $600.

Financial Aid: Resources specifically for eligible students enrolled in teacher education programs are awarded on the basis of financial need and academic merit. The institution has a Program Participation Agreement with the U.S. Department of Education for eligible students to receive Pell Grants and other federal aid. Teacher scholarships available to qualifying students. *Contact:* Financial Aid Office at: (732) 364-2200, ext. 258.

Accreditation: *Regional:* MSA. *Member of:* AACTE. *Approved by:* New Jersey State Department of Education.

Undergraduate Programs: Programs leading to the Bachelor of Arts in Education degree include elementary education,secondary education, special education, and English as a second language. All programs require the completion of a general education core, professional studies, field experiences, subject content area, and student teaching.

Graduate Programs: Post-baccalaureate programs are offered for candidates who have earned a BA or BS degree and culminate with a New Jersey certificate.

Graduate programs for certified teachers include the Master of Arts in education; Master of Arts in administration, supervision, and curriculum planning; Master of Arts in special education. A Master of Arts in instructional technology is also available.

Licensure/Reciprocity: New Jersey. Students seeking teaching certification in a state other than New Jersey should consult with that state's teacher certification office early in their program of study to insure compliance with requirements. Many state directors of teacher credentialing have signed Interstate Agreements through NASDTEC that expedite the certification process.

KEAN UNIVERSITY
College of Education
Teacher Preparation Program
1000 Morris Avenue
Union, New Jersey 07083
Phone: (908) 737-3750
Fax: (908) 737-5134
E-mail: admitme@kean.edu
Internet: http://www.kean.edu

Institution Description: Kean University, formerly known as Kean College of New Jersey, is a state institution. It was established in 1855.

The College of Education offers baccalaureate and graduate programs leading to New Jersey teacher certification.

Institution Control: Public.

Calendar: Semester (4-1-4 plan). Academic year September to May.

Official(s): Dr. Ana Maria Schuhmann, Dean.

Faculty: Full-time 42 (Early Childhood/Instruction and Educational Leadership).

Degrees Awarded: 327 baccalaureate; 352 master's.

Admission Requirements: *Undergraduate:* Graduation from an approved secondary school with 16 academic units or GED; College Board SAT or ACT composite. *Teacher education specific:* Apply by beginning of sophomore year; PRAXIS I exams; cumulative GPA of 2.75; portfolio review; faculty interview. *Graduate:* Baccalaureate degree from a regionally accredited institution. *Teacher education specific:* Official transcripts of all college/university coursework; minimum 2.75; teaching licensure when required by program pursued.

Fees and Expenses: Undergraduate: in-state $6,723 per academic year; out-of-state $9,085. Graduate: Tuition charged per credit hour. On-campus room and board: $8,920. Other expenses: $125. Books and supplies: $1,000.

Financial Aid: Resources specifically for eligible students enrolled in teacher education programs are awarded on the basis of financial need and academic merit. The institution has a Program Participation Agreement with the U.S. Department of Education for eligible students to receive Pell Grants and other federal aid. Teacher scholarships available to qualifying students. *Contact:* Financial Aid Office at: (908) 737-3190.

Accreditation: *Regional:* MSA. *Professional:* NCATE. *Member of:* AACTE. *Approved by:* New Jersey State Department of Education.

Undergraduate Programs: The following programs are 4-year bachelor degree programs leading to licensure: early childhood education, elementary education, elementary education bilingual, special education (teacher of the handicapped), teacher of the deaf, secondary education (biology, chemistry, earth science, English, mathematics, social studies, Spanish), K-12 education (art, music, physical education, health, technology). All programs require the completion of 126 semester hours including a general education core, professional studies, field experiences, subject content area, and student teaching.

KEAN UNIVERSITY—*cont'd*

Graduate Programs: The Master of Arts in Teaching programs are for those holding a baccalaureate degree who wish to obtain teaching licensure. The programs include elementary education with concentrations in reading, educational media, English as a second language, bilingual education, educational administration, counselor education, special education and speech pathology. Other graduate programs leading to the Master of Arts in Education include: counselor education, early childhood, educational administration, educational media specialist, instructional media specialist, instruction and curriculum, reading, special education, and speech pathology.

Licensure/Reciprocity: New Jersey. Students seeking teaching certification in a state other than New Jersey should consult with that state's teacher certification office early in their program of study to insure compliance with requirements. Many state directors of teacher credentialing have signed Interstate Agreements through NASDTEC that expedite the certification process.

MONMOUTH UNIVERSITY

School of Education
Department of Curriculum and Instruction
400 Cedar Avenue
West Long Branch, New Jersey 07764-1898
Phone: (800) 543-9671
Fax: (732) 263-5640
E-mail: admission@monmouth.edu
Internet: http://www.monmouth.edu

Institution Description: Monmouth University, formerly known as Monmouth College, is a comprehensive, coeducational university. that began operation in 1933.

The mission of the Department of Curriculum and Instruction is to provide undergraduate and graduate programs for future and practicing teachers.

Institution Control: Private.

Calendar: Semester. Academic year September to May.

Official(s): Dr. William B. Stanley, Dean; Dr. Bruce Normandia, Chair, Department of Curriculum and Instruction.

Faculty: Full-time 15.

Degrees Awarded: 95 baccalaureate; 135 master's.

Admission Requirements: *Undergraduate:* Graduation from an approved secondary school with 16 Carnegie units in academic subjects or GED; College Board SAT. *Teacher education specific:* 30 semester hours of college credit; PRAXIS I exams (reading, writing, mathematics); cumulative GPA of 2.75; portfolio review; faculty interview. *Graduate:* Baccalaureate degree from a regionally accredited institution. *Teacher education specific:* Official transcripts of all college/university coursework; minimum 2.75; teaching licensure when required by program pursued; PRAXIS II tests before graduation.

Fees and Expenses: Undergraduate: $16,768 per academic year. Graduate: Tuition charged per credit hour. On-campus room and board: $7,568. Other expenses: $2,291. Books and supplies: $800.

Financial Aid: Resources specifically for eligible students enrolled in teacher education programs are awarded on the basis of financial need and academic merit. The institution has a Program Participation Agreement with the U.S. Department of Education for eligible students to receive Pell Grants and other federal aid. Teacher scholarships available to qualifying students. *Contact:* Financial Aid Office at: (732) 571-3463.

Accreditation: *Regional:* MSA. *Member of:* AACTE. *Approved by:* New Jersey State Department of Education.

Undergraduate Programs: The School of Education offers a program leading to the Bachelor of Arts in Education earned in conjunction with an acceptable Bachelor of Arts degree in a liberal arts discipline: anthropology, art, communication, English, foreign language, history, science, interdisciplinary, music, political science, or psychology. A Bachelor of Science in Education can be earned in conjunction with an acceptable Bachelor

of Science degree in a liberal arts discipline: biology, chemistry, computer science, or mathematics. A Bachelor of Science program in special education is also offered. All baccalaureate programs require the completion of a general education core, professional studies, content area major, field experiences, and student teaching.

Graduate Programs: The Master of Arts in Teaching Initial Certification is for those seeking a first time teaching license in New Jersey. The program is offered with concentration in elementary, middle, or high school settings.

The Master of Arts in Teaching Advanced is a program for professional teachers holding an undergraduate degree seeking to explore their own professional development. Courses cover a wide range of various content and professional growth areas.

Licensure/Reciprocity: New Jersey. Students seeking teaching certification in a state other than New Jersey should consult with that state's teacher certification office early in their program of study to insure compliance with requirements. Many state directors of teacher credentialing have signed Interstate Agreements through NASDTEC that expedite the certification process.

MONTCLAIR STATE UNIVERSITY

Center of Pedagogy Teacher Education Program
Chapin Hall 103
Valley Road and Normal Avenue
Upper Montclair, New Jersey 07043-1624
Phone: (973) 655-5407
Fax: (973) 655-7043
E-mail: cehs@montclair.edu
Internet: http://www.montclair.edu

Institution Description: Montclair State University, formerly Montclair State College, is a public institution. It was established and chartered in 1908.

The Teacher Education Program enhances a liberal arts background and an academic major with a sequence of professional coursework and clinical experiences that emphasize critical thinking.

Institution Control: Public.

Calendar: Semester. Academic year September to May.

Official(s): Dr. Ada Beth Cutler, Dean.

Faculty: Not reported.

Degrees Awarded: 89 baccalaureate; 299 master's.

Admission Requirements: *Undergraduate:* Graduation from an approved secondary school or GED; College Board SAT or ACT composite. *Teacher education specific:* PRAXIS I test exams (reading, writing, mathematics); 30 semester hours of college credit; cumulative GPA of 2.75; two faculty recommendations; faculty interview. *Graduate:* Baccalaureate degree from a regionally accredited institution. *Teacher education specific:* Official transcripts of all college/university coursework; minimum 2.75 GPA; teaching licensure when required by program pursued; faculty interview.

Fees and Expenses: Undergraduate: in-state $6,460 per academic year; out-of-state $9,460. Graduate: Tuition charged per credit hour. On-campus room and board: $7,780. Other expenses: $2,200. Books and supplies: $850.

Financial Aid: Resources specifically for eligible students enrolled in teacher education programs are awarded on the basis of financial need and academic merit. The institution has a Program Participation Agreement with the U.S. Department of Education for eligible students to receive Pell Grants and other federal aid. Teacher scholarships available to qualifying students. *Contact:* Financial Aid Office at: (973) 655-4461.

Accreditation: *Regional:* MSA. *Professional:* NCATE. *Member of:* AACTE. *Approved by:* New Jersey State Department of Education.

Undergraduate Programs: The teacher certification areas available at the undergraduate and graduate levels are listed by college of the university: College of Education and Human Services (health education, health and physical education, home economics comprehensive, early childhood education, physical education); College of Humanities and Social Sciences (English, English as a second language, French, Italian, Latin, Spanish, social studies); College of Science and Mathematics: (biological science, earth science, mathematics, physical science); School of the Arts (art, music comprehensive); School of Business (book-keeping and accounting, comprehensive business education, data processing, economics, general business, secretarial studies, typewriting). All baccalaureate programs require the completion of a general education core, professional studies, content area major, field experiences, and student teaching. A minimum of 128 credit hours must be completed for the degree award.

Graduate Programs: Additional graduate level programs are offered in administration, counseling, educational media, reading, special education, and speech language pathology.

Licensure/Reciprocity: New Jersey. Students seeking teaching certification in a state other than New Jersey should consult with that state's teacher certification office early in their program of study to insure compliance with requirements. Many state directors of teacher credentialing have signed Interstate Agreements through NASDTEC that expedite the certification process.

NEW JERSEY CITY UNIVERSITY
College of Education
Professional Studies Building
2039 Kennedy Boulevard
Jersey City, New Jersey 07305-1597
Phone: (201) 200-2101
Fax: (201) 200-3141
E-mail: admissions@@njcu.edu
Internet: http://www.njcu.edu

Institution Description: New Jersey City University, formerly named Jersey City State College, was established as New Jersey State Normal School in 1927. It became New Jersey State Teachers College in 1955, became Jersey City State College in 1958, and adopted the present name in 1998.

The College of Education provides leadership in meeting the educational and professional needs of its students. It is dedicated to preparing reflective urban practitioners with the knowledge, skills, and dispositions to help all children learn.

Institution Control: Public.

Calendar: Semesters. Academic year September to May.

Official(s): Dr. Muriel K. Rand, Dean.

Faculty: Not reported.

Degrees Awarded: 59 baccalaureate; 460 master's.

Admission Requirements: *Undergraduate:* Graduation from an approved secondary school or GED; College Board SAT. *Teacher education specific:* Students become teacher education candidates with successful completion of requirements for placement in the Junior Practicum; cumulative GPA of 2.75; PRAXIS I test exams (reading, writing, mathematics); portfolio review; faculty interview. *Graduate:* Baccalaureate degree from a regionally accredited institution. *Teacher education specific:* Official transcripts of all college/university coursework; minimum 2.75; two letters of recommendation; acceptable score on GRE or Miller Analogy Test; faculty interview.

Fees and Expenses: Undergraduate: in-state $2,778 per academic year; out-of-state $4,754.25. Graduate: in-state $7,166.25, out-of-state $11,783.10. Other fees may apply.

Financial Aid: Resources specifically for eligible students enrolled in teacher education programs are awarded on the basis of financial need and academic merit. The institution has a Program Participation Agreement with the U.S. Department of Education for eligible students to receive Pell Grants and other federal aid. Teacher scholarships available to qualifying students. *Contact:* Carmen Panlilio, Director, Financial Aid Office at: (201) 200-3173 or e-mail at cpanlilio@njcu.edu.

Accreditation: *Regional:* MSA. *Professional:* NCATE. *Member of:* AACTE. *Approved by:* New Jersey State Department of Education.

Undergraduate Programs: The College of Education offers baccalaureate programs leading to licensure for teaching grades K-3 in elementary schools; teaching grades K-8; secondary and middle school teaching history, English, foreign languages, science, social studies, and mathematics; special education; teaching art in grades K-12; teaching music in grades K-12. The Department of Multicultural Education offers programs leading to certification for teaching English as a second language. All baccalaureate programs require the completion of a general education core, professional studies, content area major, field experiences, and student teaching. A minimum of 128 semester hours must be completed for the degree award.

Graduate Programs: The Master of Arts degree programs include: early childhood education with a focus on children from birth through 8 years of age; educational psychology; educational technology; mathematics education; music education; literacy education (elementary reading, secondary reading, reading specialist); special education; urban education (administration and supervision, basic and urban studies concentration, English as a second language concentration, bilingual/bicultural concentration).

Coursework is available to prepare students for teacher of the handicapped certification and learning disabilities teacher consultant certification.

Licensure/Reciprocity: New Jersey. Students seeking teaching certification in a state other than New Jersey should consult with that state's teacher certification office early in their program of study to insure compliance with requirements. Many state directors of teacher credentialing have signed Interstate Agreements through NASDTEC that expedite the certification process.

RAMAPO COLLEGE OF NEW JERSEY
School of Social Science and Human Services
Teacher Education Program
505 Ramapo Valley Road
Mahwah, New Jersey 07430-1680
Phone: (201) 684-7627
Fax: (201) 684-7697
E-mail: admissions@ramapo.edu
Internet: http://www.ramapo.edu

Institution Description: Ramapo College of New Jersey is a four-year state college. It was established in 1969.

The Teacher Education Program seeks to ensure that teachers are prepared to communicate effectively, establish productive relationships, and respond to the needs of individual learners, the teaching profession, and the greater community.

Institution Control: Public.

Calendar: Semester. Academic year September to May.

Official(s): Dr. John A. Mulhern, Director, Teacher Education Program.

Faculty: Full-time 9.

Degrees Awarded: 18 baccalaureate; 80 master's.

Admission Requirements: *Undergraduate:* Graduation from an approved secondary school with 16 academic units or GED; College Board SAT. *Teacher education specific: Teacher education specific:* PRAXIS I test exams (reading, writing, mathematics); apply during sophomore year; cumulative GPA of 2.75; two faculty recommendations; personal interview. *Graduate:* Baccalaureate degree from a regionally accredited institution. *Teacher education specific:* Official transcripts of all college/university coursework; minimum 2.75 GPA; teaching licensure when required by program pursued; faculty interview.

Fees and Expenses: Undergraduate: in-state $7,412; out-of-state $11,666. On-campus room and board: $8,200. Other expenses: $1,550. Books and supplies: $850.

Financial Aid: Resources specifically for eligible students enrolled in teacher education programs are awarded on the basis of financial need and academic merit. The institution has a Program Participation Agreement with the U.S. Department of

RAMAPO COLLEGE OF NEW JERSEY—*cont'd*
Education for eligible students to receive Pell Grants and other federal aid. Teacher scholarships available to qualifying students. *Contact:* Financial Aid Office at: (201) 684-7549, ext. 549.

Accreditation: *Regional:* MSA. *Member of:* AACTE. *Approved by:* New Jersey State Department of Education.

Undergraduate Programs: Undergraduate programs leading to teaching licensure are offered in collaboration with the School of Social Science and Human Services. Students seeking the elementary education endorsement may select a major in any of the disciplines in the arts and sciences. Majors in art, history, literature, mathematics, music, psychology, and science are all appropriate for pursuing the endorsement. Students do not major in elementary education.

Secondary education endorsements are available in the following disciplines: art, biology, business, earth science, elementary education, English, French, health, Italian, mathematics, music, physical science, social studies, Spanish, speech arts and dramatics.

All baccalaureate programs require the completion of a general education core, professional studies, content area major, field experiences, and student teaching. A minimum of 128 semester hours must be completed for the degree award.

Licensure/Reciprocity: New Jersey. Students seeking teaching certification in a state other than New Jersey should consult with that state's teacher certification office early in their program of study to insure compliance with requirements. Many state directors of teacher credentialing have signed Interstate Agreements through NASDTEC that expedite the certification process.

RICHARD STOCKTON COLLEGE OF NEW JERSEY

Office of Teacher Education
Jimmie Leeds Road
P.O. Box 195
Pomona, New Jersey 08240-0195
Phone: (609) 652-4288
Fax: (609) 652-5528
E-mail: admissions@pollux.stockton.edu
Internet: http://www.stockton.edu

Institution Description: Richard Stockton State College is a public institution. It was established in 1969 and offered first instruction at the postsecondary level in 1971.

The Teacher Education program is a cooperative program involving the efforts of the liberal arts faculty, an adjunct faculty of experienced practitioners, and the schools in the vicinity of the college.

Institution Control: Public.

Calendar: Semester. Academic year September to May.

Official(s): Dr. Virginia W. deThy, Director; Dr. André Joyner, Assistant Director.

Faculty: Full-time 3; adjunct 25.

Degrees Awarded: 115 baccalaureate; 22 master's.

Admission Requirements: *Undergraduate:* Graduation from an approved secondary school with 16 academic units or GED. *Teacher education specific:* Cumulative GPA of 2.5 or better; completion of educational psychology course/fieldwork with a grade of B or better; experience working with children and individuals from diverse cultures and/or disabilities; pass reading, writing, and mathematics test of the PRAXIS I exam.

Fees and Expenses: Undergraduate: in-state $136 per credit hour; out-of-state $220. Graduate: in-state $298 per credit hour, out-of-state $416. Required fees: $39 per credit hour. Housing: $3,875 per academic year; meals $2,415 per academic year. Books and supplies: $825.

Financial Aid: Resources specifically for eligible students enrolled in teacher education programs are awarded on the basis of financial need and academic merit. The institution has a Program Participation Agreement with the U.S. Department of

Education for eligible students to receive Pell Grants and other federal aid. Teacher scholarships available to qualifying students. *Contact:* Jeanne Lewis at (609) 652-4203.

Accreditation: *Regional:* MSA. *Member of:* AACTE. *Approved by:* New Jersey State Department of Education.

Undergraduate Programs: The Teacher Education Program is offered as a post-baccalaureate certification as well as a degree program. Certification can either be in elementary or secondary education. Teaching endorsements are available in: art, biological science, earth science, elementary, English, English as a second language, French, Latin, mathematics, physical science, Spanish, social studies. Students are required to observe, assist, tutor, and practice teach in elementary and secondary schools and other institutions with educational settings. The program leading to the Teacher Education Degree requires a minimum of 32 additional credits beyond the initial degree (128 semester hours).

Licensure/Reciprocity: New Jersey. Students seeking teaching certification in a state other than New Jersey should consult with that state's teacher certification office early in their program of study to insure compliance with requirements. Many state directors of teacher credentialing have signed Interstate Agreements through NASDTEC that expedite the certification process.

RIDER UNIVERSITY

School of Education
2083 Lawrenceville Road
Lawrenceville, New Jersey 08648-3099
Phone: (609) 896-5000
Fax: (609) 895-6645
E-mail: admissions@rider.edu
Internet: http://www.rider.edu

Institution Description: Rider University, formerly Rider College, is a private, independent, nonprofit college that was founded in 1865.

The School of Education prepares undergraduate and graduate students for professional careers in education, organizations, and agencies in the diverse American society.

Institution Control: Private.

Calendar: Semester. Academic year September to May.

Official(s): Dr. Patricia Louise Leonard, Chairperson.

Degrees Awarded: 132 baccalaureate; 98 master's.

Admission Requirements: *Undergraduate:* Graduation from an approved secondary school with 16 academic units. *Teacher education specific:* Sophomore students must maintain a 2.5 GPA in all courses; display a commitment to study; PRAXIS I test exams (reading, writing, mathematics); portfolio review; faculty interview. *Graduate:* Baccalaureate degree from a regionally accredited institution. *Teacher education specific:* Official transcripts of all college/university coursework; minimum 2.5; teaching licensure when required by program pursued; two letters of recommendation; faculty interview.

Financial Aid: Resources specifically for eligible students enrolled in teacher education programs are awarded on the basis of financial need and academic merit. The institution has a Program Participation Agreement with the U.S. Department of Education for eligible students to receive Pell Grants and other federal aid. Teacher scholarships available to qualifying students. *Contact:* Financial Aid Office at: (609) 896-5360.

Accreditation: *Regional:* MSA. *Professional:* NCATE. *Member of:* AACTE. *Approved by:* New Jersey State Department of Education.

Undergraduate Programs: At the undergraduate level, the School of Education offers three degree programs: Bachelor of Science in Education with a major in comprehensive business education; Bachelor of Arts in elementary education with a major in elementary education (including minors in early childhood education, and special education); Bachelors of Arts in secondary education with majors in English, mathematics, science, social studies, and world language (French, German, Spanish). All baccalaureate programs require the completion of a general education core, professional studies, content area major, field experiences, and student teaching. A minimum of 120 semester hours must be completed successfully for the degree award.

Graduate Programs: The Education Specialist degree is offered in counseling services and school psychology. The Master of Arts degree is offered in the following areas: counseling services, curriculum instruction and supervision, educational administration, reading/language arts, special education, human services administration. In addition, the graduate department provides opportunity for study leading to teacher certification and other types of educational and human services certification.

Licensure/Reciprocity: New Jersey. Students seeking teaching certification in a state other than New Jersey should consult with that state's teacher certification office early in their program of study to insure compliance with requirements. Many state directors of teacher credentialing have signed Interstate Agreements through NASDTEC that expedite the certification process.

ROWAN UNIVERSITY

College of Education
201 Mullica Hill Road
Glassboro, New Jersey 08028-1701
Phone: (856) 256-4739
Fax: (856) 256-4472
E-mail: admissions@rowan.edu
Internet: http://www.rowan.edu

Institution Description: Rowan University, formerly known as Glassboro State College, is a public institution. It was incorporated in 1921.

The College of Education offers teacher preparation programs leading to licensure in New Jersey.

Institution Control: Public.

Calendar: Semester. Academic year September to May.

Official(s): Dr. Louis Molinari, Chair, Department of Elementary Education; Dr. Holly Willet, Chair, Department of Secondary Education.

Faculty: Full-time 38.

Degrees Awarded: 369 baccalaureate; 166 master's; 7 doctorate.

Admission Requirements: *Undergraduate:* Graduation from an approved secondary school with 16 academic units or GED; College Board SAT or ACT composite. *Teacher education specific:* PRAXIS I test exams (reading, writing, mathematics); cumulative GPA of 2.5; portfolio review; faculty interview. *Graduate:* Baccalaureate degree from a regionally accredited institution. *Teacher education specific:* Official transcripts of all college/university coursework; minimum 2.75; teaching licensure when required by program pursued; PRAXIS II tests before graduation.

Fees and Expenses: Undergraduate: in-state $7,258 per academic year; out-of-state $12,654. Graduate: Tuition charged per credit hour. On-campus room and board: $7,248. Other expenses: $1,850. Books and supplies: $1,000.

Financial Aid: Resources specifically for eligible students enrolled in teacher education programs are awarded on the basis of financial need and academic merit. The institution has a Program Participation Agreement with the U.S. Department of Education for eligible students to receive Pell Grants and other federal aid. Teacher scholarships available to qualifying students. *Contact:* Financial Aid Office at: (800 435-2557.

Accreditation: *Regional:* MSA. *Professional:* NCATE. *Member of:* AACTE. *Approved by:* New Jersey State Department of Education.

Undergraduate Programs: The Department of Secondary Education provides bachelor's degree certification programs in art, English, foreign languages, mathematics, music, science, social studies, speech/arts and drama, and business education. The Department of Elementary/Early Childhood Education offers programs leading to certification to teach nursery school through eighth grade, all subjects in a self-contained classroom. The programs lead to the baccalaureate degree.

Co-Teach is a five-year program that combines undergraduate preparation in Education and Liberal Arts with graduate study that leads to certification in elementary and special education and includes an option for certification in reading.

Graduate Programs: Graduate certification programs in English as a second language, bilingual education, and a Master of Science in Teaching (initial certification program) are offered by the Department of Secondary Education. The secondary program is designed for prospective teachers in social studies, English, mathematics, foreign language (Spanish and French), and science teachers. The elementary program is designed to prepare prospective teachers for nursery school through grade eight teaching. The special education program prepares teachers for K-12 placement.

Licensure/Reciprocity: New Jersey. Students seeking teaching certification in a state other than New Jersey should consult with that state's teacher certification office early in their program of study to insure compliance with requirements. Many state directors of teacher credentialing have signed Interstate Agreements through NASDTEC that expedite the certification process.

RUTGERS, THE STATE UNIVERSITY OF NEW JERSEY

Graduate School of Education
Teacher Certification Programs
New Brunswick, New Jersey 08903
Phone: (732) 445-3770
Fax: (732) 445-0237
E-mail: admissions@rutgers.edu
Internet: http://www.rutgers.edu

Institution Description: Rutgers, The State University is a public institution and a land-grant college with campuses in New Brunswick, Newark, and Camden. The university was chartered as Queens College in 1766. The name was changed to Rutgers College in 1825 became a land-grant college in 1864. The college assumed university status in 1924.

The Office of Teacher Education offers programs leading to the baccalaureate degree. The Graduate School of Education offers certification programs to individuals seeking initial teacher certification, additional certifications, and endorsements.

Institution Control: Public.

Calendar: Semester. Academic year September to May.

Official(s): Dr. Annell L. Simcoe, Executive Director, Teacher Education.

Faculty: Full-time 58.

Degrees Awarded: 108 baccalaureate, 260 master's; 24 doctorate.

Admission Requirements: *Undergraduate:* Graduation from an approved secondary school with 16 academic units or GED; College Board SAT or ACT composite. *Teacher education specific:* PRAXIS I Test exams (reading, writing, mathematics); cumulative GPA of 2.75; portfolio review; faculty interview. *Graduate:* Baccalaureate degree from a regionally accredited institution. *Teacher education specific:* Official transcripts of all college/university coursework; minimum 2.75; teaching licensure when required by program pursued; PRAXIS II tests before certification.

Fees and Expenses: Undergraduate: in-state $7,927 per academic year; out-of-state $14,441. Graduate: in-state $373 per credit hour; out-of-state $546.85. Part-time college fee (less than 9 credits per semester) for graduate study $115.50. Other fees may apply. On-campus room and board: $8,027. Other expenses: $2,018. Books and supplies: $775.

Financial Aid: Resources specifically for eligible students enrolled in teacher education programs are awarded on the basis of financial need and academic merit. The institution has a Program Participation Agreement with the U.S. Department of

RUTGERS, THE STATE UNIVERSITY OF NEW JERSEY—*cont'd*

Education for eligible students to receive Pell Grants and other federal aid. Teacher scholarships available to qualifying students. *Contact:* Financial Aid Office at: (732) 932-7755.

Accreditation: *Regional:* MSA. *Member of:* AACTE. *Approved by:* New Jersey State Department of Education.

Undergraduate Programs: The Office of Teacher Education works in conjunction with Rutgers' faculty to offer the Bachelor of Arts, post-Bachelor of Arts, and certification programs in a variety of subject areas. The programs cover the areas of early childhood, elementary education, English, English as a second language, foreign language, mathematics, science, social studies, and special education. All baccalaureate programs require the completion of a general education core, professional studies, content area major, field experiences, and student teaching. A minimum of 120 credit hours must be completed for the degree award.

A five-year program can be undertaken during the sophomore year of the bachelor's program. After completing an additional year of teacher education, a master's degree with teacher certification in the area of specialization is awarded.

Graduate Programs: The Master of Education certification programs are offered in biological science, elementary education (K-=8), English as a second language, English, foreign language, mathematics, physical science, social studies. The Master of Education programs for certification are offered for learning disabilities teacher consultant, reading specialist, administration, and counseling psychology for student personnel services licensure.

Endorsement programs are offered for preschool-grade 3 and for bilingual/bicultural education.

Five-year teacher education programs are offered in: biological science (K-12), elementary education (K-8), English (K-12), foreign language (K-12), mathematics (K-12), physical science (K-12), social studies (K-12), social studies (K-12), special education (K-12) and elementary education (K-8). A teacher of the handicapped certificate program is also available.

Licensure/Reciprocity: New Jersey. Students seeking teaching certification in a state other than New Jersey should consult with that state's teacher certification office early in their program of study to insure compliance with requirements. Many state directors of teacher credentialing have signed Interstate Agreements through NASDTEC that expedite the certification process.

SETON HALL UNIVERSITY

College of Education and Human Services
Kozlowski Hall, 4th Floor
400 South Orange Avenue
South Orange, New Jersey 07079-2697
Phone: (973) 761-9395
Fax: (973) 245-2187
E-mail: thehall@shu.edu
Internet: http://www.shu.edu

Institution Description: Seton Hall University is a private institution affiliated with the Archdiocese of Newark, Roman Catholic Church. It was established as Seton Hall College and offered first instruction at the postsecondary level in 1856. University status was achieved in 1950.

Candidates prepare for careers in teaching and supervisory positions by pursuing baccalaureate, master's, and doctoral programs.

Institution Control: Private.

Calendar: Semester. Academic year September to May.

Official(s): Dr. Joseph V. DePierro, Dean.

Faculty: Full-time 20; adjunct 16.

Degrees Awarded: 76 baccalaureate; 129 master's; 55 doctorate.

Admission Requirements: *Undergraduate:* Graduation from an approved secondary school with 16 academic units or GED; College Board SAT preferred; ACT composite accepted. *Teacher education specific:* PRAXIS I Test exams (reading, writing, mathematics); 2.75 GPA; portfolio review; achieving program specific benchmarks; faculty interview. *Graduate:* Baccalaureate degree from a regionally accredited institution. *Teacher education specific:* Official transcripts of all college/university coursework; minimum 2.75; teaching licensure when required by program pursued; PRAXIS II tests before certification; faculty interview.

Fees and Expenses: Undergraduate: $20,181 per academic year. Graduate: $649 per credit hour. Required fees: $2,325 undergraduate; $275 graduate. On-campus room and board: $8,550. Books and supplies: $300 to $500 per academic year.

Financial Aid: Resources specifically for eligible students enrolled in teacher education programs are awarded on the basis of financial need and academic merit. The institution has a Program Participation Agreement with the U.S. Department of Education for eligible students to receive Pell Grants and other federal aid. Teacher scholarships available to qualifying students. *Contact:* Joseph DePierro, Dean at: (973) 761-9025 or e-mail at: depierjo@shu.edu.

Accreditation: *Regional:* MSA. *Professional:* NCATE. *Member of:* AACTE. *Approved by:* New Jersey State Department of Education.

Undergraduate Programs: The Bachelor of Science degree program is offered with areas of specialization in: elementary education; early childhood education endorsement; secondary education content areas; special education; special education with dual major in elementary education; 4+2 program in special education and speech pathology. All baccalaureate programs require the completion of a general education core, professional studies, content area major, field experiences, and student teaching. A minimum of 128 credit hours must be completed for the degree award.

Graduate Programs: The Master of Arts in Education program is offered with areas of specialization in: elementary education; early childhood endorsement; secondary education content areas; certification in content areas. Also offered are the Master of Arts, Education Specialist, Doctor of Education, and Doctor of Philosophy in educational leadership, management, and policy. Other graduate degrees are offered in professional development, education media specialist, English as a second language, and bilingual/bicultural education.

Licensure/Reciprocity: New Jersey. Students seeking teaching certification in a state other than New Jersey should consult with that state's teacher certification office early in their program of study to insure compliance with requirements. Many state directors of teacher credentialing have signed Interstate Agreements through NASDTEC that expedite the certification process.

WILLIAM PATERSON UNIVERSITY OF NEW JERSEY

College of Education
300 Pompon Road
Wayne, New Jersey 07470
Phone: (973) 720-2137
Fax: (973) 720-2910
E-mail: agardjames@wpunj.edu
Internet: http://www.wpunj.edu

Institution Description: William Paterson University of New Jersey is a state institution. It was established as Paterson Normal School and offered first instruction at the postsecondary level in 1855. It assumed the name of William Patterson University of New Jersey in 1997.

The College of Education serves as a major resource for educational practitioners and institutions by preparing students for entry into teaching and educationally-related professions.

Institution Control: Public.

Calendar: Semester. Academic year September to May.

Official(s): Dr. Leslie Award James, Dean.

Faculty: Full-time 24.

Degrees Awarded: 128 baccalaureate; 164 master's.

Admission Requirements: *Undergraduate:* Graduation from an approved secondary school or GED; College Board SAT or ACT composite. *Teacher education specific:* Completion of PRAXIS I exams (reading, writing, mathematics); cumulative GPA of 2.75; portfolio review; faculty interview. *Graduate:* Baccalaureate degree from a regionally accredited institution. *Teacher education specific:* Official transcripts of all college/university coursework; minimum 2.75; teaching licensure when required by program pursued; PRAXIS II tests before certification; letters of recommendation; faculty interview.

Fees and Expenses: Undergraduate: in-state $7,120 per academic year; out-of-state $11,510. Graduate: Tuition charged per credit hour. On-campus room and board: $7,630. Other expenses: $1,500. Books and supplies: $880.

Financial Aid: Resources specifically for eligible students enrolled in teacher education programs are awarded on the basis of financial need and academic merit. The institution has a Program Participation Agreement with the U.S. Department of Education for eligible students to receive Pell Grants and other federal aid. Teacher scholarships available to qualifying students. *Contact:* Financial Aid Office at: (973) 720-2202.

Accreditation: *Regional:* MSA. *Professional:* NCATE. *Member of:* AACTE. *Approved by:* New Jersey State Department of Education.

Undergraduate Programs: Teacher education certification programs are available to undergraduate students in the areas of early childhood education (P-3), elementary education (K-8), secondary education subject field (K-12), physical education, and special education. All baccalaureate programs require the completion of a general education core, professional studies, content area major, field experiences, and student teaching. A minimum of 128 credit hours must be completed for the degree award.

Graduate Programs: The Master of Arts in Teaching degree program is offered in elementary education. Other post-baccalaureate certification include the areas of elementary education (K-8), subject field (K-12), special education, and school nurse.

Master of Education degree programs include special education developmental disabilities, counseling services, education, reading, and educational leadership.

Other post-baccalaureate certification programs are offered in: bilingual education; English as a second language; reading specialist; special education; educational media specialist; associate media specialist; learning disabilities teacher-consultant; reading teacher (K-12) endorsement; student personnel services; mathematics endorsement; physical education; driver education; supervisor.

Licensure/Reciprocity: New Jersey. Students seeking teaching certification in a state other than New Jersey should consult with that state's teacher certification office early in their program of study to insure compliance with requirements. Many state directors of teacher credentialing have signed Interstate Agreements through NASDTEC that expedite the certification process.

NEW MEXICO

EASTERN NEW MEXICO UNIVERSITY

College of Education and Technology
Office of Teacher Education
Campus Station 25
Portales, New Mexico 88130
Phone: (505) 562-2491
Fax: (505) 562-2523
E-mail: Jerry.Everhart@enmu.edu
Internet: http://www.enmu.edu

Institution Description: Eastern New Mexico University is a state school with branch campuses in Roswell and Ruidoso. The university was established and chartered in 1927.

The Department of Curriculum and instruction and the Department of Educational Studies offer programs leading to New Mexico teaching licensure.

Institution Control: Public.

Calendar: Semester. Academic year August to May.

Official(s): Dr. Steven C. Russell, Dean, College of Education and Technology; Dr. Jerry Everhart, Chair, Department of Curriculum and Instruction; Dr. Alan W. Garrett, Chair, Department of Educational Studies.

Faculty: Full-time 14 (Curriculum and Instruction).

Degrees Awarded: 127 baccalaureate; 57 master's.

Admission Requirements: *Undergraduate:* Graduation from an approved secondary school or GED; College Board SAT with 1 Achievement or ACT composite. *Teacher education specific:* Must have completed 40 semester hours of general education requirements; career GPA of at least 2.0; pass the Basic Skills portion of the New Mexico Teacher Assessment Test with a score of 240 or higher. *Graduate:* Baccalaureate degree from a regionally accredited institution. *Teacher education specific:* Transcripts of all college/university coursework; minimum 2.75; teaching licensure when required by program pursued; letters of recommendation; faculty interview.

Fees and Expenses: Undergraduate: in-state $2,472 per academic year; out-of-state $8,028. Graduate: Tuition charged per credit hour. On-campus room and board: $4,415. Other expenses: $4,772. Books and supplies: $770.

Financial Aid: Resources specifically for eligible students enrolled in teacher education programs are awarded on the basis of financial need and academic merit. The institution has a Program Participation Agreement with the U.S. Department of Education for eligible students to receive Pell Grants and other federal aid. Teacher scholarships available to qualifying students. *Contact:* Financial Aid Office at: (505) 562-2194.

Accreditation: *Regional:* NCA. *Professional:* NCATE. *Member of:* AACTE. *Approved by:* New Mexico State Department of Education.

Undergraduate Programs: The Department of Educational Studies offers a variety of coursework and degree programs. The department offers a baccalaureate degree in special education as well as the coursework necessary for secondary or K-12 New Mexico teaching licensure.

The Department of Curriculum and Instruction offers a major in elementary education with minors in bilingual education and reading education. Students completing this degree are eligible to teach in grades K-8. A 24-hour emphasis area is required.

All baccalaureate programs require the completion of a general education core, professional studies, content area major, field experiences, and student teaching. A minimum of 128 credit hours must be completed for the degree award.

Graduate Programs: At the graduate level, the Department of Educational Studies offers master's degrees in education (with emphasis in education administration or secondary education), special education, school guidance and counseling, as well as an alternative secondary teaching licensure program. The Department of Curriculum and Instruction offers coursework leading to the Master of Education. The program allows for emphases in the following areas: bilingual education, English as a second language, elementary education, pedagogy and learning, and reading/literacy education.

Licensure/Reciprocity: New Mexico. Students seeking teaching certification in a state other than New Mexico should consult with that state's teacher certification office early in their program of study to insure compliance with requirements. Many state directors of teacher credentialing have signed Interstate Agreements through NASDTEC that expedite the certification process.

NEW MEXICO HIGHLANDS UNIVERSITY

School of Education
Teacher Education Program
University Avenue
Las Vegas, New Mexico 87701
Phone: (505) 454-3256
Fax: (505) 454-3311
E-mail: admission@nmhu.edu
Internet: http://www.nmhu.edu

Institution Description: New Mexico Highlands University is a state institution. It was chartered and incorporated as New Mexico Normal College in 1893. The name was changed to New Mexico Normal University in 1898 and the present name was adopted in 1941.

The School of Education (SOE) is committed to providing experiences and knowledge to students seeking a degree or licensure in education. The SOE resource is the regional collaboration between the university and the Northern New Mexico Network for Regional Educators.

Institution Control: Public.

Calendar: Semester. Academic year August to May.

Official(s): Dr. Nicholas Sanchez, Director, Teacher Education Program.

Faculty: Full-time 20.

Degrees Awarded: 91 baccalaureate; 47 master's.

Admission Requirements: *Undergraduate:* Graduation from an approved secondary school with 15 academic units or GED; ACT composite preferred. *Teacher education specific:* Completion of education foundations courses with a grade of C or better; completion of the university's core curriculum in freshman and sophomore courses; New Mexico Teacher Assessment exams; faculty interview. *Graduate:* Baccalaureate degree from a regionally accredited institution. *Teacher education specific:* Official transcripts of all college/university coursework; minimum 2.75; letters of recommendation.

Fees and Expenses: Undergraduate: in-state $2,184 per academic year; out-of-state $9,096. Graduate: Tuition is charged per credit hour. On-campus room and board: $5,798. Other expenses: $3,505. Books and supplies: $722.

Financial Aid: Resources specifically for eligible students enrolled in teacher education programs are awarded on the basis of financial need and academic merit. The institution has a Program Participation Agreement with the U.S. Department of Education for eligible students to receive Pell Grants and other federal aid. Teacher scholarships available to qualifying students. *Contact:* Financial Aid Office at: (505) 454-3431.

Accreditation: *Regional:* NCA. *Professional:* NCATE. *Member of:* AACTE. *Approved by:* New Mexico State Department of Education.

Undergraduate Programs: The School of Education offers programs leading to the baccalaureate degree. The programs feature a liberal arts and sciences curriculum with opportunities to concentrate in the educational subjects of reading, technology education, early childhood education, and bilingual education, and arts and sciences subjects including art, English, Spanish, history, political science, chemistry, life science, mathematics, computer science, business, and human performance and sport. All programs require the completion of a general education core, professional studies, content field, field experiences, and student teaching. A minimum of 128 semester hours is required for the degree award.

Graduate Programs: The Master's Degree in Education offers a variety of concentrations and emphases. The Master of Arts option in education administration prepares individuals for licensure in administration. The Master of Arts option in special education provides the opportunity to specialize in the areas of the mentally disabled, behavior disorder, and learning disabled. An option in counseling and guidance offers a variety of emphases in school counseling, rehabilitation counseling, and professional counseling.

The curriculum and instruction option offers graduate work in a variety of academic content fields, with both elementary and secondary emphases. The emphasis field may include the educational subjects of reading, technology education, early childhood education, and bilingual education, and arts and sciences subjects including art, English, Spanish, history, political science, chemistry, life science, mathematics, computer science, business, and human performance and sport.

Licensure/Reciprocity: New Mexico. Students seeking teaching certification in a state other than New Mexico should consult with that state's teacher certification office early in their program of study to insure compliance with requirements. Many state directors of teacher credentialing have signed Interstate Agreements through NASDTEC that expedite the certification process.

NEW MEXICO STATE UNIVERSITY
College of Education
Department of Curriculum and Instruction
P.O. Box 30001
Las Cruces, New Mexico 88003
Phone: (505) 646-3121
Fax: (505) 646-6330
E-mail: admissions@nmsu.edu
Internet: http://www.nmsu.edu

Institution Description: New Mexico State University is a state institution and land-grant college, with 2-year colleges at Alamogordo, Dona Ana, Carlsbad, and Grants. The university was established in 1888.

The Department of Curriculum and Instruction offers programs leading to licensure and the baccalaureate, master's, and doctoral degrees.

Institution Control: Public.

Calendar: Semester. Academic year August to May.

Official(s): Dr. Robert B. Moulton, Dean; Dr. Herman S. Garcia, Head, Department of Curriculum and Instruction.

Faculty: Full-time 21; emeritus 11.

Degrees Awarded: 258 baccalaureate; 200 master's; 23 doctorate.

Admission Requirements: *Undergraduate:* Graduation from an approved secondary school or GED; ACT composite. *Teacher education specific:* Completion of education foundations courses with a grade of C or better; completion of the university's core curriculum in freshman and sophomore courses; New Mexico Teacher Assessment exams; faculty interview. *Graduate:* Baccalaureate degree from a regionally accredited institution. *Teacher education specific:* Official transcripts of all college/university coursework; minimum 2.75; letters of recommendation.

Fees and Expenses: Undergraduate: in-state $3,372 per academic year; out-of-state $11.250. Graduate: Tuition is charged per credit hour. On-campus room and board: $5,856. Books and supplies: $760.

Financial Aid: Resources specifically for eligible students enrolled in teacher education programs are awarded on the basis of financial need and academic merit. The institution has a Program Participation Agreement with the U.S. Department of Education for eligible students to receive Pell Grants and other federal aid. Teacher scholarships available to qualifying students. *Contact:* Financial Aid Office at: (505) 646-4105.

Accreditation: *Regional:* NCA. *Professional:* NCATE. *Member of:* AACTE. *Approved by:* New Mexico State Department of Education.

Undergraduate Programs: The primary function of the undergraduate programs is the preparation of licensed teachers for elementary and secondary schools. This process includes a broad general education, professional education, and teaching specializations. The Bachelor of Science in Education program offers majors in early childhood education, elementary education, and secondary education. Endorsements are available in bilingual education, business education, foreign languages, general science, language arts, mathematics, physical education, reading, social studies, and teachers of English as a second language.

Graduate Programs: The Master of Arts with an area of concentration is offered in curriculum and instruction, bilingual education, early childhood education, language/literacy/culture, teaching English to speakers of other languages, educational learning technologies.

The Master of Arts in Curriculum and Instruction is a program designed for students holding a bachelor's degree who wish to become licensed to teach in New Mexico while earning the master's degree.

The Master of Arts in Teaching requires completion of an area of teaching content specialization and professional education in the Department of Curriculum and Instruction.

Doctoral (Ph.D.) programs are offered for those who wish to serve as directors of instruction and curriculum and in supervisory positions.

Licensure/Reciprocity: New Mexico. Students seeking teaching certification in a state other than New Mexico should consult with that state's teacher certification office early in their program of study to insure compliance with requirements. Many state directors of teacher credentialing have signed Interstate Agreements through NASDTEC that expedite the certification process.

UNIVERSITY OF NEW MEXICO
College of Education
Educational Office Building, Room 109
Albuquerque, New Mexico 87131-2039
Phone: (505) 277-7267
Fax: (505) 277-8567
E-mail: marylou@unm.edu
Internet: http://www.unm.edu

Institution Description: The University of New Mexico is a state institution with branch campuses at Gallup, Los Alamos, Valencia, and Taos plus graduate centers at Los Alamos and Santa Fe. The university was established as a normal school and chartered in 1889.

UNIVERSITY OF NEW MEXICO—*cont'd*

The College of Education offers support to students interested in careers in K-12 and adult education. The college offers within its departments a wide range of programs that lead to baccalaureate, master's, and doctoral degrees.

Institution Control: Public.

Calendar: Semester. Academic year August to May.

Official(s): Dr. Viola Florez, Dean.

Faculty: Full-time 105; part-time 70; adjunct 26.

Degrees Awarded: 324 baccalaureate; 292 master's; 43 doctorate.

Admission Requirements: *Undergraduate:* Graduation from an approved secondary school or GED; College Board SAT or ACT composite. *Teacher education specific:* Completion of 26 semester hours; 2.7 overall GPA; New Mexico Teacher Assessment exams; satisfactory writing sample; three letters of recommendation from previous teachers or supervisors in child/youth related experiences; faculty interview. *Graduate:* Baccalaureate degree from a regionally accredited institution. *Teacher education specific:* Official transcripts of all college/university coursework; minimum 3.0; letters of recommendation; faculty interview.

Fees and Expenses: Undergraduate: in-state $1,565.50 per academic year; out-of-state $5,977.20. Graduate: in-state $1,801, out-of-state $6,135.40. On-campus room and board: $5,450. Other expenses: $1,526. Books and supplies: $1,366.

Financial Aid: Resources specifically for eligible students enrolled in teacher education programs are awarded on the basis of financial need and academic merit. The institution has a Program Participation Agreement with the U.S. Department of Education for eligible students to receive Pell Grants and other federal aid. Teacher scholarships available to qualifying students. *Contact:* Office of Student Financial Aid at: (505) 277-2041.

Accreditation: *Regional:* NCA. *Professional:* NCATE. *Member of:* AACTE. *Approved by:* New Mexico State Department of Education.

Undergraduate Programs: The Bachelor of Arts in Education program is offered with concentrations in art education, bilingual education, communications arts, modern and classical languages, social studies, and teaching English to speakers of other languages.

The Bachelor of Science in Education degree program is offered with concentrations in earth science, elementary education, life science, mathematics, physical education, physical science, special education, and technology and training.

All baccalaureate programs leading to initial licensure require the completion of a general education core, professional studies, content area, field experiences, and student teaching. A minimum of 128 credit hours is required for the degree award.

Graduate Programs: The Master of Arts degree program is offered with concentrations in art, counseling, educational leadership, educational psychology, elementary education, family studies, language/literacy/sociocultural studies, organizational learning and instructional technologies, recreation, secondary education, and special education.

The Master of Science degree program is available with concentrations in health education, nutrition, and physical education.

The Education Specialist (Ed.S.) program is offered with specializations in curriculum and instruction, educational leadership, organizational learning and instructional technologies, and special education.

Doctoral degree programs include the Doctor of Philosophy (counseling, educational linguistics, educational psychology, family studies, health/physical education/recreation; multicultural teacher and childhood education; organizational learning and instructional technologies, special education) and Doctor of Education (educational leadership, multicultural teacher and childhood education, special education).

Licensure/Reciprocity: New Mexico. Students seeking teaching certification in a state other than New Mexico should consult with that state's teacher certification office early in their program of study to insure compliance with requirements. Many state directors of teacher credentialing have signed Interstate Agreements through NASDTEC that expedite the certification process.

WESTERN NEW MEXICO UNIVERSITY

School of Education
1000 College Avenue
Silver City, New Mexico 88062
Phone: (505) 538-6106
Fax: (505) 538-6155
E-mail: soerecruiter@wnmu.edu
Internet: http://www.wnmu.edu

Institution Description: Western New Mexico University is a state institution. It was established and chartered as Territorial Normal School in 1893.

The School of Education offers undergraduate and graduate programs leading to teaching licensure in New Mexico.

Institution Control: Public.

Calendar: Semester. Academic year July to June.

Official(s): Dr. Jerry Hermon, Dean.

Faculty: Full-time 21.

Degrees Awarded: 47 baccalaureate; 102 master's.

Admission Requirements: *Undergraduate:* Graduation from an approved secondary school or GED; ACT composite. *Teacher education specific:* New Mexico Teacher Assessment exams; faculty interview. completion of 26 semester hours; 2.7 overall GPA; satisfactory writing sample; three letters of recommendation. *Graduate:* Baccalaureate degree from a regionally accredited institution. *Teacher education specific:* Official transcripts of all college/university coursework; minimum 3.2 GPA for the last 64 credit hours of undergraduate work; letters of recommendation; faculty interview.

Fees and Expenses: Undergraduate: in-state $2,370 per academic year; out-of-state $8,922. Graduate: Tuition is charged per credit hour. On-campus room and board: $4,280. Other expenses: $3,000. Books and supplies: $800.

Financial Aid: Resources specifically for eligible students enrolled in teacher education programs are awarded on the basis of financial need and academic merit. The institution has a Program Participation Agreement with the U.S. Department of Education for eligible students to receive Pell Grants and other federal aid. Teacher scholarships available to qualifying students. *Contact:* Financial Aid Office at: (505) 538-6173.

Accreditation: *Regional:* NCA. *Professional:* NCATE. *Member of:* AACTE. *Approved by:* New Mexico State Department of Education.

Undergraduate Programs: Baccalaureate programs leading to initial teaching licensure are offered with concentration areas of: art education, bilingual education (Navajo, Spanish, Zuni), classical languages, elementary education, general science, language arts, mathematics, music, psychology, reading, social studies, teaching English to speakers of other languages, theatre, and wellness. All programs require the completion of a general education core, professional studies, content area, field experiences, and student teaching. A minimum of 128 credit hours must be completed for the degree award.

Graduate Programs: The Master of Arts degree program offers specialized study beyond the baccalaureate degree. It is offered in a variety of disciplines and may be completed with or without a thesis. The Master of Arts in Teaching (M.A.T.) is a non-thesis degree. The purpose of the program is to add to the competence of educators in academic, pedagogical, and research skills. Previous teaching experience is not required for the M.A.T. program

Six graduate degree programs are available: Master of Arts in counseling; Master of Arts in educational leadership; Master of Arts in Teaching-elementary education, -secondary education, -reading education.

Licensure/Reciprocity: New Mexico. Students seeking teaching certification in a state other than New Mexico should consult with that state's teacher certification office early in their program of study to insure compliance with requirements. Many state directors of teacher credentialing have signed Interstate Agreements through NASDTEC that expedite the certification process.

NEW YORK

BANK STREET COLLEGE OF EDUCATION

Graduate School of Education
610 West 112th Street
New York, New York 10025
Phone: (212) 875-4400
Fax: (212) 875-4678
E-mail: grad.courses@bankstreet.edu
Internet: http://www.bankstreet.edu

Institution Description: Bank Street College of Education is a private, independent, nonprofit college. It was established in 1916 as the Bureau of Educational Experiments in 1916. The present name was adopted in 1950.

The Graduate School of Education provides programs that blend theory with practice through close integration of academic study and field-based experiences. These programs provide adults for professional work in schools, museums, hospitals, community organizations, and public service.

Institution Control: Private.

Calendar: Semester. Academic year August to July.

Official(s): Dr. Augusta Souza Kappner, President; Dr. Jon D. Snyder, Dean.

Faculty: Full-time 86; adjunct 60.

Degrees Awarded: 380 master's.

Admission Requirements: *Graduate:* Baccalaureate degree from a regionally accredited institution. *Teacher education specific:* 3.0 GPA; sensitivity towards others; interpersonal skills relating to children and adults; commitment to teaching and learning; faculty interview.

Fees and Expenses: $798 per credit hour.

Financial Aid: Resources specifically for eligible students enrolled in teacher education programs are awarded on the basis of financial need. Teacher scholarships available to qualifying students. *Contact:* Lou Palevsky at: (212) 875-4408 or e-mail at finaid@bankst.edu.

Accreditation: *Regional:* MSA. *Professional:* NCATE. *Member of:* AACTE. *Approved by:* New York State Department of Education.

Graduate Programs: The Master of Science in Education degree certification programs are offered in infant and parent development and early intervention (birth to age 3); early childhood (birth through grade 2); early childhood (birth through grade 2 and childhood/elementary (grades 1-6); childhood/elementary education (grades 1 through 6); middle school education (grades 5 through 9); special education and general education certification; dual degree programs (with Columbia School of Social Work) leading to special education and general education certification; special education; dual language/bilingual education; literacy specialization (birth through grade 6); museum education; educational leadership.

All graduate programs include three components: coursework, supervised fieldwork and advisement, and a culminating integrative activity. This integrative activity requires students to complete a directed essay, an independent study, or portfolio.

Licensure/Reciprocity: New York. Students seeking teaching certification in a state other than New York should consult with that state's teacher certification office early in their program of study to insure compliance with requirements. Many state directors of teacher credentialing have signed Interstate Agreements through NASDTEC that expedite the certification process.

BERNARD M. BARUCH COLLEGE / CUNY

Teacher Education Program
One Bernard Baruch Way
New York, New York 10010
Phone: (646) 312=3310.
E-mail: admissions@baruch.cuny.edu
Internet: http://www.baruch.cuny.edu

Institution Description: The college was established as the School of Business and Civil Administration of City College in 1919. The college became part of the city university system and the present official name, Bernard M. Baruch College of the City University of New York, was adopted in 1968.

The education program at the college leads to the Master of Science in Education degree.

Institution Control: Public.

Calendar: Semester. Academic year August to May.

Official(s): Dr. Emily Comstock DiMartino, Director of Teacher Education.

Faculty: Not reported.

Degrees Awarded: 37 baccalaureate; 50 master's.

Admission Requirements: *Undergraduate:* Graduation from an approved secondary school or GED; College Board SAT or ACT composite. *Graduate:* Baccalaureate degree from an accredited institution. *Teacher education specific:* Official transcripts of all college/university coursework; minimum 2.75; teaching licensure when required by program pursued; New York State Teacher Certification Examination; completion of state-approved programs in child abuse education and school violence also required.

Fees and Expenses: Undergraduate: city resident $4,300 per academic year; nonresident $8,940. Graduate: Tuition charged per credit hour. Off-campus room and board: $6,800. Other expenses: $4,090. Books and supplies: $800.

Financial Aid: Resources specifically for eligible students enrolled in teacher education programs are awarded on the basis of financial need and academic merit. The institution has a Program Participation Agreement with the U.S. Department of Education for eligible students to receive Pell Grants and other federal aid. Teacher scholarships available to qualifying students. *Contact:* Financial Aid Office at: (646) 312-1360.

Accreditation: *Regional:* MSA. *Member of:* AACTE. *Approved by:* New York State Department of Education.

Undergraduate Programs: The Weissman School of Arts and Sciences offers a minor in education. The minor is designed to acquaint students with the theoretical, psychological, and sociocultural issues involved in education. Any education credits taken after spring 2001 may not count toward the professional education credits needed for New York State Teacher Certification.

Graduate Programs: The Master of Science in Education in educational administration and supervision is designed for experienced teachers who wish to develop their abilities in educa-

BERNARD M. BARUCH COLLEGE / CUNY—
cont'd

tional leadership to prepare for supervisory positions in schools or school districts. The program requires completion of 33 credit hours.

The Master of Science in Education in higher education administration offers a curriculum that emphasizes higher education management, student services, personnel management, information systems, and institutional leadership. Students in the program are required to complete 30-33 credit hours.

Licensure/Reciprocity: New York. Students seeking teaching certification in a state other than New York should consult with that state's teacher certification office early in their program of study to insure compliance with requirements. Many state directors of teacher credentialing have signed Interstate Agreements through NASDTEC that expedite the certification process.

BROOKLYN COLLEGE / CUNY

School of Education
2900 Bedford Avenue
Brooklyn, New York 11210-2889
Phone: (718) 951-5214
Fax: (718) 951-4815
E-mail: soe@brooklyn.cuny.edu
Internet: http://www.brooklyn.cuny.edu

Institution Description: Brooklyn College was established, chartered, and offered first instruction at the postsecondary level in 1930. x

The School of Education prepares students to become effective educators. It offers in conjunction with Kingsborough Community College a joint A.S degree in Educational Studies/ B.A. in Early Childhood Education.

Institution Control: Public.

Calendar: Semester. Academic year August to May.

Official(s): Dr. Deborah Shanley, Dean.

Faculty: Full-time 63; part-time 38.

Degrees Awarded: 231 baccalaureate; 588 master's.

Admission Requirements: *Undergraduate:* Graduation from an approved secondary school or GED; College Board SAT or ACT composite. *Teacher education specific:* In order to declare a major in education, a student must have completed at least 30 credits with a GPA of 2.5 or better in liberal arts and sciences courses. New York State Teacher Certification Examination; completion of state-approved programs in child abuse education and school violence also required. *Graduate:* Baccalaureate degree from a regionally accredited institution. *Teacher education specific:* Letters of recommendation; faculty interview.

Fees and Expenses: Undergraduate: resident $4,259; nonresident $8,899. Off-campus room and board: $ 6,800. Other expenses: $4,090. Books and supplies: $760.

Financial Aid: Resources specifically for eligible students enrolled in teacher education programs are awarded on the basis of financial need and academic merit. The institution has a Program Participation Agreement with the U.S. Department of Education for eligible students to receive Pell Grants and other federal aid. Teacher scholarships available to qualifying students. *Contact:* Financial Aid Office at: (715) 951-5214.

Accreditation: *Regional:* MSA. *Member of:* AACTE. *Approved by:* New York State Department of Education.

Undergraduate Programs: The School of Education offers undergraduate programs for the education of teachers in the following areas and levels: early childhood education teacher (birth-grade 2) with an option for dual certification for teaching students with disabilities in early childhood; childhood education teacher (grades 1-6); childhood education teacher (grades 1-6) with an extension for bilingual (Spanish-English) education; adolescence education (grades 7-12): biology, chemistry, English, mathematics, modern languages education, literacy, teacher of students with disabilities, and adolescence education. All programs lead to the baccalaureate degree. The pro-

grams include a general education core, professional studies, field experiences, and student teaching. Students must complete an appropriate major in another department of the college.

Graduate Programs: The college offers an advanced certificate program in educational administration and supervision as well as a master's degree and advanced certificate programs in guidance and counseling and school psychology.

Licensure/Reciprocity: New York. Students seeking teaching certification in a state other than New York should consult with that state's teacher certification office early in their program of study to insure compliance with requirements. Many state directors of teacher credentialing have signed Interstate Agreements through NASDTEC that expedite the certification process.

CANISIUS COLLEGE

School of Education and Human Services
Teacher Education Programs
2001 Main Street
Buffalo, New York 14208-1098
Phone: (716) 883-7000
Fax: (716) 888-2125
E-mail: inquiry@canisius.edu
Internet: http://www.canisius.edu

Institution Description: Canisius College is a private, independent, nonprofit college conducted in the Jesuit and Roman Catholic tradition. It was founded in 1870.

The School of Education and Human Services offers sequences in elementary/early secondary, secondary, and special education.

Institution Control: Private.

Calendar: Semester. Academic year August to May.

Official(s): Rev. Vincent M. Cooke, S.J., President.

Faculty: Student/faculty ration 18 to 1.

Degrees Awarded: 150 baccalaureate; 451 master's.

Admission Requirements: *Undergraduate:* Graduation from an approved secondary school with 16 academic units or GED; College Board SAT or ACT composite. *Teacher education specific:* 30 semester hours of college credit; cumulative GPA of 2.75; portfolio review; faculty interview; when required by program pursued; New York State Teacher Certification Examination; completion of state-approved programs in child abuse education and school violence also required. *Graduate:* Baccalaureate degree from a regionally accredited institution. *Teacher education specific:* Letters of recommendation; faculty interview.

Fees and Expenses: Undergraduate: $20,200 per academic year. Graduate: Tuition charged per credit hour. On-campus room and board: $7,790. Other expenses: $1,130. Books and supplies: $500.

Financial Aid: Resources specifically for eligible students enrolled in teacher education programs are awarded on the basis of financial need and academic merit. The institution has a Program Participation Agreement with the U.S. Department of Education for eligible students to receive Pell Grants and other federal aid. Teacher scholarships available to qualifying students. *Contact:* Financial Aid Office at: (716) 888-2300.

Accreditation: *Regional:* MSA. *Member of:* AACTE. *Approved by:* New York State Department of Education.

Undergraduate Programs: The elementary/early secondary education program leads to teaching certification for nursery school through grade 6 (N-6), plus endorsement to teach English, mathematics, science, social studies, or foreign language in grades 7-9. The N-6 endorsement will also qualify to work in pre-K, early childhood and Head Start programs. The curriculum covers the basics of teaching, reading, and diagnosing and correcting reading problems. All students gain practical experience in the classroom during one semester as student teachers. All programs lead to the baccalaureate degree.

Graduate Programs: The graduate teacher education program for elementary and secondary degrees coincides with the college's undergraduate programs and is open only to candidates who have completed one of these programs or its equivalent. Completion of the program will qualify the student with New York State permanent certification requirements for grades 7-12 in the following areas: secondary education (biology and general science, business, chemistry and general science, English, French, German, mathematics, physics and general science, social studies, and Spanish); elementary (K-6 with an early-secondary extension in 7-9) - English, French, German, mathematics, science, social studies, Spanish.

Licensure/Reciprocity: New York. Students seeking teaching certification in a state other than New York should consult with that state's teacher certification office early in their program of study to insure compliance with requirements. Many state directors of teacher credentialing have signed Interstate Agreements through NASDTEC that expedite the certification process.

CITY COLLEGE OF NEW YORK / CUNY

School of Education

NAC 6/207
160 Convent Avenue
New York, New York 10031-9198
Phone: (212) 650-7262
Fax: (212) 650-6417
E-mail: soe@ccny.cuny.edu
Internet: http://www.ccny.cuny.edu

Institution Description: City College was established as the Free Academy, the first American tuition-free municipal college in 1847.

The Department of Education offers undergraduate and graduate programs leading to teacher certification.

Institution Control: Public.

Calendar: Semester. Academic year August to June.

Official(s): Dr, Alfred S. Posamentier, Dean; Dr. Doris Cintr*oen, Chair.

Faculty: Full-time 31; part-time 38.

Degrees Awarded: 68 baccalaureate; 433 master's.

Admission Requirements: *Undergraduate:* Graduation from secondary school or GED; College Board SAT or ACT composite. *Teacher education specific:* Acceptable score on School of Education Admissions Test; 30 semester hours of college credit; cumulative GPA of 2.5; portfolio review; faculty interview; New York State Teacher Certification Examination; completion of state-approved programs in child abuse education and school violence also required. *Graduate:* Baccalaureate degree from a regionally accredited institution. *Teacher education specific:* Letters of recommendation; faculty interview.

Fees and Expenses: Undergraduate: resident $4,260; nonresident $8,899. Graduate: Tuition charged per credit hour. Off-campus room and board: $6,796. Books and supplies: $759.

Financial Aid: Resources specifically for eligible students enrolled in teacher education programs are awarded on the basis of financial need and academic merit. The institution has a Program Participation Agreement with the U.S. Department of Education for eligible students to receive Pell Grants and other federal aid. Teacher scholarships available to qualifying students. *Contact:* Financial Aid Office at: (212) 650-5819.

Accreditation: *Regional:* MSA. *Member of:* AACTE. *Approved by:* New York State Department of Education.

Undergraduate Programs: City College offers the following undergraduate degree in education: bilingual childhood education (Chinese, Haitian, Spanish); childhood education; and early childhood education.

Secondary education programs include English, fine arts, foreign language: Spanish, mathematics, music, science (biology, chemistry, earth science, and physics), social studies. All programs lead to the baccalaureate degree. The programs include a general education core, professional studies, field experiences, and student teaching. Students must complete an appropriate major in another department of the college.

Graduate Programs: Contact the School of Education for current information regarding master's degree and advanced certificate programs.

Licensure/Reciprocity: New York. Students seeking teaching certification in a state other than New York should consult with that state's teacher certification office early in their program of study to insure compliance with requirements. Many state directors of teacher credentialing have signed Interstate Agreements through NASDTEC that expedite the certification process.

COLLEGE OF MOUNT SAINT VINCENT

Department of Teacher Education

6301 Riverdale Avenue
Riverdale, New York 10471-1093
Phone: (718) 405-3284
Fax: (718) 405-3201
E-mail: megan@cmsv.edu
Internet: http://www.cmsv.edu

Institution Description: The College of Mount Saint Vincent is a private, independent, liberal arts college in the Catholic tradition and the spirit of the Sisters of Charity. It was established as the Academy of Mount Saint Vincent, a school for women, in 1847. The college became coeducational in 1974.

The Teacher Education Department prepares students for successful entry into the teaching profession and for New York State certification.

Institution Control: Private.

Calendar: Semester. Academic year August to May.

Official(s): Sr. Margaret Egan, Ed.D., Chair.

Faculty: Full-time 4; part-time 3.

Degrees Awarded: 16 baccalaureate; 124 master's.

Admission Requirements: *Undergraduate:* Graduation from an approved secondary school with 16 college preparatory units or GED; College Board SAT or ACT composite. *Teacher education specific:* GPA 2.5; academic recommendation; personal essay; New York State Teacher Certification Examination; completion of state-approved programs in child abuse education and school violence also required. *Graduate:* Baccalaureate degree from a regionally accredited institution. *Teacher education specific:* Official transcripts of all college/university coursework; minimum 3.0; two professional references; teaching licensure when required by program pursued; faculty interview.

Fees and Expenses: Undergraduate: $9,300 per academic year. Graduate: $580 per credit. Required fees: $400. On-campus room and board: $7,800.

Financial Aid: Resources specifically for eligible students enrolled in teacher education programs are awarded on the basis of financial need and academic merit. The institution has a Program Participation Agreement with the U.S. Department of Education for eligible students to receive Pell Grants and other federal aid. Teacher scholarships available to qualifying students. *Contact:* Financial Aid Office at: (718) 405-3289 or e-mail at msimotos@cmsv.edu

Accreditation: *Regional:* MSA. *Member of:* AACTE. *Approved by:* New York State Department of Education.

Undergraduate Programs: The Teacher Education Department offers 4-year programs leading to certification in the areas of early childhood (birth-grade 2); childhood education (grades 1-9); dual special education and childhood (grades 1-6); adolescence (grades 7-12); dual special education and adolescence (grades 7-12); health education (grades K-12. All programs lead to the baccalaureate degree and require completion of a general education core, professional studies, field experiences, content area, and student teaching.

Graduate Programs: Five-year programs leading to the Master of Science degree and certification include the same concentrations as for the 4-year baccalaureate programs.

The Master of Science in urban and multicultural education explores areas such as conflict resolution, contemporary health issues, second language learners, middle level education, and

COLLEGE OF MOUNT SAINT VINCENT—
cont'd

effective communication in a multicultural environment. Students may choose concentrations in English as a second language, middle level education, special education, or instructional technology.

Licensure/Reciprocity: New York. Students seeking teaching certification in a state other than New York should consult with that state's teacher certification office early in their program of study to insure compliance with requirements. Many state directors of teacher credentialing have signed Interstate Agreements through NASDTEC that expedite the certification process.

COLLEGE OF NEW ROCHELLE

Education Department
Teacher Education Programs
29 Castle Place
New Rochelle, New York 10805-2339
Phone: (914) 654-5000
Fax: (914) 654-5486
E-mail: admissions@cnr.edu
Internet: http://www.cnr.edu

Institution Description: The College of New Rochelle is a private, independent, nonprofit college. It was established as the College of St. Angela in 1904. The present name was adopted in 1910.

Teacher Education Programs provide strong preparation in teaching to the New York State Learning Standards and ensure a sound understanding of the educational needs of students across the range of developmental levels encompassed by the certificate.

Institution Control: Private.

Calendar: Semester. Academic year September to May.

Official(s): Dr. Rose Marie Hurrell, Dean.

Faculty: Full-time 12.

Degrees Awarded: 1 baccalaureate; 429 master's.

Admission Requirements: *Undergraduate:* Graduation from an approved secondary school with 15 academic units or GED; College Board SAT or ACT composite. *Teacher education specific:* Overall GPA 2.7 after 45 credits of college study; academic recommendation; New York State Teacher Certification Examination; completion of state-approved programs in child abuse education and school violence also required.

Fees and Expenses: $14,400 per academic year. On-campus room and board: $7,150. Other expenses: $3,000. Books and supplies: $600.

Financial Aid: Resources specifically for eligible students enrolled in teacher education programs are awarded on the basis of financial need and academic merit. The institution has a Program Participation Agreement with the U.S. Department of Education for eligible students to receive Pell Grants and other federal aid. Teacher scholarships available to qualifying students. *Contact:* Financial Aid Office at: (914) 654-5225.

Accreditation: *Regional:* MSA. *Member of:* AACTE. *Approved by:* New York State Department of Education.

Undergraduate Programs: The Education Department, in collaboration with other departments in the School of Arts and Sciences and area schools, provides a series of learning activities and field experiences leading to the initial New York State teacher certification in childhood education (grades 1-6), adolescence education (grades 7-12), and visual art education (grades K-12). Additional coursework and fieldwork prepare students for dual certification in the following areas: childhood/early childhood (birth-grade 2) childhood/middle childhood specialist (grades 5-9), childhood/students with disabilities, adolescence/middle childhood specialist (grade 5-9), and adolescence/students with disabilities.

The School of Arts and Sciences requires an academic major along with the teacher certification program. The following are acceptable majors for candidates in the childhood education

certification area: art history, biology, chemistry, classics, communication arts, economics, English, French, history, interdisciplinary studies, Latin, mathematics, philosophy, political science, psychology, religious studies, sociology, and Spanish.

Licensure/Reciprocity: New York. Students seeking teaching certification in a state other than New York should consult with that state's teacher certification office early in their program of study to insure compliance with requirements. Many state directors of teacher credentialing have signed Interstate Agreements through NASDTEC that expedite the certification process.

COLLEGE OF SAINT ROSE

School of Education
Department of Teacher Education
432 Western Avenue
Albany, New York 12203-1490
Phone: (800) 537-8556
Fax: (518) 454-2013
E-mail: admit@mail.strose.edu
Internet: http://www.strose.edu

Institution Description: The College of Saint Rose is a private, independent, nonsectarian college. It was established and offered first instruction at the postsecondary level in 1920.

The Department of Teacher Education seeks to develop education professionals who are reflective practitioners and who are able to create effective learning environments with the full range of their abilities and experiential backgrounds.

Institution Control: Private.

Calendar: Semester. Academic year September to May.

Official(s): Dr. Crystal Gofrs, Dean.

Faculty: Full-time 54.

Degrees Awarded: 293 baccalaureate; 436 master's.

Admission Requirements: *Undergraduate:* Graduation from an approved secondary school with 16 college preparatory units or GED; College Board SAT preferred; ACT composite accepted. *Teacher education specific:* GPA 2.5; academic recommendation; personal essay; New York State Teacher Certification Examination; completion of state-approved programs in child abuse education and school violence also required. *Graduate:* Baccalaureate degree from a regionally accredited institution. *Teacher education specific:* Official transcripts of all college/university coursework; minimum 2.75; two professional references; teaching licensure when required by program pursued; faculty interview.

Fees and Expenses: Undergraduate: $15,245. Graduate: $430 per credit hour. On-campus room and board: $7,225. Other expenses: $2,300. Books and supplies: $1,000.

Financial Aid: Resources specifically for eligible students enrolled in teacher education programs are awarded on the basis of financial need and academic merit. The institution has a Program Participation Agreement with the U.S. Department of Education for eligible students to receive Pell Grants and other federal aid. Teacher scholarships available to qualifying students. *Contact:* Financial Aid Office at: (518) 454-5168.

Accreditation: *Regional:* MSA. *Member of:* AACTE. *Approved by:* New York State Department of Education.

Undergraduate Programs: The Department of Teacher Education offers undergraduate programs preparing middle and high school teachers. These programs lead to the Bachelor of Science degree and New York State certification. The Bachelor of Science degree programs include early childhood education; early childhood/special education; childhood (elementary) education; and childhood (elementary/special education). All programs require the completion of a general education core, professional studies, content area, field experiences, and student teaching. A minimum of 122 credit hours must be completed for the degree award.

Graduate Programs: The Master of Science in Education programs are offered with concentrations in early childhood education, childhood (elementary) education; teacher education, and adolescent (secondary) education.

Licensure/Reciprocity: New York. Students seeking teaching certification in a state other than New York should consult with that state's teacher certification office early in their program of study to insure compliance with requirements. Many state directors of teacher credentialing have signed Interstate Agreements through NASDTEC that expedite the certification process.

COLLEGE OF STATEN ISLAND / CUNY

Department of Education

2800 Victory Boulevard
Staten Island, New York 10314
Phone: (718) 982-3716
Fax: (718) 982-3743
E-mail: admissions@csi.cuny.edu
Internet: http://www.csi.cuny.edu

Institution Description: The College of Staten Island, a campus of the City University of New York, was established in 1955.

The Department of Education offers a full selection of programs to prepare students for certification as teachers at all levels.

Institution Control: Public.

Calendar: Semester. Academic year August to June.

Official(s): Dr. Susan Sullivan, Dean; Dr. Kenneth Gold, Chair.

Faculty: Full-time 25; adjunct 34.

Degrees Awarded: 2 baccalaureate; 312 master's.

Admission Requirements: *Undergraduate:* Graduation from an approved secondary school or GED; College Board SAT or ACT composite. *Teacher education specific:* GPA 2.5; academic recommendation; personal essay; New York State State Teacher Certification Examination; completion of state-approved programs in child abuse education and school violence also required. *Graduate:* Baccalaureate degree from a regionally accredited institution. *Teacher education specific:* Official transcripts of all college/university coursework; minimum 3.0; two professional references; teaching licensure when required by program pursued; faculty interview. A master's degree with a minimum average of 3.0 and four years of teaching experience is required for the sixth-year professional certificate program.

Fees and Expenses: Undergraduate: $2,000 per semester. Graduate: $360 per credit. Required fees: $74 activity fee; $75 technology fee. No on campus housing.

Financial Aid: Resources specifically for eligible students enrolled in teacher education programs are awarded on the basis of financial need and academic merit. The institution has a Program Participation Agreement with the U.S. Department of Education for eligible students to receive Pell Grants and other federal aid. Teacher scholarships available to qualifying students. *Contact:* Sherman Whipkey at: (718) 982-2030.

Accreditation: *Regional:* MSA. NCATE. *Member of:* AACTE. *Approved by:* New York State Department of Education.

Undergraduate Programs: Students in the early childhood education program and the childhood education program must complete the requirements in the major in science, letters and society leading to the Bachelor of Arts degree. At least 121 credits may be required for completion. The early childhood education program is designed for students wishing to specialize in the education of children from birth to second grade. It provides the academic course content necessary for New York State certification at the early childhood level. All applicants fro initial teacher education certification in early childhood, childhood, and adolescence education must demonstrate proficiency in a language other than English.

Graduate Programs: Graduate programs leading to the Master of Science in Education are offered in childhood education, adolescence education, and special education. The department also offers a Sixth-Year Professional Certificate in education supervision and administration that is designed to prepare qualified candidates for leadership positions in schools in New York City and the metropolitan area.

Licensure/Reciprocity: New York. Students seeking teaching certification in a state other than New York should consult with that state's teacher certification office early in their program of study to insure compliance with requirements. Many state directors of teacher credentialing have signed Interstate Agreements through NASDTEC that expedite the certification process.

CORNELL UNIVERSITY

College of Agriculture and Life sciences
Cornell Teacher Education

418 Kennedy Hall
Ithaca, New York 14853
Phone: (607) 255-2207
Fax: (607) 255-7902
E-mail: lrs5@cornell.edu
Internet: http://www.cornell.edu

Institution Description: Cornell University is a private, coeducational, nonsectarian institution. The academic programs are located principally at its main campus in Ithaca, New York, and in New York City. The university was founded in 1865 by Ezra Cornell whose original endowment was augmented by a substantial land grant from the State of New York received under the Federal Land Grant (Morrill) Act of 1862.

The Teacher Education Program prepares teachers, teacher educators, and scholars in the areas of agriculture, mathematics, and science.

Institution Control: Private.

Calendar: Semester. Academic year August to May.

Official(s): Dr. Rosemary S. Caffarella, Chairperson.

Faculty: Full-time 12; part-time 1.

Degrees Awarded: 16 baccalaureate; 27 master's; 7 doctorate.

Admission Requirements: *Undergraduate:* Graduation from an approved secondary school with 16 academic units or GED; College Board SAT preferred; ACT composite accepted. *Teacher education specific:* Minimum 3.0 GPA; major in certification area; portfolio review; faculty interview; New York State Teacher Certification Examination; completion of state-approved programs in child abuse education and school violence also required. *Graduate:* Baccalaureate degree from a regionally accredited institution. *Teacher education specific:* Statement of purpose; letters of recommendation; GRE scores; 3.0 GPA; official transcripts of all previous college coursework; faculty interview.

Fees and Expenses: Undergraduate: in-state $14,634; out-of-state $23,924. Graduate: in-state/out-of-state $15,200 (all fees included). On-campus room and board: $9,580. Other expenses: $1,300. Books and supplies: $640.

Financial Aid: Resources specifically for eligible students enrolled in teacher education programs are awarded on the basis of financial need and academic merit. The institution has a Program Participation Agreement with the U.S. Department of Education for eligible students to receive Pell Grants and other federal aid. Teacher scholarships available to qualifying students. *Contact:* Rosemary Hulslanser at: (607) 255-4278 or e-mail at rh22@cornell.edu.

Accreditation: *Regional:* MSA. *Member of:* AACTE. *Approved by:* New York State Department of Education.

Undergraduate Programs: The Teacher Education Program admits up to 40 students each year. Students in the following majors are currently eligible: agriculture (agricultural engineering, animal science, food science, horticulture, plant science, soil science); biology, biology and society; biometry and statistics; chemistry; computer science; engineering; geological sciences; human biology, health, and society; mathematics; natural resources; physics. The program encourages students to complete the undergraduate major and a minor in education. The education courses count toward the certification. All programs lead to the baccalaureate degree and require the completion of a general education core, professional studies, field experiences, content area, and student teaching.

CORNELL UNIVERSITY—cont'd

Graduate Programs: Upon completion of the requirements for the bachelor's degree and certification, the student can complete a master's degree in as little as one year. The program currently serves students in mathematics, physical or biological sciences, and the agricultural fields.

Licensure/Reciprocity: New York. Students seeking teaching certification in a state other than New York should consult with that state's teacher certification office early in their program of study to insure compliance with requirements. Many state directors of teacher credentialing have signed Interstate Agreements through NASDTEC that expedite the certification process.

DAEMEN COLLEGE

Education Department
4380 Main Street
Amherst, New York 14226-3592
Phone: (716) 839-8350
Fax: (716) 839-8516
E-mail: phartwic@daemen.edu
Internet: http://www.daemen.edu

Institution Description: Daemen College (Rosary Hill College until 1976) is a private, nonsectarian college. It was established by the Order of St. Francis and chartered as Rosary Hill College, a women's college, in 1947. The present name was adopted in 1976.

The Education Department offers programs leading to baccalaureate and master's degrees.

Institution Control: Private.

Calendar: Semester. Academic year August to May.

Official(s): Dr. Patrick J. Hartwick, Chairperson.

Faculty: Full-time 7; part-time 20.

Degrees Awarded: 72 baccalaureate; 5 master's.

Admission Requirements: *Undergraduate:* Graduation from an approved secondary school or GED; College Board SAT or ACT composite. *Teacher education specific:* SAT score of 1050; maintain B- to C+ average; letter of intent; 3 letters of recommendation; faculty interview; New York State Teacher Certification Examination; completion of state-approved programs in child abuse education and school violence also required. *Graduate:* Baccalaureate degree from a regionally accredited institution. *Teacher education specific:* GRE scores; 3.0 GPA; 3 letters of recommendation; education philosophy; teacher certification; faculty interview.

Fees and Expenses: $15,120 per academic year. On-campus room and board: $7,000. Other expenses: $1,500. Books and supplies: $800.

Financial Aid: Resources specifically for eligible students enrolled in teacher education programs are awarded on the basis of financial need and academic merit. The institution has a Program Participation Agreement with the U.S. Department of Education for eligible students to receive Pell Grants and other federal aid. Teacher scholarships available to qualifying students. *Contact:* Jeff Pagano at: (716) 839-8350.

Accreditation: *Regional:* MSA. *Approved by:* New York State Department of Education.

Undergraduate Programs: The Education Department offers undergraduate degree programs leading to the Bachelor of Science in Education in the following areas: childhood education (grades 1-6); early childhood education/special education: early childhood (birth to grade 2); childhood education/special education: inclusive childhood education (grades 1-6). All programs require the completion of a general education core, professional studies, content area, field experiences, and student teaching.

Graduate Programs: The Master of Science degree programs include special education: childhood education (grades 1-6) initial certification; special education: childhood education (grades 1-6) professional certification; adolescence education-initial teacher certification.

Licensure/Reciprocity: New York. Students seeking teaching certification in a state other than New York should consult with that state's teacher certification office early in their program of study to insure compliance with requirements. Many state directors of teacher credentialing have signed Interstate Agreements through NASDTEC that expedite the certification process.

ELMIRA COLLEGE

Teacher Education
One Park Place
Elmira, New York 14901
Phone: (607) 735-1912
Fax: (607) 735-1185
E-mail: admissions@elmira.edu
Internet: http://www.elmira.edu

Institution Description: Elmira College is a private, independent, nonprofit college. It was chartered as Elmira College in 1853 and offered first instruction at the postsecondary level in 1855.

The Teacher Education programs are offered at the undergraduate and graduate levels and lead to teaching certification in New York.

Institution Control: Private.

Calendar: Semester (4-1-4 plan). Academic year September to May.

Official(s): Dr. Linda Pratt, Executive Director of Teacher Education.

Faculty: Full-time 6; part-time 2; adjunct 6.

Degrees Awarded: 87 baccalaureate; 190 master's.

Admission Requirements: Undergraduate: Graduation from an approved secondary school or GED; College Board SAT or ACT composite. *Teacher education specific:* 2.7 GPA in professional education courses and major concentrations; recommendations; essay; faculty interview; New York State Teacher Certification Examination; completion of state-approved programs in child abuse education and school violence also required. *Graduate:* Baccalaureate degree from a regionally accredited institution. *Teacher education specific:* Letters of recommendation; cumulative GPA of 2.7; copy of provisional teaching certificate; faculty interview.

Fees and Expenses: Undergraduate: $25,040. Graduate: $396 per credit hour. Required fees: $1,400. On-campus room and board: $8,080. Books and supplies; $500.

Financial Aid: Resources specifically for eligible students enrolled in teacher education programs are awarded on the basis of financial need and academic merit. The institution has a Program Participation Agreement with the U.S. Department of Education for eligible students to receive Pell Grants and other federal aid. Teacher scholarships available to qualifying students. *Contact:* Office of Financial Aid at: (607) 735-1728.

Accreditation: *Regional:* MSA. *Professional:* NCATE. *Approved by:* New York State Department of Education.

Undergraduate Programs: Baccalaureate programs offered by the Education Department include: childhood education (grades 1-6) with approved concentrations in biology, mathematics, visual and performing arts; adolescence education (grades 7-12 with an optional extension to teach a subject in grades 5 and 6 (biology, chemistry, English, French, mathematics, social studies); visual arts. All programs require completion of a general education core, professional studies, content area, field experiences, and student teaching.

Graduate Programs: The department offers a graduate program leading to the Master of Science in Education: Childhood Education (grades 1-6). The program requires the completion of a 36 credit-hour curriculum.

The Master of Science in Education: literacy (birth to grade 12) is also a 36 credit hour program. Successful completion of either program will enable graduates to seek New York State certification.

Licensure/Reciprocity: New York. Students seeking teaching certification in a state other than New York should consult with that state's teacher certification office early in their program of study to insure compliance with requirements. Many state directors of teacher credentialing have signed Interstate Agreements through NASDTEC that expedite the certification process.

FORDHAM UNIVERSITY

Graduate School of Education
113 West 60th Street
New York, New York 10023
Phone: (212) 636-6406
Fax: (212) 636-7826
E-mail: bernhardt@fordham.edu
Internet: http://www.fordham.edu

Institution Description: Fordham University is a private, independent, nonprofit institution. It was established by the Archbishop of New York as St. John's College in 1841. The present name was adopted in 1907.

The Graduate School of Education offers certification programs for students enrolled in one of the undergraduate colleges of Fordham University.

Institution Control: Private.

Calendar: Semester. Academic year August to May.

Official(s): Dr. Regis G. Bernhardt, Dean; Dr. John C. Coutz, Associate Dean.

Faculty: Full-time 43; adjunct 50.

Degrees Awarded: 483 master's; 28 doctorate.

Admission Requirements: *Undergraduate:* Graduation from an approved secondary school with 16 academic units or GED; College Board SAT or ACT composite. *Teacher education specific:* Student applicant must be pursuing an undergraduate major at Fordham University in one of the liberal arts or sciences; commit to completing all required courses in the major by the end of the junior year and to use elective credits toward fulfillment of the certification program requirements; maintain a 3.0 GPA or better; New York State Teacher Certification Examination; completion of state-approved programs in child abuse education and school violence also required. *Graduate:* Baccalaureate degree from a regionally accredited institution. *Teacher education specific:* Two reference reports; undergraduate GPA of 3.0 or better; satisfactory command of oral and written English; earned passing score on the relevant New York State Teacher Examinations; completion of state-approved programs in child abuse education and school violence also required. faculty interview.

Fees and Expenses: $25,540 per academic year. On-campus room and board: $9,235. Other expenses: $2,020. Books and supplies: $660.

Financial Aid: Resources specifically for eligible students enrolled in teacher education programs are awarded on the basis of financial need and academic merit. The institution has a Program Participation Agreement with the U.S. Department of Education for eligible students to receive Pell Grants and other federal aid. Teacher scholarships available to qualifying students. *Contact:* Joseph Korevec, Director of Admissions at: (212) 636-6401 or e-mail at korevec@fordham.edu.

Accreditation: *Regional:* MSA. *Professional:* NCATE. *Member of:* AACTE. *Approved by:* New York State Department of Education.

Undergraduate Programs: The undergraduate programs are offered at the Lincoln Center campus. In addition to the required coursework and field experiences, students must develop satisfactory professional portfolios. The majority of coursework toward certification, including student teaching, is taken during the senior year. Course selection within the major will be affected by requirements in teacher preparation. Upon completion of the undergraduate major and the certification courses, students receive baccalaureate degrees as well as institutional endorsement for New York provisional certification pre-K-6 to 7-12.

Graduate Programs: The Division of Curriculum and Teaching offers programs for college graduates with strong academic backgrounds in the liberal arts and sciences but have not had training in education and want to prepare for careers in teaching. The Master of Science in Teaching is a 40 credit-hour program and prepares students as elementary school teachers. The Master of Arts in Teaching in biology is a 46.5 credit-hour program and leads to certification in biology (grades 7-12). The Master of Arts in Teaching in English is also a 46.5 credit-hour program to prepare individuals to teach English in grades 7-12. The Master of Arts in Teaching in social studies prepares students to teach in grades 7-12 and leads to provisional New York State teacher certification in social studies.

Licensure/Reciprocity: New York. Students seeking teaching certification in a state other than New York should consult with that state's teacher certification office early in their program of study to insure compliance with requirements. Many state directors of teacher credentialing have signed Interstate Agreements through NASDTEC that expedite the certification process.

HOFSTRA UNIVERSITY

School of Education and Allied Human Services
Department of Curriculum and Teaching
243 Gallon Wing
Hempstead, New York 11550-1090
Phone: (516) 463-6700
Fax: (516) 463-6196
E-mail: hofstra@hofstra.edu
Internet: http://www.hofstra.edu

Institution Description: Hofstra University is a private, independent, nonprofit institution. It was established as Nassau College-Hofstra Memorial, an NYU Extension in 1935. It became Hofstra College in 1939 and was chartered as a university in 1963.

The Department of Curriculum and Teaching offers programs leading to certification in New York State.

Institution Control: Private.

Calendar: Semester. Academic year September to May.

Official(s): Dr. Doris Fromberg, Chairperson; Dr. Linda Davey, Assistant Chairperson.

Faculty: Full-time 22; adjunct 72.

Degrees Awarded: 64 baccalaureate; 677 master's; 12 doctorate.

Admission Requirements: *Undergraduate:* Graduation from an approved secondary school with 16 academic units or GED; College Board SAT or ACT composite. *Teacher education specific:* 30 semester hours of college credit; portfolio review; faculty interview; New York State Teacher Certification Examination; completion of state-approved programs in child abuse education and school violence also required. *Graduate:* Baccalaureate degree from a regionally accredited institution. *Teacher education specific:* Letters of recommendation; faculty interview; teaching credential if required for program pursued.

Fees and Expenses: Undergraduate: $18,412 per academic year. Graduate: Tuition charged per credit hour. On-campus room and board: $8,700. Other expenses: $950. Books and supplies: $1,000.

Financial Aid: Resources specifically for eligible students enrolled in teacher education programs are awarded on the basis of financial need and academic merit. The institution has a Program Participation Agreement with the U.S. Department of Education for eligible students to receive Pell Grants and other federal aid. Teacher scholarships available to qualifying students. *Contact:* Financial Aid Office at: (516) 463-6680.

Accreditation: *Regional:* MSA. *Professional:* NCATE. *Member of:* AACTE. *Approved by:* New York State Department of Education.

Undergraduate Programs: The Department of Curriculum and Instruction offers baccalaureate programs leading to provisional certification in early childhood (birth-grade 2); elementary education (grades 1-6); dual certification program in early

HOFSTRA UNIVERSITY—*cont'd*

childhood education and childhood education; elementary education (bilingual elementary education; mathematics, science, and technology; middle school extension into grades 7-9.

Secondary education programs are offered with concentrations in bilingual secondary education, business, English, foreign languages, mathematics, middle school extension into grades 5-6, science, social studies education. pre-K-12 Programs are offered in fine arts, music, specialization in wind conducting, speech communication, teaching English as a second language. All programs require the completion of a general education core, professional studies, content area, field experiences, and student teaching.

Graduate Programs: The Master of Arts is for those students who already have initial teacher certification in New York State. The Master of Science in Education program is for those who did not major in education as an undergraduate and wish to work toward New York State initial teacher certification. Programs are offered in elementary education, early childhood education, and dual certification for both.

The Certificate of Advanced Study is a post-master's course of study and may serve to fulfill the Professional Teacher requirement for in-service staff development.

Licensure/Reciprocity: New York. Students seeking teaching certification in a state other than New York should consult with that state's teacher certification office early in their program of study to insure compliance with requirements. Many state directors of teacher credentialing have signed Interstate Agreements through NASDTEC that expedite the certification process.

HUNTER COLLEGE / CUNY

School of Education
Department of Curriculum and Teaching

695 Park Avenue
New York, New York 10021
Phone: (212) 772-4686
E-mail: admissions@hunter.cuny.edu
Internet: http://www.hunter.cuny.edu

Institution Description: Hunter College was established as Female Normal and High School in 1870. The present name was adopted in 1914 and became coeducational in 1951. It became part of CUNY in 1961.

The Department of Curriculum and Instruction seeks to deliver comprehensive programs of study for professions who will teach and/or supervise children, adolescents, or adults in a variety of educational settings.

Institution Control: Public.

Calendar: Semester. Academic year August to May.

Official(s): Dr. Ira Kanis, Chairperson.

Faculty: Full-time 32.

Degrees Awarded: 35 baccalaureate; 583 master's.

Admission Requirements: *Undergraduate:* High school graduation with at least an 80% average or place in top 1/3 of class; College Board SAT. *Teacher education specific:* GPA 2.5; academic recommendation; personal essay; New York State Teacher Certification Examination; completion of state-approved programs in child abuse education and school violence also required. *Graduate:* Baccalaureate degree from a regionally accredited institution. *Teacher education specific:* Official transcripts of all college/university coursework; GRE scores; two letters of recommendation; teaching licensure when required by program pursued; faculty interview.

Fees and Expenses: Undergraduate: resident $4,300; nonresident $8,940. Graduate: resident $250 per credit hour; nonresident $440. Off-campus room and board: $6,796. Other expenses: $4,000. Books and supplies: $759.

Financial Aid: Resources specifically for eligible students enrolled in teacher education programs are awarded on the basis of financial need and academic merit. The institution has a Program Participation Agreement with the U.S. Department of Education for eligible students to receive Pell Grants and other federal aid. Teacher scholarships available to qualifying students. *Contact:* Financial Aid Office at: (212) 772-4820.

Accreditation: *Regional:* MSA. *Professional:* NCATE. *Member of:* AACTE. *Approved by:* New York State Department of Education.

Undergraduate Programs: The Department of Curriculum and Instruction's primary teaching responsibility is to cover the content of the elementary and secondary school curriculum and the methods by which that content is most effectively delivered. The department offers the following programs: childhood education on both the undergraduate and graduate level, and a graduate program in early childhood education (offered in conjunction with the programs in the Department of Educational Foundations and Counseling); undergraduate and graduate programs in adolescence education, Bachelor of Arts in dance K-12, Master of Arts in music preK-12, and Bachelor of Arts and Master of Arts programs in mathematics grades 7-12, and music preK-12 (offered in conjunction with the School of Liberal Arts and Sciences); school administrator and supervisor advanced certificate; graduate program in teaching English to speakers of other languages.

The Department of Special Education (in conjunction with the Departments of Curriculum and Teaching and Educational Foundations and Counseling Programs) offers dual certification programs in: blind and visually impaired; childhood special education: learning disabilities and behavior disorders, severe/multiple disabilities, deaf and hard-of-hearing, and early childhood special education.

Licensure/Reciprocity: New York. Students seeking teaching certification in a state other than New York should consult with that state's teacher certification office early in their program of study to insure compliance with requirements. Many state directors of teacher credentialing have signed Interstate Agreements through NASDTEC that expedite the certification process.

IONA COLLEGE

Department of Education

715 North Avenue
New Rochelle, New York 10801-1890
Phone: (914) 633-2502
Fax: (914) 633-2645
E-mail: doe@iona.edu
Internet: http://www.iona.edu

Institution Description: Iona College is a private, independent institution. It was established and offered first instruction at the postsecondary level in 1940.

The Education Department seeks to develop knowledgeable educators who consider the whole child in instructional planning and teaching.

Institution Control: Private.

Calendar: Semester. Academic year September to May.

Official(s): Dr. Patricia Antonacci, Chair.

Faculty: Full-time 10.

Degrees Awarded: 49 baccalaureate; 114 master's.

Admission Requirements: *Undergraduate:* Graduation from an approved secondary school with 16 academic units or GED; College Board SAT or ACT composite. *Teacher education specific:* Minimum 3.0 GPA at the time of admission which is usually the middle of the sophomore year; three letters of recommendation; provide a well-written autobiography; faculty interview; New York State Teacher Certification Examination; completion of state-approved programs in child abuse education and school violence also required. *Graduate:* Baccalaureate degree from a regionally accredited institution. *Teacher education specific:* Letters of recommendation; faculty interview.

Fees and Expenses: Undergraduate: i$18,290. Graduate: Tuition charged per credit hour. On-campus room and board: $9,700. Other expenses: $1,650. Books and supplies: $700.

Financial Aid: Resources specifically for eligible students enrolled in teacher education programs are awarded on the basis of financial need and academic merit. The institution has a

Program Participation Agreement with the U.S. Department of Education for eligible students to receive Pell Grants and other federal aid. Teacher scholarships available to qualifying students. *Contact:* Financial Aid Office at: (914) 633-2497.

Accreditation: *Regional:* MSA. *Professional:* NCATE. *Member of:* AACTE. *Approved by:* New York State Department of Education.

Undergraduate Programs: Degree programs offered at the undergraduate level include early childhood (birth-grade 2) and childhood education (grades 1-6). both programs require a concentration of 30 credits in one of the liberal arts and sciences. An Adolescence Teacher Certification Program (7-12) is offered in the areas of biology, English, French, Italian, mathematics, social studies, and Spanish. All baccalaureate programs require completion of a general education core, the liberal arts concentration, major requirements, field experiences, and student teaching.

Graduate Programs: Graduate programs in education prepare individuals for professional service in schools and are available for those interested in changing careers or embarking on a career in education, as well as for teachers and school administrators who desire career advancement. Programs offered include the Master of Science in Teaching with concentrations in childhood education (birth-grade 2); elementary education (grades 1-6)l adolescence education (grades 7-12); elementary education with a specialization in science (N-6); education: multicultural education; education: school administration and supervision; education: secondary school subjects. An Independent Teacher Certification Option program is also offered.

Licensure/Reciprocity: New York. Students seeking teaching certification in a state other than New York should consult with that state's teacher certification office early in their program of study to insure compliance with requirements. Many state directors of teacher credentialing have signed Interstate Agreements through NASDTEC that expedite the certification process.

LEHMAN COLLEGE / CUNY

Division of Education
Teacher Education Program
250 Bedford Park Boulevard West
Bronx, New York 10468
Phone: (718) 960-8000
Fax: (718) 960-8935
E-mail: admissions@lehman/cuny
Internet: http://cuny.edu

Institution Description: Lehman College (officially Herbert H. Lehman College) is a public institution. It was originally established as Hunter College in the Bronx. The college became a campus within the City University of New York and the name was changed to Herbert H. Lehman College in 1968.

Teacher preparation at Lehman is based on a firm foundation in the liberal arts and sciences. A variety of programs are available at the undergraduate and graduate levels.

Institution Control: Public.

Calendar: Semester. Academic year September to May.

Official(s): Dr. Annette Digby, Dean.

Faculty: Full-time 47.

Degrees Awarded: 51 baccalaureate; 453 master's.

Admission Requirements: *Undergraduate:* Graduation from an approved secondary school rank in top 35% or GED; College Board SAT or ACT composite. *Teacher education specific:* GPA 2.5; academic recommendation; personal essay; New York State Teacher Certification Examination; completion of state-approved programs in child abuse education and school violence also required. *Graduate:* Baccalaureate degree from a regionally accredited institution. *Teacher education specific:* Offi-

cial transcripts of all college/university coursework; GRE scores; two letters of recommendation; teaching licensure when required by program pursued; faculty interview.

Fees and Expenses: Undergraduate: resident $4,270; nonresident $8,910. Graduate: resident $285 per credit hour; nonresident $320. Off-campus room and board: $6,796. Other expenses: $4,100. Books and supplies $760.

Financial Aid: Resources specifically for eligible students enrolled in teacher education programs are awarded on the basis of financial need and academic merit. The institution has a Program Participation Agreement with the U.S. Department of Education for eligible students to receive Pell Grants and other federal aid. Teacher scholarships available to qualifying students. *Contact:* Financial Aid Office at: (718) 960-8545.

Accreditation: *Regional:* MSA. *Professional:* NCATE. *Member of:* AACTE. *Approved by:* New York State Department of Education.

Undergraduate Programs: The Department of Early Childhood and Childhood Education prepares students for initial New York State certification (birth-grade 6) to teach children at the early childhood and elementary levels, including children whose primary languages and cultures are not English; and collaborates in the preparation of teachers of special subjects (art, music) in elementary school. As of January 2004, certification titles were changed to: early childhood education; early childhood education with integrated bilingual extension; childhood education; and childhood education with integrated extension.

The Department of Middle and High School Education prepares students for Initial New York State certification to teach academic and special subjects in secondary schools (grades 7-12). All programs require the completion of a general education core, professional studies, content area, field experiences, and student teaching.

Graduate Programs: The Department of Early Childhood and Childhood Education offers two graduate sequences. The Master of Science in Education in Early childhood education provides teachers with a focus on early childhood philosophy, trends, curriculum methods, materials, and research. The Master of Science in Education in childhood education is intended for students who are currently teaching or who intend to teach children in elementary grades (nursery through sixth grade).

Licensure/Reciprocity: New York. Students seeking teaching certification in a state other than New York should consult with that state's teacher certification office early in their program of study to insure compliance with requirements. Many state directors of teacher credentialing have signed Interstate Agreements through NASDTEC that expedite the certification process.

LONG ISLAND UNIVERSITY - BROOKLYN CAMPUS

School of Education
Department of Teaching and Learning
Pratt Building 210
1 University Plaza
Brooklyn, New York 11201-9926
Phone: (718) 488-1055
Fax: (718) 488-3472
E-mail: attend@liu.edu
Internet: http://www.liu.edu

Institution Description: The institution was established and provisionally chartered as Long Island University College of Arts and sciences in 1927. The present name was adopted in 1969.

The School of Education strives to prepare an ethnically, linguistically, and socioecnomically and academically diverse student body to serve New York City public schools.

Institution Control: Private.

LONG ISLAND UNIVERSITY - BROOKLYN CAMPUS—*cont'd*

Calendar: Semester. Academic year September to May.

Official(s): Dr. J. David Ramirez, Dean; Dr. Susan Zinar, Department Chair.

Faculty: 22 full-time.

Degrees Awarded: 39 baccalaureate; 270 master's.

Admission Requirements: *Undergraduate:* Graduation from an accredited secondary school or GED; College Board SAT preferred. *Teacher education specific:* Completion of 66 general credits with an overall GPA of 2.5; achieve qualifying scores on the assessment battery; New York State Teacher Certification Examination; completion of state-approved programs in child abuse education and school violence also required; faculty recommendation. *Graduate:* Baccalaureate degree from a regionally accredited institution; 2.75 undergraduate GPA; major concentration in the liberal arts and sciences; fulfillment of all general education requirements; faculty interview.

Fees and Expenses: Undergraduate: $20,508 per academic year. Graduate: Tuition charged per credit hour. On-campus room and board: $7,770. Other expenses: $1,300. Books and supplies: $820.

Financial Aid: Resources specifically for eligible students enrolled in teacher education programs are awarded on the basis of financial need and academic merit. The institution has a Program Participation Agreement with the U.S. Department of Education for eligible students to receive Pell Grants and other federal aid. Teacher scholarships available to qualifying students. *Contact:* Financial Aid Office at:

Accreditation: *Regional:* MSA. *Professional:* NCATE. *Member of:* AACTE. *Approved by:* New York State Department of Education.

Undergraduate Programs: The Bachelor of Science in childhood urban education (grades 1-6) is offered with an optional middle childhood urban education extension (grades 7-9) and an optional bilingual education extension (7 credits). The Bachelor of Science in adolescence urban education (grades 7-12) is offered with optional adolescence/middle childhood urban education (grades 7-12) in biology, chemistry, English, mathematics, social studies, and Spanish. A Bachelor of Science in physical education in urban schools (pre K-12) is offered with optional bilingual education extension (7 credits). A Bachelor of Education in fine arts in urban schools (pre K-12) is also available.

All programs require the completion of a general education core, professional studies, subject content area, field experiences, and student teaching. A minimum of 128 semester hours must be completed for the baccalaureate degree.

Graduate Programs: Graduate programs offered in the School of Education include New York State Teacher Certification Programs for students interested in initial or professional certification and Non-Certification Programs for students interested in a graduate degree in teaching that does not grant New York State Teacher Certification.

The Master of Science in Education degree programs are offered in childhood urean education (grades 1-6), childhood/early childhood urban education (grades B-6), teaching urban adolescents (grades 7-12); teaching urban children with disabilities (grades 1-6), teaching English for speakers of other languages (all grades), bilingual education, and teaching literacy. A Master of Science in computers in education is offered as a non-certification program. A B.S./M.S.Ed. program for teacher of inclusive urban childhood and special education is also available.

Licensure/Reciprocity: New York. Students seeking teaching certification in a state other than New York should consult with that state's teacher certification office early in their program of study to insure compliance with requirements. Many state directors of teacher credentialing have signed Interstate Agreements through NASDTEC that expedite the certification process.

LONG ISLAND UNIVERSITY - C.W. POST CAMPUS

School of Education
Curriculum and Instruction
720 Northern Boulevard
Brookville, New York 11548-1300
Phone: (516) 299-2210
Fax: (516) 299-4167
E-mail: educate@cwpost.liu.edu
Internet: http://www.cwpost.liu.edu

Institution Description: The C.W. Post campus was established in 1954 and awarded its first degree (baccalaureate) in 1958.

Institution Control: Private.

Calendar: Semesters. Academic year September to May.

Official(s): Dr. Anthony A. De Falco, Chair, Curriculum and Instruction.

Faculty: Full-time 69.

Degrees Awarded: 246 baccalaureate; 756 master's.

Admission Requirements: *Undergraduate:* Graduation from an accredited secondary school with 16 academic units or GED; College Board SAT or ACT composite. *Teacher education specific:* Completion of 66 general credits with an overall GPA of 2.5; achieve qualifying scores on the assessment battery; New York State Teacher Certification Examination; completion of state-approved programs in child abuse education and school violence also required; faculty recommendation. *Graduate:* Baccalaureate degree from a regionally accredited institution; 2.75 undergraduate GPA; major concentration in the liberal arts and sciences; fulfillment of all general education requirements; faculty interview.

Fees and Expenses: Undergraduate: $20,490 per academic year. Graduate: Tuition charged per credit hour. On-campus room and board: $7,773. Other expenses: $1,000. Books and supplies: $600.

Financial Aid: Resources specifically for eligible students enrolled in teacher education programs are awarded on the basis of financial need and academic merit. The institution has a Program Participation Agreement with the U.S. Department of Education for eligible students to receive Pell Grants and other federal aid. Teacher scholarships available to qualifying students. *Contact:* Financial Aid Office at: (516) 299-2900.

Accreditation: *Regional:* MSA. *Approved by:* New York State Department of Education.

Undergraduate Programs: The Bachelor of Science programs in early childhood and childhood education are initial 4-year certification programs. Students must major in the liberal arts and science or complete a 30-credit interdisciplinary concentration. Majors can be chose from: biology, chemistry, earth and environmental science, economics, foreign languages, history, interdisciplinary studies, mathematics, philosophy, physics, political science, psychology, sociology.

The Bachelor of Science in adolescence education is for students interested in teaching at the middle school of high school level (grades 7-12). Additional baccalaureate degree programs include art education, music education, health education, physical education, speech-language pathology and audiology.

All baccalaureate program require the completion of a general education core, professional studies, subject content area, field experiences, and student teaching.

Graduate Programs: Master's degree programs include early childhood education, childhood education, teaching English to speakers of other languages, adolescence education, middle childhood education, special education, literacy: birth-grade 6, childhood education/special education, childhood education/literacy, music education, art education, teaching students with speech/language disabilities, school counseling, mental health counseling, computers in education, school administration and supervision. An autism concentration is available to those enrolled in the childhood education/special education or special education programs.

Licensure/Reciprocity: New York. Students seeking teaching certification in a state other than New York should consult with that state's teacher certification office early in their program of study to insure compliance with requirements. Many state directors of teacher credentialing have signed Interstate Agreements through NASDTEC that expedite the certification process.

LONG ISLAND UNIVERSITY - SOUTHAMPTON CAMPUS

School of Education
Teacher Education Division
239 Montauk Highway
Southampton, New York 11968-4198
Phone: (631) 283-8139
Fax: (631) 283-4000
E-mail: info@southampton.edu
Internet: http://www.southampton.edu

Institution Description: The Southampton campus was established, chartered, and offered first instruction at postsecondary level in 1963.

The Teacher Education Division offers field-based and liberal arts courses.

Institution Control: Private.

Calendar: Semester. Academic year September to May.

Official(s): Dr. R. Lawrence McCann, Director, Teacher Education Division.

Faculty: Not reported.

Degrees Awarded: 20 baccalaureate; 27 master's.

Admission Requirements: *Undergraduate:* Graduation from an accredited secondary school with 16 academic units or GED; College Board SAT or ACT composite. *Teacher education specific:* Completion of 66 general credits with an overall GPA of 2.5; achieve qualifying scores on the assessment battery; New York State Teacher Certification Examination; completion of state-approved programs in child abuse education and school violence also required; faculty recommendation. *Graduate:* Baccalaureate degree from a regionally accredited institution; 2.75 undergraduate GPA; major concentration in the liberal arts and sciences; fulfillment of all general education requirements; faculty interview.

Fees and Expenses: Undergraduate: $20,560 per academic year. Graduate: Tuition charged per credit hour. On-campus room and board: $9,210. Other expenses: $150. Books and supplies: $1,200.

Financial Aid: Resources specifically for eligible students enrolled in teacher education programs are awarded on the basis of financial need and academic merit. The institution has a Program Participation Agreement with the U.S. Department of Education for eligible students to receive Pell Grants and other federal aid. Teacher scholarships available to qualifying students. *Contact:* Financial Aid Office at: (631) 287-8321.

Accreditation: *Regional:* MSA. *Approved by:* New York State Department of Education.

Undergraduate Programs: The Teacher Education Division offers a baccalaureate program leading to teacher certification in elementary education. Students major in a liberal arts and sciences subject. A certification program is offered whereby students may minor in secondary education with a major in biology, English, or social studies. All programs require the completion of a general education core, professional studies, subject content area, field experiences, and student teaching. The area of concentration is a 36-credit requirement. The program prepares students to teach in grades K-6.

Graduate Programs: The Graduate Education Division offers master's degrees in elementary education, reading/literacy education, and certification in elementary education.

The master's degree program in special education is designed for certified teachers to allow them to earn an additional New York State approved certification in special education. Within the program, students may pursue certification in two different concentrations: teaching children with disabilities at the childhood level (grades 1-6) or at the adolescent level (grades 7-12). In addition to intensive on-campus session, students participate in a variety of field placements and in a practicum.

Licensure/Reciprocity: New York. Students seeking teaching certification in a state other than New York should consult with that state's teacher certification office early in their program of study to insure compliance with requirements. Many state directors of teacher credentialing have signed Interstate Agreements through NASDTEC that expedite the certification process.

MANHATTAN COLLEGE

School of Education
Teacher Education Program
4513 Manhattan College Parkway
Bronx, New York 10471-4098
Phone: (718) 862-7374
Fax: (718) 862-8011
E-mail: william.merriman@manhattan.edu
Internet: http://www.manhattan.ecu

Institution Description: Manhattan College is a private, independent, nonprofit institution. It was established as the Academy of the Holy Infancy (for men) in 1853. The college became coeducational in 1973.

A strong core of liberal arts and science courses is central to all programs in education offered by the School of Education.

Institution Control: Private.

Calendar: Semester. Academic year September to May.

Official(s): Dr. William Merriman, Dean, School of Education; Dr. Karen Nicholson, Chair, Education Department.

Faculty: Full-time 44; part-time 19; adjunct 25.

Degrees Awarded: 89 baccalaureate; 52 master's.

Admission Requirements: Graduation from an approved secondary school or GED; College Board SAT or ACT composite. *Teacher education specific:* SAT or ACT scores; high school course record, recommendations, personal statement; faculty interview; New York State Teacher Certification Examination; completion of state-approved programs in child abuse education and school violence also required. *Graduate:* Baccalaureate degree from a regionally accredited institution. *Teacher education specific:* Letters of recommendation; personal statement; faculty interview.

Fees and Expenses: Undergraduate: $17,100. Graduate: $435 per credit. Required fees: $1,000. On-campus room and board: $7,850. Books and supplies: $600.

Financial Aid: Resources specifically for eligible students enrolled in teacher education programs are awarded on the basis of financial need academic merit, athletic ability. The institution has a Program Participation Agreement with the U.S. Department of Education for eligible students to receive Pell Grants and other federal aid. Teacher scholarships available to qualifying students. *Contact:* Edward Keough at: (718) 862-7178 or e-mail at edward.keogh@manhattan.edu.

Accreditation: *Regional:* MSA. Accredited by: Teacher Education Accreditation Council (TEAC). *Member of:* AACTE. *Approved by:* New York State Department of Education.

Undergraduate Programs: The curriculum of the childhood education, adolescent, and dual childhood special education programs and physical education is designed for traditional undergraduate students who are pursuing their degree full-time. Each teacher preparation program has three components: the core requirements in the liberal arts and sciences, an academic concentration, and the professional education component. All programs lead to the baccalaureate degree and Initial New York State Certification. Certification can be achieved in childhood education (grades 1-6), adolescent education (grades 7-12), physical education (grades K-12), dual certification in childhood and special education (grades 1-6).

Graduate Programs: The graduate teacher education program (Master of Science in Education) is directed toward the professional preparation of teachers of disabled individuals. The dual

MANHATTAN COLLEGE—*cont'd*

program prepares teachers to work with children in grades 1-6 in the general as well as special education settings. The school leadership program (Master of Science in Education) is directed toward the professional preparation of school administrators and supervisors, assistant principals, department chairpersons, coordinators, and unit heads, Post Masters are offered in each of the programs.

Licensure/Reciprocity: New York. Students seeking teaching certification in a state other than New York should consult with that state's teacher certification office early in their program of study to insure compliance with requirements. Many state directors of teacher credentialing have signed Interstate Agreements through NASDTEC that expedite the certification process.

MEDGAR EVERS COLLEGE / CUNY
School of Liberal Arts and Education
Department of Education
1650 Bedford Avenue
Brooklyn, New York 11225
Phone: (718) 270-4918
E-mail: admissions@mec.cuny.edu
Internet: http://www.mec.cuny.edu

Institution Description: Medgar Evers College of CUNY is a four-year, coeducational institution. It was established in 1967 as a two-year community college and became a four-year college in 1969. The present name was adopted in 1970.

The Department of Education prepares students to become teachers at the early childhood, childhood, and middle childhood levels. The Department of Education was one of the first departments to be created when the college opened its doors in 1969.

Institution Control: Public.

Calendar: Semester. Academic year September to May.

Official(s): Dr. Evelyn W. Castro, Dean; Dr. Frances Lowden, Chairperson.

Faculty: Full-time 14.

Degrees Awarded: 16 baccalaureate.

Admission Requirements: *Undergraduate:* Graduation from an approved secondary school or GED. *Teacher education specific:* Pass all CUNY Assessment Tests; pass CUNY Proficiency EXAM; complete at least 60 and no more than 90 credits; maintain a 2.7 GPA; faculty interview; New York State Teacher Certification Examination; completion of state-approved programs in child abuse education and school violence also required.

Fees and Expenses: Resident $4,232; nonresident $8,872. Off-campus room and board: $6,796. Other expenses: $4,090. Books and supplies: $760.

Financial Aid: Resources specifically for eligible students enrolled in teacher education programs are awarded on the basis of financial need and academic merit. The institution has a Program Participation Agreement with the U.S. Department of Education for eligible students to receive Pell Grants and other federal aid. Teacher scholarships available to qualifying students. *Contact:* Financial Aid Office at: (718) 270-6038.

Accreditation: *Regional:* MSA. *Professional:* NCATE. *Approved by:* New York State Department of Education.

Undergraduate Programs: The Bachelor of Arts curriculum includes a minimum of 100 hours in field experience and 300 hours in clinical practicum experience. A minimum of 120 credits must be completed. Candidates are expected to complete a 27-30 credit concentration in English, mathematics, science, or social studies.

The childhood education program leads to certification in childhood education, grades 1 through 6. The middle childhood education program leads to certification in middle childhood education, grades 5 through 9. Dual certification programs include early childhood/special education for teaching students with disabilities at the early childhood level from birth through grade 2; childhood/special education for teaching students with disabilities from grades 1 through 6; middle child-

hood/special education for teaching students with disabilities at the middle childhood level from grades 1 through 6 in general and inclusive settings.

Licensure/Reciprocity: New York. Students seeking teaching certification in a state other than New York should consult with that state's teacher certification office early in their program of study to insure compliance with requirements. Many state directors of teacher credentialing have signed Interstate Agreements through NASDTEC that expedite the certification process.

MOLLOY COLLEGE
Education Department
Kellenberg Hall, Room 217
1000 Hempstead Avenue
Rockville Centre, New York 11571-5002
Phone: (516) 678-5000
Fax: (516) 256-2232
E-mail: education@molloy.edu
Internet: http://www.molloy.edu

Institution Description: Molloy College (Molloy Catholic College For Women until 1971) is a private, independent, nonprofit coeducational college. It was established in 1955.

The Education Department offers programs at the undergraduate and graduate levels leading to teacher certification.

Institution Control: Private.

Calendar: Semester (4-1-4 plan). Academic year September to May.

Official(s): Dr. Valerie Collins, President.

Faculty: Not reported.

Degrees Awarded: 25 baccalaureate; 118 master's.

Admission Requirements: *Undergraduate:* Graduation from an accredited secondary school with 16 academic units or GED; College Board SAT or ACT composite. *Teacher education specific:* SAT or ACT scores; high school course record; recommendations, personal statement; faculty interview; New York State Teacher Certification Examination; completion of state-approved programs in child abuse education and school violence also required. *Graduate:* Baccalaureate degree from a regionally accredited institution. *Teacher education specific:* Letters of recommendation; personal statement; faculty interview. credit; cumulative GPA of 2.75; portfolio review; faculty interview; teaching credential when required by program pursued.

Fees and Expenses: Undergraduate: $16,140. Graduate: Tuition charged per credit hour. Off-campus room and board: $8,000. Other expenses: $2,040. Books and supplies: $800.

Financial Aid: Resources specifically for eligible students enrolled in teacher education programs are awarded on the basis of financial need and academic merit. The institution has a Program Participation Agreement with the U.S. Department of Education for eligible students to receive Pell Grants and other federal aid. Teacher scholarships available to qualifying students. *Contact:* Financial Aid Office at: (516) 678-5000, ext. 6249.

Accreditation: *Regional:* MSA. *Member of:* AACTE. *Approved by:* New York State Department of Education.

Undergraduate Programs: Baccalaureate programs leading to teaching certification include elementary education (K-6), secondary education (7-12), special education, and music education (preK-12). All programs require the completion of 128 credit hours including a general education core, professional studies, content area (e.g., biology, communication arts, English, history, mathematics), field experiences, and student teaching.

Graduate Programs: Master of Science programs leading to initial certification include teacher of childhood education grades 1-6, teacher of adolescent education grades 7-12 in the subject areas of biology, English, mathematics, social studies, and Spanish.

Programs leading to dual initial certification include: teacher of childhood education (grades 1-6); teacher of English to speakers of other languages (preK-12); teacher of adolescent education (grades 7-12)/teacher of English to speakers of other languages (preK-12); childhood education/teaching students with disabilities in childhood education; adolescent education/ teaching students with disabilities in adolescent education (grades 7-12) in the subject areas of biology, English, mathematics, social studies, and Spanish.

Programs leading to professional certification are offered for those persons already possessing initial (provisional) certification. Areas of concentration are similar to those described above. Middle school extension endorsement programs are offered in childhood education certification to grades 7 and 8 and extension of adolescent education certification to grades 5 and 6.

Licensure/Reciprocity: New York. Students seeking teaching certification in a state other than New York should consult with that state's teacher certification office early in their program of study to insure compliance with requirements. Many state directors of teacher credentialing have signed Interstate Agreements through NASDTEC that expedite the certification process.

NEW YORK CITY COLLEGE OF TECHNOLOGY / CUNY

Occupational and Technology Teacher Education

Pearl Building 101
300 Jay Street
Brooklyn, New York 11201
Phone: (718) 260-5373
Fax: (718) 254-8542
E-mail: gnwoke@nyctc.cuny.edu
Internet: http://www.nyctc.cuny.edu

Institution Description: New York City College of Technology is a public, urban technical college within the City University of New York system. It was established in 1946.

The Occupational Teacher Education Program prepares individuals to become certified as teachers of career technical and trade subjects in vocational and comprehensive high schools. The programs at City Tech are the only such programs in the entire CUNY system that prepare K-12 teachers of technology education and specific career technical subjects.

Institution Control: Public.

Calendar: Semester. Academic year September to June.

Official(s): Dr. Godfrey I. Nwoke, Director.

Faculty: Full-time 6.

Degrees Awarded: 31 baccalaureate; 228 master's.

Admission Requirements: *Undergraduate:* Graduation from an approved high school or GED; College Board SAT or ACT composite. *Teacher education specific:* All students must take the CUNY Skills Assessment Tests in reading, writing, and mathematics; faculty interview; New York State Teacher Certification Examination; completion of state approved programs in child abuse education and school violence also required.

Fees and Expenses: Resident $4,290; nonresident $6,910. Off-campus room and board: $6,796. Other expenses: $4,090. Books and supplies: $760.

Financial Aid: Resources specifically for eligible students enrolled in teacher education programs are awarded on the basis of financial need and academic merit. The institution has a Program Participation Agreement with the U.S. Department of Education for eligible students to receive Pell Grants and other federal aid. Teacher scholarships available to qualifying students. *Contact:* Financial Aid Office at: (718) 260-5700.

Accreditation: *Regional:* MSA. *Member of:* AACTE. *Approved by:* New York State Department of Education.

Undergraduate Programs: The Bachelor of Science in Education degree program in technology teacher education prepares individuals to obtain New York State certification as kindergarten through 12th grade technology teachers. The courses focus on the broad technological systems of communication, manufacturing, and construction. As part of the communications systems sequence, the program collaborates with the Computer

Systems Technology Department to offer students an array of courses that prepare them to effectively use and manage information technology in the schools.

Licensure/Reciprocity: New York. Students seeking teaching certification in a state other than New York should consult with that state's teacher certification office early in their program of study to insure compliance with requirements. Many state directors of teacher credentialing have signed Interstate Agreements through NASDTEC that expedite the certification process.

NEW YORK INSTITUTE OF TECHNOLOGY

School of Education and Professional Services
Division of Teacher Education Programs
Wheatley Road
P.O. Box 8000
Old Westbury, New York 11568
Phone: (516) 686-7516
Fax: (516) 626-0419
E-mail: admissions@nyit.edu
Internet: http://www.nyit.edu

Institution Description: New York Institute of Technology is a private, independent, nonprofit institution with branch campuses in New York City and Central Islip.

The School of Education and Professional Services offers undergraduate and graduate programs through the Division of Teacher Education Programs.

Institution Control: Private.

Calendar: Semester. Academic year September to May.

Official(s): Dr. Jacqueline E. Kress, Dean.

Faculty: Not reported.

Degrees Awarded: 31 baccalaureate; 228 master's.

Admission Requirements: *Undergraduate:* Graduation from an approved secondary school; College Board SAT or ACT composite. *Teacher education specific:* Faculty interview; personal goal statement; New York State Teacher Certification Examination; completion of state approved programs in child abuse education and school violence also required. GRADUATE; Minimum GPA of 3.0; 3 years teaching experience; New York teaching certificate; letters of recommendation; faculty interview.

Fees and Expenses: Undergraduate: $16,625 per academic year. Graduate: $545 per credit hour. Off-campus room and board: $7,500. Other expenses: $2,550. Books and supplies: $800.

Financial Aid: Resources specifically for eligible students enrolled in teacher education programs are awarded on the basis of financial need and academic merit. The institution has a Program Participation Agreement with the U.S. Department of Education for eligible students to receive Pell Grants and other federal aid. Teacher scholarships available to qualifying students. *Contact:* Financial Aid Office at: (516) 686-7580.

Accreditation: *Regional:* MSA. *Member of:* AACTE. *Approved by:* New York State Department of Education.

Undergraduate Programs: The Bachelor of Science in childhood education focuses on the needs of children in first through sixth grades. Candidates who specialize in this age group need a strong understanding of child development to notice potential learning difficulties or to recognize gifted children.

The Bachelor of Science in middle childhood education is a teaching specialization that focuses on the needs of children in fifth through ninth grades. Emphasis is placed on teaching in multicultural environments.

The baccalaureate degree program in adolescence education focuses on the needs of children and teenagers in seventh through 12th grades with particular emphasis on high school students.

The Bachelor of Science in career and technical education program is for candidates who will work with middle and high school students to teach a variety of educational disciplines in business, health occupations, and trade subjects. All baccalaureate programs require the completion of a general education

NEW YORK INSTITUTE OF TECHNOLOGY—
cont'd

core, professional studies, content area, field experiences, and student teaching. A minimum of 120 credit hours is required for the degree award.

Graduate Programs: The Master of Science in childhood education program of studies is organized to build knowledge and skills through carefully developed course content and related field experience. It culminates with student teaching, research methods and assessment, and the planning and implementation of a field project. The program requires the completion of 45 credit hours on specified courses within a two-year period.

Licensure/Reciprocity: New York. Students seeking teaching certification in a state other than New York should consult with that state's teacher certification office early in their program of study to insure compliance with requirements. Many state directors of teacher credentialing have signed Interstate Agreements through NASDTEC that expedite the certification process.

NEW YORK UNIVERSITY

The Steinhardt School of Education
82 Washington Square East
New York, New York 10003
Phone: (212) 998-5000
Fax: (212) 995-4191
E-mail: education@nyu.edu
Internet: http://www.nyu.edu/education

Institution Description: New York University is a private, independent, nonprofit institution. It was established and chartered as the University of the City of New York in 1831.

The Steinhardt School of Education offers a variety of undergraduate majors and graduate programs leading to initial certification for teaching in the schools of New York.

Institution Control: Private.

Calendar: Semester. Academic year September to May.

Official(s): Dr. Mark Alter, Chair.

Faculty: Full-time 44; adjunct 43.

Degrees Awarded: 139 baccalaureate; 533 master's; 21 doctorate.

Admission Requirements: *Undergraduate:* Graduation from an accredited secondary school with a strong academic record from a challenging college preparatory curriculum. *Teacher education specific:* Three SAT II subject tests; letters of recommendation; New York State Teacher Certification Examination; completion of state approved programs in child abuse education and school violence also required. *Graduate: Teacher education specific:* Strong undergraduate academic record; transcripts of all college coursework; letters of recommendation. GRE exam for doctoral applicants.

Fees and Expenses: Undergraduate: $28,496 per academic year. Graduate: $20,016. Required fees: up to $1,270; graduate $1,750. On-campus room and board: $10,900 undergraduate; $15,200 graduate. Other expenses: $1,000. Books and supplies: $700.

Financial Aid: Resources specifically for eligible students enrolled in teacher education programs are awarded on the basis of financial need and academic merit. The institution has a Program Participation Agreement with the U.S. Department of Education for eligible students to receive Pell Grants and other federal aid. Teacher scholarships available to qualifying students. *Contact:* Financial Aid Office at: (212) 998-4444.

Accreditation: *Regional:* MSA. *Member of:* AACTE. *Approved by:* New York State Department of Education.

Undergraduate Programs: Undergraduate majors are offered in: early childhood education/special education (dual certification); childhood education/special education (dual certification); secondary fields (7-12) in mathematics, science, social studies, English, foreign languages, music (K-12), educational theatre (K-12, and teaching students with speech and language disabilities (K-12). Students who complete these programs are eligible for initial teacher certification from New York State.

Students take a liberal arts core, courses in their subject area, and pedagogy courses for a total of 128-133 credits, depending on the major. Students complete 100 hours of observation prior to 2-4 semesters of student teaching. Faculty-supervised placements are in any of dozens of urban schools in New York City.

Graduate Programs: Graduate majors leading to eligibility for initial or permanent teacher certification in New York State are offered in: early childhood education; childhood education; special education; secondary fields (7-12) in mathematics, science, social studies, English, foreign language, teaching English to speakers of other languages (K-12). Dual certification programs are offered in: teaching English to speakers of other languages/foreign language; literacy education, music, dance, art, and educational theatre.

Full-time and part-time study is available as well as 14-month fast-track, accelerated curricula in early childhood, childhood, special, math, science, social studies, English, and foreign language. Student without prior teaching backgrounds complete 100 hours of observation prior to extensive student teaching.

Other graduate programs at the master's and doctoral levels include educational administration, educational communication and technology, higher education, counseling and guidance, school psychology, educational psychology, sociology of education, history of education, philosophy of education, environmental conservation education, international education, arts and humanities, and many others.

Licensure/Reciprocity: New York. Students seeking teaching certification in a state other than New York should consult with that state's teacher certification office early in their program of study to insure compliance with requirements. Many state directors of teacher credentialing have signed Interstate Agreements through NASDTEC that expedite the certification process.

NIAGARA UNIVERSITY

College of Education
Niagara University, New York 14109
Phone: (716) 286-1212
Fax: (716) 286-8710
E-mail: admissions@niagara.edu
Internet: http://www.niagara.edu

Institution Description: Niagara University is a four-year, private, coeducational institution with a Vincentian tradition. It was established as College and Seminary of Our Lady of Angels in 1856.

The College of Education offers undergraduate and graduate programs leading to teacher certification in New York State.

Institution Control: Private.

Calendar: Semester. Academic year August to May.

Official(s): Dr. Debra A. Colley, Dean.

Faculty: Full-time 2; part-time 7.

Degrees Awarded: 111 baccalaureate; 290 master's.

Admission Requirements: *Undergraduate:* Graduation from an approved secondary school with 16 academic units or GED; College Board SAT or ACT composite. *Teacher education specific:* Cumulative GPA of 2.7; portfolio review; faculty interview; New York State Teacher Certification Examination; completion of state-approved programs in child abuse education and school violence also required. *Graduate:* Baccalaureate degree from a regionally accredited institution. *Teacher education specific:* Letters of recommendation; GRE or Miller Analogies Test; faculty interview.

Fees and Expenses: Undergraduate: $17,380 per academic year. Graduate: Tuition charged per credit hour. On-campus room and board: $6,500. Other expenses: $1,350. Books and supplies: $750.

Financial Aid: Resources specifically for eligible students enrolled in teacher education programs are awarded on the basis of financial need and academic merit. The institution has a Program Participation Agreement with the U.S. Department of

Education for eligible students to receive Pell Grants and other federal aid. Teacher scholarships available to qualifying students. *Contact:* Financial Aid Office at: (716) 286-8686.

Accreditation: *Regional:* MSA. *Professional:* NCATE. *Member of:* AACTE. *Approved by:* New York State Department of Education.

Undergraduate Programs: The Bachelor of Science in Early Childhood and Childhood Program leads to New York State certification in early childhood education (birth to grade 2) and childhood education (grades 1 to 6). The Bachelor of Science in middle school education 1-9 program leads to New York State certification in childhood education (grades 1 to 6) and middle childhood education (grades 5 to 9). In the middle childhood grades, candidates will be certified in a specialty area of concentration and will be able to teach that content to students in grades 5 to 9. The middle education 5-12 program leads to New York State certification in middle childhood education (grades 5 to 9) and adolescence education (grades 7 to 12).

The baccalaureate program in high school education 7-12 leads to New York State certification in adolescence education (grades 7-12) and qualified the candidate to teach a specific content area at the secondary education level.

Programs for students with disabilities include special education and childhood (grades 1-6 and grades 7-12).

All baccalaureate programs require the completion of a general education core, professional studies, content area, field experiences, and student teaching. A minimum of 120 credit hours is required for the degree award.

Graduate Programs: Teacher education programs at the master's degree level include elementary education, early childhood and childhood (birth to grade six-New York or primary/junior-Ontario); adolescence education (grades five to twelve-New York or intermediate/senior-Ontario).

Advanced Certificate Programs are offered an administration and supervision, school counseling, school psychology, and mental health counseling.

Licensure/Reciprocity: New York. Students seeking teaching certification in a state other than New York should consult with that state's teacher certification office early in their program of study to insure compliance with requirements. Many state directors of teacher credentialing have signed Interstate Agreements through NASDTEC that expedite the certification process.

NYACK COLLEGE
School of Education
Teacher Education Programs
One South Boulevard
Nyack, New York 10960-3698
Phone: (845) 358-1710
Fax: (845) 358-0874
E-mail: Bennett.Schepens@nyack.eduenroll@nyack.edu
Internet: http://www.nyack.edu

Institution Description: Nyack College is a private college affiliated with The Christian and Missionary Alliance. It was established as the Missionary Training Institute in 1882.

The School of Education offers undergraduate and graduate programs leading to teacher certification in New York State.

Institution Control: Private.

Calendar: Semester. Academic year August to May.

Official(s): Dr. Bennett Schepens, Dean.

Faculty: Full-time 9; part-time 2; adjunct 6.

Degrees Awarded: 42 master's.

Admission Requirements: *Undergraduate:* High school graduation with 16 academic units or GED; College Board SAT or ACT composite. *Teacher education specific:* Overall 2.75; New York State Certification Exams in sophomore year; approval by division faculty. *Graduate:* Baccalaureate from a regionally accredited institution. *Teacher education specific:* Two academic recommendation and one professional reference (not from faculty members); teaching certificate; faculty interview.

Fees and Expenses: $6,495 per semester. $540 per credit if less than 12 credits. On-campus room and 21-meal plan $3,300 (double) per semester. Additional fees apply.

Financial Aid: Resources specifically for eligible students enrolled in teacher education programs are awarded on the basis of financial need and academic merit. Other programs for athletics, music, distance, ministry, teaching background. The institution has a Program Participation Agreement with the U.S. Department of Education for eligible students to receive Pell Grants and other federal aid. Teacher scholarships available to qualifying students. *Contact:* Andres Valenzuela (undergraduate) or Kristen Jones (graduate) at: (845) 358-1710.

Accreditation: *Regional:* MSA. *Professional:* NCATE. *Approved by:* New York State Department of Education. The Teacher Education Programs have also been accredited by the Association of Christian Schools International for the preparation of teachers for a ministry in Christian school education.

Undergraduate Programs: Baccalaureate programs include the Bachelor of Science with an adolescent education major (grades 7-12) with specializations in English, mathematics, social studies (history, social science); biblical and theological studies; childhood education; Christian education; music education; piano performance; teaching English to speakers of other languages. All programs require the completion of a general education core, professional studies, content area, field experiences, and student teaching. A minimum of 120 credit hours is required for the degree award.

Graduate Programs: The Master of Science in Education with an inclusive education curriculum has been designed to meet the academic requirements for obtaining a professional teaching certificate in New York State. The program emphasizes meeting the educational needs of all learners. The program and course schedule are designed with the flexibility for fifth-year full-time students as well as inservice teachers who will be studying part-time. The program is also available with a extension for gifted education.

Licensure/Reciprocity: New York. Students seeking teaching certification in a state other than New York should consult with that state's teacher certification office early in their program of study to insure compliance with requirements. Many state directors of teacher credentialing have signed Interstate Agreements through NASDTEC that expedite the certification process.

PACE UNIVERSITY
School of Education
Teacher Certification
One Pace Plaza
New York, New York 10038-1598
Phone: (212) 346-1338
Fax: (212) 346-1821
E-mail: education@pace.edu
Internet: http://www.pace.edu

Institution Description: Pace University is a private, independent institution with branch campuses in White Plains and Pleasantville. It was established in 1906.

The School of Education prepares educators who are reflective professionals. The teacher preparation programs provide the academic requirements of New York State teaching certificates.

Institution Control: Private.

Calendar: Semester. Academic year September to May.

Official(s): Dr. Janet McDonald, Dean.

Faculty: Full-time 21.

Degrees Awarded: 82 baccalaureate; 175 master's.

Admission Requirements: *Undergraduate:* Graduation from an approved secondary school or GED; College Board SAT or ACT composite. *Teacher education specific:* Cumulative GPA of 2.7; portfolio review; faculty interview; New York State Teacher Certification Examination; completion of state-approved programs in child abuse education and school violence also

PACE UNIVERSITY—cont'd

required. *Graduate:* Baccalaureate degree from a regionally accredited institution. *Teacher education specific:* Letters of recommendation; GRE; faculty interview.

Fees and Expenses: Undergraduate: $21,104 per academic year. Graduate: Tuition charged per credit hour. On-campus room and board: $7,650. Other expenses: $2,780. Books and supplies; $720.

Financial Aid: Resources specifically for eligible students enrolled in teacher education programs are awarded on the basis of financial need and academic merit. The institution has a Program Participation Agreement with the U.S. Department of Education for eligible students to receive Pell Grants and other federal aid. Teacher scholarships available to qualifying students. *Contact:* Financial Aid Office at: (212) 346-1300.

Accreditation: *Regional:* MSA. *Member of:* AACTE. *Approved by:* New York State Department of Education.

Undergraduate Programs: An Initial Certificate is the minimal certificate required to teach in public schools in the State of New York. The education requirement for this certificate can be earned in Pace's single degree undergraduate (B.A.) programs, combined degree undergraduate/graduate (B.A./M.S.Ed) programs or the graduate Master of Science for Teacher (M.S.T.) program.

In the single degree programs (B.A. or M.S.T.) teacher education candidates may choose to focus on childhood education or adolescent education.

All baccalaureate programs require the completion of a general education core, professional studies, content area, field experiences, and student teaching.

Graduate Programs: To continue to teach in New York, a student must ultimately obtain a *Professional Certificate.* The education requirements for this certificate can be earned through either Pace's Combined Undergraduate/Graduate (B.A./M.S.Ed.) programs or through the graduate Master of Science in Education (M.S.Ed.) programs.

Licensure/Reciprocity: New York. Students seeking teaching certification in a state other than New York should consult with that state's teacher certification office early in their program of study to insure compliance with requirements. Many state directors of teacher credentialing have signed Interstate Agreements through NASDTEC that expedite the certification process.

QUEENS COLLEGE / CUNY

Division of Education

Powdermaker Hall, Room 054
63-30 Kissena Boulevard
Flushing, New York 11367
Phone: (718) 997-5300
Fax: (718) 997-5323
E-mail: http://www.qc.edu/admissions
Internet: http://www.qc.edu

Institution Description: The college was founded as Queens College of the City of New York in 1937. It became part of the CUNY system in 1961.

The Division of Education offers undergraduate and graduate programs leading to teacher certification in New York State.

Institution Control: Public.

Calendar: Semester. Academic year September to May.

Official(s): Dr. Eleanor Armour-Thomas, Chair, secondary education; Dr. Helen Johnson, Chair, Department of Elementary and Childhood Education.

Faculty: Full-time 27.

Degrees Awarded: 126 baccalaureate; 706 master's.

Admission Requirements: *Undergraduate:* Graduation from an approved secondary school with 16 Carnegie units or GED; College Board SAT required. *Teacher education specific:* Students must complete teacher education introductory courses; cumulative GPA of 2.75; portfolio review; faculty interview; New York State Teacher Certification Examination; completion of state-approved programs in child abuse education and school

violence also required. *Graduate:* Baccalaureate degree from a regionally accredited institution. *Teacher education specific:* Letters of recommendation; faculty interview.

Fees and Expenses: Undergraduate: in-state $4,355 per academic year; out-of-state $8,995. Graduate: in-state $2,175 per academic year; out-of-state $3,800. Off-campus room and board: $6,800. Other expenses: $4,100. Books and supplies: $760.

Financial Aid: Resources specifically for eligible students enrolled in teacher education programs are awarded on the basis of financial need and academic merit. The institution has a Program Participation Agreement with the U.S. Department of Education for eligible students to receive Pell Grants and other federal aid. Teacher scholarships available to qualifying students. *Contact:* Financial Aid Office at: (716) 997-5100.

Accreditation: *Regional:* MSA. *Member of:* AACTE. *Approved by:* New York State Board of Education.

Undergraduate Programs: The undergraduate program in elementary education prepares students for the New York State Initial Certificate in childhood education grades 1-6. The program can be taken as a co-major; students must also complete a co-major in one of the liberal arts and science programs.

The Department of Secondary Education offers undergraduate programs with specializations in art, English language/art education, foreign language, mathematics, science, social studies.

All baccalaureate programs require the completion of a general education core, professional studies, content area, field experiences, and student teaching. A minimum of 120 credit hours is required for the degree award.

Graduate Programs: The Department of Elementary and Early Childhood Education offers a Master of Arts in Teaching degree program with special areas of early childhood education (birth to grade 2) and childhood education (grades 1 to 6). A Master of Science in Education degree is offered in similar areas. An extension to the master's degrees can be obtained in bilingual education.

The Department of Secondary Education offers graduate programs leading to the Master of Science in Education with concentrations in art, English/language arts, foreign language, mathematics, science, and social studies.

Licensure/Reciprocity: New York. Students seeking teaching certification in a state other than New York should consult with that state's teacher certification office early in their program of study to insure compliance with requirements. Many state directors of teacher credentialing have signed Interstate Agreements through NASDTEC that expedite the certification process.

SAGE COLLEGES - TROY CAMPUS

School of Education

45 Ferry Street
Troy, New York 12180
Phone: (518) 244-2347
Fax: (518) 244-6880
E-mail: info-request@sage.edu
Internet: http://www.sage.edu

Institution Description: The Sage Colleges consists of four institutions: Russell Sage College, Sage Junior College at Albany, Sage Graduate School, and Sage Evening College. Russell Sage College was established in 1916. The college was rechartered with the other components as The Sage Colleges in 1995.

The mission of the School of Education is to prepare effective educators and school counselors.

Institution Control: Private.

Calendar: Semester. Academic year August to May.

Official(s): Dr. Connell G. Frazer, Dean.

Faculty: Full-time 17.

Degrees Awarded: 35 baccalaureate.

Admission Requirements: *Undergraduate:* Graduation from an accredited secondary school with 16 academic units or GED; College Board SAT or ACT composite. *Teacher education specific:*

30 semester hours of college credit; cumulative GPA of 2.75; portfolio review; faculty interview; New York State Teacher Certification Examination; completion of state-approved programs in child abuse education and school violence also required. *Graduate:* Baccalaureate degree from a regionally accredited institution. *Teacher education specific:* Letters of recommendation; faculty interview.

Fees and Expenses: Undergraduate: $19,945 per academic year. Graduate: Tuition charged per credit hour. On-campus room and board: $6,870. Other expenses: $1,120. Books and supplies: $800.

Financial Aid: Resources specifically for eligible students enrolled in teacher education programs are awarded on the basis of financial need and academic merit. The institution has a Program Participation Agreement with the U.S. Department of Education for eligible students to receive Pell Grants and other federal aid. Teacher scholarships available to qualifying students. *Contact:* Financial Aid Office at: (518) 244-2341.

Accreditation: *Regional:* MSA. *Professional:* NCATE. *Member of:* AACTE. *Approved by:* New York State Department of Education.

Undergraduate Programs: All of the Education Department's programs lead to certification in New York State. Each program incorporates extensive practical experience in schools. At the undergraduate level, field work is incorporated into each of the classes taken in the childhood education (grades 1-6) and childhood with middle childhood education (grades 5-9). The Council for Education, comprised of representatives from the School of Liberal Arts and Sciences as well as the Education Department, contribute to the format and content of the teacher preparation and guidance counseling programs. Programs at the baccalaureate level also include adolescence education with optional middle childhood extension.

All baccalaureate programs require the completion of a general education core, professional studies, content area, field experiences, and student teaching. A minimum of 120 credit hours must be completed for the degree award.

Graduate Programs: The Graduate School offers the Master of Science in Education degree program in childhood education, literacy/childhood, childhood special education. The Master of Arts in Teaching degree program is offered with concentrations in biology, English, mathematics, social studies (also with middle childhood extension).

Licensure/Reciprocity: New York. Students seeking teaching certification in a state other than New York should consult with that state's teacher certification office early in their program of study to insure compliance with requirements. Many state directors of teacher credentialing have signed Interstate Agreements through NASDTEC that expedite the certification process.

ST. BONAVENTURE UNIVERSITY
School of Education
Teacher Education Programs
Route 417
St. Bonaventure, New York 14778
Phone: (716) 375-2000
Fax: (716) 375-2005
E-mail: schled@sbu.edu
Internet: http://www.sbu.edu

Institution Description: St. Bonaventure University is a private, independent, nonprofit institution. It was established as St. Bonaventure College in 1858 and acquired university status in 1950.

The School of Education prepares students for the teaching profession in a way that is reflective of Franciscan service to others.

Institution Control: Private.

Calendar: Semester. Academic year August to May.

Official(s): Dr. Peggy Burke, Dean.

Faculty: Full-time 28; adjunct 2.

Degrees Awarded: 84 baccalaureate; 176 master's.

Admission Requirements: *Undergraduate:* Graduation from an approved secondary school of GED. College Board SAT or ACT composite. *Teacher education specific:* Cumulative 3.0 GPA; completion of a minimum of 45 credit hours (exclusive of education courses); recommendation from 2 faculty member in the School of Education; New York State Teacher Certification Examination; completion of state-approved programs in child abuse education and school violence also required. *Graduate:* Baccalaureate degree from a regionally accredited institution. *Teacher education specific:* Letters of recommendation; faculty interview.

Fees and Expenses: Undergraduate: $17,190 per academic year. Graduate: Tuition charged per credit hour. On-campus room and board: $6,430. Other expenses: $1,050. Books and supplies: $600.

Financial Aid: Resources specifically for eligible students enrolled in teacher education programs are awarded on the basis of financial need and academic merit. The institution has a Program Participation Agreement with the U.S. Department of Education for eligible students to receive Pell Grants and other federal aid. Teacher scholarships available to qualifying students. *Contact:* Financial Aid Office at: (716 375-2528.

Accreditation: *Regional:* MSA. *Member of:* AACTE. *Approved by:* New York State Department of Education.

Undergraduate Programs: The Department of Elementary Education offers students the choice of either a program in elementary education that includes a significant set of classes in special education and leads to New York certification in childhood education, grades 1-6 **or** a program that leads to dual certification in New York State—childhood education, grades 1-6 *and* students with disabilities (special education), grades 1-6. Both programs lead to additional certification in elementary education (K-6) in Pennsylvania.

The undergraduate major in physical education is designed to prepare individuals to teach physical education and provides certification to coach at the middle and high school levels. The teacher education program builds in a declared secondary concentration in biology.

All programs require the completion of a general education core, professional studies, content area, field experiences, and student teaching.

Graduate Programs: The Master of Science in Education degree programs are offered in: educational leadership; counselor education (agency, school); childhood literacy; adolescent literacy; adolescence education initial certification; health education.

Licensure/Reciprocity: New York. Students seeking teaching certification in a state other than New York should consult with that state's teacher certification office early in their program of study to insure compliance with requirements. Many state directors of teacher credentialing have signed Interstate Agreements through NASDTEC that expedite the certification process.

ST. JOHN FISHER COLLEGE
Education Department
Teacher Education Program
3690 East Avenue
Rochester, New York 14618
Phone: (716) 385-8064
Fax: (716) 385-8386
E-mail: admissions@sjfc.edu
Internet: http://www.sjfc.edu

Institution Description: St. John Fisher College is a coeducational, private, college in the Catholic tradition. The college was established in 1948.

The Education Department prepares students for teaching at the elementary, junior, and senior high school levels.

Institution Control: Private.

Calendar: Semester. Academic year September to May.

Official(s): Dr. Katharine E. Keough, President.

Faculty: Full-time 10.

Degrees Awarded: 74 baccalaureate; 134 master's.

ST. JOHN FISHER COLLEGE—*cont'd*

Admission Requirements: *Undergraduate:* Graduation from an accredited secondary school with 16 academic units or GED; College Board SAT or ACT composite. *Teacher education specific:* Cumulative GPA of 2.75; portfolio review; faculty interview; New York State Teacher Certification Examination; completion of state approved programs in child abuse education and school violence also required. *Graduate:* Baccalaureate degree from a regionally accredited institution. *Teacher education specific:* Letters of recommendation; faculty interview.

Fees and Expenses: Undergraduate: $17,750 per academic year. Graduate: Tuition charged per credit hour. On-campus room and board: $7,410. Other expenses: $800. Books and supplies; $800.

Financial Aid: Resources specifically for eligible students enrolled in teacher education programs are awarded on the basis of financial need and academic merit. The institution has a Program Participation Agreement with the U.S. Department of Education for eligible students to receive Pell Grants and other federal aid. Teacher scholarships available to qualifying students. *Contact:* Financial Aid Office at: (585) 385-8042.

Accreditation: *Regional:* MSA. *Member of:* AACTE. *Approved by:* New York State Department of Education.

Undergraduate Programs: Students can pursue a double major in elementary education and another subject of the student's choosing. They can earn a Bachelor of Science in Education and either a Bachelor of Arts or Science in another field. Student must complete all courses and practical experiences necessary for provisional certification through the double major.

Students who wish to teach at the secondary level minor in education with a major in the teaching field. Students can qualify for secondary certification in English, foreign languages (French, German, Italian, Spanish), mathematics, science (biology, chemistry, physics), and social studies (political science, history).

All programs, in addition to the major/minor requirements, must complete the general education core, four field experiences, and a 14-week student teaching experience.

Graduate Programs: The graduate programs offered through the Department of Education are: Master of Science in reading education program emphasizes a linkage between reading and special education and focuses on the application of theory to practice. The Master of Science in special education program also features linkages with reading education by including courses that emphasize teaching reading. Additionally, the program focuses on practical experiences through field work.

Licensure/Reciprocity: New York. Students seeking teaching certification in a state other than New York should consult with that state's teacher certification office early in their program of study to insure compliance with requirements. Many state directors of teacher credentialing have signed Interstate Agreements through NASDTEC that expedite the certification process.

ST. JOHN'S UNIVERSITY

School of Education
8000 Utopia Parkway
Jamaica, New York 11439
Phone: (718) 990-6161
Fax: (718) 990-5723
E-mail: admissions@stjohns.edu
Internet: http://www.stjohns.edu

Institution Description: St. John's University is a private, non-profit institution affiliated with the Roman Catholic Church, Congregation of the Mission (Vincentian Community). It was established in 1870.

The School of Education offers undergraduate and graduate programs leading to teacher certification in New York State.

Institution Control: Private.

Calendar: Semester. Academic year September to May.

Official(s): Dr. Jerrold Ross, Dean.

Faculty: Full-time 8.

Degrees Awarded: 243 baccalaureate; 14 master's.

Admission Requirements: *Undergraduate:* Graduation from an approved secondary school with 16 academic units or GED; College Board SAT or ACT composite. *Teacher education specific:* Cumulative GPA of 2.75; portfolio review; faculty interview; New York State Teacher Certification Examination; completion of state approved programs in child abuse education and school violence also required. *Graduate:* Baccalaureate degree from a regionally accredited institution. *Teacher education specific:* GRE; two letters of recommendation; faculty interview.

Fees and Expenses: Undergraduate: $20,080. Graduate: $605 per credit hour. On-campus room and board: $10,100. Other expenses: $3,800. Books and supplies: $1,000.

Financial Aid: Resources specifically for eligible students enrolled in teacher education programs are awarded on the basis of financial need and academic merit. The institution has a Program Participation Agreement with the U.S. Department of Education for eligible students to receive Pell Grants and other federal aid. Teacher scholarships available to qualifying students. *Contact:* Financial Aid Office at: (718) 990-2000.

Accreditation: *Regional:* MSA. *Member of:* AACTE. *Approved by:* New York State Department of Education.

Undergraduate Programs: The Bachelor of Science in Childhood Education is for students wishing to prepare as teachers of grades 1-6. The Bachelor of Science in Education - Dual Certificate program is for students wishing to prepare as elementary school teachers of grades 1-6 and teachers of childhood special education.

The Bachelor of Science in adolescence education program is for qualified students wishing to teach in secondary school settings (7-12) in English, mathematics, physical science, social studies, biology, or Spanish. The Bachelor of Arts with a minor in adolescence education program is for students wishing to teach in secondary settings (7-12) with a major in liberal arts or sciences (biology, English, mathematics, social studies, physics, Spanish).

All baccalaureate programs require the completion of a general education core, professional studies, content area, field experiences, and student teaching.

Graduate Programs: The Master of Science programs available include: adolescent education (7-12) with concentrations in biology, English, mathematics, social studies, and Spanish; childhood education (1-6); early childhood education (birth-2); educational administration and supervision; rehabilitation counseling; social counselor; teaching English to speakers of other languages; teaching literary (birth-6); teaching literacy (5-12); teaching children with disabilities in childhood education (1-6).

Doctoral degree programs include educational administration and supervision; instructional leadership (curriculum and instruction, learning styles, reading, technology).

Licensure/Reciprocity: New York. Students seeking teaching certification in a state other than New York should consult with that state's teacher certification office early in their program of study to insure compliance with requirements. Many state directors of teacher credentialing have signed Interstate Agreements through NASDTEC that expedite the certification process.

ST. LAWRENCE UNIVERSITY

Department of Education
Teacher Education Program
20 Atwood Hall
23 Romoda Drive
Canton, New York 13617-1445
Phone: (315) 229-5861
Fax: (315) 229-7423
E-mail: admissions@stlawu.edu
Internet: http://www.stlawu.edu

Institution Description: St. Lawrence University is a private, independent, nonprofit institution. It was established and chartered in 1856.

The Department of Education offers teacher certification programs for grades 7 through 12.

Institution Control: Private.

Calendar: Semester. Academic year August to May.

Official(s): Dr. James C. Shuman, Chair.

Faculty: Full-time 6; part-time 3; adjunct 15.

Degrees Awarded: 68 master's.

Admission Requirements: *Undergraduate:* Graduation from an approved secondary school or GED; College Board SAT or ACT composite. *Teacher education specific:* Admission into program during the sophomore year; 2.5 GPA; portfolio review; faculty interview; New York State Teacher Certification Examinations; completion of state-approved programs in child abuse education and school violence also required. *Graduate:* Baccalaureate degree from a regionally accredited institution. *Teacher education specific:* Letters of recommendation; faculty interview; teaching credential when required by the program pursued.

Fees and Expenses: Undergraduate: $27,985 per academic year. Graduate: $1,755 per 3-semester course. Required fees: $195. On-campus room and board: $7,760. Books and supplies: $600.

Financial Aid: Resources specifically for eligible students enrolled in teacher education programs are awarded on the basis of financial need and academic merit. The institution has a Program Participation Agreement with the U.S. Department of Education for eligible students to receive Pell Grants and other federal aid. Teacher scholarships available to qualifying students. *Contact:* Beth Turner at: (215) 229-5165 or e-mail at bturner@stlaw.edu.

Accreditation: *Regional:* MSA. *Approved by:* New York State Department of Education.

Undergraduate Programs: The teacher education program offers two sequences of courses—an educational studies minor that does not include student teaching, and a certification minor in education that culminates at the professional semester (student teaching) that is required for certification.. By completing the certification minor, students may be recommended for an Initial New York State Teaching Certificate. The teacher certification programs are offered for grades 7 to 12 in English, social studies, mathematics, biology, chemistry, physics, earth science, French, Spanish, and German. The university also offers a registered and approved teaching certification program for K-12 art.

Graduate Programs: The Master of Education degree program in general studies is offered in three options. An Initial/Professional Certification Option is aligned with the Regents' new standards for beginning teachers and it also meets the state's academic requirements for Professional Certification, once the teacher meets the state's additional requirements for testing, work experience, and mentoring in the public schools. The Permanent Certification Option leads leads to a New York Permanent Teaching Certificate. A Non-Certification Option is available to individuals who do not seek teaching certification.

Licensure/Reciprocity: New York. Students seeking teaching certification in a state other than New York should consult with that state's teacher certification office early in their program of study to insure compliance with requirements. Many state directors of teacher credentialing have signed Interstate Agreements through NASDTEC that expedite the certification process.

ST. THOMAS AQUINAS COLLEGE
School of Education
Teacher Education Division
125 Route 340
Sparkill, New York 10976-1050
Phone: (845) 398-4000
Fax: (845) 398-4114
E-mail: admissions@stac.edu
Internet: http://www.stac.edu

Institution Description: St. Thomas Aquinas College is a private, independent, nonprofit college. The college was founded by the Dominican Sisters of Sparkill in 1952.

The Teacher Education Division prepares students for teacher certification in New York State. The division offers undergraduate and graduate programs.

Institution Control: Private.

Calendar: Semester. Academic year September to May.

Official(s): Dr. Meenakashi Gajira, Chair.

Faculty: Full-time 12.

Degrees Awarded: 44 baccalaureate; 26 master's.

Admission Requirements: *Undergraduate:* Graduation from an approved secondary school or GED; College Board SAT preferred; ACT composite accepted. *Teacher education specific:* Application to program by sophomore year; statement of intention; 2.5 GPA; portfolio review; faculty interview; New York State Teacher Certification Examination; completion of state approved programs in child abuse education and school violence also required. *Graduate:* Baccalaureate degree from a regionally accredited institution. *Teacher education specific:* Professional and personal references; GRE of Miller Analogies Test scores; teacher licensure when required by program pursued; faculty interview.

Fees and Expenses: Undergraduate: $14,820. Graduate: $480 per credit. On-campus room and board: $8,340. Other expenses: $1,750. Books and supplies: $500.

Financial Aid: Resources specifically for eligible students enrolled in teacher education programs are awarded on the basis of financial need and academic merit. The institution has a Program Participation Agreement with the U.S. Department of Education for eligible students to receive Pell Grants and other federal aid. Teacher scholarships available to qualifying students. *Contact:* Financial Aid Office at: (845) 398-4097.

Accreditation: *Regional:* MSA. *Member of:* AACTE. *Approved by:* New York State Department of Education.

Undergraduate Programs: Students entering the initial baccalaureate level must complete general education requirements in the liberal arts and sciences. This core of courses along with a liberal arts concentration or major, gives candidates a knowledge base to teach to the New York State Learning Standards. Programs leading to the baccalaureate degree require the completion of field experiences, content major, and student teaching.

Graduate Programs: The Master of Science in Teaching program is designed for candidates who hold a bachelor's degree and wish to become teachers. The program can be completed in 18 months. Based on background and interests, candidates may select one of the three programs: Childhood Education (grades 1-6) requiring completion of 39 credits; Childhood and Special Education (grades 1-6) requiring completion of 45 credits); and Adolescent Education (grades 7-12) requiring completion of 36 credits and specializing in one of the following fields: biology, chemistry, English, physics, social studies.

The Master of Science in Education offers a curriculum leading to the following: special education - teaching students with disabilities in childhood education (grades 1-6) or in adolescence education (grades 7-12); early childhood and childhood literacy (birth-grade 6); middle childhood and adolescence literacy (grades 5-12).

Licensure/Reciprocity: New York. Students seeking teaching certification in a state other than New York should consult with that state's teacher certification office early in their program of study to insure compliance with requirements. Many state directors of teacher credentialing have signed Interstate Agreements through NASDTEC that expedite the certification process.

STATE UNIVERSITY OF NEW YORK AT ALBANY

School of Education
Ed 212

1400 Washington Avenue
Albany, New York 12222-0001
Phone: (518) 442-4985
Fax: (518) 442-4953
E-mail: cdavenport@uamail.albany.edu
Internet: http://www.albany.edu

Institution Description: The university was founded in 1844 as the first state institution in New York to train teachers and the fourth such school in the nation.

The School of Education offers an undergraduate program designed for students with well-defined interests or career objectives and graduate programs that provide opportunities for students to work with diverse student groups.

Institution Control: Public.

Calendar: Semester. Academic year September to May.

Official(s): Dr. Susan Phillips, Dean.

Faculty: Full-time 621 part-time 921 adjunct 11.

Degrees Awarded: 41 baccalaureate; 473 master's; 15 doctorate.

Admission Requirements: *Undergraduate:* Graduation from an approved high school with 18 units acceptable to the university. *Teacher education specific:* The university does not offer a teacher education program, but students major in a liberal arts and sciences subject area in which the student expects to teach. *Graduate:* Baccalaureate degree from a regionally accredited institution. *Teacher education specific:* Undergraduate GPA 3.0; competitive PRAXIS Examination score; evidence of written and oral communication; personal interview; New York State Teacher Certification Examination; completion of state-approved programs in child abuse education and school violence also required.

Fees and Expenses: Undergraduate: resident $4,350 per academic year; nonresident $10,300. Graduate: resident $6,900; nonresident $10,500. Required fees: $990. Room and board: $6,768. Other expenses: $1,550. Books and supplies: $800.

Financial Aid: Resources specifically for eligible students enrolled in teacher education programs are awarded on the basis of academic merit. The institution has a Program Participation Agreement with the U.S. Department of Education for eligible students to receive Pell Grants and other federal aid. *Contact:* Dr. Michael Green at: (518) 442-4992 or e-mail at mgreen@uamail.albany.edu.

Accreditation: *Regional:* MSA. *Accreditation:* Teacher Education Accreditation Council. *Approved by:* New York State Department of Education.

Undergraduate Programs: Undergraduate students major in a liberal arts and sciences subject area in which they expect to teach. An undergraduate teacher education program is no longer offered.

Graduate Programs: The School of Education offers graduate teacher preparation programs for initial and professional certification in New York State through its master's program for reading and special education, as well as the Master of Science in secondary education in biology, chemistry, earth science, English, French, mathematics, physics, Spanish, social studies, and teaching English to speakers of other languages. This program focuses on providing coursework that is linked to field work at school sites and seminars that enhance pedagogical and content knowledge.

Licensure/Reciprocity: New York. Students seeking teaching certification in a state other than New York should consult with that state's teacher certification office early in their program of study to insure compliance with requirements. Many state directors of teacher credentialing have signed Interstate Agreements through NASDTEC that expedite the certification process.

STATE UNIVERSITY OF NEW YORK AT BINGHAMTON

School of Education and Human Development
Division of Education

SEHD ACA, B, Room 230
P.O. Box 6000
Binghamton, New York 13902-6000
Phone: (607) 777-2365
Fax: (607) 777-6453
E-mail: educ@binghamton.edu
Internet: http:www.binghamton.edu

Institution Description: The university, also known as Binghamton University, was established as Triple Cities College in 1946. The name was changed to Harpur College in 1950 and the present name was adopted in 1965.

The Division of Education focuses on the post-baccalaureate preparation of preservice and inservice teachers. The university offers only graduate degrees in education.

Institution Control: Public.

Calendar: Semester. Academic year August to May.

Official(s): Dr. Ernest Rose, Dean; Dr. C. Beth Burch, Division Director.

Faculty: Full-time 15; adjunct 6.

Degrees Awarded: 106 master's; 4 doctorate.

Admission Requirements: *Graduate:* Baccalaureate degree from a regionally accredited institution. *Teacher education specific:* GRE; 3.0 GPA;1 letters of reference; personal statement; demonstrated experience with children; New York State Teacher Certification Examination; completion of state approved programs in child abuse education and school violence also required.

Fees and Expenses: Graduate: resident $6,900 per academic year; nonresident $10,500. Required fees: $867 per academic year. Off-campus housing only at graduate level.

Financial Aid: Resources specifically for eligible students enrolled in teacher education programs are awarded on the basis of financial need academic merit, and demonstration of personal strengths related to meeting the needs of children. *Contact:* Financial Aid and Employment Office at (607) 777-2428 or e-mail at finaid@binghamton.edu.

Accreditation: *Regional:* MSA. *Professional:* Teacher Education Accreditation Council. *Approved by:* New York State Department of Education.

Graduate Programs: The Division of Education offers preservice graduation programs leading to initial certification in childhood education and adolescence education (in English, mathematics, the sciences, and social studies). The division also has inservice graduate programs leading to professional certification in childhood education, special education, literacy, and adolescence education, as well as a graduate program in educational studies for students not pursuing certification in any of these areas.

For students desiring doctoral work, the division offers a Doctor of Education degree in educational theory and practice.

Licensure/Reciprocity: New York. Students seeking teaching certification in a state other than New York should consult with that state's teacher certification office early in their program of study to insure compliance with requirements. Many state directors of teacher credentialing have signed Interstate Agreements through NASDTEC that expedite the certification process.

STATE UNIVERSITY OF NEW YORK AT BUFFALO

Graduate School of Education

Teacher Education Institute

367 Baldy Hall
Buffalo, New York 14260-1000
Phone: (716) 645-6640
Fax: (716) 645-2479
E-mail: gse@buffalo.edu
Internet: http://www.buffalo.edu

Institution Description: The State University at Buffalo is New York's premier public center for graduate and professional education. It was established as the University of Buffalo in 1846.

Graduate School of Education is committed to providing teacher education at the post-baccalaureate level. The Teacher Education Institute and the Learning and Instruction Department are responsible for the sequence of courses that lead to New York State initial and professional certification.

Institution Control: Public.

Calendar: Semester. Academic year August to May.

Official(s): Dr. Mary H. Gresham, Dean; Dr. Julius Adams, Associate Dean.

Faculty: Full-time 70; part-time 18; adjunct 29.

Degrees Awarded: 269 master's; 35 doctorate.

Admission Requirements: *Graduate:* Baccalaureate from a regionally accredited institution. *Teacher education specific:* GPA 3.0; interview; transcripts of all undergraduate coursework; teaching credential when required by program pursued; New York State Teacher Certification Examination; completion of state approved programs in child abuse education and school violence also required.

Fees and Expenses: Graduate: resident $6,900; nonresident $10,500. Required fees. $1,009 comprehensive fee and $78 activity fee. Room: $4,854 (single room).

Financial Aid: Resources specifically for eligible students enrolled in teacher education programs are awarded on the basis of financial need and academic merit. *Contact:* Student Response Center at (716) 845-2450 or e-mail at srcenter@buffalo.edu.

Accreditation: *Regional:* MSA. *Professional:* Teacher Education Accreditation Council. *Member of:* AACTE. *Approved by:* New York State Department of Education.

Graduate Programs: The Graduate School of Education offers the sequence of courses that lead to New York State Initial and Professional Teacher Certification in early childhood, childhood, middle childhood, and adolescence education. Students can pursue certification in languages other than English (French, German, Italian, Latin, Russian), science (biology, chemistry, earth science, physics), mathematics, social studies, and English.

Additionally, students can pursue advanced degrees (master's and doctoral) and certification in the following areas: bilingual education, languages other than English (French, German, Italian, Latin, Russian), music education, literacy, social studies, science education, biology, chemistry, earth science, physics, mathematics, and English.

Licensure/Reciprocity: New York. Students seeking teaching certification in a state other than New York should consult with that state's teacher certification office early in their program of study to insure compliance with requirements. Many state directors of teacher credentialing have signed Interstate Agreements through NASDTEC that expedite the certification process.

STATE UNIVERSITY OF NEW YORK AT NEW PALTZ

School of Education

75 South Manheim Boulevard
New Paltz, New York 12561-2499
Phone: (845) 257-2800
Fax: (845) 257-2799
E-mail: schoolofed@newpaltz.edu
Internet: http://www.newpaltz.edu

Institution Description: The university was founded as New Paltz Academy in 1828.

The School of Education offers undergraduate and graduate programs leading to teaching credentials in New York State.

Institution Control: Public.

Calendar: Semester. Academic year August to May.

Official(s): Dr. Robert J. Michael, Dean; Dr. Richard Reif, Associate Dean.

Faculty: Full-time 46; adjunct 106.

Degrees Awarded: 287 baccalaureate; 430 master's.

Admission Requirements: *Undergraduate:* Graduation from an approved secondary school or GED; College Board SAT or ACT composite. *Teacher education specific:* Students must complete teacher education introductory courses; cumulative GPA of 2.75 in at least 24 credits of college coursework; portfolio review; faculty interview; New York State Teacher Certification Examination; completion of state-approved programs in child abuse education and school violence also required. *Graduate:* Baccalaureate degree from a regionally accredited institution. *Teacher education specific:* Three professional recommendations; essay; GRE scores; faculty interview; teaching credential when required by the program pursued.

Fees and Expenses: Undergraduate: resident $4,350 per academic year; nonresident $10,300. Graduate: resident $6,900; nonresident $10,500.

Financial Aid: Resources specifically for eligible students enrolled in teacher education programs are awarded on the basis of financial need and academic merit. The institution has a Program Participation Agreement with the U.S. Department of Education for eligible students to receive Pell Grants and other federal aid. Teacher scholarships available to qualifying students. *Contact:* Financial Aid Office at: (845) 257-3250 or e-mail at fao@newpaltz.edu.

Accreditation: *Regional:* MSA. *Professional:* NCATE. *Approved by:* New York State Department of Education.

Undergraduate Programs: The undergraduate secondary education competency-based teacher education program and early childhood and childhood education programs that lead to the baccalaureate degree are offered by the School of Education. The programs require the completion of a general education core, professional studies, content area, field experiences, and student teaching. A minimum of 120 credit hours is required for the degree award.

Graduate Programs: The School of Education offers graduate programs leading to the Master of Science in Education (birth-grade 6) with concentrations in reading/literacy, environmental education, early childhood, and additional specialization tracks; the Master of Science in literacy education (birth-grade 6 and grades 5-12); Master of Science for teachers in childhood (grades 1-6) and early childhood (birth-grade 2); Master of Science in Education for teachers in secondary (7-12); Master of Arts in Teaching for secondary (7-12); Master of Science in second language education; Master of Science in special education; Master of Science in educational administration.

Licensure/Reciprocity: New York. Students seeking teaching certification in a state other than New York should consult with that state's teacher certification office early in their program of study to insure compliance with requirements. Many state directors of teacher credentialing have signed Interstate Agreements through NASDTEC that expedite the certification process.

STATE UNIVERSITY OF NEW YORK AT PLATTSBURGH

Department of Educational Studies and Services

302 Sibley Hall
101 Broad Street
Plattsburgh, New York 12901-2681
Phone: (518) 564-2122
Fax: (518) 564-2045
E-mail: admissions@plattsburgh.edu
Internet: http://www.plattsburgh.edu

Institution Description: Established as Plattsburgh State Normal School in 1889, it offered first instruction at the postsecondary level in 1890. The name was changed to State Teachers College of Education in 1959 and the present name was adopted in 1961. It is also known as Plattsburgh State University.

The baccalaureate degree programs at Plattsburgh combine all that is needed for both graduation and New York State Certification. Programs also are provided leading to master's level teacher education degrees.

Institution Control: Public.

Calendar: Semester. Academic year August to May.

Official(s): Dr. John B. Clark, President.

Faculty: Not reported.

Degrees Awarded: 246 baccalaureate; 285 master's.

Admission Requirements: *Undergraduate:* Graduation from an approved secondary school or GED; College Board SAT or ACT composite. *Teacher education specific:* Students must complete teacher education introductory courses; Pre-Professional Skills Tests; cumulative GPA of 2.75; portfolio review; faculty interview; New York State Teacher Certification Examination; completion of state-approved programs in child abuse education and school violence also required. *Graduate:* Baccalaureate degree from a regionally accredited institution. *Teacher education specific:* Letters of recommendation; GRE scores; faculty interview; teaching credential when required by the program pursued.

Fees and Expenses: Undergraduate: resident $4,350 per academic year; nonresident $10,300. Graduate: resident $6,900; nonresident $10,500. On-campus room and board: $6,500. Other expenses: $1,870. Books and supplies: $850.

Financial Aid: Resources specifically for eligible students enrolled in teacher education programs are awarded on the basis of financial need and academic merit. The institution has a Program Participation Agreement with the U.S. Department of Education for eligible students to receive Pell Grants and other federal aid. Teacher scholarships available to qualifying students. *Contact:* Financial Aid Office at: (518) 564-2072.

Accreditation: *Regional:* MSA. *Member of:* AACTE. *Approved by:* New York State Department of Education.

Undergraduate Programs: Undergraduate programs leading to the baccalaureate degree and initial teaching credential include: elementary education (grades 1-6). Majors select an appropriate area of academic concentration from art, biology, chemistry, earth science, English, French, mathematics, music, social studies or Spanish. secondary education (grades 7-12) curricula include programs in English, mathematics, social studies, science (biology, chemistry, earth science, physics), and foreign language (French or Spanish). Special/elementary education (grades 1-6) program provides preparation for teaching students with mild and moderate disabilities.

All baccalaureate programs require the completion of a general education core, professional studies, content area, field experiences, and student teaching. A minimum of 120 credit hours must be completed for the degree award.

Graduate Programs: Graduate programs include the Master of Science in Teaching (childhood 1-6) and adolescence education. The Master of Science in Education is offered with specializations in early childhood (birth-grade 2); childhood (grades 21-6); adolescence (grades 7-12) with initial certificate in special education; adolescence (grades 7-12). Also offered are the Master of Science in literacy (birth-grade 6 and grades 5-12).

Licensure/Reciprocity: New York. Students seeking teaching certification in a state other than New York should consult with that state's teacher certification office early in their program of study to insure compliance with requirements. Many state directors of teacher credentialing have signed Interstate Agreements through NASDTEC that expedite the certification process.

STATE UNIVERSITY OF NEW YORK AT POTSDAM

School of Education
Teacher Education Program

44 Pierrepont Avenue
Potsdam, New York 13676
Phone: (315) 267-2000
Fax: (315) 267-2163
E-mail: teacher.ed@potsdam.edu
Internet: http://www.potsdam.edu

Institution Description: The institution was established as St. Lawrence Academy in 1816.

The Teacher Education Program offers students the opportunity to pursue undergraduate and graduate degrees and teacher certification in New York State.

Institution Control: Public.

Calendar: Semester. Academic year August to May.

Official(s): Dr. W. Amondell, Dean.

Degrees Awarded: 94 baccalaureate; 495 master's.

Admission Requirements: *Undergraduate:* Graduation from an approved secondary school or GED; College Board SAT or ACT composite. *Teacher education specific:* Students must complete teacher education introductory courses; Pre-Professional Skills Tests; cumulative GPA of 2.0; portfolio review; faculty interview; New York State Teacher Certification Examination; completion of state-approved programs in child abuse education and school violence also required. *Graduate:* Baccalaureate degree from a regionally accredited institution. *Teacher education specific:* Letters of recommendation; GRE scores; faculty interview; teaching credential when required by the program pursued.

Fees and Expenses: Undergraduate: resident $4,350 per academic year; nonresident $11,150. Graduate: resident $6,900; nonresident $10,500. On-campus room and board: $6,970. Other expenses: $1,800. Books and supplies: $900.

Financial Aid: Resources specifically for eligible students enrolled in teacher education programs are awarded on the basis of financial need and academic merit. The institution has a Program Participation Agreement with the U.S. Department of Education for eligible students to receive Pell Grants and other federal aid. Teacher scholarships available to qualifying students. *Contact:* Financial Aid Office at: (315) 267-2162.

Accreditation: *Regional:* MSA. *Professional:* NCATE. *Approved by:* New York State Department of Education.

Undergraduate Programs: Students completing a a baccalaureate education program also complete an appropriate major in the arts and sciences major. Students in the early childhood education program and the childhood education program complete one of the approved majors in liberal studies, including the courses in English, mathematics, science, social studies, modern language, and learn to address the special developmental and educational needs of children in lower and upper elementary grades.

Students in the middle and secondary education program complete an arts and sciences major appropriate to the area of certification and to learn to address the special developmental and educational needs of middle level and high school students. The emphasis on academic preparation in a content area strengthens students qualifications both for careers in teaching and graduate study in their liberal arts major.

Graduate Programs: The School of Education offers graduate programs leading toward the Master of Science in Education degrees in early childhood education, childhood education, middle and secondary education (including biology, chemistry,

English, earth science, mathematics, physics, social studies), reading, special education, information and communication technology, and general professional education.

The Master of Science in Teaching prepares persons possessing a baccalaureate degree to become provisionally certified at grades of early childhood education, childhood education, and middle and secondary education.

Licensure/Reciprocity: New York. Students seeking teaching certification in a state other than New York should consult with that state's teacher certification office early in their program of study to insure compliance with requirements. Many state directors of teacher credentialing have signed Interstate Agreements through NASDTEC that expedite the certification process.

STATE UNIVERSITY OF NEW YORK AT STONY BROOK

Professional Education Program

200 Harriman Hall
Nicholls Road
Stony Brook, New York 11794-3779
Phone: (631) 632-4137
Fax: (631) 632-9487
E-mail: pep@sunysb.edu
Internet: http//www.sunysb.edu

Institution Description: The institution was established as State University College on Long Island and offered first instruction at the postsecondary level in 1957. The present name was adopted in 1962.

The Professional Education Program offers students the opportunity to pursue teacher certification at the undergraduate and graduate levels. The program provides university-wide coordination of teacher education programs.

Institution Control: Public.

Calendar: Semester. Academic year August to May.

Official(s): Dr. Dorit H. Kaufman, Director.

Faculty: Full-time 200; part-time 4; adjunct 15.

Degrees Awarded: 71 master's.

Admission Requirements: *Undergraduate:* Graduation from an approved secondary school or GED; College Board SAT or ACT composite. *Teacher education specific:* Students must complete teacher education introductory courses; Pre-Professional Skills Tests; cumulative GPA of 2.0; portfolio review; faculty interview; New York State Teacher Certification Examination; completion of state-approved programs in child abuse education and school violence also required. *Graduate:* Baccalaureate degree from a regionally accredited institution. *Teacher education specific:* Letters of recommendation; GRE scores; faculty interview; teaching credential when required by the program pursued.

Fees and Expenses: Undergraduate: resident $4,350 per academic year; nonresident $11,150. Graduate: resident $6,900; nonresident $10,500. Required fees: $958. On-campus room and board: $7,190. Other expenses: $1,000. Books and supplies: $900.

Financial Aid: Resources specifically for eligible students enrolled in teacher education programs are awarded on the basis of financial need. The institution has a Program Participation Agreement with the U.S. Department of Education for eligible students to receive Pell Grants and other federal aid. Teacher scholarships available to qualifying students. *Contact:* Jacqueline Poscariello at (631) 632-6840.

Accreditation: *Regional:* MSA. *Professional:* NCATE. *Approved by:* New York State Department of Education.

Undergraduate Programs: Baccalaureate teacher preparation programs are offered leading to certification grades 7-12 in the subject areas of sciences and general science (biology, chemistry, earth science, physics), English, foreign languages (French, German, Italian, Russian, Spanish), mathematics, and social studies. Certification for grades pre-kindergarten through 12 can be pursued in the teaching of English to speakers of other languages (TESOL). The major components of the programs include the general education core, professional studies, 100 hours of field experience, content area, and student teaching.

Graduate Programs: The Master of Arts in Teaching: English; Master of Arts in Teaching: foreign languages; Master of Arts in Teaching: science; Master of Arts in Teaching: social studies; Master of Arts in TESOL; and Master of Arts in Teaching: mathematics lead to New York State certification for teaching in the secondary schools, grades 7-12. The programs are designed for those who have little or no previous coursework in education or formal classroom teaching experience. The degree programs consist of 42 credits in specific areas.

Licensure/Reciprocity: New York. Students seeking teaching certification in a state other than New York should consult with that state's teacher certification office early in their program of study to insure compliance with requirements. Many state directors of teacher credentialing have signed Interstate Agreements through NASDTEC that expedite the certification process.

STATE UNIVERSITY OF NEW YORK COLLEGE AT BROCKPORT

Department of Education and Human Development
Teacher Certification Programs

350 New Campus Drive
Brockport, New York 14420-2914
Phone: (716) 395-2211
Fax: (716) 395-5452
E-mail: ehd@brockport.edu
Internet: http://www.brockport.edu

Institution Description: The university was established as Brockport Normal School in 1867. The name was changed to Brockport State Teachers College in 1942 and the present name was adopted in 1948.

The Department of Education and Human Development is committed to providing programs that prepare its graduates to meet the highest professional teacher standards for certification in New York State.

Institution Control: Public.

Calendar: Semester. Academic year September to May.

Official(s): Dr. William R. Vcenis, Dean.

Faculty: Full-time 22.

Degrees Awarded: 178 baccalaureate; 309 master's.

Admission Requirements: *Undergraduate:* Graduation from an approved secondary school or GED; College Board SAT or ACT composite. *Teacher education specific:* Students must complete teacher education introductory courses; cumulative GPA of 2.75; portfolio review; faculty interview; New York State Teacher Certification Examination; completion of state-approved programs in child abuse education and school violence also required. *Graduate:* Baccalaureate degree from a regionally accredited institution. *Teacher education specific:* Three professional recommendations; essay; GRE scores; faculty interview; teaching credential when required by the program pursued.

Fees and Expenses: Undergraduate: resident $4,350 per academic year; nonresident $10,300. Graduate: resident $6,900; nonresident $10,500. On-campus room and board: $6,690. Other expenses: $1,420. Books and supplies: $810.

Financial Aid: Resources specifically for eligible students enrolled in teacher education programs are awarded on the basis of financial need and academic merit. The institution has a Program Participation Agreement with the U.S. Department of Education for eligible students to receive Pell Grants and other federal aid. Teacher scholarships available to qualifying students. *Contact:* Financial Aid Office at: (718) 395-2501.

Accreditation: *Regional:* MSA. *Member of:* AACTE. *Approved by:* New York State Department of Education.

Undergraduate Programs: Undergraduate teacher certification programs offered by the Department of Education include: adolescence education with middle school extension (grades 5-12); childhood education (grades 1-6); early childhood education

STATE UNIVERSITY OF NEW YORK COLLEGE AT BROCKPORT—cont'd

(birth-grade 2). All baccalaureate programs require the completion of a general education core, professional studies, content area, field experiences, and student teaching. A minimum of 120 credit hours must be completed for the degree award.

Graduate Programs: The Department of Education and Human Development offers the following 33- and 36-credit master's programs: elementary education; elementary education/interdisciplinary arts for children; bilingual education; childhood literacy; childhood special education; secondary English, mathematics, science (biology chemistry, earth science, physics); social studies.

An Alternate Master of Science in Education programs (54 credits) are designed specifically for those who do not possess any certification and who have little or no professional education background. These programs lead to *initial* certification and also provide the master's degree that is required in New York State for *professional* certification. Programs are in the area of adolescence education and each includes an extension to middle childhood education (grades 5-9).

Licensure/Reciprocity: New York. Students seeking teaching certification in a state other than New York should consult with that state's teacher certification office early in their program of study to insure compliance with requirements. Many state directors of teacher credentialing have signed Interstate Agreements through NASDTEC that expedite the certification process.

STATE UNIVERSITY OF NEW YORK COLLEGE AT BUFFALO

Applied Science and Education
Teacher Education Programs
114 Caudell Hall
1300 Elmwood Avenue
Buffalo, New York 14222-1095
Phone: (716) 878-4214
Fax: (716) 878-5301
E-mail: admission@buffalostate.edu
Internet: http://www.buffalostate.edu

Institution Description: The College at Buffalo, also known as Buffalo State College, was established in 1867 and offered first instruction at the postsecondary level in 1871.

The college offers a number and variety of programs to prepare individuals for the teaching profession from bachelor's to master's degree programs.

Institution Control: Public.

Calendar: Semester. Academic year August to May.

Official(s): Dr. Richard J. Lee, Dean; Dr. Richard Pademski, Dean, Graduate Studies.

Faculty: Not reported.

Degrees Awarded: 690 baccalaureate; 544 master's.

Admission Requirements: *Undergraduate:* Graduation from an approved secondary school or GED; College Board SAT or ACT composite. *Teacher education specific:* Students must complete teacher education introductory courses; cumulative GPA of 2.75; portfolio review; faculty interview; New York State Teacher Certification Examination; completion of state-approved programs in child abuse education and school violence also required. *Graduate:* Baccalaureate degree from a regionally accredited institution. *Teacher education specific:* Letters of recommendation; GRE scores; faculty interview; teaching credential when required by the program pursued.

Fees and Expenses: Undergraduate: resident $4,350 per academic year; nonresident $10,300. Graduate: resident $6,900; nonresident $10,500. On-campus room and board: $6,325. Other expenses: $1,800. Books and supplies: $900.

Financial Aid: Resources specifically for eligible students enrolled in teacher education programs are awarded on the basis of financial need and academic merit. The institution has a Program Participation Agreement with the U.S. Department of Education for eligible students to receive Pell Grants and other federal aid. Teacher scholarships available to qualifying students. *Contact:* Financial Aid Office at: (716) 878-4901.

Accreditation: *Regional:* MSA. *Professional:* NCATE. *Member of:* AACTE. *Approved by:* New York State Department of Education.

Undergraduate Programs: The undergraduate teacher preparation programs include the initial baccalaureate program that allows students to earn teaching certification while pursuing a bachelor's degree in an accredited program. Programs are offered by the various faculties in the liberal arts and sciences whereby students acquire the major requirements for the degree as well as the education foundation courses, professional studies, field experiences, and student teaching. A minimum of 123 credit hours is required for the degree award.

Graduate Programs: Initial graduate teacher preparation programs allow students to earn teaching certification while pursuing a master's degree in an accredited program. Advanced graduate teacher preparation programs are designed for students who have already earned provisional teaching certificates and who wish to pursue study in the profession while fulfilling requirements for permanent certification in New York State. Graduate programs are offered through the various departments of the college.

Licensure/Reciprocity: New York. Students seeking teaching certification in a state other than New York should consult with that state's teacher certification office early in their program of study to insure compliance with requirements. Many state directors of teacher credentialing have signed Interstate Agreements through NASDTEC that expedite the certification process.

STATE UNIVERSITY OF NEW YORK COLLEGE AT CORTLAND

School of Education
Teacher Education Program
Graham Avenue
P.O. Box 2000
Cortland, New York 13045
Phone: (607) 753-2011
Fax: (607) 753-5998
E-mail: admssn-info@cortland.edu
Internet: http://cortland.edu

Institution Description: The university was chartered as Cortland State Normal School in 1868. The name was changed to Cortland State Teachers College in 1941 and became part of the state university system in 1948.

The mission of teacher education at SUNY Cortland is to build upon the foundation of liberal learning in the development of teachers who have exceptional pedagogical knowledge and skills.

Institution Control: Public.

Calendar: Semester. Academic year August to May.

Official(s): Dr. Cynthia J. Benton, Chair.

Faculty: Full-time 161; adjunct 33.

Degrees Awarded: 822 baccalaureate; 493 master's.

Admission Requirements: *Undergraduate:* Graduation from an approved secondary school or GED; College Board SAT or ACT composite. *Teacher education specific:* Students must complete teacher education introductory courses; cumulative GPA of 2.75; portfolio review; faculty interview; New York State Teacher Certification Examination; completion of state-approved programs in child abuse education and school violence also required. *Graduate:* Baccalaureate degree from a regionally accredited institution. *Teacher education specific:* Letters of recommendation; GRE scores; faculty interview; teaching credential when required by the program pursued.

Fees and Expenses: Undergraduate: resident $4,350 per academic year; nonresident $10,300. Graduate: resident $6,900; nonresident $10,500. On-campus room and board: $6,860. Other expenses: $1,700. Books and supplies: $720.

Financial Aid: Resources specifically for eligible students enrolled in teacher education programs are awarded on the basis of financial need and academic merit. The institution has a Program Participation Agreement with the U.S. Department of Education for eligible students to receive Pell Grants and other federal aid. Teacher scholarships available to qualifying students. *Contact:* Financial Aid Office at: (607) 753-4717.

Accreditation: *Regional:* MSA. *Professional:* NCATE. *Member of:* AACTE. *Approved by:* New York State Department of Education.

Undergraduate Programs: Undergraduate programs offered include the Bachelor of Science (B.S.) or Bachelor of Arts (B.A.) in early childhood (birth-grade 2); B.S. or B.A. in early childhood/childhood (dual certification, birth-grade 6); B.S. in childhood education (certification grades 1-6). All baccalaureate programs require the completion of a minimum of 124 semester hours including the general education core, professional studies, content area, field experiences and student teaching.

Graduate Programs: The Master of Science in Teaching and the Master of Science in Education degree programs are offered in childhood education. A Master of Science in Education degree program in teaching students with disabilities (grades 1-5) is also offered.

Licensure/Reciprocity: New York. Students seeking teaching certification in a state other than New York should consult with that state's teacher certification office early in their program of study to insure compliance with requirements. Many state directors of teacher credentialing have signed Interstate Agreements through NASDTEC that expedite the certification process.

STATE UNIVERSITY OF NEW YORK COLLEGE AT ONEONTA

Division of Education
205 Fitzelle Hall
Ravine Parkway
Oneonta, New York 13820-4015
Phone: (607) 436-3500
Fax: (607) 436-3089
E-mail: admissions@oneonta.edu
Internet: http://www.oneonta.edu

Institution Description: The institution was established in 1887. The name was changed to State Teachers College in 1942, to State University Teachers College in 1948, to State University College of Education in 1959, and to the present name in 1961.

The Division of Education programs focus on the development of teachers as educational professionals, leaders, practitioners, and global citizens.

Institution Control: Public.

Calendar: Semester. Academic year August to May.

Official(s): Dr. Jeanne M. Currant, Assistant Dean.

Faculty: Full-time 14.

Degrees Awarded: 303 baccalaureate; 58 master's.

Admission Requirements: *Undergraduate:* Graduation from an approved secondary school or GED; College Board SAT or ACT composite. *Teacher education specific:* Students must complete teacher education introductory courses; cumulative GPA of 2.8; portfolio review; faculty interview; New York State Teacher Certification Examination; completion of state-approved programs in child abuse education and school violence also required. *Graduate:* Baccalaureate degree from a regionally accredited institution. *Teacher education specific:* Letters of recommendation; GRE scores; faculty interview; teaching credential when required by the program pursued.

Fees and Expenses: Undergraduate: resident $4,350 per academic year; nonresident $10,300. Graduate: resident $6,900; nonresident $10,500. On-campus room and board: $6,914. Other expenses: $2,100. Books and supplies: $850.

Financial Aid: Resources specifically for eligible students enrolled in teacher education programs are awarded on the basis of financial need and academic merit. The institution has a Program Participation Agreement with the U.S. Department of

Education for eligible students to receive Pell Grants and other federal aid. Teacher scholarships available to qualifying students. *Contact:* Financial Aid Office at: (607) 436-2532,

Accreditation: *Regional:* MSA. *Professional:* NCATE. *Member of:* AACTE. *Approved by:* New York State Department of Education.

Undergraduate Programs: The Elementary Education Department offers three undergraduate programs leading to teacher certification. Programs require the completion of a 30-hour concentration in an area consistent with New York State Learning Standards. The degree programs include early childhood education (birth-grade 2); childhood education (grades 1-6); early childhood/childhood education (birth-grade 6). These Bachelor of Science programs required the completion of a general education core, professional studies, 100 clock hours of field experience, content area, and student teaching. A minimum of 122 credit hours must be completed for the degree award.

Graduate Programs: The Master of Science in Education degree programs include: childhood education (grades 1-6); literacy education (birth-grade 6); literacy education (grades 5-12); literacy education (birth-grade 12); adolescence education (grades 7-12); family and consumer sciences education; school counselor education.

Licensure/Reciprocity: New York. Students seeking teaching certification in a state other than New York should consult with that state's teacher certification office early in their program of study to insure compliance with requirements. Many state directors of teacher credentialing have signed Interstate Agreements through NASDTEC that expedite the certification process.

STATE UNIVERSITY OF NEW YORK COLLEGE AT OSWEGO

School of Education
Department of Curriculum and Instruction
200 Poucher Hall
7060 Star Route 104
Oswego, New York 13126
Phone: (315) 341-2500
Fax: (315) 341-5438
E-mail: educate@oswego.edu
Internet: http://www.oswego.edu

Institution Description: SUNY at Oswego is a comprehensive public college with over 140 years of history and tradition. It was established and offered first instruction at the postsecondary level in 1861.

The School of Education offers undergraduate and graduate initial certification programs to fulfill the requirements of New York State.

Institution Control: Public.

Calendar: Semester. Academic year August to May.

Official(s): Dr. Linda Rae Markert, Dean.

Faculty: Full-time 25.

Degrees Awarded: 395 baccalaureate; 341 master's.

Admission Requirements: *Undergraduate:* Graduation from an approved secondary school or GED; College Board SAT or ACT composite. *Teacher education specific:* Students must complete teacher education introductory courses; cumulative GPA of 2.75; portfolio review; faculty interview; New York State Teacher Certification Examination; completion of state-approved programs in child abuse education and school violence also required. *Graduate:* Baccalaureate degree from a regionally accredited institution. *Teacher education specific:* Letters of recommendation; GRE scores; faculty interview; teaching credential when required by the program pursued.

Fees and Expenses: Undergraduate: resident $4,350 per academic year; nonresident $10,300. Graduate: resident $6,900; nonresident $10,500. On-campus room and board: $7,540. Other expenses: $1,700. Books and supplies: $800.

Financial Aid: Resources specifically for eligible students enrolled in teacher education programs are awarded on the basis of financial need and academic merit. The institution has a Program Participation Agreement with the U.S. Department of

STATE UNIVERSITY OF NEW YORK COLLEGE AT OSWEGO—*cont'd*

Education for eligible students to receive Pell Grants and other federal aid. Teacher scholarships available to qualifying students. *Contact:* Financial Aid Office at: (315) 312-2248.

Accreditation: *Regional:* MSA. *Professional:* NCATE. *Member of:* AACTE. *Approved by:* New York State Department of Education.

Undergraduate Programs: Undergraduate Initial Certification Programs are offered in adolescence education with concentrations in biology, chemistry, earth science, physics, English, French, German, Spanish, mathematics, and social studies; childhood education; teaching English to speakers of other languages; technology education; vocational education (agriculture, business, and marketing). Undergraduate non-certification majors leading to the Bachelor Science degree include wellness management and technology management. All programs lead to the baccalaureate degree and require the completion of a general education core, professional studies, content area, field experiences, and student teaching.

Graduate Programs: Graduate initial certification programs leading to the Master of Science degree include: adolescence education (7-12); childhood education (grades 1-6); vocational Education (7-12); agricultural education (all grades). The Master of Arts in Teaching is offered in art education (all grades).

Graduate initial and professional certification programs leading to the Master of Science degree are offered in child education (N-6); literacy (birth-6 and 5-12). Graduate permanent certification programs include elementary education (N-6); secondary education (7-12); technology education (K-12); and vocational-technical education (7-12).

Licensure/Reciprocity: New York. Students seeking teaching certification in a state other than New York should consult with that state's teacher certification office early in their program of study to insure compliance with requirements. Many state directors of teacher credentialing have signed Interstate Agreements through NASDTEC that expedite the certification process.

SYRACUSE UNIVERSITY

School of Education
270 Huntington Hall
Syracuse, New York 13244
Phone: (315) 443-2506
Fax: (315) 443-5732
E-mail: amredman@syr.edu
Internet: http://www.syr.edu

Institution Description: Syracuse University is a private, independent, nonprofit institution that was established in 1870.

The School of Education offers undergraduate and over 40 graduate programs leading to teacher certification and professional career enhancement.

Institution Control: Private.

Calendar: Semester. Academic year August to May.

Official(s): Dr. Louise Wilkinson, Dean.

Faculty: Full-time 55; part-time 4; adjunct 60.

Degrees Awarded: 126 baccalaureate; 164 master's; 19 doctorate.

Admission Requirements: *Undergraduate:* Graduation from an accredited secondary school with a college preparatory curriculum; College Board SAT or ACT composite; personal essay; two academic recommendations. *Teacher education specific:* Students must complete education introductory courses; cumulative GPA of 2.8; portfolio review; faculty interview; New York State Teacher Certification Examination; completion of state-approved programs in child abuse education and school violence also required. *Graduate:* Baccalaureate degree from a regionally accredited institution. *Teacher education specific:* Letters of recommendation; GRE scores; faculty interview; teaching credential when required by the program pursued.

Fees and Expenses: Undergraduate: $24,170 per academic year. Graduate: $742 per credit hour. Required fees: $960. On-campus room and board: $9,590. Other expenses: $1,098. Books and supplies: $1,162.

Financial Aid: Resources specifically for eligible students enrolled in teacher education programs are awarded on the basis of financial need and academic merit. The institution has a Program Participation Agreement with the U.S. Department of Education for eligible students to receive Pell Grants and other federal aid. Teacher scholarships available to qualifying students. *Contact:* Christopher Walsh at: (315) 443-1513.

Accreditation: *Regional:* MSA. *Professional:* NCATE. *Member of:* AACTE. *Approved by:* New York State Department of Education.

Undergraduate Programs: Baccalaureate programs offered by the School of Education include: art education, English, health and exercise science, elementary and special education, mathematics, music, physical education, science education (biology, chemistry, earth science, physics); social studies. All programs require the completion of a minimum of 124 credits including the general education core, professional studies, content area, field experiences, and student teaching.

Graduate Programs: The School of Education is composed of seven academic departments offering degrees at both the master's and doctoral levels: Counseling and Human Services; Cultural Foundations of Education; Higher Education; Instructional Design, Development and Evaluation; Reading and Language Arts, and Teaching and Leadership. The Master of Science, Doctor of Education, and Doctor of Philosophy degrees can be earned through the various academic departments.

Licensure/Reciprocity: New York. Students seeking teaching certification in a state other than New York should consult with that state's teacher certification office early in their program of study to insure compliance with requirements. Many state directors of teacher credentialing have signed Interstate Agreements through NASDTEC that expedite the certification process.

TEACHERS COLLEGE AT COLUMBIA UNIVERSITY

Department of Curriculum and Teaching
Room 305 Main Hall
525 West 120th Street
New York, New York 10027
Phone: (212) 678-3165
Fax: (212) 678-4048
E-mail: admissions@tc.columbia.edu
Internet: http://www.tc.columbia.edu

Institution Description: Teachers College is a private, independent, nonprofit graduate school affiliated with Columbia University. The college was established in 1887 and became affiliated with Columbia University in 1898.

The Department of Curriculum and Teaching prepares prospective teachers and other professionals to assume leadership roles in educational programs for learners of all ages.

Institution Control: Private.

Calendar: Semester. Academic year September to May.

Official(s): Dr. James H. Borland, Department Chair.

Faculty: Full-time 35; adjunct 14.

Degrees Awarded: 922 master's; 125 doctorate.

Admission Requirements: *Graduate:* Baccalaureate degree from a regionally accredited institution. *Teacher education specific:* Transcripts from all institutions attended; personal statement; 2 letters of reference; faculty interview. First-year doctoral students must enroll in Theory and Inquiry in Curriculum and Teaching.

Fees and Expenses: $825 per point. Required fees: $610/$939. Other fees may apply. Off-campus housing. On-campus may be available at nearby Columbia University facilities.

Financial Aid: Resources specifically for eligible students enrolled in teacher education programs are awarded on the basis of academic merit and financial need. *Contact:* Department of Curriculum and Teaching at: (212) 678-3165.

Accreditation: *Regional:* MSA. *Member of:* AACTE. *Approved by:* New York State Department of Education.

Graduate Programs: The Master of Arts programs are of two types: Preservice, or Initial Certification Programs and Inservice, or Professional Certification Programs. Preservice programs lead to certification in: early childhood education, early childhood special education, and dual certification in early childhood education and early childhood special education. Extensions are offered in gifted education and teacher of students with disabilities.

The Inservice Master of Arts programs are designed for individuals who are already certified or are initially certified to teach in New York and who seek a Master of Arts degree in curriculum and teaching, gifted education, literacy, or teacher of students with disabilities. Graduates of these programs meet the formal educational requirements for professional certification in the State of New York.

The Master of Education degree affords students the opportunity to develop an area of expertise beyond that required for classroom teaching. The degree comprises 60 points.

The Doctor of Education program requires 90 points of graduate study beyond the baccalaureate. Areas of concentration include: curriculum studies; early childhood education; early childhood policy; early childhood special education; educational leadership and school change; gifted education; learning disabilities; reading and language arts; religious education; research and inquiry in curriculum and teaching.

Licensure/Reciprocity: New York. Students seeking teaching certification in a state other than New York should consult with that state's teacher certification office early in their program of study to insure compliance with requirements. Many state directors of teacher credentialing have signed Interstate Agreements through NASDTEC that expedite the certification process.

UTICA COLLEGE

Teacher Education

1600 Burrstone Road
Utica, New York 13502-4892
Phone: (315) 792-3815
Fax: (315) 792-3714
E-mail: lfisch@utica.edu
Internet: http://www.ucsu.edu

Institution Description: Utica College is a private, nonprofit institution. It was established, chartered, and offered first instruction at the postsecondary level in 1946. The college offers programs in teacher education that lead to certification in New York State.

Institution Control: Private.

Calendar: Semester. Academic year August to May.

Official(s): Dr. Lois A. Fisch, Department Head.

Faculty: Full-time 7; adjunct 5.

Degrees Awarded: 250 baccalaureate candidates; 180 master's candidates.

Admission Requirements: *Undergraduate:* Graduation from an approved secondary school with 16 academic units or GED; College Board SAT or ACT composite. *Teacher education specific:* Students must complete education introductory courses; cumulative GPA of 2.75; portfolio review; faculty interview; New York State Teacher Certification Examination; completion of state-approved programs in child abuse education and school violence also required. *Graduate:* Baccalaureate degree from a regionally accredited institution. *Teacher education specific:* Letters of recommendation; GRE scores; faculty interview; teaching credential when required by the program pursued.

Fees and Expenses: Undergraduate: $18,848 per academic year. Graduate: $650 per credit hour. Other fees may apply. On-campus room and board: $6,800 to $9,180. Books and supplies: $800.

Financial Aid: Resources specifically for eligible students enrolled in teacher education programs are awarded on the basis of financial need and academic merit. The institution has a Program Participation Agreement with the U.S. Department of Education for eligible students to receive Pell Grants and other federal aid. Teacher scholarships available to qualifying students. *Contact:* Elizabeth Wilson at: (315) 792-3179.

Accreditation: *Regional:* MSA. *Approved by:* New York State Department of Education.

Undergraduate Programs: Students pursuing the early childhood education (birth-grade 2) program must major in a liberal arts field. Majors are available in biology, chemistry, communication arts, economics, English, government and politics, history, international studies, liberal studies, mathematics, philosophy, physics, psychology, social studies, and sociology. Students pursuing the childhood education program (grades 1-6) must also major in a liberal arts field.

The program in middle childhood education (grades 5-9) and adolescence education (grades 7-12) requires that students select a major in the subject area in which they plan to teach. All baccalaureate programs require the completion of a general education core, professional studies, content area, field experiences, and student teaching.

Graduate Programs: Four graduate programs are available for students interested in pursuing a master's degree in education. The Master of Science degree program in childhood education is designed for students who seek certification to teach children in grades 1-6. The Master of Science degree program in adolescence education is designed for candidates seeking certification to teach biology, chemistry, English, mathematics, physics, or social studies in grades 7-12. The adolescence education - apprenticeship teacher certification program is a specialized option for students in the high-need teaching areas of foreign language, mathematics, science, and technology education.

The Master of Science in Education degree program in leadership and instruction for inclusive classrooms provides certified teachers and related professionals the values, knowledge, and practices needed to work in inclusive elementary and secondary school classrooms. The Master of Science in Education degree program provides courses of study appropriate for students seeking permanent or professional teacher certification at any grade level.

Licensure/Reciprocity: New York. Students seeking teaching certification in a state other than New York should consult with that state's teacher certification office early in their program of study to insure compliance with requirements. Many state directors of teacher credentialing have signed Interstate Agreements through NASDTEC that expedite the certification process.

WAGNER COLLEGE

Education Department

One Campus Road
Staten Island, New York 10301-4495
Phone: (718) 390-3464
Fax: (718) 390-3456
E-mail: education@wagner.edu
Internet: http://www.wagner.edu

Institution Description: Wagner College is a private college supported by the Metropolitan and Upper New York Synods of the Lutheran Church in America. The college was established in 1833.

The Education Department offers undergraduate and graduate programs leading to teacher certification and professional career enhancement.

Institution Control: Private.

Calendar: Semester. Academic year August to May.

Official(s): Dr. Jeffrey Glanz, Chairman.

Faculty: Full-time 8; adjunct 14.

Degrees Awarded: 47 baccalaureate; 60 master's.

Admission Requirements: *Undergraduate:* Graduation from an approved secondary school with 16 academic units; College Board SAT or ACT composite. *Teacher education specific:* 2.75 GPA; students must complete education introductory courses; faculty interview; New York State Teacher Certification Examination; completion of state-approved programs in child abuse

WAGNER COLLEGE—cont'd

education and school violence also required. **Graduate:** Baccalaureate degree from a regionally accredited institution. *Teacher education specific:* Two letters of recommendation; minimum 2.75 GPA; interview with Department Chair; teaching credential when required by the program pursued.

Fees and Expenses: Undergraduate: $22,600 per academic year. Graduate: $780 per credit. On-campus room and board: $7,300. Books and supplies: $900.

Financial Aid: Resources specifically for eligible students enrolled in teacher education programs are awarded on the basis of financial need and academic merit. The institution has a Program Participation Agreement with the U.S. Department of Education for eligible students to receive Pell Grants and other federal aid. Teacher scholarships available to qualifying students. *Contact:* Theresa Weimer at: (718) 390-3183 or e-mail at finaid@wagner.edu.

Accreditation: *Regional:* MSA. *Member of:* AACTE. *Approved by:* New York State Department of Education.

Undergraduate Programs: Childhood education (grades 1-6) certification is valid for teaching common branch subjects to regular students and to students of special abilities in lower (1-3) and upper (4-6) elementary grades. The college also offers a registered program in K-12 theater arts education. In addition, the Education Department offers an education minor for students who wish to teach at the high school level. This could lead to either 7-12 certification sin biology, chemistry, English, mathematics, physics, social studies, or Spanish.

Students wishing to pursue certification in childhood education must complete a dual major in childhood education with a specified liberal arts discipline. The baccalaureate programs also require the completion of the general education core, professional studies, field experiences, and student teaching.

Graduate Programs: Wagner College offers five graduate programs leading to initial certification. Students without an undergraduate major in education are eligible for either childhood education (grades 1-6) or adolescent education (grades 7-12). Students with initial certification at the childhood level are eligible for early childhood education (birth-grade 2), middle level education (grades 5-9), or literacy (birth-grade 6). The early childhood and middle level programs lead to dual state certification in regular education and for students with disabilities (special education).

Licensure/Reciprocity: New York. Students seeking teaching certification in a state other than New York should consult with that state's teacher certification office early in their program of study to insure compliance with requirements. Many state directors of teacher credentialing have signed Interstate Agreements through NASDTEC that expedite the certification process.

NORTH CAROLINA

APPALACHIAN STATE UNIVERSITY

Reich College of Education
Department of Curriculum and Instruction
108 Edward Duncan Hall
730 Rivers Street
Boone, North Carolina 28608
Phone: (828) 262-2234
Fax: (828) 262-2128
E-mail: dukecr@appstate.edu
Internet: http://www.appstate.edu

Institution Description: Established as Watauga Academy in 1899, the institution offered first instruction at the postsecondary level in 1903. The name was changed Appalachian State Normal School in 1925 and to Appalachian State Teachers' College in 1929. The present name was adopted in 1967.

The Reich College of Education offers programs leading to the bachelor, master, education specialist, and doctoral degrees.

Institution Control: Public.

Calendar: Semester. Academic year August to May.

Official(s): Dr. Charles R. Duke, Dean; Dr. Doris M. Jenkins, Associate Dean; Dr. Michael G. Jacobson, Chair, Curriculum and Instruction.

Faculty: Full-time 105; adjunct 15.

Degrees Awarded: 372 baccalaureate; 207 master's; 4 doctorate.

Admission Requirements: *Undergraduate:* Graduation from an accredited secondary school or GED; College Board SAT or ACT composite. *Teacher education specific:* 2.5 GPA; letters of recommendation; PRAXIS I exams; faculty interview. *Graduate:* Baccalaureate degree from a regionally accredited institution. *Teacher education specific:* Teaching licensure when required by the program pursued; completion of all required departmental exams; letters of recommendation; faculty interview.

Fees and Expenses: Undergraduate: in-state $2,979 per academic year; out-of-state $11,900. Graduate: in-state $4,036; out-of-state $15,685. On-campus room and board: $4,435. Books and supplies: $750.

Financial Aid: Resources specifically for eligible students enrolled in teacher education programs are awarded on the basis of financial need and academic merit. The institution has a Program Participation Agreement with the U.S. Department of Education for eligible students to receive Pell Grants and other federal aid. Teacher scholarships available to qualifying students. *Contact:* Dr. Doris Jenkins at: (828) 262-6107 or e-mail at jenkinsdm@appstate.edu.

Accreditation: *Regional:* SACS. *Professional:* NCATE. *Member of:* AACTE. *Approved by:* North Carolina Department of Public Instruction.

Undergraduate Programs: The Department of Curriculum and Instruction offers undergraduate degrees in business education, early childhood: birth through kindergarten, elementary education (K-6), health education, marketing education, and middle grades education (6-9). The department also works with other departments across campus that offer teaching majors that lead to undergraduate certification at the K-12 and secondary school levels (grades 9-12). Undergraduate teaching majors must meet all the requirements for admission to the Reich College of Education. All baccalaureate programs require the completion of the general education core, professional studies, content area, field experiences, and student teaching. A minimum of 122 credit hours must be completed for the degree award.

Graduate Programs: Master of Arts degrees are available in the areas of elementary education (K-6), educational media, curriculum specialist, and middle grades education (6-9). The department also offers courses that are taken by candidates in other graduate programs (secondary and K-12) across campus who are seeking advanced licensure.

Licensure/Reciprocity: North Carolina. Students seeking teaching certification in a state other than North Carolina should consult with that state's teacher certification office early in their program of study to insure compliance with requirements. Many state directors of teacher credentialing have signed Interstate Agreements through NASDTEC that expedite the certification process.

BARTON COLLEGE

School of Education
Teacher Education Program
College Station
P.O. Box 5000
Wilson, North Carolina 27893
Phone: (252) 399-6300
Fax: (252) 399-6572
E-mail: admissns@barton.edu
Internet: http://www.barton.edu

Institution Description: Barton College is a private, four-year, coeducational institution affiliated with the Christian Church (Disciples of Christ). It was founded in 1902.

The School of Education offers baccalaureate programs leading to North Carolina teaching licensure.

Institution Control: Private.

Calendar: Semester. Academic year August to May.

Official(s): Dr. Deborah H. King, Dean.

Faculty: Full-time 7.

Degrees Awarded: 38 baccalaureate.

Admission Requirements: *Undergraduate:* Graduation from an accredited secondary school or GED; College Board SAT or ACT composite. *Teacher education specific:* 2.5 GPA; letters of recommendation; PRAXIS I exams; PRAXIS II prior to graduation; faculty interview.

Fees and Expenses: $14,278 per academic year. On-campus room and board: $5,036. Other expenses: $2,640. Books and supplies: $900.

Financial Aid: Resources specifically for eligible students enrolled in teacher education programs are awarded on the basis of financial need and academic merit. The institution has a Program Participation Agreement with the U.S. Department of Education for eligible students to receive Pell Grants and other federal aid. Teacher scholarships available to qualifying students. *Contact:* Financial Aid Office at: (252) 399-6316.

Accreditation: *Regional:* SACS. *Professional:* NCATE. *Member of:* AACTE. *Approved by:* North Carolina Department of Public Instruction.

Undergraduate Programs: Licensure areas offered by the Teacher Education Program include: elementary education (kindergarten-grade 6), B.S. degree; middle school education

BARTON COLLEGE—*cont'd*

(grades 6-9), B.S. degree; education of the deaf and hard of hearing (grades K-12), B.S. degree; secondary subjects education (grades K-12), B.S. degree; special subjects education (grades K-12), B.S. degree in art, physical education, Spanish, or English as a second language. All programs require the completion of a general education core, professional studies, content area, field experiences, and student teaching. A minimum of 126 semester hours is required for the degree award.

Licensure/Reciprocity: North Carolina. Students seeking teaching certification in a state other than North Carolina should consult with that state's teacher certification office early in their program of study to insure compliance with requirements. Many state directors of teacher credentialing have signed Interstate Agreements through NASDTEC that expedite the certification process.

BENNETT COLLEGE
Department of Professional Studies
Curriculum and Instruction Program
900 East Washington Street
Greensboro, North Carolina 27401-3239
Phone: (336) 512-2183
Fax: (336) 512-2184
E-mail: mrainey@bennett.edu
Internet: http://www.bennett.edu

Institution Description: Bennett College is a private liberal arts college for women that is affiliated with the United Methodist Church.

The Curriculum and Instruction Program is committed to the preparation of teachers as facilitators of learning through the development and understanding of learning theory and teaching practices.

Institution Control: Private.

Calendar: Semester. Academic year August to May.

Official(s): Dr. Gloria Randall Scott, President.

Faculty: Full-time 10; part-time 3; adjunct 7.

Degrees Awarded: 5 baccalaureate.

Admission Requirements: *Undergraduate:* Graduation from an accredited secondary school or GED; College Board SAT or ACT composite. *Teacher education specific:* 2.5 GPA; letters of recommendation; PRAXIS I exams; PRAXIS II prior to graduation; membership in SNCAE; personal statement; faculty interview and recommendation.

Fees and Expenses: $10,605 per academic year. On-campus room and board: $5,072. Other expenses: $1,855. Books and supplies: $765.

Financial Aid: Resources specifically for eligible students enrolled in teacher education programs are awarded on the basis of financial need and academic merit. The institution has a Program Participation Agreement with the U.S. Department of Education for eligible students to receive Pell Grants and other federal aid. Teacher scholarships available to qualifying students. *Contact:* Financial Aid Office at: (336) 517-2205.

Accreditation: *Regional:* SACS. *Professional:* NCATE. *Member of:* AACTE. *Approved by:* North Carolina Department of Public Instruction.

Undergraduate Programs: In the teacher education program, experiences are designed and implemented to prepare teachers who will be successful in areas of specialization by giving students the opportunity to develop specialized knowledge and skills. Through field experiences in public and private schools, as well as in agency settings, prospective teachers are guided in using problem solving and reflective processes to facilitate student learning.

Programs leading to the baccalaureate degree and licensure are offered in the following areas: elementary education (K-5); middle grades (6-8) language arts/mathematics; English, biology, mathematics (9-12); music (k-12); special education (K-12); mentally handicapped; learning disabled. All programs require the completion of a minimum of 124 credit hours.

Licensure/Reciprocity: North Carolina. Students seeking teaching certification in a state other than North Carolina should consult with that state's teacher certification office early in their program of study to insure compliance with requirements. Many state directors of teacher credentialing have signed Interstate Agreements through NASDTEC that expedite the certification process.

CAMPBELL UNIVERSITY
School of Education
Teacher Education
Taylor Hall, Box 369
Buie's Creek, North Carolina 27506
Phone: (910) 893-1658
Fax: (910) 893-1999
E-mail: nery@mailcenter.campbell
Internet: http://www.campbell.edu

Institution Description: Campbell University (Campbell College until 1979) is a private institution affiliated with the Baptist State Convention of North Carolina. It was founded in 1887.

The School of Education offers a variety of programs leading to a North Carolina teaching license.

Institution Control: Private.

Calendar: Semester. Academic year August to May.

Official(s): Dr. Karen Nery, Dean.

Faculty: Full-time 14; adjunct 3.

Degrees Awarded: 25 baccalaureate; 46 master's.

Admission Requirements: *Undergraduate:* Graduation from an accredited secondary school with 13 academic units or GED; College Board SAT or ACT composite. *Teacher education specific:* 2.5 GPA; PRAXIS I; PRAXIS II before student teaching; faculty interview. *Graduate:* Baccalaureate degree from a regionally accredited institution. *Teacher education specific:* Teaching licensure when required by the program; 2.7 GPA; letters of recommendation; faculty interview.

Fees and Expenses: $13,000 per academic year. Required fees: $230. On-campus room and board: $4,700. Books and supplies: $600.

Financial Aid: Resources specifically for eligible students enrolled in teacher education programs are awarded on the basis of financial need and academic merit. The institution has a Program Participation Agreement with the U.S. Department of Education for eligible students to receive Pell Grants and other federal aid. Teacher scholarships available to qualifying students. *Contact:* Financial Aid Office at: (910) 893-1658.

Accreditation: *Regional:* SACS. *Professional:* NCATE. *Member of:* AACTE. *Approved by:* North Carolina Department of Public Instruction.

Undergraduate Programs: The School of Education offers licensure programs in the following areas: elementary education, K-6; middle grades education, 6-9; secondary education, 9-12 (English, social science, mathematics, science); physical education, K-12; second languages, K-12 (French, Spanish); music, K-12; family and consumer sciences, 7-12.

All baccalaureate programs require the completion of the general education core, professional studies, content area, field experiences, and student teaching. A minimum of 120 credit hours is required for the degree award.

Graduate Programs: Advanced education degree programs are offered through the Graduate School and require admission by that body. Programs are designed for experienced practicing teachers aspiring to become master teachers and programs for those students holding a bachelor's degree but wish to obtain a license to teach. Programs are offered in elementary education, middle grades education, secondary education, and physical education.

Licensure/Reciprocity: North Carolina. Students seeking teaching certification in a state other than North Carolina should consult with that state's teacher certification office early in their program of study to insure compliance with requirements.

Many state directors of teacher credentialing have signed Interstate Agreements through NASDTEC that expedite the certification process.

CATAWBA COLLEGE
Department of Teacher Education
2300 West Innes Street
Salisbury, North Carolina 28144
Phone: (704) 637-4111
Fax: (704) 637-4444
E-mail: admission@catawba.edu
Internet: http://www.catawba.edu

Institution Description: Catawba College is a private college affiliated with the United Church of Christ. The college was established and chartered as a men's institution in 1851. It became coeducational in 1890.

The teacher education program at Catawba College is field based and has entered into a partnership with a local school to enhance the students' teacher preparation.

Institution Control: Private.

Calendar: Semester. Academic year August to May.

Official(s): Dr. James K. Stringfield, Jr., Department Chair.

Faculty: Full-time 5.

Degrees Awarded: 29 baccalaureate.

Admission Requirements: *Undergraduate:* Graduation from an accredited secondary school with 16 academic units or GED; College Board SAT preferred; ACT composite accepted. *Teacher education specific:* Application after 60 semester hours; maintain 2.5 GPA; professional portfolio; recommendation by student's major department; PRAXIS I tests; PRAXIS II before student teaching; faculty interview. *Graduate:* Baccalaureate degree from a regionally accredited institution. *Teacher education specific:* Teaching licensure when required by the program pursued; completion of all required departmental exams; letters of recommendation; faculty interview.

Fees and Expenses: Undergraduate: $16,400 per academic year. Graduate: Tuition charged per credit hour. On-campus room and board: $2,700. Other expenses: $3,445. Books and supplies: $750.

Financial Aid: Resources specifically for eligible students enrolled in teacher education programs are awarded on the basis of financial need and academic merit. The institution has a Program Participation Agreement with the U.S. Department of Education for eligible students to receive Pell Grants and other federal aid. Teacher scholarships available to qualifying students. *Contact:* Financial Aid Office at: (704) 637-4416.

Accreditation: *Regional:* SACS. *Professional:* NCATE. *Member of:* AACTE. *Approved by:* North Carolina Department of Public Instruction.

Undergraduate Programs: The Department of Teacher Education offers a major in elementary education (K-6) or middle school (6-9). The department offers a minor in secondary education (9-12) with licensure in English, mathematics, science (biology, chemistry, comprehensive science, comprehensive social studies, and a minor in special subject areas (k-12) with licensure in music and physical education. A program leading to licensure in the special field of reading (K-12) is available. All baccalaureate programs require the completion of the general education core, professional studies, content area, field experiences, and student teaching.

A person holding a baccalaureate degree from an accredited institution who wishes to prepare for a teaching license must apply through undergraduate admissions. A licensure program will be developed following evaluation of the individual's transcript.

Graduate Programs: The graduate program offers a master's program with concentration in elementary education that builds upon the strengths of the student's undergraduate major. The program requires the completion of 36 semester hours in specified courses.

Licensure/Reciprocity: North Carolina. Students seeking teaching certification in a state other than North Carolina should consult with that state's teacher certification office early in their program of study to insure compliance with requirements. Many state directors of teacher credentialing have signed Interstate Agreements through NASDTEC that expedite the certification process.

CHOWAN COLLEGE
Department of Teacher Education
200 Jones Drive
Murfreesboro, North Carolina 27855-1850
Phone: (252) 398-6500
Fax: (252) 398-1190
E-mail: admissions@chowan.edu
Internet: http://www.chowan.edu

Institution Description: Chowan College is an independent Baptist four-year college that was founded in 1848.

The mission of the teacher education program is to produce teachers who have the knowledge, skills, and attitudes to facilitate learning for all students.

Institution Control: Private.

Calendar: Semester. Academic year August to May.

Official(s): Dr. Carollyn Modlin, Chairperson.

Faculty: Full-time 6.

Degrees Awarded: 12 baccalaureate.

Admission Requirements: *Undergraduate:* Graduation from an accredited secondary school or GED; ACT composite. *Teacher education specific:* Passing scores on the PRAXIS I exams; maintain a 2.5 GPA; apply in sophomore year; faculty interview; PRAXIS II before graduation.

Fees and Expenses: $13,400 per academic year. On-campus room and board: $5,700. Other expenses: $100. Books and supplies: $750.

Financial Aid: Resources specifically for eligible students enrolled in teacher education programs are awarded on the basis of financial need and academic merit. The institution has a Program Participation Agreement with the U.S. Department of Education for eligible students to receive Pell Grants and other federal aid. Teacher scholarships available to qualifying students. *Contact:* Financial Aid Office at: (252) 398-1229.

Accreditation: *Regional:* SACS. *Professional:* NCATE. *Approved by:* North Carolina Department of Public Instruction.

Undergraduate Programs: Chowan College offers undergraduate programs leading to licensure in elementary education (K-6), mathematics, history/social studies and English education (9-12), physical education and music education (K-12). All programs lead to the Bachelor of Science degree and recommendation for teacher licensure in North Carolina. The programs require completion of the general education core, professional studies, area of specialty, field experiences, and student teaching.

Licensure/Reciprocity: North Carolina. Students seeking teaching certification in a state other than North Carolina should consult with that state's teacher certification office early in their program of study to insure compliance with requirements. Many state directors of teacher credentialing have signed Interstate Agreements through NASDTEC that expedite the certification process.

DAVIDSON COLLEGE
Department of Education
Jackson Court
102 North Main Street
Davidson, North Carolina 28036-1719
Phone: (704) 894-2130
Fax: (704) 892-2920
E-mail: admissions@.edu
Internet: http://www.davidson.edu

DAVIDSON COLLEGE—*cont'd*

Institution Description: Davidson College is a private college affiliated with The Presbyterian Church (U.S.A.). It was established as Davidson College for Men, chartered and offered first instruction at postsecondary level 1837. Women were admitted in 1972.

Institution Control: Private.

Calendar: Semester. Academic year: August to May.

Official(s): Dr. Richard Gay, Chair.

Faculty: Full-time 4.

Degrees Awarded: 11 baccalaureate.

Admission Requirements: *Undergraduate:* Graduation from an accredited secondary school with 16 academic college preparatory units or GED; College Board SAT or ACT composite. *Teacher education specific:* Proficiency in oral and written communications; PRAXIS I minimum test scores; overall 2.5 GPA; faculty recommendation; interview. PRAXIS II required prior to student teaching and graduation.

Fees and Expenses: $25,900 per academic year. On-campus room and board: $7,375. Other expenses: $1,525. Books and supplies: $1,000.

Financial Aid: Resources specifically for eligible students enrolled in teacher education programs are awarded on the basis of financial need and academic merit. The institution has a Program Participation Agreement with the U.S. Department of Education for eligible students to receive Pell Grants and other federal aid. Teacher scholarships available to qualifying students. *Contact:* Financial Aid Office at: (704) 894-2232.

Accreditation: *Regional:* SACS. *Professional:* NCATE. *Member of:* AACTE. *Approved by:* North Carolina Department of Public Instruction.

Undergraduate Programs: Through a series of articulation agreements with Duke University, Queens University of Charlotte, and the North Carolina Department of Public Instruction, Davidson College provides a course of study leading to North Carolina initial licensure/certification at the secondary level in the field of English; French (K-12); Latin (9-12); mathematics (9-12); science (9-12) with majors in biology, chemistry, physics); social studies with majors in anthropology, economics, history, political science, psychology, sociology, religion. All coursework is completed at Davidson. These baccalaureate programs require the completion of the general education core, professional studies, content area, field experiences, and student teaching.

Licensure/Reciprocity: North Carolina. Students seeking teaching certification in a state other than North Carolina should consult with that state's teacher certification office early in their program of study to insure compliance with requirements. Many state directors of teacher credentialing have signed Interstate Agreements through NASDTEC that expedite the certification process.

DUKE UNIVERSITY

Trinity College of Arts and sciences
Program in Education
Durham, North Carolina 27708
Phone: (919) 684-3914
Fax: (919) 684-9941
E-mail: askduke@admiss.duke.edu
Internet: http://www.duke.edu

Institution Description: Duke University is a private, independent, nonsectarian institution associated with the United Methodist Church. It was established in 1838.

The teacher preparation program is committed to producing liberally educated, reflective professionals who possess the intellectual background and ethical motivation to become leaders in their professions.

Institution Control: Private.

Calendar: Semester. Academic year September to May.

Official(s): Dr. Harris Cooper, Director, Program in Education.

Faculty: Full-time 8; associated faculty 17.

Degrees Awarded: 28 baccalaureate; 11 master's.

Admission Requirements: *Undergraduate:* Graduation from an accredited secondary school with 16 college preparatory units or GED; College Board SAT with 3 Achievement tests. *Teacher education specific:* Passing scores on the PRAXIS I exams; maintain a 2.5 GPA; apply in sophomore year; faculty interview; PRAXIS II before graduation. *Graduate:* Baccalaureate degree from a regionally accredited institution. *Teacher education specific:* Liberal arts and sciences subject major; recommendations; faculty interview; completion of all specific departmental requirements.

Fees and Expenses: Undergraduate: $29,345 per academic year. Graduate: Tuition charged per credit hour. On-campus room and board: $8,210. Other expenses: $3,200. Books and supplies: $900.

Financial Aid: Resources specifically for eligible students enrolled in teacher education programs are awarded on the basis of financial need and academic merit. The institution has a Program Participation Agreement with the U.S. Department of Education for eligible students to receive Pell Grants and other federal aid. Teacher scholarships available to qualifying students. *Contact:* Financial Aid Office at: (919) 684-6225.

Accreditation: *Regional:* SACS. *Professional:* NCATE. *Approved by:* North Carolina Department of Public Instruction.

Undergraduate Programs: Candidates in the elementary teacher preparation program acquire knowledge and skills that enable them to meet the changing needs of elementary children and their families. Candidates work in technology-rich environments with diverse student populations. The program leads to the baccalaureate degree and eligibility for licensure to teach at either the elementary (K-6) or secondary (9-12) level.

The early childhood certificate program is an interdisciplinary certificate designed to serve students who, in addition to their majors, may develop a concentration in childhood development by selected studies in psychology, sociology, cultural anthropology.

The secondary teacher preparation program prepares candidates to seek teacher licensure in one four areas: English, mathematics, social studies, or science.

All baccalaureate programs require the general education core, professional studies, field experiences, and student teaching.

Graduate Programs: The Master of Arts in Teaching Program provides liberal arts graduates with a program of study within their academic discipline while preparing for careers as high school teachers. The program combines graduate-level work in the teaching field with education courses and a full-year internship. Programs are offered that lead to certification in the areas of English, biology, general science (including biological anthropology and anatomy), biology, chemistry, physics mathematics, physics, social studies (history, political science, cultural anthropology).

Licensure/Reciprocity: North Carolina. Students seeking teaching certification in a state other than North Carolina should consult with that state's teacher certification office early in their program of study to insure compliance with requirements. Many state directors of teacher credentialing have signed Interstate Agreements through NASDTEC that expedite the certification process.

EAST CAROLINA UNIVERSITY

College of Education
134 Speight Building
East Fifth Street
Greenville, North Carolina 27858-4353
Phone: (252) 328-1000
Fax: (252) 328-4219
E-mail: coe@ecu.edu
Internet: http://www.ecu.edu

Institution Description: The university was established and chartered as East Carolina Teacher Training School in 1907. It became East Carolina Teachers College in 1921 and East Carolina College in 1951. University status was achieved in 1967.

The mission of the College of Education is the preparation of professional educators and allied practitioners at all levels and in all areas of the educational endeavor.

Institution Control: Public.

Calendar: Semester. Academic year August to May.

Official(s): Dr. Marilyn Sherer, Dean.

Faculty: Full-time 96; part-time 9; adjunct 31.

Degrees Awarded: 330 baccalaureate; 290 master's.

Admission Requirements: *Undergraduate:* Graduation from an accredited secondary school with 20 secondary school credits; College Board SAT or ACT composite. *Teacher education specific:* Passing scores on PRAXIS I tests in reading, writing, mathematics; minimum 2.5 GPA; personal essay; application during second semester of sophomore year of first semester of junior year; completion of 16-hour field experience; computer competencies; departmental interview. *Graduate:* Baccalaureate degree from a regionally accredited institution. *Teacher education specific:* 3.0 GPA; three letters of recommendation; GRE subject test; faculty interview.

Fees and Expenses: Undergraduate: in-state $2,814 per academic year; out-of-state $11,980. Graduate: in-state $4,036 per academic year; out-of-state $15,685. Other fees may apply. On-campus room and board: residence halls fees $2,640 to $3,540; meal plans $2,000 to $2,800. Other expenses: $2,400. Books and supplies: $800.

Financial Aid: Resources specifically for eligible students enrolled in teacher education programs are awarded on the basis of financial need and academic merit. The institution has a Program Participation Agreement with the U.S. Department of Education for eligible students to receive Pell Grants and other federal aid. Teacher scholarships available to qualifying students. *Contact:* Rose Mary Stelma, Director of Financial Aid at: (252) 328-6610 or e-mail at: stelmar@mail.ecu.edu.

Accreditation: *Regional:* SACS. *Professional:* NCATE. *Member of:* AACTE. *Approved by:* North Carolina Department of Public Instruction.

Undergraduate Programs: The College of Education offers baccalaureate degree programs through the Department of Business, Career and Technical Education (business education, marketing education, information technologies), Department of Curriculum and Instruction (elementary education, English education, history education, middle grades education, special education), and the Department of Mathematics and Science Education (mathematics education, science education). Teacher education majors may be required to complete an approved academic concentration as part of their programs of study.

The baccalaureate degree programs require the departmental general core, professional studies, content area, field experiences, and student teaching.

Graduate Programs: The Master of Arts in Education degree programs offer the education professional advanced competency coursework in professional education and the program area. The programs accepts educators who hold a baccalaureate degree and an initial teaching license. Programs are available in business education, elementary education, English, health, history, instructional technology, mathematics, marketing, middle grades, physical education pedagogy, reading, science, and special education.

The Master of Arts in Teaching degree program is designed for the individual with a non-teaching baccalaureate and leads to teaching licensure. The Master of Science Degree is offered in counselor education and vocational education. The Master of Library science degree program is also offered.

Doctoral programs in educational leadership are offered with concentrations in public school administration, higher education administration, instructional development, and library science.

Licensure/Reciprocity: North Carolina. Students seeking teaching certification in a state other than North Carolina should consult with that state's teacher certification office early in their program of study to insure compliance with requirements.

Many state directors of teacher credentialing have signed Interstate Agreements through NASDTEC that expedite the certification process.

ELIZABETH CITY STATE UNIVERSITY
School of Education and Psychology
Teacher Education Program
1704 Weeksville Road
Elizabeth City, North Carolina 27909
Phone: (252) 335-3296
Fax: (252) 335-3554
E-mail: paviltz@mail.ecsu.edu
Internet: http://www.ecsu.edu

Institution Description: The university was founded in 1891. It became Elizabeth City State Teachers College in 1939, Elizabeth City State College in 1963, and achieved university status in 1969.

The School of Education and Psychology offers undergraduate and graduate teacher education programs leading to teacher licensure.

Institution Control: Public.

Calendar: Semester. Academic year August to May.

Official(s): Dr. Paula S. Viltz, Director.

Faculty: Full-time 24; adjunct 7.

Degrees Awarded: 26 baccalaureate; 5 master's.

Admission Requirements: *Undergraduate:* Graduation from an accredited secondary school or GED; College Board SAT or ACT composite. *Teacher education specific:* 2.5 GPA; 25 hours of early field experience in an approved public school; PRAXIS I; faculty interview. *Graduate:* Baccalaureate degree from a regionally accredited institution. *Teacher education specific:* 3.0 GPA; three professional recommendations; GRE or Miller Analogies Test; personal essay; faculty interview.

Fees and Expenses: Undergraduate: in-state $2,814; out-of-state $11,980. Graduate: in-state $4,036; out-of-state $15,685. Required fees: $1,378 undergraduate, $1,202 graduate. On-campus room and board: $4,608. Books and supplies; $430.

Financial Aid: Resources specifically for eligible students enrolled in teacher education programs are awarded on the basis of financial need and academic merit. The institution has a Program Participation Agreement with the U.S. Department of Education for eligible students to receive Pell Grants and other federal aid. Teacher scholarships available to qualifying students. *Contact:* Daun Brumsey at: (252) 335-3284 or e-mail at: dlbrumsey@mail.ecsu.edu.

Accreditation: *Regional:* SACS. *Professional:* NCATE. *Member of:* AACTE. *Approved by:* North Carolina Department of Public Instruction.

Undergraduate Programs: The Teacher Education Program offers three Bachelor of Science in Education degree programs and one licensure program: elementary education (K-6), middle grades (6-9), special education (K-12) with concentrations in mental retardation and learning disabilities, secondary education licensure (9-12). A student majoring in elementary education, special education, physical education, and technology education is required to select an academic concentration in one of the following options: art, biology, English, general science, mathematics, music, psychology, social sciences. All programs require the completion of the general education core, professional studies, field experiences, and student teaching.

Graduate Programs: The Advanced Master's Degree Program in elementary education requires completion of 36 semester hours (12 semester hours of core courses, 12 semester hours in specialization courses, 9 semester hours in support courses, and 3 semester hours in elective courses. The courses require classroom, school, and community investigation geared toward improving K-12 student performance.

Licensure/Reciprocity: North Carolina. Students seeking teaching certification in a state other than North Carolina should consult with that state's teacher certification office early in their program of study to insure compliance with requirements.

ELIZABETH CITY STATE UNIVERSITY—*cont'd*

Many state directors of teacher credentialing have signed Interstate Agreements through NASDTEC that expedite the certification process.

ELON UNIVERSITY

Department of Education
Teacher Education Program

101 Haggard Avenue
Elon, North Carolina 27244-2010
Phone: (336) 278-5836
Fax: (336) 278-3986
E-mail: admissions@elon.edu
Internet: http://www.elon.edu

Institution Description: Elon University is a private institution affiliated with the Southern Conference of the United Church of Christ. It was established in 1889.

Elon's education program prepares teachers for careers in the elementary, middle, and high school grades. The program emphasizes practical hands-on experience in classrooms as well as educational theory and methods classes on campus.

Institution Control: Private.

Calendar: Semester (4-1-4 plan). Academic year August to May.

Official(s): Dr. Gerald Dillashaw, Dean.

Faculty: Full-time 11; adjunct 11.

Degrees Awarded: 77 baccalaureate.

Admission Requirements: *Undergraduate:* Graduation from an accredited secondary school or GED; College Board SAT or ACT composite. *Teacher education specific:* Passing scores on the PRAXIS I exams; maintain a 2.5 GPA; apply in sophomore year; faculty interview; PRAXIS II before graduation. *Graduate:* Baccalaureate degree from a regionally accredited institution. *Teacher education specific:* Liberal arts and sciences subject major; GRE or Miller Analogies Test; official transcripts of all coursework taken; recommendations; faculty interview; 3.0 GPA for the last 60 hours or for all major courses; completion of all specific departmental requirements.

Fees and Expenses: Undergraduate: $16,325 per academic year. Graduate: Tuition charged per credit hour. On-campus room and board: $8,670. Other expenses: $,400. Books and supplies: $800.

Financial Aid: Resources specifically for eligible students enrolled in teacher education programs are awarded on the basis of financial need and academic merit. The institution has a Program Participation Agreement with the U.S. Department of Education for eligible students to receive Pell Grants and other federal aid. Teacher scholarships available to qualifying students. *Contact:* Financial Aid Office at: (336 278-7640.

Accreditation: *Regional:* SACS. *Professional:* NCATE. *Member of:* AACTE. *Approved by:* North Carolina Department of Public Instruction.

Undergraduate Programs: Undergraduate programs offered include elementary education, middle grades education, special education, and secondary education with special subject areas in biology, chemistry, English, French, health, music, physical education, and Spanish. Programs require the completion of the general education core, professional studies, content area, field experiences, and student teaching. Baccalaureate degrees and recommendation for licensure are offered to successful candidates.

Graduate Programs: The Master of Education program is designed to enhance the professional competence of experienced classroom teachers. Candidates may select a program of study in elementary education or special education. Courses are designed to enable teachers to make immediate use of course concepts in their individual classrooms and in leadership roles.

Licensure/Reciprocity: North Carolina. Students seeking teaching certification in a state other than North Carolina should consult with that state's teacher certification office early in their program of study to insure compliance with requirements.

Many state directors of teacher credentialing have signed Interstate Agreements through NASDTEC that expedite the certification process.

FAYETTEVILLE STATE UNIVERSITY

Office of Teacher Education

G.L. Butler Building, 2nd Floor
1200 Murchinson Road
Fayetteville, North Carolina 28301-4732
Phone: (910) 672-1487
Fax: (910) 672-1941
E-mail: ote@uncfnu.edu
Internet: http://www.uncfnu.edu

Institution Description: The institution was founded in 1867. It became Fayetteville State Teachers College in 1939, Fayetteville State College in 1963, and achieved university status in 1969.

The Office of Teacher Education coordinates the teacher preparation programs that are available in the School of Education, School of business and Economics, and the College of Arts and sciences.

Institution Control: Public.

Calendar: Semester. Academic year August to May.

Official(s): Dr. Saundra N. Shorter, Chair.

Faculty: Full-time 19.

Degrees Awarded: 65 baccalaureate; 53 master's.

Admission Requirements: *Undergraduate:* Graduation from an accredited secondary school with 16 academic units or GED. *Teacher education specific:* 2.5 GPA; completion of education foundation course; PRAXIS I with minimum scores (reading, writing, math); verification of health status by the university physician; faculty interview; PRAXIS II before graduation. *Graduate:* Baccalaureate degree from a regionally accredited institution. *Teacher education specific:* 3.0 GPA; three professional recommendations; GRE or Miller Analogies Test; personal essay; faculty interview.

Fees and Expenses: Undergraduate: in-state $2,237; out-of-state $11,598. Graduate: in-state $4,036 per academic year; out-of-state $15,685. On-campus room and board: $3,820. Other expenses: $1,680. Books and supplies; $385.

Financial Aid: Resources specifically for eligible students enrolled in teacher education programs are awarded on the basis of financial need and academic merit. The institution has a Program Participation Agreement with the U.S. Department of Education for eligible students to receive Pell Grants and other federal aid. Teacher scholarships available to qualifying students. *Contact:* Financial Aid Office at: (910) 672-1325.

Accreditation: *Regional:* SACS. *Professional:* NCATE. *Member of:* AACTE. *Approved by:* North Carolina Department of Public Instruction.

Undergraduate Programs: Undergraduate programs are offered in elementary education (K-6), middle grades (6-9), secondary education (9-12), and Special Subjects (K-12). Secondary programs include English, mathematics, biology, social studies, business education, and marketing education. Special Subjects (K-12) are health, physical education, music, and Spanish. The middle grades program requires a concentration in two of four areas: language arts, social studies, science, and mathematics. In addition to the teacher education requirements of the School of Education, each subject has specialty program requirements in the School of Business and Economics and the College of Arts and sciences. The licensure levels for teachers are K-6, 6-9, 9-12, and K-12. The Office of Teacher Education coordinates the teacher preparation programs with respect to field experiences, admissions to teacher education, and student teaching assignments.

Graduate Programs: The School of Education offers a Masters Degree in Education that is designed for educators holding an initial-level license. The program consists of education courses with a concentration in areas of biology, elementary education, history, mathematics, middle grades language arts, mathematics, science, social studies, political science, reading, sociology, special education, behavioral emotionally disabled, learning disabilities, and mentally disturbed.

Licensure/Reciprocity: North Carolina. Students seeking teaching certification in a state other than North Carolina should consult with that state's teacher certification office early in their program of study to insure compliance with requirements. Many state directors of teacher credentialing have signed Interstate Agreements through NASDTEC that expedite the certification process.

GARDNER-WEBB UNIVERSITY

School of Education
Campus Box 7226
Main Street
Boiling Springs, North Carolina 28017
Phone: (704) 406-4406
Fax: (704) 406-3921
E-mail: dsimmons@gardner-webb.edu
Internet: http://www.gardner-webb.edu

Institution Description: Gardner-Webb University is a private coeducational residential university affiliated with the Baptist State Convention of North Carolina. It was founded in 1905.

The purpose of the professional education programs offered by the School of Education is to prepare educators to meet the changing needs of today's students and schools.

Institution Control: Private.

Calendar: Semester. Academic year August to May.

Official(s): Dr. Donna S. Simmons, Dean; Dr. Johnnie Hamrick, Director of Field Experiences and Student Teaching.

Faculty: Full-time 10; adjunct 8.

Degrees Awarded: 20 baccalaureate; 98 master's.

Admission Requirements: *Undergraduate:* Graduation from an accredited secondary school or GED; College Board SAT or ACT composite. *Teacher education specific:* Completion of a minimum of 30 semester hours; 2.5 GPA; declaration of intent to major in an area of licensure; passing scores on PRAXIS I examinations (reading, writing, mathematics); faculty interview. *Graduate:* Baccalaureate degree from a regionally accredited institution. *Teacher education specific:* Official transcripts of all previous academic work; scores on GRE, PRAXIS II, or Miller Analogies Test; three professional references; North Carolina teacher's license or equivalent.

Fees and Expenses: Undergraduate: $14,160 per academic year. Graduate: $230 per credit hour. Required fees apply. On-campus room: $1,310 to $2,140 per semester. On-campus meal plans: $1,085 to $1,260 per semester. Books and supplies: $1,000.

Financial Aid: Resources specifically for eligible students enrolled in teacher education programs are awarded on the basis of financial need and academic merit. The institution has a Program Participation Agreement with the U.S. Department of Education for eligible students to receive Pell Grants and other federal aid. Teacher scholarships available to qualifying students. *Contact:* Cindy Wallace at: (704) 406-4494 or e-mail at: cwallace@gardner-webb.edu.

Accreditation: *Regional:* SACS. *Professional:* NCATE. *Member of:* AACTE. *Approved by:* North Carolina Department of Public Instruction.

Undergraduate Programs: The School of Education, within the framework of the liberal arts and professional studies curriculum, offers majors in elementary education (K-6) and middle grades education (6-9). A professional education minor is available for candidates seeking 9-12 licensure in the areas of biology, chemistry, English, mathematics, and social studies, and in K-12 special subject areas in music, French and Spanish, and physical education. All bachelor degree programs require the completion of the general education core, professional studies, content area, field experiences, and student teaching.

Courses are also available for career teachers seeking teacher renewal and for persons holding a baccalaureate degree who wish to obtain teacher licensure.

Graduate Programs: Masters programs are available through the Graduate School in the areas of elementary education, middle grades education, English education, school administration, and school counseling. Successful completion of these programs fulfills the requirements for the North Carolina Teaching License.

A Doctor of Education in educational leadership is also available through the Graduate School. Successful completion of this program leads to advanced licensure in educational leadership.

Licensure/Reciprocity: North Carolina. Students seeking teaching certification in a state other than North Carolina should consult with that state's teacher certification office early in their program of study to insure compliance with requirements. Many state directors of teacher credentialing have signed Interstate Agreements through NASDTEC that expedite the certification process.

GREENSBORO COLLEGE

Department of Education
Teacher Education Program
815 West Market Street
Greensboro, North Carolina 27401-1875
Phone: (336) 271-7102
Fax: (336) 271-6634
E-mail: admissions@gborocollege.edu
Internet: http://www.gborocollege.edu

Institution Description: Greensboro College is a four-year coeducational liberal arts college affiliated with the United Methodist Church. It was founded in 1838.

Programs offered through the Teacher Education Program lead to initial licensure levels in elementary, middle grades, and secondary education.

Institution Control: Private.

Calendar: Semester. Academic year August to May.

Official(s): Dr. Rebecca Blomgren, Director, Teacher Education Program.

Faculty: Full-time 21.

Degrees Awarded: 19 baccalaureate.

Admission Requirements: *Undergraduate:* Graduation from an accredited secondary school or GED; College Board SAT or ACT composite. *Teacher education specific:* Apply before the end of the sophomore year; GPA 2.5; PRAXIS I exams (reading, writing, mathematics). faculty interview.

Fees and Expenses: $15,720 per academic year. On-campus room and board: $6,030. Other expenses: $1,300. Books and supplies; $800.

Financial Aid: Resources specifically for eligible students enrolled in teacher education programs are awarded on the basis of financial need and academic merit. The institution has a Program Participation Agreement with the U.S. Department of Education for eligible students to receive Pell Grants and other federal aid. Teacher scholarships available to qualifying students. *Contact:* Financial Aid Office at: (336) 272-7102, ext. 217.

Accreditation: *Regional:* SACS. *Professional:* NCATE. *Member of:* AACTE. *Approved by:* North Carolina Department of Public Instruction.

Undergraduate Programs: Greensboro College and the Teacher Education Program require a sequence of fieldwork hours for each licensure program. Students move from observation, to assistance, to participation in various school settings. Through the courtesy and cooperation of Guilford Public Schools and other systems in proximity to the college, observation, participation, and full student teaching privileges are available in elementary, middle, and secondary classrooms. This arrangement, coupled with successful completion of academic and professional coursework, enables graduates to meet the requirements for initial licensure in elementary education (K-6), middle grades (6-9), and secondary school (9-12) (biology, English, mathematics, and social studies) as well as in art education (K-12), music education (K-12), physical education (K-12), Spanish

GREENSBORO COLLEGE—*cont'd*

education (K-12), and special education (K-12 in specific learning disabled, mentally handicapped, behaviorally/emotionally disabled), and theatre education (K-12).

Licensure/Reciprocity: North Carolina. Students seeking teaching certification in a state other than North Carolina should consult with that state's teacher certification office early in their program of study to insure compliance with requirements. Many state directors of teacher credentialing have signed Interstate Agreements through NASDTEC that expedite the certification process.

GUILFORD COLLEGE

Education Studies

5800 West Friendly Avenue
Greensboro, North Carolina 27410
Phone: (336) 316-2420
Fax: (336) 316-2956
E-mail: mborrego@guilford.edu
Internet: http://www.guilford.edu

Institution Description: Guilford College is a private liberal arts college affiliated with the Religious Society of Friends. It was established in 1837.

The primary goal of the Education Studies Program is to develop educators who are grounded in the liberal arts. The program emphasizes understanding educational issues from a global perspective.

Institution Control: Private.

Calendar: Semester. Academic year August to May.

Official(s): Dr. Margaret Borrego, Chair, Education Studies.

Faculty: Full-time 4.

Degrees Awarded: 3 baccalaureate.

Admission Requirements: *Undergraduate:* Graduation from an accredited secondary school or GED; College Board SAT or ACT composite. *Teacher education specific:* Acceptance into the program during the sophomore year; 2.5 GPA; recommendations; PRAXIS I exams (reading, writing, mathematics); faculty interview.

Fees and Expenses: $18,700 per academic year. On-campus room and board: $5,940. Other expenses: $1,575. Books and supplies: $750.

Financial Aid: Resources specifically for eligible students enrolled in teacher education programs are awarded on the basis of financial need and academic merit. The institution has a Program Participation Agreement with the U.S. Department of Education for eligible students to receive Pell Grants and other federal aid. Teacher scholarships available to qualifying students. *Contact:* Financial Aid Office at: (336) 316-2354.

Accreditation: *Regional:* SACS. *Professional:* NCATE. *Approved by:* North Carolina Department of Public Instruction.

Undergraduate Programs: The Education Studies Program offers the Bachelor of Arts degree. The program requires a double or joint major (an education studies major and a major in another academic department), a strong interdisciplinary liberal arts core, and a cross-cultural education internship that usually includes a semester abroad. There are three licensure traces in the education studies major: elementary licensure, grades kindergarten through six; secondary licensure, grades nine through 12 (English and social studies), and K-12 licensure, grades kindergarten through 12 (French and Spanish). The degree requires the completion of 128 semester hours.

Licensure/Reciprocity: North Carolina. Students seeking teaching certification in a state other than North Carolina should consult with that state's teacher certification office early in their program of study to insure compliance with requirements. Many state directors of teacher credentialing have signed Interstate Agreements through NASDTEC that expedite the certification process.

HIGH POINT UNIVERSITY

School of Education
Teacher Education Department

833 Montlieu Avenue
High Point, North Carolina 27262-3598
Phone: (800) 345-6993
Fax: (910) 841-4599
E-mail: admiss@highpoint.edu
Internet: http://www.highpoint.edu

Institution Description: High Point University is a private institution affiliated with the United Methodist Church. It was established and offered first instruction at the postsecondary level in 1924.

The Teacher Education Program offers undergraduate and graduate programs leading to initial licensure.

Institution Control: Private.

Calendar: Semester. Academic year August to May.

Official(s): Dr. Dennis Gordon Carroll, Dean, School of Education.

Faculty: Full-time 8.

Degrees Awarded: 40 baccalaureate.

Admission Requirements: *Undergraduate:* Graduation from an accredited secondary school GED; College Board SAT or ACT composite. *Teacher education specific:* Passing scores on PRAXIS I exams (reading, writing, mathematics; 2.5 GPA; faculty recommendations; interview by Director of Teacher Education. *Graduate:* Baccalaureate from a regionally accredited institution. *Teacher education specific:* 3.0 GPA; three professional recommendations; GRE or Miller Analogies Test; personal essay; faculty interview; minimum of 3 years of K-12 teaching experience.

Fees and Expenses: Undergraduate: $14,710 per academic year. Graduate: Tuition charged per credit hour. On-campus room and board: $6,500. Other fees: $2,410. Books and supplies; $1,000.

Financial Aid: Resources specifically for eligible students enrolled in teacher education programs are awarded on the basis of financial need and academic merit. The institution has a Program Participation Agreement with the U.S. Department of Education for eligible students to receive Pell Grants and other federal aid. Teacher scholarships available to qualifying students. *Contact:* Financial Aid Office at: (336) 841-9128.

Accreditation: *Regional:* SACS. *Professional:* NCATE. *Member of:* AACTE. *Approved by:* North Carolina Department of Public Instruction.

Undergraduate Programs: Licensure programs are offered in elementary education (supporting disciplines in fine arts, language arts, mathematics, physical education, psychology, science, social studies, speech); middle grades education (discipline specializations in language arts, mathematics, science, social studies); special subjects (discipline majors in special subjects K-12 in art, physical education, French, Spanish); secondary education (biology, chemistry, English, history, mathematics); special education (fine arts, physical education, psychology/sociology, science, social studies); academically gifted. All programs lead to initial licensure and the baccalaureate degree. A minimum of 124 semester hours is required for the degree award.

Graduate Programs: The Master of Education in elementary education requires the completion of 36 hours of graduate credit, a thesis or graduate product, 3.0 GPA, and a comprehensive examination. The Master of Education in educational leadership requires the completion of 33 hours of graduate credit, internship, 3.0 GPA, and an comprehensive examination.

Licensure/Reciprocity: North Carolina. Students seeking teaching certification in a state other than North Carolina should consult with that state's teacher certification office early in their program of study to insure compliance with requirements. Many state directors of teacher credentialing have signed Interstate Agreements through NASDTEC that expedite the certification process.

JOHNSON C. SMITH UNIVERSITY

Department of Education

100 Beatties Ford Road

Charlotte, North Carolina 28216

Phone: (704) 378-1010

E-mail: admissions@jcsu.edu

Internet: http://www.jcsu.edu

Institution Description: Johnson C. Smith University is a private institution affiliated with the Presbyterian Church (U.S.A.). It was established as The Biddle Memorial Institute, a men's college, in 1867. The name was changed to Biddle University in 1876 and the present name was adopted in 1923. The university became coeducational in 1941.

While teacher education at Johnson C.Smith University is viewed as a university-wide function, the Department of Education assumes major responsibility for coordinating all programs.

Institution Control: Private.

Calendar: Semester. Academic year July to June.

Official(s): Dr. Bessie L. Gage, Department Head.

Faculty: Not reported.

Degrees Awarded: 10 baccalaureate.

Admission Requirements: *Undergraduate:* Graduation from an accredited secondary school with 16 academic units or GED; College Board SAT or ACT composite. *Teacher education specific:* Completion of 45 semester hours with a cumulative GPA of at least 2.5; passing scores on PRAXIS I exams (reading, writing, mathematics); declaration of major area; three recommendations from former professors; faculty approval.

Fees and Expenses: $13,062 per academic year. On-campus room and board: $5,046. Books and supplies: $1,250.

Financial Aid: Resources specifically for eligible students enrolled in teacher education programs are awarded on the basis of financial need and academic merit. The institution has a Program Participation Agreement with the U.S. Department of Education for eligible students to receive Pell Grants and other federal aid. Teacher scholarships available to qualifying students. *Contact:* Financial Aid Office at: (704) 378-1035.

Accreditation: *Regional:* SACS. *Professional:* NCATE. *Member of:* AACTE. *Approved by:* North Carolina Department of Public Instruction.

Undergraduate Programs: The Department of Education offers a major in elementary education leading to the Bachelor of Arts degree and teacher licensure. The degree at the secondary level may be earned in mathematics, social studies, and English. In special areas at the K-12 level, the degree may be earned in health and physical education.

Licensure only candidates who wish to pursue a teaching career may enroll and be admitted to the Teacher Education Program. Practicing teachers may also be admitted.

The department offers the professional education component that is required of all prospective teachers. The courses are offered by the Department of Education and Department of Psychology. All baccalaureate programs require the completion of field experiences and student teaching.

Licensure/Reciprocity: North Carolina. Students seeking teaching certification in a state other than North Carolina should consult with that state's teacher certification office early in their program of study to insure compliance with requirements. Many state directors of teacher credentialing have signed Interstate Agreements through NASDTEC that expedite the certification process.

LEES-MCRAE COLLEGE

Teacher Education Program

P.O. Box 128

Banner Elk, North Carolina 28604-0128

Phone: (828) 898-5241

Fax: (828) 898-8814

E-mail: admissions@bobcat.lmc.edu

Internet: http://www.lmc.edu

Institution Description: Lees-McRae College is a private, coeducational, independent college affiliated with the Presbyterian Church (U.S.A.). It was established in 1900.

The goal of the Teacher Education Program is to provide strong courses of study that promote positive and holistic development of teachers with in a reflective mentoring framework.

Institution Control: Private.

Calendar: Semester. Academic year August to May.

Official(s): Dr. Earl J. Robinson, President.

Faculty: Not reported.

Degrees Awarded: 50 baccalaureate.

Admission Requirements: Graduation from an accredited secondary school; GED considered. College Board SAT or ACT composite. *Teacher education specific:* Application during second semester of sophomore year; 2.5 GPA; passing scores on PRAXIS I exams (reading, writing, mathematics); faculty recommendation; PRAXIS II exam before graduation.

Fees and Expenses: $14,500 per academic year. On-campus room and board: $5,440. Other expenses: $2,600. Books and supplies: $760.

Financial Aid: Resources specifically for eligible students enrolled in teacher education programs are awarded on the basis of financial need and academic merit. The institution has a Program Participation Agreement with the U.S. Department of Education for eligible students to receive Pell Grants and other federal aid. Teacher scholarships available to qualifying students. *Contact:* Financial Aid Office at: (828) 898-5241.

Accreditation: *Regional:* SACS. *Professional:* NCATE. *Member of:* AACTE. *Approved by:* North Carolina Department of Public Instruction.

Undergraduate Programs: Lees-McRae offers licensure in elementary education (K 6), theatre arts (K-12), and physical education (K-12). Elementary education majors must complete an integrated concentration of studies. The program with licensure (K-6) prepares students to become teachers with distinct knowledge about the practice and theory of teaching a balanced sense of personal values and moral worth. It is also expected that students who complete the program will become teachers who reflect on all aspects of the teaching/learning process.

The baccalaureate programs require the completion of a general education core, professional studies, content area, field experiences, and student teaching. A minimum of 124 semester hours is required for the degree award.

Licensure/Reciprocity: North Carolina. Students seeking teaching certification in a state other than North Carolina should consult with that state's teacher certification office early in their program of study to insure compliance with requirements. Many state directors of teacher credentialing have signed Interstate Agreements through NASDTEC that expedite the certification process.

LENOIR-RHYNE COLLEGE

Education Programs

Teacher Education

7th Avenue at 8th Street, N.E.

P.O. Box 7288

Hickory, North Carolina 28603

Phone: (828) 328-7035

Fax: (828) 328-7338

E-mail: admissions@lrc.edu

Internet: http://www.lrc.edu

Institution Description: Lenoir-Rhyne College is a private college affiliated with the North Carolina Synod of the Lutheran Church in America. It was established in 1891.

The mission of the teacher education program is to prepare teachers who know their subject content, how to teach, and are successful with diverse populations.

LENOIR-RHYNE COLLEGE—cont'd

Institution Control: Private.

Calendar: Semester. Academic year August to May.

Official(s): Dr. Katie Fisher, Director of Teacher Education.

Faculty: Not reported.

Degrees Awarded: 21 baccalaureate; 12 master's.

Admission Requirements: *Undergraduate:* Graduation from an accredited secondary school with 12 to 16 academic units or GED; College Board SAT or ACT composite. *Teacher education specific:* Application during second semester of sophomore year; 2.5 GPA; passing scores on PRAXIS I exams (reading, writing, mathematics); faculty recommendation; PRAXIS II exam before graduation. *Graduate:* Baccalaureate degree from a regionally accredited institution. *Teacher education specific:* 3.0 GPA; three professional recommendations; GRE or Miller Analogies Test; personal essay; faculty interview; teaching licensure and experience when required by program pursued.

Fees and Expenses: $16,450 per academic year. Graduate: Tuition charged per credit hour. On-campus room and board: $5,815. Other expenses: $2,030. Books and supplies: $850.

Financial Aid: Resources specifically for eligible students enrolled in teacher education programs are awarded on the basis of financial need and academic merit. The institution has a Program Participation Agreement with the U.S. Department of Education for eligible students to receive Pell Grants and other federal aid. Teacher scholarships available to qualifying students. *Contact:* Financial Aid Office at: (828) 328-7304.

Accreditation: *Regional:* SACS. *Professional:* NCATE. *Member of:* AACTE. *Approved by:* North Carolina Department of Public Instruction.

Undergraduate Programs: Undergraduate majors leading to teacher licensure and the baccalaureate degree include birth-kindergarten education, deaf and hard of hearing education, elementary education, middle school education, and teaching English as a second language. Teacher licensure may be acquired by the liberal arts major: grades 9-12 (biology, business, English, mathematics, comprehensive science for teachers, social studies); grades K-12 (art, English as a second language, French, German, music, physical education, Spanish). Minors are available in academically gifted education, birth-kindergarten education, English as a second language, reading education.

All baccalaureate programs require the completion of a general education core, professional studies, content area, field experiences, and student teaching. A minimum of 128 credit hours is required for the degree award.

Graduate Programs: The Master of Arts Birth-Kindergarten Education program requires the completion of a core of courses in leadership and professionalism, research, child and family development, and diversity. A second tier of courses provides studies in speech, language, literacy, and communication disorders, research in curriculum and environments for young children, and focused study of typical and atypical development of the young child.

The Master of Arts in Education is designed for those who wish to pursue graduate study in the area of licensure and gain experience in order to develop leadership skills and professional competence. Successful completion of this master's degree will make the student eligible for advanced licensure in North Carolina. The programs included as specialty areas of study feature a common core of 12 credits and 24 credits in the specialty area that leads to the advanced competency license.

Licensure/Reciprocity: North Carolina. Students seeking teaching certification in a state other than North Carolina should consult with that state's teacher certification office early in their program of study to insure compliance with requirements. Many state directors of teacher credentialing have signed Interstate Agreements through NASDTEC that expedite the certification process.

LIVINGSTONE COLLEGE
Department of Professional Education
Teacher Education Program
701 West Monroe Street
Salisbury, North Carolina 28144
Phone: (704) 216-5786
E-mail: cleslie@livingstone.edu
Internet: http://www.livingstone.edu

Institution Description: Livingstone College is a private college affiliated with the African Methodist Episcopal Zion Church. The college was established in 1879.

The Teacher Education Program is designed to prepare prospective teachers as decision-makers.

Institution Control: Private.

Calendar: Semester. Academic year August to May.

Official(s): Dr. C.E. Leslie, Chair.

Faculty: Full-time 5; part-time 1; adjunct 1.

Degrees Awarded: 7 baccalaureate.

Admission Requirements: Graduation from an accredited secondary school or GED; College Board SAT or ACT composite. *Teacher education specific:* Application during second semester of sophomore year; 2.5 GPA; passing scores on PRAXIS I exams (reading, writing, mathematics); faculty recommendation.

Fees and Expenses: $15,000 per academic year. On-campus room and board: $4,700. Books and supplies: $200.

Financial Aid: Resources specifically for eligible students enrolled in teacher education programs are awarded on the basis of financial need and academic merit. The institution has a Program Participation Agreement with the U.S. Department of Education for eligible students to receive Pell Grants and other federal aid. Teacher scholarships available to qualifying students. *Contact:* Financial Aid Office at: (704) 216-5786.

Accreditation: *Regional:* SACS. *Professional:* NCATE. *Member of:* AACTE. *Approved by:* North Carolina Department of Public Instruction.

Undergraduate Programs: Degree-granting programs are offered in elementary education (K-6), physical education (K-12), music education (K-12), mathematics education (9-12), English education (9-12), and comprehensive social studies (9-12). These programs are predicated on a well-rounded general education program that emphasizes the acquisition of the necessary communication skills and general cultural background knowledge relevant to success in a highly technological and diverse world. The course content is sequentially organized to promote knowledge and understanding of subject matter. Activities are structured to develop competence in teaching and decision making. All programs require completion of field experiences and student teaching.

Licensure/Reciprocity: North Carolina. Students seeking teaching certification in a state other than North Carolina should consult with that state's teacher certification office early in their program of study to insure compliance with requirements. Many state directors of teacher credentialing have signed Interstate Agreements through NASDTEC that expedite the certification process.

MARS HILL COLLEGE
School of Education and Leadership
Teacher Education
Cascade Street
Mars Hill, North Carolina 28754
Phone: (828) 689-1151
Fax: (828) 689-1437
E-mail: dlansford@mhc.edu
Internet: http://www.mhc.edu

Institution Description: Mars Hill College is a private college affiliated with the North Carolina Southern Baptist Convention. The college was established in 1856.

The Teacher Education Program aims to prepare students for public school teaching. The program is planned to assist a prospective teacher in becoming a teaching professional.

Institution Control: Private.

Calendar: Semester. Academic year August to May.

Official(s): Dr. Dan Lunsford, Dean.

Faculty: Full-time 6.

Degrees Awarded: 52 baccalaureate.

Admission Requirements: Graduation from an accredited secondary school with 18 academic units or GED; College Board SAT or ACT composite. *Teacher education specific:* Application during sophomore year; 2.5 GPA; passing scores on PRAXIS I exams (reading, writing, mathematics); faculty recommendation; faculty interview; PRAXIS II exam before graduation.

Fees and Expenses: $15,460 per academic year. On-campus room and board: $4,700. Other expenses: $1,900. Books and supplies: $1,100.

Financial Aid: Resources specifically for eligible students enrolled in teacher education programs are awarded on the basis of financial need and academic merit. The institution has a Program Participation Agreement with the U.S. Department of Education for eligible students to receive Pell Grants and other federal aid. Teacher scholarships available to qualifying students. *Contact:* Financial Aid Office at: (828) 689-1123.

Accreditation: *Regional:* SACS. *Professional:* NCATE. *Approved by:* North Carolina Department of Public Instruction.

Undergraduate Programs: Mars Hill offers the following teacher education programs leading to North Carolina certification: elementary education (K-6); middle grades education (6-9); English; mathematics; natural sciences (biology, chemistry); social studies (history, political science); art; music; physical education; Spanish; theatre arts. A distinctive part of the elementary education/middle grades programs is the full-year internship. Students seeking secondary (9-12) or special subject (K-12) certification are required to complete a major in the area in which certification is desired.

All baccalaureate programs require the completion of a general education core, professional studies, content area, field experiences, and student teaching. A minimum of 128 credit hours is required to the degree award.

Licensure/Reciprocity: North Carolina. Students seeking teaching certification in a state other than North Carolina should consult with that state's teacher certification office early in their program of study to insure compliance with requirements. Many state directors of teacher credentialing have signed Interstate Agreements through NASDTEC that expedite the certification process.

MEREDITH COLLEGE
School of Education
Teacher Education
3800 Hillsborough Street
Raleigh, North Carolina 27607-5298
Phone: (919) 760-8600
Fax: (919) 760-2828
E-mail: hubbardl@meredith.edu
Internet: http://www.meredith.edu

Institution Description: Meredith College is a private college affiliated with the North Carolina Baptist State Convention. The college was established in 1889.

The Education Department is designed to develop the woman educator who is a reflective practitioner. Undergraduate and graduate programs are offered leading to teacher licensure.

Institution Control: Private.

Calendar: Semester. Academic year August to May.

Official(s): Dr. Linda R. Hubbard, Dean.

Faculty: Full-time 16.

Degrees Awarded: 11 baccalaureate; 10 master's.

Admission Requirements: *Undergraduate:* Graduation from an accredited secondary school with 16 academic units or GED; College Board SAT or ACT composite. *Teacher education specific:* Declaration of major area; application by second semester of sophomore year; passing scores on PRAXIS I tests (reading, writing, mathematics); 2.5 GPA; faculty interview. *Graduate:* Baccalaureate degree from a regionally accredited institution. *Teacher education specific:* 3.0 GPA; three professional recommendations; GRE or Miller Analogies Test; personal essay; faculty interview; teaching licensure and experience when required by program pursued.

Fees and Expenses: $18,065 per academic year. On-campus room and board: $5,760. Other expenses: $2,050. Books and supplies: $750.

Financial Aid: Resources specifically for eligible students enrolled in teacher education programs are awarded on the basis of financial need and academic merit. The institution has a Program Participation Agreement with the U.S. Department of Education for eligible students to receive Pell Grants and other federal aid. Teacher scholarships available to qualifying students. *Contact:* Financial Aid Office at: (919) 760-8565.

Accreditation: *Regional:* SACS. *Professional:* NCATE. *Approved by:* North Carolina Department of Public Instruction.

Undergraduate Programs: Undergraduates may choose a teacher education program in addition to their major program of study. Programs are available for initial licensure in birth through kindergarten (B-K); elementary education (grades K-6); middle grades education (grades 6-9); language arts, mathematics, science, social studies; special subject area education (grades K-12); art, music, dance, theatre, French, Spanish, physical education, occupational education); business education (grades 9-12); family and consumer sciences education (grades 7-12). Although there are common elements in each of the programs, each is a distinctly different program designed for a specific purpose. All programs require the completion of a general education core, professional studies, content area, field experiences, and student teaching. A minimum of 124 semester hours is required for the degree award.

Graduate Programs: The Master of Education degree program is structured to encourage extensive reading, independent thinking, creativity, and appropriate research. All students take a common core of courses and select a concentration in a licensure area. Licensure options include elementary education, reading, and English as a second language.

Licensure/Reciprocity: North Carolina. Students seeking teaching certification in a state other than North Carolina should consult with that state's teacher certification office early in their program of study to insure compliance with requirements. Many state directors of teacher credentialing have signed Interstate Agreements through NASDTEC that expedite the certification process.

METHODIST COLLEGE
Division of Professional Studies
Department of Education
5400 Ramsey Street
Fayetteville, North Carolina 28311
Phone: (910) 630-7027
Fax: (910) 630-7285
E-mail: jheyward@methodist.edu
Internet: http://www.methodist.edu

Institution Description: Methodist College is a private college affiliated with the United Methodist Church. The college was established and chartered in 1956.

The college is committed to meeting the need for well-trained and dedicated teachers. The unifying theme for all programs is the development of professional educators as facilitative teachers who understand and value the process of learning.

Institution Control: Private.

Calendar: Semester. Academic year August to May.

Official(s): Dr. Jaunita White Heyward, Department Head.

Faculty: Full-time 6.

Degrees Awarded: 21 baccalaureate.

Admission Requirements: Graduation from an accredited secondary school with 18 academic units or GED; College Board SAT or ACT composite. *Teacher education specific:* Cumulative

METHODIST COLLEGE—cont'd

GPA of 2.5; passing scores on the PRAXIS I exams (reading, writing, mathematics); completion of a minimum of 60 academic hours; three faculty recommendations; faculty interview.

Fees and Expenses: $15,650 per academic year. On-campus room and board: $5,940. Other expenses: $3,240. Books and supplies: $800.

Financial Aid: Resources specifically for eligible students enrolled in teacher education programs are awarded on the basis of financial need and academic merit. The institution has a Program Participation Agreement with the U.S. Department of Education for eligible students to receive Pell Grants and other federal aid. Teacher scholarships available to qualifying students. *Contact:* Financial Aid Office at: (910) 630-7192.

Accreditation: *Regional:* SACS. *Professional:* NCATE. *Member of:* AACTE. *Approved by:* North Carolina Department of Public Instruction.

Undergraduate Programs: The Teacher Education Program provides courses of study for the following teaching licenses: elementary education (K-6); middle grades education (6-9) concentrations: language arts, mathematics, social studies, science; secondary education (9-12): English, mathematics, biology, social studies; special subjects (K-12): art, French, Spanish, music, physical education, specific learning disabilities; special school personnel (K-12): school social work; add-on licenses (K-12): reading, academically gifted, Spanish or French (K-6). The programs lead to the Bachelor of Arts or Bachelor of Science degrees and require the completion of the general education core, professional studies, content area, field experiences, and student teaching. A minimum of 124 credit hours is required for the degree award.

Licensure/Reciprocity: North Carolina. Students seeking teaching certification in a state other than North Carolina should consult with that state's teacher certification office early in their program of study to insure compliance with requirements. Many state directors of teacher credentialing have signed Interstate Agreements through NASDTEC that expedite the certification process.

NORTH CAROLINA AGRICULTURAL AND TECHNICAL STATE UNIVERSITY

School of Education
Department of Curriculum and Instruction
201 Hodgin Hall
1601 East Market Street
Greensboro, North Carolina 27411
Phone: (336) 334-7712
Fax: (336) 334-7132
E-mail: admissions@ncat.edu
Internet: http://www.ncat.edu

Institution Description: The institution was established in 1891. The name became the Agricultural and Technical College of North Carolina in 1915 and the present name was adopted in 1967.

The university offers programs leading to state teacher licensure through the School of Education and coordination with the School of Agriculture, College of Arts and sciences, School of business and Economics, and School of Technology.

Institution Control: Public.

Calendar: Semester. Academic year August to May.

Official(s): Dr. Lelia Vickers, Dean; Dr. Dorothy LaFlore, Chairperson.

Faculty: Full-time 17; adjunct 4.

Degrees Awarded: 55 baccalaureate; 96 master's.

Admission Requirements: *Undergraduate:* Graduation from an accredited secondary school with 16 academic units or GED; College Board SAT score 750 or higher. *Teacher education specific:* Minimum cumulative 2.8 GPA; minimum scores on PRAXIS I exams (reading, writing, mathematics); pass 32 semester hours of coursework prior to sophomore year; interview by Teacher Education Panel. *Graduate:* Baccalaureate from a regionally

accredited institution. *Teacher education specific:* 3.0 GPA; three professional recommendations; GRE or Miller Analogies Test; personal essay; faculty interview; teaching licensure and experience when required by program pursued.

Fees and Expenses: Undergraduate: in-state $2,722 per academic year; out-of-state $12,089. Graduate: Tuition charged per credit hour. On-campus room and board: $4,968. Other expenses: $2,705. Books and supplies: $850.

Financial Aid: Resources specifically for eligible students enrolled in teacher education programs are awarded on the basis of financial need and academic merit. The institution has a Program Participation Agreement with the U.S. Department of Education for eligible students to receive Pell Grants and other federal aid. Teacher scholarships available to qualifying students. *Contact:* Financial Aid Office at: (336) 334-7973.

Accreditation: *Regional:* SACS. *Professional:* NCATE. *Member of:* AACTE. *Approved by:* North Carolina Department of Public Instruction.

Undergraduate Programs: The program in teacher education is divided into three phases: general education, subject-matter specialization, and professional. Academic degree programs leading to the Bachelor of Science degree include elementary education, special education, Agricultural education, child development (early education and family studies), family and consumer sciences education, secondary education (biology, chemistry, English, French, history, mathematics, music, physics); basic business education, secondary business education, comprehensive business education, technology education, vocational industrial education.

All baccalaureate programs require the completion of the general education core, professional studies, content area, field experiences, and student teaching. A minimum of 124 credit hours is required for the degree award.

Graduate Programs: The master's degree programs include: elementary education, instructional technology, intermediate education (grades 4-6), reading education, agricultural education, secondary education (biology, chemistry, physics, English, history, mathematics), technology education, vocational industrial education. All programs have specific course requirements.

Licensure/Reciprocity: North Carolina. Students seeking teaching certification in a state other than North Carolina should consult with that state's teacher certification office early in their program of study to insure compliance with requirements. Many state directors of teacher credentialing have signed Interstate Agreements through NASDTEC that expedite the certification process.

NORTH CAROLINA CENTRAL UNIVERSITY

School of Education
Curriculum and Instruction - Teacher Education
717 Cecil Street
Durham, North Carolina 27707
Phone: (919) 530-6466
Fax: (919) 530-5279
E-mail: sspencer@nccu.edu
Internet: http://www.nccu.edu

Institution Description: The institution was established and chartered as National Religious Training School in 1909. It became a state institution and the name was changed to Durham State Normal School in 1923, to North Carolina College for Negroes in 1925, to North Carolina College at Durham in 1947, and to the present name in 1969. The school became part of the University of North Carolina System in 1972.

The mission of the School of Education is to prepare education professionals to serve and inspire excellence in teaching, administration, counseling, communication, technology, and other related services.

Institution Control: Public.

Calendar: Semester. Academic year August to May.

Official(s): Dr. Cecilia Steppe-Jones, Dean; Dr. Sharon Spencer, Director of Teacher Education.

Faculty: Full-time 6; adjunct 3 (Curriculum and Instruction).

Degrees Awarded: 64 baccalaureate; 71 master's.

Admission Requirements: *Undergraduate:* Graduation from an accredited secondary school with 16 academic units or GED; College Board SAT or ACT composite. *Teacher education specific:* Minimum cumulative 2.8 GPA; minimum scores on PRAXIS I exams (reading, writing, mathematics); pass 32 semester hours of coursework prior to sophomore year; interview by Teacher Education Panel. *Graduate:* Baccalaureate from a regionally accredited institution. *Teacher education specific:* 3.0 GPA; three professional recommendations; GRE or Miller Analogies Test; personal essay; faculty interview; teaching licensure and experience when required by program pursued.

Fees and Expenses: Undergraduate: in-state $2,802 per academic year; out-of-state $12,171. Graduate: in-state $4,036 per academic year; out-of-state $15,685. On-campus room and board: $4,315. Other expenses: $2,415. Books and supplies: $1,000.

Financial Aid: Resources specifically for eligible students enrolled in teacher education programs are awarded on the basis of financial need and academic merit. The institution has a Program Participation Agreement with the U.S. Department of Education for eligible students to receive Pell Grants and other federal aid. Teacher scholarships available to qualifying students. *Contact:* Financial Aid Office at: (919) 530-6202.

Accreditation: *Regional:* SACS. *Professional:* NCATE. *Member of:* AACTE. *Approved by:* North Carolina Department of Public Instruction.

Undergraduate Programs: Undergraduate programs are available in elementary education leading to the bachelor's degree and K-6 licensure and middle grades education leading to licensure in grades 6-9 with two academic concentrations. Students in both programs are involved in a rigorous program of study that integrates content knowledge, pedagogy, extensive field experiences, and technology focused on preparing them to work in diverse cultural contexts.

The secondary education program includes concentrations in: English, mathematics, biology, chemistry, comprehensive social studies, physics, physical education, music, art, foreign language (French, Spanish), home economics/human science, health, and theater art.

All programs require the completion of a general education core, professional studies, content area, field experiences, and student teaching. A minimum of 124 credit hours is required for the degree award.

Graduate Programs: The Master of Education degree programs include elementary education (K-6), middle school education (6-9), special education, and communication disorders. The Master of Arts in Teaching program is offered in education technology, special education (mental behavioral/emotional, learning disabilities), and counseling (school, agency, career counseling and placement). Each program has specific course requirements.

Licensure/Reciprocity: North Carolina. Students seeking teaching certification in a state other than North Carolina should consult with that state's teacher certification office early in their program of study to insure compliance with requirements. Many state directors of teacher credentialing have signed Interstate Agreements through NASDTEC that expedite the certification process.

NORTH CAROLINA STATE UNIVERSITY

College of Education

Poe Hall
P.O. Box 7001
Raleigh, North Carolina 27695-7001
Phone: (919) 515-2231
Fax: (919) 515-5901
E-mail: kathryn.moore@ncsu.edu
Internet: http://www.ncsu.edu

Institution Description: The institution was established by the State General Assembly in 1887 and became North Carolina College of Agriculture and Mechanic Arts in 1889. The name was changed to North Carolina College of Agriculture and Engineering in 1917 and the present name was adopted in 1965.

The College of Education offers programs leading to the bachelor's, master's, and doctoral degrees.

Institution Control: Public.

Calendar: Semester. Academic year August to May.

Official(s): Dr. Kathryn M. Moore, Dean.

Faculty: Full-time 69, part-time 12, adjunct 7.

Degrees Awarded: 133 baccalaureate; 243 master's; 47 doctorate.

Admission Requirements: *Undergraduate:* Graduation from an accredited secondary school or GED; College Board SAT or ACT composite. *Teacher education specific:* 2.5 GPA to be admitted to candidacy; passing scores on PRAXIS I exams (reading, writing, mathematics); faculty interview. *Graduate:* Baccalaureate degree from a regionally accredited institution; B average in undergraduate major; three references, goal statement; GRE or Miller Analogies Test scores.

Fees and Expenses: Undergraduate: in-state $2,814 per academic year; out-of-state $11,980. Graduate: in-state $4,036 per academic year; out-of-state $15,685. On-campus room and board: $5,270. Personal expenses: $1,050. Books and supplies: $600.

Financial Aid: Resources specifically for eligible students enrolled in teacher education programs are awarded on the basis of academic merit and financial need. North Carolina Teaching Fellows Program is offered with four years of financial support for four years of teaching. *Contact:* Anona P. Smith-Williams at: (919) 515-3325 or e-mail at: anona.smith@ncsu.edu.

Accreditation: *Regional:* SACS. *Professional:* NCATE. *Member of:* AACTE. *Approved by:* North Carolina Department of Public Instruction.

Undergraduate Programs: Undergraduate programs offered by the university include licensure for middle grades teacher education (grades 6-9); secondary teacher education (grades 9-12), modern foreign language education: French and Spanish (K-12); and workforce development education (grades 7-12).

The degree awarded is Bachelor of Science or Bachelor of Arts depending upon the college in which the student is enrolled. All teacher licensure programs include three components: general studies, content area studies, and professional studies. Students enroll in the general education courses and appropriate content area courses in the disciplines administered by the relevant departments and colleges and they enroll in the professional studies courses offered by the College of Education. The minimum semester hour credits required for graduation range from 120 to 128, depending on the specialization pursued.

Graduate Programs: The College of Education offers master's and doctoral degrees leading to professional licensure. Advanced degree programs of study are offered for teachers already certified at the baccalaureate level in elementary education, English education, social studies education, mathematics education, and science education. There are also advanced programs in selected areas for those enrolling in an extended master's degree in which both the initial and advanced license is earning including special education in mental retardation, behavior disorders, and learning disabilities; and reading education. The minimum number of credits required in the master's degree program is 36 semester hours.

Doctoral degrees include the Doctor of Education and Doctor of Philosophy. The total number of credit hours required may include the master's degree and a minimum number of hours beyond the master's depending on the program, the applicant's prior education, and experience.

Licensure/Reciprocity: North Carolina. Students seeking teaching certification in a state other than North Carolina should consult with that state's teacher certification office early in their program of study to insure compliance with requirements.

NORTH CAROLINA STATE UNIVERSITY—
cont'd

Many state directors of teacher credentialing have signed Interstate Agreements through NASDTEC that expedite the certification process.

NORTH CAROLINA WESLEYAN COLLEGE

Teacher Education Program

3400 North Wesleyan Boulevard
Rocky Mount, North Carolina 27804
Phone: (252) 985-5100
Fax: (252) 977-5295
E-mail: adm@ncwc.edu
Internet: http://www.ncwc.edu

Institution Description: North Carolina Wesleyan College is a private college affiliated with the United Methodist Church. It was established and chartered in 1956.

The college offers programs leading to the baccalaureate degree and licensure in elementary education, middle grades education, and secondary education.

Institution Control: Private.

Calendar: Semester. Academic year August to May.

Official(s): Dr. Marshall A. Brooks, Chair.

Faculty: Full-time 3.

Degrees Awarded: 8 baccalaureate.

Admission Requirements: *Undergraduate:* Graduation from an accredited secondary school with 16 academic units or GED; College Board SAT or ACT composite. *Teacher education specific:* Completion of PRAXIS I exams (reading, writing, mathematics); 2.5 GPA; two recommendations; portfolio; interview by Teacher Education Council.

Fees and Expenses: $12,295 per academic year. On-campus room and board: $6,555. Other expenses: $1,400. Books and supplies: $985.

Financial Aid: Resources specifically for eligible students enrolled in teacher education programs are awarded on the basis of financial need and academic merit. The institution has a Program Participation Agreement with the U.S. Department of Education for eligible students to receive Pell Grants and other federal aid. Teacher scholarships available to qualifying students. *Contact:* Financial Aid Office at: (252) 985-5291.

Accreditation: *Regional:* SACS. *Professional:* NCATE. *Approved by:* North Carolina Department of Public Instruction.

Undergraduate Programs: Students who choose to become licensed in elementary education (grades K-6) will major in elementary education. The Bachelor of Science program requires the completion of specific courses in the humanities, social sciences, sciences, and education plus field experiences and student teaching.

The middle grades education program leading to the Bachelor of Science degree requires the completion of two concentrations selected from the following four areas: language arts, social studies, mathematics, or science. License-only and lateral entry teachers are required to complete one concentration.

Students may be licensed to teach in grades 9-12 in biology, English, history, mathematics, or social science. All students must complete a specific academic major and complete required courses in education, field experiences, and student teaching to meet licensure requirements and the Bachelor of Science degree.

Licensure/Reciprocity: North Carolina. Students seeking teaching certification in a state other than North Carolina should consult with that state's teacher certification office early in their program of study to insure compliance with requirements. Many state directors of teacher credentialing have signed Interstate Agreements through NASDTEC that expedite the certification process.

PFEIFFER UNIVERSITY

University College
Education Department

Highway 52
P.O. Box 960
Misenheimer, North Carolina 28109-0960
Phone: (704) 463-1360
Fax: (704) 463-1363
E-mail: admiss@pfeiffer.edu
Internet: http://www.pfeiffer.edu

Institution Description: Pfeiffer University, formerly Pfeiffer College, is a private institution affiliated with the United Methodist Church. It was founded in 1903.

The teacher education program is designed to educate for preparation in a specific academic discipline, a broad general education, professional competence and a thorough understanding of the responsibilities and techniques of effective teaching.

Institution Control: Private.

Calendar: Semester. Academic year August to June.

Official(s): Dr. Bettie Starr, Dean, University College.

Faculty: Teacher Education full-time 6.

Degrees Awarded: 19 baccalaureate.

Admission Requirements: *Undergraduate:* Graduation from an accredited secondary school or GED; College Board SAT or ACT composite. *Teacher education specific:* Application by end of sophomore year; 2.5 GPA; PRAXIS I exam scores (reading, writing, mathematics); satisfactory command of the English language; faculty interview. *Graduate:* Baccalaureate degree from a regionally accredited institution. *Teacher education specific:* GRE score of 800 or 40 on the Miller Analogies Test; personal essay; transcripts of all undergraduate work; teaching certificate; 2.75 GPA in all undergraduate work; three letters of recommendation; faculty interview.

Fees and Expenses: $13,550 per academic year. On-campus room and board: $5,340. Other expenses: $2,000. Books and supplies: $1,000.

Financial Aid: Resources specifically for eligible students enrolled in teacher education programs are awarded on the basis of financial need and academic merit. The institution has a Program Participation Agreement with the U.S. Department of Education for eligible students to receive Pell Grants and other federal aid. Teacher scholarships available to qualifying students. *Contact:* Financial Aid Office at: (704) 463-1360, ext. 2074.

Accreditation: *Regional:* SACS. *Professional:* NCATE. *Member of:* AACTE. *Approved by:* North Carolina Department of Public Instruction.

Undergraduate Programs: The purpose of the elementary education program (K-6) is to provide appropriate learning experiences to meet the needs, capabilities, and interests in kindergarten through grade six. The program is designed to assist individuals in acquiring the knowledge, developing skills, and forming attitudes within a learning environment and relevant learning activities. Students working toward teacher licensure must complete at least 124 semester hours required by the university, complete prescribed courses, complete cultural units and satisfy the English proficiency requirement prior to the semester in which student teaching occurs.

Graduate Programs: The Master of Science in elementary education is designed for teachers who possess elementary certification and who seek excellence in instructional design and instructional delivery systems. The purpose of the program is to provide an educational environment in which teachers who are committed to continuous learning can further their knowledge of content and refine their professional competencies. Students are expected to demonstrate abilities in analyzing, planning, and critical thinking in relation to specific problems and issues in elementary education. These skills are evaluated in each course as well as in a culminating experience.

Licensure/Reciprocity: North Carolina. Students seeking teaching certification in a state other than North Carolina should consult with that state's teacher certification office early in their program of study to insure compliance with requirements. Many state directors of teacher credentialing have signed Interstate Agreements through NASDTEC that expedite the certification process.

QUEENS UNIVERSITY OF CHARLOTTE
Division of Education
1900 Selwyn Avenue
Charlotte, North Carolina 28274
Phone: (704) 337-2580
Fax: (704) 337-2415
E-mail: eckartj@queens.edu
Internet: http://www.queens.edu

Institution Description: Queens College is a private, urban-based, diversified liberal arts college with close ties to the Presbyterian Church (U.S.A.). The college was founded in 1957.

Division objectives state that the education of teachers is threefold: they receive a liberal education, pursue in-depth their teaching specialties, and acquire the necessary professional knowledge and skills needed in teaching.

Institution Control: Private.

Calendar: Semester. Academic year August to May.

Official(s): Dr. Joyce A. Eckart, Department Head.

Faculty: Full-time 5; adjunct 3.

Degrees Awarded: 4 baccalaureate; 11 master's.

Admission Requirements: *Undergraduate:* Graduation from an accredited secondary school or GED; College Board SAT or ACT composite. *Teacher education specific:* Positive recommendations by three faculty members; overall 2.5 GPA after four semesters of coursework; satisfactory scores on PRAXIS I exams (reading, writing, mathematics). *Graduate:* Baccalaureate from a regionally accredited institution; official transcripts of all post-secondary academic coursework; cumulative GPA of 2.5; GRE scores; personal interview.

Fees and Expenses: Undergraduate: 15,650. Graduate: $235 per credit hour. Student teaching fee: $140. On-campus room and board. $6,190.

Financial Aid: Resources specifically for eligible students enrolled in teacher education programs are awarded on the basis of financial need and academic merit. The institution has a Program Participation Agreement with the U.S. Department of Education for eligible students to receive Pell Grants and other federal aid. Teacher scholarships available to qualifying students. *Contact:* Lauren Mack, Director, Financial Aid at: (704) 337-2230.

Accreditation: *Regional:* SACS. *Professional:* NCATE. *Approved by:* North Carolina Department of Public Instruction.

Undergraduate Programs: Obtaining a North Carolina initial license is possible through programs in elementary education (K-6), special subjects (grades 9-12) in French and Spanish; secondary education in the subject areas (9-12) English, mathematics, biology, history, and social studies. The education of teachers is a joint responsibility of academic departments and the education department. All baccalaureate programs require the completion of a general education core, professional studies, content area, field experiences, and student teaching. A minimum of 122 semester hours is required for the degree award.

Graduate Programs: The Education Division has developed individual programs for post-baccalaureate non-degree candidates seeking initial licensure in elementary education (K-6), secondary education (9-12), and Spanish or French. With the exception of the student teaching practicum, all education coursework can be completed in the evening.

The Master of Arts in Teaching program is for those students who hold a baccalaureate degree in a subject area and who wish to gain licensure to teach.

Licensure/Reciprocity: North Carolina. Students seeking teaching certification in a state other than North Carolina should consult with that state's teacher certification office early in their program of study to insure compliance with requirements.

Many state directors of teacher credentialing have signed Interstate Agreements through NASDTEC that expedite the certification process.

ST. ANDREWS PRESBYTERIAN COLLEGE
Department of Education
Teacher Education Program
1700 Dogwood Mile
Laurinburg, North Carolina 28352
Phone: (910) 277-5340
Fax: (910) 277-5020
E-mail: oeseduc@sapc.edu
Internet: http://www.sapc.edu

Institution Description: St. Andrews Presbyterian College is a private college affiliated with the Synod of North Carolina, Presbyterian Church (U.S.A.). It was established in 1955.

The primary objective of the Department of Education is the preparation of teachers who are professionally competent, personally and socially mature, and who are aware of their responsibilities to society.

Institution Control: Public.

Calendar: Semester. Academic year August to May.

Official(s): Dr. O. Eugene Smith, Chair.

Faculty: Full-time 3; part-time 3; adjunct 6-8.

Degrees Awarded: 6 baccalaureate.

Admission Requirements: *Undergraduate:* Graduation from an accredited secondary school or GED; College Board SAT 850 or ACT composite 17. *Teacher education specific:* Positive recommendations by three faculty members; overall 2.5 GPA after four semesters of coursework; satisfactory scores on PRAXIS I exams (reading, writing, mathematics).

Fees and Expenses: $20,525 per academic year. On-campus room and board: $5,410. Books and supplies: $800.

Financial Aid: Resources specifically for eligible students enrolled in teacher education programs are awarded on the basis of financial need and academic merit. The institution has a Program Participation Agreement with the U.S. Department of Education for eligible students to receive Pell Grants and other federal aid. Teacher scholarships available to qualifying students. *Contact:* KImberly Driggers, Director, Financial Aid at: (910) 277-5562 or e-mail at: driggers@sapc.edu.

Accreditation: *Regional:* SACS. *Professional:* NCATE. *Approved by:* North Carolina Department of Public Instruction.

Undergraduate Programs: Two majors are offered in teacher education. The major in elementary education with K-6 licensure requires the completion of specialty area requirements and professional studies method courses. The major in physical education with K-12 licensure requires the completion of specialty area courses and professional education courses. Both programs lead to the Bachelor of Science in Education degree and require completion of the general education core, professional studies, content area, field experiences, and the professional semester of student teaching.

Licensure/Reciprocity: North Carolina. Students seeking teaching certification in a state other than North Carolina should consult with that state's teacher certification office early in their program of study to insure compliance with requirements. Many state directors of teacher credentialing have signed Interstate Agreements through NASDTEC that expedite the certification process.

SAINT AUGUSTINE'S COLLEGE
Division of Education
Department of Teacher Education
Boyer Building, 200-F
1315 Oakwood Avenue
Raleigh, North Carolina 27612-2298
Phone: (919) 516-4096
Fax: (919) 516-4415
E-mail: lprice@st-aug.edu
Internet: http://www.st-aug.edu

SAINT AUGUSTINE'S COLLEGE—cont'd

Institution Description: Saint Augustine's College is a private college affiliated with the Episcopal Church. It was established as Saint Augustine's Normal School and Collegiate Institute in 1867.

Undergraduate programs leading to the baccalaureate degree and teacher licensure are offered by the Department of Teacher Education.

Institution Control: Private.

Calendar: Semester. Academic year August to May.

Official(s): Dr. Linda Price, Chair, Division of Education.

Faculty: Full-time 15.

Degrees Awarded: 4 baccalaureate.

Admission Requirements: *Undergraduate:* Graduation from an accredited secondary school with 16 academic units or GED; College Board SAT. *Teacher education specific:* Demonstrate an interest in mentoring and teaching; one-page autobiography; complete Foundations of Education course; meet cumulative PRAXIS I minimum score requirements; overall 2.5 GPA; oral and written proficiency; application by end of sophomore year.

Fees and Expenses: $9,648 per academic year. On-campus room and board: $4,960. Other expenses: $2,040. Books and supplies: $900.

Financial Aid: Resources specifically for eligible students enrolled in teacher education programs are awarded on the basis of financial need and academic merit. The institution has a Program Participation Agreement with the U.S. Department of Education for eligible students to receive Pell Grants and other federal aid. Teacher scholarships available to qualifying students. *Contact:* Financial Aid Office at: (919) 516-4131.

Accreditation: *Regional:* SACS. *Professional:* NCATE. *Member of:* AACTE. *Approved by:* North Carolina Department of Public Instruction.

Undergraduate Programs: Undergraduate programs leading to the baccalaureate degree and North Carolina teacher certification include: elementary education (K-6), exceptional children's education (K-12), physical education (K-12) and secondary education in music (K-12), biology (9-12), business (9-12), mathematics (9-12), social studies (9-12), and English education (9-12).

All programs require the completion of a general education core, professional studies, content area, field experiences, and student teaching. A minimum of 120 semester hours is required for the degree award.

Licensure/Reciprocity: North Carolina. Students seeking teaching certification in a state other than North Carolina should consult with that state's teacher certification office early in their program of study to insure compliance with requirements. Many state directors of teacher credentialing have signed Interstate Agreements through NASDTEC that expedite the certification process.

SALEM COLLEGE

Department of Education
Teacher Education
601 South Church Street
Winston-Salem, North Carolina 27108
Phone: (336) 721-2658
Fax: (336) 724-7102
E-mail: admissions@salem.edu
Internet: http://www.salem.edu

Institution Description: Salem College is a private college for women affiliated with the Moravian Church. It was established as Salem Female Academy in 1772.

The teacher education program is built upon a firm foundation in the liberal arts. The program is committed to promoting the cognitive development of each prospective teacher.

Institution Control: Private.

Calendar: Semester (4-1-4 plan). Academic year August to May.

Official(s): Associate Professor Smith, Chair and Director of Teacher Education.

Faculty: Full-time 6; adjunct 1.

Degrees Awarded: 16 master's.

Admission Requirements: *Undergraduate:* Graduation from an accredited secondary school with 16 academic units or GED; College Board SAT or ACT composite. *Teacher education specific:* Satisfactory scores on PRAXIS I exams (reading, writing, mathematics); application during the the spring of sophomore year; 2.5 GPA; faculty interview. *Graduate:* Baccalaureate degree from a regionally accredited institution. *Teacher education specific:* Letters of recommendation; GRE scores; personal essay; faculty interview.

Fees and Expenses: Undergraduate: $15,500 per academic year. Graduate: Tuition charged per credit hour. On-campus room and board: $8,870. Other expenses: $4,676. Books and supplies: $800.

Financial Aid: Resources specifically for eligible students enrolled in teacher education programs are awarded on the basis of financial need and academic merit. The institution has a Program Participation Agreement with the U.S. Department of Education for eligible students to receive Pell Grants and other federal aid. Teacher scholarships available to qualifying students. *Contact:* Financial Aid Office at: (336) 721-2808.

Accreditation: *Regional:* SACS. *Professional:* NCATE. *Member of:* AACTE. *Approved by:* North Carolina Department of Public Instruction.

Undergraduate Programs: Salem College offers teacher education programs leading to the baccalaureate degree and North Carolina licensure in: elementary education (K-6), learning disabilities (K-12), birth to kindergarten (B-K), second languages (French, Spanish) (K-12), secondary education (9-12) in biology, chemistry, English, mathematics, social studies, and English as a second language.

All programs require completion of a general education core, professional studies, content area, field experiences, and student teaching. The student must complete 36 courses for graduation.

Graduate Programs: The Master of Arts in Teaching program is for the college graduate who has a firm foundation in the liberal arts and sciences and seeks professional licensure and a master's degree. Graduate teaching licenses may be earned in either elementary education, learning disabilities, or birth-kindergarten.

The Master of Education in language and literacy is for the teacher who intends to remain in the classroom and seeks to increase his or her professional knowledge and skills. Persons who complete this degree will qualify for a graduate K-12 reading license in North Carolina.

Licensure/Reciprocity: North Carolina. Students seeking teaching certification in a state other than North Carolina should consult with that state's teacher certification office early in their program of study to insure compliance with requirements. Many state directors of teacher credentialing have signed Interstate Agreements through NASDTEC that expedite the certification process.

SHAW UNIVERSITY

Department of Education
118 East South Street
Raleigh, North Carolina 27601
Phone: (919) 546-8200
Fax: (919) 546-8301
E-mail: admissions@shawu.edu
Internet: http://www.shawu.edu

Institution Description: Shaw University is a private independent institution. It was established as Raleigh Institute in 1865. The present name was adopted in 1875.

The purpose of the Department of Education is to prepare students who will function as competent and effective professionals who are critical thinkers and problem solvers.

Institution Control: Private.

Calendar: Semester. Academic year August to July.

Official(s): Dr. Deloris Jerman, Director of Education.

Faculty: Full-time 16.

Degrees Awarded: 37 baccalaureate; 2 master's.

Admission Requirements: *Undergraduate:* Graduation from an accredited secondary school with 15 academic units or GED; College Board SAT or ACT composite. *Teacher education specific:* Satisfactory scores on PRAXIS I exams (reading, writing, mathematics); application during the the spring of sophomore year; 2.5 GPA; faculty interview.

Fees and Expenses: $14,386 comprehensive fee (includes fees, room and board). Books and supplies: $700.

Financial Aid: Resources specifically for eligible students enrolled in teacher education programs are awarded on the basis of financial need and academic merit. The institution has a Program Participation Agreement with the U.S. Department of Education for eligible students to receive Pell Grants and other federal aid. Teacher scholarships available to qualifying students. *Contact:* Financial Aid Office at: (919) 546-8240.

Accreditation: *Regional:* SACS. *Professional:* NCATE. *Member of:* AACTE. *Approved by:* North Carolina Department of Public Instruction.

Undergraduate Programs: Baccalaureate degree programs offer majors in specialty areas that lead to initial licensure as a teacher. Included are: biology education-B.S. (9-12); birth-kindergarten education-B.A. (pre-K); elementary education-B.A. (K-12); English education-B.A. (9-12); mathematics education-B.S. (9-12); social studies-B.A. (9-12); special education-mentally disabled-B.A. (K-12).

All programs require the completion of the general education core, professional studies, content area, field experiences, and student teaching. A minimum of 127 semester hours is required for the degree award.

Licensure/Reciprocity: North Carolina. Students seeking teaching certification in a state other than North Carolina should consult with that state's teacher certification office early in their program of study to insure compliance with requirements. Many state directors of teacher credentialing have signed Interstate Agreements through NASDTEC that expedite the certification process.

UNIVERSITY OF NORTH CAROLINA AT ASHEVILLE

Department of Education
148 Zageir Halll, CPO #1950
One University Heights
Asheville, North Carolina 28804-3299
Phone: (828) 251-6420
Fax: (828) 251-6999
E-mail: education@unca.edu
Internet: http://www.unca.edu

Institution Description: The institution was established as Buncombe County College in 1927. It was rechartered as Asheville-Biltmore College in 1936, The college became part of the University of North Carolina system and adopted the present name in 1969.

The primary mission of the Department of Education is to provide the professional preparation for a North Carolina Class A Teaching license with a liberal arts foundation. The licensure program is supported by extensive collaboration with area schools.

Calendar: Semester. Academic year August to May.

Official(s): Dr. Mark Sidelnick, Chair.

Faculty: 7 full-time; 10 adjunct.

Degrees Awarded: 48 baccalaureate.

Admission Requirements: Graduation from an accredited secondary school with a college preparatory academic program or GED; College Board SAT or ACT composite. *Teacher education specific:* Completion of requirements to be classified as a junior; 2.5 cumulative GPA; acceptable scores on PRAXIS I exams (reading, writing, mathematics); departmental portfolio; faculty interview.

Fees and Expenses: $1,672 in-state per academic year; $10,497 out-of-state. Required fees: $1,429. On-campus room and board: $4,978. Other expenses: $1,541. Books and supplies: $850.

Financial Aid: Resources specifically for eligible students enrolled in teacher education programs are awarded on the basis of financial need and academic merit. The institution has a Program Participation Agreement with the U.S. Department of Education for eligible students to receive Pell Grants and other federal aid. Teacher scholarships available to qualifying students. *Contact:* Scot Schaeffer, Director of Admissions and Financial Aid at: (828) 251-6841 or e-mail at: admissions@unca.edu.

Accreditation: *Regional:* SACS. *Professional:* NCATE. *Member of:* AACTE. *Approved by:* North Carolina Department of Public Instruction.

Undergraduate Programs: The Teacher Licensure Programs leading to the baccalaureate degree include: elementary education (K-6); middle school (6-9); English (9-12); mathematics (9-12); social studies (9-12); physics (9-12); earth science (9-12); biology (9-12); chemistry (9-12); reading (K-12); art (K-12); theater arts (K-12); foreign language (K-12) in French, German, Spanish, Latin (9-12). All programs require the completion of a general education core, professional studies, subject content area, field experiences, and student teaching. A minimum of 120 semester hours must be completed for the degree award.

Licensure/Reciprocity: North Carolina. Students seeking teaching certification in a state other than North Carolina should consult with that state's teacher certification office early in their program of study to insure compliance with requirements. Many state directors of teacher credentialing have signed Interstate Agreements through NASDTEC that expedite the certification process.

UNIVERSITY OF NORTH CAROLINA AT CHAPEL HILL

School of Education
Campus Box 3500
Chapel Hill, North Carolina 27599-3500
Phone: (919) 966-7000
Fax: (919) 962-1533
E-mail: ed@unc.edu
Internet: http://www.unc.edu

Institution Description: The university was authorized by the state constitution in 1776. It was chartered in 1789 and offered first instruction at the postsecondary level in 1795.

The School of Education trains teachers, administrators, and other education professionals to become leaders at all levels of education. In collaborative efforts, the school works with schools and communities to bring knowledge and skills to children and the adults who teach and care for them.

Institution Control: Public.

Calendar: Semester. Academic year August to May.

Official(s): Dr. Dixie Lee Spiegel, Senior Associate Dean.

Faculty: Full-time 59; part-time 6; adjunct 11.

Degrees Awarded: 83 baccalaureate; 125 master's; 26 doctorate.

Admission Requirements: *Undergraduate:* Graduation from an accredited secondary school or GED; College Board SAT or ACT composite. *Teacher education specific:* Admittance after sophomore year; commitment to teaching profession and to children; academic progress; passing scores on PRAXIS I exams (reading, writing, mathematics); faculty interview. *Graduate:* Baccalaureate degree from a regionally accredited institution. *Teacher education specific:* GRE; competitive GPA; recommendations; goal statement; licensure intent.

Fees and Expenses: Undergraduate: $1,407 in-state per academic year; $7,049 out-of-state. Graduate: $4,043 in-state per academic year; $15,692 out-of-state. Required fees: $1,031. On-campus room and board: $6,620. Other expenses: $2,100. Books and supplies: $800.

Financial Aid: Resources specifically for eligible students enrolled in teacher education programs are awarded on the basis of financial need and academic merit. The institution has a Program Participation Agreement with the U.S. Department of Education for eligible students to receive Pell Grants and other federal aid. Teacher scholarships available to qualifying stu-

UNIVERSITY OF NORTH CAROLINA AT CHAPEL HILL—*cont'd*

dents. *Contact:* Cheryl Kemp, Director of Student Services, School of Education at: (919) 962-8693 or e-mail at: ckemp@email.unc.edu.

Accreditation: *Regional:* SACS. *Professional:* NCATE. *Member of:* AACTE. *Approved by:* North Carolina Department of Public Instruction.

Undergraduate Programs: The School of Education offers three undergraduate programs: child development and family studies (birth-kindergarten); elementary education (kindergarten-grade 6); middle grades education (grades 6-9). All are four-year programs with the junior and senior years spent in the School of Education. All programs require the completion of a general education core, professional studies, subject content area, field experiences, and student teaching. The programs lead to a Class A North Carolina teaching license.

Graduate Programs: The Master of Arts in Teaching program is for individuals wishing to obtain initial teaching licensure in secondary education (English, mathematics, science, social studies) and K-12 special subjects (French, German, Japanese, Spanish, music). The Master of Arts is offered with majors in school psychology or in education with research areas in culture, curriculum, and change; early childhood, families, and literacy studies, and educational psychology, measurement, and evaluation. The Master of Education is offered with majors in educational psychology, school counseling, and school psychology.

Doctor of Philosophy programs are offered through the Graduate School with majors in education and the Doctor of Education degree program with majors in curriculum and instruction and educational leadership.

Licensure/Reciprocity: North Carolina. Students seeking teaching certification in a state other than North Carolina should consult with that state's teacher certification office early in their program of study to insure compliance with requirements. Many state directors of teacher credentialing have signed Interstate Agreements through NASDTEC that expedite the certification process.

UNIVERSITY OF NORTH CAROLINA AT CHARLOTTE

College of Education
Teacher Education Programs

9201 University City Boulevard
Charlotte, North Carolina 28223-0001
Phone: (704) 687-2000
Fax: (704) 687-6483
E-mail: unccadm@email.uncc.edu
Internet: http://www.uncc.edu

Institution Description: The institution was established as the Charlotte Center of the University of North Carolina in 1946. The present name was adopted in 1965.

The School of Education offers undergraduate and graduate programs leading to teacher licensure in North Carolina.

Institution Control: Public.

Calendar: Semester. Academic year August to May.

Official(s): Dr. Mary Lynne Calhoun, Dean.

Faculty: Full-time 84 (all departments).

Degrees Awarded: 210 baccalaureate; 222 master's.

Admission Requirements: *Undergraduate:* Graduation from an accredited secondary school with 16 academic units or GED; College Board SAT or ACT composite. *Teacher education specific:* Admittance after sophomore year; commitment to teaching profession; academic progress; passing scores on PRAXIS I exams (reading, writing, mathematics); faculty interview. *Graduate:* Baccalaureate degree from a regionally accredited institution. *Teacher education specific:* GRE; competitive GPA; recommendations; goal statement; licensure intent.

Fees and Expenses: Undergraduate: $3,105 in-state per academic year; $13,142 out-of-state. Graduate: $4,043 in-state per academic year; $15,692 out-of-state. On-campus room and board: $6,620. Other expenses: $5,000. Books and supplies: $900,

Financial Aid: Resources specifically for eligible students enrolled in teacher education programs are awarded on the basis of financial need and academic merit. The institution has a Program Participation Agreement with the U.S. Department of Education for eligible students to receive Pell Grants and other federal aid. Teacher scholarships available to qualifying students. *Contact:* Financial Aid Office at: (704) 687-2461.

Accreditation: *Regional:* SACS. *Professional:* NCATE. *Member of:* AACTE. *Approved by:* North Carolina Department of Public Instruction.

Undergraduate Programs: All of the following programs lead to a baccalaureate degree and/or a Class A teaching license: child and family development; birth to kindergarten education; elementary education K-6; middle grades education 6-9 with concentrations in language/communication skills, mathematics, science, social studies; secondary education 9-12 with subject concentrations in English, history, comprehensive social studies, mathematics, biology, chemistry, earth sciences, physics, comprehensive science; special education K-12 with a concentration in mental handicaps; foreign languages K-12 in French, German, Spanish; fine and performing arts; K-12 in art education, dance education, music education, theatre arts education.

All programs require the completion of a general education core, professional studies, subject content area, field experiences, and student teaching. A minimum of 120 semester hours must be completed for the degree award.

Graduate Programs: All master's programs lead to a Master of Education, Master of Arts and/or a teaching license. They include: elementary education K-6; middle grades education 6-9; secondary education 9-12; special education K-12 with concentrations in mental handicaps, behavioral-emotional handicaps, severe-profound handicaps, learning disabilities, cross-categorical disabilities, academically gifted; reading, language, and literacy K-12; teaching English as a second language K-12; instructional systems technology K-12; counseling with concentrations in school counseling and community counseling; educational administration K-12 with concentration in school administration and educational leadership

Licensure/Reciprocity: North Carolina. Students seeking teaching certification in a state other than North Carolina should consult with that state's teacher certification office early in their program of study to insure compliance with requirements. Many state directors of teacher credentialing have signed Interstate Agreements through NASDTEC that expedite the certification process.

UNIVERSITY OF NORTH CAROLINA AT GREENSBORO

School of Education
Department of Curriculum and Instruction

Curry Building, UNCG P.O. Box 26170
1000 Spring Garden Street
Greensboro, North Carolina 27402-6170
Phone: (336) 334-3433
Fax: (336) 334-4120
E-mail: soe@uncg.edu
Internet: http://www.uncg.edu

Institution Description: The institution was established and incorporated as State Normal and Industrial School for Women in 1891. The school adopted the present name in became coeducational in 1967.

The mission of the School of Education is to improve education, early childhood through older adulthood, in all educational settings.

Institution Control: Public.

Calendar: Semester. Academic year August to May.

Official(s): Dr. Dale H. Schunk, Dean.

Faculty: Full-time 55; part-time 14; adjunct 9 (all departments).

Degrees Awarded: 199 baccalaureate; 185 master's; 36 doctorate.

Admission Requirements: *Undergraduate:* Graduation from an accredited secondary school with 15 academic units or GED; College Board SAT or ACT composite. *Teacher education specific:* Admittance after sophomore year; commitment to teaching profession; academic progress; passing scores on PRAXIS I exams (reading, writing, mathematics); faculty interview. *Graduate:* Baccalaureate degree from a regionally accredited institution. *Teacher education specific:* GRE; competitive GPA; recommendations; goal statement; licensure intent.

Fees and Expenses: Undergraduate: $3,123 in-state per academic year; $14,016 out-of-state. Graduate: $4,043 in-state per academic year; $15,692 out-of-state. On-campus room and board: $4,960. Other expenses: $2,900. Books and supplies: $1,400.

Financial Aid: Resources specifically for eligible students enrolled in teacher education programs are awarded on the basis of financial need and academic merit. The institution has a Program Participation Agreement with the U.S. Department of Education for eligible students to receive Pell Grants and other federal aid. Teacher scholarships available to qualifying students. *Contact:* Financial Aid Office at: (336) 334-5702.

Accreditation: *Regional:* SACS. *Professional:* NCATE. *Member of:* AACTE. *Approved by:* North Carolina Department of Public Instruction.

Undergraduate Programs: The Department of Curriculum and Instruction houses two undergraduate programs leading to licensure for teaching and supervision. The elementary and middle grades education programs are offered in collaboration with Professional Development Schools in Guilford County. Students enter the program as juniors and become part of a student team for a two-year field-based program of internships and professional courses led by a faculty team leader. Each team has a focus that matches the faculty team leader's area of expertise. The programs lead to the baccalaureate degree and require the completion of the general education core before entering the teacher education program as juniors. A minimum of 122 semester hours must be completed for university degree awards.

Graduate Programs: The Master of Education in curriculum and instruction is offered with eleven concentrations: elementary, middle grades, instructional technology, social studies, science, Spanish, French, reading, English as a second language, mathematics, and chemistry. Each of the concentrations culminate with the development of an advanced competency portfolio that provides eligibility for candidates to earn advanced competency licensure.

Licensure/Reciprocity: North Carolina. Students seeking teaching certification in a state other than North Carolina should consult with that state's teacher certification office early in their program of study to insure compliance with requirements. Many state directors of teacher credentialing have signed Interstate Agreements through NASDTEC that expedite the certification process.

UNIVERSITY OF NORTH CAROLINA AT PEMBROKE

School of Education
Teacher Education Program
P.O. Box 1510
One Pembroke Drive
Pembroke, North Carolina 28372-1510
Phone: (910) 521-6221
Fax: (910) 521-6165
E-mail: teach@uncp.edu
Internet: http://www.uncp.edu

Institution Description: The University of North Carolina at Pembroke was formerly known as Pembroke State University. It was established in 1887.

The Teacher Education Program is a cross-disciplinary program governed by the Teacher Education Committee and administered by the Dean, School of Education.

Institution Control: Public.

Calendar: Semester. Academic year August to May.

Official(s): Dr. Warren Baker, Dean.

Faculty: Full-time 35.

Degrees Awarded: 66 baccalaureate; 95 master's.

Admission Requirements: *Undergraduate:* Graduation from an accredited secondary school or GED; College Board SAT or ACT composite. *Teacher education specific:* Admittance after sophomore year; commitment to teaching profession; academic progress; passing scores on PRAXIS I exams (reading, writing, mathematics); faculty interview. *Graduate:* Baccalaureate degree from a regionally accredited institution. *Teacher education specific:* GRE; competitive GPA; two copies of transcripts; three recommendations; goal statement; licensure intent.

Fees and Expenses: Undergraduate: $2,565 in-state per academic year; $11,930 out-of-state. Graduate: $4,043 in-state per academic year; $15,692 out-of-state. On-campus room and board: $4,364. Other expenses: $2,612. Books and supplies: $800.

Financial Aid: Resources specifically for eligible students enrolled in teacher education programs are awarded on the basis of financial need and academic merit. The institution has a Program Participation Agreement with the U.S. Department of Education for eligible students to receive Pell Grants and other federal aid. Teacher scholarships available to qualifying students. *Contact:* Financial Aid Office at: (910) 521-6255, ext. 6255.

Accreditation: *Regional:* SACS. *Professional:* NCATE. *Member of:* AACTE. *Approved by:* North Carolina Department of Public Instruction.

Undergraduate Programs: Undergraduate licensure programs leading to the baccalaureate degree include: art education, biology education, birth-kindergarten, elementary education, English education, exceptional children, mathematics education, middle grades education, music education, physical education, science education, social studies education. The program of study for teacher education majors is comprised of four components: general education, specialty area (major), professional studies, and content pedagogy. The culminating professional development experience is the senior internship (student teaching) under the direct supervision of a master teacher in a clinical setting. A minimum of 128 semester hours is required for the university degree award.

Graduate Programs: The Master of Arts degree offered by the School of Graduate Studies includes: art education, English education, mathematics education, music education, physical education, school counseling, science education, service agency counseling, and social studies education. The Master of Arts in Education degree is offered in: elementary education, middle grades education, and reading education. All programs require the completion of a specified plan of study.

Licensure/Reciprocity: North Carolina. Students seeking teaching certification in a state other than North Carolina should consult with that state's teacher certification office early in their program of study to insure compliance with requirements. Many state directors of teacher credentialing have signed Interstate Agreements through NASDTEC that expedite the certification process.

UNIVERSITY OF NORTH CAROLINA AT WILMINGTON

Watson School of Education
601 South College Road
Wilmington, North Carolina 28403-3297
Phone: (910) 962-4142
Fax: (910) 962-3609
E-mail: thomasscc@uncwil.edu
Internet: http://www.uncwil.edu

UNIVERSITY OF NORTH CAROLINA AT WILMINGTON—*cont'd*

Institution Description: The institution was established as Wilmington College in 1947. The present name was adopted in 1969 when it became a campus of the University of North Carolina.

The Watson School of Education is a community of scholars dedicated to teaching, creating, and extending knowledge through research. Its mission is to produce teachers and administrators for the public school and who are effective decision makers and reflective practitioners.

Institution Control: Public.

Calendar: Semester. Academic year August to May.

Official(s): Dr. Cathy Barlow, Dean; Dr. Mary Ann Davies, Chair, Department of Curricular Studies; Dr. John Frischetti, Chair, Department of Specialty Studies.

Faculty: Not reported

Degrees Awarded: 260 baccalaureate; 52 master's.

Admission Requirements: *Undergraduate:* Graduation from an accredited secondary school or GED; College Board SAT or ACT composite. *Teacher education specific:* Admittance after sophomore year; commitment to teaching profession; academic progress; passing scores on PRAXIS I exams (reading, writing, mathematics); faculty interview. *Graduate:* Baccalaureate degree from a regionally accredited institution. *Teacher education specific:* GRE; competitive GPA; two copies of transcripts; three recommendations; goal statement; licensure intent.

Fees and Expenses: Undergraduate: $3,362 in-state per academic year; $12,937 out-of-state. Graduate: $4,043 in-state per academic year; $15,692 out-of-state. On-campus room and board: $5,578. Other expenses: $2,116. Books and supplies: $775.

Financial Aid: Resources specifically for eligible students enrolled in teacher education programs are awarded on the basis of financial need and academic merit. The institution has a Program Participation Agreement with the U.S. Department of Education for eligible students to receive Pell Grants and other federal aid. Teacher scholarships available to qualifying students. *Contact:* Financial Aid Office at: (910) 5962-3177.

Accreditation: *Regional:* SACS. *Professional:* NCATE. *Member of:* AACTE. *Approved by:* North Carolina Department of Public Instruction.

Undergraduate Programs: Undergraduate degree programs offered by the School of Education include: education of young children, elementary education, middle grades education, special education, behavioral disorders, learning disabilities, and mental retardation.

Licensure programs include: English, foreign language (French, Spanish), mathematics, physical education, science, social studies, science, social studies,

All programs require the completion of a general education core, professional studies, subject content area, field experiences, and student teaching. A minimum of 124 semester hours must be successfully completed for the degree award.

Graduate Programs: The Master of Education degree programs are offered in elementary education, curriculum/instruction studies, language and literacy, middle grades education, secondary education, and special education. The programs in these areas address the need for conceptual and procedural foundations for decision making and for specific alternatives within the student's area of professional practice.

The Master of Arts in Teaching degree program is designed for individuals who have degrees in English, history, mathematics, or science, but have not earned teacher licensure. The program includes coursework in pedagogy, academic discipline, and an internship.

Licensure/Reciprocity: North Carolina. Students seeking teaching certification in a state other than North Carolina should consult with that state's teacher certification office early in their program of study to insure compliance with requirements. Many state directors of teacher credentialing have signed Interstate Agreements through NASDTEC that expedite the certification process.

WAKE FOREST UNIVERSITY

Department of Education
P.O. Box 7266
Winston-Salem, North Carolina 27109
Phone: (336) 758-5341
Fax: (336) 758-4591
E-mail: milner@wfu.edu
Internet: http:www.wfu.edu

Institution Description: Wake Forest University is a private institution. It was founded in 1834 as Wake Forest Institute by the Baptist State Convention of North Carolina. The school relocated from Wake Forest to Winston-Salem in 1956. The present name was adopted in 1967.

The Department of Education offers programs leading to teacher licensure in North Carolina. The department offers a wide range of professional courses and supervised internships appropriate to the professional development of students.

Institution Control: Private.

Calendar: Semester. Academic year August to May.

Official(s): Dr. Joseph D. Milner, Chair.

Faculty: Full-time 11; part-time 1; adjunct 6.

Degrees Awarded: 11 baccalaureate; 41 master's.

Admission Requirements: *Undergraduate:* Graduation from an accredited secondary school with 16 academic units or GED; College Board SAT or ACT composite. *Teacher education specific:* 2.5 GPA; admittance after sophomore year; passing scores on PRAXIS I exams (reading, writing, mathematics); faculty interview. *Graduate:* Baccalaureate degree from a regionally accredited institution. *Teacher education specific:* GRE; 3 letters of recommendation; 3.25 GPA; transcripts; teaching licensure when required by program pursued.

Fees and Expenses: Undergraduate: $24,750. Graduate: $22,200. On-campus room and board: $6,760. Books and supplies: $800.

Financial Aid: Resources specifically for eligible students enrolled in teacher education programs are awarded on the basis of financial need and academic merit. The institution has a Program Participation Agreement with the U.S. Department of Education for eligible students to receive Pell Grants and other federal aid. Teacher scholarships available to qualifying students. *Contact:* Financial Aid Office at: (336) 758-5154.

Accreditation: *Regional:* SACS. *Professional:* NCATE. *Member of:* AACTE. *Approved by:* North Carolina Department of Public Instruction.

Undergraduate Programs: Prospective elementary and secondary social studies teachers earn licensure in those broad areas and major in education. Prospective secondary teachers of English, Latin, mathematics, science, and prospective K-12 teachers of foreign languages major in that discipline and minor in education. A minor in secondary social studies education is also available. In addition to the professional program, the department provides elective courses open to all students. All programs lead to the baccalaureate degree and require the completion of a general education core, professional studies, subject content area, field experiences, and student teaching.

Graduate Programs: The Master Teacher Fellow Program is for students who have completed undergraduate degrees without entering teacher education courses and prepares them to teach through thirteen months of intensive academic coursework and heavy field experience. At the completion of the program, Fellow will have earned a Master of Arts in Education degree and a North Carolina teaching license for grades 9-12 (grades K-12 for second language).

The Master Teacher Associates Program is for students who are licensed and experienced teachers. It includes coursework and other requirements to foster extension of the candidate's development in instructional expertise, knowledge of learners, research expertise, connecting subject matter and learners, and professional development and leadership.

Licensure/Reciprocity: North Carolina. Students seeking teaching certification in a state other than North Carolina should consult with that state's teacher certification office early in their program of study to insure compliance with requirements.

Many state directors of teacher credentialing have signed Interstate Agreements through NASDTEC that expedite the certification process.

WESTERN CAROLINA UNIVERSITY
College of Education and Allied Professions
222 Killian Building
Cullowhee, North Carolina 28723
Phone: (828) 227-7311
Fax: (828) 227-7388
E-mail: cdougherty@wcu.edu
Internet: http://www.wcu.edu

Institution Description: The school was established in 1889 and became the Cullowhee Normal and Industrial School in 1905. The school became Western Carolina Teachers College and a four-year institution in 1929. The name was changed to Western Carolina College in 1953 and the present name was adopted in 1967.

The Department of Birth-Kindergarten, Elementary, and Middle Grades Education (BKEMGE) offers baccalaureate degrees leading to teacher certification.

Institution Control: Public.

Calendar: Semester. Academic year August to May.

Official(s): Dr. A. Michael Dougherty, Dean.

Faculty: Not reported.

Degrees Awarded: 179 baccalaureate; 122 master's; 7 doctorate.

Admission Requirements: *Undergraduate:* Graduation from an accredited secondary school or GED; College Board SAT. *Teacher education specific:* Admittance after sophomore year; commitment to teaching profession; academic progress; passing scores on PRAXIS I exams (reading, writing, mathematics); faculty interview. *Graduate:* Baccalaureate degree from a regionally accredited institution. *Teacher education specific:* GRE; competitive GPA; two copies of transcripts; three recommendations; goal statement; licensure when required by program pursued.

Fees and Expenses: Undergraduate: $2,606 in-state per academic year; $12,167 out-of-state. Graduate: $4,043 in-state per academic year; $15,692 out-of-state. On-campus room and board: $4,406. Other expenses: $2,474. Books and supplies: $800.

Financial Aid: Resources specifically for eligible students enrolled in teacher education programs are awarded on the basis of financial need and academic merit. The institution has a Program Participation Agreement with the U.S. Department of Education for eligible students to receive Pell Grants and other federal aid. Teacher scholarships available to qualifying students. *Contact:* Financial Aid Office at: (828) 227-7290.

Accreditation: *Regional:* SACS. *Professional:* NCATE. *Member of:* AACTE. *Approved by:* North Carolina Department of Public Instruction.

Undergraduate Programs: Undergraduate programs offered include the Bachelor of Science in Education degrees in elementary education and middle grades education. The birth-kindergarten education program is a recent addition to the undergraduate program. All programs lead to licensure and require the completion of a general education core, professional studies, subject content area, field experiences, and student teaching. A minimum of 120 semester hours must be completed for the university degree award. addition to the under

Graduate Programs: Programs leading to the Master of Arts in Education require a minimum of 30 to 48 semester hours of study. Comprehensive examinations must be passed in major and minor fields. Fields of concentration include elementary education, middle grades education (6-9);, and reading education (K-12). The Master of Arts in Teaching is for students with an undergraduate degree in a major area in which they wish to teach. The area of concentration is middle grades education and leads to initial licensure in North Carolina.

Licensure/Reciprocity: North Carolina. Students seeking teaching certification in a state other than North Carolina should consult with that state's teacher certification office early in their program of study to insure compliance with requirements.

Many state directors of teacher credentialing have signed Interstate Agreements through NASDTEC that expedite the certification process.

WINGATE UNIVERSITY
Thayer School of Education
Teacher Education Program
P.O. Box 159
Wingate, North Carolina 28174-01579
Phone: (704) 233-8000
Fax: (704) 233-8110
E-mail: admit@wingate.edu
Internet: http://www.wingate.edu

Institution Description: Wingate University is a private college affiliated with the Baptist State Convention of North Carolina. It was established in 1923.

The teacher education is offered within a curriculum that brings together a liberal arts education, values/ethics education, teacher behavior education, and adaptive teaching education.

Institution Control: Private.

Calendar: Semester. Academic year August to May.

Official(s): Dr. Sarah Harrison-Burns, Dean.

Faculty: Full-time 9,

Degrees Awarded: 17 baccalaureate; 9 master's.

Admission Requirements: *Undergraduate:* Graduation from an accredited secondary school with 16 academic units or GED; College Board SAT or ACT composite. *Teacher education specific:* Passing scores on PRAXIS I exams (reading, writing, mathematics); 2.5 GPA; faculty interview. *Graduate:* Baccalaureate degree from a regionally accredited institution. *Teacher education specific:* GRE; competitive GPA; transcripts; three recommendations; goal statement; licensure when required by program pursued.

Fees and Expenses: $14,200 per academic year. Graduate: Tuition charged per academic year. On-campus room and board: $6,000. Other expenses: $1,700. Books and supplies: $800.

Financial Aid: Resources specifically for eligible students enrolled in teacher education programs are awarded on the basis of financial need and academic merit. The institution has a Program Participation Agreement with the U.S. Department of Education for eligible students to receive Pell Grants and other federal aid. Teacher scholarships available to qualifying students. *Contact:* Financial Aid Office at: (704) 233-8209.

Accreditation: *Regional:* SACS. *Professional:* NCATE. *Member of:* AACTE. *Approved by:* North Carolina Department of Public Instruction.

Undergraduate Programs: The Thayer School of Education offers degrees in: art and education (K-12), biology and education (9-12); elementary education (K-6), English and education (9-12), history and education (9-12 social studies), mathematics and education (9-12), middle grades education (6-9 language arts, science, social studies, mathematics), music education (K-12), physical education (K-12), reading/elementary education (K-12 reading, K-6 elementary). Students take a core of required courses in the selected area of emphasis as well as the general education core and required education courses. A minimum of 125 credit hours must be completed for the degree award.

Graduate Programs: The Master of Arts in Teaching and the Master of Education degree programs are offered to qualified candidates. All programs require the completion of specified courses and other requirements. Contact the Thayer School of Education for further information.

Licensure/Reciprocity: North Carolina. Students seeking teaching certification in a state other than North Carolina should consult with that state's teacher certification office early in their program of study to insure compliance with requirements. Many state directors of teacher credentialing have signed Interstate Agreements through NASDTEC that expedite the certification process.

WINSTON-SALEM STATE UNIVERSITY
School of Education
601 Martin Luther King, Jr. Drive
Winston-Salem, North Carolina 27110-0001
Phone: (336) 750-2736
Fax: (336) 750-2375
E-mail: vargasm@wssu.edu
Internet: http://www.wssu.edu

Institution Description: The institution was established in 1892. It became Winston-Salem Teachers College in 1925 and the name was changed to Winston-Salem State College in 1963. The present name was adopted in 1969.

The mission of the Department of Education is the preparation of knowledgeable, ethical, and effective teachers.

Institution Control: Public.

Calendar: Semester. Academic year August to May.

Official(s): Dr. Manuel Vargas, Chairperson, Department of Education.

Faculty: Full-time 13; adjunct 13.

Degrees Awarded: 20 bachelor's; 5 master's.

Admission Requirements: *Undergraduate:* Graduation from an accredited secondary school or GED; College Board SAT preferred; ACT composite accepted. *Teacher education specific:* Admittance after sophomore year; commitment to teaching profession; academic progress; passing scores on PRAXIS I exams (reading, writing, mathematics); faculty interview. *Graduate:* Baccalaureate degree from a regionally accredited institution. *Teacher education specific:* GRE; competitive GPA; two copies of transcripts; three recommendations; goal statement; licensure when required by program pursued.

Fees and Expenses: Undergraduate: $2,394 in-state per academic year; $10,659 out-of-state. Graduate: $4,043 in-state per academic year; $15,692 out-of-state. On-campus room and board: $4,892. Other expenses: $2,500. Books and supplies: $1,000.

Financial Aid: Resources specifically for eligible students enrolled in teacher education programs are awarded on the basis of financial need and academic merit. The institution has a Program Participation Agreement with the U.S. Department of Education for eligible students to receive Pell Grants and other federal aid. Teacher scholarships available to qualifying students. *Contact:* Financial Aid Office at: (336) 750-3280.

Accreditation: *Regional:* SACS. *Professional:* NCATE. *Member of:* AACTE. *Approved by:* North Carolina Department of Public Instruction.

Undergraduate Programs: The Department of Education offers programs leading to the Bachelor of Science degree in birth-kindergarten, elementary, middle grades, and special education. The department provides professional courses for all teacher education programs. In addition, the program provides experiences through directed observation, participation in observation, and student teaching under the guidance of experienced cooperating teachers and university professors. Students must complete a general education core and a subject content area. Students who complete requirements for baccalaureate degrees with satisfactory performance in examinations also satisfy the requirements for licensure as outlined by the North Carolina State Department of Public Instruction.

Graduate Programs: The Master of Education in elementary education is a 36-credit hour program with 21 credit hours in the teaching field. The program is structured on a part-time basis to facilitate immediate application in the elementary classroom. The program is designed to deepen the knowledge base, teaching skills, and enrich the disposition of graduates.

Licensure/Reciprocity: North Carolina. Students seeking teaching certification in a state other than North Carolina should consult with that state's teacher certification office early in their program of study to insure compliance with requirements. Many state directors of teacher credentialing have signed Interstate Agreements through NASDTEC that expedite the certification process.

NORTH DAKOTA

DICKINSON STATE UNIVERSITY

School of Education, Business, and Applied sciences
Department of Teacher Education
290 Campus Drive
Dickinson, North Dakota 58601
Phone: (701) 483-2331
Fax: (701) 483-2409
E-mail: admissions@dickinsonstate.edu
Internet: http://www.dickinsonstate.edu

Institution Description: Dickinson State University is a regional four-year institution within the North Dakota University System. It was established in 1918.

The primary goal of the Department of Teacher Education is to prepare competent, dedicated, caring teachers to provide educational leadership for young people.

Institution Control: Public.

Calendar: Semester. Academic year August to May.

Official(s): Dr. Gary Jacobson, Chair, Department of Teacher Education.

Faculty: Full-time 8.

Degrees Awarded: 75 baccalaureate.

Admission Requirements: *Undergraduate:* Graduation from an accredited secondary school or GED. *Teacher education specific.* Completion of a minimum of 21 semester hours) pre pro fessional experience; overall 2.5 GPA; passing score on PRAXIS I exams (reading, writing, mathematics); departmental approval.

Fees and Expenses: Undergraduate: in-state $3,138 per academic year; out-of-state $7,404. On-campus room and board: $3,350. Books and supplies: $700.

Financial Aid: Resources specifically for eligible students enrolled in teacher education programs are awarded on the basis of financial need and academic merit. The institution has a Program Participation Agreement with the U.S. Department of Education for eligible students to receive Pell Grants and other federal aid. Teacher scholarships available to qualifying students. *Contact:* Financial Aid Office at: (701) 483-2371.

Accreditation: *Regional:* NCA. *Professional:* NCATE. *Member of:* AACTE. *Approved by:* North Dakota Department of Public Instruction.

Undergraduate Programs: The degree programs offered include the Bachelor of Science in Education in elementary education with concentrations in kindergarten and reading. The secondary professional education program leads to the Bachelor of Science in Education with a middle school endorsement. A minor is available in psychology.

All baccalaureate programs require the completion of a general education core, professional studies, subject content area, field experiences, and student teaching. A minimum of 128 semester hours is required for the degree award.

Licensure/Reciprocity: North Dakota. Students seeking teaching certification in a state other than North Dakota should consult with that state's teacher certification office early in their program of study to insure compliance with requirements. Many state directors of teacher credentialing have signed Interstate Agreements through NASDTEC that expedite the certification process.

MAYVILLE STATE UNIVERSITY

Division of Teacher Education
330 Third Street N.E.
Mayville, North Dakota 58257
Phone: (701) 788-4829
Fax: (701) 788-4890
E-mail: Nannette_Bagstad@@mail.masu.nodak.edu
Internet: http://www.masu.nodak.edu

Institution Description: Mayville State University is a member of the North Dakota University System. It was established and chartered as Mayville Normal School in 1889.

The Division of Teacher Education offers undergraduate programs leading to teacher certification in North Dakota.

Institution Control: Public.

Calendar: Semester. Academic year August to May.

Official(s): Dr. Nannette Bagstad, Division Head,

Faculty: Full-time 8, part-time 1; adjunct 3.

Degrees Awarded: 28 baccalaureate.

Admission Requirements: *Undergraduate:* Graduation from an accredited secondary school or GED; College Board SAT or ACT composite. *Teacher education specific:* 2.5 GPA; writing sample; electronic portfolio; passing scores on PRAXIS I exams (reading, writing, mathematics); faculty interview.

Fees and Expenses: Undergraduate: in-state $3,138 per academic year; out-of-state $7,404. On-campus room and board: $3,350. Books and supplies: $700.

Financial Aid: Resources specifically for eligible students enrolled in teacher education programs are awarded on the basis of financial need and academic merit. The institution has a Program Participation Agreement with the U.S. Department of Education for eligible students to receive Pell Grants and other federal aid. Teacher scholarships available to qualifying students. *Contact:* Shirley Hanson at: (701) 788-4767 or e-mail at: S_Hanson@mail.masu.nodak.edu.

Accreditation: *Regional:* NCA. *Professional:* NCATE. *Member of:* AACTE. *Approved by:* North Dakota Department of Public Instruction.

Undergraduate Programs: The degree programs offered include the Bachelor of Science in Education in elementary education with concentrations in kindergarten and reading. The program leads to certification to teach grades 1-8. The secondary professional education program leads to the Bachelor of Science in Education and teaching certification for grades 7-12.

All baccalaureate programs require the completion of a general education core, professional studies, subject content area, field experiences, and student teaching. A minimum of 128 semester hours is required for the degree award.

Licensure/Reciprocity: North Dakota. Students seeking teaching certification in a state other than North Dakota should consult with that state's teacher certification office early in their program of study to insure compliance with requirements. Many state directors of teacher credentialing have signed Interstate Agreements through NASDTEC that expedite the certification process.

MINOT STATE UNIVERSITY

College of Education and Health Sciences
Teacher Education Programs
500 University Avenue, West
Minot, North Dakota 58707
Phone: (701) 858-3028
Fax: (701) 858-3591
E-mail: leslie@minotstateu.edu
Internet: http://www.minotstateu.edu

Institution Description: Minot State University is a member of the North Dakota University System. It was chartered as Northwestern Normal School and offered first instruction at the postsecondary level in 1913.

The undergraduate and graduate teacher education programs are offered in a variety of subject areas at the elementary, middle school, and secondary school levels.

Institution Control: Public.

Calendar: Semester. Academic year August to May.

Official(s): Dr. Neil Nordquist, Dean; Dr. Gary Leslie, Chair, Teacher Education Programs.

Faculty: Not reported.

Degrees Awarded: 107 baccalaureate; 12 master's.

Admission Requirements: *Undergraduate:* Graduation from an accredited secondary school or GED; College Board SAT or ACT composite. *Teacher education specific:* 2.5 GPA; writing sample; personal statement; completion of speech and hearing screenings; documentation of 20 clock hours of supervised activities with children or youth; passing scores on PRAXIS I exams (reading, writing, mathematics); faculty interview. *Graduate:* Baccalaureate degree from a regionally accredited institution. *Teacher education specific:* Personal goal statement; GRE or Miller Analogies Test scores; minimum 3.0 GPA; faculty interview.

Fees and Expenses: Undergraduate: in-state $3,228 per academic year; out-of-state $7,404. On-campus room and board: $3,374. Other expenses: $3,050. Books and supplies: $750.

Financial Aid: Resources specifically for eligible students enrolled in teacher education programs are awarded on the basis of financial need and academic merit. The institution has a Program Participation Agreement with the U.S. Department of Education for eligible students to receive Pell Grants and other federal aid. Teacher scholarships available to qualifying students. *Contact:* Financial Aid Office at: (701) 858-3375

Accreditation: *Regional:* NCA. *Professional:* NCATE. *Member of:* AACTE. *Approved by:* North Dakota Department of Public Instruction.

Undergraduate Programs: Baccalaureate programs are offered in the areas of art education, business education, communication arts, education of the deaf, English education, foreign language, mathematics, music, physical science, psychology, biology, chemistry, earth science, elementary education, environmental science, history, mental retardation education, physical education, physics, social science. All programs require the completion of a general education core, professional studies, subject content area, field experiences, and student teaching. A minimum of 128 semester hours is required for the degree award.

Graduate Programs: The Master of Education program consists of a minimum of 30 semester hours of graduate credit with a required core of 16 semester hours. The elective component may reflect the needs of a particular discipline that would be reflected on the transcript and may be a continuation of graduate coursework acceptable to the Department Chair. The objectives of the program are to develop skills of scholarship and research, to increase professional competence in instructional strategies and curriculum development, and to develop perceptions of the characteristics and unique needs of the students' schools.

Licensure/Reciprocity: North Dakota. Students seeking teaching certification in a state other than North Dakota should consult with that state's teacher certification office early in their program of study to insure compliance with requirements.

Many state directors of teacher credentialing have signed Interstate Agreements through NASDTEC that expedite the certification process.

NORTH DAKOTA STATE UNIVERSITY

School of Education
Teacher Education Programs
210 FLC
1301 Twelfth Avenue North
Fargo, North Dakota 58105
Phone: (701) 231-7104
Fax: (701) 231-7416
E-mail: jim.wigtil@ndsu.nodak.edu
Internet: http://www.ndsu.nodak.edu

Institution Description: North Dakota State University is a state institution and land-grant college with a branch campus at Bottineau. The institution was established in 1890.

The Council for Teacher Education is the body within the School of Education with jurisdiction over such matters as admission, retention, student teaching, and certification.

Institution Control: Public.

Calendar: Semester. Academic year August to May.

Official(s): Dr. Virginia Clark Johnson, Dean; Dr. James Wigtil, Chair, Teacher Education Programs.

Faculty: Full-time 15; adjunct 8.

Degrees Awarded: 68 baccalaureate; 54 master's.

Admission Requirements: *Undergraduate:* Graduation from an accredited secondary school with 15 academic units or GED; College Board SAT or ACT composite. *Teacher education specific:* Application to program during or immediately following the introductory professional education course; personal statement; minimum scores on PRAXIS I exams (reading, writing, mathematics); faculty interview. *Graduate:* Baccalaureate degree from a regionally accredited institution. *Teacher education specific:* Personal goal statement; GRE or Miller Analogies Test scores; minimum 3.0 GPA; faculty interview.

Fees and Expenses: Undergraduate: in-state $3,228 per academic year; out-of-state $7, 404. On-campus room and board: $3,400. Other expenses: $3,100. Books and supplies: $700.

Financial Aid: Resources specifically for eligible students enrolled in teacher education programs are awarded on the basis of financial need and academic merit. The institution has a Program Participation Agreement with the U.S. Department of Education for eligible students to receive Pell Grants and other federal aid. Teacher scholarships available to qualifying students. *Contact:* Financial Aid Office at: (701) 231-7104.

Accreditation: *Regional:* NCA. *Professional:* NCATE. *Member of:* AACTE. *Approved by:* North Dakota Department of Public Instruction.

Undergraduate Programs: Teaching majors offered by the School of Education and leading to certification include: agricultural education, biological sciences, chemistry, comprehensive science, English, family and consumer sciences, French, earth science, German, history, mathematics, instrumental and vocal music, physical education, physics, social science, sociology, Spanish, speech communication. All programs require the completion of a general education core, professional studies, subject content area, field experiences, and student teaching. A minimum of 128 semester hours is required for the degree award.

Graduate Programs: The graduate level program in teacher education focuses on the development of educational leaders and is designed for the practitioner. Programs lead to the Master of Education or the Master of Science degree. Plans of study for either degree may emphasize curriculum and design or a wide range of education disciplines. Master programs include: agricultural education, curriculum and instruction, curriculum design, English education, family and consumer sciences education, health/physical education/recreation, history, mathematics, music, science education.

Licensure/Reciprocity: North Dakota. Students seeking teaching certification in a state other than North Dakota should consult with that state's teacher certification office early in their program of study to insure compliance with requirements. Many state directors of teacher credentialing have signed Interstate Agreements through NASDTEC that expedite the certification process.

TRINITY BIBLE COLLEGE

Elementary Education Department

50 South 6th Avenue
Ellendale, North Dakota 58436-7105
Phone: (701) 349-5760
Fax: (701) 349-5443
E-mail: hphoenix@trinitybiblecollege.edu
Internet: http://www.trinitybiblecollege.edu

Institution Description: Trinity Bible College is a private institution affiliated with the Assembly of God.

The elementary education major is combined with the biblical studies major to prepare certified, competent elementary school teachers for public, private, and Christian schools.

Institution Control: Private.

Calendar: Semester. Academic year August to May.

Official(s): Hal Phoenix, Department Head.

Faculty: Full-time 3.

Degrees Awarded: 6 baccalaureate.

Admission Requirements: *Undergraduate:* Graduation from an accredited secondary school or GED; College Board SAT or ACT composite. *Teacher education specific:* Successful completion of foundations of education course; cumulative GPA of 2.5; acceptable scores on PRAXIS I exams (reading, writing, mathematics; faculty interview.

Fees and Expenses: $8,080 per academic year. Required fees: $2,178. On-campus room and board: $4,222.

Financial Aid: Resources specifically for eligible students enrolled in teacher education programs are awarded on the basis of financial need and academic merit. The institution has a Program Participation Agreement with the U.S. Department of Education for eligible students to receive Pell Grants and other federal aid. Teacher scholarships available to qualifying students. *Contact:* Director of Student Aid at: (701) 349-5760.

Accreditation: *Regional:* NCA. *Professional:* Association of Bible Colleges. *Approved by:* North Dakota Department of Public Instruction.

Undergraduate Programs: Students are prepared in the knowledge and skills of elementary school teaching within a framework of Christian attitudes and principles. Upon successful completion of the program, students will be eligible to receive teaching certificates from the state of North Dakota and the Association of Christian Schools International. The program includes a double major: elementary education and biblical studies. It requires completion of a general education core, professional education, content area, field experiences, and student teaching. A total of 136 credits must be completed for the Bachelor of Arts degree.

Licensure/Reciprocity: North Dakota. Students seeking teaching certification in a state other than North Dakota should consult with that state's teacher certification office early in their program of study to insure compliance with requirements. Many state directors of teacher credentialing have signed Interstate Agreements through NASDTEC that expedite the certification process.

UNIVERSITY OF NORTH DAKOTA

Department of Teaching and Learning

Box 7189, UND
University Station
Grand Forks, North Dakota 58202-8135
Phone: (701) 777-3239
Fax: (701) 777-3246
E-mail: shelby_barrentine@und.nodak.edu
Internet: http://www.und.nodak.edu

Institution Description: University of North Dakota is a state institution. It was established and chartered as the University of North Dakota in 1883.

The Department of Teaching and Learning offers degree programs at the undergraduate level. Graduate programs are housed in three departments: Educational Foundations and Research, Educational Leadership, and Teaching and Learning.

Institution Control: Public.

Calendar: Semester. Academic year August to May.

Official(s): Dr. Shelby Barrentine, Department Head; Dr. Margaret Shaeffer, Director of Teaching Education.

Faculty: Full-time 22; part-time 1; adjunct 10.

Degrees Awarded: 175 baccalaureate; 124 master's; 23 doctorate.

Admission Requirements: *Undergraduate:* Graduation from an accredited secondary school with completion of core curriculum or GED; College Board SAT or ACT composite. *Teacher education specific:* 2.75 GPA; completed disposition form; passing scores on PRAXIS I exams (reading, writing, mathematics; faculty interview. *Graduate:* Baccalaureate degree from a regionally accredited institution. *Teacher education specific:* Transcripts; three favorable recommendations; faculty interview.

Fees and Expenses: Undergraduate: in-state $3,441 per academic year; out-of-state $9,860. Graduate: in-state $3,703 per academic year; out-of-state $9,888. Required fees: $715. On-campus room and board: $4,180. Books and supplies: $700.

Financial Aid: Resources specifically for eligible students enrolled in teacher education programs are awarded on the basis of financial need and academic merit. The institution has a Program Participation Agreement with the U.S. Department of Education for eligible students to receive Pell Grants and other federal aid. Teacher scholarships available to qualifying students. *Contact:* Robin Holden, Director of Student Aid at: (701) 777-3121 or e-mail at: robin_holden@mail.und.nodak.edu.

Accreditation: *Regional:* NCA. *Professional:* NCATE. *Member of:* AACTE. *Approved by:* North Dakota Department of Public Instruction.

Undergraduate Programs: The Department of Teaching and Learning offers Bachelor of Science in Education degree programs in the preparation of early childhood, elementary, middle, and secondary school teachers. Students studying elementary education are also able to pursue specialized study resulting in a combined major in visual arts, early childhood education, physical education, middle level or mathematics.

At the secondary level students must, in addition to their professional coursework, concentrate in an area typically taught in the secondary school. The following areas of concentration are available: biology, business education, chemistry, English, fisheries and wildlife biology, French, geography, geology/earth science, German, industrial technology, marketing, mathematics, physics, science, social studies, Spanish, speech communications, visual arts.

All baccalaureate programs require the completion of a general education core, professional studies, subject content area, field experiences, and student teaching.

Graduate Programs: Programs offered at the master's and doctoral levels include: early childhood education (M.S.); educational leadership (M.Ed., M.S., Ed.S., Ed.D., Ph.D.); education-general studies (M.S.); elementary education (M.Ed., M.S.); reading education (M.Ed., M.S.); special education (M.Ed., M.S.); teaching and learning (Ed.D., Ph.D.).

UNIVERSITY OF NORTH DAKOTA—*cont'd*

Licensure/Reciprocity: North Dakota. Students seeking teaching certification in a state other than North Dakota should consult with that state's teacher certification office early in their program of study to insure compliance with requirements. Many state directors of teacher credentialing have signed Interstate Agreements through NASDTEC that expedite the certification process.

VALLEY CITY STATE UNIVERSITY

Division of Education and Psychology

101 College Street S.W.
Valley City, North Dakota 58072
Phone: (701) 845-7196
Fax: (701) 845-7101
E-mail: enrollment_services@mail.vcsu.nodak.edu
Internet: http://www.vcsu.edu

Institution Description: Valley City State University is a state institution. It was established as State Normal School in 1890. It became Valley City State College in 1963 and achieved university status in 1987.

The essential function of the Division of Education and Psychology is to provide the student who plans to teach with a solid foundation in education or psychology.

Institution Control: Public.

Calendar: Semester. Academic year August to May.

Official(s): Dr. Larry Grooters, Division Chair.

Faculty: Full-time 15.

Degrees Awarded: 114 baccalaureate.

Admission Requirements: *Undergraduate:* Graduation from an accredited secondary school with college preparatory credentials; College Board SAT or ACT composite. *Teacher education specific:* 2.75 GPA; passing cores on PRAXIS I exams (reading, writing, mathematics); personal goal essay; faculty interview.

Fees and Expenses: Undergraduate: in-state $4,026 per academic year; out-of-state $8,455. On-campus room and board: $3,254. Other expenses: $2,720. Books and supplies: $700.

Financial Aid: Resources specifically for eligible students enrolled in teacher education programs are awarded on the basis of financial need and academic merit. The institution has a Program Participation Agreement with the U.S. Department of Education for eligible students to receive Pell Grants and other federal aid. Teacher scholarships available to qualifying students. *Contact:* Financial Aid Office at: (701) 845-7412.

Accreditation: *Regional:* NCA. *Professional:* NCATE. *Member of:* AACTE. *Approved by:* North Dakota Department of Public Instruction.

Undergraduate Programs: The division offers majors and minors in the following fields of study: early childhood education (major), Bachelor of Science in Education; elementary education, (major), Bachelor of Science in Education; instructional technology, (major, minor), Bachelor of Arts, Bachelor of Science; professional education sequence, (middle level), Bachelor of Science in Education; professional education series, (secondary), Bachelor of Science in Education; psychology, (major, minor), Bachelor of Arts, Bachelor of Science; reading-elementary/secondary, (minor), Bachelor of Science in Education; technology education, (composite major, minor), Bachelor of Science in Education.

All programs require the completion of a general education core, professional studies, field experiences, subject content area, and student teaching. A minimum of 128 semester hours must be completed for the degree award.

Licensure/Reciprocity: North Dakota. Students seeking teaching certification in a state other than North Dakota should consult with that state's teacher certification office early in their program of study to insure compliance with requirements. Many state directors of teacher credentialing have signed Interstate Agreements through NASDTEC that expedite the certification process.

OHIO

ASHLAND UNIVERSITY
College of Education
Department of Curriculum and Instruction
210 Bixler Hall
401 College Avenue
Ashland, Ohio 44805
Phone: (419) 289-5052
Fax: (419) 289-5999
E-mail: auadmsn@ashland.edu
Internet: http://www.ashland.edu

Institution Description: Ashland University is a private liberal arts university. It was established in 1878 and has had an historical relationship with the Brethren Church.

The mission of the College of Education is to prepare preservice and practicing teachers, administrators, and human service professionals to impact positively on students, schools, and society.

Institution Control: Private.

Calendar: Semester. Academic year August to May.

Official(s): Dr. Frank Pettigrew, Director; Dr. James Van Keuren, Chair.

Faculty: Full-time 56.

Degrees Awarded: 198 baccalaureate; 642 master's; 5 doctorate.

Admission Requirements: *Undergraduate:* Graduation from an accredited secondary school or GED; College Board SAT or ACT composite. *Teacher education specific:* Application to the program after 60 semester hours have been completed; passing scores on PRAXIS I exams (reading, writing, mathematics); 2.5 GPA; goal statement; faculty interview. *Graduate: Teacher education specific:* Bachelor's degree from a regionally accredited institution; *Teacher education specific:* Demonstrated proficiency of oral, interpersonal, and written communication skills; faculty interview.

Fees and Expenses: Undergraduate: $17,982 per academic year. Graduate: Tuition charged per credit hour. On-campus room and board: $6,632. Other expenses: $2,423. Books and supplies: $800.

Financial Aid: Resources specifically for eligible students enrolled in teacher education programs are awarded on the basis of financial need and academic merit. The institution has a Program Participation Agreement with the U.S. Department of Education for eligible students to receive Pell Grants and other federal aid. Teacher scholarships available to qualifying students. *Contact:* Financial Aid Office at: (419) 289-5002.

Accreditation: *Regional:* SACS. *Professional:* NCATE. *Member of:* AACTE. *Approved by:* Ohio Department of Education.

Undergraduate Programs: The baccalaureate programs housed in the Department of Curriculum and Instruction include middle grades: language arts, mathematics, science, social studies; adolescent/young adult: chemistry, biology, earth science, physical science, integrated science, integrated language arts, integrated mathematics, integrated business, family and consumer science, multi-age, visual arts, foreign language, music, theatre. All programs lead to Ohio certification and require the completion of a general education core, professional studies, subject content area, field experiences, and student teaching.

Graduate Programs: The Bachelor's Plus Program is a graduate program designed to provide initial teaching licensure to people who hold bachelor's degrees in fields other than education. Programs that lead to licensure include: early childhood, middle grades 4-9; secondary grades 7-12; preK-12, vocational 7-12.

The Master of Education degree programs offered include: educational technology (computer technology endorsement); talent development (gifted); intervention specialist nIld/moderate; intervention specialist moderate/intensive; middle childhood education; economic education.

Licensure/Reciprocity: Ohio. Students seeking teaching certification in a state other than Ohio should consult with that state's teacher certification office early in their program of study to insure compliance with requirements. Many state directors of teacher credentialing have signed Interstate Agreements through NASDTEC that expedite the certification process.

BALDWIN-WALLACE COLLEGE
Division of Education
275 Eastland Road
Berea, Ohio 44017-2088
Phone: (440) 826-2166
Fax: (440) 826-3779
E-mail: kkaye@bw.edu
Internet: http://www.bw.edu

Institution Description: Baldwin-Wallace College is a private college affiliated with the United Methodist Church. It was established as Baldwin Institute in 1845.

The Division of Education offers undergraduate and graduate programs leading to teacher certification in Ohio.

Institution Control: Private.

Calendar: Semester. Academic year August to August.

Official(s): Dr. Karen Kaye, Division Head.

Faculty: Full-time 17; part-time 10; adjunct 70.

Degrees Awarded: 222 baccalaureate; 139 master's.

Admission Requirements: *Undergraduate:* Graduation from an accredited secondary school or GED; College Board SAT or ACT composite. *Teacher education specific:* Successfully complete 30 semester hours of college work; cumulative 2.6 GPA; PRAXIS I scores (reading, writing, mathematics); interpersonal skills; department interview. *Graduate:* Baccalaureate degree from a regionally accredited institution. *Teacher education specific:* Professional teaching certificate; teaching experience; cumulative 2.75 GPA; two letters of recommendation. PRAXIS II exams must be taken before graduation.

Fees and Expenses: Undergraduate: $17,432 per academic year. Graduate: $443 per semester hour. On-campus room and board: $5,282. Books and supplies: $740.

Financial Aid: Resources specifically for eligible students enrolled in teacher education programs are awarded on the basis of financial need and academic merit. The institution has a Program Participation Agreement with the U.S. Department of Education for eligible students to receive Pell Grants and other federal aid. Teacher scholarships available to qualifying students. *Contact:* Financial Aid Office at: (440) 826-2108.

Accreditation: *Regional:* SACS. *Professional:* NCATE. *Member of:* AACTE. *Approved by:* Ohio Department of Education.

BALDWIN-WALLACE COLLEGE—*cont'd*

Undergraduate Programs: Bachelor's level licensure programs are offered in: early childhood education, middle childhood education, adolescent young adult/multi-age education, intervention specialist (K-12) mild/moderate educational needs. Each program has unique course requirements. All programs require the completion of a general education core, professional studies, subject content area, field experiences, and student teaching.

Graduate Programs: The Master of Arts in Education program is designed to stimulate and guide early childhood, middle childhood, adolescent young adult and multi-age teachers toward professional competency and intellectual maturity, built upon a sound philosophy of education in a liberal arts setting. Degree specializations include: reading, mild/moderate educational needs, educational technology, and pre-administration. The programs require the completion of 33-35 semester hours.

Licensure/Reciprocity: Ohio. Students seeking teaching certification in a state other than Ohio should consult with that state's teacher certification office early in their program of study to insure compliance with requirements. Many state directors of teacher credentialing have signed Interstate Agreements through NASDTEC that expedite the certification process.

BLUFFTON COLLEGE
Education Department
Teacher Education Programs
280 West College Avenue
Bluffton, Ohio 45817-1196
Phone: (419) 358-3331
Fax: (419) 358-3074
E-mail: education@bluffton.edu
Internet: http://www.bluffton.edu

Institution Description: Bluffton College is a private college affiliated with the General Conference Mennonite Church. The college was established and chartered as Central Mennonite College in 1899.

The Teacher Education Programs include undergraduate and graduate licensure programs.

Institution Control: Private.

Calendar: Semester. Academic year August to May.

Official(s): Dr. Gayle Trollinger, Chairperson.

Faculty: Full-time 8; part-time 1; adjunct 8.

Degrees Awarded: 48 baccalaureate; 16 master's.

Admission Requirements: *Undergraduate:* Graduation from an accredited secondary school or GED; College Board SAT or ACT composite. *Teacher education specific:* Candidates must have completed basic education foundation courses; personal essay with goal ambition; 2.5 GPA; faculty recommendation; passing scores on PRAXIS I basic skills tests (reading, writing, mathematics. *Graduate: Teacher education specific:* Baccalaureate degree from a regionally accredited institution; 3.0 GPA; letters of recommendation; faculty approval.

Fees and Expenses: Undergraduate: $17,260 per academic year. Graduate: Tuition charged per semester hour. Required fees: $400 technology fee. On-campus room and board: $6,030. Books and supplies: $850.

Financial Aid: Resources specifically for eligible students enrolled in teacher education programs are awarded on the basis of financial need and academic merit. The institution has a Program Participation Agreement with the U.S. Department of Education for eligible students to receive Pell Grants and other federal aid. Teacher scholarships available to qualifying students. *Contact:* Lawrence Matthews at: (419) 358-3246 or e-mail at: Matthews@bluffton.edu.

Accreditation: *Regional:* NCA. *Member of:* AACTE. *Approved by:* Ohio Department of Education.

Undergraduate Programs: The undergraduate education department offers teacher education programs leading to licensure in: early childhood (pre-K through grade 3); middle childhood (grades 4-9); adolescence to young adult (grades 7-12) in integrated language arts, mathematics, social studies, life science, physical science); nulti-age (preK-12) in foreign language, health, music, physical education, visual arts; vocational (grades 4 and up) in family and consumer sciences; intervention specialist (grades K-12) in mild/moderate educational needs; endorsements in teaching English to speakers of other languages and technology. All programs require the completion of a general education core, professional studies, subject content area, field experiences, and student teaching.

Graduate Programs: The Master of Arts in Education program is designed for both secondary and elementary teachers. The three areas of concentration include liberal arts, intervention specialist (leading to an intervention specialist license) and technology (leading to a technology endorsement).

Licensure/Reciprocity: Ohio. Students seeking teaching certification in a state other than Ohio should consult with that state's teacher certification office early in their program of study to insure compliance with requirements. Many state directors of teacher credentialing have signed Interstate Agreements through NASDTEC that expedite the certification process.

BOWLING GREEN STATE UNIVERSITY
College of Education and Human Development
444 Education Building
Bowling Green, Ohio 43403-0001
Phone: (419) 372-7901
Fax: (419) 372-2828
E-mail: jcruz@bgnet.bgsu.edu
Internet: http://www.bgsu.edu

Institution Description: Bowling Green State University is a coeducational institution that was chartered as Bowling Green State Normal College in 1910.

The College of Education and Human Development focuses on educating professionals who will have a positive impact on the development of individuals, families, communities, schools, and other institutions in society.

Institution Control: Public.

Calendar: Semester. Academic year August to May.

Official(s): Dr. José Cruz, Dean.

Faculty: Full-time 127; part-time 122.

Degrees Awarded: 757 baccalaureate; 414 master's; 18 doctorate.

Admission Requirements: *Undergraduate:* Graduation from an accredited secondary school GED; College Board SAT or ACT composite. *Teacher education specific:* Varies by licensure area; writing sample; passing scores on PRAXIS I exams (reading, writing, mathematics); faculty recommendations. *Graduate:* Baccalaureate from a regionally accredited institution. *Teacher education specific:* Varies by program; references; faculty interview.

Fees and Expenses: Undergraduate: in-state $5,940 per academic year; $12,900 out-of-state. Graduate: in-state $8,116 per academic year; out-of-state $15,076. Required fees: $1,188. On-campus room and board: $6,400. Books and supplies: $500.

Financial Aid: Resources specifically for eligible students enrolled in teacher education programs are awarded on the basis of financial need and academic merit. The institution has a Program Participation Agreement with the U.S. Department of Education for eligible students to receive Pell Grants and other federal aid. Teacher scholarships available to qualifying students. *Contact:* Song Zulch-Smit at: (419) 372-7309 or e-mail at: szulchs@bgnet.bgsu.edu.

Accreditation: *Regional:* NCA. *Professional:* NCATE. *Member of:* AACTE. *Approved by:* Ohio Department of Education.

Undergraduate Programs: Bachelor of Science in Education programs offered include: early childhood studies; middle childhood education; secondary education; intervention specialist; art education; business education; technology education; physical education; marketing education; health promotion; dance; exercise specialist; human movement science; recreation;

sport management. All programs require the completion of a general education core, professional studies, subject content area, field experiences, and student teaching.

Graduate Programs: The Master of Education degree programs are offered in: educational administration and supervision; business education; career and technology education; classroom technology; elementary education; guidance and counseling; human movement; sport and leisure studies; reading; school psychology; secondary education and intervention specialist.

The Doctor of Education degree is offered in leadership studies and the Doctor of Philosophy degree in higher education administration.

Licensure/Reciprocity: Ohio. Students seeking teaching certification in a state other than Ohio should consult with that state's teacher certification office early in their program of study to insure compliance with requirements. Many state directors of teacher credentialing have signed Interstate Agreements through NASDTEC that expedite the certification process.

CAPITAL UNIVERSITY

Education Department
Teacher Education Program
2199 East Main Street
Columbus, Ohio 43209
Phone: (614) 236-6301
Fax: (614) 236-6774
E-mail: tsanders@capital.edu
Internet: http://www.capital.edu

Institution Description: Capital University is a private, independent institution affiliated with The Evangelical Lutheran Church in America. It was established, chartered, and offered first instruction at the postsecondary level in 1850.

The goal of the Teacher Education Program is to develop competent, caring, and committed professional educators for diverse communities of learners.

Institution Control: Private.

Calendar: Semester. Academic year August to May.

Official(s): Dr. Tobie R. Sanders, Chair.

Faculty: Full-time 11; part-time 3; adjunct 15.

Degrees Awarded: 75 baccalaureate; 15 master's.

Admission Requirements: *Undergraduate:* Graduation from an accredited secondary school with 16 academic units or GED; College Board SAT or ACT composite. *Teacher education specific:* 2.5 GPA; good moral character; professional disposition; passing scores on PRAXIS I exams (reading, writing, mathematics; faculty interview.

Fees and Expenses: $18,980 per academic year. On-campus room and board: $5,950. $310 student teaching fee.

Financial Aid: Resources specifically for eligible students enrolled in teacher education programs are awarded on the basis of financial need and academic merit. The institution has a Program Participation Agreement with the U.S. Department of Education for eligible students to receive Pell Grants and other federal aid. Teacher scholarships available to qualifying students. *Contact:* Jeff Cisco at: (614) 236-6631 or e-mail at: jcisco@capital.edu.

Accreditation: *Regional:* NCA. *Professional:* NCATE. *Member of:* AACTE. *Approved by:* Ohio Department of Education.

Undergraduate Programs: The Teacher Education Program offers initial teaching license programs in 27 areas to include early childhood education, middle childhood education, intervention specialist for mild to moderate needs, art, physical education, music, health education, and a wide variety of adolescent to young adult content fields. Candidates earn a Bachelor of Arts degree and the various license programs require 124 to 136 semester hours to complete. The program requires the completion of a general education core, professional studies, field experiences, subject content area, and student teaching.

Licensure/Reciprocity: Ohio. Students seeking teaching certification in a state other than Ohio should consult with that state's teacher certification office early in their program of study to insure compliance with requirements. Many state directors of teacher credentialing have signed Interstate Agreements through NASDTEC that expedite the certification process.

CASE WESTERN RESERVE UNIVERSITY

Teacher Education Program
10900 Euclid Avenue
Cleveland, Ohio 44106-7001
Phone: (216) 368-2000
Fax: (216) 368-5111
E-mail: jeg@cwru.edu
Internet: http://www.cwru.edu

Institution Description: Case Western Reserve University is a private, independent, nonprofit institution. It was created by the federation of Case Institute of Technology and Western Reserve University in 1967.

Teacher licensure programs are offered at the undergraduate and graduate levels.

Institution Control: Private.

Calendar: Semester. Academic year August to May.

Official(s): Dr. Tim Shuckerow, Art Education; Dr. Robert Dunn, Music Education; Dr. Melanie Schuele, Communication Sciences; Dr. Phil Safford, Secondary Education.

Faculty: Not reported.

Degrees Awarded: 3 baccalaureate; 6 master's.

Admission Requirements: *Undergraduate:* Graduation from an accredited secondary school with college preparatory curriculum; writing sample; College Board SAT or ACT composite. *Teacher education specific:* Portfolio for art education; audition for music education; application to John Carroll University for other subjects; interview with advisor. *Graduate:* Bachelor's degree from a regionally accredited institution. *Teacher education specific:* Results from standardized tests; writing sample; portfolio; personal interview.

Fees and Expenses: Undergraduate and graduate: $22,500 per academic year. Required fees: $230 (undergraduate). On-campus room and board: $7,150. Other expenses: $1,150. Books and supplies: $780.

Financial Aid. Resources are awarded on the basis of financial need and academic merit. The institution has a Program Participation Agreement with the U.S. Department of Education for eligible students to receive Pell Grants and other federal aid. *Contact:* Donald W. Chenille, Director, Financial Aid at: (216) 368-3866 or e-mail at: dwc2@cwru.edu.

Accreditation: *Regional:* NCA. *Member of:* AACTE. *Approved by:* Ohio Department of Education.

Undergraduate Programs: The Bachelor of Science in art education program is conducted jointly by Case Western Reserve University and the Cleveland Institute of Art. Graduates are eligible for Multi-Age Licensure in Visual Arts. The Bachelor of Science in music education is an integrated music program conducted jointly by the Cleveland Institute of Music and Case Western Reserve University. The program requires the complete of 121 credits and graduates are eligible for the Mujlt-Age License in Music.

Teacher Licensure Programs are offered in secondary education: language arts, social studies, mathematics, sciences, and French. The program is conducted jointly with John Carroll University and the degree is awarded by Case Western Reserve University.

Graduate Programs: Graduate teacher education programs include the Master of Arts in art education, the Master of Arts in music education, the Master of Arts in communication sciences/disorders.

The doctorate in music education is designed to prepare professionals to assume positions of leadership in elementary, secondary, and collegiate instruction. Applicants must have completed three years of full-time music teaching, usually in the public schools.

Licensure/Reciprocity: Ohio. Students seeking teaching certification in a state other than Ohio should consult with that state's teacher certification office early in their program of study to

CASE WESTERN RESERVE UNIVERSITY—
cont'd

insure compliance with requirements. Many state directors of teacher credentialing have signed Interstate Agreements through NASDTEC that expedite the certification process.

CENTRAL STATE UNIVERSITY

College of Education
Department of Professional Education

1400 Brush Row Road
Wilberforce, Ohio 45384
Phone: (937) 376-6225
Fax: (937) 376-6314
E-mail: coe@centralstate.edu
Internet: http://www.centralstate.edu

Institution Description: Central State University was chartered as Combined Normal and Industrial Department of Wilberforce University in 1887. It became a became four-year institution and the name was changed to College of Education and Industrial Arts in 1941, to Central State College in 1951, and to the present name in 1965.

The goal of the Department of Professional Education is to provide students with authentic teaching and learning situations to expand their knowledge, understanding, and appreciation of the global community.

Institution Control: Public.

Calendar: Quarter (converts to semester system in 2005). Academic year September to June.

Official(s): Dr. Kaye Jeter, Dean; Dr. Johanna Hill-Thornton, Chair.

Faculty: Full-time 3.

Degrees Awarded: 26 baccalaureate; 1 master's.

Admission Requirements: *Undergraduate:* Graduation from an accredited secondary school GED; College Board SAT or ACT composite. *Teacher education specific:* 2.5 GPA; application after completion of 42 credit hours; passing scores on PRAXIS I exams (reading, writing, mathematics); interview.

Fees and Expenses: Instate $4,287 per academic year; out-of-state $9,282. On-campus room and board: $6,069. Other expenses: $1,704. Books and supplies; $950.

Financial Aid: Resources specifically for eligible students enrolled in teacher education programs are awarded on the basis of financial need and academic merit. The institution has a Program Participation Agreement with the U.S. Department of Education for eligible students to receive Pell Grants and other federal aid. Teacher scholarships available to qualifying students. *Contact:* Financial Aid Office at: (937) 376-6579.

Accreditation: *Regional:* NCA. *Member of:* AACTE. *Approved by:* Ohio Department of Education.

Undergraduate Programs: Programs leading to the baccalaureate degree and teaching licensure include: early childhood education (K-3) and multi-age (K-12) in music, visual arts, physical education, health education, intervention specialist (mild to moderate); middle childhood education (4-8) in reading and language arts, mathematics, social studies, science; adolescent to young adults and integrated social studies in life science, physical science, integrated mathematics, integrated language arts. All programs require the completion of a general education core, professional studies, subject content area, field experiences, and student teaching. A minimum of 186 quarter hours is required for the degree award.

Licensure/Reciprocity: Ohio. Students seeking teaching certification in a state other than Ohio should consult with that state's teacher certification office early in their program of study to insure compliance with requirements. Many state directors of teacher credentialing have signed Interstate Agreements through NASDTEC that expedite the certification process.

CLEVELAND STATE UNIVERSITY

College of Education
Teacher Education Programs

1983 East 24th Street
Cleveland, Ohio 44115
Phone: (216) 687-3737
Fax: (216) 687-5915
E-mail: coe@csuohio.edu
Internet: http://www.csuohio.edu

Institution Description: Cleveland State University was established as Fenn College in 1923. The present name was adopted in 1965.

The College of Education offers a variety of baccalaureate programs for teacher education and graduate programs for the advancement and enrichment of persons active in the education profession.

Institution Control: Public.

Calendar: Semester. Academic year August to June.

Official(s): Dr. James McLaughlin, Dean's Office/Special Education.

Faculty: Full-time 35 (Teacher Education).

Degrees Awarded: 172 baccalaureate; 413 master's; 12 doctorate.

Admission Requirements: *Undergraduate:* Graduation from an accredited secondary school with 16 academic units in college preparatory program or GED; College Board SAT or ACT composite. *Teacher education specific:* 2.5 cumulative GPA; score of 75 or higher on COMPASS writing proficiency test; passing scores on PRAXIS I (reading, writing, mathematics). *Graduate:* Baccalaureate degree from a regionally accredited institution. *Teacher education specific:* PRAXIS II tests before graduation; writing sample; portfolio; personal interview.

Fees and Expenses: Undergraduate: in-state $6,040 per academic year; out-of-state $11,920. Graduate: Tuition charged per credit hour. On-campus room and board: $6,240. Other expenses: $3,776. Books and supplies: $800.

Financial Aid: Resources specifically for eligible students enrolled in teacher education programs are awarded on the basis of financial need and academic merit. The institution has a Program Participation Agreement with the U.S. Department of Education for eligible students to receive Pell Grants and other federal aid. Teacher scholarships available to qualifying students. *Contact:* Financial Aid Office at: (216) 687-3764.

Accreditation: *Regional:* NCA. *Professional:* NCATE. *Member of:* AACTE. *Approved by:* Ohio Department of Education.

Undergraduate Programs: The faculty of the College of Education confers the Bachelor of Science in Education degree with majors in early childhood education, physical education, special education, and allied sports professions (exercise/fitness specialist or sport manager). In addition, undergraduate students and college graduates may earn teaching licenses in early childhood (grades preK-3), middle childhood (grades 4-9), physical education (grades preK-12), special education (grades K-12 in mild/moderate or moderate/intensive educational needs), adolescent/young adult (grades 7-12 in a variety of content areas), visual arts (grades preK-12), and foreign languages (grades preK-12 in French or Spanish.

All programs require the completion of 125 semester hours and include the general education core, professional studies, field experiences, and student teaching.

Graduate Programs: The Master of Education degree is offered in: administration, adult learning and development; counselor education, community health education, exercise science, sports management, and supervision.

Master's programs in curriculum and instruction are offered in early childhood education, educational research, educational technology, elementary education, gifted education, human performance, literacy development and instruction, pedagogy education, school health education, secondary education, and sport and exercise psychology.

Education Specialist degree programs are available in counseling and pupil personnel administration, educational administration. A Doctor of Philosophy in urban education is also offered.

Licensure/Reciprocity: Ohio. Students seeking teaching certification in a state other than Ohio should consult with that state's teacher certification office early in their program of study to insure compliance with requirements. Many state directors of teacher credentialing have signed Interstate Agreements through NASDTEC that expedite the certification process.

COLLEGE OF MOUNT ST. JOSEPH

Education Department
5701 Delhi Road
Cincinnati, Ohio 45233-1670
Phone: (513) 244-4812
Fax: (513) 244-4867
E-mail: education@mail.msj.edu
Internet: http://www.msj.edu

Institution Description: College of Mount St. Joseph is a private, coeducational institution, sponsored by the Sisters of Charity of Cincinnati, Roman Catholic Church. It was established as Mount St. Vincent Academy in 1853.

The Education Department offers teacher licensure programs at the undergraduate and graduate levels.

Institution Control: Private.

Calendar: Semester. Academic year August to May.

Official(s): Dr. Clarissa Rosas, Chair.

Faculty: Full-time 14; part-time 1; adjunct 10.

Degrees Awarded: 52 baccalaureate; 25 master's.

Admission Requirements: *Undergraduate:* Graduation from an accredited secondary school or GED; College Board SAT or ACT composite. *Teacher education specific:* Strong college preparatory curriculum in high school; 2.8 GPA; passing scores on PRAXIS I tests (reading, writing, mathematics); two letters of reference. *Graduate:* Baccalaureate degree from a regionally accredited institution. *Teacher education specific:* 2.7 GPA or GRE; two letters of reference; faculty interview; PRAXIS II tests prior to graduation.

Fees and Expenses: Undergraduate: $14,950 per academic year. Graduate: $382 per credit hour. Activity fee $140 per year; technology fee $800. On-campus room and board: room $2,800 to $5,150; meal plans $2,670 to $2,870. Books and supplies: $800.

Financial Aid: Resources specifically for eligible students enrolled in teacher education programs are awarded on the basis of financial need and academic merit. The institution has a Program Participation Agreement with the U.S. Department of Education for eligible students to receive Pell Grants and other federal aid. Teacher scholarships available to qualifying students. *Contact:* Conlin Center at: (513) 244-4418.

Accreditation: *Regional:* NCA. *Member of:* AACTE. *Approved by:* Ohio Department of Education.

Undergraduate Programs: Undergraduate programs leading to teacher licensure and the baccalaureate degree include: inclusive early childhood education; middle childhood education (concentrations in language arts, mathematics, science, social studies); adolescent and young adults education (concentrations in chemistry, biology, language arts, mathematics, science, social studies); multi-age education (concentrations in music, physical education, visual arts); intervention specialist/special education (concentrations in mild/moderate and moderate/intensive). Endorsements are offered in reading, adapted physical education, and computer technology. All programs require the completion of a general education core, professional studies, subject content area, field experiences, and student teaching.

Graduate Programs: Master of Arts in Education degree programs are offered with concentrations in art, inclusive early childhood, professional development, professional foundations, reading, special education, and school nurse licensure program. An accelerated teacher education and apprenticeship program is also available.

Licensure/Reciprocity: Ohio. Students seeking teaching certification in a state other than Ohio should consult with that state's teacher certification office early in their program of study to insure compliance with requirements. Many state directors of teacher credentialing have signed Interstate Agreements through NASDTEC that expedite the certification process.

COLLEGE OF WOOSTER

Department of Education
Morgan Hall, 930 College Mall
1189 Beall Avenue
Wooster, Ohio 44691
Phone: (330) 263-2303
Fax: (330) 263-2276
E-mail: aschnidt@wooster.edu
Internet: http://www.wooster.edu

Institution Description: The College of Wooster is a private, independent, nonprofit college affiliated with the United Presbyterian Church (U.S.A.). It was founded in 1866.

The Department of Education provides opportunities for its students to explore learning and teaching.

Institution Control: Private.

Calendar: Semester. Academic year August to May.

Official(s): Dr. Allison H. Schmidt, Chair.

Faculty: Full-time 3; part-time 1; adjunct 4.

Degrees Awarded: 10 baccalaureate.

Admission Requirements: *Undergraduate:* Graduation from an accredited secondary school with 16 academic units or GED; College Board SAT or ACT composite. *Teacher education specific:* 2.5 overall GPA; evidence of professionalism; writing and quantitative skills; passing scores on PRAXIS I (reading, writing, mathematics); faculty interview.

Fees and Expenses: $30,000 comprehensive fee per academic year.

Financial Aid: Resources specifically for eligible students enrolled in teacher education programs are awarded on the basis of financial need and academic merit. The institution has a Program Participation Agreement with the U.S. Department of Education for eligible students to receive Pell Grants and other federal aid. Teacher scholarships available to qualifying students. *Contact:* David Miller at: (330) 263-2317.

Accreditation: *Regional:* NCA. *Approved by:* Ohio Department of Education.

Undergraduate Programs: The College of Wooster offers programs for teaching licensure in the following areas: early childhood (grades preK-3/ages 3-8); middle grades (grades 6-9/ages 8-14) with concentrations in language arts, mathematics, sciences, social sciences: adolescent and young adult (grades 7-12/ages 12-21) with concentrations in chemistry, earth sciences, life sciences, physical sciences, physics, integrated language arts, integrated mathematics, integrated social studies; multi-age (grades preK-12/ages 3-21) with concentrations in French, German, Spanish, music, and visual arts. All programs require the completion of a general education core, professional studies, field experiences, and student teaching.

Licensure/Reciprocity: Ohio. Students seeking teaching certification in a state other than Ohio should consult with that state's teacher certification office early in their program of study to insure compliance with requirements. Many state directors of teacher credentialing have signed Interstate Agreements through NASDTEC that expedite the certification process.

FRANCISCAN UNIVERSITY OF STEUBENVILLE

Department of Education
1235 University Boulevard
Steubenville, Ohio 43952
Phone: (740) 283-6245
Fax: (740) 283-6401
E-mail: dikeenans@franciscan.edu
Internet: http://www.franciscan.edu

FRANCISCAN UNIVERSITY OF STEUBENVILLE—*cont'd*

Institution Description: Franciscan University of Steubenville (formerly University of Steubenville) is a private, independent, nonprofit college affiliated with the Third Order Regular of St. Francis, Roman Catholic Church. It was founded in 1946.

Education programs offered by the Department of Education prepare students for certification as elementary or early childhood educators, and provide certification to teach in specific subjects areas at middle school, high school, and multi-age levels.

Institution Control: Private.

Calendar: Semester. Academic year August to May.

Official(s): Dr. Dianne Keenan, Chairperson.

Faculty: Full-time 10; adjunct 16.

Degrees Awarded: 38 baccalaureate; 46 master's.

Admission Requirements: *Undergraduate:* Graduation from an accredited secondary school or GED; College Board SAT or ACT composite. *Teacher education specific:* 2.5 GPA; passing scores on PRAXIS I (reading, writing, mathematics); faculty interview.

Fees and Expenses: Undergraduate: $485 per credit hour. Graduate: $220 per credit hour.

Financial Aid: Resources specifically for eligible students enrolled in teacher education programs are awarded on the basis of financial need and academic merit. The institution has a Program Participation Agreement with the U.S. Department of Education for eligible students to receive Pell Grants and other federal aid. Teacher scholarships available to qualifying students. *Contact:* John Herrmann, Jr. at: (740) 283-6245.

Accreditation: *Regional:* NCA. *Approved by:* Ohio Department of Education.

Undergraduate Programs: The Department of Education offers two kinds of programs: a Degree Program and a Teacher Licensure Program. A Bachelor of Science degree is granted to students who major in education and pass the required tests. The teacher licensure programs are: early childhood (preK-3/ages 3-8); middle childhood (grades 4-9/ages 8-14); adolescent to young adult (grades 7-12, ages 12-21); multi-age (preK-12/ages 3-21); intervention specialist mild/moderate needs (grades K-12/ages 5-12). A student preparing for the middle childhood license must have two areas of concentration from the following: mathematics, language arts, science, social studies. A broad liberal arts background emphasizing the humanities and the sciences is provided. All baccalaureate licensure programs require the completion of a general education core, professional studies, field experiences, subject content area, and student teaching. Provisions have been made, within the programs of study, for education majors to study a semester at the Austrian campus if one so chooses.

Graduate Programs: Two Master of Science in Education programs are offered by the Department of Education. Contact the department for specific details.

Licensure/Reciprocity: Ohio. Students seeking teaching certification in a state other than Ohio should consult with that state's teacher certification office early in their program of study to insure compliance with requirements. Many state directors of teacher credentialing have signed Interstate Agreements through NASDTEC that expedite the certification process.

HEIDELBERG COLLEGE

Department of Education
310 East Market Street
Tiffin, Ohio 44883-2462
Phone: (419) 448-2125
Fax: (419) 448-2124
E-mail: edu@heidelberg.edu
Internet: http://www.heidelberg.edu

Institution Description: Heidelberg College is a private college affiliated with the United Church of Christ. It was established and offered first instruction at the postsecondary level in 1850.

The teacher licensure programs are based on a consructivist philosophy. Preservice and inservice teachers build or construct their knowledge as a result of a student-centered, hands on approach to learning.

Institution Control: Private.

Calendar: Semester. Academic year August to May.

Official(s): Dr. Diane Armstrong, Department Chair.

Faculty: Full-time 8; emeriti 3.

Degrees Awarded: 50 baccalaureate; 25 master's.

Admission Requirements: *Undergraduate:* Graduation from an accredited secondary school with a college preparatory course of study; College Board SAT or ACT composite. *Teacher education specific:* 2.5 GPA; passing scores on PRAXIS I (reading, writing, mathematics); faculty interview. *Graduate:* Baccalaureate degree from a regionally accredited institution. *Teacher education specific:* Portfolio; completion of all departmental required exams; faculty interview.

Fees and Expenses: Undergraduate: $13,620 per academic year. Graduate: Tuition charged per academic year. On-campus room and board: $3,537. Other expenses: $2,000. Books and supplies: $750.

Financial Aid: Resources specifically for eligible students enrolled in teacher education programs are awarded on the basis of financial need and academic merit. The institution has a Program Participation Agreement with the U.S. Department of Education for eligible students to receive Pell Grants and other federal aid. Teacher scholarships available to qualifying students. *Contact:* Financial Aid Office at: (419) 448-2293.

Accreditation: *Regional:* NCA. *Member of:* AACTE. *Approved by:* Ohio Department of Education.

Undergraduate Programs: Teacher certification programs offered by the Department of Education include: early childhood (preK-grade 3); middle childhood (grades 4-9); adolescence to young adult (grades 7-12); multi-age (German, health/physical education, music, Spanish, preK-12); intervention specialist (special education ages 5-21). Students may gain licensure in one of the first four areas listed above or (1) may add intervention specialist to any of the above or (2) may wish to seek a combination of two of the first four licenses. This will require additional coursework and may take additional time. All programs lead to the baccalaureate degree and require the completion of a general education core, professional studies, subject content are, field experiences, and student teaching.

Graduate Programs: The purpose of the Master of Arts in Education program is to develop teachers who exercise leadership within their professional communities and academic institutions. The program is designed to increase the competence of teachers, reading specialist, and school counselors based on a liberal arts core.

Licensure/Reciprocity: Ohio. Students seeking teaching certification in a state other than Ohio should consult with that state's teacher certification office early in their program of study to insure compliance with requirements. Many state directors of teacher credentialing have signed Interstate Agreements through NASDTEC that expedite the certification process.

HIRAM COLLEGE

Department of Education
113 Hilldale Hall
P.O. Box 67
Hiram, Ohio 44234-0067
Phone: (330) 569-5272
Fax: (330) 569-5290
E-mail: feather@hiram.edu
Internet: http://www.hiram.edu

Institution Description: Hiram College is a private, independent, nonprofit college affiliated with the Christian Church (Disciples of Christ). It was founded in 1850.

The Department of Education offers baccalaureate programs leading to licensure and follows the 1998 Teacher Education Standards for Ohio.

Institution Control: Private.

Calendar: Semester. Academic year August to May.

Official(s): Dr. Katherine Feather, Chair.

Faculty: Full-time 11.

Degrees Awarded: 31 baccalaureate.

Admission Requirements: *Undergraduate:* Graduation from an accredited secondary school with 14-16 academic units or GED; College Board SAT or ACT composite. *Teacher education specific:* Maintain a 3.0 GPA in the professional education courses and field of licensure; professional commitment; high scholastic attainment; passing scores on PRAXIS I exams (reading, writing, mathematics); faculty interview.

Fees and Expenses: $21,170 per academic year. On-campus room and board: $7,100. Other expenses: $2,553. Books and supplies: $630.

Financial Aid: Resources specifically for eligible students enrolled in teacher education programs are awarded on the basis of financial need and academic merit. The institution has a Program Participation Agreement with the U.S. Department of Education for eligible students to receive Pell Grants and other federal aid. Teacher scholarships available to qualifying students. *Contact:* Financial Aid Office at: (330) 569-5107.

Accreditation: *Regional:* NCA. *Member of:* AACTE. *Approved by:* Ohio Department of Education.

Undergraduate Programs: Teacher certification programs offered by the Department of Education include: early childhood (preK-grade 3): language and literacy, mathematics, social studies, art, music, drama, interdisciplinary, foreign language); middle childhood (grades 4-9); reading, language arts, mathematics, science, social studies); adolescence to young adult (grades 7-12): majors in integrated language arts, integrated mathematics, integrated social studies, life science, chemistry, physics); multi-age (ages 3-21): drama/theater, music, visual arts, foreign language). All programs lead to the baccalaureate degree and require the completion of a general education core, professional studies, subject content are, field experiences, and student teaching. Licensure in Ohio requires the successful completion of PRAXIS II tests.

Licensure/Reciprocity: Ohio. Students seeking teaching certification in a state other than Ohio should consult with that state's teacher certification office early in their program of study to insure compliance with requirements. Many state directors of teacher credentialing have signed Interstate Agreements through NASDTEC that expedite the certification process.

JOHN CARROLL UNIVERSITY

Department of Education and Allied Studies
20700 North Park Boulevard
University Heights, Ohio 44118
Phone: (216) 397-3080
Fax: (216) 397-3045
E-mail: manning@jcu.edu
Internet: http://www.jcu.edu

Institution Description: John Carroll University is a private institution affiliated with the Society of Jesus, Roman Catholic Church. It was founded in 1886.

The mission of the Department of Education and Allied Studies, built upon the ideas of a Jesuit educator, prepares educators with the knowledge and character to lead and to serve.

Institution Control: Private.

Calendar: Semester. Academic year August to May.

Official(s): Dr. Kathleen Manning, Dean.

Faculty: Full-time 24.

Degrees Awarded: 106 baccalaureate; 103 master's.

Admission Requirements: *Undergraduate:* Graduation from an accredited secondary school or GED; College Board SAT or ACT composite. *Teacher education specific:* Admission decisions are based on a broad range of criteria that emphasize varieties of scholarship and talent and academic ability; passing scores on PRAXIS I tests (reading, writing, mathematics); personal goal statement; faculty interview. *Graduate:* Baccalaureate from a regionally accredited institution. *Teacher education specific:* 2.75

GPA; written statement indicating personal interests, goals, and expectations from the degree program; Miller Analogies Test or GRE; two letters of reference.

Fees and Expenses: Undergraduate: in-state $20,906 per academic year. Graduate: Tuition charged per credit hour. On-campus room and board: $6,892. Other expenses: $1,550. Books and supplies: $1,000.

Financial Aid: Resources specifically for eligible students enrolled in teacher education programs are awarded on the basis of financial need and academic merit. The institution has a Program Participation Agreement with the U.S. Department of Education for eligible students to receive Pell Grants and other federal aid. Teacher scholarships available to qualifying students. *Contact:* Patrick Prosser at: (216) 397-4248.

Accreditation: *Regional:* NCA. *Professional:* NCATE. *Member of:* AACTE. *Approved by:* Ohio Department of Education.

Undergraduate Programs: The Department of Education offers three teaching licensure programs: early childhood (grades preK-3), middle childhood (grades 4-9); adolescent and young adult (grades 7-12). Professional and pedagogical studies provide a planned sequence of courses that develop knowledge about education and foster understanding and use of the principles of effective teaching practice. All programs lead to the baccalaureate degree and require the completion of a general education core, professional studies, subject content area, field experiences, and student teaching.

Graduate Programs: The Professional Teacher Program is designed for experienced elementary or secondary school teachers to encourage individual interest and to develop further competencies of a master teacher. A sequence of courses may be taken in a teaching field, e.g., English, or in education, wherein a number of specializations are possible. Each program requires a minimum of 30 hours. At the conclusion of studies, a successful completion of a written comprehensive examination is required for the Master of Education degree.

Licensure/Reciprocity: Ohio. Students seeking teaching certification in a state other than Ohio should consult with that state's teacher certification office early in their program of study to insure compliance with requirements. Many state directors of teacher credentialing have signed Interstate Agreements through NASDTEC that expedite the certification process.

KENT STATE UNIVERSITY

College of Education
Teacher Education Programs
306 White Hall
P.O. Box 5190
Kent, Ohio 44242-0001
Phone: (330) 672-2862
Fax: (330) 672-3549
E-mail: csnyder1@kent.edu
Internet: http://www.kent.edu

Institution Description: Kent State University is a public institution with two-year institutions at Ashtabula, Burton, East Liverpool, New Philadelphia, North Canton, Salem, and Warren. The university was founded in 1910.

The College of Education offers undergraduate and graduate programs leading to teacher licensure.

Institution Control: Public.

Calendar: Semester. Academic year August to May.

Official(s): Dr. David England, Dean.

Faculty: Full-time 94; part-time 70; adjunct 9.

Degrees Awarded: 407 baccalaureate; 440 master's; 63 doctorate.

Admission Requirements: *Undergraduate:* Graduation from an accredited secondary school with 16 college preparatory units or GED; College Board SAT or ACT composite. *Teacher education specific:* 2.75 GPA; PRAXIS I tests (reading, writing, mathematics); faculty interview. *Graduate:* Baccalaureate degree from a regionally accredited institution. *Teacher education*

KENT STATE UNIVERSITY—cont'd

specific: 2.75 GPA; completion of all required departmental exams; teaching licensure where required by program pursued; faculty interview.

Fees and Expenses: Undergraduate: in-state $3,187 per semester; out-of-state $6,165. Graduate: in-state $3,390 per semester; out-of-state $6,368. On-campus room: $1,825 per semester (double). Books and supplies: $800.

Financial Aid: Resources specifically for eligible students enrolled in teacher education programs are awarded on the basis of financial need and academic merit. The institution has a Program Participation Agreement with the U.S. Department of Education for eligible students to receive Pell Grants and other federal aid. Teacher scholarships available to qualifying students. *Contact:* Mark Evans at: (330) 672-2972 or e-mail at: mevans@kent.edu.

Accreditation: *Regional:* NCA. *Professional:* NCATE. *Member of:* AACTE. *Approved by:* Ohio Department of Education.

Undergraduate Programs: The undergraduate teacher education programs offered by the College of Education include: adolescence/young adult multi-age; early childhood; intervention specialist (gifted, mild/moderate, moderate/intensive, deaf education); vocational education (age 8 and beyond). There are also programs in the College of Arts and Sciences, Fine and Professional Arts, and the School of Technology in which students complete a major in the appropriate college and declare an education minor through the College of Education.

All programs leading to the baccalaureate degree and teacher licensure require the completion of a general education core, professional studies, subject content area, field experiences, and student teaching.

Graduate Programs: Various master's degree programs are offered by the College of Education that lead to professional and career enhancement as well as teacher licensure for those who possess a baccalaureate degree and who wish to teach in their subject area.

Licensure/Reciprocity: Ohio. Students seeking teaching certification in a state other than Ohio should consult with that state's teacher certification office early in their program of study to insure compliance with requirements. Many state directors of teacher credentialing have signed Interstate Agreements through NASDTEC that expedite the certification process.

MALONE COLLEGE

School of Education
Department of Teacher Education
515 25th Street, N.W.
Canton, Ohio 44709-3897
Phone: (330) 471-8100
Fax: (330) 471-8478
E-mail: admissions@malone.edu
Internet: http://www.malone.edu

Institution Description: Malone College is a private Christian college for affiliated with the Evangelical Friends Church-Eastern Region. The college was established in 1892.

The Department of Teacher Education offers baccalaureate and master's degree programs leading to licensure in Ohio.

Institution Control: Private.

Calendar: Semester. Academic year August to April.

Official(s): Dr. Christine A. Krol, Dean; Dr. Alice Christie, Program Director, Graduate Education.

Faculty: Full-time 29.

Degrees Awarded: 81 baccalaureate; 24 master's.

Admission Requirements: *Undergraduate:* Graduation from an accredited secondary school or GED; College Board SAT accepted; ACT composite preferred. *Teacher education specific:* Maintain a 3.0 GPA in the professional education courses and field of licensure; professional commitment; high scholastic attainment; passing scores on PRAXIS I exams (reading, writing, mathematics); faculty interview. *Graduate:* Baccalaureate degree from a regionally accredited institution. *Teacher education*

specific: 2.75 GPA; completion of all required departmental exams; teaching licensure where required by program pursued; faculty interview.

Fees and Expenses: Undergraduate: in-state $14,995 per academic year. Graduate: Tuition charged per credit hour. On-campus room and board: $6,000. Other expenses: $1,476. Books and supplies: $800.

Financial Aid: Resources specifically for eligible students enrolled in teacher education programs are awarded on the basis of financial need and academic merit. The institution has a Program Participation Agreement with the U.S. Department of Education for eligible students to receive Pell Grants and other federal aid. Teacher scholarships available to qualifying students. *Contact:* Financial Aid Office at: (330) 8159, ext. 8159.

Accreditation: *Regional:* NCA. *Member of:* AACTE. *Approved by:* Ohio Department of Education.

Undergraduate Programs: Initial teaching licensure areas offered by the Department of Teacher Education include early childhood education (preK-3); middle childhood education (4-9); adolescence to young adult (7-12) with concentrations in integrated language arts, mathematics, integrated science, integrated social studies, natural sciences); intervention specialist (K-12, mild/moderate); health education (preK-12); music education, physical education, visual arts education. All licensure programs lead to the baccalaureate degree and require the completion of a general education core, professional studies, subject content area, field experiences, and student teaching. PRAXIS II examinations must be passed before graduation.

Graduate Programs: The Master of Arts in Education with a concentration in curriculum and instruction is designed for educators who wish to strengthen their classroom instructional skill and knowledge. The program emphasizes contemporary educational issues in curriculum and instruction. The program consists of a 15-semester-hour foundation area, a 10-12 hour curriculum and instruction core, and 9-11 hours of electives to be chosen from graduate course offerings.

Licensure/Reciprocity: Ohio. Students seeking teaching certification in a state other than Ohio should consult with that state's teacher certification office early in their program of study to insure compliance with requirements. Many state directors of teacher credentialing have signed Interstate Agreements through NASDTEC that expedite the certification process.

MIAMI UNIVERSITY OF OHIO

School of Education and Allied Professions
Department of Teacher Education
176 McGuffey Hall
East High Street
Oxford, Ohio 45056
Phone: (513) 529-6317
Fax: (513) 529-7290
E-mail: witter@muohio.edu
Internet: http://www.muohio.edu

Institution Description: Miami University is a state institution that was established and chartered in 1809.

Teacher preparation and other school personnel licensure programs are housed in several departments within the division of the School of Education and Allied Professions.

Institution Control: Public.

Calendar: Semester. Academic year August to May.

Official(s): Dr. Barbara Schirmer, Dean; Dr. Raymond Witte, Associate Dean.

Faculty: Full-time 103; part-time 56; adjunct 5.

Degrees Awarded: 467 baccalaureate; 162 master's; 9 doctorate.

Admission Requirements: *Undergraduate:* Graduation from an accredited secondary school or GED; College Board SAT or ACT composite. *Teacher education specific:* Maintain a 3.0 GPA in the professional education courses and field of licensure; professional commitment; high scholastic attainment; passing scores on PRAXIS I exams (reading, writing, mathematics); faculty interview. *Graduate:* Baccalaureate degree from a regionally accredited institution. *Teacher education specific:* 2.75 GPA; completion of all required departmental exams; teaching licensure where required by program pursued; faculty interview.

Fees and Expenses: Undergraduate: in-state $6,386 per academic year; out-of-state $15,110. Graduate: in-state $6,560 per academic year; out-of-state $15,284. Required fees: $1,214. On-campus room and board: $6,290. Other expenses: $2,126. Books and supplies: $800.

Financial Aid: Resources specifically for eligible students enrolled in teacher education programs are awarded on the basis of financial need and academic merit. The institution has a Program Participation Agreement with the U.S. Department of Education for eligible students to receive Pell Grants and other federal aid. Teacher scholarships available to qualifying students. *Contact:* Chuck Knepfl, Director, Student Financial Aid at: (513) 529-8734 or e-mail at: financial aid@muohio.

Accreditation: *Regional:* NCA. *Professional:* NCATE. *Member of:* AACTE. *Approved by:* Ohio Department of Education.

Undergraduate Programs: Licensure programs include: early childhood education (pre-K-grade 3); middle childhood education prepares candidates for licensure in two of four content areas—language arts, social studies, science, mathematics— (grades 4-9); adolescent/young adult education prepares candidates for licensure in grades 7-12 in integrated English language arts, integrated mathematics, integrated social studies, science education; foreign language education (French, German, Latin, Spanish, preK-12).

The Department of Physical Education offers licensure areas in health and physical education. The School of Fine Arts offers licensure programs in visual arts education and music education.

All baccalaureate programs require completion of a minimum of 128 hours and passing scores on PRAXIS II exams. All programs also include a general education core, professional studies, subject content area, field experiences, and student teaching.

Graduate Programs: The Master of Arts in Teaching provides graduate and undergraduate students with a baccalaureate degree the opportunity to earn a teaching license and a master's degree in four semesters of full-time study. The program is restricted to the following adolescent education fields: integrated English/language arts, integrated mathematics, integrated science, and integrated social studies.

Licensure/Reciprocity: Ohio. Students seeking teaching certification in a state other than Ohio should consult with that state's teacher certification office early in their program of study to insure compliance with requirements. Many state directors of teacher credentialing have signed Interstate Agreements through NASDTEC that expedite the certification process.

MOUNT VERNON NAZARENE COLLEGE
Department of Education
Teacher Education Program
800 Martinsburg Road
Mount Vernon, Ohio 43050
Phone: (740) 392-6868
Fax: (740) 392-0511
E-mail: admissions@mvnc.edu
Internet: http://www.nvnc.edu

Institution Description: Mount Vernon Nazarene College is a private liberal arts college affiliated with the Church of the Nazarene. It was established in 1966.

The Teacher Education Program equips students to teach in pre-school, elementary, secondary, and comprehensive (kindergarten through twelfth grade) education settings.

Institution Control: Private.

Calendar: Semester (4-1-4 plan). Academic year September to May.

Official(s): Dr. Rhoda C. Sommers, Department Hear; Dr. Steve Ragan, Director of Teacher Education.

Faculty: Full-time 13.

Degrees Awarded: 65 baccalaureate; 15 master's.

Admission Requirements: *Undergraduate:* Graduation from an accredited secondary school with 18 academic units or GED; ACT composite. *Teacher education specific:* Maintain a 2.5 GPA; professional commitment; high scholastic attainment; passing scores on PRAXIS I exams (reading, writing, mathematics); faculty interview. *Graduate:* Baccalaureate degree from a regionally accredited institution. *Teacher education specific:* 2.5 GPA; completion of all required departmental exams; teaching licensure where required by program pursued; faculty interview.

Fees and Expenses: Undergraduate: $14,280 per academic year. Graduate: Tuition charged per credit hour. On-campus room and board: $4,000. Other expenses: $1,767. Books and supplies: $1,000.

Financial Aid: Resources specifically for eligible students enrolled in teacher education programs are awarded on the basis of financial need and academic merit. The institution has a Program Participation Agreement with the U.S. Department of Education for eligible students to receive Pell Grants and other federal aid. Teacher scholarships available to qualifying students. *Contact:* Financial Aid Office at: (740) 392-6868.

Accreditation: *Regional:* NCA. *Member of:* AACTE. *Approved by:* Ohio Department of Education.

Undergraduate Programs: Programs leading to Ohio licensure and the baccalaureate degrees include: Bachelor of Arts in early childhood education, middle childhood education (concentrations in language arts, mathematics, science, social studies, and reading endorsement); adolescent to young adult; integrated language arts and Bachelor of Science in integrated mathematics, integrated social studies, life science, physical science.

The multi-age education programs include the Bachelor of Arts in music, Bachelor of Arts in physical education/health education, Bachelor of Arts in Spanish, Bachelor of Arts in visual arts. The vocational education programs are for students who wish to teach in senior high school, a multi-age education, or in educational settings. The Bachelor of Arts in family and consumer sciences and the Bachelor of Arts in integrated business education are available.

All bachelor's programs require the completion of a general education core, professional studies, subject content area, field experiences, and student teaching.

Graduate Programs: The Master of Arts in curriculum and instruction program is for teachers with an Ohio teaching license who can earn a graduate degree to enhance their teaching effectiveness. The Master of Arts in Education in Professional Educator's License is for individuals with a college degree but without a teaching license. Students can ear a graduate degree while completing the requirements for licensure in Ohio.

Licensure/Reciprocity: Ohio. Students seeking teaching certification in a state other than Ohio should consult with that state's teacher certification office early in their program of study to insure compliance with requirements. Many state directors of teacher credentialing have signed Interstate Agreements through NASDTEC that expedite the certification process.

MUSKINGUM COLLEGE
Education Department
163 Stormont Street
New Concord, Ohio 43762
Phone: (614) 826-8246
Fax: (614) 826-8404
E-mail: education@muskingum.edu
Internet: http://muskingum.edu

Institution Description: Muskingum College is a private college affiliated with the Presbyterian Church (U.S.A.). The college was established, chartered, and offered first instruction at the postsecondary level in 1837.

The Education Department develops professional educators who demonstrate effective entry-year performance in meeting the challenges of teaching all students.

Institution Control: Private.

Calendar: Semester. Academic year August to May.

Official(s): Dr. Vicki A. Wilson, Department Head.

MUSKINGUM COLLEGE—*cont'd*

Faculty: Full-time 11; adjunct 3.

Degrees Awarded: 72 baccalaureate; 75 master's.

Admission Requirements: *Undergraduate:* Graduation from an accredited secondary school with 15 academic units or GED; College Board SAT or ACT composite. *Teacher education specific:* Maintain a 2.5 GPA; professional commitment; high scholastic attainment; passing scores on PRAXIS I exams (reading, writing, mathematics); faculty interview.

Fees and Expenses: $14,560 per academic year. On-campus room and board: $5,880. Other expenses: $1,340. Books and supplies: $800.

Financial Aid: Resources specifically for eligible students enrolled in teacher education programs are awarded on the basis of financial need and academic merit. The institution has a Program Participation Agreement with the U.S. Department of Education for eligible students to receive Pell Grants and other federal aid. Teacher scholarships available to qualifying students. *Contact:* Jeff Zellers at: (740) 826-8137 or e-mail at: jzellers@muskingum.edu.

Accreditation: *Regional:* NCA. *Member of:* AACTE. *Approved by:* Ohio Department of Education.

Undergraduate Programs: Licensure programs include: early childhood education (pre-K-grade 3); middle childhood education prepares candidates for licensure in two of four content areas—language arts, social studies, science, mathematics—(grades 4-9); adolescent/young adult education prepares candidates for licensure in grades 7-12 in integrated language arts, integrated mathematics, integrated social studies, integrated science, physical science, life science, earth science; multi-age (grades preK-12 in French, German, health, music, physical education, Spanish, visual arts); special education (mild/moderate disabilities); reading endorsement (grades preK-3 and 4-9).

All baccalaureate programs require completion of a minimum of 128 hours and passing scores on PRAXIS II exams. All programs also include a general education core, professional studies, subject content area, field experiences, and student teaching.

Licensure/Reciprocity: Ohio. Students seeking teaching certification in a state other than Ohio should consult with that state's teacher certification office early in their program of study to insure compliance with requirements. Many state directors of teacher credentialing have signed Interstate Agreements through NASDTEC that expedite the certification process.

NOTRE DAME COLLEGE OF OHIO

Education Department
4545 College Road
South Euclid, Ohio 44121-4293
Phone: (216) 381-1680
Fax: (216) 381-1680, ext. 5355
E-mail: education@ndc.edu
Internet: http://www.ndc.edu

Institution Description: Notre Dame College of Ohio College is a private, independent, nonprofit college.

The Education Department offers undergraduate and graduate programs leading to teaching licensure in Ohio.

Institution Control: Private.

Calendar: Semester. Academic year August to May.

Official(s): Dr. Bruce Jones, Director of Undergraduate and Graduate Education.

Faculty: Full-time: Not reported.

Degrees Awarded: 22 baccalaureate; 8 master's.

Admission Requirements: *Undergraduate:* Graduation from an accredited secondary school with 15 academic units or GED; College Board SAT or ACT composite. *Teacher education specific:* Maintain a 3.0 GPA in the professional education courses and field of licensure; professional commitment; high scholastic attainment; passing scores on PRAXIS I exams (reading, writing, mathematics); faculty interview. *Graduate:* Baccalaureate degree from a regionally accredited institution. *Teacher education specific:* 2.75 GPA; completion of all required departmental exams; teaching licensure where required by program pursued; two letters of recommendation; faculty interview.

Fees and Expenses: Undergraduate: $17,540 per academic year. Graduate: Tuition is charged per credit hour ($300 to $425). On-campus room and board: $5,962. Other expenses: $1,470. Books and supplies: $1,228.

Financial Aid: Resources specifically for eligible students enrolled in teacher education programs are awarded on the basis of financial need and academic merit. The institution has a Program Participation Agreement with the U.S. Department of Education for eligible students to receive Pell Grants and other federal aid. Teacher scholarships available to qualifying students. *Contact:* Financial Aid Office at: (216) 381-1680, ext. 5263.

Accreditation: *Regional:* NCA. *Member of:* AACTE. *Approved by:* Ohio Department of Education.

Undergraduate Programs: Areas of licensure offered by the Education Department include: early childhood education (preK-grade 3); middle childhood education (grades 4-9 with concentrations in reading and language arts, science, social studies); adolescent/young adult education (grades 7-12 with concentrations in integrated language arts, integrated mathematics, integrated science, integrated social studies, life sciences); multi-age education (preK-grade 12) in Spanish and visual arts. All programs require the completion of a general education core, professional studies, subject content area, field experiences, and student teaching.

Graduate Programs: The Master of Education program expands the educational foundation in emphasizing the preparation of master teachers. It provides a solid grounding in the philosophical foundations of classroom teaching through an in-depth exploration of pedagogical skills and their implications and through the opportunity to design and complete a final research project. The graduate options are the Master of Education with emphasis area and the Master of Education with licensure/endorsement.

Licensure/Reciprocity: Ohio. Students seeking teaching certification in a state other than Ohio should consult with that state's teacher certification office early in their program of study to insure compliance with requirements. Many state directors of teacher credentialing have signed Interstate Agreements through NASDTEC that expedite the certification process.

OHIO DOMINICAN COLLEGE

Division of Education
1216 Sunbury Road
Columbus, Ohio 43219
Phone: (614) 251-4025
Fax: (614) 252-0776
E-mail: colbyc@ohiodominican.edu
Internet: http://www.ohiodominican.edu

Institution Description: Ohio Dominican College is a private college affiliated with the Dominican Sisters of Saint Mary of the Springs, Roman Catholic Church. The college was founded in 1911.

The Division of Education offers undergraduate and graduate programs leading to teacher licensure in Ohio.

Institution Control: Private.

Calendar: Semester. Academic year August to July.

Official(s): Dr. Catherine Colby, Chair.

Faculty: Full-time 12; adjunct 15.

Degrees Awarded: 77 baccalaureate.

Admission Requirements: *Undergraduate:* Graduation from an accredited secondary school with 16 college preparatory units or GED. College Board SAT or ACT composite. *Teacher education specific:* Maintain a 3.0 GPA in the professional education courses and field of licensure; professional commitment; high scholastic attainment; passing scores on PRAXIS I exams (reading, writing, mathematics); faculty interview. *Graduate:* Baccalaureate degree from a regionally accredited institution. *Teacher education specific:* 3.0 GPA; GRE; completion of all required departmental exams; teaching licensure and one year teaching experience; three letters of recommendation; faculty interview.

Fees and Expenses: Undergraduate: $17,200 per academic year. Graduate: $440 per credit hour. On-campus room and board: $5,500 to $5,900 per year. Other fees: $1,495. Books and supplies: $665.

Financial Aid: Resources specifically for eligible students enrolled in teacher education programs are awarded on the basis of financial need. The institution has a Program Participation Agreement with the U.S. Department of Education for eligible students to receive Pell Grants and other federal aid. Teacher scholarships available to qualifying students. *Contact:* Robert mathies at: (614) 251-4778 or e-mail at: mathiasr@ohiodominican.edu.

Accreditation: *Regional:* NCA. *Member of:* AACTE. *Approved by:* Ohio Department of Education.

Undergraduate Programs: Programs leading to the Bachelor of Science in Education and Ohio licensure are offered in: early childhood education (preK-3); middle childhood education (grades 4-9); intervention specialist: mild to moderate educational needs (K-12); intervention specialist: moderate to intensive educational needs (K-12); adolescent/young adult (grades 7-12 in earth science/chemistry, integrated language arts, integrated social studies, integrated science, life science, library media; physical education, visual arts, teaching English to speakers of other languages-endorsement). All programs require the completion of a general education core, professional studies, subject content area, field experiences, and student teaching.

Graduate Programs: The Master of Education in curriculum and instruction comprises a standards-driven, research-based, reflective leadership development approach through which teachers and other school personnel develop the knowledge, skills, and dispositions deemed essential for the reflective education professional. The program is for practicing teachers and does not include the license to teach. A total of 21 credits in core courses and 15 credits in professional courses must be completed for the degree award.

Licensure/Reciprocity: Ohio. Students seeking teaching certification in a state other than Ohio should consult with that state's teacher certification office early in their program of study to insure compliance with requirements. Many state directors of teacher credentialing have signed Interstate Agreements through NASDTEC that expedite the certification process.

OHIO NORTHERN UNIVERSITY
Department of Education
Teacher Education Program
525 South Main Street
Ada, Ohio 45810
Phone: (419) 772-2000
Fax: (419) 772-1932
E-mail: m-haynes@onu.edu
Internet: http://www.onu.edu

Institution Description: Ohio Northern University is a private institution affiliated with the United Methodist Church. It was established as Northwestern Ohio Normal School in 1871. The present name was adopted in 1903.

The Teacher Education Program is designed to provide prospective teachers with the general education, subject area concentration, and professional education experiences that will enable the student to enter the profession with competency.

Institution Control: Private.

Calendar: Quarter. Academic year September to May.

Official(s): Dr. Mary Haynes, Director, Center for Teacher Education; Dr. Irma Lou Griggs, Department Chairperson.

Faculty: Full-time 6.

Degrees Awarded: 53 baccalaureate.

Admission Requirements: *Undergraduate:* Graduation from an accredited secondary school or GED; College Board SAT or ACT composite. *Teacher education specific:* Maintain a 2.5 GPA in

the professional education courses and field of licensure; professional commitment; high scholastic attainment; passing scores on PRAXIS I exams (reading, writing, mathematics); faculty interview. *Graduate:* Baccalaureate degree from a regionally accredited institution. *Teacher education specific:* 2.75 GPA; GRE; completion of all required departmental exams; teaching licensure where required by program pursued; letters of recommendation; faculty interview.

Fees and Expenses: Undergraduate $24,645 per academic year. Graduate tuition charged per credit hour. On-campus room and board: $6,030. Other expenses: $1,800. Books and supplies: $1,000.

Financial Aid: Resources specifically for eligible students enrolled in teacher education programs are awarded on the basis of financial need and academic merit. The institution has a Program Participation Agreement with the U.S. Department of Education for eligible students to receive Pell Grants and other federal aid. Teacher scholarships available to qualifying students. *Contact:* Financial Aid Office at: (419) 772-2272.

Accreditation: *Regional:* NCA. *Professional:* NCATE. *Member of:* AACTE. *Approved by:* Ohio Department of Education.

Undergraduate Programs: Teacher Education Programs leading to the bachelor's degree and state licensure include: early childhood (preK-3), middle childhood (4-9), integrated language arts (7-12), integrated mathematics (7-12), integrated science (7-12), integrated social studies (7-12), life science (7-12), physical sciences (7-12), foreign language (preK-12), health (preK-12), music (preK-12), physical education (preK-12), visual arts (preK-12), technology education (K-12).

All programs require the completion of a general education core, professional studies, subject content area, field experiences, and student teaching. Students who have successfully completed the approved teacher education program will take and pass the PRAXIS II exams and then be eligible for a provisional teacher license that will be valid for two years.

Graduate Programs: The Master of Education in Teaching degree program consists of three components: core requirements that will include emphasis in ethics and character education; area of specialization in reading; practicum. Students must complete a total of 45 quarter hours.

Licensure/Reciprocity: Ohio. Students seeking teaching certification in a state other than Ohio should consult with that state's teacher certification office early in their program of study to insure compliance with requirements. Many state directors of teacher credentialing have signed Interstate Agreements through NASDTEC that expedite the certification process.

THE OHIO STATE UNIVERSITY
School of Teaching and Learning
333 Arps Hall
1945 North High Street
Columbus, Ohio 43210-1172
Phone: (614) 292-1257
Fax: (614) 292-4818
E-mail: coe@osu.edu
Internet: http://www.osu.edu

Institution Description: The Ohio State University is a land-grant institution with regional campuses at Lima, Mansfield, Marion, and Newark. The university was established and chartered in 1870.

The School of Teaching and Learning has a strong commitment to research, teaching, and public service.

Institution Control: Public.

Calendar: Quarter. Academic year September to June.

Official(s): Dr. Peter V. Paul, Director; Dr. Barbara Lehman, Program Coordinator.

Faculty: Full-time 62.

Degrees Awarded: 355 baccalaureate; 750 master's; 96 doctorate.

Admission Requirements: *Undergraduate:* Graduation from an accredited secondary school or GED; College Board SAT or ACT composite. *Teacher education specific:* Maintain a 3.0 GPA in

THE OHIO STATE UNIVERSITY—*cont'd*

the professional education courses and field of licensure; professional commitment; high scholastic attainment; passing scores on PRAXIS I exams (reading, writing, mathematics); faculty interview. *Graduate:* Baccalaureate degree from a regionally accredited institution. *Teacher education specific:* GRE; completion of all required departmental exams; teaching licensure where required by program pursued; faculty interview.

Fees and Expenses: Undergraduate: in-state $6,651 per academic year; out-of-state $16,638. Graduate: Tuition charged per credit hour. On-campus room and board: $6,780. Other expenses: $2,985. Books and supplies: $990.

Financial Aid: Resources specifically for eligible students enrolled in teacher education programs are awarded on the basis of financial need and academic merit. The institution has a Program Participation Agreement with the U.S. Department of Education for eligible students to receive Pell Grants and other federal aid. Teacher scholarships available to qualifying students. *Contact:* Financial Aid Office at: (614) 292-0300.

Accreditation: *Regional:* NCA. *Professional:* NCATE. *Member of:* AACTE. *Approved by:* Ohio Department of Education.

Undergraduate Programs: The School of Teaching and Learning is composed of three sections and their specialty areas; Integrated Teaching and Learning (early childhood education, hearing impairment, visual impairment); Language, Literacy, and Culture (English education; foreign and second language education [TESOL], drama, language arts, literature, reading, social studies, and global education); Mathematics, Science, and Technology Education (mathematics education, science education, technology education).

All baccalaureate programs require the completion of a general education core, professional studies, subject content area, field experiences, and student teaching.

Graduate Programs: The Master of Education, Master of Arts, and Doctor of Philosophy are offered in all three sections as described above. In addition to graduate programs on the Columbus campus, graduate programs in Integrated Teaching and Learning are also offered on the regional campuses. The school also houses a Master of Education program in middle childhood and a full-time sequential program of professional courses leading to initial Ohio teacher licensure in grades four through nine.

The Integrated Teaching and Learning program is located on five campuses (Columbus, Lima, Marion, Mansfield, Newark). Students apply to one campus but may take courses and work with faculty on any campus.

Licensure/Reciprocity: Ohio. Students seeking teaching certification in a state other than Ohio should consult with that state's teacher certification office early in their program of study to insure compliance with requirements. Many state directors of teacher credentialing have signed Interstate Agreements through NASDTEC that expedite the certification process.

OHIO UNIVERSITY

College of Education
Department of Teacher Education
133 McCracken Hall
Athens, Ohio 45701-2979
Phone: (740) 593-4403
Fax: (740) 593-0569
E-mail: education@ohio.edu
Internet: http://www.ohio.edu

Institution Description: Ohio University is a state institution with separately accredited associate degree-granting regional campuses in Chillecothe, Ironton, Lancaster, St. Clairsville, and Zanesville. The university was founded in 1804.

The College of Education is committed to providing supportive and challenging experiences that foster the development of educational and human service professionals and the local, national, and international communities they serve.

Institution Control: Public.
Calendar: Quarter. Academic year September to June.

Official(s): Dr. James L. Heap, Dean.
Faculty: Full-time 55; part-time 35; adjunct 6.
Degrees Awarded: 467 baccalaureate; 149 master's; 25 doctorate.

Admission Requirements: *Undergraduate:* Graduation from an accredited secondary school or GED; College Board SAT or ACT composite. *Teacher education specific:* Maintain a 3.0 GPA in the professional education courses and field of licensure; professional commitment; high scholastic attainment; passing scores on PRAXIS I exams (reading, writing, mathematics); faculty interview. *Graduate:* Baccalaureate degree from a regionally accredited institution. *Teacher education specific:* GRE; completion of all required departmental exams; teaching licensure where required by program pursued; faculty interview.

Fees and Expenses: Undergraduate: in-state $6,336 per academic year; out-of-state $13,818. Graduate: in-state $7,708; out-of-state $14,380. On-campus room and board: : $6,777. Books and supplies: $810.

Financial Aid: Resources specifically for eligible students enrolled in teacher education programs are awarded on the basis of financial need and academic merit. The institution has a Program Participation Agreement with the U.S. Department of Education for eligible students to receive Pell Grants and other federal aid. Teacher scholarships available to qualifying students. *Contact:* Dr. Kim Brown, Director of Undergraduate Student Services at: (740) 593-4400 or e-mail at: education@ohio.edu.

Accreditation: *Regional:* NCA. *Professional:* NCATE. *Member of:* AACTE. *Approved by:* Ohio Department of Education.

Undergraduate Programs: Undergraduate programs leading to Ohio licensure and the baccalaureate degree include: early childhood education, middle childhood education, adolescent to young adult education, special education-intervention specialists program K-12, multi-age education (K-12 special fields). All programs require the completion of a general education core, professional studies, subject content area, field experiences, and student teaching.

For initial certification/licensure in the state of Ohio, individuals must pass the PRAXIS II examinations that include professional knowledge and the content knowledge test(s) for the specific license being sought.

Graduate Programs: Graduate teacher education programs are available in elementary education, middle childhood, middle childhood with licensure, reading education, adolescent to young adult education, adolescent to young adult education with licensure, mathematics education, curriculum and instruction, special education, and special education with licensure.

Licensure/Reciprocity: Ohio. Students seeking teaching certification in a state other than Ohio should consult with that state's teacher certification office early in their program of study to insure compliance with requirements. Many state directors of teacher credentialing have signed Interstate Agreements through NASDTEC that expedite the certification process.

OHIO WESLEYAN UNIVERSITY

Department of Education
214 Phillips Hall
61 South Sandusky Street
Delaware, Ohio 43015
Phone: (740) 368-3562
Fax: (740) 368-3553
E-mail: aamcclur@owu.edu
Internet: http://www.owu.edu

Institution Description: Ohio Wesleyan University is a private institution affiliated with the United Methodist Church. The university was founded in 1842.

Within a liberal arts setting, the Department of Education offers a professional program to qualify students for a teaching license when the Bachelor of Arts degree is awarded.

Institution Control: Private.
Calendar: Semester. Academic year August to May.
Official(s): Dr. Amy A. McClure, Chairperson.

Faculty: Full-time 5; part-time 3; adjunct 1.

Degrees Awarded: 25 baccalaureate.

Admission Requirements: *Undergraduate:* Graduation from an accredited secondary school or GED; College Board SAT or ACT composite. *Teacher education specific:* 2.8 GPA overall and in content area; completion of introductory courses; passing scores on PRAXIS I exams (reading, writing, mathematics); recommendations; faculty interview.

Fees and Expenses: $24,000 per academic year. On-campus room and board: $7,010. Personal expenses: $1,250. Books and supplies: $1,000.

Financial Aid: Resources specifically for eligible students enrolled in teacher education programs are awarded on the basis of financial need and academic merit. The institution has a Program Participation Agreement with the U.S. Department of Education for eligible students to receive Pell Grants and other federal aid. Teacher scholarships available to qualifying students. *Contact:* Greg Matthews at: (740) 368-3052 or e-mail at: gwmatthe@owu.edu.

Accreditation: *Regional:* NCA. *Professional:* NCATE. *Member of:* AACTE. *Approved by:* Ohio Department of Education.

Undergraduate Programs: Programs leading to the baccalaureate degree and Ohio teacher licensure include: early childhood (kindergarten to grade 3); middle childhood (grades 4-9); adolescence to young adult (grades 7-12 with concentrations in earth sciences, integrated language arts, integrated mathematics, integrated science, integrated social science, life sciences, physical sciences); multi-age (grades preK-12 with concentrations in drama/theater, foreign language [French, German, Latin, Spanish], music, physical education, visual arts). All programs require the completion of a general education core, professional studies, subject content area, field experiences, and student teaching. For initial certification/licensure in the state of Ohio, individuals must pass the PRAXIS II examinations that include professional knowledge and the content knowledge test(s) for the specific license being sought.

Licensure/Reciprocity: Ohio. Students seeking teaching certification in a state other than Ohio should consult with that state's teacher certification office early in their program of study to insure compliance with requirements. Many state directors of teacher credentialing have signed Interstate Agreements through NASDTEC that expedite the certification process.

OTTERBEIN COLLEGE
Department of Education
Teacher Education Program
College and Grove Streets
Westerville, Ohio 43081
Phone: (614) 823-1214
Fax: (614) 823-3036
E-mail: kreichley@@otterbein.edu
Internet: http://www.otterbein.edu

Institution Description: Otterbein College is a private, independent, nonprofit college affiliated with the United Methodist Church. The college was founded in 1847.

The Teacher Education program at Otterbein College is based on the philosophy that a liberal education is the best preparation for teachers.

Institution Control: Private.

Calendar: Quarter. Academic year September to June.

Official(s): Dr. Paula Knight, Chairperson, Department of Education.

Faculty: Full-time 14; part-time 14.

Degrees Awarded: 63 baccalaureate; 28 master's.

Admission Requirements: *Undergraduate:* Graduation from an accredited secondary school or GED; College Board SAT or ACT composite. *Teacher education specific:* Maintain a 2.5 GPA; strong high school academic records; professional commitment; passing scores on PRAXIS I exams (reading, writing, mathematics); faculty interview. *Graduate:* Baccalaureate degree from a regionally accredited institution. *Teacher education specific:* 2.75

GPA; completion of all required departmental exams; teaching licensure where required by program pursued; faculty interview.

Fees and Expenses: Undergraduate: $20,133 per academic year. Graduate: $254 per credit hour. On-campus room and board: $5,952.

Financial Aid: Resources specifically for eligible students enrolled in teacher education programs are awarded on the basis of financial need and academic merit. The institution has a Program Participation Agreement with the U.S. Department of Education for eligible students to receive Pell Grants and other federal aid. Teacher scholarships available to qualifying students. *Contact:* Thomas V. Yarnell at: (614) 823-1502.

Accreditation: *Regional:* NCA. *Professional:* NCATE. *Member of:* AACTE. *Approved by:* Ohio Department of Education.

Undergraduate Programs: Programs leading to the baccalaureate degree and Ohio teacher licensure include: early childhood (kindergarten to grade 3); middle childhood (grades 4-9 with two subject concentration areas); adolescence to young adult (grades 7-12 with concentrations in integrated language arts, integrated mathematics, integrated social science, life sciences, physical sciences); multi-age (grades preK-12 with concentrations in art, French, health, music, physical education, Spanish). All programs require the completion of a general education core, professional studies, field experiences, and student teaching.

For initial certification/licensure in the state of Ohio, individuals must pass the PRAXIS II examinations that include professional knowledge and the content knowledge test(s) for the specific license being sought.

Graduate Programs: A Master of Arts in Teaching degree program is available to qualified liberal arts graduates to prepare for teacher licensure in middle childhood education. A Master of Arts in Education degree program is available to certified/licensed teachers. Majors are offered in curriculum and instruction and reading.

Licensure/Reciprocity: Ohio. Students seeking teaching certification in a state other than Ohio should consult with that state's teacher certification office early in their program of study to insure compliance with requirements. Many state directors of teacher credentialing have signed Interstate Agreements through NASDTEC that expedite the certification process.

SHAWNEE STATE UNIVERSITY
Department of Teacher Education
940 Second Street
Portsmouth, Ohio 45662
Phone: (740) 351-3451
Fax: (740) 351-3603
E-mail: dtodt@shawnee.edu
Internet: http://www.shawnee.edu

Institution Description: Shawnee State University was created as Shawnee State General and Technical College by a merger of the Ohio University Regional Campus and Scioto Technical College in 1975. The name was changed to Shawnee State Community College 1978 and the present name was adopted in 1986.

The Department of Teacher Education is dedicated to preparing highly skilled educators and sports professionals and supporting professional development of practicing professionals.

Institution Control: Public.

Calendar: Quarter. Academic year September to July.

Official(s): Dr. David E. Todt, Chairperson.

Faculty: Full-time 8; adjunct 12.

Degrees Awarded: 39 baccalaureate.

Admission Requirements: *Undergraduate:* Graduation from an accredited secondary school or GED; ACT composite required. *Teacher education specific:* 2.75 GPA passing scores on PRAXIS I exams (reading, writing, mathematics); personal goal statement; faculty interview.

SHAWNEE STATE UNIVERSITY—*cont'd*

Fees and Expenses: Undergraduate: $6,336 per academic year; out-of-state $13,818. Graduate: Tuition charged per credit hour. On-campus room and board: $6,309.

Financial Aid: Resources specifically for eligible students enrolled in teacher education programs are awarded on the basis of financial need and academic merit. The institution has a Program Participation Agreement with the U.S. Department of Education for eligible students to receive Pell Grants and other federal aid. Teacher scholarships available to qualifying students. *Contact:* Pat Moore at: (740) 351-3245 or e-mail at: pmoore@shawnee.edu.

Accreditation: *Regional:* NCA. *Professional:* NCATE. *Member of:* AACTE. *Approved by:* Ohio Department of Education.

Undergraduate Programs: Programs leading to the baccalaureate degree and Ohio teacher licensure include: early childhood (grades pre-K to 3); early childhood intervention specialist (grades preK-3); middle childhood (grades 4-9); multi-age intervention specialist (grades K-12); Bachelor of Science in athletic training; Bachelor of Science in sports studies; adolescent to young adult (grades 7-12 with concentrations in integrated language arts, integrated mathematics, integrated social science, earth science, integrated science, life science, physical science); middle childhood (grades 4-9 in mathematics and science; multi-age visual arts (grades preK-12); reading endorsement. Adolescent to young adult, middle childhood, and multi-age visual arts programs are in conjunction with other liberal arts and sciences departments.

All programs require the completion of a general education core, professional studies, subject content area, field experiences, and student teaching.

Licensure/Reciprocity: Ohio. Students seeking teaching certification in a state other than Ohio should consult with that state's teacher certification office early in their program of study to insure compliance with requirements. Many state directors of teacher credentialing have signed Interstate Agreements through NASDTEC that expedite the certification process.

UNIVERSITY OF AKRON

College of Education
210 Zook Hall
302 East Buchtel Common
Akron, Ohio 44325
Phone: (330) 972-7111
Fax: (330) 972-5636
E-mail: admission@uakron.edu
Internet: http://www.uakron.edu

Institution Description: The University of Akron was established by the Universalist Church of Ohio as the nonsectarian Buchtel College in 1870. It became a public institution in 1914 with the name Municipal University. The present name was adopted in 1923. The school became state-affiliated in 1963 and a state university in 1967.

The College of Education offers a variety of programs at the undergraduate and graduate levels.

Institution Control: Public.

Calendar: Semester. Academic year September to May.

Official(s): Dr. Elizabeth Stroble, Dean.

Faculty: Not reported.

Degrees Awarded: 299 baccalaureate; 269 master's; 8 doctorate.

Admission Requirements: *Undergraduate:* Graduation from an accredited secondary school or GED; College Board SAT or ACT composite. *Teacher education specific:* Completion of 30 semester hours of coursework; 2.5 GPA; professional commitment; passing scores on PRAXIS I exams (reading, writing, mathematics); faculty interview. *Graduate:* Baccalaureate degree from a regionally accredited institution. *Teacher education specific:* 2.75 GPA; completion of all required departmental exams; teaching licensure where required by program pursued; faculty interview.

Fees and Expenses: Undergraduate: in-state $6,809 per academic year; out-of-state $14,298. Graduate: Tuition charged per credit hour. On-campus room and board: $6,268. Other expenses: $2,504. Books and supplies: $800.

Financial Aid: Resources specifically for eligible students enrolled in teacher education programs are awarded on the basis of financial need and academic merit. The institution has a Program Participation Agreement with the U.S. Department of Education for eligible students to receive Pell Grants and other federal aid. Teacher scholarships available to qualifying students. *Contact:* Financial Aid Office at: (330) 972-7032.

Accreditation: *Regional:* NCA. *Professional:* NCATE. *Member of:* AACTE. *Approved by:* Ohio Department of Education.

Undergraduate Programs: Programs leading to the baccalaureate degree and Ohio teacher licensure include: early childhood education, middle level education, secondary education, adolescent to young adult (grades 7-12) with concentrations in chemistry-physics, earth science-chemistry/physics, life science-chemistry/earth science/physics, integrated mathematics, integrated language arts, integrated language arts with reading endorsement, integrated social studies, French, Spanish, drama/theater, visual arts; technical education, physical education, outdoor education, health education, community health and wellness education, special education.

All programs require the completion of a general education core, professional studies, subject content area, field experiences, and student teaching.

Graduate Programs: Programs leading to the Master of Arts in Education, Master of Science in Education, and Master of Science in Technical Education are offered in the following departments: Curriculum and Instructional Studies (elementary or secondary education, elementary education with certification, special education, and secondary education); Counseling; Educational Foundations and Leadership (educational administration, education administration specialists, technical education); Sport Science; Wellness Education.

Licensure/Reciprocity: Ohio. Students seeking teaching certification in a state other than Ohio should consult with that state's teacher certification office early in their program of study to insure compliance with requirements. Many state directors of teacher credentialing have signed Interstate Agreements through NASDTEC that expedite the certification process.

UNIVERSITY OF CINCINNATI

Division of Teacher Education
2624 Clifton Avenue
P.O. Box 210002
Cincinnati, Ohio 45221-0002
Phone: (513) 556-3600
Fax: (513) 556-1001
E-mail: education@uc.edu
Internet: http://www.uc.edu

Institution Description: The University of Cincinnati is a state institution that was established and incorporated as Cincinnati College and Medical College of Ohio in 1819.

The Division of Teacher Education is an outgrowth of the College for Teachers established in 1905. Undergraduate and graduate programs leading to Ohio teacher licensure are offered.

Institution Control: Public.

Calendar: Quarter. Academic year September to June.

Official(s): Dr. Glenn Markle, Division Head.

Faculty: Full-time 50.

Degrees Awarded: 157 baccalaureate; 212 master's; 28 doctorate.

Admission Requirements: *Undergraduate:* Graduation from an accredited secondary school or GED; College Board SAT or ACT composite. *Teacher education specific:* Maintain a 2.5 GPA; strong high school academic records; professional commitment; passing scores on PRAXIS I exams (reading, writing, mathematics); faculty interview. *Graduate:* Baccalaureate degree from a regionally accredited institution. *Teacher education specific:* 2.75

GPA; completion of all required departmental exams; teaching licensure where required by program pursued; faculty interview.

Fees and Expenses: Undergraduate: in-state $7,623 per academic year; out-of-state $19,230. On-campus room and board: $7,113. Other expenses: $4,440. Books and supplies: $815.

Financial Aid: Resources specifically for eligible students enrolled in teacher education programs are awarded on the basis of financial need and academic merit. The institution has a Program Participation Agreement with the U.S. Department of Education for eligible students to receive Pell Grants and other federal aid. Teacher scholarships available to qualifying students. *Contact:* Financial Aid Office at: (513) 556-6982.

Accreditation: *Regional:* NCA. *Professional:* NCATE. *Member of:* AACTE. *Approved by:* Ohio Department of Education.

Undergraduate Programs: Students pursuing undergraduate degrees in early childhood education complete a concentration in a selected area. Students in middle childhood education or secondary education may enroll jointly in the College of Education and the College of Arts and sciences, earning two degrees in a program that includes a year-long internship option in the school. Graduates earn a Bachelor of Arts or a Bachelor of Science degree in arts and sciences in their selected major and a Bachelor of Science degree in education plus a teaching certificate from Ohio.

Graduate Programs: The master's degree programs within the division are designed to broaden and refine knowledge, skills, values, and attitudes of the professional education by providing a range of classroom and practical experiences. Degrees are offered in: curriculum and instruction, middle childhood education, literacy, secondary education, special education and teaching English as a second language.

The Doctor of Education degree programs are offered in curriculum and instruction, literacy secialization, language and literacy in young children with disabilities, and special education in early intervention and prevention.

Licensure/Reciprocity: Ohio. Students seeking teaching certification in a state other than Ohio should consult with that state's teacher certification office early in their program of study to insure compliance with requirements. Many state directors of teacher credentialing have signed Interstate Agreements through NASDTEC that expedite the certification process.

UNIVERSITY OF DAYTON
School of Education and Allied Professions
Department of Teacher Education
Chaminade Hall, Room 104
300 College Park Avenue
Dayton, Ohio 45469-1300
Phone: (937) 229-4411
Fax: (937) 229-4729
E-mail: soeap@udayton.edu
Internet: http://www.udayton.edu

Institution Description: The University of Dayton is a private institution affiliated with the Society of Mary, Roman Catholic Church. The university was founded in 1850 as St. Mary's School for Boys. The present name was adopted in 1920 and the school became coeducational in 1923.

The Department of Teacher Education offers undergraduate and graduate degree programs leading to teacher licensure in Ohio.

Institution Control: Private.

Calendar: Trimester. Academic year August to April.

Official(s): Dr. Thomas J. Lasley, Dean.

Faculty: Full-time 22.

Degrees Awarded: 167 baccalaureate; 433 master's; 8 doctorate.

Admission Requirements: *Undergraduate:* Graduation from an accredited secondary school with 16 academic units or GED; College Board SAT or ACT composite. *Teacher education specific:* Maintain a 2.5 GPA in the professional education courses and field of licensure; professional commitment; high scholastic

attainment; passing scores on PRAXIS I exams (reading, writing, mathematics); faculty interview. *Graduate:* Baccalaureate degree from a regionally accredited institution. *Teacher education specific:* 2.75 GPA; completion of all required departmental exams; teaching licensure where required by program pursued; faculty interview.

Fees and Expenses: Undergraduate: $18,390 per academic year. Graduate: Tuition charged per credit hour. On-campus room and board: $6,260. Other expenses: $1,200. Books and supplies: $800.

Financial Aid: Resources specifically for eligible students enrolled in teacher education programs are awarded on the basis of financial need and academic merit. The institution has a Program Participation Agreement with the U.S. Department of Education for eligible students to receive Pell Grants and other federal aid. Teacher scholarships available to qualifying students. *Contact:* Financial Aid Office at: (937) 229-4311.

Accreditation: *Regional:* NCA. *Professional:* NCATE. *Member of:* AACTE. *Approved by:* Ohio Department of Education.

Undergraduate Programs: The Department of Teacher Education offers degree programs in early childhood (grades K-3), middle childhood (grades 4-9), adolescent to young adult (grades 7-12), and intervention specialist (K-12). Special licenses can also be earned in visual arts and foreign language. Students enrolled in the College of Arts and Sciences may also enroll in the adolescent to young adult education program without transferring to the School of Education and Allied Professions. All programs require the completion of a general education core, professional studies, subject content area, field experiences, and student teaching.

Graduate Programs: Candidates who wish to pursue graduate work at the University of Dayton must be admitted to Graduate School and meet the general requirements of the School of Education and Allied Professions. The Department of Teacher Education offers the licensure and master's degree programs. Each program has specific requirements.

Licensure/Reciprocity: Ohio. Students seeking teaching certification in a state other than Ohio should consult with that state's teacher certification office early in their program of study to insure compliance with requirements. Many state directors of teacher credentialing have signed Interstate Agreements through NASDTEC that expedite the certification process.

THE UNIVERSITY OF FINDLAY
College of Education
1000 North Main Street
Findlay, Ohio 45840-3695
Phone: (419) 434-4962
Fax: (419) 434-45342
E-mail: admissions@mail.findlay.edu
Internet: http://www.findlay.edu

Institution Description: The University of Findlay, formerly Findlay College, is a private institution affiliated with the Churches of God, General Conference. The institution was established and chartered in 1882.

The College of Education offers teacher education majors and programs leading to licensures and endorsements for teaching in Ohio.

Institution Control: Private.

Calendar: Semester. Academic year August to May.

Official(s): Dr. Kenneth E. Zirkle, President.

Faculty: Full-time 19; part-time 2.

Degrees Awarded: 92 baccalaureate; 147 master's.

Admission Requirements: *Undergraduate:* Graduation from an accredited secondary school with 16 academic units or GED; College Board SAT or ACT composite. *Teacher education specific:* Maintain a 2.75 GPA in all coursework; completion of foundations courses with grades of C or better; portfolio built around goals and objectives; passing scores on PRAXIS I exams (reading, writing, mathematics); faculty interview. *Graduate:* Baccalaureate degree from a regionally accredited institution. *Teacher*

THE UNIVERSITY OF FINDLAY—*cont'd*

education specific: 2.75 GPA; completion of all required departmental exams; teaching licensure where required by program pursued; faculty interview.

Fees and Expenses: Undergraduate: $19,052 per academic year. Graduate: Tuition charged per credit hour. On-campus room and board: $7,060. Other expenses: $900. Books and supplies: $500.

Financial Aid: Resources specifically for eligible students enrolled in teacher education programs are awarded on the basis of financial need and academic merit. The institution has a Program Participation Agreement with the U.S. Department of Education for eligible students to receive Pell Grants and other federal aid. Teacher scholarships available to qualifying students. *Contact:* Financial Aid Office at: (419) 434-4791.

Accreditation: *Regional:* NCA. *Professional:* NCATE. *Member of:* AACTE. *Approved by:* Ohio Department of Education.

Undergraduate Programs: Bachelor of Arts in Education Programs include: adolescent/young adult/integrated English/language arts; adolescent/young adult/integrated social studies; middle childhood-language arts/social studies; multi-age/drama, theatre, Japanese, Spanish, visual arts.

The Bachelor of Science in Education programs include: adolescent/young adult/earth science, integrated mathematics, life science; early childhood; intervention specialist education/mIld to moderate disabilities; middle childhood-language arts-math, science, math/science, math/social studies, science/social studies; multi-age/health education/physical education.

Endorsements are offered in bilingual/multicultural, reading, and teaching English to speakers of other languages.

All programs require the completion of a general education core, professional studies, subject content area, field experiences, and student teaching.

Graduate Programs: The Master of Arts in Education degree requires the completion of 33 semester hours of graduate level classes in education and related fields. In order to be a program completer, candidates must successfully complete all aspects of the post-baccalaureate assessment plan, including all PRAXIS II tests in their area of licensure.

Licensure/Reciprocity: Ohio. Students seeking teaching certification in a state other than Ohio should consult with that state's teacher certification office early in their program of study to insure compliance with requirements. Many state directors of teacher credentialing have signed Interstate Agreements through NASDTEC that expedite the certification process.

UNIVERSITY OF RIO GRANDE

College of Professional Studies
School of Education
218 North College Avenue
Rio Grande, Ohio 45674-3131
Phone: (740) 245-5353
Fax: (740) 245-7260
E-mail: cosssie@rio.edu
Internet: http://www.rio.edu

Institution Description: The University of Rio Grande, formerly Rio Grande College/Community College is a private, independent, nonprofit institution that was founded in 1875. It is affiliated with the Free Will Baptist Church.

The mission of the School of Education is to provide a challenging environment in which students develop into professional individuals who offer service to communities.

Institution Control: Private.

Calendar: Quarter. Academic year September to June.

Official(s): Dr. Barry M. Dorsey, President.

Faculty: Full-time 13; part-time 2.

Degrees Awarded: 48 baccalaureate; 87 master's.

Admission Requirements: *Undergraduate:* Graduation from an accredited secondary school with 16 academic units or GED; College Board SAT or ACT composite. *Teacher education specific:* Maintain a 3.0 GPA in the professional education courses and

field of licensure; professional commitment; high scholastic attainment; passing scores on PRAXIS I exams (reading, writing, mathematics); personal goal essay; faculty interview. *Graduate:* Baccalaureate degree from a regionally accredited institution. *Teacher education specific:* 2.75 GPA; completion of all required departmental exams; teaching licensure where required by program pursued; faculty interview.

Fees and Expenses: Undergraduate: $10,058 per academic year; out-of-state $11,076. Graduate: Tuition charged per credit hour. On-campus room and board: $5,768. Other expenses: $2,360. Books and supplies: $1,000.

Financial Aid: Resources specifically for eligible students enrolled in teacher education programs are awarded on the basis of financial need and academic merit. The institution has a Program Participation Agreement with the U.S. Department of Education for eligible students to receive Pell Grants and other federal aid. Teacher scholarships available to qualifying students. *Contact:* Financial Aid Office at: (740) 245-7218.

Accreditation: *Regional:* NCA. *Member of:* AACTE. *Approved by:* Ohio Department of Education.

Undergraduate Programs: The School of Education offers the Bachelor of Science degree with reading endorsement in the areas of early childhood, middle childhood, adolescent to young adult, multi-age, and intervention specialist: mild/moderate. The Bachelor of Science degree is also available in sports and exercise studies. The School of Education also offers coursework for the Alternative Teacher License, renewal, and/or upgrading of certification or license.

All baccalaureate programs require the completion of a general education core, professional studies, subject content area, field experiences, and student teaching.

Graduate Programs: The graduate program offers a Master's Degree in Classroom Teaching as well as various workshops and courses that might be used for recertification, upgrade, or renewal. The program consists of four concentration: reading, learning disabilities, mathematics, and fine arts.

Licensure/Reciprocity: Ohio. Students seeking teaching certification in a state other than Ohio should consult with that state's teacher certification office early in their program of study to insure compliance with requirements. Many state directors of teacher credentialing have signed Interstate Agreements through NASDTEC that expedite the certification process.

UNIVERSITY OF TOLEDO

College of Education
Department of Curriculum and Instruction
2801 West Bancroft Street
Toledo, Ohio 43606-3390
Phone: (419) 530-4636
Fax: (419) 530-4504
E-mail: coe@utoledo.edu
Internet: http://www.utoledo.edu

Institution Description: The University of Toledo is a state institution. It was established and chartered as Toledo University of Arts and Trades in 1872.

The Department of Curriculum and Instruction offers programs leading to undergraduate and graduate degrees and teacher licensure in Ohio.

Institution Control: Public.

Calendar: Semester. Academic year September to June.

Official(s): Dr. Thomas Switzer, Dean; Dr. William Weber, Chair, Curriculum and Instruction.

Faculty: Full-time 27 (Curriculum and Instruction).

Degrees Awarded: 254 baccalaureate; 294 master's; 11 doctorate.

Admission Requirements: *Undergraduate:* Graduation from an accredited secondary school or GED; College Board SAT or ACT composite. *Teacher education specific:* Maintain a 2.5 GPA; strong high school academic records; professional commitment; passing scores on PRAXIS I exams (reading, writing, mathematics); faculty interview. *Graduate:* Baccalaureate degree from a regionally accredited institution. *Teacher education specific:* 2.75

GPA; completion of all required departmental exams; teaching licensure where required by program pursued; faculty interview.

Fees and Expenses: Undergraduate: in-state $6,145 per academic year; out-of-state $15,054. On-campus room and board: $7,044. Other expenses: $3,210. Books and supplies: $750.

Financial Aid: Resources specifically for eligible students enrolled in teacher education programs are awarded on the basis of financial need and academic merit. The institution has a Program Participation Agreement with the U.S. Department of Education for eligible students to receive Pell Grants and other federal aid. Teacher scholarships available to qualifying students. *Contact:* Financial Aid Office at: (419) 530-8700.

Accreditation: *Regional:* NCA. *Member of:* AACTE. *Approved by:* Ohio Department of Education.

Undergraduate Programs: The adolescent/young adult program is preparation for licensure for teaching grades 7-12 in a particular content areas. It is a dual-degree program designed to help prospective teachers move from being college students through their experiences as teaching interns in their role as beginning classroom teachers. Students may choose content areas from: arts, social studies, mathematics, life science, earth science, chemistry, physics.

The middle childhood licensure program leads to licensure for grades 4-9 in two subject areas in which the student desires to teach: mathematics, science, language arts, social studies.

Multi-age licensure programs are offered in: foreign language: French, German, Spanish; health; physical education, visual arts.

All programs require the completion of a general education core, professional studies, subject content area, field experiences, and student teaching.

Graduate Programs: A Master of Science degree program is offered in educational technology. For further information, contact Dr. Robert F. Sullivan, Program Coordinator at robert.sullivan@utoledo.edu.

Licensure/Reciprocity: Ohio. Students seeking teaching certification in a state other than Ohio should consult with that state's teacher certification office early in their program of study to insure compliance with requirements. Many state directors of teacher credentialing have signed Interstate Agreements through NASDTEC that expedite the certification process.

URBANA UNIVERSITY
Division of Education and Allied Programs
Teacher Education Program
North Hall
579 College Way
Urbana, Ohio 43078
Phone: (937) 484-1340
Fax: (937) 484-1322
E-mail: kengle@urbana.edu
Internet: http://www.urbana.edu

Institution Description: Urbana University is a private institution affiliated with the Swedenborgian Church. It was established and chartered in 1850.

The Division of Education and Allied Programs provides programs for prospective teachers, athletic trainers, and sports/recreation fitness specialists.

Institution Control: Private.

Calendar: Quarter. Academic year January to November.

Official(s): Dr. Daniel, Division Chair; Dr. Boldman, Director of Teacher Education.

Faculty: Full-time 20.

Degrees Awarded: 61 baccalaureate; 27 master's.

Admission Requirements: *Undergraduate:* Graduation from an accredited secondary school with 16 academic units or GED; College Board SAT or ACT composite. *Teacher education specific:* Maintain a 2.5 GPA; strong high school academic records; professional commitment; passing scores on PRAXIS I exams (reading, writing, mathematics); faculty interview. *Graduate:* Baccalaureate degree from a regionally accredited institution.

Teacher education specific: 2.75 GPA; completion of all required departmental exams; teaching licensure where required by program pursued; faculty interview.

Fees and Expenses: Undergraduate: $13,540 per academic year. Graduate: Tuition charged per credit hour. On-campus room and board: $5,410. Other expenses: $800. Books and supplies: $800.

Financial Aid: Resources specifically for eligible students enrolled in teacher education programs are awarded on the basis of financial need and academic merit. The institution has a Program Participation Agreement with the U.S. Department of Education for eligible students to receive Pell Grants and other federal aid. Teacher scholarships available to qualifying students. *Contact:* Financial Aid Office at: (937) 484-1355.

Accreditation: *Regional:* NCA. *Member of:* AACTE. *Approved by:* Ohio Department of Education.

Undergraduate Programs: The Teacher Education Program provides students with opportunities to become skilled and knowledgeable early childhood (K-3), middle childhood (4-9) or adolescent (7-12) school teachers or intervention specialists: mild/moderate (K-12). The Bachelor of Science degree programs are offered with a major in early childhood; major in middle childhood (concentrations in any two of the areas of reading/language arts, social studies, science, mathematics); major in adolescent (7-12) in the teacher fields of biological sciences, integrated science: mathematics, English, language arts, social studies.

All baccalaureate programs require the completion of a general education core, professional studies, subject content area, field experiences, and student teaching.

The Bachelor of Science degree with a major in medicine/athletic training is offered in the Sports/Leisure Studies Program.

Graduate Programs: A Post-Baccalaureate Teacher Licensure program for early childhood education (preK-3), middle childhood education (4-9), and adolescent education (7-12) or intervention specialists: mild/moderate (K-12) programs of study are open to current holders of a bachelor's degree that must have been earned at an accredited university.

Licensure/Reciprocity. Ohio. Students seeking teaching certification in a state other than Ohio should consult with that state's teacher certification office early in their program of study to insure compliance with requirements. Many state directors of teacher credentialing have signed Interstate Agreements through NASDTEC that expedite the certification process.

WILMINGTON COLLEGE
Education Department
251 Ludovic Street
Wilmington, Ohio 45177
Phone: (937) 382-6661
Fax: (937) 382-7077
E-mail: admissions@wilmington.edu
Internet: http://www.wilmington.edu

Institution Description: Wilmington College is a private college affiliated with the Wilmington Yearly Meeting of the Society of Friends. The college was founded in 1870.

The Education Department offers undergraduate and graduate programs leading to teaching licensure in Ohio.

Institution Control: Private.

Calendar: Semester. Academic year August to August.

Official(s): Dr. Michele Beery, Department Chair; Dr. Terry Miller, Director of Graduate Studies.

Faculty: Full-time 10.

Degrees Awarded: 90 baccalaureate.

Admission Requirements: *Undergraduate:* Graduation from an accredited secondary school with 16 academic units or GED; College Board SAT or ACT composite. *Teacher education specific:* Maintain a 2.5 GPA; strong high school academic records; professional commitment; passing scores on PRAXIS I exams (reading, writing, mathematics); faculty interview. *Graduate:* Baccalaureate degree from a regionally accredited institution.

WILMINGTON COLLEGE—cont'd

Teacher education specific: 2.75 GPA; biographical essay; GRE or Miller Analogies Test; completion of all required departmental exams; faculty interview.

Fees and Expenses: $17,256 per academic year. Graduate tuition charged per credit hour. On-campus room and board: $6,490. Other expenses: $1,000. Books and supplies: $1,000.

Financial Aid: Resources specifically for eligible students enrolled in teacher education programs are awarded on the basis of financial need and academic merit. The institution has a Program Participation Agreement with the U.S. Department of Education for eligible students to receive Pell Grants and other federal aid. Teacher scholarships available to qualifying students. *Contact:* Financial Aid Office at: (937) 381-6661, ext. 249.

Accreditation: *Regional:* NCA. *Member of:* AACTE. *Approved by:* Ohio Department of Education.

Undergraduate Programs: Undergraduate programs include the early childhood education major that requires a total of 70 credit hours. The middle childhood major requires the completion of 40 hours. The adolescence to young adult or multi-age majors require a total of 34 to 38 hours depending on the areas of licensure. All programs require the completion of a general education core, professional studies, subject content area, field experiences, and student teaching.

Graduate Programs: The Master in Education degree program is intended to facilitate the professional growth of practicing teachers. A common core of six courses stresses the learning theory, historical and cultural trends in education, conflict resolution and peace education, and educational research. Concentrations of five courses each are offered in reading and special education. The program highlights insights into cultural diversity, learning differences, reflective teaching, student-centered instructional methods, and democratic classroom management.

Licensure/Reciprocity: Ohio. Students seeking teaching certification in a state other than Ohio should consult with that state's teacher certification office early in their program of study to insure compliance with requirements. Many state directors of teacher credentialing have signed Interstate Agreements through NASDTEC that expedite the certification process.

WITTENBERG UNIVERSITY

Education Department

Ward Street at North Wittenberg Avenue
P.O. Box 720
Springfield, Ohio 45501-0720
Phone: (937) 327-6231
Fax: (937) 327-6340
E-mail: admission@wittenberg.edu
Internet: http://www.wittenberg.edu

Institution Description: Wittenberg University is a private, independent, nonprofit institution affiliated with the Evangelical Lutheran Church in America. The university was established in 1842.

The Education Department offers undergraduate and graduate programs leading to licensure in Ohio.

Institution Control: Private.

Calendar: Semester. Academic year August to May.

Official(s): Dr. Robert P. Walker, Department Chair.

Faculty: Full-time 12.

Degrees Awarded: 42 baccalaureate; 1 master's.

Admission Requirements: *Undergraduate:* Graduation from an accredited secondary school or GED; College Board SAT or ACT composite. *Teacher education specific:* Maintain a 2.5 GPA; strong high school academic records; professional commitment; passing scores on PRAXIS I exams (reading, writing, mathematics); faculty interview. *Graduate:* Baccalaureate degree from a regionally accredited institution. *Teacher education specific:* 2.75 GPA; biographical essay; GRE or Miller Analogies Test; completion of all required departmental exams; faculty interview.

Fees and Expenses: $24,792 per academic year. Graduate tuition charged per credit hour. On-campus room and board: $6,368. Other expenses: $700. Books and supplies: $700.

Financial Aid: Resources specifically for eligible students enrolled in teacher education programs are awarded on the basis of financial need and academic merit. The institution has a Program Participation Agreement with the U.S. Department of Education for eligible students to receive Pell Grants and other federal aid. Teacher scholarships available to qualifying students. *Contact:* Financial Aid Office at: (937) 327-7321.

Accreditation: *Regional:* NCA. *Member of:* AACTE. *Approved by:* Ohio Department of Education.

Undergraduate Programs: The major in education is offered in early childhood (grades preK-3) and middle childhood (grades 4-9), with dual licensure in early childhood and intervention specialist: mild/moderate educational needs (K-12). Licenses requiring a major in the teaching field and a minor in education are adolescence to young adult (grades 7-12) and multi-age (K-12). These programs lead to the baccalaureate degree and require the completion of a general education core, professional studies, subject content area, field experiences, and student teaching. A minimum of 130 semester hours is required for the degree award.

Graduate Programs: A Master of Arts in Education degree is offered for professional and career enhancement. Contact the Education Department for further information about the program.

Licensure/Reciprocity: Ohio. Students seeking teaching certification in a state other than Ohio should consult with that state's teacher certification office early in their program of study to insure compliance with requirements. Many state directors of teacher credentialing have signed Interstate Agreements through NASDTEC that expedite the certification process.

WRIGHT STATE UNIVERSITY

College of Education and Human Services
Teacher Education Program

427 Allyn Hall
3640 Colonel Glenn Highway
Dayton, Ohio 45435-0001
Phone: (937) 775-3333
Fax: (937) 775-5795
E-mail: mary.jean.hensy@wright.edu
Internet: http://www.wright.edu

Institution Description: Wright State University was established as a branch of Ohio State University and Miami University of Ohio in 1964. It achieved independent university status and the present name was adopted in 1967.

The College of Education and Human Services offers undergraduate programs leading to Ohio licensure. Graduate programs use the professional school model that permits a group of post-baccalaureate students to practice the art and science of teaching in a clinical environment.

Institution Control: Public.

Calendar: Quarter. Academic year September to June.

Official(s): Dr. Greg Bernhardt, Dean, College of Education.

Faculty: Full-time 95.

Degrees Awarded: 254 baccalaureate; 341 master's.

Admission Requirements: *Undergraduate:* Graduation from an accredited secondary school or GED; ACT composite. *Teacher education specific:* 2.5 GPA; professional commitment; passing scores on PRAXIS I exams (reading, writing, mathematics); personal interview. *Graduate:* Baccalaureate degree from a regionally accredited institution. *Teacher education specific:* 2.7 GPA; writing sample; completion of all required departmental exams; faculty interview.

Fees and Expenses: Undergraduate: in-state $5,682; out-of-state $11,154. Graduate: Tuition charged per credit hour. On-campus room and board: $5,861. Other expenses: $2,442. Books and supplies: $1,300.

Financial Aid: Resources specifically for eligible students enrolled in teacher education programs are awarded on the basis of financial need and academic merit. The institution has a Program Participation Agreement with the U.S. Department of Education for eligible students to receive Pell Grants and other federal aid. Teacher scholarships available to qualifying students. *Contact:* Financial Aid Office at: (937) 775-5721.

Accreditation: *Regional:* NCA. *Professional:* NCATE. *Member of:* AACTE. *Approved by:* Ohio Department of Education.

Undergraduate Programs: Teacher Education Programs are offered in the areas of: adolescent/young adult, early childhood, middle childhood, special education, reading recovery, social studies, mathematics education, science education, music education, art education, language arts, interdisciplinary arts. The programs lead to the baccalaureate degree and eligibility for teacher licensure. All programs require the completion of a general education core, professional studies, subject content area, field experiences, and student teaching.

Graduate Programs: PRAXIS II specialty exams serve as the entrance exam for the middle childhood, multi-age, and adolescent to young adult initial licensure programs. The programs are full-time programs of study. Students meeting the content requirements of Wright State's Educator Program will be enrolled in a cohort group. A Master of Education degree in classroom teaching is awarded upon successful completion of the program.

Licensure/Reciprocity: Ohio. Students seeking teaching certification in a state other than Ohio should consult with that state's teacher certification office early in their program of study to insure compliance with requirements. Many state directors of teacher credentialing have signed Interstate Agreements through NASDTEC that expedite the certification process.

YOUNGSTOWN STATE UNIVERSITY

Beeghly College of Education
Department of Teacher Education
One University Plaza
Youngstown, Ohio 44555
Phone: (330) 941-3251
Fax: (330) 941-3674
E-mail: hwpullman@ysu.edu
Internet: http://www.ysu.edu

Institution Description: Youngstown State University was founded and offered first instruction at the postsecondary level in 1908.

Undergraduate and graduate programs offered by the Beeghly College of Education lead to teacher licensure in Ohio.

Institution Control: Public.

Calendar: Semester. Academic year August to May.

Official(s): Dr. Philip Ginnetti, Dean, Beeghly College of Education; Dr. Marianne Dove, Department Head, Teacher Education.

Faculty: Full-time 19; 88 part-time.

Degrees Awarded: 225 baccalaureate; 153 master's; 2 doctorate.

Admission Requirements: *Undergraduate:* Graduation from an accredited secondary school or GED; College Board SAT or ACT composite. *Teacher education specific:* Maintain a 2.5 GPA; strong high school academic records; professional commitment; passing scores on PRAXIS I exams (reading, writing, mathematics); faculty interview. *Graduate:* Baccalaureate degree from a regionally accredited institution. *Teacher education specific:* 2.7 GPA; biographical essay; GRE or Miller Analogies Test; completion of all required departmental exams; faculty interview.

Fees and Expenses: Undergraduate: in-district $4,996 per academic year; regional $6,608; nonregional $9,748. Graduate: in-district $6,124; regional $8,596; nonregional $11,212. On-campus room and board: $5,320.

Financial Aid: Financial aid is awarded on the basis of financial need and academic merit. The institution has a Program Participation Agreement with the U.S. Department of Education for eligible students to receive Pell Grants and other federal aid. *Contact:* Elaine Rose, Director, Financial Aid at: (330) 941-3505 or e-mail at: ysufinaid@ysu.edu.

Undergraduate Programs: Undergraduate majors in teacher education are offered in early childhood education; middle childhood education (with two curriculum concentration areas from reading and language arts, mathematics, science, social studies); adolescence, multi-age, and vocational education; special education. The baccalaureate programs require the completion of a minimum of 126 semester hours. All programs require the completion of a general education core, professional studies, subject content area, field experiences, and student teaching.

Graduate Programs: The Master of Science in Education degree programs are offered in the following areas: elementary program with options in curriculum, reading specialist, early childhood education, middle grades; secondary education program with options in subject area concentration, curriculum, educational technology; special education program with options in gifted and talented education, early childhood special education, or a general option.

Licensure/Reciprocity: Ohio. Students seeking teaching certification in a state other than Ohio should consult with that state's teacher certification office early in their program of study to insure compliance with requirements. Many state directors of teacher credentialing have signed Interstate Agreements through NASDTEC that expedite the certification process.

OKLAHOMA

CAMERON UNIVERSITY

Department of Education
Teacher Education Program
Nance-Boyer Hall
2800 West Gore Boulevard
Lawton, Oklahoma 73505
Phone: (580) 581-2330
Fax: (580) 581-2865
E-mail: suf@cameron.edu
Internet: http://www.cameron.edu

Institution Description: Cameron University was established as Cameron State School of Agriculture in 1909. After several name changes over the years, the present name was adopted in 1974.

The Teacher Education Program is designed to service persons in the field of education. Undergraduate and graduate programs leading to certification licenses are offered.

Institution Control: Public.

Calendar: Semester. Academic year August to July.

Official(s): Dr. Judy Neale, Dean; Dr. Sue Fuson, Chair, Teacher Education Program.

Faculty: Full-time 18.

Degrees Awarded: 101 baccalaureate; 19 master's.

Admission Requirements: *Undergraduate:* Graduation from an accredited secondary school or GED; ACT composite. *Teacher education specific:* professional commitment; high scholastic attainment; Oklahoma Teacher Certification Test; portfolio; faculty interview. *Graduate:* Baccalaureate degree from a regionally accredited institution. *Teacher education specific:* 2.75 GPA; completion of all required departmental exams; teaching licensure where required by program pursued; faculty interview.

Fees and Expenses: Undergraduate: in-state $2,778 per academic year; out-of-state $6,678. Graduate: Tuition charged per academic year. On-campus room and board: $3,782. Other expenses: $2,266. Books and supplies: $800.

Financial Aid: Resources specifically for eligible students enrolled in teacher education programs are awarded on the basis of financial need and academic merit. The institution has a Program Participation Agreement with the U.S. Department of Education for eligible students to receive Pell Grants and other federal aid. Teacher scholarships available to qualifying students. *Contact:* Financial Aid Office at: (580) 581-2293.

Accreditation: *Regional:* NCA. *Professional:* NCATE. *Member of:* AACTE. *Approved by:* Oklahoma State Department of Education.

Undergraduate Programs: The Department of Education offers a Bachelor of Science in elementary education degree program. The program requires the completion of a general education core, professional studies, subject content area, field experiences, and student teaching. A minimum of 128 semester hours must be completed for the degree award.

Cameron University also offers programs whereby a person who already holds an appropriate degree many complete the requirements leading to an Oklahoma early childhood, elementary, secondary, or elementary-secondary teaching license.

Graduate Programs: The Master of Education degree program requires a minimum of 33 hours in approved graduate-level courses. The program includes a core of 21 hours in specified and required courses plus 12 hours in elective courses appropriate to the student's interests.

Licensure/Reciprocity: Oklahoma. Students seeking teaching certification in a state other than Oklahoma should consult with that state's teacher certification office early in their program of study to insure compliance with requirements. Many state directors of teacher credentialing have signed Interstate Agreements through NASDTEC that expedite the certification process.

EAST CENTRAL UNIVERSITY

School of Education and Psychology
Education Department
12th and Francis Streets
Ada, Oklahoma 74820
Phone: (580) 332-8000
Fax: (580) 310-5348
E-mail: soep@ecok.edu
Internet: http://www.ecok.edu

Institution Description: East Central University was established as East Central State Normal School in 1909.

The Education Department offers degree programs and teacher certification options at both the undergraduate and graduate levels.

Institution Control: Public.

Calendar: Semester. Academic year August to May.

Official(s): Dr. John Bedford, Chair, Education Department.

Faculty: Full-time 17.

Degrees Awarded: 60 baccalaureate; 106 master's.

Admission Requirements: *Undergraduate:* Graduation from an accredited secondary school with a minimum 2.7 GPA or upper 2/3 of graduating class or GED; ACT composite score of 20. *Teacher education specific: or GED; ACT composite. Teacher education specific:* professional commitment; high scholastic attainment; Oklahoma Teacher Certification Test; portfolio; faculty interview. *Graduate:* Baccalaureate degree from a regionally accredited institution. *Teacher education specific:* 2.75 GPA; completion of all required departmental exams; teaching licensure where required by program pursued; faculty interview.

Fees and Expenses: Undergraduate: in-state $2,548 per academic year; out-of-state On-campus room and board: $2,774. Other expenses: $2,700. Books and supplies: $700.

Financial Aid: Resources specifically for eligible students enrolled in teacher education programs are awarded on the basis of financial need and academic merit. The institution has a Program Participation Agreement with the U.S. Department of Education for eligible students to receive Pell Grants and other federal aid. Teacher scholarships available to qualifying students. *Contact:* Financial Aid Office at: (580) 332-8000.

Accreditation: *Regional:* NCA. *Professional:* NCATE. *Member of:* AACTE. *Approved by:* Oklahoma State Department of Education.

Undergraduate Programs: The Department of Education offers the following undergraduate degree programs: early childhood education; elementary education; special education; secondary certification programs in the majors of business education, English, family and consumer science, mathematics, science, social studies, speech and drama. K-12 Programs are also offered in art, health/exercise/physical education, music. All programs require the completion of a general education core, professional studies, subject content area, field experiences, and student teaching.

Graduate Programs: Master of Education degree programs include: elementary education, secondary education, elementary/secondary school principal, special education, counseling, reading, sports administration, library science.

Certification options include library science, psychometrist, school administration, school psychologist. These options do not lead to a degree but meet the state of Oklahoma requirements for certification. Individuals holding degrees may also seek certification in any of the program areas.

Licensure/Reciprocity: Oklahoma. Students seeking teaching certification in a state other than Oklahoma should consult with that state's teacher certification office early in their program of study to insure compliance with requirements. Many state directors of teacher credentialing have signed Interstate Agreements through NASDTEC that expedite the certification process.

LANGSTON UNIVERSITY
Education and Behavioral science
Teacher Education Program
202W Sanford Hall
Langston, Oklahoma 73050-0907
Phone: (405) 466-3382
Fax: (405) 466-3209
E-mail: drabram@lunet.edu
Internet: http://www.lunet.edu

Institution Description: Langston University is a state institution and land-grant college. It was founded in 1897 and is Oklahoma's only historically Black college.

The Teacher Education Program offers pathways to the undergraduate degree and licensure in Oklahoma.

Institution Control: Public.

Calendar: Semester. Academic year August to May.

Official(s): Dr. Darlene S. Abram, Dean; Dr. Mose Yvonne Brooks Hooks, Director, Teacher Education Program.

Faculty: Full-time 30.

Degrees Awarded: 33 baccalaureate; 16 master's.

Admission Requirements: *Undergraduate:* Graduation from an accredited secondary school or GED; College Board SAT accepted; ACT composite preferred. *Teacher education specific:* Completion of at least 30 semester hours of general education; 2.5 GPA; show evidence of adequate reading, writing, and verbal communication skills; professional commitment; portfolio assessment; faculty interview. *Graduate:* Baccalaureate degree from a regionally accredited institution. *Teacher education specify:* Minimum 2.5 GPA; GRE results; minimum score of 80 on the Langston University Writing Skills Test.

Fees and Expenses: Undergraduate: in-state $60 per credit hour; out-of-state $181. Graduate: in-state $80 per credit hour; out-of-state $229. Required fees: $181.50 flat fee; $22.50 per credit hour. On-campus room and board: $2,400 to $4,650 (room); $1,860 to $2,020 (board). Books and supplies: $550.

Financial Aid: Resources specifically for eligible students enrolled in teacher education programs are awarded on the basis of financial need and academic merit. The institution has a Program Participation Agreement with the U.S. Department of Education for eligible students to receive Pell Grants and other federal aid. Teacher scholarships available to qualifying students. *Contact:* Dr. Darlene S. Abram at: (405) 466-3382 or drabram@lunet.edu

Accreditation: *Regional:* NCA. *Professional:* NCATE. *Member of:* AACTE. *Approved by:* Oklahoma State Department of Education.

Undergraduate Programs: The Teacher Education Program includes pathways to teacher certification and the bachelor's degree, Teacher candidates in early childhood education, elementary education, and special education must have subject area concentrations that qualify them as generalists.

The Department of Special Education offers teacher education programs in the area of mild/moderate disabilities. The Department of Elementary Education seeks to guide prospective and in-service teachers in the selection of non-specialized courses in major fields of knowledge and to provide experiences leading to the development of competencies necessary for successful participation in community living and in understanding, teaching, and guiding children.

All programs require the completion of a general education core, professional studies, subject content area, field experiences, and student teaching. A minimum of 124 semester hours must be completed for the baccalaureate degree.

Graduate Programs: The Master of Education degree is designed principally for individuals who are already certified to teach or who are certifiable. The degree is for individuals who desire to increase their professional competencies in their area of teaching endorsement or to complete requirements for endorsement in areas for which certification is available only at the graduate level. Program options include elementary education, urban education, urban administration, and urban counseling. A minimum of 36 credit hours in approved graduate courses is required for the degree award.

Licensure/Reciprocity: Oklahoma. Students seeking teaching certification in a state other than Oklahoma should consult with that state's teacher certification office early in their program of study to insure compliance with requirements. Many state directors of teacher credentialing have signed Interstate Agreements through NASDTEC that expedite the certification process.

NORTHEASTERN STATE UNIVERSITY
Department of Curriculum and Instruction
202 Education Building
600 North Grand
Tahlequah, Oklahoma 74464
Phone: (918) 456-5511
Fax: (918) 458-2351
E-mail: grantke@nsuok.edu
Internet: http://www.nsuok.edu

Institution Description: Northeastern State University was established as Cherokee Female Seminary in 1846. It became coeducational and offered first instruction at the postsecondary level in 1909.

The Department of Curriculum and Instruction offers programs for the preparation of teachers and candidates for teaching licensure in Oklahoma.

Institution Control: Public.

Calendar: Semester. Academic year August to May.

Official(s): Dr. Kay Grant, Dean; Dr. roseanne Fillmore, Department Chairperson.

Faculty: Full-time 15.

Degrees Awarded: 382 baccalaureate; 137 master's.

Admission Requirements: *Undergraduate:* Graduation from an accredited secondary school or GED; ACT composite. *Teacher education specific:* professional commitment; high scholastic attainment; portfolio; faculty interview; Oklahoma Teacher Certification Test before graduation. *Graduate:* Baccalaureate degree from a regionally accredited institution. *Teacher education specific:* 2.75 GPA; completion of all required departmental exams; teaching licensure where required by program pursued; faculty interview.

Fees and Expenses: Undergraduate: in-state $2,700 per academic year; out-of-state $6,600. Graduate: Tuition charged per credit hour. On-campus room and board: $3,964. Other expenses: $1,280. Books and supplies: $900.

NORTHEASTERN STATE UNIVERSITY—*cont'd*

Financial Aid: Resources specifically for eligible students enrolled in teacher education programs are awarded on the basis of financial need and academic merit. The institution has a Program Participation Agreement with the U.S. Department of Education for eligible students to receive Pell Grants and other federal aid. Teacher scholarships available to qualifying students. *Contact:* Financial Aid Office at: (918) 456-5511, ext. 3456.

Accreditation: *Regional:* NCA. *Professional:* NCATE. *Member of:* AACTE. *Approved by:* Oklahoma State Department of Education.

Undergraduate Programs: The Bachelor of Arts in Education is offered with majors in art, English, mass communication, music (combined instrumental and vocal, instrumental, piano or vocal), social studies, Spanish, and Speech.

The Bachelor of Science in Education is offered with majors in science (biology, chemistry, physics), early childhood education, elementary education, health and physical education, family and consumer sciences education, technology education, mathematics, special education (mild/moderate disabilities).

All programs require the completion of a general education core, professional studies, subject content area, field experiences, and student teaching. Successful completion of all requirements for the baccalaureate degrees will be eligible to apply for a provisional or standard teaching certificate.

Graduate Programs: Master's degree programs are offered in areas similar to those offered as majors toward the baccalaureate degree. Contact the Department of Curriculum and Instruction for specific details and program requirements.

Licensure/Reciprocity: Oklahoma. Students seeking teaching certification in a state other than Oklahoma should consult with that state's teacher certification office early in their program of study to insure compliance with requirements. Many state directors of teacher credentialing have signed Interstate Agreements through NASDTEC that expedite the certification process.

NORTHWESTERN OKLAHOMA STATE UNIVERSITY

School of Professional Studies
Department of Teacher Education

709 Oklahoma Boulevard
Alva, Oklahoma 73717
Phone: (580) 327-8441
Fax: (580) 327-1881
E-mail: caerikson@nwosu.edu
Internet: http://www.nwalva.edu

Institution Description: Northwestern Oklahoma State University (Northwestern State College until 1974) was founded in 1897.

The Department of Education offers undergraduate and graduate programs leading to teacher certification in Oklahoma.

Institution Control: Public.

Calendar: Semester. Academic year August to May.

Official(s): Dr. James bowen, Dean; Dr. Beverly Warden, Director of Teacher Education.

Faculty: Full-time 12.

Degrees Awarded: 86 baccalaureate; 40 master's.

Admission Requirements: *Undergraduate:* Graduation from an accredited secondary school with 2.8 GPA or upper half of graduating class or GED; College Board SAT for in-state students; ACT composite for out-of-state students. *Teacher education specific:* Minimum 30 hours in general education; 2.5 GPA;; passing score on all part s of PRAXIS I (reading, writing, mathematics); proof of English proficiency; personal biography; essay; portfolio development; faculty interview; Oklahoma Teacher Certification Test before graduation. *Graduate:* Baccalaureate degree from a regionally accredited institution. *Teacher*

education specific: Completion of all required departmental exams; GRE; teaching licensure where required by program pursued; faculty interview.

Fees and Expenses: Undergraduate: in-state $2,803 per academic year; out-of-state $4,030. Graduate: Tuition charged per credit hour. On-campus room and board: $2,720. Other expenses: $1,950. Books and supplies: $800.

Financial Aid: Resources specifically for eligible students enrolled in teacher education programs are awarded on the basis of financial need and academic merit. The institution has a Program Participation Agreement with the U.S. Department of Education for eligible students to receive Pell Grants and other federal aid. Teacher scholarships available to qualifying students. *Contact:* Financial Aid Office at: (580) 327-8542.

Accreditation: *Regional:* NCA. *Professional:* NCATE. *Member of:* AACTE. *Approved by:* Oklahoma State Department of Education.

Undergraduate Programs: The Bachelor of Arts or Science in Education are four-year programs leading to a degree and a teaching certificate. Coursework is available that provides the competencies for the following certificates: elementary education, secondary education, early childhood education, special education (mild/moderate disabilities). All programs require the completion of a general education core, professional studies, subject content area, field experiences, and student teaching.

Graduate Programs: The Master of Education is an advanced professional program designed to produce better classroom teachers at the elementary and secondary levels by strengthening their mastery of both subject matter and techniques of teaching. The degree has the following options available: elementary education, secondary education, guidance and counseling (K-12), reading specialist. With the degree, the following Oklahoma certificates may be completed: school counselor, reading specialist, school psychometrist, elementary or secondary school principal; superintendent, special education.

Licensure/Reciprocity: Oklahoma. Students seeking teaching certification in a state other than Oklahoma should consult with that state's teacher certification office early in their program of study to insure compliance with requirements. Many state directors of teacher credentialing have signed Interstate Agreements through NASDTEC that expedite the certification process.

OKLAHOMA BAPTIST UNIVERSITY

Division of Teacher Education

500 West University
Shawnee, Oklahoma 74804
Phone: (405) 878-2166
Fax: (405) 878-2163
E-mail: pam.Robinson@okbu.edu
Internet: http://www.okbu.edu

Institution Description: Oklahoma Baptist University is a private institution affiliated with the Oklahoma Baptist General Convention. The university was founded in 1906.

The purposes of the teacher education program are to prepare the student to function as a professional teacher and to aid the student in developing the knowledge, skills, and attitudes necessary to assist school children in reaching their potential.

Institution Control: Private.

Calendar: Semester. Academic year August to May.

Official(s): Dr. Pam Robinson, Division Chairperson.

Faculty: Full-time 6; adjunct 2.

Degrees Awarded: 51 baccalaureate.

Admission Requirements: *Undergraduate:* Graduation from an accredited secondary school with 3.0 GPA;; ACT of at least 20 or SAT of at least 450 or GED. *Teacher education specific:* Maintain a 2.5 GPA; 3.0 in liberal arts courses; completion of 36 semester hours; professional commitment; high scholastic attainment; faculty interview. Oklahoma Teacher Certification Test before graduation.

Fees and Expenses: Comprehensive fee: $15,268 per academic year. Required fees: $414. Books and supplies: $1,000.

Financial Aid: Resources specifically for eligible students enrolled in teacher education programs are awarded on the basis of financial need and academic merit. The institution has a Program Participation Agreement with the U.S. Department of Education for eligible students to receive Pell Grants and other federal aid. Teacher scholarships available to qualifying students. *Contact:* Larry Hollingsworth at: (405) 878-2178 or e-mail at: Larry.Hollingsworth@okbu.edu.

Accreditation: *Regional:* NCA. *Professional:* NCATE. *Member of:* AACTE. *Approved by:* Oklahoma State Department of Education.

Undergraduate Programs: Degree programs are offered by the Division of Teacher Education in: elementary education; early childhood education; art education, preK-12; health and physical education, preK-12; French, preK-12; Spanish, preK-12; instrumental music education, preK-12; vocal music education, preK-12; special education, preK-12; secondary English education; secondary mathematics; secondary science; secondary social studies, secondary speech and drama.

All baccalaureate programs require the completion of a general education core, professional studies, subject content area, field experiences, and student teaching. A minimum of 128 semester hours must be completed for the degree award.

Licensure/Reciprocity: Oklahoma. Students seeking teaching certification in a state other than Oklahoma should consult with that state's teacher certification office early in their program of study to insure compliance with requirements. Many state directors of teacher credentialing have signed Interstate Agreements through NASDTEC that expedite the certification process.

OKLAHOMA CHRISTIAN UNIVERSITY
College of Professional Studies
Department of Education
2501 East Memorial
Box 11000
Oklahoma City, Oklahoma 73136-1100
Phone: (405) 425-5430
Fax: (405) 425-5208
E-mail: info@oc.edu
Internet: http://www.oc.edu

Institution Description: Oklahoma Christian University is a private, independent, nonprofit college affiliated with the Churches of Christ. It was established as Central Christian College and offered first instruction at the postsecondary level in 1950.

The university is a liberal arts institution that emphasizes spiritual growth and career preparation.

Institution Control: Private.

Calendar: Trimester. Academic year September to April.

Official(s): Dr. Dwayne Cleveland, Chair.

Faculty: Full-time 5.

Degrees Awarded: 52 baccalaureate.

Admission Requirements: *Undergraduate:* Graduation from an accredited secondary school or GED; College Board SAT or ACT composite. *Teacher education specific:* Maintain a 3.0 GPA in the professional education courses and field of licensure; professional commitment; high scholastic attainment; passing scores on PRAXIS I exams (reading, writing, mathematics); faculty interview.

Fees and Expenses: $13,034 per academic year. On-campus room and board: $4,650. Other expenses: $2,600. Books and supplies: $900.

Financial Aid: Resources specifically for eligible students enrolled in teacher education programs are awarded on the basis of financial need and academic merit. The institution has a Program Participation Agreement with the U.S. Department of Education for eligible students to receive Pell Grants and other federal aid. Teacher scholarships available to qualifying students. *Contact:* Financial Aid Office at: (405) 425-5190.

Accreditation: *Regional:* NASC. *Professional:* NCATE. *Member of:* AACTE. *Approved by:* Oklahoma State Department of Education.

Undergraduate Programs: The Teacher Education Program prepares students to meet the challenges of a teaching career and to make a difference in the lives of students taught. The program has the cooperation of nearby school districts in both urban and suburban areas that offer the opportunity to complete field experiences and student teaching in quality school settings located near the campus.

Baccalaureate programs leading to Oklahoma teacher certification include: elementary education, early childhood education, special education. A secondary education program offers concentrations in the areas of art, music, physical education, science, social studies, Spanish, teaching English to speakers of other languages. All programs require the completion of a general education core, professional studies, subject content area, field experiences, and student teaching.

Licensure/Reciprocity: Oklahoma. Students seeking teaching certification in a state other than Oklahoma should consult with that state's teacher certification office early in their program of study to insure compliance with requirements. Many state directors of teacher credentialing have signed Interstate Agreements through NASDTEC that expedite the certification process.

OKLAHOMA CITY UNIVERSITY
Department of Education
2501 North Blackwelder
Oklahoma City, Oklahoma 73106
Phone: (405) 521-5373
Fax: (405) 557-6012
E-mail: drichardson@okcu.edu
Internet: http://www.okcu.edu

Institution Description: Oklahoma City University is a private institution affiliated with the United Methodist Church. The institution was chartered as Epworth University in 1907. The name was changed to Methodist University of Oklahoma in 1911, to Oklahoma City College in 1919, and to its present name in 1924.

The general purpose of teacher education at Oklahoma City University is to prepare the student for the teaching profession and to assist the student in becoming a competent teacher.

Institution Control: Private.

Calendar: Continuous. Academic year August to May.

Official(s): Dr. Donna Castle Richardson, Chairperson.

Faculty: Full-time 4; part-time 1; adjunct 8.

Degrees Awarded: 12 baccalaureate; 46 master's.

Admission Requirements: *Undergraduate:* Graduation from an accredited secondary school or GED; College Board SAT or ACT composite. *Teacher education specific:* Minimum 2.5 GPA; passing scores on the PRAXIS I exams (reading, writing, mathematics); professional commitment; faculty interview; Oklahoma Teacher Certification Test prior to graduation. *Graduate:* Baccalaureate degree from a regionally accredited institution. *Teacher education specific:* Completion of all required departmental exams; teaching licensure where required by program pursued; faculty interview.

Fees and Expenses: Undergraduate: $6,670. Graduate: $530 per credit hour. Required fees: $600. On-campus room and board: $5,550. Books and supplies: $300.

Financial Aid: Resources specifically for eligible students enrolled in teacher education programs are awarded on the basis of financial need and academic merit. The institution has a Program Participation Agreement with the U.S. Department of Education for eligible students to receive Pell Grants and other federal aid. Teacher scholarships available to qualifying students. *Contact:* Molly Robert at: (405) 521-5211.

Accreditation: *Regional:* NCA. *Professional:* NCATE. *Approved by:* Oklahoma State Department of Education.

OKLAHOMA CITY UNIVERSITY—*cont'd*

Undergraduate Programs: The Department of Education offers an emphasis in teacher education with programs in early childhood, elementary, secondary, and elementary-secondary (K-12) leading to an Oklahoma teaching certificate. American Montessori Society certification may be attached to early childhood and elementary programs by completing the requirements for both certifications. The only majors offered by the division are early childhood education; elementary education; health and physical education; vocal music education; instrumental music education. Other certification areas require degrees in the discipline plus any other courses required to meet competency requirements in that teaching field. In addition, the division offers non-certification degrees in physical education and general studies in education.

All certification programs require the completion of a general education core, professional studies, subject area, field experiences, and student teaching. A minimum of 124 semester hours must be completed for the degree award.

Graduate Programs: Master's degree programs have been designed to meet the needs of a person who holds a bachelor's degree and wants to add another area of concentration. Candidates must complete a minimum of 36 hours of approved work (12-hour core; 12 hours of content courses, 12 hours of approved electives). Programs are offered in early childhood education and elementary education.

Licensure/Reciprocity: Oklahoma. Students seeking teaching certification in a state other than Oklahoma should consult with that state's teacher certification office early in their program of study to insure compliance with requirements. Many state directors of teacher credentialing have signed Interstate Agreements through NASDTEC that expedite the certification process.

OKLAHOMA PANHANDLE STATE UNIVERSITY

School of Education
325 Eagle Avenue
Goodwill, Oklahoma 73939
Phone: (580) 349-2611
Fax: (580) 349-2302
E-mail: rwstewart@opsu.edu
Internet: http://www.opsu.edu

Institution Description: Oklahoma Panhandle State University (Oklahoma Panhandle State College until 1974) was established in 1909.

The School of Education offers four-year bachelor degree programs in a variety of subject areas. The educational experiences offered are designed to enrich the personal lives of students and to prepare them for roles in agriculture, business, education, government, and industry.

Institution Control: Public.

Calendar: Semester. Academic year August to May.

Official(s): Dr. R. Wayne Stewart, Dean.

Faculty: Full-time 7.

Degrees Awarded: 25 baccalaureate.

Admission Requirements: *Undergraduate:* Graduation from an accredited secondary school or GED; College Board SAT accepted; ACT composite preferred. *Teacher education specific:* Minimum 30 hours in general education; 2.5 GPA;; passing score on all part s of PRAXIS I (reading, writing, mathematics); proof of English proficiency; personal biography; essay; portfolio development; faculty interview; Oklahoma Teacher Certification Test before graduation.

Fees and Expenses: Undergraduate: in-state $2,500 per academic year; out-of-state $5,142. On-campus room and board: $2,870. Other expenses: $1,400. Books and supplies: $180.

Financial Aid: Resources specifically for eligible students enrolled in teacher education programs are awarded on the basis of financial need and academic merit. The institution has a Program Participation Agreement with the U.S. Department of Education for eligible students to receive Pell Grants and other federal aid. Teacher scholarships available to qualifying students. *Contact:* Financial Aid Office at: (580) 349-1580.

Accreditation: *Regional:* NCA. *Member of:* AACTE. *Approved by:* Oklahoma State Department of Education.

Undergraduate Programs: The plans of study leading to teacher certification and the bachelor's degree include: agriculture, biology, business, chemistry, elementary education, English, health and physical education, mathematics, music, physical science, social studies. All programs require the completion of a general education core, professional studies, subject content area, field experiences, and student teaching. A minimum of 124 semester hours is required for the degree award.

Licensure/Reciprocity: Oklahoma. Students seeking teaching certification in a state other than Oklahoma should consult with that state's teacher certification office early in their program of study to insure compliance with requirements. Many state directors of teacher credentialing have signed Interstate Agreements through NASDTEC that expedite the certification process.

OKLAHOMA STATE UNIVERSITY

College of Education
School of Curriculum and Educational Leadership
333 Willard Hall
Stillwater, Oklahoma 74078
Phone: (405) 744-9465
Fax: (405) 744-6399
E-mail: coe@okstate.edu
Internet: http://www.okstate.edu

Institution Description: Oklahoma State University established as Oklahoma Agricultural and Mechanical College in 1890.

The College of Education offers a wide range of undergraduate and graduate programs to prepare individuals for careers in teaching, administration, and research in the professional fields of education.

Institution Control: Public.

Calendar: Semester. Academic year August to May.

Official(s): Dr. Ann Candler Lotven, Dean.

Faculty: Full-time 88; part-time 31; adjunct 45.

Degrees Awarded: 299 baccalaureate; 157 master's; 45 doctorate.

Admission Requirements: *Undergraduate:* Graduation from an accredited secondary school with 2.8 GPA or upper half of graduating class or GED; College Board SAT for in-state students; ACT composite for out-of-state students. *Teacher education specific:* Minimum 30 hours in general education; 2.5 GPA;; passing score on all part s of PRAXIS I (reading, writing, mathematics); proof of English proficiency; personal biography; essay; portfolio development; faculty interview; Oklahoma Teacher Certification Test before graduation. *Graduate:* Baccalaureate degree from a regionally accredited institution. *Teacher education specific:* Completion of all required departmental exams; GRE; teaching licensure where required by program pursued; faculty interview.

Fees and Expenses: Undergraduate: in-state $3,520 per academic year; out-of-state $9,420. Graduate: Tuition charged per credit hour. On-campus room and board: $6,150. Other expenses: $2,980. Books and supplies: $960.

Financial Aid: Resources specifically for eligible students enrolled in teacher education programs are awarded on the basis of financial need and academic merit. The institution has a Program Participation Agreement with the U.S. Department of Education for eligible students to receive Pell Grants and other federal aid. Teacher scholarships available to qualifying students. *Contact:* Dr. Charles Bruce at: (405) 744-7541.

Accreditation: *Regional:* NCA. *Professional:* NCATE. *Member of:* AACTE. *Approved by:* Oklahoma State Department of Education.

Undergraduate Programs: The school offers undergraduate degrees in elementary, secondary, and K-12 education, and technical and industrial education. Completion of the Bachelor of Science in elementary education qualifies the student for an Oklahoma elementary teaching license (grades 1-8). The Bachelor of Science in secondary education is available in the following areas: English, foreign language, mathematics, science, and social studies. The Bachelor of Science in technical and industrial education is designed with two distinct options: the non-certification option for students interested in adult technical education, and the certification option for students interested in secondary vocational education.

All baccalaureate programs require the completion of a general education core, professional studies, subject content area, field experiences, and student teaching. A minimum of 120 semester hours must be completed for the baccalaureate degree.

Graduate Programs: The school offers graduate programs at the master's and doctoral levels. While specialization is required, maximum program flexibility enables students to meet individual goals. Programs are designed to prepare persons to enter public or private elementary and secondary schools as curriculum directors, department heads, reading specialists, and instructional team members. Programs offered lead to the Master of Science in teaching, learning, and leadership and a Doctor of Philosophy in education.

Licensure/Reciprocity: Oklahoma. Students seeking teaching certification in a state other than Oklahoma should consult with that state's teacher certification office early in their program of study to insure compliance with requirements. Many state directors of teacher credentialing have signed Interstate Agreements through NASDTEC that expedite the certification process.

ORAL ROBERTS UNIVERSITY

School of Education

7777 South Lewis Avenue
Tulsa, Oklahoma 74171
Phone: (918) 495-6590
Fax: (918) 495-8959
E-mail: dhand@oru.edu
Internet: http://www.oru.edu

Institution Description: Oral Roberts University is a private, independent, nonprofit institution that was chartered and incorporated in 1963.

The School of Education offers a broad spectrum of undergraduate and graduate programs. The school also houses a major in International Community Development that is an interdisciplinary program in practical missions. The program emphasizes practical as well as spiritual ministry in the United States and abroad.

Institution Control: Private.

Calendar: Semester. Academic year August to May.

Official(s): Dr. David B. Hand, Dean.

Faculty: Full-time 17; part-time 18; adjunct 12.

Degrees Awarded: 41 baccalaureate; 34 master's; 4 doctorate.

Admission Requirements: *Undergraduate:* Graduation from an accredited secondary school with rank in top 40% of graduating class; 2.6 GPA or greater; GED score of 52; College Board SAT or ACT composite. *Teacher education specific:* Maintain a 3.0 GPA in the professional education courses and field of licensure; professional commitment; passing scores on Oklahoma General Education Test; faculty interview. *Graduate:* Baccalaureate degree from a regionally accredited institution. *Teacher education specific:* 3.0 GPA; GRE or Miller Analogies Test results; three academic letters of recommendation; completion of all required departmental exams; teaching licensure where required by program pursued; faculty interview.

Fees and Expenses: Undergraduate: $565 per credit hour. Graduate: $338 per credit hour. Required fees: $210 per semester. On-campus room and board: $5,900 per year. Books and supplies: $600.

Financial Aid: Resources specifically for eligible students enrolled in teacher education programs are awarded on the basis of financial need and academic merit. The institution has a Program Participation Agreement with the U.S. Department of Education for eligible students to receive Pell Grants and other federal aid. Teacher scholarships available to qualifying students. *Contact:* Scott Carr at: (918) 495-7088 or e-mail at: scarr@oru.edu.

Accreditation: *Regional:* NCA. *Professional:* NCATE. *Member of:* AACTE. *Approved by:* Oklahoma State Department of Education.

Undergraduate Programs: The School of Education offers a comprehensive program designed to train qualified teachers for early childhood, elementary, special education, and K-12 and secondary teaching assignments. The programs lead to the baccalaureate degree. All programs require the completion of a general education core, professional studies, subject content area, field experiences, and student teaching. A minimum of 128 semester hours must be completed for the degree award.

Graduate Programs: Graduate programs at the master's level offer preparation for teaching and leadership positions in Christian school education, public school administration, teaching English as a second language, and early childhood education.

The doctoral program in educational leadership prepares leaders for public and private schools, including Christian postsecondary institutions. The program includes a track that will lead to certification in public school superintendency.

Licensure/Reciprocity: Oklahoma. Students seeking teaching certification in a state other than Oklahoma should consult with that state's teacher certification office early in their program of study to insure compliance with requirements. Many state directors of teacher credentialing have signed Interstate Agreements through NASDTEC that expedite the certification process.

SOUTHEASTERN OKLAHOMA STATE UNIVERSITY

School of Education and Behavioral Sciences
Teacher Education

1405 North Fourth Avenue
PMB 4115
Durant, Oklahoma 74701-0609
Phone: (580) 745-2090
Fax: (580) 745-7473
E-mail: scanan@sosu.edu
Internet: http://www.sosu.edu

Institution Description: Southeastern Oklahoma State University (formerly Southeastern State College) was established in 1909.

Teacher education programs at the university lead to the baccalaureate and graduate degrees and teacher certification in Oklahoma.

Institution Control: Public.

Calendar: Semester. Academic year August to May.

Official(s): Dr. Joseph Licata, Dean; Dr. Ed Mauzey, Director of Teacher Education

Faculty: Full-time 47; adjunct 15.

Degrees Awarded: 165 baccalaureate; 76 master's.

Admission Requirements: *Undergraduate:* Graduation from an accredited secondary school or GED; College Board SAT or ACT composite; minimum 2.7 GPA. *Teacher education specific:* Minimum 2.5 GPA; evidence of communication skills; Oklahoma General Education Test; departmental review; professional commitment; experience working with children. *Graduate:* Baccalaureate degree from a regionally accredited institution. *Teacher education specific:* Admission to graduate study; writing sample; 3.0 GPA; completion of all required departmental exams; teaching licensure where required by program pursued; faculty interview.

SOUTHEASTERN OKLAHOMA STATE UNIVERSITY—cont'd

Fees and Expenses: Undergraduate: in-state $1,832 per academic year; out-of-state $5,366. Graduate: in-state $1,824 per academic year: out-of-state $4,920. Required fees: $672. On-campus room and board: $2,312. Books and supplies: $800.

Financial Aid: Resources specifically for eligible students enrolled in teacher education programs are awarded on the basis of financial need and academic merit. The institution has a Program Participation Agreement with the U.S. Department of Education for eligible students to receive Pell Grants and other federal aid. Teacher scholarships available to qualifying students. *Contact:* Sherry Foster at: (580) 745-2186 or e-mail at: sfoster#sosu.edu.

Accreditation: *Regional:* NCA. *Professional:* NCATE. *Member of:* AACTE. *Approved by:* Oklahoma State Department of Education.

Undergraduate Programs: Students can major in elementary education and receive certification as an elementary school teacher, or receive certification at the secondary level by combining a major in an academic field with a series of courses in education. A total of 124 semester hours is required for a bachelor's degree with a 2.5 GPA. Bachelor's degrees in education are offered in: elementary (grades 1 to middle school); elementary-secondary (grades preK-12 in art, vocal music, instrumental music, Spanish, health and physical education, special education-mild/moderate); secondary education (grades 6-12) in business, mathematics, social studies, English, science, speech/drama.

All programs require the completion of a general education core, professional studies, subject content area, field experiences, and student teaching.

Graduate Programs: Advanced degree programs of study are offered for teachers already certified at the baccalaureate level. The programs include Master of Education in: elementary education, secondary education, school administration, school counseling, and reading specialist. An advanced degree is also offered in education at the secondary level in the major content field.

Licensure/Reciprocity: Oklahoma. Students seeking teaching certification in a state other than Oklahoma should consult with that state's teacher certification office early in their program of study to insure compliance with requirements. Many state directors of teacher credentialing have signed Interstate Agreements through NASDTEC that expedite the certification process.

SOUTHERN NAZARENE UNIVERSITY

School of Education
6729 N.W. 39th Expressway
Bethany, Oklahoma 73008
Phone: (405) 789-6400
Fax: (405) 491-6381
E-mail: rtullis@snu.edu
Internet: http://www.snu.edu

Institution Description: Southern Nazarene University is a private institution affiliated with the Church of the Nazarene. It was founded in 1899.

The general purpose of professional teacher education is to orient the teacher candidates to the teaching profession within a framework of Christian principles and to assist them in becoming competent decision-makers in a democratic society.

Institution Control: Private.

Calendar: Semester. Academic year August to May.

Official(s): Dr. Rex Tullis, Chair.

Faculty: Full-time 7.

Degrees Awarded: 39 baccalaureate; 84 master's.

Admission Requirements: *Undergraduate:* Graduation from an accredited secondary school or GED; College Board SAT for admissions purposes; ACT composite required to enroll. *Teacher education specific:* Maintain a 2.5 GPA; completion of 30 semester hours of coursework; pass the Oklahoma General Education Test; professional commitment; faculty interview. *Graduate:* Baccalaureate degree from a regionally accredited institution. *Teacher education specific:* Miller Analogies Test; three recommendations; completion of all required departmental exams; teaching licensure where required by program pursued; faculty interview.

Fees and Expenses: Undergraduate: $11,310 per academic year. Graduate: Tuition charged per credit hour. On-campus room and board: $4,948. Other expenses: $4,500. Books and supplies: $850.

Financial Aid: Resources specifically for eligible students enrolled in teacher education programs are awarded on the basis of financial need and academic merit. The institution has a Program Participation Agreement with the U.S. Department of Education for eligible students to receive Pell Grants and other federal aid. Teacher scholarships available to qualifying students. *Contact:* Financial Aid Office at: (405) 491-6310.

Accreditation: *Regional:* NCA. *Professional:* NCATE. *Member of:* AACTE. *Approved by:* Oklahoma State Department of Education.

Undergraduate Programs: The university offers programs for certification in the following levels and areas: early childhood (preK-grade 3); elementary education (grades 1-8); secondary education (grades 6-12); all levels (preK-grade 12 including physical education, foreign language [Spanish], music [instrumental/general], music [vocal/general]); secondary (grades 6-12 including English, mathematics, science, social studies, speech/drama).

All programs require the completion of a general education core, professional studies, subject content area, field experiences, and student teaching.

Graduate Programs: The Master of Arts in educational leadership program is designed for teachers who want to be equipped with the necessary skills and knowledge to become effective educational administrators.

Licensure/Reciprocity: Oklahoma. Students seeking teaching certification in a state other than Oklahoma should consult with that state's teacher certification office early in their program of study to insure compliance with requirements. Many state directors of teacher credentialing have signed Interstate Agreements through NASDTEC that expedite the certification process.

SOUTHWESTERN OKLAHOMA STATE UNIVERSITY

School of Education
100 Campus Drive
Weatherford, Oklahoma 73096
Phone: (580) 772-6611
Fax: (580) 774-3795
E-mail: krose@swosu.edu
Internet: http://www.swosu.edu

Institution Description: Southwestern Oklahoma State University was established as Southwestern Normal School in 1901.

The mission of the School of Education is to provide the necessary background in professional education for the development of competencies that will contribute to successful teaching.

Institution Control: Public.

Calendar: Semester. Academic year August to May.

Official(s): Dr. Ken Rose, Dean.

Faculty: Full-time 14.

Degrees Awarded: 142 baccalaureate; 54 master's.

Admission Requirements: *Undergraduate:* Graduation from an accredited secondary school or GED; ACT composite; 2.7 minimum GPA. *Teacher education specific:* Maintain a 2.5 GPA; completion of 30 semester hours of coursework; pass the Oklahoma General Education Test; professional commitment; faculty interview. *Graduate:* Baccalaureate degree from a regionally accredited institution. *Teacher education specific:* Miller

Analogies Test or GRE; two professional recommendations; completion of all required departmental exams; teaching licensure where required by program pursued; faculty interview.

Fees and Expenses: Undergraduate: in-state $2,948 per academic year; out-of-state $6,658. Graduate: Tuition charged per credit hour. On-campus room and board: $2,910. Other expenses: $2,640. Books and supplies: $1,068.

Financial Aid: Resources specifically for eligible students enrolled in teacher education programs are awarded on the basis of financial need and academic merit. The institution has a Program Participation Agreement with the U.S. Department of Education for eligible students to receive Pell Grants and other federal aid. Teacher scholarships available to qualifying students. *Contact:* Financial Aid Office at: (580) 774-3786.

Accreditation: *Regional:* NCA. *Professional:* NCATE. *Member of:* AACTE. *Approved by:* Oklahoma State Department of Education.

Undergraduate Programs: Elementary education programs leading to the baccalaureate degree include concentrations in elementary education and early childhood. The elementary-secondary program is offered with majors in art, health/physical education/recreation, music-instrumental, music-vocal, special education. The secondary education program offers concentrations in English, history, mathematics, natural science, social studies, and technology.

All programs require the completion of a general education core, professional studies, subject content area, field experiences, and student teaching.

Graduate Programs: The Master of Education degree program is designed to provide a professional course of study for students who have acquired a bachelor's degree in education and wish to improve their proficiency and skill as educators. Areas of specialization include: early childhood, elementary, secondary, school service programs, and elementary/secondary education.

Licensure/Reciprocity: Oklahoma. Students seeking teaching certification in a state other than Oklahoma should consult with that state's teacher certification office early in their program of study to insure compliance with requirements. Many state directors of teacher credentialling have signed Interstate Agreements through NASDTEC that expedite the certification process.

UNIVERSITY OF CENTRAL OKLAHOMA

College of Education
100 North University Drive
Edmond, Oklahoma 73034-0170
Phone: (405) 974-7501
Fax: (405) 974-3851
E-mail: coewebmaster@ucok.edu
Internet: http://www.ucok.edu

Institution Description: The University of Central Oklahoma is a state institution. It was established as The Normal School of the Territory of Oklahoma in 1890.

The initial and advanced teacher preparation programs are taught by full-time faculty and highly qualified adjuncts who are field practitioners.

Institution Control: Public.

Calendar: Semester. Academic year August to May.

Official(s): Dr. Judith Coe, Dean; Dr. Pamela K. Fly, Associate Dean.

Faculty: Full-time 34; part-time 13; adjunct 13.

Degrees Awarded: 293 baccalaureate; 250 master's.

Admission Requirements: *Undergraduate:* Graduation from an accredited secondary school or GED; College Board SAT or ACT composite. *Teacher education specific:* Maintain a 2.75 GPA in the professional education courses and field of licensure; professional commitment; high scholastic attainment; passing scores on Oklahoma General Education Test; faculty interview. *Graduate:* Baccalaureate degree from a regionally accredited

institution. *Teacher education specific:* 2.75 GPA or higher; must hold standard teaching certificate; completion of all required departmental exams; faculty interview.

Fees and Expenses: Undergraduate: in-state $57.25 per semester hour; out-of-state $110.45. Graduate: in-state $75.55 per semester hour; out-of-state $129.45. Required fees: $22.45 per credit hour; $12.50 cultural and recreation. On-campus room and board: $955 to $2,169 per semester. Books and supplies: $800.

Financial Aid: Resources specifically for eligible students enrolled in teacher education programs are awarded on the basis of financial need and academic merit. The institution has a Program Participation Agreement with the U.S. Department of Education for eligible students to receive Pell Grants and other federal aid. Teacher scholarships available to qualifying students. *Contact:* Office of Student Financial Aid at: (405) 974-3334.

Accreditation: *Regional:* NCA. *Professional:* NCATE. *Member of:* AACTE. *Approved by:* Oklahoma State Department of Education.

Undergraduate Programs: The following programs leading to the baccalaureate degree and teacher certification include: allied health, art, business and marketing, early childhood, elementary, English, family and consumer sciences, foreign languages (French, German, Spanish), history/social studies, mathematics, music (vocal, instrumental), physical education, science (biology, chemistry, general science, physical science, physics), special education (mild/moderate, severe/profound), trades and industrial education.

All programs require the completion of a general education core, professional studies, subject content area, field experiences, and student teaching.

Graduate Programs: Graduate programs leading to the master's degree include: early childhood, elementary, secondary education, bilingual education/TESOL, educational administration, guidance and counseling, instructional media, special education, school psychologist, speech-language pathology, reading.

Licensure/Reciprocity: Oklahoma. Students seeking teaching certification in a state other than Oklahoma should consult with that state's teacher certification office early in their program of study to insure compliance with requirements. Many state directors of teacher credentialing have signed Interstate Agreements through NASDTEC that expedite the certification process.

UNIVERSITY OF OKLAHOMA

College of Education
820 Van Vleet Oval
Norman, Oklahoma 73109
Phone: (405) 325-1081
Fax: (405) 325-7290
E-mail: cormsbee@ou.edu
Internet: http://www.ou.edu

Institution Description: The University of Oklahoma was established in 1890.

The primary mission of the College of Education is to promote inquiry and practices that foster democratic life and that are fundamental to the interrelated activities of teaching, research, and practice in the multidisciplinary field of education.

Institution Control: Public.

Calendar: Semester. Academic year August to May.

Official(s): Dr. Joan K. Smith, Dean; Dr. Christine Ormsbee, Associate Dean for Teacher Education.

Faculty: Full-time 60; part-time 3; adjunct 25.

Degrees Awarded: 242 baccalaureate; 164 master's; 30 doctorate.

Admission Requirements: *Undergraduate:* Graduation from an accredited secondary school in top 25% of class; GED accepted. College Board SAT or ACT composite. *Teacher education specific:* 2.75 GPA; 24 hours of completed university course-

UNIVERSITY OF OKLAHOMA—*cont'd*

work; personal essay; professional commitment; passing scores on Oklahoma General Education Test; faculty interview. *Graduate:* Baccalaureate degree from a regionally accredited institution. *Teacher education specific:* 2.75 GPA; completion of all required departmental exams; teaching certification where required by program pursued; faculty interview.

Fees and Expenses: Undergraduate: in-state $69.80 freshman/sophomore per credit hour, $7470 junior/senior; out-of-state $256.45 per credit hour. Required $20.62 per credit hour. On-campus room and board: $2,292 to $2,647 per semester. Books and supplies: $1,000.

Financial Aid: Resources specifically for eligible students enrolled in teacher education programs are awarded on the basis of financial need and academic merit. The institution has a Program Participation Agreement with the U.S. Department of Education for eligible students to receive Pell Grants and other federal aid. Teacher scholarships available to qualifying students. *Contact:* Matthew Hamilton, Financial Aid Office at: (405) 325-8481 or e-mail at: mhamilton@ou.edu.

Accreditation: *Regional:* NCA. *Professional:* NCATE. *Member of:* AACTE. *Approved by:* Oklahoma State Department of Education.

Undergraduate Programs: Teacher certification program leading to the baccalaureate degree include: early childhood education (preK-grade 3); elementary education (grades 7-8); foreign language education (preK-12); language arts education (grades 6-12); mathematics education (grades 6-12); science education (grades 6-12); social studies education (grades 6-12); special education (preK-12).

All programs require the completion of a general education core, professional studies, subject content area, field experiences, and student teaching.

Graduate Programs: Graduate programs available in the College of Education include: adult and higher education; community counseling; counseling psychology; educational administration; curriculum and supervision; historical/philosophical/social foundations; instructional leadership; academic curriculum (early childhood, elementary, English, instructional leadership, mathematics, reading, science, secondary, social studies); instructional psychology and technology (education technology, educational psychology, instructional design, instructional psychology, educational technology/library information studies); special education.

Doctoral programs are offered in adult and higher education; educational administration, curriculum and supervision; historical/philosophical/social foundations.

Licensure/Reciprocity: Oklahoma. Students seeking teaching certification in a state other than Oklahoma should consult with that state's teacher certification office early in their program of study to insure compliance with requirements. Many state directors of teacher credentialing have signed Interstate Agreements through NASDTEC that expedite the certification process.

UNIVERSITY OF SCIENCE AND ARTS OF OKLAHOMA

Division of Education
Teacher Education Program
1727 West Alabama
Chickasha, Oklahoma 73018-0001
Phone: (405) 224-3140
Fax: (405) 574-1220
E-mail: facscottcv@usao.edu
Internet: http://usao.edu

Institution Description: University of science and Arts of Oklahoma (Oklahoma College of Liberal Arts until 1974) is a state institution. It was established in 1908.

The Teacher Education Program combines a well-rounded liberal arts education with a teacher preparation curriculum.

Institution Control: Public.

Calendar: Trimester. Academic year August to April.

Official(s): Dr. Vicki Ferguson, Dean.

Faculty: Full-time 12; part-time 1; adjunct 1.

Degrees Awarded: 26 baccalaureate.

Admission Requirements: *Undergraduate:* Graduation from an accredited secondary school in top 50% of class; 2.7 GPA; GED accepted; ACT composite. *Teacher education specific:* 2.5 GPA in the first 23 hours; professional education courses and field of licensure; professional commitment; high scholastic attainment; passing scores on Oklahoma General Teacher Education test; faculty interview.

Fees and Expenses: $1,548 in-state per academic year; $2,928 out-of-state. Required fees: $540. On-campus room and board: $2890 to $6,180. Books and supplies: $700.

Financial Aid: Resources specifically for eligible students enrolled in teacher education programs are awarded on the basis of financial need and academic merit. The institution has a Program Participation Agreement with the U.S. Department of Education for eligible students to receive Pell Grants and other federal aid. Teacher scholarships available to qualifying students. *Contact:* Nancy Moats at: (405) 574-1350 or e-mail at: nmoats@usao.edu.

Accreditation: *Regional:* NCA. *Professional:* NCATE. *Member of:* AACTE. *Approved by:* Oklahoma State Department of Education.

Undergraduate Programs: The Division of Education offers programs leading to the Bachelor of Science degree and teacher certification in the fields of: elementary education, early childhood, deaf education, speech-language pathology. Other options include teacher certification in the secondary areas of mathematics, science, social studies, English, and business. Also programs are offered in the preK-12 areas of art, music, and physical education. All programs require the completion of a general education core, professional studies, subject content area, field experiences, and student teaching.

Licensure/Reciprocity: Oklahoma. Students seeking teaching certification in a state other than Oklahoma should consult with that state's teacher certification office early in their program of study to insure compliance with requirements. Many state directors of teacher credentialing have signed Interstate Agreements through NASDTEC that expedite the certification process.

UNIVERSITY OF TULSA

Henry Kendall College of Arts and sciences
School of Education
600 South College Avenue
Tulsa, Oklahoma 74104-3189
Phone: (918) 631-2236
Fax: (918) 631-2133
E-mail: diane-beals@utulsa.edu
Internet: http://www.utulsa.edu

Institution Description: The University of Tulsa is a private, independent, nonprofit institution. It was established in Muskogee, Indian Territory, as Henry Kendall College in 1894. The campus was moved to Tulsa in 1907 and the present name was adopted in 1920.

The Tulsa Curriculum (general education courses taken by all students) provides a strong liberal arts-based general education and emphasizes the development of competencies in writing, languages, and mathematical sciences.

Institution Control: Private.

Calendar: Semester. Academic year August to May.

Official(s): Dr. Diane E. Beals, Dean.

Faculty: Full-time 5; adjunct 4.

Degrees Awarded: 21 baccalaureate; 20 master's.

Admission Requirements: *Undergraduate:* Graduation from an accredited secondary school or GED; College Board SAT or ACT composite. *Teacher education specific:* Maintain a 2.5 GPA in the Tulsa Curriculum; professional commitment; high scholastic attainment; passing scores Oklahoma General Education Test; faculty interview. *Graduate:* Baccalaureate degree from a regionally accredited institution. *Teacher education specific:* 3.0 undergraduate GPA; completion of all required departmental exams; GRE; teaching licensure where required by program pursued; faculty interview.

Fees and Expenses: $16,400 per academic year. Required fees: $405. On-campus room and board: $5,610. Other expenses: $1,200. Books and supplies: $400.

Financial Aid: Resources specifically for eligible students enrolled in teacher education programs are awarded on the basis of financial need and academic merit. The institution has a Program Participation Agreement with the U.S. Department of Education for eligible students to receive Pell Grants and other federal aid. Teacher scholarships available to qualifying students. *Contact:* Financial Aid Office at: (915) 631-2526 or e-mail at: finaid@utulsa.edu.

Accreditation: *Regional:* NCA. *Professional:* NCATE. *Member of:* AACTE. *Approved by:* Oklahoma State Department of Education.

Undergraduate Programs: Secondary education students complete an area of concentration while also completing approximately 30 semester hours of professional education courses. Academic majors qualifying for secondary teaching include: biology, chemistry, speech and drama, English, history, mathematics, physics, geosciences, political science.

Middle level certification areas are available in language arts, mathematics, science, and social science. Students seeking certification in elementary education complete an area of concentration consisting of a major in elementary education and a minor in a specific academic discipline.

K-12 certification can be earned in art, vocal or instrumental music, French, German, Russian, Spanish, speech language pathology, and deaf education.

All baccalaureate programs require the completion of a general education core, professional studies, subject content area, field experiences, and student teaching.

Graduate Programs: The School of Education provides two graduate academic degree programs: Master of Arts degree with majors in elementary education, secondary education, and research and evaluation; Master of Arts in Teaching degree with areas of emphasis in art, biology, English, history, and mathematics. Graduate students may pursue Oklahoma certification as part of a degree program or as an independent certification only plan.

Licensure/Reciprocity: Oklahoma. Students seeking teaching certification in a state other than Oklahoma should consult with that state's teacher certification office early in their program of study to insure compliance with requirements. Many state directors of teacher credentialing have signed Interstate Agreements through NASDTEC that expedite the certification process.

OREGON

GEORGE FOX UNIVERSITY

School of Education
Teacher Education Program
414 North Meridian Street
Newberg, Oregon 97132-2697
Phone: (503) 554-2848
Fax: (503) 554-2868
E-mail: dmyton@georgefox.edu
Internet: http://www.georgefox.edu

Institution Description: George Fox University was formed by a merger of George Fox College and Western Evangelical Seminary in 1996. The university is a private nonprofit institution affiliated with the Northwest Yearly Meeting of Friends.

The Teacher Education Program is designed to prepare teachers for the public and private schools through a curriculum that builds on a broad foundation in Christian liberal arts education and through specialization in a particular field of knowledge.

Institution Control: Private.

Calendar: Semester. Academic year September to May.

Official(s): Dr. David Myton, Dean.

Faculty: Full-time 23; part-time 12; adjunct 30.

Degrees Awarded: 20 baccalaureate; 184 master's; 4 doctorate.

Admission Requirements: *Undergraduate:* Graduation from an accredited secondary school or GED; College Board SAT or ACT composite. *Teacher education specific:* Cumulative 2.75 GPA; passing scores on California Basic Skills Test; three faculty recommendations; exemplary social and moral behavior; admission interview. *Graduate:* Baccalaureate degree from a regionally accredited institution. *Teacher education specific:* 2.75 GPA; completion of all departmental required exams (California Basic Skills Test or PRAXIS I); teaching licensure where required by program pursued; faculty interview.

Fees and Expenses: Undergraduate: $19,810 per academic year. Graduate: Tuition charged per credit hour. On-campus room and board: $6,300. Other expenses: $1,250. Books and supplies; $600.

Financial Aid: Resources specifically for eligible students enrolled in teacher education programs are awarded on the basis of financial need and academic merit. M.A.T. students may qualify for assistance specializing in high-need areas. The institution has a Program Participation Agreement with the U.S. Department of Education for eligible students to receive Pell Grants and other federal aid. Teacher scholarships available to qualifying students. *Contact:* Gayle Denham at: (503) 554-2296 or e-mail at: gdenham@georgefox.edu.

Accreditation: *Regional:* NASC. *Approved by:* Oregon Department of Education.

Undergraduate Programs: Baccalaureate programs offered in the teacher education program include elementary and secondary education. It is possible to become a middle school and/or a high school teaching by following a five-year plan that includes both an undergraduate degree in a field of study and a Master of Arts degree in teaching. In years 1-4 of the program, the student completes requirements for a major in art, biology, business, chemistry, family and consumer sciences, health, history, mathematics, music, physical education, physics, Spanish,

writing/literature, or an emphasis in theatre or speech communication. Year 5 involves completion of coursework and practicum experiences for graduation with a Master of Arts in Teaching degree.

All baccalaureate programs require the completion of a general education core, professional studies, subject content area, field experiences, and student teaching.

Graduate Programs: The purpose of the Master of Arts in Teaching program is to provide qualified early childhood, elementary, middle, and secondary teachers for public and private schools. The full-time and part-time curriculums include professional education courses and field experiences. The program offers secondary endorsements in: advanced mathematics, art, biology, business, chemistry, family and consumer sciences, language arts, music, physical education, physics, social studies, and Spanish. Basic math, drama, health education, and speech may be added as another endorsement.

Licensure/Reciprocity: Oregon. Students seeking teaching certification in a state other than Oregon should consult with that state's teacher certification office early in their program of study to insure compliance with requirements. Many state directors of teacher credentialing have signed Interstate Agreements through NASDTEC that expedite the certification process.

LEWIS AND CLARK COLLEGE

Teacher Education
MSC 14
0615 SW Palatine Hill Road
Portland, Oregon 97219-7899
Phone: (503) 768-7188
Fax: (503) 768-7055
E-mail: lcteach@lclark.edu
Internet: http://www.lclark.edu

Institution Description: Lewis and Clark College is a private, independent, nonprofit institution. It was established as Albany College in 1867. The present name was adopted in 1942.

Teacher Education at the college combines the tradition of the liberal arts with a program of professional studies directed toward developing thoughtful decision makers and leaders in the schools.

Institution Control: Private.

Calendar: Semester. Academic year August to May.

Official(s): Dr. Vernon Jones, Department Chair.

Faculty: Full-time 19.

Degrees Awarded: 37 baccalaureate; 188 master's.

Admission Requirements: *Undergraduate:* Graduation from an accredited secondary school or GED; College Board SAT or ACT composite. *Teacher education specific:* Maintain a 2.75 GPA in the professional education courses and field of licensure; professional commitment; passing scores on PRAXIS I exams (reading, writing, mathematics); faculty interview. *Graduate:* Baccalaureate degree from a regionally accredited institution. *Teacher education specific:* 2.75 GPA; completion of all required departmental exams; teaching licensure where required by program pursued; three letters of recommendation; faculty interview. PRAXIS II required for graduation and certification.

Fees and Expenses: Undergraduate $24,686 per academic year. Graduate: $550 per credit hour. On-campus room and board: $7,140. Other expenses: $1,924. Books and supplies: $800.

Financial Aid: Resources specifically for eligible students enrolled in teacher education programs are awarded on the basis of financial need and academic merit. The institution has a Program Participation Agreement with the U.S. Department of Education for eligible students to receive Pell Grants and other federal aid. Teacher scholarships available to qualifying students. *Contact:* Financial Aid Office at: (503) 768-7090,

Accreditation: *Regional:* NASC. *Member of:* AACTE. *Approved by:* Oregon Department of Education.

Undergraduate Programs: Teacher Education faculty teach several courses for undergraduates who wish to explore teaching as a career or who wish to tutor in public school classrooms and participate in college-based seminars. Experience in a public school classroom is required for admission to the MAT Intern Program in Teacher Education. Students interested in a teaching career at the middle level or high school are schooled in subjects they wish to teach. Prospective elementary teachers should take courses in multiple disciplines, including mathematics and science.

Graduate Programs: Preservice Program Options for prospective teachers leads to the Master of Arts in Teaching Degree and is designed for liberal arts graduates who wish to become teachers. Programs include: early childhood/elementary M.A.T.; middle level/high school M.A.T.; special education: deaf and hard-of-hearing auditory program.

Inservice program options for currently licensed teachers include Master of Arts in Teaching: liberal studies degree; Master of Education with special educator endorsement; Master of Education in educational administration; Continuing Teaching License; English as a second language/bilingual endorsement; language and literacy program/reading endorsement; mathematics endorsement.

Licensure/Reciprocity: Oregon. Students seeking teaching certification in a state other than Oregon should consult with that state's teacher certification office early in their program of study to insure compliance with requirements. Many state directors of teacher credentialing have signed Interstate Agreements through NASDTEC that expedite the certification process.

OREGON STATE UNIVERSITY

School of Education
Teacher Education
210 Education Hall
Corvallis, Oregon 97331-4501
Phone: (541) 737-4661
Fax: (541) 737-8971
E-mail: soe@orst.edu
Internet: http://www.orst.edu

Institution Description: Oregon State University is a state institution and land-grant college that was established in 1850.

The School of Education at Oregon State University offers an array of possibilities for persons who want to pursue a challenging career in teaching.

Institution Control: Public.

Calendar: Quarter. Academic year September to June.

Official(s): Dr. Sam Stern, Dean; Dr. Karen Higgins, Director of Teacher Education.

Faculty: Full-time 17; part-time 2; adjunct 11.

Degrees Awarded: 1 baccalaureate; 196 master's; 24 doctorate.

Admission Requirements: *Undergraduate:* Graduation from an accredited secondary school or GED; College Board SAT or ACT composite. *Teacher education specific:* Professional commitment; high scholastic attainment; passing scores on PRAXIS I exams (reading, writing, mathematics); personal narrative; faculty interview. *Graduate:* Baccalaureate degree from a regionally accredited institution. *Teacher education specific:* 3.0 GPA in last 90 quarter hours; Basic Education Skills Test; competencies

in subject matter; completion of all departmental required exams; teaching licensure where required by program pursued; faculty interview.

Fees and Expenses: Undergraduate: in-state $4,080 per academic year; out-of-state $14,340. Graduate: in-state $7,626 per academic year; out-of-state $12,810. On-campus room and board: $6,336. Books and supplies: $1,350.

Financial Aid: Resources specifically for eligible students enrolled in teacher education programs are awarded on the basis of financial need and academic merit. The institution has a Program Participation Agreement with the U.S. Department of Education for eligible students to receive Pell Grants and other federal aid. Teacher scholarships available to qualifying students. *Contact:* Kate Peterson at: (541) 737-2241 or e-mail at: financial.aid@orst.edu.

Accreditation: *Regional:* NASC. *Professional:* NCATE. *Member of:* AACTE. *Approved by:* Oregon Department of Education.

Undergraduate Programs: The School of Education offers an undergraduate double degree program in early childhood/elementary education. Two degrees can be earned concurrently— one in their chosen field and the second in education. The program leads to certification and the Bachelor of Arts or Bachelor of Science degree.

Secondary education programs are offered in agriculture, science and mathematics, business and technology, family and consumer science, foreign language, health, language arts, music, and physical education.

All baccalaureate programs require the completion of a general education core, professional studies, subject content area, field experiences, and student teaching. A minimum of 192 quarter hours is required for the baccalaureate award.

Graduate Programs: Two graduate-level Professional Teacher Education Programs are offered in early childhood and/or elementary education. The programs (Immersion and Two-Year) incorporate required coursework for the ESOL/bilingual endorsement and Master of Arts in Teaching degree. The Immersion Program is an intensive one-year preparation for licensure program based in culturally and linguistically diverse schools. Students who enter the program with a bachelor's degree are placed in either a bilingual school in Salem or an inner-city school in Portland. The Two-Year program is a part-time program with coursework offered on weekends.

The Doctor of Philosophy in Education: Teacher Leadership Program is designed for educators who are committed to providing leadership in K-12 education.

Licensure/Reciprocity: Oregon. Students seeking teaching certification in a state other than Oregon should consult with that state's teacher certification office early in their program of study to insure compliance with requirements. Many state directors of teacher credentialing have signed Interstate Agreements through NASDTEC that expedite the certification process.

PORTLAND STATE UNIVERSITY

Graduate School of Education
724 SW Harrison
P.O. Box 751
Portland, Oregon 97207
Phone: (503) 725-3511
Fax: (503) 725-5525
E-mail: edmundp@pdx.edu
Internet: http://www.pdx.edu

Institution Description: Portland State University was established and chartered as Vanport Extension Center, and offered first instruction at the postsecondary level in 1946. The name was changed to Portland State Extension Center in 1952, to Portland State College in 1955, and to the present name in 1969.

The Graduate School of Education offers programs at the master's and doctorate levels, including initial and continuing licensure and degree programs.

Institution Control: Public.

Calendar: Quarter. Academic year September to June.

Official(s): Dr. Phyllis J. Edmundson, Dean.

PORTLAND STATE UNIVERSITY—*cont'd*

Faculty: Full-time 63.

Degrees Awarded: 58 baccalaureate; 470 master's; 4 doctorate.

Admission Requirements: *Undergraduate:* Graduation from an accredited secondary school or GED; College Board SAT or ACT composite. *Teacher education specific:* Students with future teaching objectives major in the liberal arts curriculum. ***Graduate:*** Baccalaureate degree from a regionally accredited institution. *Teacher education specific:* 3.0 GPA in last 90 quarter hours; California Basic Education Skills Test; competencies in subject matter; completion of all departmental required exams; experience in working with children; faculty interview.

Fees and Expenses: Undergraduate: in-state $4,278 per academic year; out-of-state $13,674. Graduate: $274 per credit hour plus other fees. On-campus room and board: $7,950. Other expenses: $2,300. Books and supplies: $1,400.

Financial Aid: Resources specifically for eligible students enrolled in teacher education programs are awarded on the basis of financial need and academic merit. The institution has a Program Participation Agreement with the U.S. Department of Education for eligible students to receive Pell Grants and other federal aid. Teacher scholarships available to qualifying students. *Contact:* Financial Aid Office at: (503) 725-3461.

Accreditation: *Regional:* NASC. *Professional:* NCATE. *Member of:* AACTE. *Approved by:* Oregon Department of Education.

Undergraduate Programs: Baccalaureate students prepare for future teaching certification by majoring in the liberal arts and sciences. Baccalaureate degrees must be earned for admission to teacher certification programs.

Graduate Programs: The Graduate Teacher Education Program (GTEP) offers programs in early childhood education, elementary education, mid-level education, high school education, inclusive education, and educational media/librarianship. The program prepares candidates for teaching students in early childhood (preK-grade 4), elementary (grades 3-8), mid-level (grades 5-10), and high school (grades 7-12). Successful completion of the GTEP enables recommendation for a basic teaching license. Students may also prepare for endorsements in: reading, educational media, handicapped learner, severely handicapped learner, visually impaired learner, and speech impaired learner. A Master of Education degree can be earned with an additional term of planned coursework.

A master's degree in curriculum and instruction is available for students who have not completed the GTEP program, with opportunities to specialize in library/media, reading/literacy, early childhood education, or other areas of personal interest.

Licensure/Reciprocity: Oregon. Students seeking teaching certification in a state other than Oregon should consult with that state's teacher certification office early in their program of study to insure compliance with requirements. Many state directors of teacher credentialing have signed Interstate Agreements through NASDTEC that expedite the certification process.

SOUTHERN OREGON UNIVERSITY

Department of Education
Teacher Education
1250 Siskiyou Boulevard
Ashland, Oregon 97520
Phone: (541) 552-7672
Fax: (541) 552-6614
E-mail: admissions@sou.edu
Internet: http://www.sou.edu

Institution Description: Southern Oregon University, formerly Southern Oregon State College, was established as Southern Oregon Normal School in 1926.

The Teacher Education Program includes both undergraduate and graduate level programs leading to teacher certification. Undergraduate programs are mainly majors in the liberal arts and sciences with introductory education courses.

Institution Control: Public.

Calendar: Quarter. Academic year September to June.

Official(s): Dr. William Greene, Department Chair; Dr. Geoffrey Mills, Director of Teacher Education.

Faculty: Full-time 25.

Degrees Awarded: 14 baccalaureate; 182 master's.

Admission Requirements: *Undergraduate:* Graduation from an accredited secondary school with 14 college preparatory academic units or GED; College Board SAT or ACT composite. *Teacher education specific:* Students with future teaching objectives major in the liberal arts curriculum. ***Graduate:*** Baccalaureate degree from a regionally accredited institution. *Teacher education specific:* 3.0 GPA in last 90 quarter hours; California Basic Education Skills Test; competencies in subject matter; completion of all departmental required exams; experience in working with children; faculty interview.

Fees and Expenses: Undergraduate: in-state $4,153 per academic year; out-of-state $12,823. Graduate: Tuition charged per credit hour. On-campus room and board: $6,210. Other expenses: $2,700. Books and supplies: $1,100.

Financial Aid: Resources specifically for eligible students enrolled in teacher education programs are awarded on the basis of financial need and academic merit. The institution has a Program Participation Agreement with the U.S. Department of Education for eligible students to receive Pell Grants and other federal aid. Teacher scholarships available to qualifying students. *Contact:* Financial Aid Office at: (541) 552-6161.

Accreditation: *Regional:* NASC. *Professional:* NCATE. *Member of:* AACTE. *Approved by:* Oregon Department of Education.

Undergraduate Programs: The early childhood development degree is a joint bachelor's degree program offered in cooperation with Rogue Community College. While this program does not lead to teacher licensure, it prepares students for the early childhood/elementary cohort of the Master of Arts in Teaching program.

The education minor is a 24-credit program that introduces students to various aspects of precollegiate education in the United States.

Graduate Programs: The Master of Arts in Teaching program is a 12-month full-time graduate teacher preparation program. The special education initial licensure is a 12-month full-time graduate teacher preparation program leading to initial teaching license in special education.

The Master in Education degree program is a 45-credit program for currently licensed teachers. A Continuing Teaching License program is a 12-credit program for those teachers with an Oregon Initial Teaching License, a master's degree, and Oregon teaching experience who need to obtain the Oregon Continuing Teaching License. Endorsements that can be added include: English for speakers of other languages, special education, reading, and subject Areas.

Licensure/Reciprocity: Oregon. Students seeking teaching certification in a state other than Oregon should consult with that state's teacher certification office early in their program of study to insure compliance with requirements. Many state directors of teacher credentialing have signed Interstate Agreements through NASDTEC that expedite the certification process.

UNIVERSITY OF OREGON

College of Education
Area Teacher Education
Eugene, Oregon 97403-1226
Phone: (541) 346-3404
Fax: (541) 346-5815
E-mail: mgall@uoregon.edu
Internet: http://www.uoregon.edu

Institution Description: The University of Oregon is a state institution that was chartered in 1872.

Licensure and degree programs in teacher education prepare professionals to work in education and other community-based human services programs.

Institution Control: Public.

Calendar: Quarter. Academic year September to June.

Official(s): Dr. Mark Gall, Area Head.

Faculty: Full-time 13.

Degrees Awarded: 161 baccalaureate; 289 master's; 15 doctorate.

Admission Requirements: *Undergraduate:* Graduation from an accredited secondary school with 14 college preparatory academic units or GED; College Board SAT or ACT composite. *Teacher education specific:* Completion of 55 college credits with a minimum of GPA if 2.0 or better; core educational studies courses; successful experiences with children, youth, and families. *Graduate:* Baccalaureate degree from a regionally accredited institution. *Teacher education specific:* 3.0 GPA in last 90 quarter hours; California Basic Education Skills Test; competencies in subject matter; completion of all departmental required exams; experience in working with children; faculty interview.

Fees and Expenses: Undergraduate: in-state $4,914 per academic year; out-of-state $16,350. Graduate: Tuition charged per credit hour. On-campus room and board: $6,570. Other expenses: $2,350. Books and supplies: $900.

Financial Aid: Resources specifically for eligible students enrolled in teacher education programs are awarded on the basis of financial need and academic merit. The institution has a Program Participation Agreement with the U.S. Department of Education for eligible students to receive Pell Grants and other federal aid. Teacher scholarships available to qualifying students. *Contact:* Financial Aid Office at: (541) 346-3221.

Accreditation: *Regional:* NASC. *Member of:* AACTE. *Approved by:* Oregon Department of Education.

Undergraduate Programs: The integrated teaching specialization consists of core courses in educational studies and professional coursework. In core courses, students examine theories of education and human development and their applications to teaching and learning. At the end of four years, students graduate with a Bachelor of Science or Bachelor of Arts degree and a major in educational studies.

Educational Foundations is a program with a focus of specialized study in early childhood/elementary education, special education, or early childhood/early intervention.

Graduate Programs: The Graduate Elementary Teaching Program is one of the options within the teaching and learning major that leads to a teaching license in early childhood/elementary education and to a Master of Education degree.

The middle/secondary education program is a postbaccalaureate degree program leading to authorization to teach designated subjects in middle schools and high schools and to a Master in Education within the teaching and learning major.

The Sapsik'wala Program is a scholarship program to benefit and train American Indian students to become professional educators. Qualified applicants choose an elementary, middle school or high school level teacher education program.

Licensure/Reciprocity: Oregon. Students seeking teaching certification in a state other than Oregon should consult with that state's teacher certification office early in their program of study to insure compliance with requirements. Many state directors of teacher credentialing have signed Interstate Agreements through NASDTEC that expedite the certification process.

UNIVERSITY OF PORTLAND

School of Education
Teacher Education
5000 North Willamette Boulevard
Portland, Oregon 97203-5798
Phone: (503) 943-7135
Fax: (503) 943-8042
E-mail: education@up.edu
Internet: http://www.up.edu

Institution Description: The University of Portland is a private, independent, nonprofit institution affiliated with the Roman Catholic Church. It was founded in 1901.

The purpose of the School of Education is to prepare individuals in various stages of their careers to teach and lead in public and private schools.

Institution Control: Private.

Calendar: Semester. Academic year August to May.

Official(s): Dr. Maria Ciriello, Dean; Dr. Arlene Hett, Director of Teacher Education.

Faculty: Full-time 14; adjunct 18.

Degrees Awarded: 47 baccalaureate; 176 master's.

Admission Requirements: *Undergraduate:* Graduation from an accredited secondary school or GED; College Board SAT. *Teacher education specific:* Maintain a 3.0 GPA in the professional education courses and field of licensure; professional commitment; passing scores on California Basic Skills Test or PRAXIS I exams (reading, writing, mathematics); faculty interview. *Graduate:* Baccalaureate degree from a regionally accredited institution. *Teacher education specific:* Completion of all required departmental exams; teaching licensure where required by program pursued; letters of recommendation; faculty interview.

Fees and Expenses: Undergraduate: $21,800 per academic year. Graduate: $17,676. fees: Health insurance $300 per semester. On-campus room and board: $6,670. $30 Technology lab assessment fee. Books and supplies: $700.

Financial Aid: Resources specifically for eligible students enrolled in teacher education programs are awarded on the basis of financial need and academic merit. The institution has a Program Participation Agreement with the U.S. Department of Education for eligible students to receive Pell Grants and other federal aid. Teacher scholarships available to qualifying students. *Contact:* Tracy Reisinger, Director of Financial Aid at: (503) 943-7311 or e-mail at: reisinge@up.edu.

Accreditation: *Regional:* NASC. *Professional:* NCATE. *Member of:* AACTE. *Approved by:* Oregon Department of Education.

Undergraduate Programs: The School of Education offers three undergraduate degrees: elementary education, secondary education, and music education. Each degree has special requirements but all degrees lead to competence in a composite of objectives from relevant societies and licensing agencies. All programs require the completion of a general education core, professional studies, subject content area, field experiences, and student teaching. A minimum of 120 semester hours is required for the baccalaureate award.

Graduate Programs: The Master of Education degree is designed for practicing educators to continue building upon professional knowledge and experience. The advanced preparation programs require completion of a 14 hour core of professional knowledge and research courses for a total of 36 credit hours. Options are available in educational leadership, reading, special education, English speakers of other languages, initial administrator licensure, or continuing education.

Licensure/Reciprocity: Oregon. Students seeking teaching certification in a state other than Oregon should consult with that state's teacher certification office early in their program of study to insure compliance with requirements. Many state directors of teacher credentialing have signed Interstate Agreements through NASDTEC that expedite the certification process.

WESTERN OREGON UNIVERSITY

College of Education
Division of Teacher Education
345 North Monmouth Avenue
Monmouth, Oregon 97361
Phone: (503) 838-8471
Fax: (503) 838-8228
E-mail: welandg@wou.edu
Internet: http://www.wou.edu

Institution Description: Western Oregon University, formerly named Western Oregon State College, is a comprehensive regional state institution that was founded in 1856. It is part of the Oregon State University System.

The College of Education offers undergraduate and graduate degree programs leading to teacher certification in a variety of concentrations.

Institution Control: Public.

WESTERN OREGON UNIVERSITY—*cont'd*

Calendar: Quarter. Academic year September to June.

Official(s): Dr. Gary Welander, Chair, Division of Teacher Education.

Faculty: Full-time 29.

Degrees Awarded: 55 baccalaureate; 145 master's.

Admission Requirements: *Undergraduate:* Graduation from an accredited secondary school with 14 academic units or GED; College Board SAT or ACT composite. *Teacher education specific:* Maintain a 2.7 GPA in the professional education courses and field of licensure; professional commitment; high scholastic attainment; passing scores on PRAXIS I exams (reading, writing, mathematics) or California Basic Education Skills Test; faculty interview. *Graduate:* Baccalaureate degree from a regionally accredited institution. *Teacher education specific:* 2.75 GPA; completion of all required departmental exams; teaching licensure where required by program pursued; faculty interview.

Fees and Expenses: Undergraduate: in-state $4,305 per academic year; out-of-state $12,570. Graduate: Tuition charged per credit hour. On-campus room and board: $5,976. Other expenses: $2,175. Books and supplies: $1,080.

Financial Aid: Resources specifically for eligible students enrolled in teacher education programs are awarded on the basis of financial need and academic merit. The institution has a Program Participation Agreement with the U.S. Department of Education for eligible students to receive Pell Grants and other federal aid. Teacher scholarships available to qualifying students. *Contact:* Financial Aid Office at: (503) 838-8475.

Accreditation: *Regional:* NASC. *Professional:* NCATE. *Member of:* AACTE. *Approved by:* Oregon Department of Education.

Undergraduate Programs: The College of Education offers an undergraduate program (or postbaccalaureate licensure only status for degree holders) with authorization levels available in early childhood, early childhood/elementary, elementary/middle level, or middle level/high school. The programs include four terms of teacher education curriculum. All baccalaureate programs require the completion of a general education core, professional studies, subject content area, field experiences, and student teaching. A minimum of 192 quarter hours must be completed for the bachelor's degree.

Graduate Programs: The Master of Arts in Teaching program is designed to provide second career and nontraditional students an opportunity to earn initial teacher licensure, authorization at the high school level, and a graduate degree.

The Master of Science in Education is designed to assist teachers in decision making, critical and creative thinking, and problem solving as they apply to the school context. The master's program requires at least 45 quarter credits of graduate study and leads to a Continuing Teacher License or a Standard Teaching License. Content endorsements are available in biology, chemistry, French, German, health, integrated studies. language arts, mathematics (basic/advanced), physical education, social studies, Spanish. Specialty endorsements in reading and bilingual/English as a second language are also available.

Licensure/Reciprocity: Oregon. Students seeking teaching certification in a state other than Oregon should consult with that state's teacher certification office early in their program of study to insure compliance with requirements. Many state directors of teacher credentialing have signed Interstate Agreements through NASDTEC that expedite the certification process.

PENNSYLVANIA

ALBRIGHT COLLEGE

Education Department
Teacher Certification Programs
13th and Bern Streets
reading, Pennsylvania 19612-5234
Phone: (610) 921-7190
Fax: (610) 921-7530
E-mail: educationdept@albright.edu
Internet: http://www.albright.edu

Institution Description: Albright College is a private college affiliated with the United Methodist Church. It was founded as Union Seminary in 1856.

The mission of the teacher certification programs is to develop reflective practitioners who are knowledgeable and thoughtful facilitators of the learning, growth, and development of students.

Institution Control: Private.

Calendar: Semester. Academic year August to May.

Official(s): Dr. L. Susan Seidenstricker, Chairperson.

Faculty: Full-time 4; part-time 2; adjunct 12.

Degrees Awarded: 18 baccalaureate.

Admission Requirements: *Undergraduate:* Graduation from an accredited secondary school or GED; College Board SAT or ACT composite. *Teacher education specific:* Students apply after 3 semesters; 2.75 GPA; faculty interview; passing scores on PRAXIS I exams (reading, writing, mathematics). NOTE: Tests must be the new computerized tests that were implemented January 16, 2002. Tests taken prior to that date will not be accepted. *Graduate:* Baccalaureate degree from a regionally accredited institution. *Teacher education specific:* 3.0 GPA; GRE or Miller Analogies scores; completion of all required departmental exams; two recommendations; faculty interview. The Commonwealth of Pennsylvania requires passing PRAXIS II tests prior to certification.

Fees and Expenses: Undergraduate: $21,790 comprehensive fee. Graduate: Tuition charged per credit hour. On-campus room and board: $6,809.

Financial Aid: Resources specifically for eligible students enrolled in teacher education programs are awarded on the basis of financial need and academic merit. The institution has a Program Participation Agreement with the U.S. Department of Education for eligible students to receive Pell Grants and other federal aid. Teacher scholarships available to qualifying students. *Contact:* Mary Ellen Duffy at: (610) 921-7515 or e-mail at: finaid@albright.edu.

Accreditation: *Regional:* MSA. *Approved by:* Pennsylvania Department of Education.

Undergraduate Programs: Undergraduate programs leading to certification included early childhood education, elementary education, secondary education (art, biology, chemistry, English, French, German, Latin, Spanish, general science, mathematics, physics, social sciences, citizenship), and special education (cognitive, behavior, physical health disabilities). All programs require the completion of a general education core, professional studies, subject content area, field experiences, and student teaching.

Graduate Programs: The college offers graduate degree programs leading to the Master of Arts or the Master of Science degree. Candidates may elect one of five concentrations within the program: General education (including secondary content teacher certification if desired), elementary education, special education, early childhood education, English as a second language. Candidates may elect to include work toward initial or additional teacher certification within the master's degree program.

Licensure/Reciprocity: Pennsylvania. Students seeking teaching certification in a state other than Pennsylvania should consult with that state's teacher certification office early in their program of study to insure compliance with requirements. Many state directors of teacher credentialing have signed Interstate Agreements through NASDTEC that expedite the certification process.

BLOOMSBURG UNIVERSITY OF PENNSYLVANIA

College of Professional Studies
School of Education
1210 McCormick Center for Human Services
400 East Second Street
Bloomsburg, Pennsylvania 17815
Phone: (570) 389-4025
Fax: (570) 389-3894
E-mail: buadmiss@bloomu.edu
Internet: http://www.bloomu.edu

Institution Description: Bloomsburg University of Pennsylvania was established as Bloomsburg Academy in 1839. In 1927 it was known as Bloomsburg State Teachers College. The present name was adopted in 1983.

The School of Education collaborates across four colleges to provide programs that prepare teachers to apply for certification.

Institution Control: Public.

Calendar: Semester. Academic year August to May.

Official(s): Dr. Ann Lee, Dean, College of Professional Studies.

Faculty: Full-time 13 (Department of Educational Studies and Secondary Education).

Degrees Awarded: 278 baccalaureate; 206 master's.

Admission Requirements: *Undergraduate:* Graduation from an accredited secondary school with 16 academic units or GED; College Board SAT. *Teacher education specific:* Students apply after 3 semesters; 2.75 GPA; faculty interview; passing scores on PRAXIS I exams (reading, writing, mathematics). NOTE: Tests must be the new computerized tests that were implemented January 16, 2002. Tests taken prior to that date will not be accepted. *Graduate:* Baccalaureate degree from a regionally accredited institution. *Teacher education specific:* 3.0 GPA; GRE or Miller Analogies scores; completion of all required departmental exams; two recommendations; faculty interview. The Commonwealth of Pennsylvania requires passing PRAXIS II tests prior to certification.

Fees and Expenses: Undergraduate: in-state $5,844 per academic year; out-of-state $12,792. Graduate: in-state $5,578 per academic year; out-of-state $8,820. On-campus room and board: $5,000. Other expenses: $2,656. Books and supplies: $900.

BLOOMSBURG UNIVERSITY OF PENNSYLVANIA—cont'd

Financial Aid: Resources specifically for eligible students enrolled in teacher education programs are awarded on the basis of financial need and academic merit. The institution has a Program Participation Agreement with the U.S. Department of Education for eligible students to receive Pell Grants and other federal aid. Teacher scholarships available to qualifying students. *Contact:* Financial Aid Office at: (570) 389-4297.

Accreditation: *Regional:* MSA. *Professional:* NCATE. *Member of:* AACTE. *Approved by:* Pennsylvania Department of Education.

Undergraduate Programs: The College of Professional Studies houses the following programs: early childhood (N-3); elementary education (K-6), special education (N-12); education of the deaf/hard of hearing (N-12). Dual certification is available in early childhood/elementary and elementary/special education. Also housed is the secondary education program (7-12) that includes biology, chemistry, communication, comprehensive social studies, earth and space science, English, mathematics, physics, general science, as well as foreign languages K-12 (French, German, Spanish). All secondary education and foreign language education majors are dual majors in secondary education and in their discipline. All programs require the completion of a general education core, professional studies, subject content area, field experiences, and student teaching. A minimum of 128 semester hours must be completed for the bachelor's degree.

Graduate Programs: Graduate programs include special education, deaf/hard of hearing, early childhood education, elementary education, and curriculum and instruction. Teacher certification may be obtained at the graduate level in early childhood, elementary, secondary, and special education. Specialist programs are available in reading, supervision, and instructional technology.

Licensure/Reciprocity: Pennsylvania. Students seeking teaching certification in a state other than Pennsylvania should consult with that state's teacher certification office early in their program of study to insure compliance with requirements. Many state directors of teacher credentialing have signed Interstate Agreements through NASDTEC that expedite the certification process.

BUCKNELL UNIVERSITY

Department of Education
Moore Avenue
Lewisburg, Pennsylvania 17837
Phone: (570) 577-1324
Fax: (570) 577-3184
E-mail: afeurstn@bucknell.edu
Internet: http://www.bucknell.edu

Institution Description: Bucknell University is a private, independent, nonprofit institution. It was established as the University at Lewisburg in 1846. The present name was adopted in 1886.

Coursework in education is intended to prepare students to contribute to the improvement and effectiveness of education in their roles as parents, citizens, or educational professionals.

Institution Control: Private.

Calendar: Semester. Academic year August to May.

Official(s): Dr. Abe Feurstein, Chairman, Department of Education.

Faculty: Full-time 10.

Degrees Awarded: 49 baccalaureate; 24 master's.

Admission Requirements: *Undergraduate:* Graduation from an accredited secondary school or GED; College Board SAT. *Teacher education specific:* Students apply by end of sophomore year; 3.0 GPA; faculty interview; passing scores on PRAXIS I exams (reading, writing, mathematics). NOTE: Tests must be the new computerized tests that were implemented January 16, 2002. Tests taken prior to that date will not be accepted. *Graduate:* Baccalaureate degree from a regionally accredited institu-

tion. *Teacher education specific:* 3.0 GPA; GRE; completion of all required departmental exams; recommendations; faculty interview. The Commonwealth of Pennsylvania requires passing PRAXIS II tests prior to certification.

Fees and Expenses: $27,340 per academic year. Required fees: $190. On-campus room and board: $3,232.

Financial Aid: Resources specifically for eligible students enrolled in teacher education programs are awarded on the basis of financial need and academic merit. The institution has a Program Participation Agreement with the U.S. Department of Education for eligible students to receive Pell Grants and other federal aid. Teacher scholarships available to qualifying students. *Contact:* Financial Aid Office at: (510) 577-1324.

Accreditation: *Regional:* MSA. *Approved by:* Pennsylvania Department of Education.

Undergraduate Programs: The Bachelor of Art s degree with a major in education is designed for students who are interested in studying the process and structure of education and schooling but who are not necessarily interested in pursuing a career in teaching. Students interested in obtaining certification in early childhood education or elementary education should pursue the Bachelor of Science in Education degree. Students interested in secondary certification normally seek a degree in the discipline they wish to teach and may either pursue certification only or a dual major in education and the discipline. All programs require the completion of a general education core, professional studies, field experiences, and student teaching.

Graduate Programs: The Department of Education offers a master's degree or certification ins the areas of elementary and secondary principalship, supervision of curriculum and instruction, school superintendency, elementary and secondary counseling, and school psychology. The department also offers an instructional specialist option that allows students to work with members of the faculty to formulate master's degree programs in other areas of specialization, based on their professional goals and dependent upon the available course offerings.

Licensure/Reciprocity: Pennsylvania. Students seeking teaching certification in a state other than Pennsylvania should consult with that state's teacher certification office early in their program of study to insure compliance with requirements. Many state directors of teacher credentialing have signed Interstate Agreements through NASDTEC that expedite the certification process.

CABRINI COLLEGE

Division of Education
610 King of Prussia Road
Radnor, Pennsylvania 19087-3698
Phone: (610) 902-8100
Fax: (610) 902-8309
E-mail: admit@cabrini.edu
Internet: http://www.cabrini.edu

Institution Description: Cabrini College is a private institution affiliated with the Roman Catholic Church. It was chartered as an institution for women in 1957 and became coeducational in 1970.

The teacher education programs provide the knowledge and skills necessary to deal with children from all walks of life and encourage the development of a philosophy of education consistent with democratic ideals and traditions.

Institution Control: Private.

Calendar: Semester. Academic year August to May.

Official(s): Dr. Catharine O'Connell, Dean, Academic Affairs.

Faculty: Full-time 10.

Degrees Awarded: 58 baccalaureate; 122 master's.

Admission Requirements: *Undergraduate:* Graduation from an accredited secondary school or GED; College Board SAT or ACT composite. *Teacher education specific:* Students apply after 3 semesters; 2.75 GPA; faculty interview; passing scores on PRAXIS I exams (reading, writing, mathematics). NOTE: Tests must be the new computerized tests that were implemented January 16, 2002. Tests taken prior to that date will not be accepted. *Graduate:* Baccalaureate degree from a regionally accredited institution. *Teacher education specific:* 3.0 GPA; GRE or Miller Analogies scores; completion of all required departmental exams; two recommendations; faculty interview. The Commonwealth of Pennsylvania requires passing PRAXIS II tests prior to certification.

Fees and Expenses: $20,470 per academic year. Graduate: $447 per credit hour. Accelerated Degree Program $5,320 per semester. On-campus room and board: $8,550. Other expenses: $2,150. Books and supplies: $900.

Financial Aid: Resources specifically for eligible students enrolled in teacher education programs are awarded on the basis of financial need and academic merit. The institution has a Program Participation Agreement with the U.S. Department of Education for eligible students to receive Pell Grants and other federal aid. Teacher scholarships available to qualifying students. *Contact:* Financial Aid Office at: (610) 902-8420.

Accreditation: *Regional:* MSA. *Member of:* AACTE. *Approved by:* Pennsylvania Department of Education.

Undergraduate Programs: Cabrini College offers programs leading to teaching certification in Pennsylvania and reciprocating states in early childhood education, elementary education, special education, secondary education (biology, chemistry, English, English/communication, mathematics, and social studies with a concentration in history or sociology), and French and Spanish (K-12 certification in French and in Spanish offered in cooperation with Eastern College).

All programs require the completion of a general education core, professional studies, subject content area, field experiences, and student teaching. A minimum of 123 credit hours must be completed for the baccalaureate degree.

The Accelerated Degree Program is designed to meet the educational and career goals of adults who want to return to college for career advancement and personal enrichment. The program enables students to work and finish the Bachelor of Arts in as little as 18 months, depending on the number of credits students bring into the program.

Graduate Programs: The Master of Education and teacher certification is offered in early childhood, elementary, secondary, special education, and reading specialist as well as educational leadership that leads to administrative certification as a school principal. The latter program is designed to prepare principals for educational leadership through a blend of guided field experience and theoretical knowledge.

Licensure/Reciprocity: Pennsylvania. Students seeking teaching certification in a state other than Pennsylvania should consult with that state's teacher certification office early in their program of study to insure compliance with requirements. Many state directors of teacher credentialing have signed Interstate Agreements through NASDTEC that expedite the certification process.

CALIFORNIA UNIVERSITY OF PENNSYLVANIA
School of Education
250 University Avenue
California, Pennsylvania 15419-1394
Phone: (412) 938-4404
Fax: (412) 938-4564
E-mail: inquiry@cup.edu
Internet: http://www.cup.edu

Institution Description: California University of Pennsylvania is a state institution. It was established as California Academy in 1852.

The School of Education offers undergraduate and graduate programs leading to teacher certification in Pennsylvania.

Institution Control: Public.

Calendar: Semester. Academic year August to May.

Official(s): Dr. Hepner, Chair, Department of Secondary Education and Administrative Programs.

Faculty: Full-time 40.

Degrees Awarded: 300 baccalaureate; 176 master's.

Admission Requirements: *Undergraduate:* Graduation from an accredited secondary school with 16 academic units or GED; College Board SAT. *Teacher education specific:* Students apply after 3 semesters; 2.75 GPA; faculty interview; passing scores on PRAXIS I exams (reading, writing, mathematics). NOTE: Tests must be the new computerized tests that were implemented January 16, 2002. Tests taken prior to that date will not be accepted. *Graduate:* Baccalaureate degree from a regionally accredited institution. *Teacher education specific:* 3.0 GPA; GRE or Miller Analogies scores; completion of all required departmental exams; two recommendations; faculty interview. The Commonwealth of Pennsylvania requires passing PRAXIS II tests prior to certification.

Fees and Expenses: Undergraduate: in-state $6,057 per academic year; out-of-state $11,496. Graduate: Tuition charged per credit hour. On-campus room and board: $6,900. Other expenses: $1,300. Books and supplies: $700.

Financial Aid: Resources specifically for eligible students enrolled in teacher education programs are awarded on the basis of financial need and academic merit. The institution has a Program Participation Agreement with the U.S. Department of Education for eligible students to receive Pell Grants and other federal aid. Teacher scholarships available to qualifying students. *Contact:* Financial Aid Office at: (724) 938-4415.

Accreditation: *Regional:* MSA. *Professional:* NCATE. *Member of:* AACTE. *Approved by:* Pennsylvania Department of Education.

Undergraduate Programs: Bachelor of Science in Education programs are offered in: early childhood education with certification (120 credits); elementary education with certification (120 credits); elementary and early childhood education with dual certifications (129 credits); early childhood education services (120 credits); elementary education services (120 credits).

Secondary certification is offered in biology, chemistry, physics, general science, mathematics, and modern foreign languages (French and Spanish). Technology education is offered through the Department of Applied Engineering and Technology. Art certification is available for art majors through a cooperative agreement with other area colleges.

Bachelor programs in special education include: comprehensive special education; special education and early childhood education (dual major); special education and elementary education (dual major). All programs require the completion of a general education core, professional studies, field experiences, and student teaching.

Graduate Programs: The Master of Arts in Teaching Program is a two-track professional development degree program. Track I certifies degree-holding individuals as secondary education teachers in mathematics or one of six science areas. Certification is only in the areas of biology, chemistry, earth science, general science, physics, mathematics, and environmental science. Track II is a professional development for certified teachers. Regardless of certification area, the program offers all teachers an opportunity to enhance their teaching skills, earn a master's degree, or simply earn 48 credit hours. Half of the program is on educational topics and each student is allowed to develop his/her own focus area of interest using master-level classes.

Licensure/Reciprocity: Pennsylvania. Students seeking teaching certification in a state other than Pennsylvania should consult with that state's teacher certification office early in their program of study to insure compliance with requirements. Many state directors of teacher credentialing have signed Interstate Agreements through NASDTEC that expedite the certification process.

CHEYNEY UNIVERSITY OF PENNSYLVANIA
Department of Education
1837 University Circle
P.O. Box 200
Cheyney, Pennsylvania 19319-0200
Phone: (610) 399-2000
Fax: (610) 399-2415
E-mail: admissions@cheyney.edu
Internet: http://www.cheyney.edu

CHEYNEY UNIVERSITY OF PENNSYLVANIA—cont'd

Institution Description: Cheyney University of Pennsylvania is a member of the Pennsylvania State System of Higher Education. It was established in 1837.

The Department of Education is responsible for promoting opportunities for prospective teachers to develop the competence essential to successful teaching.

Institution Control: Public.

Calendar: Semester. Academic year September to May.

Official(s): Dr. Kenoe, Eke, Provost.

Faculty: Full-time 21.

Degrees Awarded: 11 baccalaureate; 133 master's.

Admission Requirements: *Undergraduate:* Graduation from an accredited secondary school or GED; College Board SAT or ACT composite. *Teacher education specific:* Students apply after 3 semesters; 2.5 GPA; faculty interview; passing scores on PRAXIS I exams (reading, writing, mathematics). NOTE: Tests must be the new computerized tests that were implemented January 16, 2002. Tests taken prior to that date will not be accepted. *Graduate:* Baccalaureate degree from a regionally accredited institution. *Teacher education specific:* 3.0 GPA; GRE or Miller Analogies scores; completion of all required departmental exams; three letters of recommendation; faculty interview. The Commonwealth of Pennsylvania requires passing PRAXIS II tests prior to certification.

Fees and Expenses: Undergraduate: in-state $5,353 per academic year; out-of-state $12,301. Graduate: Tuition charged per credit hour. On-campus room and board: $5,383. Other expenses: $1,889. Books and supplies: $1,000.

Financial Aid: Resources specifically for eligible students enrolled in teacher education programs are awarded on the basis of financial need and academic merit. The institution has a Program Participation Agreement with the U.S. Department of Education for eligible students to receive Pell Grants and other federal aid. Teacher scholarships available to qualifying students. *Contact:* Financial Aid Office at: (610) 399-2302.

Accreditation: *Regional:* MSA. *Professional:* NCATE. *Member of:* AACTE. *Approved by:* Pennsylvania Department of Education.

Undergraduate Programs: Program offerings leading to a baccalaureate degree include majors in early childhood education, elementary education, special education, and secondary education in the discipline areas of biology, chemistry, general science, English, French, Spanish, family and consumer sciences, mathematics, and the social studies. The non-teacher education programs offered by the department include clothing and textiles (with concentrations in fashion merchandising and fashion design), and hotel, restaurant, and institutional management. All teacher education programs require the completion of a general education core, professional studies, subject content area, field experiences, and student teaching. A minimum of 128 credits must be completed for the bachelor's degree.

Graduate Programs: The Master of Arts in Teaching degree is offered in elementary education. The Master of Education degree programs offered include: elementary education, special education, educational administration and supervision. Master of Science degree programs are offered in adult and continuing education and special education.

Licensure/Reciprocity: Pennsylvania. Students seeking teaching certification in a state other than Pennsylvania should consult with that state's teacher certification office early in their program of study to insure compliance with requirements. Many state directors of teacher credentialing have signed Interstate Agreements through NASDTEC that expedite the certification process.

CLARION UNIVERSITY OF PENNSYLVANIA

College of Education and Human Services

101 Stevens Hall
Clarion, Pennsylvania 16214
Phone: (814) 393-2146
Fax: (814) 393-2446
E-mail: grejda@clarion.edu
Internet: http://www.clarion.edu

Institution Description: Clarion University of Pennsylvania is a state institution. It was established and chartered as Carrier Seminary in 1867.

The College of Education and Human Services offers programs to prepare professional educators and other human services personnel. Eight specialized curricula are offered in professional education.

Institution Control: Public.

Calendar: Semester. Academic year August to May.

Official(s): Dr. Gail F. Grejda, Dean; Dr. Vickie Harry., Department Chair.

Faculty: Full-time 91; part-time 2; adjunct 4.

Degrees Awarded: 275 baccalaureate; 24 master's.

Admission Requirements: *Undergraduate:* Graduation from an accredited secondary school or GED; College Board SAT or ACT composite. *Teacher education specific:* Students apply after 3 semesters; 2.75 GPA; faculty interview; passing scores on PRAXIS I exams (reading, writing, mathematics). NOTE: Tests must be the new computerized tests that were implemented January 16, 2002. Tests taken prior to that date will not be accepted. *Graduate:* Baccalaureate degree from a regionally accredited institution. *Teacher education specific:* 3.0 GPA; GRE or Miller Analogies scores; completion of all required departmental exams; two recommendations; faculty interview. The Commonwealth of Pennsylvania requires passing PRAXIS II tests prior to certification.

Fees and Expenses: Undergraduate: in-state $4,598; out-of-state $8,048, Graduate: in-state $5,518; out-of-state: $8,830. Required fees: $1,399. On-campus room and board: $4,560. Books and supplies: $1,000.

Financial Aid: Resources specifically for eligible students enrolled in teacher education programs are awarded on the basis of financial need and academic merit. The institution has a Program Participation Agreement with the U.S. Department of Education for eligible students to receive Pell Grants and other federal aid. Teacher scholarships available to qualifying students. *Contact:* Kenneth Grugel at: (814) 393-2315.

Accreditation: *Regional:* MSA. *Professional:* NCATE. *Member of:* AACTE. *Approved by:* Pennsylvania Department of Education.

Undergraduate Programs: Baccalaureate programs offered include early childhood education, elementary education, environmental education, library science, music education, secondary education, special education, and communication sciences and disorders. Each teacher education curriculum is designed to meet the graduation requirements of the university, the certification requirements of the state, and accreditation standards of various professional groups. All baccalaureate programs require the completion of a general education core, professional studies, subject content area, field experiences, and student teaching.

Graduate Programs: Advanced degree programs are offered for teachers already certified at the baccalaureate level. These include: Master of Education (concentrations in curriculum and instruction, early childhood, English, history, library science and technology); Master of Education in reading, science education. Master of Science degree programs are also offered in communication sciences and disorders, library science; rehabilitative sciences, and special education. Certifications are also offered in environmental education, principalship, reading specialist, and instructional technology specialist.

Licensure/Reciprocity: Pennsylvania. Students seeking teaching certification in a state other than Pennsylvania should consult with that state's teacher certification office early in their program of study to insure compliance with requirements. Many state directors of teacher credentialing have signed Interstate Agreements through NASDTEC that expedite the certification process.

DICKINSON COLLEGE
Education Department
Teacher Certification Program
College and Luther Streets
Carlisle, Pennsylvania 17013-2896
Phone: (717) 245-5121
Fax: (717) 245-1442
E-mail: landauer@dickinson.edu
Internet: http://www.dickinson.edu

Institution Description: Dickinson College is a private, independent, nonprofit college that was established in 1773.

The Education Department offers baccalaureate programs leading to secondary certification in a variety of areas.

Institution Control: Private.

Calendar: Semesters. Academic year September to April.

Official(s): Dr. William Landauer, Chair.

Faculty: Full-time 6.

Degrees Awarded: 14 baccalaureate.

Admission Requirements: *Undergraduate:* Graduation from an accredited secondary school with 16 academic units or GED; College Board SAT or ACT composite. *Teacher education specific:* Students apply after 3 semesters; 2.75 GPA; faculty interview; passing scores on PRAXIS I exams (reading, writing, mathematics). NOTE: Tests must be the new computerized tests that were implemented January 16, 2002. Tests taken prior to that date will not be accepted. *Graduate:* Baccalaureate degree from a regionally accredited institution. *Teacher education specific:* 3.0 GPA; GRE or Miller Analogies scores; completion of all required departmental exams; recommendations; faculty interview. The Commonwealth of Pennsylvania requires passing PRAXIS II tests prior to certification.

Fees and Expenses: $28,615 per academic year. On-campus room and board: $7,210. Books and supplies: $750.

Financial Aid: Resources specifically for eligible students enrolled in teacher education programs are awarded on the basis of financial need and academic merit. The institution has a Program Participation Agreement with the U.S. Department of Education for eligible students to receive Pell Grants and other federal aid. Teacher scholarships available to qualifying students. *Contact:* Financial Aid Office at: (717) 245-1308.

Accreditation: *Regional:* MSA. *Member of:* AACTE. *Approved by:* Pennsylvania Department of Education.

Undergraduate Programs: The Education Department offers preparation for secondary certification (grades 7-12) in fields spanning the arts and sciences as well as K-12 certification in foreign languages. Students in the teacher education program pursue a degree in their major of choice and take a sequence of professional courses that prepares them for a career in teaching. These courses include field experiences. To cap their experience, students assume full-time teaching responsibilities in area schools for 12 weeks. All programs require the completion of a general education core.

Licensure/Reciprocity: Pennsylvania. Students seeking teaching certification in a state other than Pennsylvania should consult with that state's teacher certification office early in their program of study to insure compliance with requirements. Many state directors of teacher credentialing have signed Interstate Agreements through NASDTEC that expedite the certification process.

DUQUESNE UNIVERSITY
School of Education
Canevin Hall, Room 213
600 Forbes Avenue
Pittsburgh, Pennsylvania 15282
Phone: (412) 396-6092
Fax: (412) 396-5585
E-mail: admissions@duq.edu
Internet: http://www.duq.edu

Institution Description: Duquesne University is a private institution owned by the Congregation of the Holy Ghost, Roman Catholic Church. It was founded in 1878.

Within the ecumenical environment of the university, the mission of the School of Education is to prepare professional educators for leadership and distinction in teaching, scholarship, and service in the world's communities.

Institution Control: Private.

Calendar: Semester. Academic year August to May.

Official(s): Dr. James Henderson, Dean.

Faculty: Full-time 57.

Degrees Awarded: 146 baccalaureate; 286 master's; 22 doctorate.

Admission Requirements: *Undergraduate:* Graduation from an accredited secondary school with 16 academic units or GED; College Board SAT or ACT composite. *Teacher education specific:* Students enter the program after completion of 60 semester hours; 3.0 GPA in general education core and specified foundation courses; faculty interview; passing scores on PRAXIS I exams (reading, writing, mathematics). NOTE: Tests must be the new computerized tests that were implemented January 16, 2002. Tests taken prior to that date will not be accepted. *Graduate:* Baccalaureate degree from a regionally accredited institution. *Teacher education specific:* 3.0 GPA; GRE or Miller Analogies scores; completion of all required departmental exams; recommendations; faculty interview. The Commonwealth of Pennsylvania requires passing PRAXIS II tests prior to certification.

Fees and Expenses: Undergraduate: $18,527 per academic year. Graduate: $566 per credit hour. Required fees: $56 per credit hour. On-campus room and board: $3,585.

Financial Aid: Resources specifically for eligible students enrolled in teacher education programs are awarded on the basis of financial need and academic merit. The institution has a Program Participation Agreement with the U.S. Department of Education for eligible students to receive Pell Grants and other federal aid. Teacher scholarships available to qualifying students. *Contact:* Frank M. Dutkovich at: (412) 396-6607 or e-mail at: dutkovich@duq.edu.

Accreditation: *Regional:* MSA. *Member of:* AACTE. *Approved by:* Pennsylvania Department of Education.

Undergraduate Programs: The Leading Teacher Program offers students enrolled in early childhood and elementary certification tracks the ability to pursue 15 credits in an academic area (cognate) to enhance their knowledge base and competency in a specific academic matter. Cognates are available in the disciplines of mathematics and/or computer science, science, sociology, history, English, communications, political science, modern languages, classics, theology, philosophy, psychology, and Latin. Students enrolled in secondary education have an academic concentration equal to an academic major in the discipline.

All programs require the completion of a general education core, professional studies, subject content area, field experiences, and student teaching.

Graduate Programs: A Master of Science in Education degree may be obtained in any of the following areas: community counseling services, early childhood education, elementary education, educational studies, instructional technology, marriage and family therapy, program evaluation, reading education, school administration, school counseling, school psychology, secondary education, special education.

DUQUESNE UNIVERSITY—*cont'd*

A Doctor of Education degree may be obtained in counselor education and supervision, instructional leadership, or in an interdisciplinary doctoral program for educational leaders. The Doctor of Philosophy degree may also be earned in school psychology.

Each graduate program emphasizes the importance of field experiences, volunteer work, practica, and internships.

Licensure/Reciprocity: Pennsylvania. Students seeking teaching certification in a state other than Pennsylvania should consult with that state's teacher certification office early in their program of study to insure compliance with requirements. Many state directors of teacher credentialing have signed Interstate Agreements through NASDTEC that expedite the certification process.

EAST STROUDSBURG UNIVERSITY

School of Professional Studies

200 Prospect Street
East Stroudsburg, Pennsylvania 18301-2999
Phone: (570) 422-3377
Fax: (570) 422-3506
E-mail: shausfather@esu.edu
Internet: http://www.esu.edu

Institution Description: East Stroudsburg University is a member of the Pennsylvania State System of Higher Education. It was established as East Stroudsburg Normal School in 1893.

Teacher education programs focus on the decision-making process of teaching and learning.

Institution Control: Public.

Calendar: Semester. Academic year August to May.

Official(s): Dr. Sam Hausfather, Dean.

Faculty: Full-time 59; part-time 6; adjunct 17.

Degrees Awarded: 250 baccalaureate; 199 master's.

Admission Requirements: *Undergraduate:* Graduation from an accredited secondary school or GED; College Board SAT. *Teacher education specific:* 2.5 overall GPA; 2 math and 2 English college courses; faculty interview; passing scores on PRAXIS I exams (reading, writing, mathematics); NOTE: Tests must be the new computerized tests that were implemented January 16, 2002. Tests taken prior to that date will not be accepted. *Graduate:* Baccalaureate degree from a regionally accredited institution. *Teacher education specific:* 2.5 GPA overall; 3.0 GPA in major; completion of all required departmental exams; recommendations; faculty interview. The Commonwealth of Pennsylvania requires passing PRAXIS II tests prior to certification.

Fees and Expenses: Undergraduate: in-state $4,597; out-of-state $11,463. Graduate: in-state $5,256; out-of-state $8,406. Required fees: $1,349. On-campus room and board: $4,390.

Financial Aid: Resources specifically for eligible students enrolled in teacher education programs are awarded on the basis of financial need and academic merit. The institution has a Program Participation Agreement with the U.S. Department of Education for eligible students to receive Pell Grants and other federal aid. Teacher scholarships available to qualifying students. *Contact:* Phyllis Swinson at: (570) 422-2800 or e-mail at: pswinson@po-box.esu.edu.

Accreditation: *Regional:* MSA. *Professional:* NCATE. *Member of:* AACTE. *Approved by:* Pennsylvania Department of Education.

Undergraduate Programs: Students can be certified in the areas of early childhood education, elementary education, special education, early childhood and elementary education, integrated elementary and special education, secondary education (in the areas of English, communications, foreign language [French or Spanish], science [biology, chemistry, physics, earth and space science, general science], social studies, health and physical education, health). Extensive field experiences are incorporated throughout all four years of study, with most programs requiring a semester incorporating an integrated block of courses taught in conjunction with partner schools before the semester-long student teaching. A minimum of 120 semester hours is required for the bachelor's degree.

Graduate Programs: Initial and advanced certification programs at the master's level allow inservice educators to become leaders who apply research and practice theory to make reflective and deliberate decisions that benefit the learning of all students. The Master of Education is available in elementary education, special education, secondary education, reading, health and physical education, instructional technology, biology, general science, history, and political science. Advanced certification is also available in speech and language impaired, driver education, reading specialist, English as a second language, school dental hygiene, and school nurse.

Licensure/Reciprocity: Pennsylvania. Students seeking teaching certification in a state other than Pennsylvania should consult with that state's teacher certification office early in their program of study to insure compliance with requirements. Many state directors of teacher credentialing have signed Interstate Agreements through NASDTEC that expedite the certification process.

EDINBORO UNIVERSITY OF PENNSYLVANIA

School of Education

Edinboro, Pennsylvania 16444
Phone: (814) 732-2000
Fax: (814) 732-2420
E-mail: kadams@edinboro.edu
Internet: http://www.edinboro.edu

Institution Description: Edinboro University of Pennsylvania is a state institution. It was established and chartered as Edinboro Academy in 1856.

The School of Education offers undergraduate and programs in elementary and secondary education.

Institution Control: Public.

Calendar: Semester. Academic year August to May.

Official(s): Dr. Ken Adams, Chair.

Faculty: Full-time 23.

Degrees Awarded: 192 baccalaureate; 91 master's.

Admission Requirements: *Undergraduate:* Graduation from an accredited secondary school or GED; College Board SAT or ACT composite. *Teacher education specific:* Students apply after 3 semesters; 2.75 GPA; faculty interview; passing scores on PRAXIS I exams (reading, writing, mathematics). NOTE: Tests must be the new computerized tests that were implemented January 16, 2002. Tests taken prior to that date will not be accepted. *Graduate:* Baccalaureate degree from a regionally accredited institution. *Teacher education specific:* 3.0 GPA; GRE or Miller Analogies scores; completion of all required departmental exams; recommendations; faculty interview. The Commonwealth of Pennsylvania requires passing PRAXIS II tests prior to certification.

Fees and Expenses: Undergraduate: in-state $5,766 per academic year; out-of-state $8,116. Graduate: Tuition charged per credit hour. On-campus room and board: $5,150. Other expenses: $1,900. Books and supplies: $750.

Financial Aid: Resources specifically for eligible students enrolled in teacher education programs are awarded on the basis of financial need and academic merit. The institution has a Program Participation Agreement with the U.S. Department of Education for eligible students to receive Pell Grants and other federal aid. Teacher scholarships available to qualifying students. *Contact:* Financial Aid Office at: (888) 611-2680.

Accreditation: *Regional:* MSA. *Professional:* NCATE. *Member of:* AACTE. *Approved by:* Pennsylvania Department of Education.

Undergraduate Programs: Bachelor of Science in Education degree programs are offered in health and physical education, art education, special education, and special education/elementary education. Bachelor of Science degree programs are available in elementary education, elementary/early childhood, and elementary/special education. Programs in secondary education are offered with concentrations in the areas of biology, chemistry, earth and space science, English, general science, German, mathematics, physics, social studies, and Spanish. The Bachelor of Arts degree for all grades K-12 include art education and communication (speech/hearing disorders). All programs require the completion of a general education core, professional studies, subject content area, field experiences, and student teaching. A minimum of 128 credit hours is required for the bachelor's degree.

Graduate Programs: The Master of Education in middle and secondary instruction degree program is to provide further development of content knowledge through the academic strands while also increasing practitioners' professional skills that will enable them to gain increased classroom proficiency. The program is also structured for non-education majors who wish to pursue an advanced degree and to secure certification as a teacher.

Licensure/Reciprocity: Pennsylvania. Students seeking teaching certification in a state other than Pennsylvania should consult with that state's teacher certification office early in their program of study to insure compliance with requirements. Many state directors of teacher credentialing have signed Interstate Agreements through NASDTEC that expedite the certification process.

GENEVA COLLEGE
Department of Education
3200 College Avenue
Beaver Falls, Pennsylvania 15010
Phone: (412) 846-5100
Fax: (412) 847-6776
E-mail: admissions@geneva.edu
Internet: http://www.geneva.edu

Institution Description: Geneva College is a private college affiliated with the Reformed Presbyterian Church of North America. It was founded in 1848.

The Department of Education offers undergraduate programs leading to teaching licensure in Pennsylvania. A minor in Christian School Teaching is available for students who may wish to pursue a career in that field.

Institution Control: Private.

Calendar: Semester. Academic year August to May.

Official(s): Dr. Deborah Gayle Copeland, Chairperson.

Faculty: Full-time 5; part-time 8.

Degrees Awarded: 52 baccalaureate; 16 master's.

Admission Requirements: *Undergraduate:* Graduation from an accredited secondary school with 16 academic units or GED; College Board SAT or ACT composite. *Teacher education specific:* Students apply during the sophomore year; completion of at least 48 credit hours; 3.0 GPA; passing scores on PRAXIS I exams (reading, writing, mathematics); NOTE: Tests must be the new computerized tests that were implemented January 16, 2002. Tests taken prior to that date will not be accepted. *Graduate:* Baccalaureate degree from a regionally accredited institution. *Teacher education specific:* 3.0 GPA; GRE or Miller Analogies scores; completion of all required departmental exams; two recommendations; faculty interview. The Commonwealth of Pennsylvania requires passing PRAXIS II tests prior to certification.

Fees and Expenses: Undergraduate: $15,480 per academic year. Graduate: Tuition charged per credit hour. On-campus room and board: $4,000. Other expenses: $1,150. Books and supplies: $800.

Financial Aid: Resources specifically for eligible students enrolled in teacher education programs are awarded on the basis of financial need and academic merit. The institution has a Program Participation Agreement with the U.S. Department of Education for eligible students to receive Pell Grants and other federal aid. Teacher scholarships available to qualifying students. *Contact:* Financial Aid Office at: (724) 847-6532.

Accreditation: *Regional:* MSA. *Member of:* AACTE. *Approved by:* Pennsylvania Department of Education.

Undergraduate Programs: Baccalaureate programs are offered in elementary education and special education. Programs in secondary education are offered with concentrations in the areas of biology, chemistry, earth science, English, foreign lan-

guage, general science, mathematics, physics, and social studies. All programs require the completion of a general education core, professional studies, subject content area, field experiences, and student teaching. A minimum of 126 semester hours must be completed for the bachelor's degree.

The minor in Christian School Teaching is for prospective teachers who believe that a Christian school may be where they belong or who wish to have the background and perspective that the minor will help them develop. The minor is not intended to stand alone but to be a significant supplement to the elementary or secondary certification programs.

Licensure/Reciprocity: Pennsylvania. Students seeking teaching certification in a state other than Pennsylvania should consult with that state's teacher certification office early in their program of study to insure compliance with requirements. Many state directors of teacher credentialing have signed Interstate Agreements through NASDTEC that expedite the certification process.

GETTYSBURG COLLEGE
Education Department
300 North Washington Street
Gettysburg, Pennsylvania 17325-1486
Phone: (717) 337-6551
Fax: (717) 337-6777
E-mail: jpool@gettysburg.edu
Internet: http://www.gettysburg.edu

Institution Description: Gettysburg College is a private, independent, nonprofit institution affiliated with the Lutheran Church in America. The college was founded in 1832.

Students seeking teacher certification major in the liberal arts with a minor or concentration in education.

Institution Control: Private.

Calendar: Semester. Academic year August to May.

Official(s): Dr. Judith Brought, Chairperson.

Faculty: Full-time 4; part-time 2; adjunct 1.

Degrees Awarded: 116 baccalaureate candidates.

Admission Requirements: *Undergraduate:* Graduation from an accredited secondary school or GED; College Board SAT or ACT composite. *Teacher education specific:* C or better in all education courses; completion of 48 credit hours of full-time study; reflective essay; 3.0 GPA; passing scores on PRAXIS I exams (reading, writing, mathematics). NOTE: Tests must be the new computerized tests that were implemented January 16, 2002. Tests taken prior to that date will not be accepted. *Graduate:* Baccalaureate degree from a regionally accredited institution. *Teacher education specific:* 3.0 GPA; GRE or Miller Analogies scores; completion of all required departmental exams; two recommendations; faculty interview. The Commonwealth of Pennsylvania requires passing PRAXIS II tests prior to certification.

Fees and Expenses: $28,424 per academic year. On-campus room and board: $3,696 with variable meal plan options. Books and supplies: $800.

Financial Aid: Resources specifically for eligible students enrolled in teacher education programs are awarded on the basis of financial need and academic merit. The institution has a Program Participation Agreement with the U.S. Department of Education for eligible students to receive Pell Grants and other federal aid. Teacher scholarships available to qualifying students. *Contact:* Timothy Opgenorth at: (717) 337-6611.

Accreditation: *Regional:* MSA. *Approved by:* Pennsylvania Department of Education.

Undergraduate Programs: Programs are offered that lead to teaching certification in the areas of elementary education (K-6 or K-8 if an approved middle school), secondary education (biology, chemistry, citizenship, English, French [K-12], general science, German [K-12], Latin [K-12], mathematics, physics, social sciences, Spanish [K-12], health and physical education [K-12], and music [K-12]). All bachelor's programs require the completion of a general education core, professional studies, subject content area, field experiences, and student teaching. A minimum of 12.5 credit hours is required for the degree award.

GETTYSBURG COLLEGE—*cont'd*

Licensure/Reciprocity: Pennsylvania. Students seeking teaching certification in a state other than Pennsylvania should consult with that state's teacher certification office early in their program of study to insure compliance with requirements. Many state directors of teacher credentialing have signed Interstate Agreements through NASDTEC that expedite the certification process.

HOLY FAMILY COLLEGE

School of Education
Grant and Frankford Avenues
Philadelphia, Pennsylvania 19114-2094
Phone: (215) 637-7700
Fax: (215) 281-1022
E-mail: lsoroka@hfc.edu
Internet: http://www.hfc.edu

Institution Description: Holy Family College is an independent institution sponsored by the Congregation of the Sisters of the Holy Family of Nazareth. The college was founded in 1954.

The School of Education offers undergraduate and graduate programs designed to meet the needs of students in a variety of subject areas.

Institution Control: Private.

Calendar: Semester. Academic year August to May.

Official(s): Dr. Leonard G. Soroka, Dean.

Faculty: Full-time 22.

Degrees Awarded: 152 baccalaureate; 194 master's.

Admission Requirements: *Undergraduate:* Graduation from an accredited secondary school or GED; College Board SAT. *Teacher education specific:* Students apply during sophomore year; 2.75 GPA; passing scores on PRAXIS I exams (reading, writing, mathematics). NOTE: Tests must be the new computerized tests that were implemented January 16, 2002. Tests taken prior to that date will not be accepted. *Graduate:* Baccalaureate degree from a regionally accredited institution. *Teacher education specific:* 3.0 GPA; GRE or Miller Analogies scores; completion of all required departmental exams; statement of goals; two recommendations; faculty interview. The Commonwealth of Pennsylvania requires passing PRAXIS II tests prior to certification.

Fees and Expenses: Undergraduate: $15,490 per academic year. Graduate: Tuition charged per credit hour. Off-campus room and board: $5,892. Other expenses $900. Books and supplies: $640.

Financial Aid: Resources specifically for eligible students enrolled in teacher education programs are awarded on the basis of financial need and academic merit. The institution has a Program Participation Agreement with the U.S. Department of Education for eligible students to receive Pell Grants and other federal aid. Teacher scholarships available to qualifying students. *Contact:* Financial Aid Office at: (215) 637-5538.

Accreditation: *Regional:* MSA. *Member of:* AACTE. *Approved by:* Pennsylvania Department of Education.

Undergraduate Programs: Baccalaureate degree programs include early childhood education, early childhood/elementary education, special education/elementary education, and secondary education (concentrations in (biology, chemistry, English, French, general science, German, mathematics, physics, social sciences, Spanish). All programs require the completion of a general education core, professional studies, subject content area, field experiences, and student teaching. A minimum of 120 credit hours must be completed for the bachelor's degree.

Graduate Programs: Master's degree programs are designed to serve experienced teachers seeking to add additional certification as well as those individuals seeking certification as part of a career change. Programs include elementary education, secondary education, reading specialist, early childhood education, special education (cognitive, behavioral, physical/health), principal certification, reading supervisor. Each program has specific course requirements.

Licensure/Reciprocity: Pennsylvania. Students seeking teaching certification in a state other than Pennsylvania should consult with that state's teacher certification office early in their program of study to insure compliance with requirements. Many state directors of teacher credentialing have signed Interstate Agreements through NASDTEC that expedite the certification process.

INDIANA UNIVERSITY OF PENNSYLVANIA

College of Education
Teacher Education
104 Stouffer
1175 Maple Street
Indiana, Pennsylvania 15705
Phone: (724) 357-2480
Fax: (724) 357-5595
E-mail: coe@iup.edu
Internet: http://www.iup.edu

Institution Description: Indiana University of Pennsylvania is a state institution. It was chartered as Indiana Normal School in 1871.

The Teacher Education Program prepares students in a variety of education disciplines for teacher certification.

Institution Control: Public.

Calendar: Semester. Academic year September to May.

Official(s): Dr. John W. Butzow, Dean, College of Education; Dr. Judith Hectman, Dean, Teacher Education.

Faculty: Full-time 87; part-time 22.

Degrees Awarded: 313 baccalaureate; 141 master's; 14 doctorate.

Admission Requirements: *Undergraduate:* Graduation from an accredited secondary school or GED; College Board SAT or ACT composite. *Teacher education specific:* Minimum of 48 earned credits; 3.0 GPA; completion of speech, hearing, and TB test; personal essay; passing scores on PRAXIS I exams (reading, writing, mathematics); NOTE: Tests must be the new computerized tests that were implemented January 16, 2002. Tests taken prior to that date will not be accepted. *Graduate:* Baccalaureate degree from a regionally accredited institution. *Teacher education specific:* 3.0 GPA; GRE or Miller Analogies scores; completion of all required departmental exams; two recommendations; faculty interview. The Commonwealth of Pennsylvania requires passing PRAXIS II tests prior to certification.

Fees and Expenses: Undergraduate: in-state, $4,378 per academic year; out-of-state $10,949. Graduate: in-state $5,254 per academic year; out-of-state $8,404. On-campus room and board: $2,826 (room per semester); $4,000 (board per year). Books and supplies: $500.

Financial Aid: Resources specifically for eligible students enrolled in teacher education programs are awarded on the basis of financial need and academic merit. The institution has a Program Participation Agreement with the U.S. Department of Education for eligible students to receive Pell Grants and other federal aid. Teacher scholarships available to qualifying students. *Contact:* Christine Zuzack, Director, Financial Aid Office at: (724) 357-2218 or e-mail at: cazack@iup.edu.

Accreditation: *Regional:* MSA. *Professional:* NCATE. *Member of:* AACTE. *Approved by:* Pennsylvania Department of Education.

Undergraduate Programs: The Bachelor of Science in Education-Business Education is offered in cooperation with the College of Business and Information Technology. Teacher education programs offered in the College of Education include the Bachelor of Science in education in elementary education, elementary/early childhood (dual certification), early childhood education (education of persons with hearing loss; exceptional persons). Secondary education concentration areas include art education, music education, health and physical education, social science (anthropology, economics concentrations), English, French K-12, German, geography, history, Spanish, biology, chemistry, physics, vocational-technical education. All programs require the completion of a general education core, professional studies, subject content area, field experiences, and student teaching. A minimum of 124 semester hours must be completed for the bachelor's degree.

Graduate Programs: The Professional Studies in Education Department offers the Master of Education in education, Master of Education in early childhood education, Master of Education in literacy, and a Doctor of Education in administration and leadership studies as well as in curriculum and instruction.

The Master of Arts in Teaching English is a 36-hour degree program that involves the study of the research on teaching literature, composition, and language. The program is designed for in-service secondary English teachers who wish advanced, in-depth study in the teaching of English. It is also designed for persons with a bachelor's degree who wish to pursue initial English teaching certification.

The Department of Special Education and Clinical Services offers the Master of Education degree in education of exceptional persons and the Master of Science degree in speech-language pathology.

Licensure/Reciprocity: Pennsylvania. Students seeking teaching certification in a state other than Pennsylvania should consult with that state's teacher certification office early in their program of study to insure compliance with requirements. Many state directors of teacher credentialing have signed Interstate Agreements through NASDTEC that expedite the certification process.

KING'S COLLEGE

Education Division
Teacher Education Program
    133 North River Street
    Wilkes-Barre, Pennsylvania 18711
    Phone: (570) 208-5991
    Fax: (570) 825-8049
    E-mail: naholodi@@kings.edu
    Internet: http://www.kings.edu

Institution Description: King's College is a private, independent, nonprofit college affiliated with the Congregation of Holy Cross, Roman Catholic Church. It was established as a men's college in 1946 and became coeducational in 1970.

The mission of the Education Division is to provide future teachers with a broad-based liberal education in the Catholic tradition.

Institution Control: Private.

Calendar: Semester. Academic year August to May.

Official(s): Dr. Nicholas A. Holodick, Department Chair.

Faculty: Full-time 7.

Degrees Awarded: 53 baccalaureate; 13 master's.

Admission Requirements: *Undergraduate:* Graduation from an accredited secondary school or GED; College Board SAT. *Teacher education specific:* Students apply during sophomore year; 2.75 GPA; passing scores on PRAXIS I exams (reading, writing, mathematics). NOTE: Tests must be the new computerized tests that were implemented January 16, 2002. Tests taken prior to that date will not be accepted. *Graduate:* Baccalaureate degree from a regionally accredited institution. *Teacher education specific:* 3.0 GPA; GRE or Miller Analogies scores; completion of all required departmental exams; statement of goals; two recommendations; faculty interview. The Commonwealth of Pennsylvania requires passing PRAXIS II tests prior to certification.

Fees and Expenses: Undergraduate: $19,060 per academic year. Graduate: Tuition charged per credit hour. On-campus room and board: $7,930. Other expenses $1,520. Books and supplies: $850.

Financial Aid: Resources specifically for eligible students enrolled in teacher education programs are awarded on the basis of financial need and academic merit. The institution has a Program Participation Agreement with the U.S. Department of Education for eligible students to receive Pell Grants and other federal aid. Teacher scholarships available to qualifying students. *Contact:* Financial Aid Office at: (570) 208-5868.

Accreditation: *Regional:* MSA. *Member of:* AACTE. *Approved by:* Pennsylvania Department of Education.

Undergraduate Programs: Baccalaureate degree programs include early childhood education, elementary education, and secondary education (concentrations in biology, chemistry, English, French, general science, German, mathematics, physics, social sciences, Spanish). All programs require the completion of a general education core, professional studies, subject content area, field experiences, and student teaching. A minimum of 120 credit hours must be completed for the bachelor's degree.

Graduate Programs: Master's degree programs are designed to serve experienced teachers seeking to add additional certification as well as those individuals seeking certification as part of a career change. Programs include elementary education, secondary education, reading specialist. Each program has specific course requirements.

Licensure/Reciprocity: Pennsylvania. Students seeking teaching certification in a state other than Pennsylvania should consult with that state's teacher certification office early in their program of study to insure compliance with requirements. Many state directors of teacher credentialing have signed Interstate Agreements through NASDTEC that expedite the certification process.

KUTZTOWN UNIVERSITY OF PENNSYLVANIA

College of Education
    259 Beekey Education Center
    Kutztown, Pennsylvania 19530-0730
    Phone: (610) 683-4253
    Fax: (610) 683-4255
    E-mail: blake@kutztown.edu
    Internet: http://www.kutztown.edu

Institution Description: Kutztown University is a state institution. It was chartered as Keystone Normal School in 1866. The name was changed to Kutztown State Teachers College in 1926. The present name was adopted in 1983.

The College of Education provides the opportunity for study and career preparation in a variety of teaching fields.

Institution Control: Public.

Calendar: Semester. Academic year August to May.

Official(s): Dr. Ira K. Blake, Dean.

Faculty: Full-time 54; adjunct 13.

Degrees Awarded: 283 baccalaureate; 115 master's.

Admission Requirements: *Undergraduate:* Graduation from an accredited secondary school or GED; College Board SAT or ACT composite. *Teacher education specific:* Minimum of 48 earned credits; 3.0 GPA; completion of speech, hearing, and TB test; personal essay; passing scores on PRAXIS I exams (reading, writing, mathematics). NOTE: Tests must be the new computerized tests that were implemented January 16, 2002. Tests taken prior to that date will not be accepted. *Graduate:* Baccalaureate degree from a regionally accredited institution. *Teacher education specific:* 3.0 GPA; GRE or Miller Analogies scores; completion of all required departmental exams; two recommendations; faculty interview. The Commonwealth of Pennsylvania requires passing PRAXIS II tests prior to certification.

Fees and Expenses: Undergraduate: in-state, $5,719 per academic year; out-of-state $12,383. Graduate: Tuition charged per credit hour. On-campus room and board: $6,204. Other expenses: $2,500. Books and supplies: $1,000.

Financial Aid: Resources specifically for eligible students enrolled in teacher education programs are awarded on the basis of financial need and academic merit. The institution has a Program Participation Agreement with the U.S. Department of Education for eligible students to receive Pell Grants and other federal aid. Teacher scholarships available to qualifying students. *Contact:* Anita Faust at: (610) 683-4077 or e-mail at: faust@kutztown.edu.

Accreditation: *Regional:* MSA. *Professional:* NCATE. *Member of:* AACTE. *Approved by:* Pennsylvania Department of Education.

KUTZTOWN UNIVERSITY OF PENNSYLVANIA—cont'd

Undergraduate Programs: The College of Education offers baccalaureate programs leading to teacher certification in the fields of instructional technology, elementary education, dance, health, library science, physical education, and special education. The core of basic preparation includes a strong academic knowledge base that fosters practical application. All programs require the completion of the general education core, professional studies, subject content area, field experiences, and student teaching. A minimum of minimum of 128 semester hours must be completed for the bachelor's degree.

Graduate Programs: Master of Education programs include elementary education, reading specialist, secondary education (concentrations in biology, chemistry, English, foreign language, mathematics, social studies). Each program has specific course requirements.

Licensure/Reciprocity: Pennsylvania. Students seeking teaching certification in a state other than Pennsylvania should consult with that state's teacher certification office early in their program of study to insure compliance with requirements. Many state directors of teacher credentialing have signed Interstate Agreements through NASDTEC that expedite the certification process.

LEBANON VALLEY COLLEGE

Education Department
101 North White Oak Street
Annville, Pennsylvania 17003-0501
Phone: (717) 867-6305
Fax: (717) 867-6390
E-mail: kline@lvc.edu
Internet: http://www.lvc.edu

Institution Description: Lebanon Valley College is a private college affiliated with the United Methodist Church. The college was established and offered first instruction at the postsecondary level in 1866.

Students in the Department of Education are challenged to grow professionally and personally and are provided with the coursework and practical experiences necessary for a successful teaching career.

Institution Control: Private.

Calendar: Semester. Academic year August to May.

Official(s): Dr. Donald E. Kline, Department Head.

Faculty: Full-time 18; part-time 1; adjunct 8.

Degrees Awarded: 93 baccalaureate; 22 master's.

Admission Requirements: *Undergraduate:* Graduation from an accredited secondary school with 16 academic units or GED; College Board SAT or ACT composite. *Teacher education specific:* Students must supply a one-page personal statement describing interest in education; 2.75 GPA; passing scores on PRAXIS I exams (reading, writing, mathematics). NOTE: computerized tests that were implemented January 16, 2002. Tests taken prior to that date will not be accepted.

Fees and Expenses: $21,860 per academic year. Required fees: $650. On-campus room and board: $6,360. Other expenses: $1,080. Books and supplies: $730.

Financial Aid: Resources specifically for eligible students enrolled in teacher education programs are awarded on the basis of financial need and academic merit. The institution has a Program Participation Agreement with the U.S. Department of Education for eligible students to receive Pell Grants and other federal aid. Teacher scholarships available to qualifying students. *Contact:* Jennifer Liedtka at: (717) 867-6126 or e-mail at: liedtka@lvc.edu.

Accreditation: *Regional:* MSA. *Approved by:* Pennsylvania Department of Education.

Undergraduate Programs: The Bachelor of Science in elementary education prepares students within the context of a strong liberal arts foundation. The program encompasses the subjects of mathematics, science, language arts, reading, social studies, music, children's literature, geography, health and safety, and teaching of instructional technology for the elementary school.

Students interested in pursuing secondary teaching certification must complete an intensive program that combines chosen departmental major(s) with carefully selected education courses. Departmental majors may be certified in biology, chemistry, English, French, German, Spanish, mathematics, physics, social science, and citizenship.

The special education program graduates are certified to teach in elementary education, music education, or secondary programs and in special education programs for students with mental retardation, physical disabilities, learning disabilities, or behavior disorders in grades K-12.

All programs require the completion of a general education core, professional studies, subject content area, field experiences, and student teaching. A minimum of 120 semester hours must be completed

Licensure/Reciprocity: Pennsylvania. Students seeking teaching certification in a state other than Pennsylvania should consult with that state's teacher certification office early in their program of study to insure compliance with requirements. Many state directors of teacher credentialing have signed Interstate Agreements through NASDTEC that expedite the certification process.

LEHIGH UNIVERSITY

College of Education
A325 Iacocca Hall
111 Research Drive
Bethlehem, Pennsylvania 18015
Phone: (610) 758-3221
Fax: (610) 758-6223
E-mail: rb02@lehigh.edu
Internet: http://www.lehigh.edu

Institution Description: Lehigh University is a private, independent, nonprofit institution. It was established in 1865.

The Teacher Education Program allows students to complete an undergraduate degree, graduate with a master's degree, and Pennsylvania teacher certification.

Institution Control: Private.

Calendar: Semester. Academic August to May.

Official(s): Dr. Saly A. White, Dean; Dr.Edward S. Shapiro, Chair.

Faculty: Full-time 28; adjunct 14.

Degrees Awarded: 119 master's; 9 doctorate.

Admission Requirements: *Graduate:* Students enter the program as undergraduates. Admission to the university requires graduation from an accredited secondary institution; SAT required. *Teacher education specific:* 2.75 GPA or GRE or Miller Analogies scores; completion of all required departmental exams; recommendations; faculty interview. PRAXIS I is taken during the undergraduate period; the state of Pennsylvania requires passing PRAXIS II tests prior to certification.

Fees and Expenses: Graduate: $14,850 per academic year. Required fees: $225. On-campus room and board: $10,000. Technology fee: $100. Books and supplies: $600,

Financial Aid: Resources specifically for eligible students enrolled in teacher education programs are awarded on the basis of academic merit. *Contact:* Financial Aid Office at : (610) 738-3221.

Accreditation: *Regional:* MSA. *Member of:* AACTE. *Approved by:* Pennsylvania Department of Education.

Graduate Programs: The Five-Year Bachelor's and Master's Combined Degree Program leads to a Bachelor of Arts or a Bachelor of Science degree from the College of Business and Economics, Rosin College of Engineering and Applied science; a Master of Education degree in either secondary or elementary education, and an Instructional Teaching credential. The program engages students in professional experiences in education from the sophomore year through to their completion of the program. The minimum number of credits for the bachelor's degree is 121 and the minimum for the master's degree and certification is 30.

The university has program approval for 12 areas of certification: biology, chemistry, earth and space science, English, French, German, general science, mathematics, physics, social studies, Spanish.

In addition to the five-year bachelor's/master's combined degree program, the College of Education offers graduate degrees, certification, and non-degree programs to potential and established leaders in all aspects of educational endeavor.

Licensure/Reciprocity: Pennsylvania. Students seeking teaching certification in a state other than Pennsylvania should consult with that state's teacher certification office early in their program of study to insure compliance with requirements. Many state directors of teacher credentialing have signed Interstate Agreements through NASDTEC that expedite the certification process.

LOCK HAVEN UNIVERSITY OF PENNSYLVANIA

College of Education and Human Services

Stevenson G-34
Fairmont Street
Lock Haven, Pennsylvania 17745
Phone: (570) 893-2027
Fax: (570) 893-2006
E-mail: admissions@lhup.edu
Internet: http://www.lhup.edu

Institution Description: Lock Haven State University is an institution of the Pennsylvania State System of Higher Education. It was established and chartered as Central State Normal School in 1870.

The College of Education offers undergraduate and graduate programs in a variety of fields available for candidates for teacher certification.

Institution Control: Public.

Calendar: Semester. Academic year August to May.

Official(s): Dr. William L. Phillips, Dean.

Faculty: Full-time 17.

Degrees Awarded: 144 baccalaureate; 36 master's.

Admission Requirements: *Undergraduate:* Graduation from an accredited secondary school or GED; College Board SAT or ACT composite. *Teacher education specific:* Minimum of 48 earned credits; 3.0 GPA; completion of speech, hearing, and TB test; personal essay; passing scores on PRAXIS I exams (reading, writing, mathematics). NOTE: Tests must be the new computerized tests that were implemented January 16, 2002. Tests taken prior to that date will not be accepted. *Graduate:* Baccalaureate degree from a regionally accredited institution. *Teacher education specific:* 3.0 GPA; GRE or Miller Analogies scores; completion of all required departmental exams; three recommendations; faculty interview. The Commonwealth of Pennsylvania requires passing PRAXIS II tests prior to certification.

Fees and Expenses: Undergraduate: in-state $4,378 per academic year; out-of-state $8,946. Graduate: in-state $5,254 per academic year; out-of-state $8,408. Required fees: Undergraduate in-state $1,228; out-of-state $1,735. Graduate in-state $2,366; out-of-state $3,362. On-campus room and board: $5,032.

Financial Aid: Resources specifically for eligible students enrolled in teacher education programs are awarded on the basis of financial need and academic merit. The institution has a Program Participation Agreement with the U.S. Department of Education for eligible students to receive Pell Grants and other federal aid. Teacher scholarships available to qualifying students. *Contact:* Dr. William A. Irwin at: (570) 893-2344 or e-mail at: wirwin@lup.edu.

Accreditation: *Regional:* MSA. *Professional:* NCATE. *Member of:* AACTE. *Approved by:* Pennsylvania Department of Education.

Undergraduate Programs: The College of Education offers undergraduate programs leading to the baccalaureate degree and the teaching credential. Programs include early childhood

education, elementary education, health and physical education, and special education. The secondary education program offers concentrations in the areas of biology, chemistry, citizenship studies, earth and space science, English, English and a foreign language, French, general science, German, mathematics, physics, Spanish. All programs require the completion of a general education core, professional studies, subject content area, field experiences, and student teaching. A minimum of 128 semester hours is required for the bachelor's degree.

Graduate Programs: Graduate programs offered by the College of Education include the Master of Education in Teaching and Learning and the Master of Education in Alternative Education. Each program has specific admission and degree completion requirements. Contact the university for details.

Licensure/Reciprocity: Pennsylvania. Students seeking teaching certification in a state other than Pennsylvania should consult with that state's teacher certification office early in their program of study to insure compliance with requirements. Many state directors of teacher credentialing have signed Interstate Agreements through NASDTEC that expedite the certification process.

MANSFIELD UNIVERSITY OF PENNSYLVANIA

Teacher Education Unit

5 Academy Street
Mansfield, Pennsylvania 16933
Phone: (717) 662-4000
Fax: (717) 662-4121
E-mail: admissions@mnsfld.edu
Internet: http://www.mnsfld.edu

Institution Description: Mansfield University is a state institution. It was established as Mansfield Classical Seminary in 1854. After several name changes over the years, it became Mansfield University of Pennsylvania in 1983.

The Teacher Education Unit is responsible for all teacher certification programs regardless of the department that houses the program.

Institution Control: Public.

Calendar: Semester. Academic year August to May.

Official(s): Dr. Celeste Binns, Chair.

Faculty: Not reported.

Degrees Awarded: 116 baccalaureate; 72 master's.

Admission Requirements: *Undergraduate:* Graduation from an accredited secondary school or GED; College Board SAT or ACT composite. *Teacher education specific:* Minimum of 48 earned credits; 3.0 GPA; completion of speech, hearing, and TB test; personal essay; passing scores on PRAXIS I exams (reading, writing, mathematics). NOTE: Tests must be the new computerized tests that were implemented January 16, 2002. Tests taken prior to that date will not be accepted. *Graduate:* Baccalaureate degree from a regionally accredited institution. *Teacher education specific:* 3.0 GPA; GRE or Miller Analogies scores; completion of all required departmental exams; two recommendations; faculty interview. The Commonwealth of Pennsylvania requires passing PRAXIS II tests prior to certification.

Fees and Expenses: Undergraduate: in-state $5,922 per academic year; out-of-state $12,870. Graduate: Tuition charged per credit hour. On-campus room and board: $5,248. Other expenses: $1,874. Books and supplies: $900.

Financial Aid: Resources specifically for eligible students enrolled in teacher education programs are awarded on the basis of financial need and academic merit. The institution has a Program Participation Agreement with the U.S. Department of Education for eligible students to receive Pell Grants and other federal aid. Teacher scholarships available to qualifying students. *Contact:* Financial Aid Office at: (570) 662-4129.

Accreditation: *Regional:* MSA. *Professional:* NCATE. *Member of:* AACTE. *Approved by:* Pennsylvania Department of Education.

Undergraduate Programs: The Bachelor of Science in Education degree programs are offered in art (K—12), music (K-12), elementary education (1-6), early childhood (K-3), special edu-

MANSFIELD UNIVERSITY OF PENNSYLVANIA—*cont'd*

cation (K-12 mentally or physically handicapped), dual program in elementary and special education (1-6 elementary education and K-12 mentally/physically handicapped); social studies-history (7-12 citizenship), English (7-12), Spanish (7-12), French (7-12), German (7-12), chemistry (7-12), physics (7-12), earth and space science (7-12), mathematics (7-12).

All programs require the completion of a general education core, professional studies, subject content area, field experiences, and student teaching. A minimum of 128 semester hours must be completed for the degree award.

Graduate Programs: The master's degree programs offered through the Teacher Education Unit give students the opportunity to get a broad general preparation for a variety of endeavors. Within the programs are a specialization of 15 credit hours that may be either tailored to the student's personal and professional career goals or focus on the specialization in microcomputers. A K-12 certification as a seading specialist may be added with many courses simultaneously meeting degree and certification requirements.

Students complete a common core and work closely with graduate advisors to develop 15 semester hours of specialization relevant the students' teaching fields. The computer specialization program is designed for teachers, school administrators, and other education professionals.

Licensure/Reciprocity: Pennsylvania. Students seeking teaching certification in a state other than Pennsylvania should consult with that state's teacher certification office early in their program of study to insure compliance with requirements. Many state directors of teacher credentialing have signed Interstate Agreements through NASDTEC that expedite the certification process.

MARYWOOD UNIVERSITY

College of Education and Human Development
Education Department

2300 Adams Avenue
Scranton, Pennsylvania 18509-1598
Phone: (570) 348-6203
Fax: (570) 961-4763
E-mail: donabauman@marywood.edu
Internet: http://www.marywood.edu

Institution Description: Marywood University, formerly named Marywood College, is a private, independent, nonprofit institution, conducted by the Congregation of the Sisters, Servants of the Immaculate Heart of Mary Corporation, Scranton, Pennsylvania, Roman Catholic Church. It was founded in 1915.

The Education Department maintains a curriculum laboratory of texts, manipulative materials, and software designed for K-12 programs.

Institution Control: Private.

Calendar: Semester. Academic year August to May.

Official(s): Dr. Dona Bauman, Chair.

Faculty: Full-time 8.

Degrees Awarded: 82 baccalaureate; 77 master's.

Admission Requirements: *Undergraduate:* Graduation from an accredited secondary school with 16 academic units or GED; College Board SAT or ACT composite. *Teacher education specific:* Minimum of 48 earned credits; 3.0 GPA; completion of speech, hearing, and TB test; personal essay; passing scores on PRAXIS I exams (reading, writing, mathematics). NOTE: Tests must be the new computerized tests that were implemented January 16, 2002. Tests taken prior to that date will not be accepted. *Graduate:* Baccalaureate degree from a regionally accredited institution. *Teacher education specific:* 3.0 GPA; GRE or Miller Analogies scores; completion of all required departmental exams; recommendations; faculty interview. The Commonwealth of Pennsylvania requires passing PRAXIS II tests prior to certification.

Fees and Expenses: Undergraduate: $18,560 per academic year. Graduate: Tuition charged per credit hour. On-campus room and board: $8,134. Other expenses: $1,200. Books and supplies: $700.

Financial Aid: Resources specifically for eligible students enrolled in teacher education programs are awarded on the basis of financial need and academic merit. The institution has a Program Participation Agreement with the U.S. Department of Education for eligible students to receive Pell Grants and other federal aid. Teacher scholarships available to qualifying students. *Contact:* Financial Aid Office at: (570) 348-6225.

Accreditation: *Regional:* MSA. *Professional:* NCATE. *Approved by:* Pennsylvania Department of Education.

Undergraduate Programs: Marywood's Education Department has major responsibility for preparing students in elementary education (grades K-6) and early childhood education (N-3). The department cooperates with other departments to offer the professional education components of disciplines in art (K-12), English (7-12), mathematics (7-12), biology (7-12) foreign language (K-12), music (K-12), communication (7-12), general science (7-12), social science (7-12), early childhood education (N-3) health/;physical education (K-12), speech correction (K-12), elementary education (K-6), home economics (K-12), special education (K-12). All programs require the completion of a general education core, professional studies, subject content area, field experiences, and student teaching. A minimum of 126 semester hours must be completed for the bachelor's degree.

Graduate Programs: Fields of study at the master's level include the Master of Science in: reading education, early childhood intervention - birth to age 8, instructional technology, school leadership; Master of Arts in Teaching with elementary education certification. A library science (K-12) certification program is also available. Each program has specific course and degree requirements.

Licensure/Reciprocity: Pennsylvania. Students seeking teaching certification in a state other than Pennsylvania should consult with that state's teacher certification office early in their program of study to insure compliance with requirements. Many state directors of teacher credentialing have signed Interstate Agreements through NASDTEC that expedite the certification process.

MERCYHURST COLLEGE

Education Division

501 East 38th Street
Erie, Pennsylvania 16546-0001
Phone: (814) 824-2446
Fax: (814) 824-3074
E-mail: kbukowski@mercyhurst.edu
Internet: http://www.mercyhurst.edu

Institution Description: Mercyhurst College is a private college affiliated with the Roman Catholic Church. The college was established and offered first instruction at the postsecondary level in 1926.

The Education Division offers programs leading to teacher certification in a variety of subject areas.

Institution Control: Private.

Calendar: Semester. Academic year September to May.

Official(s): Dr. Kathleen Bukowski, Division Head.

Faculty: Full-time 9; part-time 3; adjunct 12.

Degrees Awarded: 50 baccalaureate; 38 master's.

Admission Requirements: *Undergraduate:* Graduation from an accredited secondary school with college preparatory coursework or GED; College Board SAT or ACT composite. *Teacher education specific:* Two letters of reference; apply during sophomore year; 2.5 GPA; passing scores on PRAXIS I exams (reading, writing, mathematics); NOTE: Tests must be the new computerized tests that were implemented January 16, 2002. Tests taken prior to that date will not be accepted. *Graduate:* Baccalaureate degree from a regionally accredited institution. *Teacher education specific:* 2.75 GPA; Miller Analogies Test; completion of all required departmental exams; two recommendations; faculty interview. The Commonwealth of Pennsylvania requires passing PRAXIS II tests prior to certification.

Fees and Expenses: $14,320 per academic year. Required fees: Computer fee $285. On-campus room and board: $5,958.

Financial Aid: Resources specifically for eligible students enrolled in teacher education programs are awarded on the basis of financial need and academic merit. The institution has a Program Participation Agreement with the U.S. Department of Education for eligible students to receive Pell Grants and other federal aid. Teacher scholarships available to qualifying students. *Contact:* Sheila Richter at: (814) 824-2287 or e-mail at: srichter@mercyhurst.edu.

Accreditation: *Regional:* MSA. *Approved by:* Pennsylvania Department of Education.

Undergraduate Programs: Students enrolled in the education program are exposed to the classroom environment in their freshman year through required practicum experiences. This exposure continues throughout the four years of undergraduate training. During the junior year, elementary, early childhood, elementary/early childhood, elementary/special education, and early childhood/special education majors participate in the Pre-Teaching Internships Program, a ten-week teacher aide experience that is completed in an elementary school classroom prior to student teaching.

Students who major in secondary education may receive teacher certification in the academic areas of art, biology, business, chemistry, earth and space science, English, family and consumer science, general science, mathematics, music, social studies, and world languages.

Graduates of the special education program receive a comprehensive K-12 teacher certificate covering the areas of mental retardation, behavior disorders, physical handicaps, learning disabilities, and brain injuries.

All programs require the completion of a general education core, professional studies, subject content area, field experiences, and student teaching.

Graduate Programs: The graduate program in special education is intended to provide opportunities for certified teachers in the tri-state area to refine their critical skills to the high level of proficiency required to fulfill roles of master teacher and/or consultant teacher. A total of 30 graduate credits is required. Core courses account for all of these credits. An optional master's thesis may substitute for six specialized core credits.

Licensure/Reciprocity: Pennsylvania. Students seeking teaching certification in a state other than Pennsylvania should consult with that state's teacher certification office early in their program of study to insure compliance with requirements. Many state directors of teacher credentialing have signed Interstate Agreements through NASDTEC that expedite the certification process.

MESSIAH COLLEGE

Department of Education
One College Avenue
Grantham, Pennsylvania 17027
Phone: (717) 766-2511
Fax: (717) 691-6025
E-mail: admiss@messiah.edu
Internet: http://www.messiah.edu

Institution Description: Messiah College is a Christian college committed to an embracing evangelical spirit rooted in the Anabaptist, Pietist, and Wesleyan traditions of the Christian Church. It was founded in 1909.

The mission of the Department of Education is to prepare professional leaders who are capable of independent thinking, decision-making and problem-solving in a wide variety of educational environments.

Institution Control: Private.

Calendar: Semester. Academic year August to May.

Official(s): Dr. Kevin Zook, Department Chair.

Faculty: Full-time 12; adjunct 15.

Degrees Awarded: 104 baccalaureate.

Admission Requirements: *Undergraduate:* Graduation from an accredited secondary school in top third of class; SAT score of 1000 and above or ACT score of 21 or higher; GED accepted. *Teacher education specific:* Students apply during sophomore year; 2.75 GPA; faculty approval; passing scores on PRAXIS I exams (reading, writing, mathematics); faculty interview. NOTE: Tests must be the new computerized tests that were implemented January 16, 2002. Tests taken prior to that date will not be accepted. The Commonwealth of Pennsylvania requires passing PRAXIS II tests prior to certification.

Fees and Expenses: $17,730 per academic year. Required fees: $406. On-campus room and board: $6,130. Books and supplies: $740. Other expenses: $580 travel; $1,100 personal.

Financial Aid: Resources specifically for eligible students enrolled in teacher education programs are awarded on the basis of financial need and academic merit. Discounts to alumni dependents and students whose parents are in full-time ministry. The institution has a Program Participation Agreement with the U.S. Department of Education for eligible students to receive Pell Grants and other federal aid. Teacher scholarships available to qualifying students. *Contact:* Greg Gearhart at: (717) 691-6007 or e-mail at: gearhart@messiah.edu.

Accreditation: *Regional: Approved by:* Pennsylvania Department of Education.

Undergraduate Programs: The early childhood education program prepares students to teach in preschools and grades K-3 in public and private schools. The student works in the campus Early Childhood Center, assuming responsibilities for coordinating staff schedules, directing the curriculum, and supervising the Center's total operation.

The elementary education program prepares the student to teach grades K-6 in public and private schools and includes Pennsylvania public school teacher certification. The program requires a 12-credit subject matter specialization, early and continuing field experiences, and a 12-week supervised student teaching experience in a local public school.

The 7-12 Pennsylvania certification for public school teaching at the secondary level is available in the areas of English, social studies, mathematics, biology, biology with environmental education, and chemistry.

The K-12 programs in health and physical education, foreign language (French, German, Spanish), and music education meet Pennsylvania requirements for certification in grades K-12. To be certified in art education, the student completes studies at Messiah's Philadelphia campus in connection with Temple University.

All bachelor's programs require the completion of a general education core, professional studies, subject content area, field experiences, and student teaching. A minimum of 126 semester hours must be completed for the baccalaureate degree.

Licensure/Reciprocity: Pennsylvania. Students seeking teaching certification in a state other than Pennsylvania should consult with that state's teacher certification office early in their program of study to insure compliance with requirements. Many state directors of teacher credentialing have signed Interstate Agreements through NASDTEC that expedite the certification process.

MILLERSVILLE UNIVERSITY OF PENNSYLVANIA

School of Education
Stayer Education Center
One North George Street
Millersville, Pennsylvania 17551-0302
Phone: (717) 872-3024
Fax: (717) 871-2147
E-mail: adminfo@millersv.edu
Internet: http://www.millersv.edu

Institution Description: Millersville University of Pennsylvania (formerly Millersville State College) was established as Lancaster Country Normal Institute and offered first instruction at the postsecondary level in 1855.

MILLERSVILLE UNIVERSITY OF PENNSYLVANIA—cont'd

The Department of Elementary and Early Childhood Education and the Department of Special Education offer undergraduate and graduate programs leading to teacher certification.

Institution Control: Public.

Calendar: Semester. Academic year August to May.

Official(s): Dr. Jane Bray, Chair, Department of Elementary and Early Childhood.

Faculty: Full-time 19 (Elementary and Early Childhood).

Degrees Awarded: 219 baccalaureate; 79 master's.

Admission Requirements: *Undergraduate:* Graduation from an accredited secondary school or GED; College Board SAT or ACT composite. *Teacher education specific:* Students apply during sophomore year; 2.75 GPA; faculty interview; passing scores on PRAXIS I exams (reading, writing, mathematics). NOTE: Tests must be the computerized tests that were implemented January 16, 2002. Tests taken prior to that date will not be accepted. *Graduate:* Baccalaureate degree from a regionally accredited institution. *Teacher education specific:* 3.0 GPA; GRE or Miller Analogies scores; completion of all required departmental exams; two recommendations; faculty interview. The Commonwealth of Pennsylvania requires passing PRAXIS II tests prior to certification.

Fees and Expenses: Undergraduate: in-state $5,819 per academic year; out-of-state $12,767. Graduate: Tuition charged per credit hour. On-campus room and board: $5,450. Other expenses: $1,220. Books and supplies: $700.

Financial Aid: Resources specifically for eligible students enrolled in teacher education programs are awarded on the basiInstitute

Accreditation: *Regional:* MSA. *Approved by:* Pennsylvania Department of Education.

Undergraduate Programs: The Department of Elementary and Early Childhood Education offers majors in: elementary education with certification in early childhood education; elementary education; elementary education with science option; dual major in elementary education and special education.

The Department of Special Education provides a variety of professional opportunities for students committed to the improvement of lifestyles for children, youth, and adults with disabilities. Teacher's certification is available in six areas: kindergarten through grade twelve, brain injured, learning disabled, mentally retarded, physically handicapped and/or health impaired, seriously emotionally disturbed.

All bachelor's programs require the completion of a general education core, professional studies, subject content area, field experiences, and student teaching. A minimum of 120 semester hours must be completed for the degree award.

Graduate Programs: Master's degree programs are offered in elementary education, early childhood education, and reading and language arts education. The curriculum consists of a professional core and extensive coursework in the specific program of study. Graduate students may also earn certifications in: post-baccalaureate initial teaching certification, reading specialist, English as a second language program specialist, reading supervisor, supervisor of elementary education.

Licensure/Reciprocity: Pennsylvania. Students seeking teaching certification in a state other than Pennsylvania should consult with that state's teacher certification office early in their program of study to insure compliance with requirements. Many state directors of teacher credentialing have signed Interstate Agreements through NASDTEC that expedite the certification process.

MORAVIAN COLLEGE
Education Department
1200 Main Street
Bethlehem, Pennsylvania 18018-6650
Phone: (610) 861-1558
Fax: (610) 861-3956
E-mail: admissions@moravian.edu
Internet: http://www.moravian.edu

Institution Description: Moravian College is a private, independent, nonprofit college affiliated with the Moravian Church in America. The college was formed in 1954 by the merger of Moravian Seminary for Women (founded 1742) and The School for Men at Nazareth (founded 1746).

The goal of the Education Department is to prepare teachers who are scholars as well as teachers and who are committed to the academic success of all of their students.

Institution Control: Private.

Calendar: Semester. Academic year September to May.

Official(s): Dr. Sandra Fluck, Department Chairperson.

Faculty: Full-time 6; adjunct 10.

Degrees Awarded: 9 baccalaureate; 8 master's.

Admission Requirements: *Undergraduate:* Graduation from an accredited secondary school or GED; College Board SAT or ACT composite. *Teacher education specific:* Students apply in sophomore year; 3.0 GPA in courses in the academic major and professional education courses; recommendations by major academic department and the Dean of Students; evidence of successful experiences with children or youth; evident of written and oral communication skills; passing scores on PRAXIS I exams (reading, writing, mathematics). NOTE: Tests must be the computerized tests implemented January 16, 2002. Tests taken prior to that date will not be accepted. *Graduate:* Baccalaureate degree from a regionally accredited institution. *Teacher education specific:* 3.0 GPA; GRE or Miller Analogies scores; completion of all required departmental exams; recommendations; faculty interview. The Commonwealth of Pennsylvania requires passing PRAXIS II tests prior to certification.

Fees and Expenses: Undergraduate: $22,028 per academic year. Graduate: Tuition $292 per credit hour. On-campus room and board: $7,095. Other expenses: $1,670. Books and supplies: $700.

Financial Aid: Resources specifically for eligible students enrolled in teacher education programs are awarded on the basis of financial need and academic merit. The institution has a Program Participation Agreement with the U.S. Department of Education for eligible students to receive Pell Grants and other federal aid. Teacher scholarships available to qualifying students. *Contact:* Financial Aid Office at: (610) 861-1330.

Accreditation: *Regional:* MSA. *Approved by:* Pennsylvania Department of Education.

Undergraduate Programs: Teacher certification programs are offered in art (K-12), elementary education (K-6), music (K-12), foreign language (K-12 in French, German, Latin, Spanish), secondary education (7-12 in biology, chemistry, English, general science, mathematics, physics, social science). All baccalaureate programs require the completion of a general education core, professional studies, subject content area, field experiences, and student teaching. A minimum of 124 semester hours is required for the bachelor's degree.

Graduate Programs: Post-baccalaureate teacher certification programs are field-based to provide as much pre-student teaching experience as possible. The program is designed for students holding an undergraduate degree but wish to acquire certification in their field of specialization.

The master's degree program in curriculum and instruction has been designed to fit the specific needs of classroom teachers. The 33-credit program is taught primarily in facilities within partnering districts.

The English as a second language specialist certificate program explores current knowledge and research on the process of learning English as a second language. The process of first and second language acquisition will be studied in support of literacy development of English language learners at different stages of second language acquisition.

Licensure/Reciprocity: Pennsylvania. Students seeking teaching certification in a state other than Pennsylvania should consult with that state's teacher certification office early in their program of study to insure compliance with requirements. Many state directors of teacher credentialing have signed Interstate Agreements through NASDTEC that expedite the certification process.

THE PENNSYLVANIA STATE UNIVERSITY
College of Education
275 Chambers Building
University Park, Pennsylvania 16802-3206
Phone: (814) 865-2324
Fax: (814) 865-0555
E-mail: horstv@psu.edu
Internet: http://www.psu.edu

Institution Description: The university was established in 1855 and offered first instruction at the postsecondary level in 1859. It was designated as Pennsylvania's land-grant college in 1863. The name was changed to Pennsylvania State College in 1874 and the present name was adopted in 1953.

The Penn State teacher preparation program emphasizes the continuous process of learning, extended over the entire span of the educator's professional life.

Institution Control: Public.

Calendar: Semester. Academic year September to May.

Official(s): Dr. David H. Monk, Dean.

Faculty: Full-time 99; part-time and adjunct 41.

Degrees Awarded: 670 baccalaureate; 181 master's; 80 doctorate.

Admission Requirements: *Undergraduate:* Graduation from an accredited secondary school with 15 academic units or GED; College Board SAT or ACT composite. *Teacher education specific:* Application during sophomore year; completion of 48 semester hours; minimum 3.0 GPA; approvals from academic adviser and from the professor in charge of the program area; completion of early field experiences; completion of a core of education courses; passing scores on PRAXIS I exams (reading, writing, mathematics). NOTE: Tests must be the computerized tests that were implemented January 16, 2002. Tests taken prior to that date will not be accepted. *Graduate:* Baccalaureate degree from a regionally accredited institution. *Teacher education specific:* 3.0 GPA; GRE or Miller Analogies scores; completion of all required departmental exams; two recommendations; faculty interview. The Commonwealth of Pennsylvania requires passing PRAXIS II tests prior to certification.

Fees and Expenses: Undergraduate: in-state $4,004 per semester; out-of-state $8,818. Graduate: in-state $4,760 per semester; out-of-state $9,164. Required fees: Various. On-campus room and board: $5,730 per academic year. Books and supplies: $500.

Financial Aid: Resources specifically for eligible students enrolled in teacher education programs are awarded on the basis of financial need and academic merit. Sources available to applicants committed to urban education. The institution has a Program Participation Agreement with the U.S. Department of Education for eligible students to receive Pell Grants and other federal aid. Teacher scholarships available to qualifying students. *Contact:* Dan R. Grow at: (814) 865-0488 or e-mail at: dxg2@psu.edu.

Accreditation: *Regional:* MSA. *Professional:* NCATE. *Member of:* AACTE. *Approved by:* Pennsylvania Department of Education.

Undergraduate Programs: Teacher preparation programs are offered in the following areas of certification: agriculture, art, bilingual education, biology, chemistry, communication, early childhood, earth and space science, elementary education, English, environmental education, French, general science, German, health and physical education, Latin, mathematics, music, physics, reading, Russian, social studies, Spanish, special education, speech and language impaired, vocational education. Majors are offered in elementary and kindergarten education, rehabilitation services, secondary education, special education, workforce education and development and lead to the Bachelor

of Science degree. All programs require the completion of a general education core, professional studies, subject content area, field experiences, and student teaching. Degree requirements range from 124 to 130 semester hours.

Graduate Programs: Graduate programs are offered in cooperation with the Graduate School. Degrees at the master's and doctoral levels are awarded for completion of programs in: adult education, comparative and international education, counseling psychology (Ph.D.), counselor education, curriculum and instruction; educational administration, educational psychology, educational theory and policy, higher education, instructional systems, school psychology, special education, workforce education and development.

Graduate professional certificate programs include: administrative certification, educational specialist, reading specialist.

Licensure/Reciprocity: Pennsylvania. Students seeking teaching certification in a state other than Pennsylvania should consult with that state's teacher certification office early in their program of study to insure compliance with requirements. Many state directors of teacher credentialing have signed Interstate Agreements through NASDTEC that expedite the certification process.

POINT PARK COLLEGE
Education and community Services
201 Wood Street
Pittsburgh, Pennsylvania 15222
Phone: (412) 392-3972
Fax: (412) 392-3927
E-mail: vrevilla@ppc.edu
Internet: http://www.ppc.edu

Institution Description: Point Park College is a private, independent, nonprofit institution. The college was established and chartered as Point Park Junior College in 1960. The present name was adopted in 1966.

The mission of the Department of Education and Community Services is to prepare students to successfully enter teaching professions in early childhood, elementary, and secondary education.

Institution Control: Private.

Calendar: Semester. Academic year August to May.

Official(s): Dr. Vincenne Revilla Beltram, Dean.

Faculty: Full-time 6; part-time 20.

Degrees Awarded: 42 baccalaureate; 21 master's.

Admission Requirements: *Undergraduate:* Graduation from an accredited secondary school or GED; College Board SAT or ACT composite. *Teacher education specific:* Completion of 48 semester credits; 2.75 GPA; passing scores on PRAXIS I exams (reading, writing, mathematics); NOTE: Tests must be the computerized tests that were implemented January 16, 2002. Tests taken prior to that date will not be accepted. *Graduate:* Baccalaureate degree from a regionally accredited institution. *Teacher education specific:* 3.0 GPA; completion of all required departmental exams; recommendations; faculty interview. The Commonwealth of Pennsylvania requires passing PRAXIS II tests prior to certification.

Fees and Expenses: Undergraduate: $7,590 per semester; graduate: $4,478. On-campus room and board: $4,000 per semester with fixed meal plan. Books and supplies: $800.

Financial Aid: Resources specifically for eligible students enrolled in teacher education programs are awarded on the basis of financial need and academic merit. The institution has a Program Participation Agreement with the U.S. Department of Education for eligible students to receive Pell Grants and other federal aid. Teacher scholarships available to qualifying students. *Contact:* Sandra Cronin at: (412) 392-3935.

Accreditation: *Regional:* MSA. Approved by: Pennsylvania Department of Education.

Undergraduate Programs: The Bachelor of Arts degree programs include early childhood education, elementary education (also available with a concentration in theatre arts), and secondary education with concentrations in biological sciences,

POINT PARK COLLEGE—*cont'd*

citizenship, English, mass communication, mathematics. All programs require the completion of a general education core, professional studies, subject content area, field experiences, and student teaching.

Graduate Programs: Post-baccalaureate programs are designed in each secondary education area for in-service teachers seeking additional certification and for those with non-education baccalaureate degrees planning to enter the teaching professions.

The Master of Arts in curriculum and instruction is designed to accommodate teaching professionals in those professions in higher education or in adult education and training. The Master of Arts in educational administration program prepares professional educators for leadership positions as school administrators or principals.

Licensure/Reciprocity: Pennsylvania. Students seeking teaching certification in a state other than Pennsylvania should consult with that state's teacher certification office early in their program of study to insure compliance with requirements. Many state directors of teacher credentialing have signed Interstate Agreements through NASDTEC that expedite the certification process.

ROBERT MORRIS COLLEGE

Education and Social Services
6001 University Boulevard
Moon Township, Pennsylvania 15108
Phone: (412) 262-8229
Fax: (412) 262-8494
E-mail: cellante@rmu.edu
Internet: http://www.rmu.edu

Institution Description: Robert Morris College is a private, independent, nonprofit college that was established as Pittsburgh School of Accountancy. It offered first instruction at the postsecondary level in 1921.

The Department of Education and Social Services offers programs leading to teacher certification with emphasis on programs in business and computer technology.

Institution Control: Private.

Calendar: Semester. Academic year August to May.

Official(s): Dr. Donna L. Cellante, Chairperson.

Faculty: Full-time 9; part-time 16.

Degrees Awarded: 170 baccalaureate; 142 master's.

Admission Requirements: *Undergraduate:* Graduation from an accredited secondary school or GED; College Board SAT or ACT composite. *Teacher education specific:* Students apply during sophomore year; 2.6 GPA; faculty interview; passing scores on PRAXIS I exams (reading, writing, mathematics). NOTE: Tests must be the new computerized tests that were implemented January 16, 2002. Tests taken prior to that date will not be accepted. *Graduate:* Baccalaureate degree from a regionally accredited institution. *Teacher education specific:* 3.0 GPA; completion of all required departmental exams; two letters of recommendation; faculty interview. The state of Pennsylvania requires passing PRAXIS II tests prior to certification.

Fees and Expenses: Undergraduate: $6,742 per semester. Graduate: $420 per credit hour. On-campus room and board: $2,059 (double) per semester. Books and supplies: $600 per semester.

Financial Aid: Resources specifically for eligible students enrolled in teacher education programs are awarded on the basis of financial need and academic merit. The institution has a Program Participation Agreement with the U.S. Department of Education for eligible students to receive Pell Grants and other federal aid. Teacher scholarships available to qualifying students. *Contact:* Linda Herbert at: (412) 262-8677 or e-mail at: herbert@rmu.edu.

Accreditation: *Regional:* MSA. *Approved by:* Pennsylvania Department of Education.

Undergraduate Programs: Bachelor degree programs are offered in English, communication, mathematics, and social studies (grades 7-12). Business and communication programs are offered for K-12 and elementary education for K-6. All pro-

grams require the completion of a general education core, professional studies, subject content area, field experiences, and student teaching. A minimum of 120 credit hours is required for the bachelor's degree.

Graduate Programs: Teacher certification programs at the master's level include English, communication, mathematics, social studies, and elementary education. A 30-credit Master of Science in business education and a 36-credit Master of Science in instructional leadership are available.

Licensure/Reciprocity: Pennsylvania. Students seeking teaching certification in a state other than Pennsylvania should consult with that state's teacher certification office early in their program of study to insure compliance with requirements. Many state directors of teacher credentialing have signed Interstate Agreements through NASDTEC that expedite the certification process.

SHIPPENSBURG UNIVERSITY OF PENNSYLVANIA

Department of Teacher Education
214 Shippen Hall
1871 Old Main Drive
Shippensburg, Pennsylvania 17257-2299
Phone: (717) 477-1688
Fax: (717) 477-4046
E-mail: admiss@ship.edu
Internet: http://www.ship.edu

Institution Description: Shippensburg University of Pennsylvania is a state institution. It was established as Cumberland Valley State Normal School in 1871. The name was changed to Shippensburg State Teachers College in 1927, became Shippensburg State College in 1960, and the present name was adopted in 1983.

Teacher education programs prepare professionals for teaching and leadership positions in a variety of educational settings and institutions.

Institution Control: Public.

Calendar: Semester. Academic year August to May.

Official(s): Dr. Elizabeth J. Vaughan, Department of Teacher Education.

Faculty: Full-time 25.

Degrees Awarded: 170 baccalaureate; 142 master's.

Admission Requirements: *Undergraduate:* Graduation from an accredited secondary school or GED; College Board SAT. *Teacher education specific:* GPA of 2.8 at the accumulation of 48 semester credits; faculty interview; passing scores on PRAXIS I exams (reading, writing, mathematics). NOTE: Tests must be the new computerized tests that were implemented January 16, 2002. Tests taken prior to that date will not be accepted. *Graduate:* Baccalaureate degree from a regionally accredited institution. *Teacher education specific:* 3.0 GPA; completion of all required departmental exams; recommendations; faculty interview. The Commonwealth of Pennsylvania requires passing PRAXIS II tests prior to certification.

Fees and Expenses: Undergraduate: in-state $5,679 per academic year; out-of-state $12,559. Graduate: Tuition charged per credit hour. On-campus room and board: $5,080. Other expenses: $2,091. Books and supplies: $900.

Financial Aid: Resources specifically for eligible students enrolled in teacher education programs are awarded on the basis of financial need and academic merit. The institution has a Program Participation Agreement with the U.S. Department of Education for eligible students to receive Pell Grants and other federal aid. Teacher scholarships available to qualifying students. *Contact:* Financial Aid Office at:

Accreditation: *Regional:* MSA. *Professional:* NCATE. *Member of:* AACTE. *Approved by:* Pennsylvania Department of Education.

Undergraduate Programs: The elementary education curriculum is a four-year program requiring at least 129 credit hours leading to the Bachelor of Science in Education. The basic program qualifies the student to apply for an elementary teacher certificate, thus asking the graduate eligible for employment at any level, K-6 as well as grades 7 and 8 if these grades are part of a state-approved middle school. Those students choosing the early childhood sequence receive additional certification for nursery school (N-3).

The College of Education provides programs for the preparation of teachers in the secondary schools in cooperation with the College of Arts and Sciences and the John L. Grove College of Business. Majors are offered in biology, chemistry, English, French, mathematics, physics, social studies (geography, history, political science, sociology), Spanish; business: information technology for business education, social studies-economics; Interdisciplinary: earth-space science, environmental education, general science.

Graduate Programs: The Master of Education degree is offered in educational administration and a post-master's degree program is offered leading to certification of elementary and secondary school principals. The post-master's degree program leading to the Supervisory I certificate includes certification in: communications/English, counseling, early childhood education, elementary education, environmental education, foreign languages, library science, mathematics, reading, science, social studies, special education.

The graduate programs also provide opportunities for persons who have a bachelor's degree and a teaching certificate to extend their certification to other areas.

Licensure/Reciprocity: Pennsylvania. Students seeking teaching certification in a state other than Pennsylvania should consult with that state's teacher certification office early in their program of study to insure compliance with requirements. Many state directors of teacher credentialing have signed Interstate Agreements through NASDTEC that expedite the certification process.

SLIPPERY ROCK UNIVERSITY OF PENNSYLVANIA

College of Education
103 McKay Education Building
Slippery Rock, Pennsylvania 16057
Phone: (724) 738-2007
Fax: (724) 738-2880
E-mail: isv.hertzog@sru.edu
Internet: http://www.sru.edu

Institution Description: Slippery Rock University of Pennsylvania is a state institution. It was established and chartered as Slippery Rock State Normal School in 1889. The name was changed to Slippery Rock State Teachers College in 1926, to Slippery Rock State College in 1960, and to its present name in 1983.

The College of Education offers undergraduate and graduate programs leading to teaching licensure in Pennsylvania.

Institution Control: Public.

Calendar: Semester. Academic year August to May.

Official(s): Dr. C. Jay Hertzog, Dean.

Faculty: Full-time 75; part-time 12.

Degrees Awarded: 277 baccalaureate; 65 master's.

Admission Requirements: *Undergraduate:* Graduation from an accredited secondary school or GED; College Board SAT. *Teacher education specific:* GPA of 2.8 at the accumulation of 48 semester credits; faculty interview; passing scores on PRAXIS I exams (reading, writing, mathematics). NOTE: Tests must be the new computerized tests that were implemented January 16, 2002. Tests taken prior to that date will not be accepted. *Graduate:* Baccalaureate degree from a regionally accredited institution. *Teacher education specific:* 3.0 GPA; completion of all required departmental exams; recommendations; faculty interview. The Commonwealth of Pennsylvania requires passing PRAXIS II tests prior to certification.

Fees and Expenses: Undergraduate: in-state $4,378 per academic year; out-of-state $10,946. Graduate: in-state $5,254 per academic year; out-of-state $8,408. Required fees: $1,169. On-campus room and board: $4,298.

Financial Aid: Resources specifically for eligible students enrolled in teacher education programs are awarded on the basis of financial need and academic merit. The institution has a Program Participation Agreement with the U.S. Department of Education for eligible students to receive Pell Grants and other federal aid. Teacher scholarships available to qualifying students. *Contact:* Patty A. Hiadio at: (724) 738-2044 or e-mail at: patty.hiadio@sru.edu.

Accreditation: *Regional:* MSA. *Professional:* NCATE. *Member of:* AACTE. *Approved by:* Pennsylvania Department of Education.

Undergraduate Programs: The elementary education curriculum allows student the opportunity to become competent and effective state-of-the-art teachers. Programs lead to the Bachelor of Science in Education and certification to teach kindergarten to grade 6.

Secondary education coursework is offered by the Secondary Education/Foundations of Education Department and various other departments in the College of Humanities, Fine and Performing Arts, and the College of Health, Environment, and Science. The program leads to the Bachelor of Science degree and certification to teach grades 7-12. Major content areas include: English, French, Spanish, citizenship/history, mathematics, science.

A special education program prepares educators to work with children who have special needs. The program leads to the Bachelor of Science Degree in Education and certification to teach kindergarten through grade 12. An optional dual certification in elementary education is also offered.

Graduate Programs: Master of Education degree programs are offered in elementary and secondary school counseling (48 credit hours); elementary education/early childhood with concentration options in mathematics and science, 30 credit hours (K-grade 8) and reading, 36 credit hours (K-grade 12); secondary education: basic teaching program, 36 credit hours, in mathematics, biology, chemistry, physics, earth/space science; advanced teaching program, 36 credit hours, in mathematics/science education, special education, educational technology, and/or counseling.

Licensure/Reciprocity: Pennsylvania. Students seeking teaching certification in a state other than Pennsylvania should consult with that state's teacher certification office early in their program of study to insure compliance with requirements. Many state directors of teacher credentialing have signed Interstate Agreements through NASDTEC that expedite the certification process.

SWARTHMORE COLLEGE

Department of Educational Studies
500 College Avenue
Swarthmore, Pennsylvania 19081
Phone: (610) 328-8343
Fax: (610) 328-6892
E-mail: lsmulyan1@swarthmore.edu
Internet: http://www.swarthmore.edu

Institution Description: Swarthmore College is a private, independent, nonprofit college. The college was founded by the Religious Society of Friends in 1864.

The Department of Educational Studies aims to enable students to investigate educational theory, policy, research, and practice from a variety of disciplinary perspectives.

Institution Control: Private.

Calendar: Semester. Academic year September to June.

Official(s): Dr. Lisa Smulyan, Department Head.

Faculty: Full-time 4; part-time 2; adjunct 2.

Degrees Awarded: 20 baccalaureate.

Admission Requirements: *Undergraduate:* Graduation from an accredited secondary school or GED; College Board SAT or ACT composite. *Teacher education specific:* GPA of 3.0 at the accumulation of 48 semester credits; 6 credit hours each in mathematics and English; introductory course in education; faculty interview; passing scores on PRAXIS I exams (reading, writing,

SWARTHMORE COLLEGE—*cont'd*

mathematics). NOTE: Tests must be the new computerized tests that were implemented January 16, 2002. Tests taken prior to that date will not be accepted.

Fees and Expenses: $27,272 per academic year. Required fees: $302. On-campus room and board: $8,900.

Financial Aid: Financial aid is based on financial need. The institution has a Program Participation Agreement with the U.S. Department of Education for eligible students to receive Pell Grants and other federal aid. *Contact:* Financial Aid Office at: (610) 328-8358 or e-mail at: finaid@swarthmore.edu.

Accreditation: *Regional:* MSA. *Approved by:* Pennsylvania Department of Education.

Undergraduate Programs: The Department of Educational Studies offers both introductory and upper level courses that draw on theory and research in psychology, sociology, anthropology, political science, economics, and history. Students interested in education may complete the requirements for teacher certification and/or design a special major in education and another discipline in either the course or honors program. The department supports two kinds of minors: teaching and field-based minor and educational studies minor.

Competency-based teacher certification programs are offered in biology, chemistry, civics, English, French, German, mathematics, physics, Spanish, and social science. To be certified, students must complete a major in their area of certification. As part of the certification program, students teach for a minimum of twelve weeks and receive weekly supervision from a college supervisor. Placement during practice teaching is available in a range of public and private schools, including several Friends schools in the Philadelphia area. Students desiring certification in elementary education can do so through a collaborative program with Eastern College.

Licensure/Reciprocity: Pennsylvania. Students seeking teaching certification in a state other than Pennsylvania should consult with that state's teacher certification office early in their program of study to insure compliance with requirements. Many state directors of teacher credentialing have signed Interstate Agreements through NASDTEC that expedite the certification process.

TEMPLE UNIVERSITY

College of Education
Department of Curriculum and Instruction

238 Ritter Annex
1301 Cecil B. Moore Avenue
Philadelphia, Pennsylvania 19122-6901
Phone: (215) 204-8011
Fax: (215) 204-5694
E-mail: cite@temple.edu
Internet: http://www.temple.edu

Institution Description: Temple University is an independent, state-related institution. It was established in 1884.

The Department of Curriculum, Instruction, and Technology in Education (CITE) prepares K-12 teachers for traditional and nontraditional settings.

Institution Control: Private.

Calendar: Semester. Academic year August to May.

Official(s): Dr. Thomas Walker, Chair.

Faculty: Full-time 34.

Degrees Awarded: 497 baccalaureate; 290 master's; 27 doctorate.

Admission Requirements: *Undergraduate:* Graduation from an accredited secondary school or GED; College Board SAT or ACT composite. *Teacher education specific:* Students apply during sophomore year; 2.75 GPA; faculty interview; personal goal statement; passing scores on PRAXIS I exams (reading, writing, mathematics). NOTE: Tests must be the computerized tests that were implemented January 16, 2002. Tests taken prior to that

date will not be accepted. *Graduate:* Baccalaureate degree from a regionally accredited institution. *Teacher education specific:* 3.0 GPA; GRE or Miller Analogies scores; completion of all required departmental exams; recommendations; faculty interview. The Commonwealth of Pennsylvania requires passing PRAXIS II tests prior to certification.

Fees and Expenses: Undergraduate: in-state $8,594; out-of-state $15,354. Graduate: $534 per credit hour. On-campus room and board: $7,098. Other expenses: $4,213. Books and supplies: $800.

Financial Aid: Resources specifically for eligible students enrolled in teacher education programs are awarded on the basis of financial need and academic merit. The institution has a Program Participation Agreement with the U.S. Department of Education for eligible students to receive Pell Grants and other federal aid. Teacher scholarships available to qualifying students. *Contact:* Financial Aid Office at: (215) 294-1458.

Accreditation: *Regional:* MSA. *Professional:* NCATE. *Member of:* AACTE. *Approved by:* Pennsylvania Department of Education.

Undergraduate Programs: The Bachelor of Science in Education program prepares professional teachers for elementary and secondary schools as well as business and industry. Certifications are available in elementary/early childhood education, secondary education (concentrations in English, foreign language [French, German, Hebrew, Italian, Latin, Portuguese, Spanish], mathematics, science [biology, chemistry, earth and space science, general science, physics], special education [combined program with elementary education]), vocational/technical education (business education, cooperative education, industrial education marketing education). A minimum of 125 semester credits is required for the bachelor's degree.

A five-year combined BA/MA certification program offers the opportunity for undergraduates to obtain the bachelor's degree while simultaneously pursing a Master in Education degree with certification.

Graduate Programs: The Master of Education degree enables those who hold bachelor's degrees in non-educational areas to earn teaching certification. Graduate teaching certification is available in the areas of: elementary education, English, foreign language (French, German, Hebrew, Italian, Portuguese, Spanish), mathematics, reading, science (biology, chemistry, earth and space science, general science, physics), special studies, special education, vocation education (business, cooperative, industrial, marketing, distributive education). Successful completion of the degree includes 30-36 hours of coursework depending on the specialty.

The Master of Science in Education is for individuals who wish to increase their expertise in a content area and/or prepare for higher level positions. Candidates choose among six areas: early childhood, elementary education, inclusive school practice, second/foreign language, vocational education. The program requires the completion of 33 semester hours of coursework for secondary education and 36 for elementary education.

Licensure/Reciprocity: Pennsylvania. Students seeking teaching certification in a state other than Pennsylvania should consult with that state's teacher certification office early in their program of study to insure compliance with requirements. Many state directors of teacher credentialing have signed Interstate Agreements through NASDTEC that expedite the certification process.

UNIVERSITY OF PENNSYLVANIA

Graduate School of Education
Teacher Education

1 College Hall
34th and Spruce Streets
Philadelphia, Pennsylvania 19104
Phone: (215) 898-5000
E-mail: info@admissions.upenn.edu
Internet: http://www.upenn.edu

Institution Description: The University of Pennsylvania is a private, state-aided institution. It was established as Charity School in 1740. The name was changed to University of the State of Pennsylvania in 1779 and the present name was adopted in 1791.

The Graduate School of Education offers master's and doctoral programs in a variety of areas.

Institution Control: Private.

Calendar: Semester. Academic year September to April.

Official(s): Dr. Stanton E.R. Wortham, Chair, Educational Leadership.

Faculty: Full-time 27 (Educational Leadership).

Degrees Awarded: 3 baccalaureate; 253 master's; 54 doctorate.

Admission Requirements: *Undergraduate:* Graduation from an accredited secondary school or GED; College Board SAT or ACT composite. *Teacher education specific:* Students are admitted to undergraduate study for a liberal arts subject major. *Graduate:* Baccalaureate degree from a regionally accredited institution. *Teacher education specific:* 3.0 GPA; GRE or Miller Analogies scores; completion of all required departmental exams; two recommendations; faculty interview. The Commonwealth of Pennsylvania requires passing PRAXIS II tests prior to certification.

Fees and Expenses: $29,318 per academic year. On-campus room and board: $8,642. Other expenses: $8,642. Books and supplies: $810.

Financial Aid: Resources specifically for eligible students enrolled in teacher education programs are awarded on the basis of financial need and academic merit. The institution has a Program Participation Agreement with the U.S. Department of Education for eligible students to receive Pell Grants and other federal aid. Teacher scholarships available to qualifying students. *Contact:* Financial Aid Office at: (215) 898-7526.

Accreditation: *Regional:* MSA. *Approved by:* Pennsylvania Department of Education.

Undergraduate Programs: The undergraduate major in elementary education is offered in cooperation with the College of Arts and Sciences. Students earn the bachelor's degree and teaching certification for grades kindergarten through six and are encouraged to take additional coursework in mathematics, American history, art, and music.

Graduate Programs: The Master of Science in Education programs provides a basis of specialized knowledge and prepares graduates for entry-level positions in grade K-12 schools. Teacher education programs are offered in elementary education and secondary education. Master's degree requirements vary by program, but all require a minimum of 10 course units. Preparing students for professional certification is an integral component of the programs. Most students take courses in at least one research methodology and complete a mentorship or field placements.

The Master of Science program in statistics, measurement, and research technology is designed for individuals who are preparing for careers in information rich environments, especially research and assessment organizations.

The Master of Philosophy in Education program is offered in policy research, evaluation, and measurement. The program is designed for professionals who have already earned a relevant master's degree and who wish to advance their mastery is this subject area.

The Doctor of Education and Doctor of Philosophy programs are offered for professionals in the area of teaching, learning, and curriculum and the area of reading/writing/literacy.

Licensure/Reciprocity: Pennsylvania. Students seeking teaching certification in a state other than Pennsylvania should consult with that state's teacher certification office early in their program of study to insure compliance with requirements. Many state directors of teacher credentialing have signed Interstate Agreements through NASDTEC that expedite the certification process.

UNIVERSITY OF PITTSBURGH
School of Education
5N01 Wesley W. Posvar Hall
230 S. Bouquet Street
Pittsburgh, Pennsylvania 15260
Phone: (412) 648-1769
Fax: (412) 648-1825
E-mail: soe@pitt.edu
Internet: http://www.pitt.edu

Institution Description: The University of Pittsburgh is a nonsectarian, coeducational, state-related institution. The university was established and chartered as Pittsburgh Academy in 1787. It was incorporated as Western University of Pennsylvania in 1819. The present name was adopted in 1908.

The School of Education offers graduate teacher preparation programs only. The programs are certification or certification plus the master's degree. The two programs differ in their prerequisite requirements, the teaching experience they provide, and the intensity and extent of coursework.

Institution Control: Public.

Calendar: Semester. Trimester. Academic year September to August.

Official(s): Dr. George Zimmerman, Department Chair; Dr. Anthony Petrosky, Director of Teacher Education.

Faculty: Full-time 90; part-time 61; adjunct 38.

Degrees Awarded: 22 baccalaureate; 246 master's; 55 doctorate.

Admission Requirements: *Graduate:* Baccalaureate degree from a regionally accredited institution. *Teacher education specific:* Official transcripts from all prior institutions attended; 3 letters of recommendation; statement of career goals and degree objectives; evidence of passing scores on PRAXIS I exams (reading, writing, mathematics). NOTE: Tests must be the computerized tests that were implemented January 16, 2002. Tests taken prior to that date will not be accepted.

Financial Aid: Resources specifically for eligible students enrolled in teacher education programs are awarded on the basis of financial need and academic merit. The institution has a Program Participation Agreement with the U.S. Department of Education for eligible students to receive Pell Grants and other federal aid. Teacher scholarships available to qualifying students. *Contact:* Jackie Harden at: (412) 648-7060 or e-mail at: jharden@pitt.edu.

Accreditation: *Regional:* MSA. *Member of:* AACTE. *Approved by:* Pennsylvania Department of Education.

Graduate Programs: The School of Education offers certification in early childhood education (birth - age 8, including certification in K-3rd grade), as well as elementary education that prepares individuals to teach in kindergarten through 6th grade. In secondary education, the Commonwealth of Pennsylvania requires different courses and training in different subject areas. Pitt offers programs for English/communications education, foreign language education, mathematics education, science education, and social studies education. In each of these teacher preparation programs, there are two options: the Professional Year (certificate only) and the Master of Arts in Teaching (certificate and graduate degree). Certification as a Reading Specialist is also available.

Programs in special education are offered that prepare students to teach children who are deaf and hard of hearing, those with mental and physical disabilities, and children who are blind or visually impaired, as well as preparing students who are interested in careers providing early intervention for children age birth through 5 years old with these disabilities. special education students have the choice of certification or certification plus the Master's degree.

Through its educational leadership program, the school offers programs for the Supervisor of Curriculum and Instruction Certificate, the Superintendents Letter of Eligibility, and certification as a K-Grade 12 School Principal.

Licensure/Reciprocity: Pennsylvania. Students seeking teaching certification in a state other than Pennsylvania should consult with that state's teacher certification office early in their program of study to insure compliance with requirements.

UNIVERSITY OF PITTSBURGH—*cont'd*

Many state directors of teacher credentialing have signed Interstate Agreements through NASDTEC that expedite the certification process.

UNIVERSITY OF SCRANTON

Education Department

800 Linden Street
Scranton, Pennsylvania 18510-2192
Phone: (570) 941-7421
Fax: (570) 941-5515
E-mail: lod1@uofs.edu
Internet: http://www.uofs.edu

Institution Description: The University of Scranton is a private institution conducted by the Society of Jesus, Roman Catholic Church. It was founded in 1888.

The Department of Education endeavors to contribute to the improvement of education by preparing informed, inquiring, and skilled professionals.

Institution Control: Private.

Calendar: Semester. Academic year August to May.

Official(s): Dr. Deborah Eville, Lo, Chair.

Faculty: Full-time 15; adjunct 21.

Degrees Awarded: 122 baccalaureate; 45 master's.

Admission Requirements: *Undergraduate:* Graduation from an accredited secondary school or GED; College Board SAT or ACT composite. *Teacher education specific:* Students apply during second semester of sophomore year; 2.75 GPA; faculty interview; passing scores on PRAXIS I exams (reading, writing, mathematics). NOTE: Tests must be the computerized tests that were implemented January 16, 2002. Tests taken prior to that date will not be accepted. *Graduate:* Baccalaureate degree from a regionally accredited institution. *Teacher education specific:* 3.0 GPA; completion of all required departmental exams; recommendations; faculty interview. The Commonwealth of Pennsylvania requires passing PRAXIS II tests prior to certification.

Fees and Expenses: Undergraduate: $21,208 per academic year. Graduate: $590 per credit hour. Required fees: $100. On-campus room and board: room $5,600; meals $3,800. Books and supplies: $500.

Financial Aid: Resources specifically for eligible students enrolled in teacher education programs are awarded on the basis of financial need and academic merit. The institution has a Program Participation Agreement with the U.S. Department of Education for eligible students to receive Pell Grants and other federal aid. Teacher scholarships available to qualifying students. *Contact:* William Burke at: (570) 941-7700.

Accreditation: *Regional:* MSA. *Professional:* NCATE. *Member of:* AACTE. *Approved by:* Pennsylvania Department of Education.

Undergraduate Programs: The Department of Education offers degrees in early childhood, elementary, and special education, each leading to certification. Secondary education concentrations are offered in biology, chemistry, citizenship, communication, English, French, general science, German, Latin, mathematics, physics, Spanish. Elementary education leads to state certification (K-6) and early childhood education (preK-3). All programs require the completion of a general education core, professional studies, subject content area, field experiences, and student teaching. A minimum of 127 credit hours must be completed for the bachelor's degree.

Graduate Programs: Eight master's degree programs are offered: early childhood education, elementary education, secondary education, special education, school administration (principal certification K-12) school counseling, reading, and curriculum and instruction.

The secondary education program can be pursued by those new to the field of education as well as teachers advancing their knowledge. Concentrations leading to certification with a master's degree are: biology, chemistry, communications, English, French, general science, German, Latin, mathematics, physics, and citizenship.

Licensure/Reciprocity: Pennsylvania. Students seeking teaching certification in a state other than Pennsylvania should consult with that state's teacher certification office early in their program of study to insure compliance with requirements. Many state directors of teacher credentialing have signed Interstate Agreements through NASDTEC that expedite the certification process.

VALLEY FORGE CHRISTIAN COLLEGE

Education Department

1401 Charleston Road
Pennsylvania 19460
Phone: (610) 935-0450
Fax: (610) 935-9353
E-mail: agmcclure@vfcc.edu
Internet: http://www.vfcc.edu

Institution Description: Valley Forge Christian College is a private institution affiliated with the Assemblies of God. The college was established and chartered in 1939.

The Education Department offers undergraduate programs leading to teacher certification in Pennsylvania.

Institution Control: Private.

Calendar: Semester. Academic year August to May.

Official(s): Dr. Philip McLeod, Dean; Dr. Glenn McClure, Education Chair.

Faculty: Full-time 4.

Degrees Awarded: 10 baccalaureate.

Admission Requirements: *Undergraduate:* Graduation from an accredited secondary school or GED; College Board SAT or ACT composite. *Teacher education specific:* Evidence of Christian commitment; 3.0 GPA after sophomore year; faculty interview; passing scores on PRAXIS I exams (reading, writing, mathematics). NOTE: Tests must be the new computerized tests that were implemented January 16, 2002. Tests taken prior to that date will not be accepted. The state of Pennsylvania requires passing PRAXIS II tests before certification.

Fees and Expenses: $4,360 per semester. $400 student teaching fee senior year. On-campus room and board: $4,750 to $5,560. Books and supplies: $700.

Financial Aid: Resources specifically for eligible students enrolled in teacher education programs are awarded on the basis of financial need and academic merit. The institution has a Program Participation Agreement with the U.S. Department of Education for eligible students to receive Pell Grants and other federal aid. Teacher scholarships available to qualifying students. *Contact:* Evie Meyer at: (610) 917-1417 or e-mail at: eemeyer@vfcc.edu.

Accreditation: *Regional:* MSA. *Approved by:* Pennsylvania Department of Education.

Undergraduate Programs: Programs offered by the Education Department include: early childhood education leading to the Bachelor of Science degree and certification to teach in grades N-3 (138 credits required including 30 credits of required Bible or Bible-related courses).

The elementary education program leads to the Bachelor of Science degree and certification to teach grades K-6 (142 credits required). The music education program leads to the Bachelor of Science degree with certification to teach grades K-12 (138.5 credits are required). All programs include a student teaching experience with a minimum of 60 days during the student's final semester.

Licensure/Reciprocity: Pennsylvania. Students seeking teaching certification in a state other than Pennsylvania should consult with that state's teacher certification office early in their program of study to insure compliance with requirements. Many state directors of teacher credentialing have signed Interstate Agreements through NASDTEC that expedite the certification process.

WAYNESBURG COLLEGE

Education Department
300 Miller Hall
51 West College Street
Waynesburg, Pennsylvania 15370
Phone: (724) 852-3243
Fax: (724) 627-8124
E-mail: dwoodrum@waynesburg.edu
Internet: http://www.waynesburg.edu

Institution Description: Waynesburg College is a private college affiliated with The Presbyterian Church (U.S.A.). The college was formed as Waynesburg College by a merger of Greene Academy and Madison College in 1849.

The Education Department offers teacher preparatory programs at the undergraduate and graduate levels. The graduate programs began in the fall of 2003.

Institution Control: Private.

Calendar: Semester. Academic year August to May.

Official(s): Dr. Diane T. Eoodrum, Chair.

Faculty: Full-time 5; part-time 3; adjunct 5.

Degrees Awarded: 22 baccalaureate; 2 master's.

Admission Requirements: *Undergraduate:* Graduation from an accredited secondary school or GED; College Board SAT or ACT composite. *Teacher education specific:* Students apply after 3 semesters; 2.5 GPA; faculty interview; passing scores on PRAXIS I exams (reading, writing, mathematics). NOTE: Tests must be the new computerized tests that were implemented January 16, 2002. Tests taken prior to that date will not be accepted. *Graduate:* Baccalaureate degree from a regionally accredited institution. *Teacher education specific:* 3.0 GPA; completion of all required departmental exams; two recommendations; faculty interview. The Commonwealth of Pennsylvania requires passing PRAXIS II tests prior to certification.

Fees and Expenses: Undergraduate: $13,520 per academic year. Required fees: $330 activity fee. On-campus room and board: $5,520. Books and supplies: $700.

Financial Aid: Resources specifically for eligible students enrolled in teacher education programs are awarded on the basis of financial need and academic merit. The institution has a Program Participation Agreement with the U.S. Department of Education for eligible students to receive Pell Grants and other federal aid. Teacher scholarships available to qualifying students. *Contact:* Financial Aid Office at: (724) 852-3243.

Accreditation: *Regional:* MSA. *Approved by:* Pennsylvania Department of Education.

Undergraduate Programs: The elementary education program prepares teachers for certification in regular education for grades K-6. Students take general liberal arts courses for two years before official admission into the Education Department. After two semesters of theory, the students spend their final year in methods classes, a practicum and student teaching.

Special education students in this option qualify for certification in regular elementary education (k-6) and special education (N-12). Students take 15 additional course credits in special education and complete field experiences in both areas. Special education field experiences are at both elementary and secondary levels.

Secondary education students interested in teaching in middle school or high school (7-12) must choose English, history, mathematics, biology, or chemistry for their content area specialization. These students take the same courses that a major in their content would take plus educational theory and methods. There are early field experiences for the secondary teacher candidate culminating in a semester of full-time student teaching. All baccalaureate programs require the completion of the general education core, professional studies, subject content area, field experiences, and student teaching.

Graduate Programs: The Master of Education and Master of Arts in Teaching degree programs were instituted in the fall of 2003. Contact the college for details regarding enrollment and specific course requirements.

Licensure/Reciprocity: Pennsylvania. Students seeking teaching certification in a state other than Pennsylvania should consult with that state's teacher certification office early in their program of study to insure compliance with requirements. Many state directors of teacher credentialing have signed Interstate Agreements through NASDTEC that expedite the certification process.

WEST CHESTER UNIVERSITY OF PENNSYLVANIA

School of Education
Teacher Education Program
302 Recitation Hall
South High Street
West Chester, Pennsylvania 19383
Phone: (610) 436-2956
E-mail: ugadmiss@wcupa.edu
Internet: http://www.wcupa.edu

Institution Description: West Chester University of Pennsylvania, formerly West Chester College, is a state institution. The school was chartered as West Chester Academy in 1812. It became Chester State Normal School in 1871 and the name was changed to West Chester State Teachers College in 1927. The present name was adopted in 1983.

The primary mission of the Teacher Education Program is the preparation and continuing development of educational professionals in order to meet the needs of diverse student populations in the public schools and other education environments throughout the Commonwealth of Pennsylvania.

Institution Control: Public.

Calendar: Semester. Academic year August to May.

Official(s): Dr. Yi-Ming Hsu, Chairperson, Department of Professional and secondary education.

Faculty: Not reported.

Degrees Awarded: 370 baccalaureate; 189 master's.

Admission Requirements: *Undergraduate:* Graduation from an accredited secondary school or GED; College Board SAT. *Teacher education specific:* GPA of 2.8 at the accumulation of 48 semester credits; faculty interview; passing scores on PRAXIS I exams (reading, writing, mathematics). NOTE: Tests must be the new computerized tests that were implemented January 16, 2002. Tests taken prior to that date will not be accepted. *Graduate:* Baccalaureate degree from a regionally accredited institution. *Teacher education specific:* 3.0 GPA; completion of all required departmental exams; recommendations; faculty interview. The Commonwealth of Pennsylvania requires passing PRAXIS II tests prior to certification.

Fees and Expenses: Undergraduate: in-state $5,756 per academic year; out-of-state $12,704. Graduate: Tuition charged per credit hour. On-campus room and board: $5,508. Other expenses: $2,608. Books and supplies: $800.

Financial Aid: Resources specifically for eligible students enrolled in teacher education programs are awarded on the basis of financial need and academic merit. The institution has a Program Participation Agreement with the U.S. Department of Education for eligible students to receive Pell Grants and other federal aid. Teacher scholarships available to qualifying students. *Contact:* Financial Aid Office at: (610) 436-2627.

Accreditation: *Regional:* MSA. *Professional:* NCATE. *Member of:* AACTE. *Approved by:* Pennsylvania Department of Education.

Undergraduate Programs: The Bachelor of Science in Education program in elementary education is designed to provide a broad education, an understanding of children, and the knowledge, skills, and strategies to teach all aspects of the elementary school program. The Bachelor of Science in Education - early childhood education program is designed to provide the special preparation required for early childhood education careers in public or private settings and in supervisory work in non-public early childhood programs. The Bachelor of Science in Education - special education provides comprehensive preparation to teach students with learning disabilities, mental retardation, emotional disturbances, and physical disabilities.

WEST CHESTER UNIVERSITY OF PENNSYLVANIA—*cont'd*

The Bachelor of Science in Education is awarded to those who complete the core curriculum and requirements in an area of concentration. Academic specialization is available in biology, chemistry, citizenship education, communications, earth and space science, English, French, general science, German, Latin, mathematics, physics, Russian, and Spanish. The citizenship education option includes concentrations in geography, history, and political science.

All bachelor programs require the completion of a general education core, professional studies, subject content area, field experiences, and student teaching.

Graduate Programs: The Master of Education in elementary education is offered with areas of focus in literacy, culturally responsive education, inclusion, technology, English as a second language, or an area of interest approved by the graduate coordinator. The Master of Education in special education is offered with certification in special education as well as the Master of Education in secondary education. All master's degree programs have specific course requirements.

Licensure/Reciprocity: Pennsylvania. Students seeking teaching certification in a state other than Pennsylvania should consult with that state's teacher certification office early in their program of study to insure compliance with requirements. Many state directors of teacher credentialing have signed Interstate Agreements through NASDTEC that expedite the certification process.

WIDENER UNIVERSITY

Center for Education

One University Place
Chester, Pennsylvania 19013-5792
Phone: (610) 499-4294
Fax: (610) 499-4623
E-mail: admissions.office@widener.edu
Internet: http://www.widener.edu

Institution Description: Widener University is an independent, nonprofit comprehensive teaching institution. It was established in 1821.

The Center for Education offers a variety of programs leading to the teaching credential at the undergraduate and graduate levels.

Institution Control: Private.

Calendar: Semester. Academic year September to May.

Official(s): Dr. Shelley B. Wepner, Dean.

Faculty: Full-time 24; part-time 40; adjunct 64.

Degrees Awarded: 8 baccalaureate; 158 master's; 32 doctorate.

Admission Requirements: *Undergraduate:* Graduation from an accredited secondary school with 16 academic units or GED; College Board SAT or ACT composite. *Teacher education specific:* GPA of 3.0; faculty interview; passing scores on PRAXIS I exams (reading, writing, mathematics). NOTE: Tests must be the new computerized tests that were implemented January 16, 2002. Tests taken prior to that date will not be accepted. *Graduate:* Baccalaureate degree from a regionally accredited institution. *Teacher education specific:* 3.0 GPA; GRE or Miller Analogies scores; completion of all required departmental exams; recommendations; faculty interview. The Commonwealth of Pennsylvania requires passing PRAXIS II tests prior to certification.

Fees and Expenses: Undergraduate: $20,450 per academic year. Graduate: $435 per credit hour. Required fees: Various. On-campus room and board: $7,190 to $8,700 depending on meal plan. Other expenses: $1,305. Books and supplies: $900.

Financial Aid: Resources specifically for eligible students enrolled in teacher education programs are awarded on the basis of financial need and academic merit. The institution has a Program Participation Agreement with the U.S. Department of Education for eligible students to receive Pell Grants and other federal aid. Teacher scholarships available to qualifying students. *Contact:* Mary Cay Reilly, Director, Financial Aid at: (610) 499-4174 or e-mail at: mary.c.reilly@widener.edu.

Accreditation: *Regional:* MSA. *Member of:* AACTE. *Approved by:* Pennsylvania Department of Education.

Undergraduate Programs: Students interested in obtaining teacher certification can be certified to teach elementary education, early childhood education, special education, or secondary education through the Center for Education. The secondary education program offers certification in biology, chemistry, earth and space science, French, mathematics, physics, social studies, and Spanish. Students who are certified in Spanish,English/French and are certified in elementary education can get certification in bilingual education. The completion of all the requirements for a major in French or Spanish and the completion of all teacher education requirements will permit a student to be certified as a teacher of that language upon graduation.

All baccalaureate programs require the completion of a general education core, professional studies, subject content area, field experiences, and student teaching.

Graduate Programs: The Center for Education has an extensive range of programs leading to the Master of Education degree, most of which require 30 credits. A thesis is not required. Most of the programs that lead to the master's degree are also available as certification programs. In many cases, students can obtain certification and by earning a few extra credits, earn their master's degree.

Program options include: adult education, assistant superintendent, counselor education, early childhood education, educational foundations, educational leadership, educational psychology, elementary education, English and language arts, health education, home and school visitor, human sexuality education, mathematics, middle school, reading, school nurse, school psychologist, science and technology, secondary education, social studies, special education student personnel services, supervision, technology in education.

The Center for Education offers several programs that lead to the Doctor of Education degree. These programs are for those who are interested in developing greater experience and acquiring the necessary credentials for professional advancement in a specific area of study.

Licensure/Reciprocity: Pennsylvania. Students seeking teaching certification in a state other than Pennsylvania should consult with that state's teacher certification office early in their program of study to insure compliance with requirements. Many state directors of teacher credentialing have signed Interstate Agreements through NASDTEC that expedite the certification process.

WILKES UNIVERSITY

Department of Education and Psychology
Teacher Education Program

170 South Franklin Street
Wilkes-Barre, Pennsylvania 18766-0001
Phone: (570) 408-4680
Fax: (570) 408-7872
E-mail: polachek@wilkes.edu
Internet: http://www.wilkes.edu

Institution Description: Wilkes University is a private, independent, nonprofit comprehensive college. It was founded in 1933.

The Teacher Education Program prepares future educators with the tools necessary to be successful at their craft and develop competence in knowledge pedagogy and the content areas.

Institution Control: Private.

Calendar: Semester. Academic year August to May.

Official(s): Dr. Darin Fields, Dean; Dr. Diane Polachek, Chair.

Faculty: Full-time 9; part-time 2; adjunct 15.

Degrees Awarded: 4 baccalaureate; 526 master's.

Admission Requirements: *Undergraduate:* Graduation from an accredited secondary school or GED; College Board SAT. *Teacher education specific:* GPA of 2.8 at the accumulation of 48 semester credits; completion of six credits each in mathematics and English; faculty interview; passing scores on PRAXIS I exams (reading, writing, mathematics). NOTE: Tests must be the new computerized tests that were implemented January 16, 2002. Tests taken prior to that date will not be accepted. *Graduate:* Baccalaureate degree from a regionally accredited institution. *Teacher education specific:* 3.0 GPA; completion of all required departmental exams; recommendations; faculty interview; teaching license where required by program pursued. The Commonwealth of Pennsylvania requires passing PRAXIS II tests prior to certification.

Fees and Expenses: Undergraduate: $498 per credit hour. Graduate: $249 per credit hour. Required fees: $690. On-campus room and board: $8,000. Other fees may apply.

Financial Aid: Resources specifically for eligible students enrolled in teacher education programs are awarded on the basis of financial need and academic merit. The institution has a Program Participation Agreement with the U.S. Department of Education for eligible students to receive Pell Grants and other federal aid. Teacher scholarships available to qualifying students. *Contact:* Rachael Lohman at: (570) 408-4346 or e-mail at: rachel@wilkes.edu.

Accreditation: *Regional:* MSA. *Approved by:* Pennsylvania Department of Education.

Undergraduate Programs: The Department of Education offers a Bachelor of Arts in elementary education and programs leading to certification in the areas of: biology, chemistry, citizenship education, communications, early childhood education, earth and space science, English, French, general science, mathematics, speech, and special education. All programs require the completion of a general education core, professional studies, subject content area, field experiences, and student teaching. A minimum of 121 credit hours must be completed for the baccalaureate degree.

Graduate Programs: Master of Science in Education degree programs are offered in: educational leadership, educational development and strategies, special education, instructional technology, classroom technology. Each program has specific course and program requirements.

Licensure/Reciprocity: Pennsylvania. Students seeking teaching certification in a state other than Pennsylvania should consult with that state's teacher certification office early in their program of study to insure compliance with requirements. Many state directors of teacher credentialing have signed Interstate Agreements through NASDTEC that expedite the certification process.

YORK COLLEGE OF PENNSYLVANIA

Department of Education
Country Club Road
York, Pennsylvania 17405-7199
Phone: (717) 815-1422
Fax: (717) 849-1629
E-mail: pmassa@ycp.edu
Internet: http://www.ycp.edu

Institution Description: York College of Pennsylvania is a private, independent, nonprofit, liberal arts college. The college was founded as the York Academy in 1887.

The Department of Education offers preparation programs dedicated to building the leadership capacity of regional public and private schools.

Institution Control: Private.

Calendar: Semester. Academic year August to May.

Official(s): Patrick J. Massa, Chairman.

Faculty: Full-time 7; adjunct 47.

Degrees Awarded: 155 baccalaureate.

Admission Requirements: *Undergraduate:* Graduation from an accredited secondary school or GED; College Board SAT or ACT composite. *Teacher education specific:* Completion of 48 college credits: 3.0 GPA; 6 credits each in mathematics and English; faculty interview; passing scores on PRAXIS I exams (reading, writing, mathematics). NOTE: Tests must be the computerized tests that were implemented January 16, 2002. Tests taken prior to that date will not be accepted. The Commonwealth of Pennsylvania requires passing PRAXIS II tests prior to certification. *Graduate:* Baccalaureate degree from a regionally accredited institution. *Teacher education specific:* 3.0 GPA; completion of all required departmental exams; recommendations; faculty interview; teaching license where required by program pursued. The Commonwealth of Pennsylvania requires passing PRAXIS II tests prior to certification.

Fees and Expenses: $7,500 per academic year. Graduate: $365 per credit hour. Required fees: $500. On-campus room and board: $5,570. Books and supplies: 600.

Financial Aid: Resources specifically for eligible students enrolled in teacher education programs are awarded on the basis of financial need and academic merit. The institution has a Program Participation Agreement with the U.S. Department of Education for eligible students to receive Pell Grants and other federal aid. Teacher scholarships available to qualifying students. *Contact:* Calvin Williams at: (717) 815-1226 or e-mail at: cwilliam@ycp.edu.

Accreditation: *Regional:* MSA. *Approved by:* Pennsylvania Department of Education.

Undergraduate Programs: Areas of specialization leading to the bachelor's degree and certification include: elementary education (K-6); dual elementary (K-6) and special education (N-12); secondary education (7-12) with concentrations in biology, citizenship, communication, English, general science, mathematics, social sciences. All programs require the completion of a general education core, professional studies, subject content area, field experiences, and student teaching.

Graduate Programs: The Master of Education program prepares educators for positions of administrative/instructional leadership in the public or private school setting. Areas of degree specialization include school leadership, reading, and a coursework sequence leading to certification as reading specialist. Candidates must complete four core courses as well as the program of study developed for their area of specialization.

Licensure/Reciprocity: Pennsylvania. Students seeking teaching certification in a state other than Pennsylvania should consult with that state's teacher certification office early in their program of study to insure compliance with requirements. Many state directors of teacher credentialing have signed Interstate Agreements through NASDTEC that expedite the certification process.

PUERTO RICO

UNIVERSITY OF PUERTO RICO, RIO PIEDRAS CAMPUS

Eugenio Maria de Hostos College of Education
P.O. Box 23300
University Station
Rio Piedras, Puerto Rico 00931-3300
Phone: (787) 764-2205
Fax: (787) 763-4130
E-mail: websrv@rrpac.upr.clu.edu
Internet: http://www.rrp.upr.edu

Institution Description: The campus was established in 1903.
The College of Education facilitates the preparation of learners and educator leaders. The college has the mission of contributing to the achievement of individual and collective goals of the Puerto Rican community through the formation of learners and educator leaders.

Institution Control: Public.

Calendar: Semester. Academic year August to May.

Official(s): Dr. Maria A. Trizarry, Dean; Dr. Nivia A. Fernandez, Associate Dean.

Faculty: Full-time 200; part-time 18.

Degrees Awarded: 456 baccalaureate; 30 master's.

Admission Requirements: *Undergraduate:* Graduation from an accredited secondary school; College Board SAT or ACT composite. *Teacher education specific:* Minimum 2.5 GPA; 30 hours including four basic courses; additional requirements for specialty areas. *Graduate:* Baccalaureate degree. *Teacher education specific:* Student must fulfill general requirements for admission to graduate studies; PAEG or GRE scores; interview.

Fees and Expenses: Undergraduate: $1,245 per academic year. Graduate: $2,025 per academic year. On-campus room and board: $2,340 in-state; $6,620 our-of-state. Books and supplies: $1,320. Other expenses: $1,000.

Financial Aid: Resources specifically for eligible students enrolled in teacher education programs are awarded on the basis of financial need, academic merit, talent/skills. The institution has a Program Participation Agreement with the U.S. Department of Education for eligible students to receive Pell Grants and other federal aid. Teacher scholarships available to qualifying students. *Contact:* Ms. Luz M.Santiago at: (787) 764-0000, ext. 555.

Accreditation: *Regional:* MSA. *Professional:* NCATE. *Member of:* AACTE. *Approved by:* Puerto Rico Higher Education Council.

Undergraduate Programs: Undergraduate professional programs are offered in preschool (128 credits); elementary (K-3, 4-6); special education, teaching English as a second language (139 credits); secondary education (18 areas of specialization, 124-135 credits). The programs consist of courses and experiences designed to provide the knowledge, skills, and dispositions regarding the art and science of learning and teaching. In order to accomplish target candidates' performance levels, programs integrate four components: general education, content-subject, pedagogical, and professional.

Graduate Programs: The Graduate Studies Department offers master's and doctorate programs. Master in Education is offered in the areas of: curriculum and teaching (biology, chemistry, history, mathematics, physics, Spanish); early childhood education (with majors in elementary level, pre-school level, teaching of reading); educational administration and supervision; educational research and evaluation; guidance and counseling; family ecology and nutrition; special education; teaching of English as a second language.

Doctor of Education programs are offered in three areas of specialization: educational administration and supervision; curriculum and teaching; guidance and counseling. Applicants must possess a master's degree or equivalent, including a thesis or other work of a creative nature that demonstrates competence for further graduate study.

Licensure/Reciprocity: Puerto Rico. Students seeking teaching certification outside Puerto Rico should consult with the mainland state's teacher certification office early in their program of study to insure compliance with requirements. Many state directors of teacher credentialing have signed Interstate Agreements through NASDTEC that expedite the certification process.

RHODE ISLAND

BROWN UNIVERSITY
Department of Education
Teacher Education Program
Box 1938
22 Manning Walk
Providence, Rhode Island 02912
Phone: (401) 863-3364
Fax: (401) 863-1276
E-mail: education@brown.edu
Internet: http://www.brown.edu/departments/education

Institution Description: Brown University is a private, independent, nonprofit institution. It was established and chartered as Rhode Island College in 1764.

The Brown Teacher Education Program prepares future educators to understand fundamental principles of teaching and learning and to employ that understanding to work with all children, youth, families and communities.

Institution Control: Private.

Calendar: Semester. Academic year September to May.

Official(s): Dr. Lawrence Wakeford, Department Chairman; Dr. Carin Algava, Assistant Director of Teacher Education.

Faculty: Full-time 4; adjunct 5.

Degrees Awarded: 24 baccalaureate; 25 master's.

Admission Requirements: *Undergraduate:* Graduation from an accredited secondary school or GED; College Board SAT or ACT composite. *Teacher education specific:* Sufficient coursework in teaching field; essay in response to application questions; application by November of junior year; fieldwork and seminary in secondary education; PRAXIS I; letters of recommendation. *Graduate:* Baccalaureate degree from a regionally accredited institution. *Teacher education specific:* Undergraduate transcripts; personal statement; GRE scores; writing sample (English and elementary education applicants only); personal goal statement; letters of recommendation.

Fees and Expenses: Undergraduate/graduate: $27,856 per academic year. Room and board: Variable rates. Contact Residential Life Office at (401) 863-3500 for current information.

Financial Aid: Resources specifically for eligible students enrolled in teacher education programs are awarded on the basis of financial need and academic merit. The institution has a Program Participation Agreement with the U.S. Department of Education for eligible students to receive Pell Grants and other federal aid. Teacher scholarships available to qualifying students. *Contact:* Linda Gillette (graduate program only) at: (401) 863-3184 or e-mail at: Linda_Gillete@brown.edu.

Accreditation: *Regional:* NEASC. *Approved by:* Rhode Island Department of Education.

Undergraduate Programs: Working cooperatively with other departments of the university, the Department of Education offers a teacher education program that leads to certification for teaching at the secondary level (grades 7-12). Certification programs are offered in the biological sciences, English, history/social studies. The student must complete courses toward the baccalaureate degree in general education, professional studies, subject content area, field experience, and student teaching.

Graduate Programs: The Brown University/Wheeler School Master of Arts in Teaching program in elementary education is a 12-month program leading to Rhode Island Teacher Certifica-

tion in grades 1-6. The program offers experiences and coursework that inform students of the range of educational opportunities that exist in public, private, and charter schools.

The Master of Arts in Teaching secondary education program permits students to study their disciplines broadly and in depth as they prepare themselves to help adolescents appreciate the structure and essential questions that comprise the discipline. Students pursue courses that prepare them to teach English, history/social studies, or biology/science.

Licensure/Reciprocity: Rhode Island. Students seeking teaching certification in a state other than Rhode Island should consult with that state's teacher certification office early in their program of study to insure compliance with requirements. Many state directors of teacher credentialing have signed Interstate Agreements through NASDTEC that expedite the certification process.

PROVIDENCE COLLEGE
Education Department
322 Harkins Hall
549 River Avenue
Providence, Rhode Island 02918
Phone: (401) 865-2121
Fax: (401) 865-2057
E-mail: pcadmiss@providence.edu
Internet: http://www.providence.edu

Institution Description: Providence College is a private college affiliated with the Roman Catholic Church. The college was chartered and incorporated in 1917.

The Education Department offers programs in elementary/special education and secondary education,

Institution Control: Private.

Calendar: Semester. Academic year September to May.

Official(s): Dr. Catherine L. Keating, Department Head.

Faculty: Full-time 15; part-time 14.

Degrees Awarded: 82 baccalaureate; 190 master's.

Admission Requirements: *Undergraduate:* Graduation from an approved secondary school in top 20% of class; College Board SAT (600 verbal, 600 math). *Teacher education specific:* PRAXIS I; goal statement; letters of recommendation. *Graduate:* Baccalaureate degree from a regionally accredited institution. *Teacher education specific:* PRAXIS II prior to certification; letters of recommendation; faculty interview.

Fees and Expenses: Undergraduate: $21,000 per academic year. Graduate: $750 per 3-credit course. No on-campus housing.

Financial Aid: Resources specifically for eligible students enrolled in teacher education programs are awarded on the basis of financial need and academic merit. The institution has a Program Participation Agreement with the U.S. Department of Education for eligible students to receive Pell Grants and other federal aid. Teacher scholarships available to qualifying students. *Contact:* Dr. Herbert D'Arcy at: (401) 865-1000.

Accreditation: *Regional:* NEASC. *Professional:* NCATE. *Member of:* AACTE. *Approved by:* Rhode Island Department of Education.

Undergraduate Programs: The elementary/special education major is a combined program that emphasizes preparation in both areas and leads to the baccalaureate degree. The program

PROVIDENCE COLLEGE—*cont'd*

allows students to approach the field of education in the elementary area with an understanding of ways to meet differences within the elementary school organization. Students are required to follow a prescribed program that includes integrated coursework and field experiences.

Interdisciplinary secondary education majors are offered in biology, chemistry, English, history, mathematics, social studies, French, Italian, and Spanish. Students are required to have a background of general education, specialization in the subject area, and study in the field of education.

Graduate Programs: The Providence College Graduate Studies Program offers advanced degrees as follows: Master of Arts in Teaching in: mathematics; Master of Education in: administration, counseling, literacy, secondary education, special education. Each program has specific course and departmental requirements.

Licensure/Reciprocity: Rhode Island. Students seeking teaching certification in a state other than Rhode Island should consult with that state's teacher certification office early in their program of study to insure compliance with requirements. Many state directors of teacher credentialing have signed Interstate Agreements through NASDTEC that expedite the certification process.

RHODE ISLAND COLLEGE
Feinstein School of Education and Human Development
600 Mount Pleasant Avenue
Providence, Rhode Island 02908
Phone: (401) 456-8110
Fax: (401) 456-8590
E-mail: jabucci@ric.edu
Internet: http://www.ric.edu

Institution Description: Rhode Island College is a state institution that was established as Rhode Island State Normal School in 1854.

The mission of the Feinstein School of Education and Human Development is to prepare educational and human service professionals for success in school and agency settings.

Institution Control: Public.

Calendar: Semester. Academic year September to May.

Official(s): Dr. John A. Bucci, Dean; Dr. Julie Wollman-Bonilla, Associate Dean.

Faculty: Full-time 71; part-time 23; adjunct 19.

Degrees Awarded: 360 baccalaureate; 191 master's.

Admission Requirements: *Undergraduate:* Graduation from an approved secondary school or GED; College Board SAT or ACT composite. *Teacher education specific:* PRAXIS I; goal statement; letters of recommendation. *Graduate:* Baccalaureate degree from a regionally accredited institution. *Teacher education specific:* The Rhode Island Teacher Education (RITE) Program requires a substantial amount of appropriate coursework in an academic discipline for which secondary certification is sought; PRAXIS II prior to certification; goal statement; letters of recommendation; faculty interview.

Fees and Expenses: Undergraduate: $2,990 in-state per academic year; $8,700 out-of-state. Graduate: $3,004 in-state per academic year; $6,840 out-of-state. Required fees: $675 undergraduate, $252 graduate. On-campus room and board: $5,910 to $6,420.

Financial Aid: Resources specifically for eligible students enrolled in teacher education programs are awarded on the basis of financial need and academic merit. The institution has a Program Participation Agreement with the U.S. Department of Education for eligible students to receive Pell Grants and other federal aid. Teacher scholarships available to qualifying students. *Contact:* James Hanbury at: (401) 456-8684 or e-mail at: jhanbury@ric.edu.

Accreditation: *Regional:* NEASC. *Professional:* NCATE. *Member of:* AACTE. *Approved by:* Rhode Island Department of Education.

Undergraduate Programs: Baccalaureate programs in elementary education (generalized) or elementary education (early childhood) lead to the Bachelor of Science degree in art, biology, chemistry, English, French, general science, geography, history, mathematics, physics, political science, social studies, Spanish, theatre. The Bachelor of Science degree programs include special education-elementary/middle school; special education-middle/secondary, special education-severe/profound.

The Bachelor of Science degree is offered in health education and community health. The secondary education programs lead to the Bachelor of Arts in anthropology, biology, chemistry, English, French, general science, geography, history, mathematics, physics, political science, social science, sociology, Spanish, special education.

All undergraduate degree programs require the completion of at least 120 credit hours.

Graduate Programs: The Rhode Island Teacher Education (RITE) Program is a nondegree program for students with a baccalaureate degree that leads to eligibility for certification to teach in secondary schools in Rhode Island. The program includes the sequence of professional preparation courses prescribed for the undergraduate secondary education teacher preparation program. Selected subject matter courses may also be required.

Licensure/Reciprocity: Rhode Island. Students seeking teaching certification in a state other than Rhode Island should consult with that state's teacher certification office early in their program of study to insure compliance with requirements. Many state directors of teacher credentialing have signed Interstate Agreements through NASDTEC that expedite the certification process.

ROGER WILLIAMS UNIVERSITY
School of Education
One Old Ferry Road
Bristol, Rhode Island 02809
Phone: (401) 254-3404
Fax: (401) 254-3710
E-mail: jhill@rhu.edu
Internet: http://www.rwu.edu

Institution Description: Roger Williams University is a private, independent, nonprofit college that was established in 1948.

Students who complete a teacher education program are prepared to meet the challenges they will encounter in diverse classrooms.

Institution Control: Private.

Calendar: Semester. Academic year August to May.

Official(s): Dr. Marie C. DiBiasio, Dean; Dr. Daniel A. Cabral, Associate Dean.

Faculty: Full-time 8; adjunct 12.

Degrees Awarded: 25 baccalaureate; 29 master's.

Admission Requirements: *Undergraduate:* Graduation from an accredited secondary school or GED; College Board SAT; recommendations; personal statement. *Teacher education specific:* Minimum 2.5 GPA in freshman year; two additional recommendations; personal statement of teaching; PRAXIS I tests (reading, writing, mathematics). *Graduate:* Baccalaureate degree from a regionally accredited institution. *Teacher education specific:* GRE or Miller Analogies Test; three recommendations; faculty interview.

Fees and Expenses: Undergraduate: $20,095 per academic year. Graduate: $885 per 3-credit hours. On-campus room and board: $8,935. Books and supplies: $600 per semester.

Financial Aid: Resources specifically for eligible students enrolled in teacher education programs are awarded on the basis of financial need and academic merit. The institution has a Program Participation Agreement with the U.S. Department of Education for eligible students to receive Pell Grants and other federal aid. Teacher scholarships available to qualifying students. *Contact:* Student Financial Aid Officer at: (401) 254-8100.

Accreditation: *Regional:* NEASC. *Approved by:* Rhode Island Department of Education.

Undergraduate Programs: Undergraduates participating in a Teacher Education Program must complete the requirements for a specific academic major, the university core curriculum and either the elementary or secondary education course sequence. Students currently earning a baccalaureate degree may enroll in the program as an education major, but must choose another major. Elementary undergraduates earn teacher certification in grades 1-6 and may select any other major in the liberal arts and sciences. Secondary undergraduates may enroll and earn teacher certification in grades 7-12 in one or more of the following areas: English, history, social studies, mathematics, biology, general science, foreign languages, or chemistry. Certification (K-12) in dance is also offered.

Graduate Programs: The Master of Arts in Teaching with elementary education emphasis is a 49-credit program leading to certification as a grade 1-6 teacher. The program comprises thirteen courses clustered into three curriculum levels arranged in a development sequence: Level 1-Exploring the Professions/Entering the Program; Level 2-Preparing to Teach; Level 3-Performance in the Classroom.

The Master of Arts in literacy education is a 34-credit program that leads to certification as a K-12 reading specialist/consultant. This program comprises eleven courses clustered into three curriculum levels arranged in a developmental sequence: Level 1-Explorations; Level 2-Investigations; Level 3-Professionalism.

Licensure/Reciprocity: Rhode Island. Students seeking teaching certification in a state other than Rhode Island should consult with that state's teacher certification office early in their program of study to insure compliance with requirements. Many state directors of teacher credentialing have signed Interstate Agreements through NASDTEC that expedite the certification process.

SALVE REGINA UNIVERSITY

Education Department
Teacher Education Programs
100 Ochre Point Avenue
Newport, Rhode Island 02840
Phone: (401) 847-6650
Fax: (401) 848-2823
E-mail: sruadmis@salve.edu
Internet: http://www.salve.edu

Institution Description: Salve Regina University is a private institution affiliated with the Sisters of Mercy, Roman Catholic Church. It was incorporated in 1934.

The Education Department has designed a curriculum with four major components: a general, liberal, and humanistic education; a content-oriented curriculum in the academic disciplines to be taught; a comprehensive study of pedagogy, including foundational studies; and a program of expanding field experience that culminates in student teaching.

Institution Control: Private.

Calendar: Semester. Academic year September to May.

Official(s): Dr. Alice T. Graham, Department Chair.

Faculty: Full-time 14; adjunct 13.

Degrees Awarded: 89 baccalaureate.

Admission Requirements: *Undergraduate:* Graduation from an approved secondary school or GED; College Board SAT or ACT composite. *Teacher education specific:* 2.75 cumulative GPA; PRAXIS I test scores (reading, writing, mathematics)l; portfolio presentation; faculty interview.

Fees and Expenses: $20,521 per academic year. On-campus room and board: $8,700. Other expenses: $1,640. Books and supplies: $750.

Financial Aid: Resources specifically for eligible students enrolled in teacher education programs are awarded on the basis of financial need and academic merit. The institution has a Program Participation Agreement with the U.S. Department of Education for eligible students to receive Pell Grants and other federal aid. Teacher scholarships available to qualifying students. *Contact:* Financial Aid Office at: (401) 341-2901.

Accreditation: *Regional:* NEASC. *Member of:* AACTE. *Approved by:* Rhode Island Department of Education.

Undergraduate Programs: The baccalaureate programs in early childhood. elementary, secondary, and special education prepare students for related careers in business, government, and nonprofit agencies as well as for graduate study. Students may pursue a double major either within education, or in education and another academic discipline. All programs require the completion of a general education core, professional studies, content area; field experiences, and student teaching.

Licensure/Reciprocity: Rhode Island. Students seeking teaching certification in a state other than Rhode Island should consult with that state's teacher certification office early in their program of study to insure compliance with requirements. Many state directors of teacher credentialing have signed Interstate Agreements through NASDTEC that expedite the certification process.

UNIVERSITY OF RHODE ISLAND

School of Education
Office of Teacher Education
100 Quinn Hall
8 Ranger Road
Kingston, Rhode Island 02881
Phone: (401) 874-5930
Fax: (401) 874-9102
E-mail: uriadmit@uri.edu
Internet: http://www.uri.edu

Institution Description: The University of Rhode Island is a state institution and land-grant college. It was chartered in 1888.

The School of Education offers undergraduate and graduate academic programs leading to teacher certification.

Institution Control: Public.

Calendar: Semester. Academic year September to May.

Official(s): Dr. John Boulmetio, Director.

Faculty: Full-time 23.

Degrees Awarded: 130 baccalaureate; 89 master's.

Admission Requirements: *Undergraduate:* Graduation from an approved secondary school with 18 college preparatory units or GED; College Board SAT or ACT composite. *Teacher education specific:* PRAXIS I; goal statement; letters of recommendation. *Graduate:* Baccalaureate degree from a regionally accredited institution. *Teacher education specific:* The Rhode Island Teacher Education (RITE) Program requires a substantial amount of appropriate coursework in an academic discipline for which secondary certification is sought; PRAXIS II prior to certification; goal statement; letters of recommendation; faculty interview. *Graduate:* Baccalaureate degree from a regionally accredited institution.

Fees and Expenses: Undergraduate: $6,202 in-state per academic year; $16,334 out-of-state. Graduate: Tuition charged per credit hour. On-campus room and board: $7,518. Other expenses: 41,750. Books and supplies: $800.

Financial Aid: Resources specifically for eligible students enrolled in teacher education programs are awarded on the basis of financial need and academic merit. The institution has a Program Participation Agreement with the U.S. Department of Education for eligible students to receive Pell Grants and other federal aid. Teacher scholarships available to qualifying students. *Contact:* Financial Aid Office at: (401) 874-9500.

Accreditation: *Regional:* NEASC. *Professional:* NCATE. *Member of:* AACTE. *Approved by:* Rhode Island Department of Education.

Undergraduate Programs: Students in the early childhood education program major in human development and are admitted to the teacher education component of a program that leads to a Bachelor of Science degree and initial certification for preschool and primary grades (N-2).

UNIVERSITY OF RHODE ISLAND—*cont'd*

Elementary education students follow the requirements for an arts and sciences major and receive a dual degree in elementary education and arts and sciences. Completion leads to a Bachelor of Arts degree and an initial teaching certificate for grades 1-6.

Secondary education certification programs are offered in biology, chemistry, general science, physics, English, modern languages, social studies, history, and math. Completion of a program leads to a Bachelor of Science degree and an initial teaching certificate for grades 7-12 in the area of specialization.

A physical education program leads to a Bachelor of Science degree and initial certification in K-12 physical education. A music education program, in cooperation with the Department of Music, leads to a Bachelor of Music degree and an initial certification in K-12 music.

Graduate Programs: The Master of Arts in Education program students declare adult education, elementary education, secondary education, or reading education as an area of specialization. The Master of Arts in Education with teacher certification is for students seeking initial teacher certification while working toward a master's degree in education.

The Master of Science in physical education program and the Master of Music in music education program are for students who are either certified to teach in public schools or who are enrolled in the teacher certification program.

Special endorsements are available in English as a second language and a middle school endorsement valid for service in grades 5-8 in the areas of mathematics, English, science, social studies, or foreign languages. The middle school endorsement is valid for service in grades 7 and 8 in a junior high school.

Licensure/Reciprocity: Rhode Island. Students seeking teaching certification in a state other than Rhode Island should consult with that state's teacher certification office early in their program of study to insure compliance with requirements. Many state directors of teacher credentialing have signed Interstate Agreements through NASDTEC that expedite the certification process.

SOUTH CAROLINA

ANDERSON COLLEGE

Department of Education and Kinesiology
Teacher Education
316 Boulevard
Anderson, South Carolina 29621
Phone: (864) 231-2142
Fax: (864) 231-2004
E-mail: cwooten@ac.edu
Internet: http://www.ac.edu

Institution Description: Anderson College is a private four-year liberal arts college sponsored by the South Carolina Baptist Convention. It was founded in 1911.

The purpose of the Department of Education and Kinesiology is to provide students with a scientific-based education that assists them in preparing for careers in education and human movement-related fields.

Institution Control: Private.

Calendar: Semester. Academic year August to May.

Official(s): Dr. Charles A. Wooten, Division Head; Dr. Jane S. Cahaly, Director of Teacher Education.

Faculty: Full-time 8.

Degrees Awarded: 33 baccalaureate.

Admission Requirements: *Undergraduate:* Graduation from an approved secondary school or GED, College Board SAT or ACT composite. *Teacher education specific:* Completion of all required departmental tests include PRAXIS I (reading, writing, mathematics); personal goal statement; faculty interview.

Fees and Expenses: $13,255 per academic year. On-campus room and board: $5,180. Other expenses: $4,200. Books and supplies: $1,450.

Financial Aid: Resources specifically for eligible students enrolled in teacher education programs are awarded on the basis of financial need and academic merit. The institution has a Program Participation Agreement with the U.S. Department of Education for eligible students to receive Pell Grants and other federal aid. Teacher scholarships available to qualifying students. *Contact:* Financial Aid Office at: (864) 231-2070.

Accreditation: *Regional:* SACS. *Professional:* NCATE. *Member of:* AACTE. *Approved by:* South Carolina Department of Education.

Undergraduate Programs: Programs of study leading to the baccalaureate degree include early childhood and elementary education (K-8); elementary education (1-8); special education (LD K-12) with elementary education; physical education (K-12); music education (K-12) with concentrations in instrumental or vocal/choral; secondary education (7-12) in English, social studies, biology, mathematics, Spanish. All programs require the completion of a general education core, professional studies, content area, field experience, and student teaching. A minimum of 128 semester hours must be completed for the degree award.

Licensure/Reciprocity: South Carolina. Students seeking teaching certification in a state other than South Carolina should consult with that state's teacher certification office early in their program of study to insure compliance with requirements. Many state directors of teacher credentialing have signed Interstate Agreements through NASDTEC that expedite the certification process.

BENEDICT COLLEGE

Division of Academic Affairs
Office of Teacher Education
1600 Harden Street
Columbia, South Carolina 29204
Phone: (803) 256-4220
Fax: (803) 253-5167
E-mail: admissions@benedict.edu
Internet: http://www.benedict.edu

Institution Description: Benedict College is an independent, coeducational, private college founded by the Baptist Church. It was established as Benedict Institute in 1870.

The Office of Teacher Education offers programs leading to the baccalaureate degree and teacher certification in South Carolina.

Institution Control: Private.

Calendar: Semester. Academic year to May.

Official(s): Dr. David H. Swinton, President.

Faculty: Full-time 8.

Degrees Awarded: 20 baccalaureate.

Admission Requirements: *Undergraduate:* Graduation with 18 units from an accredited secondary school or GED; College Board SAT preferred, ACT composite accepted. *Teacher education specific:* Students apply during second semester of freshman year; 2.5 GPA; practicum experiences; PRAXIS I Test (reading, writing, mathematics); completion of 60 semester hours; PRAXIS II required prior to certification.

Fees and Expenses: $10,498 per academic year. On-campus room and board: $5,434. Other expenses: $1,200. Books and supplies: $1,430.

Financial Aid: Resources specifically for eligible students enrolled in teacher education programs are awarded on the basis of financial need and academic merit. The institution has a Program Participation Agreement with the U.S. Department of Education for eligible students to receive Pell Grants and other federal aid. Teacher scholarships available to qualifying students. *Contact:* Financial Aid Office at: (803) 253-5105.

Accreditation: *Regional:* SACS. *Member of:* AACTE. *Approved by:* South Carolina Department of Education.

Undergraduate Programs: The general education program for teacher education consists of a core of subjects representing broad areas of knowledge. These courses meet the general education requirements for certification and are required in all teacher education programs. These programs include elementary education, early childhood education, secondary education, and child and family development. All programs require completion of a minimum of 125 semester hours including the general education core, professional studies, content area, field experiences, and student teaching.

Licensure/Reciprocity: South Carolina. Students seeking teaching certification in a state other than South Carolina should consult with that state's teacher certification office early in their program of study to insure compliance with requirements. Many state directors of teacher credentialing have signed Interstate Agreements through NASDTEC that expedite the certification process.

CHARLESTON SOUTHERN UNIVERSITY

School of Education
9200 University Boulevard
Charleston, South Carolina 29423
Phone: (843) 863-7355
Fax: (803) 863-7533
E-mail: education@csuniv.edu
Internet: http://www.csniv.edu

Institution Description: Charleston Southern University, formerly Baptist College at Charleston, is a private college affiliated with the Southern Baptist Convention of South Carolina. It was chartered in 1960.

The School of Education offers undergraduate and graduate programs leading to teacher certification in South Carolina.

Institution Control: Private.

Calendar: Semester. Academic year August to May.

Official(s): Dr. Gary O. Leonard, Dean.

Faculty: Full-time 9.

Degrees Awarded: 40 baccalaureate; 32 master's.

Admission Requirements: *Undergraduate:* Graduation with 18 academic units from an approved secondary school or GED; College Board SAT preferred; ACT composite accepted. *Teacher education specific:* Students apply during second semester of freshman year; 2.5 GPA; PRAXIS I Test (reading, writing, mathematics); completion of 60 semester hours; PRAXIS II required prior to certification.

Fees and Expenses: $14,426 per academic year. On-campus room and board: $7,694. Other expenses: $3,337. Books and supplies: $980.

Financial Aid: Resources specifically for eligible students enrolled in teacher education programs are awarded on the basis of financial need and academic merit. The institution has a Program Participation Agreement with the U.S. Department of Education for eligible students to receive Pell Grants and other federal aid. Teacher scholarships available to qualifying students. *Contact:* Financial Aid Office at: (843) 863-8039.

Accreditation: *Regional:* SACS. *Professional:* NCATE. *Member of:* AACTE. *Approved by:* South Carolina Department of Education.

Undergraduate Programs: The School of Education offers baccalaureate certification programs in the areas of: early childhood education (preK-4); elementary education (1-8); choral music (K-12); instrumental music (K-12); English (7-12); science (7-12); social studies (7-12); Spanish (7-12). All programs require the completion of a general education core, professional studies, content area, field experiences, and student teaching. A minimum of 125 credit hours must be successfully completed for the degree award.

Graduate Programs: Graduate education programs of study include: Master of Education in elementary education; Master of Education in secondary education; Master of Education in elementary educational administration and supervision; Master of Education in secondary education educational administration and supervision.

The School of Education offers the Master of Arts in Teaching degree in two areas of study: secondary English education and secondary social studies education. Successful completion of all program requirements leads to South Carolina certification as a teacher in grades 7 through 12.

Licensure/Reciprocity: South Carolina. Students seeking teaching certification in a state other than South Carolina should consult with that state's teacher certification office early in their program of study to insure compliance with requirements. Many state directors of teacher credentialing have signed Interstate Agreements through NASDTEC that expedite the certification process.

CLAFLIN COLLEGE

Division of Education
Department of Teacher Education
700 College Avenue
Orangeburg, South Carolina 29115-9970
Phone: (803) 535-5000
Fax: (803) 531-2860
E-mail: bbowman@claflin.edu
Internet: http://www.claflin.edu

Institution Description: Claflin College is a private college affiliated with the United Methodist Church. The college was chartered in 1869.

The mission of the Division of Education is to prepare teachers for leadership and service roles in a multicultural, global, and technological society.

Institution Control: Private.

Calendar: Semester. Academic year August to May.

Official(s): Dr. Barbara Bowman, Chair.

Faculty: Full-time 7 (Division of Education).

Degrees Awarded: 15 baccalaureate.

Admission Requirements: *Undergraduate:* Graduation from an approved secondary school or GED; College board SAT or ACT composite. *Teacher education specific:* Students apply during second semester of freshman year; 2.5 GPA; PRAXIS I Test (reading, writing, mathematics); completion of 60 semester hours; PRAXIS II required prior to certification.

Fees and Expenses: $9,654 per academic year. On-campus room and board: $5,184. Other expenses: $2,450. Books and supplies: $1,200.

Financial Aid: Resources specifically for eligible students enrolled in teacher education programs are awarded on the basis of financial need and academic merit. The institution has a Program Participation Agreement with the U.S. Department of Education for eligible students to receive Pell Grants and other federal aid. Teacher scholarships available to qualifying students. *Contact:* Financial Aid Office at: (803) 535-5334.

Accreditation: *Regional:* SACS. *Member of:* AACTE. *Approved by:* South Carolina Department of Education.

Undergraduate Programs: Students who complete the program in early childhood education (K-1) earn the Bachelor of Science degree. The second semester of the senior year is devoted exclusively to student teaching.

Students completing the elementary education program earn a Bachelor of Science degree and are certified to teach grades one through eight. A strong academic foundation in education, psychology, and health in addition to hands-on experience is provided.

The physical education program offers academic preparation for a wide range of careers in health and physical education in a public school. The Bachelor of Science degree is awarded upon successful completion of the program.

The special education/learning disabilities (K-12) program culminates in the Bachelor of Science degree. Courses in the program include Introduction to Exceptional Students; Characteristics of learning disabilities; Human Growth and Development; Curriculum and Instruction for the Mildly Handicapped; Practicum in the Instruction of Exceptional Children.

All baccalaureate programs require the completion of a minimum of 124 semester hours.

Licensure/Reciprocity: South Carolina. Students seeking teaching certification in a state other than South Carolina should consult with that state's teacher certification office early in their program of study to insure compliance with requirements. Many state directors of teacher credentialing have signed Interstate Agreements through NASDTEC that expedite the certification process.

CLEMSON UNIVERSITY
College of Health, Education, and Human Development
Eugene T. Moore School of Education
116 Edwards Hall
Clemson, South Carolina 29634
Phone: (864) 656-7640
Fax: (864) 656-2641
E-mail: cuadmissions@clemson.edu
Internet: http://www.clemson.edu

Institution Description: Clemson University is a state institution. It was established and chartered as Clemson Agricultural College in 1889.

The Eugene T. Moore School of Education offers graduate and undergraduate programs leading to teacher certification in South Carolina.

Institution Control: Public.

Calendar: Semester. Academic year August to May.

Official(s): Dr. Robert S. Barkley, Director of Admissions.

Faculty: Full-time 69.

Degrees Awarded: 300 baccalaureate; 125 master's; 14 doctorate.

Admission Requirements: *Undergraduate:* Graduation from an approved secondary school or GED; College Board SAT. *Teacher education specific:* Completion of PRAXIS I tests (reading, writing, mathematics); apply by close of sophomore year; personal goal statement; faculty interview. *Graduate:* Baccalaureate degree from a regionally accredited institution. *Teacher education specific:* Completion of all required departmental test; letters of recommendation; PRAXIS II prior to certification; faculty interview.

Fees and Expenses: Undergraduate: $6,934 in-state per academic year; $14,532 out-of-state. Graduate: Tuition charged per credit hour. On-campus room and board: $5,038. Other expenses: $3,676. Books and supplies: $780.

Financial Aid: Resources specifically for eligible students enrolled in teacher education programs are awarded on the basis of financial need and academic merit. The institution has a Program Participation Agreement with the U.S. Department of Education for eligible students to receive Pell Grants and other federal aid. Teacher scholarships available to qualifying students. *Contact:* Financial Aid Office at: (864) 656-2280.

Accreditation: *Regional:* SACS. *Professional:* NCATE. *Member of:* AACTE. *Approved by:* South Carolina Department of Education.

Undergraduate Programs: The Bachelor of Arts degree programs are offered in early childhood education, elementary education, and secondary education (English, history and geography, mathematics, modern languages, political science and economics, psychology and sociology). The Bachelor of Science degree programs include: mathematics teaching and science teaching (biological sciences, earth sciences, physical sciences). All programs require the completion of a general education core, professional studies, content area, field experiences, and student teaching. A minimum of 129 credit hours must be completed for a degree award.

Graduate Programs: The Master of Education degree is offered in the areas of elementary education, reading, secondary education, and special education. The Master of Arts in Teaching degree program is offered in middle grades education. A Transition to Teaching Certificate program is also offered to qualified candidates.

The Doctor of Philosophy degree program is offered in curriculum and instruction.

Licensure/Reciprocity: South Carolina. Students seeking teaching certification in a state other than South Carolina should consult with that state's teacher certification office early in their program of study to insure compliance with requirements. Many state directors of teacher credentialing have signed Interstate Agreements through NASDTEC that expedite the certification process.

COASTAL CAROLINA UNIVERSITY
College of Education
Kearns Hall
735 Highway 544
Conway, South Carolina 29528-6054
Phone: (843) 349-2629
Fax: (843) 349-2940
E-mail: hunt@coastal.edu
Internet: http://www.coastal.edu

Institution Description: Coastal Carolina University, formerly known as University of South Carolina - Coastal Carolina, is a state-supported institution. It was established in 1954.

The chief responsibility of the Professional Program in Teacher Education is to prepare teachers for early childhood, elementary, and middle school instruction.

Institution Control: Public.

Calendar: Semester. Academic year August to May.

Official(s): Dr. Gilbert H. Hunt, Dean.

Faculty: Full-time 26; part-time 12; adjunct 4.

Degrees Awarded: 121 baccalaureate; 29 master's.

Admission Requirements: *Undergraduate:* Graduation from an approved secondary school or GED; College Board SAT or ACT composite. *Teacher education specific:* Completion of at least 60 semester hours of study with a 2.5 GPA; passing scores on all portions of the PRAXIS I Test; two letters of recommendation; completion of education foundation courses and English 101 and 102 with a minimum grade of C. *Graduate:* Baccalaureate degree from a regionally accredited institution. *Teacher education specific:* Faculty interview; GRE or Miller Analogies Test; letters of recommendation; PRAXIS II before certification.

Fees and Expenses: Undergraduate: $5,190 in-state per academic year; $12,870 out-of-state. Graduate: $5,360 in-state per academic year; $13,160 out-of-state. On-campus room and board: $5,770. Books and supplies: $400.

Financial Aid: Resources specifically for eligible students enrolled in teacher education programs are awarded on the basis of financial need and academic merit. Students may be eligible for South Carolina Teachers Loan Program. The institution has a Program Participation Agreement with the U.S. Department of Education for eligible students to receive Pell Grants and other federal aid. Teacher scholarships available to qualifying students. *Contact:* Glenn S. Hanson at: (843) 349-2325 or e-mail at: glenn@coastal.edu.

Accreditation: *Regional:* SACS. *Professional:* NCATE. *Member of:* AACTE. *Approved by:* South Carolina Department of Education.

Undergraduate Programs: The early childhood education (pre K-4) major satisfies the educational requirements for certification. The elementary education (1-8) major meets the requirements for South Carolina certification. Middle grades education is a course of study intended to meet standards for certification.

The faculty in physical education are dedicated to the professional preparation of students as they pursue careers in teaching physical education K-12 in coaching, recreation, and leisure services management. The major satisfies the educational requirements for South Carolina certification to teach in grades K-12.

All baccalaureate programs require the completion a general education core, professional studies, content area, field experiences, and student teaching. A minimum of 120 semester hours is required for the baccalaureate degree.

Graduate Programs: The Master of Education degree programs are designed to offer professional growth and development for qualified degree candidates. The programs include early childhood, elementary education, and secondary education. Each program requires the completion of 36 semester hours. The Master of Arts in Teaching degree programs are designed to offer a route to teacher certification through graduate study as an alternative to undergraduate study.

Licensure/Reciprocity: South Carolina. Students seeking teaching certification in a state other than South Carolina should consult with that state's teacher certification office early in their program of study to insure compliance with requirements.

COASTAL CAROLINA UNIVERSITY—*cont'd*

Many state directors of teacher credentialing have signed Interstate Agreements through NASDTEC that expedite the certification process.

COLLEGE OF CHARLESTON

School of Education
66 George Street
Charleston, South Carolina 29424
Phone: (803) 953-5613
Fax: (803) 953-5407
E-mail: education@cofc.edu
Internet: http://www.cofc.edu

Institution Description: The College of Charleston is a state institution that was established in 1770.

The School of Education offers nationally accredited teacher and athletic training education programs.

Institution Control: Public.

Calendar: Semester. Academic year August to May.

Official(s): Dr. Frances C. Welch, Dean.

Faculty: Full-time 45.

Admission Requirements: *Undergraduate:* Graduation with 16 academic units from an approved secondary school or GED; College Board SAT or ACT composite. *Teacher education specific:* Completion of at least 60 semester hours of study with a 2.5 GPA; passing scores on all sections of the PRAXIS I Test; two letters of recommendation; completion of education foundation courses and other required courses *Graduate:* Baccalaureate degree from a regionally accredited institution. *Teacher education specific:* Faculty interview; GRE or Miller Analogies Test; letters of recommendation; PRAXIS II before certification.

Fees and Expenses: Undergraduate: $5,770 in-state per academic year; $13,032 out-of-state. Graduate: $4,556 in-state per academic year; $10,290 out-of-state.

Financial Aid: Resources specifically for eligible students enrolled in teacher education programs are awarded on the basis of financial need and academic merit. The institution has a Program Participation Agreement with the U.S. Department of Education for eligible students to receive Pell Grants and other federal aid. Teacher scholarships available to qualifying students. *Contact:* Financial Aid Office at: (843) 953-5540 or e-mail at: financial aid@cofc.edu.

Accreditation: *Regional:* SACS. *Professional:* NCATE. *Member of:* AACTE. *Approved by:* South Carolina Department of Education.

Undergraduate Programs: The Department of Elementary and Early Childhood Education prepares teachers to meet the educational needs of children and youth in the areas of early childhood, elementary, and middle level education. The curriculum involves coursework on-campus as well as field experiences and clinical practice in urban, suburban, and rural public school settings.

The Department of Foundations, Secondary, and Special Education prepares teacher candidates in special education and secondary education. On-campus coursework is complemented by field experience and clinical practice in a variety of local school settings. Additionally, the department offers the core foundational courses for all teacher education programs.

The Department of Physical Education and Health prepares students who have an interest in kinsiological concepts and health promotion. This undergraduate curriculum teaches students to work in a diverse community of lifelong learners and helps them acquire a depth of knowledge, research techniques, critical thinking skills, and competencies in the professional areas of athletic training, exercise science, health promotion and/or teacher education.

Graduate Programs: Graduate initial teacher education programs (Master of Arts in Teaching) as well as advanced (Master of Education) programs are offered. The Master of Arts in Education programs in early childhood, elementary, languages, science and math, and special education are designed for currently certified teachers.

Licensure/Reciprocity: South Carolina. Students seeking teaching certification in a state other than South Carolina should consult with that state's teacher certification office early in their program of study to insure compliance with requirements. Many state directors of teacher credentialing have signed Interstate Agreements through NASDTEC that expedite the certification process.

COLUMBIA COLLEGE

Department of Education
Teacher Education Programs
1301 Columbia College Drive
Columbia, South Carolina 29203
Phone: (803) 786-3558
Fax: (803) 754-3178
E-mail: susbrown@colubmiacollegesc.edu
Internet: http://www.columbiacollegesc.edu

Institution Description: Columbia College is a private liberal arts college for women that is affiliated with the United Methodist Church. It was founded in 1854.

The mission of the Department of Education is to prepare teachers as collaborative professionals who are knowledgeable in the content and practice of their respected discipline.

Institution Control: Private.

Calendar: Semester. Academic September to May.

Official(s): Dr. Susanne J. Brown, Director, Teacher Education Programs.

Faculty: Full-time 11.

Admission Requirements: *Undergraduate:* Graduation from an approved secondary school or GED; College Board SAT or ACT composite. *Teacher education specific:* Completion of at least 60 semester hours of study with a 2.5 GPA; passing scores on all portions of the PRAXIS I Test; two letters of recommendation; completion of education foundation courses and other required courses. *Graduate:* Baccalaureate degree from a regionally accredited institution. *Teacher education specific:* Faculty interview; GRE or Miller Analogies Test; letters of recommendation; PRAXIS II before certification.

Fees and Expenses: Undergraduate: $17,280 per academic year. Graduate: Tuition charged per credit hour. On-campus room and board: $5,420. Other expenses: $3,400. Books and supplies: $800.

Financial Aid: Resources specifically for eligible students enrolled in teacher education programs are awarded on the basis of financial need and academic merit. The institution has a Program Participation Agreement with the U.S. Department of Education for eligible students to receive Pell Grants and other federal aid. Teacher scholarships available to qualifying students. *Contact:* Financial Aid Office at: (803) 786-3612.

Accreditation: *Regional:* SACS. *Professional:* NCATE. *Member of:* AACTE. *Approved by:* South Carolina Department of Education.

Undergraduate Programs: The Department of Education offers undergraduate majors leading to teacher certification in early childhood, elementary, secondary, special education, and speech-language pathology. A noncertifying major in speech-language pathology also is available. The department works in collaboration with other academic departments to offer certifying majors in art, biology, chemistry, dance, English, French, mathematics, music, social studies, and Spanish. All baccalaureate programs require the completion of a general education core, professional studies, content area, field experiences, and student teaching. A minimum of 127 semester hours must be successfully completed for the degree award.

Graduate Programs: A Master of Education in divergent learning is offered to qualified candidates. Contact the Director of Teacher Education Programs for detailed information.

Licensure/Reciprocity: South Carolina. Students seeking teaching certification in a state other than South Carolina should consult with that state's teacher certification office early in their program of study to insure compliance with requirements.

Many state directors of teacher credentialing have signed Interstate Agreements through NASDTEC that expedite the certification process.

CONVERSE COLLEGE
Department of Education
580 East Main Street
Spartanburg, South Carolina 29302
Phone: (864) 596-9617
Fax: (864) 596-9526
E-mail: info@converse.edu
Internet: http://www.converse.edu

Institution Description: Converse College is a private, independent institution. It was established and chartered in 1889.

The Department of Education offers teacher education programs on the foundations of a broad liberal arts education.

Institution Control: Private.

Calendar: Semester. Academic year September to May.

Official(s): Dr. Katharine Stephens Slemenda, Chair.

Faculty: Full-time 8; adjunct 10.

Degrees Awarded: 39 baccalaureate; 171 master's.

Admission Requirements: *Undergraduate:* Graduation with 16 academic units from an accredited secondary school or GED; College Board SAT preferred; ACT composite accepted. *Teacher education specific:* 2.5 GPA; passing scores on all sections of PRAXIS I (reading, writing, mathematics); references; personal goal essay. *Graduate:* Baccalaureate degree from a regionally accredited institution. *Teacher education specific:* Approval by the Teacher Education Committee; 2.75 GPA; PRAXIS I one full semester before student teaching; PRAXIS II before final certification; 2 references; faculty interview.

Fees and Expenses: Undergraduate: $18,915 in-state per academic year. Graduate: Tuition charged per credit hour. On-campus room and board: $5,795. Other expenses: $1,850. Books and supplies: $700.

Financial Aid: Resources specifically for eligible students enrolled in teacher education programs are awarded on the basis of financial need and academic merit. The institution has a Program Participation Agreement with the U.S. Department of Education for eligible students to receive Pell Grants and other federal aid. Teacher scholarships available to qualifying students. *Contact:* Financial Aid Office at: (864) 596-9017.

Accreditation: *Regional:* SACS. *Approved by:* South Carolina Department of Education.

Undergraduate Programs: The Department of Education offers teacher education programs in the areas of: art, early childhood, elementary, comprehensive special education, emotional disabilities, deaf and hard of hearing, educational interpreting, educable mental disabilities, learning disabilities, English, French, Spanish, mathematics, music (choral and instrumental), speech and drama, science (biology, chemistry, physics), and social studies. Those who wish to teach grades 7-12 complete a 27-hour minor (29 for science teachers) in secondary education to complement an appropriate liberal arts major. The department offers two tracks: certification and noncertification. All programs require the completion of a general education core, professional studies, content area, field experiences, and student teaching. A minimum of 120 semester hours is required for the degree award.

Graduate Programs: Converse College offers the Master of Arts in Teaching degree for those seeking initial certification in the areas of: early childhood, elementary, educable disabled, learning disabilities, and secondary education (biology, chemistry, English, mathematics, social sciences). For already certified teachers, the Master of Education degree is offered in four broad areas or tracks: elementary, gifted, secondary, and special education. The Master of Music degree may be taken by either those seeking initial certification or already certified teachers. The college also offers the Educational Specialist degree in the areas of administration and supervision, curriculum and instruction, and marriage and family therapy. All graduate degree programs require a minimum of 36 semester hours of graduate study.

Licensure/Reciprocity: South Carolina. Students seeking teaching certification in a state other than South Carolina should consult with that state's teacher certification office early in their program of study to insure compliance with requirements. Many state directors of teacher credentialing have signed Interstate Agreements through NASDTEC that expedite the certification process.

FRANCIS MARION UNIVERSITY
School of Education
P.O. Box 100547
Florence, South Carolina 29501-0547
Phone: (843) 661-1362
Fax: (843) 661-1165
E-mail: admission@fmarion.edu
Internet: http://www.fmarion.edu

Institution Description: Francis Marion University is a state institution. It was established and offered first instruction at the postsecondary level in 1970.

The School of Education offers undergraduate and graduate programs leading to teacher certification in South Carolina.

Institution Control: Public.

Calendar: Semester. Academic year August to May.

Official(s): Dr. K. Wayne Pruitt, Coordinator.

Faculty: Full-time 18; part-time 8.

Degrees Awarded: 52 baccalaureate; 63 master's.

Admission Requirements: *Undergraduate:* Graduation from an accredited secondary school or GED; College Board SAT or ACT composite. Completion of at least 60 semester hours of study with a 2.5 GPA; passing scores on all sections of the PRAXIS I Test; two letters of recommendation; completion of education foundation courses and other required basic courses; *Graduate:* Baccalaureate degree from a regionally accredited institution. *Teacher education specific:* Faculty interview; GRE or Miller Analogies Test; 2 letters of recommendation; PRAXIS II before certification.

Fees and Expenses: Undergraduate: $4,947 in-state per academic year; $9,894 out-of-state. Graduate: Tuition charged per credit hour. On-campus room and board: $4,282. Other expenses: $3,454. Books and supplies: $760.

Financial Aid: Resources specifically for eligible students enrolled in teacher education programs are awarded on the basis of financial need and academic merit. The institution has a Program Participation Agreement with the U.S. Department of Education for eligible students to receive Pell Grants and other federal aid. Teacher scholarships available to qualifying students. *Contact:* Financial Aid Office at: (843) 661-1190.

Accreditation: *Regional:* SACS. *Professional:* NCATE. *Member of:* AACTE. *Approved by:* South Carolina Department of Education.

Undergraduate Programs: The School of Education offers programs leading to the baccalaureate degree and teacher certification in: art, early childhood, elementary, secondary (majors in biology, chemistry, English, French, history, mathematics, political science, sociology, Spanish), health education, physical education. All programs require the completion of a general education core, professional studies, content area, field experiences, and student teaching. A minimum of 120 semester hours must be completed for the degree award.

Graduate Programs: The Master of Arts in Teaching is offered in learning disabilities. The Master of Education degree programs include early childhood education, secondary education, learning disabilities (special education), and instructional accommodation. Each program requires the completion of specific course requirements.

Licensure/Reciprocity: South Carolina. Students seeking teaching certification in a state other than South Carolina should consult with that state's teacher certification office early in their program of study to insure compliance with requirements.

FRANCIS MARION UNIVERSITY—*cont'd*

Many state directors of teacher credentialing have signed Interstate Agreements through NASDTEC that expedite the certification process.

FURMAN UNIVERSITY

Department of Education

3300 Poinsett Highway
Greenville, South Carolina 29613
Phone: (864) 294-3086
Fax: (864) 294-3341
E-mail: admissions@furman.edu
Internet: http://www.furman.edu

Institution Description: Furman University is a private, independent liberal arts institution. It was founded in 1826.

The Department of Education prepares students for careers in public education and related professions.

Institution Control: Private.

Calendar: Semester. Trimester. Academic year September to May.

Official(s): Dr. Nelly Hecker, Chair.

Faculty: Full-time 15.

Degrees Awarded: 28 baccalaureate; 94 master's.

Admission Requirements: *Undergraduate:* Graduation from an approved secondary school or GED; College Board SAT or ACT composite. *Teacher education specific:* Completion of foundational curses; meet minimum scores on PRAXIS I tests in reading, writing, and mathematics; faculty recommendations; cumulative 2.5 GPA; documentation of at least 50 hours of independent and supervised work with children/youth. *Graduate:* Baccalaureate degree from a regionally accredited institution. *Teacher education specific:* Faculty interview; GRE or Miller Analogies Test; letters of recommendation; PRAXIS II before certification.

Fees and Expenses: Undergraduate: $22,712 per academic year. Graduate: Tuition charged per credit hour. On-campus room and board: $6,264. Other expenses: $1,639. Books and supplies: $750.

Financial Aid: Resources specifically for eligible students enrolled in teacher education programs are awarded on the basis of financial need and academic merit. The institution has a Program Participation Agreement with the U.S. Department of Education for eligible students to receive Pell Grants and other federal aid. Teacher scholarships available to qualifying students. *Contact:* Financial Aid Office at: (864) 294-2204.

Accreditation: *Regional:* SACS. *Professional:* NCATE. *Member of:* AACTE. *Approved by:* South Carolina Department of Education.

Undergraduate Programs: The Department of Education offers teaching licensure programs in the areas of: elementary education grades 1-8, early childhood education grades K-4; secondary education grades 7-12 (biology, chemistry, English, French, German, Latin, mathematics, physics, social studies, Spanish); art, drama, music, and physical science grades K-12. All baccalaureate programs require the completion of a general education core, professional studies, content area, field experiences, and student teaching. A minimum of 128 semester hours must be completed for the degree award.

Graduate Programs: The Master of Education degree programs are offered with concentrations in elementary education, early childhood education, reading, special education, school leadership; middle school (language arts, science, social studies, teaching of English as a second language). Each of the programs have specific course requirements.

Licensure/Reciprocity: South Carolina. Students seeking teaching certification in a state other than South Carolina should consult with that state's teacher certification office early in their program of study to insure compliance with requirements. Many state directors of teacher credentialing have signed Interstate Agreements through NASDTEC that expedite the certification process.

LANDER UNIVERSITY

School of Education
Marian Carnell Learning Center

320 Stanley Avenue
Greenwood, South Carolina 29649
Phone: (864) 388-8225
Fax: (864) 388-8111
E-mail: admissions@lander.edu
Internet: http://www.lander.edu

Institution Description: Lander University is a state institution. It was established and chartered in 1872.

The School of Education has the goal of developing professional instructional leaders.

Institution Control: Public.

Calendar: Semester. Academic year August to May.

Official(s): Dr. Danny L. McKenzie, Dean.

Faculty: Full-time 12; adjunct 6.

Degrees Awarded: 57 baccalaureate; 32 master's.

Admission Requirements: *Undergraduate:* Graduation from an approved secondary school or GED; College Board SAT or ACT composite. *Teacher education specific:* 2.5 GPA; passing scores on PRAXIS I; B or better in all clinical; written exam; oral interview; portfolio. *Graduate:* Baccalaureate degree in an appropriate area. *Teacher education specific:* Letters of recommendation; transcripts; portfolio; teaching certificate; faculty interview; PRAXIS II before final certification.

Fees and Expenses: Undergraduate: $4,704 in-state per academic year; $9,648 out-of-state. Graduate: $5,160 in-state per academic year; $10,632 out-of-state. Required fees: $100 health services. On-campus room and board: $4,526 to $4,746. Books and supplies: $600 per year.

Financial Aid: Resources specifically for eligible students enrolled in teacher education programs are awarded on the basis of financial need and academic merit. The institution has a Program Participation Agreement with the U.S. Department of Education for eligible students to receive Pell Grants and other federal aid. Teacher scholarships available to qualifying students. *Contact:* Stephan L. Schaiter at: (864) 388-8340 or e-mail at: sschnait@lander.edu.

Accreditation: *Regional:* SACS. *Professional:* NCATE. *Member of:* AACTE. *Approved by:* South Carolina Department of Education.

Undergraduate Programs: Three undergraduate degree programs are offered within the School of Education: early childhood education, elementary education, special education, all leading to a Bachelor of Science degree. A Montessori emphasis is available to students pursuing a degree in early childhood education. Secondary-level certification is offered in the subject areas of: art, English, mathematics, music, physical education, Spanish, social studies. In this route, the student pursues a degree in the specific subject area in which he/she will teach and the curriculum will include many education courses. All baccalaureate programs require the completion of a general education core, professional studies, content area, field experiences, and student teaching. A minimum of 125 semester credits must be completed for the degree award.

Graduate Programs: Certification in art education is available through the Master of Arts in Teaching in Art degree offered in conjunction with the Division of Fine Arts. The Master of Education degree is offered in elementary education. In addition, graduate work is offered for nondegree seeking students, including courses that provide public school teachers with opportunities to meet recertification requirements.

Licensure/Reciprocity: South Carolina. Students seeking teaching certification in a state other than South Carolina should consult with that state's teacher certification office early in their program of study to insure compliance with requirements. Many state directors of teacher credentialing have signed Interstate Agreements through NASDTEC that expedite the certification process.

NEWBERRY COLLEGE

Department of Education
Teacher Education Programs
2100 College Street
Newberry, South Carolina 29108
Phone: (803) 321-5201
Fax: (803) 321-5283
E-mail: SharonFeaster@newberry.edu
Internet: http://www.newberry.edu

Institution Description: Newberry College is a private college affiliated with the Evangelical Lutheran Church in America. The college was founded in 1856.

The goal of the Department of Education is to produce knowledgeable, effective teachers who are models and facilitators of independent lifelong learning.

Institution Control: Private.

Calendar: Semester. Academic year August to May.

Official(s): Dr. Sharon A. Feaster, Chair.

Faculty: Full-time 4; adjunct 3.

Degrees Awarded: 84 baccalaureate.

Admission Requirements: *Undergraduate:* Graduation with 18 academic units from an approved secondary school or GED; College Board SAT or ACT composite. *Teacher education specific:* Satisfactory completion of 60 semester hours of college work; 2.5 GPA; passing scores on all sections the PRAXIS I (reading, writing, mathematics); faculty recommendation.

Fees and Expenses: $22,000 per academic year. On-campus room and board: $6,000 to $7,000. Books and supplies: $750.

Financial Aid: Resources specifically for eligible students enrolled in teacher education programs are awarded on the basis of financial need and academic merit. The institution has a Program Participation Agreement with the U.S. Department of Education for eligible students to receive Pell Grants and other federal aid. Teacher scholarships available to qualifying students. *Contact:* Financial Aid Office at: (803) 321-5201.

Accreditation: *Regional:* SACS. *Professional:* NCATE. *Member of:* AACTE. *Approved by:* South Carolina Department of Education.

Undergraduate Programs: Programs are offered at the baccalaureate level for students to prepare to teach elementary education; secondary biology, English, history, and mathematics; and K-12 physical education and music. The core curriculum (50-56 semester hours) is required of all teacher education students. Programs also require the completion of professional education requirements; field of specialization requirements; and student teaching. A minimum of 126 semester credits must be attained for the degree award.

Licensure/Reciprocity: South Carolina. Students seeking teaching certification in a state other than South Carolina should consult with that state's teacher certification office early in their program of study to insure compliance with requirements. Many state directors of teacher credentialing have signed Interstate Agreements through NASDTEC that expedite the certification process.

PRESBYTERIAN COLLEGE

Education Department
503 South Broad Street
Clinton, South Carolina 29325
Phone: (864) 833-2820
Fax: (864) 833-8481
E-mail: admin@presby.edu
Internet: http://www.presby.edu

Institution Description: Presbyterian College is a private college affiliated with the Presbyterian Synod of South Atlantic. It was established and chartered in 1880.

The Education Department offers undergraduate programs leading to the baccalaureate degree and teacher certification in South Carolina.

Institution Control: Private.

Calendar: Semester. Academic year August to May.

Official(s): Dr. D. Kent Phillips, Chair.

Faculty: Full-time 5; adjunct 2.

Degrees Awarded: 29 baccalaureate.

Admission Requirements: *Undergraduate:* Graduation from an approved secondary school or GED; College Board SAT or ACT composite. *Teacher education specific:* Satisfactory completion of 60 semester hours of college work; 2.5 GPA; passing scores on all sections the PRAXIS I (reading, writing, mathematics); faculty recommendation.

Fees and Expenses: $18,360 per academic year. On-campus room and board: $6,326. Other expenses: $3,677. Books and supplies: $980.

Financial Aid: Resources specifically for eligible students enrolled in teacher education programs are awarded on the basis of financial need and academic merit. The institution has a Program Participation Agreement with the U.S. Department of Education for eligible students to receive Pell Grants and other federal aid. Teacher scholarships available to qualifying students. *Contact:* Financial Aid Office at: (864) 833-8290.

Accreditation: *Regional:* SACS. *Professional:* NCATE. *Member of:* AACTE. *Approved by:* South Carolina Department of Education.

Undergraduate Programs: Programs of study offered by the Education Department lead to the baccalaureate degree and teacher certification in the following areas: early childhood education, elementary education, music education, music choral education, music Instrumental, special education, and secondary education (biology, English, French, German, history, mathematics, Spanish, social studies, speech and drama). All programs require the completion of a general education core, professional studies, content area, field experiences, and student teaching. A minimum of 122 semester hours must be completed for the degree award.

Licensure/Reciprocity: South Carolina. Students seeking teaching certification in a state other than South Carolina should consult with that state's teacher certification office early in their program of study to insure compliance with requirements. Many state directors of teacher credentialing have signed Interstate Agreements through NASDTEC that expedite the certification process.

SOUTH CAROLINA STATE UNIVERSITY

Department of Teacher Education
Campus P.O. Box 7487
300 College Avenue, N.E.
Orangeburg, South Carolina 29117-0001
Phone: (803) 536-7098
Fax: (803) 536-4605
E-mail: zf_jkinerd@scsu.edu
Internet: http://www.scsu.edu

Institution Description: South Carolina State University was established and chartered in 1896.

The Department of Teacher Education offers undergraduate and graduate programs leading to teacher certification and programs for professional and career advancement.

Institution Control: Public.

Calendar: Semester. Academic year August to May.

Official(s): Dr. Gail Joyner-Fleming, Dean; Dr. Jesse E. Kinard, Chair, Department of Education.

Faculty: Full-time 20.

Degrees Awarded: 53 baccalaureate; 79 master's; 26 doctorate.

Admission Requirements: *Undergraduate:* Graduation from an accredited secondary school or GED; College Board SAT or ACT composite. Completion of at least 60 semester hours of study with a 2.5 GPA; passing scores on all sections of the PRAXIS I Test; two letters of recommendation; completion of education foundation courses and other required basic courses; interview. *Graduate:* Baccalaureate degree from a regionally accredited institution. *Teacher education specific:* Faculty interview; GRE or Miller Analogies Test; 2 letters of recommendation; PRAXIS II before certification.

SOUTH CAROLINA STATE UNIVERSITY—
cont'd

Fees and Expenses: Undergraduate: $5,570 in-state per academic year; $10,850 out-of-state. Graduate: Tuition charged per credit hour. On-campus room and board: $3,840. Other expenses: $3,885. Books and supplies: $1,200.

Financial Aid: Resources specifically for eligible students enrolled in teacher education programs are awarded on the basis of financial need and academic merit. The institution has a Program Participation Agreement with the U.S. Department of Education for eligible students to receive Pell Grants and other federal aid. Teacher scholarships available to qualifying students. *Contact:* Financial Aid Office at: (803) 536-7458.

Accreditation: *Regional:* SACS. *Professional:* NCATE. *Member of:* AACTE. *Approved by:* South Carolina Department of Education.

Undergraduate Programs: The Department of Teacher Education offers programs leading to the baccalaureate degree and teacher certification in early childhood, elementary, special education, and secondary education (biology, chemistry, foreign language, English, history, mathematics, political science, sociology). All programs require the completion of a general education core, professional studies, content area, field experiences, and student teaching. A minimum of 120 semester hours must be completed for the degree award.

Graduate Programs: The Master of Education degree programs include early childhood education, elementary education, reading education, and special education. Each program requires the completion of specific course requirements.

The Master of Arts in Teaching degree program is designed for those students who desire to become certified to teach in their areas of concentration.

A doctoral program is offered in supervision and leadership.

Licensure/Reciprocity: South Carolina. Students seeking teaching certification in a state other than South Carolina should consult with that state's teacher certification office early in their program of study to insure compliance with requirements. Many state directors of teacher credentialing have signed Interstate Agreements through NASDTEC that expedite the certification process.

UNIVERSITY OF SOUTH CAROLINA - AIKEN

School of Education
471 University Parkway
Aiken, South Carolina 29801
Phone: (803) 641-3483
Fax: (803) 641-3698
E-mail: education@usca.edu
Internet: http://www.usca.edu

Institution Description: The university was originally established as an off-campus center of the University of South Carolina (Columbia) in 1961.

The School of Education offers undergraduate and graduate programs leading to teacher certification. The first two years of undergraduate training consist of liberal arts, mathematics, and science education courses that are required of all students.

Institution Control: Public.

Calendar: Semester. Academic year August to May.

Official(s): Dr. Jeffrey M. Priest, Department Head.

Faculty: Full-time 22; part-time 38.

Degrees Awarded: 72 baccalaureate; 118 master's.

Admission Requirements: *Undergraduate:* Graduation from an accredited secondary school or GED; College Board SAT or ACT composite. Completion of at least 60 semester hours of study with a 2.5 GPA; passing scores on all sections of the PRAXIS I Test; two letters of recommendation; completion of education foundation courses and other required basic courses; interview. *Graduate:* Baccalaureate degree from a regionally accredited institution. *Teacher education specific:* Faculty interview; GRE or Miller Analogies Test; 2 letters of recommendation; PRAXIS II before certification.

Fees and Expenses: Undergraduate: $5,570 in-state per academic year; $10,850 out-of-state. Graduate: $266 per credit hour in-state; $568 credit hour out-of-state. On-campus room and board: $4,950. Books and supplies: $600.

Financial Aid: Resources specifically for eligible students enrolled in teacher education programs are awarded on the basis of financial need and academic merit. The institution has a Program Participation Agreement with the U.S. Department of Education for eligible students to receive Pell Grants and other federal aid. Teacher scholarships available to qualifying students. *Contact:* Financial Aid Office at: (803) 461-3476 or e-mail at: stuaid@usca.edu.

Accreditation: *Regional:* SACS. *Professional:* NCATE. *Member of:* AACTE. *Approved by:* South Carolina Department of Education.

Undergraduate Programs: The early childhood education program prepares teacher candidates to work in public and private schools with students ages 3 to 8. Graduates earn a Bachelor of Arts degree. The elementary education program is a four-year program that prepares teacher candidates to work in elementary and middle schools. The Bachelor of Arts degree is awarded upon completion of the program.

The secondary education program prepares teacher candidates for teaching in the areas of biology, chemistry, comprehensive science, comprehensive social studies, and English. Candidates earn a Bachelor of Science degree. The special education program prepares candidates to teach students who have disabilities. Candidates take specialized courses that include curriculum, pedagogy, and materials courses. A Bachelor of Arts degree is awarded upon completion of the program.

All baccalaureate programs require the completion of a general education core, professional studies, content area, field experiences, and student teaching. A minimum of 120 semester hours is required for the degree award.

Graduate Programs: The Master in Education degree in elementary education is designed to provide advanced professional studies to persons who currently hold teacher certification. The Master of Education degree in educational technology is designed to provide advanced studies to develop capabilities essential to the effective design, evaluation, and delivery of technology-based instruction and training (e.g., software development, multimedia development, assistive technology modifications, web-based development, and distance learning).

Licensure/Reciprocity: South Carolina. Students seeking teaching certification in a state other than South Carolina should consult with that state's teacher certification office early in their program of study to insure compliance with requirements. Many state directors of teacher credentialing have signed Interstate Agreements through NASDTEC that expedite the certification process.

UNIVERSITY OF SOUTH CAROLINA - COLUMBIA

College of Education
Wardlaw Building
Columbia, South Carolina 29208
Phone: (803) 777-3828
Fax: (803) 777-3035
E-mail: education@sc.edu
Internet: http://www.sc.edu

Institution Description: The University of South Carolina is a state university system of eight campuses. The Columbia campus offers undergraduate, graduate, and first-professional degree studies. The university was established in 1801.

The College of Education offers undergraduate and graduate programs leading to teacher certification in South Carolina.

Institution Control: Public.

Calendar: Semester. Academic year August to July.

Official(s): Dr. Les Sternberg, Dean. Irma Van Scoy and Michael Seaman, Associate Deans.

Faculty: Full-time 84; part-time 1; adjunct 70.

Degrees Awarded: 33 baccalaureate; 289 master's; 53 doctorate.

Admission Requirements: *Undergraduate:* Graduation from an accredited secondary school or GED; College Board SAT or ACT composite. Completion of at least 60 semester hours of study with a 2.5 GPA; passing scores on all sections of the PRAXIS I Test; two letters of recommendation; completion of education foundation courses and other required basic courses; interview. *Graduate:* Baccalaureate degree from a regionally accredited institution. *Teacher education specific:* Faculty interview; GRE or Miller Analogies Test; 2 letters of recommendation; PRAXIS II before certification.

Fees and Expenses: Undergraduate: $5,570 in-state per academic year; $10,850 out-of-state. Graduate: $5,360 per academic year; $11,648 out-of-state . On-campus room and board: $7,304. Books and supplies:$600.

Financial Aid: Resources specifically for eligible students enrolled in teacher education programs are awarded on the basis of financial need and academic merit. The institution has a Program Participation Agreement with the U.S. Department of Education for eligible students to receive Pell Grants and other federal aid. Teacher scholarships available to qualifying students. *Contact:* Edgar Miller at: (803) 777-8134 or e-mail at: ewmiller@gwm.sc.edu.

Accreditation: *Regional:* SACS. *Professional:* NCATE. *Member of:* AACTE. *Approved by:* South Carolina Department of Education.

Undergraduate Programs: Students can major in art education, music education, and physical education and receive certification in those areas for P-12 levels. New undergraduate programs began in fall 2003 in the areas of early childhood, elementary, and middle level education (double major in the content and education). All programs require the completion of 120 semester hours including the general education core, professional studies, content area, field experiences, and student teaching.

Graduate Programs: The College of Education, in cooperation with six other colleges and schools, offers graduate level degrees/certificate programs in many areas of initial and advanced certification or research specialty areas. Degree programs include the Master of Arts in Teaching, the Master of Education, Education Specialist, Doctor of Education, and Doctor of Philosophy in the fields of art, music, instruction, and teacher education areas, educational psychology and research, physical education, and educational leadership and policies. Each program has specific course requirements.

Licensure/Reciprocity: South Carolina. Students seeking teaching certification in a state other than South Carolina should consult with that state's teacher certification office early in their program of study to insure compliance with requirements. Many state directors of teacher credentialing have signed Interstate Agreements through NASDTEC that expedite the certification process.

UNIVERSITY OF SOUTH CAROLINA - SPARTANBURG

School of Education
800 University Way
Spartanburg, South Carolina 92303
Phone: (864) 503-5000
Fax: (864) 503-5727
E-mail: admissions@uscs.edu
Internet: http://www.uscs.edu

Institution Description: The university was originally established as the Spartanburg Regional Campus in 1967.

The goal of the School of Education is to prepare teachers for service to students in early childhood, elementary, middle, and secondary school settings.

Institution Control: Public.

Calendar: Semester. Academic year August to May.

Official(s): Dr. Charles Love, Dean.

Faculty: Full-time 25.

Degrees Awarded: 162 baccalaureate; 9 master's.

Admission Requirements: *Undergraduate:* Graduation from an accredited secondary school or GED; College Board SAT or ACT composite. Completion of at least 60 semester hours of study with a 2.5 GPA; passing scores on all sections of the PRAXIS I Test; two letters of recommendation; completion of education foundation courses and other required basic courses; interview. *Graduate:* Baccalaureate degree from a regionally accredited institution. *Teacher education specific:* Faculty interview; GRE or Miller Analogies Test; 2 letters of recommendation; PRAXIS II before certification.

Fees and Expenses: Undergraduate: $5,310 in-state per academic year; $11,136 out-of-state. Graduate: Tuition charged per creeit hour. On-campus room and board: $4,940. Books and supplies: $900.

Financial Aid: Resources specifically for eligible students enrolled in teacher education programs are awarded on the basis of financial need and academic merit. The institution has a Program Participation Agreement with the U.S. Department of Education for eligible students to receive Pell Grants and other federal aid. Teacher scholarships available to qualifying students. *Contact:* Financial Aid Office at: (864) 503-5340.

Accreditation: *Regional:* SACS. *Professional:* NCATE. *Member of:* AACTE. *Approved by:* South Carolina Department of Education.

Undergraduate Programs: Baccalaureate degrees are offered in early childhood education, elementary education, special education-learning disabilities, secondary education (biology, chemistry, English, French, mathematics, history, political science, Spanish), physical education, and physical education concentration in corporate fitness. All programs include a general education core, professional studies, content area, field experiences, and student teaching. A minimum of 120 semester hours is required for the degree award.

Graduate Programs: The School of Education offers the Master of Education in early childhood education, elementary education, and special education-visual impairment. Verification of a valid teaching credential from a regionally accredited institution is required for entry into the various degree programs.

Licensure/Reciprocity: South Carolina. Students seeking teaching certification in a state other than South Carolina should consult with that state's teacher certification office early in their program of study to insure compliance with requirements. Many state directors of teacher credentialing have signed Interstate Agreements through NASDTEC that expedite the certification process.

WINTHROP UNIVERSITY

Richard W. Riley College of Education
Department of Curriculum and Instruction
204 Wither's Building
701 Oakland Avenue
Rock Hill, South Carolina 29733
Phone: (803) 323-2211
Fax: (803) 323-2137
E-mail: admissions@winthrop.edu
Internet: http://www.winthrop.edu

Institution Description: Winthrop University is a state institution. It was established, chartered, and offered first instruction at the postsecondary level in 1886.

The Department of Curriculum and Instruction offers undergraduate and graduate programs leading to teacher certification in South Carolina.

Institution Control: Public.

Calendar: Semester. Academic year August to May.

Official(s): Dr. Sue Peck, Chair, Department of Curriculum and Instruction.

Faculty: Full-time 17.

Degrees Awarded: 100 baccalaureate; 97 master's.

Admission Requirements: *Undergraduate:* Graduation from an accredited secondary school or GED; College Board SAT or ACT composite. Completion of at least 60 semester hours of study with a 2.5 GPA; passing scores on all sections of the PRAXIS I Test; two letters of recommendation; completion of

WINTHROP UNIVERSITY—*cont'd*
education foundation courses and other required basic courses; interview. *Graduate:* Baccalaureate degree from a regionally accredited institution. *Teacher education specific:* Faculty interview; GRE or Miller Analogies Test; 2 letters of recommendation; PRAXIS II before certification.

Fees and Expenses: Undergraduate: $6,652 in-state per academic year; $12,348 out-of-state. Graduate: Tuition charged per credit hour. On-campus room and board: $4,630. Other expenses: $2,500. Books and supplies: $750.

Financial Aid: Resources specifically for eligible students enrolled in teacher education programs are awarded on the basis of financial need and academic merit. The institution has a Program Participation Agreement with the U.S. Department of Education for eligible students to receive Pell Grants and other federal aid. Teacher scholarships available to qualifying students. *Contact:* Financial Aid Office at: (803) 323-2189.

Accreditation: *Regional:* SACS. *Professional:* NCATE. *Member of:* AACTE. *Approved by:* South Carolina Department of Education.

Undergraduate Programs: The undergraduate certification programs include early childhood education, elementary education, and special education. The department also offers one nonlicensure degree program in family and consumer sciences. All baccalaureate programs require the completion of a general education core, professional studies, content area, field experiences, and student teaching. A minimum of 120 semester hours is required for the degree award.

Graduate Programs: At the graduate level, the department offers the Master of Education degrees in elementary education, middle level education, reading, secondary education, and special education. Each program has specific course requirements.

Licensure/Reciprocity: South Carolina. Students seeking teaching certification in a state other than South Carolina should consult with that state's teacher certification office early in their program of study to insure compliance with requirements. Many state directors of teacher credentialing have signed Interstate Agreements through NASDTEC that expedite the certification process.

SOUTH DAKOTA

AUGUSTANA COLLEGE

Teacher Education Program
2001 South Summit Street
Sioux Falls, South Dakota 57197
Phone: (605) 336-0770
Fax: (605) 336-5518
E-mail: info@augie.edu
Internet: http://www.augie.edu

Institution Description: Augustana College is a private institution affiliated with the Evangelical Lutheran Church in America.

The conceptual framework for the Teacher Education Program is grounded in a philosophy that integrates the best of Western educational thought, the wisdom of indigenous Native American culture, and emerging research on positive youth development.

Institution Control: Private.

Calendar: Semester. Academic year August to May.

Official(s): Dr. R. Kiner, Chair.

Faculty: Full-time 11; adjunct 1.

Degrees Awarded: 66 baccalaureate; 1 master's.

Admission Requirements: *Undergraduate:* Graduation from an approved secondary school or GED; College Board SAT or ACT composite. *Teacher education specific:* Completion of 15 credit hours; academic advisor's recommendation; passing scores on PRAXIS I (reading, writing, mathematics); 2.6 GPA. *Graduate:* Baccalaureate degree from a regionally accredited institution. *Teacher education specific:* Contact the Director of Graduate Study or the department chair.

Fees and Expenses: Undergraduate: $16,972 per academic year. Graduate: Tuition charged per credit hour. On-campus room and board: $3,600. Other expenses: $1,300. Books and supplies: $1,100.

Financial Aid: Resources specifically for eligible students enrolled in teacher education programs are awarded on the basis of financial need and academic merit. The institution has a Program Participation Agreement with the U.S. Department of Education for eligible students to receive Pell Grants and other federal aid. Teacher scholarships available to qualifying students. *Contact:* Financial Aid Office at: (605) 274-5216.

Accreditation: *Regional:* NCA. *Professional:* NCATE. *Member of:* AACTE. *Approved by:* South Dakota Department of Education and Cultural Affairs.

Undergraduate Programs: The Teacher Education Program offers professional preparation programs for careers in the areas of education of the deaf and hard of hearing, elementary education, secondary education, special education, and preprofessional preparation in communication disorders. All programs lead to the baccalaureate degree and require the completion of a general education core, professional studies, content area, field experiences, and student teaching. A minimum of 130 credit hours is required for the degree award.

Graduate Programs: Students may choose to complete or extend their professional preparation at the graduate level. The college offers the Master of Arts degree in the areas of teaching, elementary education, secondary education, and special education.

Licensure/Reciprocity: South Dakota. Students seeking teaching certification in a state other than South Dakota should consult with that state's teacher certification office early in their program of study to insure compliance with requirements. Many state directors of teacher credentialing have signed Interstate Agreements through NASDTEC that expedite the certification process.

BLACK HILLS STATE UNIVERSITY

College of Education
Teacher Education Program
1200 University Avenue
Spearfish, South Dakota 57799-9502
Phone: (605) 642-6550
Fax: (605) 642-6022
E-mail: admissions@bhsu.edu
Internet: http://www.bhsu.edu

Institution Description: Black Hills State University is a state institution.

The Teacher Education Program offers undergraduate and graduate programs leading to licensure to teach in South Dakota schools.

Institution Control: Public.

Calendar: Semester. Academic year July to June.

Official(s): Dr. Dean Myers, Dean, College of Education.

Faculty: Full-time 37.

Degrees Awarded: 112 baccalaureate; 54 master's.

Admission Requirements: *Undergraduate:* Graduation from an approved secondary school of GED; minimum ACT score of 20. *Teacher education specific:* Completion of 63 credit hours; academic advisor's recommendation; passing scores on PRAXIS I (reading, writing, mathematics); 2.6 GPA. professional portfolio; completion of all required tests. *Graduate:* Baccalaureate degree from a regionally accredited institution. *Teacher education specific:* Faculty interview; teaching licensure for some programs; letters of recommendation.

Fees and Expenses: Undergraduate: $5,742 in-state per academic year; out-of-state $9,420. Graduate tuition charged per credit hour. On-campus room and board: $3,823. Books and supplies: $800.

Financial Aid: Resources specifically for eligible students enrolled in teacher education programs are awarded on the basis of financial need and academic merit. The institution has a Program Participation Agreement with the U.S. Department of Education for eligible students to receive Pell Grants and other federal aid. Teacher scholarships available to qualifying students. *Contact:* Financial Aid Office at: (605) 642-6343.

Accreditation: *Regional:* NCA. *Professional:* NCATE. *Member of:* AACTE. *Approved by:* South Dakota Department of Education and Cultural Affairs.

Undergraduate Programs: The Teacher Education Program affords students the opportunity to qualify for licensure to teach in preschool, elementary school, middle school, secondary school, K-12, and special education. There are 40 teaching endorsements for those who wish to teach in an area outside their major area. K-12 education majors include: art, elementary education-special education, instrumental music, physical education, secondary education-special education, Spanish, vocal

BLACK HILLS STATE UNIVERSITY—*cont'd*

music. Secondary (7-12) majors include: biology, business, chemistry, English, English composite, history, composite, mathematics composite, physical science, speech/theatre, science composite, industrial education.

All baccalaureate programs require the completion of a general education core, professional studies, content area, field experiences, and student teaching. A minimum of 128 semester hours is required for the degree award.

Graduate Programs: Graduate courses are available to certified teachers leading to teacher endorsements and the Master of Science degree in curriculum and instruction with specializations in curriculum, reading, special education, middle school, and early childhood.

Licensure/Reciprocity: South Dakota. Students seeking teaching certification in a state other than South Dakota should consult with that state's teacher certification office early in their program of study to insure compliance with requirements. Many state directors of teacher credentialing have signed Interstate Agreements through NASDTEC that expedite the certification process.

DAKOTA STATE UNIVERSITY

College of Education
Kennedy Center, Room 150
820 North Washington Avenue
Madison, South Dakota 57042-1799
Phone: (605) 256-5177
Fax: (605) 256-7300
E-mail: tom.hawley@dsu.edu
Internet: http://www.dsu.edu

Institution Description: Dakota State University was established as Dakota Normal School in 1881.

Dakota State University and South Dakota State University have established cooperative programs for early childhood education majors from SDSU elementary or elementary/special learning and behavioral problems education majors from DSU.

Institution Control: Public.

Calendar: Semester. Academic year September to May.

Official(s): Dr. Tom Hawley, Dean; Ms.Crystal Pauli, Director of Field Services and Certification.

Faculty: Full-time 12; part-time 11; adjunct 2.

Degrees Awarded: 59 baccalaureate; 21 master's.

Admission Requirements: *Undergraduate:* Graduation in top two-thirds of secondary school or GED; 2.0 GPA. *Teacher education specific:* Completion of 48 semester hours; 2.5 GPA; declaration of major; completion of preprofessional courses and all required departmental tests; personal goal statement; faculty interview. *Graduate:* Baccalaureate from a regionally accredited institution. *Teacher education specific:* Satisfactory scores on the GRE or Miller Analogies Test; basic knowledge in the discipline as defined by the specific program; faculty interview; letters of recommendation.

Fees and Expenses: Undergraduate: $65 per credit in-state; $206.65 out-of-state. Graduate: $98.65 in-state per credit; $290.75 out-of-state. On-campus room and board: $3,307. Other expenses: $2,480. Books and supplies: $750.

Financial Aid: Resources specifically for eligible students enrolled in teacher education programs are awarded on the basis of financial need and academic merit. The institution has a Program Participation Agreement with the U.S. Department of Education for eligible students to receive Pell Grants and other federal aid. Teacher scholarships available to qualifying students. *Contact:* Rosie Jamison at: (605) 256-5152 or e-mail at: rosie.jamison@dsu.edu.

Accreditation: *Regional:* NCA. *Professional:* NCATE. *Member of:* AACTE. *Approved by:* South Dakota Department of Education and Cultural Affairs.

Undergraduate Programs: The Bachelor of Science in elementary education program offers courses designed to provide a broad background for prospective teachers. The program requires participation in field experiences prior to student

teaching. The Bachelor of Science in Education - K-12 and secondary education degrees are offered in cooperation with the appropriate academic colleges: business and information systems (business education 7-12; computer education K-12); liberal arts (English education 7-12); natural sciences (biology education 7-12; mathematics education 7-12; physical science education 7-12).

All baccalaureate programs require the completion of the general education core, professional studies, content area, field experiences, and student teaching. A minimum of 128 semester hours is required for the degree award.

Graduate Programs: Students desiring to work toward a Master of Education or Master of Arts in Teaching must apply for admission into the graduate program. Contact the College of Education for programs available and course requirements.

Licensure/Reciprocity: South Dakota. Students seeking teaching certification in a state other than South Dakota should consult with that state's teacher certification office early in their program of study to insure compliance with requirements. Many state directors of teacher credentialing have signed Interstate Agreements through NASDTEC that expedite the certification process.

DAKOTA WESLEYAN UNIVERSITY

Department of Education
Teacher Education Program
1200 West University Avenue
Mitchell, South Dakota 57301
Phone: (605) 995-2634
Fax: (605) 995-2150
E-mail: kelein@dwu.edu
Internet: http://www.dwu.edu

Institution Description: Dakota Wesleyan University is a private institution affiliated with the United Methodist Church.

The purpose of the teacher education program is to provide an organized, integrated system of study and experience for the preparation of elementary and secondary teachers.

Institution Control: Private.

Calendar: Semester. Academic year August to May.

Official(s): Dr. Kevin Lein, Department Head.

Faculty: Full-time 4; part-time 1; adjunct 18.

Degrees Awarded: 23 baccalaureate.

Admission Requirements: *Undergraduate:* Graduation in top half of class in secondary school or GED; ACT score of 18; 2.5 GPA. *Teacher education specific:* Professional statement; 2.7 GPA; faculty interview; completion of all required tests/exams.

Fees and Expenses: $15,000 comprehensive fee per academic year.

Financial Aid: Resources specifically for eligible students enrolled in teacher education programs are awarded on the basis of financial need and academic merit. The institution has a Program Participation Agreement with the U.S. Department of Education for eligible students to receive Pell Grants and other federal aid. Teacher scholarships available to qualifying students. *Contact:* Wilma Hjellum at: (800) 333-8506 or e-mail @wihjell@dwu.edu.

Accreditation: *Regional:* NCA. *Professional:* NCATE. *Approved by:* South Dakota Department of Education and Cultural Affairs.

Undergraduate Programs: Baccalaureate programs offered by the Education Department include: K-8 elementary education with 5-8 middle level; 7-12 mathematics, science-biology, social science-history education, social science composite education, business education; K-12 art education, music-vocal education, physical education, special education. Numerous endorsements are offered. All programs require the completion of a general education core, professional studies, content area, field experiences, and student teaching. A minimum of 125 credit hours is required for the degree award.

Licensure/Reciprocity: South Dakota. Students seeking teaching certification in a state other than South Dakota should consult with that state's teacher certification office early in their program of study to insure compliance with requirements. Many state directors of teacher credentialing have signed Interstate Agreements through NASDTEC that expedite the certification process.

MOUNT MARTY COLLEGE
Division of Teacher Education
1105 West 8th Street
Yankton, South Dakota 57078
Phone: (605) 668-1011
Fax: (605) 668-1607
E-mail: mmcadmit@mtmc.edu
Internet: http://www.mtmc.edu

Institution Description: Mount Marty College is a private institution affiliated with the Sisters of St. Benedict of Sacred Heart Monastery, Roman Catholic Church.

Mount Marty College combines theory and practice to ensure confident and competent teachers.

Institution Control: Private.

Calendar: Semester. Academic year August to May.

Official(s): Dr. Mark Hurtubise, President.

Faculty: Full-time 4.

Degrees Awarded: 28 baccalaureate.

Admission Requirements: *Undergraduate:* Graduation from an approved secondary school or GED; ACT composite score of 18; 2.0 GPA. *Teacher education specific:* Completion of all required tests/exams; personal goal statement; declaration of major; faculty interview.

Fees and Expenses: $14,186 per academic year. On-campus room and board: $4,670. Other expenses: $2,330. Books and supplies: $640.

Financial Aid: Resources specifically for eligible students enrolled in teacher education programs are awarded on the basis of financial need and academic merit. The institution has a Program Participation Agreement with the U.S. Department of Education for eligible students to receive Pell Grants and other federal aid. Teacher scholarships available to qualifying students. *Contact:* Financial Aid Office at (605) 668-1589.

Accreditation: *Regional:* NCA. *Member of:* AACTE. *Approved by:* South Dakota Department of Education and Cultural Affairs.

Undergraduate Programs: Education majors are offered in elementary education (K-8); special education (K-12); secondary education (7-12 with concentrations in biology, chemistry, English, history, mathematics); physical education (K-12); music education (K-12). Students have the opportunity to work in area schools from their freshman orientation class, to field experience, practicum, and into student teaching. The college offers a full semester or student teaching. Students are advised to complete additional endorsements and authorizations for marketability in order to teach additional subjects. A minimum of 128 semester hours is required for the degree award.

Licensure/Reciprocity: South Dakota. Students seeking teaching certification in a state other than South Dakota should consult with that state's teacher certification office early in their program of study to insure compliance with requirements. Many state directors of teacher credentialing have signed Interstate Agreements through NASDTEC that expedite the certification process.

SOUTH DAKOTA STATE UNIVERSITY
College of Education and counseling
Department of Teacher Education
Box 507 Wenona Hall
Brookings, South Dakota 57007
Phone: (605) 688-4321
Fax: (605) 688-5785
E-mail: sdsu_admissions@sdstate.edu
Internet: http://www.sdstate.edu

Institution Description: South Dakota State University is a state institution and land-grant college.

The Department of Teacher Education prepares students to teach in an academic major or other fields in which they are appropriately prepared. Dakota State University and South Dakota State University have established cooperative programs for early childhood education majors from SDSU elementary or elementary/special learning and behavioral problems education majors from DSU.

Institution Control: Public.

Calendar: Semester. Academic year September to May.

Official(s): Dr. Lonell Moeller, Chair, Department of Teacher Education.

Faculty: Full-time 24; part-time 2; adjunct 10.

Degrees Awarded: 54 baccalaureate; 53 master's.

Admission Requirements: *Undergraduate:* Graduation in top two-thirds of secondary school or GED; 2.0 GPA. *Teacher education specific:* Completion of 48 semester hours; 2.5 GPA; declaration of major; completion of preprofessional courses and all required departmental tests; personal goal statement; faculty interview. *Graduate:* Baccalaureate from a regionally accredited institution. *Teacher education specific:* Satisfactory scores on the GRE or Miller Analogies Test; basic knowledge in the discipline as defined by the specific program; faculty interview; letters of recommendation.

Fees and Expenses: Undergraduate: $4,538 in-state per academic year; $9,563 out-of-state. Graduate: Tuition is charged per credit hour. On-campus room and board: $3,854. Other expenses: $3,336. Books and supplies: $800.

Financial Aid: Resources specifically for eligible students enrolled in teacher education programs are awarded on the basis of financial need and academic merit. The institution has a Program Participation Agreement with the U.S. Department of Education for eligible students to receive Pell Grants and other federal aid. Teacher scholarships available to qualifying students. *Contact:* Financial Aid Office at: $605) 688-4695.

Accreditation: *Regional:* NCA. *Professional:* NCATE. *Member of:* AACTE. *Approved by:* South Dakota Department of Education and Cultural Affairs.

Undergraduate Programs: The Department of Teacher Education program is structured around three components: general studies, specialty studies, and professional studies. Areas of study include: agricultural education, art (K-12), biology, birth to age 8 education, career and technical education, chemistry, early childhood education, earth/space science, economics, education technology, English, family and consumer science, French (K-12), geography, German, history, mass communications, mathematics, music education (K-12), physical education (K-12), physics, political science, psychology, sociology, Spanish (K-12), speech/debate. In addition, endorsements can be obtained in the above areas as well as coaching and English as a new language.

All baccalaureate programs require the completion of 128 semester hours for the degree award.

Graduate Programs: Graduate programs leading to the Master's degree are offered. Contact Dr. Lonelle Moeller, Department Head of the Teacher Education Program, for detailed information.

Licensure/Reciprocity: South Dakota. Students seeking teaching certification in a state other than South Dakota should consult with that state's teacher certification office early in their program of study to insure compliance with requirements. Many state directors of teacher credentialing have signed Interstate Agreements through NASDTEC that expedite the certification process.

UNIVERSITY OF SIOUX FALLS
Fredrikson School of Education
1101 West 22nd Street
Sioux Falls, South Dakota 57105
Phone: (605) 331-6608
Fax: (605) 331-6615
E-mail: admissions@usiouxfalls.edu
Internet: http://www.usiouxfalls.edu

UNIVERSITY OF SIOUX FALLS—*cont'd*

Institution Description: The University of Sioux Falls, formerly known as Sioux Falls College, is a private institution affiliated with the American Baptist Churches, U.S.A.

The Fredrikson School of Education offers programs at the undergraduate and graduate levels leading to teacher licensure.

Institution Control: Private.

Calendar: Semester. Academic year September to May.

Official(s): Dr. Rachelle Loven, Dean; Dr. Brett Bradfield, Director of Graduate Programs.

Faculty: Full-time 6; part-time and adjunct.

Degrees Awarded: 23 baccalaureate; 39 master's.

Admission Requirements: *Undergraduate:* Graduation from an approved secondary school or GED. *Teacher education specific:* Completion of 45 credit hours; academic advisor's recommendation; passing scores on all required exams/tests; 2.5 GPA. *Graduate:* Baccalaureate degree from a regionally accredited institution. *Teacher education specific:* Contact the Director of Graduate Study for program admission requirements.

Accreditation: *Regional:* NCA. *Professional:* NCATE. *Member of:* AACTE. *Approved by:* South Dakota Department of Education and Cultural Affairs.

Undergraduate Programs: Areas of study include: art, middle school endorsement in science, biology, chemistry, birth through preschool endorsement, middle school endorsement in English/language arts, physical education endorsement, history, middle school/junior high school endorsement- mathematics, mathematics, middle school/junior high School endorsement-social studies, music, speech/theater. All baccalaureate programs require the completion of a general education core, professional studies, content area, field experiences, and student teaching. A minimum of 128 semester hours is required for the degree award.

Graduate Programs: The Master of Education program is focused in one of four areas: leadership in reading, leadership in technology, leadership in early childhood education, or leadership in schools. Each program has specific course requirements.

Licensure/Reciprocity: South Dakota. Students seeking teaching certification in a state other than South Dakota should consult with that state's teacher certification office early in their program of study to insure compliance with requirements. Many state directors of teacher credentialing have signed Interstate Agreements through NASDTEC that expedite the certification process.

UNIVERSITY OF SOUTH DAKOTA

School of Education
414 East Clark Street
Vermillion, South Dakota 57069-2390
Phone: (605) 677-5011
Fax: (605) 677-5438
E-mail: admissions@usd.edu
Internet: http://www.usd.edu

Institution Description: The University of South Dakota is a state institution that was established and chartered in 1862.

The mission of the School of Education is to prepare professional leaders in education and to develop their reflective decision-making skills through a systematic integration of theory, research, content, and field experiences.

Institution Control: Public.

Calendar: Semester. Academic year September to May.

Official(s): Dr. Rubin, Dean.

Faculty: Full-time 54; part-time 15; adjunct 3.

Degrees Awarded: 78 baccalaureate; 118 master's; 39 doctorate.

Admission Requirements: *Undergraduate:* Graduation from an approved secondary school with rank in top 60%; ACT 18 or high school GPA 2.6. *Teacher education specific:* Passing scores on all required tests; 2.5 GPA; completion of an oral communication course; faculty recommendations; personal interview; satisfactory evaluation of at least one paraprofessional experience. *Graduate:* Baccalaureate degree from a regionally accredited institution. *Teacher education specific:* GRE or Miller Analogies Test; recommendations; faculty interview.

Fees and Expenses: Undergraduate: $72.10 in-state per credit hour; $229.15 out-of-state. Graduate: $109.40 in-state per credit hour; $322.45 out-of-state. On-campus room and board: Contact Student Housing Office. Books and supplies: $800.

Financial Aid: Resources specifically for eligible students enrolled in teacher education programs are awarded on the basis of financial need and academic merit. The institution has a Program Participation Agreement with the U.S. Department of Education for eligible students to receive Pell Grants and other federal aid. Teacher scholarships available to qualifying students. *Contact:* Julie Pier at: (605) 677-5446.

Accreditation: *Regional:* NCA. *Professional:* NCATE. *Member of:* AACTE. *Approved by:* South Dakota Department of Education and Cultural Affairs.

Undergraduate Programs: Teacher Education Programs offer students opportunities to be certified in the following areas: elementary education (early childhood education; kindergarten education); middle level education; elementary/special education; secondary/special education; secondary education (concentrations in biology, chemistry, earth science, English, French, German, history, mathematics, physics, political science, Spanish, speech, theatre); special education (K-12); physical education (K-12); music education (K-12) vocal and instrumental; art education. All programs require the completion of a general education core, professional studies, content area, field experiences, and student teaching. A minimum of 128 semester hours is required for the degree award.

Graduate Programs: Master's, Specialist, and Doctoral programs are also available in teacher education and the related areas of educational administration, counseling, curriculum and instruction, physical education and recreation, and technology.

Licensure/Reciprocity: South Dakota. Students seeking teaching certification in a state other than South Dakota should consult with that state's teacher certification office early in their program of study to insure compliance with requirements. Many state directors of teacher credentialing have signed Interstate Agreements through NASDTEC that expedite the certification process.

TENNESSEE

AUSTIN PEAY STATE UNIVERSITY

School of Education

601 College Street
Clarksville, Tennessee 37040
Phone: (931) 221-7011
Fax: (931) 221-6168
E-mail: admissions@apsu.edu
Internet: http://www.apsu.edu

Institution Description: Austin Peay State University is a member of the Tennessee State University and Community College System. It was established in 1927.

The mission of the School of Education is to prepare competent, caring, and reflective professionals who seek to improve the lives of others through teaching and learning.

Institution Control: Public.

Calendar: Semester. Academic year August to May.

Official(s): Dr. Don Luck, Dean.

Faculty: Full-time 18.

Degrees Awarded: 20 baccalaureate; 96 master's.

Admission Requirements: *Undergraduate:* Graduation from an approved secondary school or GED; ACT composite. *Teacher education specific:* Completion of 60 semester hours of coursework including education foundation courses; 2.75 GPA; passing scores on PRAXIS I (reading, writing, mathematics); personal goal statement; recommendations; faculty interview. *Graduate:* Baccalaureate from a regionally accredited institution. *Teacher education specific:* 2.75 GPA; GRE or Miller Analogies Test; references; faculty interview.

Fees and Expenses: Undergraduate: $3,784 in-state per academic year; $11,936 out-of-state. Graduate: $181 per credit hour in-state; $270 out-of-state. On-campus room and board: $4,096. Other expenses: $800. Books and supplies: $1,000.

Financial Aid: Resources specifically for eligible students enrolled in teacher education programs are awarded on the basis of financial need and academic merit. The institution has a Program Participation Agreement with the U.S. Department of Education for eligible students to receive Pell Grants and other federal aid. Teacher scholarships available to qualifying students. *Contact:* Financial Aid Office at: (931) 221-7907.

Accreditation: *Regional:* SACS. *Professional:* NCATE. *Member of:* AACTE. *Approved by:* Tennessee State Board of Education.

Undergraduate Programs: The School of Education offers undergraduate programs with emphasis placed on professional preparation and other support activities. Education is divided into major coordinating and instructional areas including: early childhood, Interdisciplinary studies (elementary), secondary education, and special education. All baccalaureate programs require the completion of a general education core, professional studies, content area, field experiences, and student teaching. A minimum of 128 semester hours is required for the degree award.

Graduate Programs: Graduate areas leading to the master's and doctoral degrees include: administration and supervision, curriculum and instruction, elementary education, reading, secondary education, special education. Each program has specific course requirements.

Licensure/Reciprocity: Tennessee. Students seeking teaching certification in a state other than Tennessee should consult with that state's teacher certification office early in their program of study to insure compliance with requirements. Many state directors of teacher credentialing have signed Interstate Agreements through NASDTEC that expedite the certification process.

BELMONT UNIVERSITY

Department of Education

1900 Belmont Boulevard]
Nashville, Tennessee 37212-3757
Phone: (615) 460-6232
Fax: (615) 460-5556
E-mail: hutchins@belmont.edu
Internet: http://www.belmont.edu

Institution Description: Belmont University is a private institution affiliated with the Tennessee Baptist Convention. It was chartered and offered first instruction at the postsecondary level in 1951.

The Department of Education offers undergraduate, graduate, and post-baccalaureate licensure programs.

Institution Control: Private.

Calendar: Semester. Academic year August to May.

Official(s): Dr. Trevor Hutchins, Chairman.

Faculty: Full-time 8; part-time 4; adjunct 6.

Degrees Awarded: 5 baccalaureate; 33 master's.

Admission Requirements: *Undergraduate:* Graduation from an approved secondary school or GED; College Board SAT or ACT composite. *Teacher education specific:* Passing scores on PRAXIS I (reading, writing, mathematics); personal goal statement; recommendations; completion of education foundations courses; faculty interview. *Graduate:* Baccalaureate degree from a regionally accredited institution. *Teacher education specific:* 2.75 GPA; GRE or Miller Analogies Test; faculty interview.

Fees and Expenses: Undergraduate: $380 in-state per credit hour. Graduate: $562 per credit hour. On-campus room and board: Meal plan $1,470 per semester; board $1,375 per semester.

Financial Aid: Resources specifically for eligible students enrolled in teacher education programs are awarded on the basis of financial need and academic merit. The institution has a Program Participation Agreement with the U.S. Department of Education for eligible students to receive Pell Grants and other federal aid. Teacher scholarships available to qualifying students. *Contact:* Pamela Gill at: (615) 460-6403 or e-mail at: gillp@mail.belmont.edu.

Accreditation: *Regional:* SACS. *Professional:* NCATE. *Approved by:* Tennessee State Board of Education.

Undergraduate Programs: Undergraduate licensure programs include: K-12 (art, music education, theatre and drama, physical education, health, social work); preK-4 (emphasis on K-4 with a major in an academic discipline); 5-8 (emphasis in 5-8 with a major in an academic discipline); 7-12 (biology, chemistry, communication studies, English, French, German, history, Latin, mathematics, physics, political science, Spanish); 9-12 (psychology, sociology). All baccalaureate programs require the

BELMONT UNIVERSITY—*cont'd*

completion of the general education core, professional studies, content area, field experiences, and student teaching. A minimum of 128 semester hours is required for the degree award.

Graduate Programs: Post-baccalaureate students, with appropriate undergraduate majors, may seek licensure in a 1-2 year program depending on the grade level of the licensure.

The graduate programs in education, the Master of Education and the Master of Music Education, are designed to develop effective teachers who are scholars, skillful communicators, and competent practitioners. The curriculum leads to a specialization in elementary education or in English and within the elementary track there are further options for emphasis in gifted education, language arts, or early childhood.

Licensure/Reciprocity: Tennessee. Students seeking teaching certification in a state other than Tennessee should consult with that state's teacher certification office early in their program of study to insure compliance with requirements. Many state directors of teacher credentialing have signed Interstate Agreements through NASDTEC that expedite the certification process.

CARSON-NEWMAN COLLEGE

Education Division
Teacher Education Department
1646 South Russell Avenue
Jefferson City, Tennessee 37760
Phone: (865) 471-2000
Fax: (865) 471-3502
E-mail: admissions@cncadm.cn.edu
Internet: http://www.cn.edu

Institution Description: Carson-Newman College is a private college affiliated with the Tennessee Baptist Convention. It was founded in 1851.

The mission of the Education Division is to prepare caring and professional competent teachers who feel called to lifelong commitment to leadership, learning, and service.

Institution Control: Private.

Calendar: Semester. Academic year August to May.

Official(s): Dr. Margaret Ann Hypes, Dean.

Faculty: Full-time 13; adjunct 25.

Degrees Awarded: 71 baccalaureate.

Admission Requirements: *Undergraduate:* Graduation from an approved secondary school or GED; ACT composite. *Teacher education specific:* Passing scores on PRAXIS I (reading, writing, mathematics); personal goal statement; recommendations; completion of education foundations courses; faculty interview.

Fees and Expenses: $13,620 per academic year. On-campus room and board: $5,100. Other expenses: $2,285. Books and supplies: $700.

Financial Aid: Resources specifically for eligible students enrolled in teacher education programs are awarded on the basis of financial need and academic merit. The institution has a Program Participation Agreement with the U.S. Department of Education for eligible students to receive Pell Grants and other federal aid. Teacher scholarships available to qualifying students. *Contact:* Financial Aid Office at: (865) 471-3247.

Accreditation: *Regional:* SACS. *Professional:* NCATE. *Member of:* AACTE. *Approved by:* Tennessee State Board of Education.

Undergraduate Programs: The Teacher Education Department serves as the coordinating unit for undergraduate programs leading to licensure to teach in grades P-12. The Bachelor of Arts in liberal studies with elementary licensure or the Bachelor of Science in special education are offered. Also, the Bachelor of Arts without licensure and a Bachelor of Science in human exceptionalities are offered. Other departments on campus offer programs in preK-4 child and family studies, art (K-12), 7-12 in biology, basic business, chemistry, English, French, history, mathematics; K-12 in music, physical education, political science, Spanish; 5-12 family and consumer science.

All baccalaureate programs require the completion of the general education core, professional studies, content area, field experiences, and student teaching. A minim of 128 semester hours is required for the degree award.

Licensure/Reciprocity: Tennessee. Students seeking teaching certification in a state other than Tennessee should consult with that state's teacher certification office early in their program of study to insure compliance with requirements. Many state directors of teacher credentialing have signed Interstate Agreements through NASDTEC that expedite the certification process.

DAVID LIPSCOMB UNIVERSITY

College of Education and Professional Studies
Department of Education
3901 Granny White Pike
Nashville, Tennessee 37204-3951
Phone: (615) 279-6076
Fax: (615) 279-1804
E-mail: admissions@dlu.edu
Internet: http://www.dlu.edu

Institution Description: David Lipscomb University is a private institution affiliated with the Churches of Christ. It was established as Nashville Bible School in 1891.

The primary purpose of the Department of Education is to train and inspire students so that they master the knowledge, attitudes, and skills needed to become caring and competent educators in a diverse and technological society.

Institution Control: Private.

Calendar: Semester. Academic year August to May.

Official(s): Dr. Michael Hammond, Chair.

Faculty: Full-time 10.

Degrees Awarded: 45 baccalaureate; 10 master's.

Admission Requirements: *Undergraduate:* Graduation from an approved secondary school or GED; College Board SAT or ACT composite. *Teacher education specific:* Passing scores on PRAXIS I (reading, writing, mathematics); personal goal statement; recommendations; completion of education foundations courses; faculty interview. *Graduate:* Baccalaureate degree from a regionally accredited institution. *Teacher education specific:* 2.75 GPA; GRE or Miller Analogies Test; faculty interview.

Fees and Expenses: Undergraduate: $12,176 per academic year. Graduate: $453 per credit hour. On-campus room and board: $5,590. Other expenses: $2,700. Books and supplies: $750.

Financial Aid: Resources specifically for eligible students enrolled in teacher education programs are awarded on the basis of financial need and academic merit. The institution has a Program Participation Agreement with the U.S. Department of Education for eligible students to receive Pell Grants and other federal aid. Teacher scholarships available to qualifying students. *Contact:* Financial Aid Office at: (615) 269-1791.

Accreditation: *Regional:* SACS. *Professional:* NCATE. *Member of:* AACTE. *Approved by:* Tennessee Department of Education.

Undergraduate Programs: Students in secondary education will be expected to cohort a teaching major in the content subject or area in which they plan to teach. A student may also elect to complete state requirements for endorsement in additional high school subjects. Undergraduate students completing K-8 programs may work toward either the Bachelor of Arts or Bachelor of Science degree. All baccalaureate programs require the completion of a general education core, professional studies, content area, field experiences, and student teaching. A minimum of 132 credit hours is required for the degree award.

Graduate Programs: The Master of Education degree in instructional leadership and school administration and supervision is available for professional teacher development. Courses leading to initial teacher licensure are offered to qualified students. The Graduate Program in Education is a component of the Department of Education and the College of Education and Professional Studies.

Licensure/Reciprocity: Tennessee. Students seeking teaching certification in a state other than Tennessee should consult with that state's teacher certification office early in their program of study to insure compliance with requirements. Many state directors of teacher credentialing have signed Interstate Agreements through NASDTEC that expedite the certification process.

EAST TENNESSEE STATE UNIVERSITY
Department of Curriculum and Instruction
807 University Parkway
Johnson City, Tennessee 37614
Phone: (423) 439-1000
Fax: (423) 439-4630
E-mail: go2etsu@etsu.edu
Internet: http://www.etsu.edu

Institution Description: The university was originally established and chartered as East Tennessee State Normal School in 1909.

The faculty of the Department of Curriculum and Instruction prepares professional educators who are committed to innovation, communication, and learning.

Institution Control: Public.

Calendar: Semester. Academic year August to May.

Official(s): Dr. E.J. Dwyer, Professor, Curriculum and Instruction.

Faculty: Full-time 15; adjunct 15.

Degrees Awarded: 34 baccalaureate; 171 master's; 26 doctorate.

Admission Requirements: *Undergraduate:* Graduation from an approved secondary school or GED; ACT composite. *Teacher education specific:* Completion of 60 semester hours of coursework including education foundation courses; 2.75 GPA; passing scores on PRAXIS I (reading, writing, mathematics; personal goal statement; recommendations; faculty interview. *Graduate:* Baccalaureate from a regionally accredited institution. *Teacher education specific:* 2.75 GPA; GRE or Miller Analogies Test; references; faculty interview.

Fees and Expenses: Undergraduate: $3,839 in-state per academic year; $11,771 out of state. Graduate: $101 per credit hour in-state; $270 out-of-state. On-campus room and board: $4,565. Other expenses: $4,195. Books and supplies: $900.

Financial Aid: Resources specifically for eligible students enrolled in teacher education programs are awarded on the basis of financial need and academic merit. The institution has a Program Participation Agreement with the U.S. Department of Education for eligible students to receive Pell Grants and other federal aid. Teacher scholarships available to qualifying students. *Contact:* Financial Aid Office at: (423) 439-4300.

Accreditation: *Regional:* SACS. *Professional:* NCATE. *Member of:* AACTE. *Approved by:* Tennessee State Board of Education.

Undergraduate Programs: At the undergraduate level, the interdisciplinary studies in education major offers teacher candidates the opportunity to complete a course of study leading to licensure in elementary education K-8.

Secondary education and K-12 grade levels require a specific major field of study in addition to professional education requirements. Major areas of study are: English 7-12, health K-12, mathematics 7-12, modern language 7-12 (French, German, Spanish), music education K-12 (vocal, instrumental), science 7-12 (biology, chemistry, physics, earth science), social studies 7-12 (history, political science, geography, economics, psychology, sociology), speech communication 7-12, technology education, visual arts K-12, vocational consumer homemaking 5-12, theatre K-12.

A minimum of 132 semester hours must be completed for the degree award including a general education core, content area, professional studies, studies, field experiences, and student teaching.

Graduate Programs: The Master of Arts in Teaching-Elementary or Master of Arts in Teaching-Secondary are programs designed for students who have obtained a bachelor's degree in a field other than education. The elementary M.A.T. program covers K-8 licensure. The secondary M.A.T. covers 7-12 licensure in biology, chemistry, physics, earth science, economics, English, German Spanish, French, geography, history, government, speech communication, mathematics, vocational home economics (5-12), and vocational industrial technology (5-12).

Licensure/Reciprocity: Tennessee. Students seeking teaching certification in a state other than Tennessee should consult with that state's teacher certification office early in their program of study to insure compliance with requirements. Many state directors of teacher credentialing have signed Interstate Agreements through NASDTEC that expedite the certification process.

FREED-HARDEMAN UNIVERSITY
Teacher Education
158 East Main Street
Henderson, Tennessee 38340-2399
Phone: (731) 989-6074
Fax: (731) 989-6969
E-mail: education@fhu.edu
Internet: http://www.fhu.edu

Institution Description: Freed-Hardeman University is an independent university affiliated with the Churches of Christ. It was established and chartered in 1869.

Teacher Education programs offer students the opportunity to seek licensure by pursuing undergraduate and graduate degrees.

Institution Control: Private.

Calendar: Semester. Academic year August to May.

Official(s): Dr. John Sweeney, Dean; Dr. Elizabeth A. Saunders, Program Director, Graduate Studies.

Faculty: Full-time 18; adjunct 8.

Degrees Awarded: 18 baccalaureate; 96 master's.

Admission Requirements: *Undergraduate:* Graduation from an accredited secondary school or GED; ACT composite. *Teacher education specific:* Completion of 28 semester hours of coursework; 2.5 GPA; passing scores on PRAXIS I (reading, writing, mathematics); personal interview. *Graduate:* Baccalaureate degree from a regionally accredited institution. *Teacher education specific:* GRE or Miller Analogies Test; personal goal statement; faculty interview.

Fees and Expenses: Undergraduate: $11,046 in-state per academic year. Graduate: $215 per credit hour. On-campus room and board: $5,320. Other expenses: $1,510. Books and supplies: $1,200.

Financial Aid: Resources specifically for eligible students enrolled in teacher education programs are awarded on the basis of financial need and academic merit. The institution has a Program Participation Agreement with the U.S. Department of Education for eligible students to receive Pell Grants and other federal aid. Teacher scholarships available to qualifying students. *Contact:* Financial Aid Office at: (731) 989-6662.

Accreditation: *Regional:* SACS. *Professional:* NCATE. *Member of:* AACTE. *Approved by:* Tennessee State Board of Education.

Undergraduate Programs: Undergraduate majors include the Bachelor of Science in child and family studies (preK-4 licensure) and Bachelor of Science in arts and humanities (K-8 licensure). Secondary and K-12 programs leading to licensure include: K-12 in art, theater, music, physical education, special education; 7-12 in biology, chemistry, English, government, history, mathematics, physics, psychology. All programs require the completion of a general education core, professional studies, content area, field experiences, and student teaching. A minimum of 132 semester hours is required for the degree award.

Graduate Programs: The Master of Education program in curriculum and instruction (non-licensure) is intended for the student seeking an advanced degree without initial or add-on licensure. The Master of Education in curriculum and instruction (teaching licensure) is a program for those who have a bac-

FREED-HARDEMAN UNIVERSITY—*cont'd*

calaureate degree and are seeking a Master of Education along with initial licensure to teach or an add-on in secondary or elementary licensure.

The Master of Education programs in curriculum and instruction and administration and supervision are for students with teaching licensure who desire to complete a Master of Education with an add-on in administration and supervision (k-12). The Master of Education curriculum and instruction add-on is for students seeking a special education add-on to an existing teaching license.

Licensure/Reciprocity: Tennessee. Students seeking teaching certification in a state other than Tennessee should consult with that state's teacher certification office early in their program of study to insure compliance with requirements. Many state directors of teacher credentialing have signed Interstate Agreements through NASDTEC that expedite the certification process.

LAMBUTH UNIVERSITY

School of Education
705 Lambuth Boulevard
Jackson, Tennessee 38301
Phone: (731) 425-3264
Fax: (731) 425-3496
E-mail: sadorski@lambuth.edu
Internet: http://www.lambuth.edu

Institution Description: Lambuth University is a private liberal arts and sciences institution affiliated with the United Methodist Church. It was founded in 1843.

The School of Education offers programs leading to the bachelor's degree and teaching licensure in Tennessee.

Institution Control: Private.

Calendar: Semester. Academic year August to May.

Official(s): Dr. Rebecca Sadowski, School Head.

Faculty: Full-time 7.

Degrees Awarded: 30 baccalaureate.

Admission Requirements: *Undergraduate:* Graduation from an approved secondary school of GED. *Teacher education specific:* Passing scores on PRAXIS I (reading, writing, mathematics); application by sophomore year; personal goal statement; faculty interview.

Fees and Expenses: $11,590 per academic year. On-campus room and board: $5,178. Other expenses: $3,032. Books and supplies: $1,200.

Financial Aid: Resources specifically for eligible students enrolled in teacher education programs are awarded on the basis of financial need and academic merit. The institution has a Program Participation Agreement with the U.S. Department of Education for eligible students to receive Pell Grants and other federal aid. Teacher scholarships available to qualifying students. *Contact:* Financial Aid Office at: (731) 425-3330.

Accreditation: *Regional:* SACS. *Member of:* AACTE. *Approved by:* Tennessee State Board of Education.

Undergraduate Programs: The Elementary Certification Program offers two areas of specialization. The early grades specialization will prepare the student who wishes to teach in grades kindergarten to four, and the middle grades specialization will prepare the student to teach in grades five through eight. These specializations are realized through an interdisciplinary studies major (5-8). Each major requires successful completion of the general education core, professional education core, and the appropriate interdisciplinary study courses. The student must complete the Enhanced Student Teaching semester successfully. Both of these avenues of study result in certification in the elementary grades K-8. All baccalaureate programs require the completion of 128 semester hours.

Licensure/Reciprocity: Tennessee. Students seeking teaching certification in a state other than Tennessee should consult with that state's teacher certification office early in their program of study to insure compliance with requirements. Many state directors of teacher credentialing have signed Interstate Agreements through NASDTEC that expedite the certification process.

LEE UNIVERSITY

Helen DeVos College of Education
Teacher Education Program
120 North Ocoee Street
P.O. Box 3450
Cleveland, Tennessee 37320-3450
Phone: (423) 614-8500
Fax: (423) 614-8533
E-mail: admissions@leeuniversity.edu
Internet: http://www.leeuniversity.edu

Institution Description: Lee University, formerly Lee College, is a private college affiliated with the Church of God.

The Teacher Education Program integrates the appropriate blend and sequencing of courses and experiences that encourage development in the cognitive, social, emotional, physical, and spiritual domains.

Institution Control: Private.

Calendar: Semester. Academic year August to May.

Official(s): Dr. Charles Paul Conn, President.

Faculty: Full-time 12.

Degrees Awarded: 148 baccalaureate; 44 master's.

Admission Requirements: *Undergraduate:* Graduation from an approved secondary school or GED; ACT composite. *Teacher education specific:* Passing scores on PRAXIS I (reading, writing, mathematics); personal goal statement; recommendations; completion of education foundations courses; faculty interview. *Graduate:* Baccalaureate degree from a regionally accredited institution. *Teacher education specific:* GRE or Miller Analogies Test; personal goal statement; faculty interview;

Fees and Expenses: Undergraduate: $8,730 per academic year. Graduate: Tuition charged per credit hour. On-campus room and board: $4,950. Other expenses: $2,520. Books and supplies: $700.

Financial Aid: Resources specifically for eligible students enrolled in teacher education programs are awarded on the basis of financial need and academic merit. The institution has a Program Participation Agreement with the U.S. Department of Education for eligible students to receive Pell Grants and other federal aid. Teacher scholarships available to qualifying students. *Contact:* Financial Aid Office at: (423) 614-8300.

Accreditation: *Regional:* SACS. *Member of:* AACTE. *Approved by:* Tennessee State Board of Education.

Undergraduate Programs: Baccalaureate programs include: early childhood preK-3; 7-12 in health education, interdisciplinary studies, physical education; psychology 9-12; special education K-12; music K-12; secondary education in areas of business, biology, chemistry, English, French, history/political science, mathematics, Spanish. All programs require the completion of the general education core, professional studies, content area, field experiences, and student teaching. A minimum of 130 semester hours is required for the degree award.

Graduate Programs: The Master of Arts in Teaching is designed for those students who majored in a subject area and desire licensure to teach in that subject or others with endorsements. The Master of Education and The Master of Science in school counseling are also available.

Licensure/Reciprocity: Tennessee. Students seeking teaching certification in a state other than Tennessee should consult with that state's teacher certification office early in their program of study to insure compliance with requirements. Many state directors of teacher credentialing have signed Interstate Agreements through NASDTEC that expedite the certification process.

LEMOYNE-OWEN COLLEGE
Division of Education
807 Walker Avenue
Memphis, Tennessee 38126
Phone: (901) 774-9090
Fax: (901) 942-3572
E-mail: education@lemoyne-owen.edu
Internet: http://www.lemoyne-owen.edu

Institution Description: LeMoyne-Owen College is a private college affiliated with the United Church of Christ and the Tennessee Baptist Convention. The college was established as LeMoyne Normal and Commercial School in 1871.

The Division of Education offers work in a professional education core curriculum that, with completion of an academic major, leads to licensure for teaching.

Institution Control: Private.

Calendar: Semester. Academic year September to May.

Official(s): Dr. James G. Wingate, President.

Faculty: Full-time 16; part-time 6.

Degrees Awarded: 3 baccalaureate.

Admission Requirements: *Undergraduate:* Graduation with 21 units from an accredited secondary school or GED; ACT composite preferred; College Board SAT accepted. *Teacher education specific:* Passing scores on PRAXIS I (reading, writing, mathematics); personal goal statement; recommendations; completion of education foundations courses; faculty interview.

Fees and Expenses: $8,450 per academic year. On-campus room and board: $4,620. Other expenses: $750. Books and supplies: $800.

Accreditation: *Regional:* SACS. *Professional:* NCATE. *Member of:* AACTE. *Approved by:* Tennessee State Board of Education.

Undergraduate Programs: For elementary licensure, the academic major may be in liberal studies, English, mathematics, science, or social science. For secondary licensure, the academic major may be biology, chemistry, early childhood education, English, health fitness/wellness, history, liberal studies, mathematics, political science, social science, science. A visual arts major can support both elementary and secondary licensure. All programs require the completion of the general education core, professional core, content area, field experiences, and student teaching. The division also offers a non-licensure program in early childhood education leading to the Bachelor of Science in Education. A minimum of 120 semester hours is required for the degree award.

Licensure/Reciprocity: Tennessee. Students seeking teaching certification in a state other than Tennessee should consult with that state's teacher certification office early in their program of study to insure compliance with requirements. Many state directors of teacher credentialing have signed Interstate Agreements through NASDTEC that expedite the certification process.

MARYVILLE COLLEGE
Education Division
Teacher Education Programs
118 Anderson Hall
502 East Lamar Alexander Parkway
Maryville, Tennessee 37804-5907
Phone: (865) 981-8106
Fax: (865) 981-5907
E-mail: terry.simpson@maryvillecollege.edu
Internet: http://www.maryvillecollege.edu

Institution Description: Maryville College is a private college affiliated with the Presbyterian Church (U.S.A.). It was established as The Southern and Western Theological Seminary in 1819.

The Division of Education offers undergraduate and postbaccalaureate programs leading to teaching licensure.

Institution Control: Private.

Calendar: Semester (4-1-4 plan). Academic year September to May.

Official(s): Dr. Terry Simpson, Division Chair.

Faculty: Full-time 6; adjunct 1.

Degrees Awarded: 30 baccalaureate.

Admission Requirements: *Undergraduate:* Graduation with 15 academic units from an approved secondary school or GED; College Board SAT or ACT composite. *Teacher education specific:* Passing scores on PRAXIS I (reading, writing, mathematics); personal goal statement; recommendations; completion of education foundations courses; faculty interview.

Fees and Expenses: $19,780 per academic year. On-campus room and board: $6,180. Other expenses: $2,250. Books and supplies: $650.

Financial Aid: Resources specifically for eligible students enrolled in teacher education programs are awarded on the basis of financial need and academic merit. The institution has a Program Participation Agreement with the U.S. Department of Education for eligible students to receive Pell Grants and other federal aid. Teacher scholarships available to qualifying students. *Contact:* Financial Aid Office at: (865) 981-8100.

Accreditation: *Regional:* SACS. *Member of:* AACTE. *Approved by:* Tennessee State Board of Education.

Undergraduate Programs: Education majors include elementary education (K-8) with a concentration in child development and learning. Secondary education (7-12) majors are offered with a focus in biology, chemistry, economics/history, English, history, history/economics, history/political science, mathematics, political science/history, Spanish, music K-12 (vocal and instrumental), physical education/health K-12, and teaching English as a second language. All baccalaureate programs include a general education core, professional core, content area, field experiences, and student teaching. A minimum of 132 credit hours is required for the degree award.

Licensure/Reciprocity: Tennessee. Students seeking teaching certification in a state other than Tennessee should consult with that state's teacher certification office early in their program of study to insure compliance with requirements. Many state directors of teacher credentialing have signed Interstate Agreements through NASDTEC that expedite the certification process.

MIDDLE TENNESSEE STATE UNIVERSITY
College of Education and Behavioral Science
Department of Education
1301 East Main Street
Murfreesboro, Tennessee 37132
Phone: (615) 898-2300
Fax: (615) 898-5478
E-mail: admissions@mtsu.edu
Internet: http://www.mtsu.edu

Institution Description: Middle Tennessee State University is a member of the Tennessee State University and Community College System. It was chartered as Middle Tennessee State Normal School in 1909.

The specific objective of the Department of Education is to coordinate the teacher education programs of the university.

Institution Control: Public.

Calendar: Semester. Academic year August to May.

Official(s): Dr. Gloria Bonner, Dean.

Faculty: Full-time 107; part-time and adjunct 19.

Degrees Awarded: 110 baccalaureate; 225 master's.

Admission Requirements: *Undergraduate:* Graduation from an approved secondary school or GED; College Board SAT or ACT composite. *Teacher education specific:* Passing scores on PRAXIS I (reading, writing, mathematics); personal goal statement; recommendations; completion of education foundations courses; faculty interview. *Graduate:* Baccalaureate degree from a regionally accredited institution. *Teacher education specific:* 2.75 GPA; GRE or Miller Analogies Test; faculty interview.

MIDDLE TENNESSEE STATE UNIVERSITY—
cont'd

Fees and Expenses: Undergraduate: $3,910 in-state, $11,842 out-of-state. Graduate: $191 in-state per credit hour; $461 out-of-state. On-campus room and board: $4,248. Other expenses: $2,210. Books and supplies: $1,000.

Financial Aid: Resources specifically for eligible students enrolled in teacher education programs are awarded on the basis of financial need and academic merit. The institution has a Program Participation Agreement with the U.S. Department of Education for eligible students to receive Pell Grants and other federal aid. Teacher scholarships available to qualifying students. *Contact:* Financial Aid Office at: (615) 898-3830.

Accreditation: *Regional:* SACS. *Professional:* NCATE. *Member of:* AACTE. *Approved by:* Tennessee State Board of Education.

Undergraduate Programs: Licensure endorsement areas include grades K-8, 1-8, and special education (K-12) modified or comprehensive; early childhood education grades preK-3; and grades 5-12 or 7-12. Majors or emphases include: agribusiness, animal science, art education, business education, biology, chemistry, geoscience, English, French, geography, German, political science, health education K-12 (initial licensure only), history, marketing education, mathematics, music, physical education, physics, plant and soil science, science, social studies, Spanish, speech and theatre, technology education, theatre, home economics education. All baccalaureate programs require the completion of the general education core, professional studies, content area, field experiences, and student teaching. A minimum of 132 semester hours is required for the degree award.

Graduate Programs: A post-baccalaureate program is available for students who have already obtained a bachelor's degree and would like to pursue a teacher licensure program.

Graduate students who are working on a graduate degree program in biology, foreign languages, or mathematics may also pursue an initial Tennessee teacher license.

Licensure/Reciprocity: Tennessee. Students seeking teaching certification in a state other than Tennessee should consult with that state's teacher certification office early in their program of study to insure compliance with requirements. Many state directors of teacher credentialing have signed Interstate Agreements through NASDTEC that expedite the certification process.

MILLIGAN COLLEGE
Area of Education
Teacher Education Program
P.O. Box 309
Milligan College, Tennessee 37682
Phone: (423) 461-8927
Fax: (423) 461-9103
E-mail: admissions@milligan.edu
Internet: http://www.milligan.edu

Institution Description: Milligan College is a private, independent, nonprofit institution affiliated with the Christian Church (Independent). It was founded in 1886.

The Milligan College teacher education faculty is committed to the nurturing and development of caring and reflective teachers.

Institution Control: Private.

Calendar: Semester. Academic year August to May.

Official(s): Dr. Beverly Schmalzried, Area Chair; Dr. Billye Joyce Fine, Director, Teacher Education Program.

Faculty: Full-time 7; part-time 5; adjunct 5.

Degrees Awarded: 18 baccalaureate; 39 master's.

Admission Requirements: *Undergraduate:* Graduation from an approved secondary school or GED; College Board SAT or ACT composite. *Teacher education specific:* Church and academic references; passing scores on PRAXIS I (reading, writing, mathematics); 2.5 GPA; personal goal statement; faculty interview.

Graduate: Baccalaureate degree from a regionally accredited institution. *Teacher education specific:* 2.5 GPA; GRE or Miller Analogies Test; two references; faculty interview.

Fees and Expenses: Undergraduate: $14,750 per academic year. Graduate: $260 per semester hour. On-campus room and board: $4,600. Books and supplies: $750.

Financial Aid: Resources specifically for eligible students enrolled in teacher education programs are awarded on the basis of financial need and academic merit. The institution has a Program Participation Agreement with the U.S. Department of Education for eligible students to receive Pell Grants and other federal aid. Teacher scholarships available to qualifying students. *Contact:* Nancy Beverly at: (423) 461-8713 or e-mail at: nmbeverly@milligan.edu.

Accreditation: *Regional:* SACS. *Professional:* NCATE. *Member of:* AACTE. *Approved by:* Tennessee State Board of Education.

Undergraduate Programs: Students who wish to prepare for careers working with children from birth to nine years of age should pursue licensure in early childhood education. The middle grades education licensure program is for students who want to work with children grades five through eight. The student must major in humanities, language arts, mathematics or biology and minor in educational studies: middle grades. Students interested in teaching grades seven through twelve should seek licensure in secondary education with a major and minor in the areas of: biology, chemistry, English, French, history, mathematics, psychology, sociology, Spanish. The K-12 specialties include physical education, and music (general, vocal, instrumental).

All baccalaureate programs require the completion of the general education core, professional studies, content area, field experiences, and student teaching. A minimum of 128 semester hours is required for the degree award.

Graduate Programs: Milligan College also offers a Master of Education program for those whose undergraduate degree is not necessarily in education. The program allows the completion of the degree and teacher licensure requirements in as little as fifteen months.

Licensure/Reciprocity: Tennessee. Students seeking teaching certification in a state other than Tennessee should consult with that state's teacher certification office early in their program of study to insure compliance with requirements. Many state directors of teacher credentialing have signed Interstate Agreements through NASDTEC that expedite the certification process.

SOUTHERN ADVENTIST UNIVERSITY
Department of Education and psychology
Teacher Education Program
P.O. Box 370
Collegedale, Tennessee 37315-0370
Phone: (423) 238-2165
Fax: (423) 238-2468
E-mail: admissions@southern.edu
Internet: http://www.southern.edu

Institution Description: Southern Adventist University, formerly known as Southern College of Seventh-day Adventists, is a private college owned by the Southern Union Conference of Seventh-day Adventists. It was established in 1892.

The goal of the Teacher Education Program is to nurture the development of the holistic teacher that is reflected in the conceptual framework of the program.

Institution Control: Private.

Calendar: Semester. Academic year August to May.

Official(s): Dr. Alberto dos Santos, Chairman.

Faculty: Full-time 13; adjunct 3.

Degrees Awarded: 28 baccalaureate; 22 master's.

Admission Requirements: *Undergraduate:* Graduation from an approved secondary school or GED; College Board SAT or ACT composite. *Teacher education specific:* Passing scores on PRAXIS I (reading, writing, mathematics); personal goal statement; 2.75 GPA overall; recommendations; completion of education foundations courses; faculty interview. *Graduate:* Baccalaureate degree from a regionally accredited institution. *Teacher education specific:* 3.0 GPA; GRE or Miller Analogies Test; completion of 9 semester credits in education courses; two professional recommendations; faculty interview.

Fees and Expenses: Undergraduate: $11,840 per academic year. Graduate: $6,210 per academic year. On-campus room and board: $4,110. Books and supplies: $900.

Financial Aid: Resources specifically for eligible students enrolled in teacher education programs are awarded on the basis of financial need and academic merit. The institution has a Program Participation Agreement with the U.S. Department of Education for eligible students to receive Pell Grants and other federal aid. Teacher scholarships available to qualifying students. *Contact:* Jack Harvey at: (423) 238-2837 or e-mail at: jaharvey@southern.edu.

Accreditation: *Regional:* SACS. *Professional:* NCATE. *Member of:* AACTE. *Approved by:* Tennessee State Board of Education.

Undergraduate Programs: Teacher certification programs are offered at four levels: K-8 elementary education (B.A. in psychology and B.S. in language Arts); 5-8 middle school education (B.S. in mathematics and Science and B.S. in outdoor education; K-12 secondary education (B.Mus. in music education and B.S. in physical education and health); 7-12 Bachelor of Arts in the areas of biology, chemistry, English, history, mathematics (also B.S.); physics, religious education, French, Spanish. These baccalaureate programs require the completion of the general education core; professional core, content area, field experiences, and student teaching. A minimum of 124 semester hours is required for the degree award.

Graduate Programs: The Master of Science in education degree programs include curriculum and instruction; educational administration and supervision, Inclusive education, multi-age teaching, and outdoor teacher education. Each program has specific goals and course requirements.

Licensure/Reciprocity: Tennessee. Students seeking teaching certification in a state other than Tennessee should consult with that state's teacher certification office early in their program of study to insure compliance with requirements. Many state directors of teacher credentialing have signed Interstate Agreements through NASDTEC that expedite the certification process.

TENNESSEE STATE UNIVERSITY

College of Education
Department of Teaching and Learning
3500 John A. Merritt Boulevard
Nashville, Tennessee 37209-1561
Phone: (615) 963-5111
Fax: (615) 963-5108
E-mail: education@tnstate.edu
Internet: http://www.tnstate.edu

Institution Description: Tennessee State University is a state institution and land-grant college. The university is a member of the Tennessee State University and Community College System. It was established in 1912.

The Department of Teaching and Learning is designed primarily for providing professional education for teachers. It offers undergraduate professional courses for prospective elementary and secondary school teachers and a major in special education.

Institution Control: Public.

Calendar: Semester. Academic year August to May.

Official(s): Dr. Dean B. Roberts, Department Head.

Faculty: Full-time 18.

Degrees Awarded: 12 baccalaureate; 240 master's; 33 doctorate.

Admission Requirements: *Undergraduate:* Graduation from an approved secondary school or GED; College Board SAT or ACT composite. *Teacher education specific:* Passing scores on PRAXIS I (reading, writing, mathematics); personal goal statement; recommendations; completion of education foundations

courses; faculty interview. *Graduate:* Baccalaureate degree from a regionally accredited institution. *Teacher education specific:* 2.75 GPA; GRE or Miller Analogies Test; faculty interview.

Fees and Expenses: Undergraduate: $3,788 in-state per academic year; $11,720 out-of-state. Graduate: $247 in-state per credit hour; $517 out-of-state. On-campus room and board: $3,990. Other expenses: $2,900. Books and supplies: $1,000.

Financial Aid: Resources specifically for eligible students enrolled in teacher education programs are awarded on the basis of financial need and academic merit. The institution has a Program Participation Agreement with the U.S. Department of Education for eligible students to receive Pell Grants and other federal aid. Teacher scholarships available to qualifying students. *Contact:* Financial Aid Office at: (615) 963-5701.

Accreditation: *Regional:* SACS. *Professional:* NCATE. *Member of:* AACTE. *Approved by:* Tennessee State Board of Education.

Undergraduate Programs: The School of Education offers undergraduate programs with emphasis placed on professional preparation and other support activities. Education is divided into major coordinating and instructional areas including: early childhood, interdisciplinary studies (elementary), secondary education, and special education. All baccalaureate programs require the completion of a general education core, professional studies, content area, field experiences, and student teaching. A minimum of 128 semester hours is required for the degree award.

The university offers the Bachelor of Professional Studies with concentrations in information technology or organizational leadership and a Bachelor of Interdisciplinary Studies completely online through the Regents Online Degree Program (RODP). Other programs online include an alternative C licensure, add-on endorsement, and recertification.

Graduate Programs: The Department of Teaching and Learning offers a Master of Education degree with majors in curriculum and instruction, elementary education, and special education. A Master of Education degree may be pursued through RODP.

A Doctor of Education degree is offered with a major in curriculum.

Licensure/Reciprocity: Tennessee. Students seeking teaching certification in a state other than Tennessee should consult with that state's teacher certification office early in their program of study to insure compliance with requirements. Many state directors of teacher credentialing have signed Interstate Agreements through NASDTEC that expedite the certification process.

TENNESSEE TECHNOLOGICAL UNIVERSITY

College of Education
Department of Curriculum and Instruction
1000 North Dixie Avenue
Cookeville, Tennessee 38505
Phone: (931) 372-3223
Fax: (931) 372-6250
E-mail: u_admissions@tntech.edu
Internet: http://www.tntech.edu

Institution Description: Tennessee Technological University is a member of the State University and Community College System. The institution was established, chartered, and incorporated as Tennessee Polytechnic Institute in 1915.

The Department of Curriculum and Instruction offers undergraduate and graduate programs leading to teaching licensure.

Institution Control: Public.

Calendar: Semester. Academic year August to May.

Official(s): Dr. Darrell Garber, Dean; Dr. Larry Peach, Chairperson.

Faculty: Full-time 31.

Degrees Awarded: 74 baccalaureate; 330 master's.

Admission Requirements: *Undergraduate:* Graduation from an approved secondary school or GED; College Board SAT or ACT composite. *Teacher education specific:* Passing scores on

TENNESSEE TECHNOLOGICAL
UNIVERSITY—*cont'd*

PRAXIS I (reading, writing, mathematics); personal goal statement; recommendations; completion of education foundations courses; faculty interview. *Graduate:* Baccalaureate degree from a regionally accredited institution. *Teacher education specific:* 2.75 GPA; GRE or Miller Analogies Test; faculty interview.

Fees and Expenses: Undergraduate: $3,750 in-state per academic year; $11,682 out-of-state. Graduate: $215 in-state per credit hour; $495 out-of-state. On-campus room and board: $4,700. Other expenses: $2,380. Books and supplies: $920.

Financial Aid: Resources specifically for eligible students enrolled in teacher education programs are awarded on the basis of financial need and academic merit. The institution has a Program Participation Agreement with the U.S. Department of Education for eligible students to receive Pell Grants and other federal aid. Teacher scholarships available to qualifying students. *Contact:* Financial Aid Office at: (931) 372-3073.

Accreditation: *Regional:* SACS. *Professional:* NCATE. *Member of:* AACTE. *Approved by:* Tennessee State Board of Education.

Undergraduate Programs: The Bachelor of Science in Education is offered in the areas of: child and family studies-early childhood (preK-4) and special education (prek-1); elementary education; special education: comprehensive; special education: modified; secondary education with concentrations in English, French, German, mathematics, science, social studies, Spanish, speech communication/theatre. A minimum of 132 semester hours is required for the degree award.

Non-licensure programs are offered in multidisciplinary studies: general and child and family studies: child development and family relations.

Graduate Programs: The Master of Arts degree is offered in curriculum and instruction, educational psychology and counselor education, and instructional leadership. The educational specialist degree is offered in curriculum and instruction, educational psychology and counselor education, and instructional leadership.

The Doctor of Philosophy degree is offered in exceptional learning (concentrations in applied behavior and learning, literacy, young children and families).

Licensure/Reciprocity: Tennessee. Students seeking teaching certification in a state other than Tennessee should consult with that state's teacher certification office early in their program of study to insure compliance with requirements. Many state directors of teacher credentialing have signed Interstate Agreements through NASDTEC that expedite the certification process.

TREVECCA NAZARENE UNIVERSITY

School of Education
Department of Teacher Education
333 Murfreesboro Road
Nashville, Tennessee 37210
Phone: (615) 248-1201
Fax: (615) 248-1597
E-mail: admissions_und@trevecca,edu
Internet: http://www.trevecca.edu

Institution Description: Trevecca Nazarene University is a private institution affiliated with the Church of the Nazarene. The university was established in 1901 as the Literary and Bible Training School.

The Department of Teacher Education offers programs designed in collaboration with other departments on campus to offer an integrated programs and provide professional education components for prospective teachers.

Institution Control: Private.

Calendar: Semester. Academic year August to May.

Official(s): Dr. Esther Swink, Dean, Dr. Ruth Y. Cox, Director of Teacher Education.

Faculty: Full-time 17; part-time 7; adjunct 19.

Degrees Awarded: 24 baccalaureate; 183 master's; 22 doctorate.

Admission Requirements: *Undergraduate:* Graduation from an approved secondary school or GED; College Board SAT or ACT composite. *Teacher education specific:* Passing scores on PRAXIS I (reading, writing, mathematics); personal goal statement; pre-student teaching field experiences; recommendations; completion of education foundations courses; faculty interview; PRAXIS II before certification. *Graduate:* Baccalaureate degree from a regionally accredited institution. *Teacher education specific:* 2.75 GPA; GRE or Miller Analogies Test; faculty interview.

Fees and Expenses: Undergraduate: $438 per credit hour. Graduate: $284 per credit hour. On-campus room and board: $5,150.

Financial Aid: Resources specifically for eligible students enrolled in teacher education programs are awarded on the basis of financial need and academic merit. Other resources for missionary children (Nazarene), Nazarene pastor's children. Graduate students eligible only for federal loans. *Contact:* Financial Aid Office at: (615) 248-1242 or e-mail at: financial_aid@trevecca.edu.

Accreditation: *Regional:* SACS. *Member of:* AACTE. *Approved by:* Tennessee State Board of Education.

Undergraduate Programs: Teacher education licensure programs include: child development and learning, grades K-8; English, grades 7-12; music, grades K-12; physical education, grades K-12; biology, grades 7-12; chemistry, grades 7-12; mathematics, grades 7-12; history/government, grades 7-12); history/economics, grades 7-12. All programs of study are in conformity with the regulations for licensure of teachers in Tennessee. The baccalaureate programs require the completion of the general education core, professional studies, content area, field experiences, and student teaching. A minimum of 128 semester hours is required for the degree award.

Graduate Programs: The School of Education offers graduate programs leading to the Master of Education in educational leadership, Master of Education in instructional effectiveness; Master of Library and Information Science.

A Doctor of Education in professional practices is also available. This program requires the completion of 57 credit hours.

Licensure/Reciprocity: Tennessee. Students seeking teaching certification in a state other than Tennessee should consult with that state's teacher certification office early in their program of study to insure compliance with requirements. Many state directors of teacher credentialing have signed Interstate Agreements through NASDTEC that expedite the certification process.

UNION UNIVERSITY

Education Department
1050 Union University Drive
Jackson, Tennessee 38305
Phone: (731) 668-1818
Fax: (731) 661-5017
E-mail: info@uu.edu
Internet: http://www.uu.edu

Institution Description: Union University is a private institution affiliated with the Tennessee Baptist Convention (Southern Baptist). The school was founded in 1825.

The Education Department offers three majors with licensure in six areas for Union University students seeking a license to teach in the public schools.

Institution Control: Private.

Calendar: Semester. Academic year August to May.

Official(s): Dr. Thomas R. Rosebrough, Dean.

Faculty: Full-time 16.

Degrees Awarded: 40 baccalaureate; 96 master's.

Admission Requirements: *Undergraduate:* Graduation from an approved secondary school or GED; ACT composite. *Teacher education specific:* Passing scores on PRAXIS I (reading, writing, mathematics); personal goal statement; recommendations; completion of education foundations courses; faculty interview.

Graduate: Baccalaureate degree from a regionally accredited institution. *Teacher education specific:* GRE or Miller Analogies Test; 3.0 GPA; faculty interview; PRAXIS II prior to certification.

Fees and Expenses: Undergraduate: $14,450 per academic year. Graduate: $220 per semester hour. On-campus room and board: $4,640. Other expenses: $1,500. Books and supplies: $700.

Financial Aid: Resources specifically for eligible students enrolled in teacher education programs are awarded on the basis of financial need and academic merit. The institution has a Program Participation Agreement with the U.S. Department of Education for eligible students to receive Pell Grants and other federal aid. Teacher scholarships available to qualifying students. *Contact:* Financial Aid Office at: (731) 661-5015.

Accreditation: *Regional:* SACS. *Professional:* NCATE. *Member of:* AACTE. *Approved by:* Tennessee State Board of Education.

Undergraduate Programs: The major areas include: learning foundations, liberal studies, and special education. The learning foundations major offers the choice of licensure in early childhood education (preK-grade 4) or elementary education (grades K-8) for teaching typically developing students. The liberal studies major offers licensure in middle grades 5-8 with built-in emphases in natural and social sciences upon which the student may build further or select an additional emphasis in language arts or mathematics. The special education major prepares students to teach special needs youth in the areas of early childhood special education (birth-grade 1), modified special education (K-12), and comprehensive special education (K-12).

All programs require the completion of the general education core, professional studies, content area, field experiences, and student teaching. A minimum of 128 credit hours is required for the baccalaureate degree.

Graduate Programs: The Education Department offers programs leading to the Master of Arts in Education, Master of Education, and Education Specialist degrees. A Doctor of Education degree may also be pursued.

Licensure/Reciprocity: Tennessee. Students seeking teaching certification in a state other than Tennessee should consult with that state's teacher certification office early in their program of study to insure compliance with requirements. Many state directors of teacher credentialing have signed Interstate Agreements through NASDTEC that expedite the certification process.

UNIVERSITY OF MEMPHIS

College of Education
Department of Instruction and Curriculum
Leadership
Ball 406
Memphis, Tennessee 38152
Phone: (901) 678-2365
Fax: (901) 678-3299
E-mail: coe@.memphis.edu
Internet: http://www.memphis.edu

Institution Description: The University of Memphis, formerly known as Memphis State University, is a member of the Tennessee State University and Community College System. It was established in 1912.

The College of Education offers an extensive program for undergraduate and graduate students pursuing careers in teaching.

Institution Control: Public.

Calendar: Semester. Academic year August to May.

Official(s): Dr. Robert Cooter, Chair.

Faculty: Full-time 54.

Degrees Awarded: 137 baccalaureate; 213 master's; 27 doctorate.

Admission Requirements: *Undergraduate:* Graduation from an approved secondary school or GED; College Board SAT preferred; ACT composite accepted. *Teacher education specific:* Passing scores on PRAXIS I (reading, writing, mathematics); personal goal statement; recommendations; completion of education foundations courses; faculty interview. *Graduate:*

Baccalaureate degree from a regionally accredited institution. *Teacher education specific:* GRE or Miller Analogies Test; faculty interview; PRAXIS II before certification.

Fees and Expenses: Undergraduate: $4,234 in-state per academic year; $12,388 out-of-state. Graduate: $247 in-state per credit hour; $517 out-of-state. On-campus room and board: $5,300. Other expenses: $3,080. Books and supplies: $800.

Financial Aid: Resources specifically for eligible students enrolled in teacher education programs are awarded on the basis of financial need and academic merit. The institution has a Program Participation Agreement with the U.S. Department of Education for eligible students to receive Pell Grants and other federal aid. Teacher scholarships available to qualifying students. *Contact:* Financial Aid Office at: (901) 678-2303.

Accreditation: *Regional:* SACS. *Professional:* NCATE. *Member of:* AACTE. *Approved by:* Tennessee State Board of Education.

Undergraduate Programs: The Bachelor of Science in Education degree is offered in human development and learning (early childhood preK-4); integrative studies with concentration in elementary K-8 licensure; special education. All programs require the completion of the general education core, professional studies, content area, field experiences, and student teaching. A minimum of 132 semester hours must be completed for the degree.

Graduate Programs: Master of Arts in Teaching degree programs include: instruction and curriculum leadership with concentrations in early childhood education, elementary education, secondary education, and special education. The Master of Science degree programs include instruction and curriculum leadership with concentrations in instruction and curriculum, instructional design and technology, reading, early childhood education, special education. The Master of Science program in leadership and policy studies includes concentrations in school administration and supervision and leadership.

The Doctor of Education degree programs offered include educational leadership, community education, policy studies, higher education, and adult education.

Licensure/Reciprocity: Tennessee. Students seeking teaching certification in a state other than Tennessee should consult with that state's teacher certification office early in their program of study to insure compliance with requirements. Many state directors of teacher credentialing have signed Interstate Agreements through NASDTEC that expedite the certification process.

UNIVERSITY OF TENNESSEE AT CHATTANOOGA

College of Education Applied Professional Studies
615 McCallie Avenue
Tennessee 37403
Phone: (423) 755-4218
Fax: (423) 755-5380
E-mail: admin/utc.edu
Internet: http://www.utc.edu

Institution Description: The institution was established as Chattanooga University by the Methodist Episcopal Church in 1866. The university was merged with the University of Tennessee and Chattanooga City College in 1969.

The primary goal of the College of Education and Applied Professional Studies is to prepare qualified practitioners to be professional leaders in various roles within educational institutions and professional agencies, both public and private.

Institution Control: Public.

Calendar: Semester. Academic year August to May.

Official(s): Dr. Mary Turner, Dean; Dr. Valerie C. Rutledge, Head, Teacher Preparation Academy.

Faculty: Full-time 21 (Teacher Preparation Academy).

Degrees Awarded: 72 baccalaureate; 97 master's.

Admission Requirements: *Undergraduate:* Graduation with 16 academic unit from an approved secondary school or GED; College Board SAT score 900; ACT composite score 16. *Teacher education specific:* Passing scores on PRAXIS I (reading, writing,

UNIVERSITY OF TENNESSEE AT CHATTANOOGA—*cont'd*

mathematics); personal goal statement; recommendations; completion of education foundations courses; faculty interview. *Graduate:* Baccalaureate degree from a regionally accredited institution. *Teacher education specific:* GRE or Miller Analogies Test; faculty interview; PRAXIS II before certification.

Fees and Expenses: Undergraduate: $3,852 in-state per academic year; $11,504 out-of-state. Graduate: $228 in-state per credit hour; $565 out-of-state. On-campus room and board: $5,600. Books and supplies: $850.

Financial Aid: Resources specifically for eligible students enrolled in teacher education programs are awarded on the basis of financial need and academic merit. The institution has a Program Participation Agreement with the U.S. Department of Education for eligible students to receive Pell Grants and other federal aid. Teacher scholarships available to qualifying students. *Contact:* Financial Aid Office at: (423) 425-4677.

Accreditation: *Regional:* SACS. *Professional:* NCATE. *Member of:* AACTE. *Approved by:* Tennessee State Board of Education.

Undergraduate Programs: The Teacher Preparation Academy, a department within the College of Education and Applied Professional Studies, seeks to produce beginning teachers for public or private schools. Contact the Dr. Valerie C. Rutledge at (423) 425-4218 for specific details regarding course, degree, and teaching licensure requirements.

Graduate Programs: Master's programs are offered in initial licensure, elementary education, guidance and counseling, school leadership, secondary education (concentrations in arts, English, health education, inclusion, mathematics, physical education, sciences and environmental studies, social sciences), special education, and athletic training. All programs have specific course requirements.

The Educational Specialist in educational technology is a post-master's, sixth year degree with a focus on education technology. It is designed to generate teachers with high levels of proficiency in the use of technology in school and classroom and other educational settings. The Education Specialist school psychology program specialty is designed to prepare school psychologists who will work in school systems and other agencies to provide a comprehensive array of psychological services to individuals with special needs.

Licensure/Reciprocity: Tennessee. Students seeking teaching certification in a state other than Tennessee should consult with that state's teacher certification office early in their program of study to insure compliance with requirements. Many state directors of teacher credentialing have signed Interstate Agreements through NASDTEC that expedite the certification process.

UNIVERSITY OF TENNESSEE AT KNOXVILLE

College of Education, Health, and Human Sciences
1120 Volunteer Boulevard
Knoxville, Tennessee 37996
Phone: (805) 974-2184
Fax: (805) 974-5781
E-mail: edadmin@utk.edu
Internet: http://www.utk.edu

Institution Description: The university was established and chartered as Blount College in 1794.

The College of Education offers programs at the undergraduate and graduate levels leading to teacher licensure and advanced training in leadership and supervision.

Institution Control: Public.

Calendar: Semester. Academic year August to May.

Official(s): Dr. John Koontz, Dean.

Faculty: Full-time 150.

Degrees Awarded: 108 baccalaureate; 383 master's; 50 doctorate.

Admission Requirements: *Undergraduate:* Graduation from an approved secondary school or GED; College Board SAT or ACT composite, *Teacher education specific:* Passing scores on PRAXIS I (reading, writing, mathematics); 45, 60, or 75 credits completed depending on program pursued; 2.7 GPA; personal goal statement; recommendations; completion of education foundations courses; faculty interview. *Graduate:* Baccalaureate degree from a regionally accredited institution. *Teacher education specific:* GRE or Miller Analogies Test; overall 2.7 GPA; faculty interview; PRAXIS II before certification.

Fees and Expenses: Undergraduate: $4,056 in-state per academic year; $12,408 out-of-state. Graduate: $233 in-state per credit hour; $666 out-of-state. On-campus room and board: $4,472. Other expenses: $4,000 to $5,000 for books, supplies, and living expenses.

Financial Aid: Resources specifically for eligible students enrolled in teacher education programs are awarded on the basis of financial need and academic merit. Scholarship/loan program for residents only from Tennessee Student Assistance Corporation. The institution has a Program Participation Agreement with the U.S. Department of Education for eligible students to receive Pell Grants and other federal aid. *Contact:* Financial Aid Office at: (865) 974-3131.

Accreditation: *Regional:* SACS. *Professional:* NCATE. *Member of:* AACTE. *Approved by:* Tennessee State Board of Education.

Undergraduate Programs: Baccalaureate programs offered by the College of Education include: special education: modified and comprehensive K-12; special education: education of deaf and hard of hearing preK-12; elementary education K-8; early childhood education preK-grade 4); secondary education 7-12 (minor combined with major in teaching field; art education major coupled with a Bachelor of Fine Arts; music education; agriculture. All programs require the completion of the general education core, professional studies, content area, field experiences, and student teaching. A minimum of 120 semester hours is required for the degree award.

Graduate Programs: The college offers a Master of Science, Education Specialist, Doctor of Education, and Doctor of Philosophy in a broad range of academic disciplines.

Licensure/Reciprocity: Tennessee. Students seeking teaching certification in a state other than Tennessee should consult with that state's teacher certification office early in their program of study to insure compliance with requirements. Many state directors of teacher credentialing have signed Interstate Agreements through NASDTEC that expedite the certification process.

UNIVERSITY OF TENNESSEE AT MARTIN

College of Education and Behavior Sciences
Department of Education Studies
University Street
Martin, Tennessee 38238
Phone: (901) 587-7000
Fax: (901) 587-7029
E-mail: admitme@utm.edu
Internet: http://www.utm.edu

Institution Description: The University of Tennessee at Martin traces it origin to Hall-Moody Institute, established by the Baptists of Martin in 1900.

The Department of Education Studies offers undergraduate and graduate studies to prepare students for teaching careers.

Institution Control: Public.

Calendar: Semester. Academic year August to May.

Official(s): Dr. B.C. DeSpain, Dean.

Faculty: Full-time 31.

Degrees Awarded: 109 baccalaureate; 50 master's.

Admission Requirements: *Undergraduate:* Graduation from an approved secondary school or GED; ACT composite, *Teacher education specific:* Passing scores on PRAXIS I (reading, writing, mathematics); 60 credits completed; 2.7 GPA; personal goal statement; recommendations; completion of education foundations courses; faculty interview. *Graduate:* Baccalaureate degree from a regionally accredited institution. *Teacher education specific:* GRE or Miller Analogies Test; overall 2.7 GPA; teaching certificate for certain programs; faculty interview; PRAXIS II before certification.

Fees and Expenses: Undergraduate: $3,830 in-state per academic year; $11,480 out-of-state. Graduate: $213 in-state per credit hour; $576 out-of-state. On-campus room and board: $4,560. Other expenses: $2,500. Books and supplies: $1,000.

Financial Aid: Resources specifically for eligible students enrolled in teacher education programs are awarded on the basis of financial need and academic merit. Scholarship/loan program for residents only from Tennessee Student Assistance Corporation. The institution has a Program Participation Agreement with the U.S. Department of Education for eligible students to receive Pell Grants and other federal aid. *Contact:* Financial Aid Office at: (731) 587-7040.

Accreditation: *Regional:* SACS. *Professional:* NCATE. *Member of:* AACTE. *Approved by:* Tennessee State Board of Education.

Undergraduate Programs: Baccalaureate programs are offered in human learning, secondary education, and special education. Each of these programs is presented in three dimensions: general education, content education, and professional education. Students who successfully complete any of the undergraduate programs will be awarded the degree of Bachelor of Science in Education. A minimum of 124 semester hours is required for the degree.

Graduate Programs: The Master of Science in Education with a major in counseling has two concentrations: school counseling and mental health/community counseling. The school counselor concentration will prepare counselors to support teachers and other school personnel as well as parents in addressing the needs of students related to academic, career preparation, and personal growth and development. Students will be prepared to serve schools with grades preK through 12.

The Master of Science in Education with a major in teaching is available for those students who have obtained a bachelor's degree and who are professionally licensed to teach.

The Master of Science in Education with a major in educational administration and supervision is available to individuals who have obtained a bachelor's degree and who are professionally licensed to teach. This degree allows the candidate to complete certification requirements for the beginning administrator. The Master of Science in Education with a major in teaching for initial licensure is available for those students who have a baccalaureate degree but are not professionally licensed to teach.

Licensure/Reciprocity: Tennessee. Students seeking teaching certification in a state other than Tennessee should consult with that state's teacher certification office early in their program of study to insure compliance with requirements. Many state directors of teacher credentialing have signed Interstate Agreements through NASDTEC that expedite the certification process.

VANDERBILT UNIVERSITY

Peabody College of Education and Human Development
Wyatt Center
115 South Drive
Nashville, Tennessee 37212
Phone: (615) 322-8407
Fax: (615) 343-8501
E-mail: peabody.admissions@vanderbilt.edu
Internet: http://www.vanderbilt.edu

Institution Description: Vanderbilt University is a private, independent, nonprofit institution. The university was established and chartered as The Central University of Methodist Episcopal Church, South, 1872. The name was changed to Vanderbilt University in 1873.

The Peabody College's interests span the continuum of public and private education that encompasses preschool, postsecondary, and adult education plus lifelong learning.

Institution Control: Private.

Calendar: Semester. Academic year August to May.

Official(s): Dr. Camilla P. Benbow, Dean.

Faculty: Not reported.

Degrees Awarded: 59 baccalaureate; 102 master's; 17 doctorate.

Admission Requirements: *Undergraduate:* Graduation from with 15 academic units of college preparatory work from an approved secondary school or GED; College Board SAT or ACT composite, *Teacher education specific:* Passing scores on PRAXIS I (reading, writing, mathematics); 3.0 GPA in last two years of study; personal goal statement; recommendations; completion of education foundations courses; faculty interview. *Graduate:* Baccalaureate degree from a regionally accredited institution. *Teacher education specific:* GRE or Miller Analogies Test; overall 3.0 GPA; faculty interview; PRAXIS II before certification.

Fees and Expenses: Undergraduate: $27,720 per academic year; Graduate: $14,760. On-campus room and board: $9,864. Books and supplies: $1,310.

Financial Aid: Resources specifically for eligible students enrolled in teacher education programs are awarded on the basis of financial need and academic merit. The institution has a Program Participation Agreement with the U.S. Department of Education for eligible students to receive Pell Grants and other federal aid. *Contact:* Betty S. Lee at: (615) 322-8400 or e-mail at: betty.s.lee@vanderbilt.edu.

Accreditation: *Regional:* SACS. *Professional:* NCATE. *Member of:* AACTE. *Approved by:* Tennessee State Board of Education.

Undergraduate Programs: Peabody College offers the Bachelor of Science degree with majors in early childhood education, elementary education, secondary education, special education, cognitive studies, child development, and human and organizational development. Programs include coursework in a liberal education core, a professional core, a major area of specialization, and electives. Peabody also provides professional education courses for College of Arts and Science students who want to prepare for teacher licensure. The Bachelor of Science degree is granted on the basis of 120 semester hours of college work.

Graduate Programs: The Master of Science degree program is designed to enable students to explore personal interests or vocational options, to acquire a background for reaching at the secondary level, and/or to attain a foundation for further studies at the doctoral level. Program requirements are similar to those for the Master of Education, although Master of Science programs are more research oriented, and a thesis is required.

The Doctor of Philosophy degree is granted in recognition of high attainment in a special field of knowledge as evidenced by examinations and a dissertation representing individual research. The degree normally requires 73 hours of graduate study.

Licensure/Reciprocity: Tennessee. Students seeking teaching certification in a state other than Tennessee should consult with that state's teacher certification office early in their program of study to insure compliance with requirements. Many state directors of teacher credentialing have signed Interstate Agreements through NASDTEC that expedite the certification process.

TEXAS

ANGELO STATE UNIVERSITY

School of Education
P.O. Box 10893, ASU Station
2601 West Avenue North
San Angelo, Texas 76909
Phone: (325) 942-2052
Fax: (915) 942-2039
E-mail: admissions@angelo.edu
Internet: http://www.angelo.edu

Institution Description: Angelo State University is a state institution that was established as San Angelo Junior College in 1928. It became a four-year institution in 1965.

The School of Education offers programs leading to undergraduate and graduate degrees that prepare students for careers in teaching.

Institution Control: Public.

Calendar: Semester. Academic year September to May.

Official(s): Dr. John J. Miazga, Dean.

Faculty: Full-time 11; part-time 24.

Degrees Awarded: 155 baccalaureate; 50 master's.

Admission Requirements: *Undergraduate:* Graduation from an approved secondary school or GED; College Board SAT or ACT composite. *Teacher education specific:* Overall 2.5 GPA; no grade lower than C in major/certification area; passing scores on all three sections (reading, mathematics, writing) of the Texas Higher Education Assessment (THEA); faculty interview; personal goal statement. *Graduate:* Baccalaureate degree from a regionally accredited institution. *Teacher education specific:* 2.5 GPA; GRE or Miller Analogies Test scores; completion of all required departmental exams; teacher certification for some programs; recommendations; faculty interview.

Fees and Expenses: Undergraduate: $1,253 per academic year in-state/; $3,869 out-of-state. On-camps room and board: $5,406. Books and supplies: $700.

Financial Aid: Resources specifically for eligible students enrolled in teacher education programs are awarded on the basis of financial need and academic merit. The institution has a Program Participation Agreement with the U.S. Department of Education for eligible students to receive Pell Grants and other federal aid. Teacher scholarships available to qualifying students. *Contact:* Lyn Wheeler at: (325) 942-2246 or e-mail at: lyn.wheeler@angelo.edu.

Accreditation: *Regional:* SACS. *Member of:* AACTE. *Approved by:* Texas State Board for Educator Certification.

Undergraduate Programs: Students seeking to become teachers in elementary and middle schools major in interdisciplinary child development and learning, This leads to two levels of certification: early childhood to grade 4 or grades 4-8. Secondary certification is obtained by majoring in an academic discipline with a variety of supportive education courses. A total of 130 semester credit hours is required for graduation with a minimum of 2.5 GPA required for certification.

Graduate Programs: The School of Education offers certified teachers advanced degree programs leading to the Master of Education or Master of Arts degrees. Professional certification may be obtained leading to careers as principal, school counselor, educational diagnostician, and reading specialist. Non-certification programs in curriculum and instruction are offered in instructional technology, special education, reading, elementary classroom teaching, and secondary classroom teaching. Non-degree options are available in superintendent certification, instructional technology certification, and master reading teacher certification.

Licensure/Reciprocity: Texas. Students seeking teaching certification in a state other than Texas should consult with that state's teacher certification office early in their program of study to insure compliance with requirements. Many state directors of teacher credentialing have signed Interstate Agreements through NASDTEC that expedite the certification process.

AUSTIN COLLEGE

Austin Teacher Program
900 North Grand Avenue
Sherman, Texas 75090-4400
Phone: (903) 813-2000
Fax: (903) 813-3199
E-mail: admissions@austincollege.edu
Internet: http://www.austincollege.edu

Institution Description: Austin College is a private institution affiliated with the Presbyterian Church (U.S.A.). It was established, chartered, and offered first instruction in 1849.

The goal of the Austin Teacher Program is to prepare teachers who will have the breadth and depth of intellectual development that is afforded by a vigorous undergraduate liberal arts education.

Institution Control: Private.

Calendar: Semester. Academic year August to May.

Official(s): Dr. Tom Baker, Chair.

Faculty: Full-time 6; part-time 1.

Degrees Awarded: 3 baccalaureate; 27 master's.

Admission Requirements: *Undergraduate:* Graduation from an approved secondary school or GED; College Board SAT or ACT composite. *Teacher education specific:* Overall 2.5 GPA; no grade lower than C in major/certification area; passing scores on all three sections (reading, mathematics, writing) of the Texas Higher Education Assessment (THEA); faculty interview; personal goal statement; PRAXIS II prior to certification. *Graduate:* Baccalaureate degree from a regionally accredited institution. *Teacher education specific:* 2.5 GPA; GRE or Miller Analogies Test scores; completion of all required departmental exams; teacher certification for some programs; recommendations; faculty interview.

Fees and Expenses: $17,925 per academic year. On-campus room and board: $6,822. Other expenses: $1,000. Books and supplies: $800.

Financial Aid: Resources specifically for eligible students enrolled in teacher education programs are awarded on the basis of financial need and academic merit. The institution has a Program Participation Agreement with the U.S. Department of Education for eligible students to receive Pell Grants and other federal aid. Teacher scholarships available to qualifying students. *Contact:* Financial Aid Office at: (903) 813-2900.

Accreditation: *Regional:* SACS. *Member of:* AACTE. *Approved by:* Texas State Board for Educator Certification.

Undergraduate Programs: The Austin College Teacher Program offers prospective teachers a five-year teacher education program that terminates with the Master of Arts in teaching degree. The program strives to educate individuals who will be active learners in their personal and professional lives, who will become dedicated and creative teachers, and who will be educational leaders in their schools. Austin College is an initial certifying agency and cannot grant a Master of Arts in Teaching degree to anyone already holding any type of teaching certificate. The undergraduate portion of the program requires the completion of the general education core, professional studies, content area, field experiences, and student teaching.

Licensure/Reciprocity: Texas. Students seeking teaching certification in a state other than Texas should consult with that state's teacher certification office early in their program of study to insure compliance with requirements. Many state directors of teacher credentialing have signed Interstate Agreements through NASDTEC that expedite the certification process.

BAYLOR UNIVERSITY
School of Education
Department of Curriculum and Instruction
Waco, Texas 76798
Phone: (254) 710-3113
Fax: (254) 710-3160
E-mail: conaway@baylor.edu
Internet: http://www.baylor.edu

Institution Description: Baylor University is a private institution that is affiliated with the Baptist general Convention of Texas. It was founded in 1847.

The Department of Curriculum and Instruction offers programs preparing teachers for work in a variety of educational settings.

Institution Control: Private.

Calendar: Semester. Academic year August to May.

Official(s): Dr. Betty Conaway, Department Chairperson.

Faculty: Full-time 25.

Degrees Awarded. 249 baccalaureate, 57 master's, 25 doctorate.

Admission Requirements: *Undergraduate:* Graduation from an approved secondary school or GED; College Board SAT or ACT composite. *Teacher education specific:* Overall 2.5 GPA; no grade lower than C in major/certification area; passing scores on all three sections (reading, mathematics, writing) of the Texas Higher Education Assessment (THEA); faculty interview; personal goal statement; PRAXIS II prior to certification. *Graduate:* Baccalaureate degree from a regionally accredited institution. *Teacher education specific:* 2.5 GPA; GRE or Miller Analogies Test scores; completion of all required departmental exams; teacher certification for some programs; recommendations; faculty interview.

Fees and Expenses: Undergraduate: $18,500 per academic year. Graduate: $379 per semester hour. On-campus room and board: $5,634. Other expenses: $3,088. Books and supplies: $1,450.

Financial Aid: Resources specifically for eligible students enrolled in teacher education programs are awarded on the basis of financial need and academic merit. The institution has a Program Participation Agreement with the U.S. Department of Education for eligible students to receive Pell Grants and other federal aid. Teacher scholarships available to qualifying students. *Contact:* Financial Aid Office at: (254) 710-2611.

Accreditation: *Regional:* SACS. *Professional:* NCATE. *Member of:* AACTE. *Approved by:* Texas State Board for Educator Certification.

Undergraduate Programs: The undergraduate teacher preparation program is a collaborative network of elementary, middle, and secondary professional development schools in Waco offering teacher candidates four years of content-rich, pedagogically-intensive, and field-based coursework and professional development experiences in a culturally diverse, urban environment. The Bachelor of Science in Education degree is awarded upon completion of the program pursued.

Graduate Programs: The Master of Arts degree is designed to develop a scholarly understanding of education through theory and practice. The degree requires 33 semester hours, including the completion and defense of a thesis and a 12-hour minor in educational foundations, instructional technology, language literacy, or mathematics education.

The Master of Science in Education is designed to improve educational practice and to provide preparation for continued graduate studies in educational theory. The degree requires 36 semester hours including a 15-hour cognate specialization.

The Strickland Scholars Program is designed to prepare candidates for initial teacher certification at early childhood grade 4, middle school, or secondary as they complete a M.S.Ed. The degree requires 38-41 hours depending on which certification program is selected.

The Doctor of Education degree is a professional degree that concentrates on the use of curriculum and instruction theory, educational research, and practitioner knowledge to improve educational practice. The degree requires a minimum of 45 hours of coursework in curriculum and instruction as well as a 15-hour cognate specialization.

Licensure/Reciprocity: Texas. Students seeking teaching certification in a state other than Texas should consult with that state's teacher certification office early in their program of study to insure compliance with requirements. Many state directors of teacher credentialing have signed Interstate Agreements through NASDTEC that expedite the certification process.

CONCORDIA UNIVERSITY AT AUSTIN
College of Education
Teacher Education Program
3400 Interstate 35 North
Austin, Texas 78705-2799
Phone: (512) 486-1123
Fax: (512) 486-2000
E-mail: sandra.doering@concordia.edu
Internet: http://www.concordia.edu

Institution Description: Concordia University at Austin, formerly named Concordia Lutheran College, is a private four-year institution owned and operated by the Lutheran Church-Missouri Synod. It was founded in 1926.

The mission of the Teacher Education Program is to provide ongoing education for pre-service and in-service teachers in a collaborative, field-based, Christian environment.

Institution Control: Private.

Calendar: Semester. Academic year August to May.

Official(s): Dr. Sandra Doering, Dean.

Faculty: Full-time 7.

Degrees Awarded: 16 baccalaureate; 23 master's.

Admission Requirements: *Undergraduate:* Graduation from an approved secondary school or GED; College Board SAT or ACT composite. *Teacher education specific:* Overall 2.5 GPA; no grade lower than C in major/certification area; passing scores on all three sections (reading, mathematics, writing) of the Texas Higher Education Assessment (THEA); faculty interview; personal goal statement; PRAXIS II prior to certification. *Graduate:* Baccalaureate degree from a regionally accredited institution. *Teacher education specific:* 3.0 GPA; GRE or Miller Analogies Test scores; completion of all required departmental exams; teacher certification for some programs; three recommendations; faculty interview.

Fees and Expenses: Undergraduate: $15,410 per academic year. Graduate: $325 per credit hour. On-campus room and board: $6,350. Other expenses: $1,700. Books and supplies: $1,700.

Financial Aid: Resources specifically for eligible students enrolled in teacher education programs are awarded on the basis of financial need and academic merit. The institution has a Program Participation Agreement with the U.S. Department of Education for eligible students to receive Pell Grants and other federal aid. Teacher scholarships available to qualifying students. *Contact:* Financial Aid Office at: 512) 486-2000.

CONCORDIA UNIVERSITY AT AUSTIN—
cont'd

Accreditation: *Regional:* SACS. *Member of:* AACTE. *Approved by:* Texas State Board for Educator Certification.

Undergraduate Programs: The College of Education offers programs for elementary (early childhood through 4th grade), middle schools (grades 4-8) and secondary (grades 8-12). Upon completion of a teacher education program and successful completion of the Texas State Examinations (TexES), a graduate may apply for recommendation for the appropriate Texas State certification. All programs require the completion of a general education core, professional studies, content area, field expenses, and student teaching.

Graduate Programs: The Master of Education degree is offered with concentrations in early childhood, curriculum and instruction, and advanced literacy instruction. All programs require the completion of specified coursework.

Licensure/Reciprocity: Texas. Students seeking teaching certification in a state other than Texas should consult with that state's teacher certification office early in their program of study to insure compliance with requirements. Many state directors of teacher credentialing have signed Interstate Agreements through NASDTEC that expedite the certification process.

HOUSTON BAPTIST UNIVERSITY

College of Education and Behavioral Sciences
7502 Fondren Road
Houston, Texas 77074-3298
Phone: (281) 649-3000
Fax: (281) 649-3261
E-mail: jdbrown@hbu.edu
Internet: http://www.hbu.edu

Institution Description: Houston Baptist University (formerly Houston Baptist College) is a private institution affiliated with the Baptist general Convention of Texas. It was chartered in 1960.

The purpose of the undergraduate education program is the preparation of teachers for public and private schools from preschool through high school.

Institution Control: Private.

Calendar: Quarter. Academic year September to May.

Official(s): Dr. Joseph D. Brown, Dean.

Faculty: Full-time 12; part-time 2; adjunct 4.

Degrees Awarded: 53 baccalaureate; 353 master's.

Admission Requirements: *Undergraduate:* Graduation from an approved secondary school or GED; College Board SAT or ACT composite. *Teacher education specific:* Overall 2.5 GPA; no grade lower than C in major/certification area; passing scores on all three sections (reading, mathematics, writing) of the Texas Higher Education Assessment (THEA); faculty interview; two letters of recommendation; personal goal statement; PRAXIS II prior to certification. *Graduate:* Baccalaureate degree from a regionally accredited institution. *Teacher education specific:* 2.5 GPA; GRE or Miller Analogies Test scores; completion of all required departmental exams; teacher certification for some programs; recommendations; faculty interview.

Fees and Expenses: Undergraduate: $9,450 per academic year. Graduate: $1,050 per 3-hour course. On-campus room and board: $4,245. Books and supplies: $700.

Financial Aid: Resources specifically for eligible students enrolled in teacher education programs are awarded on the basis of financial need and academic merit. The institution has a Program Participation Agreement with the U.S. Department of Education for eligible students to receive Pell Grants and other federal aid. Teacher scholarships available to qualifying students. *Contact:* Ken Rogers at: (281) 649-3113 or e-mail at: krogers@hbu.edu.

Accreditation: *Regional:* SACS. *Member of:* AACTE. *Approved by:* Texas State Board for Educator Certification.

Undergraduate Programs: The university offers programs that lead to teacher certification in early grades (early childhood through grade four), middle school (grades four through eight), high school (grades eight through twelve), all-level music, bilingual education, English as a second language, and generic special education. Students must complete requirements in academic foundations, a teaching field, and professional teacher education.

Graduate Programs: The Master of Education degree is designed to develop leaders in school administration and in special services necessary to the successful operation of schools in Texas. The program is also designed to provide counselors for churches, business, industry, and social agencies. The degree program offers concentrations in: all-level education, educational administration, bilingual education, counselor education, educational diagnostician, early childhood through grade 4, general studies, reading specialist, secondary education. Each program has specific coursework requirements.

Licensure/Reciprocity: Texas. Students seeking teaching certification in a state other than Texas should consult with that state's teacher certification office early in their program of study to insure compliance with requirements. Many state directors of teacher credentialing have signed Interstate Agreements through NASDTEC that expedite the certification process.

LAMAR UNIVERSITY

College of Education and Human Development
Department of Professional Pedagogy
4400 Martin Luther King, Jr. Parkway
Beaumont, Texas 77710
Phone: (409) 880-8673
Fax: (409) 880-8052
E-mail: pedagogy@lamar.edu
Internet: http://www.lamar.edu

Institution Description: Lamar University is a component of the Texas State University System. It was established and offered first instruction at the postsecondary level as South Park Junior College in 1940.

The Teacher Education Program prepares students for careers in teaching and offers both undergraduate and graduate programs.

Institution Control: Public.

Calendar: Semester. Academic year August to May.

Official(s): Dr. Dorman Moore, Chair.

Faculty: Full-time 19.

Degrees Awarded: 15 baccalaureate; 103 master's.

Admission Requirements: *Undergraduate:* Graduation from an approved secondary school with 14 academic units or GED; College Board SAT. *Teacher education specific:* Successful completion of 45 semester hours with a minimum 2.5 GPA; successful completion of all departmental tests/exams; passing scores on all three sections (reading, mathematics, writing) of the Texas Higher Education Assessment (THEA); attainment of 12th grade equivalency on the Nelson-Denny reading test; faculty interview. *Graduate:* Baccalaureate degree from a regionally accredited institution. *Teacher education specific:* GRE or Miller Analogies Test; personal goal statement; faculty interview.

Fees and Expenses: Undergraduate: $3,414 in-state per academic year; $10,494 out-of-state. Graduate: Tuition charged per credit hour. On-campus room and board: $5,012. Other expenses: $3,732. Books and supplies: $662.

Financial Aid: Resources specifically for eligible students enrolled in teacher education programs are awarded on the basis of financial need and academic merit. The institution has a Program Participation Agreement with the U.S. Department of Education for eligible students to receive Pell Grants and other federal aid. Teacher scholarships available to qualifying students. *Contact:* Financial Aid Office at: (409) 880-8450.

Accreditation: *Regional:* SACS. *Member of:* AACTE. *Approved by:* Texas State Board for Educator Certification.

Undergraduate Programs: The Bachelor of Science Degree in Interdisciplinary studies is designed to meet the requirements for a Provisional Teaching Certificate. Students may receive a certificate endorsement to teach kindergarten and driver education by meeting additional curriculum requirements. In addition to completing the required academic foundations core curriculum, program students must fulfill the requirements in the area of specialization, professional education, and elective courses. A minimum of 120 semester hours is required for the degree award.

Graduate Programs: The Master of Education degree programs in counseling and development and educational administration are offered through the Department of Educational Leadership. The Master of Education degree is offered with concentrations in elementary education, secondary education, and special education. Each program has specific coursework requirements.

Licensure/Reciprocity: Texas. Students seeking teaching certification in a state other than Texas should consult with that state's teacher certification office early in their program of study to insure compliance with requirements. Many state directors of teacher credentialing have signed Interstate Agreements through NASDTEC that expedite the certification process.

LUBBOCK CHRISTIAN UNIVERSITY

School of Education
5601 19th Street
Lubbock, Texas 79407-2099
Phone: (806) 796-8800
Fax: (806) 796-8917
E-mail: admissions@lcu.edu
Internet: http://www.lcu.edu

Institution Description: Lubbock Christian University is a private, independent, nonprofit university affiliated with the Church of Christ. The institution was established in 1957.

The School of Education offers programs to prepare students for careers in teaching. Both undergraduate and graduate programs are offered.

Institution Control: Private.

Calendar: Semester. Academic year August to May.

Official(s): Dr. L. Ken Jones, President.

Faculty: Full-time 12.

Degrees Awarded: 54 baccalaureate; 35 master's.

Admission Requirements: *Undergraduate:* Graduation from an approved secondary school or GED; College Board SAT or ACT composite. *Teacher education specific:* Successful completion of 45 semester hours with a minimum 2.5 GPA; successful completion of all departmental tests/exams; passing scores on all three sections (reading, mathematics, writing) of the Texas Higher Education Assessment (THEA); faculty interview. *Graduate:* Baccalaureate degree from a regionally accredited institution. *Teacher education specific:* GRE or Miller Analogies Test; personal goal statement; faculty interview.

Fees and Expenses: Undergraduate: $11,452 per academic year. Graduate: Tuition charged per credit hour. On-campus room and board: $5,176. Other expenses: $3,426. Books and supplies: $794.

Financial Aid: Resources specifically for eligible students enrolled in teacher education programs are awarded on the basis of financial need and academic merit. The institution has a Program Participation Agreement with the U.S. Department of Education for eligible students to receive Pell Grants and other federal aid. Teacher scholarships available to qualifying students. *Contact:* Financial Aid Office at: (806) 796-7176.

Accreditation: *Regional:* SACS. *Member of:* AACTE. *Approved by:* Texas State Board for Educator Certification.

Undergraduate Programs: The Bachelor of Science Degree in Interdisciplinary studies is designed to meet the requirements for a Provisional Teaching Certificate. Students may receive a certificate endorsement to teach elementary, middle school and secondary education by meeting curriculum requirements. In

addition to completing the required academic foundations core, students must fulfill the requirements in the area of specialization, professional education, and elective courses. A minimum of 126 semester hours is required for the degree award.

Graduate Programs: The Master of Education degree programs in administration, instructional leadership, and instructional technology are offered. The Master of Education degree programs are offered in elementary education and secondary education. Each program has specific coursework requirements.

Licensure/Reciprocity: Texas. Students seeking teaching certification in a state other than Texas should consult with that state's teacher certification office early in their program of study to insure compliance with requirements. Many state directors of teacher credentialing have signed Interstate Agreements through NASDTEC that expedite the certification process.

MIDWESTERN STATE UNIVERSITY

West College of Education
Department of Education
206 Ferguson Building
Wichita Falls, Texas 76308-2099
Phone: (940) 397-4514
Fax: (940) 397-4694
E-mail: school.relations@mwsu.edu
Internet: http://www.mwsu.edu

Institution Description: Midwestern State University was established as Wichita Falls Junior College in 1922.

The Gordon T. and Ellen West College of Education offers teacher certification for elementary and secondary teachers.

Institution Control: Public.

Calendar: Semester. Academic year August to May.

Official(s): Dr. Grant Sampson, Dean; Dr. Ann Estrada, Chair, Department of Education.

Faculty: Full-time 8; emeriti 5.

Degrees Awarded: 22 baccalaureate; 51 master's.

Admission Requirements: *Undergraduate:* Graduation from an approved secondary school or GED; College Board SAT or ACT composite. *Teacher education specific:* Successful completion of 60 semester hours; satisfactory scores on all three sections (reading, mathematics, writing) of the Texas Higher Education Assessment (THEA); 3 letters of recommendation; cumulative 2.75 GPA; screening interview. *Graduate:* Baccalaureate degree from a regionally accredited institution. *Teacher education specific:* GRE or Miller Analogies Test; personal goal statement; faculty interview.

Fees and Expenses: Undergraduate: $3,414 in-state per academic year; $10,494 out-of-state. Graduate: Tuition charged per credit hour. On-campus room and board: $4,630. Other expenses: $2,253. Books and supplies: $1,165.

Financial Aid: Resources specifically for eligible students enrolled in teacher education programs are awarded on the basis of financial need and academic merit. The institution has a Program Participation Agreement with the U.S. Department of Education for eligible students to receive Pell Grants and other federal aid. Teacher scholarships available to qualifying students. *Contact:* Financial Aid Office at: (940) 397-4214.

Accreditation: *Regional:* SACS. *Member of:* AACTE. *Approved by:* Texas State Board for Educator Certification.

Undergraduate Programs: Students who wish to become elementary teachers (grades 1-8) graduate with a Bachelor of Science in interdisciplinary studies. Students who wish to become secondary teachers (grades 6-12) pursue a Bachelor of Science, Bachelor of Arts, Bachelor of Fine Arts, Bachelor of Music, or Bachelor of Business Administration with a major and/or minor in appropriate teaching fields. All programs require the completion of academic foundations and core curriculum, professional studies, field experiences, and student teaching. A minimum of 120 semester hours is required for the degree award.

MIDWESTERN STATE UNIVERSITY—*cont'd*

Graduate Programs: Graduate programs are offered leading to the Master of Education degree and may be pursued in a variety of concentrations. Contact the School of Education for detailed information.

Licensure/Reciprocity: Texas. Students seeking teaching certification in a state other than Texas should consult with that state's teacher certification office early in their program of study to insure compliance with requirements. Many state directors of teacher credentialing have signed Interstate Agreements through NASDTEC that expedite the certification process.

OUR LADY OF THE LAKE UNIVERSITY

School of Education and Clinical Studies
Education Department
411 S.W. 24th Street
San Antonio, Texas 78207-4689
Phone: (210) 434-6711
Fax: (210) 436-4036
E-mail: education@ollusa.edu
Internet: http://www.ollusa.edu

Institution Description: Our Lady of the Lake University (Our Lady of the Lake College until 1975) is a private institution affiliated with the Sisters of Divine Providence, Roman Catholic Church.

The Education Department offers undergraduate and graduate programs leading to teacher certification.

Institution Control: Private.

Calendar: Semester. Academic year August to May.

Official(s): Dr. Idalia Perez, Chair.

Faculty: Full-time 13.

Degrees Awarded: 20 baccalaureate; 57 master's.

Admission Requirements: *Undergraduate:* Graduation with 16 academic units from an approved secondary school or GED; minimum 2.75 GPA; College Board SAT or ACT composite. *Teacher education specific:* Minimum 2.5 GPA; successful completion of all departmental tests/exams; faculty interview; passing scores on all three sections (reading, mathematics, writing) of the Texas Higher Education Assessment (THEA). *Graduate:* Baccalaureate degree from a regionally accredited institution. *Teacher education specific:* GRE or Miller Analogies Test; two letters of recommendation; personal goal statement; faculty interview.

Fees and Expenses: Undergraduate: $14,650 per academic year. Graduate: Tuition charged per credit hour. On-campus room and board: $5,032. Other expenses: $2,770. Books and supplies: $900.

Financial Aid: Resources specifically for eligible students enrolled in teacher education programs are awarded on the basis of financial need and academic merit. The institution has a Program Participation Agreement with the U.S. Department of Education for eligible students to receive Pell Grants and other federal aid. Teacher scholarships available to qualifying students. *Contact:* Financial Aid Office at: (210) 434-6711.

Accreditation: *Regional:* SACS. *Member of:* AACTE. *Approved by:* Texas State Board for Educator Certification.

Undergraduate Programs: The Education Department offers a program leading to the Bachelor of Arts in communication disorders and the Bachelor of Science in Education degree with concentrations in early childhood education, elementary education, and generic special education. All programs require the completion of a general education core, professional studies, content area, field experiences, and student teaching. A minimum of 128 semester hours is required for the degree award.

Graduate Programs: The Master of Education with Nontraditional Teacher Certification is a cohort program designed for those who desire a change of career into the field of education. The three-year program allows students to graduate with a Master in Education degree and be eligible to apply for Texas teaching certification in one or more of the areas of: elementary education, generic special education, bilingual education, secondary mathematics education, secondary science education.

Licensure/Reciprocity: Texas. Students seeking teaching certification in a state other than Texas should consult with that state's teacher certification office early in their program of study to insure compliance with requirements. Many state directors of teacher credentialing have signed Interstate Agreements through NASDTEC that expedite the certification process.

PRAIRIE VIEW A & M UNIVERSITY

College of Education
Department of Curriculum and Instruction
University Drive
P.O. Box 3089
Prairie View, Texas 77446
Phone: (936) 857-2626
Fax: (936) 857-2699
E-mail: admissions@pvamu.edu
Internet: http://www.pvamu.edu

Institution Description: Prairie View A & M University, a state institution and land-grant university, is a member of the Texas A & M University System. It was established in 1876.

The purpose of the Department of Curriculum and Instruction is to provide regional, national, and international leadership study and improvement of teaching and learning in diverse educational settings.

Institution Control: Public.

Calendar: Semester. Academic year August to May.

Official(s): Dr. Constance Person, Head.

Faculty: Full-time 15.

Degrees Awarded: 63 baccalaureate; 183 master's.

Admission Requirements: *Undergraduate:* Graduation with 16 academic units from an approved secondary school or GED; minimum score on SAT 800 or ACT 18. *Teacher education specific:* Minimum 2.5 GPA; satisfactory scores on all three sections (reading, mathematics, writing) of the Texas Higher Education Assessment (THEA); successful completion of all departmental tests/exams; faculty interview. *Graduate:* Baccalaureate degree from a regionally accredited institution. *Teacher education specific:* GRE or Miller Analogies Test; letters of recommendation; personal goal statement; faculty interview.

Fees and Expenses: Undergraduate: $3,592 in-state per academic year; $10,672 out-of-state. Graduate: $48 in-state per credit hour plus $59 per credit hour; $262 out-of-state per credit hour plus $59 per credit hour. On-campus room and board: $5,945. Other expenses: $4,580. Books and supplies: $756.

Financial Aid: Resources specifically for eligible students enrolled in teacher education programs are awarded on the basis of financial need and academic merit. The institution has a Program Participation Agreement with the U.S. Department of Education for eligible students to receive Pell Grants and other federal aid. Teacher scholarships available to qualifying students. *Contact:* Financial Aid Office at: (936) 857-2424.

Accreditation: *Regional:* SACS. *Professional:* NCATE. *Member of:* AACTE. *Approved by:* Texas State Board for Educator Certification.

Undergraduate Programs: The Bachelor of Science Degree in interdisciplinary studies is designed to meet the requirements for a Provisional Teaching Certificate. Students may receive a certificate endorsement to teach kindergarten through secondary education curricula. In addition to completing the required academic foundations core curriculum, program students must fulfill the requirements in the area of specialization, professional education, and elective courses. A minimum of 120 semester hours is required for the degree award.

Graduate Programs: Programs are offered in a variety of education disciplines and lead to the degrees of Master of Arts, Master of Arts in Teaching, Master of Science in Education, Master of Education, and the Doctor of Philosophy in educational leadership. Each program has specific course requirements including a common core, program concentration, and electives.

Licensure/Reciprocity: Texas. Students seeking teaching certification in a state other than Texas should consult with that state's teacher certification office early in their program of study to insure compliance with requirements. Many state directors of teacher credentialing have signed Interstate Agreements through NASDTEC that expedite the certification process.

SAM HOUSTON STATE UNIVERSITY

College Education and Applied Sciences
Department of Curriculum and Instruction

1700 Sam Houston Avenue
Huntsville, Texas 77340
Phone: (936) 294-1146
Fax: (936) 294-3758
E-mail: edu_mdx@shsu.edu
Internet: http://www.shsu.edu

Institution Description: Sam Houston State University was chartered as Sam Houston Normal Institute in 1879.

The purpose of the teacher education programs is to prepare candidates to become exemplary teachers in secondary schools as well as both the elementary and secondary schools for those seeking all-level certification.

Institution Control: Public.

Calendar: Semester. Academic year September to May.

Official(s): Dr. Charlene Crocker, Department Chair; Dr. Daphne Eberling, High School Program Coordinator.

Faculty: Full-time 13.

Degrees Awarded: 212 baccalaureate; 133 master's; 13 doctorate.

Admission Requirements: *Undergraduate:* Graduation from an approved secondary school or GED; College Board SAT score of 900 or ACT composite score of 21. *Teacher education specific:* Overall 2.5 GPA; satisfactory scores on all three sections (reading, mathematics, writing) of the Texas Higher Education Assessment (THEA); faculty interview; personal goal statement. *Graduate:* Baccalaureate degree from a regionally accredited institution. *Teacher education specific:* 2.5 GPA; GRE or Miller Analogies Test scores; completion of all required departmental exams; recommendations; faculty interview.

Fees and Expenses: Undergraduate: $3,076 in-state per academic year; $8,740 out-of-state. Graduate: $69 in-state per credit hour; $280 out-of-state. On-campus room and board: $4,160. Other expenses: $3,026. Books and supplies: $708.

Financial Aid: Resources specifically for eligible students enrolled in teacher education programs are awarded on the basis of financial need and academic merit. The institution has a Program Participation Agreement with the U.S. Department of Education for eligible students to receive Pell Grants and other federal aid. Teacher scholarships available to qualifying students. *Contact:* Financial Aid Office at: (936) 294-1724.

Accreditation: *Regional:* SACS. *Professional:* NCATE. *Member of:* AACTE. *Approved by:* Texas State Board for Educator Certification.

Undergraduate Programs: The primary purpose of the Academic Studies Program is to prepare students for teaching positions in elementary, intermediate, and middle schools. The program offers degrees leading to certification in preschool through eighth grade in the areas of bilingual education, early childhood education, reading/language arts, special education, English as a second language, English/language arts and reading, mathematics, science, and social studies. All programs lead to the baccalaureate degree and require completion of the general education core, professional studies, content area, field experiences, and student teaching. A minimum of 128 semester hours must be completed for the degree award.

Graduate Programs: A post-baccalaureate alternate route to certification is available in programs offered in the following areas: 8-12 English language arts and reading, social studies; history, science, life science, physical science, mathematics; 4-8 social studies, science, mathematics. Each program has specific coursework requirements.

Licensure/Reciprocity: Texas. Students seeking teaching certification in a state other than Texas should consult with that state's teacher certification office early in their program of study to insure compliance with requirements. Many state directors of teacher credentialing have signed Interstate Agreements through NASDTEC that expedite the certification process.

SOUTHWESTERN UNIVERSITY

Brown College of Arts and Sciences
Education Department

1001 East University Avenue
Georgetown, Texas 78626
Phone: (512) 863-6511
Fax: (512) 863-5788
E-mail: admission@southwestern.edu
Internet: http://www.southwestern.edu

Institution Description: Southwestern University is a private, independent, nonprofit institution affiliated with the United Methodist Church. It was founded in 1840.

The Education Department believes that a strong foundation in the liberal arts is critical to the preparation of excellent teachers.

Calendar: Semester. Academic year August to May.

Official(s): Dr. Sherry E. Adrian, Chair.

Faculty: Full-time 6; part-time 1.

Degrees Awarded: 22 baccalaureate.

Admission Requirements: *Undergraduate:* Graduation in top 25% of class from an approved secondary school; College Board SAT or ACT composite. *Teacher education specific:* Overall 2.5 GPA; satisfactory scores on all three sections (reading, mathematics, writing) of the Texas Higher Education Assessment (THEA); faculty interview; personal goal statement.

Fees and Expenses: Undergraduate: $18,870 per academic year. Graduate tuition charged per credit hour. On-campus room and board: $6,540. Other expenses: $980. Books and supplies: $700.

Financial Aid: Resources specifically for eligible students enrolled in teacher education programs are awarded on the basis of financial need and academic merit. The institution has a Program Participation Agreement with the U.S. Department of Education for eligible students to receive Pell Grants and other federal aid. Teacher scholarships available to qualifying students. *Contact:* Financial Aid Office at: (512) 863-1259.

Accreditation: *Regional:* SACS. *Member of:* AACTE. *Approved by:* Texas State Board for Educator Certification.

Undergraduate Programs: Certification programs available include elementary (grades 1-8), secondary (grades 6-12), and all-level (music and physical education). The early childhood endorsement may be earned in conjunction with the elementary certificate. Generic special education certification is available in both secondary and elementary levels. Students who wish to earn secondary certification normally complete a 30-hour major and a 24-hour minor or an approved composite program, as well as 18 semester hours of professional education. All programs lead to the baccalaureate degree and require the completion of 122 semester hours.

Licensure/Reciprocity: Texas. Students seeking teaching certification in a state other than Texas should consult with that state's teacher certification office early in their program of study to insure compliance with requirements. Many state directors of teacher credentialing have signed Interstate Agreements through NASDTEC that expedite the certification process.

STEPHEN F. AUSTIN STATE UNIVERSITY

College of Education

213 McKibben Education Building
1936 North Street
Nacogdoches, Texas 75962
Phone: (936) 468-2011
Fax: (936) 468-3849
E-mail: admissions@sfasu.edu
Internet: http://www.sfasu.edu

Institution Description: Stephen F. Austin State University was chartered as Stephen F. Austin Teachers College in 1921.

The College of Education prepares students for teaching careers through its undergraduate and graduate programs.

Institution Control: Public.

Calendar: Semester. Academic year August to May.

Official(s): Dr. John Jacobson, Dean.

Faculty: Full-time 15.

Degrees Awarded: 181 baccalaureate; 179 master's.

Admission Requirements: *Undergraduate:* Graduation from an approved secondary school or GED; College Board SAT or ACT composite. *Teacher education specific:* Completion of 66 semester hours; overall 2.5 GPA; satisfactory scores on all three sections (reading, mathematics, writing) of the Texas Higher Education Assessment (THEA); faculty interview; personal goal statement. *Graduate:* Baccalaureate degree from a regionally accredited institution. *Teacher education specific:* 2.75 GPA; GRE or Miller Analogies Test scores; completion of all required departmental exams; recommendations; faculty interview.

Fees and Expenses: Undergraduate: $3,524 in-state per academic year; $10,604 out-of-state. Graduate: $42 per credit hour in-state plus $52 per hour; $253 per credit hour out-of-state plus $52 per hour. On-campus room and board: $5,080. Other expenses: $3,221. Books and supplies: $887.

Financial Aid: Resources specifically for eligible students enrolled in teacher education programs are awarded on the basis of financial need and academic merit. The institution has a Program Participation Agreement with the U.S. Department of Education for eligible students to receive Pell Grants and other federal aid. Teacher scholarships available to qualifying students. *Contact:* Financial Aid Office at: (936) 468-2011.

Accreditation: *Regional:* SACS. *Professional:* NCATE. *Member of:* AACTE. *Approved by:* Texas State Board for Educator Certification.

Undergraduate Programs: Certification at the undergraduate level is available through programs at the elementary school level (early childhood to grade 4 and grades 4 to 8) and the secondary school level (grades 8-12). A 24-hour field-based professional education component is required of all students in the baccalaureate programs. Also, students in the secondary program must complete a major in the subject area in which they plan to teach. Student teaching is accomplished in local area schools. All programs require the completion of 130 semester hours.

Graduate Programs: The Post Baccalaureate Initial Certification Program is designed for individuals holding a bachelor's degree who are seeking teacher certification. Master's degree programs include the Master of Arts in art, communication, counseling, English, history, music, school psychology. The Master of Education degree is offered in early childhood education, elementary education, special education, secondary education and educational leadership. Each program requires specific coursework.

Licensure/Reciprocity: Texas. Students seeking teaching certification in a state other than Texas should consult with that state's teacher certification office early in their program of study to insure compliance with requirements. Many state directors of teacher credentialing have signed Interstate Agreements through NASDTEC that expedite the certification process.

TARLETON STATE UNIVERSITY

College of Education
Department of Curriculum and Instruction

1333 West Washington Street
Tarleton Station
Stephenville, Texas 76402
Phone: (254) 968-9096
Fax: (254) 968-9917
E-mail: calahan@tarleton.edu
Internet: http://www.tarleton.edu

Institution Description: Tarleton State University is a land-grant college and a member of the Texas A & M University system. It was chartered as John Tarleton College in 1899.

The College of Education serves the needs of teachers who possess strong records of academic achievement and who demonstrate a continuing commitment to self-direction as learners and to the education of their students.

Institution Control: Public.

Calendar: Semester. Academic year August to May.

Official(s): Dr. Jill Burk, Dean; Dr. Ann Calahan, Head, Department of Curriculum and Instruction.

Faculty: Full-time 24.

Degrees Awarded: 112 baccalaureate; 134 master's.

Admission Requirements: *Undergraduate:* Graduation from an approved secondary school or GED; College Board SAT or ACT composite. *Teacher education specific:* 2.6 GPA; completion of basic required courses; completion of 60 semester hours; one full semester in residence; passing scores on all three sections (reading, mathematics, writing) of the Texas Higher Education Assessment (THEA); passing of the university written proficiency requirement; faculty interview. *Graduate:* Baccalaureate degree from a regionally accredited institution. *Teacher education specific:* 2.75 GPA; GRE or Miller Analogies Test scores; completion of all required departmental exams; recommendations; faculty interview.

Fees and Expenses: Undergraduate: $2,898 in-state per academic year; $11,353 out-of-state. Graduate: Tuition charged per credit hour. On-campus room and board: $4,677. Other expenses: $2,692. Books and supplies: $777.

Financial Aid: Resources specifically for eligible students enrolled in teacher education programs are awarded on the basis of financial need and academic merit. The institution has a Program Participation Agreement with the U.S. Department of Education for eligible students to receive Pell Grants and other federal aid. Teacher scholarships available to qualifying students. *Contact:* Financial Aid Office at: (254) 968-9070.

Accreditation: *Regional:* SACS. *Member of:* AACTE. *Approved by:* Texas State Board for Educator Certification.

Undergraduate Programs: The Department of Curriculum and Instruction offers the Bachelor of Science in Interdisciplinary Studies as the degree leading to teacher certification at the elementary level. Through this degree, students obtain a broad-based preparation in the academic areas that comprise the elementary school curriculum and a reading specialization. Emphases available include generalist (early childhood-8th grade), middle school math (4th to 8th grade), middle school science (4th to 8th grade), middle school math/science (4th to 8th grade), middle school language arts/social sciences (4th to 8th grade), and special education (early childhood -12th grade).

Graduate Programs: All Master in Education programs in curriculum and instruction require a minimum of 36 semester hours. Certification/supplement areas can include reading specialist, diagnostician, gifted and talented, special education. Other emphasis areas available include technology director, technology applications, teacher leadership, elementary or secondary education.

Licensure/Reciprocity: Texas. Students seeking teaching certification in a state other than Texas should consult with that state's teacher certification office early in their program of study to insure compliance with requirements. Many state

directors of teacher credentialing have signed Interstate Agreements through NASDTEC that expedite the certification process.

TEXAS A & M UNIVERSITY
Department of Teaching, Learning, and Culture
P.O. Box 4232 TAMU
College Station, Texas 77843-4232
Phone: (979) 845-3211
Fax: (979) 847-9563
E-mail: dsmith@coe.tamu.edu
Internet: http://www.tamu.edu

Institution Description: Texas A & M University is a state institution was established and offered first instruction at the post-secondary level in 1876.

The mission of the Department of Teaching, Learning, and Culture is to "prepare educators and researchers to build inclusive democratic communities in schools and society through critical and reflective research, teaching, and service".

Institution Control: Public.

Calendar: Semester. Academic year August to May.

Official(s): Dr. Donnie L. Smith, Department Head.

Faculty: Full-time 31; part-time 16.

Degrees Awarded: 508 baccalaureate; 139 master's; 52 doctorate.

Admission Requirements: *Undergraduate:* Graduation with 16 academic units from an approved secondary school or GED; College Board SAT or ACT composite. *Teacher education specific:* Completion of 60 semester hours; overall 2.5 GPA; satisfactory scores on all three sections (reading, mathematics, writing) of the Texas Higher Education Assessment (THEA); faculty interview; personal goal statement. *Graduate:* Baccalaureate degree from a regionally accredited institution. *Teacher education specific:* Three letters of recommendation; GRE or Miller Analogies Test scores; completion of all required departmental exams; biographical data; faculty interview.

Fees and Expenses: Undergraduate: $5,051 in-state per academic year; $12,131 out-of-state. Graduate: Tuition charged per credit hour. On-campus room and board: $6,030. Other expenses: $2,124. Books and supplies: $830.

Financial Aid: Resources specifically for eligible students enrolled in teacher education programs are awarded on the basis of financial need and academic merit. The institution has a Program Participation Agreement with the U.S. Department of Education for eligible students to receive Pell Grants and other federal aid. Teacher scholarships available to qualifying students. *Contact:* Financial Aid Office at: (979) 845-3236.

Accreditation: *Regional:* SACS. *Professional:* NCATE. *Member of:* AACTE. *Approved by:* Texas State Board for Educator Certification.

Undergraduate Programs: Baccalaureate programs leading to teacher certification are offered in the fields of early childhood education, middle grades (English language arts/social studies (grades 4-8) and mathematics/Science (grades 4-8); and secondary education (grades 9-12). All programs require the completion of a general education core, professional studies, subject content area, field experiences, and student teaching. A minimum of 128 semester hours must be completed.

Graduate Programs: The department offers a variety of graduate programs: two programs at the master's level (Master of Science with thesis, Master of Education) and two at the doctoral level (Doctor of Philosophy and Doctor of Education (with emphasis in science education only). All degrees are in curriculum and instruction. The Master of Science is a 32-hour (thesis option only) program beyond the baccalaureate degree.

Licensure/Reciprocity: Texas. Students seeking teaching certification in a state other than Texas should consult with that state's teacher certification office early in their program of study to insure compliance with requirements. Many state directors of teacher credentialing have signed Interstate Agreements through NASDTEC that expedite the certification process.

TEXAS A & M UNIVERSITY - COMMERCE
College of Education
2600 South Neal
P.O. Box 3011
Commerce, Texas 75429-3011
Phone: (903) 886-5081
Fax: (903) 468-3201
E-mail: Edward_Seifert@tamu-commerce.edu
Internet: http://www.tamu-commerce.edu

Institution Description: Texas A & M University - Commerce, formerly known as East Texas State University, is a state institution within the Texas A & M System. It was established in 1889.

The College of Education offers a broad selection of educator certification programs. Students may earn their initial teaching certificate as an undergraduate or graduate.

Institution Control: Public.

Calendar: Semester. Academic year September to May.

Official(s): Dr. Edward Seifert, Dean.

Faculty: Full-time 20; adjunct 11.

Degrees Awarded: 188 baccalaureate; 443 master's; 40 doctorate.

Admission Requirements: *Undergraduate:* Graduation with 16 academic units from an approved secondary school or GED; College Board SAT or ACT composite. *Teacher education specific:* Completion of 60 semester hours; overall 2.5 GPA; satisfactory scores on all three sections (reading, mathematics, writing) of the Texas Higher Education Assessment (THEA); faculty interview; personal goal statement. *Graduate:* Baccalaureate degree from a regionally accredited institution. *Teacher education specific:* Three letters of recommendation; GRE or Miller Analogies Test scores; completion of all required departmental exams; biographical data; faculty interview.

Fees and Expenses: Undergraduate: $3,620 in-state per academic year; $10,700 out-of-state. Graduate: Tuition charged per credit hour. On-campus room and board: $5,370. Other expenses: $2,730. Books and supplies: $900.

Financial Aid: Resources specifically for eligible students enrolled in teacher education programs are awarded on the basis of financial need and academic merit. The institution has a Program Participation Agreement with the U.S. Department of Education for eligible students to receive Pell Grants and other federal aid. Teacher scholarships available to qualifying students. *Contact:* Financial Aid Office at: (903) 886-5096.

Accreditation: *Regional:* SACS. *Member of:* AACTE. *Approved by:* Texas State Board for Educator Certification.

Undergraduate Programs: The Department of Elementary Education offers undergraduate degrees in early childhood-4th grade with a generalist, bilingual, or special education emphasis. Degrees in middle level education are offered in science, mathematics, mathematics/science combination, history, language arts/reading. All programs require the completion of a general education core, professional studies, subject content area, field experiences, and student teaching. A minimum of 126 semester hours is required for the degree.

The Department of Secondary and Higher Education offers an undergraduate curriculum that provides certification to teach grades 6 through 12 with students majoring in their teaching fields, trades, or industries.

Graduate Programs: The College of Education offers the following majors with their respective master's degree: higher education (Master of Science emphasizing school administration and college teaching); secondary education (Master of Science or Master of Education); learning technology and information systems (Master of Science or Master of Education) emphasizing media and technology, educational computing, library and information science); training and development (Master of Science).

A Doctor of Education degree can be earned in the areas of supervision, curriculum, and instruction.

Licensure/Reciprocity: Texas. Students seeking teaching certification in a state other than Texas should consult with that state's teacher certification office early in their program of

TEXAS A & M UNIVERSITY - COMMERCE—

cont'd

study to insure compliance with requirements. Many state directors of teacher credentialing have signed Interstate Agreements through NASDTEC that expedite the certification process.

TEXAS A & M UNIVERSITY - CORPUS CHRISTI

College of Education

6300 Ocean Drive
Corpus Christi, Texas 78412-5503
Phone: (361) 825-2660
Fax: (361) 825-2732
E-mail: dhopkins@falcon.tamucc.edu
Internet: http://www.education.tamucc.edu

Institution Description: Texas A & M University - Corpus Christi (formerly Corpus Christi State University) provides lower and upper division study. The campus was founded in 1971.

The primary purpose of the College of Education is to prepare students for a career in a selected area of professional education. The college is committed to a field-based professional development program.

Institution Control: Public.

Calendar: Semester. Academic year August to August.

Official(s): Dr. Dee Hopkins, Dean.

Faculty: Full-time 49; 5 part-time; 58 adjunct.

Degrees Awarded: 189 baccalaureate; 205 master's; 9 doctorate.

Admission Requirements: *Undergraduate:* Graduation from an approved secondary school or GED; College Board SAT or ACT composite. *Teacher education specific:* Completion of a 30 semester hours; completion of oral communication and computer literacy requirements; overall 2.5 GPA; satisfactory scores on all three sections (reading, mathematics, writing) of the Texas Higher Education Assessment (THEA); faculty interview; personal goal statement. *Graduate:* Baccalaureate degree from a regionally accredited institution. *Teacher education specific:* Three letters of recommendation; 3.0 GPA; GRE or Miller Analogies Test scores; completion of all required departmental exams; biographical data; faculty interview.

Fees and Expenses: Undergraduate: $3,252 in-state per academic year; $8,916 out-of-state. Graduate: Tuition charged per credit hour. On-campus room and board: $7,125. Other expenses: $1,994. Books and supplies: $720.

Financial Aid: Resources specifically for eligible students enrolled in teacher education programs are awarded on the basis of financial need and academic merit. The institution has a Program Participation Agreement with the U.S. Department of Education for eligible students to receive Pell Grants and other federal aid. Teacher scholarships available to qualifying students. *Contact:* Financial Aid Office at: (361) 825-2338.

Accreditation: *Regional:* SACS. *Member of:* AACTE. *Approved by:* Texas State Board for Educator Certification.

Undergraduate Programs: The College of Education offers the Bachelor of Science in interdisciplinary studies and the Bachelor of Science degree with majors in kinesiology as well as occupational training and development. Early in the field-based program, students are required to spend a significant portion of the professional development courses observing and working with experienced teachers in the local districts. A minimum of 124 semester hours of credit are required for graduation.

Graduate Programs: The Master of Science degree is offered in the fields of: counseling, curriculum and instruction, early childhood education, educational administration, educational technology, elementary education, occupational training and development, reading, secondary education, and special education. Emphasis is placed on the acquisition and application of existing knowledge and the generation of new knowledge.

The Doctor of Education degree is offered in school counseling and educational leadership (offered jointly by the Corpus Christi and Kingsville campuses).

Licensure/Reciprocity: Texas. Students seeking teaching certification in a state other than Texas should consult with that state's teacher certification office early in their program of study to insure compliance with requirements. Many state directors of teacher credentialing have signed Interstate Agreements through NASDTEC that expedite the certification process.

TEXAS A & M UNIVERSITY - KINGSVILLE

Education Department

West Santa Gertrudis
Kingsville, Texas 78363
Phone: (361) 593-2801
Fax: (361) 593-2108
E-mail: education@tamuk.edu
Internet: http://www.tamuk.edu

Institution Description: Texas A & M University - Kingsville was formerly known as Texas A & I University. It was chartered as South Texas State Teachers College in 1925.

The Education Department offers programs to prepare teachers, counselors, diagnosticians, and other educational leaders for success in a field-based preparation program.

Institution Control: Public.

Calendar: Semester. Academic year August to May.

Official(s): Dr. Michael Daniel Named, Dean.

Faculty: Full-time 22.

Degrees Awarded: 119 baccalaureate; 163 master's; 30 doctorate.

Admission Requirements: *Undergraduate:* Graduation from an approved secondary school or GED; minimum College Board SAT score 800 or ACT composite score 18. *Teacher education specific:* Completion of 60 semester hours; overall 2.5 GPA; satisfactory scores on all three sections (reading, mathematics, writing) of the Texas Higher Education Assessment (THEA); faculty interview; personal goal statement. *Graduate:* Baccalaureate degree from a regionally accredited institution. *Teacher education specific:* Three letters of recommendation; GRE or Miller Analogies Test scores; completion of all required departmental exams; biographical data; faculty interview.

Fees and Expenses: Undergraduate: $3,846 in-state per academic year; $10,926 out-of-state. Graduate: Tuition charged per credit hour. On-campus room and board: $3,966. Other expenses: $2,108. Books and supplies: $614.

Financial Aid: Resources specifically for eligible students enrolled in teacher education programs are awarded on the basis of financial need and academic merit. The institution has a Program Participation Agreement with the U.S. Department of Education for eligible students to receive Pell Grants and other federal aid. Teacher scholarships available to qualifying students. *Contact:* Financial Aid Office at: (361) 593-3911.

Accreditation: *Regional:* SACS. *Member of:* AACTE. *Approved by:* Texas State Board for Educator Certification.

Undergraduate Programs: The baccalaureate programs offered by the Education Department include: early childhood, elementary education, secondary education, bilingual education, and special education. All programs require the completion of a general education core, professional studies, subject content area, field experiences, and student teaching. A minimum of 128 semester hours is required for the degree.

Graduate Programs: Master's degree programs are offered in the areas of adult education, bilingual education, counseling and guidance, early childhood education, educational administration, English as a second language, reading specialist, and generic special education. Each program has specific coursework requirements.

Doctor of Education programs are offered in bilingual education and educational leadership.

Licensure/Reciprocity: Texas. Students seeking teaching certification in a state other than Texas should consult with that state's teacher certification office early in their program of study to insure compliance with requirements. Many state directors of teacher credentialing have signed Interstate Agreements through NASDTEC that expedite the certification process.

TEXAS CHRISTIAN UNIVERSITY

School of Education

TCU Box 76129
2800 South University Drive
Fort Worth, Texas 76129
Phone: (817) 257-7660
Fax: (817) 257-7466
E-mail: frogmail@tcu.edu
Internet: http://www.tcu.edu

Institution Description: Texas Christian University is a private institution affiliated with the Christian Church (Disciples of Christ). It was founded in 1873.

The School of Education offers studies leading to teacher certification.

Institution Control: Private.

Calendar: Semester. Academic year August to May.

Official(s): Dr. Samuel Deitz, Dean.

Faculty: Full-time 20; part-time 8; adjunct 19.

Degrees Awarded: 113 baccalaureate; 74 master's.

Admission Requirements: *Undergraduate:* Graduation with 17 academic units from an approved secondary school; College Board SAT or ACT composite. *Teacher education specific:* Completion of 54 hours of coursework; 2.5 GPA; passing scores on all three sections (reading, mathematics, writing) of the Texas Higher Education Assessment (THEA); faculty interview. *Graduate:* Baccalaureate degree from a regionally accredited institution. *Teacher education specific:* GRE or Miller Analogies Test; 3 letters of recommendation; 3.0 GPA; personal goal statement; faculty interview.

Fees and Expenses: Undergraduate: $15,740 per academic year. Graduate: $490 per credit hour. Required fees: $1,890. On-campus room and board: $5,500. Books and supplies: $1,000.

Financial Aid: Resources specifically for eligible students enrolled in teacher education programs are awarded on the basis of financial need and academic merit. The institution has a Program Participation Agreement with the U.S. Department of Education for eligible students to receive Pell Grants and other federal aid. Teacher scholarships available to qualifying students. *Contact:* Kay Derrick at: (817) 257-7858 or e-mail at: finaid@tcu.edu.

Accreditation: *Regional:* SACS. *Member of:* AACTE. *Approved by:* Texas State Board for Educator Certification.

Undergraduate Programs: The School of Education offers studies culminating in the Bachelor of Science degree. The school offers majors in early childhood education (EC-4th grade), middle school education (4th-8th grade), and secondary education (8th-12th grade). In addition, students may pursue certification in special education and English as a second language. All-level certification enables students to teach in grades K-12. Majors include art, music, physical education, and rehabilitation of the deaf. Students who major in a content area outside of the School of Education may obtain a minor in educational studies to achieve certification.

Graduate Programs: Texas Christian University offers programs leading to Initial Teacher Certification at the graduate level. The university offers a Master of Education with a major in early childhood, middle grades, or secondary education with initial certification. The Master of Education is also offered with majors in elementary education, early childhood, middle and secondary education as well as counseling, educational administration, and educational foundations. Certification in special education is also available.

Licensure/Reciprocity: Texas. Students seeking teaching certification in a state other than Texas should consult with that state's teacher certification office early in their program of study to insure compliance with requirements. Many state directors of teacher credentialing have signed Interstate Agreements through NASDTEC that expedite the certification process.

TEXAS SOUTHERN UNIVERSITY

College of Education
Department of Curriculum and Instruction

3100 Cleburne Avenue
Houston, Texas 77004
Phone: (713) 313-7011
Fax: (713) 313-7318
E-mail: coe@tsu.edu
Internet: http://www.tsu.edu

Institution Description: Texas Southern University is a state institution. It was established as Texas State University in 1947. The present name was adopted in 1951.

The mission of the Department of Curriculum and Instruction is to prepare effective teachers to serve culturally diverse populations in schools in the United States with a focus on urban school populations.

Institution Control: Public.

Calendar: Semester. Academic year September to August.

Official(s): Dr. Joy Cumming, Dean; Dr. Sumpter Brooks, Chair, Department of Curriculum and Instruction.

Faculty: Not reported.

Degrees Awarded: 16 baccalaureate; 163 master's; 17 doctorate.

Admission Requirements: *Undergraduate:* Graduation from an approved secondary school or GED; College Board SAT or ACT composite. *Teacher education specific:* Completion of 60 hours of coursework; 2.5 GPA; passing scores on all three sections (reading, mathematics, writing) of the Texas Higher Education Assessment (THEA); faculty interview. *Graduate:* Baccalaureate degree from a regionally accredited institution. *Teacher education specific:* GRE or Miller Analogies Test; 3 letters of recommendation; 3.0 GPA; personal goal statement; faculty interview.

Fees and Expenses: Undergraduate: $3,832 in-state per academic year; $10,912 out-of-state. Graduate: $42 per credit hour in-state plus $52 per hour; $253 per credit hour out-of-state plus $52 per hour. On-campus room and board: $5,920. Other expenses: $2,680. Books and supplies: $810.

Financial Aid: Resources specifically for eligible students enrolled in teacher education programs are awarded on the basis of financial need and academic merit. The institution has a Program Participation Agreement with the U.S. Department of Education for eligible students to receive Pell Grants and other federal aid. Teacher scholarships available to qualifying students. *Contact:* Financial Aid Office at: (713) 313-7011.

Accreditation: *Regional:* SACS. *Member of:* AACTE. *Approved by:* Texas State Board for Educator Certification.

Undergraduate Programs: The Bachelor of Science in interdisciplinary studies is offered in seven tracks leading to certification: bilingual education, early childhood education, English, mathematics, Spanish, special education, and reading. All programs require the completion of the general education core, professional core, content area, field experiences, and student teaching. A minimum of 124 semester hours is required for the degree award.

Graduate Programs: The Master of Education degree program is offered with a concentration in curriculum and instruction. The Doctor of Education is also offered in curriculum and instruction. Each program has specific course requirements.

The Department of Educational Administration and Foundations offers the Master of Education and the Doctor of Education degrees in educational administration.

Licensure/Reciprocity: Texas. Students seeking teaching certification in a state other than Texas should consult with that state's teacher certification office early in their program of

TEXAS SOUTHERN UNIVERSITY—*cont'd*

study to insure compliance with requirements. Many state directors of teacher credentialing have signed Interstate Agreements through NASDTEC that expedite the certification process.

TEXAS STATE UNIVERSITY - SAN MARCOS

College of Education
Department of Curriculum and Instruction
601 University Drive
San Marcos, Texas 78666
Phone: (512) 245-2150
Fax: (512) 245-7911
E-mail: MR11@txstate.edu
Internet: http://www.txstate.edu

Institution Description: Texas State University - San Marcos (formerly Southwest Texas State University) was established and chartered as Southwest Texas State Normal School in 1889. The current name was adopted in 2002.

The Department of Curriculum and Instruction offers undergraduate and graduate programs to prepare students for teaching careers.

Institution Control: Public.

Calendar: Semester. Academic year August to May.

Official(s): Dr. John Beck, Dean, College of Education; Dr. Marianne Reese, Chair, Department of Curriculum and Instruction.

Faculty: Not reported.

Degrees Awarded: 497 baccalaureate; 290 master's.

Admission Requirements: *Undergraduate:* Graduation in top 10% of class from an approved secondary school or GED; College Board SAT or ACT composite. *Teacher education specific:* Completion of 60 semester hours; overall 2.5 GPA; satisfactory scores on all three sections (reading, mathematics, writing) of the Texas Higher Education Assessment (THEA); faculty interview; personal goal statement. *Graduate:* Baccalaureate degree from a regionally accredited institution. *Teacher education specific:* 2.75 GPA; GRE or Miller Analogies Test scores; completion of all required departmental exams; recommendations; faculty interview.

Fees and Expenses: Undergraduate: $3,900 in-state, $10,510 out-of-state. Graduate: Tuition charged per credit hour. On-campus room and board: $6,500. Other expenses: $3,210. Books and supplies: $950.

Financial Aid: Resources specifically for eligible students enrolled in teacher education programs are awarded on the basis of financial need and academic merit. The institution has a Program Participation Agreement with the U.S. Department of Education for eligible students to receive Pell Grants and other federal aid. Teacher scholarships available to qualifying students. *Contact:* Financial Aid Office at: (512) 245-2315.

Accreditation: *Regional:* SACS. *Member of:* AACTE. *Approved by:* Texas State Board for Educator Certification.

Undergraduate Programs: The Bachelor of Science degree in interdisciplinary studies is designed to meet the requirements for a Provisional Teaching Certificate. In addition to completing the required academic foundations core curriculum, program students must fulfill the requirements in the area of specialization, professional education, and elective courses. A minimum of 128 semester hours is required for the degree award.

Graduate Programs: The Master of Education degree offerings from the department consist of a minimum of 36 hours without a required theses. Semester hour requirements may vary within the major and minor areas. Major areas include: educational technology; elementary education; elementary education-bilingual/bicultural; elementary education-early childhood education; reading education; secondary education; special education. Supplementary certificates are available in bilingual education, educational diagnostician, generic special education, and gifted and talented.

It is also possible to earn the Master of Arts degree with majors in elementary education and secondary education with a minimum of 30 semester hours including the thesis.

Licensure/Reciprocity: Texas. Students seeking teaching certification in a state other than Texas should consult with that state's teacher certification office early in their program of study to insure compliance with requirements. Many state directors of teacher credentialing have signed Interstate Agreements through NASDTEC that expedite the certification process.

TEXAS TECH UNIVERSITY

College of Education
Division of Curriculum and Instruction
P.O. Box 45005
Lubbock, Texas 79409-5005
Phone: (806) 742-1997
Fax: (806) 742-2179
E-mail: educ@ttu.edu
Internet: http://www.ttu.edu

Institution Description: Texas Tech University is a state institution. It was established as Texas Technological College in 1923.

The College of Education offers undergraduate and graduate programs to prepare students for teaching careers.

Institution Control: Public.

Calendar: Semester. Academic year August to May.

Official(s): Dr. Sheryl Santos, Dean; Dr. Peggy Johnson, Chairperson, Division of Curriculum and Instruction.

Faculty: Not reported.

Degrees Awarded: 80 baccalaureate; 156 master's; 23 doctorate.

Admission Requirements: *Undergraduate:* Graduation from an approved secondary school or GED; College Board SAT or ACT composite. *Teacher education specific:* Completion of 60 semester hours; overall 2.7 GPA; satisfactory scores on all three sections (reading, mathematics, writing) of the Texas Higher Education Assessment (THEA); faculty interview; personal goal statement. *Graduate:* Baccalaureate degree from a regionally accredited institution. *Teacher education specific:* 2.75 GPA; GRE or Miller Analogies Test scores; completion of all required departmental exams; recommendations; faculty interview.

Fees and Expenses: Undergraduate: $3,953 in-state, $9,617 out-of-state. Graduate: $107 per credit hour in-state; $318 per credit hour out-of-state. On-campus room and board: $6,025. Other expenses: $3,170. Books and supplies: $830.

Financial Aid: Resources specifically for eligible students enrolled in teacher education programs are awarded on the basis of financial need and academic merit. The institution has a Program Participation Agreement with the U.S. Department of Education for eligible students to receive Pell Grants and other federal aid. Teacher scholarships available to qualifying students. *Contact:* Financial Aid Office at: (806) 742-3681.

Accreditation: *Regional:* SACS. *Professional:* NCATE. *Member of:* AACTE. *Approved by:* Texas State Board for Educator Certification.

Undergraduate Programs: Eligible students at the junior level are admitted to a teacher certification program that leads to a Texas teaching certificate. The Bachelor of Science degree in interdisciplinary studies is designed to meet the requirements for a Provisional Teaching Certificate. In addition to completing the required academic foundations core curriculum, students must fulfill the requirements in the area of specialization, professional education, and elective courses. A minimum of 120 semester hours is required for the degree award.

Graduate Programs: The division offers programs leading to a Master of Education degree in curriculum and instruction, bilingual education, elementary education, language literacy education, and secondary education. Individuals seeking initial certification to teach in elementary or secondary schools must complete specified courses in education and meet other general education and teaching field requirements. Graduate program endorsements are available in bilingual education, early childhood, English as a second language, gifted and talented, information processing technologies, generic special education, and visual impairment.

Licensure/Reciprocity: Texas. Students seeking teaching certification in a state other than Texas should consult with that state's teacher certification office early in their program of study to insure compliance with requirements. Many state directors of teacher credentialing have signed Interstate Agreements through NASDTEC that expedite the certification process.

TEXAS WESLEYAN UNIVERSITY

School of Education

1201 Wesleyan Street
Fort Worth, Texas 76105-1536
Phone: (817) 531-4941
Fax: (817) 531-4425
E-mail: info@txwesleyan.edu
Internet: http://www.txwesleyan.edu

Institution Description: Texas Wesleyan University is a private, independent, nonprofit institution affiliated with the United Methodist Church. It was established and chartered as Polytechnic College, a coeducational institution, in 1891.

The School of Education offers undergraduate and graduate programs to prepare students to meet the challenging demands of the classroom.

Institution Control: Private.

Calendar: Semester. Academic year August to May.

Official(s): Dr. Harold G. Jeffcoat, President.

Faculty: Full-time 19; part-time 20.

Degrees Awarded: 43 baccalaureate; 43 master's.

Admission Requirements: *Undergraduate:* Graduation from an approved secondary school or GED; College Board SAT or ACT composite. *Teacher education specific:* Completion of 60 semester hours; overall 2.75 GPA; satisfactory scores on all three sections (reading, mathematics, writing) of the Texas Higher Education Assessment (THEA); faculty interview; personal goal statement. *Graduate:* Baccalaureate degree from a regionally accredited institution. *Teacher education specific:* 2.75 GPA; GRE or Miller Analogies Test scores; completion of all required departmental exams; recommendations; faculty interview.

Fees and Expenses: Undergraduate: $11,670 per academic year. Graduate: $250 per credit hour. On-campus room and board: $4,325. Other expenses: $2,500. Books and supplies: $700.

Financial Aid: Resources specifically for eligible students enrolled in teacher education programs are awarded on the basis of financial need and academic merit. The institution has a Program Participation Agreement with the U.S. Department of Education for eligible students to receive Pell Grants and other federal aid. Teacher scholarships available to qualifying students. *Contact:* Financial Aid Office at: (817) 531-4420.

Accreditation: *Regional:* SACS. *Member of:* AACTE. *Approved by:* Texas State Board for Educator Certification.

Undergraduate Programs: The Bachelor of Science degree in interdisciplinary studies is designed to meet the requirements for a Provisional Teaching Certificate. In addition to completing the required academic foundations core curriculum, students must fulfill the requirements in the area of specialization, professional education, and elective courses. A minimum of 124 semester hours is required for the degree award.

Graduate Programs: The Master of Education program is a 36-credit hour program designed for classroom teachers who wish to pursue a degree that focuses on developing advanced skills in teaching as well as enriching knowledge in selected content areas. Concentration areas in the program include: bilingual education, elementary science, English as a second language, reading, and non-public school leadership. The concentration areas require from 12 to 24 credit hours plus electives.

Licensure/Reciprocity: Texas. Students seeking teaching certification in a state other than Texas should consult with that state's teacher certification office early in their program of study to insure compliance with requirements. Many state

directors of teacher credentialing have signed Interstate Agreements through NASDTEC that expedite the certification process.

TEXAS WOMAN'S UNIVERSITY

College of Professional Education
Department of Teacher Education

P.O. Box 425619
Denton, Texas 76204
Phone: (940) 898-2271
Fax: (940) 898-2209
E-mail: cope@twu.edu
Internet: http://www.twu.edu

Institution Description: Texas Woman's University is a state institution that was founded in 1901.

The Department of Teacher Education offers programs to prepare students for professional careers in teaching.

Institution Control: Public.

Calendar: Semester. Academic year August to August.

Official(s): Dr. April Miller, Dean, College of Professional Education; Dr. Sid Pruitt, Chair, Department of Teacher Education.

Faculty: Full-time 15; adjunct 19.

Degrees Awarded: 205 baccalaureate; 261 master's; 27 doctorate.

Admission Requirements: *Undergraduate:* Graduation in top 50% of class from an approved secondary school or GED; College Board SAT or ACT composite. *Teacher education specific:* Completion of foundation courses; 60 hours of coursework; overall 2.75 GPA; satisfactory scores on all three sections (reading, mathematics, writing) of the Texas Higher Education Assessment (THEA); faculty interview; personal goal statement. *Graduate:* Baccalaureate degree from a regionally accredited institution. *Teacher education specific:* 3.0 GPA; GRE; completion of all required departmental exams; recommendations; faculty interview.

Fees and Expenses: Undergraduate: $2,640 in-state, $9,180 out-of-state. Graduate: $2,538 per academic year in-state; $7,824 out-of-state. Required fees: $930. On-campus room and board: $4,428. Books and supplies: $720.

Financial Aid: Resources specifically for eligible students enrolled in teacher education programs are awarded on the basis of financial need and academic merit. The institution has a Program Participation Agreement with the U.S. Department of Education for eligible students to receive Pell Grants and other federal aid. Teacher scholarships available to qualifying students. *Contact:* Financial Aid Office at: (940) 898-3050 or e-mail at: finaid@twu.edu.

Accreditation: *Regional:* SACS. *Approved by:* Texas State Board for Educator Certification.

Undergraduate Programs: The Bachelor of Science in interdisciplinary studies is designed to meet the requirements for a Provisional Teaching Certificate. In addition to completing the required academic foundations core curriculum, students must fulfill the requirements in the area of specialization, professional education, and elective courses. A minimum of 124 semester hours is required for the degree award.

Graduate Programs: Graduate degree programs include the Master of Arts or Master of Education in educational administration, elementary education, and special education. Certification programs are offered in superintendent, principal, and special education diagnostician. The Doctor of Philosophy degree is offered in special education.

Licensure/Reciprocity: Texas. Students seeking teaching certification in a state other than Texas should consult with that state's teacher certification office early in their program of study to insure compliance with requirements. Many state directors of teacher credentialing have signed Interstate Agreements through NASDTEC that expedite the certification process.

TRINITY UNIVERSITY
Department of Education
1 Trinity Place
San Antonio, Texas 78213-7200
Phone: (210) 999-7501
Fax: (210) 999-7200
E-mail: sara.sherwood@trinity.edu
Internet: http//www.trinity.edu

Institution Description: Trinity University is a private, independent, nonprofit institution. It was established, chartered, and offered first instruction at the postsecondary level in 1869.

The Department of Education provides students interested in teaching with a background in the liberal arts and sciences plus the professional education coursework and hands-on experience necessary for success in the classroom.

Institution Control: Private.

Calendar: Semester. Academic year August to May.

Official(s): Dr. Paul Kelleher, Department Head.

Faculty: Full-time 8; part-time 21.

Degrees Awarded: 15 baccalaureate; 52 master's.

Admission Requirements: *Undergraduate:* Graduation from an approved secondary school or GED; College Board SAT or ACT composite. *Teacher education specific:* Completion of 60 hours of coursework; 2.5 GPA; passing scores on all three sections (reading, mathematics, writing) of the Texas Higher Education Assessment (THEA); faculty interview. *Graduate:* Baccalaureate degree from a regionally accredited institution. *Teacher education specific:* GRE or Miller Analogies Test; 3 letters of recommendation; 3.0 GPA; personal goal statement; faculty interview.

Fees and Expenses: $717.25 per credit hour.

Financial Aid: Resources specifically for eligible students enrolled in teacher education programs are awarded on the basis of financial need and academic merit. The institution has a Program Participation Agreement with the U.S. Department of Education for eligible students to receive Pell Grants and other federal aid. Teacher scholarships available to qualifying students. *Contact:* Financial Aid Office at: (210) 999-8315 or e-mail at: financialaid@trinity.edu.

Accreditation: *Regional:* SACS. *Professional:* NCATE. *Member of:* AACTE. *Approved by:* Texas State Board for Educator Certification.

Undergraduate Programs: Students matriculating in the Trinity teacher education program complete an undergraduate degree with a major in the subject(s) they plan to teach. Students preparing to teach at the elementary school level complete the Humanities in Education curriculum. Additionally, all majors complete approximately 11 semester hours in professional education. The curriculum provides opportunities for students to engage in independent learning and problem solving. It is characterized by a variety of seminars, laboratories, and practica conducted in public and private schools in the greater San Antonio area. A minimum of 124 semester hours is required for the degree award.

Graduate Programs: The Department of Education has developed and implemented a five-year teacher education program leading to the Master of Arts in Teaching degree. Specific programs prepare students for certification in early childhood (age 3-grade 4) grades 4-8, and grades 8-12. Supplemental certificates in special education and English as a second language are also available.

A Master of Education degree program in school administration is offered in cooperation with the Center for Educational Leadership. The program prepares men and women with a background in teaching and learning, management skills, political acumen, knowledge of the change process, and a commitment to lifelong learning.

A Master of Arts in school psychology is a 60-hour program with a curriculum that includes courses on assessment, human development, counseling, behavior management, consultation, research and statistics, and educational administration.

Licensure/Reciprocity: Texas. Students seeking teaching certification in a state other than Texas should consult with that state's teacher certification office early in their program of study to insure compliance with requirements. Many state directors of teacher credentialing have signed Interstate Agreements through NASDTEC that expedite the certification process.

UNIVERSITY OF HOUSTON
College of Education
Department of Curriculum and Instruction
256 Farish Hall
4800 Calhoun Boulevard
Houston, Texas 77004
Phone: (713) 743-4950
Fax: (713) 743-9633
E-mail: admissions@uh.edu
Internet: http://www.uh.edu

Institution Description: The university was established as Houston Junior College in 1927. It became a 4-year institution and changed the name to University of Houston in 1934. Affiliation as a state institution began in 1963.

The Department of Curriculum and Instruction offers undergraduate and graduate programs leading to teacher certification.

Institution Control: Public.

Calendar: Semester. Academic year August to May.

Official(s): Dr. Robert K. Wimpelberg, Dean; Dr. Yolanda N. Padron, Department Chair.

Faculty: Full-time 45 (Curriculum and Instruction).

Degrees Awarded: 190 baccalaureate; 313 master's; 39 doctorate.

Admission Requirements: *Undergraduate:* Graduation from an approved secondary school or GED; College Board SAT or ACT composite. *Teacher education specific:* Completion of 60 hours of coursework; 2.5 GPA; passing scores on all three sections (reading, mathematics, writing) of the Texas Higher Education Assessment (THEA); faculty interview. *Graduate:* Baccalaureate degree from a regionally accredited institution. *Teacher education specific:* GRE or Miller Analogies Test; letters of recommendation; 3.0 GPA; personal goal statement; faculty interview.

Fees and Expenses: Undergraduate: $3,258 in-state per academic year; $8,922 out-of-state. Graduate: Tuition charged per credit hour. On-campus room and board: $5,870. Other expenses: $4,070. Books and supplies: $1,000.

Financial Aid: Resources specifically for eligible students enrolled in teacher education programs are awarded on the basis of financial need and academic merit. The institution has a Program Participation Agreement with the U.S. Department of Education for eligible students to receive Pell Grants and other federal aid. Teacher scholarships available to qualifying students. *Contact:* Financial Aid Office at: (713) 743-1010.

Accreditation: *Regional:* SACS. *Professional:* NCATE. *Member of:* AACTE. *Approved by:* Texas State Board for Educator Certification.

Undergraduate Programs: The Bachelor of Science degree in interdisciplinary studies is designed to meet the requirements for a Provisional Teaching Certificate. In addition to completing the required academic foundations core curriculum, students must fulfill the requirements in the area of specialization, professional education, and elective courses. A minimum of 122 semester hours is required for the degree award.

Graduate Programs: Programs for master's degrees are offered in the concentrations of: art, bilingual education, early childhood, elementary education, gifted and talented education, instructional technology, mathematics education, reading and language arts, science education, second language education, secondary education, social studies education. A Doctor of Education degree program is also available.

Licensure/Reciprocity: Texas. Students seeking teaching certification in a state other than Texas should consult with that state's teacher certification office early in their program of

study to insure compliance with requirements. Many state directors of teacher credentialing have signed Interstate Agreements through NASDTEC that expedite the certification process.

UNIVERSITY OF HOUSTON - CLEAR LAKE

School of Education

Bayou 1231
2700 Bay Area Boulevard
Houston, Texas 77058-1098
Phone: (281) 283-3600
Fax: (281) 283-2530
E-mail: admissions@uhcl.edu
Internet: http://www.uhcl.edu

Institution Description: University of Houston - Clear Lake provides upper division baccalaureate and graduate study only.

Institution Control: Public.

Calendar: Semester. Academic year August to May.

Official(s): Dr. Dennis Spuck, Dean.

Faculty: Full-time 40; part-time 63.

Degrees Awarded: 203 baccalaureate; 192 master's.

Admission Requirements: *Undergraduate:* Graduation from an approved secondary school or GED; College Board SAT or ACT composite. *Teacher education specific:* Completion of 60 hours of coursework; 2.5 GPA; passing scores on all three sections (reading, mathematics, writing) of the Texas Higher Education Assessment (THEA); faculty interview. *Graduate:* Baccalaureate degree from a regionally accredited institution. *Teacher education specific:* GRE or Miller Analogies Test; letters of recommendation; 3.0 GPA; personal goal statement; faculty interview.

Fees and Expenses: Undergraduate: $3,258 in-state per academic year; $8,922 out-of-state. Graduate: Tuition charged per credit hour.

Financial Aid: Resources specifically for eligible students enrolled in teacher education programs are awarded on the basis of financial need and academic merit. The institution has a Program Participation Agreement with the U.S. Department of Education for eligible students to receive Pell Grants and other federal aid. Teacher scholarships available to qualifying students. *Contact:* Financial Aid Office at: (281) 283-2480.

Accreditation: *Regional:* SACS. *Professional:* NCATE. *Member of:* AACTE. *Approved by:* Texas State Board for Educator Certification.

Undergraduate Programs: The Bachelor of Science degree in interdisciplinary studies is designed to meet the requirements for a Provisional Teaching Certificate. In addition to completing the required academic foundations core curriculum, students must fulfill the requirements in the area of specialization, professional education, and elective courses. Students may select any one of six certificates: generic special education, EC-4 bilingual generalist, EC-4 generalist, 4-8 social studies. A minimum of 122 semester hours is required for the degree award.

Graduate Programs: Programs for master's degrees are offered in the concentrations of: counseling, curriculum and instruction, early childhood education, educational management, instructional technology, multicultural studies in education, reading, school library and information science. Students meet certification requirements simultaneously as for the degree.

Licensure/Reciprocity: Texas. Students seeking teaching certification in a state other than Texas should consult with that state's teacher certification office early in their program of study to insure compliance with requirements. Many state directors of teacher credentialing have signed Interstate Agreements through NASDTEC that expedite the certification process.

UNIVERSITY OF HOUSTON - VICTORIA

School of Education
Department of Curriculum and Instruction

3007 North Ben Wilson
Victoria, Texas 77901-4450
Phone: (361) 570-4848
Fax: (361) 570-4257
E-mail: education@uhv.edu
Internet: http://www.uhv.edu

Institution Description: University of Houston - Victoria offers academic programs for junior, senior, and graduate-level students. It was established and offered first instruction at the postsecondary level in 1973.

One of the prime objectives of the School of Education is to acquaint its students with various cultural subgroups that characterize the school's areas of influence. The prospective student should anticipate the opportunity to work with learners in a wide variety of educational settings.

Institution Control: Public.

Calendar: Semester. Academic year September to August.

Official(s): Dr. May Natividad, Dean; Dr. Marie Plemons, Chair, Department of Curriculum and Instruction.

Faculty: Full-time 20; adjunct 4.

Degrees Awarded: 88 baccalaureate; 101 master's.

Admission Requirements: *Undergraduate:* Graduation from an approved secondary school or GED; College Board SAT or ACT composite. *Teacher education specific:* Completion of 60 hours of coursework; 2.5 GPA; passing scores on all three sections (reading, mathematics, writing) of the Texas Higher Education Assessment (THEA); faculty interview. *Graduate:* Baccalaureate degree from a regionally accredited institution. *Teacher education specific:* GRE or Miller Analogies Test; letters of recommendation; 3.0 GPA; personal goal statement; faculty interview.

Fees and Expenses: Undergraduate: $3,258 in-state per academic year; $8,922 out-of-state. Graduate: $82 per credit hour in-state.

Financial Aid: Resources specifically for eligible students enrolled in teacher education programs are awarded on the basis of financial need and academic merit. The institution has a Program Participation Agreement with the U.S. Department of Education for eligible students to receive Pell Grants and other federal aid. Teacher scholarships available to qualifying students. *Contact:* Financial Aid Office at: (361) 570-4131.

Accreditation: *Regional:* SACS. *Professional:* NCATE. *Member of:* AACTE. *Approved by:* Texas State Board for Educator Certification.

Undergraduate Programs: The Bachelor of Science degree in interdisciplinary studies is designed to meet the requirements for a Provisional Teaching Certificate. In addition to completing the required academic foundations core curriculum, students must fulfill the requirements in the area of specialization, professional education, and elective courses. Initial preparation for prospective secondary teachers is available through courses supplementing Bachelor of Arts and Bachelor of Science degrees from the School of Arts and Sciences and the Bachelor of Business Administration. A minimum of 122 semester hours is required for the degree award.

Graduate Programs: The Master of Education degree is offered in administration and supervision, curriculum and instruction, and counseling. Each program has specific goals and course requirements. Students must pass a comprehensive examination.

Licensure/Reciprocity: Texas. Students seeking teaching certification in a state other than Texas should consult with that state's teacher certification office early in their program of study to insure compliance with requirements. Many state directors of teacher credentialing have signed Interstate Agreements through NASDTEC that expedite the certification process.

UNIVERSITY OF MARY HARDIN-BAYLOR

Department of Education
900 College Street
Belton, Texas 76513
Phone: (254) 295-4572
Fax: (254) 295-4480
E-mail: admission@umhb.edu
Internet: http://www.umhb.edu

Institution Description: University of Mary Hardin-Baylor is a private institution affiliated with the Baptist General Convention of Texas. It was established as the women's division of Baylor University in 1845.

The Department of Education offers teacher education programs at the graduate and undergraduate levels that lead to teacher certification.

Institution Control: Private.

Calendar: Semester. Academic year August to May.

Official(s): Dr. Clarence Ham, Chairperson.

Faculty: Full-time 10; adjunct 2.

Degrees Awarded: 69 baccalaureate; 12 master's.

Admission Requirements: *Undergraduate:* Graduation from an approved secondary school or GED; College Board SAT or ACT composite. *Teacher education specific:* Completion of 60 hours of coursework including education foundation courses; 2.75 GPA; passing scores on all three sections (reading, mathematics, writing) of the Texas Higher Education Assessment (THEA); faculty interview. *Graduate:* Baccalaureate degree from a regionally accredited institution. *Teacher education specific:* GRE or Miller Analogies Test; letters of recommendation; 3.0 GPA; personal goal statement; faculty interview.

Fees and Expenses: Undergraduate: $325 per semester hour. Graduate: $355 per semester hour. Additional fee of $28 per credit hour. On-campus room and board: $1,825 to $1,925 per semester. Books and supplies: $900.

Financial Aid: Resources specifically for eligible students enrolled in teacher education programs are awarded on the basis of academic merit, financial need, and scholarship award for academic excellence. *Contact:* Financial Aid Office at: (254) 295-4572.

Accreditation: *Regional:* SACS. *Member of:* AACTE. *Approved by:* Texas State Board for Educator Certification.

Undergraduate Programs: Educator certificate programs leading to the baccalaureate degree and teacher certification are offered in: early childhood-grade 4 (bilingual generalist, English as a second language, generalist); grades 4-8 (bilingual generalist, English language arts, English as a second language, generalist, mathematics, science, social studies); grades 8-12 (computer science, English language arts, family and consumer sciences, health science, history, journalism, life science, mathematics, physical science, science, social studies, speech, technology applications, technology education [8-12]); all-level (art, educational diagnostician, music, physical education, reading, counseling, school librarian, technology applications). All programs require the completion of the general education core, professional studies, content area, field experiences, and student teaching. A minimum of 124 semester hours is required for the degree.

Graduate Programs: The Department of Education offers the Master of Education degree with majors in educational administration, educational psychology, reading education, and general studies. Professional certification programs are available in educational diagnostician, mid-management administrator (principal), biology, chemistry, English, reading, and master reading teacher. Certification in generic special education and early childhood education are also offered.

Licensure/Reciprocity: Texas. Students seeking teaching certification in a state other than Texas should consult with that state's teacher certification office early in their program of study to insure compliance with requirements. Many state directors of teacher credentialing have signed Interstate Agreements through NASDTEC that expedite the certification process.

UNIVERSITY OF NORTH TEXAS

College of Education
Teacher Education and administration
P.O. Box 13797
Denton, Texas 76203
Phone: (940) 565-2922
Fax: (940) 565-4952
E-mail: ndavis@coe.unt.edu
Internet: http://www.unt.edu

Institution Description: University of North Texas is a state institution. It was established and chartered as Texas Normal College in 1890.

The College of Education offers undergraduate and graduate programs for teacher preparation and professional enrichment.

Institution Control: Public.

Calendar: Semester. Academic year August to May.

Official(s): Dr. Jean Keller, Dean; Dr. John Stansell, Department Chair.

Faculty: Full-time 50.

Degrees Awarded: 324 baccalaureate; 333 master's; 53 doctorate.

Admission Requirements: *Undergraduate:* Graduation from an approved secondary school or GED; College Board SAT or ACT composite. *Teacher education specific:* Completion of 60 semester hours; overall 2.5 GPA; satisfactory scores on all three sections (reading, mathematics, writing) of the Texas Higher Education Assessment (THEA); faculty interview; personal goal statement. *Graduate:* Baccalaureate degree from a regionally accredited institution. *Teacher education specific:* 2.75 GPA; GRE or Miller Analogies Test scores; completion of all required departmental exams; recommendations; faculty interview.

Fees and Expenses: Undergraduate: $4,150 in-state, $11,050 out-of-state. Graduate: $319 per credit hour plus $21 per hour. On-campus room and board: $4,900. Other expenses: $2,170. Books and supplies: $1,010.

Financial Aid: Resources specifically for eligible students enrolled in teacher education programs are awarded on the basis of financial need and academic merit. The institution has a Program Participation Agreement with the U.S. Department of Education for eligible students to receive Pell Grants and other federal aid. Teacher scholarships available to qualifying students. *Contact:* Financial Aid Office at: (940) 565-2016.

Accreditation: *Regional:* SACS. *Professional:* NCATE. *Member of:* AACTE. *Approved by:* Texas State Board for Educator Certification.

Undergraduate Programs: The Bachelor of Science degree in interdisciplinary studies is designed to meet the requirements for a Provisional Teaching Certificate. In addition to completing the required academic foundations core curriculum, students must fulfill the requirements in the area of specialization, professional education, and elective courses. Initial preparation for prospective secondary teachers is available through courses supplementing baccalaureate degrees from other departments. A minimum of 124 semester hours is required for the degree award.

Graduate Programs: The Master of Education in curriculum and instruction is offered with concentrations in educational administration and supervision, educational curriculum and instruction, elementary education, reading, secondary education, and educational foundations. Each concentration requires the completion of goals and coursework.

A Doctor of Education and Doctor of Philosophy are offered in curriculum and instruction.

Licensure/Reciprocity: Texas. Students seeking teaching certification in a state other than Texas should consult with that state's teacher certification office early in their program of study to insure compliance with requirements. Many state directors of teacher credentialing have signed Interstate Agreements through NASDTEC that expedite the certification process.

UNIVERSITY OF ST. THOMAS
School of Education
3800 Montrose Boulevard
Houston, Texas 77006-4696
Phone: (713) 522-7911
Fax: (713) 525-2125
E-mail: admissions@stthom.edu
Internet: http://www.stthom.edu

Institution Description: University of St. Thomas is an independent, private, coeducational Catholic institution of higher learning. It was founded by the Basilian Fathers in 1947.

The goal of the School of Education is to develop classroom teachers who demonstrate the ability to be effective in a variety of field settings, both private and public.

Institution Control: Private.

Calendar: Semester. Academic year August to May.

Official(s): Dr. Joseph M. McFaddon, President.

Faculty: Not reported.

Degrees Awarded: 26 baccalaureate; 67 master's.

Admission Requirements: *Undergraduate:* Graduation from an approved secondary school or GED; College Board SAT or ACT composite. *Teacher education specific:* Completion of 60 semester hours; overall 2.5 GPA in teaching field; personal and professional qualities necessary for success as a classroom teacher; satisfactory scores on all three sections (reading, mathematics, writing) of the Texas Higher Education Assessment (THEA); faculty interview; personal goal statement. *Graduate:* Baccalaureate degree from a regionally accredited institution. *Teacher education specific:* 2.75 GPA; GRE or Miller Analogies Test scores; completion of all required departmental exams; recommendations; faculty interview.

Fees and Expenses: Undergraduate: $15,112 per academic year. Graduate: $401 per credit hour. On-campus room and board: $6,840. Other expenses: $3,325. Books and supplies: $800.

Financial Aid: Resources specifically for eligible students enrolled in teacher education programs are awarded on the basis of financial need and academic merit. The institution has a Program Participation Agreement with the U.S. Department of Education for eligible students to receive Pell Grants and other federal aid. Teacher scholarships available to qualifying students. *Contact:* Financial Aid Office at: (713) 525-2170.

Accreditation: *Regional:* SACS. *Member of:* AACTE. *Approved by:* Texas State Board for Educator Certification.

Undergraduate Programs: Teacher preparation programs are available in general and bilingual education with certification levels of elementary school (early childhood-grade 4); middle school (grades 4-8) with a concentration in reading/language arts, mathematics, science, social studies; and secondary certification (grades 8-12) in a variety of teaching fields. All-level music certification and special education certification are also available. Certification requirements vary for each level and field of concentration. All baccalaureate programs require the completion of the general education core, professional studies, content area, field experiences, and student teaching. A minimum of 126 credit hours is required for the degree award.

Graduate Programs: The majority of students in the graduate program are practicing professional educators who desire to expand their knowledge and skills within a program culminating in a graduate degree. Other students are non-degree seeking professionals who desire to update their knowledge or obtain additional expertise in a particular field. Some students are working toward initial certification after achieving a baccalaureate degree and career experience in a field other than education. The Master of Arts in Teaching and Master of Education are awarded upon completion of specified coursework.

Licensure/Reciprocity: Texas. Students seeking teaching certification in a state other than Texas should consult with that state's teacher certification office early in their program of study to insure compliance with requirements. Many state directors of teacher credentialing have signed Interstate Agreements through NASDTEC that expedite the certification process.

THE UNIVERSITY OF TEXAS AT ARLINGTON
College of Education
Teacher Education Programs
701 South Nedderman Drive
Arlington, Texas 76019
Phone: (817) 272-2591
Fax: (817) 272-2530
E-mail: gerlach@uta.edu
Internet: http://www.uta.edu

Institution Description: The institution was established as Arlington College in 1895. It became part of the University of Texas System in 1965 and the present name was adopted in 1967.

The College of Education offers undergraduate and graduate programs leading to teacher certification in Texas.

Institution Control: Public.

Calendar: Semester. Academic year September to May.

Official(s): Dr. Jeanne M. Gerlach, Dean; Dr. Ruth Davis, Department Chair.

Faculty: Full-time 50; part-time 36.

Degrees Awarded: 232 baccalaureate; 105 master's.

Admission Requirements: *Undergraduate:* Graduation from an approved secondary school; College Board SAT or ACT composite. *Teacher education specific:* 2.75 GPA; high school transcript; satisfactory scores on all three sections (reading, mathematics, writing) of the Texas Higher Education Assessment (THEA); faculty interview; personal goal statement. *Graduate:* Baccalaureate degree from a regionally accredited institution. *Teacher education specific:* 3.0 GPA; GRE or Miller Analogies Test scores; completion of all required departmental exams; recommendations; faculty interview.

Fees and Expenses: Undergraduate: $2,208 in-state per academic year; $7,872 out-of-state. Graduate: $2,484 in-state; $6,966 out-of-state. On-campus room and board: $4,828. Other expenses: $3,268. Books and supplies: $600.

Financial Aid: Resources specifically for eligible students enrolled in teacher education programs are awarded on the basis of financial need and academic merit. The institution has a Program Participation Agreement with the U.S. Department of Education for eligible students to receive Pell Grants and other federal aid. Teacher scholarships available to qualifying students. *Contact:* Financial Aid Office at: (817) 272-3561.

Accreditation: *Regional:* SACS. *Member of:* AACTE. *Approved by:* Texas State Board for Educator Certification.

Undergraduate Programs: Degree and certification programs include: early childhood through 4th grade; middle level (4th-8th grade); secondary (8th-12th grade); all-level (art, music, physical education. Students interested in teacher certification for the secondary level must select a major in an academic content area that is taught in the secondary schools. The following areas are available for secondary certification: social studies (history, government, economics, geography), mathematics, science (physics, chemistry, biology, geology), physical science (chemistry, physics), life science (biology), English language arts and reading, journalism, speech communication, theatre arts, Spanish, German, French, physical education. All programs require the completion of the general education core, professional studies, field experiences, and student teaching. A minimum of 24 semester hours is required for the degree award.

Graduate Programs: Graduate degree programs offered include: Master of Education in teaching, Master of Education in curriculum and instruction, Master of Education in curriculum and instruction with an emphasis in reading, Master of Education with principal certification, and Master of Science in physiology of exercise. Science and mathematics programs for teachers are also offered.

The Doctor of Philosophy in urban and public administration with specialization in educational leadership and policy studies is available for qualified candidates.

THE UNIVERSITY OF TEXAS AT ARLINGTON—*cont'd*

Licensure/Reciprocity: Texas. Students seeking teaching certification in a state other than Texas should consult with that state's teacher certification office early in their program of study to insure compliance with requirements. Many state directors of teacher credentialing have signed Interstate Agreements through NASDTEC that expedite the certification process.

THE UNIVERSITY OF TEXAS AT AUSTIN

College of Education
Department of Curriculum and Instruction

1 University Station
Austin, Texas 78712
Phone: (512) 471-3434
Fax: (512) 471-2471
E-mail: coe@utexas.edu
Internet: http://www.utexas.edu

Institution Description: The University of Texas at Austin was established as University of Texas, Main University in 1881.

The College of Education offers baccalaureate, master's and doctoral programs for professional preparation in the field of curriculum and instruction.

Institution Control: Public.

Calendar: Semester. Academic year September to May.

Official(s): Dr. Larry Abraham, Chair, Department of Curriculum and Instruction.

Faculty: Full-time 76; emeriti 8.

Degrees Awarded: 323 baccalaureate; 193 master's; 79 doctorate.

Admission Requirements: *Undergraduate:* Graduation from an approved secondary school; College Board SAT or ACT composite. *Teacher education specific:* 2.75 GPA; high school transcript; satisfactory scores on all three sections (reading, mathematics, writing) of the Texas Higher Education Assessment (THEA); faculty interview; personal goal statement. *Graduate:* Baccalaureate degree from a regionally accredited institution. *Teacher education specific:* 3.0 GPA; GRE or Miller Analogies Test scores; completion of all required departmental exams; recommendations; faculty interview.

Fees and Expenses: Undergraduate: $4,188 in-state per academic year; $11,268 out-of-state; Graduate: Tuition charged per semester hour. On-campus room and board: $6,082. Other expenses: $2,798. Books and supplies: $750.

Financial Aid: Resources specifically for eligible students enrolled in teacher education programs are awarded on the basis of academic merit and financial need. Graduate fellowships available for qualified students. *Contact:* Student Financial Services at: (512) 475-9857.

Accreditation: *Regional:* SACS. *Member of:* AACTE. *Approved by:* Texas State Board for Educator Certification.

Undergraduate Programs: Undergraduates earn a bachelor's degree in an approved area while fulfilling certification requirements. Students typically complete a multidisciplinary major or an academic major and supporting minor.

Graduate Programs: Earning a master's degree and receiving teacher certification are separate endeavors. Teaching certification and a master's degree can be pursued concurrently. The combined programs usually require from one to two years more than either one alone, depending on undergraduate academic preparation.

The Department of Curriculum and Instruction is organized into five clusters: early childhood education, multilingual studies, language and literacy studies (includes reading and English language/arts), curriculum studies/adult education and human and organizational learning, institutional technology, and science and mathematics education.

The Master of Education and the Master of Arts programs consist of 30-36 semester hours, depending on whether students elect to write a thesis or a report for the Master of Arts degree or take coursework only for the Master of Education degree. The programs offered for the doctoral degree are in curriculum studies, early childhood studies, instructional technology, language and literacy, and multilingual studies.

Licensure/Reciprocity: Texas. Students seeking teaching certification in a state other than Texas should consult with that state's teacher certification office early in their program of study to insure compliance with requirements. Many state directors of teacher credentialing have signed Interstate Agreements through NASDTEC that expedite the certification process.

THE UNIVERSITY OF TEXAS AT EL PASO

College of Education
Teacher Education Department

500 West University Avenue
El Paso, Texas 79968
Phone: (915) 747-5572
Fax: (915) 747-5755
E-mail: education@utep.edu
Internet: http://www.utep.edu

Institution Description: The university was established as Texas State School of Mines and Metallurgy in 1913.

The mission of the College of Education is to prepare effective teachers, counselors, diagnosticians, and school administrators to successfully address the problems of schools and other youth service agencies, especially in communities with a significant Hispanic population.

Institution Control: Public.

Calendar: Semester. Academic year August to July.

Official(s): D. Josie Tinajero, Dean.

Faculty: Full-time 22.

Degrees Awarded: 380 baccalaureate; 199 master's; 6 doctorate.

Admission Requirements: *Undergraduate:* Graduation from an approved secondary school; College Board SAT or ACT composite. *Teacher education specific:* 2.75 GPA; high school transcript; satisfactory scores on all three sections (reading, mathematics, writing) of the Texas Higher Education Assessment (THEA); faculty interview; personal goal statement. *Graduate:* Baccalaureate degree from a regionally accredited institution. *Teacher education specific:* 3.0 GPA; GRE or Miller Analogies Test scores; completion of all required departmental exams; recommendations; faculty interview.

Fees and Expenses: Undergraduate: $2,964 in-state per academic year; $8,688 out-of-state. Graduate: $2,450 in-state per academic year; $6,000 out-of-state. On-campus room and board: $2,865. Other expenses: $2,994. Books and supplies: $892.

Financial Aid: Resources specifically for eligible students enrolled in teacher education programs are awarded on the basis of financial need and academic merit. The institution has a Program Participation Agreement with the U.S. Department of Education for eligible students to receive Pell Grants and other federal aid. Teacher scholarships available to qualifying students. *Contact:* Financial Aid Office at: (915) 747-5204.

Accreditation: *Regional:* SACS. *Member of:* AACTE. *Approved by:* Texas State Board for Educator Certification.

Undergraduate Programs: Undergraduates earn a bachelor's degree in an approved area while fulfilling certification requirements. Students typically complete a multidisciplinary major or an academic major and supporting minor. Certification can be achieved in elementary education, secondary education, or all-level education. A minimum of 125 semester hours is required for the degree award.

Graduate Programs: The Master of Arts in Education is designed for students wishing to pursue research and to continue studies beyond the master's degree level. Students may work with the Department of Teacher Education, specifically in the areas of either instructional specialist or reading education to develop a plan of study. The 36 credit hour program includes the submission of a thesis.

The Master of Education degree is directed toward mastery of professional education practice. Students wishing to pursue the Master of Education degree may do so through majors in instructional specialist of reading education. Students whose professional needs are not met by these majors may major in education and plan the 36-hour program around those needs.

In the instructional specialist program students may choose to concentrate coursework in the areas of elementary education, secondary education, early childhood education, bilingual education, or health and physical education. Subject area emphases may occur within the elementary or secondary concentrations.

Licensure/Reciprocity: Texas. Students seeking teaching certification in a state other than Texas should consult with that state's teacher certification office early in their program of study to insure compliance with requirements. Many state directors of teacher credentialing have signed Interstate Agreements through NASDTEC that expedite the certification process.

THE UNIVERSITY OF TEXAS AT SAN ANTONIO

College of Education and Human Development Interdisciplinary Studies and Curriculum and Instruction

6900 North Loop 1604 West
San Antonio, Texas 78249-0631
Phone: (210) 458-4706
Fax: (210) 458-4708
E-mail: admissions@utsa.edu
Internet: http://www.utsa.edu

Institution Description: The university was established in 1969 and offered first instruction at the postsecondary level in 1973.

Undergraduate and graduate programs are offered to prepare students for careers in the teaching field.

Institution Control: Public.

Calendar: Semester. Academic year August to May.

Official(s): Dr. Miriam G. Martinez, Chair.

Faculty: Full-time 96.

Degrees Awarded. 355 baccalaureate, 278 master's.

Admission Requirements: *Undergraduate:* Graduation with 14 units from an approved secondary school; College Board SAT or ACT composite. *Teacher education specific:* 2.75 GPA; high school transcript; satisfactory scores on all three sections (reading, mathematics, writing) of the Texas Higher Education Assessment (THEA); faculty interview; personal goal statement. *Graduate:* Baccalaureate degree from a regionally accredited institution. *Teacher education specific:* 3.0 GPA; GRE or Miller Analogies Test scores; completion of all required departmental exams; recommendations; faculty interview.

Fees and Expenses: Undergraduate: $3,460 in-state per academic year; $9,124 out-of-state. Graduate: $126 in-state per semester hour; $337 out-of-state. Required fees: $781. On-campus room and board: $6,393. Other expenses: $4,216. Books and supplies: $1,000.

Financial Aid: Resources specifically for eligible students enrolled in teacher education programs are awarded on the basis of financial need and academic merit. The institution has a Program Participation Agreement with the U.S. Department of Education for eligible students to receive Pell Grants and other federal aid. Teacher scholarships available to qualifying students. *Contact:* Financial Aid Office at: (210) 458-4154.

Accreditation: *Regional:* SACS. *Member of:* AACTE. *Approved by:* Texas State Board for Educator Certification.

Undergraduate Programs: The Bachelor of Arts in interdisciplinary studies if offered with concentrations and certification in early childhood-4th grade, 4th-8th grade; bilingual education early childhood-4th grade; bilingual education 4th-8th grade; English as a second language 4th-8th grade. All baccalaureate programs require the completion of the general education core, professional studies, content area, field-based experiences, and student teaching. A minimum of 120 semester hours is required for the degree award.

Graduate Programs: The Master of Arts in Education degree programs include: curriculum and instruction, early childhood and elementary education, instructional technology, educational psychology special education, reading and literacy. Each program has specific goals and required coursework.

Licensure/Reciprocity: Texas. Students seeking teaching certification in a state other than Texas should consult with that state's teacher certification office early in their program of study to insure compliance with requirements. Many state directors of teacher credentialing have signed Interstate Agreements through NASDTEC that expedite the certification process.

THE UNIVERSITY OF TEXAS AT TYLER

College of Education and Psychology

3900 University Boulevard
Tyler, Texas 75799
Phone: (903) 566-7000
Fax: (903) 565-5705
E-mail: admissions@uttyl.edu
Internet: http://www.uttyl.edu

Institution Description: The University of Texas at Tyler provides upper division and master's degree study only. It was established as Tyler State College in 1971.

The College of Education and Psychology offers teacher preparation programs as well as graduate programs for professional enrichment.

Institution Control: Public.

Calendar: Semester. Academic year August to May.

Official(s): Dr. William C. Bruce, Associate Dean.

Faculty: Full-time 17.

Degrees Awarded: 128 baccalaureate; 55 master's.

Admission Requirements: *Undergraduate:* Graduation from an approved secondary school; College Board SAT or ACT composite. *Teacher education specific:* 2.75 GPA; high school transcript; satisfactory scores on all three sections (reading, mathematics, writing) of the Texas Higher Education Assessment (THEA); faculty interview; personal goal statement. *Graduate.* Baccalaureate degree from a regionally accredited institution. *Teacher education specific:* 3.0 GPA; GRE or Miller Analogies Test scores; completion of all required departmental exams; recommendations; faculty interview.

Fees and Expenses: Undergraduate: $2,872 in-state per academic year; $8,536 out-of-state. Graduate: $44 plus $58 in-state per semester hour; $262 plus $58 out-of-state. On-campus room and board: $5,280. Books and supplies: $700.

Financial Aid: Resources specifically for eligible students enrolled in teacher education programs are awarded on the basis of financial need and academic merit. The institution has a Program Participation Agreement with the U.S. Department of Education for eligible students to receive Pell Grants and other federal aid. Teacher scholarships available to qualifying students. *Contact:* Financial Aid Office at: (903) 566-7180.

Accreditation: *Regional:* SACS. *Member of:* AACTE. *Approved by:* Texas State Board for Educator Certification.

Undergraduate Programs: Undergraduates earn a bachelor's degree in an approved area while fulfilling certification requirements. Students typically complete a multidisciplinary major or an academic major and supporting minor. Certification can be achieved in elementary education, secondary education, or all-level education. A minimum of 124 semester hours is required for the degree award.

Graduate Programs: The Master of Arts in Education is designed for students wishing to pursue research and to continue studies beyond the master's degree level. The program requires completion of 36 credit hours that includes the submission of a thesis.

The Master of Education degree is directed toward mastery of professional education practice. Students wishing to pursue the Master of Education degree may do so through majors in various fields in a 36-hour program.

THE UNIVERSITY OF TEXAS AT TYLER—*cont'd*

The Master of Arts in Teaching program is for those students with an undergraduate major but who did not pursue a teaching credential. A Master of Science degree program is also available.

Licensure/Reciprocity: Texas. Students seeking teaching certification in a state other than Texas should consult with that state's teacher certification office early in their program of study to insure compliance with requirements. Many state directors of teacher credentialing have signed Interstate Agreements through NASDTEC that expedite the certification process.

THE UNIVERSITY OF TEXAS - PAN AMERICAN

College of Education
Department of Curriculum and Instruction
412 Education Building
1201 West University Drive
Edinburg, Texas 78539-2999
Phone: (956) 381-3627
Fax: (956) 381-2184
E-mail: education@panam.edu
Internet: http://www.panam.edu

Institution Description: The University of Texas - Pan American (formerly Pan American University) is a state institution. It was established and chartered as Edinburg Junior College in 1927 and became a four-year college in 1952. The college became Pan American University in 1971 and part of the University of Texas system in 1991.

The College of Education offers academic programs leading to teacher certification.

Institution Control: Public.

Calendar: Semester. Academic year September to August.

Official(s): Dr. Hilda Medrano, Dean; Dr. Leo Gomez, Assistant Dean.

Faculty: Full-time 15.

Degrees Awarded: 341 baccalaureate; 197 master's; 3 doctorate.

Admission Requirements: *Undergraduate:* Graduation from an approved secondary school; College ACT composite. *Teacher education specific:* 2.75 GPA; high school transcript; satisfactory scores on all three sections (reading, mathematics, writing) of the Texas Higher Education Assessment (THEA); faculty interview; personal goal statement. *Graduate:* Baccalaureate degree from a regionally accredited institution. *Teacher education specific:* 3.0 GPA; GRE or Miller Analogies Test scores; completion of all required departmental exams; recommendations; faculty interview.

Fees and Expenses: Undergraduate: $2,562 in-state per academic year; $8,666 out-of-state. Graduate: $212 in-state per semester hour; $367 out-of-state. On-campus room and board: $4,333. Other expenses: $2,826. Books and supplies: $612.

Financial Aid: Resources specifically for eligible students enrolled in teacher education programs are awarded on the basis of financial need and academic merit. The institution has a Program Participation Agreement with the U.S. Department of Education for eligible students to receive Pell Grants and other federal aid. Teacher scholarships available to qualifying students. *Contact:* Financial Aid Office at: (956) 381-2501.

Accreditation: *Regional:* SACS. *Member of:* AACTE. *Approved by:* Texas State Board for Educator Certification.

Undergraduate Programs: The College of Education offers a Bachelor of Science degree with majors in kinesiology and health and a Bachelor of Interdisciplinary Studies for elementary teachers. The college also offers undergraduate certification in elementary, secondary, and all-level art, music, and kinesiology education with options for specialized endorsements in special education, early childhood, bilingual education, and gifted education. A minimum of 124 semester hours is required for the degree award.

Graduate Programs: Master's degree programs include a Master of Education with specializations in elementary education, secondary education, special education, early childhood education, reading, educational diagnostician, bilingual education, counseling and guidance, educational administration, gifted education, supervision, and kinesiology. A Master of Arts degree in school psychology is also available.

Students may pursue work toward professional certification simultaneously with work toward a graduate degree. Candidates for the Master of Education degree should complete the academic requirements for the professional certificate as a counselor and educational diagnostician, a supervisor or an administrator, or in gifted education. Candidates for the Master of Arts or Master of Science degree should complete the academic requirements for the professional certificate in the major field selected for the degree.

An Alternative Certification Program is designed for prospective public school teachers with degrees in disciplines other than education. Certification is offered in six tracks: elementary, elementary/bilingual, elementary/ESL, secondary, secondary/ESL, and special education.

Doctoral programs are offered in supervision and leadership.

Licensure/Reciprocity: Texas. Students seeking teaching certification in a state other than Texas should consult with that state's teacher certification office early in their program of study to insure compliance with requirements. Many state directors of teacher credentialing have signed Interstate Agreements through NASDTEC that expedite the certification process.

THE UNIVERSITY OF TEXAS OF THE PERMIAN BASIN

School of Education
4901 East University Boulevard
Odessa, Texas 79762-0001
Phone: (432) 552-2020
Fax: (432) 552-2374
E-mail: tenatsch_p@utpb.edu
Internet: http://www.utpb.edu

Institution Description: The University of Texas of the Permian Basin is a four-year comprehensive university. It was founded in 1969.

The School of Education offers a teacher preparation program that is a collaborative venture between the university and local schools.

Institution Control: Public.

Calendar: Semester. Academic year September to May.

Official(s): Dr. Peter Tenatsch, Dean.

Faculty: Full-time 20.

Degrees Awarded: 3 baccalaureate; 57 master's.

Admission Requirements: *Undergraduate:* Graduation from an approved secondary school; College Board SAT or ACT composite. *Teacher education specific:* 2.75 GPA; high school transcript; satisfactory scores on all three sections (reading, mathematics, writing) of the Texas Higher Education Assessment (THEA); faculty interview; personal goal statement. *Graduate:* Baccalaureate degree from a regionally accredited institution. *Teacher education specific:* 3.0 GPA; GRE or Miller Analogies Test scores; completion of all required departmental exams; recommendations; faculty interview.

Fees and Expenses: Undergraduate: $2,788 in-state per academic year; $8,452 out-of-state. Graduate: $1,746 in-state per academic year; $5,292 out-of-state. On-campus room and board: $4,034. Other expenses: $2,410. Books and supplies: $800.

Financial Aid: Resources specifically for eligible students enrolled in teacher education programs are awarded on the basis of financial need and academic merit. The institution has a Program Participation Agreement with the U.S. Department of Education for eligible students to receive Pell Grants and other federal aid. Teacher scholarships available to qualifying students. *Contact:* Financial Aid Office at: (432) 552-2620.

Accreditation: *Regional:* SACS. *Member of:* AACTE. *Approved by:* Texas State Board for Educator Certification.

Undergraduate Programs: Undergraduates in the teacher education program earn a bachelor's degree in an approved area while fulfilling certification requirements. Students typically complete a multidisciplinary major or an academic major and supporting minor. Certification for classroom teaching is available in the following areas: early childhood-grade 4, grades 4-8, grades 8-12, all-level (early childhood-grade 12). All certification programs require the completion of the general education core, professional studies, content area, field experiences, and student teaching. A minimum of 120 semester hours is required for the degree award.

Graduate Programs: Master of Arts in Education programs are designed both as professional certification programs and as preparation for doctoral study. Research and non-research options are available. The degree requires a completion of a minimum of 36 semester hours of graduate work. Program options include: bilingual/ESL education, counseling, early childhood education, educational leadership, professional education, reading, special education.

Licensure/Reciprocity: Texas. Students seeking teaching certification in a state other than Texas should consult with that state's teacher certification office early in their program of study to insure compliance with requirements. Many state directors of teacher credentialing have signed Interstate Agreements through NASDTEC that expedite the certification process.

UNIVERSITY OF THE INCARNATE WORD

Dreeben School of Education
Teacher Education Program
4301 Broadway
San Antonio, Texas 78209
Phone: (210) 829-6001
E-mail: dsoe@uiw.edu
Internet: http://www.uiw.edu

Institution Description: University of the Incarnate Word, formerly known as Incarnate Word College, is a private institution conducted by the Sisters of Charity of the Incarnate Word, Roman Catholic Church.

The emphasis of the teacher education program incorporates a broad liberal arts education as a foundation for the more in-depth focus on academic teaching specializations and the body of knowledge associated with the teaching/learning process.

Institution Control: Private.

Calendar: Semester. Academic year August to May.

Official(s): Dr. Gilberto M. Hinojosa, Dean.

Faculty: Full-time 10.

Degrees Awarded: 36 baccalaureate; 48 master's; 11 doctorate.

Admission Requirements: *Undergraduate:* Graduation from an approved secondary school; College Board SAT or ACT composite. *Teacher education specific:* 2.75 GPA; high school transcript; satisfactory scores on all three sections (reading, mathematics, writing) of the Texas Higher Education Assessment (THEA); faculty interview; personal goal statement. *Graduate:* Baccalaureate degree from a regionally accredited institution. *Teacher education specific:* 3.0 GPA; GRE or Miller Analogies Test scores; completion of all required departmental exams; recommendations; faculty interview.

Fees and Expenses: $15,248 per academic year. Graduate: $445 plus $25 per semester hour. On-campus room and board: $5,586. Other expenses: $1,450. Books and supplies: $800.

Financial Aid: Resources specifically for eligible students enrolled in teacher education programs are awarded on the basis of financial need and academic merit. The institution has a Program Participation Agreement with the U.S. Department of Education for eligible students to receive Pell Grants and other federal aid. Teacher scholarships available to qualifying students. *Contact:* Financial Aid Office at: (210) 829-6008.

Accreditation: *Regional:* SACS. *Member of:* AACTE. *Approved by:* Texas State Board for Educator Certification.

Undergraduate Programs: Baccalaureate degrees are offered with or without certification in interdisciplinary studies (early childhood-grade 4) and all-level (art music, physical education) certification. Secondary subject area fields are offered without certification at the baccalaureate level. Secondary certification (grades 8-12) is offered at the post-baccalaureate level. Students can prepare for initial certification and teaching at the elementary level, secondary level, or kindergarten through twelfth grade (all-level). A minimum of 128 semester hours is required for the degree award.

Graduate Programs: The Master of Arts in Teaching program is offered with concentrations in the elementary and secondary education areas. The Master of Arts or Master of Education programs are offered with concentrations in adult education, early childhood education, instructional technology, international education, organizational learning, and physical education. Each program has specific goals and coursework requirements.

Licensure/Reciprocity: Texas. Students seeking teaching certification in a state other than Texas should consult with that state's teacher certification office early in their program of study to insure compliance with requirements. Many state directors of teacher credentialing have signed Interstate Agreements through NASDTEC that expedite the certification process.

UTAH

BRIGHAM YOUNG UNIVERSITY

David O. McKay School of Education

Department of Teacher Education

301 MCKB

Provo, Utah 84602

Phone: (801) 422-3695

Fax: (801) 422-0200

E-mail: msed@byu.edu

Internet: http://www.byu.edu

Institution Description: Brigham Young University is a private institution affiliated with the Church of Jesus Christ of Latter-day Saints. The university was established as Brigham Young Academy in 1875. The present name was adopted in 1903.

All teacher education licensure programs are undergraduate. Graduate programs are designed to improve the art and science of teaching or to prepare educators to function as curriculum specialists.

Institution Control: Private.

Calendar: Semester. Academic year September to April.

Official(s): Dr. K. Richard Young, Dean; Dr. Winston M. Egan, Chair, Department of Teacher Education.

Faculty: Full-time 30; part-time 9.

Degrees Awarded: 788 baccalaureate; 115 master's; 18 doctorate.

Admission Requirements: *Undergraduate:* Graduation from an approved high school; ACT composite. *Teacher education specific:* 2.85 GPA; reflective questions; autobiographical statement; completion of general education courses; passing scores on PRAXIS I (reading, writing, mathematics); interview. *Graduate:* Baccalaureate degree from a regionally accredited institution. *Teacher education specific:* 3.0 on last 60 hours of coursework; GRE; 1 year as certified teacher in elementary school classroom.

Fees and Expenses: Undergraduate: $3,150 LDS per academic year. $4,740 non-LDS. Graduate: $3,980 LDS per academic year; $5,970 non-LDS. On-campus room and board: $5,354. Other expenses: $825. Books and supplies: $825.

Financial Aid: Resources specifically for eligible students enrolled in teacher education programs are awarded on the basis of financial need and academic merit. The institution has a Program Participation Agreement with the U.S. Department of Education for eligible students to receive Pell Grants and other federal aid. Teacher scholarships available to qualifying students. *Contact:* Alva H. Merkley at: (801) 422-8308.

Accreditation: *Regional:* NASC. *Professional:* NCATE. *Member of:* AACTE. *Approved by:* Utah State Board of Education.

Undergraduate Programs: The early childhood program provides a preparation program for prospective teachers to learn about the culture of young children, develop a solid foundation in basic principles of teaching, and learning that originate in developmental theory and research, and become prescient in appropriate practices to implement these basic principles in practical settings. The elementary education program provides the opportunity for prospective teachers to learn about the culture of the elementary school and develop a solid foundation in the basic principles of teaching and learning.

The baccalaureate programs require the completion a general education core, professional studies, content area, field experiences, and student teaching. A minimum of 120 semester hours must be completed for the degree award.

Graduate Programs: The Master of Arts in teaching and learning requires the completion and defense of a thesis. The Master of Education requires the completion and defense of a professional improvement project. These degree programs require completion of a minimum of 36 semester hours.

The Doctor of Education program in reading features specific programs developed by students and faculty to help students prepare for careers as professors and reading specialists. The program requires completion of 95 semester hours including 12 dissertation hours.

Licensure/Reciprocity: Utah. Students seeking teaching certification in a state other than Utah should consult with that state's teacher certification office early in their program of study to insure compliance with requirements. Many state directors of teacher credentialing have signed Interstate Agreements through NASDTEC that expedite the certification process.

SOUTHERN UTAH UNIVERSITY

College of Education

Department of Teacher Education

351 West Center Street

Cedar City, Utah 84720

Phone: (435) 586-7700

Fax: (435) 865-8223

E-mail: barker@suu.edu

Internet: http://www.suu.edu

Institution Description: Southern Utah University is a state institution. It was established and chartered as Branch Normal School, a part of State Normal School, in 1897.

The primary mission of the College of Education is to provide students a personalized learning environment that fosters meaningful experiences. Throughout the undergraduate program, students are given a wealth of practical experience to supplement classroom education.

Institution Control: Public.

Calendar: Quarter. Academic year September to June.

Official(s): Dr. Bruce O. Barker, Dean; Dr. Lee Montgomery, Chair, Department of Teacher Education.

Faculty: Full-time 15.

Degrees Awarded: 305 baccalaureate; 48 master's.

Admission Requirements: *Undergraduate:* Graduation from an approved high school or GED; College Board SAT or ACT composite. *Teacher education specific:* Completion of general education courses; personal goal statement; passing scores on PRAXIS I (reading, writing, mathematics); interview. *Graduate:* Baccalaureate degree from a regionally accredited institution. *Teacher education specific:* 3.0 on last 60 hours of coursework; GRE or Miller Analogies Test scores; faculty interview.

Fees and Expenses: Undergraduate: $2,794 in-state per academic year; $8,058 out-of-state. Graduate: $137 in-state per credit hour; $522 out-of-state. On-campus room and board: $5,400. Other expenses: $3,480. Books and supplies: $1,036.

Financial Aid: Resources specifically for eligible students enrolled in teacher education programs are awarded on the basis of financial need and academic merit. The institution has a Program Participation Agreement with the U.S. Department of Education for eligible students to receive Pell Grants and other federal aid. Teacher scholarships available to qualifying students. *Contact:* Financial Aid Office at: (435) 586-7735.

Accreditation: *Regional:* NASC. *Member of:* AACTE. *Approved by:* Utah State Board of Education.

Undergraduate Programs: Bachelor of Arts and Bachelor of Science degrees are offered in elementary education, special education-mild/moderate, and physical education. elementary education minors are offered in art, English as a second language, early childhood, English/language arts, music, physical education, social science, science, health, K-8 mathematics, library media, physical education, reading, special education (mild/moderate). Over 30 majors and minors are approved for Utah secondary licensure. All baccalaureate programs require the completion of the general education core, professional studies, content area, field experiences, and student teaching. A minimum of 183 quarter hours is required for the degree award.

Graduate Programs: The Master of Education specialties include: educational supervisory administration license; English as a second language; gifted and talented education, instructional technology; mathematics; reading endorsement/ specialist program; special education (mild/moderate).

Graduate Educator Licensure Programs include: elementary education; secondary education; special education mild/moderate) English as a second language; reading endorsement and specialist; library/media K-12; administrative/supervisory licensure.

Licensure/Reciprocity: Utah. Students seeking teaching certification in a state other than Utah should consult with that state's teacher certification office early in their program of study to insure compliance with requirements. Many state directors of teacher credentialing have signed Interstate Agreements through NASDTEC that expedite the certification process.

UNIVERSITY OF UTAH

College of Education
200 South University Street
Salt Lake City, Utah 84112
Phone: (801) 581-8221
Fax: (801) 581-5223
E-mail: education@utah.edu
Internet: http://www.utah.edu

Institution Description: The University of Utah is a state institution. It was chartered as University of Deseret in 1850. The present name was adopted in 1892.

The College of Education prepares students for positions in public schools of higher learning and other education-related agencies. It provides a variety of programs at the undergraduate and graduate levels. Teacher education is regarded as a university-wide function and an immediate responsibility of the College of Education.

Institution Control: Public.

Calendar: Semester. Academic year September to June.

Official(s): Dr. David J. Sperry, Dean; Dr. Diana Pounder, Associate Dean for Professional Education.

Faculty: Full-time 68; part-time 71 adjunct 112.

Degrees Awarded: 97 baccalaureate; 101 master's; 14 doctorate.

Admission Requirements: *Undergraduate:* Graduation from an approved high school or GED; College Board SAT accepted; ACT composite preferred. *Teacher education specific:* Completion of general education courses; personal goal statement; passing scores on PRAXIS I (reading, writing, mathematics); interview. *Graduate:* Baccalaureate degree from a regionally accredited institution. *Teacher education specific:* 3.0 on last 60 hours of coursework; GRE or Miller Analogies Test scores; faculty interview.

Fees and Expenses: Undergraduate: $3,094 in-state per academic year; $10,704 out-of-state. Graduate: $3,428 in-state per academic year; $10,659 out-of-state. Required fees: $588. On-campus room and board: $5,114. Books and supplies: $1,086.

Financial Aid: The College of Education offers departmental, mathematics/science/foreign language, Terrell H. Bell Teaching Incentive Loan, and other scholarships. Application forms and detailed information regarding scholarships are available for the various departments within the college. *Contact:* Office of Financial Aid and Scholarships at: (801) 581-6211 or e-mail at: fawin@sa.utah.edu.

Accreditation: *Regional:* NASC. *Member of:* AACTE. *Approved by:* Utah State Board of Education.

Undergraduate Programs: Baccalaureate degree programs are offered in early childhood, elementary education, special education, and secondary education. Secondary content endorsement areas include: art, audiology, biology, chemistry, coaching, communications/speech/journalism, dance, drama, driver and safety education, English, English as a second language, French, geography, geology, German, health, history, mathematics, physical education, physics, political science, Russian, social science, social work, Spanish, speech pathology. All baccalaureate programs require the completion of the general education core, professional studies, content area, field experiences, and student teaching. A minimum of 122 semester hours is required for the degree award.

Graduate Programs: The Master of Arts, Master of Science, Master of Education, and Doctor of Philosophy degree programs include: special education license; endorsements in early childhood disabilities (mild to moderate disabilities, severe disabilities, visual impairment, hearing impairment); early childhood special education license (preK-3 with endorsements in visual impairment and hearing impairment).

The Master of Arts, Master of Science, Master of Education, and Doctor of Philosophy degree programs in teaching and learning include: early childhood license (preK-3), elementary education license (1-8), secondary license (6-12), and reading and reading specialist endorsements.

Licensure/Reciprocity: Utah. Students seeking teaching certification in a state other than Utah should consult with that state's teacher certification office early in their program of study to insure compliance with requirements. Many state directors of teacher credentialing have signed Interstate Agreements through NASDTEC that expedite the certification process.

UTAH STATE UNIVERSITY

College of Education
1400 Old Main Hall
Logan, Utah 84322-1400
Phone: (435) 797-0385
Fax: (435) 797-3900
E-mail: coe@usu.edu
Internet: http://www.usu.edu

Institution Description: Established as Agricultural College of Utah in 1888, it offered first instruction at the postsecondary level in 1890.

The goal of the teacher education programs is to provide students with the professional knowledge and teaching skills to complement the knowledge acquired in general education and in teaching majors and minors.

Institution Control: Public.

Calendar: Semester. Academic year August to May.

Official(s): Dr. Barry Franklin, Department Head, secondary education; Dr. Bernie Hayes, Department Head, Elementary Education.

Faculty: Full-time 29.

Degrees Awarded: 329 baccalaureate; 200 master's; 12 doctorate.

Admission Requirements: *Undergraduate:* Graduation from an approved high school or GED; ACT composite. *Teacher education specific:* Completion of general education courses; personal goal statement; passing scores on PRAXIS I (reading,

UTAH STATE UNIVERSITY—cont'd

writing, mathematics); interview. *Graduate:* Baccalaureate degree from a regionally accredited institution. *Teacher education specific:* 3.0 on last 60 hours of coursework; GRE or Miller Analogies Test scores; faculty interview.

Fees and Expenses: Undergraduate: $3,141 in-state per academic year; $8,946 out-of-state. Graduate: Tuition charged per credit hour. On-campus room and board: $4,230. Other expenses: $3,030. Books and supplies: $870.

Financial Aid: Resources specifically for eligible students enrolled in teacher education programs are awarded on the basis of financial need and academic merit. The institution has a Program Participation Agreement with the U.S. Department of Education for eligible students to receive Pell Grants and other federal aid. Teacher scholarships available to qualifying students. *Contact:* Financial Aid Office at: (435) 797-0173.

Accreditation: *Regional:* NASC. *Professional:* NCATE. *Member of:* AACTE. *Approved by:* Utah State Board of Education.

Undergraduate Programs: The Department of Secondary Education works with 21 university departments to provide programs leading to recommendation for secondary teacher licensure. The program includes a 35-credit set of teacher education courses and clinical experiences organized into three levels over three semesters. Successful completion of the program enables students to be recommended for secondary teacher licensure (grades 6-12) in Utah.

The Department of Elementary Education, in conjunction with the Departments of Family Studies, Human Development, and Special Education, offers programs leading to the baccalaureate degree and teacher certification include: elementary education, early childhood education, dual elementary and early childhood education, dual early childhood and special education, elementary education and mild/moderate specialization, elementary education, and deaf education. Elementary education students in the middle education program are certified to teach in a middle school, grades five through eight, as well as grades one through four.

All baccalaureate programs require the completion of the general education core, professional studies, content area, field experiences, and student teaching. A minimum of 120 semester hours must be completed for the degree award.

Graduate Programs: Master's degree programs are offered by the Department of Secondary Education to meet the needs of middle school and high school teachers. These programs include a Master of Education (36 or 40 credits), Master of Arts (30 credits), and a Master of Science (30 credits). The department also participates in the College of Education and Human Services interdepartmental doctoral program in curriculum and instruction.

The Department of Elementary Education offers Master of Arts or Master of Science degree programs. Candidates have the freedom to design programs that meet their individual needs and interests. The programs require the completion of 36 or 40 credits depending on the pre-planned program of approved graduate courses. The department also participates in an interdepartmental program leading to the doctoral degree. The program is designed for educators who wish to prepare to become curriculum specialists in public or state departments of public instruction and for those preparing to teach at the college or university level

Licensure/Reciprocity: Utah. Students seeking teaching certification in a state other than Utah should consult with that state's teacher certification office early in their program of study to insure compliance with requirements. Many state directors of teacher credentialing have signed Interstate Agreements through NASDTEC that expedite the certification process.

WEBER STATE UNIVERSITY

Jerry and Vickie Moyes College of Education
Department of Teacher Education
230 Education Building
1304 University Circle
Ogden, Utah 84408
Phone: (801) 626-7171
Fax: (801) 626-7427
E-mail: mcena@weber.edu
Internet: http://www.weber.edu

Institution Description: Weber State University was established as Weber Stake Academy by the Church of Jesus Christ of Latter-day Saints in 1889. It became a state institution in 1933.

The Department of Teacher Education offers undergraduate programs leading to teacher certification and graduate programs designed to extend the professional knowledge, skills, and attitudes of educators, including those in schools, business, industry, and higher education.

Institution Control: Public.

Calendar: Semester. Academic year September to May.

Official(s): Dr. Jack L. Rasmussen, Dean; Dr. Michael E. Cena, Department Head, Teacher Education.

Faculty: Full-time 23.

Degrees Awarded: 202 baccalaureate; 27 master's.

Admission Requirements: *Undergraduate:* Graduation from an approved high school or GED; College Board SAT or ACT composite. *Teacher education specific:* Completion of at least 45 semester hours; 3.0 GPA; personal goal statement; passing scores on PRAXIS I (reading, writing, mathematics); interview. *Graduate:* Baccalaureate degree from a regionally accredited institution. *Teacher education specific:* 3.0 on last 60 hours of coursework; GRE or Miller Analogies Test scores; faculty interview.

Fees and Expenses: Undergraduate: $2,130 in-state per academic year; $7,456 out-of-state. Graduate: $2,800 in-state per academic year; $8,600 out-of-state. On-campus room and board: $3,600 to $4,000. Books and supplies: $700.

Financial Aid: Resources specifically for eligible students enrolled in teacher education programs are awarded on the basis of financial need and academic merit. The institution has a Program Participation Agreement with the U.S. Department of Education for eligible students to receive Pell Grants and other federal aid. Teacher scholarships available to qualifying students. *Contact:* Financial Aid Office at: (801) 626-7262.

Accreditation: *Regional:* NASC. *Professional:* NCATE. *Member of:* AACTE. *Approved by:* Utah State Board of Education.

Undergraduate Programs: Baccalaureate degrees are offered in the elementary education major, elementary education and early childhood dual licensure, and composite elementary education and special education major. The latter program will allow graduates to teach in regular elementary education (grades 1-6) and/or in special education (grades K-12). All programs require completion of the general education core, professional studies, content area, field experiences, and student teaching. A minimum of 120 credit hours is required for graduation.

Students who complete secondary education licensure are prepared to teach in sixth (middle school) through twelfth grade in both their major/composite major and qualifying minor subject area. The academic teaching major and teaching minor must consist of not less than 30 and 16 credit hours respectively, or a composite major of at least 46 credit hours. A minimum of 120 credit hours is required for graduation.

Graduate Programs: The Master of Education degree program is practice-oriented with the primary focus on enhancing knowledge, skills, and attitudes of educators. The goals of the program are accomplished through courses, seminars, independent study, cooperative learning groups, individual and group assignments, and projects emphasizing a practical implementation of theory to the learning environment. The program requires the completion of 36 semester hours.

Post-baccalaureate students seeking a teaching license and who meet all Master of Education admission criteria except licensure may be admitted provided they have the equivalent of one year of full-time professional teaching experience. The teaching experience must be after the awarding of the baccalaureate degree.

Licensure/Reciprocity: Utah. Students seeking teaching certification in a state other than Utah should consult with that state's teacher certification office early in their program of study to insure compliance with requirements. Many state directors of teacher credentialing have signed Interstate Agreements through NASDTEC that expedite the certification process.

VERMONT

GREEN MOUNTAIN COLLEGE

Education Department

One College Circle
Poultney, Vermont 05764
Phone: (802) 287-8000
Fax: (802) 287-8099
E-mail: mauhspucht@greenmtn.edu
Internet: http://www.greenmtn.edu

Institution Description: Green Mountain College is a private, independent, nonprofit institution. It was established by the United Methodist Church as Troy Conference Academy, a preparatory school, in 1834.

The Department of Education offers baccalaureate programs leading to teacher certification in Vermont.

Institution Control: Private.

Calendar: Semester. Academic year September to May.

Official(s): Dr. Thomas J. Mauhs-Pugh, Chair.

Faculty: Full-time 4; adjunct 2.

Degrees Awarded: 11 baccalaureate.

Admission Requirements: *Undergraduate:* Graduation from an approved secondary school in top 50% or GED; College Board SAT 950 or ACT composite 18. *Teacher education specific:* 2.49 GPA; PRAXIS I scores (reading, mathematics, writing); completion of basic education courses; general education core; personal goal statement; recommendations; faculty interview. PRAXIS II subject matter test must be passed in order to student teach.

Fees and Expenses: $19,670 per academic year. Required fees: $440. On-campus room and board: $6,300 ($600 premium for single room). Books and supplies: $900.

Financial Aid: Resources specifically for eligible students enrolled in teacher education programs are awarded on the basis of financial need and academic merit. The institution has a Program Participation Agreement with the U.S. Department of Education for eligible students to receive Pell Grants and other federal aid. Teacher scholarships available to qualifying students. *Contact:* Doreen Kelly, Financial Aid Director at: (802) 287-8209 or e-mail at: kellyd@greenmtn.edu.

Accreditation: *Regional:* NEASC. *Approved by:* Vermont State Department of Education.

Undergraduate Programs: Approximately 80 students are enrolled in programs leading to certification in elementary education with special education endorsement, K-12 art, secondary education, secondary English, or secondary social studies. Each student is required to complete field work, methodology, and theory courses in a planned sequence in preparation for teacher certification. Students in the elementary education with special education endorsement in mild to moderate disabilities complete the elementary education program while taking additional courses and field experiences to qualify them for licensure to teach in elementary special education classes or resource rooms. All students must complete 30 credit hours in a liberal arts concentration. A minimum of 120 semester hours is required for graduation.

Baccalaureate programs are offered leading to secondary certification (grades 7-12) in English, social studies, and art (K-12). Students in these programs complete a major in the relevant discipline (art, English, history) along with a sequence of education courses and field experiences. A minimum of 120 semester hours must be completed for the degree award.

Licensure/Reciprocity: Vermont. Students seeking teaching certification in a state other than Vermont should consult with that state's teacher certification office early in their program of study to insure compliance with requirements. Many state directors of teacher credentialing have signed Interstate Agreements through NASDTEC that expedite the certification process.

UNIVERSITY OF VERMONT

College of Education and Social Services
Department of Education

300 Waterman Building
85 South Prospect Street
Burlington, Vermont 05405
Phone: (802) 656-3556
Fax: (802) 656-0855
E-mail: james.mosenthal@uvm.edu
Internet: http://www.uvm.edu

Institution Description: University of Vermont is a public university and is a land-grant and sea-grant college. It was established and chartered in 1791.

The Department of Education offers undergraduate and graduate courses leading to teacher certification and opportunities for professional studies in a variety of fields in education.

Institution Control: Public.

Calendar: Semester. Academic year August to May.

Official(s): Dr. James Mosenthal, Chairperson.

Faculty: Full-time 33; part-time 6; adjunct 6.

Degrees Awarded: 122 baccalaureate; 109 master's; 8 doctorate.

Admission Requirements: *Undergraduate:* Graduation with 16 academic units from an approved secondary school or GED; College Board SAT or ACT composite. *Teacher education specific:* PRAXIS I scores (reading, mathematics, writing); completion of basic education courses; general education core; personal goal statement; recommendations; faculty interview. PRAXIS II subject matter test must be passed in order to student teach. *Graduate:* Baccalaureate degree from a regionally accredited institution. *Teacher education specific:* 2.5 GPA in undergraduate coursework; demonstrated commitment to working with young people; major concentration in a liberal arts or sciences field; references; faculty interview.

Fees and Expenses: Undergraduate/graduate: $8,696 in-state per academic year; $21,748 out-of-state. On-campus room and board: $6,680. Books and supplies: $800.

Financial Aid: Resources specifically for eligible students enrolled in teacher education programs are awarded on the basis of financial need and academic merit. The institution has a Program Participation Agreement with the U.S. Department of Education for eligible students to receive Pell Grants and other federal aid. Teacher scholarships available to qualifying students. *Contact:* Don Honeman at: (802) 656-8793 or e-mail at: donald.honeman@uvm.edu.

Accreditation: *Regional:* NEASC. *Professional:* NCATE. *Member of:* AACTE. *Approved by:* Vermont State Department of Education.

Undergraduate Programs: The undergraduate programs offered by the Department of Education include: teacher education (art K-12 studies, early childhood preK-3, elementary education K-6, family and consumer sciences, middle level education 5-8, music K-12, physical education K-12, secondary education 7-12). All students who enroll in the teacher education programs are required to complete a 30-hour major in the liberal arts and sciences.

Students in secondary education complete a major (30 hours) and a minor (18 hours) or a broad field major (48 hours). Students in middle level education complete an individually designed interdisciplinary major. Students in early childhood, elementary education, family and consumer sciences, physical education complete a 30-hour major concentration and have the option of selecting a specific discipline or creating an individually designed interdisciplinary major concentration. A minimum of 122 semester hours is required for graduation.

Graduate Programs: The Master of Science in curriculum and instruction is designed to develop leadership in such educational settings as teaching, curriculum theory, curriculum development, and related areas of research for elementary and secondary public and private school settings. Areas of concentration include elementary, secondary, individually designed, and health and physical education. Within curriculum and instruction, the licensure Master of Education program for secondary teachers is for those students who have completed majors in humanities, the arts, social sciences, science, and mathematics and who aspire to earn both a master's degree and a license to teach in public secondary schools. Candidates will become licensed to teach in grades seven through twelve. With additional study an endorsement for the middle grades may be earned.

A doctoral program in educational leadership and policy studies is available to qualified professionals.

Licensure/Reciprocity: Vermont. Students seeking teaching certification in a state other than Vermont should consult with that state's teacher certification office early in their program of study to insure compliance with requirements. Many state directors of teacher credentialing have signed Interstate Agreements through NASDTEC that expedite the certification process.

VIRGINIA

BLUEFIELD COLLEGE

Division of Education

3000 College Drive
Bluefield, Virginia 24605
Phone: (276) 326-4242
Fax: (276) 326-4288
E-mail: gclay@bluefield.edu
Internet: http://www.bluefield.edu

Institution Description: Bluefield College is a private institution affiliated with the Baptist General Association of Virginia. The college was chartered in 1920.

The Division of Education offers undergraduate programs leading to the baccalaureate degree and teacher certification.

Institution Control: Private.

Calendar: Semester. Academic year August to May.

Official(s): Dr. Gerald E. Clay, Chairman.

Faculty: Full-time 3; adjunct 1.

Degrees Awarded: 9 baccalaureate.

Admission Requirements: *Undergraduate:* Graduation from an approved secondary school or GED; College Board SAT or ACT composite. *Teacher education specific:* Overall 2.5 GPA; no grade lower that C in major/certification area; PRAXIS I test scores (reading, writing, mathematics); faculty interview; personal goal statement.

Fees and Expenses: $10,165 per academic year. On-campus room and board: $5,410. Other expenses: $1,880. Books and supplies: $900.

Financial Aid: Resources specifically for eligible students enrolled in teacher education programs are awarded on the basis of financial need and academic merit. The institution has a Program Participation Agreement with the U.S. Department of Education for eligible students to receive Pell Grants and other federal aid. Teacher scholarships available to qualifying students. *Contact:* D. Checcio at: (276) 326-4243 or e-mail at: dcheccio@bluefield.edu.

Accreditation: *Regional:* SACS. *Member of:* AACTE. *Approved by:* Virginia State Department of Education.

Undergraduate Programs: The Division of Education offers programs leading to the bachelor's degree. The programs consist of a minimum of 126 semester hours of instruction, including courses in general education, professional studies, content area, field experiences, and student teaching. Degrees awarded with teacher licensure include: Bachelor of Science in biology, business administration, chemistry, history/social sciences, mathematics, music, social studies, visual art. The Bachelor of Arts or Bachelor of Science is offered for students desiring to teach in elementary or preK-6 and in exercise and sport science.

Licensure/Reciprocity: Virginia. Students seeking teaching certification in a state other than Virginia should consult with that state's teacher certification office early in their program of study to insure compliance with requirements. Many state directors of teacher credentialing have signed Interstate Agreements through NASDTEC that expedite the certification process.

BRIDGEWATER COLLEGE

Department of Education

Box 15
402 East College Street
Bridgewater, Virginia 22812
Phone: (540) 828-5355
Fax: (540) 828-5447
E-mail: lholsing@bridgewater.edu
Internet: http://www.bridgewater.edu

Institution Description: Bridgewater College is a private, independent, nonprofit college affiliated with the Church of the Brethren. The college was established as Spring Creek Normal School and Collegiate Institute in 1880.

The Department of Education provides a state-approved program for the preparation of elementary, secondary, and special education teachers.

Institution Control: Private.

Calendar: Semester. Academic year September to May.

Official(s): Dr. Lanny Holsinger, Chairman.

Faculty: Full-time 5; part-time 3.

Degrees Awarded: 25 baccalaureate.

Admission Requirements: *Undergraduate:* Graduation from an approved secondary school or GED; College Board SAT or ACT composite. *Teacher education specific:* Overall 2.5 GPA; PRAXIS I test scores (reading, writing, mathematics); writing sample; references; personal interview.

Fees and Expenses: $16,990 per academic year. On-campus room and board: $8,160. Other expenses: $1,890. Books and supplies: $860.

Financial Aid: Resources specifically for eligible students enrolled in teacher education programs are awarded on the basis of financial need and academic merit. The institution has a Program Participation Agreement with the U.S. Department of Education for eligible students to receive Pell Grants and other federal aid. Teacher scholarships available to qualifying students. *Contact:* Vern Fairchilds at: (540) 828-5376 or e-mail at: vfairchi@bridgewater.edu.

Accreditation: *Regional:* SACS. *Member of:* AACTE. *Approved by:* Virginia State Department of Education.

Undergraduate Programs: The liberal studies major, housed in the Department of Education, was created for students seeking elementary (preK-6) and special education (K-12) certification. Since the major is linked with pre-K-6 and special education, all requirements (major and education courses) must be met prior to graduation. The major is available in either the Bachelor of Arts or Bachelor of Science degree. During the senior year, students will enroll in the professional semester that consists of one or more student teaching experiences. The Senior Seminar will also be taken as part of the professional semester during which time students will complete development of their professional portfolio.

Students seeking certification to teach in the middle/secondary schools can obtain endorsements in the areas of: biology, chemistry, computer science, driver education, English, work and family studies, history and social sciences, mathematics, physics.

Licensure/Reciprocity: Virginia. Students seeking teaching certification in a state other than Virginia should consult with that state's teacher certification office early in their program of study to insure compliance with requirements. Many state directors of teacher credentialing have signed Interstate Agreements through NASDTEC that expedite the certification process.

COLLEGE OF WILLIAM AND MARY

School of Education
P.O. Box 8795
Williamsburg, Virginia 23187-8795
Phone: (757) 221-2317
Fax: (757) 221-2293
E-mail: amiss@wm.edu
Internet: http://www.wm.edu

Institution Description: The College of William and Mary is a state college. It was established and chartered in 1693.

The mission of the School of Education is the pursuit of excellence in the education of learners across the life-span.

Institution Control: Public.

Calendar: Semester. Academic year August to May.

Official(s): Dr. Virginia McLaughlin, Dean.

Faculty: Full-time 38; part-time 17.

Degrees Awarded: 71 baccalaureate; 88 master's; 25 doctorate.

Admission Requirements: *Undergraduate:* Graduation from an approved secondary school or GED; College Board SAT or ACT composite. *Teacher education specific:* Overall 2.0 GPA; academic status of junior; completion of 54 credit hours; PRAXIS I test scores (reading, writing, mathematics); faculty interview; personal goal statement. PRAXIS II prior to certificator. *Graduate:* Baccalaureate from a regionally accredited institution. *Teacher education specific:* 2.5 GPA; GRE test scores; completion of all required departmental exams; 3 letters of reference; personal essay; faculty interview.

Fees and Expenses: Undergraduate: $6,430 in-state per academic year; $21,216 out-of-state. Graduate: $7,502 in-state per academic year; $19,196 out-of-state. On-campus room $2,682 to $3,92; board $1,666 to $2,770. Books and supplies: $900.

Financial Aid: Resources specifically for eligible students enrolled in teacher education programs are awarded on the basis of academic merit, knowledge, skills, abilities. The institution has a Program Participation Agreement with the U.S. Department of Education for eligible students to receive Pell Grants and other federal aid. Teacher scholarships available to qualifying students. *Contact:* David Derbel at: (757) 221-2420.

Accreditation: *Regional:* SACS. *Professional:* NCATE. *Member of:* AACTE. *Approved by:* Virginia State Department of Education.

Undergraduate Programs: The program in elementary education leading to endorsement to teach grades preschool-kindergarten to grade 6 requires a dual concentration. Students are required to select a departmental or interdisciplinary concentration in the arts and sciences as a primary concentration. They are also required to declare a second concentration of 35 semester hours in elementary education. A total of 120 academic credits is required for the baccalaureate degree.

Students who plan to teach at the secondary school level declare a concentration in the subject area or areas they expect to teach. Endorsement areas are: English, foreign language (French, German, Spanish, Latin), mathematics, science (biology, chemistry, earth and space science, physics), social studies, history and Government.

All baccalaureate programs require the completion of the general education core, professional studies, content area, field experiences, and student teaching.

Graduate Programs: The Master of Arts in Education degree in curriculum and instruction is awarded upon successful completion of programs in elementary education; secondary education; reading, language and literacy; gifted education; special education (initial certification and resource collaborating teach-

ing). The Master of Education degree is awarded upon successful completion of programs in counseling, educational leadership, and school psychology.

At the doctoral level, advanced graduate students can pursue studies in counseling education and educational policy, planning and leadership, including general education administration, gifted education administration, special education administration, and higher education programs.

Licensure/Reciprocity: Virginia. Students seeking teaching certification in a state other than Virginia should consult with that state's teacher certification office early in their program of study to insure compliance with requirements. Many state directors of teacher credentialing have signed Interstate Agreements through NASDTEC that expedite the certification process.

EASTERN MENNONITE UNIVERSITY

Education Department
Teacher Education Programs
1200 Park Road
Harrisonburg, Virginia 22802-2462
Phone: (540) 432-4000
Fax: (540) 432-4444
E-mail: mrained@emu.edu
Internet: http://www.emu.edu

Institution Description: Easter Mennonite University, formerly named Eastern Mennonite College and Seminary, is a private, Christian institution operated by the Mennonite Church. It was founded in 1917.

The Teacher Education Programs offer undergraduate and graduate courses leading to certification and teaching careers in Virginia.

Institution Control: Private.

Calendar: Semester. Academic year August to April.

Official(s): Dr. Donovan D. Steiner, Chair.

Faculty: Full-time 11; adjunct 1.

Degrees Awarded: 4 baccalaureate, 19 master's.

Admission Requirements: *Undergraduate:* Graduation with a college preparatory program from an approved secondary school or GED; College Board SAT or ACT composite. *Teacher education specific:* Overall 2.5 GPA; PRAXIS I test scores (reading, writing, mathematics); faculty interview; personal goal statement. PRAXIS II prior to graduation. *Graduate:* Baccalaureate from a regionally accredited institution. *Teacher education specific:* 2.75 GPA; GRE test scores; completion of all required departmental exams; teaching experience; recommendations; faculty interview.

Fees and Expenses: $17,350 per academic year. Graduate: Tuition charged per credit hour. On-campus room and board: $5,640. Other expenses: $900. Books and supplies: $710.

Financial Aid: Resources specifically for eligible students enrolled in teacher education programs are awarded on the basis of financial need and academic merit. The institution has a Program Participation Agreement with the U.S. Department of Education for eligible students to receive Pell Grants and other federal aid. Teacher scholarships available to qualifying students. *Contact:* Financial Aid Office at: (540) 432-4137.

Accreditation: *Regional:* SACS. *Professional:* NCATE. *Member of:* AACTE. *Approved by:* Virginia State Department of Education.

Undergraduate Programs: Baccalaureate programs offered by the Education Department include: early education (preK-3) and elementary education (preK-6); secondary education (6-12) with concentrations in biology, chemistry, computer science, English, English as a second language, journalism, theatre arts, history, social science, mathematics, physics; special education (K-12) with concentrations in learning disabilities, emotional disturbance, mental retardation; all-grade education (preK-12); foreign languages: French, German, Spanish; health and physical education; music (instrumental and vocal/choral). All programs require the completion of the general education core,

EASTERN MENNONITE UNIVERSITY—*cont'd*
professional studies, content area, field experiences, and student teaching. A minimum of 128 semester hours is required for the degree award.

Graduate Programs: The Master of Education degree is awarded upon successful completion of programs in counseling, educational leadership, and school psychology. Each program has specific goals and coursework.

A Post-Baccalaureate Teaching Program is available for those who already have a bachelor's degree but wish to acquire certification to teach in their area of expertise.

Licensure/Reciprocity: Virginia. Students seeking teaching certification in a state other than Virginia should consult with that state's teacher certification office early in their program of study to insure compliance with requirements. Many state directors of teacher credentialing have signed Interstate Agreements through NASDTEC that expedite the certification process.

GEORGE MASON UNIVERSITY
Graduate School of Education
4400 University Drive
Fairfax, Virginia 22030-4444
Phone: (703) 993-1000
Fax: (703) 993-2392
E-mail: admissions@gmu.edu
Internet: http://www.gmu.edu

Institution Description: George Mason University is a state institution. It was founded by the University of Virginia as extension center for higher education in 1948.

The Graduate School of Education provides leadership in transforming schools, organizations, and communities through research, teaching, and collaboration.

Institution Control: Public.

Calendar: Semester. Academic year August to May.

Official(s): Dr. Jeffrey Gorrell, Dean.

Faculty: Full-time 74.

Degrees Awarded: 44 baccalaureate; 568 master's; 21 doctorate.

Admission Requirements: *Undergraduate:* Graduation from an approved secondary school or GED; College Board SAT or ACT composite. *Teacher education specific:* Overall 2.5 GPA; no grade lower that C in major/certification area; PRAXIS I test scores (reading, writing, mathematics); faculty interview; personal goal statement. PRAXIS II prior to certification. *Graduate:* Baccalaureate degree from a regionally accredited institution. *Teacher education specific:* 3.0 GPA on last 60 hours of undergraduate study; 3 professional letters of recommendation; personal goals statement; experience or licensure as required by some programs; GRE test scores for some programs.

Fees and Expenses: $5,122 in-state per academic year; $14,952 out-of-state. On-campus room and board: $5,881. Other expenses: 41,376. Books and supplies: $910.

Financial Aid: Resources specifically for eligible students enrolled in teacher education programs are awarded on the basis of financial need and academic merit. The institution has a Program Participation Agreement with the U.S. Department of Education for eligible students to receive Pell Grants and other federal aid. Teacher scholarships available to qualifying students. *Contact:* Financial Aid Office at: (703) 993-2353.

Accreditation: *Regional:* SACS. *Professional:* NCATE. *Member of:* AACTE. *Approved by:* Virginia State Department of Education.

Undergraduate Programs: Undergraduate special education minors are 15-credit minors in special education that provide students with background knowledge in three specializations: emotional disturbance/learning disabilities, mental retardation/severe disabilities, or early childhood special education. Completion of these minors will partially fulfill requirements for licensure in special education in Virginia. Undergraduate Initial Teacher Licensure Programs are offered in art education (preK-12), dance education (preK-12), music education (preK-12) and health/physical education. A minimum of 120 semester hours are required for these undergraduate degrees.

Graduate Programs: The Master of Education Degree programs include counseling and development, curriculum and instruction (adult education, advanced studies in teaching and learning, educational psychology, instructional psychology, multilingual/multicultural education); education leadership; special education. The Master of Arts in Teaching is available in professional studies.

Graduate Initial Teacher Licensure Programs are offered in: early childhood; elementary education (prek-6); English as a second language (preK-12); foreign language or Latin (preK-12); secondary education (6-12); special education.

Doctoral programs leading to the Doctor of Philosophy in Education are also offered.

Licensure/Reciprocity: Virginia. Students seeking teaching certification in a state other than Virginia should consult with that state's teacher certification office early in their program of study to insure compliance with requirements. Many state directors of teacher credentialing have signed Interstate Agreements through NASDTEC that expedite the certification process.

HAMPTON UNIVERSITY
School of Liberal Arts and Education
East Queen Street
Hampton, Virginia 23668
Phone: (757) 727-5332
Fax: (757) 727-5095
E-mail: admissions@hamptonu.edu
Internet: http://www.hamptonu.edu

Institution Description: Hampton University, formerly Hampton Institute, is a private, independent, nonprofit institution. It was established as Hampton Normal and Agricultural Institute in 1868.

The School of Liberal Arts and Education offers undergraduate and graduate programs that prepare students for professional teaching careers in a variety of areas.

Institution Control: Private.

Calendar: Semester. Academic year August to May.

Official(s): Dr. Marie Loclee, Dean.

Faculty: Full-time 11.

Degrees Awarded: 5 baccalaureate; 44 master's.

Admission Requirements: *Undergraduate:* Graduation from an approved secondary school or GED; College Board SAT or ACT composite. *Teacher education specific:* Overall 2.5 GPA; no grade lower that C in major/certification area; PRAXIS I test scores (reading, writing, mathematics); faculty interview; personal goal statement. PRAXIS II required prior to certification. *Graduate:* Baccalaureate from a regionally accredited institution. *Teacher education specific:* 2.5 0 GPA; GRE or Miller Analogies scores; completion of all required departmental exams; 2 letters of recommendation; faculty interview.

Fees and Expenses: Undergraduate: $12,864 per academic year. Graduate: $275 per semester hour. On-campus room and board: $6,118. Other expenses: $2,805. Books and supplies: $770.

Financial Aid: Resources specifically for eligible students enrolled in teacher education programs are awarded on the basis of financial need and academic merit. The institution has a Program Participation Agreement with the U.S. Department of Education for eligible students to receive Pell Grants and other federal aid. Teacher scholarships available to qualifying students. *Contact:* Financial Aid Office at: (757) 727-5332.

Accreditation: *Regional:* SACS. *Professional:* NCATE. *Member of:* AACTE. *Approved by:* Virginia State Department of Education.

Undergraduate Programs: The Department of Health, Physical Education and Recreation offers a professional preparation program for prospective majors and a required service program for non-majors that involves a wide variety of lifetime sports activities. The department offers undergraduate degree programs leading to the Bachelor of Science degree with teacher endorsement at the preK-12 levels. A minimum of 120 semester hours is required for graduation.

Graduate Programs: The Graduate College offers the Master of Arts in Teaching degree programs that include: early childhood K-5 (English, psychology, mathematics, marine sciences, biology, history, music); middle school grades 6-8 (English, mathematics, biology, physical science, history, music); secondary grades 9-12 (English, biology, history, mathematics, music, computer science, sociology, political science); special education (psychology/learning, behavior disorders (grades K-12).

The Master of Science in Education programs are offered in the concentrations of: applied mathematics, biology, environmental science, chemistry, computer science, physics,

A Doctor of Education program is available to qualified candidates.

Licensure/Reciprocity: Virginia. Students seeking teaching certification in a state other than Virginia should consult with that state's teacher certification office early in their program of study to insure compliance with requirements. Many state directors of teacher credentialing have signed Interstate Agreements through NASDTEC that expedite the certification process.

JAMES MADISON UNIVERSITY
College of Education
Teacher Education Programs
MSC 1907
Harrisonburg, Virginia 22807
Phone: (540) 568-2812
Fax: (540) 568-6608
E-mail: education@jmu.edu
Internet: http://www.jmu.edu

Institution Description: James Madison University (Madison College until 1977) is a state institution.

The goal of the Teacher Education Programs is to provide preparation for individuals seeking initial and advanced licenses and provide continuing professional development for practicing teachers.

Institution Control: Public.

Calendar: Semester. Academic year August to May.

Official(s): Dr. Alvin Pettus, Chairman.

Faculty: Full-time 41.

Degrees Awarded: 4 baccalaureate; 90 master's.

Admission Requirements: *Undergraduate:* Graduation from an approved secondary school or GED; College Board SAT or ACT composite. *Teacher education specific:* 2.75 GPA; satisfactory scores on PRAXIS I (reading, writing, mathematics); references; completion of universal precautions training; references. *Graduate:* Baccalaureate from a regionally accredited institution. *Teacher education specific:* Satisfactory GPA and GRE scores; official transcripts; valid teaching license; completion of all required departmental exams; written statements. PRAXIS II prior to certification.

Fees and Expenses: Undergraduate: $4,628 in-state per academic year; $11,812 out-of-state. Graduate: $23 in-state per credit hour; $554 out-of-state . Required fees: $55. On-campus room and board: $4,297. Books and supplies: $350.

Financial Aid: Resources specifically for eligible students enrolled in teacher education programs are awarded on the basis of financial need and academic merit. The institution has a Program Participation Agreement with the U.S. Department of Education for eligible students to receive Pell Grants and other federal aid. Teacher scholarships available to qualifying students. *Contact:* Martha Ringwald at: (540) 568-3357 or e-mail at: ringwama@gmu.edu.

Accreditation: *Regional:* SACS. *Professional:* NCATE. *Member of:* AACTE. *Approved by:* Virginia State Department of Education.

Undergraduate Programs: The early childhood education (preK-3) program is offered at the undergraduate level and leads to a baccalaureate degree and licensure to teach upon completion of an appropriate major and required professional education courses.

The middle education (grades 6-8) program is designed to provide preparation and experiences that form the foundation for admission to and completion of the graduate program for teacher licensure in grades six through eight. Completion of the Master of Arts in Teaching is required for licensure in middle education.

The pre-professional program in secondary education is designed to provide preparation and experiences that form the foundation for admission to and completion of the Master of Arts in Teaching program. Students must complete a major or the equivalent in the arts and sciences disciplines closely associated with the desired teaching area. Approved licensure areas include business and marketing, English, foreign languages, mathematics, natural sciences, history and social studies, and technology education.

The special education (K-12 program) provides the requisite course offerings and experiences that form the foundation for admission to the Master of Education degree program in special education.

Art education (preK-12) prepares students to teach elementary, middle school, and high school art courses. The music education program prepares musician teachers in the vocal/choral/instrumental areas. The physical and health education teacher education concentration is committed to educating leaders in the profession of teaching physical and health education.

Graduate Programs: In addition to the initial teacher licensure programs outlined above at the undergraduate level, advanced licensure programs are available in reading, school administration and supervision, school counseling, and school psychology. Graduate programs and concentrations for continuing professional development are available in art education, early childhood education, middle education, secondary education, special education, adult education/human resource development, and higher education.

Licensure/Reciprocity: Virginia. Students seeking teaching certification in a state other than Virginia should consult with that state's teacher certification office early in their program of study to insure compliance with requirements. Many state directors of teacher credentialing have signed Interstate Agreements through NASDTEC that expedite the certification process.

LONGWOOD COLLEGE
College of Education and Human Services
Department of Education, Special Education, and Social Work
201 High Street
Farmville, Virginia 23909
Phone: (434) 395-2051
Fax: (434) 395-2800
E-mail: lcadmit@longwood.lwc.edu
Internet: http://www.lwc.edu

Institution Description: Longwood College is a state-assisted, coeducational, comprehensive, residential college. It was established as Farmville Female College in 1839.

The College of Education offers undergraduate and graduate programs to prepare students for teaching careers.

Institution Control: Public.

Calendar: Semester. Academic year August to May.

Official(s): Dr. George C. Stonikinis, Jr., Chair.

Faculty: Full-time 28.

Degrees Awarded: 135 baccalaureate; 88 master's.

Admission Requirements: *Undergraduate:* Graduation from an approved secondary school or GED; College Board SAT or ACT composite. *Teacher education specific:* Overall 2.5 GPA; PRAXIS I test scores (reading, writing, mathematics); faculty interview; personal goal statement. PRAXIS II required prior to certification. *Graduate:* Baccalaureate from a regionally accredited institution. *Teacher education specific:* 2.5 0 GPA; GRE or Miller Analogies scores; completion of all required departmental exams; recommendations; faculty interview.

LONGWOOD COLLEGE—cont'd

Fees and Expenses: Undergraduate: $5,877 in-state per academic year; $11,853 out-of-state. Graduate: Tuition charged per semester hour. On-campus room and board: $5,298. Other expenses: $1,200. Books and supplies: $700.

Financial Aid: Resources specifically for eligible students enrolled in teacher education programs are awarded on the basis of financial need and academic merit. The institution has a Program Participation Agreement with the U.S. Department of Education for eligible students to receive Pell Grants and other federal aid. Teacher scholarships available to qualifying students. *Contact:* Financial Aid Office at: (434) 395-2060.

Accreditation: *Regional:* SACS. *Professional:* NCATE. *Member of:* AACTE. *Approved by:* Virginia State Department of Education.

Undergraduate Programs: The Department of Education, Special Education, and Social Work provides undergraduate programming in elementary (N,K-6), an interdisciplinary program designed primarily for students seeking license to teach multiple subjects in the elementary grades. A middle school endorsement is an interdisciplinary program designed primarily for students seeking license to teach multiple subjects in the middle grades (6-8). Arts and sciences majors seeking licensure may major in biology, chemistry, computer science, English, history, mathematics, physics, political science, and theatre arts. All-level education programs offer teacher preparation in art, instrumental music, modern languages (French, German, Spanish), physical and health education, and vocal/choral music. A program in liberal studies with the special education endorsement prepares the student for a fifth year program leading to the Master of Science in Education with a concentration in special education.

Graduate Programs: Within the Department of Education, Special Education, and Social Work there are a variety of concentrations leading to the Master of Science degree. The areas are: community and college counseling, curriculum and instruction, educational leadership, elementary education preK-6 initial licensure, guidance and counseling, literacy and culture, modern languages, school library media, and special education N,K-12 initial licensure.

The Master of Science degree is awarded to Longwood students enrolled in the special education/liberal studies five-year program. The department also offers three graduate licensure only programs in educational leadership, school library media, and special education N,K-12.

Licensure/Reciprocity: Virginia. Students seeking teaching certification in a state other than Virginia should consult with that state's teacher certification office early in their program of study to insure compliance with requirements. Many state directors of teacher credentialing have signed Interstate Agreements through NASDTEC that expedite the certification process.

MARY BALDWIN COLLEGE

Teacher Licensure

Frederick and New Streets
Staunton, Virginia 24401
Phone: (540) 887-7019
Fax: (540) 886-5561
E-mail: education@mbc.edu
Internet: http://www.mbc.edu

Institution Description: Mary Baldwin College is a private, nonprofit institution affiliated with the Presbyterian Church (U.S.A.). The college was established as Augusta Seminary in 1842.

Teacher Licensure programs integrate theory, practice, and opportunities for individual exploration within a collaborative environment.

Institution Control: Private.

Calendar: Semester (4-1-4 plan). Academic year August to May.

Official(s): Dr. Patricia Westhafer, Director, Undergraduate Residential Programs; Dr. Carol Grove, Director, MAT Program.

Degrees Awarded: 6 baccalaureate; 23 master's.

Admission Requirements: *Undergraduate:* Graduation with 16 academic units from an approved secondary school or GED; College Board SAT. *Teacher education specific:* Competence with information technologies; strong knowledge base in pedagogy and the liberal arts; professional and personal integrity; PRAXIS I test scores (reading, writing, mathematics); faculty interview; personal goal statement. PRAXIS II examination before certification. *Graduate:* Baccalaureate from a regionally accredited institution. *Teacher education specific:* 3.0 GPA in last 60 semester hours; academic major in the arts and sciences or an appropriate discipline; fluent written and spoken English; GRE or Miller Analogies scores; completion of all required departmental exams; recommendations; faculty interview.

Fees and Expenses: Undergraduate: $19,414 per academic year. Graduate: $335 per semester hour. On-campus room and board: $5,525. Other expenses: $1,615. Books and supplies: $700.

Financial Aid: Resources specifically for eligible students enrolled in teacher education programs are awarded on the basis of financial need and academic merit. The institution has a Program Participation Agreement with the U.S. Department of Education for eligible students to receive Pell Grants and other federal aid. Teacher scholarships available to qualifying students. *Contact:* Financial Aid Office at: (540) 887-7022.

Accreditation: *Regional:* SACS. *Member of:* AACTE. *Approved by:* Virginia State Department of Education.

Undergraduate Programs: Students desiring to earn licensure for teaching careers select a major in the subject of their choice and minor in education. Minor areas include early education (preK-6), middle education (6-8), secondary education (6-12) with endorsement or major in business, English, French, Spanish, mathematics, biology, chemistry, history, political science, social science; arts and languages (preK-12) with endorsement areas in art, music, theatre arts, French, Spanish. All programs require completion of the general education core, professional studies, content area, field experiences, and student teaching. A minimum of 132 credit hours is required for graduation.

Graduate Programs: The Master of Arts in Teaching degree was designed to meet the needs of both those seeking teaching credentials for the first time and experienced teachers desiring a master's degree. Depending on choice of courses, students will earn the MAT degree and licensure to teach elementary grades prek-6, middle school 6-8, or prek-8 in Virginia. Licensure is also available for special education K-12 in: learning disabilities, mental retardation, and emotional disturbance.

Licensure/Reciprocity: Virginia. Students seeking teaching certification in a state other than Virginia should consult with that state's teacher certification office early in their program of study to insure compliance with requirements. Many state directors of teacher credentialing have signed Interstate Agreements through NASDTEC that expedite the certification process.

MARYMOUNT UNIVERSITY

School of Education and Human Services
Department of Education

2807 North Glebe Road
Arlington, Virginia 22207-4299
Phone: (703) 522-5600
Fax: (703) 522-0349
E-mail: admissions@marymount.edu
Internet: http://www.marymount.edu

Institution Description: Marymount University (Marymount College of Virginia until 1986) is a private college founded by the Religious of the Sacred Heart of Mary, a Roman Catholic educational order. The institution was founded in 1950.

The Department of Education offers undergraduate and graduate programs in preparation for teaching careers and professional development.

Institution Control: Private.

Calendar: Semester. Academic year August to May.

Official(s): Dr. Alice L. Young, Chairperson.

Faculty: Full-time 12.

Degrees Awarded: 84 master's.

Admission Requirements: *Undergraduate:* Graduation from an approved secondary school or GED; College Board SAT or ACT composite. *Teacher education specific:* Overall 2.5 GPA; no grade lower that C in major/certification area; PRAXIS I test scores (reading, writing, mathematics); faculty interview; personal goal statement. PRAXIS II prior to certification. *Graduate:* Baccalaureate from a regionally accredited institution. *Teacher education specific:* 2.5 0 GPA; GRE or Miller Analogies scores; completion of all required departmental exams; recommendations; faculty interview.

Fees and Expenses: Undergraduate $16,428 per academic year. Graduate: $512 per credit hour. On-campus room and board: $7,230. Other expenses: $1,650. Books and supplies: $500.

Financial Aid: Resources specifically for eligible students enrolled in teacher education programs are awarded on the basis of financial need and academic merit. The institution has a Program Participation Agreement with the U.S. Department of Education for eligible students to receive Pell Grants and other federal aid. Teacher scholarships available to qualifying students. *Contact:* Financial Aid Office at: (703) 284-1530.

Accreditation: *Regional:* SACS. *Professional:* NCATE. *Member of:* AACTE. *Approved by:* Virginia State Department of Education.

Undergraduate Programs: Undergraduate teaching licensure programs are available in early childhood education (preK-3), secondary education (7-12), and art education (K-12). Each program is designed to prepare graduates to enter the job market as beginning professionals in their respective disciplines. Students who wish to earn licensure at the preK-3 level follow a prescribed program of studies that fulfills the requirements of their major discipline. Students may earn licensure at the secondary level in the content areas of art, biology, computer science, English, history, social science, and mathematics. The program in art education leads to K-12 licensure.

All students following a baccalaureate path to licensure must major in an academic discipline and minor in education. The programs require the completion of the general education core, professional studies, content area, field experiences, and student teaching. A minimum of 120 semester hours is required for graduation.

Graduate Programs: The Master of Education degree programs leading to licensure include: elementary education preK-6 and secondary education 6-12. The secondary education program is designed for persons who already have a B.A. or B.S. in any of the following content areas: biology, chemistry, computer science, earth and space science, English, general science, mathematics, physics, social studies. Each program has specific goals and coursework requirements.

Licensure/Reciprocity: Virginia. Students seeking teaching certification in a state other than Virginia should consult with that state's teacher certification office early in their program of study to insure compliance with requirements. Many state directors of teacher credentialing have signed Interstate Agreements through NASDTEC that expedite the certification process.

NORFOLK STATE UNIVERSITY

School of Education
Norfolk, Virginia 23504
Phone: (757) 823-8701
Fax: (757) 823-2057
E-mail: admissions@nsu.edu
Internet: http://nsu.edu

Institution Description: Norfolk State University was established as the Norfolk unit of Virginia Union University in 1935.

The central purpose of the School of Education is to provide pre-service and in-service educational programs to perspective teachers, in-service teachers, administrators, and others engaged in educational activities in other agencies.

Institution Control: Public.

Calendar: Semester. Academic year August to May.

Official(s): Dr. Jean Braxton, Dean.

Faculty: Full-time 33.

Degrees Awarded: 14 baccalaureate; 94 master's.

Admission Requirements: *Undergraduate:* Graduation from an approved secondary school or GED; College Board SAT. *Teacher education specific:* Overall 2.5 GPA; admittance at the end of 60 hours of coursework; PRAXIS I test scores (reading, writing, mathematics); faculty interview; personal goal statement. PRAXIS II prior to certification. *Graduate:* Baccalaureate from a regionally accredited institution. *Teacher education specific:* 2.5 0 GPA; GRE or Miller Analogies scores; completion of all required departmental exams; recommendations; faculty interview.

Fees and Expenses: Undergraduate: $3,584 in-state per academic year; $11,748 out-of-state. Graduate: $197 in-state per semester credit; $503 out-of-state. On-campus room and board: $5,882. Other expenses: $2,700. Books and supplies: $1,000.

Financial Aid: Resources specifically for eligible students enrolled in teacher education programs are awarded on the basis of financial need and academic merit. The institution has a Program Participation Agreement with the U.S. Department of Education for eligible students to receive Pell Grants and other federal aid. Teacher scholarships available to qualifying students. *Contact:* Financial Aid Office at: (757) 823-8381.

Accreditation: *Regional:* SACS. *Professional:* NCATE. *Member of:* AACTE. *Approved by:* Virginia State Department of Education.

Undergraduate Programs: Students seeking certification in elementary education (K-6) can pursue a degree in the liberal arts/sciences with emphases in English, mathematics, history, and psychology.

The Department of Special Education offers a sequence of courses and experiences designed for students interested in and committed to careers as special educators and related professions. The curriculum prepares graduates to teach and work with exceptional persons who may be in schools, hospitals, community centers, and other facilities and institutions.

The program in health, physical education and exercise science is designed to prepare students to become certified health and physical education teachers in grades K-12 in public schools.

Programs lead to the Bachelor of Arts or Bachelor of Science degree and require the completion of the general education core, professional studies, content area, field experiences, and student teaching. A minimum of 126 semester hours is required for graduation.

Graduate Programs: The Master of Arts in Teaching is for students with a bachelor's degree in liberal arts who seek certification in their areas of expertise. The Master of Arts program includes concentrations in urban education, administration and supervision, curriculum development and supervision, principal preparation, urban guidance and counseling, and school counseling preK-12. The Master of Arts in a subject area concentration is also offered.

Licensure/Reciprocity: Virginia. Students seeking teaching certification in a state other than Virginia should consult with that state's teacher certification office early in their program of study to insure compliance with requirements. Many state directors of teacher credentialing have signed Interstate Agreements through NASDTEC that expedite the certification process.

OLD DOMINION UNIVERSITY

Darden College of Education
5215 Hampton Boulevard
Norfolk, Virginia 23529-0050
Phone: (757) 683-3348
Fax: (757) 683-4872
E-mail: wgraves@odu.edu
Internet: http://www.odu.edu

Institution Description: Old Dominion University is a state institution. It was established as an extension center of The College of William and Mary in 1919.

OLD DOMINION UNIVERSITY—*cont'd*

The Darden College of Education offers undergraduate and graduate programs in a wide variety of studies leading to teacher certification and professional development.

Institution Control: Public.

Calendar: Semester. Academic year August to May.

Official(s): Dr. William H. Graves, Dean.

Faculty: Full-time 90; part-time 54.

Degrees Awarded: 134 baccalaureate; 646 master's.

Admission Requirements: *Undergraduate:* Graduation with 16 academic units from an approved secondary school or GED; College Board SAT. *Teacher education specific:* Overall 2.5 GPA; admission at the end of 60 hours of coursework; PRAXIS I test scores (reading, writing, mathematics); faculty interview; personal goal statement. PRAXIS II prior to certification. *Graduate:* Baccalaureate from a regionally accredited institution. *Teacher education specific:* 2.5 0 GPA; GRE or Miller Analogies scores; completion of all required departmental exams; recommendations; faculty interview.

Fees and Expenses: Undergraduate: $3,974 in-state per academic year; $11,304 out-of-state. Graduate: $202 in-state per credit hour; $524 out-of-state. On-campus room and board: $5,632. Other expenses: $2,875. Books and supplies: $800.

Financial Aid: Resources specifically for eligible students enrolled in teacher education programs are awarded on the basis of financial need and academic merit. The institution has a Program Participation Agreement with the U.S. Department of Education for eligible students to receive Pell Grants and other federal aid. Teacher scholarships available to qualifying students. *Contact:* Financial Aid Office at: (757) 683-3683.

Accreditation: *Regional:* SACS. *Professional:* NCATE. *Member of:* AACTE. *Approved by:* Virginia State Department of Education.

Undergraduate Programs: Bachelor of Science programs offered by the Darden College of Education include: educational leadership and counseling (human services counseling); early childhood, speech language pathology, and special education (speech language pathology and audiology); exercise science, sport, physical education and recreation (health and physical education, sport management, exercise science, recreation and tourism studies); occupational and technical studies (fashion, industrial technology, technology education, marketing education, training specialist).

Graduate Programs: The Interdisciplinary Studies Department provides prospective elementary, middle school, and special education teachers with a multidisciplinary liberal arts and sciences Bachelor of Science degree that leads in the fifth year to graduate study in the Darden College of Education. This fifth-year program culminates for teacher candidates in a Master of Science Degree. The early childhood program leads to a license to teach preK-grade 3.

The Master of Science in Education degree programs include: educational leadership and counseling; education, curriculum, and instruction (reading, middle school, secondary/elementary); early childhood, speech language pathology, and special education; occupational and technical studies; exercise science, sport, physical education and recreation.

Licensure/Reciprocity: Virginia. Students seeking teaching certification in a state other than Virginia should consult with that state's teacher certification office early in their program of study to insure compliance with requirements. Many state directors of teacher credentialing have signed Interstate Agreements through NASDTEC that expedite the certification process.

RADFORD UNIVERSITY

College of Education and Human Development
Teacher Education Programs
Norwood Street
P.O. Box 6960, RU Station
Radford, Virginia 24142
Phone: (540) 831-5439
Fax: (540) 831-6053
E-mail: ruadmiss@radford.edu
Internet: http://www.radford.edu

Institution Description: Radford University is a coeducational comprehensive public university. It was established as State Normal and Industrial School for Women at Radford in 1910.

The Teacher Education Programs feature field-based experiences. Undergraduate and graduate programs lead to teacher certification and professional development.

Institution Control: Public.

Calendar: Semester. Academic year August to May.

Official(s): Dr. Paul Sale, Dean.

Faculty: Full-time 44; adjunct 60.

Degrees Awarded: 48 baccalaureate; 183 master's.

Admission Requirements: *Undergraduate:* Graduation from an approved secondary school or GED; College Board SAT or ACT composite. *Teacher education specific:* Overall 2.5 GPA; involvement in extracurricular and community studies; completion of 52 hours of coursework; PRAXIS I test scores (reading, writing, mathematics); faculty interview; personal goal statement. PRAXIS II prior to certification. *Graduate:* Baccalaureate from a regionally accredited institution. *Teacher education specific:* 2.5 0 GPA; GRE or Miller Analogies scores; completion of all required departmental exams; recommendations; faculty interview.

Fees and Expenses: Undergraduate: $2,070 in-state per semester; $5,601 out-of-state. Graduate: $2,581 in-state per semester; $4,765 out-of-state. On-campus room and board: $2,793 per semester. Books and supplies: $800.

Financial Aid: Resources specifically for eligible students enrolled in teacher education programs are awarded on the basis of financial need and academic merit. The institution has a Program Participation Agreement with the U.S. Department of Education for eligible students to receive Pell Grants and other federal aid. Teacher scholarships available to qualifying students. *Contact:* Barbara Porter, Financial Aid Director at: (540) 831-5408 or e-mail at: bporter@radford.edu.

Accreditation: *Regional:* SACS. *Professional:* NCATE. *Member of:* AACTE. *Approved by:* Virginia State Department of Education.

Undergraduate Programs: Teacher education programs include: early and middle education (early childhood/early childhood special education, elementary education, middle education); K-12 education (art, music, physical and health education, special education); secondary education (biology, chemistry, earth science, English, mathematics, social studies/history). Add-on endorsements are available in computer science, driver education, mathematics-algebra I, physics.

Graduate Programs: Advanced preparation programs for school personnel are offered in: communications sciences and disorders; curriculum and instruction; educational leadership; reading specialist; school counselor; school psychologist; special education (learning disabilities, mental retardation, deaf and hard of hearing, severe and profound, high incidence disabilities). Each program has specific goals and coursework requirements.

Licensure/Reciprocity: Virginia. Students seeking teaching certification in a state other than Virginia should consult with that state's teacher certification office early in their program of study to insure compliance with requirements. Many state directors of teacher credentialing have signed Interstate Agreements through NASDTEC that expedite the certification process.

REGENT UNIVERSITY

School of Education
1000 Regent Drive
Virginia Beach, Virginia 23464
Phone: (757) 236-4479
Fax: (757) 226-4147
E-mail: alanarr@regent.edu
Internet: http://www.regent.edu

Institution Description: Regent University is a private, graduate-level institution, evangelical Christian in nature, but nondenominational. It was founded in 1977.

The School of Education does not accept first-time undergraduate-level students. Only master's and doctoral programs are offered.

Institution Control: Private.

Calendar: Quarter. Academic year September to May.

Official(s): Dr. Alan A. Arroyo, Dean.

Faculty: Full-time 21.

Degrees Awarded: 181 master's; 2 doctorate.

Admission Requirements: *Graduate:* Baccalaureate from a regionally accredited institution. *Teacher education specific:* Two recommendations; writing sample; GRE scores (verbal, quantitative, and analytical writing); faculty interview.

Fees and Expenses: Contact the institution for current tuition/fees/housing costs.

Financial Aid: Resources specifically for eligible students enrolled in teacher education programs are awarded on the basis of financial need and academic merit. The institution has a Program Participation Agreement with the U.S. Department of Education for eligible students to receive Pell Grants and other federal aid. Teacher scholarships available to qualifying students. *Contact:* Financial Aid Office at: (757) 226-4125.

Accreditation: *Regional:* SACS. *Member of:* AACTE. *Approved by:* Virginia State Department of Education.

Graduate Programs: Master of Education programs include: Christian school; cross-categorical special education; educational leadership; elementary education; individualized degree plan; joint degree; Master Teacher; teaching English to speakers of other languages. Each program has specific goals and course requirements.

The Doctor of Education program requires a minimum of 60 credit hours beyond the master's degree. Each student will designate a cognate from one of seven concentration areas: K-12 school leadership, higher education administration, staff development/adult education, educational psychology, special education, distance education, or Christian education leadership. The doctoral program may be completed in a minimum of three years.

Licensure/Reciprocity: Virginia. Students seeking teaching certification in a state other than Virginia should consult with that state's teacher certification office early in their program of study to insure compliance with requirements. Many state directors of teacher credentialing have signed Interstate Agreements through NASDTEC that expedite the certification process.

SAINT PAUL'S COLLEGE

Teacher Education Programs
115 College Drive
Lawrenceville, Virginia 23868
Phone: (804) 848-3111
E-mail: admissions@saintpauls.edu
Internet: http://www.saintpauls.edu

Institution Description: Saint Paul's College is a private college affiliated with the Protestant Episcopal Church in the United States of America. The college was founded in 1888.

Teacher Education Programs offer coursework to prepare students for teaching careers at the elementary and secondary levels.

Institution Control: Private.

Calendar: Semester. Academic year August to May.

Official(s): Dr. Claudine Coppex, Chair.

Faculty: Full-time 5; part-time 4.

Degrees Awarded: 4 baccalaureate.

Admission Requirements: *Undergraduate:* Graduation with 16 academic units from an approved secondary school or GED; College Board SAT. *Teacher education specific:* Overall 2.5 GPA; admission at the end of 60 hours of coursework; PRAXIS I test scores (reading, writing, mathematics); faculty interview; personal goal statement. PRAXIS II prior to certification.

Fees and Expenses: $9,158 per academic year. On-campus room and board: $5,188. Other expenses: $2,100. Books and supplies: $1,400.

Financial Aid: Resources specifically for eligible students enrolled in teacher education programs are awarded on the basis of financial need and academic merit. The institution has a Program Participation Agreement with the U.S. Department of Education for eligible students to receive Pell Grants and other federal aid. Teacher scholarships available to qualifying students. *Contact:* Financial Aid Office at: (434) 848-6496.

Accreditation: *Regional:* SACS. *Member of:* AACTE. *Approved by:* Virginia State Department of Education.

Undergraduate Programs: Teacher Education Programs are offered in: biology secondary education, business education, English with an endorsement in secondary education; English secondary education, history and social science with an endorsement in secondary education, mathematics secondary education, special education, general studies with an endorsement in preK-6 education, general studies with an endorsement in preK-12 special education. The Bachelor of Arts or Bachelor of Science degrees require the completion of the general education core, professional studies, content area, field experiences, and student teaching. A minimum of 120 semester hours is required for graduation.

Licensure/Reciprocity: Virginia. Students seeking teaching certification in a state other than Virginia should consult with that state's teacher certification office early in their program of study to insure compliance with requirements. Many state directors of teacher credentialing have signed Interstate Agreements through NASDTEC that expedite the certification process.

UNIVERSITY OF VIRGINIA

Curry School of Education
Teacher Education
405 Emmet Street South
Charlottesville, Virginia 22904-4272
Phone: (434) 924-0748
Fax: (434) 924-1375
E-mail: sbc7v@virginia.edu
Internet: http://www.virginia.edu

Institution Description: The University of Virginia is a state institution. The university was established and chartered under sponsorship of Thomas Jefferson in 1819.

The Curry School of Education offers professional programs designed to prepare individuals for a variety of careers related to the practice of education. The school was named for Dr. Jabez L.M. Curry, an eminent southern educator.

Institution Control: Public.

Calendar: Semester. Academic year August to May.

Official(s): Dr. David Bveneman, Dean; Dr. Sandra B. Cohen, Director, Teacher Education.

Faculty: Full-time 27; part-time 2.

Degrees Awarded: 24 baccalaureate; 357 master's; 104 doctorate.

Admission Requirements: *Undergraduate:* Graduation from an approved secondary school or GED; College Board SAT or ACT composite. *Teacher education specific:* Overall 2.7 GPA; admission at the end of 60 hours of coursework; PRAXIS I test scores (reading, writing, mathematics); faculty interview; personal goal statement. PRAXIS II prior to certification. *Graduate:* Baccalaureate from a regionally accredited institution. *Teacher*

UNIVERSITY OF VIRGINIA—*cont'd*

education specific: 2.5 0 GPA; GRE score 1000; 2 references; completion of all required departmental exams; professional goal statement; recommendations; faculty interview.

Fees and Expenses: Undergraduate: $4,556 in-state per academic year; $19,766 out-of-state. Graduate: $5,623 in-state per academic year; $18,712 out-of-state. On-campus room and board: $4,000. Books and supplies: $900.

Financial Aid: Resources specifically for eligible students enrolled in teacher education programs are awarded on the basis of financial need and academic merit. Awards and scholarships are competitive. The institution has a Program Participation Agreement with the U.S. Department of Education for eligible students to receive Pell Grants and other federal aid. *Contact:* Joanne McNergancy at: (434) 924-0759 or e-mail at: jmh8j@virginia.edu.

Accreditation: *Regional:* SACS. *Professional:* NCATE. *Member of:* AACTE. *Approved by:* Virginia State Department of Education.

Undergraduate Programs: Students wishing to pursue an academic program leading to teacher licensure are required to complete a five-year curriculum leading to the simultaneous award of both a bachelor's and master's degree. The program, sponsored cooperatively by the College of Arts and Sciences and the Curry School of Education, provides an extensive liberal arts foundation, content area preparation, and professional study in education. The bachelor's degree program provides a comprehensive background in the liberal arts, culminating in a B.A. or B.S. degree. Students complete a full major and are involved in the practical aspects of teaching during each year of the program beginning with their second year. Students are permitted to experience professional study early and continuously throughout a five-year period.

Graduate Programs: The Master of Teaching degree is for individuals who have completed a bachelor's degree and wish to qualify for a teaching license. The program require one and a half to two years of full-time study, including academic coursework in the specialization field and teacher education experiences leading to initial endorsement in one or more specialties.

The Education Specialist degree is a planned 30-credit postmaster's program in which candidates are expected to attain a broad and systematic understanding of professional education. The degree may be pursued in the following areas: administration and supervision, counselor education, curriculum and instruction, higher education, instructional technology, special education.

The Doctor of Education and Doctor of Philosophy degrees are available in the areas of: curriculum instruction, and special education; human services; leadership, foundations, and policy.

Licensure/Reciprocity: Virginia. Students seeking teaching certification in a state other than Virginia should consult with that state's teacher certification office early in their program of study to insure compliance with requirements. Many state directors of teacher credentialing have signed Interstate Agreements through NASDTEC that expedite the certification process.

VIRGINIA COMMONWEALTH UNIVERSITY

School of Education
Division of Teacher Education

Box 892020, VCU
901 West Franklin Street
Richmond, Virginia 23284-2020
Phone: (804) 828-1505
Fax: (804) 828-1326
E-mail: nddavis@vcu.edu
Internet: http://www.vcu.edu

Institution Description: Virginia Commonwealth University is a public institution. It was established in 1968 by merger of The Medical College of Virginia (established 1937) and Richmond Professional Institute (established 1917).

The Division of Teacher Education is committed to the preparation of teachers with particular emphasis placed on all learners from early childhood through secondary education settings.

Institution Control: Public.

Calendar: Semester. Academic year August to May.

Official(s): Dr. William C. Bosher, Jr., Dean.

Faculty: Full-time 49; part-time 6; adjunct 43.

Degrees Awarded: 61 baccalaureate; 216 master's; 14 doctorate.

Admission Requirements: *Undergraduate:* Graduation from an approved secondary school or GED; College Board SAT or ACT composite. *Teacher education specific:* Overall 2.5 GPA; PRAXIS I test scores (reading, writing, mathematics); faculty interview; personal goal statement. PRAXIS II prior to certification. *Graduate:* Baccalaureate from a regionally accredited institution. *Teacher education specific:* 2.8 GPA; GRE or Miller Analogies scores; completion of all required departmental exams; recommendations; faculty interview.

Fees and Expenses: Undergraduate: $3,158 in-state per academic year; $14,286 out-of-state. Graduate: $5,218 in-state per academic year; $14,286 out-of-state. Required fees: $601 undergraduate; $593 graduate. On-campus room and board: $7,440. Books and supplies: $830.

Financial Aid: Resources specifically for eligible students enrolled in teacher education programs are awarded on the basis of financial need and academic merit. The institution has a Program Participation Agreement with the U.S. Department of Education for eligible students to receive Pell Grants and other federal aid. Students in the Master of Teaching programs are eligible for the State Council for Higher Education in Virginia for scholarship support. Other programs are available for teacher education students. *Contact:* Janel Cassara at: (804) 828-6181 or e-mail at: jcassara@vcu.edu.

Accreditation: *Regional:* SACS. *Professional:* NCATE. *Member of:* AACTE. *Approved by:* Virginia State Department of Education.

Undergraduate Programs: The single undergraduate teacher education program offered at Virginia Commonwealth University is in health and physical education. The program prepares students for positions in school settings where state teacher licensure is required. The baccalaureate program requires the completion of 123 credits for graduation.

Graduate Programs: The Master of Teaching programs are for entry-level individuals. Courses and experiences are designed to prepare new teachers with the skills, knowledge and values necessary to be successful classroom practitioners. Each program requires foundations courses as well as courses in curriculum and instructional methodology. Programs range from 33 to 42 credits depending on whether licensure is included. They are offered in elementary/early childhood education, middle school education (6-9), secondary education (6-12), and special education (K-12).

A Post-Baccalaureate Certificate in Teaching Program is designed for students who have earned baccalaureate degrees in fields other than education and who wish to become teachers in one or more grades, kindergarten through 12.

The Master of Education programs include: adult education; educational administration and supervision; counselor education; curriculum and instruction, reading, special education, physical education; recreation, parks, and tourism.

A Doctor of Philosophy in education program is offered with specialized tracks in educational leadership, instructional leadership, research and evaluation, adult education, human resource development, and urban services leadership.

Licensure/Reciprocity: Virginia. Students seeking teaching certification in a state other than Virginia should consult with that state's teacher certification office early in their program of study to insure compliance with requirements. Many state directors of teacher credentialing have signed Interstate Agreements through NASDTEC that expedite the certification process.

VIRGINIA POLYTECHNIC INSTITUTE AND STATE UNIVERSITY

Department of Teaching and Learning

Blacksburg, Virginia 24061-0134
Phone: (540) 231-6000
Fax: (540) 231-9263
E-mail: vtadmiss@vt.edu
Internet: http://www.vt.edu

Institution Description: Virginia Polytechnic Institute and State University is a state institution and land-grant college. It was chartered in 1872.

The Department of Teaching and Learning provides professional education programs for prospective and experienced kindergarten, elementary, middle, secondary, and postsecondary teachers.

Institution Control: Public.

Calendar: Semester. Academic year August to May.

Official(s): Dr. Jerome A. Niles, Chair.

Faculty: Full-time 50; part-time 13.

Degrees Awarded: 54 baccalaureate; 393 master's; 44 doctorate.

Admission Requirements: *Undergraduate:* Graduation from an approved secondary school or GED; College Board SAT or ACT composite. *Teacher education specific:* Overall 2.5 GPA; admission after 57 hours of coursework; PRAXIS I test scores (reading, writing, mathematics); faculty interview; personal goal statement. PRAXIS II prior to certification. *Graduate:* Baccalaureate from a regionally accredited institution. *Teacher education specific:* 3.0 GPA; GRE or Miller Analogies scores; completion of all required departmental exams; recommendations; faculty interview.

Fees and Expenses: Undergraduate: $5,095 in-state per academic year; $15,029 out-of-state. Graduate: Tuition charged per credit hour. On-campus room and board: $4,146. Other expenses: $2,822. Books and supplies: $1,547.

Financial Aid: Resources specifically for eligible students enrolled in teacher education programs are awarded on the basis of financial need and academic merit. The institution has a Program Participation Agreement with the U.S. Department of Education for eligible students to receive Pell Grants and other federal aid. Teacher scholarships available to qualifying students. *Contact:* Financial Aid Office at: (540) 231-5179.

Accreditation: *Regional:* SACS. *Professional:* NCATE. *Member of:* AACTE. *Approved by:* Virginia State Department of Education.

Undergraduate Programs: Baccalaureate programs are offered in the areas of middle and secondary education, health and physical education, and career and technical education. The programs are designed to prepare students to teach in varied educational settings and to provide opportunities for specialization both by content and level of instruction. All students complete at least one semester of supervised field study experience and ten weeks of student teaching.

Elementary school teaching licensure (K-6) is offered in two routes: (1) Master's degree level offered in collaboration with the early childhood education program of the Department of Human Development; (2) for students who hold a bachelor's degree in an academic discipline can be completed in four semesters. Both programs are field-based and involve extensive public school field studies and internships completed in conjunction with academic coursework offered on campus.

Graduate Programs: Graduate study at the master's and doctoral levels is also available from the Department of Teaching and Learning. Programs are in the areas of elementary education, secondary education, health and physical education, special education, technology education, and career and technical education.

Licensure/Reciprocity: Virginia. Students seeking teaching certification in a state other than Virginia should consult with that state's teacher certification office early in their program of study to insure compliance with requirements. Many state directors of teacher credentialing have signed Interstate Agreements through NASDTEC that expedite the certification process.

VIRGINIA STATE UNIVERSITY

School of Liberal Arts and Education
Professional Education Program

One Hayden Street
Petersburg, Virginia 23806
Phone: (804) 524-5000
Fax: (804) 524-6506
E-mail: admissions@vsu.edu
Internet: http://www.vsu.edu

Institution Description: Virginia State University (Virginia College until 1979) is a public institution. It was established in 1882.

The mission of the Professional Education Program is to educate and prepare professional educators at the undergraduate and graduate levels for service in public and private schools.

Institution Control: Public.

Calendar: Semester. Academic year August to May.

Official(s): Dr. Leon Bey, Dean; Dr. Wayne F. Virag, Dean, Graduate Studies.

Faculty: Full-time 22.

Degrees Awarded: 77 baccalaureate; 83 master's.

Admission Requirements: *Undergraduate:* Graduation from an approved secondary school or GED; College Board SAT. *Teacher education specific:* Overall 2.5 GPA; no grade lower that C in major/certification area; PRAXIS I test scores (reading, writing, mathematics); faculty interview; personal goal statement. *Graduate:* Baccalaureate from a regionally accredited institution. 2.50 GPA; GRE or Miller Analogies scores; completion of all required departmental exams; recommendations; faculty interview; PRAXIS II prior to certification.

Fees and Expenses: Undergraduate: $4,350 in-state per academic year; $11,260 out-of-state. Graduate: $113 in-state per semester hour; $420 out-of-state. On-campus room and board: $6,008. Other expenses: $1,172. Books and supplies: $700.

Financial Aid: Resources specifically for eligible students enrolled in teacher education programs are awarded on the basis of financial need and academic merit. The institution has a Program Participation Agreement with the U.S. Department of Education for eligible students to receive Pell Grants and other federal aid. Teacher scholarships available to qualifying students. *Contact:* Financial Aid Office at: (804) 524-5990.

Accreditation: *Regional:* SACS. *Member of:* AACTE. *Approved by:* Virginia State Department of Education.

Undergraduate Programs: The education programs provide students with a strong foundation in the arts and sciences on which to build their skills in teaching. Baccalaureate programs include: agriculture, art, biology, business education, chemistry, elementary education, English, history, home economics education/human ecology, mathematics, music, physical education, physics, special education, and technology education. Program components include general studies, speciality studies, professional studies, scholarly activities, prior knowledge, and experiential background. A minimum of 120 semester hours is required for graduation.

Graduate Programs: Master's degree programs are offered in the areas of: education technology, elementary education, special education, educational administration and supervision, mathematics, vocational and technical education. Each program has specific goals and coursework requirements.

A Doctor of Education degree program is offered in educational administration and supervision.

Licensure/Reciprocity: Virginia. Students seeking teaching certification in a state other than Virginia should consult with that state's teacher certification office early in their program of study to insure compliance with requirements. Many state directors of teacher credentialing have signed Interstate Agreements through NASDTEC that expedite the certification process.

VIRGINIA UNION UNIVERSITY

School of Education and Interdisciplinary Studies

128 Martin E. Gray Hall
1500 North Lombardy Street
Richmond, Virginia 23220-1711
Phone: (804) 257-5600
Fax: (804) 257-5818
E-mail: admissions@vuu.edu
Internet: http://www.vuu.edu

Institution Description: Virginia Union University is a private institution affiliated with the American Baptist Church. It was established and offered first instruction at the postsecondary level in 1865.

The mission of the School of Education and Interdisciplinary Studies is to produce a nationally validated program to develop a community of educators who embrace student learning as their primary commitment.

Institution Control: Private.

Calendar: Semester. Academic year August to May.

Official(s): Dr. Dolores Greene, Chair.

Faculty: Full-time 5; part-time 2.

Degrees Awarded: 8 baccalaureate.

Admission Requirements: *Undergraduate:* Graduation with 16 academic units from an approved secondary school or GED; College Board SAT. *Teacher education specific:* Overall 2.5 GPA; admission by midpoint of sophomore year; no grade lower than C in major/certification area; PRAXIS I test scores (reading, writing, mathematics); faculty interview; personal goal statement.

Fees and Expenses: $10,460 per academic year. On-campus room and board: $5,236. Other expenses: $1,500. Books and supplies: $600.

Financial Aid: Resources specifically for eligible students enrolled in teacher education programs are awarded on the basis of financial need and academic merit. The institution has a Program Participation Agreement with the U.S. Department of Education for eligible students to receive Pell Grants and other federal aid. Teacher scholarships available to qualifying students. *Contact:* Financial Aid Office at: (804) 257-5882.

Accreditation: *Regional:* SACS. *Professional:* NCATE. *Member of:* AACTE. *Approved by:* Virginia State Department of Education.

Undergraduate Programs: Students who receive admission to the program must complete a combined program of study that includes 46 hours of general education courses and 47 hours in an academic discipline for teaching in grades 6-12 or 24 hours in an academic concentration for grades preK-3, preK-6, and exceptional education classrooms and 30 or more in the acquisition of courses and field-based instruction in professional studies for a total of 125 hours. In grades 6-12 or K-12 (secondary education), teacher candidates must declare an academic major in art, English, biology, business, chemistry, history/social science, mathematics, instrumental/vocal choral music, or theatre arts and an association major in teacher education. All baccalaureate programs require a minimum of 124 semester hours for graduation.

Licensure/Reciprocity: Virginia. Students seeking teaching certification in a state other than Virginia should consult with that state's teacher certification office early in their program of study to insure compliance with requirements. Many state directors of teacher credentialing have signed Interstate Agreements through NASDTEC that expedite the certification process.

VIRGINIA WESLEYAN COLLEGE

Education Department

1584 Wesleyan Drive
Norfolk, Virginia 23502-5599
Phone: (757) 455-3200
Fax: (757) 461-5238
E-mail: admissions@vwc.edu
Internet: http://www.vwc.edu

Institution Description: Virginia Wesleyan College is a private college affiliated with the United Methodist Church. The college was established and chartered in 1961.

The Education Department offers undergraduate programs that prepare students for careers in the teaching field.

Institution Control: Private.

Calendar: Semester (4-1-4 plan). Academic year August to May.

Official(s): Dr. Karen A. Bosch, Coordinator.

Faculty: Full-time 4; part-time 6.

Degrees Awarded: 38 baccalaureate.

Admission Requirements: *Undergraduate:* Graduation with 15 academic units from an approved secondary school or GED; College Board SAT. *Teacher education specific:* Overall 2.5 GPA; admission at the end of 60 hours of coursework; PRAXIS I test scores (reading, writing, mathematics); faculty interview; personal goal statement. PRAXIS II prior to certification.

Fees and Expenses: $19,200 per academic year. On-campus room and board: $6,150. Other expenses: $1,800. Books and supplies: $750.

Financial Aid: Resources specifically for eligible students enrolled in teacher education programs are awarded on the basis of financial need and academic merit. The institution has a Program Participation Agreement with the U.S. Department of Education for eligible students to receive Pell Grants and other federal aid. Teacher scholarships available to qualifying students. *Contact:* Financial Aid Office at: (757) 455-3345.

Accreditation: *Regional:* SACS. *Member of:* AACTE. *Approved by:* Virginia State Department of Education.

Undergraduate Programs: The elementary education preK-6 program is designed to provide the student with an endorsement appropriate to teaching in pre-kindergarten classrooms through sixth grade. The preK-6 with add-on middle education (6-8) is designed to provide two endorsements appropriate to teach in the elementary schools and another for the selected content areas in the middle schools. The middle education 6-8 program provides an endorsement appropriate to teaching the selected content areas in the middle schools and in grades 6 through 8.

The secondary education 6-12 program provides an endorsement to teach in the middle and high schools in the selected major from: art (K-12), music education-vocal (K-12), foreign language K-12 (French, German, Spanish), social studies, history, English, journalism, mathematics, science (biology, chemistry, earth science). The K-12 certification program provides endorsements for K-12 in the majors of art, music education-vocal, and Foreign language (French, German, Spanish).

All baccalaureate programs require the completion of the general education core, professional studies, content area, field experiences, and student teaching. A minimum of 120 semester hours is required for graduation.

Licensure/Reciprocity: Virginia. Students seeking teaching certification in a state other than Virginia should consult with that state's teacher certification office early in their program of study to insure compliance with requirements. Many state directors of teacher credentialing have signed Interstate Agreements through NASDTEC that expedite the certification process.

WASHINGTON

CENTRAL WASHINGTON UNIVERSITY
College of Education and Professional Studies
Center for Teaching and Learning
400 East University Way
Ellensburg, Washington 98926-7414
Phone: (509) 963-1461
Fax: (509) 963-1049
E-mail: cwuadmis@cwu.edu
Internet: http://www.cwu.edu

Institution Description: Central Washington University is a state institution. It was established as Washington State Normal School and chartered in 1890.

The Center for Teaching and Learning is the umbrella organization for teacher education programs spread across three colleges.

Institution Control: Public.

Calendar: Quarter. Academic year August to May.

Official(s): Dr. Rebecca Bowers, Dean; Dr. James DePaepe, Director, Center for Teaching and Learning; Dr. David Shorr, Chair, Department of Teaching and Learning.

Faculty: Full-time 27.

Degrees Awarded: 421 baccalaureate; 113 master's.

Admission Requirements: *Undergraduate:* Graduation from an approved secondary school or GED, College Board SAT or ACT composite. *Teacher education specific:* 3.0 GPA; Washington Educators Skills Test-Basic (reading, mathematics, writing); 2 recommendations; character and fitness form; fingerprinting. *Graduate:* Baccalaureate degree from a regionally accredited institution. *Teacher education specific:* Transcripts; statement of objectives; letter of recommendation; GRE; faculty interview.

Fees and Expenses: Undergraduate: $4,023 in-state per academic year; $11,799 out-of-state. Graduate: $5,862 in-state per academic year; $11,799 out-of-state. On-campus room and board: $6,402. Books and supplies: $738.

Financial Aid: Resources specifically for eligible students enrolled in teacher education programs are awarded on the basis of financial need and academic merit. The institution has a Program Participation Agreement with the U.S. Department of Education for eligible students to receive Pell Grants and other federal aid. Teacher scholarships available to qualifying students. *Contact:* Alice Fullerton at: (509) 963-1611 or e-mail at: finaid@cwu.edu.

Accreditation: *Regional:* NASC. *Professional:* NCATE. *Member of:* AACTE. *Approved by:* Washington State Superintendent of Public Instruction-Olympia.

Undergraduate Programs: Undergraduate majors/minors offered by the Department of Teaching and Learning include bilingual education, early childhood education, elementary education, reading, special education, and teaching English as a second language. Programs lead to the baccalaureate degree and require the completion of the general education core, professional studies, content area, field experiences, and student teaching. A minimum of 120 semester hours is required for graduation.

Graduate Programs: The Master of Education program is offered for those individuals who wish to become certified. Over 30 endorsement programs are offered. Other programs are offered in education administration, reading specialist, and supervision and curriculum. Each program has specific goals and coursework requirements.

Licensure/Reciprocity: Washington. Students seeking teaching certification in a state other than Washington should consult with that state's teacher certification office early in their program of study to insure compliance with requirements. Many state directors of teacher credentialing have signed Interstate Agreements through NASDTEC that expedite the certification process.

EASTERN WASHINGTON UNIVERSITY
Department of Education
302 Williamson Hall
526 Fifth Street
Cheney, Washington 99004
Phone: (509) 359-2232
Fax: (509) 359-2899
E-mail: education@ewu.edu
Internet: http://www.ewu.edu

Institution Description: Eastern Washington University (Eastern Washington State College until 1977) is a state institution. It was established as State Normal School at Cheney in 1890. The Department of Education offers undergraduate and graduate programs that prepare students for teaching careers and professional development.

Institution Control: Public.

Calendar: Quarter. Academic year August to May.

Official(s): Dr. Jerry Logan, Dean.

Faculty: Full-time 20; part-time 17; adjunct 3.

Degrees Awarded: 269 baccalaureate; 174 master's.

Admission Requirements: *Undergraduate:* Graduation from an approved secondary school or GED; College Board SAT or ACT composite. *Teacher education specific:* 2.5 GPA on most recent 45 quarter credits; Washington Educators Skills Test-Basic (reading, mathematics, writing); 2 recommendations; computer literacy; evidence of good character and fitness. *Graduate:* Baccalaureate degree from a regionally accredited institution. *Teacher education specific:* Transcripts; statement of objectives; 3 letters of recommendation; GRE; faculty interview.

Fees and Expenses: Undergraduate: $1,194 in-state per academic year; $4,146 out-of-state. Graduate: $1,924 in-state per academic year; $5,695 out-of-state.

Financial Aid: Resources specifically for eligible students enrolled in teacher education programs are awarded on the basis of financial need and academic merit. The institution has a Program Participation Agreement with the U.S. Department of Education for eligible students to receive Pell Grants and other federal aid. Teacher scholarships available to qualifying students. *Contact:* Financial Aid and Scholarship Office at: (800) 280-1256,

Accreditation: *Regional:* NASC. *Professional:* NCATE. *Member of:* AACTE. *Approved by:* Washington State Superintendent of Public Instruction-Olympia.

Undergraduate Programs: The Bachelor of Arts in Education degree can be pursued with concentrations in: art, biology, business education, chemistry, Chicano studies, child development, children's studies, early childhood education, earth sci-

EASTERN WASHINGTON UNIVERSITY—
cont'd

ence, English, English as a second language; French, German, gifted and talented education, health and fitness, history, library media, marketing education, mathematics, natural sciences, physics, psychology, reading, science, social studies, Spanish, special education, theatre. All concentrations require the completion of the general education core, professional studies, field experiences, and student teaching. A minimum of 180 quarter hours is required for graduation.

Graduate Programs: The Master of Education programs include: adult education, continuing teaching or principal certificate; curriculum and instruction, early childhood education, educational leadership; elementary teaching, foundations of education, instructional media and technology; school library media administration, literacy specialists, science education, social science education, supervising (clinic) teaching.

Licensure/Reciprocity: Washington. Students seeking teaching certification in a state other than Washington should consult with that state's teacher certification office early in their program of study to insure compliance with requirements. Many state directors of teacher credentialing have signed Interstate Agreements through NASDTEC

EVERGREEN STATE COLLEGE

Master in Teaching Program
2700 Evergreen Parkway N.W.
Olympia, Washington 98505-0002
Phone: (360) 867-6000
Fax: (360) 867-6170
E-mail: admissions@evergreen.edu
Internet: http://www.evergreen.edu

Institution Description: Evergreen State College is a public institution. It was established in 1967 and offered first instruction at the postsecondary level in 1971.

The Master in Teaching Program is offered with the opportunity to earn endorsements in various content areas.

Institution Control: Public.

Calendar: Quarter. Academic year September to July.

Official(s): Dr. Scott Coleman, Director, Master in Teaching Program.

Faculty: Full-time 11.

Degrees Awarded: 35 master's.

Admission Requirements: *Graduate:* Baccalaureate degree from a regionally accredited institution. *Teacher education specific:* 3.0 GPA; Washington Educators Skills Test-Basic (reading, mathematics, writing) and WEST-E for each endorsement area; transcripts; statement of objectives; letter of recommendation; faculty interview.

Fees and Expenses: Graduate: $4,848 in-state per academic year; $14,7469 out-of-state . On-campus room and board: $5,772. Other expenses: $3,528. Books and supplies: $780.

Financial Aid: Resources specifically for eligible students enrolled in teacher education programs are awarded on the basis of financial need, academic merit. Graduate assistantships and scholarships available to qualified candidates. The institution has a Program Participation Agreement with the U.S. Department of Education for eligible students to receive Pell Grants and other federal aid. *Contact:* Financial Aid Office at: (360) 867-6205.

Accreditation: *Regional:* NASC. *Member of:* AACTE. *Approved by:* Washington State Superintendent of Public Instruction-Olympia.

Graduate Programs: The Master in Teaching program will review and approve up to two endorsements for admission. Students may not choose both an elementary education endorsement and a secondary-level endorsement at the same time. A student who successfully completes the program and meets state-approved endorsement requirements will receive Washington's beginning-level teaching certificate (Residency Certification) in one or two endorsement areas. The areas avail-

able are: early childhood education, elementary education, middle level humanities, middle level math/science, secondary: biology, chemistry, earth science, English/language arts, history, mathematics, physics, science, social studies; All Level: bilingual education, dance, designated world languages (French, German, Japanese, Spanish), English as a second language, theatre arts, visual arts. Each endorsement area has specific goals and coursework requirements.

Licensure/Reciprocity: Washington. Students seeking teaching certification in a state other than Washington should consult with that state's teacher certification office early in their program of study to insure compliance with requirements. Many state directors of teacher credentialing have signed Interstate Agreements through NASDTEC that expedite the certification process.

GONZAGA UNIVERSITY

School of Education
Department of Teacher Education
East 502 Boone Avenue
Spokane, Washington 99258-0001
Phone: (509) 328-4220
Fax: (509) 324-5718
E-mail: admissions@gonzaga.edu
Internet: http://www.gonzaga.edu

Institution Description: Gonzaga University is a private institution sponsored by the Roman Catholic Church (Society of Jesus). It was established as Gonzaga College in 1887.

The School of Education offers undergraduate programs to prepare students for careers in teaching and graduate programs that focus on preparing K-12 educators with a variety of classroom-based experiences and theoretical applications.

Institution Control: Private.

Calendar: Semester. Academic year August to May.

Official(s): Dr. Shirley J. Williams, Dean.

Faculty: Full-time 24; emeriti 4.

Degrees Awarded: 37 baccalaureate; 190 master's.

Admission Requirements: *Undergraduate:* Graduation from an approved secondary school or GED; College Board SAT or ACT composite. *Teacher education specific:* 3.0 GPA; Washington Educators Skills Test-Basic (reading, mathematics, writing); 2 recommendations; character and fitness form; fingerprinting. *Graduate:* Baccalaureate degree from a regionally accredited institution. *Teacher education specific:* Transcripts; statement of objectives; 2 letters of recommendation; 3.0 in last 2 years of undergraduate work; statement of purpose; WEST-B test scores; GRE; faculty interview.

Fees and Expenses: $20,510 per academic year. On-campus room and board: $5,960. Other expenses: $2,750. Books and supplies: $650.

Financial Aid: Resources specifically for eligible students enrolled in teacher education programs are awarded on the basis of financial need and academic merit. The institution has a Program Participation Agreement with the U.S. Department of Education for eligible students to receive Pell Grants and other federal aid. Teacher scholarships available to qualifying students. *Contact:* Financial Aid Office at: (509) 323-6582.

Accreditation: *Regional:* NASC. *Professional:* NCATE. *Member of:* AACTE. *Approved by:* Washington State Superintendent of Public Instruction-Olympia.

Undergraduate Programs: The School of Education offers two undergraduate degrees. The Department of Special Education offers the Bachelor of Education in special education and the Department of Sport and Physical Education offers the Bachelor of Education in sport management and the Bachelor of Education in physical education.

The Department of Teacher Education offers a comprehensive teacher certification program that enables students to obtain initial as well as continuing certification at the elementary or secondary level. Available endorsement areas are early childhood special education; elementary education; secondary: biology, chemistry, physics, English, English/language arts, history, mathematics, science, social studies; all levels: drama, music-general, choral, instrumental, visual arts, designated world languages, English as a second language, health/fitness, reading, special education. All program require the completion of the university core curriculum, School of Education core, field experiences, and student teaching. A minimum of 128 semester hours is required for graduation.

Graduate Programs: The school offers graduate programs at the master's level. Certification for school counselor, principal, and superintendent are also available at the graduate level.

Licensure/Reciprocity: Washington. Students seeking teaching certification in a state other than Washington should consult with that state's teacher certification office early in their program of study to insure compliance with requirements. Many state directors of teacher credentialing have signed Interstate Agreements through NASDTEC that expedite the certification process.

HERITAGE COLLEGE

Division of Education and Psychology

Teacher Education Program

3240 Fort Road
Toppenish, Washington 98948
Phone: (509) 865-8502
Fax: (509) 865-8508
E-mail: petry_l@heritage.edu
Internet: http://www.heritage.edu

Institution Description: Heritage College is a nonprofit, independent, nondenominational institution. It is a transformation of Spokane's Fort Wright College (formerly Holy Names College) that was founded in 1907.

The Teacher Education Program is a performance-based program that prepares students for professional teaching positions.

Institution Control: Private.

Calendar: Semester. Academic year September to May.

Official(s): Dr. Larry Petry, Dean.

Faculty: Full-time 18.

Degrees Awarded: 36 baccalaureate; 217 master's.

Admission Requirements: *Undergraduate:* Graduation from an approved secondary school or GED. *Teacher education specific:* 2.8 GPA; Washington Educators Skills Test-Basic (reading, mathematics, writing); 2 recommendations; character and fitness form. *Graduate:* Baccalaureate degree from a regionally accredited institution. *Teacher education specific:* Transcripts; statement of objectives; letter of recommendation; GRE; faculty interview.

Fees and Expenses: Undergraduate: $6,729. Graduate: Tuition charged per credit hour. On-campus room and board: $6,355. Other expenses: $3,875. Books and supplies: $790.

Financial Aid: Resources specifically for eligible students enrolled in teacher education programs are awarded on the basis of financial need and academic merit. The institution has a Program Participation Agreement with the U.S. Department of Education for eligible students to receive Pell Grants and other federal aid. Teacher scholarships available to qualifying students. *Contact:* Financial Aid Office at: (509) 865-8502.

Accreditation: *Regional:* NASC. *Member of:* AACTE. *Approved by:* Washington State Superintendent of Public Instruction-Olympia.

Undergraduate Programs: The Bachelor of Arts degree is offered in interdisciplinary studies, psychology, secondary teacher grades 4-12 endorsement (English/language arts, mathematics, science). The Bachelor of Arts in Education is offered with a major in elementary education grades K-8 with endorsement options in bilingual education, early childhood, English as a second language, English, Spanish, special education. All programs require the completion of a general education core, professional core, content area, field experiences, and student teaching. A minimum of 126 semester hours must be completed for the degree award.

Graduate Programs: The Master of Education program is designed for teachers, administrators, and other specialists who pursue a degree in their field beyond the master's degree. Specializations offered include: counseling, educational administration, professional development (bilingual education/ESL, biology, reading/literacy, special education).

The Master in Teaching program is designed to provide those who already possess a baccalaureate degree with a master's degree and a residency certification.

Licensure/Reciprocity: Washington. Students seeking teaching certification in a state other than Washington should consult with that state's teacher certification office early in their program of study to insure compliance with requirements. Many state directors of teacher credentialing have signed Interstate Agreements through NASDTEC that expedite the certification process.

NORTHWEST COLLEGE OF THE ASSEMBLIES OF GOD

School of Education

5520 108th Avenue N.E.
P.O. Box 579
Kirkland, Washington 98033
Phone: (425) 822-8266
Fax: (425) 827-0148
E-mail: admissions@ncag.edu
Internet: http://www.ncag.edu

Institution Description: Northwest College of the Assemblies of God is a private institution offering undergraduate programs. The college was established and chartered as Northwest Bible Institute in 1934.

As part of their training, School of Education students observe experienced teachers at local schools.

Institution Control: Private.

Calendar: Semester. Academic year August to May.

Official(s): Dr. Gary Newbill, Dean.

Faculty: Full-time 6; part-time 3.

Degrees Awarded: 33 baccalaureate.

Admission Requirements: *Undergraduate:* Graduation with 16 academic units from an approved secondary school or GED; ACT composite. *Teacher education specific:* Washington Educators Skills Test-Basic (reading, mathematics, writing); 2 recommendations; character and fitness form; faculty interview; personal goal statement.

Fees and Expenses: $13,524 per academic year. On-campus room and board: $6,142. Other expenses: $2,000. Books and supplies: $850.

Financial Aid: Resources specifically for eligible students enrolled in teacher education programs are awarded on the basis of financial need and academic merit. The institution has a Program Participation Agreement with the U.S. Department of Education for eligible students to receive Pell Grants and other federal aid. Teacher scholarships available to qualifying students. *Contact:* Financial Aid Office at: (425) 822-8266.

Accreditation: *Regional:* NASC. *Member of:* AACTE. *Approved by:* Washington State Superintendent of Public Instruction-Olympia.

Undergraduate Programs: Baccalaureate programs are offered in secondary education with endorsements in drama, biology, health and fitness, English, history, mathematics, music (general, instrumental), reading, and social studies. The Bachelor of Arts programs offered in elementary education prepares students to become professional teachers from kindergarten through eighth grade. The program offers study in the liberal arts, Bible and theology, educational foundations, psychology, assessment, learning theory and pedagogy, and instructional methods for the varied subjects required for elementary teaching: reading, mathematics, visual arts, drama, language arts, science, health and fitness, social studies, and music. All programs require the completion of a general education core, pro-

NORTHWEST COLLEGE OF THE
ASSEMBLIES OF GOD—cont'd

fessional studies, content area, field experiences, and student teaching. A minimum of 125 semester hours is required for graduation.

Licensure/Reciprocity: Washington. Students seeking teaching certification in a state other than Washington should consult with that state's teacher certification office early in their program of study to insure compliance with requirements. Many state directors of teacher credentialing have signed Interstate Agreements through NASDTEC that expedite the certification process.

PACIFIC LUTHERAN UNIVERSITY

School of Education

121st and South Park Avenue
Tacoma, Washington 98447-0003
Phone: (253) 535-7272
Fax: (253) 535-5736
E-mail: admission@plu.edu
Internet: http://www.plu.edu

Institution Description: Pacific Lutheran University is a private institution affiliated with the American Lutheran Church. The university was established and chartered in 1890.

The School of Education offers undergraduate and graduate programs of study leading to certification for elementary, secondary, and special education teachers, administrators, reading specialists, and school librarians. The emphasis of all programs is the promotion of student learning in K-12 institutions.

Institution Control: Private.

Calendar: Semester (4-1-4 plan). Academic year September to May.

Official(s): Dr. Beck, Dean.

Faculty: Full-time 16.

Degrees Awarded: 116 baccalaureate; 53 master's.

Admission Requirements: *Undergraduate:* Graduation from an approved secondary school or GED; College Board SAT or ACT composite. *Teacher education specific:* 2.5 GPA; Washington Educators Skills Test-Basic (reading, mathematics, writing); sophomore standing; recommendations; character and fitness form. *Graduate:* Baccalaureate degree from a regionally accredited institution. *Teacher education specific:* Transcripts; statement of objectives; letter of recommendation; GRE; faculty interview.

Fees and Expenses: Undergraduate: $19,610 per academic year. Graduate: $612 per credit hour. On-campus room and board: $6,105. Other expenses: $2,158. Books and supplies: $738.

Financial Aid: Resources specifically for eligible students enrolled in teacher education programs are awarded on the basis of financial need and academic merit. The institution has a Program Participation Agreement with the U.S. Department of Education for eligible students to receive Pell Grants and other federal aid. Teacher scholarships available to qualifying students. *Contact:* Financial Aid Office at: (253) 535-7161.

Accreditation: *Regional:* NASC. *Professional:* NCATE. *Member of:* AACTE. *Approved by:* Washington State Superintendent of Public Instruction-Olympia.

Undergraduate Programs: Baccalaureate programs and teaching endorsements are authorized in the following areas and grade levels: English 4-12, English/language arts 4-12, English as a second language K-12, elementary K-8, health and fitness K-12, history 4-12, mathematics 4-12, music K-12 (choral, general, instrumental), science 4-12 (biology, chemistry, earth science, physics), social studies 4-12, special education K-12, visual arts K-12, world languages K-12 (French, German, Norwegian, Spanish). All baccalaureate programs require the completion of the general education core, professional studies, content area, field experiences, and student teaching. A minimum of 128 semester hours is required for graduation.

Graduate Programs: The Master of Arts in Education in major fields of concentration are designed to provide maximum flexibility in an experience-oriented environment. Graduate concentrations are offered in classroom teaching, residency certification, educational administration, and literacy education. Each program has specific goals and coursework requirements.

Coordinating master's degree with continuing and professional certification program is for students holding an initial or residency certificate and may coordinate the Master of Arts in Education degree with the requirements for Continuing or Professional Certification. Students must take a comprehensive examination over coursework accomplished. An oral examination over coursework and/or research must be scheduled no later than three weeks before commencement.

Licensure/Reciprocity: Washington. Students seeking teaching certification in a state other than Washington should consult with that state's teacher certification office early in their program of study to insure compliance with requirements. Many state directors of teacher credentialing have signed Interstate Agreements through NASDTEC that expedite the certification process.

SAINT MARTIN'S COLLEGE

Education Division

5300 Pacific Avenue S.E.
Lacey, Washington 98503
Phone: (360) 438-4333
Fax: (360) 438-4486
E-mail: education@stmartin.edu
Internet: http://www.stmartin.edu

Institution Description: Saint Martin's College is a private college founded by the monks of the Order of Saint Benedict. The college was established and chartered in 1895.

The Education Division's program insures that all students have knowledge in the liberal arts. During the professional sequence, students gain knowledge and skills essential to effective teaching and participate in varied field experiences in school classrooms.

Institution Control: Private.

Calendar: Semester. Academic year January to December.

Official(s): Dr. Joyce V.S. Westward, Division Dean; Dr. Paul Nelson, Director, Master's Programs.

Faculty: Full-time 12; adjunct 10.

Degrees Awarded: 23 baccalaureate; 28 master's.

Admission Requirements: *Undergraduate:* Graduation from an approved secondary school or GED; College Board SAT or ACT composite. *Teacher education specific:* 3.0 GPA; Washington Educators Skills Test-Basic (reading, mathematics, writing); recommendations; character and fitness form; *Graduate:* Baccalaureate degree from a regionally accredited institution. *Teacher education specific:* Transcripts; Washington Educators Skills Test-Basic; statement of objectives; 3 letters of recommendation; GRE; faculty interview.

Fees and Expenses: Undergraduate: $17,600 per academic year. Graduate: $519 per credit hour. On-campus room and board: $5,355. Books and supplies: $900.

Financial Aid: Resources specifically for eligible students enrolled in teacher education programs are awarded on the basis of financial need and academic merit. The institution has a Program Participation Agreement with the U.S. Department of Education for eligible students to receive Pell Grants and other federal aid. Teacher scholarships available to qualifying students. *Contact:* Amanda Robinson at: (360) 438-4397.

Accreditation: *Regional:* NASC. *Approved by:* Washington State Superintendent of Public Instruction-Olympia.

Undergraduate Programs: Students completing the elementary, secondary, or special education baccalaureate programs are eligible for state certification. Current endorsements are offered in the following fields: biology, chemistry, music, comparative religion, drama, early childhood education, English, French, history, instructional technology, instrumental music, Japanese, music (general), philosophy, physical education, political science, psychology, reading, social studies, sociology, Spanish, and special education. All teacher education programs require preprofessional courses, basic courses, and courses to complete two endorsements. A minimum of 120 semester hours is required for graduation.

Graduate Programs: The Master in Teaching program provides students with an opportunity to simultaneously earn teacher certification and a master's degree. Students choose from certifications in the areas of elementary education, secondary education, and/or special education. The number of semester hours required for the degree varies (79 to 83 credits) with the specific certification chosen.

The Master of Education program provides teachers and future school counselors the opportunity to gain advanced professional skills in the areas of classroom and pedagogical development, technology in education, guidance and counseling, reading literacy, and special education. The program requires 36 to 45 semester hours offered during the summers, evenings, and weekends.

Licensure/Reciprocity: Washington. Students seeking teaching certification in a state other than Washington should consult with that state's teacher certification office early in their program of study to insure compliance with requirements. Many state directors of teacher credentialing have signed Interstate Agreements through NASDTEC that expedite the certification process.

SEATTLE PACIFIC UNIVERSITY

School of Education
3307 3rd Avenue West
Teacher Education
Seattle, Washington 98119-1997
Phone: (206) 281-2000
Fax: (206) 281-2756
E-mail: admissions@spu.edu
Internet: http://www.spu.edu

Institution Description: Seattle Pacific University is a private institution affiliated with the Free Methodist Church of North America.

"The mission of the School of Education is to prepare educators for service and leadership in schools and communities by developing their professional competence and character within a framework of Christian faith and values."

Institution Control: Private.

Calendar: Quarter. Academic year September to May.

Official(s): Dr. William Rowley, Dean; Dr. Frank Kline, Director of Teacher Education.

Faculty: Full-time 25; part-time 2; adjunct 20.

Degrees Awarded: 30 baccalaureate; 93 master's; 12 doctorate.

Admission Requirements: *Undergraduate:* Graduation from an approved secondary school or GED; College Board SAT or ACT composite. *Teacher education specific:* 3.0 GPA; Washington Educators Skills Test-Basic (reading, mathematics, writing); recommendations; character and fitness form; *Graduate:* Baccalaureate degree from a regionally accredited institution. *Teacher education specific:* Transcripts; statement of objectives; passing scores on WEST-B; letter of recommendation; GRE; faculty interview.

Fees and Expenses: Undergraduate: $6,274 per academic year. Graduate: $325 per credit. On-campus room and board: $9,000. Books and supplies: $600.

Financial Aid: Resources specifically for eligible students enrolled in teacher education programs are awarded on the basis of financial need and academic merit. The institution has a Program Participation Agreement with the U.S. Department of Education for eligible students to receive Pell Grants and other federal aid. Teacher scholarships available to qualifying students. *Contact:* Al Blomquist at: (206) 281-2000.

Accreditation: *Regional:* NASC. *Professional:* NCATE. *Member of:* AACTE. *Approved by:* Washington State Superintendent of Public Instruction-Olympia.

Undergraduate Programs: The professional program leading to a Residency Teaching Certificate consists of three parts (in addition to the requirements for the bachelor's degree): (1) Founda-

tions Units that provide an overview of theory, pedagogy, and educational issues with limited field experiences; (2)Methods and Skills Courses that provide content breadth and depth for preparation to teach; (3)Applications Unit that provides in-depth training in methods courses along with field experiences culminating in a full-time internship.

Graduate Programs: The Master of Arts in Teaching degree integrates secondary teaching certification within a master's program. It is a special package of graduate courses that provide 4-12 secondary subject area certification. This initial certification program prepares fully qualified participants to begin teaching upon successful completion of 49 quarter credits. The five parts of the program are the Foundations Element, Application Element, Site Experiences Element, Orientation Element, and the Master's Degree Element.

Licensure/Reciprocity: Washington. Students seeking teaching certification in a state other than Washington should consult with that state's teacher certification office early in their program of study to insure compliance with requirements. Many state directors of teacher credentialing have signed Interstate Agreements through NASDTEC that expedite the certification process.

SEATTLE UNIVERSITY

School of Education
Master in Teaching Program
900 Broadway
Seattle, Washington 98122-4340
Phone: (206) 296-5759
Fax: (206) 296-2053
E-mail: bylej@seattleu.edu
Internet: http://www.seattleu.edu

Institution Description: Seattle University is a private institution affiliated with the Society of Jesus, Roman Catholic Church. The institution was established as the School of the Immaculate Conception in 1891.

The Master in Teaching is a full-time program that enables students to earn both their master in teaching degree and their teaching certification within four academic quarters of study.

Institution Control: Private.

Calendar: Quarter. Academic year September to June.

Official(s): Dr. Sue Schmitt, Dean.

Faculty: Full-time 8; part-time 2; adjunct 5.

Degrees Awarded: 173 master's; 10 doctorate.

Admission Requirements: *Graduate:* Baccalaureate degree from a regionally accredited institution. *Teacher education specific:* Washington Educators Skills Test-Basic (reading, mathematics, writing); 3.0 GPA; biographical essay; recommendations; character and fitness form; writing sample; statement of objectives; 2 recommendations; faculty interview.

Fees and Expenses: Contact the institution for current tuition/fees/housing costs.

Financial Aid: Resources specifically for eligible students enrolled in teacher education programs are awarded on the basis of financial need and academic merit. The institution has a Program Participation Agreement with the U.S. Department of Education for eligible students to receive Pell Grants and other federal aid. Teacher scholarships available to qualifying students. *Contact:* Michael Duncan at: (206) 296-5847 or e-mail at: med@seattleu.edu.

Accreditation: *Regional:* NASC. *Professional:* NCATE. *Member of:* AACTE. *Approved by:* Washington State Superintendent of Public Instruction-Olympia.

Graduate Programs: The Master in Teaching Program curriculum includes comprehensive educational theory and research following the themes of individualization, ethical responsibility, and the use of technology as an essential educational tool. Internships in community service programs put pre-service teachers in touch with the world as it is lived by their students. Successful completion of the program will enable the student to become a certified teacher in Washington state. The elementary education (K-8) candidate must have completed an undergrad-

SEATTLE UNIVERSITY—*cont'd*

uate degree with a strong liberal arts foundation, including courses in language arts, sciences, mathematics, social sciences, and the arts. The secondary certification (5-12) candidate must have completed an undergraduate or graduate degree with endorsement in: art, drama, visual art, general music, choral music, instrumental music, English, English/language arts, English as a second language, health/fitness, history, social studies, mathematics, general science, biology, chemistry, earth science, physics, world languages (Chinese, French, German, Japanese, Spanish).

Licensure/Reciprocity: Washington. Students seeking teaching certification in a state other than Washington should consult with that state's teacher certification office early in their program of study to insure compliance with requirements. Many state directors of teacher credentialing have signed Interstate Agreements through NASDTEC that expedite the certification process.

UNIVERSITY OF PUGET SOUND

School of Education

1500 North Warner Street
Tacoma, Washington 98416
Phone: (253) 879-3100
Fax: (253) 879-3500
E-mail: admission@ups.edu
Internet: http://www.ups.edu

Institution Description: University of Puget Sound is a private, independent, nonprofit institution. It was established as Puget Sound University by the Puget Sound Conference of the Methodist Episcopal Church (now United Methodist) in 1888.

The School of Education engages in the preparation and continuing development of competent professionals in education.

Institution Control: Private.

Calendar: Semester. Academic year August to May.

Official(s): Dr. Carol Merz, Dean.

Faculty: Full-time 15.

Degrees Awarded: 5 baccalaureate; 75 master's.

Admission Requirements: *Undergraduate:* Graduation from an approved secondary school or GED; College Board SAT or ACT composite. *Teacher education specific:* 3.0 GPA; Washington Educators Skills Test-Basic (reading, mathematics, writing); recommendations; character and fitness form; fingerprinting. *Graduate:* Baccalaureate degree from a regionally accredited institution. *Teacher education specific:* Transcripts; statement of objectives; WEST-B; letter of recommendation; GRE; faculty interview.

Fees and Expenses: Undergraduate: $25,190 per academic year. Graduate: $16,920 per academic year. On-campus room and board: $6,400. Other expenses: $2,300. Books and supplies: $1,000.

Financial Aid: Resources specifically for eligible students enrolled in teacher education programs are awarded on the basis of financial need and academic merit. The institution has a Program Participation Agreement with the U.S. Department of Education for eligible students to receive Pell Grants and other federal aid. Teacher scholarships available to qualifying students. *Contact:* Financial Aid Office at: (253) 879-3214.

Accreditation: *Regional:* NASC. *Professional:* NCATE. *Member of:* AACTE. *Approved by:* Washington State Superintendent of Public Instruction-Olympia.

Undergraduate Programs: The School of Education offers undergraduate students at the university guidance and instruction leading to careers in elementary and secondary school teaching, including the selection of majors and minors to meet special interests, and offers professional courses that prepare the student for admission to the Master of Arts in Teaching Program.

Graduate Programs: The Master of Arts in Teaching Program is for students who hold baccalaureate degrees in the arts or sciences. Student completing the program will meet all require-

ments for Washington state teacher certification and the academic requirements for continuing certification in the state of Washington.

The Master of Education degree offers three emphases: educational administration, counseling (school counseling, pastoral counseling, agency counseling), and learning, teaching, leadership. The programs of graduate study are administered by the director of graduate study.

Licensure/Reciprocity: Washington. Students seeking teaching certification in a state other than Washington should consult with that state's teacher certification office early in their program of study to insure compliance with requirements. Many state directors of teacher credentialing have signed Interstate Agreements through NASDTEC that expedite the certification process.

UNIVERSITY OF WASHINGTON

College of Education
Teacher Education Program

206 Miller Hall
Box 353600
Seattle, Washington 98195-3600
Phone: (206) 543-7834
Fax: (206) 221-3296
E-mail: edinfo@u.washington.edu
Internet: http://www.u.washington.edu

Institution Description: The University of Washington is a state institution and sea-grant college. It was established as Territorial University of Washington in 1861.

The College of Education awards graduate degrees only. The Teacher Education Program is a Master in Teaching degree program for elementary or secondary (specific subject) school teaching.

Institution Control: Public.

Calendar: Quarter. Academic year September to June.

Official(s): Dr. Patricia Wasley, Dean.

Faculty: Full-time 56.

Degrees Awarded: 228 master's; 37 doctorate.

Admission Requirements: *Graduate:* Baccalaureate degree from a regionally accredited institution. *Teacher education specific:* Transcripts; Washington Educators Skills Test-Basic (reading, mathematics, writing); statement of objectives; letter of recommendation; faculty interview.

Fees and Expenses: Graduate: $5,539 in-state per academic year; $14,376 out-of-state. Required fees: $390.

Financial Aid: Resources specifically for eligible students enrolled in teacher education programs are awarded on the basis of financial need and academic merit. The institution has a Program Participation Agreement with the U.S. Department of Education for eligible students to receive Pell Grants and other federal aid. Teacher scholarships available to qualifying students. *Contact:* Financial Aid Office at: (206) 543-6101.

Accreditation: *Regional:* NASC. *Professional:* NCATE. *Member of:* AACTE. *Approved by:* Washington State Superintendent of Public Instruction-Olympia.

Graduate Programs: The Master of Education degree provides intermediate-level graduate training that enhances professional knowledge and prepares students for future graduate study. The Master in Teaching degree program results in a Residency Teaching Certificate for elementary or secondary (specific subject) school teaching. The program is an integrated sequence of full-time day coursework and field experiences spanning five quarters. One quarter is a full-time placement in a school. Field experiences are in schools in the Seattle and Puget Sound area, chosen to provide a variety of situations in regard to level, school population, and location.

The Doctor of Philosophy and Doctor of Education degrees are offered by the College of Education. The Ph.D. prepares students for careers of research and teaching at the college level. Students interested in advanced professional practice directed mainly toward the application and transmission of existing knowledge usually select the Ed.D.

Licensure/Reciprocity: Washington. Students seeking teaching certification in a state other than Washington should consult with that state's teacher certification office early in their program of study to insure compliance with requirements. Many state directors of teacher credentialing have signed Interstate Agreements through NASDTEC that expedite the certification process.

WASHINGTON STATE UNIVERSITY
College of Education
Department of Teaching and Learning
Cleveland Hall
2580 N.E. Grimes Way
Pullman, Washington 99164-2114
Phone: (509) 335-1738
Fax: (509) 335-9172
E-mail: education@wsu.edu
Internet: http://www.wsu.edu

Institution Description: Washington State University is a public institution and a land grant college. It was established and chartered as Washington State Agricultural College and School of Science in 1890.

The Department of Teaching and Learning prepares teachers and other specialists for schools and colleges. The mission of the department is to prepare effective practitioners and scholars who possess the leadership and problem-solving skills necessary to meet the needs of society.

Institution Control: Public.

Calendar: Semester. Academic year August to May.

Official(s): Dr. Judy N. Mitchell, Dean, College of Education, Dr. Edwin Helmstetter, Chair, Department of Teaching and Learning.

Faculty: Full-time 31; part-time 6; adjunct 55.

Degrees Awarded: 268 baccalaureate; 220 master's; 21 doctorate.

Admission Requirements: *Undergraduate:* Graduation from an approved secondary school or GED; College Board SAT or ACT composite. *Teacher education specific:* Washington Educators Skills Test-Basic (reading, mathematics, writing); personal statement; meet minimum requirements in composition, public speaking, science, and mathematics; character and fitness form; interview;; 80 hours of work with children. *Graduate:* Baccalaureate degree from a regionally accredited institution. *Teacher education specific:* Transcripts; WEST-B; statement of objectives; letter of recommendation; faculty interview.

Fees and Expenses: Undergraduate: $4,836 in-state per academic year; $12,938 out-of-state. Graduate: $6,278 in-state per academic year; $15,514 out-of-state. On-campus room and board: $5,250. Other expenses: $3,260. Books and supplies: $950.

Financial Aid: Resources specifically for eligible students enrolled in teacher education programs are awarded on the basis of financial need and academic merit. The institution has a Program Participation Agreement with the U.S. Department of Education for eligible students to receive Pell Grants and other federal aid. Teacher scholarships available to qualifying students. *Contact:* Financial Aid Office at: (509) 335-1738 or e-mail at: education@wsu.edu.

Accreditation: *Regional:* NASC. *Professional:* NCATE. *Member of:* AACTE. *Approved by:* Washington State Superintendent of Public Instruction-Olympia.

Undergraduate Programs: The College of Education prepares individuals to teach elementary education, early childhood education, and various single subjects. To prepare in early childhood education, the candidate must satisfy the degree requirements of the Department of Teaching and Learning; to prepare in early childhood education, the candidate must satisfy the requirements of the Department of Human Development. To prepare in a single subject, the candidate must complete the baccalaureate degree/teaching option offered through the subject matter department or in general studies. Single subject endorsement preparation is available in agriculture, biology, chemistry, earth science, English language arts, world languages (French, German, Russian, Spanish), health and fitness, history, family and consumer sciences education, mathematics, music, physics, science, and social studies.

All baccalaureate programs require completion of the general education core, professional studies, content area, field experiences, and student teaching. A minimum of 120 semester hours is required for graduation.

Graduate Programs: The Master in Teaching program emphasizes preparation of teachers to work in multicultural settings. It leads to elementary certification and a master's degree. The Master of Education with secondary certification candidates may choose post-baccalaureate teacher certification only or a master's degree with certification in the areas of biology, English, language arts, history, or social studies. It is a cohort-based program.

The Doctor of Philosophy and Doctor of Education degrees are offered by the College of Education. The Ph.D. prepares students for careers of research and teaching at the college level. The Doctor of Education degree is in advanced professional practice directed mainly toward the application and transmission of existing knowledge.

Licensure/Reciprocity: Washington. Students seeking teaching certification in a state other than Washington should consult with that state's teacher certification office early in their program of study to insure compliance with requirements. Many state directors of teacher credentialing have signed Interstate Agreements through NASDTEC that expedite the certification process.

WESTERN WASHINGTON UNIVERSITY
Woodring College of Education
Teacher Education Division
516 High Street
Bellingham, Washington 98225
Phone: (360) 650-3327
Fax: (360) 650-7516
E-mail: admit@wwu.edu
Internet: http://www.wwu.edu

Institution Description: Western Washington University (Western Washington State College until 1977) is a public institution. It was established as New Whatcom State Normal School in 1893.

The Teacher Education Division offers undergraduate preparation for teaching careers and graduate programs for professional development.

Institution Control: Public.

Calendar: Quarter. Academic year September to June.

Official(s): Dr. Stephanie Salzman, Dean; Dr. Ray Wolpow, Secondary Education Department Chair; Dr. Michael Nenniger, Elementary Education Chair.

Faculty: Not reported.

Degrees Awarded: 122 baccalaureate; 177 master's.

Admission Requirements: *Undergraduate:* Graduation from an approved secondary school or GED; College Board SAT or ACT composite. *Teacher education specific:* 2.75 GPA; completion of at least 75 quarter hour credits; Washington Educators Skills Test-Basic (reading, mathematics, writing); 3 recommendations; character and fitness form. *Graduate:* Baccalaureate degree from a regionally accredited institution. *Teacher education specific:* Transcripts; statement of objectives; letter of recommendation; GRE; faculty interview.

Fees and Expenses: Undergraduate: $4,182 in-state per academic year; $12,954 out-of-state. Graduate: Tuition charged per credit hour. On-campus room and board: $5,945. Other expenses: $3,225. Books and supplies: $765.

Financial Aid: Resources specifically for eligible students enrolled in teacher education programs are awarded on the basis of financial need and academic merit. The institution has a Program Participation Agreement with the U.S. Department of Education for eligible students to receive Pell Grants and other federal aid. Teacher scholarships available to qualifying students. *Contact:* Financial Aid Office at: (360) 650-3470.

WESTERN WASHINGTON UNIVERSITY—
cont'd

Accreditation: *Regional:* NASC. *Professional:* NCATE. *Member of:* AACTE. *Approved by:* Washington State Superintendent of Public Instruction-Olympia.

Undergraduate Programs: The elementary education program leads to a recommendation for a teaching certificate with a K-8 endorsement. The program requires completion of the professional education course sequence, a major in an approved area, and one-quarter internship. Approved majors include: anthropology, biology, chemistry, earth science, economics, English, English/language arts, general science, geography, history, mathematics, physics, political science, sociology, technology.

The secondary education program is a sequenced professional program that leads to Residency Teacher Certification. Endorsement areas include: anthropology, biology, chemistry, earth science, economics, English, English/language arts, general science, geography, history, mathematics, physics, political science, sociology, technology.

All baccalaureate programs require the completion of a general education core, professional studies, content area, field experiences, and student teaching. A minimum of 180 quarter hours is required for graduation.

Graduate Programs: The Master in Teaching degree program combines the endorsement major with a graduate-level program of certification coursework to produce a program firmly backed by current research on effective teaching and conceptual framework. Approved majors include: anthropology, biology, chemistry, earth science, economics, English, English/language arts, general science, geography, history, mathematics, physics, political science, sociology, technology. All-level (P-12) majors include health/fitness, music, special education, theater, visual arts, world languages.

Licensure/Reciprocity: Washington. Students seeking teaching certification in a state other than Washington should consult with that state's teacher certification office early in their program of study to insure compliance with requirements. Many state directors of teacher credentialing have signed Interstate Agreements through NASDTEC that expedite the certification process.

WHITWORTH COLLEGE

School of Education
Department of Teacher Education
300 West Hawthorne Road
Spokane, Washington 99251-0002
Phone: (509) 777-4411
Fax: (509) 777-3785
E-mail: dsterner@whitworth.edu
Internet: http://www.whitworth.edu

Institution Description: Whitworth College is a private college affiliated with the Presbyterian Church (U.S.A.). The college was founded in 1890.

The Department of Education views the role of the teacher as a commitment to understanding and responding to the needs of children and youth.

Institution Control: Private.

Calendar: Semester (4-1-4 plan). Academic year September to May.

Official(s): Dr. Dennis Sterner, Dean.

Faculty: Full-time 16; part-time 5; adjunct 30.

Degrees Awarded: 58 baccalaureate; 80 master's.

Admission Requirements: *Undergraduate:* Graduation from an approved secondary school or GED; College Board SAT or ACT composite. *Teacher education specific:* 3.0 GPA; Washington Educators Skills Test-Basic (reading, mathematics, writing); recommendations; character and fitness form. *Graduate:* Baccalaureate degree from a regionally accredited institution. *Teacher education specific:* Transcripts; statement of objectives; letter of recommendation; WEST-B for Master in Teaching program; faculty interview.

Fees and Expenses: Undergraduate: $19,800 per academic year. Graduate: $20,000. Required fees: $260. On-campus room and board: $6,350. Books and supplies: $400.

Financial Aid: Resources specifically for eligible students enrolled in teacher education programs are awarded on the basis of financial need and academic merit. Minority scholarships available. The institution has a Program Participation Agreement with the U.S. Department of Education for eligible students to receive Pell Grants and other federal aid. *Contact:* Traci Stensland at: (509) 777-4335 or e-mail at: finaid@whitworth.edu.

Accreditation: *Regional:* NASC. *Professional:* NCATE. *Member of:* AACTE. *Approved by:* Washington State Superintendent of Public Instruction-Olympia.

Undergraduate Programs: The undergraduate teacher education program places the teacher at the intersection of five domains: subject matter, educational contents, children and youth, curriculum/instruction/assessment, and the candidate's personal worldview. Courses in the program are structured around this framework. Programs offered include: elementary K-8 certification, secondary education. speech-education minor, English as a second language as a supporting endorsement; reading as a supporting endorsement. All baccalaureate programs require a professional preliminary program, an upper division professional program, content in the teaching area, senior seminars, and student teaching. A minimum of 130 credit hours is required for graduation.

Graduate Programs: The Master in Teaching Program allows students to pursue a master's degree and teacher certification concurrently. The program is an intensive, selective, and full-time day school of 15 months duration. Both elementary and secondary certification options are available.

A Post-Baccalaureate Certification program can be developed for persons who already possess an undergraduate degree. The program is offered for full-time, part-time day or evening students. Student teaching must be done full-time during the day as must field experiences for some courses.

The Center for Gifted Education and Teacher Enrichment provides credit classes, workshops, and consulting services to teachers and parents of the gifted. A master's degree with a gifted and talented emphasis is designed to educate teachers of all grade levels in meeting the needs of the exceptionally able learner in the regular classroom and/or other settings.

Licensure/Reciprocity: Washington. Students seeking teaching certification in a state other than Washington should consult with that state's teacher certification office early in their program of study to insure compliance with requirements. Many state directors of teacher credentialing have signed Interstate Agreements through NASDTEC that expedite the certification process.

WEST VIRGINIA

ALDERSON-BROADDUS COLLEGE

Division of Education and Special Programs

College Hill
Philippi, West Virginia 26416
Phone: (304) 457-1700
Fax: (304) 457-6239
E-mail: admissions@ab.edu
Internet: http://www.ab.edu

Institution Description: Alderson-Broaddus College is a private institution affiliated with the American Baptist Churches, U.S.A. The college was established in in Virginia as Winchester Female Institute in 1871 and relocated to Philippi, West Virginia in 1909. In 1932, it merged with Alderson Junior College and the present name was adopted.

The Division of Education offers baccalaureate programs leading to teacher certification.

Institution Control: Private.

Calendar: Semester. Academic year August to May.

Official(s): Dr. Dally Digman, Chair.

Faculty: Full-time 3; part-time 7.

Degrees Awarded: 14 baccalaureate.

Admission Requirements: *Undergraduate:* Graduation from secondary school with 15 academic units or GED; College Board SAT or ACT composite. *Teacher education specific:* 2.5 GPA; passing scores on PRAXIS I (mathematics, reading, writing); completion of all required departmental exams; personal goal statement; faculty interview.

Fees and Expenses: $16,156 per academic year. On-campus room and board: $5,300. Other expenses: $2,320. Books and supplies: $900.

Financial Aid: Resources specifically for eligible students enrolled in teacher education programs are awarded on the basis of financial need and academic merit. The institution has a Program Participation Agreement with the U.S. Department of Education for eligible students to receive Pell Grants and other federal aid. Teacher scholarships available to qualifying students. *Contact:* Financial Aid Office at: (304) 457-1700.

Accreditation: *Regional:* NCA. *Professional:* NCATE. *Member of:* AACTE. *Approved by:* West Virginia Department of Education.

Undergraduate Programs: The Department of Education and Special Programs offers baccalaureate degrees in the following areas: elementary education, special education/elementary education, secondary education, recreation and leadership, recreation leadership/theoretical recreation option. A Bachelor of Science degree program is also available in physical education. All programs required the completion of a general education core, professional studies, content area, field experiences, and student teaching. A minimum of 128 semester hours is required for graduation.

Licensure/Reciprocity: West Virginia. Students seeking teaching certification in a state other than West Virginia should consult with that state's teacher certification office early in their program of study to insure compliance with requirements. Many state directors of teacher credentialing have signed Interstate Agreements through NASDTEC that expedite the certification process.

BETHANY COLLEGE

Department of Professional Studies
Teacher Preparation Program

Steinman Hall
Bethany, West Virginia 26032
Phone: (304) 829-7182
Fax: (304) 829-7192
E-mail: jdunbar@.bethanywv.edu
Internet: http://www.bethanywv.edu

Institution Description: Bethany College is a private institution affiliated with the Christian Church (Disciples of Christ). It was founded in 1844.

The major goal of the Department of Professional Studies is to provide students with a general and specialized body of knowledge that can be used to benefit society and enrich the mission of Bethany College.

Institution Control: Private.

Calendar: Semester. Academic year August to May.

Official(s): Dr. Jeffrey Dunbar, Chair.

Faculty: Full-time 5; adjunct 5.

Degrees Awarded: 16 baccalaureate.

Admission Requirements: *Undergraduate:* Graduation from an approved secondary school or GED; College Board SAT score of 900, ACT composite score of 18. *Teacher education specific:* Passing scores on PRAXIS I (reading, mathematics, writing); 2.5 GPA required; faculty recommendations and interview.

Fees and Expenses: $12,720 per academic year. On-campus room and board: $6,350. Required fees: $775. Books and supplies: $700.

Financial Aid: Resources specifically for eligible students enrolled in teacher education programs are awarded on the basis of financial need and academic merit. The institution has a Program Participation Agreement with the U.S. Department of Education for eligible students to receive Pell Grants and other federal aid. Teacher scholarships available to qualifying students. *Contact:* Jeffrey DeRubbo at: (304) 829-7840 or e-mail at: jderubbo@bethanywv.edu.

Accreditation: *Regional:* NCA. *Professional:* NCATE. *Member of:* AACTE. *Approved by:* West Virginia Department of Education.

Undergraduate Programs: The Teacher Preparation Program provides students with a liberal arts background, content preparation, and educational principles to prepare for careers in teaching at the elementary, middle and secondary school levels. Students can choose content specializations in art, biology, chemistry, English, French, general science, German, language arts, mathematics, physical education, physics, social studies, and Spanish. Students completing a major in elementary education can minor in special education. All bachelor degree programs require the completion of a liberal arts core, professional studies, content area, field experiences, and student teaching. A minimum of 128 semester hours is required for graduation.

The major in Education for Non-School Settings (a non-certification program) allows students to prepare for a variety of educational roles in non-school settings such as developing and implementing training programs in business and industry, policy planning for state and federal agencies, and instruction in foundation areas in higher education.

BETHANY COLLEGE—*cont'd*

Licensure/Reciprocity: West Virginia. Students seeking teaching certification in a state other than West Virginia should consult with that state's teacher certification office early in their program of study to insure compliance with requirements. Many state directors of teacher credentialing have signed Interstate Agreements through NASDTEC that expedite the certification process.

BLUEFIELD STATE COLLEGE

School of Professional Studies
Department of Teacher Education

219 Rock Street
Bluefield, West Virginia 24701
Phone: (304) 327-4173
Fax: (304) 327-4106
E-mail: mfarley@bluefieldstate.edu
Internet: http://www.bluefieldstate.edu

Institution Description: Bluefield State College is a public institution that was established in 1865. The present name was adopted in 1943.

The professional education courses provided by the School of Professional Studies are directed toward the mastery of skills and understandings that are needed by teachers in the public schools.

Institution Control: Public.

Calendar: Semester. Academic year August to May.

Official(s): Dr. Michele M. Farley, Department Chairperson.

Faculty: Full-time 5; part-time 2; adjunct 2.

Degrees Awarded: 32 baccalaureate.

Admission Requirements: *Undergraduate:* Open enrollment for secondary school graduates and candidates over the age of 18 or GED; ACT composite. *Teacher education specific:* Passing scores on PRAXIS I (reading, mathematics, writing); 2.5 GPA required; completion of 60 hours of voluntary service; two full-time faculty recommendations; personal interview.

Fees and Expenses: $2,806 in-state per academic year; $6,894 out-of-state. Contact the institution for current room/board rates.

Financial Aid: Resources specifically for eligible students enrolled in teacher education programs are awarded on the basis of financial need and academic merit. The institution has a Program Participation Agreement with the U.S. Department of Education for eligible students to receive Pell Grants and other federal aid. Teacher scholarships available to qualifying students. *Contact:* Thomas Ilsa at (304) 327-4022 or e-mail at: tilse@bluefieldstate.edu.

Accreditation: *Regional:* NCA. *Professional:* NCATE. *Member of:* AACTE. *Approved by:* West Virginia Department of Education.

Undergraduate Programs: The course of study for the Bachelor of Science degree in education is divided into three areas: general studies, professional education, and one or more specializations. Candidates for this degree must earn a minimum of 128 semester ours of credit in approved subjects. The K-6 elementary education program can be completed with a minimum of the following middle school content specializations: general science 5-9, English/language arts 5-9, mathematics through algebra 5-9, and social studies 5-9.

Licensure/Reciprocity: West Virginia. Students seeking teaching certification in a state other than West Virginia should consult with that state's teacher certification office early in their program of study to insure compliance with requirements. Many state directors of teacher credentialing have signed Interstate Agreements through NASDTEC that expedite the certification process.

CONCORD COLLEGE

Division of Education and Human Performance
Department of Teacher Education

Campus Box D-113M
P.O. Box 1000
Athens, West Virginia 24712
Phone: (304) 384-5155
Fax: (304) 384-5398
E-mail: admissions@concord.edu
Internet: http://www.concord.edu

Institution Description: Concord College is under the supervision of the West Virginia Board of Regents. It was established and chartered as Concord State Normal School in 1872.

The mission of the Department of Education is to prepare beginning professional educators who are informed and thoughtful decision-makers capable of teaching all students and specializations in culturally diverse settings.

Institution Control: Public.

Calendar: Semester. Academic year July to June.

Official(s): Dr. Kathryn L. Liptak, Chair; Dr. Darrin T. Martin, Director of Teacher Education.

Faculty: Full-time 11; part-time 1; adjunct 8.

Degrees Awarded: 7 baccalaureate.

Admission Requirements: *Undergraduate:* Graduation with 17 academic units from an approved secondary school or GED; College Board SAT or ACT composite. *Teacher education specific:* Passing scores on PRAXIS I (reading, mathematics, writing); 2.5 GPA required; two full-time faculty recommendations; personal interview. *Graduate:* Baccalaureate degree from a regionally accredited institution. *Teacher education specific:* 2.5 GPA; GRE official scores; proof of professional licensure; 2 letters of recommendation; faculty interview.

Fees and Expenses: Undergraduate: $1,481 in-state per semester; $3,324 out-of-state. Graduate: $183 in-state per credit hour; $316 out-of-state. On-campus room and board: Contact the institution for current rates. Books and supplies: $500.

Financial Aid: Resources specifically for eligible students enrolled in teacher education programs are awarded on the basis of financial need and academic merit. The institution has a Program Participation Agreement with the U.S. Department of Education for eligible students to receive Pell Grants and other federal aid. Teacher scholarships available to qualifying students. *Contact:* Michael Curry at: (304) 384-5160.

Accreditation: *Regional:* NCA. *Professional:* NCATE. *Member of:* AACTE. *Approved by:* West Virginia Department of Education.

Undergraduate Programs: Programs of study for the Bachelor of Science in Education include: early childhood special education (preK-K); elementary education K-6; grades 5-9 (may be combined with at least one other teaching area—English/language arts, general science, mathematics); grades K-12 (art, health, music, physical education, school library media); grades 5-12 (art, business education, English/language arts, general science, health, mathematics, physical education, social studies); grades 9-12 (biology, chemistry, oral communications). All programs require the completion of a general education core, professional studies, content area, field experiences, and student teaching. A minimum of 128 semester hours is required for graduation.

Graduate Programs: The Master of Education program is a 36-hour program specifically designed for licensed or license eligible teachers. The program consists of a 15-hour professional education core, 15-hour content specialization, and 6 hours of electives from either the professional core of the content area. Graduate students certified at the secondary level will complete a minimum of 15 hours in one or two content areas chosen in consultation with an advisor.

Licensure/Reciprocity: West Virginia. Students seeking teaching certification in a state other than West Virginia should consult with that state's teacher certification office early in their program of study to insure compliance with requirements.

Many state directors of teacher credentialing have signed Interstate Agreements through NASDTEC that expedite the certification process.

DAVIS AND ELKINS COLLEGE

Department of Education

Teacher Education Program

100 Campus Drive

Elkins, West Virginia 26241

Phone: (304) 837-1417

Fax: (304) 637-1413

E-mail: screasey@dne.edu

Internet: http://www.dne.edu

Institution Description: Davis and Elkins College is a private, independent, nonprofit college affiliated with the Presbyterian Church (U.S.A.). The college was founded in 1904.

The Teacher Education Program builds upon a strong general education and bridges the gap between theory and practice, thinking and doing, and through coursework correlated with clinical classroom experiences.

Institution Control: Private.

Calendar: Semester (4-1-4 plan). Academic September to May.

Official(s): Dr. Susan B. Creasey, Chair.

Faculty: Full-time 5.

Degrees Awarded: 16 baccalaureate.

Admission Requirements: *Undergraduate:* Graduation from an approved secondary school or GED; College Board SAT or ACT composite. *Teacher education specific:* 2.5 GPA; completion of 40-55 credit hours; passing scores on PRAXIS I (mathematics, reading, writing); completion of required basic foundation courses; two instructor recommendations; personal goal statement; interview.

Fees and Expenses: $14,668 per academic year. On-campus room and board. $5,926. Other expenses. $150. Books and supplies: $750.

Financial Aid: Resources specifically for eligible students enrolled in teacher education programs are awarded on the basis of financial need and academic merit. The institution has a Program Participation Agreement with the U.S. Department of Education for eligible students to receive Pell Grants and other federal aid. Teacher scholarships available to qualifying students. *Contact:* Financial Aid Office at: (304) 637-1373.

Accreditation: *Regional:* NCA. *Member of:* AACTE. *Approved by:* West Virginia Department of Education.

Undergraduate Programs: The major in education leads to the Bachelor of Arts degree. A student seeking multisubject certification for grades K-6 undertakes a major in education. Additional certification may be obtained in a content area by meeting West Virginia licensure requirements. A student seeking certification in a content specialization (grades 5-9, and/or 9-12) must have declared a major outside of education with a declared minor in education. All students seeking either a major or a minor in education leading to certification must meet all of the requirements for admission and retention in the Teacher Education Program. The baccalaureate program requires the completion of the general education core, professional studies, field experiences, and student teaching. A minimum of 124 semester hours is required for graduation.

Licensure/Reciprocity: West Virginia. Students seeking teaching certification in a state other than West Virginia should consult with that state's teacher certification office early in their program of study to insure compliance with requirements. Many state directors of teacher credentialing have signed Interstate Agreements through NASDTEC that expedite the certification process.

FAIRMONT STATE COLLEGE

Teacher Education Programs

Education Building

1201 Locust Avenue

Fairmont, West Virginia 26554-2470

Phone: (304) 367-4000

Fax: (304) 367-4789

E-mail: admit@fscwv.edu

Internet: http://www.fscwv.edu

Institution Description: Fairmont State College is a public institution. The college was founded as The Regency of West Virginia Normal School at Fairmont in 1865.

Undergraduate and graduate programs are offered leading to licensure and professional development for teachers.

Institution Control: Public.

Calendar: Semester. Academic year August to May.

Official(s): Dr. Dan Bradley, President.

Faculty: Not reported.

Degrees Awarded: 177 baccalaureate.

Admission Requirements: *Undergraduate:* Graduation from an approved secondary school or GED; College Board SAT or ACT composite. *Teacher education specific:* Passing scores on PRAXIS I (reading, mathematics, writing); 2.5 GPA required; two faculty recommendations; personal interview. *Graduate:* Baccalaureate degree from a regionally accredited institution. *Teacher education specific:* 2.5 GPA; GRE official scores; proof of professional licensure if required by program pursued; 2 letters of recommendation; faculty interview.

Fees and Expenses: Undergraduate: $3,130 in-state per academic year; $7,038 out-of-state. Graduate: Tuition charged per credit hour. On-campus room and board: $5,090. Other expenses: $1,850. Books and supplies: $600.

Financial Aid: Resources specifically for eligible students enrolled in teacher education programs are awarded on the basis of financial need and academic merit. The institution has a Program Participation Agreement with the U.S. Department of Education for eligible students to receive Pell Grants and other federal aid. Teacher scholarships available to qualifying students. *Contact:* Financial Aid Office at: (304) 367-4213.

Accreditation: *Regional:* NCA. *Professional:* NCATE. *Member of:* AACTE. *Approved by:* West Virginia Department of Education.

Undergraduate Programs: Teacher Education Programs include middle/adolescent education (business education, family and consumer science, technology education, social studies, mathematics); single fields (art, biology, chemistry, English, journalism, French, health, general science, technology education, oral communications, physics, school library media); middle education (grades 5-9); early/middle education; optional specialization (computer science, mathematics, special education, Spanish). All baccalaureate programs require the completion of a general education core, professional studies, content area, field experiences, and student teaching. A minimum of 128 semester hours is required for graduation.

Graduate Programs: The Office of Graduate Students offers the Master of Education with degree cores in middle childhood and special education. A Master of Arts in Teaching degree program is designed for those students who already have a baccalaureate degree in a subject area and wish to pursue a graduate degree with teaching certification. The program is a collaborative offering with Marshall University.

Licensure/Reciprocity: West Virginia. Students seeking teaching certification in a state other than West Virginia should consult with that state's teacher certification office early in their program of study to insure compliance with requirements. Many state directors of teacher credentialing have signed Interstate Agreements through NASDTEC that expedite the certification process.

GLENVILLE STATE COLLEGE
Professional Studies
Division of Education
200 High Street
Glenville, West Virginia 26351
Phone: (304) 462-7361
Fax: (304) 462-8619
E-mail: profstu@glenville.edu
Internet: http://www.glenville.edu

Institution Description: Glenville State College is a public institution. The college was established and chartered as Glenville Branch of State Normal School in 1872.

The Division of Education is committed to its mission of preparing teachers for careers in early education, elementary education, adolescent education, special education, and many different specializations.

Institution Control: Public.

Calendar: Semester. Academic year August to May.

Official(s): Dr. Debra R. Simon, Dean of Teacher Education Program.

Faculty: Full-time 10; part-time 9.

Degrees Awarded: 56 baccalaureate.

Admission Requirements: *Undergraduate:* Graduation from an approved secondary school or GED; College Board SAT or ACT composite. *Teacher education specific:* Passing scores on PRAXIS I (reading, mathematics, writing); 2.5 GPA required; two faculty recommendations; personal interview.

Fees and Expenses: Undergraduate: $2,952 in-state per academic year; $7,306 out-of-state. On-campus room and board: $4,860. Other expenses: $2,803. Books and supplies: $800.

Financial Aid: Resources specifically for eligible students enrolled in teacher education programs are awarded on the basis of financial need and academic merit. The institution has a Program Participation Agreement with the U.S. Department of Education for eligible students to receive Pell Grants and other federal aid. Teacher scholarships available to qualifying students. *Contact:* Financial Aid Office at: (304) 462-4103.

Accreditation: *Regional:* NCA. *Professional:* NCATE. *Member of:* AACTE. *Approved by:* West Virginia Department of Education.

Undergraduate Programs: The Bachelor of Arts in Education is offered with specializations in the following areas: elementary education grades K-6, early education preK-K; behavior disorders grades K-adult; middle school; special learning disabilities grades K-adult; multi-categorical special education grades K-adult; physical education (all grades). Secondary and middle school specializations are offered in music (all grades); English grades 5-9; English grades 5-adult; biological science grades 9-adult, chemistry grades 9-adult; general science grades 5-adult, 5-9; mathematics grades 5-adult, 5-9; social studies grades 5-adult, 5-9. All programs require the completion of the general education core, professional studies, content area, field experiences, and student teaching. A minimum of 128 semester hours is required for the degree award.

Licensure/Reciprocity: West Virginia. Students seeking teaching certification in a state other than West Virginia should consult with that state's teacher certification office early in their program of study to insure compliance with requirements. Many state directors of teacher credentialing have signed Interstate Agreements through NASDTEC that expedite the certification process.

MARSHALL UNIVERSITY
College of Education and Human Services
Teacher Education Programs
One John Marshall Drive
Huntington, West Virginia 25755
Phone: (304) 696-3132
Fax: (304) 696-3131
E-mail: coehs@marshall.edu
Internet: http://www.marshall.edu

Institution Description: Marshall University is a public institution and a unit of the West Virginia University System. It was established as Marshall Academy in 1837.

The College of Education and Human Services prepares teachers and other professional educators, including counselors, principals, supervisors, superintendents, and athletic trainers.

Institution Control: Public.

Calendar: Semester. Academic year August to May.

Official(s): Dr. Tony Williams, Dean.

Faculty: Full-time 69; part-time 3.

Degrees Awarded: 278 baccalaureate; 422 master's; 8 doctorate.

Admission Requirements: *Undergraduate:* Graduation from an approved secondary school or GED; College Board SAT or ACT composite. *Teacher education specific:* Passing scores on PRAXIS I (reading, mathematics, writing); 2.5 GPA; completion of specific core courses; faculty recommendations; personal interview. *Graduate:* Baccalaureate degree from a regionally accredited institution. *Teacher education specific:* 2.5 GPA; GRE official scores; proof of professional licensure if required by program pursued; letters of recommendation; PRAXIS II before certification; faculty interview.

Fees and Expenses: Undergraduate: $1,630 in-state per semester; $4,472 out-of-state. Graduate: $1,730 per semester; $5,003 out-of-state. On-campus room and board: $1,436 to $2,118 per semester. Books and supplies: $700.

Financial Aid: Resources specifically for eligible students enrolled in teacher education programs are awarded on the basis of financial need and academic merit. The institution has a Program Participation Agreement with the U.S. Department of Education for eligible students to receive Pell Grants and other federal aid. Teacher scholarships available to qualifying students. *Contact:* Jack Toney at: (304) 696-2881 or e-mail at: toney@marshall.edu.

Accreditation: *Regional:* NCA. *Professional:* NCATE. *Member of:* AACTE. *Approved by:* West Virginia Department of Education.

Undergraduate Programs: For initial teaching certification programs, all students must complete 128 credit hours. The hours are divided among general education courses, content courses, and pedagogical courses. All programs require approximately 700 hours in the field. Students must maintain a 2.7 GPA and complete content and pedagogical courses with a grade of C or better. In order to be recommended for certification, students must pass the appropriate PRAXIS II exit tests on content and pedagogy. The Bachelor of Arts is awarded upon successful completion of the program.

Graduate Programs: The Graduate School of Education and Professional Development offers programs for the Master of Arts, Master of Arts in Teaching, Educational Specialist, and Doctor of Education degrees. With the exception of the Master of Arts in Teaching, the master's degree and professional development programs do not result in initial licensure. Graduate students can achieve initial certification in secondary areas by entering the Master of Arts in Teaching program. These students have undergraduate degrees in specific content areas.

Additional teaching certifications can be obtained at the graduate level in English as a second language, general math through algebra I, middle childhood education-professional development, reading specialist, school library media, and leadership studies. Certification at the graduate level is available in several special education fields.

Licensure/Reciprocity: West Virginia. Students seeking teaching certification in a state other than West Virginia should consult with that state's teacher certification office early in their program of study to insure compliance with requirements. Many state directors of teacher credentialing have signed Interstate Agreements through NASDTEC that expedite the certification process.

SHEPHERD COLLEGE

School of Education and Professional Studies
Department of Education
Knutti Hall 108
301 North King Street
Shepherdstown, West Virginia 25443-3210
Phone: (304) 876-5237
Fax: (304) 876-3101
E-mail: jsimplic@shepherd.edu
Internet: http://www.shepherd.edu

Institution Description: Shepherd College is a public institution. It was established, chartered, and offered first instruction at the postsecondary level in 1871.

The Department of Education offers the Bachelor of Arts in elementary education and the Bachelor of Arts in secondary education programs that lead to certification in a variety of elementary and secondary areas.

Institution Control: Public.

Calendar: Semester. Academic year August to May.

Official(s): Dr. Joseph Simplicio, Dean.

Faculty: Full-time 9.

Degrees Awarded: 97 baccalaureate.

Admission Requirements: *Undergraduate:* Graduation from an approved secondary school or GED; ACT composite. *Teacher education specific:* Passing scores on PRAXIS I (reading, mathematics, writing); 2.5 GPA minimum; completion of specific core courses; faculty recommendations; personal interview.

Fees and Expenses: Undergraduate: $3,270 in-state per academic year; $8,030 out-of-state. On-campus room and board: $5,162. Other expenses: $3,100. Books and supplies: $860.

Financial Aid: Resources specifically for eligible students enrolled in teacher education programs are awarded on the basis of financial need and academic merit. The institution has a Program Participation Agreement with the U.S. Department of Education for eligible students to receive Pell Grants and other federal aid. Teacher scholarships available to qualifying students. *Contact:* Financial Aid Office at: (304) 876-5470.

Accreditation: *Regional:* NCA. *Professional:* NCATE. *Member of:* AACTE. *Approved by:* West Virginia Department of Education.

Undergraduate Programs: Baccalaureate programs offer the following specializations: art K-12; biology 9-12; business education 9-12; chemistry 9-12; elementary education multi-Subjects K-6; early education preK; English 5-12, 5-9; family and consumer science 5-12; general Science 5-12; mathematics 5-12; general mathematics through algebra I 5-9; music K-12; physical education K-12; social studies 5-12, 5-9. The academic program includes general studies, specialty studies, professional studies, and student teaching. All programs require a minimum of 128 semester hours for graduation.

Licensure/Reciprocity: West Virginia. Students seeking teaching certification in a state other than West Virginia should consult with that state's teacher certification office early in their program of study to insure compliance with requirements. Many state directors of teacher credentialing have signed Interstate Agreements through NASDTEC that expedite the certification process.

UNIVERSITY OF CHARLESTON

Department of Education
Teacher Preparation Programs
2300 MacCorkle Avenue, S.E.
Charleston, West Virginia 25304
Phone: (304) 357-4800
Fax: (304) 357-4769
E-mail: jlblackwood@ucwv.edu
Internet: http://www.ucwv.edu

Institution Description: The University of Charleston is a private, independent, nonprofit institution. The university was established as Barboursville Seminary and offered first instruction at the postsecondary level in 1888.

The goal of the Department of Education is to assist pre-service teachers in the pursuit of the role of the teacher as a committed educator, lifelong learner, and community servant.

Institution Control: Private.

Calendar: Semester. Academic year August to May.

Official(s): Dr. Jo L. Blackwood, Director of Teacher Preparation Programs.

Faculty: Full-time 8.

Degrees Awarded: 14 baccalaureate.

Admission Requirements: *Undergraduate:* Graduation with 15 academic units from an approved secondary school or GED; College Board SAT or ACT composite. *Teacher education specific:* Passing scores on PRAXIS I (reading, mathematics, writing); 2.5 GPA; two faculty recommendations; personal interview.

Fees and Expenses: $17,400 per academic year. On-campus room and board: $6,220. Other expenses: $750. Books and supplies: $720.

Financial Aid: Resources specifically for eligible students enrolled in teacher education programs are awarded on the basis of financial need and academic merit. The institution has a Program Participation Agreement with the U.S. Department of Education for eligible students to receive Pell Grants and other federal aid. Teacher scholarships available to qualifying students. *Contact:* Financial Aid Office at: (304) 357-4750.

Accreditation: *Regional:* NCA. *Professional:* NCATE. *Member of:* AACTE. *Approved by:* West Virginia Department of Education.

Undergraduate Programs: Teacher preparation programs are offered in: elementary multi-subject K-6; music K-12; general science 5-12; language arts 5-12; social studies 5-12; biology 9-12. An education student's four-year program includes three different kinds of courses: liberal arts, content (reading, math, science, social studies), and professional education courses (curriculum, instruction, assessment and theories of teaching and learning). In order to graduate with a bachelor's degree in education, students must be eligible for certification by passing scores on PRAXIS II in their subject area. All programs require 120 semester hours for graduation.

Graduate Programs: A Master of Arts in Teaching program is in the planning stage.

Licensure/Reciprocity: West Virginia. Students seeking teaching certification in a state other than West Virginia should consult with that state's teacher certification office early in their program of study to insure compliance with requirements. Many state directors of teacher credentialing have signed Interstate Agreements through NASDTEC that expedite the certification process.

WEST LIBERTY STATE COLLEGE

School of Education
308 Main Hall
P.O. Box 295
West Liberty, West Virginia 26074-0295
Phone: (304) 336-8247
Fax: (304) 336-8829
E-mail: musserbed@wlsc.edu
Internet: http://www.wlsc.edu

Institution Description: West Liberty State College is a public institution that was founded as West Liberty Academy in 1837. In 1931, the name of the institution became West Liberty State Teachers College. The present name was adopted in 1943.

The School of Education offers programs leading to the baccalaureate degree and teaching certification.

Institution Control: Public.

Calendar: Semester. Academic year August to May.

Official(s): Dr. Beth Musser, Dean.

Faculty: Full-time 7; part-time 8.

Degrees Awarded: 142 baccalaureate.

Admission Requirements: *Undergraduate:* Graduation from an approved secondary school or GED; College Board SAT or ACT composite. *Teacher education specific:* Passing scores on PRAXIS I (reading, mathematics, writing); 2.5 GPA minimum;

WEST LIBERTY STATE COLLEGE—cont'd

completion of specific core courses; faculty recommendations; personal interview. PRAXIS II tests in content area and principles of learning and teaching must be passed and are required for West Virginia licensure.

Fees and Expenses: Undergraduate: $3,138 in-state per academic year; $7,790 out-of-state. On-campus room and board: $4,730. Other expenses: $1,900. Books and supplies: $800.

Financial Aid: Resources specifically for eligible students enrolled in teacher education programs are awarded on the basis of financial need and academic merit. The institution has a Program Participation Agreement with the U.S. Department of Education for eligible students to receive Pell Grants and other federal aid. Teacher scholarships available to qualifying students. *Contact:* Financial Aid Office at: (304) 336-8016.

Accreditation: *Regional:* NCA. *Professional:* NCATE. *Member of:* AACTE. *Approved by:* West Virginia Department of Education.

Undergraduate Programs: In the School of Education, students complete a major area of study and then may elect to add on additional program area(s) for licensure purposes. Majors are offered in: elementary education/K-6 multi-subjects; art education, K-adult or 5-12; biology 9-12; chemistry 9-12; English language arts 5-12; general science 5-12; health K-adult; mathematics 5-12; music education K-adult; physical education K-adult; social sciences 5-12. Add-on programs/endorsements include: early education preK-K; English language arts 5-9; general sciences 5-9; mathematics 5-9; special education: learning disabilities K-12; special education: behavioral disorders K-12; special education: mentally impaired K-12; special education: multicategorical K-12.

All programs require the completion of a general education core professional studies, field experiences, and student teaching. A minimum of 128 semester hours is required for graduation.

Licensure/Reciprocity: West Virginia. Students seeking teaching certification in a state other than West Virginia should consult with that state's teacher certification office early in their program of study to insure compliance with requirements. Many state directors of teacher credentialing have signed Interstate Agreements through NASDTEC that expedite the certification process.

WEST VIRGINIA STATE COLLEGE

Department of Education
Teacher Education Program
Wallace 629
P.O. Box 1000
Institute, West Virginia 25112-1000
Phone: (304) 766-3253
Fax: (304) 756-3285
E-mail: education@wvsc.edu
Internet: http://www.wvsc.edu

Institution Description: West Virginia State College is a public institution. The college was established and chartered in 1891.

The Teacher Education Program awards the Bachelor of Science in Education degree for satisfactory completion of a variety of content specializations.

Institution Control: Public.

Calendar: Semester. Academic year August to May.

Official(s): Dr. Robert L. Hamisin, Jr., Chair.

Faculty: Full-time 10.

Degrees Awarded: 81 baccalaureate.

Admission Requirements: *Undergraduate:* Graduation with 17 academic units from an approved secondary school or GED; College Board SAT or ACT composite. *Teacher education specific:* Passing scores on PRAXIS I (reading, mathematics, writing); 2.5 GPA minimum; completion of specific core courses; faculty recommendations; personal interview.

Fees and Expenses: Undergraduate: $2,665 in-state per academic year; $6,334 out-of-state. On-campus room and board: $4,400. Other expenses: $1,601. Books and supplies: $900.

Financial Aid: Resources specifically for eligible students enrolled in teacher education programs are awarded on the basis of financial need and academic merit. The institution has a Program Participation Agreement with the U.S. Department of Education for eligible students to receive Pell Grants and other federal aid. Teacher scholarships available to qualifying students. *Contact:* Financial Aid Office at: (304) 766-3131.

Accreditation: *Regional:* NCA. *Professional:* NCATE. *Member of:* AACTE. *Approved by:* West Virginia Department of Education.

Undergraduate Programs: Teacher Education Program options include: elementary K-6 that will lead to certification to teach in self-contained early and elementary classroom setting grades K-6; specific learning disabilities K-12 and 5-12 that is an endorsement onto a regular education major; mentally impaired K-12 and 5-12 is an endorsement onto a regular education major that certifies to teach students with mild-moderate degrees of mental impairment; adolescent content specialization. All programs require the completion of a general education core; professional studies, content area, field experiences, and student teaching. A minimum of 121 semester hours must be completed for the baccalaureate degree.

Licensure/Reciprocity: West Virginia. Students seeking teaching certification in a state other than West Virginia should consult with that state's teacher certification office early in their program of study to insure compliance with requirements. Many state directors of teacher credentialing have signed Interstate Agreements through NASDTEC that expedite the certification process.

WEST VIRGINIA UNIVERSITY

College of Human Resources and Education
Teacher Education Program
602 Allan Hall
P.O. Box 6122
Morgantown, West Virginia 26506-6122
Phone: (304) 293-34441
Fax: (304) 293-3080
E-mail: HREadmn@wvu.edu
Internet: http://www.wvu.edu

Institution Description: West Virginia University is a public institution and land-grant college. It was established as Agricultural College of West Virginia in 1867. The present name was adopted in 1870.

The College of Human Resources and Education offers baccalaureate, five-year, and graduate programs to prepare students for careers in teaching and for professional development. A branch of the university is located at Parkersburg.

Institution Control: Public.

Calendar: Semester. Academic year August to May.

Official(s): Dr. Anne Nardi, Dean.

Faculty: Full-time 76.

Degrees Awarded: 67 baccalaureate; 474 master's; 35 doctorate.

Admission Requirements: *Undergraduate:* Graduation from an approved secondary school or GED; College Board SAT or ACT composite. *Teacher education specific:* Passing scores on PRAXIS I (reading, mathematics, writing); 2.5 GPA; completion of specific core courses; faculty recommendations; personal interview. *Graduate:* Baccalaureate degree from a regionally accredited institution. *Teacher education specific:* 2.5 GPA; GRE official scores; proof of professional licensure if required by program pursued; letters of recommendation; PRAXIS II before certification; faculty interview.

Fees and Expenses: Undergraduate: $3,548 in-state per academic year; $10,768 out-of-state. Graduate: Tuition charged per credit hour. On-campus room and board: $5,822. Other expenses: $2,320. Books and supplies: $740.

Financial Aid: Resources specifically for eligible students enrolled in teacher education programs are awarded on the basis of financial need and academic merit. The institution has a Program Participation Agreement with the U.S. Department of

Education for eligible students to receive Pell Grants and other federal aid. Teacher scholarships available to qualifying students. *Contact:* Financial Aid Office at: (304) 293-5242.

Accreditation: *Regional:* NCA. *Professional:* NCATE. *Member of:* AACTE. *Approved by:* West Virginia Department of Education.

Undergraduate Programs: For those students who do not yet have a bachelor's degree, the Five-Year Teacher Education Program is available. Students who are interested in teaching in elementary education (including early childhood education or multi-categorical special education) or a secondary education teacher in mathematics, science, social studies, English, or a foreign language, will graduate with a bachelor's degree in their field of concentration and a master's degree in education.

Students interested in teaching art, music, physical education, or agricultural environmental education may enroll in baccalaureate programs in their field of concentration. All bachelor degree programs require the completion of the general education core, professional studies, content area, field experiences, and student teaching. A minimum of 128 semester hours is required for graduation.

Graduate Programs: Students who already have a bachelor's degree and wish to be certified as either an elementary teacher or a secondary teacher in mathematics, science, social studies, or foreign language may enroll in one of several post-baccalaureate options, including special education.

The primary purpose in elementary (early/middle) education is to provide increased knowledge, skill, and competence in working with children. The program has three major areas of emphasis: general education, subject area/grade level curriculum and methods, and electives. The program in secondary education provides the opportunity to work with students in junior, middle, and high schools. The program emphasizes both pedagogical and content knowledge.

The doctoral degree program is designed to prepare candidates to teach at college or university levels, work with school districts or other agencies in curriculum areas, or to hold leadership positions that emphasize teaching and learning.

Licensure/Reciprocity: West Virginia. Students seeking teaching certification in a state other than West Virginia should consult with that state's teacher certification office early in their program of study to insure compliance with requirements. Many state directors of teacher credentialing have signed Interstate Agreements through NASDTEC that expedite the certification process.

WEST VIRGINIA WESLEYAN COLLEGE

Department of Education
Teacher Education Program
59 College Avenue
Buckhannon, West Virginia 26201
Phone: (304) 473-8045
Fax: (304) 473-8347
E-mail: rupp_l@wvwc.edu
Internet: http://www.wvwc.edu

Institution Description: West Virginia Wesleyan College is a coeducational, residential, liberal arts college affiliated with the United Methodist Church. It was established as West Virginia Conference Seminary in 1890.

The Department of Education offers programs in elementary and secondary education leading to certification and careers in teaching.

Institution Control: Private.

Calendar: Semester. Academic year August to April.

Official(s): Dr. Lynn Rupp, Department Head.

Faculty: Full-time 12; part-time 5; adjunct 4.

Degrees Awarded: 37 baccalaureate.

Admission Requirements: *Undergraduate:* Graduation with 15 academic units from an approved secondary school or GED; College Board SAT or ACT composite. *Teacher education specific:* Passing scores on PRAXIS I (reading, mathematics, writing); 2.5 GPA; completion of 45 semester hours of college work; two letters of recommendation; autobiographical statement; dispositions evaluation; evidence of a current negative T.B. test; personal interview.

Fees and Expenses: $19,850 per academic year. On-campus room and board: $5,350. Other expenses: $3,000. Books and supplies: $1,000.

Financial Aid: Resources specifically for eligible students enrolled in teacher education programs are awarded on the basis of financial need and academic merit. The institution has a Program Participation Agreement with the U.S. Department of Education for eligible students to receive Pell Grants and other federal aid. Teacher scholarships available to qualifying students. *Contact:* Financial Aid Office at: (304) 473-8080.

Accreditation: *Regional:* NCA. *Professional:* NCATE. *Member of:* AACTE. *Approved by:* West Virginia Department of Education.

Undergraduate Programs: Programs are offered in elementary teaching (K-6), secondary teaching (9-12 or 5-12 depending on the field or fields), or combined education (grade level non-specified, available in art, music, physical education, and physical education-grade level non-specified/health-K-12). Students majoring in elementary education may declare optional endorsements as minors. Those completing a program in secondary education may declare their teaching fields as minors. The teaching fields include art (5-12), biology (9-12), chemistry (9-12), English (5-12), general science (5-12), mathematics (9-12), physical education (5-12), physics (9-12), social studies (5-12). All baccalaureate programs require the completion of the general education core, professional studies, content area, field experiences, and student teaching. A minimum of 120 semester hours is required for graduation.

Licensure/Reciprocity: West Virginia. Students seeking teaching certification in a state other than West Virginia should consult with that state's teacher certification office early in their program of study to insure compliance with requirements. Many state directors of teacher credentialing have signed Interstate Agreements through NASDTEC that expedite the certification process.

WISCONSIN

ALVERNO COLLEGE
School of Education
3400 South 43rd Street
P.O. Box 343922
Milwaukee, Wisconsin 53234-3922
Phone: (414) 382-6100
Fax: (414) 382-6354
E-mail: admissions@alverno.edu
Internet: http://www.alverno.edu

Institution Description: Alverno College is a private, Catholic, independent, nonprofit college. It was established as St. Joseph Normal School in 1887.

The college offers weekday and weekend programs in a variety of majors and minors.

Institution Control: Private.

Calendar: Semester. Academic year August to May.

Official(s): Dr. Mary Diez, Graduate Dean.

Faculty: Full-time 12; part-time 22.

Degrees Awarded: 31 baccalaureate; 61 master's.

Admission Requirements: *Undergraduate:* Graduation with 17 academic units from an approved secondary school or GED; ACT composite. *Teacher education specific:* Passing scores on PRAXIS I tests (reading, mathematics, writing); 2.5 GPA minimum; personal goal statement; recommendations; completion of basic foundation courses; faculty interview. PRAXIS II required prior to certification. *Graduate:* Baccalaureate degree from a regionally accredited institution. *Teacher education specific:* Teaching licensure for some programs; faculty interview.

Fees and Expenses: Undergraduate: $13,688 in-state per academic year. Graduate: $464 per credit hour. On-campus room and board: $5,250. Other expenses: $2,500. Books and supplies: $1,000.

Financial Aid: Resources specifically for eligible students enrolled in teacher education programs are awarded on the basis of financial need and academic merit. The institution has a Program Participation Agreement with the U.S. Department of Education for eligible students to receive Pell Grants and other federal aid. Teacher scholarships available to qualifying students. *Contact:* Financial Aid Office at: (414) 382-6046.

Accreditation: *Regional:* NCA. *Professional:* NCATE. *Member of:* AACTE. *Approved by:* Wisconsin Department of Public Instruction.

Undergraduate Programs: The School of Education offers baccalaureate programs in the following areas: art education, broad field science education, broad field social studies, early childhood/elementary, middle/secondary education, mathematics education, English/language arts; music education. The middle/secondary education program, offered as a minor, prepares students for certification for grades 6-12. Students seeking secondary certification choose the subject(s) they would like to teach in middle or high school.

Alverno's education students spend over 100 hours actively involved in classroom practice. Alverno maintains ties with over 150 schools in the Milwaukee area to provide field experience and student teaching opportunities for its education students.

Graduate Programs: The Master of Arts program, focusing on teaching, learning, and assessment, is designed for teachers in K-12 schools and in technical and community colleges. It is also available for persons working in the area of instructional design, training, and human-resource or organizational development in business, government, and not-for-profit agencies. Courses are available in Alverno's Weekend College. The curriculum consists of a common set of core courses and courses specific to teach specialization. Teachers who have the appropriate bachelor's or master's degree and have an initial teaching license may complete coursework for an additional license in this area, as part of the Master of Arts degree program or within a separate program.

Licensure/Reciprocity: Wisconsin. Students seeking teaching certification in a state other than Wisconsin should consult with that state's teacher certification office early in their program of study to insure compliance with requirements. Many state directors of teacher credentialing have signed Interstate Agreements through NASDTEC that expedite the certification process.

BELOIT COLLEGE
Department of Education
700 College Street
Beloit, Wisconsin 53511
Phone: (608) 363-2325
Fax: (608) 363-2194
E-mail: klinek@beloit.edu
Internet: http://www.beloit.edu

Institution Description: Beloit College is a private, independent, nonprofit, liberal arts college that is nonsectarian but historically related to Congregationalism. It was established and chartered in 1846.

The Department of Education is committed to an articulated, integrated program of theory and practice that promotes social responsibility through shared scholarship.

Institution Control: Private.

Calendar: Semester. Academic year August to May.

Official(s): Dr. Kathleen Greene, Chair.

Faculty: Full-time 4; part-time 2; adjunct 9.

Degrees Awarded: 2 baccalaureate.

Admission Requirements: *Undergraduate:* Graduation from an approved secondary school or GED; College Board SAT or ACT composite. *Teacher education specific:* 2.5 GPA; passing scores on PRAXIS I tests (reading, mathematics, writing); demonstrated proficiency in speaking and listening skills; essay; optional interview.

Fees and Expenses: $23,016 per academic year. Activity fee: $220. On-campus room and board: $5,268. Books and supplies: $450.

Financial Aid: Resources specifically for eligible students enrolled in teacher education programs are awarded on the basis of financial need and academic merit. The institution has a Program Participation Agreement with the U.S. Department of Education for eligible students to receive Pell Grants and other federal aid. Teacher scholarships available to qualifying students. *Contact:* Jane Hessian at: (608) 363-2663 or e-mail at: hessian@beloit.edu.

Accreditation: *Regional:* NCA. *Member of:* AACTE. *Approved by:* Wisconsin Department of Public Instruction.

Undergraduate Programs: The Bachelor of Arts degree is offered with a major in education studies. The program offers an integrated curriculum that provides connections between theory and practice among courses and programs. bilingual/bicultural certification, coaching certification, teacher certification, and teaching English as a second language are available. The major in education studies requires the completion of a general education core, professional studies, content area, field experiences, and student teaching. A minimum of 124 semester hours is required for graduation.

Licensure/Reciprocity: Wisconsin. Students seeking teaching certification in a state other than Wisconsin should consult with that state's teacher certification office early in their program of study to insure compliance with requirements. Many state directors of teacher credentialing have signed Interstate Agreements through NASDTEC that expedite the certification process.

CARDINAL STRITCH COLLEGE

College of Education
6801 North Yates Road
Milwaukee, Wisconsin 53217-7516
Phone: (414) 410-4434
Fax: (414) 410-4377
E-mail: jcaldwell@stritch.edu
Internet: http://www.stritch.edu

Institution Description: Cardinal Stritch College is an independent, four-year liberal arts institution sponsored by the Sisters of St. Francis of Assisi, Roman Catholic Church. It was founded in 1937.

The mission of the College of Education is to transform lives and communities by preparing teachers for learning and service.

Institution Control: Private.

Calendar: Continuous. Academic year August to July.

Official(s): Dr. Anthea L. Bojar, Dean, Dr. Joanne Caldwell, Associate Dean.

Faculty: Full-time 22.

Degrees Awarded: 42 baccalaureate; 420 master's; 22 doctorate.

Admission Requirements: *Undergraduate:* Graduation with 16 academic units from an accredited high school or GED; rank in upper 50% of graduating class; College Board SAT or ACT composite. *Teacher education specific:* Passing scores on PRAXIS I tests (reading, mathematics, writing); faculty interview; personal goal statement. *Graduate:* Baccalaureate degree from a regionally accredited institution. *Teacher education specific:* 2.75 GPA minimum (3.0 for Master of Science in Education Leadership); official transcripts; personal interview.

Fees and Expenses: Undergraduate: $14,540 per academic year. Graduate: $445 per credit hour. On-campus room and board: $5,130. Other expenses: $2,810. Books and supplies: $672.

Financial Aid: Resources specifically for eligible students enrolled in teacher education programs are awarded on the basis of financial need and academic merit. The institution has a Program Participation Agreement with the U.S. Department of Education for eligible students to receive Pell Grants and other federal aid. Teacher scholarships available to qualifying students. *Contact:* Peter Holbrook, Vice President for Enrollment Management at: (414) 410-4041 or e-mail at: pjholbrook@stritch.edu.

Accreditation: *Regional:* NCA. *Member of:* AACTE. *Approved by:* Wisconsin Department of Public Instruction.

Undergraduate Programs: Baccalaureate programs are offered in secondary education and elementary education. All programs require the completion of a general education core, professional studies, content area, field experiences, and student teaching. A minimum of 128 semester hours is required for the degree award.

Graduate Programs: The Master of Arts degree programs include: teaching (initial teaching certification); reading/language arts; special education (with certifications available in cognitive disability, learning disabilities, emotional disturbance, or combined certification in the first three categories).

The Master of Education degree concentrations include education, instructional technology, and ministry.

The Master of Science program is offered with concentrations in instructional technology and educational leadership. Extended certifications at the graduate level (post-baccalaureate certification) may be pursued in special education, reading, computer education, and English as a second language.

A Doctor of Education program is offered in leadership for the advancement of learning and service.

Licensure/Reciprocity: Wisconsin. Students seeking teaching certification in a state other than Wisconsin should consult with that state's teacher certification office early in their program of study to insure compliance with requirements. Many state directors of teacher credentialing have signed Interstate Agreements through NASDTEC that expedite the certification process.

CARROLL COLLEGE

Department of Education
100 North East Avenue
Waukesha, Wisconsin 53186
Phone: (262) 547-1211
Fax: (262) 524-7139
E-mail: cc.info@cc.edu
Internet: http://www.cc.edu

Institution Description: Carroll College is a private, nonprofit college affiliated with the Presbyterian Church (U.S.A.).The college was founded in 1841.

The curriculum offered by the Department of Education prepares students for graduate school and success in professional careers.

Institution Control: Private.

Calendar: Semester (4-1-4 plan). Academic year September to May.

Official(s): Dr. Lynette Zuroff, Department Chair.

Faculty: Full-time 6.

Degrees Awarded: 88 baccalaureate.

Admission Requirements: *Undergraduate:* Graduation from an accredited high school or GED; College Board SAT or ACT composite. *Teacher education specific:* Passing scores on PRAXIS I tests (reading, mathematics, writing); faculty interview; personal goal statement.

Fees and Expenses: Undergraduate: $17,380 per academic year. On-campus room and board: $5,360. Other expenses: $2,162. Books and supplies: $786.

Financial Aid: Resources specifically for eligible students enrolled in teacher education programs are awarded on the basis of financial need and academic merit. The institution has a Program Participation Agreement with the U.S. Department of Education for eligible students to receive Pell Grants and other federal aid. Teacher scholarships available to qualifying students. *Contact:* Financial Aid Office at: (262) 524-7296.

Accreditation: *Regional:* NCA. *Member of:* AACTE. *Approved by:* Wisconsin Department of Public Instruction.

Undergraduate Programs: Baccalaureate programs offer majors in elementary education, secondary education areas, health and physical education with non-teaching concentrations in community health or sport management, social science for secondary education, teaching English to speakers of other languages. Students interested in teaching in the secondary schools major in the content areas they want to teach and take classes in teacher education.

There are two ways that students may obtain a Class II Teaching Certificate for grades 5-12: (1) select a broad field major in English literature and writing, mathematics, or social sciences; (2) have both a major and a minor in areas that lead to teacher education. Majors include: biology, chemistry, commu-

CARROLL COLLEGE—cont'd

nication studies, English, history, political science, Spanish (K-12), teaching English to speakers of other languages (K-12). Minors include areas similar to the major areas plus computer science, health and physical education (K-12), psychology reading (K-12), special education (K-12).

All programs require the completion of a general education core, professional studies, content area, field experiences, and student teaching. A minimum of 128 semester hours is required for graduation.

Licensure/Reciprocity: Wisconsin. Students seeking teaching certification in a state other than Wisconsin should consult with that state's teacher certification office early in their program of study to insure compliance with requirements. Many state directors of teacher credentialing have signed Interstate Agreements through NASDTEC that expedite the certification process.

CONCORDIA UNIVERSITY WISCONSIN

School of Education
Teacher Certification Program
12800 North Lake Shore Drive
Mequon, Wisconsin 53097-2402
Phone: (262) 243-5700
Fax: (262) 243-4351
E-mail: admissions@cuw.edu
Internet: http://www.cuw.edu

Institution Description: Concordia College Wisconsin is a private school owned and operated by The Lutheran Church-Missouri Synod. It was founded as a Lutheran training school in 1881.

The School of Education has the mission of helping students develop in mind, body, and spirit for service to Christ and the world.

Institution Control: Private.

Calendar: Semester (4-1-4 plan). Academic year August to May.

Official(s): Dr. Marsha Konz, Dean of Graduate Studies; Dr. Ross Stueber, Director of Graduate Education.

Faculty: Full-time 17.

Degrees Awarded: 87 baccalaureate; 41 master's.

Admission Requirements: *Undergraduate:* Graduation with 16 academic units from an accredited high school or GED; ACT composite preferred; College Board SAT accepted. *Teacher education specific:* Passing scores on PRAXIS I tests (reading, mathematics, writing); faculty interview; personal goal statement. *Graduate:* Baccalaureate degree from a regionally accredited institution. *Teacher education specific:* 3.0 GPA minimum; official transcripts; personal interview.

Fees and Expenses: Undergraduate: $15,650 per academic year. Graduate: Tuition charged per credit hour. On-campus room and board: $5,930. Other expenses: $2,150. Books and supplies: $800.

Financial Aid: Resources specifically for eligible students enrolled in teacher education programs are awarded on the basis of financial need and academic merit. The institution has a Program Participation Agreement with the U.S. Department of Education for eligible students to receive Pell Grants and other federal aid. Teacher scholarships available to qualifying students. *Contact:* Financial Aid Office at: (262) 243-4427.

Accreditation: *Regional:* NCA. *Professional:* NCATE. *Member of:* AACTE. *Approved by:* Wisconsin Department of Public Instruction.

Undergraduate Programs: The Teacher Certification Program offers certifiable majors in: biology, broad field science, broad field social science, business education, English, German, history, mathematics, Spanish. Minor areas may be added in: biology, English as a second language, German, mathematics, Spanish, theater. All baccalaureate programs require the completion of a general education core, professional studies, content area, field experiences, and student teaching. A minimum of 126 semester hours is required for graduation.

Graduate Programs: The graduate program is designed to prepare graduate students for leadership roles in professional education careers. The Master of Science in Education degree requires 30 semester hours of credit including a thesis or project. A non-thesis 36 credit-hour program is also offered. Concentrations are offered in administration, art education, counseling, curriculum and instruction, early childhood, family studies, and reading.

Licensure/Reciprocity: Wisconsin. Students seeking teaching certification in a state other than Wisconsin should consult with that state's teacher certification office early in their program of study to insure compliance with requirements. Many state directors of teacher credentialing have signed Interstate Agreements through NASDTEC that expedite the certification process.

EDGEWOOD COLLEGE

Education Department
855 Woodrow Street
Madison, Wisconsin 53711
Phone: (608) 663-4861
Fax: (608) 663-3291
E-mail: schmied@edgewood.edu
Internet: http://www.edgewood

Institution Description: Edgewood College is a private college affiliated with the Roman Catholic Church. The college was founded originally as St. Regina Academy in 1881.

The Education Department offers a variety of teaching majors, minors, and areas of concentration for the preparation of teachers.

Institution Control: Private.

Calendar: Semester (4-1-4 plan). Academic year September to May.

Official(s): Dr. Joseph Schmiedicke, Chair.

Faculty: Full-time and part-time 56.

Degrees Awarded: 61 baccalaureate; 31 master's.

Admission Requirements: *Undergraduate:* Graduation with 16 academic units from an accredited high school or GED; College Board SAT or ACT composite. *Teacher education specific:* Passing scores on PRAXIS I tests (reading, mathematics, writing); faculty interview; personal goal statement. *Graduate:* Baccalaureate degree from a regionally accredited institution. *Teacher education specific:* 2.75 GPA minimum; official transcripts; personal interview.

Fees and Expenses: Undergraduate: $15,100 per academic year. Graduate: $425 per credit. On-campus room and board: $5,420. Other expenses: $2,253. Books and supplies: $750.

Financial Aid: Resources specifically for eligible students enrolled in teacher education programs are awarded on the basis of financial need and academic merit. The institution has a Program Participation Agreement with the U.S. Department of Education for eligible students to receive Pell Grants and other federal aid. Teacher scholarships available to qualifying students. *Contact:* Financial Aid Office at: (608) 663-2206.

Accreditation: *Regional:* NCA. *Professional:* NCATE. *Member of:* AACTE. *Approved by:* Wisconsin Department of Public Instruction.

Undergraduate Programs: Teaching majors for middle and secondary education include: biology, broad field science, computer science, chemistry, performing arts, English, French, history, mathematics, religious studies, social studies broad field with history concentration, Spanish. Teaching minors for elementary and elementary/middle level education include: early childhood education, English/communication arts, English, French, history, natural science teaching, performing arts, science education, social science, Spanish. All baccalaureate programs have general education and professional core prerequisites. A minimum of 120 semester hours is required for graduation.

Graduate Programs: The Master of Arts in Education degree program is designed to prepare students for advancement in classroom teaching, educational administration, special education, and other aspects of the education profession in schools and other organizations and agencies with educational programs. Students entering the master's program may seek the master's degree, teacher certification and licensure, both a master's degree and a license, or no degree (taking courses that match individual educational needs). The program includes coursework in educational leadership, curriculum design, instructional implementation, and actions research, with specializations in curriculum instruction, instructional technology, educational administration, special education, and general professional development.

Licensure/Reciprocity: Wisconsin. Students seeking teaching certification in a state other than Wisconsin should consult with that state's teacher certification office early in their program of study to insure compliance with requirements. Many state directors of teacher credentialing have signed Interstate Agreements through NASDTEC that expedite the certification process.

MARIAN COLLEGE OF FOND DU LAC
School of Education
45 South National Avenue
Fond du Lac, Wisconsin 54935
Phone: (920) 923-7600
Fax: (920) 923-7154
E-mail: education@mariancollege.edu
Internet: http://www.mariancollege.edu

Institution Description: Marian College of Fond du Lac is a private, nonprofit institution affiliated with the Congregation of the Sisters of St. Agnes, Roman Catholic Church. The college was established in 1936.

The School of Education is committed to the education and development of caring, competent, reflective teachers and educational administrators.

Institution Control: Private.

Calendar: Semester. Academic year August to May.

Official(s): Dr. Larry A. Robinson, Dean of Education; Dr. Christine Erickson, Undergraduate Program Director for Teacher Education.

Faculty: Full-time 17.

Degrees Awarded: 36 baccalaureate; 213 master's.

Admission Requirements: *Undergraduate:* Graduation with 16 academic units from an accredited high school or GED; ACT composite preferred; College Board SAT accepted. *Teacher education specific:* Passing scores on PRAXIS I tests (reading, mathematics, writing); faculty interview; personal goal statement. *Graduate:* Baccalaureate degree from a regionally accredited institution. *Teacher education specific:* 3.0 GPA minimum; 3 recommendations; official transcripts; teaching licensure where required for the program pursued; personal interview.

Fees and Expenses: Undergraduate: $15,025 per academic year. Graduate: $249 per credit. On-campus room and board: $5,240. Other expenses: $1,230. Books and supplies: $700.

Financial Aid: Resources specifically for eligible students enrolled in teacher education programs are awarded on the basis of financial need and academic merit. The institution has a Program Participation Agreement with the U.S. Department of Education for eligible students to receive Pell Grants and other federal aid. Teacher scholarships available to qualifying students. *Contact:* Financial Aid Office at: (920) 923-7614.

Accreditation: *Regional:* NCA. *Professional:* NCATE. *Member of:* AACTE. *Approved by:* Wisconsin Department of Public Instruction.

Undergraduate Programs: Licensure programs are offered in: early childhood education, middle childhood through early adolescence grade 1 through 8 (minors in computer education, English/language arts, environmental science, social studies, mathematics, natural science, foreign languages [French, German, Spanish]; athletic coaching); early childhood through adolescence education programs in business education, choral and instrumental music; middle-secondary education (majors in biology, broad field social studies, broad field science, chemis-

try, English, foreign language [Spanish], history, mathematics; minors in biology, chemistry, environmental science, mathematics).

All programs require the completion of the general education core, professional studies, content area, field experiences, and student teaching. A minimum of 128 semester hours is required for the baccalaureate degree award.

Graduate Programs: Graduate programs are offered in the areas of teacher development (master educator, educational technology, students at-risk, alternative education licensure); educational leadership (principal, director of instruction, school business manager, director of special education and pupil services; certificate programs (educational technology, students at-risk, leadership institute). The master's program combines a nontraditional instructional format with an off-site delivery system designed to meet the needs of the adult learner.

Licensure/Reciprocity: Wisconsin. Students seeking teaching certification in a state other than Wisconsin should consult with that state's teacher certification office early in their program of study to insure compliance with requirements. Many state directors of teacher credentialing have signed Interstate Agreements through NASDTEC that expedite the certification process.

MARQUETTE UNIVERSITY
School of Education
Teacher Education Program
615 North Eleventh Street
P.O. Box 1881
Milwaukee, Wisconsin 53201-1881
Phone: (414) 288-7710
Fax: (414) 288-7197
E-mail: go2marquette@marquette.edu
Internet: http://www.marquette.edu

Institution Description: Marquette University is an independent, coeducational institution affiliated with the Society of Jesus, Roman Catholic Church. It was founded in 1881.

The School of Education is committed to prepare teachers and educational specialists who uphold the Jesuit traditions of *cura personalis* (care for the whole person), social justice, academic excellence, ethical behavior, and service to the urban community.

Institution Control: Private.

Calendar: Semester. Academic year August to May.

Official(s): Dr. Mary P. Hoy, Dean; Dr. William Pink, Assistant Dean.

Faculty: Full-time 16, part-time 15.

Degrees Awarded: 32 baccalaureate; 61 master's; 6 doctorate.

Admission Requirements: *Undergraduate:* Graduation with 16 academic units from an accredited high school or GED; ACT composite preferred; College Board SAT accepted. *Teacher education specific:* Passing scores on PRAXIS I tests (reading, mathematics, writing); 2.5 GPA in 45 semester hours of coursework; faculty interview; personal goal statement. *Graduate:* Baccalaureate degree from a regionally accredited institution. *Teacher education specific:* GRE or Miller Analogies Test scores; official transcripts; personal interview.

Fees and Expenses: Undergraduate: $20,724 per academic year. Graduate: Tuition charged per credit hour. On-campus room and board: $6,900. Other expenses: $1,650. Books and supplies: $900.

Financial Aid: Resources specifically for eligible students enrolled in teacher education programs are awarded on the basis of financial need and academic merit. The institution has a Program Participation Agreement with the U.S. Department of Education for eligible students to receive Pell Grants and other federal aid. Teacher scholarships available to qualifying students. *Contact:* Financial Aid Office at: (414) 288-7390.

Undergraduate Programs: Students who complete the teacher education program graduate with a double major in education and a major in an academic content area. The Bachelor of Arts or Bachelor of Science is conferred by the college in which the

MARQUETTE UNIVERSITY—cont'd

student's major department is located. Bachelor of Arts teaching majors include: business education, communication studies, English, French, German, history, journalism, political Science, psychology, religious studies, sociology, Spanish, theatre arts. The Bachelor of Science teaching majors include: biology, chemistry, mathematics, physics. All baccalaureate programs require the completion of a general education core, professional studies, content area, field experiences, and student teaching. A minimum of 128 semester hours is required for graduation.

Graduate Programs: The Secondary Teacher Certification/Master's Degree in instructional leadership is designed to meet the needs of working professionals with a bachelor's degree in fields certifiable for secondary teaching in Wisconsin to earn both an initial Wisconsin secondary teaching license (grades 6-12) and a master's degree. The program prepares teachers to uphold the Jesuit traditions of care for the person, social justice, academic excellence, ethical behavior, and service to the urban community.

A Doctor of Education program offers concentrations in educational policy and leadership and counseling.

Licensure/Reciprocity: Wisconsin. Students seeking teaching certification in a state other than Wisconsin should consult with that state's teacher certification office early in their program of study to insure compliance with requirements. Many state directors of teacher credentialing have signed Interstate Agreements through NASDTEC that expedite the certification process.

MOUNT MARY COLLEGE

Department of Education

2900 North Menomonee River Parkway
Milwaukee, Wisconsin 53222
Phone: (414) 258-4810
Fax: (414) 256-0182
E-mail: schwale@mtmary.edu
Internet: http://www.mtmary.edu

Institution Description: Mount Mary College is a private college for women affiliated with the Roman Catholic Church. The college was established in 1877 as Saint Mary's Institute in Prairie du Chien. In 1929, the college moved to Milwaukee and the present name was adopted.

Mount Mary's education curriculum offers a solid foundation to prepare students for a variety of teaching experiences including elementary, middle school, and high school level education.

Institution Control: Private.

Calendar: Semester. Academic year August to May.

Official(s): Dr. Eileen Schwalbach, Director.

Faculty: Full-time 5; part-time 3.

Degrees Awarded: 8 baccalaureate; 22 master's.

Admission Requirements: *Undergraduate:* Graduation from an accredited secondary school or GED; College Board SAT or ACT composite. *Teacher education specific:* Passing scores on PRAXIS I tests (reading, mathematics, writing); faculty interview; 2.75 GPA on a minimum of 40 semester credits at the college level; personal goal statement. *Graduate:* Baccalaureate degree from a regionally accredited institution. *Teacher education specific:* 2.75 GPA minimum; 3 recommendations; official transcripts; teaching licensure where required for the program pursued; personal interview.

Fees and Expenses: Undergraduate: $15,270 per academic year. Graduate: $425 per credit. On-campus room and board: $5,100. Other expenses: $2,398. Books and supplies: $900.

Financial Aid: Resources specifically for eligible students enrolled in teacher education programs are awarded on the basis of financial need and academic merit. The institution has a Program Participation Agreement with the U.S. Department of Education for eligible students to receive Pell Grants and other federal aid. Teacher scholarships available to qualifying students. *Contact:* Financial Aid Office at: (414) 256-1258.

Accreditation: *Regional:* NCA. *Member of:* AACTE. *Approved by:* Wisconsin Department of Public Instruction.

Undergraduate Programs: Mount Mary offers the following types of certification: early childhood/middle childhood (preK-6); middle childhood/early adolescence (5-9), early adolescence/adolescence (6-12), early childhood/adolescence (preK-12). Content areas available include: art (preK-12); bilingual (Spanish, preK-12, 6-12); biology (6-12); broad field science (6-12); chemistry (6-12); English (6-12); French (preK-12, 6-12); history (6-12); mathematics (6-12); music (choral 6-12); music (general 6-12); social studies (6-12); Spanish (preK-12, 6-12). Prospective teachers complete 100 hours of approved clinical experience prior to student teaching. All baccalaureate programs require the completion of a minimum of 128 semester hours.

Graduate Programs: A Post-Baccalaureate Certification Program offers teaching certificates to individuals looking for a career change. Certification for grades preK-6, 6-12, 1-9, or preK-12 can be earned by students who complete a major in one of the certification areas and meet all requirements specified by the Department of Education.

The Master of Arts in Education program is designed to help early childhood, elementary, middle school, and high school teachers to strengthen their knowledge base, broaden their repertoire of instructional skills, and pursue professional development opportunities. The graduate program requires completion of 36 credits and is offered with special emphases in art, adaptive education, English, music, and reading.

Licensure/Reciprocity: Wisconsin. Students seeking teaching certification in a state other than Wisconsin should consult with that state's teacher certification office early in their program of study to insure compliance with requirements. Many state directors of teacher credentialing have signed Interstate Agreements through NASDTEC that expedite the certification process.

SILVER LAKE COLLEGE

Education Department
Teacher Education Program

2406 South Alverno Road
Manitowoc, Wisconsin 54220-9319
Phone: (920) 684-6691
Fax: (920) 684-7082
E-mail: mnugent@sl.edu
Internet: http://www.sl.edu

Institution Description: Silver Lake College is a private college affiliated with the Roman Catholic Church. The college was established and chartered in 1935.

The Education Department offers undergraduate and graduate programs leading to teaching certification and professional development.

Institution Control: Private.

Calendar: Semester. Academic year August to May.

Official(s): Sister Mary Ann Nugent, Director; Dr. Patrice A. Hicks, Department Chair.

Faculty: Full-time 12; part-time 14.

Degrees Awarded: 25 baccalaureate; 61 master's.

Admission Requirements: *Undergraduate:* Graduation with 16 academic units from an accredited high school or GED; College Board SAT or ACT composite; *Teacher education specific:* Passing scores on PRAXIS I tests (reading, mathematics, writing); 2.75; successful clinical experiences; faculty interview; personal goal statement. *Graduate:* Baccalaureate degree from a regionally accredited institution. *Teacher education specific:* 2.75 GPA minimum; 3 recommendations; official transcripts; teaching licensure where required for the program pursued; personal interview.

Fees and Expenses: Undergraduate: $14,350 per academic year. Graduate: $295 per credit. On-campus room and board: $6,143. Other expenses: $2,116. Books and supplies: $610.

Financial Aid: Resources specifically for eligible students enrolled in teacher education programs are awarded on the basis of financial need and academic merit. The institution has a Program Participation Agreement with the U.S. Department of Education for eligible students to receive Pell Grants and other federal aid. Teacher scholarships available to qualifying students. *Contact:* Financial Aid Office at: (920) 686-6122.

Accreditation: *Regional:* NCA. *Member of:* AACTE. Approved by: Wisconsin Department of Public Instruction.

Undergraduate Programs: Students in the elementary/middle education or secondary/middle programs must pursue an approved content minor in any of the following areas: biology, computer education, computer science, early childhood, English, history, mathematics, psychology, religious studies, natural science, social science, Spanish. All programs lead to the baccalaureate degree and require the completion of a general education core, professional studies, field experiences, content area, and student teaching. A minimum of 120 semester hours is required for graduation.

Graduate Programs: The graduate education curriculum is designed to help classroom teachers and potential school administrators acquire the knowledge, skills, and dispositions needed for effective leadership. Wisconsin Professional Educator Licenses are available in school administration (principalship, director of instruction, director of special education and pupil services, school business administrator) and teaching (reading teacher, special education). All master's programs require the completion of specified goals and coursework.

Licensure/Reciprocity: Wisconsin. Students seeking teaching certification in a state other than Wisconsin should consult with that state's teacher certification office early in their program of study to insure compliance with requirements. Many state directors of teacher credentialing have signed Interstate Agreements through NASDTEC that expedite the certification process.

UNIVERSITY OF WISCONSIN - EAU CLAIRE

School of Education
Department of Curriculum and Instruction
153 Brewer
Eau Claire, Wisconsin 54701
Phone: (715) 836-3671
Fax: (715) 836-2380
E-mail: ask-uwec@uwec.edu
Internet: http://www.uwec.edu

Institution Description: Established as Eau Claire State Normal School in 1916, the school became Eau Claire State Teachers College in 1927. After several name changes, the present name was adopted in 1971.

The mission of the School of Education is commitment to the initial preparation and continued support of professional educators.

Institution Control: Public.

Calendar: Semester. Academic year August to May.

Official(s): Dr. Katherine Rhoades, Associate Dean.

Faculty: Full-time 18.

Degrees Awarded: 196 baccalaureate; 57 graduate.

Admission Requirements: *Undergraduate:* Graduation with 17 academic units from an accredited high school or GED; ACT composite preferred; College Board SAT accepted. *Teacher education specific:* Passing scores on PRAXIS I tests (reading, mathematics, writing); faculty interview; personal goal statement. *Graduate:* Baccalaureate degree from a regionally accredited institution. *Teacher education specific:* 3.0 GPA minimum; 3 recommendations; official transcripts; teaching licensure where required for the program pursued; personal interview.

Fees and Expenses: Undergraduate: $4,305 in-state per academic year; $14,352 out-of-state. Graduate: $249 in-state per credit; $795 per credit. On-campus room and board: $3,980. Other expenses: $2,238. Books and supplies: $400.

Financial Aid: Resources specifically for eligible students enrolled in teacher education programs are awarded on the basis of financial need and academic merit. The institution has a Program Participation Agreement with the U.S. Department of Education for eligible students to receive Pell Grants and other federal aid. Teacher scholarships available to qualifying students. *Contact:* Financial Aid Office at: (715) 836-3373.

Accreditation: *Regional:* NCA. *Member of:* AACTE. *Approved by:* Wisconsin Department of Public Instruction.

Undergraduate Programs: Programs in the Department of Curriculum and Instruction are designed to lead to licensure by the state of Wisconsin. Programs offered include: middle childhood through early adolescence (ages 6-13), early adolescence through adolescence (ages 10-21); early childhood through adolescence (ages 6-21). All baccalaureate programs require the completion of a general education core, professional studies, content area, field experiences, and student teaching. A minimum of 120 semester hours is required for graduation.

Graduate Programs: The Master of Arts in Teaching is available with concentrations in history, biology, English, and mathematics. The Master of Science in Teaching is available in the areas of biology, elementary education, English, history, history/social science, mathematics, and reading specialist. The Master of Education - Professional Development is offered in teaching of English to speakers of other languages. An additional certification is available in reading.

Licensure/Reciprocity: Wisconsin. Students seeking teaching certification in a state other than Wisconsin should consult with that state's teacher certification office early in their program of study to insure compliance with requirements. Many state directors of teacher credentialing have signed Interstate Agreements through NASDTEC that expedite the certification process.

UNIVERSITY OF WISCONSIN - LA CROSSE

School of Education
Teacher Education
Morris Hall
1725 State Street
La Crosse, Wisconsin 54601
Phone: (608) 785-8122
Fax: (608) 785-6695
E-mail: admissions@mail.uwlax.edu
Internet: http://www.uwlax.edu

Institution Description: The institution was chartered as State Normal School in 1905. The name was changed to State Teachers College in 1926 and changed again to Wisconsin State College—La Crosse in 1951. The present name was adopted in 1971.

The Teacher Education faculty are committed to the preparation of education professionals for preK-12 schools that service a variety of diverse populations.

Institution Control: Public.

Calendar: Semester. Academic year August to May.

Official(s): Dr. Ronald S. Rochon, Director.

Faculty: Not reported.

Degrees Awarded: 142 baccalaureate; 44 graduate.

Admission Requirements: *Undergraduate:* Graduation with 17 academic units from an accredited high school or GED; top 35% of graduating class; College Board SAT or ACT composite. *Teacher education specific:* Passing scores on PRAXIS I tests (reading, mathematics, writing); faculty interview; personal goal statement. *Graduate:* Baccalaureate degree from a regionally accredited institution. *Teacher education specific:* 2.75 GPA minimum; 3 recommendations; official transcripts; teaching licensure where required for the program pursued; personal interview.

Fees and Expenses: Undergraduate: $4,358 in-state per academic year; $14,404 out-of-state. Graduate: $223 in-state per credit hour; $769 out-of-state. On-campus room and board: $4,146. Other expenses: $2,079. Books and supplies: $375.

UNIVERSITY OF WISCONSIN - LA CROSSE—
cont'd

Financial Aid: Resources specifically for eligible students enrolled in teacher education programs are awarded on the basis of financial need and academic merit. The institution has a Program Participation Agreement with the U.S. Department of Education for eligible students to receive Pell Grants and other federal aid. Teacher scholarships available to qualifying students. *Contact:* Financial Aid Office at: (608) 785-8604.

Accreditation: *Regional:* NCA. *Professional:* NCATE. *Member of:* AACTE. *Approved by:* Wisconsin Department of Public Instruction.

Undergraduate Programs: Baccalaureate programs offered by the School of Education include: early childhood through middle childhood (ages birth to 11 years old and grades preK to grade 6); middle childhood through early adolescence (ages 6 to 13 and grades 1-9); early adolescence through adolescence (ages 10-21 and grades 6-12); early childhood through adolescence (ages birth through 21 and all grades and requires a certifiable content area major in art, music, foreign language, health education, or physical education. All programs require the completion of a general education core, professional studies, content area, field experiences, and student teaching. A minimum of 120 semester hours is required for graduation.

Graduate Programs: The Master of Education for Professional Development program is for educators who seek to improve their professional knowledge and skills. Teachers who wish to add a license in educational media may enroll in this concentration. Individuals with a bachelor's degree but no teaching license may also apply to earn a master's degree while completing the coursework necessary for a teaching license.

The Master of Science in Education-Reading program is designed to improve the classroom teacher's ability to teach reading or to provide the expertise needed to qualify for a position as a reading teacher, reading specialist, or reading coordinator at elementary, middle level, or high schools.

The Master of Science in Education-Special Education program prepares teachers sof students identified as emotionally disturbed and/or cross-categorical. The degree enables students to be eligible for certification to teach at the elementary/middle level (K-9) or at the middle level/secondary level (6-12).

Licensure/Reciprocity: Wisconsin. Students seeking teaching certification in a state other than Wisconsin should consult with that state's teacher certification office early in their program of study to insure compliance with requirements. Many state directors of teacher credentialing have signed Interstate Agreements through NASDTEC that expedite the certification process.

UNIVERSITY OF WISCONSIN - MADISON

School of Education
Department of Curriculum and Instruction
500 Lincoln Drive
Madison, Wisconsin 53706
Phone: (608) 262-1234
Fax: (608) 262-1429
E-mail: education@.wisc.edu
Internet: http://www.wisc.edu

Institution Description: The institution was chartered as the University of Wisconsin in 1848. It became part of the University of Wisconsin system and the present name was adopted in 1973.

The general mission of the Department of Curriculum and Instruction is to advance knowledge of and professional practice in teaching and learning.

Institution Control: Public.

Calendar: Semester. Academic year September to May.

Official(s): Dr. Charles W. Read, Director, School of Education; Dr. Carl A. Grant, Chair, Department of Curriculum and Instruction.

Faculty: Full-time 42; emeriti 9.

Degrees Awarded: 190 baccalaureate; 132 master's; 55 doctorate.

Admission Requirements: *Undergraduate:* Graduation with 16 academic units from an accredited high school or GED; College Board SAT or ACT composite. *Teacher education specific:* Passing scores on PRAXIS I tests (reading, mathematics, writing); faculty interview; personal goal statement. *Graduate:* Baccalaureate degree from a regionally accredited institution. *Teacher education specific:* 3.0 GPA minimum; 3 recommendations; official transcripts; teaching licensure where required for the program pursued; personal interview.

Fees and Expenses: Undergraduate: $5,136 in-state per academic year; $19,136 out-of-state. Graduate: $399 in-state per credit hour; $1,282 out-of-state. On-campus room and board: $6,130. Other expenses: $2,130. Books and supplies: $820.

Financial Aid: Resources specifically for eligible students enrolled in teacher education programs are awarded on the basis of financial need and academic merit. The institution has a Program Participation Agreement with the U.S. Department of Education for eligible students to receive Pell Grants and other federal aid. Teacher scholarships available to qualifying students. *Contact:* Financial Aid Office at: (608 262-3060.

Accreditation: *Regional:* NCA. *Member of:* AACTE. *Approved by:* Wisconsin Department of Public Instruction.

Undergraduate Programs: Programs in the Department of Curriculum and Instruction are designed to lead to licensure by the state of Wisconsin. Programs offered include: middle childhood through early adolescence (ages 6-13), early adolescence through adolescence (ages 10-21); early childhood through adolescence (ages 6-21). All baccalaureate programs require the completion of a general education core, professional studies, content area, field experiences, and student teaching. A minimum of 120 semester hours is required for graduation.

Graduate Programs: Graduate study in the Department of Curriculum and Instruction is distinguished from undergraduate study in its depth of subject matter and its more intense consideration of professional problems and issues. Departmental graduate programs include: art education, bilingual education, curriculum theory and research, early childhood education, education communications and technology elementary education, English as a second language, English education, English/language arts, foreign language education; health education; International studies in curriculum/pedagogy/teacher education, literacy studies, mathematics education, multicultural education, music education, reading education (literacy studies), science education, social studies, teacher education.

Graduate study beyond the master's degree level is primarily research-oriented. The Doctor of Philosophy degree is granted upon evidence of general proficiency, distinctive attainment in a special field, and a demonstrated ability for independent investigation as reflected in a thesis.

Licensure/Reciprocity: Wisconsin. Students seeking teaching certification in a state other than Wisconsin should consult with that state's teacher certification office early in their program of study to insure compliance with requirements. Many state directors of teacher credentialing have signed Interstate Agreements through NASDTEC that expedite the certification process.

UNIVERSITY OF WISCONSIN - MILWAUKEE

School of Education
Department of Curriculum and Instruction
P.O. Box 413 Education
Milwaukee, Wisconsin 53201
Phone: (414) 229-4181
Fax: (414) 229-6348
E-mail: soedean@@uwm.edu
Internet: http://www.uwm.edu

Institution Description: The institution was formed by the merger of Wisconsin State College, Milwaukee and the University of Wisconsin's Milwaukee Extension Center in 1956.

The goal of the Department of Curriculum and Instruction is to prepare teachers at the early childhood, elementary, and secondary levels who are able to provide maximum educational opportunities for children in the urban community.

Institution Control: Public.

Calendar: Semester. Academic year August to May.

Official(s): Dr. Alonzo Thurman, Dean; Dr. Elizabeth Bolt, Assistant Dean; Dr. William Kritek, Associate Dean.

Faculty: Full-time 76; adjunct 150.

Degrees Awarded: 144 baccalaureate; 141 master's; 8 doctorate.

Admission Requirements: *Undergraduate:* Graduation with 17 academic units from an accredited high school; rank in the top 50% of class; minimum score of 21 on ACT composite. *Teacher education specific:* Passing scores on PRAXIS I tests (reading, mathematics, writing); completion of 58 credits of coursework including required basic foundation courses plus math and English proficiencies. *Graduate:* Baccalaureate degree from a regionally accredited institution. *Teacher education specific:* Minimum 2.75 GPA; English proficiency for non-native speakers; faculty interview.

Fees and Expenses: Undergraduate: $4,355 in-state per academic year; $17,108 out-of-state. Graduate: $6.652 in-state per academic year; $21,017 out-of-state. Required fees: $308 per semester. On-campus room and board: $4,954. Books and supplies: $712.

Financial Aid: Resources specifically for eligible students enrolled in teacher education programs are awarded on the basis of financial need and academic merit. The institution has a Program Participation Agreement with the U.S. Department of Education for eligible students to receive Pell Grants and other federal aid. Teacher scholarships available to qualifying students. *Contact:* Financial Aid Office at: (414) 229-4541 or e-mail at: finaid@uwm.edu.

Accreditation: *Regional:* NCA. *Professional:* NCATE. *Member of:* AACTE. *Approved by:* Wisconsin Department of Public Instruction.

Undergraduate Programs: The Department of Curriculum and Instruction offers teacher education programs in early childhood, middle childhood through early adolescence, and early adolescence through adolescence. Students must complete specific course requirements in four core areas: fine arts, humanities, natural science and mathematics, and social science. Courses in educational foundations and methods are also required. Student teaching is a full-day, full public school semester.

Students in elementary and early childhood education may complete a certification program leading to certification to teach in classrooms in which two languages are used for instruction. Secondary education majors and minors are offered in computer science, English, teaching of English to speakers of other languages, foreign language (French, German, Latin, Russian, Spanish), mathematics, natural sciences, science (biology, chemistry, earth science, physics), social studies (anthropology, economics, geography, history, political science, psychology, sociology).

All baccalaureate programs require successful completion of 120 semester hours.

Graduate Programs: The Master of Science in Curriculum and Instruction is comprised of 33 hours. The program requires completion of a thesis or a capstone graduate seminar. Areas of focus include early childhood education, middle childhood through early adolescence, early adolescence through adolescence, reading, urban education, bilingual education, curriculum planning and instructional improvement, and school-based custom designed programs.

The Doctor of Philosophy in urban education curriculum and instruction specialization program is comprised of 54 hours, including courses in urban education, research, the specialization, and a minor. Specialization areas include a content area, educational level, general area (e.g. curriculum and instruction, teacher education), and the special area (e.g., urban curriculum design, teacher leadership).

Licensure/Reciprocity: Wisconsin. Students seeking teaching certification in a state other than Wisconsin should consult with that state's teacher certification office early in their program of study to insure compliance with requirements. Many state directors of teacher credentialing have signed Interstate Agreements through NASDTEC that expedite the certification process.

UNIVERSITY OF WISCONSIN - OSHKOSH

College of Education and Human Services
NE113 COEHS
800 Algoma Boulevard
Oshkosh, Wisconsin 54901
Phone: (920) 424-3324
Fax: (920) 424-0858
E-mail: ford@uwosh.edu
Internet: http://www.uwosh.edu

Institution Description: The university was established as Oshkosh Normal School in 1871. The name was changed to Oshkosh Teachers Colleges in 1925, to Wisconsin State College—Oshkosh in 1949, to Wisconsin State University—Oshkosh in 1964, and to the present name in 1971.

The College of Education and Human Services offers undergraduate and graduate programs that prepare students for teaching careers and professional development.

Institution Control: Public.

Calendar: Semester. Academic year September to August.

Official(s): Dr. Craig Fiedler, Dean; Dr. Michael Ford, Associate Dean.

Faculty: Full-time 50; part-time 10; adjunct 40.

Degrees Awarded: 193 baccalaureate; 164 master's.

Admission Requirements: *Undergraduate:* Graduation with 15 academic units from an accredited high school; College Board SAT or ACT composite. *Teacher education specific:* Passing scores on PRAXIS I tests (reading, mathematics, writing); completion of 40 credits; general education and professional coursework; portfolio; letters of recommendation; personal statement; faculty interview. *Graduate:* Baccalaureate degree from a regionally accredited institution. *Teacher education specific:* Minimum 3.0 GPA; educational program specific requirements; letters of recommendation; faculty interview.

Fees and Expenses: Undergraduate: $4,043.50 in-state per academic year; $14,088.70 out-of-state. Graduate: $5,534.70 in-state per academic year; $15,854.80 out-of-state. Required fees: $100. On-campus room and board: $4,078. Books and supplies: $400.

Financial Aid: Resources specifically for eligible students enrolled in teacher education programs are awarded on the basis of financial need and academic merit. The institution has a Program Participation Agreement with the U.S. Department of Education for eligible students to receive Pell Grants and other federal aid. Teacher scholarships available to qualifying students. *Contact:* Beatrice Contreras at: (920) 424-3377 or e-mail at: contreras@uwosh.edu.

Accreditation: *Regional:* NCA. *Professional:* NCATE. *Member of:* AACTE. *Approved by:* Wisconsin Department of Public Instruction.

Undergraduate Programs: The college offers six majors: elementary education, human services, natural sciences, social science, special education, and dual (elementary and special education). Although the college does not offer a secondary education major as such, it does provide programs leading to licensure to teach at the secondary levels (6-12, 9-12, K-12). The college offers twelve minors within the education major: elementary language arts, elementary social science, elementary science, library science, reading, English as a second language, bilingual education-Spanish, bilingual education-Himong. All baccalaureate programs require the completion of a general education core, professional studies, content area, field experiences, and student teaching. A minimum of 120 semester hours is required for graduation.

UNIVERSITY OF WISCONSIN - OSHKOSH—
cont'd

A Cooperative Urban Teacher Education program is available for talented students who wish to become teachers. Black, Hispanic, Native Americans, and Asian students are encouraged to consider the cooperative program that was created by a joint effort of the University of Wisconsin-Oshkosh and the Milwaukee Area Technical College.

Graduate Programs: The Professional Education Program has been designed to provide an undergraduate degree in four years and graduate credit and licensure in five years. The Master of Science in Education program is offered with concentrations in reading (reading teacher, reading specialist), counseling (school, community, higher education), curriculum and instruction, special education, and educational administration. The Master of Science degree is offered in educational leadership.

Licensure/Reciprocity: Wisconsin. Students seeking teaching certification in a state other than Wisconsin should consult with that state's teacher certification office early in their program of study to insure compliance with requirements. Many state directors of teacher credentialing have signed Interstate Agreements through NASDTEC that expedite the certification process.

UNIVERSITY OF WISCONSIN - PLATTEVILLE

School of Education
One University Plaza
Platteville, Wisconsin 53818-3001
Phone: (608) 342-1131
Fax: (608) 342-1133
E-mail: education@uwplatt.edu
Internet: http:www.uwplatt.edu

Institution Description: The university was established as Platteville Normal School in 1886. It became Platteville State Teachers College in 1927 and Wisconsin State College, Platteville in 1951. The present name was adopted in 1971.

The School of Education offers a variety of undergraduate and graduate courses to prepare students for teaching careers.

Institution Control: Public.

Calendar: Semester. Academic year September to May.

Official(s): Dr. Alison Bunte, Department Head; Dr. John Nkemnji, Director, Teacher Education.

Faculty: Full-time 21; part-time 14; adjunct 8.

Degrees Awarded: 107 baccalaureate; 54 master's.

Admission Requirements: *Undergraduate:* Graduation from an accredited high school; minimum score of 22 on ACT composite; top 50% of graduating class. *Teacher education specific:* Passing scores on PRAXIS I tests (reading, mathematics, writing); completion of 40 credits of coursework including required basic foundation courses; two recommendations; admission portfolio; faculty interview. *Graduate:* Baccalaureate degree from a regionally accredited institution. *Teacher education specific:* Minimum 2.75 GPA; faculty interview. PRAXIS II required prior to certification.

Fees and Expenses: Undergraduate: $4,251 in-state per academic year: $14,297 out-of-state. Graduate: $5,406 in-state per academic year; $16,018 out-of-state. On-campus room and board: $3,990. Books and supplies: Textbook rental included with undergraduate tuition.

Financial Aid: Resources specifically for eligible students enrolled in teacher education programs are awarded on the basis of financial need and academic merit. The institution has a Program Participation Agreement with the U.S. Department of Education for eligible students to receive Pell Grants and other federal aid. Teacher scholarships available to qualifying students. *Contact:* Sheila Trotter at: (608) 342-1836 or e-mail at: trotter@uwplatt.edu.

Accreditation: *Regional:* NCA. *Professional:* NCATE. *Member of:* AACTE. *Approved by:* Wisconsin Department of Public Instruction.

Undergraduate Programs: The Bachelor of Science degree program in early childhood/middle childhood (birth-age 11) requires the completion of courses in general education, elementary education, minor studies (early childhood), and professional studies. The Bachelor of Arts in middle/secondary education or Bachelor of Science degree in an academic major requires completion of courses in general education, major/minor, professional education. Special field concentrations leading to the Bachelor of Arts or Bachelor of Science include agriculture, art, foreign language, music, technology, and physical education. The Bachelor of Science degree program in early adolescence (ages 10-14) is also offered. All baccalaureate licensure programs require the completion of a major and a professional education component and 120 or more semester hours depending on the program pursued.

Graduate Programs: The goal of the Master of Science in Education is the development of an individual program plan based on professional development goals prepared by the student in consultation with the advisor. The programs include teaching-elementary, middle, secondary, vocational/technical emphases. All candidates must demonstrate research and writing proficiency. Students may elect 30 credits of approved graduate coursework that includes a thesis or seminar paper *or* 36 credits of approved graduate coursework. All programs consist of core courses and an area of knowledge.

Licensure/Reciprocity: Wisconsin. Students seeking teaching certification in a state other than Wisconsin should consult with that state's teacher certification office early in their program of study to insure compliance with requirements. Many state directors of teacher credentialing have signed Interstate Agreements through NASDTEC that expedite the certification process.

UNIVERSITY OF WISCONSIN - RIVER FALLS

College of Education and Professional Studies
Teacher Education Department
410 South 3rd Street
River Falls, Wisconsin 54022
Phone: (715) 425-3230
Fax: (715) 425-3242
E-mail: admit@uwrf.edu
Internet: http://www.uwrf.edu

Institution Description: The university was established as River Falls Normal School in 1875. It became River Falls State Teachers College in 1926 and the present name was adopted in 1971.

Teacher education has been a major commitment of the university since its inception. Professional organizations within the College of Education and Professional Studies offer students opportunities to become actively involved in the education profession.

Institution Control: Public.

Calendar: Semester. Academic year September to May.

Official(s): Dr. Connie Foster, Dean; Dr. Florence Monsour and Dr. Tim Holleran, Co-Chairs, Teacher Education Department.

Faculty: Full-time 14.

Degrees Awarded: 187 baccalaureate; 85 master's.

Admission Requirements: *Undergraduate:* Graduation with 17 academic units from an accredited high school; rank in the top 40% of class; minimum score of 22 on ACT composite. *Teacher education specific:* Passing scores on PRAXIS I tests (reading, mathematics, writing); completion of 58 credits of coursework including required basic foundation courses plus math and English proficiencies. *Graduate:* Baccalaureate degree from a regionally accredited institution. *Teacher education specific:* Minimum 2.75 GPA; autobiographical essay stating professional goals; 2 recommendations. faculty interview.

Fees and Expenses: Undergraduate: $4,225 in-state per academic year; $14,270 out-of-state. Graduate: $5,406 in-state per academic year; $16,108 out-of-state. On-campus room and board: $3,968. Other expenses: $2,112. Books and supplies: $200.

Financial Aid: Resources specifically for eligible students enrolled in teacher education programs are awarded on the basis of financial need and academic merit. The institution has a Program Participation Agreement with the U.S. Department of Education for eligible students to receive Pell Grants and other federal aid. Teacher scholarships available to qualifying students. *Contact:* Financial Aid Office at: (715) 425-3141.

Accreditation: *Regional:* NCA. *Professional:* NCATE. *Member of:* AACTE. *Approved by:* Wisconsin Department of Public Instruction.

Undergraduate Programs: The Bachelor of Science degree is granted after successful completion of of the program. The secondary education major (broad area art education, music education, comprehensive physical education) leads to comprehensive certification in early childhood-adolescence (grades K-12). Secondary certification: early adolescence-adolescence (6-1) can be acquired with concentrations in agriculture, biology, chemistry, computer systems, earth science, English, teaching English to speakers of other languages, journalism (minor only), mathematics, modern languages, physics, physical science, science (broad field), social studies (broad area), and speech communication. All programs require the completion of a general education core, professional studies, content area, field experiences, and student teaching. A minimum of 120 semester hours is required for the degree award.

Graduate Programs: Master's degree programs are offered in middle childhood through early adolescence education, counseling, school psychology, reading, agricultural education, and early adolescence through adolescence education. Each program has specific goals and required coursework.

Licensure/Reciprocity: Wisconsin. Students seeking teaching certification in a state other than Wisconsin should consult with that state's teacher certification office early in their program of study to insure compliance with requirements. Many state directors of teacher credentialing have signed Interstate Agreements through NASDTEC that expedite the certification process.

UNIVERSITY OF WISCONSIN - STOUT

School of Education

Office of Teacher Education

One Clock Tower Plaza

Menomonie, Wisconsin 54751

Phone: (715) 232-1088

Fax: (715) 232-1244

E-mail: hassd@uwstout.edu

Internet: http://www.uwstout.edu

Institution Description: The university was established as Stout Manual Training and Domestic Science School in 1893. The name was changed to Stout Institute in 1908, to Stout State College in 1955, to Stout State University in 1964, and to the present name in 1972.

The Office of Teacher Education is responsible for all clinical programs and offers a variety of undergraduate courses preparing students for careers in teaching.

Institution Control: Public.

Calendar: Semester. Academic year September to May.

Official(s): Dr. Judy Jax, Dean; Dr. Mary Hopkins-Best, Coordinating Chair.

Faculty: Full-time 30; part-time 15; adjunct 33.

Degrees Awarded: 215 baccalaureate; 101 master's.

Admission Requirements: *Undergraduate:* Graduation from an accredited high school or GED; rank in the top 40% of class; minimum score of 22 on ACT composite. *Teacher education specific:* Passing scores on PRAXIS I tests (reading, mathematics, writing); completion of 58 credits of coursework including required basic foundation courses plus math and English proficiencies. *Graduate:* Baccalaureate degree from a regionally accredited institution. *Teacher education specific:* Minimum 2.75 GPA; autobiographical essay stating professional goals; 2 recommendations. faculty interview.

Fees and Expenses: Undergraduate: $5,051 in-state per academic year; $15,407 out-of-state. Graduate: Tuition charged per credit hour. On-campus room and board: $3,732. Books and supplies: $500.

Financial Aid: Resources specifically for eligible students enrolled in teacher education programs are awarded on the basis of financial need and academic merit. The institution has a Program Participation Agreement with the U.S. Department of Education for eligible students to receive Pell Grants and other federal aid. Teacher scholarships available to qualifying students. *Contact:* Beth Resech, Director, Financial Aid at: (715) 232-1695.

Accreditation: *Regional:* NCA. *Member of:* AACTE. *Approved by:* Wisconsin Department of Public Instruction.

Undergraduate Programs: The curriculum in the early childhood program is designed to prepare graduates to work in settings with young children and their families. The Bachelor of Science degree is awarded after successful completion of 124 to 129 credits.

The Bachelor of Science degree in family and consumer sciences education provides career options for a variety of educational settings. The programs require 124 to 127 credits. The teaching certification in marketing education can be pursued with the option of teaching certification in business education. The program requires completion of 124 credits. The technology education program consists of 124 credits. Students study fields such as communication, construction, manufacturing, and transportation. The vocational, technical and adult education program prepares teachers for post-high school settings such as junior colleges, public and private colleges, and industrial training programs. A minimum of 124 credits is required for graduation.

All programs require completion of a general education core, professional studies, major studies, area content concentration, and student teaching.

Graduate Programs: The Master of Science degree is designed to prepare individuals to work as professional teachers or to enhance the skills they already have. The requirements include completion of at least 30 semester hours. If a student does not have a teaching undergraduate degree, he/she must complete all certification and graduate coursework before being recommended for certification.

The Master of Science degree program in guidance and counseling provides a basic preparation in school counseling. Students may choose either the elementary or secondary option. A Master of Science degree in industrial/technology education is designed for individuals with undergraduate preparation in industrial arts, industrial education, technology education, and related fields.

The Master of Science degree program in school psychology provides students with specialized training in both psychology and education. This is a 30-credit program. The Master of Science degree program in vocational and technical Education is designed to increase professional competence of those who plan to serve in high school or post-high school programs. Learning experiences include internship, outreach courses, and independent study.

Licensure/Reciprocity: Wisconsin. Students seeking teaching certification in a state other than Wisconsin should consult with that state's teacher certification office early in their program of study to insure compliance with requirements. Many state directors of teacher credentialing have signed Interstate Agreements through NASDTEC that expedite the certification process.

UNIVERSITY OF WISCONSIN - WHITEWATER

College of Education
2030 Winther Hall
800 West Main Street
Whitewater, Wisconsin 53190
Phone: (262) 472-1101
Fax: (262) 472-5716
E-mail: education@uww.edu
Internet: http://www.uww.edu

Institution Description: The university was established as Whitewater Normal School in 1868. The name was changed to Whitewater State Teachers College in 1925. The present name was adopted in 1971.

The College of Education is committed to the principles of excellence in teaching education and leadership in maintaining and extending an effective system of schools for a free society.

Institution Control: Public.

Calendar: Semester. Academic year August to May.

Official(s): Dr. Jeffrey C. Barnett, Dean; Dr. Larry Kenney, Associate Dean.

Faculty: Full-time 76; part-time 45; adjunct 13.

Degrees Awarded: 298 baccalaureate; 190 master's.

Admission Requirements: *Undergraduate:* Graduation from an accredited high school or GED; rank in the top 40% of class; College Board SAT or ACT composite. *Teacher education specific:* Passing scores on PRAXIS I tests (reading, mathematics, writing); completion of 40 credits of coursework including required basic foundation courses plus math and English proficiencies; 350 hours of experience with children; portfolio. *Graduate:* Baccalaureate degree from a regionally accredited institution. *Teacher education specific:* Minimum 2.75 GPA; autobiographical essay stating professional goals; 2 recommendations. faculty interview.

Fees and Expenses: Undergraduate: $3,939 in-state per academic year; $13,783 out-of-state. Graduate: $4,870 in-state per academic year; $15,480 out-of-state. On-campus room and board: $3,700. Books and supplies: Textbook rental $110.

Financial Aid: Resources specifically for eligible students enrolled in teacher education programs are awarded on the basis of financial need and academic merit. The institution has a Program Participation Agreement with the U.S. Department of Education for eligible students to receive Pell Grants and other federal aid. Teacher scholarships available to qualifying students. *Contact:* Carol Miller, Director, Financial Aid at: (262472-1130 or e-mail at: millerc@uww.edu.

Accreditation: *Regional:* NCA. *Professional:* NCATE. *Member of:* AACTE. *Approved by:* Wisconsin Department of Public Instruction.

Undergraduate Programs: Students can major in early childhood education, elementary education, or secondary education as well as in special education and in K-12 programs in art, music, and physical education. All licensure programs require between 120 and 146 credits with a 2.75 GPA required for licensure. All programs have a minimum of three field experiences culminating with student teaching for a full semester. All students in teacher education are required to have a minimum of 350 hours in teaching experiences with children.

Graduate Programs: The College of Education offers master's degree programs in communicative disorders, counselor education, curriculum and instruction, library media, safety, school business management, school psychology, reading and special education. A joint master's program in school administration is offered in cooperation with the University of Wisconsin-Madison.

Licensure/Reciprocity: Wisconsin. Students seeking teaching certification in a state other than Wisconsin should consult with that state's teacher certification office early in their program of study to insure compliance with requirements. Many state directors of teacher credentialing have signed Interstate Agreements through NASDTEC that expedite the certification process.

VITERBO UNIVERSITY

School of Education
Teacher Education Program
815 South Ninth Street
La Crosse, Wisconsin 54601
Phone: (608) 796-3000
Fax: (608) 796-3050
E-mail: admission@viterbo.edu
Internet: http://www.viterbo.edu

Institution Description: Viterbo University, formerly Viterbo College, is a private, independent, nonprofit college founded by the Franciscan Sisters of Perpetual Adoration of La Crosse, Roman Catholic Church. It was founded in 1890.

The mission of Viterbo University is to provide a quality liberal arts and a career-oriented professional education rooted in the Catholic tradition. The base of liberal arts studies provides a background knowledge of the traditional liberal arts disciplines and the opportunity to integrate that background into the student's teaching major/minor.

Institution Control: Public.

Calendar: Semester. Academic year August to May.

Official(s): Dr. Susan Batell, Dean, School of Education and Director of Teacher Education Program.

Faculty: Full-time 14.

Degrees Awarded: 31 baccalaureate; 371 master's.

Admission Requirements: *Undergraduate:* Graduation with 16 academic units from an accredited high school or GED; ACT composite preferred; College Board SAT accepted. *Teacher education specific:* Passing scores on PRAXIS I tests (reading, mathematics, writing); completion of 40 credits of coursework including required basic foundation courses plus math and English proficiencies; 2.5 GPA; faculty approval. *Graduate:* Baccalaureate degree from a regionally accredited institution. *Teacher education specific:* Minimum 2.75 GPA; autobiographical essay stating professional goals; 2 recommendations. faculty interview.

Fees and Expenses: $15,320 per academic year. Graduate: Tuition charged per credit hour. On-campus room and board: $5,100. Other expenses: $2,300. Books and supplies: $650.

Financial Aid: Resources specifically for eligible students enrolled in teacher education programs are awarded on the basis of financial need and academic merit. The institution has a Program Participation Agreement with the U.S. Department of Education for eligible students to receive Pell Grants and other federal aid. Teacher scholarships available to qualifying students. *Contact:* Financial Aid Office at: (608) 796-3900.

Accreditation: *Regional:* NCA. *Professional:* NCATE. *Member of:* AACTE. *Approved by:* Wisconsin Department of Public Instruction.

Undergraduate Programs: Undergraduate curricula are designed to help the prospective teacher develop the competencies necessary for teaching in the following programs: elementary education 1-6; elementary/middle school education 1-9 (majors in English, English/language arts, history, mathematics, religious studies, science, Spanish). middle/secondary school education 6-12; pre-kindergarten-12 (majors in art K-12, business education, music general K-12 and choral 6-12, Spanish, theatre arts). All programs require the completion of a general education core, professional studies, content area, field experiences, and student teaching. A minimum of 128 semester hours is required for graduation.

Graduate Programs: The Master of Arts in Education provides professional teachers with a meaningful avenue for personal growth and development. It is designed to provide teachers with skills in reading, evaluating, and conducting classroom action research. Courses are offered in convenient formats to meet the needs of practicing teachers.

Licensure/Reciprocity: Wisconsin. Students seeking teaching certification in a state other than Wisconsin should consult with that state's teacher certification office early in their program of study to insure compliance with requirements. Many state directors of teacher credentialing have signed Interstate Agreements through NASDTEC that expedite the certification process.

WYOMING

UNIVERSITY OF WYOMING

College of Education
Teacher Education
University Station
P.O. Box 3435
Laramie, Wyoming 82071
Phone: (307) 766-2230
Fax: (307) 766-2018
E-mail: edquest@uwyo.edu
Internet: http://www.uwyo.edu

Institution Description: The University of Wyoming is a state institution and land-grant university. It was established and chartered as the University of Wyoming in 1886.

Institution Control: Public.

Calendar: Semester. Academic year September to May.

Official(s): Dr. Kay Persichitte, Director of Teacher Education.

Faculty: Full-time 57; part-time 15; adjunct 4.

Degrees Awarded: 274 baccalaureate; 51 master's; 13 doctorate.

Admission Requirements: *Undergraduate:* Graduation from an accredited high school or GED; College Board SAT 960; ACT composite 20. *Teacher education specific:* grade of C or better in required prerequisite courses; 2.5 GPA; first aid certification; substitute teaching certification. *Graduate:* Baccalaureate degree from a regionally accredited institution. *Teacher education specific:* Faculty interview; personal goal statement.

Fees and Expenses: Undergraduate: $84 in-state per credit hour; $279 out-of-state. Graduate: $142 in-state per credit hour; $408 out-of-state. Required fees: $284 undergraduate per semester. On-campus room and board: $5,546. Books and supplies: $600.

Financial Aid: Resources specifically for eligible students enrolled in teacher education programs are awarded on the basis of financial need and academic merit. The institution has a Program Participation Agreement with the U.S. Department of Education for eligible students to receive Pell Grants and other federal aid. Teacher scholarships available to qualifying students. *Contact:* Office of Student Financial Aid at: (307) 766-2116 or e-mail at: finaid@uwyo.edu.

Accreditation: *Regional:* NCA. *Professional:* NCATE. *Member of:* AACTE. *Approved by:* Wyoming Professional Teaching Standards Board.

Undergraduate Programs: The College of Education allows students to earn a degree in either elementary education or secondary education. Elementary education majors select an areas of concentration that allows for further expertise in a particular area. secondary education majors complete extensive coursework in one of 16 content areas. A degree program is also offered that offers dual certification in elementary and special education. All students complete the Wyoming Teacher Education Professional Education coursework which offers extensive field experiences and courses that foster human learning, diversity, and exploration of multiple ways to provide positive teaching and learning environments.

Graduate Programs: Advanced degree programs of study are offered for teachers already certified at the baccalaureate level include: Master of Science in counselor education with an option for school counseling; Master of Arts in principal and superintendent certification; Master of Arts in curriculum and instruction, and Master of Arts in special education.

The Doctor of Education and Doctor Philosophy degrees are offered in educational leadership and curriculum and instruction. An Education Specialist degree is offered in special education.

All graduate programs have specific goals and course requirements.

Licensure/Reciprocity: Wyoming. Students seeking teaching certification in a state other than Wyoming should consult with that state's teacher certification office early in their program of study to insure compliance with requirements. Many state directors of teacher credentialing have signed Interstate Agreements through NASDTEC that expedite the certification process.

Institution Index

This index lists all institutions in alphabetical order followed by their location information, including city and state.